CW01370269

The Dictionary of Urbanism

The Dictionary of Urbanism

Robert Cowan

Illustrated by
Lucinda Rogers

Streetwise Press

THE DICTIONARY OF URBANISM
First published in 2005 by Streetwise Press

© 2005 Robert Cowan (text); Lucinda Rogers (illustrations).

Copyright for the text remains with the author Robert Cowan and copyright for the illustrations remains with the illustrator Lucinda Rogers. All rights reserved. No part of this publication may be reproduced, stored in a retrieval system, or transmitted by any means, electronic, mechanical, photocopying, recording or otherwise, without the prior permission of the author and/or illustrator via the publisher.

A CIP catalogue record for this book is available from the British Library.

ISBN 0 9544330 0 9

Published by Streetwise Press Limited, High Street, Tisbury, Wiltshire SP3 6HA
Printed and bound in Great Britain by Biddles Limited, King's Lynn, Norfolk

Contents

Preface	vii
Acknowledgements	ix
The word on the street	xi
A note on the entries	xviii
A–Z	1
References	459
List of places illustrated	468

Preface by Sir Peter Hall

Dictionary-making seems to come in historical waves, doubtless impelled by some obscure deep economic cause: Dr Johnson had his immediate imitators and competitors, as did the Oxford Dictionary a century ago. And the same doubtless applies to the specialist variants: my shelves show no dictionary of planning since the 1960s. So Rob Cowan's new labour of love fills an obvious gap, intellectually as well as physically.

Some might dismiss dictionary-making as an adjunct to crossword-solving. But good, that is thoughtful, dictionaries can do much better than that: by probing alternative and shifting meanings, they can investigate the most basic question of all, what we actually mean by the words we use. Often of course we use them carelessly, with little evident meaning. Sixty years ago Orwell (1941) devastatingly dissected the use of cliché in political discourse – but it is alive and well, as a look at professional jargon will show.

The late Aaron Wildavsky (1973) famously asserted, in the title of one of his papers, that 'If planning is everything, maybe it's nothing'. Perhaps unconsciously, he recalled the words of Friedrich von Hayek (1944): 'It is of the utmost importance to the argument of this book for the reader to keep in mind that the planning against which all our criticism is directed is solely the planning against competition – the planning that is to be substituted for competition… But as in current usage "planning" has become synonymous with the former kind of planning, it will sometimes be inevitable for the sake of brevity to refer to it simply as planning, even though this means leaving to our opponents a very good word meriting a better fate.'

Not everyone would agree – even two decades after von Hayek belatedly helped generate an intellectual revolution. But his words are still worth pondering. And one could surely echo them for 'sustainability', the most overworked political buzzword of the 1990s. Deconstruction of meaning is one of the most important aids to clarity of thought, and dictionary makers are uniquely qualified for this task.

But this dictionary goes far beyond that: it is also an invaluable guide to every aspect of the urban scene, popular as well as professional, iconoclastic as well as legalistic. So welcome to this refreshing reintroduction to a significant genre.

Peter Hall
London

References

Orwell, G. (1941) 'Politics and the English Language' in *Shooting an Elephant and Other Essays*, Secker and Warburg, London.
Wildavsky, A. (1973) 'If planning is everything, maybe it's nothing', *Policy Sciences* 4.
Hayek, F.A. (1944) *The Road to Serfdom*, George Routledge, London.

To Liz, Jessie and Andrew

ACKNOWLEDGEMENTS

Two people are due the very warmest thanks. Tim Mars and Cy Fox have each made a significant contribution to the dictionary. They have been enormously generous with their time, their editorial judgement and their knowledge of urbanism.

Michael Edwards and Michael Hebbert have made valuable detailed comments on the text. Many others have helped generously with ideas, information, practical help and encouragement: Robert Adam, Marie Adran, Sherin Aminossehe, Nigel Barker, Tim Brindley, Eric Brodie, Steve Carr, Matthew Carmona, Amanda Claremont, Andrew Cowan, Jessie Cowan, Jim Cowan, Liz Cowan, Mary Cowan, Karen Dufour, Carol Enright, Adrian Forty, Leslie Gallery-Dilworth, Edward Green, Ben Guy, Robert Huxford, Matt Lally, Graham Lane, Sebastian Loew, Margaux Mallett, Ian Manson, Paul O'Keeffe, Roger Kirkham, John Pounder, Lucinda Rogers, Alexandra Rook, Rob Shipway, Malcolm Simmonds, Anne Skinner, Guus Smeets, Rosemarie Smeets, Gordon Sorensen, Jake Stafford, Jonathan Taylor, Marcus Wilshere, Ken Worpole and Kate Worsley. Very many thanks to them all.

*When we deal with cities we are dealing with
life at its most complex and intense*
JANE JACOBS

The word on the street

urbanism 1 The study or appreciation of the processes of change in towns and cities; making towns and cities work; town (UK) or city (US) planning. **2** The process of becoming urban. **3** The product of town planning or development. **4** Patterns of social life characteristic of urban areas. **5** Architecture in an urban context. **6** A building's characteristic of having internal spaces that create something of the sense of being in a street, square or other external urban space. *See this dictionary for a fuller entry.*

What is the difference between *arcology* and *archaeology*? Why did Hitler use *Baedeker*? What are the *blue banana* and the *blue carrot*? Who was *Bungalow Briggs*? Who lives in *Cactusville*? Who or what would you call *café creep*? What is the difference between a *car ban*, a *car barn* and *kan-ban*? Who asked: *Can Man Plan*? Who is *white van man*? Where is the *city of magnificent distances*? What is the difference between *disurbanisation* and *desuburbanisation*? What is wrong with *dingbats*? Where are *Dulburb, Dullborough, Dullsville* and *Dulston*? Who suffers from *link wilt*? What are *muesli*, *spotted dick* and *Spam Valley*?

Is there a connection between *noli me tangere design* and a *Nolli diagram*? What is the difference between *personalisation* and *personification*, or between *planning permission* and *planning consent*? What is *rear-view marketing*? What difference is there between *urban regeneration* and *urban renewal*, or between *topology* and *typology*? Who or what is a *rural buffer*? When is a *square* not a square? What or where is *subtopia*? When does *suburbia* become *slurbia*? What are *twocking* and *triple convergence*? Is there a difference between an *urbanite* and an *urbanist*?

'Every language is a world,' George Steiner declared. Welcome to the world of urbanism: the world of people who think, talk and write about towns and cities in all their ever-changing complexity; who plan, manage, design, administer, celebrate, build, govern, study, engineer, survey, embellish and portray them; and who campaign, teach and sing about them. That, come to think of it, is everyone.

The language of urbanism is a rich one. We communicate about the built environment with an astonishing wealth of words and concepts, from dry legalistic formulae to street slang. There is the language of statute (like *conservation area*), professional practice (like *park and ride*), design (like *massing*), academia (like *proxemics*), polemic (like *gnomescape*), politics (like *positive parochialism*), the arts (like *lipstick on the face of the gorilla*), popular culture (like *Stepford Wives*), marketing (like *kerb appeal*), science (like *ecosystem*), slang (like *derry*), theology (like *strangeness*) and warfare (like *mouse-hole*). The categories overlap, intersect, collide and merge into one another, and into the everyday language that we all use in talking about the places where we live and work.

Specialists develop specialist languages. They do so because they need to talk about specialised matters, but that is only partly the reason. Language is constantly evolving, and any group – whether a family, a tribe or a profession – that is to some extent living in a world of its own, isolated from other groups, will adopt some ways of speaking and writing that are unique to itself.

Different types of specialist often fail to understand each other, and fail to communicate with non-specialists. It is even worse than that. Each specialism has a language that its own practitioners only partly understand. They pick it up gradually throughout their training and career, but learning the language is not easy. First, meanings change. Second, any one term may have several different meanings, even though those who use the term may not be aware of it.

Academics coin new terms for new concepts, or for repackaging old ones. Politicians find new terms to make their ideas seem fresh. Drafters of legislation need them for new laws. Polemicists need them to get their ideas noticed and to ridicule their opponents. But many terms appear seemingly from nowhere.

At conferences of urban specialists of one kind or another it is common to hear a word or phrase that an attentive listener can be fairly sure has never before been heard by most or all of the audience. The speaker is not trying to confuse anyone. He or she is probably using a term that is current in their own office or among fellow members of their own particular specialism. Occasionally, searching for the right expression to express a thought, the speaker appropriates a word or metaphor that just happens to come to mind. Unfamiliar though it may be, the term may yet be understood in its context. If it is not understood, it merely joins the other 98 per cent of the content of the average conference presentation that passes by the audience without making any lasting impression at all. Occasionally an unfamiliar word or phrase will – consciously or not – stick in someone's memory. It may even enter their vocabulary, and possibly eventually that of their office, of their specialism, of their broad professional field or, ultimately, of the common language.

This dictionary records current meanings and tracks how some of them have changed over the years. It may encourage people who write official documents to define their terms. The development plans of a few local authorities already do it. Generally, though, the writers leave their readers to puzzle out meanings for themselves, and the unfamiliar language helps to exclude many of them from joining the debate. Sometimes this is deliberate. More often it just does not occur to the writers that they are communicating in anything other than plain English.

'Ignorance is power,' a Liverpool councillor once told me. 'If you don't understand what someone is saying, it probably means that they don't either, so you are doing them a favour by pointing it out.' That may well be true, but this book is for those who would rather not risk a punch on the nose.

In 2000 the Department of the Environment, Transport and the Regions published the report of a research project that its Sustainable Development Research Panel has commissioned with the title 'Towards a language of sustainable development'. The oddly-worded brief was '...to identify a coherent language for the education of Sustainable Development...' The researchers identified the problem as being that, although the term 'sustainable development' was well known, too few people were acting in a sustainable fashion.

The researchers saw their job as being either to find better ways of explaining the term, or to find an alternative term that would provoke people into action. The project's aim was to find or develop a language that would help government departments and other agencies educate people into behaving in ways that would support sustainable development. 'This culture shift will not happen overnight,' the report declared. 'Indeed the creation of a new and relevant language for sustainable development will not alone automatically lead to the desired culture change'.

It is extraordinary that anyone could have suspected for a moment that it might. Sustainable development is not a specialist topic that can be communicated in a few carefully chosen phrases. At that time the government's definition of sustainable development, as quoted in the report, encompassed 'better education, learning resources, training, health services, safer communities,... limiting global environment threats, protecting human health and safety, wildlife, landscapes and historic buildings from natural and man-made hazards,... preserving natural resources... and [enabling everyone to] share in higher living standards and greater job opportunities.'

The challenge is not to persuade people that those are worthy aims, but to help them make choices that support a sensible set of priorities. The best language for English-speaking people to use in discussing what those priorities might be and what choices will support them is plain English. After a year's work (during which they consulted focus groups), the researchers failed to achieve to their satisfaction the aims of explaining sustainable development or finding an alternative term. This led them to the fatal error of concluding that the concept of sustainability was too complex to communicate through words alone.

So they invented a translucent plastic three-sided pyramid. Each face of the pyramid would bear an image representing, respectively, society, economy and environment (which their research concluded were the three elements of sustainability). Eureka! 'The Sustainable Pyramid is translucent, so that when it is viewed through the base, all three elements are seen coming together,' the researchers wrote. 'The power of the pyramid lies in its simple approach to communicating what is otherwise too complex to articulate in words.' They recommended that the pyramids should be manufactured and distributed in a variety of sizes as 'creative learning tools', and that 2-D versions could be marketed as jigsaw puzzles ('large pieces for young children, small pieces for adults').

The researchers could not have been more wrong. Communication is not like that. A concept 'too complex to articulate in words' is unlikely to be understood by looking up the backside of a mass-produced plastic pyramid.

Most languages are collections of dialects. The language of urban specialists is itself a collection of different dialects spoken by, for example, planners and architects. As with all dialects, there is a limited degree of mutual understanding between their speakers. Within each dialect group the degree varies from speaker to speaker, depending on the extent to which each has been exposed to other groups.

All languages and dialects change continuously. They change for a variety of reasons. First, they absorb words and ways of speaking from other languages and dialects. Second, new linguistic complexities emerge, often for no identifiable reason at all, and become standard, making the group of speakers progressively less intelligible to outsiders. Third, a group of speakers will sometimes cement its own identity – and distance itself from being understood by outsiders – by deliberately adopting usages special to itself.

The language and dialects of urbanism change for all these reasons and more, though the processes are hard to follow. For example, if you hear the phrase 'horses for courses' spoken at a conference on urban regeneration, the speaker is likely to be a planner, or possibly an engineer, but not at all likely to be an architect. Is this because the concept of means being appropriate to ends is particularly important in planning? Or because planning attracts people with a particular propensity for thinking in such terms? Or has the particular phrase become part of planners' dialect by chance, giving them a warm sense of belonging when they use it, whereas for architects it has not?

To take another example: if you hear the phrase 'urban intervention', the speaker (unless an academic) is likely to be an architect. Practising planners, though they spend much of their lives talking about what architects would call 'urban interventions', hardly ever use the term. The details may not matter. The important point is that what might at first seem to be a common language has much that is not held in common at all.

Cities are the most complex of artefacts. They are matched in complexity by language. In the language of urbanism the two complex structures – of language and cities – collide, with the variously illuminating, exasperating or entertaining consequences that this book records.

Some urbanists regret the lack of precision with which their subject is discussed. American new urbanists such as Andres Duany see part of their mission as being to provide precise definitions of urban elements. Terms such as avenue, boulevard, drive, lane, road and street once had specific meanings, they say, but are now used more or less interchangeably. Yet each element has a specific role in helping a particular urban place to function in a specific way. Abandoning the precise definition, the new urbanists argue, deprives planners and urban designers of the ability to make intelligent use of the available urban elements. If these elements are the words, they explain, then there is a grammar and syntax for joining them together.

The new urbanists' solution is to compile lexicons. These prescribe precise definitions for each urban element, explaining in words and diagrams exactly what each element is, and how it should be used in each of a range of precisely defined urban and semi-urban contexts. There are some ways of arranging urban elements that will work in a specific context and some that will not, the new urbanists say, and it is the duty of those who understand the difference to explain it.

Such an attitude makes sense for a group of people with a fully worked-out view of how to create the type of urbanism appropriate for a particular context and culture. This dictionary has a different aim. Recognising that all languages change continuously, it describes how words and phrases are actually used. The aim is to help people understand what they are hearing and reading, and to show how clear thinking and effective communication depend on defining our terms wherever there is a danger of ambiguity.

Urbanism has faced the problem of how to define its terms for at least a century. The garden city movement defined what a garden city was with some precision, but the more successful the pioneers were in building the movement's credibility, the more house-builders gave the name 'garden city' to developments that met few, if any, of the pioneers' criteria. The same thing happened when the garden city movement moved on to advocate new towns. At first a 'new town' was one designated under the New Towns Act – Stevenage, Bracknell and the like. These government-sponsored initiatives were the new town movement's idea of good planning. To the public and the sponsors of a wide variety of kinds of developments, though, new town was a convenient term to apply to a scheme of any sort. Consequently the term bore the weight, not just of public disapproval of the towns developed under the New Towns Act – which was itself considerable – but of a wide variety of other urban discontents.

Language is seductive, and like all good things it is in danger of being borrowed and debased. Half a century later, the British advocates of urban villages were aware of the problem from the start. They dismissed as too complicated the idea of establishing a detailed test (a 'sieve', as the abandoned prototype was called) of what could and could not be called an urban village. Instead they published a simple list of criteria. The urban village concept was successful in attracting professional as well as Royal approval, but before long the Urban Villages Forum was complaining that housing developments meeting none of the urban village criteria were appropriating the name and threatening the movement's credibility.

A few years on, the same is happening with 'urban extension'. The term is used approvingly by the UK government and the Prince's Foundation, among others, to describe well-planned developments at the edge of urban areas. But already sharp developers are using the term to give spurious credibility to ill-conceived examples of suburban sprawl.

It was the realisation that unregulated labels are public property that led, for example, to the term 'architect' being regulated by statute and the term 'planning for real' being copyrighted. In the latter case the originators of the participation method had become concerned that the term was being applied sometimes to cynical exercises that merely went through the motions. They now insist that it can be used only to describe programmes run by people with the appropriate training. But for few other urbanistic terms is such an option available or, probably, desirable.

Perhaps the most important question to consider in discussing the language of urbanism is the extent to which specific words relate to specific things. The answer, as the entries in this dictionary show, is that the relationship is often not very close at all. Avenue, boulevard and street sometimes have inconsistent meanings. A square may or may not have four sides. A new town or an urban village may or may not conform to any official definition. The meaning of amenity may be whatever is in a particular planner's head at the time. Sustainability may be used in any one of the 500 different senses identified by Heather Cruickshank, or in another sense entirely. Renewal may or may not be a synonym for regeneration.

A great deal of discussion about urbanism uses abstract words as though they were concrete things. Amenity, community, quality, sustainability and urban renaissance, for example, are spoken of almost as if they were physical substances so familiar that there is no need to define them. Such use of language may make life simpler for the specialists who speak and write it, but it does not match the complexity of the urban experience. Language does not offer a simple relationship between words and things. If it did, there would be no need for language to be so complex. Nor would a dictionary of urbanism be so long, or such fun to write.

Speaking and writing effectively about urbanism depends on defining terms for specific contexts. Urban movements need their lexicons. Planning documents need their glossaries. But individual words can not do the hard work for us. Specifying in a plan that development must be sustainable, for example, is no more useful as guidance to a developer than describing a piece of music as beautiful tells us anything about what it sounds like.

Communication depends on taking the trouble to explain what we mean. The rich resources of the language of urbanism are there to tempt us from empty abstractions and from the sterile wastes of professional jargon. This dictionary is offered as evidence that we are spoiled for choice.

Robert Cowan
London

A note on the entries

Words printed in SMALL CAPITALS refer the reader to other entries, where further information on the topic or a related topic will be found. Dates in brackets immediately after a name – such as Patrick Geddes (1905) or (Geddes, 1905) – refer to a work listed at the back of this book. Bracketed dates that do not follow a name serve to date an example or a publication, but do not reference it. Semicolons are used in listing different ways of describing meanings that are the same or similar. Bold numerals indicate different meanings of the same term.

Many of the terms described in this dictionary are used internationally. There are many, though, that relate to the law or practice of a particular country. Unless otherwise indicated, references to statutes and regulations are to law and practice in England; England and Wales; or the United Kingdom (UK). For example the letters (US) indicate that the meaning is specific to the United States. Terms in languages other than English are included only when they are used (at least occasionally) by English speakers and writers. Acronyms are included only when they make words.

A few of the entries are distinctly rural. This reflects the fact that urban and rural issues are inextricably mixed. Large parts of rural Britain are within *city regions*. According to many definitions *urban design* includes design in villages. And at the government's Urban Summit in 2002, deputy prime minister John Prescott defined the event's remit as including villages and rural areas.

Many of the entries could be classified as slang, being very informal words or phrases that readers would be unwise to use in professional writing or polite company. But to mark them as such in this dictionary might suggest that all the other entries are part of the mainstream language – or at least of a specialist language of urbanism. In reality, a large proportion of the entries are likely to cause bafflement, confusion or offence if used in the wrong context. So instead of classifying each problematic entry as slang, jargon, dialect, legalese, obfuscation, technospeak, govspeak, regenbabble or anything else, readers are advised that in communicating with words, context is everything.

The dictionary is not prescriptive. It describes how words are used, on the basis of the evidence of the contexts in which they have appeared. It does not lay down how the words *should* be used or define correct meanings. A word means whatever the person who speaks or writes it intends it to mean. The only real test is whether that meaning is understood.

The scandal of urbanism is how often that test is failed. Like any language, the specialist languages of urbanism are full of multiple meanings, changing meanings and neologisms. Like any foreign or specialist language, they are heard by many people who only dimly understand what they are hearing, and spoken by some who find themselves using words and phrases they barely understand. Catherine Croft (2002) reports 'a cheerfully laconic guide' at the Urbis centre in Manchester explaining that, in his words, 'the building responds organically to the surrounding streets. I don't know what that means, but it's what it says on the website.'

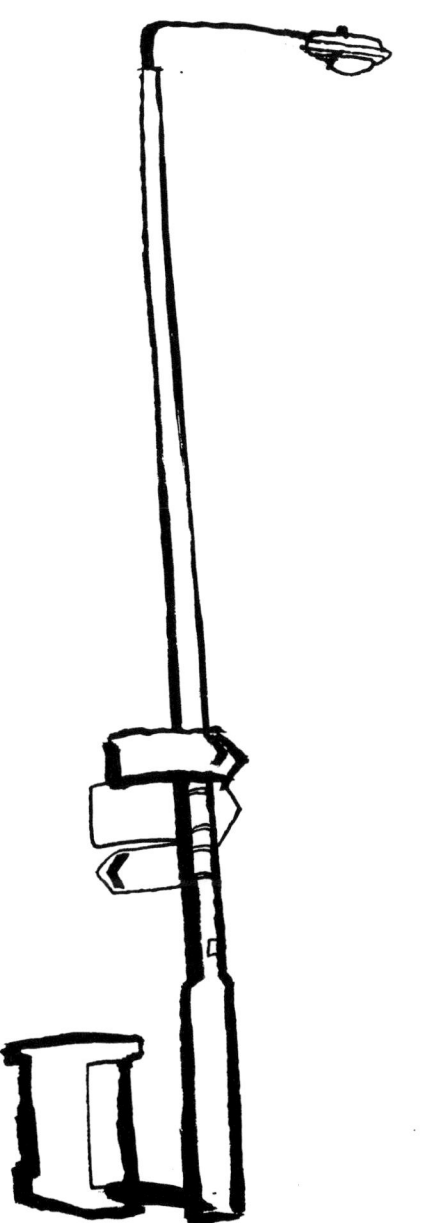

www.urbanwords.info

Readers are invited to contribute to the evolving dictionary by way of the website www.urbanwords.info. Please post your suggested amendments and additions there, supported by references wherever appropriate.

All adopted changes to the dictionary will appear in the website's continuously updated online supplement, which will be incorporated into the printed dictionary's next edition. The website will carry a growing body of information: more terms, improved definitions, more meanings, and more examples of uses, both current and historic.

A

Aalborg Charter The outcome of the first European Conference on Sustainable Cities and Towns, held in Aalborg, Denmark in 1994. The charter declares that: 'Our towns have existed within and outlasted empires, nation states and regimes, and have survived as centres of social life, carriers of our economies, and guardians of culture, heritage and tradition... Our present urban lifestyle, in particular our patterns of division of labour and functions, land-use, transport, industrial production, agriculture, consumption and leisure activities, and hence our standard of living, make us essentially responsible for many environmental problems humankind is facing... Present levels of resource consumption in the industrialised countries can not be achieved by all people currently living, much less by future generations, without destroying the natural capital... Sustainable human life on this globe cannot be achieved without sustainable local communities'.

abandoned city See INVADED CITY.

Abbess of Chicago PATRICK GEDDES' name for JANE ADDAMS, no doubt due to the somewhat monastic nature of her settlement HULL HOUSE.

Abbey of Thélème An ideal city conceived by François Rabelais (c1495–1553).

ABC community A SATELLITE settlement to Stockholm, Sweden, providing for three functions: Arbete (workplace), Bostad (dwelling) and Centrum (centre) (Hall, 1998).

ABC principle (Netherlands) The practice of locating intense passenger-generating activity at 'A' locations on public transport nodes; activity needing a great deal of space and few people at 'C' locations where public transport is worse; and activity lying between these extremes at intermediate 'B' locations.

Abercrombie, Patrick (Sir) (1879–1957) Town and regional planner. Abercrombie led the development of town and regional planning practice in the UK for 60 years. Trained as an architect, he joined the Department of Civic Design at Liverpool University. In 1915 he succeeded STANLEY ADSHEAD as professor of civic design there. For 20 years Abercrombie combined academic life at Liverpool with private practice as a town and regional planner. He prepared the first comprehensive regional plan (for the Doncaster area, 1922) and the Sheffield Civic Survey (1924) (which, like most of his work, showed the influence of PATRICK GEDDES) and the East Kent regional plan (1925). Abercrombie was a founder of the Council for the Preservation of Rural England (see CAMPAIGN TO PROTECT RURAL ENGLAND) in 1926. His County of London Plan identified communities based on London's villages and former market towns. His GREATER LONDON PLAN (1944, published in 1945) proposed dispersing a million people from the city's inner areas. This would be accommodated, not in further suburban sprawl (a green belt would prevent further growth), but in new towns. Land values would be controlled. Abercrombie had become a professor at University College London. He completed

Patrick Abercrombie

his Clyde Valley Regional Plan in 1946. Abercrombie's background as an architect showed in all his work. 'To him a planning commission was very much like an architectural commission,' Peter Hall (1994) writes. 'He produced a one-shot, partly intuitive design solution to a problem. You will look in vain throughout Abercrombie's work for forecasts, projections, generation and evaluation of alternatives; in other words, for all the paraphernalia of planning as we have known it since the 1950s. You will look in vain for any costings, let alone cost-benefit analysis... Nor will you find much reference to the need to monitor and correct the plan...' Abercrombie was president of the Town Planning Institute and was awarded the Royal Gold Medal of the RIBA.

ableist design That which assumes that the users of a building or environment will be able-bodied.

abutter (US) The owner of property abutting or bordering a street. See also FRONTAGER.

abyss, the The east end of London, so called in and after the 1880s (Ackroyd, 2000). See THE PEOPLE OF THE ABYSS.

Acacia A popular name for suburban streets. In imaginary street names Acacia usually denotes suburban ordinariness. Example: 'The oiks from the press were allowed a peep inside the Royal Train yesterday in an attempt to portray the Queen and Prince Philip as Mr and Mrs Windsor of Acacia Close... On the windows were net curtains – a must in Acacia Avenue' (from the *Independent* in 2002); 'Through the census website the secrets of No 1 Acacia Avenue, Anytown, can be clicked up on-screen' (from the *Guardian* in 2003). Bananaman, hero of the eponymous 1980s television cartoon series, lived at 29 Acacia Road. The picture behind the opening titles showed this to be – contrary to what 'Acacia' usually denotes – a street of small terraced houses close to the city centre, their front doors opening directly on to the pavement. The 1980s London A–Z has 13 examples of the road name Acacia Road, and 11 of Acacia Avenue. Other Acacias in London (including Close, Court, Gardens and Drive but never Acacia Street) bring the total to almost 50. The Merseyside area has three Acacia Avenues and five Acacia Groves. Leeds has one Acacia Avenue. Glasgow has no Acacias. The fashion for the name dates from the period of suburban expansion in the 1920s and '30s. Most of the ornamental deciduous trees known as acacia that are common in suburban streets are not true acacias but the hardier *false acacia* or *black locust* (*Robinia pseudoacacia*). See also THE AVENUE and ARCADIA.

accent A small element of a building's form designed to attract attention.

access A means of approaching or entering a building, place or facility. The word derives from the Latin *accessus*, meaning *arrived*. See also VIVA.

access audit A systematic assessment of the conditions faced in a particular place by people on foot or in wheelchairs. Access audits cover matters such as the location and condition of dropped kerbs; controlled crossings; pavement width and obstructions; surface conditions; signage; lighting; personal security; and the maintenance of vegetation. See also MOBILITY and PEDESTRIAN AUDIT.

access control See NATURAL ACCESS CONTROL.

access management Providing for access to land from the network of roads and footways.

access statement Accompanies a planning application to show how the proposal will accommodate people with a wide range of needs, including those with disabilities.

accessibility The ease with which a building, place or facility can be reached by people and/or goods and services. Accessibility can be shown on a plan or described in terms of pedestrian and vehicle movements, walking distance from public transport, travel time or population distribution. See also PUBLIC TRANSPORT ACCESSIBILITY and UNIVERSAL DESIGN.

accessible housing Built or adapted to a standard that makes it suitable for most people with impaired MOBILITY.

accessory apartment (US) A separate, self-contained living unit within a house.

accessory dwelling unit (US) Residential accommodation ancillary to a house. Granny flats and flats in converted houses are examples.

accessory use One subordinate to a site's principal use.

accident See BIASED TERMINOLOGY.

accommodation schedule A list of the building types, uses and floor areas provided (now or in future) by a development.

accommodation works Preliminary works on a development site, such as diverting services.

accompanied journey A transport survey carried out by questioning travellers in the course of their journeys.

ACE ARTS, CULTURE AND ENTERTAINMENT.

achieve High densities of development, particularly of housing, are often spoken of as being 'achieved'. This use of the word is sometimes controversial, as opponents of high densities argue that it implies approval of such densities.

Ackerman, F Lee (1878–1950) A leading advocate of GARDEN CITIES in the USA (Miller, 1989).

acquiring authority One with compulsory purchase rights.

Action for Cities A UK government programme launched in 1988.

action plan A description of intended action in relation to a specific issue or a small site.

action planning Participation techniques, including

community planning weekends, REGIONAL/URBAN DESIGN ACTION TEAMS and URBAN DESIGN ACTION TEAMS, which enable local people and invited teams of professionals to explore design ideas for particular areas over one or several days.

action research That in which the researcher is also an active participant in the process that is being studied. The researchers are often able directly to apply the results to their own work practices.

Active Communities Development Fund Lottery funding to enable more people – particularly in deprived areas – to take part in sport.

Active Communities Unit (ACU) A part of the Home Office supporting efforts to make people more active in their communities, particularly focusing on volunteering, training and mentoring.

active community exemption A system by which residents are compensated for their time and efforts in supporting regeneration programmes without losing their entitlement to benefits.

active engagement Being involved in the life of a public space through social contact with other people. Compare PASSIVE ENGAGEMENT.

active water feature The term denotes a man-made, ornamental body of moving water in a shopping mall (and no doubt also a hotel foyer or office atrium, and so on), according to Joel Garreau (1994). See also BLUE WATER.

activity mapping A technique of showing on a map how people use a place.

activity node A concentration of activity at a particular point.

activity spine A street or streets along which activity is concentrated.

actor A person or organisation taking a significant part in a process such as regeneration. Also known as a *societal actor*.

Adam, Robert (1728–92) Architect. The son of William Adam, another distinguished Scottish architect, he studied classical Roman architecture during a Grand Tour of France and Italy. Back in Great Britain he developed the highly influential 'Adam style', featuring delicate neo-antique ornament internally and externally. His work included the urban complex of the Adelphi in London, now largely destroyed.

Adams, Douglas (1952–2001) Writer. See THE HITCHHIKER'S GUIDE TO THE GALAXY.

Adams, Thomas (1871–1940) The first British planning consultant and an inveterate founder of planning institutes. Adams began his working life as a farmer near Edinburgh. He became interested in politics and land issues, and in 1900 moved to London to write. The following year he became full-time secretary of the Garden City Association (founded in 1899). As secretary-manager of the first Garden City Company he was responsible for launching Letchworth. He left in 1906 for private practice, becoming, in the estimation of his biographer Michael Simpson, the first Briton to earn his living entirely from planning. Adams called his cooperative social philosophy 'associated individualism'. In 1909 he became town planning advisor to the Local Government Board. He was a founder of the Town Planning Institute (the only founder not to be qualified in another profession) and its inaugural president. He moved to Canada in 1914 as town planning advisor to the federal government, helped to found the Town Planning Institute of Canada and was the institute's inaugural president. In 1923 Adams was appointed general director of plans and surveys of the New York regional plan. He was a founder of the American City Planning Institute (later the American Institute of Planners). Back in the UK he founded the Town and

Thomas Adams

Country Planning Summer School in 1933 and was president of the Institute of Landscape Architects (now the Landscape Institute). Michael Simpson wrote of Adams in a biographical essay (in Cherry, 1981): 'his goals were irritatingly imprecise and his vision disappointingly limited, resulting in cautious, opportunist, ameliorative, trend-modifying plans... He failed to understand the social consequences of modern economic life... He assumed too uncritically that the interests of... the political and economic elite were unbiased and coincident with the interests of the community.' LEWIS MUMFORD made similar criticisms of Adams' NEW YORK REGIONAL PLAN.

adaptability The capacity of a building or space to respond to changing social, technological, economic and market conditions. Adaptability is recognised as an important objective of urban design. Charles Darwin wrote of the natural world: 'It is not the strongest of the species that survive, nor the most intelligent, but the one most responsive to change.'

adaption Defined by the BURRA CHARTER as modifying a place to suit proposed COMPATIBLE USES.

adaptive plan One aimed at implementing measures necessary to ensure that the present course is maintained as far as possible (Blowers, 1976). Compare AMELIORATIVE PLAN.

Jane Addams

Addams, Jane (1860–1935) Social worker, social reformer, writer and international peace activist. After visiting TOYNBEE HALL in the slums of London, Addams founded HULL HOUSE in 1889 as a SETTLEMENT to revive community life in a poor area of Chicago. Originally housed in a single building, it expanded to a whole city block with a dormitory for residents. Addams advocated *municipal housekeeping*, urging women to take as much care of their cities as of their own homes. She was awarded the Nobel Peace Prize for her work with the Women's International League for Peace and Freedom. PATRICK GEDDES called her 'the Abbess of Chicago', no doubt due to the somewhat monastic nature of Hull House.

Addison Act The Housing, Town Planning etc Act 1919, named after its promoter, the health minister Christopher Addison. The Act undertook that the government would bear any costs incurred by local authorities beyond a specified amount for every house they built. This open-ended commitment led to spiralling costs to the exchequer, as local authorities simply passed rising building costs on to the government. Addison resigned and the government limited the number of houses to be built under the terms of the Act to 176,000. See also CHAMBERLAIN ACT, GREENWOOD ACT and WHEATLEY ACT.

Addison, Christopher (1869–1951) Politician. As a government minister he promoted the Housing, Town Planning etc Act 1919.

additionality Benefits of a regeneration project that would not have taken place without it. Compare DEADWEIGHT.

address *v.* To be designed to relate to. Architects sometimes speak of a building they have designed 'addressing' adjacent buildings, meaning that it reflects the form of its neighbours in some way. See also RESPOND.

address street One which premises have as their address. The opposite is an urban ring road or a street lined by the backs of buildings.

adjacency See PROPINQUITY.

adobe Sun-dried mud brick used as a building material.

Adshead, Stanley (1868–1946) Architect and civic designer. In 1910 he became the first Lever Professor of Civic Design at Liverpool University (the first chair of its kind anywhere).

advertisement Defined by the Town and Country Planning (Control of Advertisements) Regulations 1992 as 'a sign, board, notice or word (whether illuminated or not) announcing the selling of goods or services, or giving public information'.

advocacy planning Planners or other professionals acting on behalf of local communities. The term and the practice were current in the 1960s and '70s in the USA. Advocacy services were provided by, among others, a network of *community design centres* supported by the American Institute of Architects. Eventually, Graham Towers (1995) claims, 'what had begun as a radical movement became primarily a means of providing more work for private architectural practices'.

aedile A municipal officer in ancient Rome who was in charge of public buildings, and other public facilities and services. Some of the graffiti found at Pompeii call on people to vote for particular candidates for the post. The term derives from the Latin for a building.

aerial differentiation See RESIDENTIAL DIFFERENTIATION.

aerotropolis A city based on an airport.

AESOP The Association of European Schools of Planning.

aesthetic *adj.* Relating to possessing a sense of beauty; relating to perception of the senses; relating to visual appearance and effect – of a building, for example. The architect RICHARD ROGERS (2001) has written: 'Civil servants and politicians in this country will always shy away from any discussion of even the most common-place aesthetic values... Again and again while writing the Urban Task Force's report... I was strongly advised not to use words like "beauty", "harmony", "aesthetic" and even "architecture" if I wanted the report to be taken seriously by those who counted. And sure enough those words hardly appear, replaced by less alarming euphemisms: "good design", "planning" or, better still, "construction".'

aesthetic control The debate about the role of planning in relation to design in the 1970s and '80s centred on the control of the aesthetic qualities of development. This led to confusion, with planners failing to explain why aesthetic matters were a valid concern of public policy. Only in the 1990s did the debate focus on how design could contribute in practical ways to making successful places. In 1980 UK government planning policy declared that 'planning authorities should recognise that aesthetics is an extremely subjective matter. They should not therefore impose their tastes on developers'. In 1992 government guidance noted that 'aesthetic judgements are to some extent subjective and authorities should not impose their taste on applicants'. By 1997 the government had nothing to say about the subjectivity of aesthetic matters, decreeing bluntly that 'local authorities should reject poor design' (quoted in Carmona, Heath, Oc and Tiesdell, 2003). The term *aesthetic control* is now rarely used.

affordable housing Housing for rent set within the reach of households with low incomes, and/or housing for sale on a shared ownership basis (predominantly provided by local authorities and housing associations or trusts), or low cost market housing. One US definition specifies affordable as meaning available at a mortgage payment or rental of no more than 25 per cent of the starting salary of a local elementary school teacher. The term often conveys little when it is used (as it often is) without relating it to an income level. The income level at which affordability becomes an issue depends on local circumstances. Sir Peter Hall (2001) reported that the highly prosperous ski resort and conference town Aspen, Colorado, decided that it needed to build affordable housing for doctors and lawyers. Providing affordable housing is often set as a PLANNING OBLIGATION.

affordable public transport The DETR (2000b) suggested that the degree to which public transport is affordable is determined by the extent to which the financial cost of journeys put an individual or household in the position of having to make sacrifices to travel, or the extent to which they can afford to travel when they want to.

After London A book by Richard Jefferies, published in 1884, describing the resurgence of nature in post-apocalypse England and its ruined capital. The flooded city's centuries of waste transform it into a toxic swamp. See also RATS.

age of greed, the LE CORBUSIER's name for the age in which he lived.

ageing (also aging) *adj.* Old, but not sufficiently old or significant to be considered HISTORIC; showing its age. Example: 'The streetscape is let down by the ageing seats and lighting which detract from their historic surroundings.'

agency The capacity of people to make choices about their lives. Compare ALIENATION.

age-value The value that a building has by virtue of giving those who see or use it a sense of the passage of time, as opposed to HISTORIC-VALUE. The two concepts are used in discussing the conservation of historic buildings.

agglomération (French) A CONURBATION.

agglomeration A cluster of cities or urban areas, not necessarily contiguous. Example: 'The giant Rhine-Rühr agglomeration is essentially an aggregation of separate smaller cities' (2002). See also POLYCENTRIC and compare CONURBATION.

aggregates Sand, gravel, crushed rock and other materials used for roadstone or for making concrete, mortar or asphalt.

aging in place Growing old at home rather than in an institution. Also called *staying put*.

Aglaura A fictional city described in Italo Calvino's INVISIBLE CITIES (1972). The city in reality and the Aglaura of memory seem inextricably confused.

agora (Greek) The market place and civic space of cities in ancient Greece, surrounded by buildings and colonnades. Compare FORUM.

agreement for sale An agreement to sell land at a future date, subject to conditions.

agribusiness Industrialised agriculture.

agricultural belt A stretch of farmed countryside around and between urban areas.

agri-environment scheme A programme for managing a piece of land sustainably, for example by conserving or recreating landscapes and wildlife habitats.

Ahwanhee principles The original set of principles of the CONGRESS FOR THE NEW URBANISM.

air rights Rights to build above, rather than on, a piece of land.

air space That above and around a building. The legal ownership of land extends from the centre of the earth infinitely far into space. As William Empson writes in his 1928 poem 'Legal Fiction': 'Law makes long spokes of the short stakes of men/... Your rights extend under and above your claim/ Without bound.../ ...down where all owners meet, in Hell's/ Pointed exclusive conclave, at earth's centre/ ...And up, through galaxies...'

air-rights building A building that does not stand directly on the ground, being built over railway lines or a road, for example.

Akroyd, Colonel Edward Millowner. He built two of the earliest planned mill villages at COPLEY and AKROYDON.

Akroydon A model village built outside Halifax, Yorkshire, by textile manufacturer Edward Akroyd after 1859. The 'A' is pronounced as in 'bay'.

alabaster cities An image from the fourth stanza of the song 'America the Beautiful': 'O beautiful for patriot dream/ That sees beyond the years/ Thine alabaster cities gleam/ Undimmed by human tears!'

Albany Mall New York State's seat of government: a vast inward-looking modernist complex of marble-clad buildings, topped with a series of office towers. In the view of art critic Robert Hughes (1980), Albany Mall 'is designed for one purpose and achieves it perfectly: it expresses the centralization of power, and one may doubt if a single citizen has even wandered on its bleak plaza... and felt the slightest connection with the bureaucratic and governmental processes going on in the towers above him... Its meaning is utterly simple; there are no ambiguities... What speaks from these stones is not the difference between American free enterprise and, say, Russian socialism, but the similarities between the corporate and the bureaucratic states of mind, irrespective of country or ideology.' Building the Albany Mall was the project of state governor Nelson Rockefeller.

Albert Square The fictional east London square in and around which the soap opera EASTENDERS is set.

Albertopolis A group of cultural sites in South Kensington, London, including the Victorian and Albert Museum, Science Museum, Natural History Museum and Albert Hall. The land was bought on the initiative of PRINCE ALBERT following the success of the Great Exhibition of 1851. The area was called Albertopolis in the 1850s, but the name went out of use until it was revived for a development proposal planned by NORMAN FOSTER in the 1990s. An alternative name for the area is Coleville, after Sir Henry Cole, who played a leading role in implementing Albert's plan (Quinion, 1998).

Alconbury The former US air base at Alconbury in Cambridgeshire was the subject of an important legal case on the question of whether the government violates human rights when it decides planning issues in which it has an interest.

Aldis, Owen Real estate property manager. He was influential in promoting tall buildings in Chicago in the years after 1875.

Alexander, Christopher (b1936) Architect and theorist. Born in Vienna, he was raised and educated in England, and after 1963 was professor of architecture at Berkeley, California. His book *Towards a New Architecture of Humanism*, published in 1963, calls for regional decentralisation and low-rise, high-density housing. *A Pattern Language: towns, buildings, construction*, published in 1977, describes well-established ways of building that people can draw on in designing for themselves. See A CITY IS NOT A TREE and A NEW THEORY OF URBAN DESIGN.

Alexandra Road A housing scheme designed for the London Borough of Camden by Neave Brown and built in 1969–79. The MEGASTRUCTURE, incorporating a pedestrian street with car parking and vehicle circulation beneath, stretches for a quarter of a kilometre. Its back overhangs the main railway line out of Euston station. The scheme was listed in 1993.

alienation People's loss of capacity to make choices about their lives. Compare AGENCY.

Alifbay A fictional country in which lies a city so sad that its name has been forgotten, in Salman Rushdie's *Haroun and the Sea of Stories* (1990). The rich live in skyscrapers, the middle classes in concrete houses and the poor in shacks constructed with rubbish glued together by despair.

alignement (French) The BUILDING LINE.

allée (French) A pathway lined with trees.

Allee (German) An AVENUE. See also STALIN-ALLEE.

allee Defined by ANDRES DUANY (2000) as 'a rural thoroughfare, free of enfronting buildings except at the terminus, where trees in alignment define the space'. In time, he suggests, an allee may become urbanised, evolving into an AVENUE.

Allen, Augustus (1806–64) **and John Kirby** (1819–38), brothers, founders of HOUSTON, Texas, in 1836.

alley A narrow LANE or passage. The word comes from the Latin *ambulare*, meaning 'to walk', by way of an Old French word. See also AREAWAY, BACK OPENING, BLOOD ALLEY, CHARE, ENTRY, GASSE, GINNEL, JIGGER, JOWLER, LANE, MUGGERS' ALLEY, OCCUPATION ROAD, PASSAGE, PEND, RUELLE, SCORE, SHUTE, SILICON ALLEY, SLYPE, SNICKET, THROUGATE, TRANCE, TUNNEL-BACKS, TWITTEN, TWITTING, VENNEL and WYND.

alleygating Installing gates to close the back alleys between terraces of houses as a means of deterring crime. The term came into currency in the UK in the late 1990s.

allotment A garden plot in an area of similar plots. Each plot is rented by an individual, usually from the local authority. David Crouch and Colin Ward have written: 'The word "allotment" is curiously abstract: a legalistic term meaning simply "a portion", but it is shorthand for a number of images of people, places and activities.

It is loaded with assumptions, attitudes and experience that bring us back into our own culture, whether or not we are plot-holders. The word occupies an obscure corner in contemporary culture, but an absolutely interesting one. It may imply something out of the way, passing out of ordinary experience... But it is also tinged with nostalgia for the world we think we have lost, an image of humility from the days when our grandparents would urge us to "Use it up and wear it out/ Make do or do without." Yet it also implies the idea of something "worthwhile" to occupy the weekend, a concern with the quality of the food we eat, an attractive alternative culture' (quoted in Spring, 1990).

Almere A new town in the Netherlands begun in the late 1960s on reclaimed land east of Amsterdam.

Alseopolis See LETCHWORTH.

Alsop, Will (b1947) Architect. See BIG ARCHITECTURE, ECSTATIC ARCHITECTURE, ICON, INHABITED WALL, RURAL CITY and THREE GRACES.

alternative See BIASED TERMINOLOGY.

alternative dispute resolution (ADR) A range of procedures for resolving disputes, including arbitration and mediation. ADR services are provided in the UK by, among others, the Centre for Dispute Resolution, the City Disputes Panel and the Royal Institution of Chartered Surveyors.

alternative energy Produced by means other than by burning fossil fuels or by nuclear power. Sources include the sun, tides, waves, wind, geothermal energy, biomass and landfill gas.

Alton Estate A housing estate built in the 1950s by the London County Council on the edge of Richmond Park at Roehampton in three parts: Ackroyden, Alton East and, finally, Alton West. The last, begun in 1954, was the most dramatically modernist, evoking the UNITÉ D' HABITATION by LE CORBUSIER.

Altruria A fictional island described by William Dean Howells in *A Traveller from Altruria* (1907). The old industrial cities have been abandoned and people now live in small villages. Compare GARDEN CITY.

Alva and Irva See ENTRALLA.

ambient noise Continuing, unwelcome background sound.

amelioration Avoiding or lessening the negative effects on the environment of a development or other project.

ameliorative plan One that seeks to overcome problems and restore the system to what is thought of as a normal state (Blowers, 1976). Compare ADAPTIVE PLAN.

aménagement de ville (French) Development, with an emphasis on equipping the town with services.

aménagement du territoire (French) Strategic social and economic planning with a spatial dimension and an emphasis on providing infrastructure.

amenity Something that contributes to an area's environmental, social, economic or cultural needs. The term's meaning is a matter for the exercise of planners' discretion, rather than being defined in law. See DETRIMENTAL TO AMENITY.

amenity green space Defined by the Urban Green Space Taskforce (2002) as comprising residential squares and public spaces around buildings. See URBAN GREEN SPACES.

amenity lighting That which illuminates buildings or generally contributes to making the street scene more attractive. Compare STATUTORY LIGHTING.

American Beauty A film, directed by Sam Mendes and released in 1999, about a man (played by Kevin Spacey) who suffers a mid-life crisis in American SUBURBIA and discovers the astounding beauty of everyday things, such as a plastic bag blowing about – dancing, it seems to him – in the wind. The residents of suburbia are shown to be living a lie. Before the hero can escape to a new life, his neighbour and wife both decide, independently, to shoot him. The neighbour gets there first. See also TWELVE.

American City Planning Institute See CITY PLANNING.

American grid A European term for a layout in which diagonal streets run through an otherwise regular grain of rectangular blocks.

American Planning Association (APA) A non-profit public interest and research organisation representing practicing planners, officials and citizens involved with urban and rural planning issues. The APA resulted from a merger in 1978 between the American Institute of Planners, founded in 1917, and the American Society of Planning Officials, established in 1934. The American Institute of Certified Planners is the APA's professional and educational institute, certifying planners who have met specific educational and work criteria and passed the certification exam.

Amos, Francis (Jim) (1924–2003) Town planner. He was city planning officer of Liverpool from 1966 to 1973, when he was appointed chief executive of Birmingham. As president of the Royal Town Institute (1971–72) he was an early proponent of PLANNING AID.

Amourot One of the 54 cities of Thomas More's UTOPIA. The name means 'shadowy town' (that is, like Utopia, unreal). Amourot's buildings are 'so uniform, that a whole side of a street looks like one house. The streets are 20 feet broad; there lie gardens behind all their houses; these are large but enclosed with buildings, that on all hands face the streets; so that every house has both a door to the street and a back door to the garden'. The town was designed by Utopus, but 'he left all that belonged to the ornament and improvement of it, to be added by those that should come after him, that being too much for one man to bring to perfection'.

amusement centre Defined by the Scottish Office (1998) as a building used for such activities as a bingo hall or club, prize bingo centre, amusement-with-prizes machines (for example, fruit machines) and amusement-only machines (pin tables and video games).

analytic hierarchy process A method of assessing value (of a development, for example) by taking account of tangible and intangible costs and benefits (Rouse, 2001).

anarchitecture A movement active in New York in the early 1970s, hoping to promote new ways of looking at cities by exhibiting images of neglected urban spaces. The word combines *anarchy* and *architecture*.

anarchy 1 Organisation without authority. The anarchist writer COLIN WARD (1973) has argued that an anarchist society 'is always in existence, like a seed beneath the snow, buried under the weight of the state and its bureaucracy, capitalism and its waste, privilege and its injustices, nationalism and its suicidal loyalties, religious differences and their superstitious separatism.' Ward suggests that his own account of anarchism, 'far from being a speculative vision of a future society... is a description of a mode of human organisation, rooted in the experience of everyday life, which operates side by side with, and in spite of, the dominant authoritarian trends of our society... Anarchists are people who make a social and political philosophy out of the natural and spontaneous tendency of humans to associate together for their mutual benefit.' Elsewhere Ward (1996) has quoted a well-known anarchist saying: 'Government is a confidence trick by which citizens pay for being prevented from initiating anything.' 2 Disorder.

anastylosis Restoring a ruin with the original fallen fragments.

anatemoplanset (Russian) See BORIS SAKULIN.

anchor A location's main retail or other attraction.

ancient monument A SCHEDULED MONUMENT or any other monument which in the opinion of the secretary of state is of public interest by reason of its historic, architectural, traditional, artistic or archaeological interest. Monument in this context has a wider meaning than in normal use: it can refer to a building, structure or site, and does not have to be something set up as a monument. *Scheduled* means it is on the official list (so called because the original list was a schedule to an Act of Parliament) and enjoys statutory protection.

And how much for your grandmother? A paper by the geographer John Adams (1974) ridiculing the efforts of transport planners to quantify absolutely everything in carrying out cost-benefit analysis.

Anderson, Sherwood Novelist. See MAIN STREET.

Andreae, Johann Valentin (1585–1654) Author of CHRISTIANOPOLIS.

Angel effect A place being put on the map by the creation of a work of public art. Anthony Gormley's 'Angel of the North' is supposed to have done this for Gateshead. See also BILBAO EFFECT.

animated space A place in which an attempt is made to overcome barrenness and sterility by the addition of anything that suggests life, according to Joel Garreau (1994).

animateur See TOWN CHAMPION.

Ankh-Morpork The lawless metropolis of Terry Pratchett's Discworld fantasy books. In 2002 the Somerset market town of Wincanton put up road signs announcing that it was twinned with Ankh-Morpork.

Annan, Thomas (1829–87) Photographer. He documented the slums of Glasgow in the 1860s and '70s.

annexation (US) A town or city extension.

annular city One laid out in the form of one or more rings. See ARAMANTH and CROITAS SOLIS, for example.

anonymity Lacking a known name or distinct identity. Oscar Newman (1973) cited anonymity as a factor that increased the risk of crime in housing developments.

Anson, Brian (b1935) Architect, campaigner and community planner. In 1967 he joined the team at the Greater London Council planning the COMPREHENSIVE REDEVELOPMENT of the Covent Garden area. Two years later he had become convinced that the GLC's approach was wrong. He lost his job, burnt his architectural models, drawings and writings, and joined the local community in campaigning successfully against the

GLC's plans. He later taught architecture, and worked as a COMMUNITY PLANNER and PLANNING AID worker.

anthropogenic Caused by human activity.

anthropogeography The study of the distribution of human communities in relation to their geographical environment.

anthropos A single person. EKISTICS classifies anthropos as both a 'unit' and an 'element'.

anti-city LEWIS MUMFORD'S (1961) term for MASS SUBURBIA.

anti-fascist defence wall See BERLIN WALL.

anti-landscaping A landscape treatment that allows local wildlife to grow naturally, rather than imposing a designed landscape with imported trees and plants (Galilee, 2003).

anti-monument A building designed not to be ICONIC or monumental. RICHARD ROGERS used the term to describe the BEAUBOURG in Paris.

anti-place James Howard Kunstler's (2000) term for SUBURBIA.

anti-snob law (US) A colloquial name for a law passed in Massachusetts in 1969 to prevent the ('exclusionary') use of zoning as a means of keeping poor and black households out of an area.

anti-social behaviour That which is likely to disrupt the life of the neighbourhood. Examples include vandalism, threatening behaviour, making noise, writing graffiti and the fouling of public places by dogs.

anti-social behaviour order (ASBO) An injunction served by the police or a council on a person over 10 years old causing harassment, alarm or distress to a household or a neighbourhood.

Anti-Uglies A group of student protestors about low standards of contemporary architecture, led by the pop-artist and actress Pauline Boty (1938–66), active in the UK in the 1950s. One of the targets of their protests was BRACKEN HOUSE, designed by Sir Albert Richardson and completed in 1958, which later became the first post-war building to be listed.

anti-urbanism 1 The belief that cities or towns are an unacceptable setting for human life. **2** The belief that existing, large or dense cities are unacceptable.

Anti-urbanism and *anti-urbanist* are usually pejorative terms. Most of those accused of that attitude would deny it, saying that they object to certain kinds of cities, not cities in general. EBENEZER HOWARD, for example, is often called anti-urban because he was convinced that the big cities of his time had no future, though he sought civic qualities in smaller towns and his GARDEN CITIES. Even FRANK LLOYD WRIGHT, who advocated extreme decentralisation, called his favoured form of development BROADACRE CITY. A follower of JANE JACOBS might accuse LEWIS MUMFORD of being an anti-urbanist, while a follower of Mumford might accuse Frank Lloyd Wright of the same.

The well-known line from Abraham Cowley's 1666 poem 'The Garden' expresses an anti-urban sentiment: 'God the first garden made, and the first city Cain'. (Cain was the first murderer.) The poet Shelley wrote in 1819 that 'Hell is a city much like London – a populous and smoky city'. The novelist DH Lawrence agreed. 'London seems to me like some hoary massive underworld, a hoary ponderous inferno,' he wrote in a letter. 'The traffic pours through the rigid grey streets like the rivers of hell' (quoted by Knevitt, 1986). HENRY GEORGE (1886) wrote: 'This life of great cities is not the natural life of man. He must, under such conditions, deteriorate, physically, mentally, morally. Yet the evil does not end there. This is only one side of it. This unnatural life of the great cities means an equally unnatural life in the country. Just as the wen or tumour, drawing the wholesome juices of the body into its poisonous vortex, impoverishes all other parts of the frame, so does the crowding of human beings into great cities impoverish life in the country.' Andrew Saint has noted that the founders of the NATIONAL TRUST, OCTAVIA HILL,

> ❝ **THE CONCENTRATION OF HUMAN BEINGS IN TOWNS IS CONTRARY TO NATURE, AND THIS ABNORMAL EXISTENCE IS BOUND TO ISSUE IN SUFFERING, DETERIORATION AND GRADUAL DESTRUCTION TO THE MASS OF POPULATION** ❞
>
> *Sir Henry Campbell-Bannerman*

Robert Hunter and Hardwick Rawnsley, 'all held that tenacious English belief in the superior morality of the countryside to the city'. The prime minister Sir Henry Campbell-Bannerman observed in 1907 when receiving the freedom of the City of Glasgow (hardly tactfully, considering the occasion) that 'the concentration of human beings in towns... is contrary to nature, and... this abnormal existence is bound to issue in suffering, deterioration and gradual destruction to the mass of population' (quoted in Cherry, 1982). The historian Oswald Spengler (1880–1936) wrote in *The Decline of the West*, published in 1918 (but written before the war): 'In place of a world, there is a *city*, a *point*, in which the whole life of broad regions is collecting while the rest dries up. In place of true-type people, born of and grown of the soil, there is a new sort of nomad, cohering unstably in fluid masses, the parasitical city dweller, traditionless, utterly matter-of-fact, religionless, clever, unfruitful, deeply contemptuous of the countryman and especially the highest form of countryman, the country gentleman'.

RALPH NEVILLE (1909), a prominent lawyer recruited by Ebenezer Howard as the first chairman of the Garden City Association, wrote that in a metropolis 'the multitude of impressions received by the brain and the rapidity of their impressions tend to induce shallowness of thought and instability of purpose. An increase of emotionalism and a loss of steadfastness are marked characteristics of town dwellers.' The survival of the race, Neville declared, would depend on freeing the working classes from the cities. FJ OSBORN (1938)

> **“ GARDEN CITIES – REALLY VERY NICE TOWNS IF YOU WERE DOCILE AND HAD NO PLANS OF YOUR OWN ”**
>
> *Jane Jacobs*

wrote: 'Great cities mean a choice between two appalling evils; a concrete landscape and four flights of stairs for mother and baby, or an hour of agonising strap hanging in a tube for father.' Such comments led to Osborn and other garden city and new town pioneers being accused (as contemporary urban decentralists often are today) of being anti-urban. Osborn (1939) retorted that his critics were not real urbanists at all. 'Just as many people have doubted whether a nation which watches professional footballers is a nation of sportsmen and athletes,' he wrote, 'so I doubt whether the swarm of art addicts and lecture eaters who make up high-brow London constitute a true urban culture... Such habits have little to do with creative culture, resound in nothing resembling a community, produce no tradition and no collective memories.' The architect CHARLES REILLY (1938) was typical of the critics in referring to 'a garden city with all that implies in pettiness and snobbishness and the village outlook'. Jane Jacobs (1961) wrote of Ebenezer Howard: 'He not only hated the wrongs and mistakes of the city, he hated the city and thought it an outright evil and an affront to nature that so many people should get themselves into an agglomeration. His prescription for saving the people was to do the city in.' Jacobs dismissed garden cities as 'really very nice towns if you were docile and had no plans of your own'.

In Ayn Rand's 1947 bestselling novel THE FOUNTAINHEAD, Dominique Francon (whose character was much like herself in a bad mood, Rand said) is repulsed by, if not New York, then all contact with its people. 'She had always hated the streets of a city. She saw the faces streaming past her, the faces made alike by fear... fear of themselves, fear of all and of one another, fear making them ready to pounce upon whatever was held sacred by any single one they met... she had kept herself clean and free in a single passion – to touch nothing.' She can not even bear the thought of her lover, the modernist architect Howard Roark, touching the hand of the vendor when he buys a packet of cigarettes. Her attitude brings to mind the words of the sociologist RICHARD SENNETT (1990): 'What is characteristic of our city-building is to wall off the differences between people,' he writes, 'assuming that these differences are more likely to be mutually threatening than mutually stimulating. What we make in the urban realm are therefore bland, neutralising spaces, spaces which remove the threat of social contact: street walls faced in sheets of plate glass, highways that cut off poor neighbourhoods from the rest of the city, dormitory housing developments.' For a very different view of passing strangers to that of Dominique Francon/Ayn Rand, see EDWIN MORGAN.

To the poet Robinson Jeffers (1887–1962), a city represented an intolerable concentration of people. In 'November Surf' he imagines 'The cities gone down, the people fewer and the hawks more numerous,/ The rivers mouth to source pure; when the two-footed/ Mammal, being someways one of the nobler animals, regains/ The dignity of room, the value of rareness.' Jeffers wrote elsewhere: 'when the cities lie at the monster's feet there are left the mountains'. LOUIS SULLIVAN (1949) wrote that he felt 'swallowed up' when he moved to the city of Boston. 'The effect was immediately disastrous. As one might move a flourishing plant from the open to a dark cellar, and imprison it there, so the miasma of the big city poisoned a small boy acutely sensitive to his surroundings. He mildewed; and the leaves and buds of ambition fell from him. In those about him, already city-poisoned, even in his own kin, he found no solace, and ceased openly to lament. Against the big city his heart swelled in impatient, impotent rebellion. Its many crooked streets, its filthy streets, lined with stupid houses crowded together shoulder-to-shoulder like selfish hogs upon these trough-like lanes, irritated him, suffocated him; the crowds of people, and wagons, hurrying here and there so aimlessly – as it appeared to him – confused and overwhelmed him, arousing amazement, nausea and dismay.'

Morton and Lucia White (1962) claimed: 'The fact that our most distinguished intellectuals have been on the whole sharply critical of urban life helps explain America's lethargy in confronting the massive problems of the contemporary city in a rational way.' Jonathan Raban (1974) reported that 'in America the city is widely regarded as the sack of excrement which the country has to carry on its back to atone for its sins. Radio, television, magazines, colleges mount ritual talk-ins in which the word "urban", pronounced in the hushed and contrite tone of a *mea culpa*, is monotonously followed by the two predicates, "problems" and "renewal". On these joyless occasions, it is made clear that the problems have no real solutions, and that the notion of rehabilitation is a piece of empty piety, a necessary fiction in which no-one really believes.' Stephen Barber (2002) cites the 1995 Japanese film *Tokyo Fist*, directed by Shinya Tsukamoto, as a vision of how a city can degrade its population. 'The film's cityscapes show vast, empty corporate towers, illuminated at night, while their human components are contained into the minuscule, flickering images of surveillance cameras or blindly perform their insane corporeal floods of movement across the opaque, screeching terrain,' Barber writes. The film reflects 'the city's sensory engulfing of its inhabitants, whose forms dissolve, disappear and resurge.' BILL HILLIER (1996) has argued that 'for much of the twentieth century, nineteenth-century anti-urbanism provided the paradigm for urban design and planning'. Councillor Richard Leese, leader of Manchester City Council, declared at the URBAN SUMMIT in 2002 that 'we need to change the fundamental culture of this country, which is an anti-urban culture.'

You would expect the devil to rejoice in cities' least pleasant attributes. So it makes sense that the devilish narrator in Glen Duncan's 2002 novel *I, Lucifer* calls Manhattan in summer 'my kind of place, my kind of time'. Lucifer exults in the scene. 'Cab grilles snarl in the boomerang light. The subway's foetid lung exhales. Winos strip to the earliest sartorial strata – salmon pink t-shirts and sepia string vests, emblems of the pasts [that] drinks and I have stolen. Garbage trucks chow down on the city's ordure – what a sight: the slow-chewing maw with its stained teeth and heady halitosis. Beautiful. The sun-hot sidewalks give up their ghosts of piss and dogshit. Treacle-coloured roaches conduct their dirty business while pot-bellied rats cloak-and-dagger through the shadows. The pigeons look like they've been dipped in gasoline and blow-dried.' Lucifer congratulates himself on a job well done. See also CITYCIDE and URBICIDE, and compare GREENERY, NEVER TRUST AIR YOU CAN'T SEE and POST-URBANISM.

anytown A place lacking a distinct identity. The architect RICHARD ROGERS (1998) has written of 'homogenous "anytowns", with their sprawling out-of-town housing estates, business parks and retail centres'.

anywhere development Development that looks and feels like it could be anywhere, lacking any local distinctiveness.

Apache land (Glasgow) Any rough part of the city. Called after the tribe of native Americans, as portrayed in Western films.

apartheid planning See WILLIAM GRAHAM.

apart-hotel A hotel in which a significant part consists of apartments, run on a hotel basis, rather than rooms or suites.

apartment 1 Self-contained living accommodation, usually on one floor, with other households' accommodation above and/or below. In England such accommodation used to be called a FLAT, but apartment is becoming more general. The term was first used in France to describe suites of rooms in aristocratic houses (Kostof, 1992). **2** (Scotland) A bedroom or living room in a house or flat. A three-apartment flat in Scotland may have five rooms, counting the kitchen and bathroom, the same as a five-room flat (or apartment) in England. See also UNIT.

Apollo Pavilion See VICTOR PASMORE.

Apology for the Builder, An A tract, published in 1685, possibly written by NICHOLAS BARBON. It attempted, John Summerson (1962) notes, 'to overthrow the prejudice against urban expansion and to show that suburban building, far from being a menace to the public welfare, is a healthy and necessary development, which enhances existing land values near the centre of the town, provides new markets, settles the equilibrium between town and country, and creates revenue and potential cannon-fodder for the government.' Summerson adds: 'The point of view is thoroughly nineteenth century, and makes one realise vividly that the mentality which we habitually associate with the Victorian epoch is merely an expansion of concepts crystallised and sanctified in the age of Charles II, Locke, Wren and Barbon.'

appeal See PLANNING APPEAL.

appearance The combination of the aspects of a place or building that determine the visual impression it makes. The concept is important in development control.

applied social art See CIVICS.

applied sociology See CIVICS.

appreciative inquiry A technique for managing change in an organisation based on finding what works in the organisation and building on that.

appropriate A favourite word of planners, often used in relation to the need for development to respect the CHARACTER of the place. Example: 'Development should be appropriate to its setting.' Such use of the word rarely conveys much meaning. The words '...where appropriate' are commonly added to the wording of a planning policy where the drafters get cold feet about imposing it. The effect may be to make the policy unenforceable and to allow lawyers to argue at length about what the phrase means in a particular context.

Gottfried Semper complained in 1852 that 'notwithstanding our many technical advances, we remain far behind [our ancestors] in formal beauty, and even in the feeling for the suitable and the appropriate' (quoted in Hvattum, 1995). Charles McKean (1994) writes of 'architect after architect' in the mid-nineteenth century discussing 'the question of the correct deployment of new materials, of appropriateness and of "an architecture of the time"'. He notes that '"appropriateness" was of greater consequence than the imposition of a universal style.'

approved development programme (England) Government funding for social housing paid through the HOUSING CORPORATION.

Aramanth The mythical city of William Nicholson's children's novel *The Wind Singer*, published in 2000. The hero redeems the city, which has lost its soul. The circular walled city is composed of districts arranged in concentric rings. 'The outermost ring, in the shadow of the walls, was formed by the great cube-shaped apartment blocks of Grey District. Next came the low-rise apartments that made up Maroon District, and the crescents of the small terraced houses of Orange District... Nearest the central sector of the city lay the broad ring of Scarlet District, a region of roomy detached houses, each with its own garden, laid out in a pleasing maze of twisting lanes.' In the heart of the city is the White District, where the emperor has his palace. 'Here were the great houses of the city leaders, built in marble or polished limestone, beautiful and austere.' The Wind Singer is a wooden tower in its centre. See also HIGH DOMAIN.

arcade 1 A covered passageway, usually lined with shops. **2** A covered area with a series of attractions (such as an *amusement arcade*). **3** A series of arches and their supporting columns or piers, either open or closed with masonry or other material. The word comes from the Latin for arch.

Arcades Project, The An unfinished investigation by the cultural critic Walter Benjamin (1892–1940), based on his study of the PASSAGES of nineteenth-century Paris.

Arcadia An ideal rustic setting. A plan for the landscape of the River Thames in London between Teddington and Kew was published in 2003 with the title *Arcadia in the City*. Arcadia, a mountainous district in the Peloponnese, was celebrated in Ancient Greece as a region where people led a simple pastoral life, and enjoyed music and dancing. The Roman poet Virgil wrote of Arcadia in his *Eclogues*. Tom Stoppard's play *Arcadia* concerns mathematics, CHAOS THEORY and nineteenth-century theories of LANDSCAPE DESIGN. See also CITY OF ARCADIA.

arcadian (also Arcadian) In, or reminiscent of, an ideal rustic setting; pastoral. Example: 'A billboard shows an image of the new Ford Explorer set in an Arcadian landscape of waterfalls and lush trees, captioned "the best the world has to offer"' (from the US in 2001). Urban designers (in the influential ESSEX DESIGN GUIDE, for example) use the term to describe a quality that some suburban development seems to aspire to.

archaeological priority zone An area designated as being known (through past finds, excavations or historical evidence) to be archaeologically important.

archaeological remains Buildings, structures, works, caves and excavations, or their remains, above or below ground, of archaeological interest, including ANCIENT MONUMENTS.

archaeology The study of the past through material remains.

archi:tekt The description of himself used by Stan Green, the self-styled leader of Britain's non-regulated ARCHITECTURAL DESIGNERS in 2002. Green was once prosecuted for describing himself as an ARCHITECT when he was not qualified or registered as such. He hoped that the novel spelling would protect him against that risk (Booth, 2002a).

Archigram An architectural group (and newsletter) set up in 1960 to promote the design of MEGASTRUCTURES and other technological solutions to the problems of living. A proposal for a WALKING CITY was one of the most celebrated. The group's name reflected the hope that the journal would be simple and urgent like a telegram – an archi(tecture)-gram. The original members were Peter Cook, Warren Chalk, Dennis Crompton, David Greene, Ron Herron and Mike Webb. Cook (1966, quoted in Jarvis, 2001) wrote in an editorial in *Archigram 7*: 'Cars, homes, workplaces, fun palaces... are not determinate as artefacts so why should they be determinate as zones, symbols or parts of a hierarchy?... There may be no buildings at all in *Archigram 8*.' The group only ever built, ironically, a playground in Milton Keynes, but Archigram was credited as a major influence on hi-tech architecture. Archigram was awarded the Royal Gold Medal for Architecture in 2002.

architect 1 A person who designs buildings and supervises their construction. **2** A person registered with the Architects Registration Board. **3** One who plans, devises or creates something of significance. Example: 'Cyril Stein, architect of the Hilton chain'; this indicates that he created the chain, not that he designed the hotels. Some designers of buildings enjoy the nominal association with the Great Architect or the Architect of the Universe (God).

In the UK the title 'architect' is protected by Act of Parliament. It is illegal for anyone to call himself or herself an architect who is not registered with the Architects Registration Board, and only people who are properly qualified can register. This means that in the UK 'qualified architect' is a tautology (legally, an unqualified architect can not exist); but then so is 'registered architect', which is a phrase many architects use. The protection relates to the name, not the activity. Anyone is free to design buildings and supervise construction work in the UK, and many non-architects do. Nor is there any prohibition against a non-architect describ-

anywhere development

ing their building as 'architecture'. The architects' professional bodies in the UK are the Royal Institute of British Architects (RIBA) and the Royal Incorporation of Architects in Scotland (RIAS). There is no requirement for an architect to belong to them, and many do not. Members can put RIBA or RIAS after their names, but only if they are also registered architects. Using these letters is held in law to constitute claiming to be an architect. Similarly, American architects practising in the UK are not allowed to use the letters AIA (to indicate their membership of the American Institute of Architects) after their names if they are not registered with the ARB.

Architects used to expect to lead the building team. Now they find their traditional role carved up and swallowed by surveyors, design-and-build package operators, project managers, suppliers of building components, standard computer-aided design programs, and several species of engineer. A survey by the Royal Institute of British Architects in the early 1990s showed that, in the words of Frank Duffy (who commissioned it when he was RIBA president): 'the most able architects did not feel impelled to measure systematically the application of their design skill to what happened subsequently to their clients' operations. In other words, "success" is being measured all too often, even by our best architects, by internal efficiency, by peer group judgements, by introverted architectural criteria.' Job satisfaction for architects, it seemed, was measured in terms of other architects admiring photographs of their newly completed projects in architectural journals, or drawings of unbuilt projects at specialist architectural exhibitions.

Architects have a range of allegiances. First, to their own integrity as artists or designers: to the way they design and how they think a particular building should be designed. Second (assuming they do not have a patron who gives them a free hand), to the client: the person or people who determine the building's mix of functions, a host of other requirements, and its budget; and who may choose the other specialists that the architect has to work with the project, such as engineers, quantity surveyors, landscape architects, interior designers and many others. The client may also have their own foibles and prejudices to which the architect must respond. Third, the architect must decide what consideration to pay to other people who will be affected by the development: people (other than the client) who use it, who see it, who are shaded or obstructed by it, whose space is defined by it, or who experience the immediate impact of the traffic, the pollution or the noise it creates. In responding to these needs the architect will be guided and directed to some extent by the policy and regulations of central and local government, through design guidance, planning control, building regulations and environmental health legislation, for example. Processes of public consultation and participation may also help to set the scene. But much will depend on the architect's attitudes to these wider responsibilities. Fourth, the architect must decide what consideration to pay to people in other places who will be affected by what is designed: those who will suffer the more distant effects of the traffic, pollution, waste or noise it creates; those whose opportunities the development planner reduces; and those whose resources it consumes. Finally, the architect must decide what consideration to pay to people in the future. Once the building is complete, the architect's role ends. But at that moment the building's life begins. The building will decay, be altered, be damaged; its clients will sell up, move away or die; new uses may be found for it; its surroundings and context will change continuously. Decisions made by the architect will help to determine how well the building adapts, and how well it satisfies something beyond the designer's artistic intuition and the client's immediate needs. In the past two decades these fifth and sixth considerations have been labelled as the stuff of sustainability, but that is no more than a new word for the old question of whose interests a particular design serves. Architects make their choices in deciding the sort of professional practices they work for, the sort of clients they serve, and how they go about designing a particular building.

JOHN RUSKIN declares in *Lectures on Architecture and Painting*: 'No person who is not a great sculptor or painter can be an architect. If he is not a sculptor or painter, he can only be a builder.' Ambrose Bierce's *Devil's Dictionary* (published 1869–1906) defines an architect as 'One who drafts a plan of your house, and plans a draft of your money'. The word architect, dating from around 1555–65, derives from the Greek *arkhitekton*, which means leading or master builder. See also ARCHITECTURAL DESIGNER and ARCHI:TEKT.

architect-designed *adj.* An estate agent's description of any modern house of original and unusual design. The term was more commonly used when the public was less distrustful of architects.

architective A child engaged in finding out about architecture. The term was coined by organisers of an education project in the 1990s. The word combines *architecture* and *detective*.

architectonic *adj.* Relating to the technical means of supporting a building, as distinct from SCENOGRAPHIC.

architect-planner A person combining the skills of an architect and a planner. Such professionals were more common in the early days of planning, before the SCHUSTER REPORT of 1950 led to the training of planners with more concern for social sciences than for physical aspects of development. Concern about the decline of the architect-planner helped to inspire the urban design movement in the UK in the 1970s and '80s. By the 1990s an architect-planner would be more likely to call themselves an URBAN DESIGNER.

architectural (also environmental) possibilism
See ARCHITECTURAL DETERMINISM.

architectural (also environmental) probabilism
See ARCHITECTURAL DETERMINISM.

architectural The Architects' Registration Board, the statutory body that controls the use of the word ARCHITECT in the UK, asked the government in 2002 to give it control over the word architectural as well. The board explained that its move was a response to complaints about misleading advertisements.

architectural designer One who designs buildings but is not registered as an ARCHITECT, and so can not legally use the latter term. See also ARCHI:TEKT.

architectural determinism The belief that human behaviour can be influenced significantly by the form and configuration of buildings. According to Winston Churchill: 'There is no doubt whatever about the influence of architecture and structure upon human character and action. We make our buildings and afterwards they make us. They regulate the course of our lives' (quoted in Worpole, 2000). George Ferguson said as president of the Royal Institute of British Architects (echoing an earlier statement by CABE): 'You will enjoy life more if you are living in a well-designed place. Your children will learn better in a well-designed school. You'll get better quickly by being in a well-designed hospital' (quoted in Moye, 2003).

Quite what is the relationship between buildings and behaviour is controversial. The reality is no doubt that, if the physical form of a place does not actually make things happen, it does create the potential for things to happen, and it can prevent things from happening. People do not walk through walls. The relationship is also expressed in the terms *architectural (or environmental) possibilism* and *architectural (or environmental) probabilism*, meaning respectively that the physical environment creates opportunities for behaviours or that it makes certain behaviours probable. Human behaviour in cities is shaped by a complex combination of factors (see COMPLEXITY) and in most cases it is simplistic to consider any one of them in isolation.

Maurice Broady (1966) explains why in his view a belief in architectural determinism is unjustified. 'Architectural design, like music to a film, is complementary to human activity,' he writes. 'It does not shape it. Architecture, therefore, has no kind of magic by which men can be redeemed or society transformed. Its prime social function is to facilitate people's doing what they wish, or are obliged to do.' The architect achieves this, Broady suggests, by designing a physical structure that is able to meet known and predictable activities as conveniently and economically as possible. 'However, human behaviour is like runny jelly – not formless, but wobbly and changeable; and since he can not predict its changes, the designer also has to allow as best he can for such new demands as may come to be made of his buildings. More positively, perhaps, it is open to him to provide clues in the potential environment which he is creating which might serve as foci for these new activities or suggest them. He may even be able, as Mackintosh did for the modern movement, to set forth in design ideas and suggestions which may then directly influence a society's aesthetic and, through that, its whole *Weltanschauung* [worldview]. But even this is far from architectural determinism: and the conclusion, I believe, is that architects should be more modest and realistic about their ability to change the world through design.'

“ WE MAKE OUR BUILDINGS AND AFTERWARDS THEY MAKE US. THEY REGULATE THE COURSE OF OUR LIVES ”

Winston Churchill

Heidi de Mare and Anna Vos (1993) conclude from studies of urban rituals in Italy and the Netherlands that urban use 'is largely independent of the urban structure... The existence of an impressive public city life depends neither on the presence of spatial facilities, nor on the climate. The driving force behind public behaviour is generated elsewhere.' BILL HILLIER (1996) defines architectural determinism as the idea 'that buildings can have systematic effects on human behaviour, individually or collectively'. He argues that not only is architectural determinism false, but so is its opposite: the proposition that it does not matter at all how environments are designed since they are behaviourally neutral. Each, he suggests, follows from asking the wrong questions. He notes: 'Unlike environmental determinism, architectural determinism survived Darwin.'

The new urbanist ANDRES DUANY (2003) accuses architects who believe that physical design is incapable of affecting human behaviour of being 'seriously hampered' in their powers of observation. 'The manipulation of behavior in a modern shopping mall is a conclusive example of this phenomenon,' he writes. 'Architects often have difficulty allowing for [it], perhaps from inexperience in urbanism. Clearly, urbanism can affect behavior far more than an individual building.' In Duany's view, blindness to behavioural determinants is not physiological. 'It is ideological, and endemic only among the current architectural avant-garde. This was not always so. The potential to affect human behavior was one of the defining premises of the modern movement.' The adherents of that movement should have learnt from its disastrous failures, he suggests, that 'design has such a powerful affect on human behavior that it can transform, in very short order, a viable neighborhood society into a self-destructive one'. As they did not learn that lesson, 'this power, since so ably documented by Oscar Newman and William Whyte, was thus abdicated to the mall developers'. See NON-PLACE URBAN REALM and SPRAWLSCAPE.

architectural liaison officer Most people with the title are attached to police forces, ensuring that the police's perspective on CRIME PREVENTION is taken into account in the planning and design process.

architectural style Defined by the classical architect Robert Adam (b1948) (*Building Design*, 2003) as 'a combination of recognisable elements'. The architect William Lethaby (1857–1931) wrote: 'There are only two modern styles of architecture: one in which the chimneys smoke, and the other where they do not'.

architectural technologist A specialist in the technology of the design and construction of buildings. The final word in the name of the British Institute of Architectural Technologists (BIAT) was formerly *technicians*. In 2002 BIAT, grappling with the problem of professional demarcation, introduced a new technician membership grade. This, it said, was 'a necessary professional qualification to distinguish architectural technicians from architectural technologists'. BIAT explained: 'Architectural technologists provide architectural design services and solutions. They are specialists in the science of architecture, building design and construction, and form the link between concept and construction. They negotiate the construction project and manage the process from conception through to completion.' Architectural technicians, on the other hand, 'are specialists in the application of technology to architecture, building design and construction... working alongside fellow architectural technicians in support of architectural technologists, architects, engineers, surveyors and other professionals within the construction industry.' These definitions of 'technician' and 'technologist' seemed unlikely to dispel any confusion immediately. The new technician members of BIAT would be called 'technician members of the British Institute of Architectural Technologists'. But some of BIAT's existing members still called themselves technicians, from the days before the change to technologists. These technicians, as they called themselves, were members of BIAT, but not 'technician members'. BIAT warned that they might be required to stop calling themselves technicians.

architectural workshop The Newcastle Architecture Workshop was founded in 1977 with a brief to examine the architectural contribution to environmental education. It became a prototype for a national network of similar organisations, though none of the others survived the 1980s. A workshop was originally defined as being a physical entity or centre, being multi-disciplinary, having a staff and a structure or organisation, and carrying out specific tasks related to education, community involvement and community technical aid. Under the influence of the RIBA, the definition was widened in 1985 to refer not only to such a resource centre but also to 'an alliance of professionals who share the aims of built environment education'. The definition was further widened in the following year: 'The term architecture workshop does not necessarily imply a fixed physical form. An architecture workshop can be a gathering of adults or young people, or a combination of both. This gathering can last a couple of hours, days, weeks, or be designated to convene at regular intervals, or maintain a constant presence at some location.' A 1986 report listed 27 architectural workshops, without specifying how many were centres. A national review of the programme for the Department of the Environment (Newcastle Architecture Workshop, 1990) concluded that 'the term architectural workshop ultimately referred to a plethora of projects, alliances, summer school events and centres... There was confusion about the role of an architecture workshop, whether it related specifically to buildings and architecture, or whether it embraced a wider viewpoint, taking in the social and economic environment.' Only the original architectural workshop, in Newcastle, survived into the 1990s.

architectural zoo A collection of buildings with an assortment or confusion of designs.

architecture 1 The profession of designing buildings. **2** The style of buildings. **3** The design of interior and exterior space. **4** The design of the built environment. The University of Westminster's undergraduate prospectus for 2002 defined architecture as 'the design of the built world around us, ranging from urban design and rural landscape to interior design and furniture.' The architect Eero Saarinen defined architecture as 'the total of man's man-made physical surroundings' (quoted in Knevitt, 1986). WILLIAM MORRIS described architecture as 'the moulding and altering to human needs of the very face of the earth itself' (quoted in Briggs, 1962). **5** Buildings designed with a view to aesthetic appeal. Nikolaus Pevsner's (1943) opening words to his *An Outline of European Architecture* have become well known. 'A bicycle shed is a building; Lincoln Cathedral is a piece of architecture. Nearly everything that encloses space on a scale sufficient for a human being to move in is a building; the term architecture applies only to buildings designed with a view to aesthetic appeal' (see USELESSNESS). Roger Scruton (1979) argues that the architect Alberti, and other thinkers of the early Renaissance, would find inimicable 'the idea that there should be architecture on the one hand, conforming to aesthetic standards and setting itself the highest aims, and building on the other, a mere craftsman's activity of no aesthetic consequence, designed only to satisfy a function'.

LE CORBUSIER (in *Vers une Architecture*) defined architecture as 'the masterly, correct and magnificent play of masses brought together in light'. The architect BERNARD TSCHUMI says that 'architecture is not a knowledge of form; it's a form of knowledge', meaning that an architect's first step in designing a building should be to think about what will happen in it, not to determine its final form. The architectural writer Reyner Banham (1960) defines architecture as 'the ordering of space'. Aldo Rossi (1982) writes: 'Aesthetic intention and the creation of better surroundings for life are the two permanent characteristics of architecture.' The difficulty of communicating about architecture is reflected in a comment attributed to the musician Thelonius Monk: 'Talking about music is like dancing about architecture.'

In 1999 representatives of various professions lobbied the government over the name of the new body which would replace the Royal Fine Art Commission. Architects argued that it should be called the 'Architecture Commission'. Planners and urban designers, on the other hand, preferred the 'COMMISSION FOR ARCHITECTURE AND THE BUILT ENVIRONMENT'. Their preferences largely reflected their contrasting definitions of the word 'architecture', not different views on what the commission's brief should be. These differing perspectives often confuse discussions about design in an urban context. The architectural critic Charles Jencks explains it like this: 'The truth of city building is that good architecture and good urbanism are opposed... good architects, like good artists, are primarily concerned with the language of form, while good urbanists must have an equal commitment to the things that erode such a language: compromise, democracy, pluralism, entrepreneurial skills and patience.' Too many architects use that as an excuse for creating bad urbanism. After all, the design of any building requires the architect to balance any commitment to an artistic conception of form with other needs – those of the climate, the ground conditions, the client and the budget at the very least. The case of Portsmouth's Tricorn Shopping Centre points to the dangers. That complex, built in the 1960s in brutalist style, scored highly in opinion surveys of Britain's most unpopular buildings. Its architect argued against proposals to demolish it. 'The reason it has become a disaster,' he wrote, 'is not because of its architecture but because it was built in the wrong place at the wrong time...' The surgeon makes no apology for carrying out the right operation on the wrong patient. Oriol Bohigas (1999), the architect who conceived Barcelona's Spaces and Sculpture programme, argues that it is essential for architects to take a creative leap. 'Good architecture can not avoid being a prophecy, in conflict with actuality.' If

> **"ARCHITECTURE IS NOT A KNOWLEDGE OF FORM. IT'S A FORM OF KNOWLEDGE"**
> *Bernard Tschumi*

he is right, architecture will always be a risky business for those who practice it and those who live with it.

The term architecture is also used with an indefinite article, meaning a type of or approach to architecture. Example: 'We need an architecture that takes issues of sustainability seriously.'

architecture and planning centre A building or organisation which provides a focus for a range of activities and services (such as discussions, information, exhibitions, training, collaboration and professional services) relating to design and planning.

architecture for speed-reading Buildings designed to make an impression on passing motorists. The term was used by Chester A Liebs (Hall, 1998).

architecture intérieure des villes (French) INTERIOR URBAN DESIGN.

architecture of silence, the The architect James Dunnett's (2000) approving term for what he sees as LE CORBUSIER's vision of the city as, in Dunnett's words, 'a place of meditation, of cultural creativity inspired by the example of Cubist art'.

arcology A means of using technology and architecture to create urban habitats that conserve resources and blend harmoniously with the environment; the marriage of architecture and ECOLOGY. See ARCOSANTI.

Arcosanti A self-contained community and proposed megastructural city in the Arizona desert designed by architect PAOLO SOLERI, intended to demonstrate the principles of ARCOLOGY. Soleri explained in a 1993 interview (quoted in Pawley, 1998): 'In nature, as the organism evolves, it increases in complexity and also becomes more compact and miniaturized. The city too must become a more compact and miniaturized container for social, cultural and spiritual evolution. Nobody has ever understood that the megastructures we proposed at Arcosanti are in fact ministructures: that putting things together is a miniaturization, not a "megaturization". My solution is an urban implosion, rather than an explosion.'

area 1 A two-dimensional surface defined by an exact or approximate boundary, or having certain identifiable characteristics. **2** A sunken space next to a building which gives light to the basement; the front 'yard' in Georgian (and similar) terraced housing.

area action plan A DEVELOPMENT PLAN DOCUMENT that provides a planning framework for an area of significant change or conservation.

area appraisal An assessment of an area's land uses, built and natural environment, and social and physical characteristics.

area at risk from flooding An area that the ENVIRONMENT AGENCY advises is liable to river flooding on average at least once every 50 years.

area committee Set up by a council to devolve decision-making locally.

area development framework See URBAN DESIGN FRAMEWORK.

area improvement As early as 1959 Tom Brennan was advocating careful improvement as an alternative to comprehensive development in Glasgow. 'The corporation could let it be known that these areas were not being allowed to deteriorate until they joined the list of places awaiting demolition,' he wrote (Brennan, 1959). 'It should be made clear as forcefully as possible that, on the contrary, they are to be reconstructed and repaired; that they would be profitable districts in which to consolidate or expand business, that because their future was assured they would be good districts in which to try out new kinds of services or establish new ventures, and that they would be very pleasant places in which to live.' It was years before Brennan's advice (like that of PATRICK GEDDES decades earlier) was heeded in Glasgow or anywhere else.

area investment framework A statement of regeneration priorities submitted to a regional development agency for funding.

area of outstanding natural beauty (AONB) An area, designated under the National Parks and Access to the Countryside Act 1949 because of its outstanding scenic beauty, for whose protection a local authority has special responsibility. The primary purpose is to conserve and enhance the area's natural beauty, including flora, fauna, and geological and physiographic features.

area of special advertisement control Declared by a local authority to restrict the display of advertisements on the grounds of AMENITY or public safety, as defined in the Town and Country Planning (Control of Advertisement) Regulations 1992. The designation is subject to confirmation by the secretary of state.

area of special scientific interest The equivalent in Northern Ireland of a SITE OF SPECIAL SCIENTIFIC INTEREST in England and Wales.

area variance (US) A zoning variance permitting a departure from a zoning ordinance in relation to matters of layout.

areaway (US) A passageway between buildings; one giving access to a basement (often under – and lit by glass blocks in – the pavement/sidewalk). See also ALLEY.

arisings Defined by the Scottish Office (1996b) as the amount of waste created within a given area over time (for convenience in waste planning, usually a year) requiring recovery or final disposal by various means.

Richard Arkwright

Arkwright, Richard (Sir) (1732–92) See CROMFORD.

arm's length management organisation (ALMO) Manages a council's housing at arm's length, with the benefit of extra government funds.

Armadillo, The The local nickname for Glasgow's Clyde Auditorium, whose distinctive roof of eight overlapping aluminium-clad shells makes it resemble that animal. Designed by NORMAN FOSTER and Partners, it was built in 1997. See ZOOMORPHIC ARCHITECTURE.

Armageddon The city that the Bible (Revelation, chapter 16, verse 16) prophesies will be where the armies will gather for the final great battle at the end of time. The name is an English version of the Hebrew har-Megiddon. The ancient city was a great strategic importance, controlling a trade and military route between Egypt and Mesopotamia. It was fought over and ruined many times. The ruins, currently being excavated, are at Megiddo in northern Israel.

armature 1 (urban design) The spatial organisation of an area. Example: 'New York will endure even when other American cities like Los Angeles and Phoenix implode, because New York's physical armature is so sturdy' (James Howard Kunstler). **2** (architecture and construction) A supporting framework.

Arndale Centre The name of a series of town and city centre shopping centres built in the north of England by the Arndale company, mainly in the 1960s. The name came from the first name of one of the founders of the company, Arnold Hagenbach, and the surname of the other, Sam Chippendale. The Arndale company, founded in Bradford in 1950, began its life developing SHOPPING PARADES.

Arnstein's ladder A diagram showing a hierarchy of citizen participation, devised by Sherry Arnstein (1969) and published in the *Journal of the American Institute of Planners*. The ladder has eight rungs. They are, from the bottom, manipulation, therapy, informing, consultation, placation, partnership, delegated power, and citizen control. Arnstein classifies the lowest two rungs as non-participation, the next three as degrees of tokenism, and the top three as degrees of citizen power. The concept of the ladder has been influential in illuminating the nature of public participation, particularly in planning.

around the way (US) From the neighbourhood.

arrondissement (France) A subdivision of one of France's three largest cities, Paris, Lyons and Marseilles. Each *arrondissement* has its own mayor and council. Paris has 20 arrondissements, of which the 'First' is in the centre of the city.

art deco A style of design (in architecture, and the fine and applied arts) that evolved in the 1920s and '30s. It shows the influence of Egyptian, Greek, Roman, Mayan and Eastern design, sometimes with geometric forms, and streamlining and other industrial influences. The style was often used for hotels, theatres and office buildings. The Chrysler Building in New York, designed by William van Alen and completed in 1930, is a famous example. Miami Beach, Florida, has the Art Deco National Historic District, consisting of dozens of hotels and apartment buildings, mostly built in the 1930s. The furore over the unexpected demolition of the art deco FIRESTONE FACTORY in London in 1980 led to LISTING in the UK being extended to many more pre-1939 buildings. In the 1920s and '30s the style tended to be called *style moderne* or *modernistic*. *Art deco* was coined in the 1960s by the critic and historian Bevis Hillier, abbreviating the name of the Exposition Internationale des Arts Decoratifs Industriels et Modernes, held in Paris in 1925. The writer and critic Robert Grant (1998) suggests that art deco was the last genuine architectural and decorative style with its own vocabulary, order and discipline.

arterial road A main road leading into the heart of a town or city; one that links major destinations. Joseph Rykwert (2000) notes that the anatomical term was applied to transport in the nineteenth century. The idea that the chief function of roads and streets is the circulation of traffic became central to how engineers, among others, thought about towns and cities.

Article 4 direction A power available under the General Development Order 1988 (subject to the approval of the secretary of state) allowing a planning authority to restrict PERMITTED DEVELOPMENT rights. This extends planning control to certain kinds of development that do not normally require planning permission. Article 4 directions are most commonly used in conservation areas.

articulate To express clearly. The term is often used by architects in attempting to describe their buildings. Examples: a) 'The façade articulates the building's structure'. b) 'Architects, for the first time in several decades, are being solicited for their power to physically articulate new visions' (Rem Koolhaas). c) The architect Robert Venturi wrote in 1966 that he liked architectural elements that were 'distorted rather than "straightforward", ambiguous rather than "articulated" ' (quoted in Taylor, 1998).

The word comes from the Latin *articulare*, meaning to utter distinctly.

articulation Expression. See ARTICULATE.

artificer A person who is engaged in the construction of buildings.

artist in demolition BARON HAUSSMANN used this phrase to describe himself (Goodman, 1972).

Artists' Plan A plan for Paris, drawn up in 1797, on which HAUSSMANN later based his transformation of the city.

Artizans' and Labourers' Dwellings Act 1875 The Act, promoted by home secretary RA Cross, enabled unhealthy areas to be cleared as a whole, and the land acquired for redevelopment by other bodies, including housing trusts (Miller, 1989).

arts and crafts A design movement that began in the UK as a reaction to the de-humanising effects of nineteenth century industrialisation and flourished between around 1875–1915. Arts and crafts designers and architects advocated high standards of craftsmanship and the use of natural materials.

arts, culture and entertainment (ACE) A generic term (used in planning, for example) for activities that contribute to intellectual, artistic and social life.

Arup, Ove (Sir) (1895–1988) Engineer. Arup worked closely with many leading architects (initially BERTHOLD LUBETKIN and the Tecton team) and was responsible for making Utzon's Sydney Opera House buildable. The firm he founded has remained famous for inter-disciplinary working.

asbestos Once widely used as a building material, asbestos has been known since at least 1898 to present a major risk to the health of people working with it or being exposed to airborne fibres from damaged pieces of the material. Blue and brown asbestos have been banned in Great Britain since 1985 and white asbestos since 1999. In the UK around 3,000 people a year (mainly building workers, carpenters, plumbers and electricians) die from the effects of asbestos. The need to remove asbestos or to make it safe has had a significant impact on the cost of refurbishing buildings constructed between 1950 and 1980.

Asbury, Herbert See THE GANGS OF NEW YORK.

a-schematic See URBAN SCHEMA.

Ashfield, Lord See ALBERT STANLEY.

ashlar Masonry made of square-cut stones.

aspatial community of interest People with common interests who do not live or work in the same place as one another.

aspect The direction a building, building façade or slope faces. Example: 'The house has a southern aspect.'

asphalt A street paving material made of bitumen and sand (or stone dust) aggregate.

asphalt literature A name given by some of its exponents to some writing on urban themes, produced in Berlin in the 1920s. This verse by Frank Warschauer is characteristic: 'Man without stars, you, asphalt-faced/ how you carry the greasy evenings around you,/ grey mist, stale air, petrol's corroding stream,/ tar fumes, stink of filth and decay from basements,/ night without wind and day without light,/ away,/ man without stars, you, asphalt-faced' (quoted in Willett, 1978).

aspirational space The area or areas to which a person would like to move.

aspirational target A target (for the proportion of development to be on BROWNFIELD sites, for example) which central or local government finds expedient to adopt, even though it knows it is almost certainly impossible to achieve.

Assault on Precinct 13 A film, directed by John Carpenter, set in an abandoned police station in the gang-ridden urban wastelands of east Los Angeles. See also ESCAPE FROM NEW YORK.

assemblage (US) A bulk sale of the properties in an area, negotiated between owners and a developer. Usually the sellers get relatively high prices, and the developer acquires the land relatively quickly and easily for redevelopment.

asset base The strengths of an area prior to a regeneration project.

asset sale The sale of public assets, such as land or housing, to the private sector.

asset-based development Carried out usually by a community-based organisation by making use of assets such as land or buildings.

assimilation 1 The incorporation of a minority group into society. **2** The absorbtion of pollutants.

assimilative capacity The ability of an ecosystem to absorb pollutants harmlessly.

Assist An organisation formed in the Govan area of Glasgow in the early 1970s to promote and support the improvement of tenement housing. Assist grew from an architectural student project by Raymond Young. The council's approach to the new concept of improving tenements at that time was to rehouse the tenants, carry out the work, and let the flats to new tenants. Young, supported by his tutor Jim Johnson, wanted to improve the homes for the existing tenants. Coping with a variety of ownerships, needs and preferences depended on the flexibility that Assist provided by supporting the residents' own efforts with a free technical service, operating from a local shopfront office. Assist's success led to a major programme of community-based housing associations improving tenements throughout Glasgow and further afield.

assisted area A region designated for aid to industry by the UK government on the basis of unemployment and other economic criteria.

Association of London Government Represents the capital's 33 councils. It funds voluntary groups and administers the travel pass scheme allowing elderly people to travel free on public transport.

assured tenancy Providing tenants with less legal protection than a secured tenancy, they are commonly used by housing associations.

asylum-without-walls See SERVICE-DEPENDENT GHETTO.

at least it's not Basildon An unofficial public relations slogan for Liverpool – studiously avoiding hyperbole – jokingly thought up by some employees of the city council in the 1980s in response to the GLASGOW'S MILES BETTER campaign. Basildon, a NEW TOWN in Essex, was no doubt seen as the epitome of a place without history or distinctive character – both of which Liverpool, for all its social and economic problems, has in plenty. See also BOOSTERISM and THE WORLD IN ONE CITY.

at sixes and sevens In disorder. The phrase arises from a long-running dispute about the order of precedence for the City of London's Livery Companies. It was finally settled in 1515 by agreeing that the Merchant Taylors and the Skinners would take sixth or seventh place in alternate years, which they have done ever since.

Atget, Eugène (1856–1927) Photographer. He is remembered for his photographs of Paris.

at-grade junction A road junction at which at least one road meets another on the same level.

Athens The world's first true GLOBAL CITY, according to Sir Peter Hall (1998).

Athens Charter 1 The manifesto of modernist architecture and town planning by CIAM, written on an Aegean cruise in 1933. **2** The Athens Charter for the Restoration of Historic Monuments of 1931 set the scene for international agreements on heritage practice and law. See HISTORIC MONUMENT, KRAKOV CHARTER and VENICE CHARTER.

Athens of the North 1 Edinburgh. Example: 'Tourists want to come to the Athens of the north, rather than the HIV capital of Europe' (Welsh, 1996). A character in Tom Stoppard's 1972 play *Jumpers* describes Edinburgh as 'the Reykjavik of the South'. **2** Belfast (so called in a BBC radio programme in 2002). **3** Manchester, according to Benjamin Disraeli. He wrote in his novel *Coningsby*: 'What art is to the ancient world, science is to the modern. Rightly understood, Manchester is as great a human exploit as Athens.' See MODERN ATHENS, and compare VENICE OF THE NORTH.

> **"WHAT ART IS TO THE ANCIENT WORLD, SCIENCE IS TO THE MODERN. RIGHTLY UNDERSTOOD, MANCHESTER IS AS GREAT A HUMAN EXPLOIT AS ATHENS."**
>
> *Benjamin Disraeli*

Atlantis The capital city of the continent of the same name which supposedly sank under the Atlantic thousands of years ago. Plato was the first to tell its story. Spiro Kostof (1991) cites Plato's Atlantis as the classical source for the west's conception of a city and its territory as a series of concentric rings. The central acropolis was surrounded by five circles of land and water. See also THE ORDERING OF TOWNS.

A-Town Atlanta, Georgia.

atrium A covered space, usually several storeys high, within a building. Kostof (1992) cites Crystal Court in the IDS Centre, Minneapolis (1968–73) as one of the earliest examples. They have since become a common feature of commercial buildings. The Latin word atrium derives from *ater* meaning black: the atrium of a Roman house was a central family room whose walls were blackened by the smoke of cooking fires (Hall, 1998).

audit An assessment of the extent to which conditions conform to specified standards. Common subjects of audits include accessibility, child safety, crime and disorder, cycling, gender, pedestrians, public transport, local environmental quality, pavement management and road safety. See also ACCESS AUDIT and PEDESTRIAN AUDIT.

Auld Reekie (Scots) Edinburgh. The phrase means *old smokey*. Compare BIG SMOKE and THE SMOKE and see also MODERN ATHENS.

aural privacy Freedom from unwanted NOISE.

Aurelius, Marcus See TIME.

Auspasia A fictional city whose inhabitants are the world's most talkative. It is described in Georges Duhamel's *Letters from Auspasia* (1922).

Austin, Alice Constance See LLANO DEL RIO.

autarkic Self-sufficient, as in an *autarkic house*. See also AUTONOMOUS HOUSE.

autarky Self-sufficiency.

authenticity The quality of a place where things are what they seem: where buildings that look old are old, and where the social and cultural values that the place seems to reflect did actually shape it. The 2000 KRAKOW CHARTER states that 'the purpose of conservation of historic buildings and monuments... is to maintain their authenticity and integrity'. The charter defines authenticity as 'the sum of substantial, historically ascertained characteristics: from the original up to the current state, as an outcome of the various transformations that have taken place'. Robert Adam (2003) comments: 'An existing building or place is, by [that] definition, only authentic up to the moment someone identifies it as being of worth. Anything that happens after that is not authentic.' The design guide for the PRINCE OF WALES' town extension at POUNDBURY notes that 'traditionally, roofs in the district were often provided with two courses or so of heavy, split stone tiles at the eaves', presumably as a precaution against the high winds. 'This would be an attractive and authentic detail to reproduce [in the new building]'. In this case the detail is authentic in that it was a local tradition, but inauthentic to the extent that its use today is not for the original practical reason. Compare RETRO DESIGN and URBAN FALSE MEMORY SYNDROME, and see FACADISM, NEIGHBOURHOOD, OZZIE AND HARRIET, RICHMOND RIVERSIDE and WILLIAMSBURG.

autobarn Defined by the humorist Ian Martin (2002) as 'a unique home in a rural location equipped for home/office use, suiting early retirers; a barn conversion designed by local architects to "blend in" with neighbouring converted barns'.

automobile city A city (or part of one) where the car is the dominant mode of movement. Compare WALKING CITY.

automopolis A city dominated by the motor car. Example: '3,400 die on the roads [in the UK] every year, but both politicians and citizens shruggingly accept this as the price of living in a modern automopolis'.

autonomous house One that draws only to a small degree, if at all, on mains services such as water, heat and power. See also AUTARKIC.

autonomy Self-government; self-determination. PAUL GOODMAN wrote: 'The chief principle of anarchism is not freedom but autonomy, the ability to initiate a task and do it in one's own way' (quoted in Ward, 1991). See also URBAN AUTONOMY.

Autopia An exhibit by General Motors at the 1939 World's Fair showing a future made for the car.

autopia One of the FOUR ECOLOGIES of LOS ANGELES identified by Reyner Banham (1973). He saw the city's freeway system in its totality as 'now a single comprehensible place, a coherent state of mind, a complete way of life.'

autoport A term used by LE CORBUSIER for large underground car parks.

autoroute (France) A MOTORWAY.

available See CRAVED.

ave (US) An avenue.

avenue 1 A wide street. **2** A road lined with trees. **3** A drive leading to a country house. The word comes from the Latin *advenire*, meaning to come to. See also ALLEE.

avenue office building (US) A conventional office building fronting a mixed-use thoroughfare, with parking at the rear of the building rather than being associated with a specialised office park.

Avenue, The Greater London has 70 examples of this street name, and a further 38 of Avenue Road. The Merseyside area has eight examples of The Avenue, two of them in Liverpool. Leeds has six, and Glasgow none. See also ACACIA ROAD.

Averlino, Antonio See SFORZINDA.

Avola A new town in Sicily, designed by the architect Fra Angelo Italia to a hexagonal grid plan. It replaced the nearby hill town of Avola, destroyed in an earthquake.

award-winning *adj.* A term commonly used in the media in an ironic sense to describe a building suffering irredeemable failure due to faulty design or construction. See, for example, PRUITT-IGOE.

awareness space The parts of a town or city that a particular person knows about.

awareness-raising day A day devoted to a range of activities aimed at interesting the people of an area in planning and design issues as part of a programme of public participation.

away The architect and environmentalist William McDonough has commented: 'There used to be something called "away". We used to throw things "away", but now we all know that whatever we discard has consequences. We can't throw things "away" any more' (Williams, 2002).

axial map A diagram showing the fewest and longest straight lines which pass through all the CONVEX SPACES of a settlement (Hillier, 1988).

axial plan A layout based on long, straight streets.

axiality The quality of being based on an axial plan.

axis A line about which a layout (of a place, building or part of a building) is arranged. LE CORBUSIER wrote in *Vers une Architecture*: 'An axis is perhaps the first human manifestation; it is the means of every human act. The toddling child moves along an axis, the man striving in the tempest of life traces for himself an axis. The axis is the regulator of architecture.'

Carol Ann Duffy

A–Z A street atlas. The London A–Z street atlas was compiled by Phyllis Pearsall in 1936. Pearsall, a bohemian painter and writer (who had once shared a boarding house with the novelist Vladimir Nabokov), roamed the streets for 18 hours a day checking the details. A–Z street atlases are now published for most cities and larger towns in the UK (see also FINGER-PRINTING).

In her poem 'The Map-Woman', published in 2002, Carol Ann Duffy describes a woman whose 'skin was a map of the town/ where she'd grown from a child... birthmark, tattoo – / the A–Z street-map grew, a precise second skin,/ broad if she binged, thin when she slimmed,/ a précis of where to end or go back or begin.' Years later the map-woman returns, 'thinking/ she knew the place like the back of her hand,/ but something was wrong. She got lost in arcades,/ in streets with new names, in precincts/ and walkways, and found what was familiar/ was only a façade.' That night, as she sleeps, 'her skin sloughed like a snake's'. In the morning she lays out the map – 'her own small ghost' – on the floor, and leaves it, and the town, behind her. Not quite, though: 'deep in the bone/ old streets tunnelled and burrowed, hunting for home.'

B

Babel 1 A great and diverse city. **2** A city doomed by its sinfulness. Peter Ackroyd (2000) writes that the image of the city as a kind of hell 'became a cliché in the poetry of the nineteenth century; its citizens resembled a "Satanic throng" while the atmosphere was that of a "brown Phitonian gloom". The sulphurous smell of coal dust and smoke provoked images of Satan, while the manifold and manifest vices of the city represented all the works of the devil incarnate. Images of Babel and Sodom abound...'. See BABYLON.

baby boom A peak in the birth rate. One occurred in the UK between around 1948 and 1954.

baby boomer A person born in a baby boom; a member of a *boomer generation*.

Babylon 1 A great and diverse city. This use was common in the nineteenth century (when BABEL and Babylon seem to have been used interchangeably). The novelist Henry James wrote at Christmas 1876 from London of the 'darkness, solitude and sleet in midwinter' within a 'murky Babylon' (quoted in Ackroyd, 2000). NEW BABYLON was a vision of the urbanism of the future Constant Nieuwenhuys. The German painter Max Beckmann, arriving at New York in 1947 to live in America after a grim wartime exile in Amsterdam, wrote in his diary: 'Arrival in the misty dawn. Manhattan peopled with sleepy giants in damp fog... Yes, New York is truly wonderful, only it stinks of burnt fat like the roasted enemy caught by some savage tribe. All the same – fantastic, utterly fantastic – Babylon is a kindergarten by comparison and the tower of Babylon has here become the mass erection of a monstrous (senseless?) will. So I like it.' **2** A city devoted to conspicuous luxury, and sometimes wickedness and corruption. This use was common in the middle ages. Example: 'London is pre-eminently the Wicked City – the Modern Babylon' (from 1938). The composer Charles Ives (1874–1954) called Manhattan 'Babylon' and 'hell-hole', though he celebrated its cacophonous vitality in his Fourth Symphony. The architect Ian Buruma suggested that the destruction of the WORLD TRADE CENTER in 2001 was seen by America's critics as representing 'an act of divine punishment equivalent to that meted out to Babylon' (quoted in Melhuish, 2002). **3** The ancient capital of Babylonia in Mesopotamia, rebuilt after 689 BC by Nebuchadnezzar II. Its hanging gardens were one of the Seven Wonders of the World. The Bible records Babylon as having been destroyed as a punishment for the evil of its people. The tower of Babel may have been located there. **4** A village in New York State, USA. **5** A Rastafarian term for the bureaucratic, legalistic and oppressive structures of western society.

Babylon is the Greek form of *Babel*. The word meant 'gate of the gods'. It was here that the gods were supposed to come down to earth (Smith, 1974). Babylon sounds like the Hebrew for 'mixed up'.

back entry See ENTRY.

back jigger (Liverpool) A back ALLEY (see that entry for regional variants). See JIGGER.

back opening (Suffolk) An ALLEY (see that entry for regional variants). Compare OPENING.

back streets 1 The smaller residential streets behind the main streets of a town or city. **2** Slums, or near-slums. Example: 'His mother was determined that being brought up in the back streets would not handicap him for life.'

back yard See also CASSIE.

back-double See TURNING.

background building A building that is not a LANDMARK or OBJECT BUILDING. Andrew Saint has written: 'Until the nineteenth century, [houses and flats] were interspersed only occasionally with grander forms and scales of building. A difficulty today is that, especially in major city centres, we have lost the sense that most buildings should be ordinary. We want incidence, sensation, individualism. The logical outcome of this is incoherence.' See also PROSE.

backland development The development of sites at the back of existing development, such as back gardens.

back-to-backs Small TERRACED HOUSES built in double rows, with their back and side walls being party walls (except at the ends of the terrace), so that only the front elevation has a door and windows. The term is sometimes used, confusingly, to refer to THROUGH-TERRACE houses. The first recorded, consciously-designed, pair of back-to-backs was built in Bermondsey, London, in 1706. Back-to-backs were particularly common in certain northern cities. Health reformers excoriated them because of the lack of through ventilation. Though building them was illegal in Manchester after 1844 and in Liverpool after 1861, they continued to be a common type of house in Leeds, where they were being built as late as 1937 (Burnett, 1986). Restrictions on building back-to-backs were lifted by the Thatcher government in 1980. Some builders took advantage of the relaxation by building groups of very small STARTER HOMES.

Bacon, Edmund Urban planner and architect. He worked as executive director of the Philadelphia Planning Commission for the reforming mayor RICHARDSON DILWORTH and until he retired in 1970. His influential book *Design of Cities* was published in 1968. See URBAN DESIGN.

Bacon, Francis See THE NEW ALTANTIS.

bad-neighbour use One likely to be offensive to its neighbours due to matters such as noise, smell and traffic.

Baedeker raids Air raids by German bombers on English historic towns, chosen for psychological impact rather than strategic importance, carried out in 1942 in retaliation for British raids on German cities. The Germans picked their targets with the help of *Baedeker*, a series of guidebooks published originally by Karl Baedeker (1801–59). See also JOHN BETJEMAN.

bag lady A homeless woman who carries her possessions around with her in bags. See VAGRANT.

baile (Scots, pronounced bailey) A town.

bailiff A person who acts to enforce court orders, including evicting squatters and taking away the goods of people who have not paid their rent. The UK Lord Chancellor's Department announced in 2003 that the post was to be renamed *enforcement agent*. The term bailiff derives from the Latin for 'carrier'.

Baines, Frank (Sir) (1879–1933) Architect. Working for the Office of Works in the 1914–18 war, he designed WELL HALL in Woolwich and ROE GREEN VILLAGE at Hendon.

Baixa, Lisbon See Marquis of POMBAL.

Baker, Kenneth (Lord Baker) (b1934) Politician. See SECRETARY OF STATE.

fess A balance in age structure and/or social class among the people living in an area.

balkanisation The division of an urban area into a large number of local government units. The analogy is with the many historically warring states in the Balkans. Also called *metropolitan fragmentation*.

ballet See CHOREOGRAPHY

Ballungsräume (German) A CONURBATION.

BANANA Acronym for 'build absolutely nothing anywhere near anything'. NIMBYISM taken to absurdity. The term originated in the USA.

banana, the (also the blue banana) The roughly banana-shaped, urbanised region variously described as encompassing London and Milan, or Cardiff, Birmingham and Milan.

banking Apart from PROSTITUTION, virtually the only function of a modern city, according to FRANK LLOYD WRIGHT (Twombly, 1973).

banlieue (French) Suburbs. Since many French cities have very large working class housing estates (*grand ensembles*) as their suburbs, the term carries connotations similar to INNER CITY in England. This is the cause of much confusion. See also FAUBOURG and QUARTIERS DE BANLIEUE.

banlieuesard (French) A suburbanite.

Barbican, The A major mixed-use development in the City of London, comprising more than 2,000 flats for 6,500 people built in the 1960s, and the Barbican Arts Centre, completed in the 1980s. The scheme, designed by Chamberlin Powell and Bon, is notable for its formal planning, hard landscaping, large secluded garden courtyard and three 40-storey residential towers of distinctive rectangular plan. Unfortunately the development forms a large specialised ENCLAVE, disrupting and cut off from the network of surrounding streets, with pedestrian access only at second floor level, designed as part of the City of London's only partially completed aerial pedestrian network.

Barbon, Nicholas (c1640–1698) Builder, developer, insurer and economist. Barbon began his career by rebuilding his father's house, which had been burnt in the Great Fire of 1666. As a major developer of streets and squares in London he standardised systems of mass-produced building. The building of Red Lion Square provoked a pitched battle with the students of Gray's Inn. KARL MARX later drew on his work as an economist.

Barcelona The capital of Catalonia, Spain, has become one of Europe's most celebrated examples of design-led regeneration. An early major expansion of Barcelona was based on the city's preparations for the 1888 World Exposition. Streets and boulevards were laid out on a grid proposed by the planner and engineer ILDEFONS CERDÁ thirty years earlier. Street blocks with chamfered corners created its characteristic public spaces where streets cross. The city's recent resurgence began with a determination, at the end of decades of Franco's dictatorship in 1976, to celebrate the city's political, cultural and civic identity, and the power of its local neighbourhood organisations. An energy and enthusiasm for new design reflected a feeling of release after the long neglect of urban and Catalan culture.

A major programme of urban design was an important part of the city's strategy. The mayor, Pasqual Maragall, identified the aim as being 'to recover the lost dignity of our urban landscape, and create an atmosphere of controversy and discussion in a Catalan society threatened by conformism, ideological uniformism and the fear of confrontation'. A series of projects created 160 small public spaces. Maragall wrote: 'Cities do not live solely by a sort of liturgy of remembrance. For this reason we preferred to run the risk of creating spaces that bore a strong personal stamp of their authors, rather than maintaining the environmental mediocrity that we had inherited'. The city planning department was headed by JOAN BUSQUETS. The architect and urban designer Oriol Bohigas, who conceived Barcelona's Spaces and Sculpture programme, describes his approach to regenerating a city. 'Start with the open spaces and not the buildings,' he wrote. 'In rehabilitating the empty spaces, which are potentially social spaces, and in giving them a distinct, formal identity, you have a quicker and more direct influence on the neighbourhood.'

The programme's overall impact on the city and its international image has been overwhelmingly positive. But some of the new parks and spaces soon required major remedial work. In most cases it was not hard to find the reason for the failure: factors such as an intended use not materialising, inadequate maintenance, insufficiently robust materials, and failure to design something that would mature over time rather than have an instant impact. The renewal programme was given added impetus by Barcelona being chosen to host the 1992 Olympics. The facilities for the games were built where they could contribute to regeneration. The Olympic village, for example, was built on derelict industrial land by the sea. Barcelona has received international recognition for its efforts, and in 1999 became the first city to be awarded the RIBA's Royal Gold Medal for Architecture.

Bohigas (1999) summed up how he saw Barcelona's

"PUBLIC SPACE IS THE CITY"
Oriol Bohigas

approach: 'a) The city is a political phenomenon. In Barcelona it was the continuity of a common ideology and programmes carried out by the city's three socialist mayors that made possible the coherent transformation of the city. b) The city is the indispensable physical domain for the modern development of a coherent commonality. It is not the place of the individual, but the place of the individuals who together make up a community. c) Public space is the city. d) The city provides the enriching presence of tensions and chance. e) The city should be understood as the sum of its neighbourhoods or identifiable fragments. f) The space of collective life must not be a residual space but a planned and meaningful space, designed in detail, to which the various public and private constructions must be subordinated. If this hierarchy is not established the city ceases to exist, as can be seen in so many suburbs and peripheral zones of European cities which have turned away from their urban values. g) The city must be legible. If the citizens do not have the sense of being carried along by spaces that communicate their identity and enable them to predict itineraries and convergences, the city loses a considerable part of its capacity in terms of information and accessibility. In other words, it ceases to be a stimulus to collective life. h) The urbanistic instruments for the reconstruction and the extension of a city can not be limited to normative and quantitative general plans. It is necessary to go further and give concrete definition to the urban forms. A series of one-off urban projects will have to be imposed. It is necessary to design the public space – that is, the city – point by point, area by area, in architectural terms. i) If architecture is an art, a cultural effort, it must be an act of innovation towards the future, an opposition to established customs. Good architecture can not avoid being a prophecy, in conflict with actuality.'

bareland condominium (US) A vacant piece of land that is subdivided.

Barlow Commission The Royal Commission on the Geographical Distribution of the Industrial Population. Chaired by Sir Anderson Montague Barlow, it reported in 1940. The Commission was concerned by 'the continued drift of the population to London and the Home

Counties', and by what it saw as the capital's excessive size and concentration of talent. Its recommendations included a more effective planning system and planned decentralisation to new and expanded towns.

Barnard, George (1819–1902) Photographer. He recorded the devastation of cities in the American Civil War.

Barnett, Canon Samuel Augustus (1844–1913) Social reformer, founder of the university SETTLEMENT Toynbee Hall in London's east end, advocate of 'practicable socialism' and author of THE IDEAL CITY. He was the husband of HENRIETTA BARNETT.

Henrietta Barnett

Barnett, Henrietta (Dame) (1851–1936) A cosmetics heiress turned social worker and social reformer, she founded HAMPSTEAD GARDEN SUBURB.

barong-barong See SQUATTER SETTLEMENT.

baroque Spiro Kostof (1991) identifies some of the characteristics of the baroque aesthetic in urban design (as revealed in the work of PIERRE CHARLES L'ENFANT): a) A total, grand spacious urban ensemble pinned on focal points distributed throughout the city. b) These focal points suitably plotted in relation to the drama of the topography, and linked with each other by swift, sweeping lines of communication. c) A concern with the landscaping of the major streets. d) The creation of vistas. e) Public spaces as settings for monuments. f) Dramatic effects, as with waterfalls and the like. g) All of this superimposed on a closer-grained fabric for daily, local life. Kostof traces baroque planning to at least as far back as the Hellenistic city of PERGAMON (Turkey) in the third and second centuries before Christ.

baroque-tech An architectural style exuberantly expressing hi-tech elements. Hugh Pearman (2002) has used the term to describe RICHARD ROGERS' Lloyd's of London building.

barraca See SQUATTER SETTLEMENT.

Barragán, Luis (1902–88) Mexican architect. He designed the unbuilt satellite city of LOMAS VERDES.

barrage A structure built across a river to store water, control flooding, generate electricity or improve the setting of a city.

Barratt, Lawrie (Sir) (b1927) House builder. His company Barratt Homes became one of the UK's largest house builders in the 1970s. MARGARET THATCHER bought a new Barratt house in a gated development in Dulwich in the 1980s when she was prime minister, though she slept there for no more than a couple of nights.

Barrattification (also Barrattisation) Covering an area with the standard products of volume house-builders (such as Barratt Homes).

barriada See SQUATTER SETTLEMENT.

barrier An obstacle to movement. Identifying barriers is part of LYNCHIAN ANALYSIS.

barrio (Spanish) Neighbourhood. See SQUATTER SETTLEMENT.

basecase What is expected to happen if no specific regeneration initiative is carried out.

baseline indicator A measure of conditions at the outset, against which subsequent progress can be measured.

baseline study Carried out at the start of a project as a basis for monitoring subsequent progress. See also BENCHMARKING.

basis point One hundredth of one per cent. The measure is used in calculating interest (in property development, for example).

Bassett, Edward M (1863–1948) Lawyer and public servant. He has been credited with the invention of ZONING, developing the first comprehensive zoning ordinance in the US to regulate the use, height and area of buildings in 1916. He has been called the Father of City Planning (Goodman, 1972) and is said to have coined the term FREEWAY. See also HIGHWAY and PARKWAY.

basti See BUSTEE.

bastide A medieval French new town. The term comes from the Latin *terrae bastitae*, meaning a rural landholding with one or more buildings, by way of the medieval French *bastir*, to build.

Bata See ZLIN.

Bath The entire city is a WORLD HERITAGE SITE. It has been noted since Roman times for its medicinal springs and is famed for its eighteenth-century architecture. The Georgian city was developed in around 70 years, beginning in 1730. 'John Wood the elder conceived what we should now call an "urban plan",' writes

Sophie Jeffreys (1998). After his death in 1754 his son and other local architects continued to design in the same spirit. Jeffreys notes: 'The elder Wood's original conception included showpieces: a Forum, a Circus, promenades, assembly rooms, squares and churches that were connected by terraced streets providing accommodation for visitors, artisans and tradesmen.' Amenities such as schools, the hospital and the prison were located centrally. 'The plan was truly urban and included no "green space" within the city. There were neither turfed squares nor city parks. Today people admire the tall plane trees in the centre of the Circus that cast their shadow on the grassy cushion beneath them. Originally, however, the centre was cobbled and Wood envisaged an equestrian monument of George II as the centrepiece. Bath, as Wood conceived it, was built on the premiss that human beings are urban in their nature and content to dwell in purely architectural surroundings.' See JOHN WOOD.

BATNEEC Acronym for *best available technology not entailing excessive cost*. The concept is used in environmental protection legislation.

bats These flying mammals are common in urban areas, though their habitats are under threat. All bats and their roosts in the UK are protected under national and international legislation. Building works need a licence if bats are present. It is often necessary to check old buildings for the presence of bats before conservation work is carried out.

Battery Park City A huge office development in lower Manhattan, New York, designed by Cesar Pelli and built in the 1980s. Battery Park itself was built on land reclaimed from the Hudson River, using material excavated for the foundations of the WORLD TRADE CENTER, destroyed by terrorist action in September 2001.

Bau (German) Building.

Baudelaire, Charles (1821–67) Poet and critic. See FLÂNEUR.

Bauer, Catherine (1905–1964) Urban planner, housing specialist, writer and teacher. In the 1930s she was influential in shaping legislation on public housing in the USA. Bauer was a close collaborator of LEWIS MUMFORD, who wrote in 1958 that she had 'openly declared that she would never have promoted public housing if she could have anticipated that it would become the monstrous caricature that it has actually become' (Hughes, 1971). She sometimes used her husband's name, calling herself Catherine Bauer Wurster.

Baufläche (German) A development zone

Bauforum (German) Several Hamburg Bauforum events (also known as city development forums) have been held since 1985 to generate ideas on major development areas in the city. Typically, 15 teams of architects explore different approaches to the same problem, in public, over four or five days. Open brainstorming sessions help to formulate ideas and concepts before overall strategies and individual projects are defined. Each event is followed by an architectural competition for particular sites.

Baugenehmigung (German) Building or planning permission.

Baugesetzbuch (German) A building code.

Baugrenze (German) A set-back line.

Baugrundstück (German) A development site.

Bauhaus, The A school of art that operated first in Weimar then in Dessau, Germany, in 1919–33. Extending the principles of the arts and crafts movement, the Bauhaus pioneered modernist design and architecture. It was closed by the Nazis in 1933. The German name means House of Building. Robert Hughes (1980) explains that the name 'carried intentional overtones of the Bauhütten or lodges where, in the middle ages, masons and designers at work on mediaeval cathedrals were housed'. Walter Gropius (1965, quoted in Kolb, 1990) later explained that, according to the Bauhaus educational programme, a modern building 'must be true to itself, logically transparent and virginal of lies and trivialities, as befits a direct affirmation of our contemporary world of mechanisation and rapid transit.' It must represent 'not the personal whims of a handful of architects avid for innovation at all cost, but simply the inevitable logical product of the intellectual, social and technical conditions of our age.' The modern building must be free of reference to historical styles. 'A breach has to be made with the past, which allows us to envisage a new aspect of architecture corresponding to the technical civilization of the age we live in; the morphology of dead style has been destroyed; and we are returning to honesty of thought and feeling.'

Baulinie (German) A building line.

Bauman, Zygmunt (b1925) Sociologist. See SOCIAL EXCLUSION.

Bauordnungen (German) Building regulations.

Bay City (also Bay) San Francisco.

Bayko A children's construction toy, developed by Charles Plimpton in the 1930s and popular in the 1950s. Plastic (originally bakelite) elements, held together by metal rods and ties, were used to build models of suburban-style houses with brick walls, PEBBLEDASHED bays and tiled roofs.

Bazalgette, Joseph (Sir) (1819–91) Civil engineer. He designed and built London's drainage system in 1845–75 (using 318 million bricks, he estimated).

B-boys New York street dancers who developed BREAK DANCING in the 1970s. The name is said variously to stand for *beat boys*, *boogie-boys* and *break-boys*. See also HIP HOP, KOOL HERC and RAP.

BDAMPFISHES (or DAMPFISHES) A mnemonic used in assessing historic buildings for LISTING. The letters stand for *B*rief description (or *B*uilding type), *D*ate,

Architect, Materials, Plan, Façade, Interiors, Subsidiary features, History, Extras and Sources. An earlier version did not have the B.

beacon council A local authority that is demonstrating excellence and innovation as part of the government's Beacon Council scheme.

Beacontree (pronounced *beckontree*) A suburban housing estate built between 1921 and 1934 in Essex by the London County Council. Housing 90,000 residents, it was the world's largest planned suburb. To FJ OSBORN, Beacontree represented much of what the garden city movement was opposed to. Osborn (1926), who had spent six years developing Welwyn Garden City, expressed his frustration at the movement's lack of progress. 'We pet our two ewe lambs [Letchworth and Welwyn garden cities] in public with almost indecent fondness, but we show no realisation that they are already threatened with old-maidish sterility. Are we not too large-minded and tolerant of housing schemes and garden suburbs and town planning schemes which contradict our central ideas? Beacontree, for instance, should send a thrill of horror into the marrow of our bones. Arterial road schemes, the whole point of which is that they will enable London to spread from Hunstanton to Peacehaven, are held up to admiration by their creators as triumphs of planning. Our advocacy of new towns failed in its endeavour to resist the pressure of the great municipalities to increase their size and rateable value.'

Bean Town Boston, Massachusetts, so called as the home of Boston baked beans.

Beaulieu A walled town in New England described in Ralph Adams Cram's *Walled Towns* (1919). The town is free of motor cars and each house has a garden of an acre or more. Land owners who neglect their land pay extra tax.

beautility The marriage of beauty and utility, coined by an advocate of the CITY BEAUTIFUL MOVEMENT (Cullingworth, 1997).

> **" WHEN I'M WORKING ON A PROBLEM, I NEVER THINK ABOUT BEAUTY. I THINK ONLY HOW TO SOLVE THE PROBLEM. BUT WHEN I AM FINISHED, IF THE SOLUTION IS NOT BEAUTIFUL, I KNOW IT IS WRONG "**
>
> *Buckminster Fuller*

beauty The quality that gives AESTHETIC pleasure. The designer, engineer and architect BUCKMINSTER FULLER wrote: 'When I'm working on a problem, I never think about beauty. I think only how to solve the problem. But when I am finished, if the solution is not beautiful, I know it is wrong.'

Beaux Arts 1 A style of florid neoclassical architecture and formal planning that flourished between around 1885 and 1920s, being used particularly for public buildings and grand urban development. It was inspired by the traditional teaching of the École des Beaux Arts in Paris (founded in 1819). See also CHARRETTE, JEAN-NICHOLAS-LOUIS DURAND and THE LONDON PLAN. **2** (French) Fine arts.

Beaver Committee See FOG.

Bebauungsdichte (German) The density of development.

Bebauungsplan (German) A local development plan.

Beck, Henry (1903–74) An engineering draughtsman with London Underground. In 1933 he redesigned the map of the London tube system as a diagram, providing the basis for every subsequent version and many others worldwide. Inspired by diagrams of electrical circuits, Beck showed every line as meeting at an angle of either 45 or 90 degrees, and made no attempt to indicate the actual distance between stations.

Beckmann, Max (1884–1950) German painter. See BABYLON, CITY and UNREAL CITY.

Bedford Falls The fictional, idyllic, small town in New York state in which Frank Capra's 1946 film *It's a Wonderful Life* is set. The town owes much to its protagonist, the modest and decent George Bailey (played by James Stewart). Early in the film the young George tells his father of his ambition to study architecture. 'You know what I've always talked about,' he says. 'Build things. Design new buildings. Plan modern cities.' And later: 'I'm gonna build airfields, I'm gonna build skyscrapers a hundred stories high, I'm gonna build bridges a mile long.' He abandons those ambitions on the sudden death of his father, when it becomes clear that unless he steps in to run the family business, a building and loan association, it be closed by the machinations of a rival, the scheming Mr Potter, denying ordinary the people the chance to buy a decent home. Later Potter drives the association into bankruptcy. George contemplates suicide, but his guardian angel dissuades him by summoning up a vision of what Bedford Falls might have been like without him. As with any instance of COMPLEXITY, small changes (including Bailey's absence) can lead to major consequences. Potter has taken over the town, filled it with bars and gambling joints, and renamed it Pottersville. Several of the inhabitants face a grim life due to George's absence. The hero is persuaded that his life has value, and he decides not to end it. The screenplay was based on a short story *The Greatest Gift*, written by Philip Van Doren Stern and first published on a Christmas card.

Bedford Park A GARDEN SUBURB in Chiswick, west London, designed primarily by the architect Norman Shaw and built 1875–83 in Queen Anne style. 'The disposition of clumps of houses in winding, tree-lined roads produced a predominantly rural atmosphere which was almost unique in suburban housing of the period,' writes John Burnett (1986). One resident, WB Yeats, called its picturesque streets 'the pre-Raphaelite movement at last affecting life' (Glazebrook, 1967).

bedpan man A resident of the area north of London around the railway line from *Bed*ford to London's St *Pan*cras station. The term emerged briefly in the 2001 UK general election campaign as a stereotype of a prosperous, contented person. In fact, the advent of the Thameslink Cross-London line means that Bedford trains no longer go to St Pancras, but Bedkingscross (Thameslink) man does not have quite the same ring about it. Compare MONDEO MAN, PEBBLEDASH PEOPLE and WHITE VAN MAN.

bedroom community (US) The UK equivalent is DORMITORY TOWN.

bedroom culture Teenagers with their own television, hi-fi and computers spending significant amounts of time in their bedrooms.

Bedzed Beddington Zero Energy Development, a mixed-tenure development of houses and workspaces by the PEABODY TRUST. It was built in 2001 on the site of a disused sewage works at Beddington in the London Borough of Sutton, on energy-saving principles. Peabody claims that it is the first large-scale housing scheme to be carbon-neutral.

Beeching cuts The industrialist Lord (Richard) Beeching was given the job of reviewing the UK's rail network in the 1960s. His controversial recommendations led to many branch lines (amounting to around a third of the network) being closed, on the grounds that they were underused and uneconomic. The programme of closures was criticised for ignoring its social costs. The issue had been aired as early as 1953 in the Ealing comedy film (the first to be made in colour) *The Titfield Thunderbolt*, written by Tibby Clarke and directed by Charles Crichton. The railway line between Titfield and Mallingford is to be closed and replaced by a bus service. The villagers decide to run the line themselves, but the bus company arranges for their engine to be wrecked shortly before a government inspector is due to assess their service. Undaunted, the locals borrow an early Victorian locomotive (the Thunderbolt) from a museum and beat the bus in a race to show which is faster. The film's location was a line near Bath that had been closed to passengers in 1925 and was closed to goods traffic in 1951.

Beersheba A fictional city described in Italo Calvino's INVISIBLE CITIES. Its inhabitants believe that everything that is best in the city is mirrored in another Beersheba that is suspended in the heavens; and everything that is least admirable about Beersheba is mirrored in another version, filthy, stinking and rubbish-strewn, underground.

behavioural mapping Recording in graphic form the results of observations of patterns of human behaviour.

behavioural studies Studies of the relationship between behaviour and the environment, particularly focusing on people's perception of a place.

beigefield A site partly despoiled by an aggregates company, which then claims the right to planning permission for housing development on the grounds that, while not a BROWNFIELD site, it is nearly so. The term was in use by 2000.

Bel Geddes, Norman (1893–1958) Industrial and theatrical designer. See FUTURAMA.

Bellamy Clubs Formed in the USA in the 1880s to discuss how to bring about the vision portrayed in Edward Bellamy's utopian novel LOOKING BACKWARD.

Bellamy, Edward (1850–98) The author of LOOKING BACKWARD.

belong to (Scotland) To come from. Ian Spring (1990) writes: 'The natives of many cities may come from that city, but it is a peculiarly Glaswegian (or perhaps Scottish) habit to "belong" to your home town.' Will Fyffe made a play on the phrase in his popular song: 'I belong to Glasgow,/ Dear old Glasgow Town./ But what's the matter with Glasgow?/ For it's going round and round./ I'm only a common or working chap,/ As anyone here can see,/ But when I get a couple of drinks on a Saturday,/ Glasgow belongs to me.'

Belper An early cotton-spinning town in Derbyshire built by the industrialist JEDEDIAH STRUTT in the years after 1776.

beltway (US) An orbital motorway. 'Inside the Beltway' is Washington shorthand for the seat of power. See RING ROAD.

benches The anthropologist Franco La Cecla describes benches as the litmus paper of a country's democracy and tolerance. Too often, though, they are regarded as undesirable features that attract undesirable people. Colin Ward (2002), who quotes La Cecla, writes of 'the sin of unprofitable sitting', which is how it seems to him to be regarded by those who manage shopping centres, railway stations, and other public or semi-public places. See THE FIVE BS.

benching (US) Stepping the height of buildings to avoid creating an overly dominant single-height skyline.

benchmarking Using an example of good practice as a standard against which to measure performance. The term comes from a surveyor's benchmark cut in a wall or pillar as a basis for measuring heights. See also BASELINE STUDY.

bending main programmes Focusing spending by local agencies and the government on places where it is most needed.

Benefactor, The See WE.

Benefactors A play by Michael Frayn, premiered in 1984 and set in 1968, featuring an idealistic architect enthusiastic about replacing Victorian terraces with tower blocks. The comedy explores the marital tensions of the architect and his wife (who opposes such redevelopment), and their neighbours (the husband moves to squat in a threatened house and campaigns against tower blocks).

Benjamin, Walter (1892–1940) Cultural critic. See THE ARCADES PROJECT and FLÂNEUR.

Benoit-Lévy, Georges Town planner and theorist. His book *The Garden City*, published in France in 1904, advocated GARDEN SUBURBS.

Bentham, Jeremy See PANOPTICON.

Berlin airlift After the second world war Berlin, though surrounded by the communist state of East Germany, was a separate territory under the control of the allied powers (France, Great Britain, the USA and the USSR). East Germany and the USSR took every opportunity to undermine western control and to restrict the west's influence. The western allies supplied West Berlin by air for more than a year in 1948–49 after the Soviet Union blockaded it in an attempt to gain control of the whole city. More than 200,000 flights brought in food and all other essential supplies, including coal for domestic heating and the city's power stations. See also BERLIN WALL and ICH BIN EIN BERLINER.

Berlin Express A 1948 film made by a Hollywood studio and directed by Jacques Tourneur, setting a political mystery story against the background of the ruins of Europe's cities (the film was shot on location). Stephen Barber (2002) writes of a scene in Berlin: 'As the characters wander at night through the moribund city, the ruins are transformed into an extraordinarily beautiful and lush terrain of startling shapes and intense shadows, richly rendered in monochrome contrasts… The city has largely turned to dust, its surviving inhabitants invisibly starving among the wreckage.' Barber comments: 'The obliteration of the German cities is made to appear beneficial, while the rare surviving buildings possess an insidious aura of horror.'

Berlin Wall Built in 1961 by the East German authorities to isolate West Berlin from East Germany, which surrounded it. Barbed wire and trenches were begun on 13 August 1961, and the nine-foot high concrete wall, reinforced by a death strip and guard-dog runs, was started a few days later. In the years to come, dozens of people would be killed trying to cross. The wall, with a total length of 165 kilometres, was a symbol of political oppression. The East German regime referred to it as the Anti-Fascist Defence Wall. President Kennedy declared in his famous speech in Berlin: 'I know of no town, no city, which has been besieged for 18 years that still lives with the vitality and force, and the hope and the determination of the city of West Berlin. While the Wall is the most obvious and vivid demonstration of the failures of the communist system, for all the world to see, we take no satisfaction in it… All free men, wherever they may live, are citizens of Berlin and therefore, as a free man, I take pride in the words "Ich bin ein Berliner"' (see BERLINER). The East German authorities breached the wall in 1989, in what was celebrated as a historic moment in the ending of the Cold War between the west and the eastern bloc. The reunification of East and West Germany, and later the move of the Federal German capital from Bonn to Berlin, followed.

Berliner 1 (German and English) A native of Berlin. **2** (German) A jam doughnut. The two meanings have given rise to occasional amusement at President Kennedy's famous declaration to the people of Berlin: 'Ich bin ein Berliner' (see BERLIN WALL).

Berlioz, Hector (1803–69) Composer. See EUPHONIA.

berm A long mound of earth, grassed or planted, designed to absorb and deflect noise from roads, restrict pedestrian movement or mask unsightly uses such as car parking. *Berm walls* are also used to increase the insulation of buildings. New urbanists generally disapprove of berms, valuing connectivity and preferring to mask parking by buildings (Duany, 2000). See THE FIVE BS.

Berman, Ed Social entrepreneur. See CITY FARM and INTER-ACTION.

Bernick, Michael See TRANSIT VILLAGE.

bespoke development Carried out for a particular client, rather than being speculative. Compare SPECULATIVE DEVELOPMENT.

best available technology See BATNEEC.

best value The process through which local authorities work for continuous improvement in the services they provide. The aim is to ensure that the cost and quality of services are of a level acceptable to their electorate. The Labour government introduced the best value system in 1998 as an alternative to compulsory competitive tendering. Local authorities are required to challenge why a particular service is needed; compare performance across a range of indicators; consult on the setting of new performance targets; and show that services have been procured through a competitive process. Councils are subject to independent best value audits by the Best Value Inspectorate, an offshoot of the Audit Commission.

best value performance plan Sets out a local authority's objectives, programme and achievements of its BEST VALUE work.

best value review Based on the 'four Cs': challenge, compare, consult and compete.

Betjeman, John (Sir) (1906–84) Poet. Working for the Ministry of Information during the 1939–45 war, he claimed to have considered writing a book called *Information of Use to the Enemy*, intended to guide the Luftwaffe to Britain's ugliest buildings. See BAEDEKER RAIDS, METROLAND and JOKE TOWN.

John Betjeman

béton brut (French) Raw concrete. The concrete's surface is left as it was when the formwork (shuttering) was removed, often with the grain of the wood visible. First used self-consciously by LE CORBUSIER at the Unité d'Habitation (out of expediency), it is now a standard part of the architectural repertoire. Examples include the National Theatre in London and Clifton Cathedral. The finish was often used in brutalist architecture, though this was not the reason for the style's name (see BRUTALISM). The Liverpool poet Adrian Henri imagined in his poem *Healthy Cities* a city in which the sound of the bulldozer would be banished and severe sentences imposed 'on anyone designing a building/ finished in shuttered concrete.'

Better City, The A book by Dana Bartlett, published in 1907, which described how Los Angeles could become 'a city without slums'. He explained how, with cheap fares and rapid transit, 'instead of the pent-up millions in other cities, that from necessity or choice know only a contracted indoor existence, here will be found only healthy, happy families, scattered over a vast area' (quoted in Girouard, 1985).

betterment levy A short-lived attempt to recoup increases in the value of land for the community in general through the Land Commission Act 1967.

Bettman, Alfred Lawyer and city planner. He was an important influence on the development of planning in the USA in the 1920s.

biased terminology Terms whose use implies, often unintentionally, a particular point of view.

In 1996 the City of West Palm Beach, Florida, adopted a new transportation language policy that employees and others who dealt with the city were asked to follow. The city administrator, Michael Wright, explained that 'much of the current transportation language was developed in the 1950s and '60s. This was the golden age of automobiles and accommodating them was a major priority in society. Times have changed, especially in urban areas where creating a balanced, equitable, and sustainable transportation system is the new priority.' Wright's official memo gave some examples: 'The word "improvements" is often used when referring to the addition of through lanes, turn lanes, channelization, or other means of increasing motor vehicle capacity and/or speeds. Though these changes may indeed be "improvements" from the perspective of motor vehicle users, they would not be considered "improvements" by other constituents of the city.'

Wright continued: 'For example, a resident may not think that adding more lanes in front of the resident's house is an "improvement". A parent may not think that a channelized right turn lane is an "improvement" on their child's pedestrian route to school. City staff referring to these changes as "improvements" indicates that the city is biased in favor of one group at the expense of others. Suggested objective language includes being descriptive (for example, use through lanes, turn lanes, etc.) or using language such as "modifications" or "changes".' Other examples of biased terminology included *enhance, enhancement, deteriorate* and *upgrade*. The West Palm Beach memo explained: ' "Upgrade" is a term that is currently used to describe what happens when a local street is changed to become a collector, or when a two-lane street is expanded to four lanes. "Upgrade" implies a change for the better. Though this may be the case for one constituent, others may disagree... Objective language includes "expansion", "reconstruction", "widened" or "changed".' Another biased term was *level of service*. This, Wright explained, 'is a qualitative measure describing the operational conditions of a facility or service from the perspective of a particular set of users (motor vehicle users, cyclists, pedestrians and so on). If the set of users is not specified, then it is a mystery as to which set is being considered. The bias enters the picture when it is assumed that, unless otherwise specified, level of service implies for motor vehicle users. The objective way to use this term is to add the appropriate modifier after "level of service" '. This would involve using phrases such as 'the level of service for motor vehicle users' and 'the level of service for pedestrians'. To save using the modifier frequently for the same users in the same document, it would be acceptable to use it only at the beginning of the document and periodically after that, the memo advised. *Alternative* was another problem word. 'Promoting "alternative" modes of transportation is generally considered a good thing at the city. However, the word "alternative" begs the question "alternative to what?" The assumption is alternative to automobiles. "Alternative" also implies that these "alternative" modes are non-traditional or non-conventional, which is not the case with the pedestrian, cycle nor transit modes. If we are discussing "alternative" modes of transportation in the city, then use direct and objective language such as "non-automobile" modes of transportation. Alternatively, one can add an appropriate modifier.'

The memo also disapproved of the word *accident*. '"Accidents" are events during which something harmful or unlucky happens unexpectedly or by chance. "Accident" implies no fault. It is well known that the vast majority of "accidents" are preventable and that fault can be assigned. The use of "accident" also reduces the degree of responsibility and severity associated with the situation and invokes an inherent degree of sympathy for the person responsible. Objective language includes "collision" and "crash".' Similarly, the memo continued, '"protect" means shielding from harm. However, when we discuss "protecting" land for a right of way for a road, the intent is not to shield the land from harm, but to construct a road over it. Objective words include "designate" and "purchase".'

Finally, Wright noted that it was important to make the city's transport systems operate as *efficiently* as possible. 'However,' he wrote, 'we must be careful how we use "efficient" because that word is frequently confused with the word "faster". Typically, "efficiency" issues are raised when dealing with motor vehicles operating at slow speeds. The assumption is that efficiency increases when changes are made that increase the speeds of the motor vehicles. This assumption is highly debatable. For example, high motor vehicle speeds lead to urban sprawl, motor vehicle dependence, and high resource use (land, metal, rubber, etc.) which reduces efficiency. Motor vehicles burn the least fuel at about 30 miles per hour; speeds above this result in inefficiencies. In urban areas, accelerating and decelerating from stopped conditions to high speeds result in inefficiencies when compared to slow and steady speeds. There are also efficiency debates about people's travel time and other issues as well...'

bicycle and sidecar housing A house in kit form with an extendable pod to one side.

bidonville See SQUATTER SETTLEMENT.

Big A 1 BIG ARCHITECTURE. **2** Atlanta, Georgia.

Big Apple New York. The nickname owes its current familiarity to a publicity campaign launched by the city's Convention and Visitors Bureau in 1971. The term *big apple* in New York has been said to have been used traditionally to refer to racecourses, a mobsters' boss, the height of an actor's ambition, or anything else thought to be the leading one of its kind. It was used in jazz lyrics to refer to New York at least as early as the 1930s (Pye, 1991) and to any large northern city before that. The application of the nickname to New York is also said to derive from the fact that the Spanish word *manzana* means both *grid* and *apple*. Also known as Big Burg, Big Town and GOTHAM.

big architecture Master planning. The term is sometimes used pejoratively in relation to some architects who are accused of not understanding the difference between the design of buildings on the one hand and urban design on the other. It is also used to describe their own masterplanning by some architects (Will Alsop is one) who feel that the term ARCHITECTURE can properly be used to describe design at any scale. See also MASTER PLAN and TOTAL ARCHITECTURE.

Big B Baltimore.

big bang development A development project of sufficient size to attract further development that would otherwise be unlikely to take place in the area.

Big Bang The deregulation of financial markets in the UK in 1986, which led to greatly increased demand for office and trading space, and consequently development, in London.

big body An SUV.

big box A building designed to cover a large area cheaply, usually with extensive car parking next to it. Sometimes also known as a *tin shed*.

Big Burg New York. See also BIG APPLE and BIG TOWN.

Big C Chicago. See also BIG TOWN and WINDY CITY.

big city (US) Mike Davis (2002) suggests that in the early twentieth century the term was a euphemism for the 'teeming Papist masses', and that today it equates with a Black-Latino 'underclass'. He comments: 'Contemporary debates about the city – as about drugs and crime – are invariably really about race.'

big city syndrome A tendency for a city to act as though it were independent of any region because of its successful economy. Herrschel and Newman (2002) cite Leeds in the 1990s as an example.

Big D 1 Dallas. **2** Detroit.

Big Easy New Orleans. The nickname perhaps derives from *speakeasy*, the name for an illegal drinking house at the time of prohibition. The term became well known as the title of a novel by James Conaway, set in New Orleans, published in 1970.

big gubment (US) Government intervention. The phrase is a derisive evocation of how 'big government' is referred to by those who are thought mindlessly to oppose it.

Big M Memphis, Tennessee.

Big Orange Los Angeles.
Big Smoke (or Big Smokey) Pittsburgh, Pennsylvania, notorious in its steel-making days for its toxic atmosphere. See also AULD REEKIE, SMOG and THE SMOKE.
Big T Tucson, Arizona.
Big Town 1 New York. **2** Chicago.
Big V Las Vegas.
Biggleswick Garden City A fictional setting of *Mr Standfast*, the third of John Buchan's Richard Hannay novels, published in 1919. Hannay lodges in a 'badly built and oddly furnished' cottage with the Jimsons, a caricature of odd and oddly dressed garden city residents. Tancred Jimson wears grey flannels, a soft collar, an orange tie and a soft black hat. His wife Ursula favours a gown 'modelled on a chintz curtain' (see DRESS SENSE). John Buchan had been staying in LETCHWORTH in 1915 after having been invalided out of the war (Miller, 1989).
Bilbao effect The supposed consequence of a landmark building singlehandedly bringing about the regeneration of a city. The Guggenheim Museum in

Frank Gehry

Bilbao, designed by FRANK GEHRY, is famously said to have had this effect. Gehry warns: 'It's not like instant coffee. You can't put hot water in and make it happen. I get approached a lot for those sort of projects but I'm not interested when I feel they haven't got their act together' (quoted in Blackler, 2003). See also ANGEL EFFECT.

Bilboaise To seek to attract international attention by constructing a dramatic landmark building (see BILBAO EFFECT). Example: 'These days it seems that every city competing to be a City of Culture must be Bilboaised with a signature building' (2002).
bill of rights See RIGHTS.
billing authority A local authority that produces bills for council tax. This excludes county councils.
bimbo architecture Buildings designed to attract customers but lacking architectural INTEGRITY. The analogy is with a 'bimbo' (a female model) at a trade fair. The term was used by RIBA president Maxwell Hutchinson (1989), but it did not catch on. 'Bimbo architecture,' he wrote, 'has a big smile and a pretty face, but nothing between the ears. It scoops up just enough dressing-up clothes to create an impression. It is "hi-tech" architecture without the tech and with an exclamation mark after the "hi".'
bindle stiff (US) A VAGRANT. The *bindle* is the bundle the vagrant carries. See also SWAGMAN.
bing (Scotland) A spoil heap.
bioclimatic design Takes account of local climatic conditions to ensure minimum reliance on non-renewable energy sources.
bioclimatic skyscraper See KEN YEANG.
biodiversity The variety of forms of life, specifically the (desirable) genetic range.
biological analogy Relating the development of urban areas to that of biological organisms.
biomass Biological matter such as straw or wood which is burned as a relatively environmentally friendly fuel. Burning it does produce the greenhouse gas carbon dioxide, but planting biomass as a crop immediately after harvesting ensures that the new crop takes up carbon dioxide.
biome A balanced ecological community.
biosphere The planet's natural systems. The term was coined by the physicist Vladimir Ivanovitch Vernadsky, according to Barbara Ward and René Dubos (1972). Ward and Dubos contrasted the biosphere of living things with the *technosphere* of mankind's inventions.
Biotop (German) A habitat.
bird See FLYING RAT, GUTTER BIRD, THE LONDON PIGEON WARS and SEAGULL.
Birkenhead See BIRKENHEAD PARK, ONE-EYED CITY and REILLY GREEN.
Birkenhead Park Designed by JOSEPH PAXTON in 1843, it was the world's first park provided at public expense. Its layout and design were extremely influential on, among others, New York's CENTRAL PARK.
Birmingham Urban Design Study The study by FRANCIS TIBBALDS, published in 1990, was the basis of Britain's first comprehensive urban design strategy. It drew on the 1970 San Francisco Plan (Punter and Carmona, 1997).

birtway A toll motorway. The term was coined by the press in 2002 after the government's transport advisor John Birt, formerly director general of the BBC, recommended building a network of them. *Birttrack* was suggested as an alternative.

biscuit-tin development Large, featureless box-like buildings.

Bitter Cry of Outcast London, The A pamphlet protesting at poverty and squalor in London. Published in 1883, it is thought to have been written by the Reverend Andrew Mearns.

black The word has a variety of meanings when used to describe people. Such meanings relate to one or more of the following: **1** Skin colour. **2** Ethnic origin. **3** Being discriminated against. The London-based organisation Race on the Agenda, for example, defined the term 'black' in 2001 as meaning 'those people of African, Asian, Caribbean and South East Asian descent and other groups who are discriminated against on the grounds of their race, culture, colour, nationality or religious practices'. The Black Environment Network (BEN), a UK-wide organisation pioneering the participation of ethnic minorities in the built and natural environment, says that it uses the word black symbolically, 'recognising that black communities are the most visible of ethnic communities'.

Black Act, The A name used for the Building Act 1774 (which regulated building in London) by those who resented its controls.

black ban (Australia) A ban by a labour union on its members working on a particular project of whose social or economic consequences they disapprove. Compare GREEN BAN.

black country An industrial area; an area ravaged by highly polluting industry.

Black Country, the A region bordering Birmingham in the English Midlands consisting of the boroughs of Dudley, Sandwell, Walsall and Wolverhampton. Its name is widely supposed to derive from the soot laid down in its long years of heavy industrial production. It is more likely, though, to have been inspired by the region's thick coal seam. This was in many places only a few feet below the surface, making the soil black.

black economy Economic activity hidden from official records, regulations and the tax authorities. Compare INFORMAL ECONOMY.

Black Road A housing improvement scheme in Macclesfield, Cheshire, in the 1970s, supported by architect and local resident Rod Hackney. The terraced houses, scheduled for clearance, were improved instead. The residents did much of the work themselves to minimise costs. The project inspired other community enterprise and self-build schemes, and launched Hackney's career as a community architect, entrepreneur and president of the RIBA. See COMMUNITY ARCHITECTURE.

blacktop The city street.

Blade Runner A cult film directed by Ridley Scott, based on the novel by PHILIP K DICK, *Do Androids Dream of Electric Sheep?* The term *blade runner* (meaning a professional killer) was taken from a book by William S Burroughs Jnr. The film presents a dystopian future set in Los Angeles. It was shot mainly at night, and it seems always to be raining. At ground level are crumbling nineteenth-century buildings and unremitting urban squalor. Towering above them are the modernistic ziggurats where anyone of any influence lives. Ridley Scott ended the film with a vision of unremitting gloom. This, the studio bosses decided, was not what cinemagoers wanted. They added a narration to explain what was going on, and an upbeat ending, in which the main characters drive out of the city into a startlingly green landscape (using outtakes from STANLEY KUBRICK's film *The Shining*). The film was a commercial failure until in 1990 the original version – without the commentary and the happy ending – was shown by accident. The audience's enthusiasm led eventually to the original director's cut being released and becoming a classic. Afficionados debate whether or not Rick Deckard, the film's supposedly human hero (played by Harrison Ford), is actually a replicant (an android) himself. Ridley Scott has confirmed that he is, though the film itself is ambiguous. One of *Blade Runner*'s dramatic interiors was shot in a building designed by an architect inspired by EDWARD BELLAMY's book *Looking Backward*.

Blair, Tony (b1953) UK prime minister. See CHEWING GUM, COMMUNITARIANISM, COMMUNITY, LIVEABILITY, OFFWORLD, STAKEHOLDER and URBAN RENAISSANCE.

Bletchley A Buckinghamshire railway town expanded under the EXPANDED TOWNS programme. It was later incorporated into the new city of MILTON KEYNES.

blight Planning legislation in 1944 defined 'blighted' land as having obsolete buildings or bad layout. The Act provided powers for such land to be redeveloped. See PLANNING BLIGHT.

blight notice Served on a local authority by the owner of a house or small business requiring it to buy the property at the sort of price it would have fetched had it not been blighted by planning.

blind competition A competition (architectural or urban design, for example) in which the judges do not know the identity of the entrants.

blind-eyed city JANE JACOBS' (1961) description of a place without animated streets and too few EYES ON THE STREET. Compare ONE-EYED CITY.

blitz 1 The bombing of cities by the Luftwaffe (German air force) in the Second World War. **2** Any highly destructive act. From the German *Blitzkrieg* meaning lightning war.

Blitz and Blight Act The UK Town and Country Planning Act 1944.

blob architecture 1 Works of architecture that do not relate to their context or express their practical function to any great degree. Anthony Alofsin (source unknown) wrote (reviewing an exhibition of the work of FRANK GEHRY): 'Blobs are the newest thing in American architecture... Blobs... tend to emphasise exterior packaging rather than interior innovation. The creative breakthroughs that came from rethinking and challenging the human conditions of habitation and work (so important for modernist architects) rarely occur among the skin practitioners or blob architects, to whom sculptural void is an entity in itself and, like art, unconcerned with the pragmatics of daily life.' Robert Huxford of the Institution of Civil Engineers describes *blob development* as 'an urban area characterised by a traditional fine grain grid and mixed use, into which developers have dropped large and apparently prestige buildings that are at least three times the height and four times the width of local buildings. Considerable attention is paid to the buildings themselves, but the designers' mental concentration lapses when addressing the surrounding spaces, so that the development appears to be part of a different town rather than an evolution of the existing fabric.' Example: '[The Irish Republic] is still a small country, and it's not in the mood for the showy flamboyance of the blob-builders and bombastic shapemakers' (Deyan Sudjic in 2002). **2** Buildings without corners. Example: 'Why all this no-corner architecture now? Blob architects [explain] that computer-aided design systems linked to robotic production processes have made it no more difficult to design, detail and fabricate curved shapes than orthogonal ones' (2002).

blobitecture A contraction of BLOB ARCHITECTURE (Hellman, 2002).

block 1 The area bounded by a set of streets and undivided by any other significant streets. The term is used both to refer to the area itself and as a measure of distance along a street, as in 'walk three blocks to the north'. The term is of US origin (being particularly appropriate in towns laid out on a rectangular GRID) and now in use in the UK. See also SUPER BLOCK. **2** A large building, often subdivided, as in *tower block*.

block club (US) A group of residents living on the same block or set of blocks who watch out for potential problems. See also NEIGHBOURHOOD WATCH.

block interior The piece of land surrounded by a PERIMETER BLOCK.

Block, Alexander (c1868–1955) A lawyer, he was a leading member of the Russian garden city movement before the revolution. He settled in WELWYN GARDEN CITY in 1933 (Cooke, 1978).

Blockbebauung (German) Perimeter development.

blockbusting (US) Housing speculators moving black residents into blocks formerly occupied exclusively by white people, in the hope of profiting from the buying and selling of property as the alarmed white residents sell up and move out. Thomas J Sugrue (1996) notes that the blockbusters' tactics included 'selling a house in an all-white block or neighbourhood to a black family, or using devious techniques like paying a black woman to walk her baby through a white neighbourhood to fuel suspicion of black residential takeover.... Some brokers brazenly displayed a house for sale in a white neighbourhood to a black family, waited a day for rumours to spread, and then inundated residents with leaflets and phone calls, informing them that "Negroes are taking over this block or area" and that they "had best sell now while there is still a chance of obtaining a good price".' See also WHITE FLIGHT.

block-home One that is built defensively in the style of a bunker.

Blood Alley West India Quay in London's docks, so nicknamed in the nineteenth century due to the number of injuries suffered by dockers (McGrath, 2003).

Bloomsday 16 June 1904. That day, on the which the entire action of James Joyce's novel *Ulysses* takes place, is celebrated every year in locations all over the world by Joyce scholars and enthusiasts. *Ulysses* is set in Dublin, which Joyce (1882–1941) observes minutely. He had left the city in 1904 at the age of 24 to live abroad, returning only for two brief visits, but Dublin provides the setting for most of his writing. Many Bloomsday celebrations recreate the day in the life of the three principal characters: Leopold Bloom, an advertising agent, his wife Molly, and the young poet and teacher Stephen Daedalus.

Bloxham, Tom (b1963) Developer. In the 1990s Bloxham pioneered the rehabilitation of old buildings for living, working and retail uses in central areas in the north west of England, particularly Manchester and Liverpool, through his company Urban Splash.

blue banana, the (also the banana) The roughly banana-shaped, urbanised region variously described as encompassing London and Milan, or Cardiff, Birmingham and Milan.

blue belt The London Rivers Association in 1998 proposed that the River Thames should be designated as blue belt to protect it against unsympathetic development. Mayor KEN LIVINGSTONE later proposed designating the river as SPECIAL BLUE RIBBON ZONE. Compare GREEN BELT

Blue Book A report of a House of Commons select committee or a Royal Commission.

blue carrot See SEZAIN.

blue ribbon A river or canal CORRIDOR.

blue ribbon network A spatial policy covering London's waterways and waterspaces, and land alongside them.

blue water 'The stuff you put in the fountain of your mall to offset the ugliness of the pennies that people throw in, as well as the grout that washes off,' according to Joel Garreau (1994). Compare BLUEWATER.

blueprint A plan that sets out in some detail the form of a development; a master plan. Originally the technology of production meant that the print on such plans was blue.

Blueprint for Survival A proposal for a SUSTAINABLE, decentralised society published in *The Ecologist* in 1972.

blueprint plan Shows an end-state that it is hoped will be achieved at a certain time in the future.

blue-sky scenario A development concept that is not constrained by previous ideas or other limitations.

Bluewater An out-of-town shopping mall in Kent, England, opened in 1999. Compare BLUE WATER.

blueway An urban waterway. Compare GREENWAY and REDWAYS.

bobo A bourgeois-bohemian. In his book *Bobos in Paradise*, David Brooks argues that the new culture of today's creative people represents a blending of bourgeois and bohemian values. Compare BOHO.

bodge (or botch) To mend something incompletely. The word comes from the Middle English word meaning to repair or patch (Quinion, 2003).

bodge culture Carrying out development with no concern for the standards of its design or construction. Deputy prime minister JOHN PRESCOTT used the phrase at the Urban Summit in 2002.

bodgie (Australia) A member of a street gang.

Bofill, Ricardo Architect and urban designer. He is noted for applying the GRAND MANNER, monumental baroque urban forms and neo-classical architecture to working-class housing, often using prefabricated concrete. 'The aim,' Spiro Kostof (1991) suggests, 'is to exalt daily life by situating it in extraordinary settings. But since there is no public life to speak of in these transfixed environments, they can achieve little else than to embalm domesticity.' See also WOW FACTOR.

Bogeyland See TOYLAND.

Bohemian index Used by RICHARD FLORIDA to measure the number of artists, writers and performers (and hence, he suggests, the creativity and acceptance of diversity) of an area.

Bohigas, Oriol See BARCELONA.

boho A bohemian. Compare BOBO.

boiled frog syndrome Accepting and adjusting to increasing health and ecological hazards in order to satisfy a desire for material comforts and easier living. Thomas Saunders wrote about it in *The Boiled Frog Syndrome* (2002). The analogy is with a frog jumping into a pan of water that is being slowly heated. The frog, apparently, adjusts its body temperature to that of the water until it is boiled alive.

boiler (US) A CAR.

bollard-led development A pejorative term for streetscape improvements that provide new paving and street furniture, such as bollards, but little else. GORDON CULLEN (1971) regretted that his ideas on townscape had encouraged 'a superficial civic style of bollards and cobblestone'.

Bologna The Italian town has been celebrated since the 1970s for its ambitious and effective conservation programme, carried out originally by a communist administration. The aim has been to protect communities as well as buildings. Bologna is also noted for its policies of putting pedestrians first. The writer and philosopher TE Hulme (1911) wrote that Bologna was the perfect town, particularly for a philosopher to wander in.

bombing GRAFFITI artists writing their names in as many places in as short a time as possible.

Bonfire of the Vanities, The Tom Wolfe's novel, published in 1988, presents a satiric vision of New York's class, political and racial structure in the 1980s. The story follows what happens when a Wall Street bond-trader and his mistress kill a young man from a housing project in a road accident, after getting lost in the South Bronx.

'Utterly empty, a vast open terrain. Block after block – how many? – six? eight? a dozen? – entire blocks of the city without a building left standing. There were streets and curbing and sidewalks and light poles and nothing else. The eerie grid of a city was spread out before him, lit by the chemical yellow of the street lamps. Here and there were traces of rubble and slag. The earth looked like concrete, except that it rolled down this way... and up that way... the hills and dales of the Bronx... reduced to asphalt, concrete, and cinders... in a ghastly yellow gloaming.' See YUPPIE.

bonusing (US) Allowing development of a higher density than originally zoned in return for the developer offering a specific public benefit.

book-town movement A network of towns that specialise in second-hand bookshops and associated cultural activities, including HAY-ON-WYE in England, Stillwater in the USA and Montolieu in the south of France.

boom-box A GHETTO-BLASTER.

boomburb A rapidly growing EDGE CITY. The Fannie Mae Foundation defined a boomburb in 2000 as an area that currently has more than 100,000 residents and has maintained double-digit rates of population growth in each recent decade, but is not the largest city in its metropolitan area. A boomburb is spread out at low density and almost never has a dense CENTRAL BUSINESS DISTRICT.

boomer generation See BABY BOOMER.

boomtown A town experiencing dramatic economic growth. Also *Boomville* (used in a newspaper report in 2001 to describe Leeds, for example).

booster A person who promotes the reputation of a particular town or city. HL Mencken (1925) described a booster as 'one who devotes himself to advertising his town, usually by gaudy methods'. Mark Lee Luther, based in Los Angeles in the 1920s, wrote a novel called *The Boosters*, published in 1924. The hero, an architect, travels to Los Angeles to make his fortune and meets his first booster on the train. An early example of a booster was Daniel Denton, who wrote a pamphlet extolling the virtues of New York on a visit to London in 1670 (Pye, 1991).

boosterism (US) Strategies for improving a city's image. Rarely has boosterism resorted to a slogan as desperate as this 2002 example: 'Coventry: two vowels, six consonants, hundreds of opportunities'. A less fanciful example is: 'Oldham, home of the tubular bandage'. The unofficial 'Walsall: not as bad as you'd think' (2003) has the merit of honesty, like Liverpool's unofficial 'AT LEAST IT'S NOT BASILDON'. A modern equivalent term is *place marketing*. See also BRANDING.

booter (US) A parking enforcement officer, clamping illegally parked vehicles with a Denver boot.

Charles Booth

Booth, Charles (1840–1916) Social reformer and author of the seventeen-volume *Life and Labour of the People in London*, published 1889–1902.

Booth, William (1829–1912) Founder of the Salvation Army. He was the author of IN DARKEST ENGLAND, AND THE WAY OUT.

borderlands Geographical spaces or social structures where new patterns of life develop at the borders of dominant cultures. Compare EDGELANDS and URBAN (or RURBAN) FRINGE.

boreen (Ireland) A LANE.

Borie, Henry-Jules An advocate (in a book published in 1865) of high-rise, high-density development in Paris, with roof gardens, roof-top schools and internal courtyards roofed with iron and glass (Rykwert, 2000).

borrowed sun Sunlight reflected off a tall building on to a space below.

Boston bum (US) A VAGRANT who considers themselves superior to other vagrants.

Boswash The urban area from Boston to New York and Washington on the east coast of the USA. Also called *Bosnywash* and the *Bos-Wash corridor*.

bottom-drawer plan 1 A document on which a local authority bases planning decisions despite the document not having gone through the procedures necessary to validate a statutory plan. **2** A plan whose originators are keeping it hidden, while they go through processes of consultation in the pretence that no significant decisions have yet been taken.

Boty, Pauline (1938–66) Artist and actress. See ANTI-UGLIES.

boulevard 1 (UK) A broad street lined with trees. **2** (US) A broad street. The tree-lined promenade on the site of Paris' former city walls were called boulevards after the Grand Boulevart, a former bastion.

boulevard à redans (French) A boulevard whose BUILDING LINE is indented at regular intervals, providing alternate building blocks and tree clusters. The form was developed by the Paris planner Eugène Hénard in the early twentieth century.

boundary definition Defined by OSCAR NEWMAN (1973) as 'mechanisms for creating boundaries which define a hierarchy of increasingly private zones, from public street to private apartment'. See also TERRITORIALITY.

Boundary Street Estate The London County Council's first estate of flats, built in Shoreditch from 1893 to replace slum housing. Twenty-three blocks of walk-up flats housed 5,000 people. It was widely influential, attracting visitors from all over the world (Harwood and Saint, 1991).

bounded dialogue See DIALOGUE.

bounded rationality An idea of rationality that accepts that there are always limitations and constraints on knowledge. The term has been used to describe the basis of planners' decisions.

Bourdieu, Pierre (b1930) Sociologist. See HABITUS and SOCIAL CAPITAL.

boutique skyscraper One highly designed for the specific needs and context of its site, as opposed to being built to a more or less standard design.

Bowling Alone A book by ROBERT D PUTNAM on 'the collapse and revival of American community', published in 2001. Putnam identifies a person bowling alone (whether actually alone or in a team but watching the night's television on a set above the lane) as typifying the collapse of community. He argues that over the past thirty years Americans have become alienated from one another and from social and political institutions. This disengagement, he says, damages personal

Robert D Putnam

health, local communities and national well-being. The loss of SOCIAL CAPITAL is reflected in lower educational performance and higher rates of crime, teenage pregnancy, child suicide, low birth weight babies and infant mortality. Putnam identifies a variety of technological, social and economic causes. Among them are: a) Time pressure, especially on two-career families. b) Changes in family structure, with more people living alone. c) Suburban sprawl. d) Electronic entertainment, especially television, privatising leisure time. See also SAGUARO SEMINAR.

box builder A pejorative term for someone who puts up a building with little concern for its design or appearance. See also NODDY BOX.

Boyle family A family of artists (parents Mark and Joan, son Sebastian and daughter Georgia) well known since the 1960s for their 'earthpieces' – three-dimensional facsimiles of the earth's surface made of glass fibre and resin. The subjects, including small areas of street or pavement surface, indistinguishable from the real thing, are sometimes chosen at random. They call themselves Boyle family without the definite article.

Brace, Charles Loring Social reformer. See DANGEROUS CLASSES.

Brache (German) Derelict or vacant land.

Bracher, Samuel See WHITEWAYS.

Bracken House Designed by Sir Albert Richardson in 1953 as offices and printing works for the *Financial Times* in the City of London, it was completed in 1958. Its threatened demolition in 1986 led to it becoming the first building in England or Wales less than 30 years old to be listed. It was later remodelled by the architects Michael Hopkins and Partners. See ANTI-UGLIES.

Brahe, Per (1620–80) As head of the Generalship of Finland he planned at least a dozen towns, including Helsinki (Kostof, 1991).

branch economy A local economy dominated by branches of companies whose headquarters are located elsewhere. In places with such economies companies tend to show less commitment to civic life and urban regeneration.

brand *v.* To make a locality distinctive in relation to places with which it is competing. The term was borrowed from the marketing of products and services in the 1990s. In marketing parlance, milk and bread are commodities, while cigarettes, beer and cars (for example) are sold as brands with the emphasis on image, status and identity. See also REBRAND.

brand-bombing Placing multiple franchisees of the same business in and around a particular shopping centre with the intention of squeezing out non-franchise competitors (De Costa, 2002).

Brandon Estate Housing built in Southwark by the London County Council in 1960. Unusually for its time it was a mixed development of new housing (high-rise flats, old people's homes and maisonettes) and rehabilitated Victorian houses.

Brasilia Capital of Brazil. The city, conceived in 1956, was designed by the architect Lucio Costa after he won a competition. Costa had not intended to enter: he did so at the last minute, drawing a complete and highly-detailed plan freehand on five small pieces of paper. This is known as 'heroic' or 'seat of the pants' planning. Thomas Deckker (2000) writes: 'Astonishingly, there is no evidence that Costa, in marked contrast to the other entrants, made any calculations at all for any part of the plan.' Brasilia was listed as a World Heritage Site in 1987.

Brassaï Photographer of Paris in the years after 1932. His favourite subjects included GRAFFITI. Brassaï was a pseudonym taken from his home town of Brassó in Hungary.

brasserie bulge See CAFÉ CREEP.

Brave New World See FORDISM.

break A small change in direction in a plan or elevation of one or more buildings.

break dancing A form of street dancing in which the body is stretched to its limits. It developed in New York in the 1970s as part of HIP HOP culture. See B-BOYS, KOOL HERC and RAP.

break the china *v.* To damage buildings and structures while fighting in an urban area. Example: 'When you go in and sort out an urban area you are not out to break the china. We want to win hearts and minds but we will have to use force' (a British air marshall in Iraq in 2003). See also FIBUA, MOUSEHOLE and MOUT.

breakfast See MUESLI and TOAST RACK.

breakthrough street A new street cut through a block in a gridded plan.

Brecht, Bertolt (1898–1956) Poet and playwright. See MAHAGONNY, READER FOR THOSE WHO LIVE IN CITIES and STEELTOWN.

Brentham Probably the first GARDEN SUBURB, begun in Ealing, west London, in 1901. The layout was by BARRY PARKER and RAYMOND UNWIN.

Bressey Report The Greater London Highway Development Survey, published in 1937, prepared by the engineer SIR CHARLES BRESSEY with SIR EDWIN LUTYENS as architectural consultant. The report advocated large street-blocks to reduce the 'extravagantly large' area occupied by streets, alleys and courts. It urged that 'the building lines adjacent to roundabouts, as well as the buildings themselves, should form integral parts of a well-considered architectural design'. In Lutyens' words, 'beyond essential police and traffic considerations, roundabouts should be planned in relation to their gradients. To achieve well-designed skylines, careful consideration should be given to the prosceniums of the streets that converge upon them. Wherever possible, it is advisable that the design of any one roundabout should be controlled by a single mind.' The report recommended that roads should be laid out as PARKWAYS, 200 or 300 feet wide, fringed by greens and open spaces. Few of its proposals were implemented.

Bressey, Charles (Sir) (1874–1951) Engineer. With the architect Sir Edwin Lutyens he prepared a regional highway plan for London (the GREATER LONDON HIGHWAY DEVELOPMENT SURVEY), published in 1937.

Brick City Newark, New Jersey.

bricks and mortar approach Urban regeneration strategies based on encouraging physical development. At the URBAN SUMMIT in 2002, chancellor Gordon Brown rejected the approach – which he described as 'subsidising property developers' – as misguided.

bricolage Something (a building, for example) made from whatever materials are available. The word derives from the French *bricole*, a trifle.

Bride of Denmark, The The former private pub in the basement of the Georgian offices of the Architectural Press (publisher of the *Architectural Review* and *Architects' Journal*) in Queen Anne's Gate, London, from 1946 to the early 1990s. It was equipped with fixtures and fittings scavenged from pubs that had been blitzed or were being demolished or refurbished. The Bride was the scene of many a discussion among the leading writers, architects and urbanists of the day, including IAN NAIRN and GORDON CULLEN, both on the staff of the Architectural Press. Celebrated visiting architects were invited to inscribe their names on a pair of mirrors with a diamond stylus. The Bride of Denmark was named after Queen Anne, bride of Prince George of Denmark.

bridging group Defined by the DETR (1998b) as 'a community organisation that has grown to a point where it can take on running substantial projects, or a professional voluntary organisation that has actively involved the community in its management and raised the status of volunteers'.

bridleway (or bridlepath) A highway on which the public has a right of way on foot, horseback, leading a horse or on a bicycle (and sometimes driving animals along it).

Brigadoon 1 A fictional village in the Scottish Highlands, featured in the eponymous 1955 film, directed by Vincenti Minnelli. In 1753 the parson prays that Brigadoon will avoid being corrupted by local witches, by falling into a sleep from which its inhabitants will awaken only one day in every 100 years. This is granted on the condition that the village will disappear for ever if any villager leaves it. The film tells the story of what happens when two American tourists find Brigadoon in 1953. **2** Any place that comes to life only under certain conditions. Example: 'Italian beach resorts are essentially miniature neighbourhoods on the sand, perfectly organised and regulated Brigadoons that come to life for a few months every year' (2003).

Briggs, RA See BUNGALOW BRIGGS.

Bright Lights, Big City See YUPPIE.

brightfield (US) Defined by the US Department of Energy in 2001 as 'an abandoned or contaminated property (brownfield) that is redeveloped through the incorporation of solar energy'. The department explains that its brightfield concept 'addresses economic development, environmental cleanup and air quality challenges by bringing pollution-free solar energy and high-tech solar manufacturing jobs to brownfield sites.'

brightfield site (UK) A lively urban place whose rich identity has developed over time. The term has been used by community activists in Spitalfields, London, inspired by William Taylor's (2000) book *This Bright Field*. The implication is that an urban site is not fair game for indiscriminate development just because its previous uses classify it as BROWNFIELD. Taylor prefaces his book with a poem by RS Thomas, 'The Bright Field'. The Welsh poet's sight of a field momentarily bathed in sunlight leads him to reflect on what is of value. 'Life is not hurrying/ on to a receding future, nor hankering after/ an imagined past.' See also TRANSACTION ENCOUNTER.

Brighton See CITY BY THE SEA and CITYCIDE.

Brightsite A campaign established by the Groundwork Trust in the 1980s to improve the physical environment of commercial and industrial buildings.

BrindleyPlace (sic) A new commercial quarter of Birmingham, begun in 1994. TERRY FARRELL was its masterplanner.

Britain and the Octopus A book by the architect Clough Williams-Ellis, published in 1928, in which he fulminated against the 'octopus' of urban development.

British Urban Regeneration Association (BURA) A membership charity that promotes good practice.

Brizzie Brisbane, state capital of Queensland, Australia.

Broadacre City (or Broadacres) FRANK LLOYD WRIGHT's proposed ideal city. He first exhibited a model of it in 1935. It would not have been a city in any conventional sense, being a dispersal of development across the countryside. Every person would have at least one acre of land, which they would spend some or all of their time farming. The most powerful person in Broadacre City would be the county architect. Broadacre City would have no centre, and no distinction between town and country. Its basic unit is the family in its homestead. Wright explained in *When Democracy Builds* in 1945 that it was to be called Broadacre City 'simply because it is broadly based upon the spacing of the minimum of an acre, or several, to an individual'.

broad-brush plan See FINE-GRAINED PLAN.

Broadwater Farm An AWARD-WINNING housing estate in the London Borough of Haringey, built in the late 1960s, consisting of slab and tower blocks linked at first floor level by pedestrian decks. Broadwater Farm became notorious in 1985 when riots broke out following a police raid on a flat in which the tenant died. Police constable Keith Blakelock was hacked to death in the two days of rioting and arson that followed. The estate has since been the focus of community development initiatives and government-funded improvement schemes, and it has been renamed. See SO GOOD THEY NAMED IT TWICE.

broken windows Neglecting to repair broken windows reinforces the impression that no one cares about a place. This, wrote George Kelling and James Wilson in the USA in 1982, encourages GRAFFITI and VANDALISM, which makes the street less welcoming, which encourages petty crime, which in turn leads to serious crime (Kelling and Wilson, 1982). The idea has led to the development of the *zero tolerance* approach to policing. See also CRIME PREVENTION.

Bromborough Pool A pioneer model village on the Wirral, Cheshire, built by Price's Patent Candle Company in 1853–8 (Miller, 1989). John Burnett (1986) suggests it has a good claim to be 'the first garden village'. In 1843 Price's had perfected a method of refining fats by distillation, producing the first candle made of paraffin wax.

Brookside A soap opera set in a suburban cul-de-sac in Liverpool, produced by Phil Redmond, first televised in 1982. 'Brookside' has become derogatory shorthand for such anywheresville modern suburban culs-de-sac. Brookside Close was a speculative housing development in which the television company bought houses when they were first offered for sale. Regular meetings between the production team and the real-life residents made coexistence possible. In 1991 Brookside Parade was built as an extension to the set, by converting a disused college block in Liverpool into the appearance of a modern shopping precinct. When Manchester and Liverpool organised a photo-opportunity in 2003 to show Manchester's support for Liverpool's bid for European Capital of Culture status in 2008, Manchester was represented by two actors from the soap opera CORONATION STREET (made in the city) and Liverpool by two from Brookside. See also EASTENDERS, OZZIE AND HARRIET and THE SIMPSONS.

brough (Scots) A town. See also BURGH.

brown land Land (in an urban area) that is no longer in permanent use. Also known as *brownfield and brownfield land*.

brownfield *adj* and *n*. PREVIOUSLY DEVELOPED LAND. The term became widely current in the 1980s. Used as a noun or an adjective (describing land or a site) brownfield was introduced as a contrast to *greenfield* (land that has not been developed). The enthusiasm for building on brownfield sites is a response to a variety of different motives. These include: a) It saves building on the countryside, which is valued for its own sake, and is agricultural land (though this is less important than it was, as around 10 per cent of agricultural land in south-east England is EU set-aside, likely to remain unproductive in the long term). b) Brownfield sites are thought by many to be suitable for relatively dense, resource-efficient, urban development compared to new development on greenfield sites. c) Many of the people who live in the countryside (especially those who do not have children seeking affordable homes) are vehemently opposed to further development.

A brownfield site may well be green, not brown, if its buildings have been demolished and vegetation has taken over. Mike Davis (2002) writes: 'Environmentalists have belatedly tried to appreciate that the "brownfield" sites of post-industrial Europe are actually biological oases – "green islands" – whose species diversity typically exceeds not only the rest of the city but the surrounding factory-farmed, genetically modified countryside as well.' Redundant sites on the edges of cities or in the countryside (sites of former isolation hospitals or military airfields, for example) are often classified as 'brownfield' rather than 'greenfield', as they have been built on before. This, it is said, makes them suitable to be developed again. The result is often a new stretch of suburban sprawl, poorly connected to economic and movement networks, which has no sense of identity, and none of the features that contribute to making a place robust and adaptable to change.

Brownfield land is often difficult to develop because of fragmented ownership, poor servicing and transport, contamination and a poor environment. By 2002 the UK government preferred the term *previously developed land*. Brownfield was defined by the US Department of Energy in 2001 as 'an abandoned, idled or under-used industrial and commercial site where expansion or redevelopment is complicated by real or perceived environmental contamination; it also has an active potential for redevelopment or reuse.' Compare GREENFIELD and URBAN GREENFIELD. See also UNDERUTILIZED PARCEL and URBAN FIRST.

brownlining Avoiding building on contaminated sites or BROWNFIELD land. A variant of REDLINING.

Brum Birmingham. See BIRMINGHAM URBAN DESIGN STUDY, BRINDLEYPLACE and BULL RING.

Brummagem The nickname of Birmingham, England. The word derives from *Bromwycham,* an old name for Birmingham. The word brummagem also meant cheap and showy, deriving from the sort of goods and counterfeit coins supposedly made there. 'One has no great hopes for Birmingham,' Jane Austen wrote in *Emma*, published in 1816. 'I always say there is something direful in the sound.'

brummie A native of Birmingham.

Brundtland Report *Our Common Future,* issued by the World Commission on Environment and Development report in 1987. Gro Harlem Brundtland chaired the commission. See SUSTAINABLE.

Brunswick Centre A mixed-use development of council housing, shopping, a cinema and underground car park in a concrete megastructure in Bloomsbury, London. Designed by Patrick Hodgkinson and built in 1968–72, it was inspired by unexecuted designs of the Italian architect ANTONIO SANT'ELIA. In the original scheme the housing was intended to be private. Camden Council took it over when other sources of investment could not be found, necessitating many design changes and cheaper finishes. At the time similar dramatic redevelopments of Bloomsbury's streets and squares were being carried out by the University of London. See LESLIE MARTIN.

brutalism 1 Buildings of stained concrete that appear to be brutally unsympathetic to passers-by. This is the popular use of the term. Example: 'It's not concrete, it's not depressing and it's not brutalist' (headline over a story in the *Guardian* arts section about a new bus station, 2000). **2** A modernist style of architecture promoted by the advocates of *new brutalism*. The movement, founded in 1954, emphasised the form and massing of buildings, truth to materials, and a sense of history. 'Its name is easily open to misconception,' Elain Harwood (2000) writes, 'partly because of confusion with Le Corbusier's term for rough concrete, BÉTON BRUT, yet what mattered was not the materials – "brutalist" buildings could as easily be of brick or stone as concrete – but a new vitality and imagination in design, classical planning and a rejection of all that was suburban or petty.' William Curtis (1996) has written of the new brutalists as 'a younger generation sensing the devaluation of the heroic vision of the earlier modern movement into something smooth and ersatz, and seeking a visual language to give body to their own rough awakening to the social realities of the post-war years'.

Bryce, James (1838–1922) A member of Parliament and supporter of PATRICK GEDDES, he wrote *The Menace of Great Cities* (1913). He was the first president of the UK Sociological Society.

Brynmawr rubber factory Celebrated for its innovative reinforced concrete construction, it was the first post-war building in Wales to be listed. It was demolished after standing empty for many years.

B-Town Berkeley, California.

Buchan, John (1875–1940) Novelist. See BIGGLESWICK GARDEN CITY.

Colin Buchanan

Buchanan, Colin (Sir) (1907–2002) Engineer and town planner. Buchanan trained as a civil engineer. He worked at the Ministry of Town and Country

Planning and its successor, the Ministry of Housing and Local Government, from 1946 to 1954, when he became an inspector for special public enquiries. In 1960 he was appointed special adviser on urban road planning to the minister of transport, Ernest Marples. The result was the Ministry of Transport's *Traffic in Towns*, published in 1963 and the most influential and widely read planning report of its time. At the time it was praised for proposing to create 'environmental areas' (see ALKER TRIPP and TRAFFIC CALMING) in which pedestrians would be protected from motor traffic, though now the report is often criticised for going too far to accommodate traffic, and of proposing to carve up town centres with roads. Buchanan was president of the Town Planning Institute in 1964, professor of transport planning at Imperial College, London, director of the School of Advanced Urban Studies at the University of Bristol, and founder in 1964 of a planning consultancy. He was a member of the ROSKILL COMMISSION of Inquiry into the location for a third London airport. Its report, published in 1970, was accompanied by his note of dissent.

bucket (US) A CAR.

Buckingham, James Silk (1786–1855) The GARDEN CITY ideas of EBENEZER HOWARD were influenced by Buckingham's plan for a model town called Victoria, published in 1849 as *National Evils and Practical Remedies, with the Plan of a Model Town*. Buckingham proposed a layout with a one-mile square plan form, with major diagonal and radial avenues. The whole town would be illuminated by a central towering beacon. A development company would manage the estate, own all the buildings and be the sole employer (Miller, 1989). Its name, chosen in honour of the queen, also denotes a victory over social evils.

Bucksbaum, Martin Pioneering developer of shopping centres. He built his first in Cedar Rapids, Iowa, in 1956. He referred to the new suburban shopping malls as 'the new downtowns' (Adamson, 2000).

buddleia (also buddleja) A fast-growing plant common on derelict urban sites. Its purple (or sometimes orange), honey-smelling flowers attract butterflies and bees. It was named after the botanist Adam Buddle (d1715). See also ROSEBAY WILLOW HERB.

budgie-box A pejorative term for a small house built as the standard product of a volume house-builder. See also BOX BUILDER and NODDY BOX.

build quality The degree to which a building is well constructed, as distinct from its qualities of fulfilling its intended function (FUNCTIONALITY) or making an impact on the senses.

building 1 The act or process of constructing. **2** Something that is built. A building is defined by the Royal Institute of British Architects for the purposes of its design awards schemes as 'any structure, whether new, restored, rehabilitated or converted, which includes an element of executed design work'. In 2002 the RIBA awarded the prestigious Stirling Prize for 'the architects of the building thought to be the most significant of the year' to the designers of Gateshead's Millennium Bridge. Some architects protested that a bridge was not a building: one former RIBA president defined a building as a structure containing a toilet. Before 1999 the RIBA's definition of a building specified that the structure must be walled (Chapman, 2002). In 2003 an underpass taking the A43 under the M1 near Towcester was nominated for 'the prime minister's better public building award'. The US Department of Housing and Urban Development's Office of Community Planning and Development defines a building as 'any structure which includes provision for a heating or cooling system, or both, or for a hot water system'.

building element A feature (such as a door, window or cornice) that contributes to the overall design of a building.

building envelope guidelines One or more diagrams with dimensions showing the recommended site and massing of one or more buildings. See ENVELOPE.

building exploratory A centre for explaining, interpreting and providing information on the built environment. Hackney's, opened in the 1990s, is the UK's first. Its developing exhibition about the built environment was put together by Hackney people across a wide range of ages and abilities in the late 1990s. Helped by artists, Hackney residents use their ideas and skills to make interactive models and educational games, produce exhibits and displays, and record their views and knowledge on computer databases, on video and in print.

building facelift scheme A grant scheme jointly funded by a local authority and the private and voluntary sectors aimed at improving building façades.

building line The line formed by the frontages of buildings along a street. The building line can be shown on a plan or section.

building preservation notice Served by a local authority to give an unlisted building temporary LISTED status for six months, while the secretary of state decides whether or not to confirm the listing.

building regulations A system of control through which statutory standards on matters such as safety and energy conservation are enforced by local authorities. Writing of the Building Acts of the past, Andrew Saint (2001) notes that 'there are many features of London, as of other cities, which derive their character from building regulations. They represent the *passive* tradition of urbanism as opposed to the *active* model represented by design. A passive tradition will be sluggish, unimaginative and reactive. But it is likely to command a measure of public understanding and acceptance, because

Boundary Street Estate

people know where they stand. Most important, it can be enforced. At its highest, the building regulation is the key tool of a municipal democracy for urban order. In principle, it should surely not be about style at all, but about specification – about performance and dimension.'

building shoulder The top of a building's main façade.

building stable communities See HOMES FOR VOTES.

build-to-line A line on a plan indicating the required position of a building's façade. Specifying a build-to-line can ensure the continuity of the street frontage and avoid SETBACKS that create spaces of uncertain function and responsibility.

built environment The entire ensemble of buildings, neighbourhoods and cities with their infrastructure.

built environment professional A generic term for architects, planners, urban designers, landscape architects, highway engineers, surveyors and others. DENISE SCOTT BROWN (2002), being an architect, planner and urban designer herself, understands how different the various professionals sometimes are. 'Put a group of urban designers, architects and planners in a sightseeing bus and watch them as the cameras click,' she suggests. 'Where do the architects click? At buildings or clusters of buildings, or at objects – bridges, sculptures, pylons. The urban designers click where things come together – buildings against bridges, pylons beside small houses. The planners are too busy talking to each other to look out of the window.'

built form Buildings and structures.

built up Largely developed with building and streets or roads. Compare RURAL.

bulbout A bulb-shaped extension of the kerb, usually at an intersection, designed to slow the speed at which vehicles turn a corner. A NECKDOWN is similar. See TRAFFIC CALMING.

bulk The combined effect of the arrangement, volume and shape of a building or group of buildings. Also called MASSING.

bulky goods Defined by the Scottish Office (1998) as goods generally sold from retail warehouses where the goods are of such a size that they would normally be taken away by car and not be manageable by customers travelling by foot, cycle or bus, or that large, flat areas would be required to display them (such as furniture in room sets), or not large individually, but part of a collective purchase that would be bulky, such as wallpaper or paint.

Bull Ring, The Britain's first fully enclosed and air-conditioned shopping mall, in central Birmingham. Designed by Sidney Greenwood in association with TJ Hirst, it opened in 1964 and closed for redevelopment in 2000. 'For the average woman it will provide a real fillip – the kind of spree that, until now, only London can afford her,' the *Birmingham Post* promised in 1964. Instead it became a byword for the worst sort of megastructural city centre development. A redevelopment scheme was published in 1988 but criticised by Birmingham for People as 'an aircraft carrier parked in the city'. A succession of alternative proposals followed before the Bull Ring eventually closed for redevelopment 12 years later. The new Bull Ring opened in 2003.

bullet repayment Repaying interest only on a loan until the capital is due to be paid at the end.

Buls, Charles (1837–1914) As mayor of Brussels, and in his 1893 book *The Design of Cities*, he put the case for making the most of historic cities and their streets.

bum *n*. **1** A pejorative term for a shiftless, homeless person. See VAGRANT. **2** A worthless person.

bummler box (Geordie) A small house.

Bunbury An edible town that features in L Frank Baum's book *The Emerald City of Oz* (1910).

Bundesausbaugebiet (German) A development area.

Bundesausbauort (German) A development centre.

bungaloid growth A derogatory term used in the 1920s and '30s to describe low-density, BUNGALOW (sometimes PLOTLAND) development.

bungalow A house of only one storey. Mark Girouard (1985) notes that bungalows on the Anglo-Indian model were built all over the hotter zones of the British Empire from the early nineteenth century to the 1930s. The first bungalows in the UK were built as seaside holiday homes. The first to be so named was built near Westgate-on-Sea in Kent in 1869 (Burnett, 1986). Others in various places along the Kent coast followed in the 1870s. They were what previously would have been called 'cottages' under a new name, Girouard suggests. 'The name was probably chosen for the sake of novelty, in order to sell them, for visually the little houses bore little resemblance at all to Indian bungalows.' The name caught on though, and many English bungalows were built with Indian features such as a veranda and a big roof. Girouard records bungalows as reaching the east coast of America in the 1880s and spreading to the mid-west (more than 100,000 bungalows being built in and around Chicago between 1920 and 1930) and California, where they were also highly popular.

The bungalow, built around 1913, in which DH Lawrence lived when he wrote his Australian novel *Kangaroo*, is preserved today not only because of its literary connection but as 'the oldest surviving example in New South Wales (and probably Austalia) of the California bungalow' (quoted in Maddox, 2003). Lawrence, though, was unimpressed by the type, writing in *Kangaroo* of Sydney's suburbs 'loused over with small promiscuous bungalows around which lay an aura of rusty tin cans'. Bungalows are particularly common in central Scotland, many of them dating from the 1920s and '30s. In Edinburgh there are large area of bungalows even near the city centre. Glasgow's are mainly in the city's outlying villages (a consequence of the city's planning policies). Two surveys in 2002 showed that almost a third of Britons considered a bungalow to be their ideal home. Bungalow is a Hindi word.

bungalow bliss (Ireland) The widespread building of bungalows. The term was current in the 1990s when the practice was being criticised for despoiling the landscape with new houses in non-traditional forms and materials.

Bungalow Briggs RA Briggs, who built the first bungalow development at East Grinstead in 1887 (Burnett, 1986).

bungalow court (US) **1** Around 10 or 20 bungalows, usually built for rent and often for summer visitors, grouped round a pedestrian court. The form of development first appeared in 1909 and became popular in California (Girouard, 1985). **2** Defined approvingly by ANDRES DUANY (1998) as small, detached, one- or two-bedroom cottages each with its own YARD, usually developed in clusters of four to eight. They share a common walkway and sometimes also a common parking pad.

Bungalow Town A development of 200 bungalows built by PH Harrison in the 1900s between Lancing and Worthing in Sussex (Burnett, 1986).

bungalow town An early term for what were later called PLOTLANDS (Ward, 1998).

bunk off To play truant.

bunk on To ride on public transport without paying.

bunker A development that internalises its services (catering, recreation and retailing, for example), excluding passers-by. Examples include gated communities and many larger public or private institutions.

bunker architecture Buildings designed to exclude outsiders.

bunker mentality Thinking about a particular subject without considering relevant related subjects. Also SILO mentality.

Bunnybury A city of marble inhabited by rabbits in *The Emerald City of Oz* (1910).

burb Suburb. Example: 'So long as the majority of the British bourgeoisie prefers to struggle home to burbs that whisper a fib about maypoles and morris men, our inner cities will continue to be bywords for dereliction' (Meades, 2003).

Burbank, Truman See SEAHAVEN ISLAND.

bureaucracy 1 Administrative systems run by officials. **2** Inefficient, inflexible and excessively secretive administration. The French word *bureau* originally referred to the baize covering of a desk, then to the writing-desk itself, and later to the office.

bureaucratic managerialism The anarchist writer COLIN WARD (1990) argued that an alliance between Fabians and radical conservatives at the end of the nineteenth century led to the takeover of socialism by bureaucratic managerialism, leading to the worst types of town planning, unsuccessful council housing, and collectivism.

bureaucratic proceduralism A concern with carrying out bureaucratic procedures, to the exclusion of other concerns. Town planning in the UK has been accused of this in recent years.

burgage A long, narrow (usually about 30 feet wide) plot of land held by a burgess in a medieval town.

burgagium (Latin) BURGAGE.

burgess In the middles ages the term referred to a resident of a borough, and in some cases one with particular privileges.

Burgess, Ernest (1886–1966) See URBAN ECOLOGY.

burgh (Scotland) The English equivalent (pronounced approximately the same) is borough.

Burghs, the Pittsburgh, Pennsylvania.

Burle Marx, Roberto (b1909) Garden and landscape designer, known for his private gardens, public plazas and the Copacabana Beach promenade. He calls his style Burlesque-Marxist. His gardens are, in the opinion of the critic Richard Weston (2002) 'arguably Brazil's major contribution to the adventure of modern art'.

Daniel Burnham

Burnham, Daniel Hudson (1846–1912) Chicago-based architect, planner, entrepreneur and a leader of the CITY BEAUTIFUL MOVEMENT. He was responsible for the 1909 Chicago Plan and for completing L'ENFANT's Washington Plan. His most widely quoted remark ('Make no little plans, they have no magic to stir men's blood. Make big plans, aim high in hope and work, remembering that a noble, logical diagram once recorded will never die') is now considered apocryphal, according to Joseph Rykwert (2000).

Burns, John (1858–1943) Politician. He was appointed president of the Local Government Board in 1905. 'I was born in a slum and this made me a town planner,' he said. 'Having slept in Windsor Castle and Pentonville [Prison, as a consequence of his political activism], I think I am an authority on housing.' Burns was responsible for the first town planning legislation. The aim of the Housing and Town Planning Act 1909 was, he told the House of Commons, 'to secure the home healthy, the house beautiful, the town pleasant, the city dignified and the suburb salubrious.'

Burns, Wilfred City planning officer of Newcastle-upon-Tyne (1960–68) and later the UK government's chief planner. He favoured slum clearance and comprehensive redevelopment as a way of breaking up and dispersing communities which he considered vicious, apathetic and depraved. See SLUM and T DAN SMITH.

Burra Charter A statement of conservation principles, and a set of definitions of terms and concepts, adopted by Australia ICOMOS (International Council of Monuments and Sites) at Burra Burra in 1979.

Burroughs, Edgar Rice Writer. See TARZANA.

Burton, James (1761–1837) A major developer and builder of the streets and squares of Georgian London. He was the father of the architect Decimus Burton who, in the words of John Summerson (1962), 'does not deserve to be so *very* much more famous than his extraordinary father'.

bus The word is a shortening of *omnibus*. George Shillibeer introduced London's first (horse-drawn) bus service in 1829, and the motor bus was introduced to the capital in 1905. The French used the term *voiture omnibus* (carriage for all) after 1828. In London after 1829 the French term was shortened to omnibus ('*voiture* was obviously foreign rubbish, but *omnibus* was classical and we could live with that,' comments Michael Quinion, 2003) and subsequently to bus ('one of our weirdest linguistic inventions, since it consists just of part of a Latin suffix, *-ibus*, with no root in it at all,' Quinion notes). The politician Margaret Thatcher

> **❝ IF YOU ARE SEEN ON A BUS AFTER THE AGE OF 30 YOU ARE A LOSER IN LIFE ❞**
>
> *Margaret Thatcher*

is supposed to have said: 'If you are seen on a bus after the age of 30 you are a loser in life'. David Begg, chairman of the Integrated Transport Commission, said in 2002 that 'if you see a white man in a suit standing at a bus stop you assume he has lost his driving licence'.

bus rapid transit An express bus service with infrequent stops, fast loading, unloading and fare collection. The buses may use bus-only lanes or buses-only streets, and they may be able to make traffic lights turn green as they approach. In some cases the buses stop at platforms, avoiding the need for stairs and wheelchair lifts.

bush, the (Australia) The countryside.

business architecture Buildings designed primarily to meet the needs of business.

business excellence model See STREET EXCELLENCE MODEL.

business improvement district A town or city centre area, or other commercial district, in which property owners agree by ballot to the levy of a mandatory tax to fund environmental improvements and management schemes. The first was declared in Minneapolis in 1970.

business incubator A building or part of a building designed, adapted or managed to accommodate new businesses.

business park A development of mainly office buildings. See PARK.

business tourism Short-term travel and visits by people travelling in the course of their work (or, at least, at their employer's expense).

Busquets, Joan Planner, urban designer and architect. He was professor of town planning at the University of Barcelona after 1979, and city planner of BARCELONA from 1983 to 1989. He later became professor of planning and urban design at Harvard. Sir Peter Hall (2003) has called him 'the man who remade Barcelona' and 'the world's most successful town planner'.

Joan Busquets

bustee SQUATTER SETTLEMENT. The word derives from the Hindi/Urdu word *basti*, a small town (Vidal and Gupta, 1999).

Buxton, Major See CHALK PIT CASE.

-by The suffix, as in *Grimsby* and *Whitby*, derives from the Old Norse for town. See also BYLAW HOUSING.

bye-law housing See BYLAW HOUSING.

Byers, Stephen (b1953) Politician. See SECRETARY OF STATE.

Byker Estate Council housing in Newcastle-upon-Tyne designed by the British-born, Swedish architect Ralph Erskine and built 1973–1980. The scheme incorporated the *Byker Wall*, a sinuous, continuous medium-rise block intended to protect the rest of the estate from the noise and pollution of an urban motorway that was not, in fact, built. The Victorian terraced housing of the Byker area was demolished in phases, allowing the architects (who set up a shop-front office in the area) to consult the tenants about the design of their new homes. The Byker Wall is notable for, among other things, its brightly coloured timber balconies. The style was dubbed 'high shambolic' by the architectural critic Reyner Banham. By 1999 the partial redevelopment of the Byker Wall was being proposed. Vandalism and graffiti were blamed on a high density of children, the lack of youth facilities, inadequate lighting and the number of spaces not overlooked by the flats. The Byker estate won many architectural awards and in 2003 the government announced its intention to list it.

by-lane A side lane leading off a street.

bylaw (also by-law and bye-law) housing Terraced housing built, mostly between 1880 and 1914, to the minimum standards specified in local bylaws. The houses were laid out in parallel streets without trees or public spaces, and usually the front door opened to the pavement. Most of these THROUGH-TERRACES had a yard (sometimes a small garden) opening on to an alley at the back. The bylaws were successful in ensuring that housing could no longer be built in cramped, unhealthy courts. Mervyn Miller (1989) notes that suburbs built according to model bylaws were 'healthier than the chaotic network of slum courts and alleys, but to the aesthetically sensitive a deadly reflection of unthinking conformity with prescribed standards, and further inducing the uncontrolled outwards sprawl of the major urban areas' (compare HAMPSTEAD GARDEN SUBURB). Bylaw housing now sells for large sums in parts of London. The prefix by- derives from the Old Norse for town. The suffix -by in *Grimsby* and *Whitby* has the same origin.

bypass A road built so that traffic can avoid a congested town centre. The earlier spelling *bye-pass* was current in 1935, as evidenced by the signs erected in that year for the Silvertown Bye-pass in east London. See also HITCHHIKER'S GUIDE TO THE GALAXY.

byroad A secondary or side road.

by-street One that is obscure.

byway A highway used by the public mainly for walking, cycling or horse riding, but for which there is a public right to use any kind of wheeled vehicle. As a result, a number have been badly damaged by the recreational use of four-wheel drive vehicles.

cappuccino culture

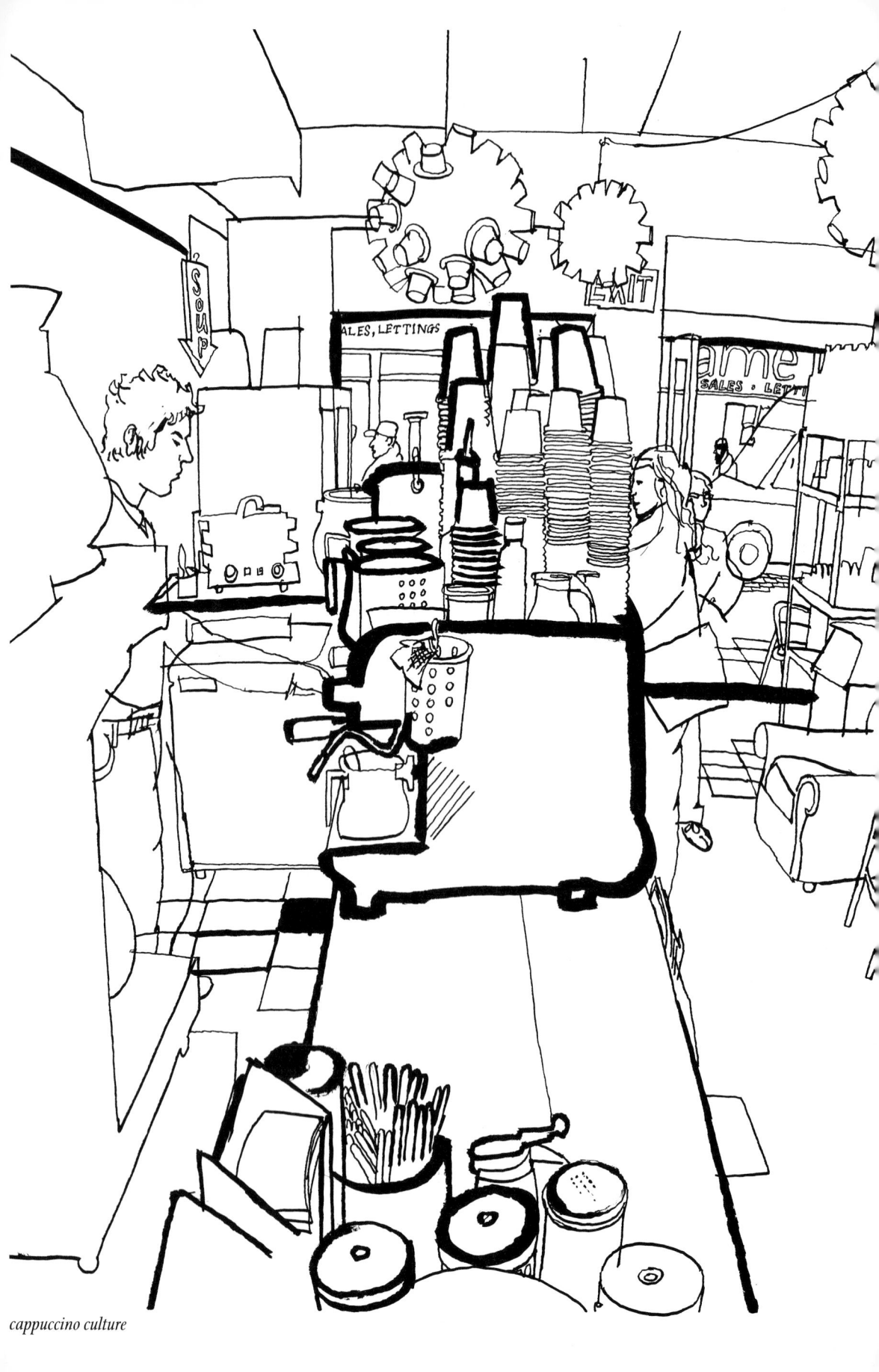

C

CABE COMMISSION FOR ARCHITECTURE AND THE BUILT ENVIRONMENT.

Cabet, Etienne (1788–1856) Utopian socialist. His novel *Voyage to Icaria*, published in 1840, describes the utopian city of ICARA, whose housing is mass-produced. He left France for England and later the USA, where he and his followers, the Icarians, founded a series of utopian settlements.

cabin fever 1 A malaise caused by living or working in isolation. In modern cities it may be a consequence of increased TELEWORKING: even when workers can work in isolation, ways may have to be found to meet their psychological need for being with other people. Stir-crazy (*stir* being prison) has a similar meaning. **2** Suffocating conditions. Example: '…escaping the cabin fever of marriage and family life.' The term is of North American origin.

cacatopia See KAKATOPIA.

Cactusville 1 The home town of Desperate Dan, a character in the *Dandy* comic since 1938. The comic strip shows Cactusville to be an incongruous mixture of the American Wild West and Dundee, Scotland, where the *Dandy* is published. **2** (US) A small, out-of-the way place of no interest. Examples: 'I fell in love with New York and knew right then I could never return to Cactusville'; 'With the car having only seven inches of ground clearance, you'd better be sticking to well-traveled fire roads if you venture off the pavement and into Cactusville'. Compare SMALLVILLE, and see also ONE-EYED CITY and WOOP WOOP.

CAD jockey A pejorative term for an architect or technician who uses a computer-aided design system. Example: 'Making architectural students spend time working in practices was not intended to provide cheap draughtsmen (or, nowadays, CAD jockeys)' (2003).

cadastral map 1 One that shows individual properties (particularly a map showing the findings of a CADASTRAL SURVEY). **2** One that is to a large scale. The word cadastral derives from the Greek *kata stikhon*, meaning line by line.

cadastral survey Carried out in order to prepare a CADASTRE.

cadastre An assessment of the extent and value of land for purposes of taxation.

Cadbury, George (1839–1922) Chocolate manufacturer and philanthropist. Cadbury built the model industrial village of Bournville outside Birmingham in the West Midlands for his workers. He was a supporter of EBENEZER HOWARD.

Cadw The short name of the Welsh Historic Monuments Agency. The Welsh word means 'to preserve'.

Caerleon A legendary city in Wales where King Arthur sometimes held court. See also CAMELOT.

Caernarfon A planned, walled town on the North Wales coast built by King Edward I. Caernarfon illustrated the authority of England in Wales. 'Behind the castle a town was built, enclosed with tough walls, with four gates and a harbour in the lee of the fortress,' Jan Morris (1984) writes. 'This was not merely an English garrison town, but an English colony too. English merchants were encouraged to settle there by exclusive trading rights, while Welshmen were forbidden to live within the city gates.'

café See CAPPUCCINO CULTURE.

café creep Tables from cafés spilling out on to the pavement without authorisation. This is one example of public space being annexed or diminished by adjacent businesses. The term, and the related terms *brasserie bulge* and *trattoria trickle*, are used by the American urban planner Jerold Kayden (2000).

café latte See CAPPUCCINO CULTURE.

calcium chloride Formerly used as a setting agent in concrete, it can cause steel reinforcing to corrode and buildings to collapse.

Caliph's Design, The The title of a pamphlet of art criticism (subtitled *Architects! Where is your Vortex?*) by the painter and writer WYNDHAM LEWIS, published in 1919. Lewis was campaigning for a modernist aesthetic and arguing that the artist's vision should shape the environment directly. He hoped to produce, Paul Edwards (2000) explains, 'a place where senses are stimulated and life can be lived to the full, instead of the "effusive meanness" of the urban scene inherited from the Victorians'. Lewis recounts 'The Parable of

The Caliph's Design': 'One day the Caliph rose gingerly and stealthily from his bed of gold and placed himself at a window of his palace. He then took a pen of turquoise, and for some hours traced hieroglyphs upon a piece of paper. They consisted of patches and of lines, and it was impossible to say what he was doing. Apparently exhausted by the effort, he sank back upon his bed of gold and slept heavily for 10 hours. Waking up in the small hours of the morning, he summoned a messenger and despatched him in search of Mahmed and Hassan, respectively the most ingenious engineer and the most experienced architect in his dominions. The Caliph... addressed them as follows: "I am extremely dissatisfied with the shape of my city, so I have done a design of a new city, or rather of a typical street in a new city. It is a little vorticist bagatelle that I threw off while I was dressing this morning."' The Caliph gives his engineer and architect until the following morning 'to invent the forms and conditions that would make it possible to realize my design', under threat of death if they should fail. 'After a half-hour of complete paralysis of their brilliant faculties, they pulled themselves together. By ten o'clock the following morning a series of the most beautiful plans that had yet been made in Baghdad (retaining with a scrupulous fidelity the masses and directions of the potentate's design) were ready for their master. And within a month a strange street transfigured the heart of that cultivated city.'

call option See OPTION.

callampas See SQUATTER SETTLEMENT.

call-in The secretary of state can *call in* for his own decision any development proposal which he regards as sufficiently important.

Calvino, Italo (b1923) Novelist. See INVISIBLE CITIES.

camber A slight curvature (in a road surface or the underside of a beam, for example).

Camelot King Arthur's legendary capital city. See also CAERLEON.

Cameron, Charles (1745–1812) English architect of Scottish descent. He designed many buildings in ST PETERSBURG in the years after 1772.

Campaign to Protect Rural England With a claimed total of 50,000 supporters, the CPRE campaigns locally and nationally. It has been influential in making the case for development needs to be met on urban BROWNFIELD SITES rather than in the countryside. It was founded in 1926 as the Council for the Preservation of Rural England at a time when agriculture was in trouble, land was cheap and large areas of the countryside were being covered by unplanned development. The CPRE's founders were PATRICK ABERCROMBIE (president of the Town Planning Institute), Guy Dawber (president of the RIBA) and the Earl of Crawford and Balcarres (chairman of the Fine Arts Commission). Its equivalent in Wales was founded in 1929. The 'Preservation' in its name was later changed to 'Protection'. The current name was adopted in 2003, partly as some people were confusing the 'Council' with a local authority.

Campanella, Tomaso (1568–1639) See CITY OF THE SUN.

Campbell, Kelvin (b1952) Urbanist and urban designer. Born in South Africa, he is a founder of the London-based urban design and planning practice Urban Initiatives. He was joint leader of the team on whose work the UK government's guide *By Design: urban design in the planning process* was based, and joint author of RE:URBANISM. He is a past chairman of the URBAN DESIGN GROUP. See MIXED USE and THE THREE MAGNETS.

campus 1 An area with buildings laid out in a park-like setting. In the view of the new urbanist Andres Duany (2000), 'campuses are justified for educational institutions which are heavily pedestrian, but not for offices which should be integrated into the thoroughfare network'. **2** A university site, whether in parkland or not.

can (US) A CAR.

Can Man Plan? A book of light verse, much of it on urbanistic themes, by FJ OSBORN, published in 1959. Osborn's answer to the title poem's question is yes, but no one can plan man.

Canaletto (Giovanni Antonio Canal) (1697–1768) Painter. His paintings of Venice found buyers in visitors to the city, including Englishmen on the Grand Tour, merchants and princes. In 1746, the number of visitors having fallen due to the War of the Austrian Succession, Canaletto moved to London, where he spent 10 years painting that city. Even today his paintings of London influence how people see and value certain views (of the Thames and St Paul's Cathedral, for example), and they have been cited in recent controversies about proposals to build tall buildings in the capital.

Canary Wharf A new financial office district built in London Docklands from the 1980s. The site was originally a wharf handling trade from the Canary Islands. See also PAUL REICHMANN.

Cancer of Empire A book by the English journalist William Bolitho on the slums of Glasgow, published in 1924. Compare WORKSHOP OF THE EMPIRE.

Cantril Farm A council estate on the outskirts of Liverpool, rebranded 'Stockbridge Village' as part of an attempt to regenerate it in the 1980s. See SO GOOD THEY NAMED IT TWICE.

cap An upper limit for a variable rate loan, created by means of an insurance policy.

capability The likelihood that a borrower will be able to meet the interest payments on a loan and in due course repay the capital.

capacity building Development work that strengthens the ability of individuals and community organisations to build the structures, systems, networks and skills needed to take part effectively in managing processes of change.

capital The World Bank identifies four types of capital: physical capital (the quality of the built environment), human capital (the health and quality of life of people in the urban environment), environmental capital (the quality of undeveloped spaces) and SOCIAL CAPITAL (a measure of people's ability to live, work and contribute productively to urban communities).

capital holiday A period in the early years of a loan in which interest only is paid.

capital markets Markets for long-term debt and equity shares. Compare MONEY MARKETS.

capital of all music New York, according to EL Doctorow in CITY OF GOD.

capital of capital New York, due to its dominant position in the world of global finance (Bender, 2002).

capital of exhausted trees New York, according to EL Doctorow in CITY OF GOD.

capital of money London, as portrayed in Tobias Hill's 2003 novel *The Cryptographer* (set in the near future when a new virtual currency has replaced all the world's other currencies).

capital of the mind Edinburgh in the eighteenth century, according to James Buchan's 2003 book with that title. The city was the home of, among other notable writers and thinkers, the philosopher David Hume (1711–76).

capital of the nineteenth century Paris, according to the cultural critic Walter Benjamin (1892–1940) (Hall, 1998). See QUEEN CITY OF THE WORLD.

capital of the twentieth century 1 DETROIT, according to Jerry Herron (2001). 'Nowhere else has American modernity so completely had its way with people and place alike. Reputedly "historic" towns, like Philadelphia, New Orleans and San Francisco, merely seem *old* by comparison. Others, such as New York, Los Angeles and Miami, are not American at all, but more like small, poorly run foreign countries with insufficient fresh water and arable land. And Chicago, no less than its sun-belt reflex, Houston, has been forced to compensate with high-rise architecture for the general lack of autochthonous culture. This makes Detroit the revealed "Capital of the Twentieth Century", and likely the century ahead, because this is the place, more than any other, where the native history of modernity has been written.' **2** LOS ANGELES, according to Allen Scott and ED SOJA.

capital of the world New York, according to its mayor RUDI GIULIANI in 1998.

capital punishment A slogan applied to London by northern cities in 2002 to highlight what they saw as the capital's high cost of living and poor quality of life.

capital web A network of infrastructure and public space structuring urban development, as advocated by the urban designer DAVID CRANE.

Capone, Al Gangster. See MOBTOWN.

cappuccino culture A pejorative term for affluent people living urban lifestyles in central areas. (Cappuccino is espresso coffee topped with steamed and frothed milk, often sprinkled with chocolate.) Example: 'Regeneration must be about more than cappuccino culture'. The term became current in the late 1990s, coinciding with the growth of coffee bars serving cappuccino and similar coffees in town and city centres (*cappuccino* being a reference to the white cowl of a monk, which the frothed milk on top of the coffee is thought to resemble).

Often the 'culture' is evoked without that word having to be used. 'It is new housing that might look appealing in estate agents' brochures – all croissants and cappuccinos and fluffy white dressing gowns on the sun-drenched terrace,' Jonathan Glancey (2003) writes of development proposals for THAMES GATEWAY. Jon Rouse, chief executive of CABE, reported in 2003 that his organisation had been accused of being the 'cappuccino-drinking elite' (De Castella, 2003). In 2001 *Building Design* columnist Ian Martin summed up his view of the architect RICHARD ROGERS' urban vision: 'plenty of covered squares for people to have frothy coffee while they watch clowns on stilts'. Comedians Alan Gilby and Steve Wells, commenting in 2001 on the growth of London's financial district, noted that it was two years since 'the first cappuccino was poured in Brick Lane' (Melhuish, 2001). By 2001 cappuccino was too common to be regarded so often as being particularly characteristic of the affluent or sophisticated. Jokey or pejorative references to cosmopolitan urbanites were more likely to cite *café latte* (which made its appearance also on paint charts). (Café latte is steamed milk added to espresso coffee). Example: 'Brick Lane... buzzes with young urbanites, nipping into "coffee@" to grab a café latte on their way to work' (2002). In 2002, though, a survey of househunters and estate agents found that people deciding where to live were applying 'the cappuccino test', a check on the number of coffee bars in an area (Littlejohn, 2002).

LE CORBUSIER described cafés in 1923 (in *Vers une Architecture*) as 'fungus that eats up the pavements of Paris'. FJ OSBORN (Hughes, 1971) expressed his contempt in a letter to LEWIS MUMFORD in the 1950s or '60s. 'The best of the intelligensia... have moved to the outer suburbs,' Osborn wrote. 'Such intelligentsia as is left is... of the over-urbanised café-lounging, quasi-communist, quasi-technocratic type – right out of touch, not only with the sanity of the countryside but with the psychology of ordinary, home-centred workers.' Max Hutchinson (1989), discussing the London County Council's housebuilding programmes of the 1950s, writes that 'the young architectural lions no longer discussed fine art over a glass of Madeira at the Athenaeum but modern jazz over an espresso at the local coffee bar'. The writer VS Pritchett (1997) observes (writing in 1956): 'Until the espresso bars started there was a certain affinity between London coffee and crime.' Lewis Keeble declared in the 1964 edition of his definitive textbook *Principles and Practice of Town and Country Planning* that 'the population of Britain does not consist of people with a frustrated hankering after a café society' of the sort 'to be found in the centres of continental towns' (quoted in Hague, 2001).

The first recorded coffee-houses in England opened in Oxford in 1650. Their equivalents in Paris were known as *maisons de café*, abbreviated by 1700 to *cafés* (Girouard, 1985). Peter Ackroyd (2000) records that London's first coffee house was the Jamaica Tavern, set up in St Michael's Alley, off Cornhill, in 1652, and that 'by the turn of the century there were some two thousand of them in the capital... There were coffee houses for every trade and every profession.' Many remain, having evolved into public houses, including the Jamaica Tavern.

James Howard Kunstler (2001), is unusual in associating coffee with suburbanites. Suspicious of the coffee-drinking habits of the enemies of new urbanism, he writes of 'hardcore suburban growth cheerleaders, in their narcotic raptures of consumerism and gourmet coffee...'

Capra, Frank (1897–1991) Film director. See BEDFORD FALLS.

car Also known informally in the USA as a *boiler, bucket, can, crate, heap, iron* or *jalopy*.

car alarm An electronic device that sounds loudly to let its absent owner know that it is malfunctioning.

car ban A regulation excluding cars from a particular area.

car barn Garaging for cars provided in the central part of a housing block. The form reduces the degree to which parking disrupts the continuity of the street frontage. Car barns were included in the design for the millennium village at Allerton Bywater near Leeds, published in 2001.

car city A city (or part of one) where the car is the dominant mode of movement. Compare WALKING CITY.

car club 1 People giving each other lifts to work. Also known as *car share*. **2** A scheme in which people living in a specific area rent cars from a pool. **3** An association of people who share a pool of cars in collective ownership. Also known as *city car clubs* and *car share clubs*.

car culture Ways of thinking, designing, planning and developing that favour cars over other forms of transport and land use.

car dependency Having no choice of transport apart from a car. Example: 'We want to reduce car dependency, not car ownership' (a UK government minister in 1998, quoted in Adams, 1998).

car platform A hardstanding in front of a house where a car can be parked.

car port (also carport) A covered stand for a car, open on at least two sides.

caravan sites Subject to both the planning system and a separate licensing system.

carbon-neutral development Producing no net carbon dioxide emissions.

carcass The basic structure of a building. The speculative builders of some of the largest Georgian terraces would sell the carcasses for owners to complete to their own taste. Sometimes the carcasses of buildings are left uncompleted for years following a property slump. In the 1860s, after a slump following a development boom, *Building News* described London's Notting Hill as 'a graveyard of buried hopes... naked carcasses, crumbling decorations, fractured walls, slimy cement' (Ackroyd, 2000).

car-centric Based on car-borne movement.

carceral city A part of a city where poor and destitute people live, excluded from other parts by security measures or regulations (Dear and Flusty, 1998).

carchitecture Buildings and landscapes that have been shaped by the motor car.

cardboard city Any place where a large number of homeless people live in cardboard boxes and structures made of other found material. A well-known example was under the roads and walkways of London's South Bank for many years.

cardo (Latin) The north-south main street of a Roman town, crossing the east-west *decumanus*. Spiro Kostof (1991) notes that the terms are modern: there is no solid ancient authority for them in those senses (the Romans applied the terms to the main coordinates of CENTURIATION). See also VIA PRINCIPALIS.

care and repair Schemes that help older homeowners with repairs, improvements and adaptations.

care in the community A government programme aiming to provide services and support for people who are affected by problems of ageing, mental illness, mental handicap, or physical or sensory disability, enabling them to live as independently as possible, rather than in institutions.

While the aim may be laudable, the programme has been criticised for inadequate alternative provision, and the suspicion that saving money is the primary objective. The programme has led to the closure of many hospitals, including up to 150 large psychiatric hospitals, many of which had historic buildings and extensive grounds. Many have now been converted or redeveloped, often having been classified as BROWNFIELD. Meanwhile the 'care in the community' is often judged to be lacking.

careful urban renewal The name given to the approach adopted by the Internationale Bauausstel-

car

lung (IBA) in the Kreuzberg area of Berlin in the 1980s, following public protest against proposed redevelopment. A set of basic principles was agreed in 1983. They included: renewal must be carried out with local people; the building stock must be preserved; technical and social planning must go hand in hand; the area's special character must be maintained; renewal should be gradual; and public facilities such as streets, squares and green areas must be renewed and extended (Kleihues, 1990).

carmaggedon The disastrous effect of excessive dependence on the car. The term has been used by the geographer John Adams.

Carpenter, Edward (1844–1929) Socialist philosopher. His rural commune at Millthorpe near Sheffield, based on a 'healthy, democratic, vegetarian… simple life', influenced many of the GARDEN CITY pioneers (Miller, 1989).

carpet An artificial, raised surface that allows pedestrians and sometimes vehicles to move over features (such as roads or railway lines) that might otherwise obstruct them.

carpool The sharing of a ride by two or more people in a car.

Carport Cardiff and Newport, south Wales, and the corridor between them.

carrefour à gyration See ROUNDABOUT.

carriage arch An archway in a street frontage that provides access to the rear of the buildings without completely disrupting the BUILDING LINE.

carriageway The part of a road intended for use by vehicular traffic. See FOOTWAY.

carrying capacity An area's ability to support development or human activities without unacceptable consequences, in view of its limited resources (such as food that can be grown and available energy) and other matters (such as biodiversity). Capacities are defined as *critical* (the most important), *constant* and *tradeable* (less important).

cartoon architecture A pejorative term for buildings designed for instant, simple effect. See SPRAWLSCAPE.

cash-in-lieu for parking (US) A policy allowing a cash payment to be made to a parking fund instead of providing parking spaces.

cashstake The amount of their own money that is being put into a development by the person or organisation that is borrowing the rest.

cassie (Ireland) A back yard.

Castra Sanguinarius and **Castrum Mare** Two fictional ancient Roman cities, at war with one another, cut off from the world and time in the heart of Africa. They feature in Edgar Rice Burroughs' novel *Tarzan and the Lost Empire* (1929). See also TARZANIA.

Catal Hüyük The location in Turkey of a shrine in which a wall-painting, dating from some time after 6,500 BC, may show the oldest extant graphic representation of a town plan, according to Spiro Kostof (1991). See also UR and URUK.

catchment The area of land drained by a watercourse.

catchment area See DRAW AREA.

category D village Certain former colliery villages in the north east of England were categorised as 'category D' in development plans of the 1960s and '70s, indicating that without their mining jobs they were no longer viable. The intention was that they would be allowed to decline: new capital expenditure was limited to the maintenance of existing facilities and large numbers of houses were to be demolished. The highly controversial policy was eventually abandoned.

Cathne A fictional city in Africa built of gold. This City of Gold is at war with Athne, the City of Ivory. Both feature in Edgar Rice Burroughs' *Tarzan and the City of Gold* (1933). See also CASTRA SANGUINARIUS.

Cathy Come Home Jeremy Sandford's BBC television play, broadcast in 1966, dramatised the social costs of homelessness. Shelter, the recently formed campaign for homeless people, benefited from the publicity and from the general assumption that the newly discovered problem could be solved by determined action. It was not to be, and Shelter has become a permanent part of the landscape of voluntary organisations. In 2000 the play was voted by producers, writers and critics as the second-best television programme ever (after the sitcom series *Fawlty Towers* and before *Dr Who*).

causey A pavement; a cobbled street. A variant of *causeway*, the term is now used mainly in Scotland and the north of England.

causey edge (Yorkshire) A KERB.

ceety (Scots) A CITY.

Celebration A new town built on new urbanist principles by the Disney Corporation near Disney World at Orlando, Florida. Celebration's website explains that it has been is 'conceived as a small southeastern town with pre-1940s architecture'. When complete, it is expected to have around 12,000 residents. The master plan is by the architects Cooper, Robertson and Partners, and Robert AM Stern Architects. A number of internationally architectural stars have designed individual buildings in the downtown, including VENTURI, SCOTT BROWN and Associates, Phillip Johnson, Michael Graves and Cesar Pelli. ALDO ROSSI designed the first three buildings in the office park. Celebration's design principles are enforced by a strict code, devised by Urban Design Associates.

'There once was a place where neighbours greeted neighbours in the quiet of summer twilight,' one of its early advertising campaigns warbled. 'Where children chased fireflies. And porch swings provided easy refuge from the care of the day. The movie house showed cartoons on Saturday. The grocery store delivered. And there was one teacher who always knew you had that "special something". Remember that place? Perhaps from your childhood. Or maybe just from stories. It held a magic all its own. The special magic of an American home town. Now, the people at Disney – itself an American family tradition – are creating a place that celebrates this legacy. A place that recalls the timeless traditions and boundless spirit that are the best parts of who we are' (quoted in Ross, 2000).

The new urbanist *New Urban News* (2001) has written of Celebration: 'The visually striking town centre opened its doors five years ago – the first complete new urban town centre – perhaps the first new US downtown in three quarters of a century. While its success is debatable, one thing is for sure – it can't be judged by conventional real estate analysis alone. Critics point out that the downtown was highly expensive, is poorly located for retail, and caters more to tourists than residents. On the other hand, Celebration's downtown forms a powerful civic heart for the community and gives residents the choice of doing some of their shopping by foot.' See also THE STEPFORD WIVES.

Celesteville The idyllic capital city founded by King Babar in Jean de Brunhoff's children's story *Babar the King*, published in 1939. It is named after his wife, Queen Celeste.

Celestial City The religious writer and preacher John Bunyan's name for heaven in his allegory *Pilgrim's Progress*, published in two parts in 1678 and 1685. See also CITY OF GOD and URBAN DESIGN FRAMEWORK.

Céline, Louis-Ferdinand (1894–1961) Novelist. See URBAN DESTRUCTION.

cell system A traffic management method based on allowing private access traffic into, but not across, a town centre, and requiring it to leave by the same route (Pharoah, 2001).

cellular structure Urban development based on neighbourhoods that are to some extent self-contained. Nigel Taylor (1998) writes that '[the] "cellular" concept was evident in the master plans for all the post-war "Mark 1" new towns and was also central to Abercrombie's 1944 plan for Greater London.' It was this approach to structuring urban areas that CHRISTOPHER ALEXANDER criticised in his essay 'A city is not a tree' (see CITY IS NOT A TREE, A).

census A population count. The UK census is a count of the whole population that takes place every 10 years. It provides information on which planning for housing, transport, health, employment and other matters is based.

central activities zone Designated by the Greater London Authority (2001) as the area within central London where planning policy will promote finance, specialist retailing, tourism and cultural activities.

central activity area (CAA) (Australia) The term was used by Australian urban designers in the 1980s in place of CENTRAL BUSINESS DISTRICT, on the grounds that the centre of a city should be occupied by more activities than just business. The term did not stick and CBD is again in general use in Australia.

central business district (CBD) The commercial area of a town or city centre. In the UK this American term was widely current in the 1970s, fell largely into disuse, and in the 1990s made a modest comeback. Jane Jacobs (1961) noted that 'planning jargon... no longer speaks of "downtowns" but instead of "CBDs"... A central business district that lives up to its name, and is truly described by it, is a dud.' See CENTRAL ACTIVITY AREA.

central city In EBENEZER HOWARD's original conception, a SOCIAL CITY would consist of a *central city* of 58,000 people surrounded by SIX GARDEN CITIES of 32,000 each, giving a total population of 250,000. Compare CENTRE CITY.

central London The 1971 Census of Population defined the 'Conurbation Centre' of London as consisting of the City of London and 'the West End' (most of which is in Westminster). In the 1981 census that same area was called 'London City Centre'. The property agents who operate in this territory refer to it instead as 'the Central Area', which comprises not only THE CITY and the West End, but also 'Midtown', which lies between the two. The London Planning Advisory Committee (London's strategic planning agency until 2000) preferred to speak of a 'Central Activities Core Zone' (or 'Central Core Zone') and a wider 'Central Statistical Area'. But LPAC also referred to 'Central London', which it defined either as the Cities of London and Westminster, or as the area bounded by the main railways stations, according to circumstance. On the other hand, when the City of London's planners refer to the 'Central Core', they mean the central core of the City (the financial district), not of London as a whole. In 2001, documents relating to the Mayor of London's Spatial Development Strategy referred to 'Central London', to the 'Central Area' (which did not include Canary Wharf) and to the 'Central Area (including Canary Wharf)'. In 2003 the mayor of London and the London Tourist Board announced that parts of central London were being rebranded 'Cityside', apparently on the grounds that the name would be more familiar to American tourists (see REBRAND).

Central Park, New York Proposed by ANDREW JACKSON DOWNING, it was designed in 1858 by FREDERICK LAW OLMSTED and CALVERT VAUX, inspired by the example of BIRKENHEAD PARK.

central place theory Describes settlement patterns in terms of spheres of influence.

central reservation (UK) An island in the centre of a street or intersection to separate opposite travel lanes and to protect pedestrians. The US term is *median*. See also TRAFFIC CALMING.

centre city The central part of a city or CONURBATION. Compare CENTRAL CITY.

centre for the built environment A building or organisation that provides a focus for a range of activities and services (such as discussions, information, exhibitions, training, collaboration and professional services) relating to design and planning. By 2002 CABE was using this term for what were also called *architecture centres* and ARCHITECTURE AND PLANNING CENTRES.

centre of culture The title given to a UK city shortlisted for the award of EUROPEAN CAPITAL OF CULTURE.

Centre Point An office tower on London's Oxford Street (constructed in 1961–5 as the world's tallest prefabricated building, now listed), designed by RICHARD SEIFERT with the engineers Pell Frischmann. For many years it remained vacant. Critics claimed that the owner, developer Harry Hyams, was keeping it empty because it was worth more as an empty asset than it would have been tenanted. He successfully established through a libel action that this was not so. On one occasion the empty building was occupied by squatters protesting against the lack of homes.

centre-ville (French) City centre.

centrifugal fragmentation The tendency for cities to spread out and form areas dominated by single uses.

centuriation The most common Roman method of land survey, basing a grid on two roads at right angles to each other. A *centuriae* was one of the hundred smallholdings that fitted into each of the resulting grid squares.

Cerdá y Señer, Idelfonso (1815–75) Planner, engineer and politician, famous mainly for his BARCELONA extension plan.

certainty Precise knowledge of an outcome. In the specialist language of property development, *partial uncertainty* is a condition where there is knowledge of what the alternative outcomes are likely to be, but not of the relative probability of each of them occurring. In a condition of *total uncertainty*, on the other hand, it is not even possible to identify what the alternatives might be.

certificate of immunity from listing Issued by a local authority in response to a request from a building owner or developer who wants to be sure that their property will not be listed.

certificate of lawfulness Provided by the local authority at the request of a developer to confirm that planning permission is not required for a particular development (because consent is given automatically by the GENERAL DEVELOPMENT ORDER, for example).

Cervero, Robert See TRANSIT VILLAGE.

ceuffordd (Welsh) A subway.

Chadwick, Edwin (Sir) (1800–1890) Sanitary reformer and civil servant. Born near Manchester, he and his family moved to London at the age of 10. He began his career as a lawyer and journalist. Chadwick became convinced that poverty and ill-health were not just problems for the individuals who suffered them, but issues on which government action was urgently needed. He became secretary to the utilitarian philosopher Jeremy Bentham (1748–1832). After 1832, as assistant commissioner to the Royal Commission set up to enquire into the working of the outdated Poor Laws, Chadwick investigated slum life in London. His work contributed to the Poor Law Amendment Act 1834 and the formation of a centralised administration, and he himself served as secretary to the Board of Commissioners. His 1842 three-volume *Survey into the Sanitary Condition of the Labouring Classes in Great Britain* made the case for the public health legislation that was passed in 1848. Chadwick was pensioned off from public service shortly afterwards, but he continued campaigning for reform, often against determined opposition.

Chadwick, George See SYSTEMS APPROACH.

Chalk Pit Case A significant legal case relating to the status of *third parties* at planning inquiries. A Major Buxton, objecting to a proposal to dig chalk on a site near his home in Essex, found that he had no legal status at the inquiry.

Chalk, Warren See ARCHIGRAM.

Chamberlain Act The Housing Act 1923, named after its promoter (later prime minister) NEVILLE CHAMBERLAIN. Following the financial debate brought about by the open-ended subsidies of the ADDISON ACT of 1919, the Chamberlain Act offered a low government subsidy to local authorities, conditional financial aid to private builders, and local authority mortgages for those with sufficient savings to buy their own home. More than 400,000 homes were completed under the terms of this act by the outbreak of the second world war. See also WHEATLEY ACT.

Chamberlain, Joseph (1836–1914) Politician. As mayor of Birmingham in the 1870s, he was noted for promoting municipal enterprise. Father of Neville.

Chamberlain, Neville (1869–1940) Politician. He was lord mayor of Birmingham 1915–16 (when he was a noted supporter of planning in the city), health secretary in 1923 and 1924–29, and prime minister 1937–1940 (appointing the BARLOW COMMISSION). See CHAMBERLAIN ACT.

Chambless, Edgar See ROADTOWN.

chameleon building One designed to fit unnoticed into its setting. Compare BACKGROUND BUILDING and QUIET ARCHITECTURE.

champion See DESIGN CHAMPION, STREET CHAMPION and TOWN CHAMPION.

Chandigarh The new capital of the Punjab, India,

designed successively by Albert Mayer, Matthew Nowicki and LE CORBUSIER in the 1950s and '60s.

Chandler, Bill See HI-LO.

change agent A person or organisation able to bring about change.

change delivery Managing the processes of urban change.

change of use See DEVELOPMENT.

changed See BIASED TERMINOLOGY.

chaos theory The new science of chaos explains how simple processes in nature can produce structures and effects of amazing COMPLEXITY, without randomness. A popular image of this is the idea (suggested by the American meteorologist and mathematician Edward Lorenz in 1979) that the flap of a butterfly's wings in Brazil might set off a tornado in Texas. That image is based on the phenomenon, important in the study of chaos, of very small differences in the input to a system leading to very large differences in output. The science of chaos is relevant to a wide range of non-linear relationships (those in which there is not a proportional relationship between the elements). Some complex systems show similar patterns at very different scales (such patterns are called *fractals*, a term coined by the mathemetician Benoit Mandelbrot [b1924] who pioneered their study). Chaos theory has been used in the study of, among other things, economic growth, population trends and the structure of the universe. Examples of chaotic behaviour in the field of urbanism include traffic congestion. The term 'chaos' in this scientific sense was coined by the mathematician James Yorke in in 1975. See also ARCADIA.

character 1 Locally distinctive patterns of development, landscape and use; a combination of all the aspects of a place that together make it distinct from anywhere else. The concept, used widely in planning, urban design and conservation, can cover everything from architectural style to land uses, and from topography to smell. The objective of creating or maintaining distinct character is the single most common feature of design policies in local authority development plans. Often the policy says no more than that development should be 'appropriate' to its local context, without giving any clear idea as to what that might mean. How a place's character is defined in any official context will help determine in whose interests it is planned and developed.

The architect REM KOOLHAAS (1996) has doubts about attempts to build character in places. 'Architecture can't do anything that culture doesn't,' he writes. 'We all complain that we are confronted by urban environments that are completely similar. We say we want to create beauty, identity, quality, singularity. And yet, maybe in truth these cities that we have are desired. Maybe their very characterlessness provides the best context for living.' For a fuller discussion of the issue, see LOCAL DISTINCTIVENESS.

The term *character* was first used in relation to architecture in the eighteenth century as the expression of a building's purpose, the evocation of a mood or the expression of a place (Forty, 2000). *Building News* suggested in 1858 that 'it is the duty of our architecture to translate our character into stone' (Ackroyd, 2000). John McKean (1994) notes that the brief to designers of new housing under Edinburgh's High Street Improvement Act 1866 demanded that they 'maintain the Scottish character' and that 'such a theme was surely equally forceful in Glasgow... at this moment of antiquarian and historicist awareness.' The author Tom Douglas MacDonald wrote in the 1930s of the towns of Angus in Scotland: 'They have character in the sense in which the word connotes a certain quality of strength of boldness and substantiality. And they have also character in the second sense, in which it means a quality of uniqueness or difference by virtue of which each is a town by itself and in no danger of being confused with any other' (quoted in Bold, 1984). Some writers suggest that the character of a place is the equivalent of a human personality. That makes it possible to write a city's biography (rather than a history), as M Pye (1991) has done for New York and Peter Ackroyd (2000) for London. Ackroyd, for example, sees certain activities as happening in particular places in London consistently over many hundreds of years, despite there being no evident functional reason for it. Patrick Geddes wrote in 1915: 'Each place has a true personality... a personality too much asleep it may be, but which it is the task of the planner, as master-artist, to awaken' (quoted in Webber, 1988a). **2** In lending money (for property development, for example) character is the sum of the characteristics of a borrower which indicate how proficient and experienced he or she is in carrying out developments and managing finance.

character appraisal Techniques (particularly as developed by English Heritage) for assessing the qualities of conservation areas.

character area An area with a distinct character, identified as such so that it can be protected or enhanced by planning policy. The degree of protection is less strong than in a CONSERVATION AREA.

character assessment An area appraisal emphasising historical and cultural associations.

characterisation 1 Defining and understanding the characteristics of a place; CHARACTER APPRAISAL. **2** The product of such a process.

chare (Newcastle) An ALLEY (see that entry for regional variants).

charity mugger (also chugger) A person (employed by an agency) who accosts passers-by in the street and tries to persuade them to contribute to a particular charity. See MUG.

Charles Hire The capital city of Aprilis, one of the three fictional islands of New Britain, south of the

Cape of Good Hope. Its houses are painted in black, red and yellow stripes. The city's story is told by Pierre Duplessis in *Memoirs of Sir George Wollap* (1787–88). The other cities of New Britain are Burnel, Cuningham, Edinburgh, Jarvis, Rasilinette and Springle.

Charleville A new town north east of Reims, France, built in 1608–20 to a grid plan.

charrette (also charette) 1 An event (ranging from a couple of hours to several days) that brings together a range of people to discuss design issues. A charrette may or may not use techniques of collaborative design. The word originates in the name for the small cart that at one time collected Parisian architecture students' drawings to take them to the Ecole des Beaux Arts to be assessed. The students, as ever, left their projects until the last moment, and may even have added the finishing touches 'en charrette'. The word for the cart became transferred to their intensive (often all-night) design sessions. The term has been widely used in North America in the last two decades, had limited currency in the UK by 1998 and has become more widely used since then. The term has also been applied on occasion to longer design processes. Kevin Starr (1990) writes of 70 Los Angeles architects working in 'a voluntary eleven-month charrette throughout 1924 dealing with the whole question of public buildings and spaces in downtown Los Angeles'. Also known as a *design workshop*. **2** Design work carried out to a tight deadline.

Charter of Krakow See KRAKOV CHARTER.

Chartist Cooperative Land Society Formed in 1845 by Feargus O'Connor to build model communities with cottages and smallholdings. The first of six such communities was built at HERONSGATE near Rickmansworth in 1845. The scheme collapsed in 1851.

Chattanooga Identified in 1969 as the USA's most polluted city, Chattanooga was named in 1990 by the US Environmental Protection Agency as the country's most improved.

chautauqua (pronounced *shetarqua*) A form of popular event held in the late nineteenth and early twentieth centuries, combining education and entertainment, and often held outdoors or in tents. Some chautauquas were held in England to discuss and promote the GARDEN CITY movement. From its beginnings at the Methodist Episcopal camp at Lake Chautauqua, New York, in 1874, the Chautauqua Institute developed lecture series, summer schools and home study courses.

Chaux A model town begun in northeastern France in 1775 to a design by Claude Nicolas Ledoux. In the original plan, the town had a tree-lined, oval ring road and radiating avenues. Half of it was built (Kostof, 1991).

Chavez Ravine A housing development in Los Angeles built in the 1940s and '50s for hispanic people. Its reputation as a socialist endeavour contributed to its fate when it was cleared to make way for a car park in the late 1950s (Fraser, 2001).

checkerboard (US) **1** A street layout based on square blocks. Compare GRIDIRON. **2** The pattern of city layout proposed by Thomas Jefferson in 1816, with buildings and green space in alternate squares, in the hope of preventing the spread of yellow fever.

Chelm A fictional town whose inhabitants take logical reasoning to extremes, as described in Samuel Tenenbaum's *The Wise Men of Chelm*. The people walk in the streets while horses and carts use the pavements, for example, the streets being wider and people more important.

Chelyabinsk-40 A secret military city in the Soviet Union that suffered a nuclear catastrophe in 1957 (Davis, 2002).

chemin des anes, le See STREET OF ASSES.

chequer A block in a gridded plan. The term was used in medieval New Sarum (Salisbury) in Wiltshire.

cherry-pick *v.* To select for development those sites which are easiest or most profitable, instead of selecting more difficult sites or developing the whole area comprehensively.

Cheryomushki The housing estate on the edge of Moscow that is the setting for Dmitri Shostakovich's musical 'Paradise Moscow', written in 1958–9. 'There is no north, it's all south-facing, both sides,' one of the characters observes. 'That's modern construction workers for you' (Croft, 2001a).

chewing gum Unsightly, highly adhesive, blackened blobs of discarded gum pose a significant maintenance problem on the pavements of many town and city centres. Chewing gum was banned in Singapore for 10 years up to 2003 for this reason, and is now available there only from pharmacies. At the time of the Urban Summit in 2002, prime minister Tony Blair announced that the government would introduce on-the-spot fines for dropping gum, to be levied by council street-cleaners. The following day the government admitted that the plan was impractical.

Chi Chicago.

chic *adj.* Fashionable; stylish; elegant; sophisticated. The word is borrowed from the French.

Chicago overcoat A coffin.

Chicago school 1 Sociologists working in Chicago in the early twentieth century, particularly pioneering the study of cities. **2** Economists working in Chicago in the late twentieth century developing theories of monetarist economics.

Chicago Tribune competition Organised by the Chicago Tribune newspaper in 1922 to choose a design for its new skyscraper headquarters. The wide range of designs by many of the world's best architects made the event something of a festival of architecture. Although many of the leading modernist architects entered, including Walter Gropius, Adolf Loos and Max Taut, the winner was a neo-gothic design by John Mead Howell and Raymond Hood. The Chicago Tribune Tower was built in 1925.

Chicago World's Fair The World's Columbian Exposition of 1893 was held to celebrate the 400th anniversary of Columbus' discovery of America. The neo-classical city that was created for the occasion on the former marshes on Chicago's south side helped to inspire the CITY BEAUTIFUL MOVEMENT.

chicane Extensions of the kerb (or other means) which change a straight roadway into a zig-zag or serpentine path to slow vehicles. See TRAFFIC CALMING.

chi-chi *adj.* Fashionable and superficial. The term is often mildly pejorative.

chi-chi-up To make look fashionably chic. Example: 'The shopping street had been chi-chied-up, but the surrounding area was just urban sprawl' (2003, in conversation).

chief planning adviser A part-time post in the UK DETR occupied, sporadically, by a non-civil servant. The last incumbent (1994–97) was David Lock, who succeeded SIR PETER HALL.

child Defined by the United Nations as a person under the age of 18.

child poverty A focus on children living in POVERTY has the benefit, in terms of social policy, of avoiding the issue of whether or not the subjects are to blame for their condition. The Child Poverty Action Group has a long-running campaign. The Social Exclusion Unit (2000) defines child poverty as 'children living in households where the main source of income is a means-tested benefit'.

Children of the City See WOLFGANG SUSCHITZKY.

chimney of the world, the Manchester in the late 1830s (in consequence of the number of factory chimneys belching smoke), according to Major General Charles James Napier, who also called it 'the entrance to hell, realised' (quoted in Johnson, 2001).

Chipitts The Chicago-Pittsburgh corridor.

Chocolate City Washington DC.

choker A narrowing of a street (by means of kerb extensions, landscaping or islands in the street) to reduce traffic speed. See TRAFFIC CALMING.

Chopper City New Orleans, Louisiana. See also BIG EASY, CLICK-CLICK and CRESCENT CITY.

choreography (also urban choreography) Directing the people who shape the development of towns and cities in time and space; the art of managing the process of making places. The phrase is a metaphor for PROACTIVE PLANNING. When in 1999 it appeared in a draft report to be published by the Royal Town Planning Institute, it was decided that the association with ballet might offend some of the institute's rugged northern members, so the phrase was deleted. Jane

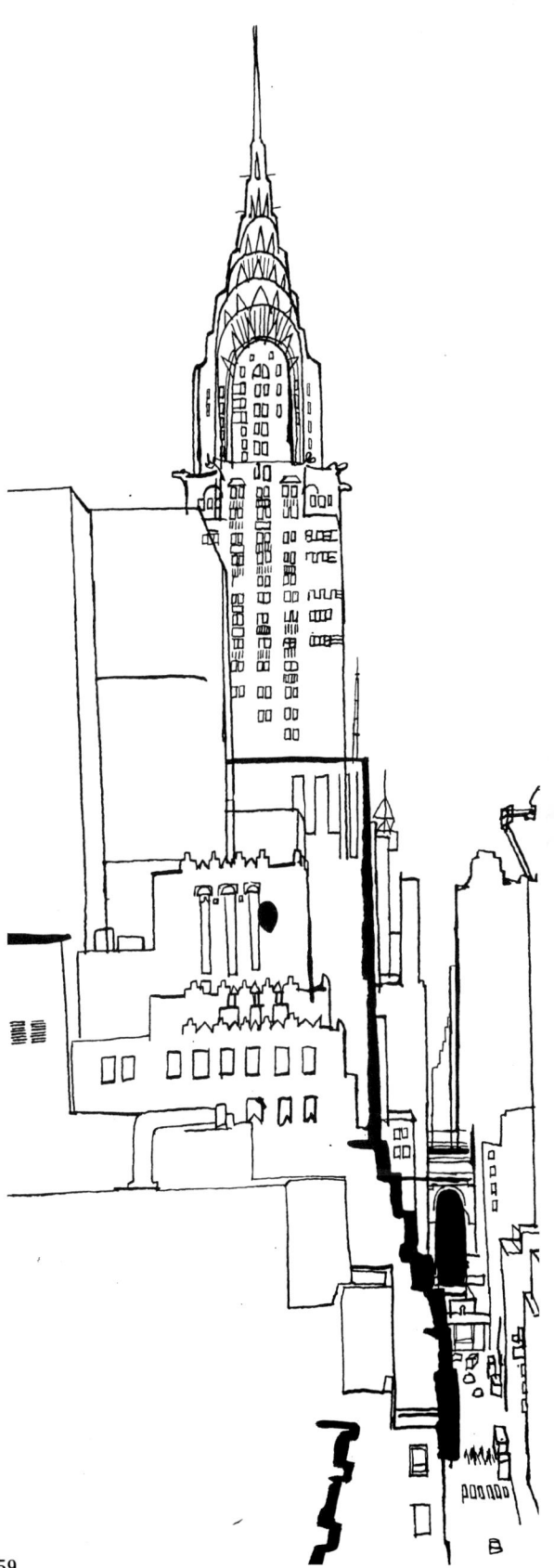

Jacobs (1961) described the vitality of old cities as 'an intricate ballet in which the individual dancers and ensembles all have distinctive parts which miraculously reinforce each other and compose an orderly whole.' Hugh Pearman (2002) writes that three buildings in Newcastle-upon-Tyne masterplanned by Terry Farrell 'perform a frozen dance around the public space'. See also EXPERIENTIAL ENVIROTECTURE.

Chosen City, The A book by the journalist Nicholas Schoon (2001). He argues that almost all GREENFIELD development should be confined to a restricted number of masterplanned TOWN EXTENSIONS. People's desire for plenty of private space indoors and outdoors, for security and easy access to their own car – desires all closely associated with the flight to the suburbs and the countryside – can all be accommodated in the city, he writes.

Christchurch, New Zealand See GARDEN CITY.

Christianopolis The fictional small city featured in Johann Valentin Andreae's *Description of the Republic of Christianopolis*, written in Latin and published in 1619. The city is square in form, seven hundred feet across, and its three districts are devoted respectively to food, exercise and beauty.

Chrysler Building See ART DECO.

Church Commissioners The organisation that manages the property of the Church of England.

Churches Aloft A movement in the USA in the 1920s aimed at restoring churches to cities' skylines by building them in the upper parts of skyscraper office blocks.

CIAM (Congrès Internationaux d'Architecture Moderne) A series of meetings, initiated by the Swiss architectural critic and theorist Sigfried Giedion in 1928, which discussed and promoted modernism in architecture. LE CORBUSIER was among its leading members. The national sub-group in the UK was MARS (Modern Architectural Research Society). CIAM drew up the ATHENS CHARTER at its fourth congress in 1933. See PARIS II.

Cicero See MOBTOWN.

cidade (Portuguese) A city.

Cidade de Deus See CITY OF GOD.

Cinderella effect One well-designed tall building attracting a number of poorly designed buildings (its ugly sisters) to its immediate area.

cinema See FILM.

Circle City Corona, California, founded in 1886 and since absorbed by Los Angeles. Its centre was originally bounded by a circular boulevard.

Circleville, Ohio. A town whose centre was originally planned (in 1810) on a circular plan.

circulation Movement in or around a building or area. The term is a metaphor from physiology. Perhaps its earliest published use in this sense was by VIOLLET-LE-DUC in 1872 (Forty, 2000).

circus An open circular or semi-circular space surrounded by buildings. See also POLYGON and SQUARE.

citadel A fortress protecting a city. Plymouth boasts a spectacular example.

cité (French) The old part of a city or the nucleus of a town (Rykwert, 2000).

cité-jardin (French) A GARDEN CITY or GARDEN SUBURB.

cities of the plain Sodom and Gomorrah. The alleged proclivity of the Sodomites is well understood. What the Gomorrahites got up to remains a mystery. Either way, the Old Testament God disapproved and both cities were destroyed. The American author Jack London (pen name of John Griffith, 1876–1916), who wrote of the appalling living conditions in the east end of London in THE PEOPLE OF THE ABYSS, published in 1902, suggested on one occasion that if he could be God for an hour he would destroy London and its people 'like Sodom and Gomorrah'. Generally, though, his experience in London convinced him of the need for revolutionary socialism.

citified *adj.* A sometimes pejorative term for (a person) having adapted to city life.

citistat The collective world city. The term is used by Michael Dear and Steven Flusty (1998). They define it as consisting of *commodities* (centres of command and control), *cyburbia* ('the collection of state-of-the-art data transmission, premium pay-per-use, and interactive services generally reliant on costly interfaces') and *cyberia* ('an electronic outland of rudimentary communications including basic phone service and telegraphy', as used by those who are not locked into the electronic world).

citizen 1 An inhabitant of a town, city or nation. **2** A wedge used by criminals for opening safes. The term was current in the nineteenth century, as were a series of terms for wedge of different sizes: a *citizen's friend* (smaller than a *citizen*) and two larger wedges, an *alderman* and a *lord mayor*.

citizen control See ARNSTEIN'S LADDER.

citizen engagement PUBLIC PARTICIPATION.

citizenry The citizens collectively.

citizens' jury Around 12–16 people, selected to be representative of a community, who consider an issue in depth (usually over three to five days) and draw up a set of conclusions. Citizens' juries were first used widely in the UK in the 1990s.

citizenship The state of having the rights and duties of an inhabitant of a town, city or nation. Citizenship became a non-statutory part of the personal, social and health education curriculum in primary schools in September 2000. The government wanted children to be instructed in democracy, human rights, the media and conflict resolution. Schools were expected to create student councils and organise voluntary or community work for pupils. A consultation document in 2001 proposed that a short-course qualification should be a 'GCSE in Citizenship Studies' as opposed to 'Citizenship', so that pupils who did not obtain the required grade could not be described as having failed citizenship (Streetwise, 2001).

città (Italian) A town or city

Cittabella Known as the City of Holes, it features in Lia Wainstein's *Voyage to Drimonia* (1965). Its inhabitants walk oddly as they are trying to negotiate the numerous and often dangerous holes of various sizes that are a common feature of the terrain.

city 1 A large town; a place with a cathedral; a place with a city charter. *A New Urbanist Lexicon* (McLaughlin, 2000) defines a city as 'the aggregate of two or more towns, specialized districts and connective transportation and open space corridors.'

'The city,' says John Norquist (2002), mayor of Milwaukee, 'is the only natural form of government. Empires decline, cities endure.' DAVID ENGWICHT (2003) describes cities as 'an invention to maximise exchange opportunities and minimise travel'. BILL HILLIER has called a city 'a mechanism for generating contact'. RICHARD SENNETT (1978) describes a city as 'a human settlement in which strangers are likely to meet'. The architect LÉON KRIER has described the invention of the city as 'a spiritual and technical achievement the historical significance of which surpassed by far the discovery of fire or the invention of the wheel' (Kunstler, 2003). Henning Bech (1992) describes the city as 'a large, dense and permanent cluster of heterogenous human beings in circulation'. 'Cities,' writes Mike Davis (2002), 'have incredible, if largely untapped, capacities for the efficient use of scarce natural resources. Above all, they have the potential to counterpoise public affluence (great libraries, parks, museums, and so on) as a real alternative to privatised consumerism, and thus cut through the apparent contradiction between improving standards of living and accepting the limits imposed by ecosystems and finite natural resources.' In the words of Donald L Miller (1996): 'A great city is not a work of inspired scene painting, static and splendid. It is a living drama with a huge and varied cast and a plot filled with conflict, tension, spectacle, and significance... A city's greatness is the result of an uneasy balance between order and energy, planning and privatism, diversity and conformity, vice and reform, art and enterprise, high culture and low culture, the smart and the shabby, the permanent and the temporary.' Shakespeare writes in *Coriolanus*: 'The people are the city'. The writer Jonathan Raban (1974) notes that a city is 'a community of people who are strangers to each other.' The novelist Peter Ackroyd (2001) calls the city 'the creature of human desire and the manifestation of human appetite'. Italo Calvino writes in INVISIBLE CITIES: 'Cities, like dreams, are made of desires and fears, even if the thread of their discourse is secret, their rules are absurd, their perspectives deceitful, and everything conceals something else.' In the words of JANE JACOBS (1961): 'To approach a city, or even a city neighbourhood, as if it were a larger architectural problem, capable of being given order by converting it into a disciplined work of art, is to make the mistake of attempting to substitute art for life. The results of such profound confusion between art and life are neither life nor art. They are taxidermy... dead, stuffed cities.' LEWIS MUMFORD (1961) writes: 'What is a city? The city... is the point of maximum concentration for the power and culture of a community. It is the place where the diffused rays of many separate beams of life fall into focus... Here is where human experience is transformed into viable signs, symbols, patterns of conduct, systems of order... Cities are a product of time. They are the moulds in which men's lifetimes have cooled and congealed, giving lasting shape, by way of art, to moments that would otherwise vanish with the living and leave no means of renewal or wider participation behind them... Through its complex organisation of time and space... life in the city takes on the character of a symphony: specialised human aptitudes, specialised instruments, give rise to sonorous results which, neither in volume nor in quality, could be achieved by any single piece.' Peter Hall (1998) has called cities 'places for people who can stand the heat of the kitchen: places where the adrenaline pumps through the bodies of the people and through

> **❝ A CITY'S GREATNESS IS THE RESULT OF AN UNEASY BALANCE BETWEEN ORDER AND ENERGY ❞**
> *Donald L Miller*

the street on which they walk; messy places, sordid places sometimes but places nevertheless superbly worth living in, long to be remembered and long to be celebrated.' Ralph Waldo Emerson wrote in his *Journal* (1864): 'The test of civilisation is the power to draw the most benefit out of cities.' CANON BARNETT wrote in THE IDEAL CITY, published around 1893–4 (the exact date is not known): 'We have as our neighbours in a city, not the trees and the beasts, but fellow human beings. We can from them learn greater lessons, and with them do greater deeds. We can become more human.' In 1929 the Russian planning theorist MIKHAIL OKHITOVICH argued that new forms of transport made the traditional compact city redundant. The city should be thought of as an organism, not a place. 'The city is a specific socially determined human entity, not a territorially determined one,' he wrote. 'It is an economic and cultural complex.'

He recognised that this was a novel definition of a city. 'If you like a quarrel about terminology, let this complex also be a city. Let us call it, shall we say, the Red City of the Planet Communism. If one talks about the essence, then this new complex will not be called a point, a place or a city, but a process, and this process will be called disurbanisation' (quoted in Cooke, 2001). The sociologist ROBERT PARK (1952) regarded a city as primarily a state of mind. It was 'a body of customs and traditions, and of the organized attitudes and sentiments that inhere in these customs and are transmitted with this tradition. The city is not, in other words, merely a physical mechanism and an artificial construction. It is involved in the vital processes of the people who compose it; it is a product of nature and particularly of human nature.' Thomas Flanagan (quoted in Lynch, 1960) called the city 'the landscape of our confusions'. To LE CORBUSIER a city was 'the grip of man on nature'. In 1918, in the chaotic aftermath of world war, Max Beckmann (1884–1950), the twentieth century's greatest German painter, felt his place was in the city (Frankfurt, in his case at that time): 'I need to be with people. In the city, that is where we belong these days. We must be part of all the misery that is coming. We have to surrender our heart and our nerves, we must abandon ourselves to the horrible cries of pain and deluded people... They say that the air in the country is cleaner... But the great orchestra of humanity is still in the city' (Beckmann, 1997).

Max Beckmann

PATSY HEALEY (1988) has written that 'it is no longer possible to conceptualise "the city" as a compact entity, with its built form containing a discrete set of economic, social and political relations. "Cities" are open collections of relations, each with multiple spatial referents, which diffusely intersect with each other, and variously link to the world beyond an urban region. What "binds" urban regions in the contemporary context is likely to be labour markets, land and property markets, infrastructure investments, and the image and culture of an area formed historically and in relation to national and international tendencies. Spatial organisation, "urban structure" as such, is merely a produced pattern rather than a "binding" quality of cities.' Notions of central places, of hierarchies of centres or of any particular urban structure lose their relevance in this context, Healey argues. 'One set of relations may indeed have a spatial patterning which is nodal and hierarchical. Another may have a pattern more like a lattice, a third an ANNULAR form. All three may intersect, perhaps at a motorway junction, or a regional city centre.'

To the critic Reyner Banham (1965, quoted in Jarvis, 2001), cities were a form of human settlement rooted in the past. 'Cities', he wrote, 'could be regarded as the archaeological remains of a civilisation that ought to have died when gizmos came in. They represent the kind of enormously massive infrastructural deposits that were left behind by handicraft civilisations for whom... the only way to get anything halfway clever done was to pile men up in vast unhygienic heaps... On such man warrens were built the only concepts of civilisation that we know.' The humourist PJ O'Rourke wrote of Saigon (in *Give War a Chance*, published in 1992) that it was 'like all the other great modern cities of the world. It's the mess left over from people getting rich.'

The US novelist Toni Morrison wrote in *Jazz*, published in 1991: 'How soon country people forget. When they fall in love with a city it is forever, and it is like forever. As though there was never a time when they didn't love it. The minute they arrive at the train station or get off the ferry and glimpse the wide streets and the wasteful lamps lighting them, they know they are born for it. There, in a city, they are not so much new as themselves: their stronger, riskier selves.' ALDO ROSSI has written: 'Cities are in reality great camps of the living and the dead where many elements remain like signals, symbols, cautions. When the holiday is over, what remains of the architecture is scarred, and the sand consumes the street again. There is nothing left but to resume with a certain obstinacy the reconstruction of elements and instruments in expectation of another holiday.'

The thirteenth-century word *city* was at first used for a settlement of any size. FJ OSBORN told LEWIS MUMFORD in a letter in 1971 (Whittick, 1987) that he had been comparing the naming of settlements in various translations of the Bible. 'I was studying the New English Bible's variations from the 1611 and 1881–5 versions in the references to towns and countryside,' Osborn wrote. 'One thing that became clear is that all versions use the term "city" in two senses: a) the ordinary English sense of a built-up town; and b) an "inhabited place" or district or region of any size, containing towns and villages (as in your USA sense in "township" and sometimes even "city", which we never use here). Nineveh,

> **"CITIES COULD BE REGARDED AS THE ARCHAEOLOGICAL REMAINS OF A CIVILISATION THAT OUGHT TO HAVE DIED WHEN GIZMOS CAME IN"**
>
> *Reyner Banham*

which Jonah describes as "three days' journey across" and having a total population of 120,000, was clearly a state containing a big city in our sense, but the whole thing is referred to as a "city".'

The Urban Task Force wanted to know what sort of terms to use in trying to persuade the general population of the advantages of living in urban areas. Their researchers organised focus group workshops to find out. They reported (URBED *et al*, 1999) that the reaction 'to the idea of a *city* or *city living* was very positive at all the workshops...' The term INNER CITY, on the other hand, was seen as being very negative.

Mike Davis (2002) notes that in political debate in the USA the word 'city' is generally avoided, being thought to have connotations alarming to the typical suburban voter. In the presidential campaign of 1992, he writes, 'the word "city" – now color-coded and worrisome to the candidates' common suburban heartland – was expunged from the exchanges. Thus the thousand-pound gorilla of the urban was simply and consensually conjured out of sight.' Davis comments: 'The big cities, once the very fulcrum of the Rooseveltian political universe, have been demoted to the status of a scorned and impotent electoral periphery' (see also BIG CITY). **2** A complex of buildings or a distinct urban area. For example, a complex of 18 disused industrial containers (with more planned to follow), piled three high on a site in London's docklands in 2001 to create low-cost artists' studios, was called Container City. WHITE CITY is another example. **3** An urban settlement. Herbert Girardet (1999) in *Creating Sustainable Cities* uses the word city 'to encompass all human settlements'. In the US, Joseph Rykwert (2000) points out, 'any urban grouping can take it upon itself to assume the "city" title'. **4** Used after another word, *city* denotes an intensity of experience or use, without necessarily any urban connotation. Examples: 'Meat City' and 'Bargain City' (shops), and DEPRESSION CITY. The Scots for city is *ceety*.

city action team One of the groups of civil servants set up to coordinate the work of government departments in inner city areas from 1985, until the job was taken over by the Government Offices for the Regions.

city air makes you free An old German proverb.

City and the Stars, The A novel by Arthur C Clarke, published in 1968. The city was Diaspar. 'Men had built cities before, but never a city such as this. Some had lasted for centuries, some for millennia, before time had swept away even their names. Diaspar alone had challenged Eternity, defending itself and all it sheltered against the slow attrition of the ages, the ravages of decay, and the corruption of rust. Since the city was built, the oceans of Earth had passed away and the desert had encompassed all the globe. The last mountains had been ground to dust by the winds and the rain, and the world was too weary to bring forth more. The city did not care; Earth itself would crumble and Diaspar would still protect the children of its makers, bearing them and their treasures safely down the stream of time'. Diaspar is the last refuge of humanity: it takes one man to break through its stifling inertia and discover its secret.

city architect 1 The head of a local authority's architecture service. **2** A CIVIC ARCHITECT. Compare TOWN ARCHITECT.

city beautiful movement A movement in the late 19th and early 20th centuries aimed improving cities through municipal reform and beautification rather than through social reform. The example of the World's Columbian Exposition in Chicago in 1893 inspired city beautiful initiatives in many other places. In the words of Spiro Kostof (1987), the movement's 'premise was that overall plans... would bring order to the disquieting jungle of American towns, an order based on uniformity, on the classical style in public architecture, on reverence for natural beauty'. SIR PETER HALL (1998) argues that 'the city beautiful movement, both in its original European manifestation under Haussmann and his less illustrious imitators, and then in its American transmogrification, provided the model for urban regeneration in any self-respecting city between about 1850 and about 1920.' (The modernist movement, Hall adds, effectively replaced it between 1930 and 1980.) See also DANIEL BURNHAM and WHITE CITY.

city bug A pejorative term for a city dweller.

city built on bones ST PETERSBURG, the building of which is believed to have cost between 30,000 and 100,000 lives of Swedish prisoners of war, conscripts, peasants and criminals (Glancey, 2003).

city bull-dog A police constable (an early eighteenth-century term).

city by the sea 1 Brighton (designated a city in 2000, as it calls itself). Compare CITY IN THE SEA and see also CITYSIDE. **2** Long Beach, Long Island, in the 2003 film 'City by the Sea', directed by Michael Caton-Jones. In the film seaside ruins provide a metaphorical backdrop to derelict lives.

city challenge A programme under which local partnerships were able to bid competitively for government funding to regenerate a specific deprived area using a comprehensive approach. MICHAEL HESELTINE launched the initiative in his second term as environment secretary in 1991.

city college (US) A city prison. Historically the term referred to Newgate prison in London.

city design URBAN DESIGN; CIVIC DESIGN. PATRICK GEDDES used the term in *Cities in Evolution* in 1915. LEWIS MUMFORD wrote to Geddes in 1921 that he hoped the latter would 'give American city planning a push in the direction of civics and city design' (quoted in Novak, 1995).

city development forum See BAUFORUM.

city farm A farm in an urban area, often intended mainly as a facility for children. The UK's first was set up by INTER-ACTION in London's Kentish Town in 1972. The Urban Green Spaces Taskforce (2002) estimated that there were around 65 city farms in the UK.

city father A prominent citizen.

City Fruitful A development in Dordrecht, Holland, combining greenhouse horticulture and urban planning.

city grant Introduced in 1988 to replace Urban Development Grant and Urban Regeneration Grant.

city growth strategy initiative A series of pilot projects by the Small Business Service promoting regeneration in inner urban areas though business and enterprise.

City Housing Corporation Founded in 1924 to build garden cities in the USA.

city in the country near the sea Exeter. The city gave itself this marketing slogan in the 2000s in the hope of attracting visitors with varied preferences.

city in the park A modernist slogan promoting the vision of high-rise buildings in wide green spaces. Spiro Kostof (1991) observes: 'We tore down the old city and built the new in an impoverished celebration of the modernist "city in the park" – without the park.'

City in the Sea A poem by Edgar Allan Poe in which a sinful city disappears beneath the waves. The poem 'Star Swirls' by Robinson Jeffers, written in 1954, presents a similar image. The polar ice-caps and mountain glaciers are melting, tides are every year a little higher: 'They will drown New York, they will drown London' (a fate Jeffers thought the cities richly deserved). Compare CITY BY THE SEA. See also URBAN DESTRUCTION.

city is not a tree, A An essay by the architect CHRISTOPER ALEXANDER (1965). Alexander analyses the structures of what he calls *natural cities* (that arose more or less spontaneously over many years) and *artificial cities* (deliberately created by designers and planners). The structure of both types consists of a large collection of many small systems making up a large and complex system. In artificial cities, he writes, the structure takes the form of a tree, and in natural cities the form of what he calls a 'semilattice'. His definitions of *tree* and *semilattice* describe how the two structures relate *elements* of the city and *sets* (collections of elements). He defines semilattice according to this axiom: 'A collection of sets forms a semilattice if, and only if, when two overlapping sets belong to the collection, the set of elements common to both also belongs to the collection'. The axiom for a tree is: 'A collection of sets forms a tree if, and only if, for any two sets that belong to the collection either one is wholly contained in the other, or else they are wholly disjoint.' The practice of segregating uses is based on a fundamental misunderstanding of how cities work.

'Does a concert hall ask to be next to an opera house? Can the two feed on one another? Will anybody ever visit them both, gluttonously, in a single evening, or even buy tickets from one after going to a performance in the other?' Alexander argues that designers conceive cities as trees because they are trapped by a mental habit, perhaps even trapped by the way the mind works. 'They can not encompass the complexity of a semilattice in any convenient mental form, because the mind has an overwhelming predisposition to see trees wherever it looks and can not escape the tree conception... Designers, limited as they must be by the capacity of the mind to form intuitively accessible structures, can not achieve the complexity of the semilattice in a single mental act.'

Alexander suggests that such thought processes 'stem essentially from the organism's need to reduce the complexity of its environment by establishing barriers between the different events that it encounters. It is for this reason – because the mind's first function is to reduce the ambiguity and overlap in a confusing situation and because, to this end, it is endowed with a basic intolerance for ambiguity – that structures like the city... are... persistently conceived as trees'. This, he says, is disastrous. 'When we think in terms of trees we are trading the humanity and richness of the living city for a conceptual simplicity which benefits only designers, planners, administrators and developers. Every time a piece of city is torn out, and a tree made to replace the semilattice that was there before, the city takes a further step towards dissociation.'

city lite Development designed to have something of an urban feel, without offering the real urban experience of traditional cities (Bender, 2002).

city manager A person responsible for managing the

city

affairs of the city; a local authority chief executive who runs a council alongside a directly elected mayor.

city of a hundred towers Pavia, Italy.

city of a million dustbins London in NINETEEN EIGHTY-FOUR, according to George Orwell's novel.

city of a thousand wells See ISAURA.

City of Ambition The title of a famous photograph of New York by Alfred Steiglitz, taken in 1910.

city of angels LOS ANGELES.

City of Arcadia An affluent, mainly residential suburb of Los Angeles, California (motto: 'A Community of Homes'). Development was begun in the 1930s by Elias Jackson 'Lucky' Baldwin, who became its first mayor, and Arcadia expanded greatly in the 1940s and 1950s. Annual highlights are the Sponge Toss ('it's wild and wet'), sponsored by the Arcadia Association of Realtors, and the City of Arcadia Lucky Baldwin Day Community Picnic Pumpkin-carving Contest. See ARCADIA.

city of architecture and design 1999 Glasgow organised a year-long festival of architecture and design after being awarded the title in the Arts Council's Arts 2000 initiative. Its aim was to 'pull architecture and design out of the professional ghetto and to provide a full programme of events and exhibitions that will involve the whole community and leave a lasting legacy'. The celebrations included exhibitions: *Alexander Thomson: the unknown genius* pulled in the crowds, while *Vertigo: the strange new world of the contemporary city* did not. Homes for the Future was a development of 100 houses of self-consciously radical design (considering they were developed by UK housebuilders) in the city's east end. THE LIGHTHOUSE, an architecture and design centre in the converted and enlarged former Glasgow Herald building (detailed by the young CHARLES RENNIE MACKINTOSH when he was an assistant to a local architectural practice) was intended as a permanent legacy of the year. Another was the transformation of five gap sites around the city by teams of artists and architects in collaboration with local communities. Some of these have not worn well.

city of bells Strasbourg.

city of big shoulders Chicago. See also WINDY CITY.

City of Bits A book by William Mitchell, published in 1995, about 'the urban consequences of the digital world'. The City of Bits, he wrote, will be 'unrooted to any definite spot on the surface of the earth, shaped by connectivity and bandwidth constraints rather than by accessibility and land values, largely asynchronous in its operation, and inhabited by disembodied and fragmented subjects who exist as collections of aliases and agents'. See also E-TOPIA. Compare CITY OF PARTS.

City of Brass A fictional dead city in the deserts of north Africa where King Solomon once imprisoned evil spirits in brass bottles. It is described in *The Arabian Nights* (fourteenth-fifteenth centuries).

city of brotherly love Philadelphia.

city of cities A POLYCENTRIC city. The concept of Sydney, Australia, as a city of cities was proposed in 2002. The idea was to plan it as a 'conglomerate', with both a single identity and six individual components with their own identities. The Manchester/ Liverpool/ Leeds/ Preston 'conglomerate' in England was cited as a possible model (Stapleton, 2002).

city of clones Atlanta, Georgia, according to the architect REM KOOLHAAS. See also CLONE CITY.

city of David Jerusalem. See DAVID'S CITY.

city of democracy BROADACRE CITY, according to FRANK LLOYD WRIGHT.

City of Destruction The epitome of worldliness and irreligiousity in John Bunyan's *Pilgrim's Progress*. Compare CELESTIAL CITY.

city of djinns Delhi, according to the travel writer William Dalrymple in his 1993 book *City of Djinns*. Dalrymple saw Delhi as 'a city disjointed in time, a city whose different ages lay suspended side by side in aspic, a city of djinns'. A djinn is an invisible spirit or genie.

City of Dreadful Height, The An essay by Thomas Hastings, published in 1927, warning against the increasing density of development in New York's Manhattan.

city of dreadful joy Los Angeles, according to Aldous Huxley in 1926.

city of dreadful knights Cardiff, so named in 1922 when prime minister Lloyd George was accused of having procured knighthoods for three of the city's citizens in return for payment.

City of Dreadful Night, The A long poem by James Thomson, published in 1874, despairingly evoking a half-ruined city that is a vision of a living hell.

city of dreaming spires Oxford. Compare CITY OF PERSPIRING DREAMS.

city of dreams Vienna in the years before the first world war. Compare PROVING-GROUND FOR WORLD DESTRUCTION.

city of efficient consumption The city that the anarchist writers PAUL AND PERCIVAL GOODMAN imagined as the logical consequence of the consumer society. The city centre would be a single vast supermarket.

city of exacerbated differences A plan by the architect REM KOOLHAAS for China's Pearl River Delta. Koolhaas (1996) describes it as 'not a single city but a region inhabited by a cluster of very diverse cities such as Hong Kong, Shenzhen, Guangzhou, Guangdong, Zhuhai and Macau. Together, they may represent a new model of the megalopolis in the sense that their coexistence, their functioning, their legitimacy is determined by their extreme mutual difference.'

city of free choice A city of the future (also called Maximum Security with Minimum Regulation) imagined by the anarchist writers PAUL AND PERCIVAL GOODMAN.

Each citizen would be obliged to work for three years in a production centre. That would be enough to provide the basic needs for everyone, and after those three years everyone would be entitled to have their basic needs met for the rest of their lives. Anyone who wanted more could work to pay for it.

city of garantism A proposal by CHARLES FOURIER (1772–1837) for a new city planned in three concentric bands: commercial at the centre, surrounded by industry and, beyond that, agriculture. The three bands were to be separated by hedges (Kostof, 1991).

City of God 1 The Christian church; the Kingdom of Christ. See also HOLY CITY. **2** A novel by EL Doctorow with a religious theme, set in New York, published in 2000 (see also CAPITAL OF ALL MUSIC and CAPITAL OF EXHAUSTED TREES). **3** A film directed by Fernando Meirelles and Katia Lund, released in 2002, set in the brutal, poverty-stricken world of the Brazilian slums (favelas). The Cidade de Deus (City of God) is a housing project outside Rio de Janeiro. The film was adapted from the novel (based on fact) by Paolo Lins.

City of God, The A book written by St Augustine between 412 and 427, contrasting the City of this world with the City of God. The earthly City and the heavenly City (the society of the elect) are commingled in this world, St Augustine asserts, and the state can be part of the City of God only by submitting to the church in all matters of religion. The book had an enormous influence on medieval philosophy and theology.

city of gods Angkor Thom, Cambodia, built 1181–1219.

city of gold 1 London (Ackroyd, 2000), so called because of its great wealth. **2** Johannesburg, South Africa, the industrial centre of the world's most important gold-producing region. Compare GOLDEN CITY. **3** The fictional city of CATHNE in Edgar Rice Burroughs' novel *Tarzan and the City of Gold* (1933). See CITY OF IVORY.

city of hard labour New York, according to LE CORBUSIER in 1925 (Dunnett, 2000). See also CITY OF PANIC.

city of heaven See URANOPOLIS.

city of holes See CITTABELLA.

city of ivory The fictional city of Athne in Edgar Rice Burroughs' *Tarzan and the City of Gold* (1933). See CITY OF GOLD.

city of light 1 Paris. **2** Lyons, which has carried out a programme of lighting buildings in the city centre and promoting the lighting design industry.

City of Light A novel by Lauren Belfer, published in 1999. The city is Buffalo in 1901. The light is that provided by the Niagara Frontier Power Company.

city of lilies Florence, which has a lily as its emblem.

City of Lost Souls A 2001 film, directed by Takashi Miike, set in Tokyo.

city of magnificent distances Washington, so called because of its layout, as described by Charles Dickens.

city of nations London, so called because of its cosmopolitan character.

city of numbers See DIGITOPOLIS.

city of panic Any of the American skyscraper cities, according to LE CORBUSIER in 1925 (Dunnett, 2000). See also CITY OF HARD LABOUR.

city of parts ALDO ROSSI's (1982) concept of a city as a whole being constituted of many pieces complete in themselves. The distinctive character of each city, and thus also of the urban aesthetic, he suggests, is the dynamic that is created between its different areas and elements, and among its parts. Compare CITY OF BITS.

city of perspiring dreams Cambridge, according to Frederic Raphael in *The Glittering Prizes*, published in 1976. Compare CITY OF DREAMING SPIRES.

City of Quartz A book by Mike Davis on metropolitan America and, in particular, the African-Americans of Los Angeles.

city of saints 1 Montreal, whose streets are named after saints. **2** SALT LAKE CITY, Utah, the city of the Church of the Latter Day Saints (the Mormons).

city of seven hills 1 Rome. **2** Sheffield.

city of shadows A fictional underground city that lies beneath the Mediterranean, described by Léon Groc in *The City of Shadows* (1926). Circular in form, it is served by six roads that radiate from the centre. The city is many centuries old, and its people are no longer able to see.

city of sleep, the See MORPHOPOLIS.

City of Spades A novel by Colin McInnes set in the bohemia of London's SOHO in the 1950s.

city of steel See STAHLSTADT.

city of strife Milan. 'The history of the Lombard plain is a history of invasion and war,' wrote the historian JH Plumb (1961). 'For more than a thousand years some of Europe's bloodiest battles were fought on it. If Florence belonged to Minerva, Milan belonged to Mars.'

city of suicides See SUICIDE CITY.

city of the [nineteenth] century Chicago, according to Donald L Miller, who wrote a book with that title.

city of the apes A fictional city, described in *The Arabian Nights* (fourteenth-fifteenth centuries), whose inhabitants have to leave it every night to avoid being killed by the apes who regularly invade.

city of the beautiful towers San Gimignano, Tuscany.

city of the blind All of the fictional city's inhabitants were struck blind in an epidemic of a mysterious disease, which also strikes every visitor. Now it seems that the city is being used as a rubbish dump for some other place. José Saramago describes it in *Ensaio Sobre a Cegueira* (1995).

city of the deformed See SPOROUNDIA.

city of the firsts Kokomo, Indiana, a city known for industrial innovation.

city of the future BRASILIA. See also THE CONTEMPORARY CITY.

city of the Golden Gate San Francisco (after the eponymous strait which connects San Francisco Bay with the Pacific Ocean, and which is spanned by the Golden Gate Bridge).

city of the immortals A ruined city of irrational design in Ethiopia. Troglodytes inhabit a complex series of underground passages and rooms. Jorge Luis Borges describes it in his story 'The immortal' in *The Aleph* (1949).

city of the stars Beverly Hills, Los Angeles, where the film stars live. See also TINSELTOWN,

city of the sun 1 Baalbeck. 2 Heliopolis. 3 Rhodes. See CIVITAS SOLIS and NEW JERUSALEM.

City of the Sun, The A book by the friar Tomaso Campanella (1568–1639), published after 1602, describing an ideal republic. The City of the Sun is set out in seven concentric circles, each named after a planet.

city of the trees Caras Galadhon in JRR Tolkien's novel *The Lord of the Rings*. Compare CITY OF TREES.

city of the world London. See SMOKE and WORLD CITY.

city of three kings Cologne, where the Magi were said to have been buried.

city of trees 1 MILTON KEYNES in Buckinghamshire, so named by its development corporation in 1971. 2 London. Compare CITY OF THE TREES.

city of truth An allegorical city described in Bartolommeo Delbene's book of that name, published in 1609.

city of villages 1 London, according to the Greater London Authority in 2002. 2 San Diego, California. The concept has also been associated with strategic planning initiatives in Auburn, Alabama; Concord, New Hampshire; and Ottawa, Ontario (which also calls itself a *community of communities*). See VILLAGE.

city of women See GYNAECOPOLIS.

city of words DICTIONOPOLIS.

city of X See X.

city on a hill See NEW JERUSALEM.

City Plan, The A quarterly journal published by the American City Planning Institute from 1915 to 1918. It was revived from 1925 to 1934 as *City Planning* and again in 1935 as the *Planners' Journal*. In 1944 it became the *Journal of the American Institute of Planners* (ACPI having dropped the City in its name in 1938). When the institute merged with the American Society of Planning Officials in 1978 the journal became the *Journal of the American Planning Association*.

City Planners, The A poem by Margaret Atwood. See URBAN DESTRUCTION.

city planning (US) The UK equivalent is TOWN PLANNING. The term was new when the First National Conference on City Planning was held in Washington DC in 1909. The following year FREDERICK LAW OLMSTED JUNIOR described city planning as 'the attempt to exert a well-considered control on behalf of the people of a city over the development of their physical environment as a whole' (quoted in Nolen, 1916). The American City Planning Institute was founded in 1917. See also EDWARD M BASSETT.

City Pride Initiative Launched in 1993 by JOHN GUMMER as environment secretary. Birmingham, London and Manchester were invited to produce a prospectus for their cities that combined a vision of the future with practical measures for its achievement. In Birmingham and Manchester the city councils undertook the task. In London, with no city-wide authority, the promotional body London First brought together a City Pride Partnership of 10 bodies. Its prospectus, the last of the three, was published in 1995.

city region A city and its hinterland. In 1996 the City Region Campaign called for Britain's local government system to be restructured on the basis of 53 city regions. A region based on Plymouth would include all Cornwall and West Devon. In advocating regional survey, PATRICK GEDDES (1918) wrote : 'Town and country can then again be considered together as city regions'. See also THE HUNDRED MILE CITY and URBAN REGION.

city roast (coffee, US) A rather darker roast of coffee than is normal in America. A *full city roast* is slightly darker still. See also CAPPUCCINO CULTURE.

city safari An organised trip for tourists to unusual places (often of cultural interest) in a rundown urban neighbourhood. Safaris take visitors to places they would not otherwise know about or perhaps dare to visit. The idea was conceived in Rotterdam in the early 1990s. See also CONCRETE JUNGLE.

city sherry Pale ale (bitter). A late nineteenth-century term.

city slicker An urban dweller with excessively sophisticated tastes.

city stage The gallows. An eighteenth- and early nineteenth-century term.

city state (historic) A sovereign city and its dependencies.

city that never sleeps, the New York.

city that reads, the The title Kurt L Schmoke, mayor of Baltimore, Maryland, said he aspired to for his city when running for office in 1987. Schmoke promoted a major literacy programme in recognition, he said, of the nature of jobs in an information-driven economy.

city wilderness, the A phrase current in the USA in the nineteenth century, summing up the worst aspects of urban life.

City, The A play written in 1909 by the American Clyde Fitch (1865–1909) attacking political corruption.

City, the The financial and commercial centre of a city. The term comes from London's financial centre, the City of London (which is a small, administratively distinct part of Greater London governed by the City of London Corporation). Compare CENTRAL LONDON.

city-centre syndrome The problem of a city having a lively centre which is flanked by neighbourhoods sharing none of that success.

citycide Columnist Julie Burchill's term for a town 'condemning itself to destruction' by seeking designation as a city. Burchill (2001) was commenting on Brighton's designation in 2000. 'Frankly, wanting to be a city seems to me about as sensible and life-affirming as wanting to be a wart... While England's only Grade I listed pier

> **"FRANKLY, WANTING TO BE A CITY SEEMS TO ME ABOUT AS SENSIBLE AND LIFE-AFFIRMING AS WANTING TO BE A WART"**
> *Julie Burchill*

continued to fall into the sea, while the seagulls grew fat and fierce from all the uncollected rubbish left to rot in the streets..., while lidos closed and Brighton comprehensive schools became a byword for bullying and underachievement, money was thrown ceaselessly at the city bid... The excitement of certain local politicians over the city bid was a revelation to behold; people who had been unable to garner any extra enthusiasm or cash in order to improve such bagatelles as health or education were now wetting themselves with righteous fervour at the thought of getting new headed notepaper.'

city-line PATRICK GEDDES (1915d) wrote of the possibility that 'the not very distant future will see practically one vast city-line along the Atlantic Coast for five hundred miles, and stretching back at many points, with a total of, it may be, as many millions of population.'

CityMatters A computer software tool used to calculate ACCESSIBILITY.

Citynet The short name of the Regional Network of Local Authorities for the Management of Human Settlements. Citynet promotes the exchange of expertise and experience among urban local governments, development agencies and non-government organisations in the Asia-Pacific region.

cityologist One who studies cities.

cityscape The form and appearance of a city. The term, derived from LANDSCAPE, was coined in the USA in 1850. See also TOWNSCAPE.

Cityside The name given in a rebranding exercise in 2003 by the mayor of London and the London Tourist Board to parts of central London, apparently on the grounds that the name would be more familiar to American tourists.

city-state (US) A CITY REGION.

citystate A city region under unified municipal administration. The designation has been proposed by American new urbanists.

ciudad (Spanish) A city.

ciudad lineal (Spanish) A linear city. See ARTURO SORIA Y MATA.

civic Relating to a town or city, or its citizens.

Civic Amenities Act 1967 See CONSERVATION AREA.

civic amenity site A euphemism for a place where residents can bring waste material for recycling or disposal; a rubbish dump.

civic architect An architectural mentor to a local authority; a council employee with a wide-ranging brief to improve the local authority's impact on design (as opposed to being the head of the council's architecture service). The position (although with the title *city architect*) was first created by Leeds City Council in the 1990s.

civic art (US) The name of a formal approach to urban design current around 1910–30, exemplified by the book *Civic Art* by Werner Hegemann and Elbert Peets, published in 1922. Modern new urbanists generally approve of the civic art approach.

civic booster See BOOSTER.

civic boosterism See BOOSTERISM.

civic centre 1 The location of municipal offices. **2** The municipal offices themselves. **3** A building or complex of buildings housing council offices and other public functions.

civic creativity Described by Charles Landry (2000) as 'imaginative problem-solving applied to public-good objectives'.

civic design 1 A synonym for URBAN DESIGN. In the early decades of the twentieth century it tended to refer to formal masterplanning, and also to town planning generally. The School of Civic Design at the University of Liverpool, founded in 1910, was the first university department of town planning. The Lever Chair of Civic Design at the University of Liverpool, founded in 1912 and endowed by the first Viscount Leverhulme (WILLIAM HESKETH LEVER), became the Lever Chair of Town and Regional Planning in 1988. Stanley Adshead held it from 1912 to 1914 (from 1909–1912 it had been a lectureship, which he had also held). He was followed in the chair by PATRICK ABERCROMBIE (1915–1935) and WILLIAM GRAHAM (later Lord Holford) (1936–1947). The Town Planning Institute was founded in 1913 'to advance the study of Town Planning and Civic Design'. The term's use declined with the increasing currency of *urban design* from the 1970s. A few practitioners use it today, intending an emphasis on the design of public places, or on urban design as a collaborative process. **2** The design of public or civic buildings. The term was used in this sense in relation to the campaign by the COMMISSION FOR ARCHITECTURE AND THE BUILT

ENVIRONMENT in 2001 for higher standards of design for public buildings.

civic engagement Defined by ROBERT D PUTNAM as people's connections with the life of their communities.

civic planning (US) The term was used by Runes and Schrickel (1946) to include town planning, city planning and regional planning.

civic pride The urge to express a feeling of belonging to a particular town or city.

civic renewal Defined by ROBERT D PUTNAM as 'working towards realising a... sustained process of social and political engagement' (Palmer, 2001).

civic ruin PATRICK GEDDES' term for comprehensive redevelopment, by contrast with his approach of conservative surgery.

civicentre PATRICK GEDDES' suggested term for a centre of survey and social action in a city.

civicness A sense of being a place with an urban identity.

civics The study of the life of towns and cities. The term was coined in the USA in the early 1880s. PATRICK GEDDES (1905) defined civics as 'applied sociology' and 'that branch of sociology which deals with cities', and as 'the science of cities'. He argued that if civics became merely 'applied social art', on the other hand, it would be 'open to ridicule as a Utopian hope.'

civil architecture That which does not have a military purpose. JOHN RUSKIN defined it in *The Seven Lamps of Architecture* as including 'every edifice raised by nations or societies, for the purposes of common business or pleasure'.

civil engineer A person who designs or supervises the construction of public works such as roads and bridges. See also ENGINEER.

civil engineering The art or science of designing, planning and building fixed public works. Originally the term distinguished this from *military engineering*. See also ENGINEERING.

civil renewal The UK government announced in 2002 that 'civil renewal' would be the new remit of the Home Office's Active Community Unit. The unit's new aims were defined as: a) To build the capacity of local people to lead community development. b) To promote community involvement and citizenship. c) To develop productive partnerships between government and the community and voluntary sectors at local, regional and national levels. d) To develop a modern legal and regulatory framework for the sectors and encourage good practice. Compare URBAN RENEWAL.

civil society Defined by the London School of Economics as 'the set of institutions, organisations and behaviour situated between the state, the business world, and the family.'

Civilia A proposal for a new high-density city on derelict urban land outlined by *The Architectural Review* in 1971. Deyan Sudjic (1992) recalls: 'It was presented in the form of a strangely compelling set of photographic montages, collaging images of new plate-glass universities with shots of Brasilia'.

civilised The Glasgow housing association director Rob Joiner (2002) describes a civilised person as someone who lives in a city.

civilised city See QUALITY OF LIFE.

civility Politeness.

civitas 1 Citizenship with shared responsibility. **2** The city as a righteous assembly of people (Kostof, 1991).

Civitas Solis The City of the Sun. An imagined New Jerusalem described in the seventeen century by Thomas Campanella. The city was laid out in seven concentric circles (Girouard, 1985).

clachan (Scots) A VILLAGE; a HAMLET.

cladding Non-structural material used for the outside facing of a building.

CLAIRE (Contaminated land: applications in real environments) A public/private partnership, set up in 1999, involving government, regulators, industry, research organisations and technology developers in promoting the SUSTAINABLE remediation of land.

clamps See SEVEN CLAMPS.

clarity of joint Defined by KEVIN LYNCH (1960) as 'high visibility of joints and SEAMS (as at a major intersection, or on a sea-front); clear relation and interconnection (as of a building to its site, or of a subway station to the street above).'

Clarke, CW As engineer to Easington Council, he put forward the proposal for what became Peterlee new town. See also PETER LEE and BERTHOLD LUBETKIN.

Clarke's law of exponential density decay The relationship between the density of development and distance from the city centre, as explained by Colin Clarke (1951, quoted in Echenique, 2001).

Clash, The A punk band active in the 1970s and '80s. Their singles include 'White Riot', 'London's Burning' and 'City of the Dead' (all 1977), 'Clash City Rockers' (a 1978 song about, among other things, 'burning down the suburbs with a half-closed eye') and 'London Calling' (1979). See HIGH RISE and URBAN DESTRUCTION.

CLASP The Consortium of Local Authorities' Special Programme system of building. Developed for building schools in the 1950s by Donald Gibson, among others, Clasp was used successfully for a wide variety of building types. The early buildings at York University are notable examples. Its lightweight steel construction was designed particularly for sites with mining subsidence. Henry Swain (1924–2002), Nottinghamshire's county architect, was one of the system's pioneers.

class Classification of people according to social and economic criteria.

Classic Slum, The A book by Robert Roberts, published in 1971, describing poverty in Salford before the First World War. See also SLUM.

city of a million dustbins

classical 1 Reflecting ancient Greek and Roman architecture. The term was first applied to architecture in the seventeenth century. See also NAZI ARCHITECTURE. **2** The antithesis of romantic. The meaning of classical in relation to the arts in general dates from the late eighteenth century. **3** Displaying clarity and logic in form, and following recognised models. This use of the term emerged in the twentieth century.

classical-lite A bland style of architecture with some vaguely classical features.

classification Sorting buildings, spaces or landscapes into different types according to specific criteria.

Clean Air Act See FOG.

clean purchase Buying a piece of land without taking on any uninsured liability for risks that may arise from matters such as contamination and subsidence.

clean-sweep planning The wholesale demolition and rebuilding of an urban area.

clean-up Making contaminated land fit for development or other re-use.

clear zone An area in which traffic is reduced and streets are made more pleasant for pedestrians.

clearance 1 A procedure, parallel to the processes of obtaining planning permission or listed building consent, required of bodies that enjoy Crown immunity and are exempt from those processes. Government bodies are required to notify local authorities of their proposals for development and for any proposed alterations to listed buildings. **2** SLUM CLEARANCE.

clearance area See SLUM.

clearances See HIGHLAND CLEARANCES.

clever CCTV A closed-circuit television system that uses computerised pattern recognition to identify car number plates or faces in crowds.

Click-Click New Orleans, Louisiana, so called because of its high murder rate. See also BIG EASY, CHOPPER CITY and CRESCENT CITY.

client 1 A person who commissions professional services. In relation to architecture, Andres Duany (2003) suggests, clients – as distinct from PATRONS – 'are not so much sophisticated as savvy. By making themselves available for contact with architects during the design process, they acquire a modicum of sophistication.' Duany comments: 'The resulting buildings can be quite good and sometimes excellent. Clients underwrite most of the decent houses in America. Sometimes an individual within government will rise to the level of client.' Compare CUSTOMER, PATRON and VICTIM. **2** A user of a social services agency. From the Latin for 'dependent' or 'follower'.

climate The average weather conditions over a long period for a place or area.

Clinton, William Jefferson (Bill) (b1946) US president. See COMMUNITARIANISM and COMMUNITY.

clip-on revivalism Building façades with historically-inspired features bearing no apparent relation to the building as a whole. See also FACADISM.

Clockwork Orange chic An ironic term for a threatening urban place, like those featured in the novel (by Anthony Burgess) and film (directed by Stanley Kubrick) *A Clockwork Orange*. Example 'The Elephant and Castle shopping centre suffers from Clockwork Orange chic, only accessible by interminable, dimly lit subways. There is a whiff of ultra violence' (2003). See MUSIC and THAMESMEAD.

Clone City 'The city formed by the mindless, market-driven proliferation of built environments' according to Miles Glendinning and David Page, whose book *Clone City: crisis and renewal in Scottish architecture* was published in 1999. The phrase 'clone city' refers to the idea that modern cities are becoming increasingly the same as one another, regardless of local conditions, culture and climate. Scottish scientists were the first to create a mammal (Dolly the sheep) by cloning. The architect REM KOOLHAAS has described Atlanta (in his book *S, M, L, XL*) as 'a city of clones'.

close 1 A CUL-DE-SAC. **2** (Scotland) The hallway and common parts leading off each street entrance in a tenement block. **3** (Scotland) All the flats served by a particular tenement close (in the same way that *street* can refer both to the thoroughfare and to the houses on it).

closed landfill Land previously used for the deposit of waste.

close-in neighbourhood (US) A residential area close to the city centre.

closet (Yorkshire) A TOILET.

Clousden Hill Farm A cooperative community founded near Newcastle-upon-Tyne in 1896. It was inspired by the anarchist writings of PETER KROPOTKIN (Quail, 1978). See also CO-OPERATIVE COLONY.

Clouston, Brian See LANDSCAPE ARCHITECT.

cloverleaf intersection A motorway junction whose slip roads look from the air like clover leaves. 'Our national flower is the concrete cloverleaf,' LEWIS MUMFORD wrote.

cluster A geographic concentration of interconnected companies, specialist suppliers, service providers, firms in related industries and associated institutions in particular fields that compete but also cooperate.

cluster block A series of buildings (usually housing) linked together. See DENYS LASDUN and POOLEYVILLE.

Cluster City A proposed development form designed by Peter Smithson in 1952.

cluster zoning (US) Allows for development to be concentrated on part of a site, leaving the rest for less intensive use such as recreation.

clustering Groups of similar people living close to one another. See also CONGREGATION.

clutterbuster A person employed to remove disfiguring and unauthorised signs and street furniture, either physically or by other means.

Clydeforth PATRICK GEDDES' term for the conurbation in the central belt of Scotland between the Rivers Clyde and Forth.

coach-lamps Reproductions or evocations of historic coach-lamps are cited as characteristic of the taste of people who buy the standard products of volume housebuilders.

Coal City A fictional underground city in central Scotland described in Jules Verne's *The Black Indies* (1877). The city stands beside an underground lake in a network of natural caverns. Its main industry is coal mining.

Coalfields Enterprise Fund Start-up funding for enterprises in former coalfield areas.

Coalfields Regeneration Trust A charity supporting social and economic regeneration in former coalfield areas. It was launched in 1999 in response to the Coalfields Task Force Report.

Coalfields Task Force Set up by the government in the 1990s to tackle the problems of former coal-mining communities.

coals in the bath The supposed result of tenants being unfamiliar with or uninterested in the proper function of a bath. The phrase, current in the UK and North America in the twentieth century at least up to the 1960s, was used as shorthand for the idea that improved housing (particularly council housing) was wasted on some tenants. The saying 'you can take the people out of the SLUM, but you can't take the slum out of the people' reflected a similar feeling. (Variants of that phrase include 'you can take the boy out of the country but not the country out of the boy', and Dorothy Parker's 'you can take the girl out of the chorus but not the chorus out of the girl'). Later 'a Jaguar on the drive' expressed the same hostility through the opposite accusation: that their expensive cars showed many council tenants not to be in need of the public housing they had been provided with. See also TWO JAGS.

coarse grain The quality of an area's LAYOUT of building BLOCK and plots having large and infrequent subdivisions. Compare FINE GRAIN.

coarse mesh See MESH.

Cobbett, William (1763–1835) Writer and reformer. His book *Rural Rides* described conditions in the countryside from 1821. See the GREAT WEN.

COBRA Conservation-based research and analysis. Kate Clark defines the concept as 'the research, analysis, survey and investigation necessary to understand the significance of a building and its landscape, and thus inform decisions about repair, alteration, use and management' (quoted in Gard'ner, 2003).

Coca-Colazation The GLOBALISATION of lifestyles, called after the global soft drink brand. Also *McDonaldization*.

Cocacolonisation The term was used in the 1950s to describe the domination of Europe and other parts of the world by the USA.

cockney *n*. One who was born within the sound of the bells of St Mary-le-Bow in Cheapside, London; a person from inner east London. Peter Ackroyd (2000) notes the suggestion that the word derives from a cock-shaped weathervane that once topped the belfry of St Mary-le-Bow. Ben Weinreb and Christopher Hibbert (1983) suggest that a cockney is derived from the Middle English *cokeney*, a cock's egg, meaning a misshapen one as sometimes laid by young hens. They write that the term once meant an effeminate person or a simpleton, particularly a weak man from a town as opposed to a tougher countryman. Cockney was applied to Londoners from the seventeenth century and has since lost its pejorative connotation.

cocktail belt The prosperous outer suburbs of a city where people supposedly socialise at cocktail parties.

cocoon effect People being isolated from their surroundings by the vehicles they are travelling in.

Coen, Jan Pieterszoon Founder of Batavia, now Jakarta, capital of the Dutch East Indies, in 1619 (Kostof, 1991).

coffee See CAPPUCCINO CULTURE.

cognition 1 The process of acquiring knowledge and understanding (of the urban environment, for example). **2** The results of this process.

cognitive map A mental map reflecting the individual's understanding of the place. Example: 'The expansion dotted the boroughs with recognizable place names and gave New Yorkers an extensive cognitive map, shaped by stations rather than local streets or natural topography. (I should say *two* cognitive maps – one for each subway company, each of which denied, in effect, the existence of the city served by the other.)' (Bender, 2002).

coherent structure An attribute of an urban place whose parts relate in an easily understandable way to each other and to the whole. A place with a coherent structure is likely to be legible (see LEGIBILITY). The architect CHARLES REILLY evoked the possibility of a coherent structure (but without using the term) on the scale of a city in a lecture he gave in 1934 (printed in Reilly, 1938). 'Perhaps the greatest of all the gifts the Italian Renaissance gave to architecture was [the] civic sense which has made it possible to conceive a town, if such a one has not yet been built on any scale, which is not only a complete organism with its separate parts and individual buildings expressing their separate functions, but one in which all such parts and structures have an hierarchic relation to the other and are consciously designed as subordinate parts in their proper order of subordination to the conception of the whole.' Reilly suggested that SIR CHRISTOPHER WREN'S plan for the rebuilding of London after the Great Fire was perhaps the nearest approach on paper to this renaissance ideal, while the cities of Washington and New Delhi were the nearest in practice.

cohesive community One in which different kinds of people live happily side by side. The Home Office defines a cohesive community as 'one where there is a common vision and a sense of belonging for all communities; the diversity of people's different backgrounds and circumstances is appreciated and positively valued; those from different backgrounds have similar life opportunities; and strong and positive relationships are being developed between people from different backgrounds in the workplace, in schools and within neighbourhoods'. Following the disturbances in Burnley, Oldham and Bradford in the summer of 2001, a series of reports were published. These identified problems including deep polarisation and fragmented communities living parallel lives. The importance of 'community cohesion' was identified as being crucial to promoting greater knowledge, respect and contact between various cultures, and to establish a greater sense of citizenship. *Social cohesion* has a similar meaning. See also SEGREGATION.

cohort survival model A means of projecting changes in population by focusing on the survival rates of successive five-year age cohorts (groups).

co-housing 1 A small group of homes around a community building, forming a village designed and managed by the residents. **2** Housing owned jointly by its occupiers and with some communal facilities (Duany, 2000).

Coin Street A formerly derelict five-hectare site near Waterloo on London's South Bank, where a successful community campaign evolved into a not-for-profit development organisation. The campaign began in the early 1970s, when Waterloo's long-established residential community realised that commercial pressures could soon overwhelm it. If the Coin Street sites were redeveloped for offices and hotels, as developers were proposing, local facilities and social networks would not survive. Coin Street Community Builders have created a riverside walkway; a park; a designer craft-market; a major, mixed-use refurbishment scheme; and cooperative housing schemes which have won awards for their architecture. The achievement has taken more than two decades, including two of Britain's longest-ever planning inquiries (in the run-up to one of which the local action group was operating through 24 working groups, each concentrating on a particular aspect of the campaign). The initiative might have been doomed to failure by the lack of any one of its ingredients: a strong sense of community; various regeneration grants available for community development; effective leadership; unpaid support from sympathetic professionals; physical proximity to the centres of power and the media; the Housing Corporation's particular grant regimes; and the ownership of half the site by the GREATER LONDON COUNCIL. The way the community campaign was transformed into a development vehicle was a matter of some local controversy.

Coketown The fictional, grim, northern industrial town portrayed by Charles Dickens in his 1854 novel *Hard Times*. 'It was a town of red brick, or of brick that would have been red if the smoke and ashes

Charles Dickens

had allowed it; but, as matters stood it was a town of unnatural red and black like the painted face of a savage. It was a town of machinery and tall chimneys, out of which interminable serpents of smoke trailed themselves for ever and ever, and never got uncoiled. It had a black canal in it, and a river that ran purple with ill-smelling dye, and vast piles of building full of windows where there was a rattling and a trembling all day long, and where the piston of the steam-engine worked monotonously up and down, like the head of an elephant in a state of melancholy madness. It contained several large streets all very like one another, and many small streets still more like one another, inhabited by people equally like one another, who all went in and out at the same hours, with the same sound upon the same pavements, to do the same work, and to whom every day was the same as yesterday and tomorrow, and every year the counterpart of the last and the next.' PATRICK GEDDES and LEWIS MUMFORD both used Coketown as a generic name for the PALEOTECHNIC city at its worst (Novak, 1995).

cold bridge A part of a building's structure that unintentionally conducts heat from the inside of a building to the outside (in effect carrying coldness into the building), causing condensation on internal surfaces and consequent damage from dampness. The failure to avoid cold bridges has been the cause of failure in many modern buildings.

Coleman, Alice (b1923) Geographer. Coleman, a professor at King's College London, was a virulent critic of planners and architects in the 1970s and '80s. She presented evidence (of the incidence of litter, urine, human faeces, vandalism and their supposedly direct correlation with rates of children in care, for example) that she claimed established a link between social malaise and the design and layout of modern housing estates. As an advocate of ideas of DEFENSIBLE SPACE in the 1980s, she advised adapting unsuccessful housing estates by such means as removing pedestrian walkways and building houses on pieces of left-over land. Her book *Utopia on Trial*, published in 1985, attacked professional orthodoxies that she said contradicted common sense. 'The brave new Utopia,' she wrote, 'is essentially a device for treating people like children, first by denying them the right to choose their own housing, and then by choosing for them disastrous designs that create a needless sense of social failure'. Utopia, according to Coleman, is a house with its own front door. Flats are inherently dystopian, and the more of them that are sharing a common entrance, the more dystopian they will inevitably become (Coleman, 1985; see also JOHN TURNER). Coleman was influential with both local and central government. She attracted the support of prime minister Margaret Thatcher, who liked her iconoclastic approach. A number of academics, such as BILL HILLIER, were critical of her methods, as she was of theirs.

Coleville See ALBERTOPOLIS.

collaboration Any arrangement of people working together, such as between departments, between councillors and officials, within partnerships, between local authorities, between local authorities and developers, and with the public. The term became widely used in the 1990s as an alternative to PUBLIC PARTICIPATION, which some people feel gives the unfortunate sense that 'the public' is participating in someone else's process, rather than there being a collaboration between equal partners.

collaboratory *n.* A collaboration among different functional sectors (government, business, academia, voluntary organisations and others), and among different jurisdictions within a geographical region. John Egers (2003) suggests that such associations 'are fast becoming the new model for successful urban organization in the global age, and the only local political arrangement likely to make it possible for besieged municipalities to survive in the increasingly intense global competition that lies ahead'.

Collage City A critique of modernist architecture and urban design by COLIN ROWE and Fred Koetter, published in 1975.

collateral Security for a loan (in property development, for example).

collateral warranty Gives the purchaser or tenant of a building the right to sue the contractor or professional team for negligent construction or design.

collective memory Italian architect ALDO ROSSI's concept of what he saw as an element that is often reflected in a city's form, and should be reflected in new development.

Collective Plan A modernist plan for reconstructing Berlin, prepared by a team led by the architect Hans Scharoun in 1946. It was based on a high-speed grid system of 64 clover-leaf interchanges. Apart from the medieval core, which would be saved as an urban museum, the city's fabric that had survived the war would have been swept away. The plan was rejected (Kostof, 1991).

collector road (US) One that collects traffic from LOCAL ROADS and connects smaller towns with each other and to arterial roads.

Collège des Ecossais See PATRICK GEDDES.

collision See BIASED TERMINOLOGY.

colonisation Permanent structures replacing temporary ones, as sometimes happens with a market. Also called *concretion*.

colony (India) A housing estate (Vidal and Gupta, 1999).

Colossus of Roads, The The engineer and road-builder THOMAS TELFORD (1757–1834), so called by the poet Robert Southey, punning on the ancient Colossus of Rhodes, one of the seven wonders of the world. See also PONTIFEX MAXIMUS.

combinational urbanism Defined by the new urbanist Stef Polyzoides as a North American planning technique in which a set of building and urban codes ensures that subsequent incremental development fulfils an initial vision of desirable development. Compare COMPOSITIONAL URBANISM.

combined heat and power A system that generates electricity, and uses what would normally be waste heat to heat water for domestic use. It can be on either a small scale (such as single building) or on a very large scale – the most notable UK example being Dolphin Square and Churchill Gardens in Pimlico which were heated by Battersea power station on the other side of the Thames. Compare COMMUNAL HEATING and DISTRICT HEATING, and see POWELL AND MOYA.

Comeback City Cleveland, Ohio, according to its BOOSTERS' determinedly optimistic view of its attempts in the 1990s to stem the outward tide of its population.

comedians See SMILE.

comfortable concentration camp The feminist

writer Betty Friedan's description of the affluent US suburban home where, she said, middle-class housewives were economically dependent and socially isolated (Markus and Cameron, 2002).

commercial leisure development Defined by the Scottish Office (1998) as a development that needs to be accessible to a large number of people, such as a multi-screen cinema or bowling alley.

commercial waste Waste from premises used for a trade, business, sport, recreation or entertainment.

commissar's tudorbethan Public housing built in a debased historicist style, particularly by the LONDON COUNTY COUNCIL in the 1950s. Alan Powers recalls the architect Colin St John Wilson using the term.

Commission for Architecture and the Built Environment CABE has defined its role as 'the champion for architecture in England, promoting high standards in the design of buildings and the spaces between them'. Created in 1999 to replace the Royal Fine Art Commission, it continues the RFAC's work reviewing designs and providing advice, but with a wider remit.

Chris Smith, secretary of state for culture, media and sport, told a conference how the name had been chosen. 'We were warned off "environmental design" because to some people that means air-conditioning,' he said. '"Urban design" would have excluded the villages and perhaps small towns... The press made its own choice and adopted "The Architecture Commission"... However, we were repeatedly reminded by the Urban Design Alliance that, for some people, "architecture" is read in a very narrow sense: simply the design of individual buildings.' Smith was surely right that, to most people, 'urban' would have excluded villages and perhaps small towns, though such places were included in the DETR's then-current definition of urban design. The press that 'made its own choice' was the architectural press. And architecture means the design of individual buildings not to some, but to most people, and possibly to most architects as well.

CABE rhymes with *babe*, except when enunciated by Lord St John of Fawsley (chairman of its predecessor, the RFAC) who pronounces it *Carbay*. (Lord St John also gives the correct Latin pronunciation to the late twentieth-century word *video*.)

Commission for the New Towns An independent public body set up under the New Towns Act 1959 to take on the ownership and management of land and buildings in any new town whose development corporation had finished its work and been wound up. The commission was incorporated into English Partnerships in 1999.

Committee on the Appearance of Housing Estates The committee reported in 1948 on the dullness of much contemporary housing design and layout (Burnett, 1986).

committees The rhyme 'In all the parks/ In all the cities/ There are no statues to committees' is sometimes recited by architects, among others, in complaining about planning committees. See SIGNATURE PROFESSION.

commodification Transforming things into commodities that can be bought and sold. Example: '...the insatiable demand of global capitalism to commodify everything, including civic and national identity, into an element in marketplace competition. "National heritage" is now just a mask for global commodification. Heritage islands are dotted within... mass-produced sprawl' (Glendinning, 2000).

commoditie, firmenes and delight The essentials of architecture, as defined by Sir Henry Wotton in 1624. The phrase was Wotton's translation of one coined by Vitruvius in the first century BC: 'firmitatis, utilitatis, venustatis'. *Commoditie* may be translated as usefulness. Morris Hickey Morgan translated the phrase in 1914 as 'durability, convenience and beauty'. In 2001 the Construction Industry Council was using the three concepts as the basis for developing a set of performance indicators for buildings. Its equivalent terms were *functionality, build quality* and *impact*. See also DESIGN QUALITY INDICATOR.

common A piece of land that belongs to local people collectively, and which is open for public use.

Common Ground A voluntary organisation, founded in 1984, supporting projects which develop LOCAL DISTINCTIVENESS through people's experience of, among other things, local custom, landscape, natural history, settlement patterns, architecture, art, social history, folklore, legend and literature.

common interest ownership A form of multi-ownership private housing in Australia and the USA. Types include CONDOMINIUM, housing cooperative and PLANNED COMMUNITY.

common land Land subject to grazing rights or other common rights for owners of nearby properties, or other open, uncultivated land. Common land is registered with county councils under the Commons Registration Act 1965.

Common Purpose A organisation that runs educational programmes in cities throughout the UK, 'bringing together talented, energetic people from diverse backgrounds who would not usually meet... to forge links bringing new vision to the running of their city... and giving them a chance to learn what makes it tick'.

commonhold A form of tenure in that gives an individual a freehold interest in part of a multi-occupied building and a defined collective interest in the building's common parts.

commonplace *n.* Sue Clifford (1997) of COMMON GROUND suggests that promoting LOCAL DISTINCTIVENESS depends on 'liberation from preoccupation with the beautiful, the rare, the spectacular to help people explore what makes the commonplace particular and to build ways of demonstratively expressing what they value in their everyday lives... This should be an inclusive process, encouraging local people to debate what is important to them as well as luring the experts to appreciate a broader view.'

Commonwealth of Oceana A description of a utopia, written by James Harrington and published in 1656.

communal garden Shared by the occupants of a group of buildings but not accessible to the public in general. Most London squares, for example, were developed with the centre of the square as a locked communal garden.

communal heating A system providing heating for a group of housing (but a less extensive area than a DISTRICT HEATING system). Compare COMBINED HEAT AND POWER.

commune 1 A group of people, not all of whom are related, living together and sharing, often following an unorthodox lifestyle. **2** (France) A traditional unit of decentralised municipal government. **3** In medieval Europe the term was used to describe a body of people whose aim was to govern themselves. London, like many other European cities at the time, declared itself a commune – a self-governing republic within the kingdom – in 1190 when King Richard the Lionheart was away on a crusade.

communicative planning A theoretical approach to town planning based on a democratic interactive process in which different groups of participants come to understand each other's perspectives. Technical processes are demystified and forces of oppression unmasked. Patsy Healey is among its leading proponents.

Communist Manifesto, The A call by KARL MARX and FRIEDRICH ENGELS for worldwide revolution, published in 1848. Among much else, the manifesto proposed a 'combination of agriculture with manufacturing industries; gradual abolition of the distinction between town and country, by a more equable distribution of population over the country'.

communitarianism A philosophical movement proposing a new ethical base for politics, restoring community through a revival of mutual responsibility. Led by AMITAI ETZIONI, the movement attracted the interest of Bill Clinton and TONY BLAIR in the 1990s.

communitas (Latin) In the late middle ages the term was used to describe the residents of a town as a whole.

Communities Against Drugs Home Office funding for programmes to reduce the availability of drugs and tackle problems associated with their use.

Communities First A partnership-based regeneration programme run by the Welsh Assembly.

Communities Scotland The Scottish Executive's regeneration and housing agency. Its responsibilities include the regulation and inspection of social landlords.

community *n.* **1** A grouping of people with common interests. The DETR (1998) defined community as 'any group of individuals with a common bond above the family unit and below the first level of municipal administration. It is primarily those people living or working in a defined area... in general the people intended to benefit from regeneration and local services.' The New Economics Foundation (2000) describes a community as 'a web of relationships defined by a significant level of mutual care and commitment'. AMITAI ETZIONI defines community as combining two elements: first, 'a web of affect-laden relationships among a group of individuals, relationships that often crisscross and reinforce one another (rather than merely one-on-one or chainlike individual relationships); and, second, 'a measure of commitment to a set of shared values, norms and meanings, and a shared history and identity – in short to a particular culture'. Gerald Fug defines community as 'a capacity to live in a world composed of different people without explosive tension, to be able to interact with unfamiliar strangers and not to see them as a mob, and to foster negotiation rather than neighbourliness' (Rook, 2002). Researchers for the URBAN TASK FORCE found that community meant different things to different people. The older of the people they talked to, many of whom lived in the suburbs, tended to emphasise more formal local organisations and knowing neighbours when describing strong communities. For the younger people the researchers talked to, more of whom lived in urban areas, community was more about shared interests and identity than about knowing individual neighbours well (Urban Task Force, 1999a). Michael Beaman (2001) has described the concept of community in London's north Kensington. 'Everybody used the word [community] and everybody assumed they meant the same thing by it, but none of them did. [The Caribbean community] was... organised around people [who] had been driven out by gentrification and were living up as far as the North Circular [Road]... based on the extended family. We had a large Moroccan population whose community was founded on a bunch of people who left one valley in Morocco about 40–50 years ago... This community were frankly at each other's throats half of the time, and unless you knew which side of the village granddad lived on 100 years ago, you never understood what they were going on about. We had a large population from the horn of Africa. There it was pure politics, which side of the Somalian divide you were on. Finally, you had the white Anglo-Saxon community [which was] completely polarised. [There was] the working class population on one side of Ladbroke Grove which had been there a long time... and the fairly well-heeled denizens of the east side of Ladbroke Grove who for the most part had this rather quaint idea of community... this idea that somehow because they lived close to each other they were all friends and all chummy, and that... it gave them, the white educated middle class people, the right to speak for the others.' MICHAEL YOUNG and PETER WILLMOTT (1957) called for housing and planning policy to be less destructive of community networks, which they saw as being of great social value. WILFRED BURNS (1963), city planning officer of Newcastle-upon-Tyne and later the UK government's chief planner, took a different view. 'In a huge city, it is a fairly common observation that the dwellers in a slum area are almost a separate race of people with different values, aspirations, and ways of living...' Burns wrote. 'One result of slum clearance is that a considerable movement of people takes place over long distances, with devastating effect on the social groupings built up over the years. But, one might argue, this is a good thing when we are dealing with people who have no initiative or civic pride. The task is surely to break up such groupings even though the people seem to be satisfied with their miserable environment and seem to enjoy an extrovert social life in their own locality' (see also SEGREGATION). ROBERT GOODMAN (1972), himself a community planner, warned against some professionals' romantic view of the concept of community. 'In architectural school, "community" was good because it allowed you to put a lot of buildings together in ways that would visually "define" interesting spaces; our models for this were the medieval hill towns of Italy. But in the ghettos many families were trying to get away from a sense of forced community – a community where people were packed together with other families because our economic system gave them no other choices.' **2** A place and its people. New urbanists specify that a community must be 'a sustainable human habitat which is complete and compact' (Duany, 2000). **3** (especially US) A place where people live. In this sense the term does not imply any particular closeness or interaction between the residents. **4** A group of people living under the same government. Example: 'It is a high priority for this government to sort out the planning system because of the important effect it has on the community as a whole' (from the UK in 2002). Jeremy Bentham is said to have been the first, in the phrase 'the good of the community', to apply the term to the people of the country as a whole (Potter, 1950). **5** The opposite of an institution (such as a hospital or prison). For example, people with mental illnesses who before the 1980s might have been in a mental hospital are now described as living 'in the community', which means no more than that they are not in an institution.

In 1955 George A Hillery identified 94 definitions of community (concluding that the definitions had nothing in common apart from relating to people). Sociologists and other commentators have been adding more ever since. *The community* is one of the most overused phrases in urbanism. Planners consult and plan for 'the community' even when it does not exist in any meaningful sense. They are anxious to give their work legitimacy by referring to the people on the receiving end, and it is easier to treat them as an undifferentiated mass than to recognise their often conflicting interests. In a particular place traders may have common interests, cyclists may have common interests, car drivers may have common interests and parents of young children may have common interests. But some traders ride bikes, some cyclists also drive a car, and some people are child-caring, cycling, car-driving traders. The art of planning lies in working out how development can contribute to building on common interests and reconciling conflicts. That process, with its mixture of technical and political aspects, is nearly always obscured and confused by speaking of 'the community'.

Community is often used interchangeably with NEIGHBOURHOOD. Some commentators have suggested that *community* tends to be used to refer to poor black or ethnically mixed populations, and that *neighbourhood* tends to refer to poor white populations. 'Opportunity, Responsibility and Community' was an election slogan of Bill Clinton in 1991 and TONY BLAIR in 1997 (recalling the motto of the World State in Aldous Huxley's 1932 novel *Brave New World*: 'Community, Identity, Stability'). In 1998 George W Bush, running for governor of Texas, converted it to a two-word slogan by dropping 'community'. Ottawa, Ontario calls itself a *community of communities*. The word *community*, deriving from the Latin *communitas* meaning fellowship, dates from the fourteenth century. See also GHOST COMMUNITY.

community action The people of an area working together to bring about change. The term was widely used in the UK in the 1960s and early '70s, often to describe processes involving confrontation with public authorities or the private sector.

community advocacy The government's green paper *Planning: delivering a fundamental change*, published in 2001, used the term to describe PLANNING AID. See also ADVOCACY PLANNING.

community appraisal (or audit) A survey of the needs and resources of the people of a particular area, often carried out by the people themselves. See also PLACECHECK.

community architecture 1 The design of buildings and space for which a community organisation is the client. One of the high points of the community architecture movement was the rehabilitation of Glasgow's nineteenth-century tenement housing by COMMUNITY-BASED HOUSING ASSOCIATIONS in the 1970s and '80s, following the example of ASSIST. **2** The design of buildings and space where local residents or future users are closely consulted on the design.

The term (with both meanings) became current in the mid 1970s. In the 1980s community architecture bathed briefly in the spotlight of fashion, was jumped on as a bandwagon by professionals looking for new clients in a recession, then cast aside as yesterday's news (see BLACK ROAD). By the late 1990s the term was little heard, though not because any less of that sort of work was being done. Graham Towers (1995) defined the principles of community architecture more widely. They were, he suggested, user participation; taking account of user needs; appreciating the wider urban context; cooperation; multiple skills; an integrated design process; building re-use; modest scale; and quality before innovation. The architect Herman Hertzberger emphasised how different this approach was. He wrote: 'Architecture was never very humane in the past. Pyramids, temples, cathedrals and palaces were the instruments of oppression rather than of freedom. The architect's work throughout history has been dedicated more to the glory and celebration of the reputation of a few than to the improvement of the living conditions of everyone.'

Community Architecture Group Set up in 1981 as part of the Royal Institute of British Architects 'to promote popular participation in the built environment'.

community areas policy A planning policy adopted by the Labour-controlled GREATER LONDON COUNCIL in 1984 to protect working-class communities on the fringes of London's commercial centres from the speculative property development, and to support developments for social needs and employment. The communities were supported through planning, housing and employment policies, and grants for community projects. The policy was described as an example of POPULAR PLANNING.

community audit 1 An assessment of the characteristics of the people who live in an area. **2** An assessment of an area carried out by the people who live there.

Community Champion A government fund supporting community champions and other means of community capacity-building.

community champion A local leader who plays a major role in initiating action to improve an area.

community charge The official name for the poll tax, introduced in the 1990s. See COMMUNITY.

community chest 1 A fund collected for the general benefit. **2** Money raised from a levy on new development to pay for improvements identified by local people. **3** A funding programme providing small grants to community groups and social enterprises through the Neighbourhood Renewal Unit. **4** One of two of stacks of cards in the board game 'Monopoly'. The other stack is *chance*.

community cohesion See COHESIVE COMMUNITY.

community council A voluntary group that represents local views to public bodies. Local authorities have a duty to consult community councils on local issues and services.

community design centre 1 Provides professional skills for people unable to afford market rates, and often in ways that help the users learn about the relevant processes for themselves. **2** (US) A local service offering design expertise to an under-served community and providing students with a chance of becoming involved in real projects. Ruth Durack (2002) records that community design centres flourished in USA in the 1960s and '70s. In the 1980s cutbacks in federal funding of social programmes caused most of them to close. By the end of the 1990s, Durack notes, 'design schools had renewed their interest in community engagement... [and] the concept of service-learning [had] gained credence in a wide range of disciplines as a way of applying new theoretical approaches to real-world problems, while encouraging students to engage in public life.' By 2002 there were more than 50 university-supported community design centres in the USA. See ADVOCACY PLANNING.

community development Developing communities of interest within local areas.

community development project A series of 12 local projects set up by the Home Office in 1969 with the aim of tackling DEPRIVATION, as it was called. Each project was based in a local authority, with the support of a local university. The Home Office wanted to test ways of a) improving the ways in which local authorities delivered their services, b) improving communications between the local authority and residents and c) promoting community self-help projects. Many of the people who worked for the projects did not believe that deprivation could be tackled by such means. They preferred a more politically radical approach, often based on Marxist analysis of class struggle, involving helping local people to confront the local authority as representing the LOCAL STATE. By 1977 the government had abandoned the programme.

community economic development Action to develop the local economy involving local people controlling the process or owning assets.

Community Empowerment Fund Funding from the government's Neighbourhood Renewal Unit to help community and voluntary groups become involved in LOCAL STRATEGIC PARTNERSHIPS.

community empowerment Helping the people in an area acquire the skills, information and confidence necessary to participate effectively in managing or resisting change.

community engagement Helping local people to become invoved in the processes of change.

community enterprise Action by local people, often involving economic development, in pursuit of social objectives. Defined by the DETR (1998b) as an enterprise having social aims, being financially viable, and being owned and run by local people. In the 1980s some community-based initiatives adopted this term, in place of terms such as COMMUNITY ACTION that were politically out of favour with the Thatcher government.

community entrepreneur A person who initiates and develops projects involving and benefiting a local community. See also SOCIAL ENTREPRENEUR.

community forest A well-wooded landscape that can include farmland, settlements, leisure facilities, natural areas and public open space. A programme of creating community forests was launched in 1989 to diversify land and restore areas of industrial dereliction in the countryside around towns. The deputy chair of the COUNTRYSIDE AGENCY, Pam Warhurst, was reported in *New Start* (2001) as saying that a community forest did not have to be full of trees. A community forest was what happened when people 'greened up' their towns and cities in whatever way they saw fit.

community forum An organisation that brings together a wide range of local interests to discuss the future of the place.

Community Forum Set up in 2002 to advise the government's Neighbourhood Renewal Unit.

community foundation A locally based, grant-making trust with a permanent endowment which funds voluntary and community groups.

Community Fund Lottery funding for groups supporting disadvantaged communities.

community governance Running public services with the involvement of local people.

community heating Centrally heated steam or hot water distributed through a network of pipes to heat a large area of commercial, industrial or domestic buildings, or for industrial processes.

Community Housing Taskforce A government unit formed in 2001 to support the transfer of council homes to housing associations.

community indicators A set of measures used in a COMMUNITY APPRAISAL.

community information network Any of the many ways communities have devised to communicate with one another, locally, nationally or internationally, ranging from local resource centres to funded online projects. UK Communities Online was formed in 1997 to support this work.

community interest company A form of company whose profits and assets would be used for the public good. Such companies were proposed by the UK government in 2003 as a means of financing urban regeneration.

community investment Defined by the Joseph Rowntree Foundation (2001a) as 'increasing the ability of communities to manage change effectively for themselves'.

Community Land Act 1975 Enabled local authorities and the LAND AUTHORITY FOR WALES to buy development land at current use value and sell it at market value. The Act also introduced a *development land tax*. The scheme was abolished in 1979 by Margaret Thatcher's incoming government.

community land scheme Introduced in the Community Land Act 1975 (providing powers to acquire compulsorily) and the Development Land Tax Act 1976 (taxing development values).

Community Learning Chests Funding from the government's Neighbourhood Renewal Unit to help communities acquire skills and knowledge to enable them to contribute to the renewal process.

Community Legal Service Partnership A local network of organisations providing legal services to communities in particular need.

community loan fund Provides flexible, low-cost credit to support the regeneration of a local neighbourhood by helping community organisations and businesses excluded by mainstream banks.

community of communities Ottawa, Ontario calls itself a community of communities, meaning that the city as a whole constitutes a COMMUNITY as well as being made up of smaller distinct communities. Ottawa has also called itself a CITY OF VILLAGES.

community plan 1 One prepared by the people of a particular area. **2** One prepared by a local authority and other organisations to promote, plan and provide for the well-being of local communities.

community planner 1 One who works with community organisations, helping them to plan their local area and to use the planning process to their own benefit. This meaning, the equivalent of community architect, was current in the 1970s and '80s, but is now less commonly used. **2** One employed in local government to prepare a community planning strategy.

community planning 1 The process by which a local authority and other organisations come together to promote, plan and provide for the well-being of the communities they serve. In 2000 the Local Government Association asked its members to 'develop a community planning process' and 'prepare community planning strategies', working with local residents to define priorities. This use dates from the late 1990s. **2** Planning by, for or with local community organisations. **3** A process of involving a wide range of local people in planning a particular area in an event held over a few days, usually with the help of specialists and facilitators.

community planning forum 1 An event at which a wide range of people who live and work in a place take part in planning its future. **2** An organisation or standing committee of local people with this function.

community politics Based on local issues and community-based organisations.

community profiling Examining the needs and resources of an area with the active involvement of local people.

community reinvestment (US) URBAN REGENERATION.

community renewal Urban renewal initiatives involving community-based organisations; NEIGHBOURHOOD RENEWAL. The magazine *Regeneration and Renewal* in 2001 headed its news sections respectively *community renewal* and *physical regeneration*.

community safety Crime prevention seen in its local context. Community safety policies focus on such issues as PASSIVE SURVEILLANCE, NEIGHBOURHOOD WATCH and active citizenship.

Community Services Fund Government grants to help community groups provide transport, alterations to community buildings, and other facilities or services in small rural communities.

community services Provided by the local authority, other public bodies, statutory undertakers, voluntary groups and private organisations to meet local needs, including education, health, water, gas, electricity and sewerage.

community spirit A shared feeling of belonging to a group of people with common interests in a place.

community strategy Local authorities have a duty to prepare a community strategy for their whole area. The strategy sets out a long-term vision that has been agreed with all the main local STAKEHOLDERS, including public, private and community sector organisations, through a LOCAL STRATEGIC PARTNERSHIP. Community strategies should promote the economic, social and environmental well-being of their areas and contribute to the achievement of SUSTAINABLE development. They must have four main components: a) A long-term vision for the area which focuses on the outcomes that are to be achieved. b) An action plan identifying shorter-term priorities and activities that will contribute to the achievement of long-term outcomes. c) A shared commitment to implement the action plan and proposals for doing so. d) Arrangements for monitoring the implementation of the action plan, for periodically reviewing the community strategy, and for reporting progress to local communities.

community strengths assessment A method of assessing the capacity of communities to take leading roles in regeneration and local action. The approach, developed by Bradford Council, sees effective community involvement and leadership as being built primarily through the collective activity of local community and voluntary groups.

community technical aid Defined by the Department of the Environment in the 1980s as 'the provision of low- or no-cost technical assistance to non-profit community-based development projects.' See also COMTECHSA.

community technical aid centre The base for a community technical aid service. The TOWN AND COUNTRY PLANNING ASSOCIATION's Community Technical Aid Centre in Manchester, set up in the late 1970s, was one of the first. Several more, under a variety of different names, followed in the 1980s. The movement was supported and promoted by the Association of Community Technical Aid Centres (ACTAC), set up in 1983. In 1989 ACTAC listed the aims of community technical aid centres as being: to give technical and professional support to local people who want to develop their community's facilities, environment, resources and skills; to support a wide range of community groups on social, environmental, economic, housing, cultural and other issues; to work with communities in flexible ways that enable them to make the best use of both the centre's resources and skills, and their own; to help people to develop the confidence, understanding, skills and resources they need to tackle the issues their community feels are important.

community unit A neighbourhood bounded by FREEWAYS, as proposed in 1943 by the Los Angeles County Regional Planning Commission. Sir Peter Hall (1998) comments: 'It was a concept essentially no different from that which SIR ALKER TRIPP and PATRICK ABERCROMBIE were developing, quite independently, for London at the same time'.

community well-being The phrase is sometimes used as a alternative for social sustainability.

community without propinquity A term used by the American planner MELVIN WEBBER for what he also called NON-PLACE URBAN REALM or MEGALOPOLIS, where communities of interest are more important than communities of people living near one another.

Community, Identity, Stability The World State's motto in Aldous Huxley's 1932 novel *Brave New World*.

community-based housing association One that is run by its residents, who control the improvement of their own homes, and the building and letting of new ones. Some of the most successful examples improved Glasgow's tenements in the 1970s and '80s. See ASSIST and COMMUNITY ARCHITECTURE.

community-based regeneration Defined by the DETR (1998) as 'any activity carried out by the community for the community, in order to improve its social and economic lot'.

Commutaria The ideal commuter village, described in Elspeth Ann Macey's story 'Awayday' in *Absent Friends and Other Stories* (1955). Located on a commuter railway line between Portsmouth and London's Waterloo station, the village offers each commuter exactly what he or she wants. This is fiction: the trains always run exactly on time.

commuter belt A suburban area from which residents commute to the centre of the town or city.

commuter One who travels a significant distance from home to work. The word was first recorded in 1865 in the USA. The longest daily commuting time of any European city in 2002 was London, with an average of 51 minutes each way. Ogden Nash explained (in 'The Banker's Special' in *Versus*, published in 1949) that a commuter is one who never knows how a play or show concludes, because he has to leave early to catch a train to get him back to the country in time to catch a train to bring him back to the city.

commutershed The area from which a town or city's commuters are drawn. Example: 'Commutersheds can be shrunk through improving the balance between jobs and housing' (from the US, 2002). Compare PEDSHED and WATERSHED.

commuterville A commuter or dormitory town or suburb. Example: '[Urbana, Illinois, home of the novelist Richard Powers] is part lefty university town and part plush commuterville, with wide streets and pretty white houses' (2003).

compact An estate agents' euphemism for *small*.

compact city An approach to planning based on intensive development within existing urban areas, or on cities with relatively high densities and limits to their growth. 'If sustainability is the new religion,' Tim Mars (1998) writes, 'then planners are its priests and the compact city is the new Jerusalem.' Some advocates of compact cities see medieval cities as being examples of these. Leonardo Benevolo (1993) has put the case for traditional compact cities as being the most environmentally sustainable. 'In Europe it is everywhere apparent that the re-establishment of environmental balance depends not on natural processes but human industry, and in this the city re-acquires importance', he writes. 'Reconstruction of a comprehensive environment begins in the historic centres – rather than in the countryside – which survive as a model of a balanced and ordered setting of human dimensions. The seemingly densest cities – Venice, Bologna, Bruges, Prague – are in fact tightly bound worlds of buildings, parks and water, punctuated with direct and inspiring openings to the protected open spaces in their immediate vicinity.' The planning academic Patsy Healey disputes this. She has written that 'the compact city, which contained the production and consumption, material and cultural needs of a community within a clearly identifiable built form, has rarely been an accurate model of the economy and society of most urban areas, and makes very little sense in the open, loosely interconnected local economics and societies of today' (Healey, 1988).

Aristotle wrote in *Politics:* 'All cities that have a reputation for good government have a limit of population' (quoted in Hughes, 1971). The writer and philosopher TE Hulme (1911) argued that 'there is a great misconception as to what really constitutes a town. The usual idea is that city and country are a pair of opposites, and that the progress of events tends to spread the one and destroy the other. Nothing of the kind. The country is not the raw material out of which the town has been evolved. In the beginning was something I can vaguely call desert. Out of this matrix at one period of history civilisation had evolved two perfect correlatives of artificial and deliberate construction: the compact walled town, and the country. That was the ideal state.' Cyril Connolly wrote in *The Unquiet Grave*, published in 1945: 'No city should be too large for a man to walk out of it in a morning.'

company titles scheme (Australia) A housing cooperative. See COMMON INTEREST OWNERSHIP.

company town One built or dominated by one or a few companies.

comparative method Used to value land or property by reference to examples in the market. Compare CONTRACTOR'S TEST.

comparison goods Durable items such as furniture, clothing and electrical goods for which a shopper is likely to compare similar items in different shops before buying. Compare CONVENIENCE SHOP.

comparison shopping Defined by the Scottish Office (1998) as shopping not classified as convenience shopping, which the purchaser will compare on the basis of price and quality before a purchase is made, such as clothes, fashion, gift merchandise, electrical goods or furniture.

compatible use Defined by the BURRA CHARTER as one that involves no change to the culturally significant fabric, changes which are substantially reversible, or changes with a minimal impact. See ADAPTION and CULTURAL SIGNIFICANCE.

complex A group of related buildings, often in a single structure.

Complexity and Contradiction See ROBERT VENTURI.

complexity The state of being composed of many interconnected parts. The relatively new science of complexity theory uses the analogy of the sand pile. Sometimes when a small amount of sand is added, the pile will remain almost undisturbed. Occasionally, though, a small addition will result in the pile suffering a substantial collapse. Similarly with a city, change is continuous: patterns of employment, retailing, property prices, trade, traffic and many other aspects of life are constantly changing in response to an enormous number of interrelated determinants and influences. In this context, public policy can not treat a part of a city as if it were unconnected to the city and district as a whole. In the language of complexity theory, a city is a complex adaptive system that displays emergent behaviour. As John Holland observes, 'a city's coherence is somehow imposed on a perpetual flux of people and structures. Like the standing wave in front of a rock in a fast-moving stream, a city is a pattern in time' (quoted in Johnson, 2001).

In a complex system a large number of independent elements interact. The system acquires collective properties of its own – a life of its own, you might say – through those elements clashing with or accommodating each other. As the system becomes more complex, new collective properties emerge (the process is called *emergence*) and new ways of understanding them need to be found. Small events can result in unexpectedly large changes. Complexity theory studies these emergent structures: molecules forming cells, neurons forming brains, birds forming flocks, species forming ecosystems, producers and consumers forming economies, and developments forming cities. It is the structure of the networks that we must understand, not their details. The structures can be understood only as being constantly in transition as they respond to ever-changing conditions. Influencing complex systems is a matter of managing change, not of achieving equilibrium. A system in equilibrium is one in which its elements have ceased to interact. Apart from somewhere like Pompeii, that is a condition not found in cities.

Much of the least successful town planning and urban design is a consequence of visualising a condition of equilibrium and trying to achieve it. The drawings may be impressive, the scheme may even be executed exactly as planned, but the result will never be what was hoped or expected. People are often tempted to analyse situations of complexity in terms of simple cause and effect. For example, the Social Exclusion Unit (2000) has written: 'The cycle of decline for a neighbourhood almost always starts with lack of work. This generates other social problems – crime, drugs, low educational attainment and poor health – all of which reinforce one another and speed local decline'. In fact, the cause of a neighbourhood's decline is probably in most cases as complex and inter-related as what the Social Exclusion Unit recognises as the process of the neighbourhood's continuing decline. See also BEDFORD FALLS, CHAOS THEORY and TIPPING POINT.

composition urbaine (French) Urban design.

compositional urbanism Defined by the new urbanist Stef Polyzoides as a European planning technique in which a single public or private agency implements a broadly-based physical vision of development in large-scale increments. Compare COMBINATIONAL URBANISM.

comprehensive (re)development The architect CHARLES REILLY (1938) explained why he thought that 'the clearance of whole sectors of [towns] on a huge scale is necessary'. He explained: 'The new fast traffic on the one hand can not be canalised and treated as it should be to make the most of its efficiency except by radical replanning, and the new standard of life demanded by all alike can not be achieved except by rebuilding on a great scale. We all know how a new block of tenements here and another there create great slum areas in between and how when these areas are rebuilt, congestion and want of proper town planning will by that time have turned the first tenements back into slums.'

The writer Ian Jack recalls how large areas of Glasgow's tenements were swept away in the 1960s. 'Those were the days when not just streets but whole districts were staked out on maps and marked for destruction via a coloured overlay of "comprehensive redevelopment" or cloverleaf traffic intersections,' Jack writes. 'I remember the pen-and-wash drawings..., spindly, untenemental ladies walked their dogs through greensward and potential trees while something like the Empire State Building towered in the background, white and noble against a friendly sky' (quoted in Spring, 1990).

comprehensive area strategy A document setting out the long-term vision for an area, a plan of how this vision will be achieved, and details of the programme.

comprehensive development area One declared under the Town and Country Planning Act 1947 as an area 'to be developed or redeveloped as a whole, to deal with extensive war damage, poor layout, obsolete development, or to facilitate the relocation of population or industry, the replacement of open space, or for any specified purpose'. Local authorities had greater powers to control development and acquire land in a CDA. Urlan Wannop and Roger Leclerc (1987) noted that comprehensive development areas tended to be brutally insensitive, not only in their impact on mature communities, but also in destroying the local economy, and the social and economic value of much of the housing and urban structure. In Glasgow, for example, the local authority cleared housing much faster than it replaced it, and most of the new housing was built on remote fields at the city's edge.

compulsory competitive tendering A requirement on local authorities introduced in the 1980s. The Labour government replaced it by BEST VALUE in 1998, partly on the grounds that CCT encouraged local authorities to focus on the cost of services and ignore the quality.

compulsory purchase The forced purchase of land or private property by central government, a local authority or a government agency for public benefit at a price set by the district valuer.

COMTECHSA (Community Technical Services Agency) Founded in Liverpool in 1979, COMTECHSA was the first COMMUNITY TECHNICAL AID agency controlled by its client groups.

concave space One which contains some points that can not be seen from all other points in it. An L-shaped space is an example. Compare CONVEX SPACE.

concealable See CRAVED.

concentrated deconcentration Dispersing economic development from congested urban regions and reconcentrating it in less developed regions. The approach has been applied in RANDSTAD HOLLAND and the European Spatial Development Perspective (Hall, 2002).

concentric zone theory In the 1920s the Chicago-based theorist EW Burgess developed the theory that urban spatial structure could be understood as a series of concentric zones around the city centre. See also ATLANTIS, CITY OF GARANTISM, DOUGHNUT CITY, GARDEN CITY and VILA PITOTO.

concept plan Shows the basic principles on which a development will be based.

concept statement Sets out some of the design objectives and context appraisal results that may later become part of a DEVELOPMENT BRIEF.

concessionaire A consortium that contracts to design, build, operate and maintain a development.

concrete A building material formed by mixing cement, sand and gravel with water. Adrian Forty (2001) writes: 'Despite what the cement manufacturing industry would have us believe, truly speaking, concrete is not a material at all, but a process... Of all the ingredients... the most important and the most decisive for the final result is labour. To a greater degree than other materials – products of nature, or of other industrial technologies – concrete is the product of human labour and, for better or for worse, the evidence of its manual treatment in the few hours between its liquid and its set state decides the fate of the building for ever.' Forty neatly summarises the twentieth century's indecisive treatment of structural concrete: 'covered up until 1950, uncovered in the '70s and '80s, and then, in the '90s, a renaissance of exposed concrete.' See also BRUTALISM.

Concrete Bob Robert McAlpine (1847–1934), the head of the well-known family building firm, who pioneered the use of that material from 1876.

concrete cancer See HIGH-ALUMINA CEMENT and see also GLASS CANCER.

concrete collar Birmingham's ring road. See HERBERT MANZONI.

concrete forest An area of high concrete buildings packed tightly together. The phrase has been used to describe the densest parts of Hong Kong.

concrete jungle A popular term for a place where people feel unsafe and where they have difficulty in finding their way around. Also *urban jungle*. See also CITY SAFARI.

concretion Permanent structures replacing temporary ones, as sometimes happens with a market. Also known as *colonisation*.

condition See PLANNING CONDITION.

conditional contract An agreement for the sale of a piece of land that will be activated if a condition, such as the granting of planning permission, is fulfilled. Compare OPTION.

conditional use (US) A use permitted under a ZONING ORDINANCE, but only on certain conditions. A filling station in a residential area is a typical example.

condominium (US) A building containing units that are individually owned; a form of home-ownership in which home-owners have a freehold interest in their homes and a tenant-in-common interest in the common areas. The term means having control over a property jointly with one or more owners. The equivalent in Australia is *strata title*. See COMMON INTEREST OWNERSHIP.

Conference of Socialist Planners A short-lived organisation (not an event) formed in the 1970s, inspired by the more influential Conference of Socialist Economists (which itself had an interest in urban planning issues).

configuration Shape; three-dimensional built form; the relation of one part to another; layout (of streets or development). For example, SPACE SYNTAX ANALYSIS focuses on the 'configuration' of the URBAN GRID. BILL HILLIER (1996), the pioneer of space syntax analysis, defines configuration as 'relations taking into account other relations.' From the Latin *configurare*, to form.

conflict resolution The processes of managing, planning and designing cities often depend on building on common interests and, where possible, resolving conflicts between individuals, groups and organisations. Four alternative ways of resolving conflicts are: *fighting, problem-solving, negotiation,* and *creative collaboration* (DE BONO, 1985). All of them can be used (sometimes in combination) in the processes of regenerating cities, either as part of the formal democratic political process or outside it. a) *Fighting* is the familiar process through which developers, planning authorities, action groups and anyone else polarise the issues and dig themselves into entrenched positions, until a public inquiry, political decision or war of attrition finally produces a winner. This approach ignores the possibility of finding and building on any common ground there may be between the conflicting parties. b) *Problem-solving* is more constructive than fighting. It relies on identifying deviations from what is considered normal, and putting them right. This approach suits professions or politicians with narrow perspectives, and task forces with tight remits. However the assumption that we know where we want to end up may restrict more creative possibilities. c) Successful *negotiation* leads to compromise: a resolution of conflict based on the elements that neither side finds objectionable. In the right circumstances this can be a creative solution. d) *Creative collaboration* resolves conflicts by creating something which makes the most of the circumstances, but which no one may have imagined before. It does not start from assumptions as to what the problem or the solution might be. What is created may be something tangible, like a building or an urban space; or it may be an idea, a process, a strategy, a set of guidelines, or some other means of getting to grips with a complex system such the whole or part of a city. See also CONSENSUS.

congestion 1 A condition where the large number of vehicles using a road or roads at a particular time contributes to unacceptably low traffic speeds or unacceptable social, economic or environmental costs. Congestion is a subjective measure. Most of the drivers

> **"CONGESTION IS A SIGN THAT YOU HAVE A HEALTHY, GROWING ECONOMY AND HAVE REFRAINED FROM OVER-INVESTING IN ROADS"**
>
> *Robert Cervero*

who cause it choose to use roads that they know will be congested. The weight of traffic is not so great as to persuade them to travel at a different time, take another route, use another mode of transport, or not to make the journey (or they may believe they have no realistic alternative). For some other potential drivers, on the other hand, congestion acts as a natural means of rationing road use: they find it less acceptable than possible alternatives and so avoid the congested road. ROAD PRICING provides a potential alternative means of rationing road use, by adding a monetary cost to the many other factors in decisions about whether or not to use a particular road. If a significant number of people are discouraged from using the road by the price, they may be replaced by a slightly smaller number of road users, who are attracted by the reduction in congestion and are not put off by the cost. Congestion is a measure of the slowness of travel people will tolerate. Any perceptible increase in speeds, due to such means as improved roads or traffic management, attracts drivers who might otherwise have found an alternative. Any decrease in speeds will persuade some drivers to find an alternative. Congestion therefore represents a 'tolerated equilibrium'. James Howard Kunstler (2001) writes of driving in Atlanta, Georgia. 'You dared not venture out anymore to a restaurant on a Friday evening in Buckhead, the Beverly Hills of Atlanta, unless you wanted to spend half the night listening to books-on-tape in your suv. Routine mid-day trips to the supermarket now required the kind of strategic planning used in military re-supply campaigns under wartime conditions. Mothers with children were spending so many hours on chauffeuring duty that they qualified for livery licenses. Motorists were going mad, literally behind the wheel: one berserker tired of waiting at an intersection shot out the signal light with a handgun. The people of Atlanta were clearly driving themselves crazy with driving.' Robert Cervero, author of *Suburban Gridlock*, has described congestion as 'a sign that you have a healthy, growing economy and have refrained from over-investing in roads'. See also PLANNED CONGESTION. **2** Overcrowding. Example: 'City planning through removing the labouring classes from the congested districts promotes industrial efficiency' (from the USA, 1909).

The word congestion (meaning clogging) dates from around 1590. See also GRIDLOCK.

congestion charging Making road users pay according to the extent of use in a particular area, the class of road, the time of day or the type of vehicle. The aim may be to reduce the number of vehicles and level of congestion in a congested area, and/or to raise money to pay for public transport.

conglomerate A CONURBATION; a POLYCENTRIC city. See CITY OF CITIES.

congregation Groups of similar people living close to one another by choice. Compare SEGREGATION and see CLUSTERING.

Congress for the New Urbanism The Congress for the NEW URBANISM was convened in 1993 (meeting in Alexandria, Virginia) and drew up its charter in 1996. The charter outlines a set of prescriptive principles to guide public policy, development practice, urban planning and design, aimed at restoring existing urban centres and towns within coherent metropolitan regions, reconfiguring sprawling suburbs into communities of real neighbourhoods and diverse districts, conserving natural environments, and preserving the built heritage. The charter declares that: a) The neighbourhood, the district and the corridor are the essential elements of development and redevelopment in the metropolis. Neighbourhoods should be compact, pedestrian-friendly and mixed-use. Districts generally emphasise a special single use. Corridors (ranging from boulevards and railway lines to rivers and parkways) are regional connectors of neighbourhoods and districts. b) Many activities of daily living should occur within walking distance. c) Schools should be within walking or cycling distance for children. d) Neighbourhoods should have a broad range of housing types and price levels. e) Appropriate building densities and land uses should be within walking distance of public transport. f) Concentrations of civic, institutional and commercial activity should be embedded in neighbourhoods and districts, not isolated in single-use complexes. g) Graphic urban design codes can guide change. h) A range of parks should be distributed within neighbourhoods. i) Conservation areas and open spaces should be used to define and connect different neighbourhoods and districts. j) A primary task of all urban architecture and landscape design is the physical definition of streets and public spaces as places of shared use. k) Individual architectural projects should be seamlessly linked to their surroundings. This does not imply that new buildings should mimic historic forms. l) The design of streets and buildings should reinforce safe environments, but not at the expense of accessibility and openness. m) Streets and squares should be safe, comfortable and interesting to the pedestrian. n) Architecture and landscape design should grow from local climate, topography, history and building practice. o) Civic buildings and public gathering places require important sites and distinctive form. p) All buildings should provide their inhabitants with a clear sense of location, weather and time.

connected city approach An approach to improving urban areas by focusing on the connections between people who bring about change, connections between elements of the built environment, and connections in the movement network (Cowan, 1997b). This approach was the basis of the URBAN DESIGN ALLIANCE'S PLACE-CHECK method.

connectivity 1 The degree to which a place is connected by routes to other places and to which its own parts are connected to each other. **2** The degree to which a city's financial and business services are connected to those in other cities. A 2002 report by Loughborough University named London as the world's most connected city in terms of its financial and business services. The assessment, measuring the connections between 316 cities, was made on the basis of information about the office networks of 100 global business services companies. New York came second and Hong Kong third. See WORLD CITY.

consensus An agreement that satisfies the primary interests and concerns of all parties. British prime minister Margaret Thatcher defined consensus as 'the absense of leadership'. This may have been a pose: she was as skilful as anyone at building political consensus when she needed it.

consensus building Reaching agreements in ways that satisfy the primary interests and concerns of all parties. The *Consensus Building Handbook* (Sage Publications, 1999) suggests that the process works best when four conditions are met. Participants need the right kind of facilitation or mediation assistance to manage the process; they need to agree a set of ground rules at the start; they need to give themselves sufficient time to build their capacity to work in this way; and they need a written guide to building consensus. See also CONFLICT RESOLUTION.

conservation 1 Maintaining the most valued aspects of a building or place while sensitively accommodating change. The BURRA CHARTER defines conservation as all the processes of looking after a place so as to retain its cultural significance. It includes maintenance and may, according to circumstances, include preservation, restoration, reconstruction and ADAPTION, and it will be commonly a combination of more than one of these. Robin Maguire has identified four values of conservation: a) The academic or archaeological value of an object as a historical document. b) Its aesthetic value. c) The value of continuity and identity, which is affected by the rate of environmental change. d) Ecological values, embodied in the broader concept of conservation and of the wise use of resources. See also FORENSIC CONSERVATION. **2** The protection of living things and their habitats, and the careful use of natural resources.

conservation area One designated by a local authority under the Town and Country Planning (Listed Buildings and Conservation Areas) Act 1990 as possessing special architectural or historical interest. The council will seek to preserve or enhance the character and appearance of such areas. Conservation areas were first introduced by the Civic Amenities Act 1967.

conservation area advisory group A group of people with specialist knowledge, which meets regularly or occasionally to advise a local authority on the merits of planning applications, or other planning and design issues in a conservation area.

conservation area character appraisal A published document defining the special architectural or historic interest that warranted the area being designated.

conservation area consent Permission to demolish an unlisted building in a conservation area.

conservation area partnership A scheme for administering ENGLISH HERITAGE grants in a conservation area.

conservation by demolition Demolishing a building or buildings in order to create open space or space for development that will enable the area to be improved in a way that will allow other existing buildings to be refurbished and found new uses. The term was used by the Manchester and Liverpool developer Urban Splash in the 1990s.

conservation deficit The difference between the capital costs of a scheme and the increase in the value of the property, where the former is greater than the latter; the difference between the cost of restoring a historic building and its market value, where the former is greater than the latter.

conservation officer A local authority officer dealing with the conservation of historic buildings. The first conservation officer was appointed in Chester in 1971, following a recommendation in a 1968 report to the council by the architect Donald Insall, *Chester: a study in conservation*. Their original professional body the Association of Conservation Officers, formed in the mid-1970s, widened its remit to become the Institute of Historic Building Conservation in the 1990s.

conservation plan A document setting out what is significant and of value in a heritage asset, and how the place will be protected. ENGLISH HERITAGE suggests that a conservation plan can be particularly relevant for places of exceptional heritage value, in split ownership, or with more than one type of heritage, and for major monuments and their settings, large complex objects such as ships, and historic sites with associated collections.

conservation-officer Georgian A term of derision for a style of architecture designed to satisfy the local authority's requirements for a new building that fits into a historic context. Compare KENTUCKY FRIED GEORGIAN and PLANNING OFFICER'S GEORGIAN, and see GEORGIAN.

conservative surgery See PATRICK GEDDES.

conserver gains A principle proposed by the social policy researcher Meyer Hillman as an alternative to the *polluter pays* principle. Governments would reward people who take steps to avoid adversely affecting society or the environment (Karpf, 2002).

consistency See MONOTONY.

consistent poverty The state of being poor for an extended period of time. This was suggested in 2002 as needing to be given greater emphasis as an indicator of POVERTY.

Consortium Developments In 1983 a number of the big housebuilders joined forces to propose a series of large-scale, free-standing, privately developed new communities. The idea was that it might be easier to obtain planning permission for full-blown new settlements (with schools, shops and other facilities) than it was proving to obtain permission for new housing schemes on greenfield sites tacked on to existing towns and villages. To the Thatcher government, strongly supportive of market forces, this could have been a convenient way of accommodating the large number of new houses that forecasts showed were needed. But the government was unwilling to overrule the outraged local opposition that each site provoked. Consortium Developments' ambitious programme came to nothing, and names such as Foxley Wood and Tillingham Hall joined the list of places that never were. Advocates of new towns were divided over whether to welcome the proposals, on the grounds that they were free-standing new settlements, or to disapprove of them as being unlikely to be socially or economically balanced communities.

conspicuousness The degree to which a route or other urban element is obvious and identifiable.

constraints map Shows features that may limit how a particular site or area can be developed.

constructed experience That which is provided by a themed environment. Example: 'Las Vegas has pioneered the constructed experience. Walk along the strip and in one journey you can take in versions of Venice, Paris and the Pyramids.'

consult *v.* 'To seek another's approval of a course already decided on,' according to Ambrose Bierce's *Devil's Dictionary* (published 1869–1906).

consultant A person who hires her- or himself out as a specialist. Large numbers of built environment professionals are consultants, many of them working for local authorities (which have funds for specific projects but no longer for an adequate complement of professional staff) and the development industry (which enjoys the flexibility that using consultants provides). See also PLANNING CONSULTANT.

consultation Finding out people's views. See ARNSTEIN'S LADDER and CONSULT.

consultation fatigue An unwillingness of people to respond to being consulted, usually due to past experience of being consulted with no noticeable effect.

consumer-driven industry One that responds readily to what consumers want. The house-building industry is accused of not being consumer-driven. Compare PRODUCER-DRIVEN INDUSTRY.

consumption The rate at which resources are used up. The concept is important in discussions of sustainability.

Container City See CITY.

containment The physical enclosure of an urban area (of a city by a wall or a town centre by a ring road, for example).

containment site A landfill site where the rate of release of leachate into the environment is extremely low. Polluting components in wastes are retained within such landfills for sufficient time to allow biodegradation and attenuation processes to have occurred, thus preventing the escape of polluting species at unacceptable concentrations (Scottish Office, 1996b).

contaminated land Polluted land that needs treatment before it can be developed or otherwise re-used. For example, the former South Eastern Gas Works, which became the site for the MILLENNIUM DOME, required extensive and expensive remediation.

contaminative use A use that is likely to contaminate the site (with solvents, oils or heavy metals, for example). Examples include gas works, hospitals, scrap yards and railway land.

contemporary *adj.* **1** Characteristic of the present; current; modern. **2** Of a modern or modernist style. Example: 'Planning permission has been granted for a contemporary house next to Richmond Park.' **3** Belonging to the same period of time.

The much-used term *contemporary architecture* can be ambiguous, as it can mean architecture by living architects or architecture in a modern style. On the other hand, as the contemporary (in the first but not the second sense) architect Robert Adam points out, the phrase 'a series of lectures by contemporary architects' (advertised some time ago by the RIBA), must refer to those who design in a modern style, as there is no need to point out that the lecturers are not dead.

Contemporary City, The The first plan by LE CORBUSIER for a complete environment, published in 1925 as *A Contemporary City for Three Million People*. The architect was offended when his vision was referred to as a city of the future. On the contrary, he said, it ought to be built at once (Banham, 1960).

contemporary style The style of architecture of, among others, the buildings of the 1951 Festival of Britain. The actual term was coined by the architect Theo Crosby later, in 1954. Elain Harwood (2000) notes that 'in its combination of classical proportions and modern details, traditional materials, quirky shapes, spindly metalwork and bright colour, the Festival idiom... was humane and its buildings were built in this charming style.'

context The setting of a site or area. The architect Eliel Saarinen (1956) writes: 'Always design a thing by considering it in its larger context – a chair in a room, a room in a house, a house in an environment, and an environment in a city plan'. Adrian Forty (2000a) suggests that the roots of the concepts of context, contextual and contextualism lay in Milan in the mid-1950s. Ernesto Rogers wrote editorials for *Casabella Continuità*, criticising modernist architects' 'tendency to treat every scheme as a unique abstract problem, their indifference to location, and their desire to make of every work a prodigy'. Forty dates the probable 'first significant appearance within the vocabulary of architecture' of the term context to CHRISTOPHER ALEXANDER's *Notes on the Synthesis of Form* of 1964. Its meaning there was as a synonym for *environment*, rather than having the connotations it has since acquired.

context (or site and area) appraisal A detailed analysis of the features of a site or area (including land uses, built and natural environment, and social and physical characteristics) which serves as the basis for an urban design framework, development brief, design guide, or other policy or guidance.

context dependency A situation in which the context of a regeneration initiative needs to be taken into account in order to predict the output.

contextual architecture That which takes regard of its setting.

contextualism Adrian Forty (2000a) dates its introduction into the architectural vocabulary to 1966 in the urban design studio that COLIN ROWE was teaching at Cornell University. It seems likely, Forty suggests, that the term was borrowed from the literary New Criticism movement, even though its sense there was entirely different. He quotes Rowe as defining his approach as being 'a mediation between the city of Modern architecture – a void with objects – and the historical city – a solid with voids.'

contextualization The word COLIN ROWE had originally intended to use instead of CONTEXTUALISM.

contingent valuation A method of measuring the social and environmental costs and benefits of buildings and structures (Rouse, 2001).

continuing professional development (CPD) Members of the Royal Town Planning Institute, for example, are obliged to carry out personal CPD programmes according to a professional development plan. Recommended forms of CPD include 'structured reading' ('an invaluable, individually focused, low-cost activity') and 'structured learning for work' (identifying and solving problems in the workplace). Professionals come in three categories: those who do not need the discipline of being required by their institute to carry out structured CPD, those who merely go through the motions and never learn anything from it, and those who benefit from it.

Continuous Movement A project by the design group Superstudio (founded in Florence by Adolfo Natalini and Cristiano Torelado and active 1966–78) dating from the late 1960s, with the subtitle *An architectural model for total urbanisation*. Gerrard O'Carroll and Mark Barcia (2003) write that the project 'blanketed the planet with an uninterrupted, all-enveloping and linear mega-grid resembling a colossal, horizontal and glacial skyscraper that engulfed city, mountain, canyon, river and forest'. Its grids 'subsumed objects, people, cities and life itself under a fascistic and totalitarian apotheosis of architecture.' O'Carroll and Mark Barcia suggest, remarkably, that this total urbanisation would have been 'non-repressive'. On the other hand, the intent may have been satirical. In 1972 Superstudio proposed flooding Florence to the depth of the base of the dome of the cathedral.

contracommuting Travelling to work in the opposite direction to the main flow of traffic. Contracommuters have quicker journeys and make good use of road and rail capacity.

contract zoning (US) Rezoning a property subject to the terms of a contract.

contractor's test Used to value land or property by reference to the cost of building works. Compare COMPARATIVE METHOD.

Contrasts A book, published in 1836, in which the architect AWN Pugin promoted a revival of gothic style, contrasting the ugliness and squalor of contemporary towns with their medieval equivalents. Pugin argued that architecture could not be judged apart from the society that produced it. That insight, Michael Lewis (2002) writes, 'instantly and permanently changed the terms of architectural debate'.

controlled heterogeneity A mix of design approaches in an area that is nonetheless given coherence by planning or design codes. The term has been used to describe the new urbanism at SEASIDE.

controlled parking zone An area in which on-street parking is managed, usually through a system of permits.

controlled waste Household, commercial and industrial waste.

controversy Creating an atmosphere of controversy and discussion in a society threatened by conformism, ideological uniformism and the fear of confrontation was one of the aims of the major programme of urban design carried out in BARCELONA in the post-Franco era.

CONU Control others, not us. A relative of NIMBY.

conurbation A large urban area made up of several towns or cities that have coalesced. The term, popularised by the geographer Jean Gottman, is one of the few coined by PATRICK GEDDES (around 1910) to have entered general usage. Geddes (1915) writes: 'Some name for these city-regions, these town aggregates, is wanted. Constellations we can not call them; conglomerations is, alas! nearer the mark at present, but it may sound unappreciative; what of "Conurbations?"' He identifies and names (including some coinages of his own) seven conurbations in Britain: Clyde-Forth, Tyne-Wear-Tees, Lancaston, West Riding, South Riding, Midlanton, Waleston (each of them based on a coalfield) and Greater London. He calls these seven conurbations the New Heptarchy. The French and German equivalents are *agglomération* and *ballungsräume*.

convenience shop Where food and household goods are generally bought daily or weekly. Compare COMPARISON GOODS.

convenience shopping Defined by the Scottish Office (1998) as shopping for food, drinks, tobacco, newspapers, magazines and confectionery, purchased regularly for relatively immediate consumption.

conventional suburban development (CSD) A term used by new urbanists to describe areas of car-based development devoted mainly to single uses: residential, offices or shopping. CSD is seen as the antithesis of PLANNED NEIGHBORHOOD DEVELOPMENT.

conversation A continuing discussion between developers and their designers, on the one hand, and the public, on the other, about a proposed development scheme.

convex space One in which any point in the space (or on its perimeter) can be seen from any other point in it.

A square is an example. Compare CONCAVE SPACE.

convexity The two-dimensional structure of an urban space is *convex* if all points are visible from all other points. The concept is used in SPACE SYNTAX ANALYSIS.

conviviality The liveliness of a place. IVAN ILLICH (1973) used the term to designate the opposite of industrial productivity. Conviviality, he writes, is 'individual freedom realised in personal interdependence' and 'autonomous and creative intercourse among persons, and the intercourse of persons with their environment; and this in contrast with the conditioned response of persons to the demands made on them by others, and by a man-made environment.'

Conzen, MRG (1907–2000) Urban morphologist. After studying at the University of Berlin in the 1920s, MRG Conzen ('Con' to his friends and family) came to England in 1933. Working at the University of Newcastle-upon-Tyne, he played a major part in the development of urban MORPHOLOGY (the study of urban form) in both the UK and Germany. He emphasised three elements of urban form: town plan, building types and land use. *Alnwick, Northumberland*, published in 1960, is one of his most influential books. See also MORPHOTYPE.

Cook, Peter (b1936) See ARCHIGRAM.

cookbook engineering A pejorative term for an approach to highway and traffic engineering based on the unthinking application of codes, regulations and standards.

cookie-cutter development (US) A pejorative term for development (usually housing) built to standardised plans in regular subdivisions, whatever the site or setting. The analogy is to a cookie-cutter making cookies (biscuits) all in the same shape. Also *cookie-cutter approach*. Example: 'There is no cookie-cutter approach to developing a smart community.'

Cooley, Charles Horton (1864–1929) Sociologist. See NEIGHBOURHOOD, PRIMARY GROUP and REGIONAL PLANNING ASSOCIATION OF AMERICA.

Cooperative City An imaginary, utopian city in Maine, USA, described in Bradford Peck's *The World, a Department Store: a story of life under the cooperative system* (1901). The city, with a population of 100,000, was founded by a businessman with the aim of creating a Christian heaven on earth. Money, unemployment and religious dogmatism have been abolished. The city's form is a square grid with three-storey (plus basement) apartment blocks, parkways and public gardens. Transport is provided by taxis and electric trains.

cooperative colony An experimental community of the type inspired by the cooperative movement in England at the end of the nineteenth century. There were eight such colonies in 1899 (Quail, 1978) including CLOUSDEN HILL FARM and WHITEWAYS. See also ROCHDALE PIONEERS.

Copley, West Yorkshire One of the earliest planned mill villages, built in 1847–53 by the benevolent mill-owner Colonel EDWARD AKROYD.

copy The new urbanist ANDRES DUANY (2003) argues that, for architects, copying buildings is a key to successful urbanism. 'Most good cities today are composed principally of competent copies, marred by just a few failed (usually modernist) original buildings,' he writes. 'Bad cities simply reverse the ratio. Test it yourself. Travel to a city and ask any host to help you find a bad building built prior to 1930 (a period when buildings were invariably "copied").' The visitor may well spend all day driving around in a vain search, he says. 'Now, look for a bad building built after 1960 (the era of "originality"). You will probably find one just by turning your head. Then, to confirm the point, try finding a good building designed after 1960. You will again usually find yourself on a long drive.' Duany comments: 'It is no mean achievement that the artistic avant-garde has been able to saddle the neutral, technical term of "copy" with an intrinsically negative connotation... What architects actually do is *emulate*, otherwise known as participating in a tradition.'

Corbett, A Cameron See HYGEIA.

corbie-steps (Scotland) Crow-steps (on a gable that has stepped rather than sloping sides).

core Kevin Lynch (1960) uses the term to describe a NODE which has a particular concentration of uses: 'the focus and epitome of a DISTRICT, over which their influence radiates and of which they stand as a symbol'.

core city In 1995 the councils of seven major English regional cities began working together to set out a vision of the role big cities could play in national and regional life. These cities – Birmingham, Bristol, Leeds, Liverpool, Manchester, Newcastle and Sheffield (later joined by Nottingham) – formalised their association as the English Core Cities Group. The cities saw themselves as competing against other European and world cities for investment and jobs, rather than each other. This was the case even where cities were in the same region. They claimed that, for example, Manchester and Liverpool very rarely competed against each other for resources.

core income The less risky income from a property development. The riskier income is the TOP SLICE. See also SLICED INCOME APPROACH.

Cork A city floating on a large piece of cork in the Atlantic Ocean, as described by Lucian of Samosata in *True History* (second century). Having feet of cork, its inhabitants are able to walk on water.

corner boy (US) One who hangs around on street corners.

corner shop 1 A local shop on a street corner. **2** A CONVENIENCE SHOP, even if it is not (as many of them have been traditionally) on a corner.

corner visibility triangle (US) A triangular area of pavement bounded on two sides by the kerbs to allow road users to see one another.

cornice An ornamental moulding projecting along the top (or high on the façade) of a building.

cornice line A horizontal projection running the width of a building or street block at the top of the building or above one of the higher floors.

cornucopian A person who believes that people will find a way out of their environmental problems while maintaining economic growth and rising standards of living, through ingenuity, and scientific and technological expertise (Cherry, 1982). The word comes from the Latin for horn of plenty. Compare ECOCENTRISM and see also ENVIRONMENTAL TECHNOCENTRISM.

Corona See CIRCLE CITY.

Coronation Street A television soap opera (nicknamed 'Corrie' or 'The Street'), set in a fictional street of terraced houses in Salford. It has been running since 1960. The street was supposedly built in 1902, to celebrate the imminent succession of King Edward VII. The pub was named The Rover's Return to mark the return from the Boer War of a scion of the family that owned the brewery. It was later renamed The Rovers Return (without the apostrophe) to celebrate the homecoming of the local survivors of the First World War. The set for Coronation Street was modelled on the real Archie Street in Salford, which appeared in the closing credits of the first episode. The first scriptwriter (who had pleaded to be allowed to write about a world that he knew, rather than the adventure of the action hero Biggles to which he had been assigned) proposed to call it Florizel Street. The television company executives thought this too unfamiliar. The alternative titles Coronation Street and Jubilee Street were discussed at length one evening in a pub. Jubilee Street was preferred – or so all the parties to the decision believed, apart from the one whose job it was to inform the *TV Times* of the name of the new programme. So it was listed as Coronation Street, which it has remained ever since. Granada Television nearly shelved the project in its early days as being 'incomprehensibly northern'. See also BROOKSIDE, EASTENDERS, OZZIE AND HARRIET and THE SIMPSONS.

corporate finance Finance, provided for a property development, for example, for which the principal security is not the property. Compare PROJECT FINANCE.

corporate modernism The outward forms of MODERNIST ARCHITECTURE adapted to the needs of large organisations, without any of the modern movement's supposedly social aims.

corporate plan Sets out a local authority's strategic objectives and how they will be achieved.

corporate planning An approach to local authority management developed in the 1970s, sometimes giving town planners a leading role in managing a local authority's various services.

corporate strategy An official expression of the overall aims of a local authority or other organisation.

corridor A linear feature (such as a road, canal or railway) and the land alongside it. *Corridor studies* provide the basis for planning such areas. Corridors are regarded as one of the fundamental organising elements of NEW URBANISM, connecting and separating neighbourhoods and districts (Duany and Plater-Zyberk, 1994). *A New Urbanist Lexicon* (McLaughlin, 2000) defines a corridor as 'a linear configuration that connects disparate areas of countryside through natural systems, or disparate neighborhoods through transportation systems.'

corridor street LE CORBUSIER's dismissive term for the traditional, building-lined, traffic-filled street that he promised his visionary cities would replace.

Corrie A nickname for CORONATION STREET.

Cortina man See MONDEO MAN.

cosmopolis A multi-cultural city; a cosmopolitan metropolis; a place that has world city status and is multi-culturally diverse. ED SOJA has applied the term to LOS ANGELES (Dear and Flusty, 1998). The *National Geographic* applied the term to London in 2000. The Greater London Authority (2001) has called London 'the most cosmopolitan city in the world, with every major language spoken'. In the London Borough of Lambeth alone the children in its schools spoke 110 different languages in 2000, the council recorded. An estimated 180 languages are spoken in New York. Example: 'Now we are in the centre of Cosmopolis [London]. Within a stone's throw of where we stand you can eat as you choose the mañana of Spain, the banat of Hungary, the Yong Mei Koon of China, the Privatdozent of Germany, the dhobi of India, the pouss-pouss of Armenia or the poulet rôti of France. Yong Mei Koon consists of dried newts' legs with crystallized pork fat and shredded toughened bamboo. The others consist of anything you like to think of' (Shanks, 1938).

Cosmopolis A novel by Don DeLillo (b1936), set in New York.

cosmopolitan *n*. A city dweller who can make a life with those who are not like themselves (Sennett, 2001).

cost effectiveness analysis Comparing the costs of alternative ways of producing the same or similar outputs of a regeneration programme without giving them monetary value.

cost of variability The most a person or group is willing to pay to have a benefit (from a regeneration project, for example) that is certain, rather than one that is uncertain.

Costa, Lucio (1902–98) Architect and planner. In the 1950s he planned the Brazilian capital of BRASILIA.

cost-benefit analysis A method of assigning monetary values to all the factors to be taken into account in making a decision, so that they can be fairly compared. The use of such analysis – which may involve placing a monetary value on a human life or a Norman church, for example – is controversial. See also AND HOW MUCH FOR YOUR GRANDMOTHER?, PATRICK ABERCROMBIE and ROSKILL COMMISSION.

Costford See PROSPECT HILL.

Cotati, California A six-sided, radial city founded in 1893 by Thomas Page (1815–72). He named the streets after his six sons.

Cottonopolis MANCHESTER, world centre of the cotton industry, during the industrial revolution.

cottoun (Scots) A HAMLET.

Council for European Urbanism Founded in Bruges, Belgium, in 2003 to promote NEW URBANISM, the council dedicated itself to 'the well-being of the people of Europe by the re-creation of humane cities, towns and countryside'. It identified European cities, towns and countryside as being under threat from a) Waste of land and cultural resources. b) Social segregation and isolation. c) Monofunctional development. d) Loss of local, regional and national cohesion, character and distinctiveness. The council set out its 12 'challenges for European urbanism' in the DECLARATION OF BRUGES.

council housing Houses or flats built (or, less often, bought) by local authorities for renting. Alison Ravetz (1980), writing of the influence of RAYMOND UNWIN on the standards and design guidelines for council housing built under the Housing Act 1919, notes that 'the early estates, though laid out according to the principles he set, were usually executed by borough engineers, who lost much of his architectural subtlety and social idealism in the process.' When government subsidies to local authorities were cut in the early 1920s, 'the graceful style of the earliest council houses, which clearly showed their garden city origins, gave way, to crudely utilitarian styles.' By the 1930s estate layouts had become fossilised into large-scale geometric patterns. Ravetz identifies three motivations for the UK's early council housing: first, the utopian ideal inspired by the garden cities; second, the post-war housing crisis of 1918; third, the imposition by the state of higher housing standards which made it uneconomic for private developers to house working-class people. 'For socialists it was a matter of conviction that publicly owned, "socialised" housing should be a permanent social service,' Ravetz writes. 'But for governments, both Labour and Tory, it was a temporary expedient to be used only until the market returned to its "normal" condition, or for certain special needs. Governments were addicted to the idea that one day the housing problem would be "solved" and their intervention no longer needed.'

After 1979, MARGARET THATCHER's government no longer saw any significant role for local authorities as providers of housing. The government put its faith instead in the private market; in the RIGHT TO BUY (giving council tenants the right to buy their homes at substantial discounts; and in HOUSING ASSOCIATIONS (providing social housing). See also ADDISON ACT, CHAMBERLAIN ACT and WHEATLEY ACT.

counter-intuitive planning 1 The process by which 'all the things we tend to like about places are designed out by the processes that deliver them', as David Lunts describes it. **2** An appropriate approach to planning in a system of complexity, where whatever is predicted *intuitively* is unlikely to happen as outcomes are rarely the straightforward consequences of a few, simple causes.

counter-urban Tending towards dispersal from major urban areas.

counter-urbanisation The movement of population from cities to smaller towns and rural areas.

country Rural, as opposed to urban, places. Raymond Williams (1983) suggests that in England the widespread specialised use of *country* as opposed to *city* began in the late sixteenth century with increasing urbanisation and especially the growth of London. The poet Donagh MacDonagh (b1912) expresses his disdain for life in the country in 'Dublin made me': 'Dublin made me, not the secret poteen still/ the raw and hungry hills of the West/ The lean road flung over profitless bog/ Where only a snipe would nest/ …I disclaim all fertile meadows, all tilled land/ The evil that grows from it and the good,/ But the Dublin of old statutes, this arrogant city,/ Stirs proudly and secretly in my blood.' See COUNTRYSIDE.

country belt A stretch of countryside around and between towns.

country lore Knowledge of rural ways. A survey in 2000 showed Britain's children to be thoroughly urbanised. Two-thirds of the sample did not know where acorns came from and 39 per cent did not know in which season harvest takes place. Many urban primary schools do, in fact, still celebrate harvest festival. But these vaguely charitable events in which tins of peaches are given to bemused local pensioners (as one commentator has described them) do little to make the connection between the consumption and production of the food we eat.

country music See URBAN MUSIC.

country town A small town in a rural area. Compare COUNTY TOWN.

countryside Land outside built-up areas. The countryside is an artifact. As Hugh Brody (1998) writes: 'Farmland in God's sole care is forest and savannah.' The sociologist WILLIAM WHYTE predicted in 1957 – wrongly – that the viability of the rapidly expanding suburbs was likely to be short-lived. The new suburbanites had moved out of the city to be near the countryside, he said, but they would soon find that it had been eaten up by still more suburbs. Most thinking about urbanism implies an attitude to the countryside. The vision of FRANK LLOYD WRIGHT was of development spread across the countryside at very low densities with the occasional mile-high tower for visual relief (see BROADACRE CITY). Similarly EA Gutkind advocated extreme decentralisation to rural communities in *The Expanding Environment* (see POST-URBANISM). They and others like them have regarded the countryside as an asset to be inhabited, not preserved. That is an attitude rarely voiced today in the UK, where the political strength of the countryside lobby discourages the government from allowing development outside urban areas where it can possibly be avoided (see CAMPAIGN TO PROTECT RURAL ENGLAND). Tony Travers (2001) argues that, 'it is not the efforts of the Urban Task Force so much as the very romanticism about rural and suburban life that has led to a desire to protect the countryside from bulldozers and to reassess the need to make towns and cities more desirable'. The countryside lobby defends the countryside, but not all country dwellers are opposed to all development. Patterns of rural development will inevitably change as the rural economy restructures itself in the face of dramatic changes in agriculture. Further development will be needed if the children of country dwellers are to avoid having to move away for want of affordable housing. In the USA some commentators and campaigners are alarmed by the spread of development across the countryside, and particularly by unplanned, low-density sprawl. Others, by contrast, are confident that the countryside can continue to absorb the present rate of growth comfortably. Attitudes towards people in the countryside range widely. Some people see no reason why rural areas should be protected from people at all, so long as development is based on small communities and ecological principles. At the other extreme, perhaps, was the poet Robinson Jeffers (1887–1962), for whom almost any human presence was an affront to the natural environment. Prime Minister Stanley Baldwin evoked his idea of the English countryside in 1924: 'The tinkle of the hammer on the anvil in the country smithy, the corncrake on a dewy morning, the sound of the scythe against the whetstone, and the sight of a plough team coming over the brow of a hill... The wild anemones in the woods in April, the last load at night of hay being drawn down a lane as twilight comes on... and above all the most subtle, most penetrating and most moving, the smell of wood smoke coming up in an autumn evening' (quoted in Barnett, 1998). Compare John Major's evocation of SUBURBS. See RURAL.

Countryside Agency The body which superseded the Countryside Commission and is responsible for advising the government and taking action on issues relating to the social, economic and environmental well-being of the countryside in England. It is concerned with urban as well as rural issues as so many of them are closely related.

countryside design summary A descriptive analysis explaining the essential design relationship between the landscape, settlement patterns and buildings. From this analysis the document draws principles that can be applied to development in the area and sets out the implications of the choices open to designers. As supplementary planning guidance prepared by a local authority, the summary can encourage a more regionally and locally based approach to design and planning. It can also provide the context for individual communities to prepare VILLAGE DESIGN STATEMENTS.

countryside policy area (Northern Ireland) A rural area in which there are limits to what may be built.

countryside stewardship (England) A programme of protecting, enhancing, restoring and recreating targeted landscapes, their wildlife habitats and historical features, and to improve opportunities for public enjoyment of the countryside. It operates throughout England outside ENVIRONMENTALLY SENSITIVE AREAS.

County of London Plan (1943) The first of the town plans that PATRICK ABERCROMBIE prepared for the capital during the war.

county town A town from where the local government of a county is conducted. Compare COUNTRY TOWN.

couples in, families out A saying that describes the movement of people in cities: couples without children move in towards the centre, while those with children move out to find more space and better schools. See MOBILITY.

cours (French) A drive laid out for the purposes of pleasure.

court 1 A piece of open land partially or completely enclosed by buildings or walls. **2** A short street enclosed by buildings on three sides.

court housing Two rows of houses facing one another with a paved area between them, opening at one end on to a street. Some of the worst urban slum housing took this form until the nineteenth century.

court of miracles A back ALLEY, particularly in Paris, where underworld figures and beggars met. Beggars who simulated infirmities to attract sympathy would seem to be miraculously cured when they were back in the alley, out of the public gaze. VICTOR HUGO describes one such alley in his novel *Notre-Dame de Paris*.

covenant An obligation on the owner of a piece of land. See POSITIVE COVENANT and RESTRICTIVE COVENANT.

Covent Garden Designed by Inigo Jones in the 1630s as the first London square, it later became the site of London's central fruit and vegetable market. The market moved out to Nine Elms in 1974, leading to a long-running planning battle over the area's future.

The GREATER LONDON COUNCIL proposed a major redevelopment, including offices, hotels, housing and a conference centre served by a six-lane highway on the site of Maiden Lane. A coalition of local residents, community activists and conservationists campaigned to save the existing fabric and for housing, shops and workplaces. They were successful in saving the market and other buildings for, while the GLC's plan was approved by the secretary of state for the environment, Geoffrey Rippon, he sabotaged its implementation by simultaneously spot-listing more than 100 buildings. Covent Garden has since become a tourist honeypot, and high rents have forced out many of the uses that the campaigners had hoped to preserve or attract.

CowParade A city-wide display of glass-fibre life-size model cows, each individually decorated or adorned. The project raises money for charity. The first CowParade was in Zurich in 1998. Others have been held in Chicago, New York and London. See also MOOSE CITY.

Craig, James (1744–95) Architect. He planned Edinburgh's New Town, winning the design competition in 1766.

Cramlington A new town near Blyth built by local authorities on Tyneside.

Crane, David Urban designer, architect and academic. He was influential through his advocacy of the use of a capital web of infrastructure and public space to structure urban development. He worked on KEVIN LYNCH's Image of the City Project at MIT (1955–56), and was professor of architecture and urban design (among other posts) at the University of Pennsylvania in the late 1950s and '60s, and professor of architecture at Rice University (1972–78).

Crash A novel by JG Ballard (b1930), published in 1995, about accident victims who become obsessed with car crashes. The book, Ballard explains in his introduction, presents 'the car as a sexual image,… as a total metaphor for man's life in today's society'. He describes *Crash* as 'a warning against that brutal, erotic and overlit realm that beckons more and more persuasively to us from the margins of the technological landscape.' David Cronenberg, seeing *Crash* as an exploration of the link between danger and creativity, made a film of the book, with the same name, in 2000.

crash See BIASED TERMINOLOGY.

crate (US) An old CAR.

CRAVED An acronym, used in crime prevention, for factors that influence a target's risk of criminal attack: concealable, removable, available, enjoyable and disposable. Compare VIVA.

crawsteps (Scots) Steps on the gable of a building.

creando pensamus (Latin) We think by creating. A motto of PATRICK GEDDES, who also used the alternative *pensando creamus*, we create by thinking. See also VIVENDO DISCIMUS.

creative city The creative city approach to urban strategy, in the words of Charles Landry (2000), 'uses a place's imaginative capacity as an asset and planning tool' in the belief that 'by generating an environment where people are given greater scope to think, plan and act creatively our cities can be made more liveable and vital'.

creative class Defined by RICHARD FLORIDA (2002) as including people in science and engineering, architecture and design, education, arts, music and entertainment, whose economic function is to create new ideas, new technology and/or new creative content. Around this core, the creative class also includes a broader group of *creative professionals* in business and finance, law, health care and related fields. These people engage in complex problem-solving that involves a great deal of independent judgement and requires high levels of education or human capital.

creative destruction The continuous process of rebuilding a city, as described in Max Page's 2002 book *The Creative Destruction of Manhattan, 1900–1940*. Page

❝IT'LL BE A GREAT PLACE IF THEY EVER FINISH IT❞

O Henry on New York

quotes the writer O Henry's comment on New York City: 'It'll be a great place if they ever finish it'. See also URBAN DESTRUCTION.

creative loft A combined live/work unit for young entrepreneurs.

creative partnership An organisation linking schools and cultural organisations.

creative town, the Huddersfield, where an EU pilot project has focused on nurturing creativity in individuals and the whole town.

credit union A mutual banking scheme in which people, often in areas suffering poverty, pool their savings; a locally based organisation providing financial services, often to poor people. In some cases credit unions have proved to be one of the more dynamic legacies of the cooperative movement, providing a client-friendly alternative to the big banks.

Crescent City New Orleans, Louisiana. See also BIG EASY, CHOPPER CITY and CLICK-CLICK.

crib (Scots) A KERB.

crib-stane (Scots) A KERBSTONE.

Crichel Down Rules Rules specifying that land in the UK originally acquired by, or under threat of, compulsory purchase but which has since become surplus to requirements, should be offered back to the previous landowner, before being sold to a third party. They were drawn up in 1954 following the purchase and subsequent sale of land at Crichel Down in Dorset.

crime pattern analysis A method used by the police to analyse patterns of criminal activity in an area.

crime prevention See ANONYMITY, ARCHITECTURAL LIAISON OFFICER, BLOCK-HOME, BOUNDARY DEFINITION, BROKEN WINDOWS, BUNKER ARCHITECTURE, ALICE COLEMAN, CUL-DE-SAC, CRAVED, CRUSTY SPACE, DEFENSIBLE SPACE, ENVIRO-CRIME, FEAR GENERATOR, FOOTPADS' PARADISE, FORTRESS LA, FORTRESS MENTALITY, RUDOLPH GIULIANI, GUARDIAN, HONEYPOT, JITTERY SPACE, LUXURY LAAGER, MILIEU, NATURAL ACCESS CONTROL, NEIGHBOURHOOD WATCH, OSCAR NEWMAN, PEOPLING, PLACE MANAGER, PLANNING OUT CRIME, POCKET GHETTO, PREVENTER, QUALITY OF LIFE CRIME, ROUTE ACTIVITY THEORY, SCANSCAPE, SPACE SYNTAX, STRONGPOINT OF SALE, SURVEILLANCE, TARGET HARDENING, TERRITORIALITY, TERRITORIAL REINFORCEMENT, VIVA and WORLD CITADEL.

critical load The amount of emitted pollutant that will cause harm.

critical regionalism An approach to architecture emphasising local identity and inspired by practice in places other than the cultural capitals of the western world. Such self-consciously cultivated regionalism is 'critical' in that its practitioners try to avoid, in the words of Kenneth Frampton (1988), 'falling into sentimentality, or into the false perpetuation of exhausted modern forms, or into the empty vagaries of historicism'. Frampton saw critical regionalism, not as form of vernacular revival, but as a way of consciously evolving a local culture of architecture in opposition to the forces of universal civilisation and universal technology. Although Frampton has been the chief proponent of critical regionalism, the term was coined by Alex Tzonis and Liliane Lefaivre in 1981. Frampton, who based his own inspiration for the basic idea to an essay of 1961 by Paul Ricoeur, later had doubts about the term. 'I have come to realise that the suffix *ism* presupposed style', he wrote. 'This ending is therefore etymologically antithetical to the cultural syndrome I would like to evoke. I do not want to deny style, but at the same time I do not wish to imply its necessary presence in advance.'

critical renewal (also critical reconstruction) An approach to regeneration developed in the 1980s in Berlin's International Building Exhibition (Internationale Bauausstellung), a series of demonstration projects. The nineteenth century pattern of urban street BLOCKS and squares was used as a framework for modern architecture. The term was used by Josef Kleihues (1990). See also CAREFUL URBAN RENEWAL.

Crittall, Francis Window manufacturer. See SILVER END.

Croitas Solis (1623) The city consists of seven concentric fortified circles, named after the planets, and four streets following the points of the compass. At the centre is the Temple of Knowledge and Metaphysics. Campanella's description of the city's laws and customs makes it sound to Jonathan Raban (1974) like 'a puritanical, ecologically sound kibbutz'.

Cromford, Derbyshire The first industrial mill town, built in the two decades after 1771 by the cotton-spinning pioneer Sir Richard Arkwright (1732–92). See also BELPER.

Crompton, Dennis See ARCHIGRAM.

Crooklyn Brooklyn, New York.

Crosland, Anthony (1918–77) Politician. See SECRETARY OF STATE and THE PARTY'S OVER.

Cross, RA As home secretary in the government of BENJAMIN DISRAELI he promoted the ARTIZANS' AND LABOURERS' DWELLINGS ACT 1875.

cross-cutting strategy A strategy that is applied to several subject areas or departments.

crosswalk (US) The UK term is *pedestrian crossing*.

Croton Water System The aqueducts, dams and reservoirs built to supply water to Manhattan. It has been hailed as one of the great engineering feats of the nineteenth century.

crowd dynamics Defined by Keith Still as the study of how and where crowds form and move above the critical density of more than one person per square metre (the density above which there is potential for overcrowding and injury).

crowded See OVERCROWDED.

crowd-soaking Standing in a crowd to enjoy the experience of being with and observing other people. See also FLÂNEUR.

Crown Street Regeneration Project The redevelopment of the 1960s comprehensive redevelopment of 40 acres of Glasgow's GORBALS district, began in 1990. Its masterplanner, the architects CZWG, drew on urban design principles inspired by Glasgow's traditional patterns of building.

crusty space That which is surrounded by walls and checkpoints (Dear and Flusty, 1998).

cryonic conservaction (sic) The humorist Ian Martin's fanciful term for building unbuilt masterpieces by dead architects. For example, CHARLES RENNIE MACINTOSH's House for an Art Lover, completed in 1996, was built in Glasgow more than 90 years after he designed it. In 2003 a developer proposed building on the site of the WORLD TRADE CENTER a skyscraper hotel to a design of 1908 by ANTONIO GAUDI.

Crystal Palace 1 A prefabricated structure of glass and iron built in Hyde Park for the Great Exhibition of 1851 to JOSEPH PAXTON's design. The great exhibition hall was, suggests Deyan Sudjic (1992), a new architectural type. 'It was a condensation of many different kinds of urban space – promenade, piazza and forum – into a single gigantic object.' After the exhibition the structure was re-erected in Sydenham, where it was destroyed by fire in 1936. **2** The district in Sydenham, south-east London, where Paxton's Crystal Palace was re-erected. Crystal Palace Park is now home to the National Recreation Centre. **3** The glass-roofed commercial, shopping and exhibition complex described in Ebenezer Howard's original GARDEN CITY proposal. Neither of the two garden cities that were built had such a feature.

Crystal Way A glass-covered street proposed for London by William Moseley in 1855 (Miller, 1989).

C-Town Cleveland, Ohio.

Cubitt, Thomas (1788–1855) One of the first large-scale building contractors, Cubitt built large parts of Bloomsbury, Belgravia, Pimlico and Clapham in London.

Cubitt, William See ENGINEER.

CUDAT Community Urban Design Assistance Team. A UK name for the equivalent of the US REGIONAL/URBAN DESIGN ASSISTANCE TEAM, though RUDAT is the more common UK term.

culchie (Ireland) A country person, so called by city dwellers. Compare SHAM and JACKEEN.

cul-de-sac (plural *culs-de-sac* or *cul-de-sacs*) A street open at only one end, usually with a turning area at the other. The cul-de-sac has been a very popular form of housing layout in recent decades due to their perceived privacy and security. The question of whether culs-de-sac tend to have higher or lower incidences of burglary and personal assault remains hotly disputed. Urban designers tend to disapprove of them on the grounds that they fail to contribute to making a PERMEABLE network of connected streets, creating instead isolated, car-dependent enclaves. Large-scale planning based on culs-de-sac creates URBAN SPRAWL. The word comes from the Old French, meaning the bottom of a bag. See also BROOKSIDE, CLOSE and MEWS.

Culdesac A small town in Idaho.

Cullen, Gordon (1914–94) Influential urban designer, draughtsman and writer. Cullen developed the TOWNSCAPE approach to urban design, the technique of SERIAL VISION, and the methods of recording townscape called 'the notation' and 'the scanner'. In the 1930s he worked as an assistant in various architectural offices, including BERTHOLD LUBETKIN's practice Tecton. From 1946 to 1956 he was a writer and illustrator at the Architectural Press (publisher of the *Architectural Review* and *Architects' Journal*), which was active in promoting the concept of townscape. In 1959–62 he was a consultant on development plans for Delhi, Calcutta, Liverpool, Bolton and Northampton, and in 1965 to Buckinghamshire County Council (on the development of villages). He was later a planner or consultant for proposals at Llantrisant, Peterborough, Ware (see VIVAT WARE), Telford, the Isle of Dogs in London's Docklands, and Glasgow city centre.

Cullen explained some of the ideas behind the notation in his 1967 book *A Town Called Alcan*. 'In these days the observant layman is concerned about the apparent loss of control over the physical environment,' he wrote. 'There may be a hundred reasons for this but the principal one seems to be the speed of development, the rate of change, which is outstripping the capacity of the human mind to absorb, digest and subsequently incorporate discoveries, new products and fresh social patterns into a coherent environment.' Cullen suggested that in 1750 the rate of change might have been such that the mind could comprehend it and sublimate all the factors into a humanised landscape. 'With the increased speed of change this perfection or sublimation receded and its alternative, which we may call end-gaining, obtained part possession of the field. An example of the difference between the two? Sublimation: if the child cries you find out why it is crying and put it right; to do this you use experience, intelligence, compassion and patience. End-gaining: if the child cries hit it till it stops. The application of the latter attitude to problems of traffic, housing, power supplies and so on is not difficult to observe around us.' See also BOLLARD, THE BRIDE OF DENMARK and MAW.

Cullingworth Report Published in 1967 following an inquiry chaired by the housing and planning specialist Barry Cullingworth, its recommendations on tackling substandard housing in Scotland shaped the Housing (Scotland) Act 1969. The Act established the TOLERABLE STANDARD as a more flexible equivalent of unfitness in England and Wales.

cultural bombing The deliberate targeting of culturally valuable targets as a strategy of war. Miles Glendinning (2000) notes that the first deliberate mass bombing of a historic city was the Royal Air Force attack that incinerated over 80 per cent of the timber-built Hanseatic old town of Lübeck in 1942. The attack was an experiment to test whether bombing timber-framed buildings could start an inferno large enough to be used as an easy aiming point for later waves of bombers. Hitler launched the Luftwaffe's BAEDEKER RAIDS in retaliation. See also OPERATION GOMORRAH.

cultural capacity The degree of change that a particular community will accept.

cultural crucible Peter Hall (1998) proposes six prime examples of 'the city as cultural crucible', having a period of intellectual and artistic glory: Athens (500–400 BC), Florence (1400–1500), London (1570–1620), Vienna (1780–1910), Paris (1870–1910) and Berlin (1918–1933). See also INNOVATION.

cultural elitism See THEORY OF LOOSE PARTS.

cultural environment (Denmark) Historic buildings and monuments, other relics of the past, and cultural connections in the landscape and townscape (Holmgren and Svensson, 2001).

cultural landmark Described by the New York organisation Place Matters as 'a catchword for those places with compelling associations with the lives of important people, historical events or cultural history'.

cultural landscape Land, and the memories, perceptions, stories, practices and experiences that give it meaning. UNESCO defines it as representing the 'combined works of nature and of man' and identifies three main categories: *designed landscapes, organically evolved landscapes* and *associative landscapes* (the latter having a particular association, such as England's Lake District with the Lake poets).

cultural planning Defined by Colin Mercer as 'the strategic and integral planning and use of CULTURAL RESOURCES in urban and community development' (Biancini, 2000).

cultural resources Defined by Colin Mercer (Biancini, 2000) as the arts and other aspects of local resources, including '...the cultures of youth, ethnic minorities and other communities of interest; the heritage, including archaeology, gastronomy, local dialects and rituals; local and external perceptions of a place, as expressed in jokes, songs, literature, myths, tourist guides, media coverage and conventional wisdom; the natural and built environment, including public and open spaces; the diversity and quality of leisure, cultural, eating, drinking and entertainment facilities and activities; and the repertoire of local products and skills in the crafts, manufacturing and services'.

cultural significance Defined by the BURRA CHARTER as aesthetic, historic, scientific or social value for past, present or future generations.

culture 1 The arts. **2** Ways of living that are transmitted socially rather than biologically. The impact of urban development on the cultural (in addition to the social, economic and environmental) conditions of people is increasingly taken into account in considering what is SUSTAINABLE. Sir Edward Burnett Tylor (1832–1917) defined culture as 'that complex whole which includes knowledge, belief, art, morals, law, custom and any other capabilities and habits acquired by man as a member of society'. The poet TS Eliot (1948) defined culture as a 'peculiar way of thinking, feeling and behaving'.

culture of poverty The supposedly distinctive values and attitudes of poor people that are passed down from generation to generation, reducing the chance that people will find their way out of poverty. The culture's characteristics were said in the 1960s to include a lack of social organisation and disengagement from political and civic life. The term was originated by the anthropologist Oscar Lewis, according to COLIN WARD (1989). Ward notes that Lewis used the term to describe how people adapt to their situation, rather than suggesting that they are incapable of escaping from it.

Culver City See PER CENT FOR ART.

culvert A covered channel, pipe or drain that is below ground level or that carries a watercourse beneath a building, structure or embankment.

Cumbernauld A Mark Two NEW TOWN near Glasgow, designated in 1955. The town was designed so that its MEGASTRUCTURAL town centre was within easy pedestrian access of every home. This was a departure from the approach, followed in the earlier UK new towns, of basing the town on NEIGHBOURHOODS. See NODDYTOWN.

cumulative impact Defined by the Scottish Office (1998) as the combined effect of all out-of-centre developments, developed and proposed, on a town centre, or the effect of such developments on all strategic centres, including the town centre.

Cunningham, Walter Mapmaker. His woodcut map of Norwich in *The Cosmographical Glasse* (1559) is the earliest surviving printed map of any English town (Kostof, 1991).

cupressocyparis leylandii A tree, often used in hedges, that grows rapidly to a great height. It is known as the *scourge of suburbia* and a cause of *hedge rage* due to the way it can take the light and block views from neighbouring houses. It is responsible for a number of assaults and a plethora of writs. Councils now have the power to cut them back to two metres high.

curb See KERB.

Curitiba A rapidly expanding Brazilian city renowned in the 1980s and '90s for its integrated transport and planning policies. Curitiba's 1965 master plan limited central area growth, encouraged commercial and service sector growth along two transport arteries, and promoted local community self-sufficiency. Traffic types are separated on the city's roads, with buses having priority. Denser development is concentrated on bus routes.

curtain twitching Holding back a net curtain a little to see better what is going on in the street. This is cited as a characteristic of small-minded, inquisitive suburbanites.

curtilage The site area; the area of land attached to a building, used for the enjoyment of a house and that in some necessary or reasonably useful way serves the purpose of the building. The word derives from the French *courtillage*, a diminutive of *cort*, a COURT.

customer A person who buys a product or service. In relation to housing design in the USA, Andres Duany (2003) suggests, 'the customer has no contact with the designer. He or she (usually) arrives at a decision to acquire a dwelling in a state of innocence at best, but more usually having been manipulated through the experience of comparison shopping. Only lightly attuned to the rigors of architecture, a customer is vulnerable to kitsch. Since this option is usually provided competitively in the vicinity, it tends to undermine serious architecture.' Duany comments, characteristically:

'This situation is exacerbated because most "good" architects disparage, shun, and remain ignorant of this huge stratum of housing, just as they have been taught to do in the architecture schools.' Compare CLIENT, PATRON and VICTIM.

Cuttenclip A village made of paper, inhabited by living paper people, described in L Frank Baum's *The Emerald City of Oz* (1910). The village is surrounded by a wall to stop it blowing away.

Cutteslowe wall A seven-foot high spiked wall built in the 1930s by the developer of an estate of private housing in the Oxford suburb of Cutteslowe to separate it from an adjoining council estate. The wall became notorious as visible evidence of social division. See also BERLIN WALL and PEACE WALL.

Cuzco The capital city of the Incas, known as the Sacred City of the Sun.

cyberia The sphere of people who are not locked into the electronic world (Dear and Flusty, 1998). See CITISTAT.

cybernetics The science of organising knowledge relating to complex systems. It was developed and named by NORBERT WIENER.

cyberplace A real, physical place in a digitally connected world.

cyberspace An abstract communications space that exists everywhere and nowhere. See also ELECTRONIC VILLAGE.

cyburbia 1 Described by the architectural critic Michael Sorkin as an interconnected grid of exurban office buildings and internet telecommuters for which time and space are increasingly obsolete, and by Dear and Flusty (1998) as 'the sphere of people who are locked into the electronic world'. **2** A virtual online community with suburban values, compared to the anonymity of cyberspace. **3** A landscape of suburban office parks. Alan Loomis has credited the term to Walter Wriston.

cycle track (UK) Legally defined as 'a way constituting or comprised in a highway, being a way over which the public have... a right of way on pedal cycles... with or without a right of way on foot.'

cyclopath Defined by the humorist Ian Martin (2002) as 'an environmental campaigner suffering from a behavioural disorder on two wheels'.

D

da Vinci, Leonardo (1452–1519) The polymath of the Italian renaissance was, among everything else, a city planner. His projects included the design for a system of pedestrian streets above a network of alleys and waterways for Milan in about 1490. Beasts of burden, carriages and the lower classes would use the lower level, while the upper level would be reserved for the upper classes. Patrice Boussel notes that 'in his plans for civic improvement, Leonardo gave priority to financial and political factors; the well-being of inhabitants was of secondary consideration' (Boussel, undated). ALDO ROSSI (1982) suggests that Leonardo's plan was the inspiration for the Adam brothers' 1768–72 development of the Adelphi district in London. Da Vinci designed a new city at Romorantin in France that was never built.

Dalton, Nick See SPACE IS THE MACHINE.

Daly, Herman (b1938) Economist. He has been particularly concerned with the relationship of the economy and the environment, and the relationship of the economy to ethics. He received the RIGHT LIVELIHOOD AWARD in 1996.

DAMPFISHES See BDAMPFISHES.

Dancing in the Street A pop record by Martha Reeves and the Vandellas, made in Detroit by MOTOWN records and released in 1964. It begins: 'Calling out around the world, are you ready for a brand-new beat? Summer's here and the time is right for dancing in the street.' Richard Williams (2002) writes that the song became part of the informal soundtrack to black uprisings throughout the cities of the United States. 'A call to dance was taken as a call to arms, not least because Martha Reeves's tone was strong and confrontational, shouting out the lyric over a particularly crunching backbeat, punctuated by aggressive brass fanfares.' Ironically, as Williams points out, the riots of 1967 helped to persuade Motown records to abandon downtown Detroit and move to Hollywood. See also DOWNTOWN and SUMMER IN THE CITY.

dangerous classes Categories of people in an urban UNDERCLASS. The term comes from the social reformer Charles Loring Brace's book *The Dangerous Classes of New York*, published in 1872. Some commentators have argued that some recent social policies treat certain minority groups as dangerous classes (though they are not called that) and use them as scapegoats for social ills.

Darbishire, Henry (1825–99) Architect. He designed MODEL housing for, among others, George Peabody (see PEABODY TRUST).

dark design Designing places with particular attention to how they work at night.

dark green See SHALLOW GREEN.

dark Satanic mills William Blake's phrase from his poem 'Jerusalem' became a key image for crusaders against the evils of the industrial revolution. Kathleen Raine (1970) observed that to Blake the dark Satanic mills of the industrial landscape were built in the image of the mechanistic philosophy whose product they were.

DATAR (Délégation à l'aménagement du territoire et l'action regionale) The French regional planning agency.

David's City 1 (Old Testament) The part of Jerusalem captured by King David from the Jebusites. **2** (New Testament) Bethlehem (also referred to in the New Testament as 'David's town').

Davidoff, Paul Lawyer, city planner and proponent in the 1960s of ADVOCACY PLANNING.

Dawley A new town in the west midlands of England, designated in 1963. Five years later it was enlarged as Telford new town.

Day of the Triffids, The A best-selling novel by John Wyndham, published in 1951, in which killer vegetables take over the world after most of the population has been blinded by gazing at a comet shower. The hero, Bill Masen, feels a sense of release in witnessing the destruction of civilisation in London. See URBAN DESTRUCTION.

day tripper A pejorative term for a consultant with a lucrative contract who makes visits to a regeneration project without showing any personal commitment. See also NEW DEAL FOR CONSULTANTS.

daylight Combined skylight and sunlight. Also called *natural light*.

daylight indicators Angle controls used to establish the permissible heights of a building in relation to nearby buildings, to ensure that new and existing buildings receive adequate daylight.

Dayton, Ohio A model company town built by the National Cash Register Company in the late nineteenth century. Dayton later became famous as the birthplace of the pioneers of flight, Orville and Wilbur Wright, and in 1995 as the location (at the air force base a few miles out of town) of the Bosnian peace talks. Dayton was picked for that historic role, Anthony Bailey (1995) suggests, because it is in the back of beyond. 'Stranded there, unable to play to their supporters, the delegates of the homicidal ex-Yugoslav factions might actually make peace'.

'D' word, the See DENSITY.

De Carlo, Giancarlo (b1919) Architect and urban designer. He has been noted for his work in Urbino since the early 1950s, particularly on the university's development plan. In the 1960s he developed the concept of the CITY REGION in Italy. He was awarded the RIBA's Royal Gold Medal for Architecture for 1993.

De Chirico (1827–1901) Painter. Many of his works were inspired by the squares and arcades of the Italian cities of Ferrara and Turin. *Melancholy and Mystery of a Street*, painted in 1914, is typical: a single figure (and the shadow of another) inhabits an otherwise empty space, lonely and haunted in the late afternoon sun.

De Mandeville, Bernard See FABLE OF THE BEES.

De Nerval, Gérard (1808–55) Poet. See FLÂNEUR.

De Redver A landowning family who founded and planned the southern English towns of Lymington, Yarmouth, Newport (Isle of Wight) and Portsmouth in the twelfth century.

De Sanctis, Francesco (1693–1740) Designer of the baroque Spanish Steps in Rome.

De Vauban, Sébastien Le Prestre (1633–1707) A military planner of towns for LOUIS XIV of France.

De Voland, Franz Engineer. He drew the plans for Odessa and many other new cities in southern Russia in the late eighteenth century (Kostof, 1991).

dead architecture Places where people do not congregate. The phrase has been used by CHRISTOPHER ALEXANDER (Forty, 2000).

Dead Cities 1 A collection of essays by Mike Davis, published in 2002, finding insights into the process of change in episodes of URBAN DESTRUCTION by riot, aerial bombardment, planned demolition and ecological overload. **2** An album by the band the Future Sound of London, issued in 1996. The music evokes the romance (to young people and committed urbanists) of gritty urban life. In the words of one reviewer (Bennun, 1996): 'Cities, the exciting ones, are lustrous on the surface and filthy just beneath it. If they have a veneer of calm, it will soon be violated by sudden noise and action... The effect [of the music] is deliciously ominous... Somebody is in for a rotten time, and it isn't going to be you. This vicarious intoxication with hell on earth sharpens an already jagged and fractured record... *Dead Cities* is acrid smoke, dangerous shadows, cratered pavements and glass shattering on tarmac. Our own cities are just trash enough to give this fantasy an edge of realism.'

dead-end street See CUL-DE-SAC.

deadweight Expenditure to promote a desired regeneration activity that would have occurred even without it. Compare ADDITIONALITY.

Dean Clough Mills A vast redundant carpet factory in Halifax, converted to workplaces and cultural facilities by Sir Ernest Hall as a 'practical utopia' in the 1980s.

Dean of Guild rules The system of building control in Scotland.

Dean's December, The A novel by Saul Bellow in which the protagonist, a liberal academic, realises the uselessness of urban renewal programmes to the people they are meant to benefit (Ward, 1989).

death 'or middle age as it is known in Govan', according to Rab C Nesbitt in Ian Pattison's novel about a life of poverty in Glasgow, *A Stranger Here Myself*, published in 2000.

death by consultation Opportunities to create successful development being missed due to badly managed, ineffective, long-drawn-out or untimely discussions with interested parties.

death of distance, the The dramatic decrease in the significance of physical distance due to the communications revolution. The phrase was used by Frances Cairncross in 1995 (Hall, 1998).

de-bantustan v. To make less like a *bantustan*. Bantustans were the South African homelands created by the apartheid regime in the 1970s and '80s to deny black South Africans their rights. Example: 'The regeneration programme is intended to de-bantustan this estate by connecting it into the surrounding area' (tenant of West Indian origin on a rundown London housing estate in 2003).

Debord, Guy (1931–94) French political and cultural theorist. As a leading member of the Situationist International his book *On the Poverty of Student Life*, published in 1967, has been described as 'the text that launched a thousand cobblestones' (in the student demonstrations of the following year). See also DÉRIVE and PSYCHOGEOGRAPHY.

debris surge (also debris storm) (US) The spread of material from a collapsing building. See also URBAN DESTRUCTION.

debt security A contractual obligation to repay corporate borrowing.

decanting Moving tenants from their homes to allow improvements to be carried out or to match the size of households to the size of houses more exactly. The term applies whether or not the tenants are to move back after the work has been done (sometimes referred to as *double decanting*). It was more widely used before the 1980s, since when it has been thought better suited to describing inert substances and containers than people and their homes. FJ OSBORN wrote in 1949: '"Decanting" people, as it is called, so as to keep each house exactly filled and no more, would not be human if it were practicable, which it is not in a country that still values freedom' (Hughes, 1971).

decentralisation 1 The planned movement of people and workplaces from congested inner urban areas to less congested outer areas, detached smaller towns, NEW TOWNS, villages or rural locations. **2** (Especially US) Spontaneous movement from the centre to the immediate outskirts of an urban area (Pepper, 1978).

decentralised concentration A model of urban development defined by Hildebrand Frey (1999) as 'a multi-nucleated city or even city region in which uses concentrated in the mono-core of the compact city are dispersed into a smaller number of smaller centres forming the nuclei of urban districts, towns or villages.'

decentrists Advocates of regional planning, such as LEWIS MUMFORD, CLARENCE STEIN, HENRY WRIGHT and CATHERINE BAUER who proposed decentralising development from big cities.

deceptively spacious An estate agents' euphemism describing a house that is so deceptive as to not appear spacious at all (Jennings, 2001).

decide 'To succumb to the preponderance of one set of influences over another set,' according to Ambrose Bierce in *The Devil's Dictionary* (1881–1911).

deck access A means of providing access to flats or maisonettes whose doors are above ground level by means of a corridor open to the air on one side. See ALISON AND PETER SMITHSON.

Deckard, Rick See BLADE RUNNER.

Declaration of Bruges Passed in 2003 at the inaugural meeting of the COUNCIL FOR EUROPEAN URBANISM, the declaration set out its 12 'challenges for European urbanism': 1) Poorly integrated housing: slab and tower blocks and low-density sprawl. 2) Unintegrated public and commercial functions: business parks and out-of-town shopping and entertainment centres. 3) Disposable buildings and short life-cycle developments. 4) Degradation of public places. 5) Public realm made from left-over space. 6) Car-dominated transport. 7) Indiscriminate road and street design. 8) Disconnected street networks. 9) Autocratic planning methods and over-regulation. 10) Destruction of villages through decay, abandonment or suburbanisation. 11) Disruptive infill and dysfunctional zoning in urban areas. 12) Non-contextual guidelines and regulations in historic areas.

decocity A city that, giving a low priority to environmental issues (like most modern cities), is not becoming an ECOCITY. The term (from de-ecocity) was coined by the architect and planner Koichi Nagashima in 1996.

deconcentration See DECENTRALISATION.

deconstruction The term was coined by the French philosopher Jacques Derrida in the 1960s to describe a way of understanding how meaning relates to writers, readers and texts. The term was later applied to a particular approach to design (but not necessarily in a way that Derrida would recognize or understand). Deconstructionist design values change, unpredictability, tension and randomness rather than their opposites. The architect REM KOOLHAAS (1994) has called deconstruction 'corny at best – an obvious, quickly tiring metaphor for fragmentation.' David Kolb (1990) has suggested that deconstructivist buildings would lose their point if there were very many of them. 'They need contrast with an accepted language,' he writes. 'If a deconstructivist mode itself became to accepted language, the buildings would lose their inner tension... Deconstruction does not allow us to make places but only to dance on the borders of the almost-places we have.'

decorated shed ROBERT VENTURI's name for, in the words of Trachtenberg and Hyman (1986), 'a structurally and formally trivial, utilitarian construction given a superficial layer of explicit symbolism and applied ornaments'. Venturi favoured such buildings. His views were influential on the development of POST-MODERN ARCHITECTURE. Compare DUCK.

decriminalised parking enforcement Making parking offences a matter for a local authority, rather than the criminal law, through creating a *special parking area*.

de-designation Ending an area's designated status. For example, a conservation area can be de-designated if demolitions and alterations mean that there is no longer much worth conserving.

deemed planning permission A PLANNING PERMISSION accompanying an approval by a government department. In relation to an advertisement, permission is deemed to have been given if the planning authority makes no objections.

deep green See SHALLOW GREEN.

deep plan One in which parts of the floor area are far from a source of natural light and always need to be lit artificially. Compare SHALLOW PLAN.

Deeplish Study A pilot project improving houses in Deeplish, Rochdale, launched in 1966 as an alternative to slum clearance.

Défense, La Built as a new office district for Paris in the 1960s and '70s, partly to keep office towers out of the city centre. The name derives from a war memorial on the site.

defensible space Space over which the occupiers of adjacent buildings can exercise effective supervision and control. The American commentator Oscar Newman, who coined the term in 1972, argued that a lack of defensible space in violent areas could be remedied by, among other things, design measures which increased overlooking, and encouraged a sense of personal or community ownership of space. Newman's ideas were highly influential at the time in both the USA and the UK, though they were also widely criticised for being too deterministic. See ANONYMITY, BOUNDARY DEFINITION, ALICE COLEMAN and TERRITORIALITY, and compare SPACE IS THE MACHINE.

deficit financing Financing a development project on the basis that the cash flows in the early years are less than the interest payable on the debt.

definition The demarcation of specific parts of a building by lines, textures, colours or other means.

definitive map Shows rights of way. The Act of Parliament under which county councils and unitary authorities prepare them intended them to be definitive, but their coverage is incomplete.

deformed grid A pattern of streets that intersect at irregular angles. Also called a *deformed block structure*. The deformed GRID is an important concept in SPACE SYNTAX ANALYSIS. A regular grid is defined as being made up of outward-facing islands of buildings, each surrounded by continuous space. The structure of that space can be 'deformed' in two ways. First, it is linearly or axially deformed if lines of sight and access do not continue right through the grid from one side to the other. Second, it is convexly deformed if two-dimensional spaces continuously vary in their dimensions and shape, making a pattern of wider and narrower spaces (Hillier, 1996). Compare INTERRUPTED GRID.

degradation See URBAN DEGRADATION.

deindustrialisation A decline in manufacturing activity.

Deinocrates An architect of the time of Alexander the Great, around 350 BC. The town plan of Alexandria has been attributed to him.

Delaney, Alan (b1958) Photographer. His photographs of London were published in *London After Dark* (1993).

Delbene, Bartolommeo See CITY OF TRUTH.

delegated power See ARNSTEIN'S LADDER

deleterious material A building material that may fail or cause harm if not used properly. Such materials are often listed in development documents.

delf (especially Yorkshire) A quarry; an excavation.

Delft model The much-quoted method of allocating affordable housing in the Dutch town of Delft.

delight See COMMODITIE, FIRMNESS AND DELIGHT.

delight detector The Construction Industry Council's informal name for the system of performance indicators for design quality that it was developing in 2002.

delight rating *v.* Assessing the extent to which a building or place is likely to delight users and passers-by.

Delirious New York A book by the architect REM KOOLHAAS, published in 1978. Koolhaas describes it as 'a Blueprint for the Culture of Congestion' and 'a Retroactive Manifesto for Manhattanism'. James Dunnett (2000) writes that the word 'delirious' was borrowed from Salvador Dali. See also MANHATTANISE.

de-listing Removing a building's listed status on the grounds that it no longer qualifies or that it was listed in error.

delivery Something being made to happen (in an urban regeneration programme, for example). Example: 'The master plan looked fine: the problem was delivery'.

delivery architect One who oversees the detailed design and construction of a building, but was not responsible for the initial design. Compare TROJAN HORSE.

delivery mechanism (or structure) A means of making development happen, through a partnership, a development trust or a joint venture company, for example.

delivery plan Sets out what a regeneration project aims to achieve and how it will achieve it.

delivery room A collaborative event focused on delivering urban regeneration.

Delouvrier, Paul (1914–95) Prefect of Paris under president Charles de Gaulle in the 1960s and '70s. He determined the region's polycentric structure, with five new towns, three circumferential motorways and new railway lines, 'doing for the suburbs of Paris what HAUSSMANN had done 100 years earlier for the city' (Hall, 1998).

Deltametropolis A declaration made in 1998 by the alderman responsible for planning in Amsterdam, Rotterdam, The Hague and Utrecht stating the intention to transform the collection of villages, towns and cities known as the Randstad into an interconnected urban constellation (Frieling, 2001).

demand-responsive transport Transport services whose route or timing responds to individual customers indicating where or when they need to travel.

dematerialise To become invisible. The word is sometimes used of buildings by their architects and other apologists. Alicio Pivaro (2003) noticed an example in a caption to an exhibit in the architecture room at the Royal Academy's summer exhibition. 'We are told the rather huge Wienerberg Twin Towers by Fuksas "dematerialise", she writes. 'Captain Kirk [of the television science fiction series *Star Trek*] dematerialises. These enormous buildings most certainly do not.'

Democracity A 200–foot model of a prototype American metropolis of the future, created by the industrial designer Henry Dreyfuss and displayed as the central exhibit at the 1939 New York World's Fair. 'The model, which visitors viewed from above while riding on a circular, mechanically-conveyed walkway, showed a concentrically-planned riverfront city of multi-storey buildings contained within a perimeter ring road,' Paul Adamson (2000) records. 'Radial boulevards turned to high-speed motorways at the city's perimeter, and snaked into the surrounding countryside, where they spawned discrete satellite developments among parks and farmlands.' See also FUTURAMA.

democracy Government by the people. 'Democracy,' wrote Ivan Illich, 'is only possible when no one travels faster than the speed of a bicycle.' See also PARTICIPATIVE DEMOCRACY and REPRESENTATIVE DEMOCRACY.

> "DEMOCRACY IS ONLY POSSIBLE WHEN NO ONE TRAVELS FASTER THAN THE SPEED OF A BICYCLE"
>
> *Ivan Illich*

democratic 1 Relating to government by the people. **2** Relating to popular culture; non-elitist. Examples: 'Cultural policy has widened to embrace a broader "more democratic" conception of culture which includes all kinds of everyday social and leisure activities that take place in cities'; 'Gehry's work can be seen as democratic in the sense that Disneyland is democratic, motivated by an intention to entertain and ultimately to sell'; 'There is a potential contradiction between the "democratic" ideas of the Congress of New Urbanism and the élitism of the new urbanist communities.' **3** Open for public use. Example: 'Bus shelters are the smallest democratic spaces.'

demography The study of population change.

demonstration cities See MODEL CITIES PROGRAM.

demunicipalisation Reducing the power and influence of local government.

dendritic layout A road layout with a tree-like structure of dead ends connected to branches. See also CITY IS NOT A TREE, A.

densification Increasing the density of an urban area, by means such as redevelopment, backland development or building on urban greenfield sites. Opponents sometimes call it TOWN CRAMMING. The term became current in the UK in the 1990s.

density The mass or floorspace of a building or buildings in relation to an area of land. Density can be expressed in terms of PLOT RATIO (for commercial development); habitable rooms per hectare (for residential development); site coverage plus the number of floors or a maximum building height; space standards; or a combination of these. David Rudlin (1998) has noted the wide range of densities of actual or proposed housing. He quotes examples of 20 persons per hectare (detached housing in Hertfordshire), 100 (the minimum density for a bus service), 120 (recommended by RAYMOND UNWIN in *Nothing Gained by Overcrowding* in 1912), 240 (the minimum density for a tram service), 247 (defined by PATRICK ABERCROMBIE as low density in 1944 Greater London Plan), 320 (Victorian and Edwardian terraces in Hertfordshire), 336 and 494 (defined by Abercrombie in 1944 respectively as medium and high density), 600 (Hulme, Manchester, as it was in the 1930s), 1,000 (planned density for Singapore in the 1970s) and 5,000 persons per hectare (actual density in Kowloon). (A density of one person per hectare is the same as one of 0.405 persons per acre.) Allan Jacobs and Donald Appleyard (1987) suggest that 'a minimum net density (people or living units divided by the size of the building site, excluding public streets) of about 15 dwelling units (30–60 people) per acre of land is necessary to support city life.' Oregon's Department of Land Conservation and Development records that the density of urban population in the USA decreased by 23 per cent from 1970 to 1990. Tony Travers (2001) suggests that 'the British appear generally to see density as an evil, irrevocably muddled up with overcrowding and nineteenth-century slums'. The architect Barry Munday wrote in 2002 that 'perhaps the biggest barrier to achieving higher densities is winning the hearts and minds of the public. In all our work with existing communities density quickly becomes a difficult issue and we have learned to avoid using the D-word. It is more constructive to talk about what makes good places' (Munday, 2002).

The architect Raymond Hood argued in the 1930s that high densities and urban congestion could contribute to the life of a city rather than being unfortunate consequences (Goldberger, 1981). In the often bitter debate about housing densities, the opponents of high density sometimes question whether its advocates live in such conditions themselves. FJ OSBORN (1953) wrote: 'We have a file (thus far secret) labelled WHERE THEY LIVE, in which we record particulars of the areas and persons per residential acre of the palaces, country homes, town houses, villas, farmsteads, windmills, clubs and shooting lodges of the advocates of flat-mindedness and high density for the urban masses. If they persist in this advocacy, and if our file is ever stolen by some proletarian spokesman, class war may come into planning controversies'. The Ministry of Housing and Local Government announced in 1962: 'Over the next 20 years we are going to need at least six million more houses. That is a formidable problem with two inescapable consequences; we need higher densities especially in the pressure areas. We need not one or the other, but both – more land and higher densities' (MHLG, 1962).

density bonus (US) An increase in density, over and

above that originally zoned, allowed to a developer in return for a specific public benefit.

density pyramid Development that increases in density the nearer it is to the centre, a railway station or other transport node. *Density cone* would seem to be a more appropriate term.

Dent, Arthur See THE HITCH-HIKER'S GUIDE TO THE GALAXY.

Denton, Daniel See BOOSTER.

Denver boot A device for clamping illegally parked vehicles. See also BOOTER.

Department of the Environment Created by prime minister Edward Heath in 1970, with Peter Walker as its first secretary of state. Originally the DoE had responsibility for transport, but this was later hived off into a separate department. It became the Department of the Environment, Transport and the Regions after the election of the Blair government in 1997. The name, but few of the original functions, survived in the Department of Environment, Farming and Rural Affairs after the 2001 election of a second Blair government. See also DETR.

depressed area An area suffering severe economic decline. The phrase was in official use in the 1930s.

Depression City John Walsh (2000) identifies this as 'one of a number of wholly imaginary localities invented in the early 1980s, as the symbolic dwelling places of people in certain states of mind'. The term originated, he suggests, as the obverse of FUN CITY. It was used to describe, for example, the editorial offices of a national newspaper following the company's takeover by a publisher of pornography in 2000.

deprivation POVERTY; the lack of what are generally considered the essentials of an acceptable quality of life, such as employment and satisfactory housing. The term was particularly common in the 1970s and '80s. The most deprived 10 per cent of wards (as officially defined) in England are in cities, former coal mining areas and seaside towns. The phrase can be used to describe more than just a lack of material things. The poet Philip Larkin (1922–85) may have had emotional deprivation in mind when he wrote (in *Required Writing*): 'Deprivation is for me what daffodils were to Wordsworth.' See MULTIPLE DEPRIVATION.

deprofessionalise Reduce the dominance of professionals. Example: 'If it's your profession, you don't want to deal with an ignorant bunch of tenants. We need to deprofessionalise, but it's the last thing the government will agree to' (Colin Ward, 2002).

depth 1 The distance from one side of a building to another. **2** A relative measure of how many changes of direction and/or how many continuous lines of sight there are between two points on a network of routes.

deregulation The relaxation of central, local or public agency rules and regulations, particularly in the interests of business.

derelict 1 *n.* A VAGRANT. **2** *adj.* Abandoned; dilapidated. The word comes from the Latin meaning to abandon.

derelict land 1 Unused land bearing evidence of previous uses. **2** That which is so damaged by industrial or other development that it is incapable of beneficial use without treatment.

derivative plot A small plot created by dividing a larger one.

dérive Drifting; the drift. A method of helping to understand a city by wandering through it without any predetermined route. It was devised by the political art-action alliance the Situationists (who worked between 1957 and 1972). The SITUATIONIST theorist GUY DEBORD wrote in 1956: 'In a *dérive* one or more persons during a certain period drop their usual motives for movement and action, their relations, their work and leisure activities, and let themselves be drawn by the attractions of the terrain and the encounters they find there' (Debord, 1981). Compare FLÂNEUR and see WALKING.

dero A homeless person, tramp or VAGRANT. The word derives from DERELICT.

derry A derelict building.

Derry See STROKE CITY.

desertification The process of making urban wastelands.

design *n.* **1** An outline sketch or plan of the form or structure of something to be constructed or carried out; instructions, particularly in the form of drawings, for making an object, a building or a development. **2** Work executed from those instructions (Forty, 2000). **3** The features and details of a building or designed area; the physical form and appearance of development. **4** An inventive arrangement. The Treasury Taskforce (2000) defined design as 'the process in which intelligence and creativity are applied to a project in order to achieve an efficient and elegant solution'. The architect and urban designer John Worthington has quoted a definition of design as 'the meaningful and elegant allocation of resources'. The architect William Mitchell has defined it as 'the art of offering visions of the future'. **5** The structure of a work of art.

Design has been described as an iterative process that begins with the designer coming up with an initial idea on the basis of incomplete information, and refining that idea in the light of further information (including the contributions of collaborators) as it becomes available. This is sometimes said to contrast with planning, a linear process in which gathering and analysing the information precedes the stage at which the plan is drawn up. See SURVEY, ANALYSIS, PLAN.

Adrian Forty (2000a) suggests that the concept of design has enabled architects to separate the mental activity of design from the practice of construction. This may make architecture easier to teach as an academic rather than a practical subject, but it may also help marginalise architects from their former role of supervision construction (see, for example, DESIGN AND BUILD). The term design, or its equivalent, emerged in most of the European languages around the sixteenth century, according to Mike Cooley (1988). The reason, he suggests, is not that design was a new activity, but that 'it was being separated out from wider productive activity and recognised as a function in its own right... Above all, the term indicated that *designing* was to be separated from *doing*.' The word, from the Latin word meaning to mark out and from the Italian *disegno*, drawing, dates from the second half of the fourteenth century. See also URBAN DESIGN.

design advisory panel A group of people (often architects) with specialist knowledge, which meets regularly or occasionally to advise a local authority on the design merits of planning applications or other design issues.

design and build An arrangement whereby a single contractor designs and builds a development, rather than a contractor building it to the design of an independent architect. Design and build generally produces buildings that are relatively cheap and easy to build, using the methods with which the builder is most familiar. Standards of design are often low.

design audit An independent assessment of a design, carried out for a local authority by consultants, another local authority or some other agency.

design brief 1 A brief to a designer. **2** A document, prepared by a district or unitary authority, a developer, or jointly by both, providing guidance on how a site of significant size or sensitivity should be developed. Site-specific briefs are also called a variety of other names, including *planning briefs* and DEVELOPMENT BRIEFS. As design is now recognised as an integral part of planning, there is no need for separate planning and design briefs in the planning process.

design chain The design element of the product supply chain (the process of supplying a product).

design champion A person responsible for ensuring that a particular organisation – a local authority, regional development agency, health authority or government department, for example – promotes high standards of design throughout its work. Compare STREET CHAMPION and TOWN CHAMPION.

design code A document (usually with detailed drawings or diagrams) setting out with some precision the design and planning principles that will apply to development in a particular place. It provides developers with a template within which to design their schemes or individual buildings. The code may cover a group of buildings, a street or a whole area. Design codes are an important element of NEW URBANISM. New urbanists argue that only certain ways of building will produce successful urbanism in any particular place, and that it makes sense to agree, write down and enforce that approach. New urbanist design codes are often set out in PATTERN BOOKS.

Design codes (also known as urban codes and urban design codes) vary in the level of detail they prescribe. Many are enforceable by legally binding agreements (through conditions of sale of a piece of land, for example), while others are no more than general advice that may carry some weight in the planning process. An example of the latter is the Poole Design Code (elsewhere this would be called a DESIGN GUIDE), adopted in 1998 to augment the council's local plan. Other documents may have similar effects to design codes without being named as such. The documents that prescribe highway standards – and that have had an enormous and often baleful influence of the design of places – are examples of this. The UK government began promoting the use of design codes in 2004 (partly at the instigation of the PRINCE'S FOUNDATION), in the hope of raising design standards in its major programme of building SUSTAINABLE COMMUNITIES.

The use of design codes has been traced back at least as far as the Romans and, in the UK, to the regulations governing the rebuilding of London after the Great Fire of 1666. Design codes shaped cities such as SIENA (see URBAN DESIGN FRAMEWORK) and Georgian cities such as BATH and Edinburgh. See also CELEBRATION, COMBINATIONAL URBANISM, CONGRESS FOR NEW URBANISM, CONTROLLED HETEROGENEITY, COOKBOOK ENGINEERING, ENCLOSURE, POUNDBURY, QUAE PUBLICAE UTILIA, SEASIDE, STOREY/STORY, TYPOLOGICAL CODE and URBAN VILLAGE.

design coordinator One who manages the design process in a development project, particularly liaising between the developer and the local authority.

design day A one-day event at which local people play a part in determining design issues.

design dividend An Australian method of using urban design criteria to show that better-designed buildings and spaces perform better in terms of both commercial and social value (Rouse, 2001).

design for disassembly Designing a building so that later it can be dismantled with as many of its components as possible being reused elsewhere.

design game A method of investigating design issues with the use of paper cut-outs.

design guidance A generic term for documents providing guidance on how development can be carried out in accordance with the planning and design policies of a local authority or other organisation. There are four types of guidance that can usually be distinguished from one another. 1) Guidance relating to specific places. There are three main types of these: URBAN DESIGN FRAMEWORKS (for areas), DEVELOPMENT BRIEFS (for sites) and MASTER PLANS (for sites). These may include more detailed guidance in the form of DESIGN CODES. 2) Guidance relating to specific topics. These, usually called DESIGN GUIDES, cover topics such as shopfronts, house extensions, lighting and cycling. 3) Guidance relating to specific policies. Examples are policies on conservation areas, transport corridors, waterfronts, promenades and green belts. 4) Guidance relating to a whole local authority area. These may give general urban design guidance for the whole district or county.

design guide A document providing guidance on how development can be carried out in accordance with the planning and design policies of a local authority or other organisation. Design guides are issued by some counties, and by many district and unitary authorities, among others. A local authority design guide will often relate to a specific topic such as shopfronts or house extensions, or may relate to all kinds of development in a specific area.

Design in Town and Village Published by the Ministry of Housing and Local Government in 1953, the report was 'the only substantive government text on design ever published' (Punter and Carmona, 1997) until the publication in 2000 by the Department of the Environment, Transport and Regions (in collaboration with the Commission for Architecture and the Built Environment) of *By Design: urban design in the planning system, towards better practice.*

design plan A concept advocated by Tony Hall in a book *Design Control: towards a new approach*, published in 1996. Hall argues that local authorities should draw up policy statements in the form of design plans to reveal their full intentions towards the design of the physical environment and convey them to the public in a form intelligible to lay people. The principles on which the concept is based include: a) Design briefs should derive from design plans (statements of wider urban design policy). b) Design plans should be driven by objectives. c) Objectives are more precise formulations of more general goals, and their achievement can be measured. d) Goals should correspond with value statements used in the political process. e) Goals should be of two types: general principles that should, in the opinion of the planning authority, govern all design; and goals specific to the particular plan area. f) A design plan should consist of: a statement of the objectives; criteria for the achievement of the objectives (performance standards) and advisory material on how the objectives might be fulfilled; advisory material giving guidance on how the objectives might be fulfilled without necessarily limiting the possible options; and procedures that will, or may, be necessary in the process of fulfilling the objectives.

design policy Relates to the form and appearance of development, rather than the land use.

design principle An expression of one of the basic design ideas at the heart of an urban design framework, design guide, development brief or design code. Each such planning tool should have its own set of design principles.

design professional A generic term for people with a wide range of skills including architects, urban designers and landscape architects. The term's use in recent years reflects the erosion of the boundaries between the traditional professions.

design quality indicator A method of assessing the quality of buildings in terms of 'build quality', 'functionality' and 'impact'. It was developed by the Construction Industry Council and launched in 2002. See COMMODITIE, FIRMENES and DELIGHT.

design standards Produced by districts and unitary authorities, usually to quantify measures of health and safety in residential areas.

design statement A written report, supported by illustrative material, accompanying a planning application. The statement shows how the applicant has analysed the site and its setting, and formulated and applied design principles to achieve good design for buildings and public spaces. Its scope and level of detail is determined by the nature of the development, the site and its context. Design statements are an important means of raising standards of design in new development. They can improve dialogue between developers (and their designers) and the local planning authority and the local community.

design workshop A participative event, ranging in length from a couple of hours to several days, which brings together a range of people (often local people and professional advisors) to discuss design issues. A workshop may or may not use techniques of collaborative design. Also known as a CHARRETTE.

designate See BIASED TERMINOLOGY.

design-blind Oblivious to the value of good design. Example: 'Housebuilders seem to be beginning to mind about being seen as design-blind' (2002).

designer 1 *n.* A person who devises designs. The word dates from the 1640s. **2** *adj.* Carrying the label of, or easily identified as the work of, a particular designer.

designer region The focus of coordinated action for a particular purpose such as waste management or public transport (Herrschel and Newman, 2002). See REGION.

design-fed regeneration *adj.* A process in which design skills are available without designers taking an inappropriately dominant role. The term has been used to describe an alternative process to DESIGN-LED REGENERATION.

design-led development (or regeneration) Development whose form is largely shaped by strong design ideas. These ideas may range from an architect's design for a landmark building to a masterplan or development brief. Those who use the phrase perhaps see design-led development in contrast to development that is market-led, policy-led or community-led. These types, they fear, may leave design as an afterthought. The concern is justified but the concept of design-led development can be simplistic. Successful development needs to be rooted in commercial reality and to respond to public policy and local needs. Planning at its best balances these in a way that makes the most of opportunities for design, establishing appropriate design principles early in the process, and developing them into a design framework (through briefs and masterplans, for example) at each stage. That avoids the situation in which design takes the lead, but the designers' proposals are later torpedoed by unforeseen commercial, policy or political factors. The supposed summit of design-led development is the vision of a landmark building transforming a whole area by its presence alone (the POMPIDOU CENTRE in Paris and the Guggenheim Museum in Bilbao – see BILBAO EFFECT – are frequently cited examples). The exceptional conditions that make this possible without a more conventional planning and design process are rare. Compare DESIGN-FED REGENERATION.

design-led planning Planning based on the use of URBAN DESIGN FRAMEWORKS, DESIGN CODES, DEVELOPMENT BRIEFS and master plans.

desire line The shortest, most direct route between facilities or places. Even when obstacles or difficulties are in the way, people will still try to follow the desire line, so it makes sense to accommodate desire lines in a plan as far as practicable.

desk study Carried out by reference to documents that are already available, rather than by fresh investigations. See also WINDSCREEN SURVEY.

Despina An imaginary city in Asia described by Italo Calvino in INVISIBLE CITIES (1972). It can be approached from the sea or from across the desert. The distant view of Despina will remind the camel-driver of a ship, whereas to the sailor the city appears as a camel hung with bags of merchandise. Their vision of the city depends on where they have come from.

Destruction of Sodom and Gomorrah A 1852 painting by John Martin (1789–1854) showing the two cities being consumed by fire and molten lava as punishment for their evil inhabitants. Lot and his family have been allowed to escape on the condition that they do not look back. His wife disobeys and can be seen transformed into a pillar of salt. See also CITIES OF THE PLAIN and URBAN DESTRUCTION.

destruction See URBAN DESTRUCTION.

desuburbanisation Suburbs losing population to small towns in the city's hinterland (Drewett, 1980). See also DISURBANISATION.

detached town garden Groups of rented gardens laid out in the seventeenth and eighteenth centuries on the outskirts of towns. Where there was great pressure for open land in the town centre, they enabled their tenants to spend their leisure time in a country setting. Each plot, covering about one sixth of an acre, would typically have had a path system among lawns and beds. Many also had brick or stone summerhouses and glasshouses. The few detached town gardens that were not built on in the nineteenth century were taken on by the suburban dwellers, who eventually turned them into allotments (Rutherford, 2002)

detailed master plan Usually drawn to a scale of 1:500. See MASTER PLAN.

detailed planning application Seeks permission for all aspects (or all aspects not yet approved) of a development.

deteriorate See BIASED TERMINOLOGY.

determinism See ARCHITECTURAL DETERMINISM.

DETR The DEPARTMENT OF THE ENVIRONMENT, TRANSPORT AND THE REGIONS, which was replaced in 2001 by the Office of the Deputy Prime Minister, the Department of Transport, and the Department of the Environment, Transport and Rural Affairs. See also DEPARTMENT OF THE ENVIRONMENT.

detrimental to amenity Detracting from an area's environmental, social, economic or cultural qualities. It is a stock phrase often used by planning authorities in refusing planning permission. Often its use masks a failure to consider (or at least to explain) more specifically the reasons for the decision.

Detroit The city whose name has become shorthand for 'the American automobile industry'. In the words of Dan Hoffman (2001): 'Nowhere else do we find a city so completely dedicated to a single industry and the obsessions of modern technology.' Patrick Schumacher and Christian Rogner (2001) write: 'Detroit stands devastated, overburdened by the infrastructural, architectural and human sediment of its Fordist past: central parts of Detroit are empty. Large buildings stand as ruins. Offices, schools, train stations and vast urban territories have been abandoned. Urban planning proposals counter this drastic situation with equally drastic measures: the demolition of entire urban quarters and their conversion into parks. Greenbelts are proposed to cut the vast, fragmented field into recognisable "communities", sealing the ultimate fate of Detroit as a suburb of its own suburbs. Detroit's extended suburbs are alive and well, forming a polycentric conurbation where typically post-Fordist service industries settle at a safe distance from inner-city wastelands.'

Jerry Herron (2001) writes that what some might see in today's Detroit as ruin, others might call history. He notes that the city stands accused of having failed to make liveable places. On the contrary, Herron argues, the city 'did produce places to get to. We got there, by choice, on paved highways. And it is the extraordinary wealth created by this city, Detroit, that made the trip possible for numbers of individuals unprecedented in the long histories of human societies. That is what the city did. Now, to presume its putative exhaustion is evidence of anything but the city's successful design is like blaming the gas tank for getting empty or the tires for wearing out when somebody drives the family car. The problem is not that so many people used the city to get to where they wanted to go, which was someplace else. The problem is that not everybody was allowed to come along for the ride, so that a population who has been excluded from its entitlements now often inhabits the structural apparatus of modernity.' See INNOVATION and MOTOWN.

Detroitism The dramatic growth of a modern industrial city, as exemplified by Detroit in the first half of the twentieth century.

detrunk To remove a road's trunk status, allowing it to be lined with buildings with active frontages, and giving pedestrians and cyclists greater priority.

de-urbanisation The process of an area becoming less urbanised. Example: 'With a decrease of 50 per cent of its citizens since the early 1950s, the city of Detroit is experiencing an ongoing process of aggressive de-urbanization' (Daskalakis and Perez, 2001).

developable Capable of being developed.

developer's brief 1 Prepared by the owner of a site as the basis for appointing a developer. **2** Prepared by a developer as the basis for appointing consultants. Compare DEVELOPMENT BRIEF.

developer's fit-out Constructing an office building with suspended ceilings and raised floors, but without partitions. This is a more advanced fit-out than SHELL AND CORE.

developing corporation In 1933 FREDERIC OSBORN called for 'developing corporation' to build new towns. The New Towns Act 1946 set up individual DEVELOPMENT CORPORATIONS to build a series of new towns.

development Statutorily defined under the Town and Country Planning Act 1990 as 'the carrying out of building, engineering, mining or other operation in, on, over or under land, or the making of any material change in the use of any building or other land'. Most forms of development require planning permission. The word *development* (though not its urbanistic meaning) dates from the late 1740s. Compare EVOLUTION.

development appraisal A structured assessment of the characteristics of a site and an explanation of how they have been taken into account in drawing up development principles.

development brief A document providing guidance on how a specific site of significant size or sensitivity should be developed in line with the relevant planning and design policies. It will usually contain some indicative, but flexible, vision of future development form. A development brief usually covers a site most of which is likely to be developed in the near future. The terms 'planning brief' and 'design brief' are also sometimes used. These came into use at a time when government policy was that planning and design should be kept separate in design guidance. The term 'development brief' avoids that unworkable distinction. Compare DEVELOPER'S BRIEF.

development capital Money to finance a company's expansion.

development charge (US) Payment required as a condition for permission to develop.

Development Control Charter, The One of the UK government's citizen's charters.

development control The process through which a local authority determines whether (and with what conditions) a proposal for development should be granted planning permission.

development corporation See NEW TOWN and URBAN DEVELOPMENT CORPORATION, and compare DEVELOPING CORPORATION.

development form See FORM.

development framework See DEVELOPMENT BRIEF.

development parcel A piece of land, usually under a single ownership, suitable for development.

development period The time taken to plan, build and let or sell a development.

development plan Prepared by a local authority in the UK planning system prior to 2004 to describe the intended use of land in an area and provide a basis for considering planning applications. Every area was covered either by a UNITARY DEVELOPMENT PLAN or by a development plan comprising more than one document (a STRUCTURE PLAN and a LOCAL PLAN, and sometimes also other plans relating to MINERALS and waste). The development plan set out the policies and proposals against which planning applications were assessed. Its context was set by national and regional PLANNING POLICY GUIDANCE. They were often too detailed to provide flexibility or too general to provide specific direction. They took years to produce and were often out of date as soon as they were finally adopted.

development plan document (England and Wales) A spatial planning document prepared by a plan-making authority and subject to independent examination.

development planner 1 One who works on the preparation of a local authority's development plan. **2** One who works on the planning of a specific development on behalf of a developer.

development rights (UK) The right of a landowner to develop, and to reap any consequent increase in the value of the land, was effectively nationalised by the Town and Country Planning Act 1947. The justification was that the betterment (the increase in land value) rightfully belonged to the community that created it, although a £350 million fund was provided to compensate landowners in some cases. Increases in land value were taxed by a 100 per cent betterment clause. The system came into operation in 1949. It was discontinued two years later following the defeat of Clement Attlee's Labour government, though development rights have remained nationalised ever since. Compare COMMUNITY LAND ACT.

development team 1 The people working together to bring about a particular development. **2** Local authority officers working collaboratively in dealing with development proposals rather than each carrying out their own section's responsibilities individually.

development trust Defined by the DETR (1998) as being a community-led enterprise with social objectives, sharing benefits within the community (mutuality), creating opportunities for local people (empowerment), and acquiring an asset base.

development value The difference between the value of land in its existing or past use, and its current market value for development; the potential for increasing the value of land or buildings by developing them by means of building work or change of use.

de-zoning (US) Relaxing zoning regulations to promote mixed uses.

Di Giorgio, Francesco (1439–1501) Architect and military engineer. Spiro Kostof (1991) notes that he was the first designer to show how a radial system of streets, a bastioned periphery wall and a public space in the centre could be made to work together.

diabetes See URBAN DIABETES.

diagnosis, design and development Sometimes referred to as the three Ds of the regeneration process. See also ECONOMY, EFFICIENCY AND EFFECTIVENESS.

diagnostic survey The first step in PATRICK GEDDES' approach to planning.

Diagon Alley A magical shopping street in London described by JK Rowling in *Harry Potter and the Philosopher's Stone* (1997) and her subsequent Harry Potter books. Witches and wizards enter the street by tapping a brick wall with their wands to make a hole open up, or by other magical means. See also PRIVET DRIVE.

diagonal diverter A physical barrier that connects two diagonally opposite kerbs, running across an intersection, making motor vehicles slow down and turn. Cyclists, pedestrians and emergency vehicles may be able cross. See also TRAFFIC CALMING.

dialogue 1 A means of communication between people involved in a process of public or STAKEHOLDER participation. The facilitator Richard Harris identifies two forms. In *bounded dialogue* the parameters of the dialogue are pre-determined by the initiator, and may be tightly drawn and non-negotiable. In *open dialogue* all stakeholders decide the parameters of the dialogue together. **2** The supposed active relationship between a building and its setting. Example: 'Materials have been chosen carefully – like the Corncockle red sandstone – to start a "dialogue" with the city [Glasgow]' (the author is probably quoting the building's architect).

dialogue research (Denmark) Defined by Holmgren and Svensson (2001) as 'action-oriented research, conducted in dialogues between professionals and residents, without their taking sides in the actual urban renewal project and without their taking part in its implementation.'

Diary of a Nobody, The See CHARLES POOTER.

Diaspar The city, more than a thousand million years old, described in Arthur C Clarke's novel THE CITY AND THE STARS.

diaspora city London, so called for its cultural diversity. See also COSMOPOLIS.

Dick Whittington syndrome A tendency of people in rural areas to have exalted expectations of what city life will offer them. Dick Whittington (a historical figure who died in 1423, as well as a popular subject for pantomimes) walked to London with his cat and became Lord Mayor.

Dick, Philip K (1928–82) Science fiction writer. The film BLADE RUNNER was based on his novel *Do Androids Dream of Electric Sheep?*

Dickensian Poor, squalid or exploitative, like conditions portrayed in the novels of Charles Dickens (1812–70).

Dictionopolis The City of Words, from where all words originate. Ruled by King Azaz the Unabridged, it is described in Norton Juster's *The Phantom Tollbooth* (1962). Compare DIGITOPOLIS.

Dido Building Carthage A painting of 1815 by JMW Turner, showing the classical city under construction in the morning sunlight.

diffusion theory The theory states that the city originated in Mesopotamia in the fourth millennium BC, spreading from there to the Indus Valley and China, and westward to Greece. Spiro Kostof (1991) writes that 'these days almost nobody believes [in it].' See also UR and URUK.

dig and dump Dealing with a contaminated site by removing the soil.

digital city Defined by Helen Couclelis (2003) as 'a comprehensive, web-based representation or reproduction of aspects or functions of a specific real city, open to non-experts'. This definition, she notes, does not cover urban computer games and representations of fictitious cities (such as SIMCITY) since they do not represent any specific real city. 'The digital city is not a traditional geographic information system representation or urban model,' she writes, 'since these are not directly open to non-experts, nor can it be identified with the many useful telematics applications, such as intelligent transportation systems, developed to assist urban management or to make some urban function run smoother (these are not representations or reproductions of urban aspects or functions). However, all these forms of urban digitality (the games, geographic information systems, models, intelligent technologies and so on) may be related to the digital city as defined here.' Couclelis points to two characteristics of digital cities. First, they are place-based (that is, they are actual places). Second, they are meant to be accessible to the public in the broad sense rather than to any particular groups of experts, professionals, special interests or urban managers.

Digitopolis The City of Numbers, which supplies numbers to the world, as described in Norton Juster's *The Phantom Tollbooth* (1962). Compare DICTIONOPOLIS.

diktat A pejorative term for a regulation. Example: 'A planner has to find a way through a minefield of English Heritage diktats.'

dilapidated Ruined. Pedants have been known to insist that its origin – from the Latin *dilapidare*, combining *di-* (asunder) and *lapis, lapidis* (stone) – means that the word can be used only when referring to stone buildings or structures.

dilapidation A state of ruin.

dilapidations 1 Damage caused to a building during a tenancy. **2** Money paid at the end of the tenancy to pay for this.

Dilworth, Richardson K (1898–1974) Politician and lawyer. As district attorney and later mayor (1956–62) of Philadelphia, he made a reputation for reforming the city's administration in the face of deep-seated political corruption. See also EDMUND BACON.

dinas (Welsh) A city. Compare TREF and PENTREF.

dingbat (US) A building raised on columns to maximise parking underneath, to the detriment of the pedestrian frontage. NEW URBANISTS use the term. Compare PILOTI.

dinky Acronym for dual income, no kids yet. See YUPPIE.

directional differentiation Defined by KEVIN LYNCH (1960) as 'asymmetries, gradients and radial references which differentiate one end from another (as on a path going uphill, away from the sea, and toward the centre); or one side from another (as with buildings fronting a park); or one compass direction from another (as by the sunlight, or by the width of north-south avenues).'

disability Statutorily defined in the UK as 'a physical or mental impairment, which has a substantial and long-term adverse effect on a person's ability to carry out normal day-to-day activities'. Some campaigners prefer to define disability as 'the loss or limitation of opportunities that prevent people who have impairments from taking part in the life of the community on an equal level with others due to physical and social barriers'. The first definition puts the emphasis on the impairment, the second on the barriers.

disadvantage The lack of opportunities associated with POVERTY and SOCIAL EXCLUSION.

disadvantaged *adj.* Poor; socially excluded. See POVERTY and SOCIAL EXCLUSION.

Disappeared A city under the sea, described in VICTOR HUGO's story 'The Underwater City' in *The Story of the Centuries* (1859).

Disappearing City, The A book by the architect FRANK LLOYD WRIGHT, published in 1932. Modern communications would make existing cities disappear, he believed, to be replaced by BROADACRE CITY.

discharge A flow of water from a watercourse, culvert, pipe or drain into another watercourse.

discontinuance order Served by a planning authority to remove an unacceptable advertisement.

discretion The power to decide. Local authorities in the UK have discretion in relation to many planning matters that in other countries are subject to non-discretionary regulations.

disencumber To clear away buildings and structures that are thought to compromise the setting of a significant work of architecture. Debate about the wisdom of the practice of disencumbering raged in the nineteenth century. CAMILLO SITTE, for one, was opposed to it. The French equivalents are *dégagement* or *isolement*, the German *Freilegung* (Kostof, 1992).

disfigured city One that is unplanned and occupied mainly by poor people. Compare FIGURED CITY.

disjointed incrementalism An approach to planning developed by Charles Lindblom in the late 1950s, intended as a more realistic alternative to supposedly rational and comprehensive planning (Taylor, 1998).

Disney Corporation An enthusiastic patron of NEW URBANISM, as in its development of CELEBRATION.

Disney World A theme park in Florida, opened in 1971.

Disney, Walter (Walt) (1901–66) Animator, film producer and purveyor of fantasy.

disneyfication A pejorative term for the practice of transforming a place into a commercialised, themed version of a popular image of somewhere historic or imaginary. The term is inspired by the Disney Corporation's Disneyland and Disney World.

Disneyland 1 A theme park in California created by the film producer Walt Disney (1901–66) in 1955. Margaret Crawford (1992) discusses its influence on the development of shopping malls. 'While enclosed shopping malls suspended space, time, and weather,' she writes, 'Disneyland went one step further and suspended reality. Any geographic, cultural, or mythical location, whether supplied by fictional texts (Tom Sawyer's Island), historical locations (New Orleans Square), or futuristic projections (Space Mountain), could be reconfigured as a setting for entertainment.' Shopping malls, Crawford explains, easily adapted this

diversity

appropriation of 'place' in creating specialised theme environments. In Scottsdale, for example, 'the Borgata, an open-air shopping mall set down in the flat Arizona desert, reinterprets the medieval Tuscan hill town of San Gimignano with piazza and scaled-down towers (made of real Italian bricks).' Further Disneyland parks opened near Tokyo in 1983 and near Paris in 1992. **2** A commercialised, themed place made in the popular image of somewhere historic or imaginary. Richard Rogers accused the Prince of Wales in 1989 of having a 'Disneyland approach' to architecture.

dispersal Creating less centralised forms of human settlement. A national policy of extreme dispersal has been considered (and rejected) on at least one occasion in the USA. 'In 1947,' writes Martin Pawley (2002a), 'a presidential advisory commission on universal military training, concerned at the difficulty of defending the US against Soviet nuclear weapons, proposed that the whole of the habitable land surface of the country be developed along a 25-mile square grid of superhighways. Within this grid an industrial complex was to be located at the centre of each square, while the population would be housed in low-density linear residential zones along the highways.' William Cobbett called for 'the dispersal of the wen' (London) in 1821. See FRANK LLOYD WRIGHT, EBENEZER HOWARD, NEW TOWN, FJ OSBORN, POST-URBANISM, REGIONAL PLANNING ASSOCIATION OF AMERICA and TOWN AND COUNTRY PLANNING ASSOCIATION.

dispersalist One who advocates the dispersal of population from urban centres.

dispersed high density A concept of housing development described by Lionel March in *Homes Beyond the Fringe*, published in 1967. Semi-detached, two-storey houses would be laid out in a hexagonal grid of extended courtyards (Dunnett, 2000).

displacement 1 The effect by which a regeneration project has unintended positive or negative effects on other, nearby areas. **2** One group of people or uses taking the place of another in an area. Examples include wealthier residents moving into a gentrifying area and restaurants replacing shops on a high street. See GENTRIFICATION.

disposable See CRAVED.

disposition Defined by Richard McLaughlin (2000) as the horizontal placement of structures on building lots.

dispute resolution professional A person who guides others in resolving disputes through using various techniques of collaboration, consensus building, mediation or negotiation.

Disraeli, Benjamin (Earl of Beaconsfield) (1804–81) Novelist and statesman. See SYBIL.

dissociation Lack of contact with others. See also SOCIABILITY.

distance-decay effect The reduced consumption of goods and services by people who live furthest from them.

distanciation The effect of the communications media in reducing the effects of time and space.

distinctive See MARKETING.

distributor road (UK) A residential distributor road distributes traffic within a large estate and links the highway network with other residential roads. It is generally suitable as a local bus route and designed to discourage stopping on the carriageway. Frontage development is discouraged, with the result that the road is often lined with high walls or close-boarded fencing, and sometimes also planting or earth mounding tob act as a screen. Such roads may suffer from not being overlooked (see NATURAL SURVEILLANCE).

district 1 An area dominated by a single activity. Such districts are regarded as one of the fundamental organising elements of NEW URBANISM (Duany and Plater-Zyberk, 1994). *A New Urbanist Lexicon* (McLaughlin, 2000) defines a district as 'an urbanised area organized around a predominant human activity'. Although districts preclude the full range of activities of a NEIGHBOURHOOD, McLaughlin writes, their primary activity is supported by typically neighbourhood-scale uses. Examples are theatre districts, medical facilities and college campuses. Generally, though, a district is thought of as being larger than a neighbourhood. KEVIN LYNCH (1960) defined districts as 'the medium-to-large sections of city, conceived of as having two-dimensional extent, which the observer mentally enters "inside of", and which are recognisable as having some common, identifying character'. The URBAN TASK FORCE (1999b) described a district 'in a city-scale urban area' as having a population of 9,000–40,000 people and a radius of two to six kilometres. Hildebrand Frey (1999) has suggested that an urban district might be formed of four or five neighbourhoods, with a total population of 25,000–35,000, and that ideally four or five districts should form a town. **2** A unit of administration.

district centre Defined by the Scottish Office (1998) as a shopping centre or group of shops, separate from the town centre, usually containing at least one food supermarket or superstore and non-retail services, such as banks, building societies and restaurants serving suburban areas or smaller settlements.

district heating A system by which the heating for all the buildings in an area is provided from a single source. Compare DISTRICT HEATING and COMBINED HEAT AND POWER.

district park Defined by Llewelyn-Davies (2000) as 'a landscape setting (of around 20 hectares) with a variety of natural features providing for a wide range of activities, including outdoor sports facilities and playing fields, children's play for different age groups, and informal recreation pursuits'. Compare REGIONAL PARK.

disturbance payment Payable to people who lose their home through local authority action and are not entitled to compensation, and to housing association tenants who are decanted while their homes are improved. Compare HOME LOSS PAYMENT.

disurbanisation 1 A decrease in the proportion of people living in urban settlements. **2** The changes that occur in social structures when people move away from towns and cities. Compare DESUBURBANISATION and URBANISATION.

Disurbanisers, The A group of Russian constructivist architects who in the 1920s and '30s promoted linear plans (for Moscow and Stalingrad, among other places).

disurbanism 1 Development lacking urban characteristics. **2** The act of creating such development. BILL HILLIER (1996) describes disurbanism as 'the breaking of the relation between buildings and public space; the breaking of the relation between scales of movement; and the breaking of the interface between inhabitant and stranger'. See RED CITY OF THE PLANET OF COMMUNISM.

disurbia The word, standing for *dense, industrial and self-contained suburban region,* has been credited by Alan Loomis to Mark Baldassare.

diversity Variety. 'Sameness stultifies the mind,' Richard Sennett (2001) writes, 'diversity stimulates and expands it.' Jane Jacobs (1961) identified four conditions for generating exuberant urban diversity: 1) The district, and as many of its internal parts as possible, must serve more than one primary function. 2) Most blocks must be short. 3) The district must mingle buildings that vary in age and condition. 4) There must be a sufficiently dense concentration of people.

diverter A barrier that makes traffic turn. See also TRAFFIC CALMING.

divide (US) A boundary between two drainage basins. The UK term is a WATERSHED.

Dixon of Dock Green The eponymous hero of the BBC TV series, played by Jack Warner. When it began in the mid-1950s the series reflected the general trust between urban communities and the police. By the time it was taken off in 1976 that trust had been eroded and Dixon's style of policing seemed anachronistic, compared for example to that of the brutal, hard-drinking detective inspector Charlie Barlow (played by Stratford Johns) in the 1960s–'70s TV series Z CARS.

Dobry Report The government inquiry chaired by George Dobry QC published its *Review of the Development Control System* in 1974. The report's recommendations were not implemented.

Dobson, John (1787–1865) Architect. He did much to shape Newcastle after 1810, often in collaboration with the developer and builder Richard Grainger.

Docklands light railway The driverless LIGHT RAIL system serving the London dockland redevelopment. Construction began in 1984.

dockney An urban professional living in London's docklands and working in the City (Whimster, 1992). The word, briefly current in the 1980s, has echoes of COCKNEY and YUPPIE. Compare MOCKNEY.

DoCoMoMo The organisation devoted to the documentation and conservation of works of architecture of the modern movement.

dog fouling The geographer ALICE COLEMAN used the incidence of dog fouling as a quantifiable indicator of urban disfunction. Ingesting dog faeces can cause the disease *toxocariasis* in humans (usually children), following infestation with the larvae of *toxocara canis*, sometimes leading to blindness.

dog's breakfast See MUESLI.

Dome See MILLENNIUM DOME.

Domesday Book A survey of England, begun by King William I in 1086. It provides an important source of information about medieval towns.

Dom-Ino LE CORBUSIER's first design for a system-built, reinforced-concrete house, published in 1914. The name derives from the six dots its columns made on a plan.

don't worry, you won't know we were there A phrase used by builders who have no intention of being there, according to Robert Huxford.

donut effect See DOUGHNUT EFFECT.

doomwatcher One who warns of the prospect of environmental catastrophe.

doors open day A day on which free access is given to buildings, gardens and sites not normally open to the public. See OPEN HOUSE.

doorstep green A small, public space provided by a programme funded by the New Opportunities Fund's Doorstep Greens programme.

Doppelhaus (German) A semi-detached house.

Dorf (German) A village.

dormitory suburb An area of suburban housing without significant shopping or other facilities, or workplaces. See GARDEN SUBURB.

dormitory town or village (UK) A place many of whose working residents commute to a nearby town or city. The US equivalent is *bedroom community*.

dorsale The north-west European corridor stretching from Birmingham to Milan and including London, Amsterdam, Cologne, Frankfurt, Basle and Zurich. See also BLUE BANANA.

doss 1 *n.* Sleep. **2** *n.* A crude bed. **3** *v.* To sleep in any convenient place. Also *doss down*.

doss house A hostel for homeless people; a cheap lodging house.

dosser A pejorative term for a homeless person who sleeps on the streets or in a hostel. See VAGRANT.

double (US) A semi-detached house.

double coding Designing a building with two levels of meaning: a level of abstraction for the architectural connoisseur, and a level of accessible and popular symbolism for the unsophisticated viewer. Double coding is said to be a characteristic of much POST-MODERN ARCHITECTURE.

double decanting See DECANTING.

double-yolk city region A region centred on two cities (for example, Manchester and Liverpool in the north west). Sir Peter Hall used the term in 2001. See also CITY REGION.

doughnut (or donut) effect The downtown area of a city being abandoned as people and activities move out to the suburbs, leaving a 'hole in the middle' like a ring doughnut. See also WHITE FLIGHT.

doughnut city A proposed form of city in which the central business district would be replaced by a park or airport, and business, light industry and residential areas would be wrapped in bands around it and separated by green belts of parks and golf courses, and cut through by the spokes of rapid transit. It was proposed in 1949 as a form well suited to reducing vulnerability to nuclear attack in a book *Must We Hide?* (Kostof, 1991). See also TARGET ATTRACTIVENESS.

Dover See DULLBOROUGH.

Dower Report John Dower reported in 1945 to the Ministry of Town and Country Planning on his assessment of possible sites for the first NATIONAL PARKS in England and Wales.

Down and Out in Paris and London George Orwell's account of his experience working in menial jobs and sleeping rough in the two capitals, published in 1933.

down-and-out *n.* A destitute, homeless person. See VAGRANT. Also an adjective.

downdraught Wind moving down the face of a building due to the building's mass diverting a lateral wind.

Downing, Andrew Jackson (1815–1852) Landscape designer and architect. His PATTERN BOOK *Cottage Residences*, compiled with Alexander Jackson Davis and inspired by JOHN CLAUDIUS LOUDON, was published in 1842. In 1848 he proposed what eventually became New York's CENTRAL PARK. He was working with FREDERICK LAW OLMSTED on its design when he drowned after a steamboat exploded.

downside risk See RISK.

downstream Later in the development process, as opposed to UPSTREAM. For example, building is *downstream* of design. Example: 'The design professions have moved upstream into conceptual work, aiming to influence major decisions on strategy and policy... Surveyors have moved upstream into strategy to influence the regeneration process and capture downstream work' (Roberts, 2001).

downtown (US) The town or city centre. *Uptown* and *downtown* referred originally to Manhattan. *Downtown* was the southern end of the island, downstream of the rivers. Martin Bucksbaum, pioneer of suburban shopping centres in the USA in the 1950s, called them 'the new downtowns' (Adamson, 2000).

Downtown A pop song, written by Tony Hatch, giving a positive view of city centre life. 'Listen to the music of the traffic in the city... The lights are much brighter there, you can forget all your troubles, forget all your cares and go Downtown...' It sold three million copies when recorded by Petula Clark in 1964. See also SUMMER IN THE CITY.

downzoning (US) Changing the zoning of an area to a use of lower intensity.

dowry A sum of money paid by a local authority to a housing association that is taking over council housing whose outstanding repairs will cost more than the market price.

Doxiadis, Constantinos (1913–75) Architect and urban designer. He was the founder of EKISTICS.

drag (US) A street or road. See MAIN DRAG.

Drag City (US) A boring place.

drama PATRICK GEDDES' concept of life as a drama led him to describe it variously as an *autodrama*, *biodrama*, *cosmodrama*, *politodrama*, *pschodrama* and *technodrama*. See also TIME.

Drancy A garden city begun in 1920 as one of a series aimed at decentralising population from Paris.

draw area (US) The area from which the customers or users of a shop, shopping centre or other attraction come.

drawing 1 A representation of ideas in symbolic form. Types of drawing include analytical drawing, cartoon, design, diagram, doodle, elevation, gestural drawing, narrative drawing, map, observational drawing, plan, projection (axonometric, isometric, oblique, orthographic), schematic drawing, scribble, sequence drawing, sketch, speed drawing, storyboard and technical drawing. **2** The act of creating such a representation. A drawing can be a means of communication (helping to make ideas, thoughts and feelings available to others); manipulation (helping the creative process of developing thoughts); and perception (helping to order sensations, feelings, ideas and thoughts) (*Power Drawing*, 2001). The artist Saul Steinberg called drawing 'a way of reasoning on paper' (quoted in Knevitt, 1986).

Drayneflete A fictional town whose development over the centuries is chronicled in Osbert Lancaster's satirical story *Drayneflete Revealed*, published in 1949.

dream sketch Translation of the German term *Stadttrauemliche Studie*, describing a sketch visualising how the layout and massing of development can transform an area (Hebbert, 2000).

dreamscape The totality of what someone aspires to.

dress sense The history of male, built-environment professionals' preferences in clothing will probably never be written. Its chapters would record, among other trends, planners' choice of sports jacket and cavalry twill trousers in the 1960s. It would discuss architects' preference for bow ties (said to be explained by the need to avoid a necktie dangling over the drawing board, but rare even among tie-wearing, drawing-board users by the 1980s), for coloured spectacles in the 1980s (sometimes with brightly coloured shoes) and, along with other types of designers, for dressing entirely in black – though not if they are classicists – since the 1980s (examples: 'There ought to be black-polo-necked Gauloise-smoking students at planning schools and there aren't' [from a discussion about Scottish planners' lack of design skills, 2001]; 'We need to convince architects to move on from the black polo-neck jumper' [from an article urging architects to communicate better with people beyond the profession, 2002]). The history would record conservation planners' preference for waxed Barbour jackets; engineers' preference for short-sleeved shirts; landscape architects' choice of shirts with floppy collars; and urban designers' choice of blue shirts with button-down collars in the 1990s (darker blue at the end of the decade), moving towards dark grey and black shirts (with collars not buttoned down) by 2002.

In that year town planners noted in the technical press that the wearing of beards in their profession had declined significantly. An entry in the satirist Ian Martin's fictional diary column in *Building Design* (Martin, 2003) reads: 'Friday: Invited to merge with a major engineering and transport consultancy. Decline, as I refuse to wear a jumper over a shirt and tie.' Surveyors and estate agents have a close and sometimes antagonistic relationship with one another (many estate agents being surveyors). One surveyor summed up common stereotypes in 2003. 'We see estate agents as unscrupulous men in shiny suits,' he said. 'They see surveyors as fuddy-duddies dressed in tweed.'

Mike Davies, project architect of the MILLENNIUM DOME, dresses entirely in red. George Ferguson, RIBA president from 2003, habitually wears red trousers. The architect Mart Stam's trousers are recalled in the title of a book written by the collaborative Crimson with Michael Speaks and Gerard Hadders (1999), *Mart Stam's Trousers: stories from behind the scenes of Dutch moral modernism*. The title comes from an interview with PETER SMITHSON, in which he tells of of a photograph of MIES VAN DER ROHE and LE CORBUSIER. Seen in the photograph is what is said to be Mart Stam's trouser-clad leg, the rest of his body having been obliterated from the picture. The authors offer this as an example of how the history of modernism has been falsified.

The retired architect BRIAN ANSON visited the Architectural Association (a leading school of architecture in London), where he had taught many years earlier, in 2002. 'With time on my hands, I sat in the bar... a bar I once knew as a bloody battleground of debate on the meeting between architecture and the poor – and nearly wept to see that the AA was now a place where students didn't actually need portfolios: they were their own portfolios. The architecture is now the self, the style, the fashion.' By contrast Howard Roark, the egotistical architect hero of Ayn Rand's novel *The Fountainhead*, is willing to dress like everyone else (Gary Cooper plays him in the 1949 film wearing a beautifully tailored business suit): what he will not compromise on is his architecture. Another fictional 'architect of distinction' in *The Fountainhead*, Gordon L Prescott, wears a beige turtleneck sweater (though this is out of the office, at a meeting of a new architects' group).

For a columnist on the *Seattle Times*, the experience of interviewing the celebrated architect REM KOOLHAAS led to a realisation of the importance of wearing shoes that were APPROPRIATE (though he did not use that word). 'The conversation had a curious effect on me,' O Casey Corr (1999) writes. 'I studied Koolhaas' clothes: grey stretch-flannel pants, rumpled shirt, no tie, and dark nylon jacket. He completed the Euro Guy Intellectual look with dark, square-toed shoes. It worked. At the end of the interview, he left to get coffee. I left for a store and bought shoes that were dressy, but not too dressy. They had to work with the "context" of my slacks.' Jonathan Raban (1974) suggests that a concern with uniforms (common ways of dressing) is an urban characteristic. 'Uniforms aren't important in villages,' he writes. 'They are seen as the mark of irredeemable townees, signs of an obsession with symbols which the countryman finds incomprehensible and absurd.' The architect Michael Morrison (2002) has spoken of conservation architects' fascination with white gloves. These architects, he says, tend to place undue weight on scientific data produced by the sort of specialists who wear white gloves when handling delicate artefacts. 'It is much easier to define the needs of a single object than of a complex multi-functional system', and too often the architects lose sight of the bigger picture. 'In the extreme, the measures to preserve the contents of a building may be destroying the fabric of the building itself.'

The Scottish architect Richard Murphy has said that getting work 'is luck, especially with competitive interviews – it depends what aftershave you are wearing sometimes' (*Building Design*, 2003). Ruth La Ferla (2003), writing in the *New York Times* about the competitors for the design for the WORLD TRADE CENTER site, asked: 'Why do architects wear round, thick-framed glasses?' She traced the fashion back to LE CORBUSIER and the desire of architects to 'trademark their faces, much as they trademark a building'. La Ferla noted that Rafael Viñoly, one of the shortlisted competitors, 'appeared in photographs wearing two pairs of spectacles on his head – something of a fashion signature'. Competition-winner Daniel Libeskind's frames, meanwhile, were 'a particularly severe example of so-called statement glasses, meant to confer a

George Orwell

degree of gravitas, but hinting all the while that he (or she) has raffishly artistic leanings'. Spectacles with a pronounced geometric shape were a natural style choice in a profession focused on structure and form, La Ferla suggested, and they were so prevalent as an insignia of the architect's profession that ordinary people often tried to copy them. She quoted a New York eyewear retailer: 'You never hear customers saying, "Make me look like a lawyer". It's always "Give me that architect type of look".' Winning the competition made Libeskind so famous that the press reported that shops in New York were selling out of his trademark elk-skin cowboy boots (Gates, 2003).

In Thomas More's fictional UTOPIA all people dressed alike, except that men dressed differently from women, and married people from unmarried. There were no changing fashions, nor was there any difference between summer and winter clothes. People wore leather clothes or skins at work, with undyed woollen cloaks over them outside working hours. In the early days of LETCHWORTH GARDEN CITY, in the first years of the twentieth century, 'rational dressers' (who spurned conventional dress), including 'no-hatters' (who refused to wear hats) and toga-wearers, gave the place a reputation for eccentricity that the garden city company did its best to play down. JOHN BUCHAN's 1919 novel *Mr Standfast* makes fun of Tancred and Ursula Jimson, residents of Biggleswick Garden City (based on Letchworth, where Buchan had lived). Tancred wears grey flannels, a soft collar, an orange tie and a soft black hat. His wife Ursula favours a gown 'modelled on a chintz curtain'. These were no doubt the sort of people George Orwell had in mind when he wrote some years later of 'that dreary tribe of high-minded women and sandal wearers and bearded fruit-juice drinkers who come flocking towards the smell of "progress" like bluebottles to a dead cat.' Wearers of sandals (which were another symbol of eccentricity in the early garden city days) and beards are still regarded as stereotypes of environmentalism.

The skyscraper designer Harvey Wiley Corbett, writing in 1928, urged fellow architects to learn from the design of clothes. 'We have vertical stripes on our clothes because we think they add to our appearance. And, conversely, how are ugly clothes – clothes that we do not want copied, the uniforms of convicts – how are such clothes designed? They have broad horizontal stripes. No one would willingly wear anything so hideous. In his buildings, too, man has liked lines that accentuate heights and carry the eye upward' (quoted in Bender, 2002). Alan Powers (2003) records what happened when the partners of architects Connell, Ward and Lucas were arraigned by their fellow modernists of the MARS GROUP in the 1930s for submitting a neo-classical design for Newport Civic Centre (their excuse being that after winning they hoped to convert the clients to modernism). 'They turned up in evening dress. They happened to be going to a party, and even modern architects dressed that way then, but it was an appropriate two-finger gesture towards the design police of their own side.' Walt Disney's EPCOT was originally intended to have a strict dress code. (LE CORBUSIER said he could spot an architect by the way they rearranged their place setting during dinner, but that is another matter.)

There seems to be less to say about female, built-environment professionals' preferences in clothing: the women seem less inclined to wear professional uniforms. How ordinary women dress in the street, on the other hand, was the subject of a project carried out in 2002 by the San Francisco artist and photographer Sarah Hughes. Her exhibition 'Safe and sexy: personas and codes of public space' documented women in public space and how they modified their appearance, persona and identity in order to establish a sense of comfort and/or sensuality. In particular Hughes examined how the influences of society, government structures, economics, age, race and geographical location effect how women present themselves in public spaces. For the photographs (taken in each woman's neighbourhood or in another area that they frequented), she asked the women to choose two outfits, one in which they felt comfortable and safe, and one in which they felt attractive and sexy. Hughes saw the juxtaposition of the two photographs as illustrating the chameleon-like roles and personas that women subconsciously and consciously play on a daily basis in the urban environment (see also GENDER).

Dreyfuss, Henry (1904–72) Industrial designer. See DEMOCRACITY.

driveable (also drivable) (of a city) Easy to drive in, thanks to such factors as smooth road surfaces, free-flowing traffic, low fuel prices and a pleasant climate. Compare LIVEABLE.

Drop City 1 A settlement in Colorado, built in the 1960s. It featured geodesic domes made from the roofs of abandoned cars (Pawley, 2002c). **2** A novel by TC Boyle, published in 2003, taking its name from that of the fictional 1970s commune in California in which it is set.

drop lock loan A means of managing the interest rate on a property development and providing the developer with predetermined sums of money over an agreed period of time.

dropped housing estate One that seems to relate in no way to its surroundings, looking as though it has just been dropped on to its site.

dropped kerb/curb (UK/US) A short stretch of kerb set at a slope to allow people in wheelchairs or with buggies to cross the road.

drowned worm A type of suburban layout in which roads curve this way and that, seemingly at random, in a desperate attempt to create some variety. See also LOOPS AND LOLLIPOPS and TRAIN-WRECK LAYOUT.

dual city One with extremes of social inequality.

Duany Plater-Zyberk A Miami-based architectural and town planning practice led by ANDRES DUANY and ELIZABETH PLATER-ZYBERK. The practice is a leading exponent of NEW URBANISM.

Duany, Andres (b1949) Architect and town planner. In 1980 with his wife ELIZABETH PLATER-ZYBERK he co-founded the architectural and town planning practice Duany Plater-Zyberk. Duany is the most prominent advocate and propagandist for NEW URBANISM. He sees his mission as being to promote neo-traditional design and planning (new applications of traditional approaches) in the face of modernism (in the professions and the media), marxism (in the universities) and anti-urban environmentalism.

Born to a Cuban family, Duany lived as a child in Barcelona in Franco's Spain. 'I don't think I would be as confirmed in the pleasures and assets of cities if I hadn't been wandering about Barcelona as a kid,' he says (Lehrer and Zinmeister, 2002). After studying at Yale University, he had early success designing high-rise apartment blocks in Miami Beach, Florida. Duany was converted to traditional urbanism – 'after a couple of weeks of real agony and crisis,' he recalls (Lehrer and Zinmeister, 2002) – by hearing a lecture by LÉON KRIER. See also ALLEE, ARCHITECTURAL DETERMINISM, BERM, BUNGALOW COURT, CAMPUS, CLIENT, CO-HOUSING, COMMUNITY, COPY, CORRIDOR, CUSTOMER, DISTRICT, ENCLOSURE, FIVE BS, FLEX HOUSE, FRAGMENT, GENETIC BLUEPRINT, GENTRIFICATION, GREENFRONTING TOWNHOUSE, NEIGHBOURHOOD, NORTH DALLAS SPECIAL, PATRON, REMNANT, SEASIDE, SECTOR, SIMULTANEOUS FLUSH, STREET GRID, SUBURB, SUBURBAN SPRAWL, TYPE, TYPOLOGICAL CODE, URBANISM, VICTIM, VILLAGE and WALKING DISTANCE.

Andres Duany

Dubelir, Grigorii (1874–1942) Russian specialist in planning and highway design.

duck The architect ROBERT VENTURI distinguished between *ducks* and DECORATED SHEDS. A duck is a building that formally tries to symbolize its function (such as a roadside stand in the shape of a duck selling ducks) (Trachtenberg and Hyman, 1986). Venturi favoured decorated sheds.

Dulburb See DULSTON.

Dullborough The fictional version of Dover in Richard Aldington's 1929 autobiographical novel *Death of a Hero*.

dullsville A nickname for any place lacking in interest, based on the US practice of coining placenames by adding -VILLE to some characteristic feature. Compare PITSVILLE.

Dullsville One of the development scenarios in the computer game SIMCITY.

Dulston The place in north London where people live after they die (those who do not go to south London's DULBURB, that is) in Will Self's novel *How the Dead Live*. Published in 2000, the book portrays parts of London as cities of the dead. Dulston was based on Dalston and Dulburb on Clapham. See also MAGNETIC CITY.

dumbbell interchange A motorway junction with a roundabout at the end of the slip roads on either side, so that it looks like a dumbbell from the air. Compare CLOVERLEAF INTERSECTION.

dumbbell plan The most common layout of tenement blocks in the US between 1877 and 1901. The name derives from the shape (in plan) of the lightwell, designed to provide light to all bedrooms at minimal cost to the developer.

Dumills, the An imaginary family of Londoners of the future featured in Peter Hall's book *London 2000*, published in 1963.

dummerer (US) A beggar who pretends to be mute (dumb).

dump the chintz A slogan used by the Swedish furniture and household goods store IKEA, hoping to persuade people to discard conventional ideas about furnishing and decorating in their homes. Some commentators, impatient of the popular suspicion of modern architecture, have suggested that an equivalent slogan should be applied to design in cities.

duplex (US) **1** An apartment on two floors. **2** Two dwellings, one above the other. **3** A property legally zoned as a two-family dwelling. **4** A SEMI-DETACHED HOUSE.

Durand, Jean-Nicolas-Louis (1760–1834) An architect and teacher in nineteenth century Paris whose approach later shaped the teaching at the École des Beaux Arts.

dwell time The length of time a train, bus or other vehicle waits at a station or stop.

dymaxion BUCKMINSTER FULLER used the name for various of his designs and inventions, including the Dymaxion House and the Dymaxion Car. It was coined by Waldo Warren, a professional namer of merchandise, by combining *dynamic* with *maximum*.

dystopia A bad place; the opposite of UTOPIA. The Latin word, derived from the Greek for *bad* and *place*, was coined by John Stuart Mill.

Dzerzhinsk The Russian city was said in 2003 to be the world's most polluted.

E

Earth Abides A novel by the naturalist and historian George R Steward, published in 1949, chronicling the gradual decay of San Francisco in the years after its population has been wiped out by the plague. See also THE SCARLET PLAGUE and URBAN DESTRUCTION.

earth-bund A BERM.

Earthly Paradise, The A best-selling cycle of poems by WILLIAM MORRIS telling Greek and medieval stories. The first volume was published in 1868. In it Morris urged his readers to 'Forget six counties overhung with smoke,/ Forget the snorting steam and piston stroke,/Forget the spreading of the hideous town;/ Think rather of the pack horse and the down,/And dream of London, small, and white, and clean,/ The clear Thames bordered by its garden green.'

Earthquake A 1974 film, directed by Mark Robson, in which Los Angeles is destroyed. Charlton Heston stars as one of the heroic survivors.

East End The unfashionable part of a city. Example: 'I would have no West Ends and East Ends' (GEORGE LANSBURY in 1934, quoted in Cherry, 1982). Compare WEST END and see REBRAND.

East St Louis See SPRINGFIELD.

East Thames Corridor See THAMES GATEWAY.

EastEnders A soap opera set in Albert Square in the fictional borough of Walford in London's East End. It was first televised in 1985. There was a real Albert Square in the East End of London in the nineteenth century (close to the Shadwell basin) – home to 'sailors and brothel keepers', according to the 1871 census – which was later demolished. London currently has two real Albert Squares, neither of them in the East End, and 33 Albert Roads. Most of them are named after PRINCE ALBERT. See also BROOKSIDE, CORONATION STREET, OZZIE AND HARRIET and THE SIMPSONS.

eaves line The line where a wall and roof meet.

ecclesiastical exemption Ecclesiastical buildings are exempt from listed building and conservation area controls if the religious denomination has an acceptable system of control of its own (as the Church of England does, among others).

echelon parking Parking at an angle (often 45 degrees) to the street. This can make moving in and out of the parking space easier than parking at right angles, and it takes up less of the width of the street. Compare PARALLEL PARKING.

eco- (prefix) Concerned with the habitat of living organisms.

eco-cement A cement that absorbs more carbon dioxide in its creation than it produces, unlike Portland cement. Invented by the Australian John Harrison, it replaces the unusual lime with magnetite (Quinion, 2003).

ecocentrism Trust in in the potential for environmental problems to be solved through understanding and working with the ECOSYSTEM. Compare CORNUCOPIAN and ENVIRONMENTAL TECHNOCENTRISM.

ecocity A city that is aiming at a high degree of sustainability.

ecofreak See ECONUT.

École des Beaux Arts See BEAUX ARTS.

ecological desert A derogatory term for green but featureless open space of minimal ecological value. Also known as URBAN PRAIRIE.

ecological footprint The area of the earth's surface required to maintain present levels of production with current technology; the land surface required to feed an inhabited area, supply it with forest products, and reabsorb its carbon dioxide and other waste. London's ecological footprint, for example, is calculated to be 125 times its surface area. That, at 20 million hectares, is greater than the entire area of productive land in the UK. The concept has been developed by the writer and filmmaker Herbert Girardet, among others.

ecological metabolic cycle theory An approach to design by the architect KISHO KUROKAWA and the METABOLIC GROUP. Service components are located on the exterior of a building so they can be replaced easily (Bareham, 2001).

ecological skyscraper One that makes better use of resources than skyscrapers generally do. KEN YEANG (2003), the leading designer and exponent of such buildings, concedes that 'skyscrapers are as unecological as any building can be'.

ecologism Fundamentalist ENVIRONMENTALISM. Michael Quinion (1997) suggests that ecologism 'has a strong spiritual component that seeks to preserve the environment in absolute terms without concern for the place of human beings within it and in particular without making allowance for the potential needs of future generations.'

ecology The relationships between living things and their physical environment. As the scientific term *oecology*, the word dates from the 1870s, mainly through translation from the German zoologist Haeckel, Raymond Williams (1983) suggests. The eco- comes from the Greek *oikos*, meaning household. The word's popular use dates from the 1960s, from when Williams also dates *ecocrisis, ecocatastrophe, ecopolitics* and *ecoactivist*.

Eco-media City A concept used by the architect KISHO KUROKAWA in masterplanning cities, focusing on ecological systems and multi-media industries.

economic vitality The phrase is sometimes used as an alternative for economic sustainability.

economics of agglomeration The tendency for similar businesses to cluster together.

economy, efficiency and effectiveness The three Es of regeneration, sometimes used as criteria for success. See also DIAGNOSIS, DESIGN AND DEVELOPMENT.

econut One who is obsessively concerned about ecological and environmental issues. Also *ecofreak*.

eco-park An area of green-belt land opened up for food production, recreation and public access. The concept was proposed by the TOWN AND COUNTRY PLANNING ASSOCIATION in 2002.

ecopoesis (also ecopoiesis) The bringing into being of an ecology that did not previously exist (Quinion, 1998). Compare TERRAFORM and WORLDSCAPE.

ecopolis A SUSTAINABLE city.

eco-school A school committed to focusing on environmental issues and applying that experience in the day-to-day running of the school, particularly as part of the eco-schools programme launched in the UK in the late 1990s.

ECOSERT European Cooperation for Sustainable Environmental Regional Development through Tourism. ECOSERT aims to attract visitors to places other than the usual tourist hot-spots, and to develop rural assets in ways that stimulate the rural economy while conserving the cultural and natural heritage. See HONEYPOT and SUSTAINABLE TOURISM.

ecosystem Living organisms and their physical environment. An ecosystem can be at any scale, from a single log or pond to the whole earth.

Ecstacity An installation in which the architect Nigel Coates presented an urban vision at the Venice Biennale in 2000.

ecstatic architecture Buildings designed to lift the viewers out of themselves by the uncommon experience generated by their unorthodox and seemingly irrational form. The term was coined by architectural writer Charles Jencks to describe what another writer, Alan Powers, calls 'post-Cartesian architecture'. Jencks' term

Daniel Libeskind

covers modern architects such as FRANK GEHRY, DANIEL LIBESKIND, Coop Himmelblau and WILL ALSOP, and forerunners such as Borromini and Gaudi.

ecumenopolis The largest of the 15 EKISTIC units, having a population of 50 billion.

Eden Vale The capital of the utopia of Freeland, described in Theodor Hertzka's *Freeland* (1890). Transport in the spacious, pollution-free city is by means of vehicles powered by springs that are pre-wound by steam power.

edge KEVIN LYNCH (1960) defines edges as 'the linear elements not used or considered as paths by the observer. They are the boundaries between two phases, linear breaks in continuity: shores, railroad cuts, edges of development, walls. Such edges may be barriers, more or less penetrable, which close one region off from another; or they may be seams, lines along which two regions are related and joined together'.

edge city A place in the suburbs of a metropolis (particularly in the USA) that has developed into a major centre for office employment and shopping, taking advantage of easy accessibility by car and low land values. Suburbs which housed people who originally commuted to the city centre now provide customers and workers for new centres. The result can hinder attempts to regenerate urban areas and to promote public rather than private transport. In 1991 journalist Joel Garreau defined them in his book *Edge City* as settlements of at least five million square feet of office space and 600,000 square feet of shopping, with more people working than living there. James Howard Kunstler (2001) writes of Atlanta: 'Atlanta was becoming a collection of fabulous edge cities which, the cognoscenti would tell you, was what the future would be all about – brilliant sparkling satellite pods of corporate high-rise dynamism embedded in a wonderful matrix of leafy, tranquil dormitory suburbs, all tied together by a marvellously efficient personal transportation system... Wait a minute. This sounded like that old bullshit from LE CORBUSIER... Towers in a Park connected by freeways... [or, as JANE JACOBS satirised the idea in 1961,] towers in a parking lot.' See also BOOMBURB.

edge thinking The tendency for a local authority to neglect the edges of its area, due to the fact that some of the benefits of any improvements will be enjoyed by residents of a neighbouring authority.

edgelands The anonymous places between town and country; the URBAN (or RURBAN) FRINGE. Compare BORDERLANDS.

edge-of-centre Defined by the Scottish Office (1998) as 'a location within easy walking distance of a town centre, and usually adjacent to the town centre, and providing parking facilities that serve the centre as well as the store, thus enabling one trip to serve several purposes'.

edit *v.* To make amendments to the structure of the city.

edited community (US) One strictly segregated by wealth or race.

eds and meds (US) Educational and medical facilities.

education for sustainable development The UK's Panel for Education for Sustainable Development wrote in 1998 that 'education for sustainable development enables people to develop the knowledge, values and skills to participate in decisions about the way we do things individually and collectively, both locally and globally, that will improve the quality of life now without damaging the planet for the future.' The phrase had largely replaced the term ENVIRONMENTAL EDUCATION by the late 1990s.

edutainment A facility supposedly combining education and entertainment.

Edwardian Dating from the reign of King Edward VII (1901–10).

Edwards, Arthur Trystan (1884–1973) The author of *Good and Bad Manners in Architecture* (1924), which called for buildings to be designed to fit in with their context.

effective housing supply Defined by the Scottish Office (1996a) as the part of the established land supply that is expected to be free of constraints in the five year period under consideration and will therefore be available for the construction of houses.

effectiveness The extent to which a project, programme or policy achieves its objectives.

efficiency The relationship between outputs and inputs; the ratio of output to input.

Egan, John (Sir) Industrialist, government advisor and chairman of the Confederation of British Industry. He chaired the task force whose influential report Rethinking Construction, published in 1998, called for more modern building techniques and better cooperation between clients and builders in public building projects. In 2002 Egan was referred to as the government's 'construction tsar'. The following year he was appointed to review the skills and training of the built environment professions (see SUSTAINABLE COMMUNITY).

Eggs Up A village, described in Carl Sandburg's *Rootabaga Stories* (1922), whose inhabitants once tried to build a skyscraper that would reach the moon. Finding that the moon had moved, they pulled it down and built another, only to face the same problem again. Since then they have been trying to think of a way of keeping the moon in the same place.

Egoville An imaginary city described by Bob Jarvis (1983) in which there is no memory of time and space. Every record decays. 'The inhabitants use a complex system of pronouns that refer back to the original states without describing them; photography, map-making and pictorial art are unknown... Each moment is a discovery, and only carefully learned, regular patterns of behaviour allow recall of such essential elements as home, workplace and social facilities. Indeed, some deviant elements exploit this lack of locational recall, indulging in a perpetual ecstasy of discovery, never returning to any one place, preferring instead continual new and dislocated environmental experience.' Egoville is contrasted with ROBOPOLIS to help in understanding the real world, which is somewhere between the two.

Eichler, Joseph (1900–74) Developer and builder of housing and planned communities in Palo Alto, California in the 1950s. He was noted for his refusal to follow the common local practice of discriminating against minority groups in selling houses.

Einfamilienhaus (German) A detached house (literally 'one-family house').

Einstein, Albert (1879–1955) Physicist. Einstein wrote: 'The world we have created today as a result of our thinking thus far has problems which can not be solved by thinking the way we thought when we created them.' His comment is quoted by the CONGRESS FOR THE NEW URBANISM.

Einstein's Dreams See HEIGHT.

Einwohnerdichte (German) Population density.

ekistic elements The five ekistic elements are nature, ANTHROPOS, society, SHELLS, networks and synthesis.

ekistician One who practices EKISTICS.

ekistics The problems and science of human settlements. The movement, and a journal of the same name, was founded in Greece in the 1940s by the architect and planner Constantinos Doxiadis (1913–75). Ekistics is particularly concerned with how different disciplines work together. The term is derived from the ancient Greek word for 'concerning the foundation of a house, a habitation, a city or a place'. Also *ekistic* and *ekistical* (adjs.), and *ekistically* (adv.).

El Dorado The Golden City of Manoa, believed by the Spaniards and Sir Walter Raleigh to lie on the banks of the Amazon or Orinoco rivers.

El, the The nickname for Chicago's and New York's elevated railways. The first section of New York's opened in 1870.

Eland House Premises of the Office of the Deputy Prime Minister (and formerly the Department of the Environment, Transport and the Regions) in Victoria, London. See MARSHAM STREET.

Eldon Square Shopping Centre Built to the north of Newcastle city centre in the late 1970s involving the complete demolition of Eldon Square, part of Grainger and DOBSON's grand development of 1825–40, and its replacement by a blank, brown-brick box. At the time it was criticised for its impact on the original city core. No one dreamed that far worse would follow with the growth of out-of-town shopping.

Eldonians, The Descendants of Irish immigrants of the 1840s living today near Eldon Street in Liverpool's Vauxhall area. The Eldonians have been spectacularly successful since the 1980s in rebuilding their neighbourhood physically, socially and economically. The close-knit community had been threatened with the demolition of their homes and relocation to outlying estates, and the major local employer, a sugar refinery, had closed. They won the right to stay; refurbished some of their homes; built cooperative housing and homes for elderly people in the Eldonian Village; set up a garden market, a development trust and a local enterprise agency; and persuaded the Merseyside Development Corporation to extend its boundaries. In the early days of their campaign the Eldonians flourished in the teeth of opposition from Liverpool City Council. At that time the Labour council, controlled by the Militant Tendency, was ideologically opposed to housing cooperatives and community enterprise. Margaret Thatcher's government, committed to doing everything it could to frustrate Militant's plans, found that supporting the Eldonians through the Department of the Environment served as a useful weapon.

electronic city In the view of LÉON KRIER (2001), 'traditional patterns of streets and squares are the optimal means of networking pieces of real estate of whatever size. Electronic networking completes spatial networks of public spaces but it does not replace them. To believe the latter is a philosophical error of the same degree as believing that the wheel could replace the leg.'

electronic pedestrian One equipped with such equipment as a mobile phone, personal stereo, laptop computer and/or camcorder.

electronic village One in which the majority of the businesses and residents are connected to a local data network. See also CYBERPLACE.

electrosmog Unwanted electromagnetic emissions from structures such as overhead electricity cables and mobile phone masts. The extent to which such pollution is a danger to health is a matter of controversy. See also SMOG.

Elektropolis Berlin, the capital of the world's electrical industry between 1880 and 1913 (Hall, 1998).

element KEVIN LYNCH (1960) defined five elements that contribute to IMAGEABILITY and 'act as building blocks for the designer': PATH, EDGE, DISTRICT, NODE and LANDMARK.

elevation 1 An external face of a building. **2** A diagrammatic drawing of this. **3** The height of a site above sea level.

elevational control Planning control over the elevations of buildings.

Elevational Control The title of a 1966 UK government circular.

elevator (US) The UK term is *lift*. The first Otis elevator was installed in a store in New York City in 1857, and elevators were widely used by the 1880s. The elevator was a crucial technology, making high buildings – and eventually the SKYSCRAPER – possible.

eleven miles an hour The average speed of traffic in central London in both 1900 and 2000.

Eliot, Thomas Stearns (TS) (1888–1965) Poet. See CULTURE and UNREAL CITY.

Elizabeth A new capital of England, to be located in marshland in Yorkshire, proposed by *Prospect* magazine in 2002.

elsewhereness 1 A sense that a place is somewhere else to where it actually is. Example: 'The shopping mall's medieval theme created a disturbing sense of elsewhereness.' **2** The sense a place evokes as being the same as many other places.

Elstow Garden Villages See GARDEN VILLAGE.

embedded Integrated. Example: 'Shopping centres embedded on main drags should thrive. Many centres in secondary locations are doomed' (from the US in 2003).

embodied energy That which is used in extracting, producing, manufacturing, transporting, constructing, maintaining, demolishing and disposing of buildings and their materials, and thus embodied in the building itself.

embodied energy analysis Assessment of the total energy likely to be used in the construction and operation of a proposed development.

embourgeoisement 1 (places) GENTRIFICATION. **2** (people) Working-class people moving into suburban areas and adopting middle-class lifestyles. The term has been adopted from the French.

Embra (Glasgow) Edinburgh.

Emerald City The capital of Oz, described in L Frank Baum's *The Wonderful Wizard of Oz* (1900), *The Emerald City of Oz* (1910) and others of Baum's books. Its streets and pavements are of marble ornamented with emeralds. Its features include a GREEN BELT of lawns and rare trees.

emergence A new phenomenon arising spontaneously in a complex system (a city, for example). See COMPLEXITY.

eminent domain The power to condemn and compulsorily purchase property.

emmet (Cornwall) **1** A tourist. This use has been current since about the 1960s (Quinion, 2000). Compare GROCKLE. **2** An ant.

Empire Windrush The ship SS Empire Windrush brought nearly 500 migrants to London from Jamaica in 1948 at the start of the migration that was to have a major impact on the nature and culture of the UK's urban population.

employment See JOBS.

employment zone A deprived area where additional government funds are available to help long-term unemployed people to find work.

empowerment Creating opportunities for people living in a particular area to become actively involved in the processes of change.

empty nester A parent whose children have left home.

Emscher Park A 70-kilometre long area of parks (some of them based on industrial relics), new housing and rehabilitated buildings in the Emscher district, a former industrial area of the northern Ruhr in Germany. The park was the product of an International Building Exhibition (regeneration programme) of 1989–2000.

emulate See COPY.

enable Increase the ability of people to manage their own lives. The opposite of *disable*. See TOWN CHAMPION.

enabling development 1 Commercial development whose profitability makes possible a related development or restoration of social, historic or environmental value. **2** Development (such as building an access road) that is necessary for carrying out another development.

enclave A part of a town or city without significant through MOVEMENT; an area disconnected from the continuous urban fabric. See ESTATE, OFFWORLD, PARK, PRECINCT, PRECINCTISATION and RESERVATION.

enclavism A pejorative term for designing an urban area as a series of distinct enclaves rather than as continuous urban form.

enclosure 1 The creation of a sense of defined space by means of surrounding buildings or planting. The new urbanist ANDRES DUANY describes a horizontal-to-vertical ratio of greater than 6:1 (that is, the distance between facing buildings is more than six times their height) as 'a cause for concern'. In his view 'a ratio of between 3:1 and 1.5:1 is best' (Shallcross, 2000). HAUSSMANN's rebuilding of Paris followed a building height of 17.54 metres for streets of more than 10 metres wide, as specified in the city's 1784 building code. Cornice height for building of streets less than eight metres wide was set at 12 metres, giving a similar horizontal-to-vertical (width/height) ratio of 1:1.5 (Hall, 1998). **2 (also inclosure)** The process by which fields were created in England from the former pattern of open fields held in common, and from formerly unfarmed land. Land was enclosed from the thirteenth century, and on a large scale under Acts of Parliament between 1750 and 1820.

encounter field The natural pattern of background space use and movement created by a town plan and the distribution of buildings within it (Hillier, 1988).

encroachment Development on land that was formerly part of a street or other public space.

end user A person who uses a building or place after it is newly built or renewed.

endgabble Defined by the humorist Ian Martin (2002) as 'complicated drivel at the end of a stylised terrace'. Compare GABLE END.

end-gaining See GORDON CULLEN.

end-of-pipe activity Something that is done at the end of a regeneration process, such as evaluation and monitoring.

end-on perspective The view of a small linear settlement (such as a village set out along a road) that makes it unobtrusive in the landscape to most people who will see it.

energy Fifty per cent of the energy consumed throughout the world is said to be used in constructing and operating buildings. Michael Hough (1995) has argued that the availability of cheap energy has been an overriding determinant of urban form. 'Attitudes and perceptions of the environment expressed in town planning since the Renaissance, have, with some exceptions, been more concerned with utopian ideals than with natural process as determinants of urban form. Examples of cities and institutions all over the world attest to the aesthetic and cultural baggage of a past era, transported to hostile climatic environments and wholly inappropriate to them. Cheap fossil fuel, together with a misguided sense of civic pride, or expressions of power and wealth, has enabled the inorganic structures of planning theory to persist and maintain the illusion that the creation of benign outdoor climates has little relevance to urban development.'

energy efficiency The result of minimising the use of energy by transport, through the planning of settlements, and through the way in which buildings are constructed and arranged on site.

energy recovery Recovering useful energy in the form of heat and/or electric power from waste.

enforcement DEVELOPMENT CONTROL is effective only if it is enforced. Councils take enforcement action to ensure that any unauthorised development either gets PLANNING PERMISSION, or is altered, removed or (if it is an operation rather than a building) stopped.

enforcement agent See BAILIFF.

Engels, Friedrich (1820–95) Philosopher, Manchester-based manufacturer, and chief collaborator and patron of KARL MARX. Engels' *Condition of the Working Class in England* was published in 1845.

engineer One who is engaged in a branch of ENGINEERING. In recent decades no group of people has had a greater influence on the shape of cities than HIGHWAY ENGINEERS. Other types of engineer play a major role in the practical aspects of making buildings, structures and systems work. They include civil, electrical, heating, mechanical, structural, and traffic.

William Cubitt declared in his presidential address to the Institution of Civil Engineers (ICE) in 1850: 'The engineers have always been the real sanitary reformers, as they are the originators of all onward movements. All their labours tend to the amelioration of their fellow men.' The engineer (and former chairman of the URBAN DESIGN ALLIANCE and ICE president) Mark Whitby (2001) has noted that 'a special urban design role [for engineers] dates from the nineteenth century with the need to address the problems of public health and sanitation. It required city-wide planning and gave birth to municipal engineering. It was a dimension of civil engineering that grew steadily in response to an increasing demand for highways, power and housing.' After the second world war, Whitby explains, activities became progressively more specialised. 'Transport became a principal focus for engineers. Municipal engineering became increasingly divorced from planning, and the tendency for technical officers to have both planning and engineering qualifications declined.' The late fourteenth-century word comes from the medieval Latin *ingeniator*, probably meaning one who contrives.

engineered architecture A structure, designed by architects in collaboration with engineers, of a type that would usually be considered an piece of engineering. The term was used in 2002 to describe the Gateshead Millennium Bridge, whose design won the Stirling Prize for its architects Wilkinson Eyre.

engineering The use of mathematical and scientific principles to achieve practical ends in relation to structures, systems and machines.

English Cities Fund Government funding to support the regeneration of BROWNFIELD sites on the edges of town and city centres.

English Estates An offshoot of the Development Commission, it was later taken over by ENGLISH PARTNERSHIPS.

English Heritage The government's statutory adviser on the historic environment.

English Partnerships Created in 1994 to support land reclamation, property development and 'the creation of strategic development packages for employment, housing, recreation and green space', particularly by working with local authorities. Its regional offices were incorporated into the new REGIONAL DEVELOPMENT AGENCIES in 1999.

Engwicht, David (b1950) Campaigner, planner and urban designer, describing himself as 'a professional generalist'. Since 1987 Engwicht has pioneered TRAFFIC CALMING, first in Australia and later worldwide. His local campaign CART (Citizens Against Route 20) later became CART (Citizens Advocating Responsible Transportation). In 1992 he wrote *Towards an Eco-City: calming the traffic*, which was published in the US and Canada as *Reclaiming Our Cities: better living with less traffic*. Engwicht claims to have invented the WALKING BUS and the RED SNEAKER ROUTE.

enhance See BIASED TERMINOLOGY.

enhanced building (Northern Ireland) One designed to be resistant to attack by terrorists.

enhancement Improvement.

enjoyable See CRAVED.

Enoch The first city, according to the Bible. It was built by Cain and named after his eldest son (Genesis 4:17). See also UR and URUK.

enquiry (UK) See INQUIRY.

enquiry by design A form of urban design and planning CHARRETTE or workshop in which STAKEHOLDERS in a proposed development, including local authorities, residents, developers, landowners, voluntary groups, employers and retailers, collaborate in producing a master plan through a workshop that can last up to a week. The term was introduced to the UK in 1999 by ENGLISH PARTNERSHIPS and the PRINCE'S FOUNDATION, drawing on experience from the USA and Australia.

ensanche (Spanish) A planned expansion of a town or city.

Enskede A GARDEN SUBURB of Stockholm, Sweden, begun in 1908 by Olof Hallman.

enterprise neighbourhood The UK government announced in 2002 that it would remove the obligation to pay stamp duty on property transactions in 2,000 'enterprise neighbourhoods'.

enterprise zone The power to declare enterprise zones was introduced in the Local Government, Planning and Land Act 1980 by MICHAEL HESELTINE. The aim was to encourage development by exempting industrial and commercial property from rates, simplifying planning procedures through zoning, and providing 100 per cent tax allowances for capital spending. More than 30 zones were designated, each with a 10-year life. The Isle of Dogs enterprise zone in London Docklands prompted the development of CANARY WHARF. The enterprise zone concept is sometimes traced back to the proposal in 1969 by Paul Barker, PETER HALL and Cedric Price for a *plan-free zone* (though Peter Hall has denied that this was anything like what they had in mind) and, more accurately, to a concept proposed by Peter Hall in 1977. The enterprise zone concept was copied in the USA under the Reagan administration.

entertainment management zone Designated in a development plan to enable planning, licensing, policing, transport and street management to be managed and coordinated in an area where there is an active evening economy.

Entralla The fictional central European city that is the setting for Edward Carey's 2003 novel *Alva and Irva: the twins who saved a city*. One character describes it as 'the most insignificant, piffling, little zilch of a spot, where nothing happens, where everybody speaks one of the most obscure languages in the world so that the rest of the world will not understand them'.

entry (also back entry) (Cheshire, Belfast and elsewhere) An ALLEY (see that entry for regional variants); a narrow lane between houses.

entry treatment Features such as pillars, archways, or special pavement surface or colour, signalling to drivers that they are entering a residential area. See TRAFFIC CALMING.

Entwicklung (German) Development.

envelop *v.* To encase within a building. Example: 'Incredibly, a substantial Elizabethan tower house has been discovered "enveloped" in a bakery, when the latter was about to be demolished.'

envelope *n.* **1** The physical outer layer of a building's fabric (the cladding and the roof, for example). **2** An imaginary outline of the MASSING of a proposed building (see BUILDING ENVELOPE GUIDELINES).

envelope scheme A programme directed at improving the outer fabric of an area's buildings, leaving internal improvements to be carried out independently.

enviro-crime One that inflicts damage on the environment. Examples at a local level include GRAFFITI and VANDALISM.

environics The study of ways of influencing behaviour by controlling the environment.

environment 1 The physical surroundings, including land, air and water, in which people, plants and animals live. In the language of planners and urban designers, 'the local environment' means the characteristics of a place. The environment of something usually means its surroundings. (Surroundings, being a word in commoner currency, is often a better one to use.) In the language of professionals, the environment is divided into the *built environment* and the *natural environment*. (When Nigel Taylor [1998] writes that 'the effects of town planning actions on the environment were not a major concern of planning theorists throughout the 1970s', presumably he means the natural, not the built environment). The built environment is supposed to be the concern of *built environment professionals* (such as planners, urban designers, architects and surveyors), while the natural environment is the habitat of the flora and non-human fauna. The distinction is of limited use. Cities, towns and villages can be understood fully only in the light of their land form, watercourses, green areas, ecology, plant and wildlife, climate and much else that no one has built. Similarly the natural environment turns out not to be very natural at all, but a series of complex relationships between natural processes and the human-made landscapes in which they operate. **2** In everyday language 'the environment' and 'environmental' generally refer to green issues such as energy use, biodiversity and pollution. **3** Matters relating to the quality of places. Example: 'A structure plan covers population, employment, housing, transportation as well as the "environment" (recreation, conservation)...' (1976).

The title DEPARTMENT OF THE ENVIRONMENT was convenient, though vague. Renaming it the Department of the Environment, Transport and the Regions in 1997 made a nonsense of it. The confusion deepened in 2001 when the DETR was broken up and two new departments created: the Department of Transport, Local Government and the Regions (whose responsibilities included the built environment) and the Department of the Environment, Food and Agriculture (including the natural environment).

An Environment Society was formed (with PATRICK GEDDES as secretary) in Edinburgh in 1884. In Arnold Bennett's novel *The Card*, published in 1911, Denry Machin pictures marriage as 'a perpetual afternoon tea alone with an elegant woman, amid an environment of ribboned muslin'. The word comes from the French *environner*, meaning to encircle. It was coined by Thomas Carlyle, according to Bill Bryson (1990).

Environment Agency Created in 1995 to coordinate aspects of environmental protection and enhancement in England and Wales. The agency took over the work of HM Inspectorate of Pollution, the National Rivers Authority and the local waste regulation authorities.

Environment City Leicester, as it has called itself, reflecting the various environmental programmes promoted by the city council.

environmental amenity See AMENITY.

environmental appraisal Formal assessment of the likely impact of a proposed development on the natural environment.

environmental assessment 1 (UK) A process, involving the systematic review of a proposed development, which leads to an ENVIRONMENTAL STATEMENT. Information is presented by the would-be developer in a form that provides a focus for public scrutiny and enables the development's likely effects (and the scope for modifying or mitigating them) to be evaluated before a planning decision is given. EU directives require a full assessment of the environmental impact of certain categories of major development. *Environmental impact analysis* is the equivalent US term. **2** (US) A study carried out to determine whether or not an ENVIRONMENTAL IMPACT STATEMENT is needed.

environmental assessment audit Carried out to check that an ENVIRONMENTAL ASSESSMENT that has been carried out by a developer is accurate.

environmental capital 1 An area's environmental assets. **2** The name of a method of assessing the impact of a proposed development and identifying the conditions under which the impact would be environmentally neutral or beneficial. The approach focuses on the benefits, rather than on the things that produce the benefits. The method was developed in the 1990s. Compare SOCIAL CAPITAL.

environmental conditioning The shaping of people's behaviour by the physical and social surroundings.

environmental determinism The belief that the environment influences behaviour, and hence that undesirable behaviour can be prevented by changing the environment. See also ARCHITECTURAL DETERMINISM and NON-PLACE URBAN REALM.

environmental education Urban environmental education was defined by the DEPARTMENT OF THE ENVIRONMENT in 1979 as helping people 'perceive, understand, analyse and finally improve their built environment. It should be centrally concerned with aiding people to participate more effectively in shaping their local environment.' Twenty years later the phrase had been largely replaced by EDUCATION FOR SUSTAINABLE DEVELOPMENT. See also ARCHITECTURE AND PLANNING CENTRE, ARCHITECTURE WORKSHOP, URBAN STUDIES CENTRE and COLIN WARD.

environmental fit The relationship of a development to its setting.

environmental geography The study of the surroundings in which people, plants and animals live, and how they interact.

environmental graphic design (US) Defined by the SEGD (formerly the Society for Environmental Graphic Design) as the design of graphic elements in the environment, involving graphic design, interior design, architecture, landscape architecture and industrial design.

environmental health officer A local authority official concerned with the effect on public health of environmental hazards such as pollution, noise and low standards of hygiene.

environmental homogenisation The process by which places become increasingly like one another.

environmental impact assessment A technique for identifying the environmental effects of development projects. The EU requires an EIA for certain public and private projects.

environmental impact statement The US equivalent of ENVIRONMENTAL STATEMENT in the EU. Environmental impact statements have been required in the USA for all significant development projects since 1969 (Kostof, 1991).

environmental integrity The phrase is sometimes used as an alternative for environmental sustainability.

environmental justice Defined by the Sustainable Development Commission in 2002 as 'equal access to a clean environment and equal protection from possible environmental harm irrespective of race, income or class or any other differentiating feature of socio-economic status'. The commission notes that the term, 'coined in America, has traditionally been confined to the disproportionate impact of pollution sources on poorer communities. However, the term is now being widened to include less tangible aspects of quality of life including community confidence, cohesion and safety, civic pride, empowerment and environmental education.'

environmental noise Defined by the European Environmental Noise Directive as 'unwanted or harmful outdoor sound created by human activities, including noise emitted by means of transport, road traffic, rail traffic, air traffic and from sites of industrial activity'.

environmental planning 1 Planning the built and natural environment. **2** Planning the natural environment.

environmental statement A document (one output of an ENVIRONMENTAL ASSESSMENT) submitted with a planning application that is likely to have particularly significant environmental effects. It sets out an assessment of a project's likely environmental effects and shows how harmful effects can be mitigated. The US term *environmental impact statement* is sometimes also used in the UK.

environmental technocentrism Trusting in the potential for technical solutions to be found to environmental problems. See CORNUCOPIAN and compare ECOCENTRISM.

environmentalism An active concern for the impact of environmental change, particularly in relation to issues such as countryside protection, GLOBAL WARMING, BIODIVERSITY and the depletion of natural resources; a concern for the effect of people on places (Brown, 2000). Compare EUTHENICS.

environmentalist One who has an active concern for the impact of environmental change. In the context of the debate on compact or dispersed cities, Michael Breheny (2001) defines environmentalists loosely as 'protagonists of the compaction approach – who want to reduce house-building, protect the countryside, and intensify use of existing cities and towns'.

environmentally enhanced vehicle One that is relatively quiet and low in emissions.

environmentally sensitive area An area designated for its high landscape, wildlife and historic value, and which is threatened by agricultural practices. Financial incentives are offered to farmers to adopt agricultural practices which safeguard and enhance the rural environment and improve public access.

envision To envisage; to conceive a VISION of. Envision, generally a US term, has recently been used in the UK to describe the processes of drawing up visions that will become the basis of a plan (and it is used in other contexts as well). Envisage was an import into English from French near the beginning of the nineteenth century. Envision became current in around 1920 (Quinion, 2001).

eopolis A village (Mumford, 1961).

eotechnic The period of human history when people lived off the earth's renewable resources. LEWIS MUMFORD coined the term to describe the 'dawn age of modern technics' which, he argued, came before the PALEOTECHNIC and NEOTECHNIC ages described by PATRICK GEDDES. The eotechnic age saw the development of wood and water technology.

Epcot A futuristic theme park. WALT DISNEY originally intended it as an 'experimental prototype community of tomorrow', with 20,000 residents and a strict dress code, and without retired people, home ownership, pets, drunkenness or cohabitation. It opened, without the residents, in 1982 as part of DisneyWorld. See also FUTURE WORLD and DRESS SENSE.

eperopolis Defined by EKISTICS as a settlement with a population of 7,500 million. A *small polis* has 1,000 million.

ephemeralization The fate of architecture in the invisible global city, according to Martin Pawley (1998), is to 'ephemeralize'. 'Like DISPERSAL, ephemeralization is a resultant force. It is the end product of a process of species selection brought about by an environment that is more and more informationalized. Urban dispersal multiplied by information technology means TERMINAL ARCHITECTURE.'

episode A section of a street (experienced over a short period of time as the observer moves along the street).

e-planning Providing planning services electronically, for example by making it possible to apply for planning permission and submit a planning appeal online.

Equilibrium A film, directed by Kurt Wimmer and released in 2003, set in the totalitarian, walled state of Libria, a superpower born in the aftermath of a nuclear war. The architecture is bare and austere, and all forms of art have been prohibited, though a rebel group has preserved some works of art underground. The film was shot in Berlin, where Wimmer found a suitable range of uncompromising settings, provided by buildings ranging from those of the Nazis to examples of modernism.

equilibrium model A description of the development process in terms of relationships between aspects of demand such as rents and yields. Compare EVENT-SEQUENCE MODEL and STRUCTURE MODEL.

equity 1 Fairness in access to resources; impartiality. **2** Money and resources provided by those who share in a property development's risk and profit. **3** A capital stake in a property.

equity participation An arrangement by which the lender financing a property development takes a share in the increase in the property's value in exchange for charging a lower rate of interest.

equity planner (US) The term was coined by Norman Krumholz and Pierre Clavel in 1994 to describe 'professional urban planners who, in their day-to-day practice, have tried to move resources, political power and political participation away from the business elites

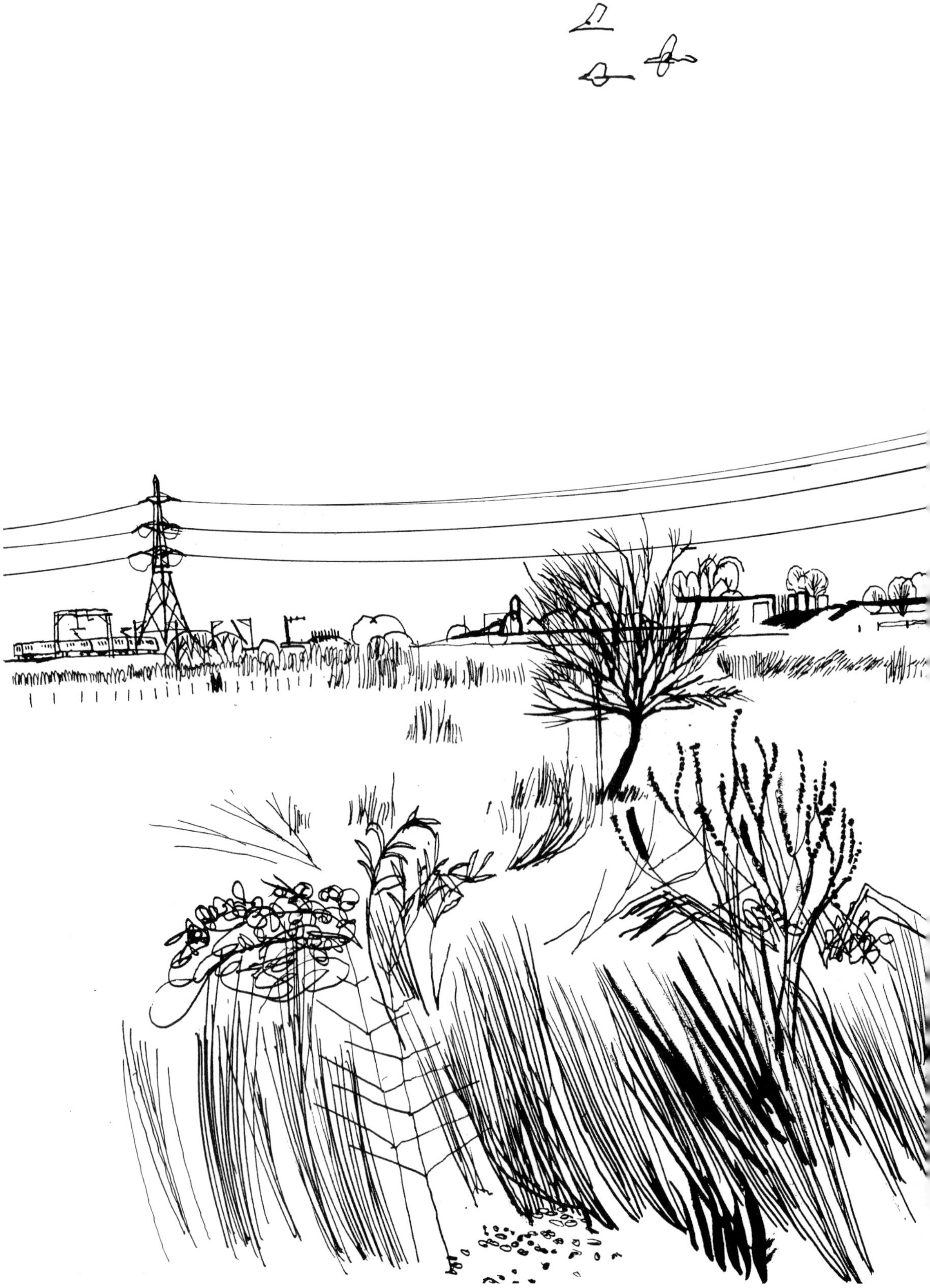

edgelands

that frequently benefit from public policy and toward the needs of low income or working-class people of their cities' (quoted in Cullingworth, 1997). In short, they seek to achieve greater equity.

equity security Shares of company stock representing non-contractual claims on the company's residual cashflow.

equity-sharing arrangement A means of sharing the financial interest in a property development.

erf (Dutch) **1** A small, highly traffic-calmed, area. Shortened from WOONERF to describe a zone that is not solely residential. **2** A yard.

Erhaltungssatzung (German) A preservation statute.

Ersilia A city whose inhabitants rebuild it in successive different locations. The relationships between the people are represented by strings stretched between the houses. When there are too many strings for the streets to be passable, the people dismantle the city and rebuild it somewhere else. The strings and their supports alone remain as a reminder of the relationships that once made the city live. Italo Calvino describes Ersilia in INVISIBLE CITIES (1972).

eruv A zone in which orthodox Jews are permitted to carry out tasks normally forbidden in public places on the Sabbath, such as carrying keys or pushing a wheelchair. The UK's first ever eruv was created in north London in 2003, after planning permission was granted for the series of metal poles (wooden where they cross Hampstead Heath) with thin transparent wire that mark the boundary of the 10 square kilometre zone.

escalator 1 A moving staircase. **2** The process by which young people move to an inner urban area, move out to the suburbs as they become older and better off, and are replaced by more young people.

Escape from New York A film, directed by John Carpenter, released in 1981 and starring Kurt Russell, set in a derelict Manhattan of the near future (1997) controlled by a criminal underclass. See also ASSAULT ON PRECINCT 13.

esplanade A level open area for walking on. From the Latin for 'make level'.

ESPON European Spatial Planning Observatory Network.

ESPRID European Spatial Planning Research and Information Database.

essay in civilisation, an The aspiration of LORD REITH for the post-war new town's programme, for which he was responsible.

essential workers Those who provide essential services in urban areas but may have difficulty in finding affordable places to live with convenient reach of their work. Nurses, firefighters, catering staff and even planners are among those who have been cited as examples. Some housing policies discriminate in favour of essential workers. See also PREFAB.

Essex Design Guide Published in 1973 by Essex County Council, the *Essex Design Guide for Residential Areas* encouraged housing developers to think more about the streets and places they were making, and to respond to the local VERNACULAR. With any design guidance there is a danger of some developers following it mindlessly. In the absence of similar guidance for other places, developers throughout the country could be found offering planners development proposals faithfully reflecting the Essex vernacular. The guide was updated in 1998. Recognising that designing solely residential areas was itself often not good practice, it became the *Essex Design Guide for Residential and Mixed-use Development*. See also SOUTH WOODHAM FERRERS.

estate 1 A large area of development (for example, HOUSING ESTATE, *industrial estate*); an ENCLAVE, disconnected from the continuous urban fabric, where few people go who do not have specific business there. See also PARK and RESERVATION. **2** All the land owned by a particular landowner (for example, *the Grosvenor Estate, the Crown Estate*). **3** An area of properties under a common ownership.

Muthesius (1982) notes of the historic, privately owned estates in English towns: 'the leading "estates" in the country were often the most important developers of "estates" of houses in the towns. The use of the same word in both contexts is significant and seems peculiar to the English set-up'.

estate agent (UK) A person engaged in valuing, leasing and selling property. The term was established by 1900 (Muthesius, 1982). The US term is *realtor*. Opinion polls show estate agents to be held at a similarly low level of public esteem as politicians and tabloid journalists.

estate agreement (also estate contract) See NEIGHBOURHOOD AGREEMENT.

estate culture Research published by the Joseph Rowntree Foundation (2000) identified an *estate culture* on certain social housing estates. Its features include tolerating crime, drugs and anti-social behaviour; accepting low personal achievement and educational attainment; low aspirations and expectations; different norms from mainstream society; and strong pressure from peers to conform to those norms.

estate management board A tenant-run organisation responsible for the management of a SOCIAL HOUSING estate.

estate village Built mainly to house the workers on the estate of a large landlord.

estoppel A rule of evidence or other legal obstruction to a person contradicting something he or she has already established by word or deed. It relates particularly to the purchase of rights.

Eternal City, the Rome.

ethnic Relating to nations, races and culturally distinct groups. The word derives from the Greek for *nation*.

ethnic community without propinquity An ethnic group maintaining its identity and institutions even though its members have dispersed.

ethnic minority A culturally distinct group of people comprising less than half of the population of a place.

ethnic village An area within a city occupied by a particular ethnic group,

ethnicity The culture and way of living of a particular ethnic group.

ethnography The study of culture, particularly of minority ethnic groups.

ethnoscape The urban landscape created by a particular ethnic group or groups. This sense of the term seems to have been adapted from anthropology. The anthropologist Arjun Appadurai (1991) defines an ethnoscape as 'the landscape of persons who make up the shifting world in which we live: tourists, immigrants, refugees, exiles, guestworkers and other moving groups and persons [who] constitute an essential feature of the world and appear to affect the politics of and between nations to a hitherto unprecedented degree.'

E-topia The title of a book, published in 1999, in which William Mitchell predicts the 'soft transformation' of the environment brought about by the new computer age. Mitchell identifies a set of principles for more effective cities: a) Dematerialise (a lot of physical construction will no longer be needed). b) Demobilise (reduced need to travel with consequent savings in fuel consumption and pollution). c) Mass customisation (automatic delivery to precise individual specification and requirement). d) Intelligent operation (minimising waste of energy and resources). See also CITY OF BITS.

Etruria Model housing at Stoke-on-Trent built by the pottery manufacturer Josiah Wedgwood in 1769–70.

Etzioni, Amitai (b1929) American sociologist and advocate of COMMUNITARIANISM.

Euclid The New York village gave its name to the Euclid case, in which the Supreme Court approved the concept of comprehensive ZONING in 1926 (Cullingworth, 1997).

Euclidian zoning (US) Makes MIXED USES illegal. See EUCLID.

euergetism Providing civic amenities and subsidies to urban residents regardless of need (Clark, 2000); private liberality for public benefit (Veyne, 1990). Thomas Kraebel (2002) writes that euergetism is 'a new idea in classical studies', being included in the authoritative *Oxford Classical Dictionary* only in its most recent, third edition. He notes that 'in the ancient world status depended to a large extent on the sums of money one was able to spend for the benefit of the entire urban community, normally in the form of building projects'. Ray Laurence (1999) writes that 'local elites were involved in [euergetism] not simply for display to their own city, but also to those who visited it'.

eugenics The study of methods of selective breeding in the belief that it is possible and desirable to 'improve' the genetic qualities of humans. Eugenics was advocated by some urban reformers at the end of the nineteenth century and named in 1883 by its founder, Francis Galton. Enthusiasts in the twentieth century included the birth control pioneer Marie Stopes and the novelist Aldous Huxley (despite his terrifying portrayal of state-organised eugenics in *Brave New World*). Opponents of eugenics included leaders of the labour movement (to whom slum clearance seemed a preferable means of dispersing the breeding grounds of new generations of people without hope) and the Roman Catholic Church. Eugenics was practised in Campanella's imaginary CITY OF THE SUN (1602–23).

euphemism A term by which something offensive or unattractive is made to sound pleasant. See LANDSCAPED GARDENS, TOWN SQUARE, PARKWAY, URBAN VILLAGE and VILLAGE.

Euphonia A fictional city in Germany's Harz Mountains wholly devoted to music, described by Hector Berlioz in *Euphonie, or the Musical City* (1852). Each street is reserved for people who play a particular instrument or sing in a certain manner, and is named accordingly. Visitors to Euphonia are welcome only if highly qualified musically.

eu-politogenics One of PATRICK GEDDES' terms (the other was plain *politogenics*) for the science of good cities.

Euralille The transport hub around the TGV station

> **"EURALILLE LOOKS AND FEELS AS IF A LUNAR RESEARCH STATION HAS CRASH-LANDED ON TO A SMALL, RESPECTABLE FRENCH MARKET TOWN. THIS IS MEANT AS A COMPLIMENT"**
>
> *New York Times*

in the northern French town of Lille, masterplanned by the architect Rem Koolhaas. The *New York Times* (11 September 1994) commented: 'Euralille looks and feels as if a lunar research station has crash-landed on to a small, respectable French market town. This is meant as a compliment.'

eurometropolis A city region of European significance. Also *eurometropolitan*. The French city of Lille, for example, claims this status for itself.

European Capital of Culture A title awarded annually by the EU to a city (not necessarily a national capital) bidding to hold a year-long programme of events. In the UK a city on the shortlist is awarded the status of *Centre of Culture.*

European Regional Development Fund Support from the EU for economic development through industrial diversification.

European Social Fund Support from the EU for economic and social development.

European Spatial Development Perspective A non-statutory document produced by the Informal Council of Ministers, setting out principles for the spatial development of the EU.

European structural funds These funds from the EU include the European Social Fund, the European Regional Development Fund and other funds supporting community initiatives.

Euston Arch The entrance arch to London's Euston Station was built in 1836–9 to a design by Philip Hardwick in Greek classical style. The arch was demolished in 1961 after an unsuccessful campaign by conservationists to allow for, allegedly, extending the length of platforms as part of the rebuilding of Euston Station. The extra platform lengths never materialised, making the demolition unnecessary (except, perhaps, as a propaganda exercise to demonstrate that the railways were not a clapped-out

> **"CONCERN FOR SUCH RELICS WILL SAP NATIONAL VITALITY"**
>
> *Harold Macmillan*

piece of Victoriana but part of the go-ahead, hi-tech modern age). Prime minister Harold Macmillan is said to have felt that 'concern for such relics would sap national vitality'. This unnecessary act of official vandalism gave momentum to the conservation movement. 'For the first time,' comments Deyan Sudjic, 'nineteenth-century architecture – previously seen as no more than frivolous eclecticism – was treated as an artistic achievement of the first rank.' Some of the stone became a terrace in the Bromley garden of the demolition contractor. Another 4,000 tons was used by British Waterways to fill a huge hole that appeared in a riverbed in East London. Architectural historian Dan Cruickshank (1994) has written hopefully that 'judging by the amount of the arch that has already been discovered in good condition, reconstruction of this great monument to the railway age appears to be technically possible'. Similar arches were constructed to mark the terminus of the line first at Birmingham and, subsequently, at Holyhead. The Holyhead arch remains.

euthenics 1 The study of the effects of place on people (Brown, 2000). **2** Improving people's surroundings to enable them to thrive. The word, coined around 1900–5, derives from the Greek word meaning to prosper. Compare ENVIRONMENTALISM.

euthenist One who practices euthenics.

eutopia A good place; an achievable ideal city; the opposite of KAKATOPIA. PATRICK GEDDES (1915) used the term. Compare UTOPIA.

Eutopitecture PATRICK GEDDES used the term, probably meaning the structure and design of utopias, in a letter to LEWIS MUMFORD in 1923 (Novak, 1995).

evaluation 1 Retrospective analysis of a project, programme or policy to assess how successful it has been, and what lessons can be learnt. **2** A process that seeks to order preferences (Hall, 2002).

Evangelistic Bureaucrat, The A book by Jon Gower Davies, published in 1972, describing how politicians, planners and housing managers in Newcastle wrecked large swathes of the city and destroyed local communities in pursuit of the holy grail of 'urban renewal'.

Event-Cities A book by the architect Bernard Tschumi, published in 1994, exploring ways in which architecture can contribute to shaping cities.

Bernard Tschumi

eventrement (French) Evisceration. BARON HAUSSMANN's term for the demolition he practiced in Paris (Kostof, 1991).

event-sequence model A description of the development process in terms of the relationships between the people involved. Compare EQUILIBRIUM MODEL, EVENT-SEQUENCE MODEL and STRUCTURE MODEL.

everyday space Public space where people live and work.

everyday urbanism Described in a book of that name (edited by John Chase, Margaret Crawford and John Kaliski, published in 1999) as 'small, temporary, unintentional, nondescript, though often frequented spaces, next to unified, expensive, permanent, and grand public developments that resemble ghost towns'. The authors celebrate 'the lived realities of the city... from inner-city neighborhoods to street-corner miniparks, idiosyncratic garden environments to middle-class trash alleys, vacant lots to sidewalks and front yards, temporary street performers to an auto-body repair lot that transforms into a drive-in restaurant during dinner hours'.

Doug Kelbaugh (2000) describes these authors' advocacy of everyday urbanism as 'non-utopian or atopian, conversational, and nonstructuralist. It is non-utopian because it celebrates and builds on everyday, ordinary life and reality, with little pretence about the possibility of a perfectible, tidy or ideal built environment... Its openness to populist informality that makes everyday urbanism conversational. It is non-structuralist because it downplays the direct relationship between physical design and social behavior. It, for instance, delights in the way indigenous and migrant groups informally respond in resourceful and imaginative ways to ad hoc conditions and marginal spaces. Appropriating space for commerce in parking and vacant lots, as well as private driveways and yards for garage sales can be more urban design by default than by intention. Form and function are seen to be structurally connected in a very loose way that highlights culture more than design as a determinant of behavior. Vernacular and street architecture in vibrant, ethnic neighborhoods are held up as one instructive model or, at least, a point of departure.'

Everytown A fictional city whose centre is destroyed by bombs in the 1936 film *Things To Come*, directed by ALEXANDER KORDA.

evolution The conservationist Tamás Fejérdy has expressed his reservations about the universal use of the word 'development' in the context of urban sites. To Fejérdy, Dennis Rodwell (2002) notes, development suggests something forced. Fejérdy considers evolution to be a more appropriate word to use in many instances, whether geographic or socio-economic: conservation and development need to be harmonised, not placed in conflict.

exaction (US) DEVELOPMENT CHARGE.

examination in public A more informal alternative to a PUBLIC INQUIRY, used for structure and regional plans.

Excellence Challenge Government funding to help young people who would not otherwise be able to take part in higher education.

Excellence in Cities Programme (England) A government programme to raise standards in city schools.

excess condemnation (US) Compulsorily purchasing not only the land needed for a particular development but also additional land nearby that will later be sold at a profit due to the increase in value resulting from the area's improvement.

exchange Exchanging things (goods, information, money, favours, gossip, ideas and anything else) is a prime function of a town or city. Many cities developed specialised exchanges, housed in purpose-built buildings like Manchester's Cotton Exchange and Cardiff's Coal Exchange.

exchange value Market value, as distinct from a value in use as a commodity (*use value*).

exchequer cost One that falls or will ultimately fall on taxpayers.

exchequer revenue That which will reduce claims on taxpayers.

exclusive An estate agents' euphemism for *expensive* (that is, excluding people who can not afford to pay). See also LUXURY, MARKETING and PRESTIGIOUS.

executive housing Detached housing built at low densities and offering (or pretending to offer) the sort of lifestyle to which a business executive might be expected to aspire.

existence value The value people ascribe to something they want to continue to exist, despite rarely or never seeing or making use of it. Examples might include wilderness, biodiversity, the village shop or pub, and rural bus services.

existentialism See MATERIALITY.

exit strategy Arrangements intended to ensure that the work or regeneration programme, initiative or agency is not undone when it ceases to exist. Also called a *forward strategy*.

exopolis The inside-out city or city region, with traditionally downtown functions carried out at EDGE CITIES; literally 'the city without'. The term is used by the theorist ED SOJA.

expanded town A town with a major expansion programme carried out under the Town Development Act 1952. The largest were Andover, Basingstoke and Swindon.

Expanding Environment, The A book by EA Gutkind, published in 1953. See POST-URBANISM.

expansion See BIASED TERMINOLOGY.

experiential envirotect One who choreographs people's use of the environment. The term was used by Phillip Thiel (1961).

experiential envirotecture A design process, devised by Phillip Thiel, which uses the language of theatrical design, stage craft, dance notation and TV script writing to shape the urban experience (Jarvis, 2001). See also CHOREOGRAPHY.

expert system A model or simulation of decision-making processes which is intended to draw conclusions from data in the way that an objective professional might.

expert witness A person who appears at a public inquiry to give a professional view in support of one side of the case or the other. See also PLANNING CONSULTANT.

Expiation City An imaginary Christian city where people go to atone for their sins. PS Ballanches describes it in *Expiation City* (1907).

exploration licence A licence, issued by the government, that permits a geophysical survey to be carried out in an area where the geology suggests that oil or gas may be present.

express consent Planning permission expressly given (in the case of various advertisements, notices and signs), as opposed to being deemed to have been given through the local authority's not making any objection. The phrase has nothing to do with speed.

expression The way in which a building reveals its use, its structure or the intentions of its designer(s).

extended family A social grouping, consisting of spouses, parents, children and other people related by descent, marriage or adoption, that is wider than a nuclear family.

extended suburbanisation The growth of relatively low density development in towns or villages to house commuters to or former residents of a nearby urban centre.

External City, the Rome.

Externality 1 A benefit that is a secondary consideration. **2** A cost that is imposed on someone else or the environment (pollution, for example) which does not therefore feature on the internal balance sheet.

extra-mural *adj.* Outside the walls (of a town or city). The opposite of *intra-mural*.

extrovert buildings Those which look out on to the street (shops, for example).

exurb The outer reaches of a city, beyond traditional suburbs. Example: 'Letchworth established a dubious template for what is now termed exurb. Low-density, low-rise, land-hungry developments are a problem, not a solution' (Meades, 2003).

exurbanisation The process of people moving out of cities, often to commuter villages.

exurbia A suburb that has developed a degree of independence from the city. The writer AC Spectorsky coined the term in 1955. Three decades later the same phenomenon, on a larger scale, was being described as EDGE CITY and X-URBIA.

eyes on the street People whose presence in adjacent buildings or on the street make it feel safer. Jane Jacobs (1961) writes: 'the sidewalk must have users on it fairly continuously... to add to the number of effective eyes on the street'. See NATURAL SURVEILLANCE.

F

Fabianism An English movement promoting gradual social and political change. Founded in 1884, the Fabian Society was influential in promoting MUNICIPAL SOCIALISM. It was named after the Roman general Quintus Fabius Maximus Verrucosus Cunctator (died 203 BC) whose motto was 'slow but sure'.

Fable of the Bees A utopian story by Bernard de Mandeville, published in 1714.

fabric The physical material of a place.

façade The principal face of a building. The architect William Lethaby put the case for the design of a building's public face to be an issue of legitimate public concern. 'The faces of buildings which are turned outwards towards the world are obviously of interest to the public, and all citizens have a property in them. The spectator is in fact part owner. No man builds to himself alone. Let the proprietor do as he likes inside his building, for we need not call on him. Bad plays need not be seen, books need not be read, but nothing but blindness or the numbing of our faculty of observation can protect us from buildings in the street' (quoted in Worpole, 2000).

façadism A generally pejorative term for one of three approaches to development: a) Retaining a façade and building new behind it. English Heritage notes that the impact will depend on whether replacing the body of the building destroys valuable roofscapes, back elevations or side views, and whether one or more historic buildings are left to front a single large, new structure behind. b) Rebuilding a façade, in the original or new materials, and in the original form or STRETCHED (or otherwise altered) to fit the needs of the new building behind it. c) Building a façade that bears little relationship with the new building behind it, in order to fit in with the existing streetscape. Such a façade will often be intended to match the style of neighbouring buildings or to be in some supposedly historic or NEO-VERNACULAR style. See AUTHENTICITY and RICHMOND RIVERSIDE.

facilitator A person who designs, organises and runs meetings and participatory events.

facilities benefit assessment (US) An impact fee levied on new development.

facilities management Managing buildings, structures and their systems.

factory camp A term used by Robert Goodman (1972) to describe the nineteenth-century city.

factory shop Defined by the Scottish Office (1998) as a shop adjacent to a production unit, specialising in the sale of manufacturers' products direct to the public.

factory-outlet centre Defined by the Scottish Office (1998) as a group of shops, usually in out-of-centre locations, specialising in selling seconds and end-of-line goods at discounted prices.

faience Glazed TERRACOTTA.

fair trade town One that is committed to fair trade initiatives, aimed at building trade networks with disadvantaged producers in developing countries, promoting better trading conditions and raising awareness. Residents voted Garstang in the borough of Wyre as a fair trade town in 2000, claiming it as the world's first.

Faith in the City A report by the Church of England, published in 1985, championing poor and deprived inner-city communities and criticising some of the Conservative government's policies. Prime minister Thatcher was furious at what she saw as evidence of the church's incorrigible left-wing bias. It was followed in 1990 by LIVING FAITH IN THE CITY.

> **"BAD PLAYS NEED NOT BE SEEN, BOOKS NEED NOT BE READ, BUT NOTHING BUT BLINDNESS OR THE NUMBING OF OUR FACULTY OF OBSERVATION CAN PROTECT US FROM BUILDINGS IN THE STREET"**
>
> *William Lethaby*

Faludi, Andreas Planning theorist. Nigel Taylor (1998) describes him as 'the leading theorist of rational planning in Britain in the early 1970s'.

Family and Kinship in East London The classic study by sociologists MICHAEL YOUNG and PETER WILLMOTT (1957) of life in an old working-class community in Bethnal Green, east London, and one of the new housing estates in Essex to which its people were being rehoused. In Bethnal Green the authors found remarkably close ties between mothers and daughters. Their research persuaded them to 'expect the stressing of the mother-daughter tie to be a widespread, perhaps universal, phenomenon in the urban areas of all industrial countries, at any rate in the families of manual workers.' For Bethnal Green families these ties provided a support network without which 'the wives are left without the help of grandmothers, the old without the comfort of children and grandchildren'. Young and Willmott pointed to the social cost of disrupting these networks. 'The question for the authorities,' they wrote, 'is whether they should do more than they are at present doing to meet the preference of people who would not willingly forgo these advantages, rather than insisting that more thousands should migrate beyond the city. To supply good houses for families with young children as well as flats for others is not a simple operation in a congested town; we do not pretend that it is. It would mean sacrificing some of the many projected open spaces, earmarked in the plans for future public gardens and parks, for the only reason which could justify so grave a step, that on balance people would much rather have houses than spaces. It would mean putting some factories rather than residences in high flatted buildings. It might mean gradually moving out to the country some of the vast railway yards, the unwelcome inheritance of another transport age, which at present sprawl smokily across the face of the city – and using the sites for houses instead. It would certainly mean saving as many as possible of the existing houses, where these are structurally sound, by installing within the old fabric new bathrooms, lavatories, and kitchens.' Young and Willmott conceded that the problems were formidable. 'But if the purpose of rehousing is to meet human needs, not as they are judged by others but as people themselves assess their own, it is doubtful whether anything short of such a programme will suffice. Not everyone could, under this or any other plan, hope to stay where he is. People will have to move about within their own district, if not outside it, as the slums beyond salvage are cleared and replaced. But re-shuffling the residents could be accomplished by moving as a block the social groups, above all the wider families, to which people wish to belong. Movement of street and kinship groupings as a whole, members being transferred together to a new setting, would enable the city to be rebuilt without squandering the fruits of social cohesion.' Compare WILFRED BURNS.

FAR (US) Floor area ratio: the developable floor area as a multiple of the site area.

Farley, Paul (b1965) Poet. See SO GOOD THEY NAMED IT TWICE.

farmers' market An informal urban outlet for farm produce. Peter Hall wrote in 2002 that 'farmers' markets appear to be the key to any serious regeneration exercise', though when he and Colin Ward had written about them in 1998 'no one had heard of them'.

Farrell, Terry (Sir) (b1938) Urban designer and architect. He set up the practice of Farrell Grimshaw with Nicholas Grimshaw in 1965, designing in a high-tech modernist style. After setting up Terry Farrell and Partners in 1980, he made a name for himself as the leading British POSTMODERNIST architect. His taste for monumentalism had its jokey beginnings in the giant egg-cups on the façade of his building for the breakfast television company TVam. At the end of the 1980s the practice (by then disavowing the title 'postmodernist') designed major London buildings, including Embankment Place above Charing Cross Station and the government intelligence headquarters at Vauxhall Cross. In the 1990s Farrell won a string of large commissions abroad, many in the Far East. With a passion for building in the context of a city, he has been a leader of the urban design movement in the UK since the 1970s.

fascism See ALBERT SPEER, STRIPPED CLASSICISM, NAZI ARCHITECTURE and HANS BERNHARD REICHOW.

father of city planning See EDWARD W BASSETT.

Fathy, Hassan (1900–89) Egyptian architect. One of the outstanding architects of his generation in Africa, he sought to show that it was possible to build for the poor and taught people to build for themselves. His book *Architecture for the Poor*, published in 1973, describes his experience in planning and building a village using mud bricks and employing traditional Egyptian architectural features, such as enclosed courtyards and domed and vaulted roofing. He worked closely with the people to tailor his designs to their needs. Fathy received the RIGHT LIVELIHOOD AWARD in 1980. 'How do we go from the architect/constructor system to the architect-owner/builder system?' he asked. 'One man can not build a house, but ten men can build ten houses very easily, even a hundred houses. We need a system that allows the traditional way of cooperation to work in our society. We must subject technology and science to the economy of the poor and penniless. We must add the aesthetic factor because the cheaper we build the more beauty we should add to respect man.' See also JOHN TURNER and COLIN WARD.

fattest city Houston, Texas, was named by *Men's Fitness* magazine in 2002 for the third year running as America's fattest city. Its citizens' exceptional weight

façadism

was ascribed to the city's humid climate, poor air quality and lack of outdoor recreation, and their love of junk food. Second and third places were taken by Chicago and Detroit.

fatto urbano See URBAN ARTIFACT.

faubourg (French) Suburb. See also BANLIEUE.

fauna The animals of a particular place. Fauna was a Roman god who protected shepherds. Compare FLORA.

favela See SQUATTER SETTLEMENT.

fear See ANTI-URBANISM.

fear generator A place (such as abandoned building) that becomes the focus for ANTI-SOCIAL BEHAVIOUR. The term is used in discussions of CRIME PREVENTION.

feasibility The appropriateness of development in relation to economic and market conditions.

federal empowerment zone (US) Focuses private, non-profit and public initiatives within a designated area of economic decline.

Federal Housing Administration Supporting bank lending on new private housing in the years after 1934, the FHA insisted on particular street layouts and construction standards. See also SEWARD MOTT.

fee simple estate Complete ownership of a property.

feel James Howard Kunstler (2001) writes that 'whenever the word *feel* is used in real estate development propaganda, it should be understood that the place will be a cartoon of the thing it is purported to feel like'.

felicific calculus An assessment of the likely balance of costs and benefits of a development proposal in terms of human happiness.

fenestration The arrangement of windows on a façade.

feng shui (pronounced – by some – fong shway) The ancient Chinese art of placement. The architect Norman Foster consulted a feng shui adviser in designing the Hong Kong and Shanghai Bank in Hong Kong, and

> **"FENG IS CORRECTLY TRANSLATED AS 'SENSE' AND SHUI MEANS 'MORE MONEY THAN'"**
>
> Victor Lewis-Smith

the art became fashionable in the UK in the 1990s. The eighteenth-century term means wind-water. The belief is that wind and water shaped the natural landscape, which in turn influences the universal spiritual breath. Feng shui is thought to be a means of ensuring that any change to the form of our surroundings will affect that breath for good rather than ill. The London *Evening Standard* columnist Victor Lewis-Smith has suggested that *feng* is correctly translated as 'sense' and *shui* means 'more money than'.

Ferriss, Hugh (1889–1962) Architectural illustrator. His dramatic, imaginative drawings of how the massing of skyscrapers could be arranged under New York's 1920 zoning regulations influenced what was built.

festival marketplace A shopping centre with public space, small shops, stalls and cafes, designed as a venue for leisure as well as shopping. US developer James Rouse (with architect Benjamin Thompson and mayor Kevin White) pioneered them in 1976 in creating one from Boston's historic Faneuil Hall. The transformation of London's Covent Garden market is another successful example.

festivalisation A pejorative term for introducing tourist and leisure attractions to an area. Example: 'They were accused of actively promoting the festivalisation of the South Bank so as to cash in on London's flourishing tourist and leisure business across the river.'

fever den An area of housing so bad and overcrowded as to harbour high levels of disease. The term was current in the nineteenth century.

fibua (UK) A military acronym for *fighting in built-up areas*. The US equivalent is *mout* (military operations in urban terrain). See also BREAK THE CHINA and MOUSEHOLE.

Fichter, Robert See JOHN TURNER.

field of wheat (Cockney rhyming slang) A street.

field pattern The way in which a landscape is divided by hedges and walls.

fieldwork The study of an area (urban or rural) at first hand. See also STREETWORK.

figure/ground (or figure and ground, or NOLLI) diagram 1 A plan showing the relationship between built form and publicly accessible space (including streets and the interiors of public buildings such as churches) by presenting the former in black and the latter as a white background, or the other way round. Katherine Shonfield (1998) writes: 'The great strength of this method of describing space is that it throws into full relief both the spaces themselves and the network of interconnections of these public places, and shows you precisely where such interconnection is aborted or cut off.' **2** A diagram distinguishing developed from undeveloped land. The term derives from the analogy of the composition of a picture, in which a figure or figures are set against a background. In urban design the space can be considered the figure, against the ground of the buildings, or the other way round.

figured city One that is planned, and is occupied by affluent people.

film See AMERICAN BEAUTY, ASSAULT ON PRECINCT 13, BEDFORD FALLS, BERLIN EXPRESS, BRIGADOON, CITY BY THE SEA, CITY OF GOD, CITY OF LOST SOULS, CLOCKWORK ORANGE CHIC, DISNEYLAND, EARTHQUAKE, EQUILIBRIUM, ESCAPE FROM NEW YORK, EVERYTOWN, FOG, THE FOUNTAINHEAD, THE FUGITIVE FUTURIST, GANGS OF

NEW YORK, GET CARTER, GRIDLOCK, HIGH TREASON, INDEPENDENCE DAY, ALBERT KAHN, KENSINGTON GORE, LONDON, MAIDENHEAD TOWN HALL, METROPOLIS, MULTIPLEX, NEW MOSCOW, NIGHT AND THE CITY, ROAD WARRIOR, EMIL AND MAX SKLADANOWSKY, STALK, STEPFORD WIVES, STEELTOWN, THAMESMEAD, THINGS TO COME, TOKYO FIST, UNREAL CITY, URBAN DESTRUCTION, JEAN VIGO and ZABRISKIE POINT.

filtering The process by which affluent people move from older to newer housing, usually further out of town or city, to be replaced by poorer people. The process was described by Homer Hoyt.

filtering up The supposed process by which it has at times been assumed that building homes, at whatever level of the market, will benefit people in the poorest housing. Compare TRICKLE-DOWN EFFECT.

finance lease A scale-and-leaseback arrangement made with a financial institution.

financial institution An insurance company or pension fund.

finding of no significant impact (FONSI) (US) One of the possible conclusions of an ENVIRONMENTAL ASSESSMENT.

fine grain The quality of an area's LAYOUT of building BLOCKS and plots having small and frequent subdivisions. Compare COARSE GRAIN.

fine mesh See MESH.

fine particles The technical term for invisible microscopic dust particles, measuring less than one millionth of a metre, which can be breathed deep into the lungs. Diesel engines are believed to be the main source of this pollutant.

fine-grained plan One that includes a considerable amount of detail, in contrast to a *broad-brush plan*.

Finger Plan The 1948 plan for Copenhagen encouraged development along radial railway lines, with wedges of open space between them. A well-known diagram superimposes the outline of a human hand over the area of existing and planned development, with the new axes of growth represented by the fingers.

fingerprinting Including insignificant errors in a street plan in order to be able to detect when the plan is being copied. See also A–Z.

Finnish Village Action (Kylatoiminta) The movement was founded in 1976 by Lauri Hautamäki to promote rural revival. By 1985 2,000 village committees had been set up. Now covering more than two thirds of Finland's villages, they initiate projects in the areas of culture, leisure, communications, services, housing and economic development. Since 1995, when Finland joined the EU, the village committees have taken an active role in executing regional and rural policy. The movement received the RIGHT LIVELIHOOD AWARD in 1992.

fire road (US) A dirt mountain road wide enough for a truck or fire engine. See CACTUSVILLE.

Fireman Sam See PONTYPANDY.

Firestone Factory A tyre factory on London's Great West Road, designed by Wallis Gilbert and Partners in ART DECO style, built in 1928, and demolished by its owners over the 1980 August bank holiday weekend to prevent its being protected by listing. The subsequent furore led to listing being extended to many more pre-1939 buildings.

firmness See COMMODITIE, FIRMNESS AND DELIGHT.

First Garden City Ltd A company formed in 1903 to build the first garden city (LETCHWORTH), taking over from the GARDEN CITY PIONEER COMPANY.

first-year fail A design so incompetent that it would fail as a first-year project on an architecture or urban design course.

fish bowl An event at which local people observe professionals planning and designing their area, without becoming actively involved.

Fitch, Clyde (1865–1909) Playwright. See THE CITY.

fitness for purpose An obligation that a contractor or developer may take on, guaranteeing that the development will meet its occupier's requirements.

fitpad (Scots) A footpath.

fitting in A favourite phrase of planners. Example: 'Development should fit in with its context.' The Prince of Wales (2001) said that he feared that 'so much of the modernist aesthetic is based on the notion of standing out rather than fitting in.'

five Bs Bricks, banners, balloons, BENCHES and BERMS. 'The five Bs do not create streetlife,' ANDRES DUANY warns. 'It is the available shopping that provides it.'

Five Towns, The The fictional 'Five Towns' of the novels of Arnold Bennett (1867–1931) were based on the six Staffordshire towns of Burslem, Fenton, Hanley, Longton, Stoke and Tunstall, centres of the pottery industry.

five-per-cent philanthropy See PHILANTHROPY AT FIVE PER CENT.

fixation line One that marks a change in the form of development due to the influence of an existing or former linear feature, such as a city wall or railway line, constituting a barrier to development. The concept is used in morphological analysis. See also *fringe belt*.

fixed hazardous object A tree (in the parlance of US traffic engineers objecting to their presence in streets, according to the urban designer Paul Murrain).

Flächennutzungsplan (German) A zoning plan.

Flagg, Ernest (1857–1947) Architect, most notably of the 600-foot high Singer Building in New York, completed in 1908. He later argued that legal limits should be imposed on SKYSCRAPERS, specifying that they should be no more than 100 feet high unless they occupied less than three-quarters of their sites.

flagship project One intended to have the highest profile of all the elements of a regeneration scheme. See also GRAND PROJECT.

flâner (French) To stroll, observing.

flânerie (French) Strolling in a public place.

flâneur/flaneur (French/English) **1** One who strolls in the crowd observing life without being seen. The cultural critic Walter Benjamin (1892–1940) wrote extensively on the flâneur, drawing initially on references in Baudelaire. Benjamin sees the Baudelairean flâneur as being on the borders of joy and melancholy, enjoying the spectacle of urban life yet unsettled by its fragmentary nature. He finds himself having to make his own narrative from those fragments (Huang, 2000 and Shields, 1994). 'For the perfect flâneur,' Baudelaire writes, 'it is an immense joy to set up house in the heart of the multitude, amid the ebb and flow. To be away from home, yet to feel oneself everywhere at home; to see the world, to be at the centre of the world, yet to remain hidden from the world – such are a few of the slightest pleasures of those independent, passionate, impartial natures which the tongue can but clumsily define.'

Benjamin was himself devoted to flânerie. Hannah Arendt (1973) writes: 'The extent to which this strolling determined the pace of his thinking was perhaps most clearly revealed in the peculiarities of his gait, which Max Rychner described as "at one advancing and tarrying, a strange mixture of both". It was the walk of the flâneur, and it was so striking because, like the dandy and the snob, the flâneur had his home in the nineteenth century, an age of security in which children of upper-middle-class families were assured of an income without having to work, so that they had no reason to hurry.' Arendt comments: 'Just as the city taught Benjamin flânerie, the nineteenth century's secret style of walking and thinking, it naturally aroused in him a feeling for French literature as well, and this almost irrevocably estranged him from normal German intellectual life.' Benjamin observes that 'an intoxication comes over the man who walks long and aimlessly through the streets. With each step, the walk takes on greater momentum; ever weaker grow the temptations of shops, of bistros, of smiling women, ever more irresistible the magnetism of the next street corner, of a distant mass of foliage, of a street name' (see Benjamin, 1938 and Tester, 1994).

The geographer Doreen Massey (1994) writes that 'the flâneur is irretrievably male... the notion of a *flâneuse* [in the nineteenth and early twentieth centuries] is impossible... because of the one-wayness and the directionality of the gaze'. JM Coetzee describes such a man (without using the word 'flâneur') in his 1999 novel *Disgrace*. The central character, a professor of communications, 'has always been a man of the city, at home amid a flux of bodies where eros stalks and glances flash like arrows.' **2** An idler; a PROMENADER; one who delights in strolling in public places, observing life and being seen.

The word flâneur is sometimes used in discussions of urban design to describe one sort of user of public spaces. Examples: 'In a world of Starbucks and Niketowns... no longer is the urban flâneur someone who can discover – at least in new public realm – the strange, the unexpected, or the arousing' (Sennett, 2001); 'as a flâneur of Paris for 16 years, he knows where to find the very best of everything – silver, sheets, plum slivovitz. He can tell you where to rent an entire castle for a party or even where to get Skippy peanut butter' (2003). The songwriter WF Hargreaves (1846–1919) satirises one type of flâneur in a song written in 1915: 'I'm Burlington Bertie/ I rise at ten thirty and saunter along like a toff,/ I walk down the Strand with my gloves on my hand,/ Then I walk down again with them off.' The poet Gérard de Nerval, when asked why he was walking in the Palais-Royal leading a lobster on a ribbon, replied: 'It doesn't bark, and it knows the secrets of the sea.' See also CROWD-SOAKING, DÉRIVE, PASSEGGIATA and WALKING.

flanking transmission Sound transmitted between rooms through a wall.

flat (UK) Self-contained living accommodation on one floor, with other separate accommodation above and/or below. *The Builder* magazine advocated flats as a solution to the problem of URBAN SPRAWL in 1849. Before then, flats were not thought of as accommodation for families. The first result of this interest was a block of upper-middle-class flats, built by Henry Ashton in London's Victoria Street between 1852 and 1854 (Burnett, 1986). In 1853 *The Builder* reported that a Mr Mackenzie had built 'residences on flats' (sic) (Dixon and Muthesius, 1978). When the English rent a flat abroad on holiday they generally refer to it as an APARTMENT, and apartment is replacing flat back in England as well. By the late 1990s probably no newly built accommodation for private sale was advertised as a 'flat'. A flat perhaps has implications of being the kind of home occupied by people unable to afford a house. Apartment, on the other hand, is thought to suggest sophistication and cosmopolitan living (and can be on more than one floor). See also UNIT.

Flatiron building A celebrated New York skyscraper designed by Daniel Burnham and built in 1903. Its name derived from its narrow triangular floor plan, itself determined by the intersection of Broadway with the later GRID of Manhattan streets. See TWENTY-THREE SKIDDOO.

flats over shops A grant scheme supporting efforts to bring empty homes above shops back into use.

flatted terrace A terrace of housing with individual flats on the ground floor and first floor. *London flats* and *Tyneside flats* are examples.

flex house (US) Defined approvingly by ANDRES DUANY (1998) as a conventional house with the front of the building (at the position of the conventional garage) available as a commercial space or as an ancillary rental unit. The rear alley accommodates the additional parking requirement. Duany also defines two other types that provide useful flexibility. The *flex apartment house* is an otherwise conventional apartment building with the ground floor available as a commercial space, either independently or in association with the apartment above (by way of an internal stair). The *flex rowhouse* has the ground floor available as a commercial space, either independently leased or in association with the residential unit above. A rear alley or parking lot accommodates the additional parking requirement.

flexcity The urban form of a place that is undergoing restructuring through deindustrialisation and the rise of the information economy. ED SOJA has applied the term to LOS ANGELES.

flexibility The word entered currency as a general architectural principle around the early 1950s as a way of dealing with the contradiction that arose between the expectation that, as Adrian Forty (2000a) puts it, 'the architect's ultimate concern in designing buildings was with their human use and occupation, and the reality that the architect's involvement in a building ceased at the very moment that occupation began.'

flexible An estate agents' euphemism describing, according to Charles Jennings (2001), a part of a house unsuited for any fixed purpose. In the phrase *flexible accommodation*, he explains, it indicates that the previous owners have tried every ground-floor room as dining room before giving up and putting the property on the market. See also DECEPTIVELY SPACIOUS.

flexible tenure A type of shared ownership housing in which the occupier takes whatever stake in the ownership they can afford.

flexism Defined by Michael Dear and Steven Flusty (1998) as 'a pattern of econo-cultural production and consumption characterized by near-instantaneous delivery and rapid redirectability of resource flows'.

flivver (US) **1** A Ford car. **2** Nickname of the Ford Model T, which in 1913 became the world's first car to be mass-produced. **3** A small, cheap car.

Floating City A proposal of 1961 by the architect Kisho Kurokawa. The project was an example of METABOLISM.

floccinaucinihilipilification Setting something (for example, a piece of land, or design – see KITCHEN CULTURE) at little or no value. The word was created in the eighteenth century from Latin words for little or no value: *flocci, nauci, nihili* and *pili. Antidisestablishmentarianism*, popularly thought of as the longest word in the English language, is shorter (though neither matches the longest in the *Oxford English Dictionary*, *pneumonoultramicroscopicsilicovolcanoconiosis*). The German language of urbanism and environmentalism is, as ever, rich in long compound words, such as *Umweltverträglichkeitsprüfung* (environmental impact assessment).

flood A flow of water over land that is usually dry. One person in 10 in the UK lives on FLOOD PLAIN. Development pressure increasingly leads to houses being built on land that was previously left undeveloped. More intense urbanisation reduces the ground's ability to soak up precipitation and increases the likelihood of flooding. Climate change may add unpredictable weather patterns to the equation.

flood plain (also floodplain) All land adjacent to a watercourse over which water flows in time of flood, or would flow but for the presence of flood defences.

floor area ratio (US) Total floorspace as a proportion of total land area. See also PLOT RATIO.

floorplate The area of a single floor of a building.

floorspace *Gross external floorspace* is calculated according to the overall dimensions of a building or buildings, including the thickness of external walls. It consists of the total floorspace in the development, excluding floors completely or mainly below ground level. It includes the gross floor area of covered car parking and structures on the roof (such as lift and tank rooms), and servicing areas and other ancillary uses not below or mainly below ground level. *Gross internal floorspace* is the total floor area of a building, including internal walls, partitions, piers, columns, chimney breasts and stairwells. The thickness of perimeter walls and any floor area where the floor-to-ceiling height is less than 1.5 metres are excluded from the calculation.

flora The vegetable species of a particular place. Flora was the Roman goddess of flowers. Compare FAUNA.

Florence of the West, The Chicago in the late nineteenth century, according to the novelist Theodore Dreiser. He celebrated 'this singing flame of a city, this all America, this poet in chaps and buckskin, this rude, raw Titan…! By its shimmering lake it lay, a king of shreds and patches, a maundering yokel with an epic in its mouth, a tramp, a hobo among cities, with the grip of Caesar in its mind, the dramatic force of Euripides in its soul. A very bard of a city this, singing of high deeds and high hopes, its heavy brogans buried deep in the mire of circumstance.' See also ATHENS OF THE NORTH and VENICE OF THE NORTH.

Florida, Richard Professor of economic development at Carnegie Mellon University and author of *The Rise of the Creative Class: how it is transforming work, leisure, community and everyday life*, published in 2002. See CREATIVE CLASS.

flowing space Space that continues under buildings (raised on PILOTIS) or, in appearance, between the inside and outside of a building (through glass walls). The concept was developed by modernist architects.

fluffy *n.* A person who engages in or supports peaceful mass protest against capitalism and globalisation. The term became current in the 1990s. Compare SPIKEY.

Flurstück (German) A plot.

fly *v.* To be economically viable. Example: 'The market appraisal will ensure that the development can fly.'

flying rat A term sometimes used by campaigners against pigeons in urban areas to describe those BIRDS.

flyposting Sticking up posters without permission.

fog Dense water vapour hanging in the air near the ground, reducing visibility. Peter Ackroyd (2000) reports that London's notorious fogs were variously described as black, bottle-green, pea-soup yellow, rich lurid brown, grey, orange and dark chocolate. These fogs – or rather *smogs* (smoke plus fog) were the result of the almost universal burning of coal for heating homes, offices, public buildings and factories. Paris, by contrast, burned wood and was smog free. Nathaniel Hawthorne wrote of the fog, Ackroyd notes, as 'very black indeed, more like a distillation of mud than anything else; the ghost of mud, the spiritualised medium of departed mud, through which the departed citizens of London probably tread in the Hades whither they are translated.' Charles Dickens called the fog 'London's ivy'. Jonathan Raban (1974) suggests that for Victorian writers, the fog was 'the supreme symbol of the city's capacity to make people disappear inside it'. To Dickens in particular, Raban writes, London was 'an ectoplasmic soup from which characters can be fished out then dropped back at will'. Ernie Diamond was a carpenter at London's film studios from 1926 to 1973. He recalled how, in the early days, filming was a seasonal trade due to fog. 'November, and around Christmas – you couldn't make films,' he told Colin Sorensen (1996). 'The fog got into the studio for about three months.' The Beaver Committee on Air Pollution was set up in response to the London fog (smog) of December 1952, which killed an estimated 12,000 people. The government of the day was sensitive to criticisms that it had contributed to the severity of the problem by exporting the high-quality coal and reserving the 'dirty coal' with a high sulphur content for use in the UK. It responded by pretending that many of the deaths had been due to a flu epidemic, which later research showed had not taken place. The Beaver Committee's report led to the Clean Air Act 1956. The Smoke Abatement League of Great Britain had campaigned for such legislation since at least 1909. In the autumn of that year more than 1,000 people died as a result of smogs in Edinburgh and Glasgow. Ironically the Clean Air Act finally became law when coal burning was declining in favour of gas and electricity.

FONSI (US) A *finding of no significant impact* following an ENVIRONMENTAL ASSESSMENT.

food desert An urban area poorly served by affordable shops.

food poverty Defined by the DETR (1998) as 'being unable to afford healthy food, especially where fuel and other basic needs take priority. Food poverty is exacerbated by lack of access to shops selling healthy food, disproportionately affecting poorer communities less able to travel to out-of-town superstores.'

footfall A measure of the number of people passing a particular point.

foothills One of the FOUR ECOLOGIES of LOS ANGELES identified by Reyner Banham (1973). The foothills are the wealthy suburbs such as Beverly Hills and Bel Air.

footloose industry One whose location is not tied to a particular area.

footpads' paradise An ideal place for MUGGERS, for whom footpads is an old term. The phrase is said to have been used to describe POUNDBURY by the police, when they first saw plans of its proposed street and footpath layout, which has many alternative routes (see PERMEABILITY). That fear turns out to have been unfounded, as Poundbury seems to enjoy a low rate of crime.

footpath A highway on which the public has a right of way on foot only. The Scots for footpath is *fitpad*.

footprint 1 The total ground floor area of a building or buildings on a site (excluding temporary buildings and open spaces with direct external access between the wings of a building). **2** The area providing goods and services to, and receiving waste and pollution from, a town or city.

footway A surface reserved for pedestrians. See CARRIAGEWAY.

Forbidden City A complex of some 800 buildings in the centre of the Chinese capital Beijing. The Forbidden City, now a museum, was begun in 1406 as the palace of the emperor and the seat of government. Entrance was forbidden to ordinary people without special permission.

fordism (also Fordism) Forms of capitalist organisations typified by Henry Ford's car assembly-line mass-production plants. Richard Sennett (2001) has described fordism as 'a kind of military micro-management of a worker's time and efforts which a few experts could dictate from the top.' In discussions of urbanism POST-FORDISM is a more common phrase. Aldous Huxley's novel *Brave New World* is set in the year AF632 – that is, 632 years after the birth of Henry Ford (1863–1947). In the novel Ford has become a deity and the whole world follows his industrial philosophy.

foreign transaction See TRANSACTION.

forensic conservation Defined by Martin Weaver (1995) – to whom the term is credited – as 'conservation practised scientifically and to such a standard that the practitioner could appropriately present any aspect of the work as expert testimony or evidence in a court of law'.

Forest Hill Gardens A New York model GARDEN SUBURB built on Long Island after 1909 by the Russell Sage Foundation. FREDERICK LAW OLMSTED and his brother were the planners. Peter Hall (1998) notes its long-lasting influence on American suburban development, but comments that Forest Hill Gardens was 'an aesthetic, not a social triumph…; intended to be a social mixture, it almost immediately became entirely upper middle class'. See NEIGHBOURHOOD.

forest park A forest used for both recreation and the production of timber.

form The layout (structure and urban grain), density, scale (height and massing), appearance (materials and details) and landscape of development. 'In architecture, form is a noun; in industry, form is a verb,' BUCKMINSTER FULLER observed. The definition of form was an important preoccupation of nineteenth-

> **"IN ARCHITECTURE, FORM IS A NOUN; IN INDUSTRY, FORM IS A VERB"**
>
> *Buckminster Fuller*

century aesthetics. Architectural modernists in the twentieth century adopted the term, Adrian Forty (2000a) suggests, partly because 'it implied that the true substance of architecture lay beyond the immediately perceptible world of the senses… and it gave to architects a description for that part of their work over which they held exclusive and unequivocal control.'

form follows function A much-quoted saying of the American architect Louis Sullivan. The architect RICHARD ROGERS (*The Times*, 1991) has echoed it: 'Form follows profit is the aesthetic principle of our times.' The architectural writer Paul Finch (2000) commented on the MILLENNIUM DOME: 'Form swallows function'.

formal Relating to a building's architectural properties, rather than to its usefulness.

formal surveillance Police, security personnel and street wardens looking out for crime and anti-social behaviour. Compare NATURAL SURVEILLANCE and ORGANISED SURVEILLANCE.

formalism An approach to architecture in which a building's functions are subservient to its external appearance and image; designing with a preconceived idea of the building's form. Example: 'If a building is forced into a preconceived shape, its proper functioning is almost bound to be compromised. Housing design has suffered from such formalism' (2002). See also SHAPEMAKER.

formulaic solution The same approach to urban regeneration (for example) applied in different places, such as relying on a major landmark building to attract attention, visitors and further development.

Forshaw, JH As the London County Council's chief architect, he collaborated with PATRICK ABERCROMBIE on plans for London in the 1940s.

fort up To fortify; to install defensive measures against crime (on a housing development, for example).

fortified planting A usually pejorative term for raised flowerbeds in pedestrian spaces.

fortress city One in which social breakdown has led to forms of building (and other means) designed to exclude people considered threatening. See also BUNKER ARCHITECTURE and SCANSCAPE.

fortress LA A term used by the urban commentator Mike Davies to describe buildings in Los Angeles designed to protect their occupiers against threats from an unstable city. See also BUNKER ARCHITECTURE, DEFENSIBLE SPACE, HARD ARCHITECTURE and SCANSCAPE.

fortress mentality A way of thinking that leads to excessive efforts to make a building or place resistant to crime or ANTI-SOCIAL BEHAVIOUR. Compare TARGET HARDENING.

forum (Latin) A central open space in a Roman city, surrounded by buildings and colonnades. Compare AGORA.

forward planning Preparing development plans, as opposed to development control planning, which applies them. In that sense it is not the tautology it seems.

forward strategy See EXIT STRATEGY.

Foster, Norman (Sir) (Lord Foster of Thames Reach) (b1935) Architect. His first practice was

Team 4, a double husband-and-wife team with Wendy Foster, RICHARD ROGERS and Sue Rogers. Like Rogers, he became known initially for his high-tech style, expressing new forms of building technology. He has been awarded the Royal Gold Medal for Architecture and membership of the Order of Merit. See also ALBERTOPOLIS, THE ARMADILLO, FENG SHUI, FOSTERITO, JUMBO JET, MILLENNIUM TOWER, PRINCE OF WALES, STANSTED and WILLIS FABER DUMAS BUILDING.

Fosterito One of the glazed entrance canopies to the underground stations of the Bilbao metro, built in the 1990s. They are named after their designer, NORMAN FOSTER.

Foulness See MAPLIN.

Fountainhead, The A bestselling novel by Ayn Rand, published in 1943. It uses a portrait of an architect as genius and hero (and rapist, though the author does not hold that against him) as a vehicle for Rand's espousal of her philosophy of authoritarian egotism. A film of the book, starring Gary Cooper as the architect Howard Roark, was released in 1949. See URBAN DESTRUCTION.

four Cs See BEST VALUE REVIEW.

four ecologies Reyner Banham (1973) identified four 'ecologies' of Los Angeles: SURFURBIA, THE FOOTHILLS, THE PLANES OF ID and AUTOPIA.

Fourier, Charles (1772–1837) Philosopher, economist and utopian socialist. He argued that human actions should be guided by pleasure, not reason. He proposed a city of three circles, divided from each other by GREEN BELTS. People would live in PHALANSTERIES (pleasure palaces).

four-slicing Dividing the income from a development so that the first charge on it is to the local authority or land owner as ground rent, the second covers the developer's costs, the third contributes the developer's profit, and the fourth 'top slice' may be split between those who share the equity.

Fourth World The world's very poorest countries. Compare THIRD WORLD.

Foveaux A novel by Kylie Tennant (b1912), published in 1939, about life in the slums of Sydney, Australia between 1912 and 1935.

foyer 1 A facility providing accommodation and training for young people under one roof as a way of tackling both homelessness and unemployment, two issues that are often closely linked. The idea was developed, and the term coined, in France, and introduced to the UK in the 1980s. **2** (French) A home.

fractal analysis See CHAOS THEORY.

fractured metropolis An urban form created by an old city splitting apart. Suburban villages and rural countries are transformed into a new kind of city with sprawling residential areas and long corridors of commercial development. Jonathan Barrett (1995) used the term as the title of a book.

fragment Defined by ANDRES DUANY (2000) as a developable area that is too small to be a complete neighborhood unless conjoined to an adjacent area. ALDO ROSSI has explained: 'In Italian *frammento*, fragment, means a small chip broken from a larger body. Following this definition fragments can he regarded as objects of hope; a multitude or accumulation of broken objects should not, therefore, be considered to amount to a scrap-heap. In this light, if changes are not effected, if disorder continues to be accepted, and if no thoughtful provisions are made, the scrap-heap may well turn out to be the city of the future instead. Among the many other meanings of *frammenti*, fragment is the literary and artistic term used to describe the remains of a larger work. The fragments of a book, for instance, or the fragments that are the known works of a poet, the greater part of whose oeuvre has been lost. Whether given their physical definition (broken objects, detached elements) or general meaning (the surviving parts a whole), fragments belong without doubt to the world of architecture. They belong as solid, built elements, and as theoretical elements. The first, being concrete, are more readily recognizable than the second, where fragments constitute the remains of a ruined general theory.' Compare REMNANT.

fragmentation See DECONSTRUCTION.

Fragmented Metropolis, The A book by R M Folgelson, published in 1967, on Los Angeles between 1850 and 1970.

Frankfurt Museum Quarter Frankfurt invested heavily in new museums in the 1980s when the prosperous banking centre realised that it was short on cultural assets. Six of the new museums were adapted by adventurous architects with large budgets from a series of villas beside the River Main. One of the new museums, its building and collection paid for by the city, is the German national museum of architecture (Deutsches Architekturmuseum).

Freedom of the City, The A book by Ken Worpole and Liz Greenhalgh, published in 1996, on how to bring life back to public space. The authors argue that: a) Urban public spaces provide the settings for more democratic and convivial forms of citizenship to develop. Their protection and enhancement is vital to a higher quality of urban life. b) Successful public spaces are created by popular use, over time, and under differing conditions. Management and programming are as important as the physical fabric. c) Public spaces need not only management but forms of staffing dedicated to conspicuous care. d) Over-zealousness with regard to the enforcement of health and safety measures can hinder the development of a better quality of life and more local, informal activity and enterprise. e) New public spaces should be designed in close consultation with neighbouring communities and potential users.

Flexibility and adaptability are the key ingredients. Proposals for new spaces should include detailed plans as to how the space is to be funded, managed, programmed and staffed in the long term. f) Successful public space is defined by use more than by legal ownership.

freehold A form of tenure based on the exclusive ownership of property for an indefinite period. Compare LEASEHOLD.

Freeland An imaginary utopian city and state described by THEODOR HERTZKA in his 1890 book *Freeland*.

freeport A zone that is treated in some ways as though it were foreign territory. No tariffs or duties are levied in goods coming in, and processing is subject to reduced taxation and regulation. The concept was experimented with in the UK after having been proposed by PETER HALL in the 1970s.

free-rider One who benefits from an improvement scheme (through a BUSINESS IMPROVEMENT DISTRICT, for example) without contributing financially.

freeway (US) A high-speed, controlled-access, toll-free road, as opposed to a TURNPIKE where the driver has to pay. The first, the Arroyo Seco Parkway (later the Pasadena Freeway) opened in 1940. The term was coined by the lawyer EDWARD M BASSETT, who defined a freeway as a strip of public land devoted to movement over which the abutting property owners have no right of light, air or access (compare HIGHWAY). Equivalents are *motorway* (UK), *autobahn* (Germany) and *autostrada* (Italy).

freeway art Public art intended to be viewed from a major road. Also known as *kinetic art* or *speedway sculpture*.

freezer clause A clause in a land option agreement specifying that if a tax (such as capital gains tax, or a new tax such as a GREENFIELD TAX) is applied or increased, the land owner may either freeze the tax at a percentage slightly above current rates, or withdraw from the option for a specified period (or possibly for ever). The result may be that the land will not be brought forward for development.

Freiburg A university town in south west Germany, close to the French and Swiss borders, it is now known as a model of SUSTAINABLE planning. Rebuilding since heavy bomb damage in the 1939–45 war has been the opportunity for restoring historic buildings, creating pedestrian streets and investing in public transport, including six tram lines. The Green Party has been politically influential. Freiburg was one of the ZÄHRINGER TOWNS.

Freifläche (German) Open space.

Freo Fremantle, Western Australia.

Freudenstadt A mining town in Germany's Black Forest, designed by Heinrich Schickhardt and founded in 1599. It is square in plan with radial streets.

friche urbaine (or friches industrielles) (French) Urban wasteland. See URBAN FALLOW LAND.

frictional costs Adverse consequences of the failure of organisations involved in urban regeneration to work together.

fringe belt An area (in the form of a whole or partial belt) where the character of the urban form reflects the fact that the development took place at the periphery of the town or city. The fringe belt (which may be associated with a FIXATION LINE) may still be at the periphery, or development may have since extended beyond it. The concept is used in morphological analysis.

fringe city See X-URBIA.

front and back door housing The housing association director Rob Joiner (2002) claims that when Glasgow people say they want housing with a front door and a back door, they do not necessarily mean it literally, but they mean that they want a house or flat that does not feel as though it is accessed from an unattractive common area. '"A front and a back door" is a social description of the type of house that people want,' he has said, 'not an architectural one'.

front setback The distance between a BUILDING LINE and a building's FAÇADE.

front-loading (England and Wales) The pre-production processes (including those relating to STATEMENTS OF COMMUNITY INVOLVEMENT, LOCAL DEVELOPMENT SCHEMES and annual monitoring reports) involved in preparing LOCAL DEVELOPMENT DOCUMENTS.

frontage development Buildings whose entrances front on to a road or street.

frontager An owner or occupier of a building that fronts on to a particular space.

Fruin analyis A method of analysing pedestrian movement devised by JOHN FRUIN.

Fruin, John A leading authority on pedestrian planning who researched crowds in the 1970s.

fuck-box The writer Alan Bennett's contemptuous term for a suburban house.

fuel poverty The inability to afford adequate fuel for essential domestic uses. While low income is the primary cause, fuel poverty is often exacerbated by poor insulation standards and/or insufficient or expensive heating systems. In the UK fuel poverty is particularly widespread in Scotland, a country with low incomes and a cold, wet climate. The Scottish Executive reported in 2002 that a third of Scots (mainly elderly people and households on benefits) lived in fuel poverty. The DETR (2001) defined fuel poverty as 'the need to spend more than ten per cent of income on heating to achieve an adequate level of warmth'.

Fugitive Futurist, The A film, made in 1924, set in a future London. The Thames has been drained and converted into a railway, and Tower Bridge has become a monorail station (Sorensen, 1996).

Fuller, Richard Buckminster (1895–1983) Designer, engineer and architect. His many designs and inventions included the GEODESIC DOME and he published proposals for domes large enough to enclose a city. He wrote an *Operating Manual for Spaceship Earth*, published in 1969.

Fun City The term was applied to New York in 1966 by a *Herald Tribune* journalist at the start of Mayor John Lindsay's tenure of office (Walsh, 2000). See DEPRESSION CITY.

function Adrian Forty (2000a) dates the first use of the term in relation to architecture to the Venetian Friar Carlo Lodoli in the 1740s. Decoration should be based on the inherent properties of materials, Lodoli argued. The American sculptor and art theorist Horatio Greenough is usually credited as the first English speaker to apply 'function' to architecture (in the 1840s), Forty notes. Best known, though, is the American architect Louis Sullivan's 1920s aphorism 'form follows function'. Forty comments: 'At no point did Sullivan's "function" have anything to do with utility or the satisfaction of user needs; it was instead entirely based in metaphysics, the expression of organic essence.' The term played a new role in modern architecture from the 1930s. In 1932, for example Hitchcock and Johnson published their book *The International Style* to accompany the New York Museum of Modern Art exhibition. Their purpose, Forty argues, 'was to win approval for modernism in the United States by cleansing it of its political content, characterising as "functional" those aspects of European modernism they wished to discard – its scientific, sociological and political claims. But in order to present modern architecture as a purely stylistic phenomenon, they had to invent a fictitious category of "functionalist" architecture to which they consigned all work with reformist or communist tendencies.' In fact, Forty observes, 'their charactization of the "functionalists" as those to whom "all aesthetic principles of style are… meaningless and unreal" bore so little relation to what had been happening in Europe that they succeeded in finding only one architect, Hannes Meyer, who fitted the description.'

function, disposition and configuration The three elements that determine a particular building type, according to some NEW URBANISTS. In this context the *function* is the uses permitted within a building and its lot. The *disposition* is the placement of a building on its lot. The *configuration* is the building's three-dimensional form.

functional city CIAM used the term (without defining it precisely) as the focus of its discussions in the 1930s.

functional urban area Defined by measures such as patterns of journeys to work rather than by administrative boundaries.

functional urban region Defined by Roy Drewett (1980) as 'a nodal region consisting of two urban zones: the urban centre, or core, and a set of contiguous areas in a bounded hinterland, or ring'.

functional zone A part of a town or city with one dominant land use.

functionalism The term was introduced in print by Alberto Sartoris in 1932 to describe the progressive architecture of the 1920s. It was in general use by the mid-1930s. Sartoris had intended to use the term 'rational architecture', but changed it on LE CORBUSIER's advice (Banham, 1960). Early architectural modernists in the 1930s had pragmatic reasons for calling their style functionalist. Reyner Banham (1960) suggests that, in the face of political opposition (in Germany and Russia) and economic hardship (in France and the USA), 'it was better to advocate or defend the new architecture on logical and economic grounds than on grounds of aesthetics or symbolisms that might stir nothing but hostility. This… was certainly a misrepresentation. Emotion had played a much larger part than logic in the creation of the style; inexpensive buildings had been clothed in it, but it was no more an inherently economical style than any other'. The critic Nikolaus Pevsner, a vigorous proponent of modernist architecture in the 1930s and '40s, was happy to apply the term functionalist to gothic as well as modern architecture. This did not imply that either type of architecture was merely functional. Each expressed values, and symbolised

Hannes Meyer

ideals and beliefs. These related to Christianity in the case of gothic, and to science, technology and modern life in the case of modernism (Fuller, 1988).

functionality The quality of being usable, of fulfilling an intended function. Urban designers and architects cite it as a necessary attribute of a building or space. Compare BUILD QUALITY.

fundi See REALO.

furbish See REFURBISH.

Futurama General Motors' display, designed by the industrial designer Norman Bel Geddes, at the 1939 World's Fair in New York. Paul Adamson (2000) records: '[The] 36,000 square foot exhibit, set inside a futuristic, free-formed concrete shell-like structure, consisted of a model representing a prototypical section of the American lanscaped, laced with roadways of varying sizes connecting cities to the country and to one another in a seamless flow of continuous energy... The segregation of city and country would be complete. "Cities," [Bel Geddes] wrote, "become centres for working and country districts for living."' The Futurama model was said to include 50,000 cars. See also DEMOCRACITY.

future mall (US) A SHOPPING MALL fronting a MAIN DRAG. Such places written of in 2003 as being likely to survive, whereas malls in secondary locations would not.

future proof *v.* To design a building taking into account the possibility of higher rainfall and more severe storms in the future as a consequence of global climate change. *The Sustainable Housing Design Guide for Scotland*, published in 2000, recommended that housing developments should be future proofed by such means as checking the water table, increasing the capacity of guttering and pipework, and using robust roofing details.

future search A participation technique enabling groups of people to identify common interests, discuss ideas and share information and experience. OPEN SPACE is a similar technique.

Future World 1 Disney's futuristic theme park, which opened in 1989. See also DISNEYLAND and EPCOT. **2** An exhibition of houses built at Shenley Lodge in Milton Keynes in the 1990s to demonstrate energy-saving ideas.

Futurism An international art movement founded by the Italian poet FT Marinetti in 1909 (and lasting until around 1915), dedicated to speed, noise, machines and the dynamic forces of urban life. Many of its Italian exponents later joined the fascist movement. Marinetti wrote in the *Initial Manifesto of Futurism*, published in 1909: 'We declare that the world's splendour has been enriched by a new beauty: the beauty of speed. A racing motor car, its frame adorned with great pipes, like snakes with explosive breath... a roaring motor car, which seems to run on shrapnel, is more beautiful than the Victory of Samothrace... We shall sing of the great crowds in the excitement of labour, pleasure or rebellion; of the multicoloured and polyphonic surf of revolutions in modern capital cities; of the nocturnal

FT Marinetti

vibrations of arsenals and workshops beneath their violent electric moons; of the greedy stations swallowing smoking snakes; of factories suspended from the clouds by their strings of smoke; of bridges leaping like gymnasts over the diabolical cutlery of sunbathed rivers; of adventurous liners scenting the horizon; of broad-chested locomotives prancing on the rails, like huge steel horses bridled with long tubes; and of the gliding flight of aeroplanes, the sound of whose propeller is like the flapping of flags and the applause of an enthusiastic crowd' (translated by Caroline Tysdall). See THE NEW CITY, ANTONIO SANT'ELIA, MARIO SIRONI, TRAM and THE FUTURIST CITY.

Futurist City, the Proposed in the *Futurist Manifesto of Architecture* of 1914: 'big hotels, railway stations, immense roads, colossal ports, covered markets, brilliantly lit galleries, freeways, demolition and rebuilding schemes'.

futurity Concern for future quality of life.

Fyson, Anthony See URBAN STUDIES CENTRE.

grade-separated intersection

G

gaff A person's home or patch.

gagger A beggar. See also VAGRANT.

Gaia The scientist James Lovelock's (b1919) theory that the planet Earth behaves as a living organism.

gait (or gate) (Scots) A way or road.

Galactic Hyperspace Planning Council See THE HITCH-HIKER'S GUIDE TO THE GALAXY.

galactic metropolis A central city and its satellites.

Gallatin, Albert (1761–1849) President Jefferson's secretary of the treasury. In 1808 he wrote the *Report on Roads and Canals*, proposing a federally sponsored transport system.

galleria A large covered space used as a shopping centre. The term derives from the Galleria in the Vatican (used to display sculpture, not merchandise), according to design writer Stephen Bayley.

Galleria Vittore Emmanuele Milan's shopping arcade, built in 1865–67, has been a major influence on the design of arcades and shopping malls.

galleting Small chips of stone pushed into the pointing mortar of a flintwork wall.

Gandelsonas, Mario See X-URBIA.

Gangs of New York A film directed by Martin Scorsese, released in 2002, based on Herbert Asbury's 1928 book *The Gangs of New York*. 'I rule this district by a spectacle of fearsome acts,' says a one-eyed man, tapping his glass eyeball with the blade of a knife...

Gangs of New York, The A book (subtitled 'an informal history of the underworld') by Herbert Asbury, published in 1928, in which the film *Gangs of New York* was based. 'In the main,' Asbury wrote, 'the gangster was a stupid roughneck born in filth and squalor and reared amid vice and corruption. He fulfilled his natural destiny.'

gap funding Using public investment in high-risk projects to make up the difference between the extra cost of developing difficult sites and possible market values if the projects are unsuccessful.

gap site A site comprising a gap in otherwise continuous urban fabric.

gap town One located in a gap in a ridge. Gap towns were likely historically to be on significant routes.

garbitecture Big-box buildings whose external appearance makes some perfunctory attempt to conceal dull reality behind.

garbo (or garbologist) (Australia) A municipal rubbish (garbage) collector.

garden 1 (UK) A plot of land next to a house planted with grass and/or other plants. See also LAWN. The US equivalent is YARD, and the Scots for garden is YAIRD. **2** (US) The part of the YARD that is given over to planting other than grass.

Garden City 21 A proposal by a consortium of developers and local authorities to build a 10,000-home development west of Stevenage in the 1990s. Hertfordshire County Council removed the site from the green belt in the county structure plan, but withdrew its support for the scheme in 1999 following a change of political control. The scheme's proposers argued that the greenfield development was SUSTAINABLE as it would be well connected to public transport and the town's facilities.

garden city The central element of EBENEZER HOWARD's vision of an alternative socio-economic system. In 1919 the Garden City and Town Planning Association adopted this definition of a garden city: 'A town designed for healthy living and industry; of a size that makes possible a full measure of social life, but not larger; surrounded by a rural belt; the whole of the land being in public ownership or held in trust for the community'.

WG Moore (1949) credits the first use of the term to AT Stewart in the USA in 1869. In the late nineteenth century, before Howard launched what was to become the garden city movement, the term garden city had already been applied to BEDFORD PARK in London; Chicago; Christchurch in New Zealand; a development on Long Island, New York; and many other US towns and suburbs. WELWYN and LETCHWORTH were given the name when they were founded by Ebenezer Howard in the early twentieth century. After that, many other places, often no more than low-density housing developments with some trees, took the name too, their developers considering it a selling point. (Compare the use of URBAN VILLAGE at the end of that century.)

FJ OSBORN recorded that Howard always said he did not know of the Garden City on Long Island, New York, when he chose that name for his own scheme, though Osborn conceded that Howard might have heard the name and forgotten it (Hughes, 1971). LEWIS MUMFORD (1961) commented: 'The title that Howard chose for this new urban conception proved unfortunate: not only because it had been pre-empted much earlier by the dingy railroad metropolis of Chicago, but also because the existence of gardens, though integral to the new city, was not its distinctive feature, since it characterized even more copiously many a contemporary suburb... It was in its urbanity, not its horticulture, that the Garden City made a bold departure from the established method of building and planning'. FJ Osborn wrote in 1945 that 'garden city does not etymologically cover Howard's idea; but it is in itself a pleasant term, we haven't found a better one, and if we did it might still be perverted if planning writers remain inefficient. So I've set myself to correct the perversions and restore the term to its original clear meaning, while accepting "satellite town" as an alternative in the case of garden cities and genuine country towns in the region of a large metropolis or regional capital' (Hughes, 1971).

The term garden city was appropriated again when Manchester presented its bid to host the 1996 Olympic Games. The bid committee's brochure promised 'self-contained garden city accommodation in special temporary residential blocks' that Deyan Sudjic (1992) described as 'wretched eight-storey-high pre-fabs that looked as if they were made from bolted-together segments of container lorry.' The 1997 plan of the Singapore Urban Development Authority included as one of its aims 'to reinforce the garden city image'.

There are more than a dozen places in the USA called Garden City. They range in size from Garden City, South Dakota, with a population of 93 in 1990 to three with populations of more than 20,000, in Kansas, Miami and New York. Compare VERTICAL GARDEN CITY.

Garden City Association Founded in 1899 to promote the garden city concept devised by EBENEZER HOWARD. It became the TOWN AND COUNTRY PLANNING ASSOCIATION in 1941.

Garden City by the Sea Peacehaven in Sussex, as proclaimed by its developer Charles Neville in the 1920s. The historian Dennis Hardy (1991) notes that Peacehaven was as far from the ideals of the garden city movement as any development.

garden city movement By 1913 the term was being used to describe a wider range of development than just garden cities, most of it being of a GARDEN SUBURB type (Hardy, 1991). See THE GARDEN CITY.

Garden City Pioneer Company Formed in 1902 to build the first garden city, with Ebenezer Howard as its managing director. See FIRST GARDEN CITY LTD.

Garden City, The A book by GEORGES BENOIT-LÉVY, published in France in 1904, advocating GARDEN SUBURBS. See GARDEN CITY MOVEMENT.

garden festival Inspired by the German experience, garden festivals were held in Liverpool, Stoke-on-Trent, Glasgow, Gateshead and Ebbw Vale between 1984 and 1992. Created on derelict, inner city land, there were intended to kick-start urban regeneration.

garden party (Glasgow) An open-air drinking session in a park or on waste ground by alcoholics and others with nowhere else to drink.

garden suburb A suburban area of low-density housing with gardens on tree-lined streets, sometimes with businesses serving only the local population. Simon Pepper (1978) noted that FJ OSBORN preferred the term *dormitory* or *residential suburb* and, where industry was incorporated, *industrial suburb*. See also BEDFORD PARK, GEORGES BENOIT-LÉVY, BRENTHAM, ENSKEDE, FOREST HILL GARDENS, GARTENSTADT STAAKEN, GLENDALE, HAMPSTEAD GARDEN SUBURB, JOHN NETTLEFOLD, CHARLES PEARSON, WELL HALL and WYTHENSHAWE.

garden village A leafy model development laid out at low density. John Burnett (1986) suggests that BROMBOROUGH POOL, built in 1853–8 on the Wirral, Cheshire, has a good claim to be 'the first garden village'. MERVILLE GARDEN VILLAGE, a suburb of Belfast, was built as a housing estate in the 1940s and '50s. Highlands Garden Village, a 27-acre infill development in Denver, Colorado, built around 2000, is noted for its comprehensive approach to resource conservation (*New Urban News*, 2001). In 2002 a Bedfordshire local authority gave outline planning permission for a development to be called Elstow Garden Villages. It would consist of three 'villages' with a total population of 14,000 people, grouped round a central area. The developer claimed to have been inspired by Ebenezer Howard's GARDEN CITY MOVEMENT.

gardens Planted grounds provided for display and recreation.

Garnier, Tony (1869–1948) Architect and town planner. See INDUSTRIAL CITY.

Gartenstadt Staaken Berlin's first GARDEN SUBURB, designed by Paul Schmitthemmer in 1914–17. Spiro Kostof (1991) calls it 'a synthesis of British garden city theory and German neo-medieval design'.

Gary An industrial town in Indiana, founded in 1906 and named after Elbert Gary, chairman of US steel (Rykwert, 2000).

gas-and-water socialism The municipal control of utilities. The term was used in the late nineteenth century, as a slightly derogatory version of MUNICIPAL.

Gaskell, Elizabeth (1810–65) Novelist. See MARY BARTON.

Gasse (German) A lane; an alley.

gated estate (or community or development) An area of private housing closed off from public streets, surrounded by a high wall or fence and protected by an electronically operated or guarded gates to make the residents feel more secure.

Anna Minton (2002) reports that at least 80 per cent of new urban development in the USA is thought to be gated. She notes the negative effects of gating: a) It promotes class and racial segregation. b) People feel safer behind gates, but their fear of the outside world increases. c) Crime within gated communities does not decline. d) Crime is encouraged by pinpointing rich enclaves. e) Public law enforcement is hampered by lack of visibility inside gates. f) A proliferation of gated communities removes recreational space, amenities and services from the public realm. g) Having their own services, gated residents do not wish to pay local taxes as well. This threatens local government and democracy, and undermines public services such as health, education and transport.

The Social Market Foundation (2002) comments: 'Gated communities have grown enormously in popularity in the US. Their growth is mirrored at the other end of the spectrum by a relative increase in those living in poverty in socially deprived ghettos. The number of gated communities in the UK remains small but is growing fast, with many new estates promising a gated boundary. Critics argue that such communities are a visible and powerful reminder of the breakdown of inclusive societies, allowing the wealthy to withdraw from normal social interaction, thereby exacerbating the social ills they leave behind. On the other hand, defenders see them as a positive step in the revitalisation of communal living, offering not only an attractive option for those on higher incomes, but a new model for social housing.'

In what seems to be a new dimension of gatedness, Mike Davis (2002) writes of the new development of Lake Las Vegas, which includes 'lakefront villas in a private gated subdivision *within* a larger guarded-gated residential community". It stands to reason that when a significant proportion of the population lives in gated communities, some of the residents within the gates will be criminally minded. Gated estates are not new: there were 150 in central and western districts of London in 1875, John Burnett (1986) records. Many of the Georgian squares of London (such as Bloomsbury Square) were originally gated. See also OFFWORLD and PARABLE OF THE SOWER.

gatekeeper 1 A person whose negative attitudes makes an organisation involved in urban regeneration less accessible and less effective at working in partnership. See also LINK WILT. **2** A trusted member of the community who can liaise between officials and the public. The UK government used the term in this sense in 2002 to describe members of a proposed network of people who would be called on in case of a major terrorist attack.

gateway capital One serving a broad but sometimes thinly populated territory, and having a wider range of services than its size would suggest (Hall, 2002).

Gaudi A pan-European network of architecture centres and related organisations. Its name is an acronym for *government, architecture, urbanism as democratic interaction*.

Gaudi, Antonio (1852–1926) Architect. His best-known work is the unfinished Church of the Sagrada Familia in Barcelona.

Gavin-Lowry model A mathematical model used to predict the distribution of people and service industries in an urban area.

Gavron, Nicky Politician. A community activist in north London in the 1970s, she later became a local councillor. She chaired the London Planning Advisory Committee from 1994 to 2000, developing a consensual approach, and led the Local Government Association's local planning reform working group. As a member of the Greater London Assembly, she was appointed by mayor KEN LIVINGSTONE as his deputy, with a major role in preparing the London plan.

gay ghetto An area with a concentration of gay people.

gay index A measure of the number of gay people living in an area. RICHARD FLORIDA (2002) uses the index as one measure of an area's diversity and likely creativity. It is, he writes, 'a reasonable proxy for an area's openness to different kinds of people and ideas'.

Gazzard's Law of Urban Vitality The law, formulated by the Australian architect Don Gazzard (1988), states that it takes 100 Australians to create the same urban activity as 10 Italians. (It has been estimated that in Italy there are 472 inhabitants per café.)

The architect ROBERT VENTURI (1966) also commented on the need for urban design to recognise cultural distinctions. 'Americans feel uncomfortable sitting in a square,' Venturi wrote. 'They should be working at the office or at home with the family looking at television.'

GEAR Glasgow Eastern Area Renewal, set up in 1974, was one of the first of a new wave of inner city renewal programmes. See also STONEHOUSE.

gearing (UK) The debt on which interest is payable expressed as a ratio of the shareholder's funds. The higher the proportion of debt, the higher is the gearing. See also LEVERAGE.

Geddes, Arthur (1895–1968) The younger son of PATRICK GEDDES, he assisted his father in his planning work in India. He later lectured in geography at the University of Edinburgh.

Geddes, Patrick (Sir) (1854–1932) A biologist, botanist, ecologist, geographer, town planner, educator and social philosopher, Geddes saw himself primarily as a sociologist. His aim was to show how social processes and the environment interacted, and how the processes of urban and social change could be managed in the interests of the social development of the individual. He was, he wrote, 'a student of living nature in evolution'. Geddes pioneered the use of the concept of the region (and the technique of regional survey) as the basis for social, economic and environmental analysis. 'He saw both cities and human beings as wholes; and he saw the processes of repair, renewal, and rebirth as natural phenomena of development,' his disciple LEWIS MUMFORD (1947) wrote. 'His ideal of the best life possible was always the best that was latent in a particular site and situation at a particular moment in the development of a particular family, group or community: not an abstract ideal that could be imposed by authority or force from the outside'.

Born in west Aberdeenshire, Scotland, in 1854, Geddes studied biology under Thomas Huxley in London. He became a demonstrator at University College, London (where he met Charles Darwin on one occasion), and tried unsuccessfully to interest JOHN RUSKIN in his ideas on statistics. Back in Scotland, he organised practical, low-cost improvements in Edinburgh's historic, decayed ROYAL MILE, living with his wife and first child in a slum tenement himself, and involving fellow residents and volunteers in the process. He developed the technique he called 'conservative surgery'. This was an incremental approach to area improvement which involved the people who lived and worked there and, unlike much practice then and since, ensured that they were able to remain there and benefit from the improvements. By 1898 the improvements in Edinburgh had extended to more than 30 courts and closes. He converted more slum housing in Edinburgh into Scotland's first (and Britain's first self-governing) student halls of residence.

Geddes promoted public education through international expositions and summer schools. In 1884 he helped found an Environment Society in Edinburgh, soon renamed the Edinburgh Social Union. He tried to promote a cultural renaissance in Edinburgh in the 1890s based on the ARTS AND CRAFTS movement. With J Arthur Thomson he wrote *The Evolution of Sex*, published in 1889. In Dublin he organised a programme of urban renewal. For many years he was a part-time professor of botany at Dundee University. In 1897 he went to Cyprus in an attempt to promote economic development. He was commissioned to prepare plans for an estate in Dunfermline that had been donated to the town by the philanthropist Andrew Carnegie. His report, *City Development: a study of parks, gardens and culture-institutes*, published in 1905, presented an inspiring vision of how local people could participate in and learn from the process of town planning and regeneration. As usual in his work, his recommendations were based on a comprehensive survey.

Geddes helped to inspire the founding of the Sociological Society in 1903. In India he developed his ideas of planning as a process, not of creating model developments on new sites, but of renewing existing places for, with, and through the people who lived there. In Indian towns and cities he found zealous public health officials destroying workplaces and social networks along with the slums they cleared, and hardly noticing when the people were pushed into even more overcrowded conditions somewhere else. He showed that a more selective approach could improve living conditions while maintaining the neighbourhood's economic and social balance. Geddes (1915a) wrote: 'The policy of sweeping clearances should be recognised for what I believe it is; one of the most disastrous and pernicious blunders in the chequered history of sanitation.' Decades of painful experience were to pass before that lesson was learned elsewhere.

In his later years, Geddes founded a Collège des Ecossais (Scots College) at Montpellier in the south of France, intended as a living embodiment of his educational theories. He became increasingly obsessed with what he called his 'thinking machines', gridded diagrams showing the classifications of and relationships between the topics and concepts that were central to his thought. He failed to convince more than a handful of his followers that this endlessly refined system provided the key to understanding human life and its environment. Having refused the honour once, he was knighted at the end of his life.

Planning, Geddes insisted, was 'the development of a local life... capable of improvement and development in its own way and upon its own foundations, not something which can be done from above, on general principle easily laid down, which can be learned in one place and imitated in another'. Geddes (1910) wrote: 'Architecture and town planning... are not the mere products of the quiet drawing-office... they are the expressions of the local history, the civic and national changes of mood and contrasts of mind.' He wanted to present a contrary view to 'those town planners who design a shell, and then pack their snail of a would-be progressive city into it, not discerning that the only real and well-fitting shell is that which the creature at its growing periods throws out from its own life. This is no doctrine of *laissez-faire*; it is simply the recognition that each generation, and in this, each essential type and group of it, must express its own life, and thus make its contribution to its city in its own characteristic way.' The local focus was just the start. 'Local knowledge and understanding are essential to the town planner, together with consideration and tact when dealing with the individual requirements of the citizens. Other requirements are powers of social appeal and a civic enthusiasm that will enable him to arouse neighbourhood after neighbourhood to participate in schemes of improvements instead of remaining indifferent to them. Only in this way can he gradually inspire the city as a whole' (Geddes, 1918). The process must be collaborative, he insisted. 'Each of the various specialists remains too closely concentrated upon his single specialism, too little awake to those of other. Each sees clearly and seizes firmly one petal of the six-lobed flower of life and tears it apart from the whole'. The core of his method was that planning must be based on diagnostic survey. 'It requires long and patient study,' he wrote. 'The work can not be done in the office with ruler and parallels, for the plan must be sketched out on the spot, after wearying hours of perambulation.' His training as a botanist never left him. 'This is a green world,' Geddes wrote, 'with animals comparatively few and small, and all dependent on the leaves. By leaves we live. Some people have strange ideas that they live by money. They think energy is generated by the circulation of coins. Whereas the world is mainly a vast leaf colony, growing on and forming a leafy soil, not a mere mineral mass: and we live not by the jingling of our coins, but by the fullness of our harvests.'

Geddes could be a difficult person to work with, driven by one enthusiasm after another and failing to understand why his colleagues did not always pick up the pieces. But he inspired passionate admirers. 'Prophets are proverbially without honour in their own country,' wrote the poet Hugh MacDiarmid (1966), who attended one of his meetings in Edinburgh, 'but even so the neglect or ignorance of Sir Patrick Geddes in Scotland goes to an uncommon degree and throws a very disconcerting light on our whole national condition, since he was one of the outstanding thinkers of his generation, not merely in Britain but in the world, and not only one of the greatest Scotsmen of the past century but in our entire history.' COLIN WARD (1996) summed Geddes up as 'an erratic, disorganised and overbearing genius who anticipated every one of our late-twentieth century preoccupations, from the energy crisis to women's liberation'. Lewis Mumford found his insensitivity and willfulness infuriating. 'And yet I love him; I respect him; I admire him; he is still for me the most prodigious thinker in the modern world' (quoted in Novak, 1995). See CHARACTER, CITY REGION, CITY-LINE, CIVIC RUIN, CIVICENTRE, CLYDEFORTH, CONURBATION, DRAMA, EOTECHNIC, EU-POLITOGENICS, EUTOPITECTURE, ROBERT GRIEVE, HAUSSMANNISE, HOLISM, HOUSE-PROVINCE, IDEALOTOPIA, KAKATOPIA, KROPOTKIN, LANDSCAPE ARCHITECT, FRANK MEARS, MEGALOPOLIS, NEOTECHNIC AGE, NEW HEPTARCHY, OUTLOOK TOWER, PALEOTECHNIC, PATHIOPOLIS, PLACE WORK FOLK, PLACE-SENSE, POLITOGENICS, QUARTER, REGIONCITY, REVIVANCE, SHOLOPOLIS, SHORT'S OBSERVATORY, STRATEGOLOPOLIS, SURVEY BEFORE PLAN, TIME, TYRANNOPOLIS, URBAN VILLAGE and VALLEY SECTION.

Jan Gehl

Gehl, Jan (b1936) Architect and urban designer. Gehl is noted in particular for his close analysis and understanding of what makes successful streets and public spaces. His work has been highly influential. Gehl's books include *Life between Buildings*, published in 1971, and *Public Spaces and Public Life* (1987). Trained in Copenhagen, he has been a visiting professor at architecture, landscape architecture and planning schools in, among other places, Toronto (1972–73), West Australia (1978), and Berkeley, California (1983 and 1985). 'A good city is like a good party,' Gehl says. 'People don't want to leave early. They want to stay.'

Gehry, Frank (b1929) Architect, born in Canada and based in the USA. His early works in a deconstructivist style explored the sculptural effects of unusual materials. Some of his celebrated later buildings have been hailed as contributing to the regeneration and international image of their cities by their effectiveness as landmarks. See BILBAO EFFECT, BLOB ARCHITECTURE and DECONSTRUCTION.

Gemeinde (German) A municipality.

Gemeinschaft (German) COMMUNITY. The sociologist E Toennies identified two kinds of community in the 1950s. *Gemeinschaft* is characterised by warm, close relationships. *Gesellschaft* (natural community or association) by relationships of convenience. Toennies' work has had considerable influence on the debate about the meanings of 'community'.

gender The categories of female and male. (In discussions of urbanism, the term 'sex' tends to be used to refer to the biological division into female and male, and 'gender' to the social divisions that are derived from it.) Gender is believed to have a significant influence on how people experience the world around them. Women experience the built environment differently from men because they operate differently within it, due to economics and their social roles. They are at home more, they shop more, they push children in buggies and walk to school more, and they feel less safe on the streets. Fewer women than men have access to cars, twice as many women use public transport, they have lower average incomes and they live longer than men.

Women make up half the population, but are dramatically under-represented in the planning and urban design professions (Cavanagh, 1998). The writer Beatrix Campbell (1993) has described the different reactions of men and women living in bad housing and difficult social conditions. Men may react by finding a local situation to dominate, often through violent behaviour or crime, she suggests. Women, by contrast, are more likely to become involved in cooperative, socially useful activities, such as in community organisations. A number of woman writers, planners and designers have made efforts to increase the influence of women both in the professions and as people whose particular needs should be taken account of in the planning process. PATRICK GEDDES advocated an important role for women in action to improve society and the environment.

Asked in 1920 about the future of women in architecture, EDWIN LUTYENS replied drolly: 'It depends which architect she marries' (Dalley, 2002). The aptitude of women for architecture has a matter of controversy ever since. A number of scientific studies have concluded that, on average, men are better able to manipulate space, while women have a greater capacity for emphasising with people. Some people see this as an explanation of why such a small proportion of architects are women, and as a reason for believing that women are unlikely to become great architects.

Such an analysis is limited and reflects a limited view of the job of an architect. The process of design involves understanding the human needs that the building is intended to meet; communicating with the client; and collaborating with a wide range of other people in the design team and beyond, in addition to conceiving and manipulating three-dimensional space. Many unsuccessful buildings and places stand as evidence that their designers, however skilled they may have been at manipulating space, failed to understand the needs that the building was to have met, failed to communicate effectively with the client, or failed to get the best out of the design team.

Asked recently to name its favourite building, the predominately male architecture profession in the UK voted in first place MIES VAN DER ROHE's pavilion for the 1929 Barcelona exhibition. That is a gem indeed (it was demolished after the exhibition but has since been recreated), but it is architecture that is close to sculpture: a building without a context or a specific function. Too many architects try to emulate it in inappropriate circumstances, treating context and function as unfortunate obstacles on the road to artistic creation. Whatever the respective aptitudes of the two genders may be, the chances are that women and men have an equal potential for designing buildings and spaces.

gender audit An assessment of how the built environment provides differently for people of different genders, or of how policies or practice create (or may create) such differences.

General Permitted Development Order The GPDO grants permission for certain defined classes of development, mainly of a minor character. The most commonly used class permits a wide range of small extensions or alterations to dwelling houses.

generalised needs index The government's statistical measure of comparative housing needs, used as the basis for allocating funds to councils.

generalist The writer LEWIS MUMFORD described a generalist (which is how he saw himself) as 'one who sought to bring together in a more intelligible pattern the knowledge that the specialist had, by over-strenuous concentration, sealed into separate compartments' (quoted in Novak, 1995). The planning campaigner FJ

OSBORN called himself 'a specialist in things in general'.
Generalverkehrsplan (German) A general transport plan.
generation M Mature people, particularly as entrepreneurs.
generic town planner One with a range of skills rather than a specific specialism.
generica Types of development that are the same everywhere, often being part of a large company's corporate identity; an area largely made up of these. The term is used by NEW URBANISTS. Example: 'We were lost in generica. I didn't know what city it was' (from the USA, 2002).
genetic blueprint The American new urbanist ANDRES DUANY has called the sprawl model of urban planning 'the genetic blueprint for our own self destruction as a nation'. See NEW URBANISM, SUBURB, SUSTAINABLE, URBAN DESTRUCTION and URBAN SPRAWL.
genius loci (Latin) The spirit of the place. The Romans believed that every independent being and every place had its *genius*, which determined its character. Urban designers have tried to identify the genius loci and express it through their designs. Example: 'The site was like an amphitheatre, allowing a design in which the formal order would not be imposed architecturally but arise directly from the genius loci.' Aldo Rossi (1982) describes the genius loci as 'the local divinity, an intermediary who presided over all that was to unfold in it'. The novelist Peter Ackroyd (2001) has written: 'There is such a thing as the genius loci... and it is possible that certain districts actively modify the behaviour of people who live in them. Much art and literature may spring from this strange but persistent influence.' WILLIAM MORRIS asked in a letter to the *Daily News* in 1885, protesting about contemporary developments in Oxford: 'what speciality has Oxford if it is not the genius loci which our modern commercial dons are doing their best to destroy?' The architect Daniel Libeskind, discussing his plans for the WORLD TRADE CENTER site and other projects in 2003, spoke of listening to 'the voice of the site' (quoted in Dyckhoff, 2003).
gentle architecture TERRY FARRELL wrote in 1984 that the term 'implies that which is accessible to a wide range of people; is non-alienating in contextual handling and external expression of internal use and entrance ways; is unassertive and familiar in colour, form, imagery and formality of arrangement, sane and humane in terms of non-extreme theoretical or technological interpretations; and is above all an anxiety-free architecture which doesn't feed off any crisis cultivation' (quoted in Terry Farrell and Partners, 2002). Compare SOFT ARCHITECTURE.
gentleman of the road A tramp; a hobo. See VAGRANT.
gentrification The process of people with higher incomes moving into a residential area and carrying out improvements. In a market economy public improvements to an area are always likely to eventually lead to gentrification. Bill Kraus has written: 'Cities are gentrified... in sequence: first by the risk-oblivious (artists), then by the risk-aware (developers), finally by the risk adverse (dentists from New Jersey)' (quoted in Duany, 2001). Sukhvinder Stubbs (2002) observes: 'Many councils believe that run-down areas can not be regenerated while predominantly poor people continue to live there. Socio-economic mixing is deemed essential for successful regeneration. It's what used to be called "gentrification".' A poem 'The Planner and the Architect' by the cartoonist and writer Louis Hellman in the *Architects' Journal* in 1970 described, in the style of Lewis Carroll's 'The Walrus and the Carpenter', the gentrification (though without using that word) of the Barnsbury area of London. The planner and the architect organise improvements to the rundown, but the tenants wonder how they will be able to pay the increased rents. The poem ends: '"I weep for you," the Planner said:/ "I deeply sympathise."/ With sobs and tears he bought a house/ One of the largest size,/ Next door to the Architect/ And the chaps who Advertise./ "O locals," said the Architect,/ "You see a job well done;/ How do you like your district now?"/ But answer came there none – / And this was scarcely odd, because/ They'd moved out every one.' The term gentrification was used by the sociologist Ruth Glass (in relation to London) as early as 1964.
gentry People who move into an area as part of the process of GENTRIFICATION.
genuflection The design of one building being excessively deferential to another. Example: 'The new building picked up in a loose way on a number of attributes of its striking neighbouring buildings, without any attempt at genuflection.' The word comes from the Latin for 'knee' and 'bending'.
geodemography The study of how population characteristics relate to places; the practice of linking demographics to place. Geodemography has been used to identify small areas where characteristics of the local population suggest that there might be a market for types of house that the housing industry has not previously built there. Researchers in the USA have used it to identify people who live in suburban areas who would be likely to enjoy living in urban neighbourhoods.
geodesic dome A spherical structure formed from a network of triangles. It was conceived by BUCKMINSTER FULLER, who designed one 20 storeys high for the US pavilion at Expo '67 in Montreal. Fuller proposed roofing whole cities in transparent geodesic domes. Geodesic, from the Latin, means 'earth-dividing'. A geodesic line is the shortest distance between two points on a sphere.

geographic information system (GIS) A computer system for storing, mapping and analysing geographic data.

geography The study of the physical features of the earth and of human activities relating to these. The word derives from the Greek for *earth* and *writing*. See also HUMAN GEOGRAPHY and HUMANISTIC GEOGRAPHY.

geology The study of the earth's composition and structure.

geometrics The vertical and horizontal curves and straights that form the alignment of a road.

geomorphology The study of the origins and character of the landform, including glacial effects and geological origins.

George, Henry (1839–97) American economist. In his best-selling *Progress and Poverty* (1881), George advocated basing all taxation on the value of land, regardless of its use or improvement, and eventually taking all ground rent for public purposes. The idea of claiming the unearned increment of urban land values for public purposes became a cornerstone of EBENEZER HOWARD'S GARDEN CITY concept. Site value rating still has its advocates today. Henry Law of the Land Value Taxation Campaign argues that the absence of any tax on the site value of land distorts the use of land. 'The only holding cost of unused land is revenue foregone, and when owners have expectations of higher values in the future, they are willing to give up present income and allow land to stand vacant, under-used and under-developed in the interim. Thus regeneration is deferred, often for decades.' Law concludes: 'If any government were to set out with the deliberate aim of provoking urban decay, it would introduce a tax system much like the one we have in Britain today' (Law, 2002).

Georgian Buildings dating from the reigns of the first four Kings George (1714–1830). 'The Georgian period,' John Summerson (1962) suggests, 'begins with the building boom which followed the Treaty of Utrecht and continues to the end of the boom signalled by Waterloo. Or again, it begins with the rise of the Palladian movement and ends with the whole classical tradition tottering.' See also CONSERVATION-OFFICER GEORGIAN, KENTUCKY FRIED GEORGIAN and PLANNING OFFICER'S GEORGIAN.

Georgian Group A conservation campaign founded by Lord Derwent in 1937, in response to a threat to demolish JOHN NASH's Carlton House Terrace in London. Lord Derwent stated its aim as being to highlight the need 'to protect the nation's steadily diminishing Georgian heritage and... to rescue from demolition squares, terraces and individual buildings of beauty and importance.'

geosophy The study of how humans understand their world.

Gerckens, Laurence See TWENTIETH-CENTURY CITY.

German Village A detailed mock-up of typical Berlin apartments constructed in the desert of Utah in 1943 so that the military could investigate the most effective methods of bombing residential districts of Hitler's capital. 'Berlin's most far-flung, secret and orphan suburb,' as Mike Davis (2002) calls it, was designed by the modernist German-Jewish architect Eric Mendelsohn (though not in modernist style, of course). A similar mock-up of typical homes in Japanese cities was built nearby. See also URBAN DESTRUCTION.

Germania Adolf Hitler's name for his proposed rebuilding of Berlin, to the design of ALBERT SPEER, as the capital of the Third Reich and supposedly the world's greatest and most beautiful city.

Geschossfläche (German) Floor-space.

Get Carter A celebrated British gangster film directed by Mike Hodges and released in 1971. Michael Caine plays small-time London crook Jack Carter, who goes to Newcastle to find out who killed his brother. The film was made on location in Gateshead and Newcastle and is memorable for its evocation of urban Tyneside. The Get Carter Appreciation Society still visits its gritty urban locations and stages word-for-word re-enactments of the film. The society protested when in 2000 a multi-storey car park, one of the film's notable locations, was threatened with demolition. The film is adapted from the novel *Jack's Return Home* by Ted Lewis, published in 1970. See also MAIDENHEAD TOWN HALL.

get the job The first principle of architecture, according to the American architect Henry Hobson Richardson (1838–86).

Geuze, Adriaan (b1960) Landscape architect and urban planner. Geuze is the founder and principal of West 8 Landscape Architects in Rotterdam and founder of the Surrealist Landscape Architecture Foundation.

Gewerbegebiet (German) A commercial zone.

ghettification The formation of ghettoes; transforming a place into a ghetto.

ghetto 1 A part of a city where a particular group is concentrated or segregated. Ghetto was the name of the part of Venice where the Jews lived in the sixteenth century, possibly because it had been the site of an iron foundry (getto) or as a shortening of borghetto (suburb) (Flavell and Flavell, 1999). The term is not used exclusively to refer to people who are poor: examples include *upper-class ghetto* and *ghettos of the old* (retirement communities). **2** A place where something is particularly concentrated. See GHETTO HERITAGE, CAMILO VERGARA and WHITE FLIGHT.

ghetto heritage Historic monuments considered in isolation rather than in their context.

ghetto shift (US) A particular social or ethnic group moving from inner urban ghettos to blue-collar suburbs (Davis, 2002).

ghetto-blaster A large transistor radio for outside use, often carried on the shoulder. The term *boom-box* has sometimes been used as a supposedly non-stigmatising synonym.

EXPERIENCE WAITLESSNESS.
Delta
DELTA.COM/NYC
AviStar Haynes
'S Self Park
Free Car Wash
"PARK"
faster safer better

ghetto-griot (US) An urban poet; a rapper. See RAP.

ghost community The people who will live in a particular area that is being planned, but who have not yet been identified.

ghost town A town left almost deserted, usually after its economic base has collapsed.

giant glass stump The Prince of Wales in his 1984 Hampton Court speech called a proposed office block designed by MIES VAN DER ROHE for Mansion House Square in the heart of the City of London 'a giant glass stump better suited to Chicago'. The design had been commissioned by developer and architectural patron Lord Palumbo. Opposition to the proposal (and to the demolition of the site's Victorian buildings and the obliteration of a medieval lane) ensured that it was not built. Lord Palumbo commissioned a design by James Stirling instead, which was eventually built (and the site's Victorian buildings demolished).

Gibberd, Frederick (Sir) (1908–84) Architect and town planner. He was architect-planner of Harlow new town after 1947 and the architect of Liverpool Roman Catholic Metropolitan Cathedral. His book *Town Design* was published in 1953.

Gibson, Donald (Sir) (1908–1991) Architect and town planner. As Coventry city architect after 1938 he conceived ambitious plans to redevelop the city centre, publicised in the Coventry of Tomorrow exhibition of May 1940. Six months later two massive bombing raids destroyed much of the city centre. Gibson took the chance to impose the radically new street pattern that he already had in mind. The pedestrian precinct and ring road became – regrettably – a model for much post-war development. See also CLASP and PERCY JOHNSON-MARSHALL.

Giedion, Sigfried (1883–1968) Swiss architectural historian. His influential book *Space, Time and Architecture* was published in 1941. He was the founding secretary of CIAM (the Congrés Internationaux d'Architecture Moderne).

Gindroz, Raymond Urban designer and NEW URBANIST. He has helped pioneer the development of participatory planning methods for neighbourhoods, downtowns and regional plans.

ginnel (Yorkshire) An ALLEY (see that entry for regional variants).

giro drop (UK) An unoccupied flat used as an address for the purposes of fraudulently receiving welfare payments.

Giuliani, Rudolph (Rudi) (b1944) Republican mayor of New York in the 1990s and until the beginning of 2002, widely credited with making the city cleaner, safer and more prosperous. 'Zero tolerance' of crime was among the policies he pursued with celebrated zeal. When he took office in 1994, there were 2,000 murders a year in New York City. The number was down to 643 when he stood down in 2001. Giuliani also introduced league tables to shake up public services. Mike Davis (2002) comments tartly: 'The media generally viewed the fascistic bullying of squeegee men, pan handlers, cabbies, street vendors and welfare recipients as a small price to pay for the triumphs of having brought Disney (the ultimate imprimatur of suburban safety) to Times Square and tourism back to New York.'

Tony Travers (2002) of the LSE has written: 'The key to Giuliani's success was his decision to tell the police to adopt an aggressive approach to so-called nuisance crimes. Squeegee men, minor drug-dealers, fare-dodgers, aggressive beggars, drunks and even people urinating in the street were hauled in for their misdemeanours. Once arrested, many were found to have committed other crimes.' The number of people summonsed for these 'quality of life' infractions grew from 150,000 to more than 500,000 in 1994. Travers explains: 'Lobbyists for the dispossessed were incensed by the new, tough, approach... But the wider population were so fed up with the carnage and chaos on their streets that they silently assented to Giuliani's radical policies.' (The zero tolerance approach seemed unlikely to be adopted in London, Travers thought. Londoners did not yet feel that crime was quite bad enough to warrant it, they were not sufficiently trustful of the police, and their liberal instincts were too strong.)

In 2000 Mayor Giuliani withdrew from the race (against Hillary Clinton) to become a senator from New York on announcing that he was suffering from cancer. His reputation soared in response to his leadership of the city following the terrorist attacks on the WORLD TRADE CENTER on 11 September 2001. When he was awarded an honorary knighthood in London in 2002, the British press called him 'Rudi the Rock' and 'the Mayor of the World'.

Glasgow See THOMAS ANNAN, ANTI-URBAN, APACHE LAND, AREA IMPROVEMENT, THE ARMADILLO, ASSIST, BELONG TO, BUNGALOW, CANCER OF EMPIRE, CHARACTER, CITY OF ARCHITECTURE AND DESIGN 1999, COMMUNITY ARCHITECTURE, COMMUNITY-BASED HOUSING ASSOCIATION, COMPREHENSIVE REDEVELOPMENT, COMPREHENSIVE DEVELOPMENT AREA, CROWN STREET REGENERATION PROJECT, DEATH, GARDEN PARTY, GEAR, THE GORBALS, GOTHAM, GRID, ROBERT GRIEVE, HIGH RISE, HING, HOMES FOR THE FUTURE, PERCY JOHNSON-MARSHALL, MICHAEL KELLY, THE LIGHTHOUSE, OSCAR MARZAROLI, MEAN CITY, MERCHANT CITY, MOCKINTOSH, EDWIN MORGAN, NO MEAN CITY, PATTER, PERSONIFICATION, ROOM AND KITCHEN, GEOFF SHAW, SINGLE END, SMILE, SPAM VALLEY, STREET GAME, WOLFGANG SUSCHITZKY, UNTHANK, URBAN, JOHN RUSKIN, VILLA, WALKING, WALLY CLOSE, WINDAE-HINGER and WORKSHOP OF THE EMPIRE. 'Glasgow' is also the title of a poem written by Alexander Smith in 1857. Ian Spring (1990) calls it 'an excessive evocation of the first era of industrial society'. Smith declares: 'Draw thy fierce streams of blinding ore,/ Smite on a thousand anvils, roar/ Down to the harbour-bars;/ Smoulder in smoky sunsets, flare/ On rainy nights, with street and square/ Lie empty to the stars./ From terrace proud to alley base/ I know thee as my mother's face.'

Glasgow's Miles Better A campaign to improve Glasgow's IMAGE, launched in 1982. It involved plastering the mantra 'Glasgow's Miles Better' on London's buses and taxis until politicians and media people began automatically to repeat it whenever prompted by the word 'Glasgow'. See also AT LEAST IT'S NOT BASILDON and BOOSTERISM.

glass cancer A name given to *nickel sulphide inclusion*, an occasional cause of problems in glazing. Nickel and sulphur impurities combine in glass during manufacture, and may later (sometimes years later) expand, causing the glass to explode. See also HIGH-ALUMINA CEMENT.

Glaswegian A person from Glasgow. See also WEEDJIE.

Glendale, Ohio. A GARDEN SUBURB designed by Robert C Phillips and begun in 1851.

global city A city that serves as a base for organisations that shape the global economy. The sociologist Saskia Sassen (2000) has defined a global city as 'a complex organizational entity that concentrates the multiple resources needed for the management, coordination, specialized servicing, and governance of the global economic operations of firms and markets'. See also ATHENS and GLOBALISATION.

global village The Canadian communications theorist MARSHALL MCLUHAN argued in *The Gutenberg Galaxy*, published in 1960, that 'when man lives globally to the notes of a tribal drum [radio] on a planet that is no more than a village in scope and extent, he can not avoid the all-at-oneness of pattern which is the auditory and tribal type of structure'. McLuhan developed the idea in a letter in the same year: 'Today with electronics we have discovered that we live in a global village, and the job is to create a global *city*, as center for the village margins. The parameters of this task are by no means positional. With electronics any marginal area can become center, and marginal experiences can be had at any center. Perhaps the city needed to coordinate and concert the distracted sense programs of our global village will have to be built by computers in the way in which a big airport has to coordinate multiple flights' (Molinaro *et al*, 1987). McLuhan acknowledged the inspiration of the painter and writer WYNDHAM LEWIS. Lewis had written in *America and Cosmic Man*, published in 1947, that 'plural sovereignty... – now that the earth has become one big village, with telephones laid on from one end to the other, and air transport, both speedy and safe – must be a little farcical...' Zelimar Koscevic (2002) writes that the term global village appeared in print in Zagreb in 1924 (though in what language is not clear).

globalisation The growing interdependence of activities and countries worldwide; the reduction of local differences. The sociologist Anthony Giddens has described globalisation as 'a decoupling of space and time', with instantaneous communications, knowledge and culture that can be shared around the world simultaneously. The degree to which globalisation is inevitable or desirable, and the question of who benefits and who suffers from it, are hotly debated. For example, Robert Hunter Wade (2002), professor of political economy at the LSE, argues that globalisation in many ways has been a matter of the USA engineering its dominance. This, he says, has at times been for the general good, but often the global superpower's clout has been used solely in the interests of its richest citizens and most powerful corporations. In Wade's view, much of the talk about globalisation has obscured the power relations and the USA's exercises of statecraft. 'The increasing mobility of information, finance, goods and services frees the American government of constraints while more tightly constraining everyone else,' he writes. 'Globalisation enables the US to harness the rest of the world to its own rhythms and structure. Of course these arrangements do not produce terrorism. But they are deeply implicated in the very slow economic growth in most of the developing world since 1980, and in the widening world income inequality. Slow economic growth and vast income disparities breed cohorts of partly educated young people who grow up in anger and despair. Some try by legal or illegal means to migrate to the west; some join militant ethnic or religious movements directed at each other and their own rulers. But now the idea has spread among a few vengeful fundamentalists that the US should be attacked directly.' Wade concludes: 'The US and its allies can stamp out specific groups by force and bribery. But in the longer run, the structural arrangements that replicate a grossly unequal world have to be redesigned, so that markets working within the new framework produce more equitable results.'

In the words of University College London's Development Planning Unit (2001): 'Cities display profound differences in economic, social and cultural assets and political processes. Yet there is a growing consensus of what cities should be like. This consensus is based on the neo-liberal ideologies of efficiency, productivity, and competition and the needs of the market. Cities are competing, both within countries and around the world, to attract investment. In doing so, they are tending towards specialisation, particularly in the provision of services that exploit the new international communications and information technologies; biotechnology; and financial services.' The authors argue that certain cities become increasingly vulnerable to external shocks (such as the Asian economic crisis of the late 1990s) as they grow responsive to the global economy. 'The influence of cities is such that urban economic recessions are felt throughout the country and beyond. In addition, the global market is built on comparative advantages, which by definition are unequally distributed. While some cities prosper, others are left behind and can not compete in the global economy, thereby creating inequalities and imbalances within countries.' They conclude: 'There are conflicting aspects to globalisation. Some are positive, innovative and dynamic aspects, while others are negative, disruptive and marginalise people.' RICHARD SENNETT (2001) suggests that globalism makes some buildings into a form of international currency. 'The neutrality of new buildings... results from their global currency as investment units; for someone in Manila easily to buy or sell a hundred thousand square feet of office space in London, the space itself needs the uniformity, the transparency, of money.'

The process of globalisation has been traced back at least as far the first circumnavigation of the world in 1519 to 1521, and through the rapid growth in world trade and investment in the late nineteenth century, the establishment of the International Date Line and world time zones, the near-global adoption of the Gregorian calendar between 1875 and 1925, the adoption of international standards, the growth of multinational companies after the second world war, the growth of air travel, the end of the cold war, the growth of telecommunications and the development of the internet. President Ulysses S Grant declared in his 1873 inaugural address: 'As commerce, education, and the rapid transition of thought and matter by telegraph and steam have changed everything, I rather believe that the great maker is preparing the world to become one nation, speaking one language' (quoted in Bender, 2002). Globalisation is the opposite of LOCALISATION.

glocalisation Combining respect for the global system with an emphasis on local identity. The term is used by people trying to combat the negative effects of GLOBALISATION.

gloon The word means *town* in the language of the fictional Vril-ya Country, as described by Lord Lytton in *The Coming Race* (1871). Vril-ya Country, which seems to lie beneath Newcastle-upon-Tyne, is inhabited by large winged creatures that live according to the maxim: 'No happiness without order, no order without authority, no authority without unity.'

gnomescape A derisive term for the sort of suburban landscape where residents have plaster gnomes in their front gardens. See NATO.

go bush (Australia) To get away from built-up places. Usually camping/living in non-serviced and relatively natural locations.

goals-achievement matrix A technique for evaluating alternative plans, devised by M Hill in the late 1960s.

gob-on *n.* Meaningless detail on a building. Jon Rouse, chief executive of the COMMISSION FOR ARCHITECTURE AND THE BUILT ENVIRONMENT, used the phrase in 2001, giving as examples carriage lamps and functionless chimneys. See also STICK-ON.

God 'Man makes plans, and God laughs,' according to a Yiddish proverb.

God of the City See GEORG HEYM.

go-faster stripes The most superficial design treatment. The phrase comes from the stripes that can be stuck on a car, supposedly to enhance the impression of speed or of being streamlined.

Going, Going A poem by Philip Larkin (1922–85) mourning the loss of traditional England in the face of urban growth.

Golborne Neighbourhood Council Britain's first neighbourhood council, elected in 1971 to serve part of London's north Kensington.

Golden City A town near Denver in Colorado, USA. It first grew in the gold rush of the 1850s but is thought to have been named after Thomas Golden, an early settler. In 1872 the town's name was shortened to Golden. Compare CITY OF GOLD.

golden section Based on a line divided so that the ratio of the smaller to the larger part is the same as the ratio of the larger part to the whole. The ratio is 1:1.618 or 0.618:1. The mathematics were known to the ancient Greeks. Some architects have used the ratio in designing, often claiming that it is the most beautiful proportion. In nature the ratio is related to the Fibonacci series of numbers. It is also called the *golden mean*, *golden ratio* and *golden proportion*.

The Royal Town Planning Institute used a diagram of the golden section as the basis of a new logo, unveiled in 2001 to symbolise its New Vision for Planning. The figure, the institute explained, 'encapsulates the balance between art and science which we seek to promote; it occurs in both the natural and man-made environments with which we deal; ...and it relates to the concept of visual harmony and balance'. The Duchy of Cornwall's design guide for POUNDBURY notes that the proportions of 'the more formal landmark houses' in the Prince of Wales' model community are 'related to the golden mean'. The guide specifies that columns, verandah and porch openings, and the vertical axes of window panes 'shall be approximate to the golden mean'.

Goldsmith, Edward (b1928) Ecological campaigner. Since 1969 he has edited *The Ecologist*, a magazine that came to prominence in 1972 with its issue 'Blueprint for Survival', which sold half a million copies in 17 languages. This prompted the formation of the UK's Green Party, the first in the world. His book *The Way: an ecological world-view* was published in 1992. 'The industrial society in which we live, and that we take to be normal, desirable and permanent, is in fact aberrant, destructive and necessarily short-lived,' Goldsmith writes. 'Rather than further increase our dependence on it, we should, on the contrary, reduce such dependence and set out systematically to phase it out.' He received the RIGHT LIVELIHOOD AWARD in 1991.

Gomorrah One of the Biblical 'CITIES OF THE PLAIN'. See also BABEL, DESTRUCTION OF SODOM AND GOMORRAH and URBAN DESTRUCTION.

gondola of the people A tram. The phrase is credited to the cultural historian Richard Hoggart.

Good and Bad Manners in Architecture See ARTHUR TRYSTAN EDWARDS.

good city form The urban designer KEVIN LYNCH defined seven criteria in *Good City Form*, published in 1984. They are: a) *Vitality*: the degree to which the form of the settlement supports the vital functions, the biological requirements and capabilities of human beings; above all, how it protects the survival of the species. This is an anthropocentric criterion, Lynch notes, 'although we may some day consider the way in which the environment supports the life of other species, even where that does not contribute to our own survival'. b) *Sense*: the degree to which the settlement can be clearly perceived and mentally differentiated, and structured in time and space by its residents, and the degree to which that mental structure connects with their values and concepts: the mental capabilities, and our cultural constructs. c) *Fit*: the degree to which the form and capacity of spaces, channels, and equipment in a settlement match the pattern and quantity of actions that people customarily engage in, or want to engage in; that is, the adequacy of the behaviour settings, including their adaptability to future action. d) *Access*: the ability to reach other persons, activities, or places, including the quantity and diversity of the elements that can be reached. e) *Control*: the degree to which the use and access to spaces and activities, and their creation, repair, modification and management are controlled by those who use, work, or reside in them. f) *Efficiency*: the cost, in terms of other valued things, of creating and maintaining the settlement, for any given level of attainment of the environmental dimensions listed above. g) *Justice*: the way in which environmental benefits and costs are distributed among persons, according to some particular principle such as equity, need, intrinsic worth, ability to pay, effort expended, potential contribution, or power. Justice is the criterion that balances the gains among person, while efficiency balances the gains among different values.

Lynch explained that the last two criteria (efficiency and justice) apply to each of the other five. The first five 'are meaningless until costs and benefits have been defined by specifying the prior basic values. In each case, one asks: first, what is the cost (in terms of anything else we choose to value) of achieving this degree of vitality, sense, fit, access, or control? And, second, who is getting how much of it?'

good design The term is widely used though rarely defined. Good design will always be at least to some extent a subjective matter, though it becomes more objective when there are agreed principles or criteria, as may be set out in a DEVELOPMENT PLAN or, in more detail, in a DEVELOPMENT BRIEF.

In 1994 the Royal Fine Art Commission published a short book *What Makes a Good Building?* The commission claimed that the criteria it set out were 'objective values exhibiting facts which are not coloured by the feelings or opinions of the person making a judgement,' though it was hard to see how those criteria could be applied objectively. The commission noted that architects 'see the imposition of design criteria or guidelines as a threat to their freedom as artists' but that 'if more architects were willing to impose design criteria on themselves, they would be in a better position to challenge the demands of planning officers and amenity groups.' It quoted LEONARDO DA VINCI's aphorism: 'Strength is born of constraint and dies in freedom.'

The RFAC's criteria for a good building were: a) *Order and unity*. Order through symmetry, balance, repetition, the grid, the bay and the frame. In the best architecture a satisfying and indivisible unity is a consequence of this search for order. b) *Expression* of the function of the building. c) *Integrity* or honesty to the principles of construction. d) *Plan and section*. Intelligence, ingenuity and innovation in the siting, planning and organisation of a building. e) *Detail* brings us into close contact with a building where we can admire the beauty of the materials and the skill of the craftsman or engineer. f) *Integration*. Fitting a building into its surroundings harmoniously through appropriate siting, massing, scale, proportion, rhythm and materials. g) *Siting* is to do with the way a building fits into the grain of the city and how it relates to other buildings and to the street. h) *Massing* is the three-dimensional disposition of the different parts of a building and includes height, bulk and silhouette. The height of a new building should respect the height of existing buildings and its bulk should not greatly exceed the bulk of adjoining buildings. i) *Scale* in architecture is, first, the dimensions of a building and all its parts relative to the dimensions of a human being and, second, the dimensions of a building relative to the dimensions of another building. A building can be of human or inhuman scale, and in or out of scale with another building. Scale is exactly measurable and whether a building is in or out of scale with a human being or another building is a fact and not a matter of opinion. j) *Proportion* is the relation between one part of a building and another, and between any one part and the whole. Proportion is measurable and something about which it is possible to be objective. Proportion is also to do with the ratio of solid to void in the facade of a building. k) *Rhythm* is the arrangement and size of the constituent parts of a facade and is therefore to the facade what grain is to the city as a whole. Rhythm of street facades usually consists of repeated vertical elements. Buildings with strong horizontal emphasis tend to disrupt the street rhythm. l) *Materials* determine the colour and texture of a building, and the choice of material can either sharpen or soften the differences between the various parts.

The housing association director Rob Joiner (2002) has described good (and well-designed) public housing as 'housing you thought was private sector housing'. Some practitioners and commentators point to a divine origin for the laws of architecture. The Scottish architect Alexander 'Greek' Thomson claimed that 'the laws which govern the universe, whether aesthetical or physical, are the same which govern architecture... The laws of architecture were not invented by man, but were discovered by slow degrees' (quoted in Watkin, 1994). Those who have made similar claims in recent years include the PRINCE OF WALES and the neo-classical architect QUINLAN TERRY. See also GOOD URBAN DESIGN.

good enough to approve? An approach to DEVELOPMENT CONTROL based on asking whether a planning application is good enough to approve, rather than asking (as some say planners traditionally do) whether it is it *bad enough to refuse*.

Good Life, The UK 1970s television situation comedy. The series was a suburban comedy of manners in which a couple (played by Richard Briers and Felicity Kendall) who have dropped out of the rat race to pursue self-sufficiency are contrasted with their bemused, conformist neighbours (Paul Eddington and Penelope Keith). See also OZZIE AND HARRIET and TERRY AND JUNE.

good urban design The DETR/CABE (2000a) guidance *By Design* defines good urban design as that which creates: a) A distinct sense of place responding to local context. b) Continuity of frontages and clearly defined public space. c) Safe, attractive and functional public space. d) An accessible, well-connected, pedestrian-friendly environment. e) A readily understandable, easily navigable environment. f) Flexible and adaptable public and private environments. g) A varied environment offering a range of uses and experiences.

Goodman, Paul (1911–72) Anarchist writer. Brother of Percival. See AUTONOMY, CITY OF EFFICIENT CONSUMPTION, CITY OF FREE CHOICE, THE NEW COMMUNE and VACATION LAND.

Goodman, Percival (1904–89) Architect, planner, teacher and painter. Brother of Paul. See CITY OF EFFICIENT CONSUMPTION, CITY OF FREE CHOICE, THE NEW COMMUNE and VACATION LAND.

Goodman, Robert Radical architect and planner. He was a founder of Urban Planning Aid and an organiser of the Architects' Resistance in the late 1960s. His book *After the Planners* was published in 1972.

goodsline A pipeline or conduit for moving goods in capsules.

goo-stop (BLACK COUNTRY dialect) A traffic light. The term is a variant of go-stop.

Gopher Prairie See MAIN STREET.

Gorbals, The A district of Glasgow, south of the city centre across the River Clyde, best known in the first half of the twentieth century as a classic slum and for its reputation for gang violence. Beginning as a medieval village, it was Glasgow's first suburb by the eighteenth century. At its peak, the Gorbals housed 100,000 people in a square mile of squalid, overcrowded tenements.

The area was redeveloped (and most of the population exported) in the 1960s to an ambitious modernist plan providing mainly tower blocks and systems-built slab blocks. The architects of the new Gorbals included Basil Spence and Robert Matthew. A character in Jeff Torrington's novel *Swing Hammer Swing*, published in 1992 and set in the 1960s, comments: 'Most of the old Gorbals had been levelled by now. Housing planners had taken up their slum-erasers and rubbed out the people who'd lived there.'

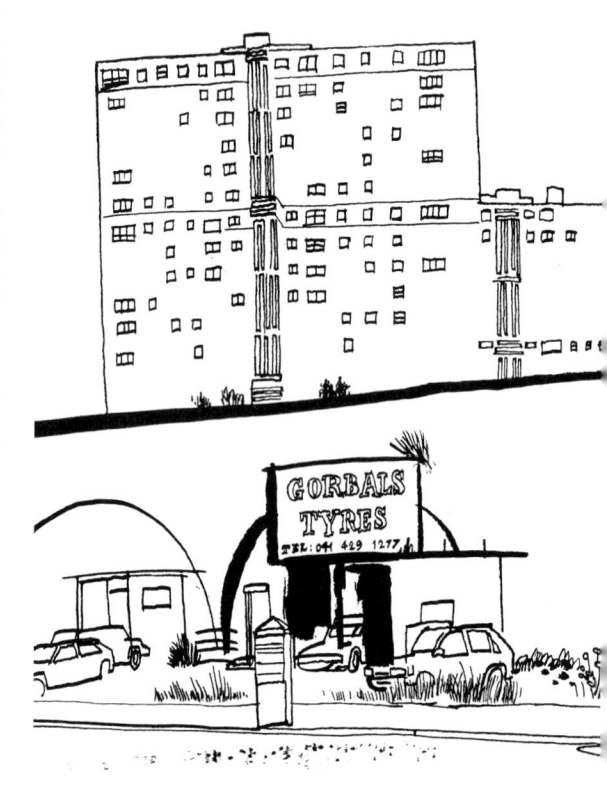

Writing in 1960, IAN NAIRN argued that the 'incredibly dignified' Glasgow style 'culminated around 1850 in two places. About Kelvingrove there will be little argument, but I tremble to mention the other one, because it is of all places, the Gorbals. I can hear the cries of outraged planners already: "Really, this fellow Nairn has gone too far this time". But I would plead with them really to go and have a look at the Gorbals, while it is still there. It was laid out on a grid, with immensely dignified, four-storey, stone-built terraces. There are far too many people living there, and the state of the backyards and the communal staircases with their lavatories on the half-landings are intolerable and must be altered. However, the actual outside appearance, in other circumstances, would be applauded as a splendid piece of urban design. Parts are past repair... but Kingston, the part west of the railway, could easily be salvaged, not as a stop-gap or cut-rate measure but because of the innate qualities of the buildings.'

The redevelopment was spectacularly unsuccessful. Revisiting the area in 1967, Ian Nairn wrote: 'The old pattern is thrown away without a thought to its virtues... Unless the city wakes up to a sense of its own greatness, Glasgow is headed for disaster... There are fearsome road proposals and fearsome rehousing proposals.' A further redevelopment by the CROWN STREET REGENERATION PROJECT followed after 1990. This project has been widely praised, but its official brochure in 2000 showed that the lesson has been learnt that time is the real test of whether a regeneration project is successful. 'Fifty years must pass,' it said, 'before a true judgement can be made as to whether the project has achieved its aim of creating a robust, balanced and integrated community.' See ANTI-URBANISM, ASSIST, NO MEAN CITY and UNTHANK.

Gordon, Alex (Sir) (1917–1999) A Scottish-born, Cardiff-based architect, Gordon was an early advocate of what is now termed SUSTAINABLE DEVELOPMENT. As RIBA president in 1972, two years before the world oil crisis, he promoted an approach to design summed up in his slogan 'long life, loose fit, low energy'.

Gordon, Rodney Architect. He designed the BRUTALIST Tricorn shopping centre in Portsmouth in the 1960s while working with the Owen Luder Partnership. The Tricorn topped more than one list of the UK's most unpopular buildings before being demolished in 2004.

Gordy, Berry (b1929) Record producer and music industry entrepreneur. See MOTOWN.

gore A triangular piece of land. From the Old English *gara*, meaning a triangular piece of land or a spear. See also KENSINGTON GORE.

gorod sad (Russian) A garden city.

gossip group Houses in the Greenwich Millennium Village were designed in horseshoe-shaped *gossip groups* of 30–50 houses. This was taken to represent the number of people who recognise each other without forced intimacy (Llewelyn-Davies, 2000).

Gotham 1 New York. The nickname was popularised in 1807–08 by *Salmagundi*, a series of satirical essays by Washington Irving and others. See also BIG APPLE. **2** Any town or city that is the subject of satire. The nickname was borrowed from the Nottinghamshire village of Gotham, whose inhabitants were supposed to be fools (although possibly they were only pretending to be, so as to avoid the expense of accommodating a royal visitor). An anonymous *Chronicles of Gotham*, published in 1856, lambasted the authorities in Glasgow for neglecting the city (McKean, 1994).

Gotham City The fictional setting of the Batman comic adventures.

Gothamite A New Yorker.

gothic A style of architecture that originated in north western France around 1140. It is characterised by such features as pointed arches, large windows, flying buttresses and pinnacles. By the fifteenth-century in Italy and France, and the sixteenth in England, the fashion for gothic had faded in the face of classicism. In the early eighteenth century the style was revived. Michael Lewis (2002) writes: 'A style of architecture that stood condemned for three centuries as the apex of barbarism and irrationality was rehabilitated – at first playfully, then seriously and finally dogmatically... The gothic revival is rather more than a fashion craze for pointed arches and pinnacles. During its years of greatest influence, it subjected every aspect of art, belief, society and labour to intense intellectual scrutiny, using the middle ages as a platform from which to judge the modern world.' Lewis agrees that this seems a considerable burden to place on the back of what was, after all, just a style of architecture. 'But the gothic always stood for ideas larger than itself. The eighteenth century admired it for its suggestive quality of decay and melancholy, the early nineteenth century for the religious piety it expressed, the late nineteenth for its superb engineering. In the course of the revival the gothic was attached to social movements of every sort – from political liberalism to patriotic nationalism, from Roman Catholic solidarity to labour reform. Lewis notes: 'Like Marxism, which also drew lessons from medieval society, the gothic revival offered a comprehensive response to the dislocations and traumas of the industrial revolution. In the broadest view, it is the story of Western civilization's confrontation with modernity.'

gothick 1 (up to the 1750s) The architectural style now known as GOTHIC. **2** (nineteenth century) A description of any gothic revival building that was particularly naïve, flimsy or historically incorrect (Lewis, 2002).

Gott, Samuel See NOVA SOLYMA.

Gottwaldov See ZLIN.

governance See URBAN GOVERNANCE.

govspeak The impenetrable language of government departments.

Gowers Report The report *Houses of Outstanding Historic and Architectural Interest*, published in 1950, led to the Historic Buildings and Ancient Monuments Act 1953.

grade (or gradient) The slope along a length of road.

grade separation Movement occupying different levels (a pedestrian deck above streets, or roads crossing over a motorway, for example). The opposite is movement being *at grade*.

grade-separated intersection A road junction at which at least one road passes over another.

grading uses Arranging a mix of several different uses so that only 'compatible' uses are next to each other. For example, offices might be next to housing, workshops next to offices, and general industrial uses next to workshops.

graf kat (US) A graffiti artist.

graffiti (plural of *graffito*) RICHARD SENNETT (1990) describes the origins of the modern explosion of graffiti. 'In a city that belongs to no one, people are constantly seeking to leave a trace of themselves, a record of their story. In the 1970s, New York was awash with these traces. Huge numbers, initials, and nicknames identifying the writer appeared inside and outside subway cars, insignia made with cans of pressurized spray paint and felt-tipped pens. Neither obscene, nor political as in the posters of a previous

> **"IN A CITY THAT BELONGS TO NO ONE, PEOPLE ARE CONSTANTLY SEEKING TO LEAVE A TRACE OF THEMSELVES, A RECORD OF THEIR STORY"**
>
> *Richard Sennett*

decade, they were just names and tags like LA11 written everywhere, the work of slum-kids. The scale of this graffiti was what at first made the impression: there was so much of it, and so much of it was big, covering doors and windows and bench backs and metal plates of subway cars, the functional parts of these walls ignored, all covered over as surface on which to write. From the walls of subway cars the names spread to the walls of buildings outside the slums, and the fixed walls were similarly appropriated. These endless monster labels might be rather grandly described as the making of a theatrical wall, the subway cars treated as a neutral backcloth to be brought to life by dramatic gestures in paint. The kids were indifferent, however, to the general public, playing to themselves, ignoring the presence of other people using or enclosed in their space.' The photographer BRASSAÏ photographed figurative graffiti in Paris for more than 30 years, and he devised a system for classifying and decoding them. 'These abbreviated signs are none other than the origins of writing,' he wrote (Brassaï, 1993). 'These animals, monsters, demons, heroes, phallic deities are the elements of mythology, no less. Rising to the lofty heights of poetry or plunging to the depths of triviality ceases to make any sense in this region where the laws of gravity no longer apply'.

Graham, William (Sir) (Lord Holford of Kemp Town) (1907–1975) South African-born town planner and architect, president of the Town Planning Institute and the Royal Institute of British Architects. Holford was professor of civic design at Liverpool University, and adviser to the Ministry of Town and Country Planning (drawing up the Town and Country Planning Act 1947). He was responsible with Charles Holden for a plan for the City of London (1946–7). He produced a report on the development of Canberra (1957–8) and was a member of the jury for the new city of Brasilia in 1957.

He produced plans for both Durban and Cambridge which were condemned as *apartheid planning* – racial in the case of Durban, town/gown at Cambridge. As a consultant he is best remembered for his 1955–6 design of the precincts of St Paul's Cathedral in London. Almost universally loathed, the buildings were demolished in 2001. Holford was knighted in 1953, and in 1965 became the first architect or planner to be made a life peer.

William Graham

grand ensemble (French) A term describing large, post-war housing estates on the periphery of French cities.

Grand Manner, the The urbanism of a powerful state authority, characterised by, in the words of Spiro Kostof (1991), 'ramrod-straight avenues, vast uniformly bordered squares, and a suitable accompaniment of monumental public buildings.' The Grand Manner 'speaks of ceremony, processional intentions, a regimented public life. The street holds the promise of pomp: it traverses the city with single-minded purpose and sports accessories like triumphal arches, obelisks and free-standing fountains. All this architectural drama subsumes the untidiness of our common routines. Shielded by the spacious envelopes, most of us continue to manage our plain existence, ready to gather into attendant crowds when the high business of the Grand Manner City needs its popular complement.'

grand projet (French) **1** Any of the series of big development projects built in Paris mainly under the presidency of François Mitterrand. The programme was a vote of confidence in the ability of FLAGSHIP PROJECTS, with big budgets and the freedom for architects to express themselves, to boost the international prestige and cultural dynamism of the French capital. The projects were intended to be completed in time for the celebrations marking the 1989 bicentennial of the French revolution. **2** Any other major project, in any country, of which the government has high expectations (see JUBILEE LINE EXTENSION).

grande ensemble (French) A housing estate.

Granite City Aberdeen, largely built of that stone (see also THE SILVER CITY); St Louis.

granny flat A small extension to a house, intended for an elderly relative. A US equivalent is *mother-in-law apartment*.

gravitational pull The effect of an urban settlement or major development attracting activity (shopping, for example) from the surrounding area.

gray area (US) A rundown area at the edge of town or city centre; a TWILIGHT AREA. Paul D Spreiregen (1965) wrote: 'The gray areas are not quite slums – they are the service quarters of the city, the places where small businesses may begin and, often, where major ones thrive.'

Gray, Alasdair (b1934) Novelist and painter. See UNTHANK.

Gray, Bennie (b1945) Urbanist, entrepreneur and developer. Since 1976 Gray has pioneered arts-and-media-led regeneration through converting large derelict buildings for new mixed uses through his SPACE Organisation. The Custard Factory in Birmingham, UK, is the best known of his projects.

grayfield (US) A failing shopping centre.

Great Society, The The concept of the Great Society was being discussed by social reformers such as John Dewey in the USA in the 1920s, inspired by Graham Wallas' book *The Great Society*. President LYNDON JOHNSON revived the phrase in a speech to students at the University of Michigan in 1964. 'Your imagination, your initiative, and your indignation will determine whether we build a society where progress is the servant of our needs, or a society where old values and new visions are buried under unbridled growth,' Johnson declared. 'For in your time we have the opportunity to move not only toward the rich society and the powerful society, but upward to the Great Society.' The Great Society became the name of Johnson's programme of social reform, only a few of whose aims were achieved.

Great Stink, the The smell caused by pollution of the River Thames in London in 1858. It finally convinced the authorities that measures must be taken to deal with the capital's sewage. See BAZALGETTE.

great unwashed, the A derisive term for poor people. *The Great Unwashed* was the title of a book by Thomas Wright, published in 1868, about the lives of the urban poor.

Great Wen, The London, so called by WILLIAM COBBETT in the 1820s. A wen is a disfiguring cyst of the skin, caused by a blocked sebaceous gland. Cobbett demanded that the Great Wen be dismantled in order that civilisation might have a second chance (Raban, 1974). Compare MONSTROUS CARBUNCLE.

Greater London Authority (GLA) Established in 2000 to provide city-wide strategic government for London, the GLA covers the 32 London boroughs and the Corporation of London. It is responsible for planning, regeneration, transport, the police and fire services. The GLA is headed by a directly elected mayor, who is scrutinised by the Greater London Assembly. See also KEN LIVINGSTONE.

Greater London Council (GLC) (1965–1986) The GLC replaced the LONDON COUNTY COUNCIL (which covered a smaller area). As well as the administration arguments for enlargement, the then Conservative government hoped to dilute the politically 'red' inner boroughs which made up the LCC with 'blue' outer boroughs so as to produce a Tory majority on the new council. When it turned a virulent shade of red under KEN LIVINGSTONE, it was duly abolished by the Thatcher government.

Greater London Development Plan The first statutory strategic plan for Greater London, prepared by the GREATER LONDON COUNCIL. It was submitted for approval in 1969 and approved in 1976. Compare THE LONDON PLAN.

Greater London Highway Development Survey See BRESSEY REPORT.

Greater London Plan (1944, published in 1945) The second of PATRICK ABERCROMBIE's plans for the capital, supported by the Ministry of Housing and Local Government. Abercrombie planned for a system of arterial roads, slum clearance, rebuilding of bombed areas, a green belt, and new towns and town expansions.

Greatness of Cities, The A book by Giovanni Botero, published in the sixteenth century, discussing the relationship between cities and political power.

green 1 *n.* An informal, grassed public space, often providing a focus to local or village life. **2** *v.* To apply ecological principles. **3** *v.* To improve a place through soft landscaping.

green architecture Designing buildings with particular concern for their environmental impact, for example by requiring little energy in their construction and use, and using renewable materials. J Farmer (1996) defines green architecture as 'buildings which use lightly the earth's resources, and are expressive also of a way of living which thinks itself in partnership with nature'. See also GREEN DESIGN.

green ban The refusal by unionised building workers to work on contracts which they saw as detrimental to the environment. The movement was started by the New South Wales Builders' Labourers' Federation, led by Jack Mundey, in Australia in the early 1970s. At least one green ban was declared in the UK, in Birmingham in 1976. Compare BLACK BAN.

green belt (UK) A special policy defining an area within which only a highly restrictive schedule of changes constituting development under the planning acts will normally be permitted (Elson, 1986). The government defines the purpose of a green belt as being to check the growth of a large built-up area, to prevent neighbouring towns merging into one another, or to preserve the special character of a town. Green belts have been one of the most popular instruments of the UK planning system. They have a long history. In 1580 Queen Elizabeth I of England decreed that 'the Queen's Majestie, perceiving the state of the City of London... doth charge and strictly command all manner of persons, of what quality so ever they be, to desist and forbear from any new building of any house or tenement within three miles from any of the gates of the said City of London.' The ideas of green belts was central to the GARDEN CITY concept. In EBENEZER HOWARD's original proposal, published in 1898, each garden city would be surrounded by an 'agricultural belt'. This would provide the city's food and open space, and keep it compact. Alfred Marshall wrote in 1899 proposing a 'national fresh air tax' to create green belts for agriculture and leisure between towns (Mumford, 1961). 'We need to prevent one town from growing into another, or into a neighbouring village,' Marshall wrote. In 1910 RAYMOND UNWIN spoke approvingly of the *green girdle* that he had seen on a visit to Chicago the previous year. George Pepler proposed a green girdle round London in 1911. Unwin called for a green belt round London in 1921. The green belt was introduced in the London and Home Counties Green Belt Act 1938, and applied throughout England in 1955. Sir PETER HALL has called green belts 'a civilised form of apartheid'. COLIN WARD has written: 'The rich can buy their way into the green belt, the commuting middle classes can leapfrog over it into new settlements or old country towns and villages beyond it. But the poor are trapped for lack of mortgage-worthiness' (Ward, 1989). John Prescott (see TWO JAGS) once told an interviewer when he was environment secretary: 'The green belt is one of New Labour's finest achievements, and we're going to build on it.' That prospect came nearer in 2002 when the Royal Town Planning Institute announced that the development of green belt sites should be considered to relieve the demand for housing in the south-east of England. 'The green belt shouldn't be regarded as sacred,' the RTPI's president Michael Haslam said. 'It may be more sustainable to take a bite out of the inside of the green belt as an urban extension, rather than build housing 10 miles outside the town on the other side of the green belt.' See also GREEN WEDGES, RURAL BUFFERS and STRATEGIC GAPS.

green chain A series of linked but separate open spaces and the footpaths between them.

Green City 1 FREIBURG, so called because of its green planning, transport and environmental policies. **2** London, so called because of its parks and gardens.

green consumerism People taking account of environmental issues in deciding what to buy and in making other decisions about their lifestyles.

green design The Architectural League of New York (2001) has written of what it calls green design: a) There is no such thing as a GREEN ARCHITECTURE or a green aesthetic. Instead there are countless ways design can address and synthesize green issues. b) Green design is not merely a matter of add-ons or product specification. It involves more than insulation, low-emissivity glass, non-polluting paints, and water-conserving toilets. Rather, it influences the form of the whole building and is one of its major generators from the first moments of the design process. c) Pursuing a green agenda is no constraint on creativity but instead a major stimulus towards an architecture that is innovative, significant and relevant. d) Greenness is not incompatible with the highest levels of architectural excellence. Europe's leading architects are also among its best exponents of green design. e) Green design acknowledges the dynamic intersection of buildings with immediate natural setting and ambient forces. It is these interactions on which the design process focuses as much as on the resultant form of the building. This way of working draws on and parallels the most up to date insights from science. f) Many green buildings represent the leading edge of engineering design, such as predictive modeling techniques. Their functioning depends on neural network software and a myriad of sensors. Such buildings, which are produced through close collaboration with engineers from the first moments with design, need to be far more precisely engineered than conventional buildings.

green girdle See GREEN BELT.

green goddess 1 A fire engine of the fleet kept by the government for use in national emergencies, and seen on the streets of Britain during fire-fighters' strikes. **2** A tram of Liverpool Corporation's fleet (of which locals are said to have been proud), in use until the 1950s.

Green Heart The area within the urbanised horseshoe of the Netherlands' RANDSTAD.

green industry Businesses that produce goods or services that are less than usually harmful to the environment.

green island See BROWNFIELD.

green lane 1 An unpaved lane, usually rural, which may be a FOOTPATH, BRIDLEWAY, ROAD USED AS A PUBLIC PATH or unclassified. **2** An urban street enhanced by a programme of planting and environmental improvements.

green map An annotated map showing the location of environmental initiatives in an area. Green maps are produced as part of the Green Map System, a global collaboration whose aim is to identify, promote and link each city's eco-resources. The UK's first green map, published in the 1990s, was for Liverpool: it categorised initiatives under *food* and *eating out; shopping* and *green businesses; nature* and *open spaces; transport;* and *information* and *institutions*.

green necklace A series of linked areas of parkland round an urban area.

green paper A government discussion document. Compare WHITE PAPER.

Green Spaces and Sustainable Communities Grants from the New Opportunities Fund to help communities improve and care for their natural environment.

green travel plan The basis for reducing the impact of a land use that generates a significant amount of traffic.

green up See COMMUNITY FOREST.

green wave A pattern of coordinated traffic signals that allows a vehicle to travel through a series of green lights.

green way A linked series of more or less continuous pieces of open land suitable for continuous walking, riding or cycling.

green wedge A designation in a development plan of land which should not be developed, usually to protect strategic open land. Like RURAL BUFFERS and STRATEGIC GAPS, they are less formal than GREEN BELTS.

Green, David See TAYLER AND GREEN.

Greenbelt A *green belt town* in Maryland designed by CLARENCE STEIN and built by the US Resettlement Administration. See also GREENBROOK and Greendale.

greenbelt towns (or cities) Planned by the US Resettlement Administration in the 1930s.

Greenbrook A *green belt town* in New Jersey built by the US Resettlement Administration. See also GREENBELT and GREENDALE.

green-collar sector People with jobs in environmentally beneficial activities such as public transport, recycling, refurbishment and renewable energy.

Greendale 1 A *green belt town* in Wisconsin designed by CLARENCE STEIN built by the US Resettlement Administration. See also GREENBELT and GREENBROOK. **2** The home village of the television animated character Postman Pat, first broadcast in the late 1970s. His post office (which closed in 2003) was based on that in Greenside, near Kendall in Cumbria, where the series' creator John Cuncliffe lived.

Greene, David See ARCHIGRAM.

greenedge (US) A belt of open space round an urban area.

greenery The writer Frank O'Hara declared: 'One need never leave the confines of New York to get all the

> "I CAN'T EVEN ENJOY A BLADE OF GRASS UNLESS I KNOW THERE IS A SUBWAY HANDY, OR A RADIO STORE, OR SOME OTHER SIGN THAT PEOPLE DO NOT TOTALLY REGRET LIFE"
>
> *Frank O'Hara*

greenery one wishes. I can't even enjoy a blade of grass unless I know there is a subway handy, or a radio store, or some other sign that people do not totally regret life.' See also NEVER TRUST AIR YOU CAN'T SEE.

greenfield land That which has not previously been developed. Though government policy is generally to avoid developing greenfield land, in many cases it can not be avoided. And the government recognises that in some cases developing a greenfield site may be – in its terms – the SUSTAINABLE option. A greenfield site already within the urban fringe, compromised by its surroundings, and well integrated into the urban fabric, may offer development opportunities that are better than a poorly located but previously developed site. For example the previously developed site might be in a rural area with poor access to transport and other infrastructure. Compare BROWNFIELD.

greenfield tax A special tax on the development of greenfield sites has been proposed (but not, so far, introduced), as a way of discouraging greenfield development and making the development of BROWNFIELD (previously developed) sites more likely.

greenfronting townhouse (US) Defined approvingly by Andres Duany (1998) as a conventional attached type on a small lot with the addition of a shared square, green or close at the front. A variant is a shared area within the inner block, usually a playground.

Greenheart Metropolis RANDSTAD HOLLAND, so called by the planner Gerald Burke (Hall, 2002).

greenhouse effect The raising of temperatures at the earth's surface due to the build-up of gases in the atmosphere (such as carbon dioxide and methane) letting through short-wave energy from the sun but absorbing long-wave radiation from the earth (a similar effect to a greenhouse). Minimising the greenhouse effect (and the global warming it causes) by reducing the emission of carbon dioxide and other gases is one of concerns of SUSTAINABLE DEVELOPMENT.

greenie (Australia) An environmentalist.

greening Improving the appearance and function of an urban area through soft landscaping.

Greensward The design by FREDERICK LAW OLMSTED and CALVERT VAUX for New York's Central Park.

Greentown Group A group of people who took up the Town and Country Planning Association's idea of creating a new community in the 1970s. They were unsuccessful in their attempts to negotiate for a site in Milton Keynes. See THIRD GARDEN CITY.

Greenville An imaginary URBAN VILLAGE described in the first report of the Urban Villages Group (1992).

greenwash To present an action as being more ecologically or environmentally sensitive than it actually is.

greenway A network of spaces providing a route through an urban area for people (on foot and bicycles) and wildlife.

Greenwood Act The Housing Act 1930, which promoted slum clearance.

Gregory XIII, Pope (1502–85) See QUAE PUBLICE UTILIA.

Grenfell-Baines, George (Sir) (1908–2003) Architect. A pioneer of collaborative working, he founded the inter-disciplinary Building Design Partnership, which became the UK's largest architectural practice.

grey space A open space that is not green (a street or an area of paving, for example).

grey water Water from sinks, basins and baths, which can be treated more easily and less intensively than sewage, or stored and used to flush toilets in some systems.

greyfields housing concept A proposal for studio homes around car parks, put forward by the architect David Prichard in 2003. Relocateable, cylindrical, factory-made studio homes would be erected around the perimeter of suburban car parks for rent to young single people and key workers. In more central areas the units might be stacked in multi-storey modules.

grid A network of streets intersecting at approximately right angles; an urban layout consisting of, in the words of Bill Hillier (1988), 'a series of islands of outward-facing buildings, each surrounded by a ring of open space that forms part of an interconnected net.' Grid planning has been practised for at least 4,000 years (Rykwert, 2000). Spiro Kostof (1987) notes that in the USA using a grid system was the simplest way to survey land and divide it for settlement. John McKean (1994) writes of Glasgow's nineteenth-century 'gridded city of dwellings, with its evenness of image. Individual buildings silently mass into walled streets. Apart from the clue of a rolling topography, within this urban artefact – the grid – we locate ourselves primarily by abstract processes: reading, thinking, remembering – they are all in the head.' McKean quotes Camillo Sitte writing that 'a network [grid] of streets always serves only the purposes of communication, never of art, since it can never be comprehended sensorily, can never be grasped except in plan.' The nineteenth century word may be a shortening of the thirteenth century GRIDIRON. Also called a *gridiron plan*.

grid square 1 A square on a map or plan representing an area on the ground. **2** An area formed by a grid of roads. Tim Mars (1998) notes that 'the residential areas of MILTON KEYNES were deliberately not called "villages" or even "neighbourhoods" but "grid squares" – a neutral, technical term for parcels of land carved up by the grid roads.'

gridiron A street layout based on rectangular blocks; (US) a pattern of long, narrow street blocks (Kostof, 1991). The thirteenth-century word may have meant an iron griddle (*griddle* deriving from the Latin word for a small piece of wickerwork). HW Fowler (1926) argues that the word derives from a variant of griddle, with no implication that it is made of iron. Compare CHECKERBOARD.

gridlock 1 A traffic jam, especially one involving a series of connecting streets. The term was coined in 1971 and has been in general use since 1980 (Bryson, 1994), and in the UK particularly since the 1990s. The US romantic comedy film 'Pie in the Sky', released in 1996, is centred on a young man who was conceived in a traffic jam and has been obsessed with gridlocks ever since. *Lock* was a nineteenth-century term for a traffic jam (Ackroyd, 2000). **2** Severe traffic congestion. Example: 'A devastating report into the government's transport strategy has revealed that Britain's roads will remain gridlocked and its railways in chaos at least for the rest of this decade' (broadsheet newspaper, 2002); 'Gridlocked airports threaten the economic growth of the South East' (tabloid newspaper, 2003 – the gridlock in this case refers to the supposed inability of the airports to handle the required amount of air traffic, not to congestion on the roads around them).

Grieve, (Sir) Robert (b1910) Town and regional planner. Between 1943 and 1946 he played a major role in producing the Clyde Valley Plan, one of the UK's most admired (and disastrous) regional plans. He was a planner at the Scottish Office, and chief planner from 1960–65. He then became professor of town and regional planning at Glasgow University, and the first chairman of the Highlands and Islands Development Board. Grieve was chairman of the Royal Fine Arts Commission for Scotland. PATRICK GEDDES was a major influence on him. Grieve (undated) recalled 'a scene in Glasgow a few months before the death of Geddes on 17 April 1932... On that evening I got off a bus at the top of Buchanan Street on my way to evening classes... Immediately north of where I stood lay an extensive area of the worst kind of slum, the Cowcaddens – now mercifully gone. And out of it, as I looked up the street before crossing, came a long procession of small stunted men with little cardboard banners... "we want work"... "we want bread". Silently, on the experimental rubber blocks of the street, they passed out of the darkness of the notorious Cowcaddens down into the bright lights of the central shopping area, not with the raised fists and rhythmic shouting of today – their physical stamina did not look up to that. And, silently, they were gone. I was 20 then. I knew nothing about Geddes; and was not going to hear anything about him at the "tech" where I was bound. But I had seen a ghostly manifestation of what he called the PALAEOTECHNIC Era.' Such visions inspired Grieve throughout his long career: he chaired a comprehensive inquiry into Glasgow's housing in his 78th year in 1988.

Robert Grieve

Griffin, Walter Burley (1876–1961) Architect and town planner. An American, he planned the Australian capital of Canberra on anthroposophical lines in 1911 (although the city was not built until after the first world war).

grinding See SKATEBOARD.

grockle (Devon and other tourist areas) A tourist. The term has been current since the 1960s. Its origin is obscure (Quinion, 2000). Compare EMMET.

Gropius, Walter (1883–1969) Architect. He founded the BAUHAUS and from the 1930s practised in the USA.

gross internal area The enclosed functional space of a building, measured to the internal face of its external walls.

Grosstadt (German) A city.

ground plan The plan of the ground floor of a building.

ground rent A sum of money (usually nominal and paid annually) charged by a freeholder of a property to a leaseholder.

Ground Zero The site of the WORLD TRADE CENTER, destroyed by terrorist action on 11 September 2001. *Ground zero* is the place at which (or immediately below or above which) a nuclear or other bomb explodes.

groundscraper A building with a large floorplate. The term, with its intentional echo of *skyscraper*, became current in the 1980s to describe banking buildings that provided large trading floors and buildings with wide and deep office floorspace. By the time it was used at the House of Commons urban affairs subcommittee in 2002, the term had become sufficiently unfamiliar for the magazine *Regeneration and Renewal* (2002) to hail it as a new coinage. The reporter noted that the chair of the subcommittee, Gwyneth Dunwoody, 'denounced it with contempt'. The architect Sir Terry Farrell uses the term to describe some of his buildings. His practice describes them as 'iconic structures that are horizontally integrated into their environment' (Terry Farrell and Partners, 2002).

groundwater Water that forms the part of the natural water cycle which is present within underground strata (aquifers).

groundwater source A point of abstraction of water, such as a well, borehole or spring.

Groundwork A series of community-based, comprehensive environmental regeneration and neighbourhood renewal projects. Groundwork Trusts have operated throughout much of England, Wales and Northern Ireland since the early 1980s.

group repair scheme Introduced by the Local Government and Housing Act 1989 to promote exterior improvements to housing blocks.

growth cap (US) A ceiling to the amount of building that can take place in any one year (Kostof, 1991).

growth coalition (US) A public-private partnership promoting inward investment and economic development.

growth pole A geographical area or sector of the economy designated (or destined) for economic growth; a point in historic time and in space when entrepreneurial forces vigorously generate economic growth The *pôle de croissance* concept (relating to economic sectors rather than geographical areas) was developed by the French economist François Perroux in 1955 (Hall, 2002).

Gruen, Victor (1867–1930) Austrian-born, US architect and planner. He pioneered the modern shopping centre in the 1950s and '60s. See URBAN DESIGN.

Grünflächen (German) Green space.

Grünzüge (German) A green belt.

guardian A person whose presence discourages crime. Also called a *preventer*. See CRIME PREVENTION.

guerrilla architecture That which subverts planning controls and building regulations.

guidance See DESIGN GUIDANCE.

guided busway A special track which only buses can use. Buses are slightly modified to use the track, but cars and other vehicles will not fit it. The track enables buses to move faster and more quietly than on a normal road.

guided trail A route whose features of interest are signposted or indicated by other means.

Gummer, John (b1939) Politician. The last and most interventionist of a long line of Conservative secretaries of state for the environment, he was appointed in 1993 by John Major. Gummer tried to use the planning system to protect town centres against the commercial forces that preferred out-of-town development, he gave official recognition to urban design through the Department of the Environment's Quality In Town and Country initiative, and he became committed to helping tackle worldwide environmental problems.

Gummer's Law The nickname of a measure introduced by JOHN GUMMER in 1997, making it easier for planning permission to be granted to new country houses of 'exceptional quality'.

Gutkind, EA (1886–1968) Author of *The Expanding Environment*, published in 1953. See POST-URBANISM.

gutter bird A PIGEON.

Gwynn, John (1713–86) Architect and civil engineer. His LONDON AND WESTMINSTER IMPROVED, published in 1766, proposed major new streets.

Gynaecopolis The City of Women, fictional capital of the state of New Gynia or Viraginia, described by Joseph Hall in *Mundus alter et idem* (1613).

gypsy (or gipsy) 1 A person of Romany origin. Romany gypsies, with their distinctive culture, language and itinerant lifestyle, arrived in Europe following migration from northern India, and are now found as far afield as America and Australia. The word gypsy derives from the supposition, made when gypsies first appeared in England in the sixteenth century, that they had originated in Egypt. The Gypsy Council argues that the Gypsy people are a recognised ethnic group, and deserve the same respect as other ethnic and racial groups by having their name spelled with a capital. **2** Statutorily defined in the UK as a 'person of nomadic life, whatever their race or origin', but excluding people travelling with fairs or circuses. See also TRAVELLER.

gyratory A rotary intersection, especially one with multiple lane markings and complex filtered multiphase traffic lights, where the normal ROUNDABOUT priority rules do not apply.

gyratory circus See ROUNDABOUT.

H

Habermas, Jürgen (b1929). Sociologist and philosopher. David Kolb (1990) has described Habermas' attitude to the concept of *place*, and in particular his use of the concept of *lifeworld*. 'The lifeword,' Kolb writes, 'is that background of beliefs, values, and practices that provides a horizon of meaning for our actions. It is a cultural construct that must be renewed and handed along to provide community identity.' In the view of Habermas, buildings embody and help form the distinctive practices and values of a community, and so they are one way of transmitting the lifeworld. But today, Kolb explains, 'the reproduction of the lifeworld has been dominated by imperatives stemming from the workings of the economic system. Lifeworld meanings are being thinned out, and so places become thinner as well... More and more the act of building becomes determined only by systemic considerations of profit and efficiency.' For Habermas, Kolb writes, there is no architectural or design solution to this problem. 'It requires new institutions for community decision-making, and a form of democratic social control of the economy that keeps the system from overwhelming the lifeworld. But even if we imagine such sweeping changes to have been accomplished, there would still be something different about modern places that would keep them from being equivalent to those old villages and towns.' The autonomy of the community in evaluating and changing its values and practices must be safeguarded. 'This means that no place should impose a past upon us,' Kolb notes. 'Tradition can not simply dictate how we build. Habermas has no use for nostalgic programs that prescribe covert returns to unliberated modes of life.' See PUBLIC SPHERE.

habitable room A room used for living purposes, excluding kitchens with floor area of less than 13 sq m (140 sq ft), bathrooms, toilets, corridors and halls.

habitat A characteristic living place. From the Latin, meaning 'it lives'.

Habitat The United Nations Conference on Human Settlements, held in 1976 in Vancouver, and the subsequent United Nations Human Settlements Programme (UN-HABITAT). The conference affirmed the move away from large-scale, clean-sweep urban renewal but is perhaps best remembered for Moshe Safdie's Ziggurats of prefabricated concrete dwellings. UN-HABITAT's mission is to promote SUSTAINABLE urbanisation through policy formulation, institutional reform, capacity-building, technical cooperation and advocacy, and to monitor and improve the state of human settlements worldwide. It has three 'preventive strategies' (to slow down the pace of rural-urban migration; strengthen local authorities outside rapidly growing cities; and enhance rural livelihood and security) and two 'adaptive strategies and interventions' (to fight poverty but not the poor; and fight squatting and not squatters).

habitus A person's sense of their own and others' place and role in the world and the built environment (Hillier and Rooksby, 2002). The term is used by the French sociologist Pierre Bourdieu (b1930).

hack (US) A taxi or other vehicle for hire. From *Hackney cab*, from the London borough of that name.

Hackney Building Exploratory See BUILDING EXPLORATORY.

hairy building A skyscraper in Kuala Lumpur designed by KEN YEANG, lavishly planted at every level with bougainvillea.

Halifax Ecocity Project An ecological design initiative aiming to provide self-sustaining infrastructure for a neighbourhood of up to 1,000 people in Adelaide, South Australia.

Hall, Edward T (b1914) Anthropologist. See INVOLVEMENT RATIO and PROXEMICS.

Hall, John Developer. See METROCENTRE.

Hall, Peter (Sir) Planning academic and writer. He has been professor of planning at Berkeley, California, and at the Bartlett School of Architecture and Planning, University College London. From 1991–94 he was special adviser on strategic planning to the secretary of state for the environment in the UK. He was chairman of the TOWN AND COUNTRY PLANNING ASSOCIATION (1995–1999) and a member of the URBAN TASK FORCE (1998–1999). His many books include *London 2000* (1963, revised 1969), *The World Cities* (1966, 1977,

1983); *Urban and Regional Planning* (1975, 1982); *Great Planning Disasters* (1980); *Cities of Tomorrow* (1988); *London 2001* (1989); *Sociable Cities* (with Colin Ward, 1998) and *Cities in Civilization* (1998). He was awarded the Royal Town Planning Institute's Gold Medal in 2003.

Peter Hall

hamlet A group of houses in the countryside; a small village without a church. A hamlet is defined in *A New Urbanist Lexicon* (McLaughlin, 2000) as 'a compact urban settlement within the countryside, with the essential characteristics of a complete neighborhood but with few, if any, commercial services.' The word derives from the Middle Low German *hamm* by way of the Anglo-French diminuitive *hamelet*. The Scots for hamlet is *clachan* or *cottoun*. Compare VILLAGE.

Hampstead Garden Suburb The north London suburb was founded in 1907 by HENRIETTA BARNETT as a social experiment in providing a model settlement for people of all classes. The concept grew out of a threat to develop on the edge of Hampstead Heath, which was defeated when Barnett campaigned successfully for an extension to the heath. The GARDEN SUBURB, to be built on the edge of the extension, would show that there was an alternative to the usual dull streets of suburban villas. Barnett outlined the proposal in 1905 and formed a company the following year. The scheme was intended for people of all classes and incomes; the cottages and houses would be at no more than an average to eight to the acre; the fronts of the houses would be at least 50 feet apart; plots would be divided by hedges or trellises, not walls; the roads would be lined with trees; and public gardens would be free to all tenants. The Hampstead Garden Suburb Trust appointed RAYMOND UNWIN as architect and surveyor in 1906. He and his partner, BARRY PARKER, prepared the plan and designed many of the early houses. EDWIN LUTYENS, appointed as consulting architect, designed many of the principal buildings. The Hampstead Garden Suburb Act 1906 provided the necessary powers to build the suburb in a former radically different to the usual BYLAW HOUSING. The experiment had a major influence on the layout and design of suburbs, though it never fulfilled its intended role of housing working-class commuters, becoming instead a middle-class area. A further part of the suburb was laid out after 1918 to the design of JCS Soutar, with few of the qualities or aspirations of the original.

handover The act of passing responsibility for a new building to its first owner.

hands-on planning A process or workshop event involving members of the public playing an active part in planning an area, using large-scale plans.

hang-out shelter See YOUTH SHELTER.

Happy Colony, The A book by Robert Pemberton describing the imaginary model city of Queen Victoria Town in a proposed group of agricultural settlements in New Zealand (Girouard, 1985).

Happy Ever After See TERRY AND JUNE.

haptic *adj.* Relating to the sense of touch; tactile. The word, deriving from the Greek word meaning to touch, is occasionally used in relation to buildings or public sculpture. It is more widely used in relation to virtual-reality computer systems that reproduce a sense of touch.

hard architecture Buildings designed in response to real or imagined threats in a harsh urban environment. The term was used in the 1960s by the environmental psychologist Robert Sommer, author of *Hard Architecture*. See also BUNKER ARCHITECTURE, CRIME PREVENTION, DEFENSIBLE SPACE, FORTRESS LA and SCANSCAPE.

hard end use A use involving buildings for reclaimed land. Compare SOFT END USE.

hard ground An acoustically reflecting outdoor surface such as paving materials or water.

hard landscaping See LANDSCAPING.

hard space The parts of an area that are identified in a design process as being worth keeping, as distinct from the *soft spaces* that are suited for redevelopment.

hard to let (UK) A term applied to social rented housing for which it is difficult to find tenants. It became an official designation for some council housing in the 1970s. Some commentators objected that the term seemed to imply that potential tenants might be to blame for being too fussy, and preferred instead to call such housing *hard to live in*. See also PROBLEM ESTATE and VANDALISM.

Hardman, Edward Chambré (1898–1988) Photographer. He chronicled Liverpool.

hard-to-reach groups Categories of people who do

not readily participate in processes of public consultation. Such people were also referred to in the 1990s as *hard-to-hear*, and in 2002 were reported as being referred to as *hard-to-find* (Rook, 2002).

hardware The buildings and infrastructure of a regeneration programme, as opposed to the *software* such as education programmes and public relations campaigns.

hardwire To connect something into specific systems. Example: 'Streets and spaces must be hardwired into built environment and financial programmes.'

harling (Scotland) Roughcasting (an external finish for walls). See also PEBBLEDASH.

harmony See AESTHETIC.

Harriman, Edward H (1848–1909) A builder of railways and 13 new towns in California, particularly in the early years of the twentieth century.

Harrington, James See COMMONWEALTH OF OCEANA.

Harris, Arthur 'Bomber' (Sir) (1892–1984) As the air marshall leading RAF Bomber Command in the second world war, Harris was at the centre of controversies, then and since, about the policy that he implemented of bombing German cities (such as Dresden and Hamburg – see OPERATION GOMORRAH) to instil terror into their populations rather than with purely military or strategic objectives. See also URBAN DESTRUCTION.

Harris-Ullman model An explanation of urban land use patterns in terms of development from multiple nuclei.

Hastie, William A Scottish planner who was in charge of Russia's imperial city planning service between 1808 and 1832.

Hastings, Hubert de Cronin (1902–86) As proprietor of the Architectural Press he actively promoted the *Architectural Review*'s advocacy of the TOWNSCAPE approach. He coined the term WORM'S EYE VIEW.

HAT HOUSING ACTION TRUST.

haudin (Scots) A house; a holding; a home.

Häuserreihe (German) A terrace of houses. Compare TERRASSENHÄUSER.

Haussmann, Georges-Eugène (Baron) (1809–91) Civil servant and lawyer. As prefect of the Seine Départment under Napoleon III in 1853–70 he transformed Paris. He exerted enormous powers to clear areas and control redevelopment, creating Paris' distinctive urban landscape. Spiro Kostof (1991) notes that the design prescriptions that controlled Haussmann's Paris extended to the smallest details. Pilasters on façades could not be more than 40 centimetres in depth, balconies required official permission and could not project more than 80 centimetres, and so on. Richard Sennett (1990) notes that Haussmann confronted a congested city a thousand years old whose twisted streets were a breeding ground for, in his mind, the unholy trinity of disease, crime, and revolution. 'He imagined a traditional means of repression in the face of these dangers,' Sennett writes. 'The cutting of straight streets through a congested Paris was to make it easier for people to breathe, for police, and if necessary, troops to move. The new streets of north-eastern Paris were to be lined with apartments over elegant shops, in order to attract the bourgeoisie into previously working-class districts; he imagined a kind of internal class colonization of the city.' See also ARTIST IN DEMOLITION, CITY BEAUTIFUL MOVEMENT, PAUL DELOUVRIER, ENCLOSURE, EVENTREMENT, ORDER, PLAN DES ARTISTES, QUARTIER and ALBERT SPEER.

Georges-Eugène Haussmann

Haussmannise To restructure an urban area with major new streets, as practised by BARON HAUSSMANN in Paris. Example: 'A fearful tangle and slum in parts, though of magnificent situation and fine features, and now being Haussmannised' (Patrick Geddes in 1914).

Hav The imaginary Mediterranean city described in Jan Morris's novel *Last Letters from Hav*, published in 1985. The book tells of, among other marvels, the annual Roof-Race. The city's most athletic youths run round the old town at roof level, 'involving jumps over more than thirty alleyways, culminating in a prodigious leap over the open space in the centre of the Bazaar, and ending desperately in a slither down the walls of the castle gate to the finish.' The author explains: 'As the horserace is to Siena, as the bull-running is to Pamplona, as Derby Day is to the English or even perhaps Bastille Day to the French, so the day of the Roof-Race is to the people of Hav. It is not known for sure how this fascinating institution began, though there are plenty of plausible theories. The race was certainly being run in the sixteenth century, when Nicander Nucius described it in passing as "a curious custom of these people"; and in 1810 Lady Hester Stanhope, the future "Queen of Palmyra", was among the spectators: she vociferously demanded the right to take part herself, and was only dissuaded by her private physician, who said it would almost certainly be the end of her. In later years the Russian aristocracy made a regular fete of it, people coming all the way from St Petersburg simply for the day, and lavish house-parties were organized in the villas of the western hills. Enormous stakes were wagered on the outcome; the winner, still covered with dust and sweat, was immediately taken to the Palace in the Governor's own carriage for a champagne breakfast and the presentation of the traditional golden goblet.'

havens for hoodlums The phrase was coined by the *St Pancras Chronicle* in 1983. An article criticised low-rise, high-density housing, built by the London Borough of Camden, that was proving difficult to manage.

Hawks, Tony The world's best-known exponent of SKATEBOARDING, he has developed an international business based on the sport.

Hayek, Friedrich (1899–1992) Political theorist and economist. Hayek was an influential advocate of free markets and critic of all kinds of state planning. Margaret Thatcher was among his admirers.

Hay-on-Wye A Welsh border town specialising in second-hand bookshops and associated cultural activities. Richard Booth began selling books there in 1961, after he had moved into his family's half-ruined castle. On 1 April 1977 Booth declared Hay-on-Wye an independent state, with himself its king. See also BOOK-TOWN MOVEMENT.

header A brick laid at right angles to the face of a wall. Compare STRETCHER.

headline rent The level set before any inducement is made to a prospective tenant.

head-turner A high-profile event organised as part of a regeneration initiative. Example: 'You need a head-turner every two or three years to keep up the momentum.'

headway The interval between public transport vehicles travelling in the same direction and on the same route.

Healey, Patsy Planning theorist. See COMMUNICATIVE PLANNING, MASTER PLAN and MODERNITY.

health Defined by the World Health Organisation as 'a state of complete physical, mental and social well-being, and not merely the absence of disease or infirmity'.

health action zone A deprived area in which local authorities, the national health service, the voluntary and private sectors and local communities work in partnership to promote health, regeneration, employment, education and housing.

Health of Towns Association A private campaigning body founded in 1844.

Health of Towns Commission A Royal Commission appointed in 1843.

healthy city Defined as 'one that is continually creating and improving those social environments and strengthening those community resources which enable people mutually to support each other in performing all functions of life and achieving their maximum potential' (NHS Executive *et al*, 2000). See also HYGEIA.

healthy living centre A building or service promoting healthy lifestyles and tackling social exclusion in a deprived area. Such centres provide gyms, childcare, adult education and health services.

heap (US) An old CAR.

heat island See URBAN HEAT ISLAND.

Heaven Inspired See HI-LO.

heaven The writer and painter Wyndham Lewis (1947) wrote that heaven must be 'a rootless, irresponsible city (for everyone is agreed that Heaven is a city, so what the confirmed agriculturalist will do it is difficult to see), where the spirit is released from all the too-close contacts with other people... but where everything is superficially fraternal.'

heavy rail High-capacity, relatively infrequently stopping forms of railway.

hedge rage See CUPRESSOCYPARIS LEYLANDII.

Hegemann, Werner See CIVIC ART.

height The height of a building or structure can be expressed in terms of a maximum number of floors; a maximum height of parapet or ridge; a maximum overall height; any of these maximum heights in combination with a maximum number of floors; a ratio of building height to street or space width; height relative to particular landmarks or background buildings; or strategic views.

LÉON KRIER has advocated limiting the number of *floors* of buildings, but not their *height*. 'The most beautiful and pleasant cities which survive in the world today have all been conceived with buildings of between two and five floors. There is no ecologically defensible justification for the erection of utilitarian SKYSCRAPERS; they are built for speculation, short-term gain or out of pretentiousness. Paradoxically, the imposition of a universal height limit for buildings of between two and five floors does not exclude very tall buildings or monumental buildings. St Paul's Cathedral in London is a skyscraper on one level. The Eiffel Tower has only three floors. The Capitol in Washington, Nôtre-Dame de Paris, the Forbidden City in Beijing and even the Seven Wonders of the World respected these limits. Thus, building heights should not be limited metrically (such regulations are always arbitrary and lead to a stultifying uniformity) but by the number of floors: between two and five, depending on the character of the village or city, the nature, status and use of the building, the width of roads and squares, and the prestige of the site.' The opening (verbless) sentence of Aldous Huxley's novel *Brave New World*, published in 1932, associates high buildings with a dystopian future: 'A squat grey building of only 33 storeys.' WH Auden explained in a two-line poem: 'Why are the public buildings so high? How come you don't know?/ Why, that's because the spirits of the public are so low'. Noel Coward wrote (in *Law and Order*, 1928): 'I don't know what London's coming to. The higher the building, the lower the morals'. Alan Lightman's 1993 novel *Einstein's Dreams* describes a world (among many other worlds) in which people live high up to benefit from the fact that time flows slightly more slowly farther from the centre of the earth. 'Many are not content simply to locate their homes on a mountain. To get the maximum effect, they have constructed their houses on stilts. The mountaintops all over the world are nested with such houses, which from a distance look like a flock of fat birds squatting on long skinny legs. People most eager to live longest have built their homes on the highest stilts. Indeed, some houses rise half a mile high on their spindly wooden legs. Height has become status...' But a few residents in each city have stopped caring whether they age a few seconds faster than their neighbours. 'These adventuresome souls come down to the lower world for days at a time, lounge under the trees that grow in the valleys, swim leisurely in the lakes that lie at warmer altitudes, roll on level ground... When the others rush by them and scoff, they just smile.' (In the same novel Lightman imagines a city where each neighbourhood lives in a different age; another city where people have no memories; a world where there is no time, only images; another world where time is circular and events perpetually repeat themselves; another where time flows backward; another without cause and effect; and strangest of all, a world where time is a flock of nightingales.) See also HIGH RISE and TALL BUILDING.

Heimatschutz (German) Protection of the homeland. The term is important historically in German discussion of HERITAGE.

Heimatstadt (German) The city as home.

helicopter view An overall, holistic view of a regeneration concept. Compare PARACHUTE.

heliotropic design Orienting buildings taking account of the position of the sun.

Helix City A proposal of 1961 by the architect Kisho Kurokawa. The project was an example of METABOLISM. The name derives from the helical shape of its multi-storey buildings.

hell See CB PURDOM and THE CHIMNEY OF THE WORLD.

hell with the lid off Pittsburgh, Pennsylvania, in its heyday as a steel-making city.

Hell's Hundred Acres The SOHO district of New York at the end of the nineteenth century, according to the City Fire Department which was appalled at the many sweatshops (Tiesdell, Oc and Heath, 1996).

Hemingway, Ernest (1898–1961) Writer. See A MOVEABLE FEAST.

Hénard, Eugène (1849–1923) Planner. See BOULEVARD À REDANS.

Henderson, Nigel (1917–85) Photographer. His work included many evocative images of the streetlife of East London, where he lived from 1945 to 1953.

Herbert, Edwin (Sir) Chairman of the Royal Commission on whose recommendations the GREATER LONDON COUNCIL and new London boroughs were created in 1965.

Herc, Kool (b circa 1954) Disc jockey. A pioneer of RAP music, Kool Herc came to New York's Bronx district in 1967 from Jamaica. Born Clive Campbell, he was nicknamed Hercules at school because of his physical strength and chose Kool Herc as his tag in his days as a GRAFFITI artist. He is credited with inspiring BREAK DANCING.

heritage 1 Something inherited from the past. **2** Something whose particular value might make it worth keeping.

Under the government of John Major, the inappropriately named Department of National Heritage had the responsibilities that were later taken on by its successor, the Department of Culture, Media and Sport in 1997. The landscape architect Kathryn Gustafson (1999) has asked: 'Why does heritage have to mean history? The testimony of our culture, that is heritage.' The architectural historian Andrew Saint has called heritage 'a term which in its modern usage combines imprecision, sentimentality and chauvinism'. David Lowenthal has described what he sees as a clear distinction between heritage and history. Unlike history, he writes, heritage 'is not a testable, or even a reasonably plausible account of some past, but a declaration of faith in that past. Heritage is not history, even when it mimics history. History seeks to convince by truth and succumbs to falsehood. Heritage exaggerates, omits, candidly invents and frankly forgets, and thrives on ignorance and error... Heritage is immune to critical reappraisal because it is not erudition but catechism; what counts is not checkable fact but credulous allegiance' (quoted in Markus and Cameron, 2002). Robert Grant noted in 1998 that 'at Safeway, the label "Heritage" denotes a superior grade of meat; at B&Q, a simulated mahogany shelving system' (Grant, 1998).

Robert Adam (2003) takes a close look at the definition of the term heritage in the KRAKOW CHARTER. The charter declares: 'Heritage is that complex of man's work in which a community recognises its particular

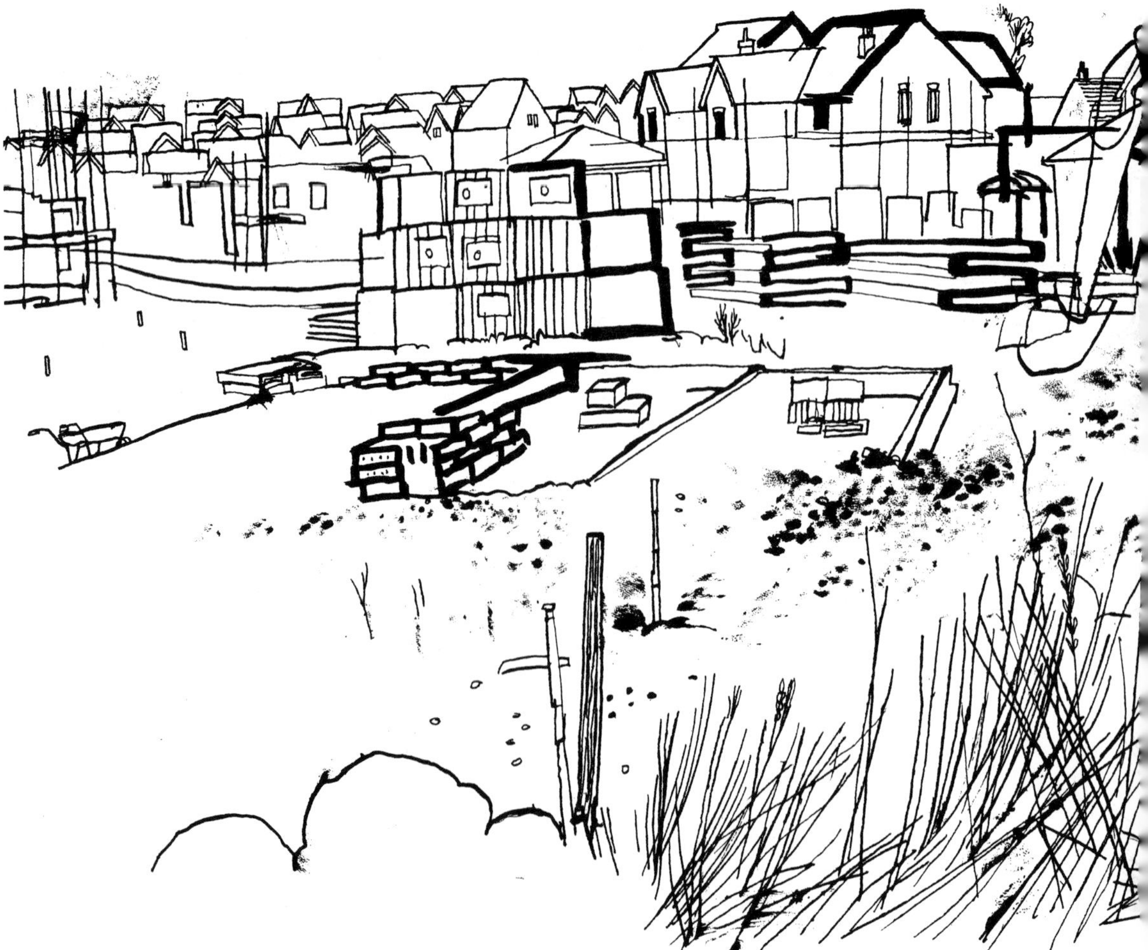

housebuilding

and specific values and with which it identifies. Identification and specification of heritage is therefore a process related to the choice of values.' Adam comments: 'There are two things to note about this. The first is the lack of any reference to age, time or the passage of time and the generality of the definition. Heritage is effectively anything with which a community can be said to identify. The only history involved is the practical expedient that for a community to identify with a "complex of man's work" it has to exist and so must have some history, even if only a year or two. The second is the lack of any indication of just how a community identifies its heritage in practice... The charter marks out built heritage as a place for experts or civil servants who, through their knowledge of their speciality or position are qualified to represent the whole community.'

Heritage is a thirteenth-century word, deriving from the Latin *hereditare*, to inherit. See also GHETTO HERITAGE and NATURAL ESTATE.

heritage coast An area of coastline designated for recreation and conservation.

heritage dividend Economic and social benefits of conserving historic buildings and places, by encouraging tourism, for example.

Heritage Economic Regeneration Scheme English Heritage and local authority funding for conservation schemes supporting regeneration in conservation areas.

heritage industry An often perjorative term for those who earn their living protecting the HERITAGE.

heritage land An area of land of strategic importance which, because of its combined value for landscape, historical interest and nature conservation, needs to be protected and sensitively managed.

Heritage Lottery Fund (England) Set up to fund, from proceeds of the National Lottery, projects to preserve or widen public access to the physical heritage.

heritage mortician A pejorative term for a conservationist who restores a building to a state from which it will not be allowed to change. See also RESTORATION.

heritagise A pejorative term for making a building or place look old.

Hero City Santiago de Cuba, Cuba, where the first insurrection against the dictator Batista took place in 1953.

Heronsgate Built in 1845 as the first of six estates founded by Feargus O'Connor's CHARTIST COOPERATIVE LAND SOCIETY. The estate, near Rickmansworth, was also called O'Connorsville.

Herron, Ron See ARCHIGRAM.

Hertzka, Theodor Economist. His book *Freeland: a social anticipation*, published in 1891, described a utopian city and state whose land and means of production would be state-owned. A number of Freeland associations pursued his ideas, without practical result.

Heseltine, Michael (**Lord Heseltine**) (b1933) Politician. His various posts included deputy prime minister and two terms of office as secretary of state for the environment (appointed in 1979 and 1990). See CITY CHALLENGE, IT TOOK A RIOT, LOCKING AWAY JOBS IN FILING CABINETS, MARSHAM STREET, MERSEYSIDE TASK FORCE, REGIONAL ECONOMIC PLANNING COUNCILS, RIGHT TO BUY, THAMES GATEWAY, URBAN DEVELOPMENT CORPORATION, URBAN REGENERATION and URBAN RENAISSANCE.

hetero-architecture An architecture of great diversity, whose informality allows a wide range of marginalized groups to feel at home. Charles Jencks (1993) identifies Frank Gehry, Eric Owen Moss and Charles Moore as being among its visible leaders, but he suggests that 'there is also a vernacular and frank version of the same genre as well as the populist versions of Jon Jerde and Disneyland'.

heterophilia The love of difference; the desire to seek out new experience.

heteropolis A city with a great diversity of ethnic groups, lifestyles and languages. Charles Jencks describes Los Angeles as such a city in his 1993 book *Heteropolis*.

Heym, Georg (1887–1912) German expressionist poet. Some of his most powerful poems imagine oppressive cities being swept away by war or superhuman forces, such as his 'God of the City' who shakes a 'slaughterer's fist' as fire devours a street. Heym drowned in an ice-skating accident.

hierarchy of settlements An ordering of settlements according to their size or function.

hierarchy of space(s) Urban space conceived as a series of connected spaces; a series of linked spaces of differing size, function and activities. BILL HILLIER has suggested that urban theorists' concept of the hierarchy of space is a misreading of reality, replacing what should be a dynamic view of space with one that is essentially static.

hierarchy principle Specifies that waste should be dealt with according to the following hierarchy: reduce; re-use; recover (recycle, compost or convert to energy); landfill. See also PROXIMITY PRINCIPLE.

high architecture The design of a LANDMARK or OBJECT BUILDING.

high cross A village or town cross.

High Domain The fictional city – 'the most beautiful city built by man' – of William Nicholson's children's novel *Slaves of the Mastery*, published in 2001. Sited on an island in a lake and reached by a causeway, High Domain 'seemed to be built out of light and colour alone'. The buildings 'jostled close one against the next, but their thousand roofs seemed to float, each one sustained by a weightless shimmering umbrella'. In the later afternoon sun 'the domed roofs, seeming to drink it, were gorged with light, flushed rose-pink, emerald-green, blood-red'. The upper stonework of the soaring city walls was pierced with intricately patterned holes, so that from a distance 'the great walls seemed no more substantial than a curtain of amber lace'. See also ARAMANTH.

high-quality public transport That which is able to compete with private vehicles in terms of convenience, speed, price and reliability. The term is used to include light rail, guided bus ways and particularly high-quality bus networks.

high rise 1 *n.* and *adj.* A building (usually housing) of around five or more storeys. Joan Ash (1980) noted that in British statute 'high rise' was defined as a minimum of four storeys before the 1939–45 war and five storeys afterwards. The world's tallest block of flats is probably the 70-storey, 195m high Lake Point Tower in Chicago. Half the floors of the 100-storey, 343m John Hancock Centre in Chicago are residential. The architect CHARLES REILLY (1938) put the case for building high. 'Granted that we are at heart a country-folk and do not make good town-dwellers, and that there will always be a number of people who can not be happy unless they live under their own roofs, even if they have to travel a couple of hours each day to reach them, and that we must, therefore... go on building suburbs of small houses, we shall never under that system provide for all the amount of sun and air and opportunity for exercise the new generation is so rightly demanding, nor an adequate urban life. That can only be done by building higher.' Reilly was convinced that 'by grouping the blocks together it is clear that all the advantages and more that the eighteenth-century squares gave to the well-to-do in open space, trees and grass, can now be given to everyone.' He advocated tenement blocks of between five and 10 storeys, laid out in rings, each ring separated from the next by a belt of grass and trees, or parkland and playing fields. Allotments and gardens 'with their unavoidable untidiness' would be 'kept to special places on the town plan'. FJ OSBORN was an early and consistent critic of high-rise housing. He wrote (1949): 'It is amazing that there has been no discussion in parliament or the press of the financial or social folly of the present wave of flat building. At ceremonial openings bouquets are thrown, and mayors and chairmen of housing committees are conscious of haloes. Speeches and women's columns gloat lovingly over the central heating, the lifts, the laundries and the gadgets. Nobody wonders how a family of children will get along in a flat of three or four rooms on an upper floor. Nobody seems concerned for the money and manpower poured into these Babylonic towers.' Osborn (1952) wrote in the same journal: 'Fantastic subsidies for high-density 10-storey blocks of flats in the centres of our cities... It would seem that the TOWN AND COUNTRY PLANNING ASSOCIATION should seek the advice of psychologists in order to explain what delusions of grandeur, what expression of a frustrated ego lie deep in a policy which stands condemned equally on economic as on human

> **"THE COUNTRY CAN NOT AFFORD THIS POLICY, THE PEOPLE DO NOT WANT THIS POLICY: IN A DEMOCRACY THAT OUGHT TO BE AN IRRESISTIBLE COMBINATION"**
>
> *FJ Osborn*

grounds... The country can not afford this policy, the people do not want this policy: in a democracy that ought to be an irresistible combination.' Osborn wrote in a letter to LEWIS MUMFORD in 1945 (Hughes, 1971): 'I don't think philanthropic housing people anywhere realise the irresistible strength of the impulse towards the family house and garden as prosperity increases: they think that the suburban trend can be reversed by large-scale multi-storey building in downtown districts, which is not merely a pernicious belief from a human point of view, but a delusion. In a few years the multi-storey technique will prove unpopular and will peter out. Damage will be done to society by the trial, but probably all I can do is hasten the day of disillusion. If I have underestimated the complacency of the urban masses, the damage may amount to a disaster.'

A developer's architect (quoted in Horsey, 1990) recalled his part in creating in 1961 a housing estate of 10 slab blocks of 20 storeys each. The site was a reclaimed chemical waste dump at Sighthill in Glasgow. 'My managing director came along one day with a piece of tracing paper, with what turned out to be the final shape [of the Sighthill housing estate]... and said, "How many dwellings can you put on this site?" I said, "You've got access roads, daylight and sunlight to consider." He said, "Just put multis on it and some low rise." So in a day I knocked together some thoughts... then he took me over to Sighthill in his Jaguar, and said, "What do you think?" I said, "Jesus Christ!"' The architect was dismayed to find he had designed homes for several thousand people without having seen the site. (In 2001 Sighthill was in the news. Its flats were difficult to let, and nearly 400 vacancies had been allocated to asylum seekers. The murder of one Turkish refugee highlighted hostility to asylum seekers and the resentment of some of Sighthill's other tenants to what they saw as their own neglect.) 'Up in Heaven', a 1980 song by the punk band THE CLASH, reflected the widespread condemnation of high-rise housing at that time. 'The wives hate their husbands and their husbands don't care/ The children daub slogans to prove they lived there/ A giant pipe organ up in the air/ You can't live in a home which should not have been built/ By the bourgeois clerks who bear no guilt.' The first high flats in London, rising to 14 storeys, were Queen Anne's Mansions, St James's Park, begun in 1873 (Burnett, 1986). See PROSPECT HILL and SKYSCRAPER. **2** (US) *n*. A bicycle with small wheels, a long seat and high handlebars.

high road 1 A locally important ROAD. **2** A road for general traffic.

high shambolic See BYKER ESTATE.

high street 1 *n*. The most important shopping and commercial street of a traditional town. MAIN STREET is the US equivalent. High Street is the most common street name in Britain. (The next most common are Station Road, London Road and Church Road. The longest road name is Bolderwood Arboretum Ornamental Drive, in the New Forest. The worst-named road is, according to a television quiz show in 2002, Goosemuck Lane in East Lindsey, Lincolnshire.) **2** *adj*. Located in a high street, as in *high street store*. **3** *adj*. Popular or mainstream, as in *high street fashion*.

High Treason A film, made in 1929, presenting a vision of London in 1940. It was directed by Maurice Elvey and designed by Andrew Mazzei.

high-alumina cement An ingredient added to concrete to speed its setting. The concrete is prone to deteriorate if it is not made carefully, and the use of high-alumina cement has been the cause of some highly publicised building failures. Its effect is sometimes called *concrete cancer*. See also GLASS CANCER.

Highbury Initiative In 1988, international specialists worked intensively over a period of 48 hours on the opportunities and problems of Birmingham city centre with people who knew the city intimately. Eighteen months later a second event brought together many of the same 90 people to review progress. The initiative had a significant influence on city centre policy and action, particularly in establishing new pedestrian roads and spaces and in breaking the 'concrete collar' of the ring road. Highbury was the name of the historic mansion where the event was held.

highland clearances The enforced simultaneous eviction of all the inhabitants of a settlement in the Highlands and Islands of Scotland to make way for sheep or deer. The clearances took place throughout the region mainly between 1790 and 1855. Many of the evicted people swelled the urban populations of Scotland's cities or migrated to Canada, the USA, Australia and New Zealand. Others were settled on coastal allotments or in new fishing villages. The landlords called the mass evictions *removals*. Eric Richards (2000) notes that 'by 1843 the word "clearance" had emerged as the general and derogatory term to denote the unsavoury methods of Highland landlords'.

high-occupancy toll (US) Payment by a solo driver using a lane otherwise reserved for high-occupancy vehicles.

high-occupancy vehicle 1 One with enough occupants to warrant priority use of road space. How many that is (it can be as few as two) will be a matter of local policy. **2** One with two or more people in it.

high-occupancy vehicle lane One reserved for vehicles containing two or more people.

high-order shop One that specialises in selling products of a particular type and of relatively high value. High-order shops are often clustered together as people buying their COMPARISON GOODS want to compare alternatives. Customers are likely to come from further away and less frequently than they would for a LOWER-ORDER SHOP.

high-rise building See HIGH RISE.

high-rise subsidy The UK government subsidy for building council flats above six storeys was abolished in 1967.

high-road building A durable, independent building that steadily accumulates experience and becomes in time wiser and more respected than its inhabitants, according to the classification by Stewart Brand (1994). See LOW-ROAD BUILDING and NO-ROAD BUILDING.

highway 1 A public road. **2** A road (public or private) to which the public has access. **3** A road classified as a highway in a hierarchy of road types. EDWARD M BASSETT defined a highway as a strip of public land devoted to movement over which the abutting property owners have the right of light, air and access (compare FREEWAY and PARKWAY).

highway engineer For decades, planning and development were dominated by highway engineers. First design the roads, the engineers told us, and you can safely leave the other aspects of planning and design until later. We are living with the consequences. Roads strangle and divide towns and cities. New patterns of movement help to create lifeless streets and spaces that cast each passer-by in the role of intruder. They spawn dull, big-box buildings which turn their backs on their surroundings. The highway engineers can protest that they were merely trying to accommodate the expanding demand for road capacity. Our collective blame lies in allowing them to blind us to the need to achieve a balance between, first, the comfort, convenience and attractiveness of our surroundings; second, our need to walk; third, the effectiveness of public transport; and, fourth, the easy flow of traffic. We were blinded by science. The highway engineers had three advantages: a single, clear objective (unimpeded traffic flow); an ability to discuss it in quantifiable terms (such as numbers of parking spaces, dimensions of roads and traffic speeds); and their willingness to deal with one element of the complex urban system in isolation. Attitudes have changed over the past 10 years. Urban design is at last on the political and professional agenda (including that of many highway engineers). The need to see things whole and to balance conflicting objectives are widely accepted. But the urban design movement, for all its achievements, lacks the highwaymen's most potent weapons: clear objectives and quantifiable measures.

Highwayless Town, the RADBURN, New Jersey.

Hilberseimer, Ludwig (1885–1967) Architect and urbanist, based at the BAUHAUS in Dessau (1929–38) and later in Chicago. In 1924 he proposed an 'ideal city' composed of high slab blocks and motorways. In the late 1940s he devised plans for development on a decentralised polynuclear pattern. Paul Adamson (2000) describes the basis of Hilbersheimer's strategy as 'a formal typology of multiple self-sustaining industrial and residential centres spread more or less evenly across the exurban landscape.'

Hill, Octavia (1838–1912) A pioneer of housing management and a founder of the NATIONAL TRUST. She contrasted her sympathetic, people-centred approach to the problems of poverty and poor housing to the 'sanitary engineering' of the housing reformers and the philanthropic trusts. See also ANTI-URBANISM.

Hillier, Bill Architectural theorist and morphologist. See THE SOCIAL LOGIC OF SPACE, SPACE IS THE MACHINE and SPACE SYNTAX ANALYIS.

Hillman, Meyer Social policy researcher and environmental campaigner. See CONSERVER GAINS and STRANGER DANGER.

HI-LO A classification of development projects proposed by the Australian urban designer Bill Chandler (2001). HI projects are Heaven Inspired, excellence having been aspired to and achieved. LO projects are instances of Lost Opportunity, where mediocrity has been accepted and excused.

hing (Glasgow) To hang out of a window (leaning on the window sill) having a leisurely conversation with someone in an adjacent window or in the street below. See also WINDAE-HINGER.

hinterland The area economically dependent on a town or city. The word is, Bill Bryson (1990) points out, one of the inexplicably few English words to have been borrowed from modern German. The German word means back country.

hip hop A subculture, including RAP, GRAFFITI and BREAK DANCING, that developed in New York's South Bronx district in the 1970s.

Hippodamus (5th century BCE) Greek town planner and architect. He is credited as being the first to plan cities according to geometric layouts. His highly influential work included planning the port of Piraeus and the city of Rhodes.

historic Important in history. Compare AGEING.

historic district (US) The equivalent of a UK CONSERVATION AREA.

historic monument Robert Adam (2003) writes that 'the 1931 ATHENS CHARTER does not define "monuments" but in the text monuments can be "of artistic, historic or scientific interest" (although by its title the Charter is concerned only with Historic Monuments) and most references are specifically to "ancient monuments". It is safe, therefore, to assume that the word "monument" in the 1931 Charter pretty well accords with common usage in Britain: a building or object of some antiquity and of particular and significant interest or something that records an important person or event.' The first Article of the 1964 VENICE CHARTER defines 'historic monument'. It says: 'The concept of an historic monument embraces not only the single architectural work but also the urban or rural setting in which is found the evidence of a particular civilization, a significant development or an historic event. This applies not only to great works of art but also to more modest works of the past which have acquired cultural significance with the passing of time.' In Robert Adam's view, the implications of this definition are clear: 'monuments can be "modest works" the significance of which can be gained culturally by no more than the passage of time. What these modest works might constitute is open ended. Historic monuments can now be much more than buildings or objects of particular and significant historic interest – it is implied, however, that they must at least be reasonably old.' Adam goes on the consider how the term 'monument' is defined in a third charter. 'Age may seem to be an obvious precondition for a charter on heritage – but not so in the 2000 KRAKOW CHARTER.' He finds the Krakow Charter's definition of 'monument' 'highly revealing'. The charter states: 'A monument is an entity identified as of worth and forming a support to memory. In it, memory recognises aspects that are pertinent to human deeds and thoughts, associated with the historic time line. This may still be within our reach, even though not yet interpreted.' Adam comments: 'Once you have got through the curious terminology, this definition finally reduces monuments to pretty well anything. History is reduced to an association with "the historic time line" and even this is qualified as something that "may still be within our reach" and so is, one can only assume, quite recent and "not yet interpreted", which I take to mean not yet even the subject of any historical consideration. In fact, the only reasonably objective qualification is that a monument is "identified as of worth" but there are no criteria and identification alone seems to be enough.' Robert Adam finds 'further and conclusive evidence of mission creep' in the definition of HERITAGE, the word which has displaced the word 'monument' in the title and text of the Krakow Charter.

historic preservation (US) Defined by Richard C Collins (1980) as 'the act of retaining the tangible elements of our national heritage' and by W Brown Morton III (2000) as 'a dynamic and deliberate process through which we decide what to keep from the present for the future, and try to keep it'.

historical 1 Pertaining to history. **2** Authentic.

historicism Drawing heavily on historical precedent in designing buildings.

historic-value The evidence a building provides of a moment in history, as opposed to AGE-VALUE. The term was used by ALOIS RIEGL.

hit the ground A building is said to 'hit the ground' that it stands on. How a tall building hits the ground – as opposed to what impact it makes on the skyline – is often discussed as a distinct aspect of urban design.

hitch-hiker A person who travels by accepting rides from passing drivers. The term originated in the USA in the 1920s.

Hitch-hiker's Guide to the Galaxy, The A comic science fiction saga by Douglas Adams (1952–2001), broadcast on BBC radio in 1978, published as a book in 1979, and later made into a television series. The narrator is Ford Prefect, a roving reporter for the guide. He is an alien who chose his name (the Ford Prefect was a British car) thinking it would be 'nicely inconspicuous', having identified cars as the dominant life form on earth. Prostetnic Vogon Jeltz of the Galactic Hyperspace Planning Council tells the people of Earth: 'As you will no doubt be aware, the plans for development of the outlying regions of the Galaxy require the building of a hyperspatial express route through your star system, and regrettably your planet is one of those scheduled for demolition.' On a more mundane level, the earthling Arthur Dent has already heard from Mr Prosser of the local planning department that his own house is to be demolished to make way for a bypass. 'It's not as if it's a particularly nice house,' Prosser says as Dent lies down in front of the bulldozer. Dent replies: 'I'm sorry, but I happen to like it.' Says Prosser: 'You'll like the bypass.'

Hitler, Adolf See POL POT.

hobo (US) A homeless person who wanders from place to place; a tramp. The term was first recorded in around 1889. See VAGRANT.

hobohemia (US) The world of hoboes. A combination of *hobo* and *bohemia*. See VAGRANT.

Hobrecht, James As police president of Berlin, he prepared a plan for the city in 1858–62, laying it out in large street blocks. Mark Girouard (1985) notes that it was intended that these blocks should be subdivided by minor roads, but in fact they were developed in a series of courtyards running back from the street frontage. Girouard writes: 'A curious contrast developed: on the frontages, endless vistas of six-storey tenements, all exactly seventy-two feet high, vanishing into the distance to either side of wide streets; behind them a warren of high, enclosed courtyards, humming with people and machinery.'

Hochhaus (German) A tower block.

hodopoei (Ancient Greece) Commissioners of roads. They were required to keep the roads in order, using an assigned body of slaves.

hoile (Yorkshire) A shed or small room, as in *coal-'oile* (coal cellar, coal house or coal shed) and *back-'oile* (back room or shed).

Holabird, William (1854–1923) Architect. As a leader of the Chicago School of architecture he was a noted designer of skyscrapers.

Holford, Lord See WILLIAM GRAHAM.

holism The theory that the universe consists of complete systems, from atoms to complex lifeforms and human settlements; the study and treatment of wholes, as opposed to parts; the opposite of REDUCTIONISM. Example: 'The idea that everything progresses in a regular linear progression has broken down with an increased awareness of holism, with its belief in the intrinsic connectedness of everything' (Landry, 2000). PATRICK GEDDES (1915d) wrote (explaining the concept but not using the term holism): '...unemployment and employment... disease and folly... vice and apathy... indolence and crime... All these are not separately to be treated, as our too specialised treatments of them assume, but are logically connected, inseparably connected, like the symptoms of a disease.' The term was coined by General Smuts from the Greek *holos*, whole. It is sometimes spelled *wholism*. Compare COMPLEXITY.

holistic Defined by the Local Government Association (2000) as 'linking land use, transport, housing and the provision of health, education and other services in the public and private sectors'.

Hollar, Wenceslaus (1607–77) Artist. His architectural etchings are a unique source of information about seventeenth-century London.

hollowing out The process by which the centre of a town or city becomes less densely used and inhabited as activity moves out to the suburbs.

Hollywood See TINSELTOWN.

Holme, Thomas (1624–95) Surveyor. With William Penn he planned Philadelphia.

Holy City 1 Allahabad. **2** Jerusalem. **3** Mecca. **4** Rome. **5** VARANASI – among many other examples. See also CITY OF GOD.

home equity The homeowner's share of the value of a home.

home guard (US) A VAGRANT who stays within a town or city. See also WALLY.

home loss payment Payable in recognition of the hardship of losing a home by compulsory dispossession to both owner occupiers (in addition to any compensation) and tenants. Compare DISTURBANCE PAYMENT.

historic monument

home zone A small, highly TRAFFIC-CALMED, residential area, often with road and pavement integrated into a single surface, where pedestrians and cyclists have priority over cars. The Department of Transport, Local Government and the Regions (2001) proposed the following definition. 'A home zone should have a significant level of residential use. It can consist of one or more roads or parts of roads. They should have no more than low flows of motor traffic after the local traffic authority has done whatever is needed to create the home zone. Any traffic should be kept to low speeds appropriate to the mix of uses in the home zone. The intention should be to make sure that, for example, children can play games or that people can stand talking in safety, even if they have to move occasionally to allow vehicles to pass. It would follow that any road or part of a road proposed for designation as a home zone should either have very low traffic speeds already, or have measures applied to lower speeds'. Mike Biddulph (2001) describes a home zone as 'a residential street in which the living environment clearly predominates over any provision for traffic.'

A home zone will almost certainly make a particular street, or part of a street, more pleasant for the people who live in it. But creating a zone in isolation may make some parts of the wider area less pleasant to live in, due to traffic that would have driven through the zone diverting to less obstructed routes. Traffic-calming measures need to be considered in the context of a strategic approach to taming traffic over a wider area.

Biddulph (2001) credits the road safety campaigner Barbara Preston with coining the term home zone in the early 1990s, when the idea was to create areas where drivers would bear the burden of proof for any accidents involving pedestrians. The term was used by the Children's Play Council from 1998. The concept was adapted in the UK from the Dutch WOONERF. An early example of the home zone concept, though not the name, can be seen in the shared road surface at the Brow in Runcorn new town, built in 1969 (Biddulph, 2000). Compare QUIET LANE.

Homebuy A scheme in which a buyer takes out a mortgage for 75 per cent of the value of a home and a housing association provides the remainder. The housing association receives 25 per cent of the value of the home when it is sold.

HOMEFREGYFITOP How many fried eggs can you fit on a plan? This approximate acronym was used by Australian NEW URBANISTS in 2001 making fun of typical plans for one of their favoured forms of development. The plans use concentric circles to indicate the elements of a district. The commercial centre is coloured red, areas of medium density housing and mixed uses are orange, and low-density development is yellow.

homeless *adj.* Lacking a place to live. The word needs more precise definition in any particular context. People living in bed and breakfast hotels, hostels, overcrowded conditions, temporarily with friends or relatives or with an abusive partner, for example, are often considered homeless, and as such may be eligible for rehousing under the housing acts.

homeless, the Homeless people. Campaigners against homelessness tend to avoid the term 'the homeless' on the grounds that it suggests homelessness is an inherent characteristic of people who suffer from it.

homes for heroes The well-known phrase is generally attributed to Lloyd George, who did promise in 1918 'habitations that are fit for the heroes who have won the war' (quoted in Swenarton, 1981). He declared in that same year: 'What is our task? To make Britain a fit country for heroes to live in.' The architect WR Lethaby had called in 1916 for 'houses fit for sane people to live in' (Lethaby, 1922).

Homes for the Future A demonstration project of 300 houses built beside Glasgow Green to celebrate Glasgow's year as CITY OF ARCHITECTURE AND DESIGN in 1999. The master plan was by Page and Park Architects with Arup Associates. Prominent architects designed 10 residential blocks.

homes for votes A scandal of the late 1980s in which Dame Shirley Porter, leader of Westminster City Council, and her deputy sold empty council homes at a discount in politically marginal wards, in the hope of improving the party's electoral prospects. The theory was that incoming owner occupiers were more likely to be Conservative voters than homeless people living in bed and breakfast or existing council tenants who might otherwise be rehoused in the same properties. At their instigation the council's housing committee decided in 1987 to sell 500 homes a year under a policy called 'building stable communities'. After an investigation by the Audit Commission, Porter, heiress to the Tesco empire, and her deputy were ordered to reimburse the council's financial loss of £26 million. A decade of legal wrangling led to the ruling being confirmed by the House of Lords in 2001.

homesteading See URBAN HOMESTEADING.

homeworking Working from home. *Teleworking* is homeworking based on information technology.

homogenise To make places the same as one another. Example: 'Maintaining local distinctiveness is a challenge when globalisation threatens to homogenise our towns and cities.'

honeypot 1 A place that is particularly attractive, especially to tourists. **2** Defined by SECURED BY DESIGN as a place 'that encourage[s] people to congregate'. One of the Secured by Design principles is that designers should avoid creating such places.

hood (US) The neighbourhood.

hoodie 1 The hood to a hooded top, as worn by urban

youths in the 2000s. In 2004 Manchester Magistrates' Court banned four youths from wearing their hoodies up, as a part of a series of ANTI-SOCIAL BEHAVIOUR ORDERS. The magistrates hoped this would 'prohibit their association with gang culture'. See also DRESS SENSE. **2** (US) A person of the neighbourhood.

Hook A new town at Hook in Hampshire was planned by the London County Council. Even though the town was never built, its plan (published in 1961) was influential, particularly in its ideas of pedestrian and vehicle movement. Sebastian Loew (1996) notes that the plan aimed for URBANITY: it called for 'a coherent structure, easy to understand... compact without sacrificing standards of open space... Urban character in terms of buildings, landscape and the relationship between them... although the town would be predominantly horizontal' (London County Council, 1961). Loew writes: 'Admittedly the masterplan is based on the separation of land uses, particularly in relation to industry, but any other approach would probably have been unacceptable at the time, when industry still meant 'heavy'. Otherwise the plan was ahead of its time: it gives priority to pedestrian movement and provides all essential services along pedestrian routes, it chooses compactness for the inner area, and it establishes firm design criteria without specifying architectural details.'

hooligan A person who runs wild in the street. The word may derive from Patrick Hooligan, a London criminal of the 1890s.

Hooper, Daniel See SWAMPY.

hooray Henry The male equivalent of a SLOANE RANGER.

hoose (Scots) A house.

HOPE (US) Housing Opportunities for People Everywhere, an official programme that seeks to attract higher income people to low-income neighbourhoods (Minton, 2002).

horizontal alignment The direction and course of a roadway on a plan.

Horizontal City, The A 1940 design by the Italian rationalist architect Giuseppe Pogatschnig (1896–1945), an ardent fascist. Jacqueline Gargus (1981) comments that the scheme shows 'the limitations of his functionalist-rationalist way of generating design: clustered around a town centre, residential blocks infinitely repeat themselves with no modifications, no attempts to make special places that give character to the urban fabric.'

horizontal cooperation Between organisations at the same level, such as departments. Compare VERTICAL COOPERATION.

horizontal mixed uses See MIXED USES.

Horsfall, Thomas Cogan A Manchester-based manufacturer of playing cards and an early advocate of town planning. His 1904 book *The Example of Germany* urged that Britain should emulate German cities, which enjoyed well-planned public transport and high standards of urban design, and whose burgomasters had powers to specify wide streets, parks and street trees. 'In the edgy climate of Edwardian Britain,' notes Michael Hebbert (2000), 'this clinched the political argument for town planning legislation.'

horsiculture Fields used for keeping horses, often on marginal land at the edge of cities. The term echoes *horticulture*.

hot spot 1 An area of high property values. **2** A small area of high-density development.

hot-block A street or street block where illegal activities take place.

hot-desking Using the facilities of an office building without having a designated permanent desk. The practice was introduced by IBM in the 1980s (Hall, 1998). Also known as *hotelling, location-independent working* and *virtual office* (Quinion, 1997).

hotel Defined in planning law as an establishment falling within Class C1 of the Town and Country Planning (Use Classes) Order 1987, providing temporary accommodation and at least one meal a day for visitors, including bed-and-breakfast and guest houses.

Hôtel de Ville (France) A town hall in a larger town. Compare MAIRIE.

hoteling (US) HOT-DESKING.

Hotlanta Atlanta, Georgia.

house 1 A dwelling, sometimes particularly as distinct from a FLAT. **2** (Scotland) A tenement flat. **3** In some house types in Leeds, England, the living-room was traditionally known as the *house* (Burnett, 1986).

house in multiple occupation (HMO) A house or flat that provides permanent accommodation, not self-contained, for people who do not form more than one household.

housebuilding An activity that in recent decades has been too often a matter of building estates or developments that consist of houses and little else, leaving the residents to rely on their cars or on often inadequate bus services. For several decades after the second world war – in which many homes were destroyed by bombing and repairs were neglected – the numbers of houses built was a major political issue in the UK. In the early post-war years most houses were built by local authorities, but by 1959 more homes were being built by the private sector. The peak rate of housebuilding in the UK in recent decades was hit in 1968, when more than 400,000 new dwellings were built. At that time the rate of building new houses was a politically important gauge of a government's success.

In the 1980s MARGARET THATCHER's government discouraged councils from building houses, leaving the job mainly to the private market, but the market was held back by the difficulty in finding suitable sites and obtaining planning permission. Though the numbers of houses built decreased dramatically, the electorate did not seem to mind after all. In 2002/03 184,000 homes were built, 89 per cent of them by the private sector. In the 2000s the UK government (and in particular the Treasury under chancellor of the exchequer Gordon Brown) became concerned that the low level of housebuilding in the south east of England was preventing the labour market from responding to the booming regional economy. The government sought to remedy this by promoting a major housebuilding programme under the slogan 'SUSTAINABLE COMMUNITIES'. The relative proportions of homes built on GREENFIELD and BROWNFIELD sites remains controversial. New SOCIAL HOUSING in the UK is now built mainly by REGISTERED SOCIAL LANDLORDS rather than by local authorities.

household Defined in the UK census as one person living alone, or a group of people (who may or may not be related) living at the same address with common house-keeping, sharing either a living room or sitting room, or at least one meal a day.

household fission Households shrinking in size due to such factors as children setting up on their own sooner; separation and divorce; and old people living independently for longer.

household waste Defined by the Scottish Office (1996b) as waste from a domestic property, caravan, residential home, university, school or other educational establishment, or premises forming part of a hospital or nursing home (but excluding clinical waste).

house-province The term was used by PATRICK GEDDES (1905) to refer to the 'province covered with houses' spreading across south-east England.

houser A housing reformer. The term was current in the USA in the early twentieth century. JANE JACOBS (1961) argued that '"housers", narrowly specialising in "housing" expertise', were a vocational absurdity. 'Such a profession makes sense only if it is assumed that "housing" *per se* has important generalized effects and qualities,' she wrote. 'It does not.'

housing action area Introduced by the Housing Act 1974 to promote the gradual improvement of an area of poor housing, particularly in the interests of the people already living there. Replaced by HOUSING RENEWAL AREAS in 1989.

housing action trust A body set up to take over the control of an area (or areas) or types of housing from a local authority, with the approval of a majority of the tenants, and responsible to the environment secretary. The initiative was launched by environment secretary NICHOLAS RIDLEY in 1988, but the first proposed HATs were voted down by the tenants. Many tenants were suspicious that the initiative was motivated primarily by the government's desire to transfer housing from local authorities, and they were angry that funds for essential improvements were being made conditional on a change of ownership. Nor, not surprisingly, did they think it democratic for (as the government at first intended) abstentions in the tenants' vote on the HAT proposal to be counted as votes in favour of it. It was two or three years before the first successful HAT scheme emerged from this unpromising start. This method has since been superseded by transfers to housing associations. See LIVERPOOL HOUSING ACTION TRUST.

housing association A non-profit making organisation, registered with the Housing Corporation, whose purpose is to provide, build, improve or manage houses for sale or rent. Housing associations began to be set up in the nineteenth century by housing reformers as purely voluntary philanthropic endeavours. Since the 1960s they have become increasingly reliant on state funding and consequently state control to the extent of becoming almost a direct arm of central government. Their lack of local political control and supposed effectiveness persuaded central government in the 1980s to enable them to take over from local authorities as the main providers of SOCIAL HOUSING.

housing benefit Paid (usually through local authorities) to help people in low incomes to pay their rent.

Housing Corporation (UK) Created in 1964 to encourage *coownership*, it evolved to support and regulate housing associations.

housing development An area of new houses, often without other uses or facilities.

housing estate A planned residential area, often without other uses or facilities. Jonathan Raban (1974) described one of the worst of its kind. 'Four miles to the west of Southampton city centre, they built a housing estate called Millbrook, a vast, cheap storage unit for nearly 20,000 people. Laid out on a sloping plain, it has 50 acres of grassland at its centre, a great, useless, balding greenspace of sickly turf and purely symbolic value. What one sees first are the tower-blocks, 24 storeys high, of pre-stressed concrete and glass, known, I am told, as "slab block/scissors-type", should anyone order more.' Raban observes: 'The roads are service roads; they loop purposelessly around the estate in broad curves that conform to no contours. There is no street life on them: an occasional pram pushed by a wind-blown mother, a motorbiking yobbo or two, a dismal row of parked Ford Anglias, an ice-cream van playing "Greensleeves" at half-tempo, a mongrel snapping at its tail.'

housing management renewal area Coordinates housing action by local authorities and other agencies.

Housing Manual Published in 1919 to illustrate the standards set out in the TUDOR WALTERS REPORT. The manual favoured groups of cottages with gardens rather than terraced housing, at low densities on curving or geometrically shaped tree-lined road layouts.

housing market area Defined by the Scottish Office (1996a) as a geographical area which is relatively self-contained in terms of reflecting people's choice of location for a new home; that is, a large percentage of people settling in the area will have sought a house only in that area.

housing mix The range of housing in an area or a development in terms of such factors as its type, size, affordability, accessibility and tenure.

housing module See PREFAB.

housing pathfinder partnership The first nine were set up in 2002 to promote regeneration in Manchester, Salford, Burnley, Rochdale, Stoke, Birmingham, Sheffield, Liverpool and Hull.

housing quality indicator system A measurement and assessment tool designed to allow potential or existing housing schemes to be evaluated on the basis of quality rather than simply cost.

housing Residential accommodation.

housing strategy and investment statement An annual statement of a local authority's housing objectives and financial bid to central government.

Houston The Texan oil city has long had a reputation of having no control over development. Deyan Sudjik (1992) challenges this. 'Houston, supposedly the most unplanned Western city of all, is in fact nothing of the kind. It is perfectly true that Houston has no zoning legislation, unlike every other major city in the United States. The voters of Houston rejected the idea as recently as 1962, but though they might change their minds one day, the city is certainly not without planning, and it has an armoury of regulations that achieve very much the same ends. What makes Houston – the Third Coast as it presumptuously calls itself – different is the extent to which development control is in the hands of the private landowners and developers who have made fortunes out of the city's explosive growth. Right up until the 1960s, Houston was run from regular meetings at a suite in the Lamar Hotel by a clique that

> **"IN HOUSTON, A PERSON WALKING IS SOMEONE ON HIS WAY TO HIS CAR"**
>
> *Anthony Downs*

made the decisions, formed the committees and fired the mayors.' Taxes and services were kept at survival level, Sudjik writes, with infrastructure investment put off until crisis point was reached. 'They used tax money to bail out their flooded suburbs and to provide water and sewers for private developments. Hints of the skulduggery that accompanied the city's foundation in 1836, when a couple of carpetbaggers from New York, Augustus and John Kirby Allen, bought the swamps on which Houston is built sight unseen, continue to surface. Land use in Houston is controlled by restrictive covenants in the title deeds that cover most of the city's developed land. There are ten thousand such covenants dealing with use, size, cost and height, administered by 630 civic clubs which function exactly like private zoning boards, backed up the city itself, which has acquired the power to enforce private covenants.' Anthony Downs has written: 'In Houston, a person walking is someone on his way to his car.'

how the other half lives The phrase, relating to poor people, entered the language in 1890 when Jacob Riis published *How the Other Half Lives*, his best-selling book on urban poverty in the USA.

Howard, Ebenezer (Sir) (1850–1928) Founder of the GARDEN CITY movement. Howard is credited as a founding father of town planning, though his real aim was much more ambitious: to introduce a practical means of radical social and economic reform in Britain. He published his proposal in 1898 in *Tomorrow: a peaceful path to real reform* (which in later editions became *Garden Cities of Tomorrow*). Howard considered the large cities of his time to be 'ulcers on the very face of our beautiful island'. He wrote in *Tomorrow*: 'These crowded cities have done their work. They were the best which a society largely based on selfishness and rapacity could construct, but they are in the nature of things entirely unadapted for a society in which the social side of our nature is demanding a larger share of recognition.' Howard dreamt of a society based on cooperation. His idea was to create 'garden cities' in the countryside. People would be attracted from the old cities, whose densities would decline, allowing them to be re-planned on garden city lines. Garden cities would have a population of no more than 32,000 each. They would combine the best of country life with the best of city life, without the disadvantages of either. The freehold of each garden city would be collectively owned, so the rise in land values brought about by the creation of the city would be retained as part of the community's wealth, rather than being siphoned off by developers and speculators. The larger urban units of the future, which Howard called 'social cities', would be federated clusters of garden cities.

As Howard had hoped, the magnetic attraction of the big cities did eventually fade. But this was not because of the rival attraction of garden cities (in the UK only two, LETCHWORTH and WELWYN, were built, and neither went very far toward fulfilling their inventor's hopes). The populations of the cities fell because people voted with their feet (and their cars), attracted by the lower densities in suburbs, villages and small towns.

Howard earned his living as a stenographer. Throughout his life he was an inventor, not only of garden cities but also of a stenography machine that, like his other inventions, failed to make his fortune. The son of shopkeepers, he was born in London. He left school at 14 to become a clerk, before teaching himself shorthand. In his twenties he emigrated to the USA as a homesteader in Nebraska, but he failed to make a success of it and returned home after a year.

Howard invented garden cities after years of considering social and economic problems, and studying his contemporaries' many proposals for resolving them. Reading Edward Bellamy's utopian novel LOOKING BACKWARD concentrated his mind, though he soon decided that achieving Bellamy's vision would be neither practical nor desirable. Howard believed that cooperative civilisation could be developed from small communities in a decentralised society, not from the existing cities with their extremes of wealth and poverty. He believed neither that any government could be persuaded to build garden cities nor that it should do so. 'If you wait for the government to do it,' he said, 'you will be as old as Methuselah before they start' (Osborn, 1970). He put his faith in action by wealthy people who combined support for the garden city idea with a desire to speculate in land and a philanthropic willingness to take a relatively low return on their capital. Fishman (1977) comments: 'For Howard, the garden city was an environment in which capitalism could be peacefully superseded. Most of his supporters, however, looked to the garden city as the place where capitalism could be most easily preserved.'

The modest stenographer drove the garden city movement with energy and infectious confidence. The dramatist and critic George Bernard Shaw (quoted in Hardy, 1991) wrote: 'He was one of those heroic simpletons who do big things whilst our prominent wordlings are explaining why they are Utopian and impossible.' In 1901 the Garden City Association began looking for a site and raising the money to build a first garden city. Two years later Howard and the wealthy allies he had recruited (including GEORGE CADBURY and WH LEVER) bought land at Letchworth in Hertfordshire, 35 miles north east of London, on which to build the first garden city.

With the development of Letchworth progressing slowly, Howard continued his propaganda for garden cities. In 1919 he found a site at Welwyn in Hertfordshire, between London and Letchworth, which he decided would be suitable for a second garden city. He managed to buy it only by persuading his agent to lend him the money for the deposit. As at Letchworth, the work of building the city was funded through philanthropic land speculation. As Welwyn slowly developed, Howard retired there, learning Esperanto, practising spiritualism and continuing his unsuccessful attempt to make his fortune by inventing a stenographic machine. He was granted a modest Civil List pension in 1913 and knighted in 1927.

Jane Jacobs (1961) has been one of the most trenchant critics of Howard's ideas and their impact on planning. 'Howard set spinning powerful and city-destroying ideas,' she wrote. 'He conceived that the way to deal with the city's functions was to sort and sift out of the whole certain simple uses, and to arrange each of these in relative self-containment. He focused on the provision of wholesome housing as the central problem, to which everything else was subsidiary; furthermore he defined wholesome housing in terms only of suburban physical qualities and small-town social qualities. He conceived of commerce in terms of routine, standardised supply of goods, and as serving a self-limited market.' Jacobs argued that Howard conceived of good planning as a series of static acts. 'In each case the plan must anticipate all that is needed and be protected, after it is built, against any but the most minor subsequent changes. He conceived of planning also as essentially paternalistic, if not authoritarian.' Other hostile critics have also accused Howard of ANTI-URBANISM and having a suburban mentality. The town planner and writer THOMAS SHARP (1932) wrote: 'Howard's new hope, new life, new civilisation, Town-Country, is a hermaphrodite; sterile, imbecile, a monster; abhorrent and loathsome to the Nature which he worships.'

Sir Peter Hall and Colin Ward (1998) are among Howard's admirers. '*Tomorrow*... was destined to become the most influential and important book in the entire history of twentieth-century town planning,' they write. 'His ideas are still completely relevant to the creation of civilised and sustainable new communities for the coming century.'

Ebenezer Howard

howff (Scots) A resort.

Hoyt, Homer See FILTERING.

H-Town HOUSTON, Texas.

hub and spoke Patterns of transport networks in some cities. Radial routes are the spokes.

HUD (US) The federal Department of Housing and Urban Development.

Hugo, Victor (1802–85) Poet, novelist and dramatist. In the 1830s he campaigned against the destruction of works of medieval architecture, arguing that, among other things, the cost of maintaining them was more than outweighed by the revenue from the tourism they encouraged. See also COURT OF MIRACLES and LES MISÉRABLES.

Hull House The SETTLEMENT in Chicago founded by JANE ADDAMS in 1889. Charles Hull had been a previous owner of the building.

Hulme A district of Manchester that was redeveloped in the 1960s and '70s (replacing nineteenth-century terraced housing) and again in the 1990s, each time with what was thought to be the best modern architecture and urban design. More than 3,000 deck-access flats were completed by 1971. Four years later the council was moving the tenants out, having accepted that the housing had failed. After Manchester City Council demolished the entire Hulme estate in the early 1990s, it commissioned planners to design layouts for new housing development on the site. 'The first designs came back with the same mistakes as in the 1960s, such as roads not leading anywhere,' the then council leader Graham Stringer (1995) remembered. 'It turned out to be a journey of discovery about how the city council makes decisions.' The council decided to investigate what made the city's most popular neighbourhoods successful, and to use the answers as design principles for Hulme. The result was the *Guide to Development in Hulme*, published in 1994, which set out the approach to urban design which Hulme Regeneration (a collaboration between public and private sectors, and local people) followed. The development is generally thought to be a reasonably successful example of NEW URBANIST design.

human ecology The interaction of people and their environment.

human geography The study of human activity in relation to the world's physical features; the study of where and how people live. Compare HUMANISTIC GEOGRAPHY.

Human Neighbourhood Project An initiative by the Human City Institute in support of local neighbourhood renewal projects.

human scale Development is of a human scale if its size, position and details relate to passers-by in a way that makes them feel comfortable rather than intimidated.

humanistic geography The study of people's emotional ties to place. Compare HUMAN GEOGRAPHY.

Hume, David (1711–76) Philosopher. See CAPITAL OF THE MIND.

Hummer The product name of a gas-guzzling civilian off-road vehicle. It has the same basic design and components as the US Army's standard truck the *Humvee* (High Mobility Multi-purpose Wheeled Vehicle, or HMMWV). Sales of the Hummer were boosted by the Iraq war of 2003, when owners were said to feel patriotic driving a similar vehicle to those seen on their television screens, carrying the stars and stripes in the Iraq desert.

Hundred Mile City, The A book by Deyan Sudjic (1992) describing the characteristic modern city as having 'a force field stretching for a hundred miles in each direction, over towns and villages and across tracts of what appears to be open country, far from any existing settlement that could conventionally be called a city. This is the hundred mile city... The airline door is the new city gate, the shopping mall and the museum are its civic spaces'.

hustreet A street reserved for humans only and prohibited to machines. The term (also *husquare* and *hu-avenue*) was coined by CONSTANTINOS DOXIADIS. A *mecstreet* is reserved for machines only (also *mecsystem* and *mecarea*).

hybrid vehicle One where a conventional engine is used to generate electricity to power an electric motor and to charge batteries. Such vehicles are relatively low in fuel consumption and pollution and, when running on battery power alone, generate no harmful emissions.

hydrogen The motor industry is looking for practical means of making cars non-polluting by using hydrogen as a fuel. Electric motors would be powered by fuel cells, electrochemical devices that convert to electricity the energy released when hydrogen and oxygen combine. The only emission from vehicles powered by this means would be water vapour. Pollution can be created, though, in making the electricity needed to extract the hydrogen from the water to provide the fuel. The whole process would be non-polluting only if this electricity were generated by such means as wind or wave power.

hyem (Geordie) Home.

Hygeia The name of two proposals for new towns (named after the Greek goddess of health): one published by JOHN BOUNAROTTI PAPWORTH in 1827, the other by BENJAMIN RICHARDSON some 50 years later. Among the supposedly health-giving features of Richardson's Hygeia (population 100,000) was a prohibition on cellars and carpets. A Cameron Corbett MP (later Lord Rowallan) advertised the Corbett Estate, his suburban development in Hither Green, south London, as a 'modern Hygeia' and a 'Garden of Eden'. See HEALTHY CITY and NEW JERUSALEM.

hypercar The concept of a motor car made highly efficient by the use of a range of new technologies. The term was coined by the futurist Amory Lovins (Quinion, 1997).

hypermarket A very large SUPERMARKET, with more than 4,500 sq metres floorspace, often combining features of a department store and largely serving car-borne customers. The term, dating from the late 1960s, derives from the French *hypermarché*.

hypermobility Very high levels of transport use. See also ZERO-FRICTION SOCIETY.

hyper-segregation Extreme segregation of a city's population in GHETTOES.

hyper-urbanisation Fast and massive URBANISATION. Example: 'The globe is undergoing hyper-urbanisation. Large cities are being built from scratch, some built from scratch in the last ten years' (2002).

hyper-urbanist A pejorative term for one who advocates extremes in the DENSITY or extent of urban living. Example: 'It is a smack in the eye for the hyper-urbanist restaurant reviewers who have taken over the cerebral cortex of the architectural profession in recent years' (Pawley, 2002b).

hypothecation Linking the process of raising revenue to the expenditure. Examples would include spending the product of road fund tax on road building, or using planning application fees to pay for a local authority's planning service.

Hythloday, Ralph The fictional narrator-hero of Thomas More's novel UTOPIA.

I

I and the City A self-portrait painted in 1913 by the German expressionist artist LUDWIG MEIDNER. Superhuman forces seem to be violently shaking both him and the city around him. Such images of the city as heaving with either energy or impending disaster are common in expressionist painting and poetry of the time.

iatrogenics Ameliorating a problem that was itself caused by previous treatment or action. Example: 'Some funding goes towards iatrogenics, such as when finance to improve the public realm is provided as a planning gain from projects that themselves inhibit people from walking.'

Ibansk A fictional, vast city that, according to Alexander Zinoviev's satire *Yawning Heights* (1976), covers a large part of Europe and Asia. Its architecture is so fine that even LE CORBUSIER said he could not improve on it. Most of the inhabitants are called Ibanov.

Icara The capital of the utopian republic of Icaria, featured in ETIENNE CABET's novel *Voyage to Icaria* (1840). Its architecture is inspired by that of the best of the world's cities. The houses, mass-produced, no more than four storeys high and each with a garden, are in the centre of the city, and the factories and businesses on the outskirts.

Icarians Followers of the utopian socialist ETIENNE CABET.

icon 1 *n.* Something particularly significant and distinctive; an iconic building or structure; a LANDMARK. Example: 'Washington's Mall must be one of the most recognisable icons of America.' The building called The Deep – 'the world's only submarium' – was described by its architect TERRY FARRELL and Partners in 2002 as 'an icon for Hull'. A colleague of the architect WILL ALSOP described his practice's competition-winning, proposed 'fourth grace' building for Liverpool's waterfront (see THE THREE GRACES) in 2002 as an icon. He explained: 'None of the other schemes were icons. They were landmarks.' In Birmingham, though, the new Selfridges store by the architect Future Systems was described in 2003 in the architectural press (probably quoting its developer) as both iconic and a landmark: an 'iconic landmark... a vivid focal point for the new Bullring centre'. The increasing popularity of the word, which sometimes seems to be used to describe any building not specifically designed to be self-effacing, makes it likely that a new term will soon be adopted for buildings or structures of real significance. *Super-icon* was heard in 2003. **2** *adj.* Notable. Example: 'We need icon buildings and icon regeneration in Birmingham' (2003).

iconic *adj.* Representing something particularly significant and distinctive. Examples: 'Views can be enhanced by buildings [such as] the first iconic glistening building at Canary Wharf before it was compromised by its recent lumpy brothers'; 'Most people outside Liverpool are familiar with a number of its iconic structures: the buildings of the Pier Head, the Albert Dock, St George's Hall or the two cathedrals.' There is no general agreement on what constitutes an iconic building. In the words of one writer (Pardey, 2001): 'It only takes one iconic building to make a great city, as Sydney proved in the 1960s, so London should be thankful that it has three in the Tower, St Paul's and the Houses of Parliament. Our age does not yet promise a fourth.' Most people, though, would judge that in London the Lloyd's Building and 1 Canada Square at Canary Wharf (in addition to a fourth classic, Tower Bridge) make the grade. In the wake of the destruction by terrorists of the WORLD TRADE CENTER, a London developer was quoted (in Garlick and Loney, 2001) as arguing that his company's proposed skyscrapers (designed by Lord Foster for a site at Elephant and Castle) were not likely to be a target for terrorists as they were not 'iconic' buildings. In 2003 the architect WILL ALSOP presented a plan for Bradford to be split into 24 areas, each of a square mile and having either an 'iconic building', a park or a piece of public art. See also ANTI-MONUMENT and STATUE.

iconic city One that is recognised for its strong, positive identity. Example: 'The mayor says he needs a replacement icon for the world's most iconic city' (discussing plans for the WORLD TRADE CENTER site, 2003). Jon Rouse, chief executive of CABE, urged Plymouth in 2002 to improve 50 public spaces to turn it from dereliction into an iconic city.

iconographic building An ICONIC BUILDING. Example: 'The council's cabinet member for planning and regeneration said he was seeking an "iconographic" building for Croydon, not "just another grey shoe box".'

Ideal City, The A pamphlet by CANON BARNETT, undated but published around 1893–4, describing his social vision and the means that the civic leaders of Bristol, in particular, should take to achieve it. Barnett envisaged the ideal city as having a population of a quarter or half a million citizens.

idealotopia The ideal place. PATRICK GEDDES used the term in the 1920s.

iDeath A small town in the USA where almost everything, including the buildings, is made of the sugar produced by cooking watermelons. It is described in Richard Brautigan's *In Watermelon Sugar* (1964).

identity point A place or feature designed to help visitors get their bearings.

ideology The legal authority Patrick McAuslan (1980) pointed out that Britain's planners operated a planning system made up of laws created at different times for different purposes. Three main ideologies – sets of values, attitudes and assumptions – lay behind these laws, each relating to a different set of ideas about the relationship between cities and their citizens. McAuslan identified the three categories of planning law as: first, legislation designed primarily to protect private property rights in the face of government intervention; second, legislation designed primarily to provide the legitimacy for action to advance the public interest; and third, legislation designed as a vehicle for the advancement of public participation. Any one of these sets of legislation might be the basis for a coherent planning system. Unfortunately the British planning system, he argued, was based on all three of them.

ideopolis A city of knowledge-based industries. Will Hutton (2002) identifies the key elements of a city's status as an ideopolis as airports, universities and the capacity to create new businesses to exploit new ideas. Hutton (2003) also suggests that London is the only UK city to fit the model, but that Manchester has the right attributes to become the next one.

Igloo Regeneration Fund Private-sector funding for partnership projects at the edge of city centres. Igloo insists on high standards of design and sustainability.

Igloo, the Minneapolis, Minnesota.

IJburg A new town on six artificial islands in the IJ-Lake, near Amsterdam in the Netherlands.

Iladelph Philadelphia, Pennsylvania.

Illich, Ivan (b1926) Writer and teacher. Illich was been a strong critic of the debilitating influence of PROFESSIONS on the ability of people to influence and change their environment. See CONVIVIALITY and WALKING.

îlot (French) An island. A historical name for a block in a gridded plan. See also CHEQUER and INSULA.

image 1 The overall visual impact of a place. **2** The overall impression that people have of a place. KEVIN LYNCH wrote in *The Image of the City*, published in 1960: 'Dickens helped to create the London we experience as surely as its actual builders did.' **3** The associations, positive or negative, that the *name* of a place evokes.

> **"DICKENS HELPED TO CREATE THE LONDON WE EXPERIENCE AS SURELY AS ITS ACTUAL BUILDERS DID"**
> *Kevin Lynch*

These can be altered by changing the name (see SO GOOD THEY NAMED IT TWICE) or by a public relations campaign to adjust the associations (see GLASGOW'S MILES BETTER).

imageability A place's capacity for creating a strong visual image. KEVIN LYNCH, who developed the concept, defined it as 'that quality in a physical object which gives it a high probability of evoking a strong image in any given observer' (Lynch, 1960).

Imagine Chicago An organisation that runs pioneering education and community development programmes, and has helped to form partnerships of community organisations, schools and cultural institutions in 40 neighbourhoods. Its projects include the Urban Imagination Network, Reading and Writing a City, Choices for Changes and Citizen Leaders.

imagineer 1 To conceive a vision for a place. **2** To create a place in the image of another.

impact Paul Finch (2002) of CABE has complained that the use of the word in relation to the effect of a building on its surroundings has an undeservedly negative implication. 'It sounds like a car crash. Why not try effect, or benefit, or contribution?' See also BIASED TERMINOLOGY.

impact fee (US) A charge payable by a developer as a condition for permission to develop, to provide new or expanded public capital facilities needed to serve that development, or to mitigate its social or environmental costs. Impact fees are widely used in the USA to do the job that is done less satisfactorily in the UK by the system of PLANNING OBLIGATIONS (which is slow, unpredictable and tends to compensate rather than necessarily mitigating directly). The Urban Task Force (1999b) recommended introducing impact fees in the UK but admitted that it did not know how the system might work.

Impact fees are programmed and calculated by projecting needs for facilities around 20 years ahead; identifying areas of service (such as parks, water supply or fire protection); adopting a standard of service to be provided; working out what facilities are needed;

imposed environment

and drawing up a capital improvement programme (identifying the gap between the need for facilities or services, and the money available to pay for them). The level of impact fee is based on what is needed to fill the gap.

impasse (French) A close; a dead-end street.

impenetrable See PENETRATE.

impermeable Not allowing through-movement. Impermeable urban form has few or no routes through it. Also *impermeability*. The opposite is PERMEABLE.

implementation Making things happen. The complement of *policy*, a statement of what should happen. The American urban planner Jerold Kayden (2000) writes: 'To plan is human, to follow up, divine'. See also MONITORING.

imposed environment One in which the citizen has only a passive part to play. See THEORY OF LOOSE PARTS.

imposition Treating the surface or some other aspect of a building in a way that takes no account of the building's function or construction.

impost (US) See DEVELOPMENT CHARGE.

improvement A positive change in the condition of a building or place. John Summerson (1962) records a specific use of the term in GEORGIAN London. At the lowest level, he writes, it might be said that 'an "improvement" occurred whenever a sufficient number of influential men were so far inconvenienced as to be induced to act in accordance with the public spirit with which they believed themselves endowed. Their own interest and that of the public being seen to coincide, they set about obtaining from Parliament powers to carry an "improvement" into effect with the minimum of expense to themselves.' But that is too cynical an interpretation, Summerson suggests: 'a disinterested "spirit of improvement" did exist among a great many people in Georgian London.' The improvements included Lighting and Paving Acts and many Road Acts. A Captain Hall wrote in the 1830s that the word 'improvement' in America seemed to mean 'an augmentation in the number of houses and people and above all in the amount of cleared land' (quoted in Shama, 2003). See also BIASED TERMINOLOGY, REFURBISH, REVAMP, URBAN REGENERATION, URBAN RENAISSANCE, URBAN RENASCENCE, URBAN RENEWAL, URBAN RESURRECTION and URBAN REVITALISATION.

impure public goods Goods (such as roads) that are not paid for directly when they are consumed or used, but that are not completely free like air. Peter Hall (1972) notes: 'They are spatially distributed, and those located conveniently in relation to them will enjoy a more generous supply and/or a lower cost supply.'

In Darkest England and the Way Out The title of a book, published in 1890, in which General Booth, founder of the Salvation Army, described the living conditions of the 'submerged tenth' of the population and proposed 10 expedients to remedy 'pauperism and vice'.

in the heart of An estate agents' euphemism for, according to Charles Jennings (2001), 'in immediate proximity to the principal thoroughfare of; girdled by a vicious one-way system; has a branch of Woolworths at rear.'

incapsulation (or encapsulation) The condition of a community of migrants, living in a city but retaining a distinct identity.

incense of thanksgiving The eighteenth-century poet John Dyer's phrase celebrating the smoke rising over the growing towns of the West Riding in Yorkshire's landscape (Mullan, 2000).

incentive zoning (US) Allowing development of a higher density than originally zoned in return for the developer offering a specific public benefit.

incineration Burning waste at high temperatures with sufficient air to achieve complete combustion.

inclined plaza Outdoor stairs of sufficient size to serve as a significant public space. Spiro Kostof (1991) suggests Rome's Spanish Stairs and the main entrance staircase of New York's Metropolitan Museum of Art as examples. See also TREPPENSTRASSE.

inclosure See ENCLOSURE.

inclusionary zoning (US) A requirement for development with a specific social benefit (such as housing for people on relatively low incomes) to be provided as a condition of approval of a project (perhaps involving building at higher densities than would otherwise be allowed). Also called *linkage*.

inclusive city One that empowers communities and supports SUSTAINABLE livelihoods for people who would otherwise suffer poverty.

inclusive design Aims to create places without barriers that involve people in undue effort, separation or special treatment, and to enable everyone to take part in mainstream activities independently. See MOBILITY.

inclusive development One in which residents or users with a variety of backgrounds live or work side by side. Example: 'It is an inclusive development, with the affordable housing located in different parts of the area instead of being clustered in the least attractive corner.'

income deprivation A measure of POVERTY. It is sometimes defined as referring to households with below half mean (or median) income, or people in the UK claiming Income Support or income-based Jobseeker's Allowance.

incrementalism Doing things in small stages. Also known as 'the science (or art) of muddling through', STEALTH PLANNING or SALAMI DECISION-TAKING.

incubator See BUSINESS INCUBATOR.

in-curtilage parking Parking within a building's site boundary, rather than on a public street or space.

Independence Day A film, directed by Roland Emmerich and released in 1996, in which gigantic alien spacecraft hover over major cities before destroying them – until the American good guys find the aliens' weakness and annihilate them. See also URBAN DESTRUCTION.

independent design audit An assessment of a design, carried out for a local authority by consultants, another local authority or some other agency.

indicative master plan Guidelines for developing a site or area which have little design input and few precise, definite proposals; a PLANNING BRIEF.

indicative sketch A drawing of building forms and spaces which is intended to guide whoever will later prepare the actual design. The architect, planner and urban designer DENISE SCOTT BROWN (2002) notes a problem. 'How does an urban designer show something that's indicative without constraining the future architect? Try constraining architects. Ask them to do one thing and they'll do the opposite. Ask them to put the front door here because it will relate to others on the street, and they will put it around the corner because they're the architect.'

indicator A means of measuring the condition of something of interest, such as changes in complex environmental systems.

indicator species One whose presence is usually evidence of the presence of some particular phenomenon. See WALKERS.

indirect (or secondary) impact 1 An effect on a development that does not take place in a direct or obvious way. **2** An effect of a development that takes place somewhere other than the development itself.

induced traffic Vehicle movements that are a response to the building of a new road.

inductive space A street or other linear space the interesting nature of whose form or activities encourages people to move along it (Smith, 1974).

industrial and provident society An organisation such as a workers' cooperative, housing association, social and sports club, or other local, non-profit organisation.

industrial archaeology The study of the material remains of the means of production of industrial society.

industrial area Defined as an area allocated as a preferred location for general industrial use (Class B2 under the Town and Country Planning [Use Classes] Order 1987) and warehousing use (B8).

industrial business park Defined by the Greater London Authority (2001) as 'a strategic employment site designed to accommodate general industrial, light industrial, and research and development uses which require a higher quality environment and less heavy goods access than a preferred industrial location, and which can be accommodated next to environmentally sensitive uses.'

industrial city One heavily dependent on manufacturing industry. Spiro Kostof (1991) suggests that the rise of the industrial city (mainly in the eighteenth century, but as early as 1500 and even before that) was characterised by the urban landscape being fundamentally transformed 'when urban land came to be seen as a source of income, when ownership was divorced from use, and property became primarily a means to produce rent'. Compare PRE-INDUSTRIAL CITY.

Industrial City, The An imaginary city of 35,000 people designed by French modernist architect and town planner Tony Garnier while still a student, exhibited in 1904 and later revised. The city was zoned, with only one of the zones being for industry. Its road network would have created serious congestion, according to Reyner Banham (1960).

industrial estate A planned area devoted to a variety of industrial uses. See ESTATE.

industrial heritage Historic buildings, structures or artefacts thought to be worth conserving.

industrial suburb See GARDEN SUBURB.

industrial village PETER KROPOTKIN's vision of a form of cooperatively owned, decentralised development which would replace urban factories.

Industriegebiet (German) An industrial zone.

inertia See VIVA.

infill development Building on a relatively small site between existing buildings.

influentogram See BORIS SAKULIN.

informal economy Work not recorded in official statistics. This includes not just paid work in the BLACK ECONOMY but also various types of casual work for which the earnings are too small to have to be declared, as well as mutual exchanges, banks, LETS schemes and voluntary work.

information district A place with a concentration of new cultural and other industries, depending on both informal face-to-face contact and a high capacity of on-line linkages to the wider world (Graham and Marvin, 1995).

information economy Economic activity based on scientific, technical and design-related knowledge.

Information of Use to the Enemy See JOHN BETJEMAN.

informational city The economist Manuel Castells' concept of a form of late twentieth-century development based on information technologies.

informed conservation Knowledge about CONSERVATION set out in a systematic way, by such means as a management plan or a conservation plan for a particular area, for example.

informing See ARNSTEIN'S LADDER.

infrastructure Physical networks of road, rail, canal and navigable waterway, seaports and airports, water and gas mains, drainage and sewerage, electricity supply and telecommunications systems. See URBAN INFRASTRUCTURE.

inhabited bridge One with buildings on it. JOHN GUMMER as environment secretary in the 1990s promoted the idea of building an inhabited bridge over the Thames (the old London Bridge being a famous example of an inhabited bridge). A competition was run and a major exhibition held at the Royal Academy, but no such bridge was built.

Will Alsop

inhabited wall A long building that also acts as a wall. The architect WILL ALSOP proposed in 2002 that an inhabited wall should be built around the central area of the Yorkshire town of Barnsley, defining the centre and raising densities. Some parts of the town beyond the wall might be returned to agriculture, he suggested. See also BYKER ESTATE.

Initiative for a Competitive Inner City The US not-for-profit organisation, founded by business guru Michael Porter in 1994, also develops strategies in rundown parts of English cities.

injurious to amenity (or to the interests of amenity) A phrase commonly used by planners to describe (in the vaguest terms) the supposed effects of a development proposal of which they do not approve. It is often used as a stock phrase when planners refuse a planning application.

Innenbereich (German) An inner zone.

Inner Area Studies Government-sponsored studies of Liverpool, Birmingham and Lambeth commissioned by Conservative environment secretary Peter Walker in 1972.

Inner Cities Religious Council A government-backed body created in 1992 to involve the Christian, Hindu, Jewish, Muslim and Sikh faiths in regeneration policy.

inner city In the 1960s planners talked about the 'unstable zones of transition' and 'TWILIGHT AREAS' between town and city centres and the suburbs beyond. By the 1970s, urban problems were being defined as problems of the inner city. Some of the resulting programmes of action may have been valuable, but the phrase 'inner city' suggested that the problems could be tackled on the basis of particular areas or types of area, rather than as part of the urban system as a whole. Typically an inner city area was defined as one of poor housing, high unemployment, unstable communities and social problems. When these characteristics started to be identified on large run-down council estates on the edge of cities, and later even seemed to be concentrated in small places, these too were eventually, and confusingly, classified as inner city areas.

In 1989 COLIN WARD suggested that the term was being used as a euphemism for the urban poor. 'The "inner city" is an idea rather than a place,' he wrote. 'We insist on using the words as a kind of shorthand for poor people, often indeed for those immigrant minorities for whom poor city districts are, as they have been throughout history, a "zone of transition", a point of entry into the urban economy.' Only in the 1990s did policy-makers reluctantly conclude that the term had outlived its usefulness. It survived in popular use, in the media and among politicians. This is probably because the inner areas of cities, in contrast to peripheral estates, are where poverty and urban malaise are a visible affront to people who do not normally suffer them personally. On General Election night 1987, MARGARET THATCHER visited Conservative Party central office to celebrate being returned to power. 'We've got a big job to do in some of those inner cities,' she was famously heard to say. Her comment was no doubt prompted by her party's poor showing

> **"THE 'INNER CITY' IS AN IDEA RATHER THAN A PLACE. WE INSIST ON USING THE WORDS AS A KIND OF SHORTHAND FOR POOR PEOPLE "**
>
> *Colin Ward*

in those areas. It is uncertain whether her mind was on inner city residents' social needs, or if she was telling her party organisation not to rest on its laurels and to bring out the inner city vote next time, or both. In 1999 the URBAN TASK FORCE wanted to know what sort of terms to use in trying to persuade the general population of the advantages of living in urban areas. Their researchers organised focus group workshops to find out. They reported (URBED *et al*, 1999) that 'the term inner city was seen as very negative'. The researchers noted comments such as 'the inner city is where it is difficult to park your car'... 'and where you might not find it when you come back!' and 'the inner city is where the people who take the drugs live'. The inner city was also seen as being somewhere else: no-one would accept that they lived in the inner city.

The term made an official comeback in 2001 when the UK government launched an initiative to find the Inner City 100: 'the fastest-growing businesses in inner cities across the UK'. The publicity material seemed to use *inner city* and *deprived area* interchangeably. In 2003 the shadow home secretary Oliver Letwin announced that the Conservatives must become 'the party of the inner cities'. The term inner city was in use as early as 1909, when the novelist Ford Madox Ford wrote of the well-planned roads of a German city being 'straight enough to act, as it were, the part of airshafts into the inner city' and of 'a great avenue of ancient trees encircling the whole inner city' (Ford, 1909).

inner city partnerships Established by the UK's Inner Urban Areas Act 1978.

inner city task forces Eighteen were set up in the UK in the late 1980s.

Inner City Trust Founded by the Prince of Wales in 1987 to raise funds for regeneration projects, the trust was unsuccessful, probably due to conflicts with the prince's other parallel interests.

inner town An 'INNER CITY' area in a place that is not a city. Example: 'The British National Party will regenerate Burnley's inner-town wards' (2002).

Inner Urban Areas Act 1978 The result of a major refocusing of government policy from new and expanded towns to INNER CITY areas. The new and expanded towns were blamed for attracting people and jobs from the old cities, making them less viable. In reality, the flight from the cities would have happened without the new and expanded towns (they were responsible for only 10 per cent of out-migration): people and employers found (and still find) new homes and premises in a range of different settings beyond the cities. In 1978, though, the review of what planning policies were doing to the inner cities was long overdue. The act promoted urban regeneration by partnerships.

innovation and good practice grant A research programme funded by the Housing Corporation.

innovation Peter Hall (1998) proposes four prime examples of 'the city as innovative milieu': MANCHESTER (1760–1830), DETROIT (1890–1925), Tokyo-Kanagawa (1850–1950) and San Francisco/Palo Alto/Berkeley (1950–1990). See also CULTURAL CRUCIBLE.

inquiry 1 An investigation into the facts of a particular situation. **2** (UK) The hearing at which an inspector considers an appeal is a planning *inquiry*. The question asked by a visitor to the council's development department is a planning *enquiry*.

The term *inquiry* dates from 1400–50. Both spellings derive originally from the Latin *inquirere*, meaning to seek for. *Enquiry* comes by way of the late Middle English term *enquery*. See also PUBLIC INQUIRY.

inside-out city See EXOPOLIS.

in-situ concrete Poured on site, rather than prefabricated.

institute for the built environment A proposal for a new body to be created by merging the Royal Institute of British Architects and the Royal Institution of Chartered Surveyors, and perhaps other professional bodies. The proposal has been sympathetically considered by the institutes themselves, reflecting the dissolving boundaries between the professions.

'The idea has been around for ages,' RIBA president David Rock said in 1999. 'It's going to happen sometime.' Many other architects can be expected bitterly to oppose what they will see as fraternising with the traditional enemy. See also URBAN DESIGN ALLIANCE.

institutional investor A financial institution such as a bank, insurance company or pension fund.

institutional sclerosis An inability of nations and regions to adapt organisationally and culturally. The term was used by the economist Mancur Olson (Florida, 2002).

institutional uses Uses falling within Classes C2 (residential institutions) and D1 (non-residential institutions) of the Town and Country Planning (Use Classes) Order 1987.

insula (Latin) An island. A historical name for a block in a gridded plan. See also CHEQUER and ÎLOT.

intangible heritage Characteristics (such as traditions or historical associations) that make a place valued, apart from any valuable buildings it might have.

integrated action plan (Republic of Ireland) Prepared by local authorities, such plans cover both physical development and wider socio-economic issues.

integrated procurement system An arrangement by which the design and construction of a development are the responsibility of a single contractor or organisation.

integration 1 The process of making whole, or the state of being entire and unsegregated; drawing together different areas of policy, different social, economic and environmental perspectives, and the concerns and action of all agencies involved in government and development, and drawing on a wide range of professional skills. **2** A building fitting into its surroundings. **3** A term with a specialised use in SPACE SYNTAX ANALYSIS.

integrity 1 A building's quality of expressing honestly through its appearance, its use, its structure or the intentions of its designer(s). **2** A building's quality of being soundly constructed, in good condition and complete.

integument A town or city extension.

intelligent building One whose fabric changes in response to changes in the environment.

intelligent transportation system One co-ordinating all available modes of transport with the aid of sophisticated electronic control systems; electronic systems for parking, vehicle navigation, road pricing, traffic speed control, ROAD TRAINS and others aspects of transport.

intelligibility The degree to which what can be seen in a particular location allows the wider area to be understood without conscious effort (Hillier, 1996). See LEGIBILITY.

intensity pyramid See DENSITY PYRAMID.

Inter-Action An environmental action initiative and probably the UK's first technical aid service, founded in London by the American Ed Berman in 1968. Inter-Action also set up the UK's first CITY FARM, in London's Kentish Town in 1972.

Interbau The first of two major programmes of model development held in Berlin. Interbau, beginning in 1957, was followed by the IBA in 1980–84.

interdisciplinary Involving people with different skills and experience working closely together in teams. Compare INTER-PROFESSIONAL, MULTIDISCIPLINARY and MULTI-PROFESSIONAL.

interest capitalisation Rolling up the interest on a development project and adding it to the project costs.

interest group People with a common interest who take collective action to achieve it.

interest rate collar An arrangement that provides an upper and lower limit to the interest payable on a loan. The borrower is protected against unacceptably high rates in exchange for protecting the lender against unacceptably low rates.

interface The threshold between two elements of the built environment. Sometimes it will be marked by walls or fences.

interface area Where two of Northern Ireland's more or less segregated communities, one nationalist and one loyalist, adjoin. Example: 'In the interface area even a glance can be taken the wrong way and can lead to confrontation' (from Belfast in 2002). See also PEACE WALL.

intergenerational equity (US) A fair distribution of the costs associated with developing an area between people who move to the area at different times; allowing future generations fair access to resources; the degree to which people at different times benefit from change. Also called *intertemporal fairness*. Compare SPATIAL EQUITY.

interim use A short-term use for a site in the period before it is redeveloped.

interior urban design A translation of *architecture intérieure des villes*, a term used by the architect Jean-Michel Vilmotte to express the idea that architecture can create a setting for urban life.

interiorscaping Designing the arrangement of plants in a building. Also *plantscaping*.

intermediate housing Housing for KEY WORKERS.

intermodal Involving several forms (modes) of transport.

intermodal change Between one form of transport and another.

internalise 1 To create a building that looks inwards instead of having active frontages that face surrounding streets. Most shopping malls are internalised in this sense. **2** To reflect the full costs of an activity, including consequent and external impacts (such as pollution), in its price. Example: 'Petrol would need to cost £25 a gallon to internalise the real cost of motoring'. **3** To reduce the amount of external social contact, for example by valuing privacy more highly, and relying more on home-based activities like television and home computers for entertainment.

international planning aid Defined by Clive Harridge and Ian Silvera (2001) as 'aimed at enabling community participation in planning and development by those in need through the international exchange of information, expertise and support on a voluntary basis.' See PLANNING AID.

international style, the Early modernist architecture. The term is credited to Alfred H Barr (Banham, 1960). Marshall Berman (1988) describes how, as he sees it, the 1932 exhibition 'The International Style', organised by Henry Russell Hitchcock and Philip Johnson at New York's Museum of Modern Art, defined its subject. 'A building in "The Style",' he writes, 'is cubic, geometrically organised, constructed in steel, glass and reinforced concrete, regular in form, flat at the top and (with a few specified exceptions) pure white. It is to be conceived as a thing in itself, as if it were the only building in the world, and designed from the inside out, in terms of an abstract, idealised conception of its functions, with no concessions to the landscape or cityscape around it.' Hitchcock and Johnson agreed

> **"THESE MODERNISTS COMBINE A CELEBRATION OF THE IDEA OF THE MODERN WORLD WITH AN ALMOST TOTAL LACK OF FEELING FOR THE ACTUAL PEOPLE IN IT"**
>
> *Marshall Berman*

with Le Corbusier, Berman suggests, that socio-political revolution could be avoided only if architects and designers were given the freedom and power to change the world. 'Looking back on this modernism… we can admire the high seriousness, the moral purity and integrity, the strength of its will to change. At the same time, it is impossible to miss some ominous undertones: a lack of empathy, an emotional aridity, a narrowness of imaginative range.' Berman concludes: 'These modernists combine a celebration of the idea of the modern world with an almost total lack of feeling for the actual people in it.'

internodal village A model for suburban development proposed by Elmer W Johnson in *Chicago Metropolis 2020*, published in 2001.

interpretation Explaining the historical, economic, social and cultural background to a building or place.

inter-professional Involving people from different professions working closely together in teams. Compare INTERDISCIPLINARY, MULTIDISCIPLINARY and MULTI-PROFESSIONAL.

INTERREG An initiative funded through the European Regional Development Fund, supporting transnational cooperation in spatial planning.

interrupted grid One whose irregularity comes from buildings and other structures being placed so as to interrupt some lines of sight. BILL HILLIER (1996) suggests that this is a characteristic of Graeco-Roman and American, rather than European cities. See also DEFORMED GRID and GRID.

intertemporal fairness (US) A fair distribution of the costs associated with developing an area between people who move to the area at different times. Also called *intergenerational equity*.

inter-urban (or interurban) 1 *adj.* Between towns and cities. The geographer Jean Gottmann used the term in the 1960s to refer to largely residential areas that were not suburbs of a specific city. **2** *n.* (US) An electric light railway system.

intervention 1 An action that has an impact on the built environment. The term is often used by architects and academics in describing development in an urban context, but rarely by anyone else. **2** The act of coming between two things.

intimate distance The distance (0 to 45 cm) at which intense feelings are expressed. The term featured in the work of EDWARD T HALL. *Personal distance* (0.45 to 1.30m) is the conversation distance between close friends and family; *social distance* (1.30 to 3.75m) the distance for doing business and talking with strangers; and *public distance* the distance used in more formal situations. The urban designer JAN GEHL uses the concepts in his own work.

intra-locational equity Allowing people in different places fair access to resources.

intra-mural *adj.* Within the walls (of a town or city). The opposite is *extra-mural*.

introductory tenancy A legal agreement enabling local authorities to evict unruly residents in the first year of a tenancy.

introversion A building looking inwards, rather than outwards towards the street.

intrusion An element that disrupts the townscape or landscape.

invaded city One whose public spaces have been taken over by cars. An *abandoned city* is one whose public spaces are deserted due to the number of cars that have invaded them, and a *reconquered city* one whose public spaces have been recovered from the cars. The three terms are used by the urban designer JAN GEHL.

invented place One that is almost wholly designed to have a specific character. Model communities such as POUNDBURY and themed shopping malls are examples. See also SIMULACRUM.

inventorisation Keeping lists, for instance, of buildings of historical or cultural value.

investment property Owner-occupied or rented land or buildings.

invisible Neglected by standard processes of government or professional practice. Also *invisibility*. Example: 'The issue of walking suffers from invisibility. No one is responsible for it in local government and it depends on cross-disciplinary working' (2002).

Invisible Cities A book by the novelist ITALO CALVINO, published in 1972. It relates how each time Marco Polo returns from his travels he tells Kublai Khan about the strange qualities of the cities he has visited. Kublai wonders which of them is likely to be the city of the future. Marco suggests no more than that the fragments might make an image of the perfect city. 'If I tell you that the city toward which my journey tends is discontinuous in space and time, now scattered, now more condensed, you must not believe the search for it can stop.'

invisible city, the LEWIS MUMFORD'S (1961) term for the functions that were the reason for traditional cities having developed, but that in the modern world do not require the physical presence of everyone involved in them.

invisible tenure Owner occupiers, private renters and social housing tenants living indistinguishably in the same development, unlike orthodox development where the tenure is usually easy to identify. The term became current in 2001.

involvement ratio The term used by the anthropologist Edward T Hall for the amount of sensory involvement that people in different cultural groups tend to have with each other. 'Highly involved people apparently require higher densities than less involved people, and they may also require more protection or screening from outsiders,' Hall (1966) wrote. 'It is absolutely essential that we learn more about how to compute the maximum, minimum and optimum density of the different cultural enclaves that make up our cities.' Critical commentators such as Robert Goodman (1972) wondered whether such an approach might not perpetuate the environments different cultural groups had found themselves forced into. See also GAZZARD'S LAW OF URBAN VITALITY.

inward investment That which comes from sources outside the area.

Irem Zat El-Emad (Irem with the Lofty Buildings) A fictional uninhabited city in the Yemen, built by a king on the lines of a description of Paradise he had read. After more than 300 years of building and preparation, the king's retinue was destroyed by an unbearable sound from the heavens when it was one day's travel from the city. The story is told in *The Arabian Nights* (fourteenth to fifteenth centuries).

iron (US) A CAR.

ironworks Metal covers, providing access to services, set into the street or pavement surface.

Irvine 1 The fastest-growing city in California in the 1970s. John Punter (1995) has noted that 'it has often been cited as one of the best-planned cities in America, although two of the three levels of planning and control are in fact private'. The city was largely developed by the Irvine Company, which prepared design controls for each successive tract of land, prescribing precise standards of layout and house type, and details of architecture and materials. 'In the search for a more connected, livelier, denser, more mixed and socially inclusive, less car-dependent and ultimately more sustainable set of communities that is going on throughout suburban America, Irvine does not have much to teach us,' Punter writes. 'But it remains a fascinating, if claustrophobic, example of privatised design control and a perfect expression of NIMBYism in one of the fastest-changing urban landscapes of the world.' **2** A new town in Ayrshire, Scotland.

Isaura An imaginary city of a thousand wells, built over an underground lake in Asia. There is disagreement, as Italo Calvino explains in INVISIBLE CITIES (1972), as to whether the city's gods live in the lake itself or in the complex apparatus for raising water from it.

Islamabad The new capital of Pakistan, begun in the 1960s. The principal buildings – stark concrete forms geometrically perforated – were designed by the American architect Louis Kahn.

-ism (suffix) See CRITICAL REGIONALISM.

isochrone A line linking points of equal time of travel to a central point.

isogriv A map reference line. The term is even more useful than you might think: Joel Wapnick of Canada used it in his winning move in the final of the 1999 World Scrabble Championships.

Isokon The Isokon building in Hampstead, London, was a block of serviced flats, designed in modernist style by Wells Coates and built as an experiment in social housing (albeit for a rather exclusive group of tenants – modernist architects like WALTER GROPIUS) in 1933. The term Isokon was coined by Jack Pritchard, the building's client, to denote functional design and standardisation in housing, furniture and fittings.

isometric permeability PERMEABILITY in all directions.

It took a riot The opening words of a paper outlining proposals for urban action presented to the UK cabinet by environment secretary MICHAEL HESELTINE, following the inner-city riots of 1981. Prime minister MARGARET THATCHER was not amused.

It's a Wonderful Life See BEDFORD FALLS.

Italia, Fra Angelo Architect. He designed the new town of AVOLA in Sicily in 1693.

iter (Latin) A path or right of way.

iterative dialogue A process in which the client and the designer develop a design by repeatedly reviewing and improving it.

Ives, Charles (1874–1954) Composer. The second movement of his polytonal, polyrhythmic Fourth Symphony is an evocation of MANHATTAN in rush hour.

joke town

J

jackeen (Ireland) A Dubliner, so called by country people. Compare CULCHIE.

Jacobs, Jane (b1916) Writer and urban activist. She is best known for her *The Death and Life of Great American Cities*, one of the most influential in the history of planning and urbanism. Written in 1958–60 and published in 1961, it attacked contemporary planning practice and passionately advocated traditional, mixed-use

Jane Jacobs

neighbourhoods. Never before had the essential COMPLEXITY of urban life been so revealingly described. Jacobs has been one of the most effective advocates of the STREET as the focus for urban life. From 1952 to 1968 she was associate editor of *Architectural Forum*. She was a member of the New York Community Planning Board, campaigning to save Greenwich Village and other neighbourhoods. She moved to Toronto, Canada in 1968. Her other books include *Cities and the Wealth of Nations* (1989) and *Systems of Survival* (1992). See ANTI-URBANISM, EBENEZER HOWARD, EYES ON THE STREET, HOUSER and MOTHER JACOBS.

Jagannath See JUGGERNAUT.

Jaguar See COALS IN THE BATH and TWO JAGS.

jalopy (US) A car.

jam jar (London rhyming slang) A car.

jargon The specialised use of language, particularly when it involves neologisms, unfamiliar words or familiar words used in unfamiliar ways or with specialist meanings. The term also refers to language that is convoluted, imprecise and unintelligible to people outside a limited group. Specialised language can help specialists understand one another, but it is often used as an excuse for communicating in ill-defined concepts or to deliberately mislead. In the world of urbanism, the use of jargon prevents different kinds of specialists from understanding one another, and excludes non-specialists from understanding such matters as planning, urban design and regeneration, or being involved in them.

George Steiner (1975) has argued that developing specialised language is a natural way by which humans establish their identity. 'The proliferation of mutually incomprehensible tongues stems from an absolutely fundamental impulse in language itself,' he wrote. 'I believe that the communication of information, of ostensive and verifiable "facts", constitutes only one part, and perhaps a secondary part, of human discourse... Different tongues... realise needs of privacy and territoriality vital to our identity. To a greater or lesser degree, every language offers its own reading of life.' True as this may be, it does not excuse letting jargon go unchallenged.

jay-walk To cross or walk in a street carelessly. From *jay*, a stupid person.

JCT standard form of contract The Joint Contract Tribunal's traditional form of contract, agreeing that the main contractor will carry out building work specified by the developer's designers and other professionals.

Jefferies, Richard (1848–87) See AFTER LONDON.

Jeffers, Robinson (1887–1962) Poet. See ANTI-URBANISM, CITY IN THE SEA, COUNTRYSIDE and URBAN DESTRUCTION.

Jeltz, Prostetnic Vogon See THE HITCH-HIKER'S GUIDE TO THE GALAXY.

Jencks, Charles (b1939) Architect, landscape architect, writer and commentator. See ARCHITECTURE, ECSTATIC

ARCHITECTURE, HETERO-ARCHITECTURE, HETEROPOLIS, POSTMODERN ARCHITECTURE and POSTMODERNISM.

Jenkin, Patrick (Lord Jenkin) (b1933) Politician. See SECRETARY OF STATE.

Jenney, William Le Baron (1832–1907) Architect, engineer and town planner. He has been called the father of the American SKYSCRAPER (developing the steel-frame technology in the 1880s) and the founder of the CHICAGO SCHOOL of architecture (with DANIEL BURNHAM, WILLIAM HOLABIRD and LOUIS SULLIVAN among his pupils).

Jerde, Jon (b1940) A leading designer of shopping and leisure malls, including Mall America.

jerkwater town (US) An insignificant or inferior place. The term refers to the means by which early locomotives were replenished with water in remote areas where there were no facilities for doing this, probably by the locomotive scooping water from troughs between the tracks without stopping (Quinion, 2003). See also ONE-HORSE TOWN.

jerry v. To jerry-build. Example: 'I bet I've made more money... than you have with all your jerrying' (Bennett, 1911).

jerry-built Built to the lowest standards. The term was first applied to building around 1830 (Burnett, 1986). *The Builder* magazine wrote in 1885 of the contemporary jerry-builder that 'he found a solitude and leaves a slum' (quoted in Raban, 1974). The derivation is unclear. Possibilities include *jury rigged* (makeshift rigging for a ship, dating back to at least the early 1600s); a nineteenth-century firm of Liverpool builders; and Jericho (whose walls fell down at the blast of a trumpet) (Quinion, 1998).

Jerusalem See NAVEL OF THE WORLD.

Jerusalem of temperance Preston, Lancashire, in the nineteenth century. The town was a centre of the temperance (alcohol-avoidance) movement.

jhuggi (India) A SQUATTER SETTLEMENT; a shanty town.

jigger (Liverpool) An ALLEY (see that entry for other regional variants). Also *back jigger*.

jitney A small passenger vehicle that can be stopped by users at any point on its route. The planner MELVIN WEBBER (2003) has written: 'The ideal transit system to serve the Western metropolis has not yet been invented. The closest we have come so far is a shared taxi or jitney – an automobile used in public-transit mode. The effective transit system that does evolve will surely be more like a shared taxi than a train – adaptable to low-density, dispersed settlement patterns; capable of providing random-access – from anywhere to anywhere; approximated door-to-door, no-wait, no transfer service; thus providing short trip-times and lower dollar-costs than automobiles allow.' Jitney is an old term (whose derivation is obscure) for a nickel, so perhaps the word has been applied to the vehicle in relation to the low fare.

jittery space That which is ostentatiously saturated with surveillance devices (Dear and Flusty, 1998).

jitty (East Midlands) An ALLEY (see that entry for other regional variants).

jobs Deyan Sudjic (1992) writes: 'The city is... reshaped by the changing pattern of employment, which more than anything else is behind the dispersion of the city and its ever larger geographical spread... Work places are simultaneously moving closer and further away from people's homes. Some people are commuting longer and longer distances, while others have the chance to live in outer suburbia and still be in reach of business parks.' Michael Breheny (2001) writes: 'Remarkably, nowhere in the urban compaction in Britain debate do jobs get a mention. Even the otherwise worthy Task Force Report fails to mention jobs. Unless it is possible to imagine an URBAN RENAISSANCE without thriving urban economies, this is a glaring error... The new geography of jobs is profoundly decentralised... This... can be explained by the growth in services, particularly personal services, following an increasingly decentralised population. Other services have, in turn, pursued the increasingly decentralised and able workforce... Homes and jobs are becoming increasingly uncoupled, with ever more complex journey to work patterns...' Powerful economic and social forces are providing virtually all of the new jobs in suburban, small-town and rural areas. 'Surely, this must undermine the prospects for urban renaissance. Unless we can imagine cities thriving without significant economies – perhaps based on high-quality residential and leisure environments – then this counter-urbanisation of jobs has to be reversed. The crucial question is whether the public sector can change any of this. A relatively powerful planning system has failed to prevent this process in recent decades. There is no evidence to suggest that this will change, or change to any serious degree. The advocates of urban renaissance will have to think again... The Treasury has denied the Department of the Environment, Transport and the Regions the massive scale of investment that LORD ROGERS states is required to deliver an urban renaissance. Politicians have to keep up with the pretence that rapid progress can be made. Not to do this would lead to an electoral nightmare.'

Joe Brown (UK) (rhyming slang) Town. Dating from the 1960s, it probably derives from the name of the English pop singer.

Joe (also Joanna) Suburban (US) A colloquial term for an uninformed participant in the public planning process, less active but more responsive to education than the NIMBY (Duany, 2000).

John Citizen A typical citizen.

John, Murray The town clerk of Swindon who masterminded its expansion. See EXPANDED TOWN.

Johnson, Elmer See INTERNODAL VILLAGE.

Johnson, Jim Architect. See ASSIST.

Johnson, Lyndon (1908–73) US president. The historian Thomas Bender (2002) calls him 'the last president to consider cities and their people an essential part of America'. Johnson was born in Texas, not far from Johnson City, which his family had helped settle. He became president in 1963 on Kennedy's assassination, after a long and successful career in Congress, and won the presidency in his own right the following year. In his first years of office he put through one of the most extensive legislative programmes in US history. The GREAT SOCIETY programme became Johnson's agenda for Congress in 1965. Its measures included aid to education, attack on disease, Medicare, urban renewal, beautification, conservation, development of depressed regions, a fight against poverty, control and prevention of crime and delinquency, and removal of obstacles to the right to vote. Congress rapidly enacted Johnson's recommendations. But despite the new anti-poverty and anti-discrimination programmes, black ghettos exploded into riot, and his presidency became mired in the disasters of the Vietnam war. Little of the Great Society programme survived, and Johnson died with a deep sense of failure.

Johnson, Philip (b1906) Architect. As the first director of the department of architecture at New York's Museum of Modern Art, after 1932 he introduced the work of European modernist architects to the USA and named the INTERNATIONAL STYLE. His Glass House, built for himself in 1949, was a MODERNIST classic. He collaborated with Mies van der Rohe on the design of the Seagram Building in New York in 1958. By contrast his AT&T headquarters in New York, built in 1984 and likened to an overgrown Chippendale tallboy, was a striking example of POST-MODERNISM.

Johnson, Samuel (1709–84) Author and lexicographer. 'When a man is tired of London,' Dr Johnson wrote in 1777, 'he is tired of life; for there is in London all that life can afford.' A native of Lichfield, Dr Johnson was famously fond of his adopted city, and his comment is often quoted. But he was not blind to the many defects of this wealthy capital in which a large proportion of the people lived in poverty. His early poem *London* (1738) testifies that this was a place 'where all are slaves to gold,/ Where looks are merchandise, and smiles are sold'.

Johnson-Marshall, Percy (1915–93) Planner and architect. He studied with CHARLES REILLY and PATRICK ABERCROMBIE at the University of Liverpool. Until his war service in 1941 he worked with Donald Gibson on replanning and rebuilding Coventry. After the war Johnson-Marshall worked at the Ministry of Town and Country Planning, where he was involved in framing the Town and Country Planning Act 1947. He became a planner at the London County Council, working on comprehensive development areas, including the showpiece LANSBURY ESTATE. In 1959 he joined the Department of Architecture at the University of Edinburgh, and later became professor of urban design and regional planning. After 1964 his private practice worked on regional and town plans across the world. Johnson-Marshall was associated with disastrous redevelopment schemes at the GORBALS in Glasgow and the Elephant and Castle in London, and with the wrecking of Edinburgh's George Square.

Percy Johnson-Marshall

joined-up working Defined by the DETR in 2000 as 'the coordination of the activities and budgets of organisations, groups and/or agencies, working towards a common goal or vision, with the aim of providing best value for money.' The term is adapted from *joined-up thinking*, a favourite of the Labour government in the late 1990s.

Joint Centre for Urban Design The school of urban design at Oxford Brookes University (formerly Oxford Polytechnic). The school's approach is demonstrated in the book RESPONSIVE ENVIRONMENTS.

joint venture A development project involving a collaboration between two or more parties that share the risks and rewards. The joint venture might be a limited liability company, a partnership or a partnership arrangement with profit division.

joke town One whose name alone is used to raise a laugh. UK examples include the new city of MILTON KEYNES (possibly in reaction to its lavish, bucolic and smug self-promotion in the early years); the north

London suburb of Neasden (satirised in the magazine *Private Eye*); the south London suburbs of Penge (probably due to the sound of the word) and Surbiton (possibly because it sounds like suburb-town); the town of Slough (not helped by Bunyan's SLOUGH OF DESPOND, and later condemned in John Betjeman's 1937 poem 'Slough': 'Come friendly bombs, and fall on Slough!/ It isn't fit for humans now'; and the town's image suffered further from its portrayal in Ricky Gervais' 2002 television comedy series *The Office*); and Pratt's Bottom (due to what the name evokes – though it refers to a valley bottom). Whether in any of these cases the ribaldry is justified by a notable lack of distinction is a matter of opinion.

journey substitution Doing something else instead of making a journey: shopping on the internet instead of going to the supermarket, for example.

jowler (Liverpool) A lane between the backs of terraced houses. See ALLEY for other regional variants.

Joyce, James (1882–1941) Writer. See BLOOMSDAY.

Joyville 1 A place of joy. Compare PITSVILLE. **2** A state of feeling joyful. **3** There are places names Joyville in Connecticut, Maine and Texas.

Jubilee Line Extension Andrew Saint (2001) has described the extension to London's underground railway system as uniting 'practical democratic utility with stirring architecture'. It is, he writes, 'worth all London's other GRAND PROJETS put together. There lies a rare and proper model for urban renaissance and civic identity.' Others have criticised the priority accorded to the project merely to service the MILLENNIUM DOME site at North Greenwich while the rest of the tube network was starved of funds.

juggernaut 1 A lorry whose excessive size has an unacceptable impact on the environment. **2** Any other unacceptable, overwhelming force. Example: 'Wilfred Thesiger resented the juggernaut of western "civilisation" and its inexorable movement to squash what he believed was the colour and diversity of the earth's peoples.' The Hindi word is a variant of Jagannath (meaning lord of the world), a title of the god Vishnu. It was once believed that his devotees threw themselves under the wheels of a cart bearing his image.

jumbo jet Asked to choose his favourite building for a television programme, the architect LORD FOSTER chose the Boeing 747, popularly known as the jumbo jet because of its size and passenger-carrying capacity. If it is a building, it is unusual in having no fixed context of other buildings, a design opportunity that some architects would relish. The enormously successful plane was designed by Joseph F Sutter. The first made its maiden flight in 1969, and the 1,000th was delivered in 1993. It has been estimated that a 747 taking off uses the same amount of fuel as 27,000 cars driven the same distance down the runway.

jumbo office building One of at least one million square feet.

Jünger, Ernst (1895–1998) Novelist. See ON THE MARBLE CLIFFS.

Jungle, the A large decayed area of Philadelphia.

Jungle, The A polemical novel by Upton Sinclair on the poverty-stricken lives of a Chicago stockyard worker and his family, published in 1906. One critic noted that the book's portrayal of the stockyards made Chicago 'a fearsome combination of Babel, bedlam and hell'. Sinclair summed up the stockyards as 'the hog-squeal of the universe'.

junior debt One that does not have first charge on a security. Compare SENIOR DEBT.

junkscape The chaotic environments created by modern consumer society. The architect REM KOOLHAAS has used the term.

K

Kahn, Albert (1860–1940) Financier and philanthropist. From 1909 he commissioned cinematographers to film the world's cities, fearing that, in the words of Stephen Barber (2002), they 'had already begun to disintegrate and vanish'. The project continued for two decades until Kahn was bankrupted in the financial crash of 1929.

kailyaird (Scots) A kitchen garden; a back garden.

kakatopia (also cacatopia) The worst place. Joseph Rykwert (2000) records Jeremy Bentham as being the first to use the term (in 1818). PATRICK GEDDES (1915d) used the term to describe a place characterised by the worst of PALAEOTECHNIC disorder; the opposite of EUTOPIA.

kampong A SQUATTER SETTLEMENT.

kan ban (Japanese) A Japanese method of inventory control: the phrase means 'just in time'. In fast-track building construction it involves delivering materials, components and even the design of details to the site just when they are needed.

Karfik, Vladimir (b1901) Company architect to Bata at ZLIN in 1930–48. He also designed a Bata shoe factory, a hotel and housing at East Tilbury, Essex, in 1932.

Karl Marx Hof A celebrated social (and socialist) housing development built in Vienna in 1927, influencing the design of inter-war council flats in London and Liverpool.

Kayden, Jerold American urban planner. See CAFÉ CREEP.

keelie A Glaswegian.

keeping in keeping The term describes a new building that is of similar appearance to its neighbours, or a planning policy encouraging such development. Sometimes the term is used sympathetically (example: 'He believed firmly in "keeping in keeping" and made seamless, but spirited, additions to a number of important Arts and Crafts houses' [Powell, 2001]), but more often it is used derisively.

Kelling, George See BROKEN WINDOWS.

Kelly, Michael As provost of Glasgow in the mid 1980s, he coined the celebrated slogan 'Glasgow's Miles Better'. See BOOSTER.

ken (Liverpool) A house.

Kennedy, John Fitzgerald (1917–63) US president. See BERLIN.

> **"MOST CITIES ARE NOUNS. NEW YORK'S A VERB"**
>
> *John F Kennedy*

keno capitalism The spatial manifestations of the post-modern urban condition. The term is used by Michael Dear and Steven Flusty (1998). 'Conventional city form,' they write, 'is sacrificed in favour of a non-contiguous collage of parcelized, consumption-orientated landscapes devoid of conventional centres yet wired into electronic propinquity and nominally unified by the mythologies the disinformation superhighway.' They suggest LOS ANGELES as a mature form of this post-modern metropolis and Las Vegas as a youthful example. Keno capitalism takes its name from the game of Keno. 'The result is a landscape not unlike that formed by a keno gamecard. The card itself appears as a numbered grid, with some squares marked during the course of the game and others not, according to some random draw... The consequent urban aggregate is characterised by acute fragmentation and specialization – a partitioned gaming board subject to perverse laws and peculiarly discrete, disjointed urban outcomes.' Given the pervasive presence of crime, corruption and violence in the global city (not to mention geopolitical transitions, as nation states give way to micro-nationalisms and transnational mafias), Dear and Flusty write, 'the city as a gaming board seems an especially appropriate twenty-first-century successor to the concentrically ringed city of the early twentieth'.

Kensington Gore 1 A fashionable street in Kensington, London. **2** Fake blood used in films. See GORE.

Kentucky Fried Georgian A contemptuous term for the sort of neo-classical details some homeowners apply to their homes. The analogy is with the products of the fast-food chain Kentucky Fried Chicken. Compare CONSERVATION-OFFICER GEORGIAN and PLANNING OFFICER'S GEORGIAN, and see GEORGIAN.

kerb (also curb) The edge of a pavement, often marked by a kerbstone (curbstone); a line of kerbstones where footway and carriageway meet. From the Latin *curvus* meaning bent, by way of the French *courbe*. The Scots for kerb is *crib*.

kerb appeal/curb appeal (UK/US) The immediate quality of a house that attracts potential buyers. The supposed commercial importance of this aspect can encourage developers to lavish attention on the front façade of a house rather than consider its overall design and setting.

kerb radius/curb radius (UK/US) At a junction, the radius of the curb/kerb will determine how fast vehicles are likely to turn the corner and how much road space a pedestrian crossing will have to walk over. In general, the smaller the radius the safer the pedestrian.

Kerngebiet (German) A business zone.

Kerouac, Jack (1922–69) Possibly the only writer in America to have a street named after him, according to J Jobe Smith (2003), in contrast to France, where boulevards and avenues are named for writers. Jack Kerouac Street, Smith notes, is 'behind a pub in San Francisco's North Beach, an alley about the length of a London taxicab.'

Kersh, Gerald (1911–68) Novelist. See VICE.

key 1 *n.* A list of symbols on a map, plan or diagram with explanations. See also SCALE. **2** *adj.* A favourite adjective of planners, among many other people. Originally meaning *essential*, frequent use has devalued it in many cases to *important* or sometimes merely *relevant*, as in *key variables*, *key considerations* and *key constraints*. Today it is also used detached from its noun, as in 'this policy is key'.

key settlement A village or town that the local planning authority has chosen for expansion.

key worker One who works in an occupation vital to the local economy, but who may not be able to afford the cost of local housing without the help of special housing allocation policies or subsidies. Examples may include teachers, health care workers, police officers, catering workers and even (as was suggested in London in 2001) town planners.

Khirokitia See STREET.

kidult An adult who enjoys childish recreations. Developers of THEMED SPACES value them as a valuable extension of the market that children represent.

kill the street See RUE-CORRIDOR.

killer vegetables See DAY OF THE TRIFFIDS.

Killingworth A new township built by local authorities on Tyneside.

kinaesthetic experience That which results from moving through space.

Kinder Scout See BENNY ROTHMAN.

kine slice (North Staffordshire) Supposedly the local pronunciation of *council house*.

kinetic art See FREEWAY ART.

King Arthur See CAERLEON and CAMELOT.

King, Rodney The black motorist whose savage beating by police officers led to the Los Angeles riots of 1992. An all-white jury acquitted four officers of charges associated with the assault, despite being shown video footage of King being hit 56 times with a baton. Fifty-four people died in the rioting that followed.

King, Tom (b1933) Politician. See SECRETARY OF STATE.

kiosk A miniature building for temporary occupation. The British red telephone box, designed by Giles Gilbert Scott in the 1920s (probably inspired by a tomb by SIR JOHN SOANE), is a celebrated example. The term is of Turkish origin.

Kirkby (the second k is silent) The attempt to create a new town on the outskirts of Liverpool began with high hopes and great idealism. Barbara Castle opined that the founders of the Labour party would have given years of their lives to be present at its foundation. But the project turned to disaster when the planned industrial base failed to appear, leaving residents without access to jobs and with almost no facilities or transport links to Liverpool. Since 1974 Kirkby has been part of Knowsley Borough.

Kirkby kiss A head-butt in the face.

kiss and ride One spouse driving another to a station to take the train to work. Compare PARK AND RIDE.

kitchen culture The expectation that design can be procured at little or no cost; the FLOCCINAUCINIHILIPILIFICATION of design. The analogy is with a householder who buys a new kitchen from a supplier who offers to design it for no extra charge.

kitsch A pejorative term for something designed or assembled by a person considered to have vulgar taste. The term is applied to some buildings that incorporate a seeming jumble of popular motifs.

knitting Designing or carrying out small-scale development that draws together disconnected parts of the urban fabric. Also called *stitching*.

knowing urban design Described by Carmona, Heath, Oc and Tiesdell (2003) as 'the process by which different concerns are intentionally shaped, balanced and controlled through development and design proposals, plans and policies'. Compare UNKNOWING URBAN DESIGN.

knowledge management Ensuring that the people involved in an organisation or project have the information and skills they need.

Kohr, Leopold (1909–94) Kohr was an early advocate of the concept of the human scale and the idea of a return to life in small communities, both later popularised by his friend, Fritz Schumacher in the best-selling book *Small is Beautiful*. Kohr consistently advocated the effectiveness of the small autonomous unit in solving human problems. He argued that massive external aid crippled the vital communal identity of developing countries and stifled local initiatives and participation. He called for centralised structures to be replaced by a system of small communities solving local problems with their own material and intellectual resources. Kohr received the RIGHT LIVELIHOOD AWARD in 1983.

kondratieff cycle An approximately 50-year cycle of economic upturn and downturn identified by the Russian economist Kondratieff in the 1920s. One suggested explanation is that the cycle reflects the way new technologies first disrupt economic patterns and later promote growth.

Rem Koolhaas

Koolhaas, Rem (b1944) Architect. His practice is the Office for Metropolitan Architecture. His projects include the master plan and Grand Palais for Lille, France. He is the author of *Delirious New York: a retroactive manifesto*, published in 1978, and *S, L, M, L, XL* (Small, Large, Medium, Large, Extra Large, referring to his interest in design at every scale). See ARTICULATE, CHARACTER, CITY OF CLONES, CITY OF EXACERBATED DIFFERENCES, DECONSTRUCTION, DELIRIOUS NEW YORK, DRESS SENSE, EURALILLE, JUNKSCAPE, LINEAR VOID, LOCAL DISTINCTIVENESS and NEW URBANISM.

Korda, Alexander (Sir) (1893–1956) See EVERYTOWN and THINGS TO COME.

Kostof, Spiro (1936–1991) Historian of architecture and urbanism. He was professor of architectural history at the University of California at Berkeley and author of, among other books, *The City Assembled* and *The City Shaped*.

Krakov Charter The Charter of Krakow on the Principles for Conservation and Restoration of Built Heritage of 2000. See ATHENS CHARTER, HERITAGE, HISTORIC MONUMENT and VENICE CHARTER.

Krier block A type of layout with no private or semi-private outdoor space, designed to force a more intense use of the public realm (Duany, 2000). The concept is used by LÉON KRIER.

Krier, Léon (b1946) Architect, town planner and urban designer. Born in Luxembourg, he studied architecture at the University of Stuttgart. He lived in the UK for 20 years before moving to the south of France. He has been a major influence on urban design and was probably responsible more than anyone for inspiring the NEW URBANISM movement. 'The challenge of the future,' he writes, 'will be the urbanisation of suburbia, the redevelopment of sprawl.' He was the masterplanner of the Prince of Wales' model development at POUNDBURY.

According to Krier (2001): 'Traditional architecture is not an ideology, religion or transcendental system. It can not save lost souls or give meaning to empty lives. It is part of technology rather than style; it is a body of knowledge and know-how allowing us to build practically, aesthetically, socially and economically satisfying cities and structures in the most diverse climatic, cultural and economic situations.' He is suspicious of architects' claims for the role of inspiration. 'As is the case with all good things in life – love, good manners, language, cooking – personal creativity is required only rarely.' As for the relationship

Léon Krier

between architects – or any other artists – and their public: 'As long as artists arbitrarily assume the right to decide what is or is not art,' Krier writes, 'it is logical that the public will just as arbitrarily feel that they have the right to reject it.' He once declared: 'If ever I was to head this Royal Institute of British Architects I would probably enter this building, in the thick of the night, and with my own hands I would plaster up that memorial wall which is covered in names (the list of Royal Gold Medallists inscribed in the entrance hall of the RIBA building in London), for most of these names have, more than any other names, contributed to the destruction of European cities and culture.' The younger brother of Rob, Léon Krier worked with the architect James Stirling in London from 1968 to 1974. He was professor of architecture at Princeton University in 1977 and Eero Saarinen Professor at Yale in 2002.

Krier, Rob (b1938) Urban designer, architect, sculptor and theorist. His book *Urban Space* (1984) challenged modernist theories of urbanism. He was a professor of architecture at the technical university in Vienna from 1976 to 1994, and has practised in Vienna and (in partnership with Christoph Kohl) Berlin. His sculpture is mainly for public spaces. Elder brother of Léon.

Kropotkin, Peter (1842–1921) Russian anarchist writer and social thinker who emigrated to England. He proposed *mutual aid* (his book with that title was published in 1902) in place of Darwinian struggle for existence. His book *Fields, Factories and Workshops* (1898) and other writings helped confirm EBENEZER HOWARD in his view that state intervention would not achieve his vision of new communities. Kropotkin advocated INDUSTRIAL VILLAGES. He took part in the Edinburgh Summer Meetings organized by PATRICK GEDDES.

Krupp The German steel-maker built model company villages near Essen after 1860.

Kubin, Alfred (1877–1959) Artist and writer. See PERLE.

Kubitschek, Juscelino (1902–76) Politician. As president of Brazil he founded the new capital Brasilia.

Kubrick, Stanley (1928–99) Film director. See BLADE RUNNER and THAMESMEAD.

Kurokawa, Kisho (b1934) Architect. See ECO-MEDIA CITY, ECOLOGICAL METABOLIC CYCLE THEORY, FLOATING CITY, HELIX CITY and METABOLIC GROUP.

L

L'Enfant, Pierre Charles (1754–1825) French-born American engineer, architect and soldier. He drew up plans for the new federal capital of Washington, DC in 1791 at the request of George Washington, but they were ignored until 1889 and put in effect only after 1901.

labyrinthine (or labyrinthian) *adj.* Difficult to find one's way around due to the lack of points where visitors can see where they have come from or where they are going to. Examples: 'She was wandering up and down, from Bermondsey into Southwark, from Southwark into Lambeth, through labyrinthine streets where snotty-nosed children played at hop-scotch on pavements horrible with banana skins and decaying cabbage leaves' (George Orwell, *A Clergyman's Daughter*, 1935); 'Step a hundred yards from Piccadilly [in Dickens' London] and you reached Seven Dials, which it was only safe to penetrate in the company of two top-hatted policemen. Here were houses so rotten that the bricks sweated, alleys so labyrinthine that after an hour's hard walking you found yourself back at the same point, and dens, where… the populace resorted to theft and murder as a reasonable alternative to starvation' (Wolfe, 1938).

Lady Metroland A character in Evelyn Waugh's novel *Decline and Fall*, published in 1928. The title presumably reflected the essentially *arriviste* character of Lord and Lady METROLAND.

Lagado The capital of the fictional Pacific island of Balnibarbi, described in Jonathan Swift's *Travels into Several Remote Nations of the World* (1726). Its houses, oddly constructed, are all in bad repair, following an unsuccessful project to make buildings that would last for ever. Those few people who opposed that project were eventually forced to demolish their homes and rebuild according to the new method. Another unsuccessful project involved building houses from the top down.

Lake Wobegon The fictional small Minnesota town featured in Garrison Keillor's radio broadcasts and subsequent book *Lake Wobegon Days*, published in 1985. 'It is a quiet town, where much of the day you could stand in the middle of Main Street and not be in anyone's way – not forever, but for as long as a person would want to stand in the middle of a street'.

lamella block A form of housing in long buildings designed to maximise sunlight. The name is of Swedish origin.

Lanark See UNTHANK.

Lanchester, Henry Vaughan (1863–1953) Architect and town planner. HV Lanchester's work included consulting on the design of New Delhi in 1912 and planning other Indian cities. He was a founding member of the Town Planning Institute and was awarded the Royal Gold Medal for Architecture.

land (Scotland) A tenement.

land assembly Acquiring the necessary plots of land in order to make a site available for development.

Land Authority for Wales Created in 1975 to buy, develop and service land.

land availability A measure of how much development land is available for a particular use or uses.

land bank A series of sites, owned by a developer, house builder or housing associations, being held for future development.

Land Commission Established by the Land Commission Act 1967 to buy land for public purposes. It was abolished when the Labour government lost power in 1971.

Land Nationalisation Society Formed in 1881, the society was a forerunner of the GARDEN CITY movement, which it helped launch in 1899.

land raising The deposit of waste on and above the existing contours of the ground.

land reclamation Any process of improving land for reuse.

land use The activity that takes place in a particular building or area.

land value taxation See HENRY GEORGE.

landcover Buildings, structures, surfaces and vegetation.

landfill capacity The volume available in a landfill site for the disposal of waste, sometimes split by waste type. Also called *void space*.

landfill Disposing of waste on land. Britain's more than 10,000 landfill sites take 90 per cent of all domestic waste, in addition to industrial and commercial waste.

landfill gas The end product of degradation of biodegradable wastes in a landfill site. The gas is usually around 65 per cent methane and 35 per cent carbon dioxide, with traces of other gases and vapours.

landfill site An area where waste is dumped prior to being covered with a layer of soil.

landfill tax The Landfill Tax Credit Scheme was introduced in 1996 to encourage the recycling of materials normally destined for landfill. The tax raises the cost of disposing waste in landfill sites. Landfill operators can pay part of the tax to registered environmental projects near their sites – one of the first times HYPOTHECATION has been accepted by the Treasury.

landform The shape of the land. Landform can be described in terms such as elevation and slope.

landmark A conspicuous building or structure; one that stands out from the background buildings; a point of reference in the urban scene.

Lands Tribunal The UK's highest court dealing with land and property valuation and compensation.

landscape The form and appearance of land, including its shape, colours and elements, the way these components combine in a way that is distinctive to a particular locality, the way they are perceived, and an area's cultural and historical associations. The Landscape Institute (2002) defines landscape as 'human perception of the land conditioned by knowledge and identity with a place'. The landscape architect Anne Whiston Spirn (1996) writes: 'Landscapes evolve continually in time, in predictable and unpredictable ways, in response to natural processes and changing human processes. The forms we see on the surface of the landscape are a sum of all these processes, both natural and cultural: the patterns they produce are juxtaposed, interwoven and overlain. This surface structure is thus in flux. Underlying this surface, however, there is a more enduring structure, with distinctive rhythms, to which all organisms within that landscape respond... Deep structure can be masked, but it can not be erased entirely. When surface structure obscures or opposes deep structure, it will require additional energy, materials and information to sustain... Design attuned to deep structure goes beyond the conventional understanding of regionalism with its focus on the use of indigenous materials and vernacular settlement and building forms. Attending to deep structure entails a response not only to the physical structure of land form, plants, and plant communities, but also to the temporal structure, to the rhythmic daily and seasonal changes of light, temperature, and water, and to the evolution of the landscape, its past, present and future.' Punter and Carmona (1997) quote the view of Anne Beer (1993) that the British concept of landscape can be encapsulated in the word *scenery* (as opposed to regarding landscape as a natural entity), which gives landscape architects a largely cosmetic role. Raymond Williams (1983) notes that the Old English word *landscipe* was a region or tract of land, and that the word was later adopted from the Dutch *landschap* as a term in painting. In the seventeenth century a landscape was a delightful artifice: Joseph Addison wrote in the 1690s that on his travels to Italy he hoped 'to compare the Natural Face of the Country with the Landskips that the Poets have given us of it' (Mullan, 2000). Compare WORLDSCAPE.

landscape appraisal A description and analysis of a landscape and its character.

landscape architect A person who is skilled in designing the external environment. The landscape architect Kathryn Gustafson defined her professional remit grandly as 'everything below the sky'. FREDERICK LAW OLMSTED was probably the first person to call himself a landscape architect. In the UK, THOMAS MAWSON was among the first. Tom Turner (1984) has suggested that 'the crucial event was [Mawson's] competing with, and working with, PATRICK GEDDES on the Dunfermline Competition in1903–4. Certainly, when Mawson published the first edition of *The Art and Craft of Garden Making* [in 1900] he did not describe himself as a landscape architect, simply as a garden architect, whereas in the later editions he does describe himself as a landscape architect.' Turner concluded: 'I suspect that he took the title from Patrick Geddes, who was the first person to use it. Geddes at the time was a professor of biology.' Brian Clouston (2002), leader of one of the UK's largest landscape architecture practices until the late 1990s, argues against landscape architects thinking of themselves as artists. 'Landscape design is a creative practice,' he writes. 'It is about making things work by design. Design is a collaborative venture. The creation of a landscape will need a client, budget, brief and liaison with other design and technical professionals. Actual work on the ground is done by the contractor. The finished work is then passed over to the client/owner managers. It will mature over time and will be influenced by the hand of nature.' Clouston notes that during 30 years of practice as a landscape architect he was involved in the creation of hundreds of new landscapes. 'I can not claim authorship or ownership of any... I trust those who may have been unsure will now renounce the title of artist when making landscapes.'

landscape architecture The landscape architect Cornelia Hahn Oberlander has defined landscape architecture as 'the art and science of planning and designing external space for human use and enjoyment'.

landscape assessment The descriptive analysis and classification of landscape.

landscape capacity The amount of change that a particular area is able to accommodate without unacceptable consequences.

landscape character The distinct nature of an area of land in terms of such elements as its shape, geology, soils, vegetation, land uses and settlement patterns.

landscape character type A category of landscapes with similar character.

landscape condition The physical state of the landscape.

landscape effects Changes to the landscape resulting from development or other causes.

landscape element A distinct feature of the landscape, such as a hill, road, lake, wood or hedge.

landscape evaluation Assessing a landscape in terms of a set of criteria relating to how it is valued in other than monetary terms.

landscape factor One of the aspects of a landscape that contributes to its overall effect.

landscape feature A landmark in the landscape.

landscape framework A document setting out how an area's landscape can be used as the basis for development.

landscape gardening Laying out and planting a large garden for visual effect. The term is said to have been coined by HUMPHRY REPTON.

Landscape Institute Founded in 1929 as the Institute of Landscape Architects, it received the Royal Charter in 1997.

landscape quality A judgement of a landscape in terms of how it compares with other landscapes or with how it could be.

landscape resource The overall value and usefulness of a landscape.

landscape sensitivity The degree to which a landscape can accommodate change without compromising its valued character and quality.

landscape upgrade Developer-speak for bushes, according to Joel Garreau (1994).

landscape value An assessment of how much a particular landscape is valued (in other than monetary terms) in comparison with other landscapes or to a set of criteria.

landscaped gardens An estate agents' euphemism for construction waste covered with a layer of turf and a rose bush, according to Robert Huxford.

landscaper One who designs landscapes; a landscape architect.

landscaping *n.* and *v.* The General Development Order defines landscaping as 'the treatment of land (other than buildings) for the purpose of enhancing or protecting the amenities of the site and the area in which it is situated and includes screening by fences, walls or other means, the planting of trees, hedges, shrubs or grass, the formation of banks, terraces or other earthworks, the layout of gardens or courts, and the provision of the amenity features'. Landscaping is generally divided into *hard landscaping* (elements made of materials such as brick, stone and paving) and *soft landscaping* (planting). Many landscape architects dislike the term landscaping, believing it reduces their role to cosmetics. John Punter, an academic authority who stresses the importance of landscape to urban design, has described landscaping as 'the garnish sprinkled on bad development to try to hide it.'

landscapism Studying, improving and creating landscapes.

Landschaft (German) A landscape.

Landschaftsplan (German) A landscape plan.

Landschaftsraum (German) Landform.

landscrape *v.* To clear a site or area of its symbolic, political and material residues. James Corner (2001) uses the term in relation to Detroit's vacant areas, echoing the more familiar verb *landscape*. 'The scraped ground then becomes an empty field of absence that accommodates multiple interpretations and possibilities,' he writes.

landscraper 1 A horizontal MEGASTRUCTURE; a GROUNDSCRAPER. **2** A building that is wholly or partly underground, or that merges with the contours of the land.

landshaft (Russian) See PEYZAZH.

land-take The amount of land required for a development.

land-use planning The codification and control of land use in new development according to plans which then form the basis of DEVELOPMENT CONTROL decisions (Hall, 1995). Land-use planning is concerned with what land is used for, rather than other characteristics of development, such as what it looks like. A distinction is often made between land-use planning and *physical planning*. Land-use planning focuses on policy, and is expressed in words and two-dimensional diagrams. Physical planning is expressed in drawings and diagrams showing three dimensions. Planning generally combined the two in its early days, but in time town planning and land-use planning became almost synonymous. The URBAN DESIGN movement in the UK has largely been a campaign to rediscover physical planning.

landward town (Old Scots) A farm or country house with adjoining cottages.

lane 1 A narrow road (see also QUIET LANE). The Scots for lane is LOAN or TRANCE. An Irish variant is *boreen*. **2** A passage or (in Carlisle) ALLEY (see that entry for regional variants). **3** One of the strips (marked or not) into which a CARRIAGEWAY can be divided. **4** (Galloway, Scotland) A slow-moving river.

Langley, Batty (1696–1751) Carpenter, surveyor and architect. He was the author of around 20 PATTERN

BOOKS and guides for builders between 1726 and 1751. In 1734 he submitted a proposed design ('indescribably gauche', in the opinion of John Summerson, 1962) for the Mansion House in London.

Language of Landscape, The A book by the landscape architect Anne Whiston Spirn, published in 1999. She argues that there is a language of landscape with its own syntax, grammar and metaphors, and that we imperil ourselves by failing to read and speak this language.

languages See COSMOPOLIS.

Lansbury A bomb-damaged part of Poplar in London's east end rebuilt as a model neighbourhood as an exhibit in 'living architecture' for the Festival of Britain in 1951. The exhibition site included housing, pubs, a shopping centre, market and clock tower. It was named after GEORGE LANSBURY.

Lansbury, George (1859–1940) Politician, and women's rights and peace campaigner. As mayor of Poplar he worked to improve living conditions of people who were poor, unemployed and badly housed. In 1921 he and most of Poplar's councillors were imprisoned for four months for exceeding government limits for spending on poor relief. He was leader of the Labour party (1931–35). The LANSBURY is named after him. See also EAST END.

lanwair Land, water and air. CONSTANTINOS DOXIADIS coined the term to describe a transport network conceived as a unified system.

Laparelli, Francesco (1521–70) The designer of Valletta, Malta.

large scale voluntary transfer The selling off of 500 or more council homes to a housing association. The move must be approved through a ballot of the tenants. See also HOUSING ACTION TRUST.

large-lot zoning (US) Zoning which sets a minimum size for a lot (plot) of land.

Larkin, Philip (1922–85) Poet. See GOING, GOING.

Larsson, Yugve Swedish politician. He played a major role in the planning of Stockholm in the 1930s and '40s.

Lasdun, Denys (Sir) (1914–2001) Architect. His design for the National Theatre expressed the floors as 'strata'. He explained: 'Strata express the visual organisation of social spaces in geometrical terms; they recall the streets and squares of the city and contour lines of the hills; and, at a more profound level, they bear witness to the roots of an architectural language inspired by natural geological forms' (quoted in Rowntree 2001). This approach can also be seen in his buildings for the University of East Anglia outside Norwich, particularly the ziggurats of student rooms. Lasdun also designed CLUSTER BLOCKS of housing in east London, linking four 14-storey blocks to a central stair and lift tower. Diana Rowntree (2001) called it 'probably the most interesting built example of Le Corbusier's "streets in the air"'.

Last Exit to Brooklyn A novel by Hubert Selby (1928–2004), published in 1964, chronicling life in Brooklyn (partly on a housing PROJECT). It was the subject of a landmark obscenity trial in the UK in 1966, when an order banning it was overturned.

latchkey child One who lets him- or herself in to their home after school as no parent is there (usually being out at work). The term is used by newspapers reporting on changes in family life. A children's book *The Latchkey Children* by Eric Allen, published in 1963, tells the story of four children in Pimlico, London, who fight officialdom to save the tree in the playground of the flats where they live.

latent defect One that can not be discovered by inspecting the building.

Latham Report *Constructing the Team* was the report, published in 1994, of a review committee chaired by Sir Michael Latham. Its proposals concerned the management of the construction process and, in particular, the role of project managers.

Latin Quarter A district of the LEFT BANK in Paris, so named from being the centre of the city's university life since the middle ages.

latti (POLARI, the argot of theatre, circus and the gay community) A house; lodgings.

Law, Sylvia (1931–2004) Town planner. In the 1970s she became the first woman president of the Royal Town Planning Institute. She chaired the RTPI working party that produced the 1976 report *Planning for the Future*.

lawn An area of grass (see also GARDEN and YARD). In Ramsgate, England, curiously, a lawn is a terrace of houses (Muthesius, 1982).

Laws of the Indies Regulations governing Mexico and Latin America, drawn up by the Spanish invaders in 1573. The laws covered the layout of towns, among other matters.

lawyer See PLANNING LAWYER.

Layfield, Frank (Sir) (1921–2000) Planning lawyer and judge. He presided over the public inquiries into the Greater London Development Plan and Sizewell B nuclear reactor.

layout The way buildings, routes and open spaces are placed in relation to each other. Two scales of layout can be categorised as structure (large scale) and urban grain (small scale). See also COARSE GRAIN and FINE GRAIN.

layout structure The framework or hierarchy of routes that connect in the local area and at wider scales.

Le Bon, Gustave (1841–1931) French author of the book *The Crowd*, published in 1895, on the psychology of crowds. The modern era is the era of the crowd, he writes, and the survival of the state depends on a strong leader who can hypnotize the crowd. Mussolini was among those who acknowledged his influence.

Le Corbusier (Charles-Edouard Jeanneret)

(1887–1965) Swiss-born architect, town planner, visionary and painter. One of the greatest architects and most influential town planners of his time, he helped give a generation of architects and planners the confidence to demolish large parts of cities and rebuild them according to modernist principles, seeing themselves as visionaries whose time had come. 'Corb's was a vision that *took*,' Michael Sorkin (2000) writes, 'and it continues to be the default for large-scale housing around the world.' Le Corbusier, a pseudonym meaning 'the crowlike one', was a name adopted from his maternal grandfather. At 13 he was apprenticed to a watchcase engraver, following his father's craft. He soon turned to architecture. He studied in Paris with Auguste Perret, the engineer, architect and pioneer of reinforced concrete. In 1914 Jeanneret designed a system for building what he called the DOM-INO house. The English GARDEN CITY approach to housing layout and its cooperative ideas (rather than its decentralisation proposals) were an early inspiration. He moved to Paris permanently in 1916. His Plan for a CONTEMPORARY CITY, published in 1922, was intended to demonstrate the principles of urbanism. Land uses (offices, housing, industry and so on) were strictly zoned, and accommodated on a symmetrical grid of roads. The centre of the city would be a multi-level transport interchange, surrounded by 24 60-storey office skyscrapers. The buildings, all of them mass-produced, were set in parks. The Contemporary City would depend on centralised authority exercised by an elite through large organisations. All the housing would be cooperatively owned and run by its residents. Le Corbusier presented his next vision in the PLAN VOISIN (named after its sponsor and happening to be the French for neighbour) for Paris in 1925. The business district on the Right Bank would be demolished and replaced by skyscrapers, open spaces and motorways. Motor traffic would be at ground level, with pedestrians on three upper levels. 'Imagine all this junk,' he wrote of historic Paris in *Urbanisme* in 1925, 'which till now has lain spread out over the soil like a dry crust, cleaned off and carted away.' Le Corbusier became a leader of CIAM, the International Congress of Modern Architecture. Around 1930 he embraced syndicalism, the ideology based on the idea of independent groups of workers owning and managing the means of production. In 1930 he formally adopted his pseudonym, Le Corbusier, and became a French citizen. Le Corbusier's next urban vision was of the Radiant City (*La Ville Radieuse*). At its centre would be high-rise blocks of flats called *unités*. Each would house 2,700 people and provide leisure facilities, workshops, meeting rooms, a school, a laundry and a food shop. The plan would be laid down by technical experts on the basis of 'truth', not 'opinion', and realised through the government's absolute authority. Le Corbusier wrote in *The City of Tomorrow* in 1924: 'I was assisting at the titanic reawakening of a comparatively new phenomenon... traffic. Motors in all directions, going at all speeds. I was overwhelmed, an enthusiastic rapture filled me... the rapture of power. The simple and ingenious pleasure of being in the centre of so much power, so much speed. We are a part of it... we have confidence in this new society... Its power is like a torrent swollen by storms; a destructive fury. The city is crumbling, it can not last much longer; its time is past. It is too old. The torrent can no longer keep to its bed.' The Radiant City was his vision of how the syndicalist society would

Le Corbusier

be realised in urban form. Although the scheme was libertarian at its most local level, every aspect of production was organised from the top. The plan would be devised by technical experts, confident in the rightness of their own values and detached from the political process. In 1950 he was appointed architectural adviser for Chandigarh, the new capital of Punjab. There he built the beginnings of the city of his dreams, without giving close attention to its social and economic setting. Later he developed ideas for linear cities. Le Corbusier died at the age of 77 after suffering a heart attack while swimming. JANE JACOBS (1961, quoted in Taylor, 1998) commented on what she saw as Le Corbusier's disastrous influence. 'Le Corbusier's dream city has had an immense impact on our cities. It was hailed deliriously by architects, and has gradually been embodied in scores of projects, ranging from low-income public housing to office building projects... His city was like a wonderful mechanical toy... his conception, as an architectural work, had a dazzling clarity, simplicity and harmony. It was so orderly, so visible, so easy to understand. It said everything in a flash, like a good advertisement... But as to how the city works, it tells... nothing but lies.' Thomas Deckker (2000) has written: 'Le Corbusier's vision was of the solitary observer of a well-ordered urban life: it contained no view on what constituted urban culture nor on how it was formed or transmitted; the centre of the Ville Radieuse was just landscape.' See also THE ARCHITECTURE OF SILENCE and MACHINE AGE.

Le Waleys, Henry (Sir) Town-planning advisor to Edward I in the late thirteenth century (Kostof, 1991).

leachate Liquid that seeps through a landfill, extracting substances from the deposited waste. See also LONDON ORBITAL.

Leadville A book by Edward Platt, published in 2000, with the subtitle 'a biography of the A40'. It tells the story of the A40 running through west London, from its early days as a leafy suburban arterial to the blighted canyon of today.

League of American Wheelmen A lobby for better roads active in the 1890s. The wheelmen were cyclists.

leakage Benefits of a regeneration initiative that are enjoyed outside the target area or group.

leaky space Architectural space that is only partly enclosed by walls.

Learning from Las Vegas An influential book by ROBERT VENTURI, DENISE SCOTT BROWN and S Izenour, published in 1972. It celebrates the richness of unplanned urban form and helped lay the foundations for POSTMODERN design. The authors argued that the pop architecture of Las Vegas strip development was a vernacular that could inspire a new, popularly accessible architecture. 'If you ignore signs as "visual pollution", you are lost,' they write. 'If you look for "spaces between buildings" in Las Vegas, you are lost. If you see the buildings of urban sprawl as forms making space, they are pathetic – mere pimples in an amorphous landscape. As architecture, urban sprawl is a failure; as space, it is nothing. It is when you see the buildings as symbols in space, not forms in space, that the landscape takes on quality and meaning. And when you see no buildings at all, at night when virtually only the illuminated signs are visible, you see the Strip in its pure state.'

lease and leaseback A landowner (often a local authority) leasing a property to a developer, who leases it back to the landowner on a shorter lease. The guaranteed rent enables the developer to finance the development project.

lease guarantee An agreement between a developer and a funder, specifying that if the development is not let within a specified period, the developer will be paid a profit from the funder but will then lease the property back until it is let commercially. See also PROFIT EROSION.

leasehold A form of tenure giving the right to occupy property for a fixed term. Compare FREEHOLD.

Ledoux, Claude-Nicolas (1736–1806). French architect. He designed buildings (not executed) for his ideal city of Chaux.

Lee, Peter (1864–1934) A leader of the Durham miners after whom Peterlee new town was named in 1948.

Lefaivre, Liliane See CRITICAL REGIONALISM.

Lefevbre, Henri (1901–91) French philosopher and sociologist. In the early 1960s he collaborated with the Situationist International and became an important influence on the radical students who in 1968 occupied the Sorbonne and the Left Bank in Paris. He expounded the idea that everyone has a 'right to the city'. He analysed urban space in terms of the 'perceived space' of everyday life, the 'conceived space' of the people who plan, control and manage it, and the 'lived space' of the people who imagine new ways of living in it. Lefevbre's discussions of how urban space is used and experienced has been highly influential on later theorists such as ED SOJA. See SITUATIONISM.

Left Bank (Rive Gauche) 1 A district of Paris on the south side of the River Seine (the left bank if you are going with the river's flow) associated with the capital's intellectual life. The term refers to a bohemian lifestyle as well as the geographical location. **2** A generic term for a place supposedly having some undefined, fashionable quality. In 2002 Manchester City Council named an area of its city centre 'the Left Bank', and prepared a regeneration framework for it. Hereford, on the River Wye, has a Left Bank Village, developed in the late 1990s. It is advertised as 'a stylish, contemporary complex' of restaurants, bars, specialist shops, conferencing and banqueting suites, arts and entertainment facilities, and 'luxury accommodation'. Compare RIGHT BANK and see LATIN QUARTER.

legibility The quality of a place being welcoming, understood easily by its users, easy for visitors to orient themselves in, and presenting a clear image to the wider world. The concept was developed by KEVIN LYNCH in the 1950s and '60s and is now widely used in urban design. The Catalan architect Orial Bohigas (1999) has written: 'The city must be legible. If the citizens do not have the sense of being carried along by spaces that communicate their identity and enable them to predict itineraries and convergences, the city loses a considerable part of its capacity in terms of information and accessibility. In other words, it ceases to be a stimulus to collective life.' The complex structure of a traditional city may be relatively easy to understand intuitively, however illegibly labyrinthine it may appear on a plan.

Conversely, a city whose structure looks clear and logical on a plan may be difficult to find one's way around.

The writer COLIN WARD (1989) notes that in the past 'a city fancier knew without seeing that there must be a lorry-driver's snack bar round the next corner, as accurately as any predecessor centuries earlier would locate a coaching inn. A poor traveller would know where he could find cheap lodgings and the prospect of casual work. An itinerant salesman would know that a shop on that particular site would not pick up enough trade to be safe for credit. A lecher knew, without any red lights, where the red-light district was. Drinkers knew where to find their particular kind of bar. Criminologists could take one look at a place and predict the patterns of offences. Wholesalers and hucksters, junk men and junkies, model airplane enthusiasts and people selling leotards to dancing academies all developed a city sense which is a guide to the specialised functions for which cities originally arose.' Ward complains: 'The buildings of the rebuilt city do not talk any more, at least not in a language that makes sense to the citizen'.

Some people, of course, are better at reading the city than others. In Conan Doyle's *The Sign of Four*, Dr Watson soon loses his bearings. 'Sherlock Holmes was never at fault, however, and he muttered the names as the cab rattled through squares and in and out by tortuous by-streets' (quoted in Ackroyd, 2000). In Raymond Chandler's 1940 novel *Farewell, My Lovely*, a potential client phones the private eye. '"You have been recommended to me as a man who can be trusted to keep his mouth shut. I should like you to come to my house at seven o'clock this evening... My name is Lindsay Marriott and I live at 4212 Cabrillo Street, Montemar Vista. Do you know where that is?" "I know where Montemar Vista is, Mr Marriott". "Yes. Well, Cabrillo Street is rather hard to find. The streets down here are all laid out in a pattern of interesting but intricate curves."'

Rayner Banham (1971) wrote: 'Like earlier generations of English intellectuals who taught themselves Italian in order to read Dante in the original, I learned to drive in order to read Los Angeles in the original.' Joseph Rykwert (2000) notes that the US Defence Department's gargantuan Pentagon building in Washington is well-known for its labyrinthine complexity. 'It has been said that a telegraph boy making a delivery got lost in it and emerged 25 years later as a full colonel.' See also INTELLIGIBILITY, NAVIGABLE and GRID.

legible city One that is welcoming, can be understood easily by its users, is easy for visitors to orient themselves in, and presents a clear image to the wider world. KEVIN LYNCH (1960) describes a legible city as 'one whose districts or landmarks or pathways are easily identifiable and are easily grouped into an overall pattern'. Bristol has been a pioneer in this field. It launched its Legible City initiative in the late 1990s to make the city centre easier for visitors to find their way around and to reinforce its quarters' distinct identities.

Lego A children's toy system. Some styles of building (particularly POST-MODERN) have been castigated, and sometimes admired, for seeming to emulate the bold, glossy, brightly coloured appearance of a model made of Lego bricks (see also TOYTOWN). Example: 'It [the 1990s transport interchange and retail scheme at Hammersmith Broadway, London] is a mess, so appalling... it's as if someone had some pieces left over from a Lego set' (2003). The name was coined in 1934 when the Danish toymaker Ole Kirk Christiansen held a competition among his staff to name his company, with a bottle of wine as the prize. Christiansen won the prize himself, making the word from the Danish for 'play well' – *leg godt*. The fact that *lego* means *I assemble* in Latin is apparently a coincidence. Lego bricks were introduced in 1953, the Lego system the following year and the Lego Town Plan range in 1955, the year in which Lego was introduced to the UK. The distinctive stud-and-tube coupling system (made at first in wood, and later of plastic) was invented in 1957. The British Association of Toy Retailers in 1999 voted Lego Toy of the Century.

LEG-UP Local enterprise grants for urban projects, a Scottish Development Agency programme.

Leitch Report Published in 1977, the report advised the government on methods of assessing the need for trunk roads.

Leonia An fictional city in Asia that is re-made every day. Nothing that can be thrown out is re-used. As Italo Calvino explains in INVISIBLE CITIES (1972), the mountains of rubbish it expels threaten to engulf it.

leprous Resembling leprosy; having a flakey surface. George Orwell used the word as a metaphor for rotting slum houses more than once in his book *Down and Out in Paris and London*, published in 1933. He described one narrow street in Paris as 'a ravine of tall, leprous houses, lurching towards one another in queer attitudes, as though they had all been frozen in the act of collapse'.

Lerup, Lars See STIM.

less is more The famous dictum of MIES VAN DER ROHE, recorded in the *New York Herald Tribune* in 1959. Another architect, ROBERT VENTURI, famously retorted: 'Blatant simplification means bland architecture. Less is a bore.' FRANK LLOYD WRIGHT observed: 'Less is only more when more is no good.'

Letchworth The first GARDEN CITY, founded by EBENEZER HOWARD in 1903. Although not the start of as great a revolution as Howard had hoped, the influence of Letchworth has been immense. A hundred years on, Jonathan Meades (2003) writes: 'Letchworth became the model for Britain's housing and still exerts an influence on planning. The winsome charm of its Arts and Crafts houses has caused subsequent generations to overlook its flaws: we are blinded by its douce Merry Englishness and its sham rusticity.' The pioneers of the first garden city at first called their site 'garden city', but as others were also intended a more distinctive name was needed. A vote was held among shareholders and residents in 1904. Mervyn Miller (1989) writes: 'The alternatives offered included Garden City; Letchworth [a local name], both with and without the appendage Garden City...; Wellworth, a truly awful combination of [three local place names]; Homesworth; and Alseopolis. This last attempted to recify the mixed derivation of RURISVILLE by using pure ancient Greek. The concept of the Platonic ideal of a democratic city appealed to supporters of the movement, but Alseopolis had a distinctly mid-western American twang which would have been incongruous in Hertfordshire... Letchworth (Garden City) was chosen. The appendage quickly disappeared and Letchworth predominated; in 1919 when the second garden city adopted the name WELWYN GARDEN CITY to distinguish it from the nearby historic town of Welwyn many forgot that Letchworth was the precursor.'

Lethaby, William (1857–1931) Architect. See ARCHITECTURAL STYLE and FAÇADE.

LETS A local employment and trading system. A LETS is a trading network with its own score-keeping system, which enables participants to trade with each other without using cash. The system was designed in 1983 by Michael Linton. It is seen as, among other things, a means of promoting community development and supporting local economic life. See also TIME BANK.

level of service See BIASED TERMINOLOGY.

levels of scale The idea that all elements of the built environment are both part of something larger and made up of smaller parts.

Lever House An air-conditioned, curtain-walled glass skyscraper on a single-storey raised podium, built in New York in 1950–52. Its design, by SOM and Gordon Bunshaft, became the model for dozens of similar office towers throughout the world.

Lever, William Hesketh (Viscount Leverhulme) (1851–1925) Soap manufacturer and philanthropist. Lever built the model industrial village of PORT SUNLIGHT on the Wirral in Cheshire for his workers and LEVERBURGH on Harris in an attempt to revive the fishing industry in the Outer Hebrides. He was a supporter of EBENEZER HOWARD.

leverage Using public investment to stimulate private investment in property, land or other urban action.

Leverhulme, Viscount See WILLIAM HESKETH LEVER.

Levittown 1 A development of 17,000 houses, with schools, shopping centres and other community facilities, built in the late 1940s at Nassau County, Long Island, New York, by the housebuilder Abraham Levitt, and his sons William and Alfred. **2** A similar formulaic scheme built by the same developers between Philadelphia and Trenton, New Jersey, in the early 1950s. **3** Derogatory shorthand for any mass-produced suburban housing.

Lewis, David Urban designer, architect and painter. Born in South Africa and trained in England, he founded UDA Architects in Pittsburgh, Pennsylvania in 1964. He was a pioneer of urban design and of the American Institute of Architects' REGIONAL/URBAN DESIGN ASSISTANCE TEAMS (RUDATs). See URBAN DESIGN.

Lewis, Sinclair (1885–1951) Novelist. Martin Seymour-Smith (1975) calls him 'one of the worst writers to win a Nobel Prize'. See MAIN STREET.

Lewis, Wyndham (1882–1957) Writer and painter. See THE CALIPH'S DESIGN, GLOBAL VILLAGE, MAIN STREET, MAGNETIC CITY, THIRD CITY and VILLAGE.

leylandii See CUPRESSOCYPARIS LEYLANDII.

Libeskind, Daniel (b1956) Architect. Born in Poland, he became a US citizen in 1965. In 2003 he was appointed masterplanner for the redevelopment of the site of the WORLD TRADE CENTER. See DRESS SENSE, ECSTATIC ARCHITECTURE and GENIUS LOCI.

LIBOR The London Inter-Bank Offered Rate. Interest charged on property finance is generally expressed as a margin over the LIBOR.

Libria See EQUILIBRIUM.

Lichfield, Nathaniel See PLANNING BALANCE SHEET.

Life and Labour of the People in London The seventeen-volume report of the survey by the social reformer and author Charles Booth (1840–1916), published 1889–1902.

life-cycle analysis Examines the environmental impact of each stage of the life of a building material in the light of its raw materials, impact on biodiversity, toxic emissions, water consumption, energy consumption in manufacture and use, and output of waste.

life-cycle costing Assessing the total cost of a building over its operating life, including the construction, maintenance and running costs. Compare WHOLE-LIFE COSTING.

lifestyle A set of arrangements of daily life. The term is used particularly by people marketing housing to delude prospective buyers or tenants into believing that their lives will be totally transformed in their new home. An *urban lifestyle* is often contrasted to a suburban one.

lifetime home Designed to be adaptable to meet a household's changing needs, and to be accessible and safe for people to live in at all stages of their life.

lifetime neighbourhood A place which meets the needs of people of all ages.

Letchworth

lifeworld The background of beliefs, values, and practices that provides a horizon of meaning for our actions (Kolb, 1990); the patterns of everyday life. See JÜRGEN HABERMAS.

lifing A method proposed in the 1940s for keeping track of a building's obsolescence by allocating it a life expectancy figure. Buildings whose life was almost over would be given low values, making them cheap for local authorities to buy and redevelop.

lift A device for lifting people or goods from one floor of a building to another. The first use of the term to describe such a device was in the catalogue of the 1851 Great Exhibition, according to Flavell and Flavell (1999). See OTIS.

Lifting the Burden A white paper published in 1985 as part of the Thatcher government's campaign to deregulate economic activity. Planning control was held to be part of the unnecessarily heavy burden on business.

light pollution Excessive levels of lighting, illuminating areas beyond what is intended or necessary. Its effects include frustrating city-based astronomers' observations of the night sky.

light rail Trams and other relatively low-capacity, frequently stopping forms of railway.

light trespass Artificial lighting in places where it causes a nuisance.

Light, Francis Born in Suffolk in 1740, he planned George Town, Penang, Malaysia. Father of William.

Light, William (1786–1839) Colonel Light's plan for Adelaide, Australia, with its green belt and satellite expansion, was a forerunner of Ebenezer Howard's GARDEN CITY concept. Son of Francis.

Lighthouse, The Created to celebrate Glasgow's year as City of Architecture and Design in 1999, the facility now calls itself 'Scotland's centre for architecture and design in the city'. The building is a conversion and extension by Page and Park Architects of CHARLES RENNIE MACKINTOSH's 1893 Glasgow Herald Building. See ARCHITECTURE CENTRE.

Lightmoor See THIRD GARDEN CITY.

lightning conductor 1 A means of protecting a building against damage due to being struck by lightning. **2** An individual with an interest in improving an area who, though not normally active, will provide a link to other people when a particular issue arises or information needs to be disseminated. **3** The aspect of a development proposal most likely to attract public attention. Example: 'Although the proposed new street frontage is only one aspect of the architecture, it was always going to be the lightning conductor as far as discussing the merits of the project was concerned.'

like-for-like Matching the existing or original material when carrying out repairs to a historic building.

Lillington Gardens A council housing estate built on Vauxhall Bridge Road in Westminster in the 1960s. Designed by architects Darbourne and Darke, it pioneered a new informality in place of the rigours of modernism.

Limits to Growth The influential report on the global environment by the Club of Rome, published in 1972.

Lindblom, Charles See DISJOINTED INCREMENTALISM.

line of steel A row of cars closely parked at the side of a road. See also PARALLEL PARKING.

linear Long and narrow in form.

linear (also lineal) city A city in LINEAR form, as opposed, for example, to CONCENTRIC or POLYCENTRIC form. See ARTURO SORIA Y MATA and CONTINUOUS MOVEMENT.

linear void An area designated on a plan to be kept empty. REM KOOLHAAS, for example, proposed creating five linear voids in the planning framework for the new town of Melun-Senart. 'A system of bands, linear voids, is inscribed on the site like an enormous Chinese figure,' Koolhaas writes (quoted in Corner, 2001). 'We propose to invest most of the energies needed for the development of Melun-Senart in the protection of these bands, in maintaining their emptiness.' James Corner (2001) notes that Koolhaas proposed a 'reservoir of void' in his Point City/South City plan, which reallocated density and distribution of settlement across the Netherlands, and that the Dutch landscape architect Adriaan Geuze and his consultancy West 8 have proposed a similar strategy of 'empty scenarios' for the RANDSTAD and its Green Heart.

link wilt The weakening of working relationships between organisations involved in urban regeneration. See also GATEKEEPER.

linkage (US) A requirement for development with a specific social benefit (such as housing) to be provided as a condition for approval for a major development project. Also called *inclusionary zoning*.

lipstick on the face of the gorilla See PER CENT FOR ART.

lip-sync architecture The architect and critic Michael Sorkin's term for inauthentic architecture. The analogy is with singers miming to recorded music. Sorkin (1991) suggests that 'in London, as in so many other cities, the choice seems to be between just such varieties of the ersatz, different versions of the faked climax. It is only a poverty of imagination that gives rise to the argument that precedented forms are the only natural medium of urban design – that prefers Leo Krier or Quinlan Terry lip-syncing Al Speer or Beau Nash's greatest hits.'

Lipton, Stuart (Sir) Property developer and first chairman of the COMMISSION FOR ARCHITECTURE AND THE BUILT ENVIRONMENT. He began as an estate agent. As a property developer he imported fast-track US construction methods, employed talented architects and put quality before cheapness. Lipton's companies have included Sterling Land, Greycoat and Stanhope. He developed STOCKLEY PARK (a business park on reclaimed land near Heathrow) and Broadgate, an office complex on the east edge of the City of London.

Lisa of Lambeth The 1897 novel by Somerset Maugham (1874–1965) is a naturalistic account of life in the London slums.

Lisbon See Marquis of POMBAL.

listed building See LISTING.

listed building consent Permission from a local authority to demolish or alter a listed building. The consent can be subject to conditions.

listed building management guidelines An informal memorandum of understanding between the owner and manager of a listed building, the local planning authority and, usually, English Heritage.

listed building purchase notice Served on a local authority by a building owner in a case where the refusal of LISTED BUILDING CONSENT has left the site 'incapable of reasonably beneficial use'.

listing A generic term for a number of legal procedures used to protect the architectural heritage. The word comes from the statutory lists of buildings of 'special architectural or historical interest' that the relevant secretary of state is required to complete. Consent must be obtained before any alterations are made that might affect the special character of a listed building. The secretary of state is required to compile lists of buildings of special architectural or historic interest for the guidance of local authorities in the exercise of their planning functions under the Planning (Listed Buildings and Conservation Areas) Act 1990 and the Town and Country Planning Act 1990. Buildings are graded to show their relative architectural or historic interest: Grade I (buildings of exceptional interest); Grade II* (particularly important building of more than special interest); and Grade II (buildings of special interest). Listing was introduced during the 1939–45 war as a means of noting the degree of importance of historic buildings, in case of damage by enemy action.

little Hitler See POL POT.

live edge Provided by a building or other feature whose use is directly accessible from the street or space which it faces. A blank wall creates the opposite effect. Live edges are among the standard features that urban designers identify in surveying an area.

liveable (also livable) Fit to live in; providing a good QUALITY OF LIFE; being a good place to live in. Also *liveability* and *livability*. The US Environmental Protection Agency has rated urban areas for liveability according to such factors as crime rates, unemployment and how much people on average give to charity, producing an overall average score. The assessment factors used by the US organisation Places Rated include transport, higher education, climate mildness, the arts and health care. The US urban designer Donald Appleyard published his book *Livable Streets* in 1980. The term was introduced to the UK in the 1990s. Prime minister Tony Blair announced his commitment to promoting liveability in the 2001 general election campaign, describing it as 'a shorthand for all the things which improve our daily experience of life where we live'. It could be supported, he suggested, by such initiatives as closed-circuit television and neighbourhood wardens. Achieving livability has been identified as one of the aims of the Greater London Authority (2001). In 2003 the term arose when the House of Commons ODPM Housing, Planning, Local Government and the Regions Committee took evidence from CABE. Andrew Bennett MP, the committee chairman, asked Jon Rouse, chief executive of CABE, about 'this buzz word "liveability"'. Rouse replied: 'We did not invent that and you will never find us using it. It is an awful word.' Asked what 'liveability' meant, Rouse said: 'I think it is quality of life as experienced outdoors by people'. He explained that he preferred the term 'quality of life'. See also SPRINGFIELD and compare DRIVABLE.

lived space See HENRI LEFEVBRE.

livelihood Defined as 'the capabilities, assets (including material and social resources) and activities required for a means of living' (Rakodi and Lloyd-Jones, 2002) in discussions of the 'livelihoods approach' to tackling poverty.

Liverpool See AT LEAST IT'S NOT BASILDON, BROOKSIDE, CANTRIL FARM, THE ELDONIANS, GRANBY STREET COOPERATIVE, GREEN GODDESS, GREEN MAP, EDWARD CHAMBRÉ HARDMAN, THREE GRACES, KIRKBY, EDWIN LUTYENS, NEW TOWN, NIMBY, ONE-EYED CITY, REDBURN, REDEVELOPMENT, CHARLES REILLY, SCOUSE, SMILE, SO GOOD THEY NAMED IT TWICE, ST MARTIN'S COTTAGES, TOXTETH DIAMONDS, TWILIGHT AREA, URBAN REGENERATION, WELLER STREETS HOUSING COOPERATIVE, THE WORLD IN ONE CITY and Z CARS.

Liverpool Housing Action Trust The organisation formed to take over all but four of the city's tower blocks from the city council, demolishing 47 of them and refurbishing the other 20. See HOUSING ACTION TRUST.

live-work space Flexible units that accommodate both functions.

living architecture Places where people linger and random encounters occur. The architect CHRISTOPHER ALEXANDER uses the phrase (Forty, 2000).

living centre The term used by the South East England Regional Assembly in 2002 in place of TRANSPORT DEVELOPMENT AREA, to stress that the main aim of such a designation is to make a good place to live.

Living City, The Frank Lloyd Wright's last book, published in 1958. The living city was, as ever, Wright's proposed BROADACRE CITY.

Living Faith in the City The Church of England's 1990 follow-up to its 1985 report FAITH IN THE CITY.

Livingstone, Ken (b1945) Politician. He was elected mayor of London in 2000, standing as an independent after failing to win the Labour party's nomination, becoming the first directly elected mayor of a UK city. Livingstone identified public transport as his most important challenge. He was leader of the Labour-controlled Greater London Council from 1981, earning himself the nickname Red Ken for his radical politics, until it was abolished by the Thatcher government in 1986. He was a member of parliament from 1987 to 2000.

lizzie tramp (US) **1** A wandering person travelling in a car. **2** A hitchhiker. See TIN LIZZY and VAGRANT.

llan (Welsh) A church. Hence the prefix Llan- to many Welsh place names.

Llanfairpwllgwyngyllgogerychwyrndrobwyll-llantysiliogogogoch The name of the small town in Anglesey in North Wales (usually shortened to Llanfair PG) is commonly cited as the world's longest. It translates from the Welsh as 'the church of St Mary in the hollow of white hazel trees near the rapid whirlpool by St Tysilio's of the red cave'. It seems likely that it was coined as a ploy to attract tourists. Other places across the world have emulated it by giving themselves even longer names. Like Llanfair PG, these are usually nothing more than a description of the place or a précis of its history, run into a single word.

Llano del Rio A proposed socialist feminist city of 10,000 inhabitants described by Alice Constance Austin in 1916. In order to eliminate the domestic drudgery that oppressed women, the houses would have no individual kitchens (Markus and Cameron, 2002).

Llaregyb The small Welsh coast town that is the setting for *Under Milk Wood*, a 'play for voices' by Dylan Thomas, published in 1954. Llaregyb is a place where nothing very significant ever happens: it is no accident that the name spells, more or less, *bugger all* backwards. See also CACTUSVILLE, SMALLVILLE and WOOP WOOP.

Llewellyn Park The first of New York's picturesque suburbs, built by Llewellyn S Haskell in 1853. Peter Hall (1998) calls it 'one of the most important developments in the history of Anglo-American urbanism'.

LO See HI-LO.

loan (Scots) A LANE; a common green.

loan:value ratio The value of the loan expressed as a proportion of the value of the project.

lobscouse See SCOUSER.

local 1 *n.* A person from a particular place. See also VOCAL LOCAL. **2** *adj.* Relating to a particular place. The word derives from the Latin *locus*, place.

Local Agenda 21 A decision of the Rio Summit (the United Nations Conference on Environment and Development) in 1992 led to the publication of Agenda 21, an action plan for SUSTAINABLE development. Local authorities were expected to consult with their populations and produce a Local Agenda 21 action plan (identifying what sustainable development meant for their area) by 1996.

local area of special character An area of architectural or townscape value designated for protection and enhancement, despite not meeting the criteria for designation as a CONSERVATION AREA.

local centre A focus of shopping and small-scale commercial activities outside a town or city centre.

local design statement A document explaining what aspects of the physical form of an area local people value and the design principles on which they hope future development will be based. See also DESIGN STATEMENT.

local development document (England and Wales) A statutory DEVELOPMENT PLAN DOCUMENT or a non-statutory SUPPLEMENTARY PLANNING DOCUMENT contained in a LOCAL DEVELOPMENT FRAMEWORK.

local development framework (England and Wales) A portfolio of LOCAL DEVELOPMENT DOCUMENTS that together provide a framework for delivering the spatial planning strategy for an area. Local development frameworks replace the STRUCTURE PLANS, LOCAL PLANS and UNITARY DEVELOPMENT PLANS of the pre-2004 planning system.

local development scheme (England and Wales) Sets out a local authority's programme for preparing LOCAL DEVELOPMENT DOCUMENTS.

local distinctiveness The positive features of a place and its communities which contribute to its special CHARACTER and SENSE OF PLACE. The concept of local distinctiveness, developed by COMMON GROUND in the 1990s, was incorporated into UK government planning guidance in Planning Policy Guidance Note 1 in 1997. The idea had been discussed by Michael Hough in his 1990 book *Out of Place: restoring identity to the regional landscape* (Hough, 1990). 'Local distinctiveness,' writes Sue Clifford, Common Ground's joint coordinator, 'is about the conspiracy of nature and culture to intensify variegation and it is about anywhere. It is about detail, patina, authenticity and meaning, the things which create identity. Importantly it focuses on locality (neighbourhood, parish), not the region. It is about accumulations and assemblages, about accommodation and change, not about compartmentalisation and preservation. It must include the invisible as well as the physical: symbol, festival, legend, custom, language, recipe, memory may be as important as street and square. Places are not just physical surroundings. They are a web of rich understandings between people and nature, peoples and their histories, people and their neighbours. People understand places and value them because they mean something to them. Little things (detail) and overlapping clues to previous lives and landscapes (patina) may be the very things which breath significance into the streets or fields.' Unfortunately the response of many house-builders and other developers is fairly cynical: a little flint detailing on the front elevation of a standard house type, for example, may be offered in the hope of making a scheme acceptable to the planners. Stephen Owen (1997) has argued that the key to local distinctiveness is to recognise that every aspect of what we now see as locally distinct about a place was once a response to something. 'The local distinctiveness displayed by attractive villages and small towns evolved mainly through *local responses* to local circumstances,' he says. 'For instance, building was often a specific response to known local need or demand (the "clients" were local and known); the "producers" of the physical fabric (landowners, builders and sometimes the local inhabitants themselves) often lived and worked locally; the form of settlements usually responded to the character of the local natural environment such as the shape of land, shelter, hydrology and vegetation; changes to the physical fabric of settlements occurred at a slow pace and were small in scale and extent; building materials were usually quarried, manufactured, felled or gathered locally; site development and building technology were applied to overcome the constraints imposed by individual sites and responded to their individual characters. In summary, most needs and problems that gave rise to distinctive changes in the physical fabric and setting of villages and small towns were addressed as they occurred, *in situ*. It is also important to emphasise that local responsiveness was the medium through which *change* took place.' If we are concerned with local distinctiveness today, says Owen, we should aim for a similar responsiveness to that which created the places we value. We must make places that respond 'to the local physical environment (the built fabric, such as characteristic street layouts, consistent use of building forms, and the use of local building materials), the natural environment (such as the shape and structure of land, patterns of sunlight, shade, shelter, vegetation and hydrology), and to local social and economic need (such as employment, particularly for people on low incomes and with low educational achievement), homes (at affordable prices for people on low incomes) and services (such as primary schools, bus services and shops).' The question is: how can we make places that are responsive in that way? The answer, says Owen, is that responsiveness 'can be achieved through local community involvement (including the identification of needs, knowledge of local physical character), local production of development (including appropriate site development and building technology, use of local materials, and small scale of development), and through localising the planning system (including determination of the scale and pace of change, integration of design with social and economic issues, enhancement of design skills, localisation of state power, and increased understanding of the local physical environment).'

As long ago as 1852 JOHN RUSKIN was regretting that all towns were coming to look the same, with the visitor's first view being of a railway station of more or less standard design (Timms and Kelley, 1985). The philosopher John Stuart Mill warned in *On Liberty*, published in 1859: 'Europe... is decidedly advancing toward the Chinese ideal of making all people alike.'

The architect REM KOOLHAAS (2000) has complained that many places are failing to make themselves distinctive. 'Most old cities – Paris, New York, Amsterdam – are now sclerotic machines that dispense known qualities in ever greater quantities, instead of laboratories of the uncertain,' he has said. 'They function now by virtue of their predictability... From uniqueness, individuality and unpredictability to the ponderous repetition of branding within one generation – this incredible acceleration has clearly had an effect on the city that hasn't been sufficiently recognised.' But Koolhaas (2002) has also suggested that local distinctiveness may not always be achievable or even desirable. 'Architecture can't do anything that the culture doesn't,' he told an interviewer. 'We all complain that we are confronted by urban environments that are completely similar. We say we want to create beauty, identity, quality, singularity. And yet, maybe in truth these cities that we have are desired. Maybe their very characterlessness provides the best context for living.' He cited Singapore as an example of a city that over the past 40 years had succeeded in removing any trace of AUTHENTICITY. 'It is a culture of the contemporary. And many Asian cities are like this now, seeming to exist of nothing but copies – in many instances bad copies – of Western architecture. But actually, if you look closely you can perform another reading – you can see, for instance, that these copies are dealing differently with layering and with problems of density.' The architect Michael Sorkin (2002) has spoken of 'the continued creation of urban difference as one of the engines that will drive the possibility of cities being democratic'. He suggests that 'the artistic component of urban design' may be important in 'opposing, on the one hand, the depredations of multinational culture and, on the other, a kind of localism that has been completely wrested from its originating context of meaning'. Without artistic leaps of the imagination, Sorkin clearly feels, urban designers' evocation of local distinctiveness may have little value (for Andrew Saint's contrasting view, see PERSONALISATION).

local enterprise company The LECs were set up in Scotland in the early 1990s to run youth and employment training services.

Local Government Act 2000 Legislation introducing directly elected mayors and cabinet-style government, and encouraging councils to prepare strategies to increase people's social, economic or environmental well-being.

local government ombudsman A service that investigates complaints about local government administration.

local housing company A social landlord registered with the Housing Corporation to take over former council homes, after the tenants have voted to change from local authority control to a new non-profit landlord. A high proportion of tenants and councillors sit on the company's board.

local list A non-statutory list of buildings of local architectural or historic interest compiled by the local authority.

local nature reserve An area of local nature interest that is primarily managed for nature conservation.

local neighbourhood renewal strategy Defined by the DETR in 2000 as 'strategies identifying local priority neighbourhoods, diagnosing their problems and designing an appropriate local response' as part of a COMMUNITY STRATEGY.

local open land Parks and other open spaces within and on the edge of a built-up area.

local park Officially defined as a publicly accessible open space of around two hectares, providing for children's play, court and field games, sitting-out and nature conservation.

local people The people who live in a particular area, and are on the receiving end of planning and development processes. The phrase is a favourite of planners and others as an alternative to the ambiguous term COMMUNITY.

local plan The detailed, local element of what, with a STRUCTURE PLAN, constitutes the development plan for an area. Local plans are the means by which local authorities express the land-use implications of their policies. A local plan allocates land for specific uses by means of a written statement and a proposals map showing precise boundaries. Produced by districts and unitary authorities, local plans set out detailed policies and specific proposals for the development and use of land, and guide most day-to-day planning decisions. Design policies in a local plan set the framework for a local authority's design control and guidance.

local planning authority A local authority that has statutory planning powers.

local road (US) One that provide access to private properties or public facilities that generate low volumes of traffic.

local state Some Marxist academic writers in the 1970s described planning from the perspective of their analysis of local government as the local manifestation of the state. In a capitalist society, they argued, the state was an instrument by which the bourgeoisie dominated the working class. Local government planning, accordingly, was a means by which the local state exercised its control, and planners who believed they were helping to create a more just society were the state's innocent dupes. The term is still used, though more rarely. Example: 'Council house is a reference to the form of tenure on which it is occupied. You rent it from the local state' (2003). See also STATE and KARL MARX.

local strategic partnership Brings together the local authority, all service providers (such as schools, the police, and health and social services), local businesses, community groups and the voluntary sector to develop a

COMMUNITY STRATEGY to cover the local authority area, to coordinate the work of more local or more specific partnerships, and to develop *neighbourhood renewal strategies* 'in areas in which DEPRIVATION is a significant factor' (in the words of the 2000 Urban White Paper).

local transaction See TRANSACTION.

local transport plan A five-year plan which sets out a local authority's transport strategy. Introduced in 1998 by a government claiming to pursue integrated transport policy, local transport plans represent a major missed opportunity to integrate transport and land-use planning. The system replaced the annual *transport policies and programmes* system.

localisation Protecting local differences; the opposite of GLOBALISATION. See LOCAL DISTINCTIVENESS.

localism Focusing on a particular local area. Example: 'There is further localism within the borough. People are apt to look for their friends and their club within a close range' (1954).

locality A geographical expression of PLACE, which does not imply that it has any particular meaning for anyone. See REGION.

locality budgeting Coordinating budgets between all government departments and agencies relevant to a particular area.

Location of Offices Bureau Created in 1963 to promote the decentralisation of office employment from the cities. The LOB's remit was reversed in the 1970s when the government decided that the process had already gone too far. The bureau was later closed.

location, location, location The three most important determinants of property value, according to estate agents' droll mantra.

lock 1 A device to enable boats to go 'uphill' and 'downhill' on canals and navigable waterways. **2** A nineteenth-century term for a traffic jam (Ackroyd, 2000). Compare GRIDLOCK.

locking away jobs in filing cabinets MICHAEL HESELTINE as environment secretary in 1979 used the phrase in accusing planners of unnecessarily delaying proposals for economic development.

lock-up garage One that is not on the same site as the user's home or workplace.

lock-up shop One without living accommodation.

locus ALDO ROSSI (1982) uses the term to describe the relationship between a specific location and the buildings that are in it.

loft 1 (UK) A room or space immediately below a roof. **2** (US) An upper floor. **3** A large open space on an upper floor used for warehousing, manufacturing or commerce, or such a space converted to one or more apartments. Loft living was pioneered in Greenwich Village, New York, in the 1970s. The word comes from the Old English *lyft*, meaning air. See also SOHO LOFT.

loft district An area where former warehousing, manufacturing or commercial premises are being or have been adapted as apartments.

lofted house (Scotland) One of more than one storey.

Logue, Edward (1921–99) Urban administrator. From 1960–68 he was city development administrator in Boston, where his projects included the Faneuil Hall Marketplace. He ran the New York State Urban Development Corporation from 1968 to 1975, and was director of the South Bronx Development Corporation in the late 1970s.

Lomas Verdes An unrealised proposal for a satellite city north of Mexico City, designed by the Mexican architect LUIS BARRAGAN in 1964–73.

London See AFTER LONDON, CENTRAL LONDON, THE CITY, CITY OF GOLD, CITY OF THE WORLD, CITY OF TREES, CITY OF VILLAGES, COSMOPOLIS, FOG, REBRAND, SEX, THE SLOUGH OF DESPOND, SMOG and SMOKE.

London An experimental film by Patrick Keiller, released in 1993, exploring the urban landscape.

London and Westminster Improved A book by John Gwynn, published in 1766, calling for development in the capital to be controlled according to a plan. Gwynn proposed more than 100 street, square and embankment improvements. 'The amazing thing about this plan is its complete grip on reality,' John Summerson (1962) writes. 'Nothing in it is utopian and, in fact, a very large proportion of his suggestions were carried out within a hundred years of the publication of the book.' Summerson notes 'one conspicuous defect in this extraordinary performance'. This was 'Gwynn's naïve belief that London could be called to a halt at Marylebone Road on the north and Hyde Park on the west.'

London cottage flat TERRACED HOUSING divided horizontally, so that the ground floor and first floor are separate flats. Also called *half-house flats* and *maisonettes*. TYNESIDE FLATS are similar.

London County Council (1889–1965) London's first strategic authority, created in 1890, to replace the METROPOLITAN BOARD OF WORKS. It covered what are now the inner London boroughs. It was replaced in 1964 by the Greater London Council. Joseph Rykwert (2000) records that by the 1950s the LCC had the world's largest architects' office, with some 5,000 professionals, mostly designing housing estates. The architectural critic J M Richards called the LCC 'a great empire in which the concrete never sets'.

London Development Agency The Greater London Authority's economic development arm.

London Orbital A book by Iain Sinclair, published in 2002, describing a walk around the M25, London's orbital motorway. See also LEADVILLE.

London Overture, A A work for orchestra by the composer John Ireland (1879–1962). One of its themes is said to have been inspired by a bus conductor calling 'Piccadilly!' See also LONDON SYMPHONY.

London Pigeon Wars, The A novel by Patrick Neate, published in 2003, in which the central character finds himself irresistible to pigeons that he comes across in Trafalgar Square, with catastrophic results. The book is an imaginative exploration of the relationship between human and avian sharers of urban space (*flying rats,* as some people call them).

London peculiar A London fog, as described by Charles Dickens.

London Plan, The 1 An alternative name for the *Spatial Development Strategy for London,* prepared by the London mayor and published in draft in 2002. It deals with matters that are of strategic importance to Greater London. Boroughs' local plans must be in 'general conformity' with it. **2** A plan prepared in 1942 by the Royal Academy Planning Committee, chaired by SIR EDWIN LUTYENS and including SIR PATRICK ABERCROMBIE among its members. One of its suggestions was the removal of Charing Cross Station and Hungerford Bridge and their replacement by a grand processional bridge by which passengers arriving at Waterloo Station would cross the Thames. Compare GREATER LONDON DEVELOPMENT PLAN.

London Symphony Composed by Ralph Vaughan Williams (1872–1958) in 1914, and revised by 1920. Vaughan Williams wrote: 'A better title would be *Symphony by a Londoner*; that is today, the life of London (including possibly its various sights and sounds) has suggested to the composer an attempt at musical expression; but it would be no help to the hearer to describe these in words. The music... must stand and fall as "absolute" music.' (quoted in Cox, 1967). There are, though, direct London references: Westminster chimes, a cry of 'sweet lavender', sounds of a mouth-organ and the jingle of hansom cab bells. See also A LONDON OVERTURE.

London, Jack (pen name of John Griffith, 1876–1916) American writer. See CITIES OF THE PLAIN, THE PEOPLE OF THE ABYSS and THE SCARLET PLAGUE

Londonderry See STROKE CITY.

lone ranger (US) **1** An unaccompanied car driver. **2** Someone who is doing something on their own. Example: 'I went along to the meeting to see if I was the lone ranger in my area, but there were about 40 people there.' The Lone Ranger was the hero of the eponymous radio and television Western series in the 1940s and '50s. Compare SLOANE RANGER.

long grid A gridded street layout with long principal streets and short cross streets.

long life, loose fit, low energy See ALEX GORDON.

Löns, Hermann (1867–1914) Writer. He satirised city life and celebrated the open landscape. In his story *The Devil's Doing,* the devil disguises himself as a developer to destroy an area of heartland by building factories, while the peasants are forced to move to the city, where they degenerate. Thomas Nevin (1996) writes: 'A generation after his death, his work was enlisted to serve the cheerless nostalgia of National Socialism.' Löns was an important influence on the novelist Ernst Jünger (1895–1998) (see ON THE MARBLE CLIFFS).

Looking Backward A utopian novel by Edward Bellamy, published in 1888. Julian, the central character, wakes up in the future to find that Boston in the year 2000 has become a utopian socialist community. 'At my feet lay a great city. Miles of broad streets, shaded by trees and lined with fine buildings, for the most part not in continuous blocks but set in larger or smaller enclosures, stretched in every direction. Every quarter contained large open squares filled with trees, along which statues glistened and fountains flashed in the late-afternoon sun. Public buildings of a colossal size and architectural grandeur unparalleled in my day raised their stately piles on every side'.

Julian's host tells him that the 'excessive individualism' of the nineteenth century has been replaced by a concern for the city's appearance. 'Nowadays,' he explains, 'there is no destination of the surplus wealth so popular as the adornment of the city, which all enjoy in equal degree.' Among the city's features are a shopping arcade: 'A continuous waterproof covering had been let down so as to enclose the sidewalk and turn it into a well-lighted and perfectly dry corridor, which was filled with a stream of ladies and gentlemen dressed for dinner.'

The book's social and economic ideas were an early influence on EBENEZER HOWARD. WILLIAM MORRIS, who considered the vision of *Looking Backward* to be bleakly machine-oriented, wrote NEWS FROM NOWHERE in reaction to it.

Loop, the The lakefront inner-city core of Chicago, defined by its elevated circular railway track.

loops and lollipops A pejorative term for residential road layouts consisting of culs-de-sac joined to curving collector roads, leading nowhere. See also DROWNED WORM and TRAIN-WRECK LAYOUT.

loose parts See THEORY OF LOOSE PARTS.

loose-fit building One that is easily adaptable to a variety of uses. Example: 'Buildings can be loose-fit and adaptable: indeed they must be, for we need to be able to knock them about, nail pictures in, renew them.' See ALEX GORDON.

Los Angeles The writer HL Mencken called it '19 suburbs in search of a metropolis' (quoted in Knevitt, 1986). Dorothy Parker is supposed to have called it '72 suburbs in search of a city'. The name is short for El Pueblo de Nuestra Señora la Reina de los Angeles de Porciuncula. See also AUTOPIA, THE BETTER CITY, BLADE RUNNER, CAPITAL OF THE TWENTIETH CENTURY, CITY OF QUARTZ, COSMOPOLIS, EARTHQUAKE, FLEXITY, THE FOOTHILLS, FOUR ECOLOGIES, THE FRAGMENTED

METROPOLIS, KENO CAPITALISM, PLAINS OF ID, EDWARD SOJA, SOYLENT GREEN, SURFURBIA and THERE'S NO THERE THERE.

Lost Opportunity See HI-LO.

lost river One that has been culverted or otherwise hidden under urban development.

lot (US) A plot of ground.

LOTS Living over the shop. Programmes for bringing unused or under-used, upper-floor properties back into use.

Lou' St Louis, Missouri.

Loudon, John Claudius (1783–1843) The author of an influential architectural copybook, the *Encyclopaedia of Cottage, Farm and Villa Architecture and Furniture*, published in 1833. 'More than any other individual,' writes John Burnett (1986), 'he was responsible for the break-up of the long Georgian domination of English house style and for what John Summerson describes as "the descent into chaos". From one point of view, the English bourgeoisie had abandoned "taste" for "fashion" and had lapsed into a sentimental antiquarianism: from another, they had rejected their dependence on traditional, aristocratic dictates, and had announced their individuality in a variety of distinctive architectural styles.'

Louis XIV (1638–1715) King of France. A great town planner, according to LE CORBUSIER. 'This despot conceived great projects and realised them,' Le Corbusier wrote. 'Over the country his noble works still fill us with admiration. He was capable of saying, "we wish it", or "such is our pleasure".'

Lovelock, James (b1919) Scientist. See GAIA.

Lovin' Spoonfuls A pop group. See SUMMER IN THE CITY.

low-cost home ownership Initiatives funded by the housing corporation helping people buy their own homes wholly or partially.

low demand A description of homes that are difficult to let or sell people as do not want to live in them.

low-cost market housing Provided by the private sector, without public subsidy and not involving a housing association, and sold or let at less than the average open market price for housing of that type.

low-density housing The DETR defined low-density housing development in 1999 as being at less than 20–25 dwellings per acre.

low-emission zone An area closed to vehicles that fail to meet a specified emission standard.

low-order shop One selling relatively cheap and frequently bought goods; a CONVENIENCE SHOP. Customers are likely to come from nearer and more frequently than they would to a HIGH-ORDER SHOP.

low-road building An 'unrespectable, mercurial, street-smart', utilitarian structure such as a shopfront, shed, garage or factory building, as classified by Stewart Brand (1994). Compare HIGH-ROAD BUILDING and NO-ROAD BUILDING.

Lowry, LS (1887–1976) A painter of bleak industrial landscapes and townscapes in and around Salford and Manchester, populated by stick-like figures. Lowry was a rent collector for a property company.

Lubetkin, Berthold (1901–90) The most talented of the modernist architects working in England in the 1930s, best-known for the penguin pool at London Zoo and the Highpoint One flats in Highgate, London (1935). His projects with the architectural practice Tecton included the SPA GREEN ESTATE in Finsbury, London. He prepared plans for the new town of PETERLEE (1947–8). When they were rejected, Lubetkin abandoned architecture and planning, and took up pig farming instead. Towards the end of his life he declared: 'There are only four kinds of artistic activity: fine art, music, poetry and ornamental pastry cooking, of which architecture is a minor branch.' He was awarded the Royal Gold Medal for Architecture in 1982. See also SPATIAL VORTEX and TOWN PLANNING.

Berthold Lubetkin

lucky charm A NEW URBANISTS' pejorative term for an asterisk, blunt arrow or zigzag line of the type usually drawn in marker pen, often used in diagrams by designers of CONVENTIONAL SUBURBAN DEVELOPMENT. The new urbanists' objection is to these symbols' crudity and coarse scale.

ludic Playful. The word is part of the jargon of critical theory.

Luftwaffe The German airforce. 'You have to give this much to the Luftwaffe,' the PRINCE OF WALES told the Corporation of London at its planning and communication committee's annual dinner in 1987. 'When it knocked down our buildings, it didn't replace them with anything more offensive than rubble.' See also BLITZ and URBAN DESTRUCTION.

LULU A locally unwanted land use.

lumpy investment (US) Payment for infrastructure of a sort that can not be provided in small increments.

Lutyens, Edwin (Sir) (1869–1944) Architect. His designs for country houses (several of them in collaboration with the garden designer Gertrude Jekyll, and many of them in ARTS AND CRAFTS style) and neo-classical commercial buildings such as the Midland Bank at Poultry, London, were highly influential. Lutyens was consultant architect to HAMPSTEAD GARDEN SUBURB and designed many of its principal buildings. He built council flats on Page Street in Pimlico (1928–30) with a distinctive chequered surface treatment of windows and stucco and brickwork panels. Of his design for a vast Roman Catholic Cathedral in Liverpool, only the crypt (1933–41) was built (a much smaller cathedral designed by FREDERICK GIBBERD was later built above it). Lutyens was chief architect for the New Delhi planning commission in 1913–30. He was architectural consultant for the Greater London Highway Development Survey (the BRESSEY REPORT, published in 1937). See also GENDER.

luxury *adj.* When used by estate agents in relation to APARTMENTS, the term seems to denote little more than the attribute of having a carpeted entrance hall. See also EXCLUSIVE, MARKETING and PRESTIGIOUS.

luxury laager A gated, high-security area of expensive homes.

Luzhkov, Yuri Politician. As mayor of Moscow after 1992 he promoted the reconstruction of St Basil's Cathedral and other historical monuments.

Lynch, Kevin (1918–1984) Urban designer and planner. Lynch studied with FRANK LLOYD WRIGHT at TALIESIN from 1937 to 1939. He studied and later taught at the Massachusetts Institute of Technology from the late 1940s, becoming in professor of city planning in 1963. Lynch's work on the theory of city form was highly influential. Studies carried out in collaboration with Gyorgy Kepes led to Lynch's book *The Image of the City* (1960). This established the concept of LEGIBILITY (ease of understanding) as a major theme in urban design. Lynch's methods of analysing and graphically notating

Kevin Lynch

urban form are the most commonly used by urban designers today. He worked widely as a consultant. His other books include *What Time is This Place* (1972) and *Growing Up in Cities* (1977) and GOOD CITY FORM (1984). See also CLARITY OF JOINT, CORE, DAVID CRANE, DIRECTIONAL DIFFERENTIATION, DISTRICT, EDGE, ELEMENT, IMAGE, IMAGEABILITY, LEGIBLE CITY, MOTION AWARENESS, NAMES, ORDER, PATH, TIME SERIES, URBAN COUNTRYSIDE, VISUAL PLAN and VISUAL SCOPE.

Lynchian analysis KEVIN LYNCH's widely used method of CONTEXT APPRAISAL.

Lyons, Eric Architect. See SPAN.

M

Mac and Mick A nickname of MacTaggart and Mickell, a Scottish housebuilding firm established in 1925. The company is well known for designs that draw on local vernacular styles.

machine age The first machine age followed the industrial revolution. The second saw technology being brought into the home. LE CORBUSIER identified the first machine age (1830–1930) as that in which the machine had oppressed man. He predicted that the second, by contrast, would see mankind in harmony with the machine.

machizukuri (Japanese) The word conveys the concepts of town planning, community design and development, according to Japanese planner Catherine Huws Nagashima (1998), who has advocated its addition to English usage. *Machi* means town, in the sense of the community and its well-being as well as the physical settlement. *Zukuri* is derived from the verb *tsukuru*, meaning to make, build or create.

macjob A low-grade job in the service sector, such as serving fast food in a branch of McDonalds.

Mackintosh, Charles Rennie (1868–1928) Architect, designer and artist. See CRYONIC CONSERVACTION [sic], THE LIGHTHOUSE and MOCKINTOSH.

MacMansion A large, ostentatious house built to a tasteless design. The mac- prefix from the fast-food chain McDonalds is being used to denote a lack of good taste. Example: 'This is the sort of MacMansion likely to be built in Footballers' Wives country' (2003).

macro scale Relating to an area larger than a town or city.

Mad Max See ROAD WARRIOR.

Madurodam The world's largest model village, in the Hague, Netherlands. Founded in 1952 as an exhibition of models of historic buildings, Madurodam now includes modern architecture as well, and is used to promote interest in planning and design. A committee of local schoolchildren helps to run the town. The scale is 1:25.

Maertens, Hermann A German architect who in 1877 published a book on how urban design should be influenced by the way people experience buildings and space.

maestref (Welsh) A suburb.

magazine architecture Designed primarily to look good in photographs in glossy magazines, rather than to meet the needs of its users (Brand, 1994).

Magic City, The A story for children by E Nesbit (author of *The Railway Children*), based on the premise that any construction by children comes to life, somewhere. An eleven-year-old builds a city from anything he can find and, sure enough, it comes to life.

Magical Urbanism A book by Mike Davis on the dynamics of Latino culture in the USA, published in 2000.

magistrale A street that serves as a ceremonial axis. Spiro Kostof (1991) notes that the term means main or arterial road in the Slavic languages. It entered the vocabulary of East German architects and planners with the Soviet occupation, and was routinely used in the 1950s and '60s to refer to the principal city-centre avenue.

magnet school Designated in a blighted area with the aim of raising educational standards and attracting people on relatively high incomes to the area.

Magnetic City A walled city (also called the Third City) peopled by the dead in Wyndham Lewis's three-volume novel *The Human Age*, published 1928–55. The city is a kind of half-way house to heaven. Lewis describes it early in *Childermass* (the first volume of the trilogy): 'The sheer profile of the city is intricate and uneven. Above the walls appears, naissant, armorial, and unreal, a high-hatched out-cropping of huddled balconies, black rufous brown vermilion and white; the upper stages of wicker towers; helmet-like hoods of tinted stucco; tamarisks; the smaragdine and olive of tropical vegetations; tinselled banners; gigantic grey sea-green and speckled cones, rising like truncated eggs from a system of profuse nests; and a florid zoologic symbolism — reptilian heads of painted wood, filled-out tinfoil or alloy, that strike round beneath the gusts of wind, and pigs made of inflated skins, in flight, bumped and tossed by serpents, among the pennants and embossed banners. The severe crests of bulky ziggurats rise here and there above this charivari of roof-life, perceived beyond and between the protecting walls. It is without human life, like a city after a tragic exodus.' Compare DULSTON.

Magnificent Mile, the North Michigan Avenue, Chicago's chief commercial street.

Magnitogorsk A new industrial city built in the Urals in the 1930s. See STEELTOWN.

Kurt Weill

Mahagonny A city of bars and brothels founded in the desert by a group of criminals in the opera *The Rise and Fall of the City of Mahagonny* (libretto by Bertold Brecht, music by Kurt Weill), first performed in 1927. *Mahagonny* is a political satire on the self-destructiveness of capitalism.

Maidenhead Town Hall The Berkshire town's 1950s town hall, made famous as the hospital in Carry On films with a medical theme, became the centre of a local political row in 2002 when the council announced its intention to demolish it. See also GET CARTER.

mail (French) A MALL.

mail-order house Built from prefabricated parts ordered from a mail-order catalogue. This method of acquiring a house was popular in North America in the twentieth century.

main drag (US) The principal street of a town. Compare MAIN STEM.

main stem (US) The most popular street in a town or city for vagrants. Compare MAIN DRAG and MAIN STREET, and see VAGRANT.

main street (US) The most important shopping and commercial street of a traditional town. The equivalent of the UK HIGH STREET. In the words of Spiro Kostof (1987): 'Main Street, of course, is much more than a place name to Americans. It is a state of mind, a set of values. It is what defined the heartland of the nation for generations… In railroad towns it ran parallel to the industrial axis along the tracks or, less often, at right angles to it. It was usually not more than two or three blocks long, wider than the rest of the town's streets, and open to farmland at either end… It was always something of a myth, the simple insular life of Main Street, USA, easygoing and genuine – the sentimental setting of Rod Serling's *Twilight Zone* and Andy Hardy movies, where decency and common sense always ruled. So, like all myths, it could be challenged sometimes, and even disowned. On Main Street novelists like Sherwood Anderson and SINCLAIR LEWIS could find ignorance and bigotry and closed-mindedness. Still, Main Street remains one of the central landscapes of American life' (see also ROUTE 66). In a rare UK example, Main Street was the name given to the 'neighbourhood spine' street proposed by English Partnerships and the Prince's Foundation in 2002 in their plan for a model URBAN EXTENSION to be developed at the edge of Northampton. The principal route through the area, it was to be fronted by townhouses and apartments of three to four storeys, which at ground level would be adaptable over time from residential to retail, office, workspace or community uses.

Main Street A novel by SINCLAIR LEWIS, published in 1920. The book is critical of the life of the fictional small town of Gopher Prairie (based on the author's home town of Sauk City, Minnesota). The writer HL Mencken (1921) warned that *Main Street* should not be treated by big-city sophisticates as simply a satire on small-town American life. Big towns, like Mencken's own Baltimore, deserved similar treatment. 'They are all pretty much alike – huge, overblown villages, run by lodge-joiners and greengrocers, some of them disguised as bankers, publicists and pedagogues.' The writer Cy Fox notes that 27 years later WYNDHAM LEWIS (no relation) wrote that the size of cities in America meant nothing culturally. Modern industrial techniques, Wyndham Lewis (1948) wrote, 'spawn a city several times the size of Babylon in two or three decades. From personal observation I should… class Detroit, Chicago, St Louis, Buffalo as monstrous manufacturing villages.'

Main Street is almost all right A slogan used by the architects ROBERT VENTURI and DENISE SCOTT BROWN (1984) in defending popular culture. 'Why must architects continue to believe that when "the masses" are "educated" they'll want what the architects want?' they asked. They urged architects to learn instead from the cultures around them.

mainline 1 A principal railway route. **2** A motorway and its associated LAND-TAKE.

main-main intersection (US) The place where the busiest roads in an area meet. Often this will be an attractive location for retail development.

mainstream funding From the core budgets of local authorities and other agencies rather than from other sources of regeneration funding.

mainstreaming 1 Reallocating mainstream resources to deprived areas. **2** Integrating a new policy into normal practice.

maintenance Defined by the BURRA CHARTER as the continuous protective care of the fabric, contents and setting of a place (as distinct from *repair* which, the charter states, involves restoration or reconstruction, and should be treated accordingly).

maintenance-free A description of a building material or component that is likely to have to be replaced in its entirety if it breaks.

mairie (France) Town hall. In larger towns it is often called the *Hôtel de Ville*.

maisonette A two-storey dwelling with at least one other dwelling either above or beneath it. FJ OSBORN remarked that maisonettes 'as the French rightly said [combine] the disadvantages of flats and houses' (Hughes, 1971).

major centre An important shopping and service centre, typically smaller in scale than a metropolitan centre, with a mix of both comparison and convenience shopping (Greater London Authority, 2001).

major development Retail development with a gross floorspace of more than 2,500 sq m (26,910 sq ft) or other commercial development with a gross floorspace of more than 3,000 sq m (32,292 sq ft); residential development providing 30 or more dwellings; or development involving the change of use of one hectare or more of land.

major repairs allowance The main government housing subsidy for local authorities. It is based on the cost of maintaining council homes.

majority minority city One in which ethnic minorities collectively account for a majority of the population.

make no little plans 'Make no little plans, they have no magic to stir men's blood' is often quoted as a saying of the US planner DANIEL BURNHAM, though Joseph Rykwert (2000) notes that the remark is now considered apocryphal.

making-down Dividing and sub-dividing dwellings to become ever more overcrowded (McKean, J, 1994).

mall 1 (UK/US) A shopping and/or leisure centre where users are segregated from vehicles. The word, which may have been first applied to a shopping centre in 1967, previously meant a pleasant place for strolling. The first malls, recorded in the late sixteenth century, were strips of grass laid out for playing the ball game *pall-mall* or *pell-mell* (meaning ball-to-mallet) – which required such a setting – with lanes of traffic on each side. The street Pall Mall and the adjacent avenue THE MALL were examples in London. Malls later became used for promenading. Mark Girouard (1985) traces the roots of contemporary malls to the twelfth century, 'to the covered selds of Cheapside, or the great halls of Flanders'. Their immediate ancestor, he writes, is a Kansas City shopping centre of 1923. See DISNEYLAND and JON JERDE. **2** (India) An avenue (Vidal and Gupta, 1999).

Mall A novel by Eric Bogosian, published in 2000, satirising suburban American culture. The lives of the central characters (including Mal, who has just shot his mother and set fire to his house) converge on a shopping mall.

Mall, The A ceremonial street between Admiralty Arch and Buckingham Palace in London, parallel to Pall Mall, originally laid out to enable pell-mell to be played without disrupting the traffic on Pall Mall. See MALL.

mallification The progressive replacement of open, public streets and places by private covered, enclosed spaces. Example: 'Progressive urbanists bemoaned the mallification of the American city.' See MALLING.

malling The process by which increasingly large parts of urban areas are occupied by SHOPPING MALLS.

mallopolis An urban region and network of consumption dominated by shopping malls. The term is credited to the economist James Millar.

Malraux, André See SECTEUR SAUVEGARDÉ.

Mammon The false god of wordly riches. The author and journalist Simon Jenkins once described his home city of Birmingham as 'a city that sold its soul to Mammon and lost the receipt'. He later (Jenkins, 2003) conceded that it had recognised its error.

man on the Clapham omnibus, the An ordinary person. The phrase dates from when 'man' was used to refer to people of both sexes. In fact twice as many women as men use public transport.

management board A group of individuals from various partners set up to oversee the delivery of a regeneration programme and its strategic direction.

management contract A contract under which work is carried out by subcontractors managed by a contractor who may not carry out any of the building work directly.

managerialism An approach to planning based on the concept of planners and other local authority officers as managers of the development process.

Manaus See PARIS OF THE AMAZON.

Manchester The world's first industrial city, and the first to be served by railways. Alexis de Toqueville described the Lancashire landscape in 1835. 'From this foul drain the greatest stream of human industry flows out to fertilize the world,' he wrote. 'From this filthy sewer pure gold flows. Here humanity attains its most complete development and its most brutish; here civilisation works its miracles, and civilised man is turned back almost into a savage' (quoted in Johnson, 2001). Hippolyte Taine described the city as he found it on a visit in around 1859. 'A sky turned coppery red by the setting sun; a cloud, strangely shaped resting up on the plain; and under this motionless cover a bristling of chimneys by hundreds, as tall as obelisks. Then a mass, a heap, blackish, enormous, endless rows of buildings; and you are there, at the heart of a Babel built of brick' (quoted in Girouard, 1985). The historian AJP Taylor (1957) imagined Manchester as 'the last and greatest of the Hanseatic towns – a civilisation created by traders without assistance from monarchs of territorial aristocracy'. The BBC radio producer DG Bridson (1971), remembering the city in the 1930s, wrote that 'during the slow strangulation of the cotton trade, with unemployment growing from year to year, Manchester had an almost embattled air – that of the waning capital of a grimly autonomous Northern republic.' In recent decades the city has established itself as the regional capital of north-west England. See CHIMNEY OF THE WORLD.

Manchester Ship Canal Begun in 1887 and opened in 1894, the 56-kilometre canal from the Mersey brought ocean-going ships to the inland city, making it one of Britain's busiest ports.

Mandelbrot, Benoit (b1924) Mathematician. See CHAOS THEORY.

Mandelstam, Osip (1891–1938) Russian poet. See RAILWAY PROSE.

Manhattanise To make a place more like Manhattan with its concentration of skyscrapers. *Manna-hata* (hilly island) was the island's native American name (Burrows and Wallace, 1998).

Manifesto of Futurist Architecture 1 Published in 1914, the manifesto was signed with the name of the architect ANTONIO SANT'ELIA, though only part of it was written by him. **2** Another document with the same title was written by the Italian Futurist painter Umberto Boccioni in 1914, but it remained unpublished until the manuscript came to light in 1972. It had probably been suppressed by Marinetti, the Futurist leader and poet, in favour of the other one, published over the name of Sant'Elia. 'We live in a vortex of architectural forces,' Boccioni wrote. 'Up to yesterday, construction developed as a series of successive panoramas. House followed house, street followed street. Today our architectural environment is beginning to play upon all our senses: from the light-filled underground chambers of department stores, from the multi-levelled metropolitan railway tunnels, to the immense soaring of American skyscrapers... The future is preparing a sky for us that will be unbridled by architectural armour' (quoted in Zevi, 1981b).

manipulated city One in which private interests achieve what they want through making use of the city's political, administrative and legal frameworks.

manipulation See ARNSTEIN'S LADDER.

Mannheim The first city whose streets were numbered in one direction and alphabetised in the other (in the seventeenth century), according to Joseph Rykwert (2000).

mansard roof A roof with two pitches on each side of the ridge, the lower one steeper than the upper. The double pitch makes more usable space in the attic storey. A mansard roof is often used to disguise the apparent height of a building, frequently ineptly. It is named after the French architect François Mansart [sic] (1598–1666). See PERCEIVED HEIGHT.

Mansion House Square A new square for the City of London proposed by the developer PETER PALUMBO in the 1980s as a setting for the Mansion House and a new office building designed in the 1960s by LUDWIG MIES VAN DER ROHE. The public inquiry was a classic confrontation between conservationists (Victorian buildings would be demolished and a medieval street alignment obliterated) and modernists, many of whom felt obliged to support Mies's dated and obsolete design. Planning permission for the square and the Mies building was refused. In 1998 Palumbo developed No. 1 Poultry with a building by James Stirling, Michael Wilford and Associates (see PRINCE OF WALES).

manufactured home (US) One built in a factory and installed on site under the regulations of a code of the Department of Housing and Urban Development (also called a *panellised home*); a permanently sited 'mobile home'. The term was coined to distinguish them from conventional housing, in order to prevent manufactured housing being allowed in areas zoned for single-family dwellings. Factory-built homes were called mobile homes in the USA before 1976. Compare MODULAR HOME.

Manzoni, Herbert (Sir) (d1972) City engineer of Birmingham, 1935–69. As Birmingham's engineer and planning officer, he planned the 'concrete collar' of the inner ring road that so disastrously carved up

> **"I'M NOT INTERESTED IN SMALL SOLUTIONS, ONLY BIG ONES"**
>
> *Herbert Manzoni*

the centre of the city in the 1960s. 'I'm not interested in small solutions, only big ones,' he said (Upton, 2001). Colin Ward (1989) notes that Manzoni 'was not an ignorant technocrat spiralling up the local authority promotion circuit. He was a cultivated and dedicated public servant devoted to his city and using the best wisdom of the period to solve its traffic problems. (In retrospect, we could cynically conclude that more fortunate cities had an engineer who was lazy, close to retirement or addicted to golf, as traffic would then have been managed through one-way systems, park-and-ride provision or neglect, and the physical fabric of the city would have remained intact.)'

map A representation of the surface features of a place or an area of the earth's surface. See also MENTAL MAP.

map amendment (US) Amending a ZONING map to permit a use prohibited by the zoning ordinance.

Maplin The coastal site in Essex proposed at various times for a new airport to serve London. Until the 1970s the site was known as Foulness.

mapping 1 Creating a map. **2** Describing space (not necessarily using a map).

Maragall, Pasqual See BARCELONA.

Marble Farm, The A book by Nathaniel Hawthorne in which he proposed that 'all towns should be made capable of purification by fire, or of decay, within each half-century'. Otherwise, he wrote, it would be impossible to take advantage of constantly evolving new ways of building. See also ON THE MARBLE CLIFFS and URBAN DESTRUCTION.

March of Bricks and Mortar, The Cruickshank's cartoon, published in 1829, showing development cascading across the countryside.

mardi gras Any festival named after the Brazilian and Sydney Mardi Gras.

Margaretenhöhe The largest of the settlements built by the steel-makers Krupp. It was designed by George Metzendorf in 1906 (Rykwert, 2000).

margin The interest rate payable over a base rate as a reward for taking a risk.

margins The fringes of an area. See also BORDERLANDS and EDGELANDS.

marker See URBAN MARKER.

market forces The phrase was generally replaced by *consumer preferences* in the 1990s. Those leading the change probably felt that the new phrase implied multiple, personal choices rather than abstract economic forces.

market town One whose main original function was as a place where farmers and others bought and sold goods.

Market Towns Initiative Government funding to enable local communities in market towns to carry out a health check and implement an action plan.

marketecture Buildings designed to reflect their users' products or services. An example is the headquarters of a manufacturer of roof windows, whose windows are its own products, set in a roof/wall. An earlier example was the Prussian iron foundry at Sayn, designed by Karl Ludwig Althans and built in 1825. The iron and glass structure in gothic style showed off the product it made (Lewis, 2002).

marketing The language used by those who market developments include such devalued terms as *distinctive*, EXCLUSIVE, LUXURY, *prestigious* and *unique*. Such adjectives, intended to convey a sense of distinctiveness without specifying what is distinctive, are used in marketing housing of standard design, as Robert Huxford has noted.

marriage of town and country The aim of garden cities, according to EBENEZER HOWARD. FJ OSBORN (1966), always suspicious of people he saw as metropolitan intellectuals (see CAPPUCCINO CULTURE) wondered 'whether Howard's use of the image "The Marriage of Town and Country", attractive as we know it is to the merely literate multitude, is deterrent to more cultivated or scientific minds. If he had used instead some such phrase as "The Symbiosis of the Urbano-Mechanistic and Vegetative Ecologies", would he more quickly have interested the sociologists and economists?' See also URBAN AND REGIONAL PLANNING.

MARS Group The Modern Architectural Research Group, formed in 1933, became the official British delegation to CIAM.

MARS Plan The Master Plan for London, published by the MARS GROUP in 1942 (developed from an earlier plan prepared in 1937), proposing the redevelopment of London as a broad east-west corridor with fingers of residential development protruding north and south, divided by green wedges. John Gold (2000) writes: 'Its best known element, a striking image of a linear city with spines of residential development located north and south of a central transport corridor [is] frequently cited as representing the uncompromising visionary stance said to have characterised the thinking of the inter-war modern movement towards the future city. Yet this plan is almost always presented as a discrete exercise. There is rarely any sense that it was the culmination of a discontinuous series of separate exercises and was shaped, directly and indirectly, by different authors with varying views and intentions.' All the same, the published plan, as Gold explains, 'superimposed a new gridded pattern on London – or, at least, the space occupied by London – to produce a dramatically reconstructed city of ten million people... Almost the entire city would have been swept away, apart from a few historic buildings of national significance. At the heart of the new pattern was an east-west corridor, some 25 miles long and two wide, containing London's vital industrial, commercial and administrative functions. Radiating north and south would... be 16 strips of urban development, each roughly one mile across and bordered by belts of protected countryside that would prevent sprawl and allow inhabitants easy access to open space.' The commitment of the MARS group to its own plan was shortlived: it

Marsh, Benjamin The American author of what Barry Cullingworth (1997) suggests may be the first textbook of planning: *Introduction to City Planning*, published in 1909.

Marsh, George Perkins (1802–1882) Linguist, diplomat and conservationist. See SUSTAINABLE.

Marshall, Alfred (1842–1924) Economist. EBENEZER HOWARD was influenced by an article, published in 1884, in which Marshall pointed to the potential that the rail network offered for decentralising industry to rural sites. These could be bought by committees, Marshall suggested, which would benefit from the increase in land values.

Marshall, Sir Frank Commissioned in 1977 by the Greater London Council to carry out a review of its role. He was a former leader of Leeds City Council.

Marsham Street The Westminster headquarters of the DEPARTMENT OF THE ENVIRONMENT until the late 1990s, designed by the government architect Eric Bedford with Robert Atkinson & Partners and built 1963–71. The three slab blocks linked by a podium (nicknamed the Toast Rack) were widely considered an eyesore on London's skyline, particularly as they provided a backdrop to the Palace of Westminster. In 1992 environment secretary MICHAEL HESELTINE announced that the building (some of whose concrete was breaking up) would be demolished. One of his successors in the post, JOHN GUMMER, later held an urban design competition for its replacement, but the abandoned building lay empty for some years.

Martha Reeves and the Vandellas See DANCING IN THE STREET.

Martin, John (1789–1854) Nineteenth-century painter of apocalyptic scenes. John Summerson (1994) writes that Martin's 'The Fall of BABYLON' (1819) and 'Belshazzar's Feast' (1820) 'were furnished with buildings of the most powerful kind: vast cubic masses playing against each other, interminable colonnades of some unacknowledged order, temples of inconceivable solemnity and exotic style.' Summerson notes that the Scottish architect Alexander 'Greek' Thomson, a generation younger than Martin, 'took these apocalyptic forms and – what is so surprising – made them work.' See DESTRUCTION OF SODOM AND GOMORRAH.

Martin, Leslie (Sir) (1908–2000) Architect. As chief architect to the London County Council, Martin was responsible for the overall design of the ROYAL FESTIVAL HALL on London's South Bank. Later, as professor of architecture at Cambridge, he was an important influence on the development of architecture as a graduate-based profession. Alan Powers (2000a) writes that designing buildings with a stepped section almost became Martin's trademark, offered as an alternative to high-rise for high-density housing. 'In the studies for Bloomsbury – the basis for Patrick Hodgkinson's BRUNSWICK CENTRE – the stepped section became an infinite extrusion. It could also be wrapped around to generate endless courtyard forms... taken to extremes in Martin's notorious proposals, published in 1965, for replacing most of the government offices in Whitehall. Opposition... was one of the significant turning points in the conflict between modern architecture and conservation, decisively settled in favour of the latter with help from the oil crisis.'

Karl Marx

Marx, Karl (1818–83) German economic and social theorist, and founder of revolutionary communism. Marx argued that capitalism carried the seeds of its own decay, making revolution inevitable. See also FRIEDRICH ENGELS and the COMMUNIST MANIFESTO, and compare ROBERTO BURLE MARX.

Marxism The theory and political practice deriving from the writings of KARL MARX and FRIEDRICH ENGELS. In much of the twentieth century Marxism was supposedly the basis of the political systems under which a third of the world's population lived. It was also the basis of a great deal of social, economic and political thought, not least about processes of urban change. Marxists argue that capitalist cities are shaped in the class interests of the owners of capital. Marxism has been a strong tradition in worldwide academic discussion of urbanism. In the UK this has been less overt since the 1980s, when the Thatcher government attempted to expunge it from higher education and research. See also LOCAL STATE.

Mary Barton A novel by ELIZABETH GASKELL, published in 1848, depicting working-class life in contemporary

Manchester. The city fathers' furious reaction to the implied criticism was reflected in a review in the *Manchester Guardian* on the occasion of the publication of the third edition in 1849. 'It is a libel on the masters, merchants and gentlemen of this city, who have never been exceeded by those of any other part of the kingdom in acts of benevolence and charity, both public and private,' the reviewer thundered. 'It appears very strange that no notice whatever is taken of what has been done by the masters for improving the conditions of the workmen – for instance, of the day and Sunday schools attached to many mills and, where this is not the case, of the inducements held out for their becoming subscribers to extensive libraries founded expressly for their benefit, or to mechanics' institutions. Nothing is said of the parks which have been purchased, and laid out exclusively for their recreation and enjoyment, where thousands of happy and intelligent faces may be seen on Saturday afternoons and on holidays, delighting themselves in innocent games or athletic exercises, nor (when the mills are stopped for the want of a market) of the many instances in which the masters advance their workpeople a weekly sum for their subsistence.'

Marzaroli, Oscar (1933–88) Photographer. His black and white photographs of Glasgow document the transformations being wrought upon the city by post-war developments, especially the clearance of large areas of working-class tenements and their replacement by high-rise blocks of flats.

mask architecture Façade architecture (McKean, C, 1994). The term was in use in the nineteenth century. See also FAÇADISM and SKIN ARCHITECTURE.

masonry Stone or brick.

mass suburbia Large-scale, undifferentiated suburbs.

mass transit (US) The UK term is *public transport*.

massing The combined effect of the arrangement, volume and shape of a building or group of buildings. Also called *bulk*.

master plan (also masterplan) 1 A diagram or scheme showing how a site or area can be developed. This is the definition used by the URBAN DESIGN GROUP. Such a master plan charts the masterplanning process and explains how a site or a series of sites will be developed. It will describe how the proposal will be implemented, and set out the costs, phasing and timing of development. A master plan, generally drawn at a scale of 1:1250, will usually be prepared by or on behalf of an organisation that owns the site or controls the development process. As with all design guidance, the purpose of a master plan is to set out principles on matters of importance, not to prescribe in detail how development should be designed. But it should show in some detail how the principles are to be implemented. If the master plan shows an area designated for mixed-use development, for example, it should show a layout that will support such uses (such as by configurations of space that will promote an adequate pedestrian flow). Some master plans indicate the approximate three-dimension form recommended or specified for a development, while others indicate the layout in two dimensions. **2** A DEVELOPMENT BRIEF or an URBAN DESIGN FRAMEWORK, but more formal and architectural than these usually are. **3** URBAN DESIGN GUIDANCE. In this widely used definition master plan is a generic term, covering anything from a detailed brief of what is likely to be built to a vague indication of a possible framework.

The DTLR/CABE design guidance *By Design*, published in 2000, did not use the term *master plan* at all. The authors preferred the terms *urban design framework* and *development brief*. Master plan, they thought, tended to have unfortunate associations with prescriptive plans that envisaged a specific end state, rather than setting out a flexible framework for a process of development.

After 2000, though, there was a flood of master plans. *Towards an Urban Renaissance*, the report of the Urban Task Force (1999b), saw master plans as a means of focusing on the visual impact of three-dimensional form. (Masterplanning was a mainstream activity in urban design before the Urban Task Force, though. In 2001, 48 per cent of urban design practices listed in *Urban Design Quarterly* advertised themselves as offering masterplanning as one of their services. In 1993 the proportion had been 33 per cent.) The Urban Task Force described a master plan as 'a synthesis of the design-led approach to urban development... a sophisticated visual "model"'. The task force contrasted spatial masterplans to 'conventional two-dimensional zoning plans' which, it wrote, 'tend simply to define areas of use, density standards and access arrangements'. The spatial masterplan, on the other hand, 'establishes a three-dimensional framework of buildings and public spaces' as well as determining the distribution of uses. This sounds like a development brief (for a site) and urban design framework (for an area), but the task force seemed to want to distinguish it from these. 'A spatial masterplan,' its report suggested, 'when accompanied by design guidelines in the form of supplementary planning guidance or a more informal code or brief, should provide sufficient detail to allow statutory bodies and project sponsors to evaluate their performance against design and development objectives.' The Urban White Paper of 2000, the government's response to the Urban Task Force's report, advocated the use of master plans. It described a master plan in the vaguest of terms, as 'setting out a vision for an area undergoing change and a strategy for implementing that vision'.

The urban designer Sir Terry Farrell has defined masterplanning as 'a way of stating desired outcomes and setting out to achieve them in physical, material terms' (Williams, 2001). The planning academic Patsy

Healey (1988) writes of the importance of the 'master plan' to planning in the immediate postwar period. 'The social and economic goals of urban planning... were presented as self-evident, and the management of city building as a technical rather than political task. The "Master Plan" provided the ideal form to express and organise what had to be done... [In the 1950s] it involved collecting and organising information about the existing conditions of places, and how many people were to be accommodated in them, converting these via standards of space use, engineering principles and alternative conceptions of urban form into spatial strategies and action programmes. Thus urban planning *was* urban design. The main task of planning was to design better cities, and the main debates were about urban form'. By 1988, though, Healey could write that 'in Britain, we have largely abandoned the master plan concept, although in many other parts of the world it is still widely used, if only as an ideal.' In her view 'the preparation of a master plan, with its programme of action to achieve precisely defined outcomes, seems a peculiarly inappropriate vehicle for expressing the strategic dimensions of managing environmental change. The articulation of directions is a political process rather than a technical one; strategy is about influencing a few key events and relations, rather than setting the framework for every action...'

Master Plan for London Published by the MARS GROUP in 1942. See MARS PLAN.

match funding The balance of funding required to implement a regeneration project over and above that contributed by a major funder.

Matcham, Frank (1854–1920) Architect. He designed or completely redesigned more than 120 theatres in the UK between 1879 and 1912, of which around 24 remain.

material 1 *adj.* Substantial, as in *material change of use*. If a change of use is not material, it does not constitute DEVELOPMENT. **2** *n.* The *materials* of which a building is made are subject to planning control.

material consideration A consideration that must be taken into account, where relevant, in a decision on a planning application. They include policies and guidance, and all the fundamental factors involved in land-use planning (including the form and appearance of buildings).

materiality The ability of a building's materials to generate a particularly heightened response in people who use the building. Adrian Forty (2002b) writes that the word has been around for '10 years at the most'. He suggests that critics find it useful 'to have a word that tells us that [the building] is made of some rather nice materials, yet add the gravity of a philosophical concept'. The philosophy, apparently, is existentialism, which some critics suggest is the inspiration for those architects whose buildings are said to have the quality of materiality – even though, as Forty points out, those architects may never have come into contact with that philosophy.

matrilocal *adj.* Kinship and neighbour relations in which the most significant social relationship is between the mother and the married daughter (Parker, 1973).

matrix approach Presenting the results of an appraisal, often as part of a matrix of costs and benefits, not all of which may be valued in monetary terms.

Matthew, Robert (Sir) (1906–1975) As architect to London County Council (1946–53) he was an important influence on the design of housing estates. Later he was Scotland's leading architect/planner, and in the 1970s he was a pioneer of urban conservation. Matthew designed Pakistan's new capital of Islamabad.

Maugham, Somerset (1874–1965) Writer. See LISA OF LAMBETH.

maw A deep, dark space which people may be intrigued to look into, though perhaps a little apprehensively. The term was used by GORDON CULLEN (Smith, 1974).

Mawson, Thomas (1861–1933) Lancashire-born landscape architect and town planner. He was the first president of the Institute of Landscape Architects and president of the Town Planning Institute.

maxigrid See SUPERGRID.

maximum city New York, according to the title of a 'biography' of the city by Michael Pye (1991).

Maximum Security with Minimum Regulation See CITY OF FREE CHOICE.

Max-Neef, Manfred Chilean economist. In his 1981 book *From the Outside Looking In: experiences in barefoot economics* he describes his experiences as an economist attempting to practise 'economics as if people matter' among the poor in South America. He set up the Centre for Development Alternatives, promoting local self-reliance in Chile, and in 1993 he stood as a minority candidate in the Chilean Presidential election. 'There are two separate languages now – the language of economics and the language of ecology, and they do not converge,' Max-Neef writes. 'The language of economics is attractive, and remains so, because it is politically appealing. It offers promises. It is precise, authoritative, aesthetically pleasing. Policy-makers apply the models, and if they don't work there is a tendency to conclude that it is reality that is playing tricks. The assumption is not that the models are wrong but that they must be applied with greater rigour.' He received the RIGHT LIVELIHOOD AWARD in 1983.

May, Ernst (1886–1970) Trained by RAYMOND UNWIN in England, he developed a series of satellite towns as city planner and architect of Frankfurt in the 1920s (Hall, 2002).

Mayor of the World See RUDOLPH GIULIANI.

McAlpine, Robert See CONCRETE BOB.

McDonaldization The GLOBALISATION of lifestyles, called after the global fast-food chain. Also *Coca-Colazation*.

McHarg, Ian (1920–2001) Landscape architect, ecological planner and educator. Born in Scotland, McHarg was apprenticed at the age of 16 to a landscape architect and began attending the Glasgow College of Art. After wartime service in the army he studied landscape architecture and city planning at Harvard. Later he created a department of landscape architecture (which he headed from 1955 to 1986) at the University of Pennsylvania and worked as a consultant. By the early 1960s, McHarg was bringing his holistic approach to the public with his television series 'The House We Live In', featuring discussions about the relationship between humans and their environment. His influential book *Design With Nature*, published in 1969, argues that the shaping of land for human use ought to be based on an understanding of natural processes. The book discusses the effects of what is now called sprawl and advocates a means of SUSTAINABLE development. 'McHarg's method' consists of a multidisciplinary analysis of a region's ecological sensitivity and assesses a site's suitability for different types of development and use. McHarg helped to develop the methodology for environmental impact assessments for the US Environmental Protection Agency.

McLoughlin, Brian Author of *Urban and Regional Planning: a systems approach*, published in 1969. It was a standard textbook of the SYSTEMS APPROACH to planning.

McLuhan, Marshall (1911–80) Canadian communications theorist. See GLOBAL VILLAGE.

Marshall McLuhan

McMansion (US) A large house built to a standard design in a populist style. The allusion is to McDonald's fast food.

McUrbia (US) An area of homogenous suburbs. Alan Loomis has credited the term to Kenneth Helphand.

McWorld The urban designer Douglas Kelbaugh (2002) writes of 'McWorld, code for the multi-national, corporate market with little if any allegiance to local place and community'.

mean *adj.* **1** Unimportant; inferior. See NO MEAN CITY. **2** Unkind; spiteful. **3** Miserly. **4** Bad-tempered; cantankerous; tough. Streets that are mean in this sense need not be mean in physical form. The *Guardian* wrote in 2003 of the troubled Chapeltown area of Leeds: 'Villas, mature trees, Victorian parks; time and again the allegedly "mean streets" are the former favoured places of the late nineteenth-century middle class.' Raymond Chandler wrote in a 1950s essay 'The Simple Art of Murder': 'Down these mean streets a man must go who is not himself mean, who is neither tarnished nor afraid'. Paul O'Keeffe suggests that the sentence appears to refer to a world where no one can walk down a dark street in safety because law and order are things we talk about but refrain from practising. **5** Hard to cope with. The word comes from the Old English word for *common*.

Mean City A novel by Ron McKay set in Glasgow's gangland, published in 1995. Compare NO MEAN CITY.

Mean Streets A film by Martin Scorsese, released in 1973, set in the Italian-American community of New York's Lower East Side. Scorsese recalled: 'While we were [shooting] in the Lower East Side, a slate would come up saying *Mean Streets* and people would get angry and say, "There's nothing wrong with these streets!" And I'd say, "No, it's only a preliminary title." I kept hoping to change it, but it turned out as that' (quoted in Tate Modern, 2001).

Mean Streets, Tales of A book by Arthur Morrison, published in 1894, about the east end of London.

meaning The value that a place has for particular people. Sue Clifford (1990) writes: 'We seem to be trapped in the pedantry of "facts" and "objectivity", forgetting that we called them into existence to help us not to rule us. Our cities and suburbs may need topographers to describe, historians and economists to analyse, planners to synthesise, and so on, but if we allow power and logic alone to make places, the likelihood of conceiving meaningless spaces is high.'

Mearns, Andrew See THE BITTER CRY OF OUTCAST LONDON.

Mears, Frank (1880–1953) Architect. He worked closely with PATRICK GEDDES, whose daughter he married.

meat axe See ROBERT MOSES.

Mecca 1 The chief holy city of Islam and birthplace of Mohammed, in what is now Saudi Arabia. **2** New York City.

mecca A place that is a centre of attraction or a goal for a particular group of people.

mecca of anti-sprawl Portland, Oregon, in the words (intended ironically) of Harry W Richardson and Peter Gordon (2001), advocates of suburban sprawl. Portland is well-known for its planning policies aimed at preventing sprawl.

Mecco The fictional capital of Meccania, described in Gregory Owen's *Meccania, the Super-State* (1918). Like Meccania's other towns, Mecco is built to a circular plan. Its central ring accommodates public buildings, with cultural institutions in the next ring round it. The outer ring provides housing, strictly zoned according to the state's rigid social classes. The lowest two classes, the semi-skilled and industrial workers, are housed in an adjacent satellite area. The state controls all aspects of life and practices EUGENICS.

Medellín, Colombia. A centre of Colombia's drug cartels, Medellín is one of the world's most violent cities.

median (US) An island in the centre of a street or intersection to separate opposite travel lanes and to protect pedestrians. The UK term is *central reservation*. See also TRAFFIC CALMING.

mediappeal A possible process combining MEDIATION with a planning appeal decision. If the mediation fails, the mediator decides. Chris Shepley, the government's then chief planning inspector for England and Wales, used the term in 2000.

mediate 1 To resolve disputes with the help of a neutral mediator. **2** To resolve perceived differences between architectural elements. Example: 'The wall in architecture represents the tension between inside and outside, mediated through material, shadow, thinness and thickness' (from the *Architects' Journal*). **3** To divide a plot of land lengthwise.

mediation 1 A confidential process for resolving disputes with the help of a neutral mediator. The solution is produced by the parties themselves, and they are encouraged to see each other as united in achieving a solution. The parties do not have to reach a settlement: at any stage any party can walk away. The mediator will never impose a solution. Mediation can be appropriate before a planning application has been put to the council's planning committee; when the council has refused an application (either before or after the applicant has appealed); or when a planning application has been granted but with conditions with which the applicant does not agree (either before or after the applicant has appealed). Before mediation, the parties produce a short written explanation of their side of the argument. **2** The division of a plot of land lengthwise.

Medina community A neighbourhood renewal initiative focused on improving rundown housing estates, employment training, and working with religious groups. The concept of Medina communities, developed in the UK in the 1990s, is based on the Islamic duty of neighbourliness. The name refers to the community of Muslims, Christians and Jews founded in the seventh century in the city of Medina.

mega-city 1 A conurbation of exceptional size; a MEGALOPOLIS or SUPERCITY. The term has been used to describe the PEARL DELTA SUPERCITY. **2** A city with a population of more than five million.

mega-grid See CONTINUOUS MOVEMENT.

megalith 1 A very large prehistoric stone, standing alone or part of a larger structure. **2** A very large building. Tony Travers said of the twin towers of the WORLD TRADE CENTER: 'They were megaliths, not tall buildings. They were one step beyond what we think of as a tall building' (quoted in Garlick and Loney, 2001).

megalopolis 1 An urban region consisting of several large cities. Peter Hall (2002) writes of a megalopolis in England stretching from London through the Midlands to Cheshire. The term was coined around 1830. PATRICK GEDDES helped to bring the term into currency in modern discussions of urbanism. In 1918 he wrote of 'the megalomania of every Megalopolis'. In Greek the word referred to a large planned town. LEWIS MUMFORD told the writer Anthony Bailey (1967): 'These days the word [megalopolis] is generally used by urban experts who are trying to convince other experts that it's some new kind of city, instead of the urbanoid mishmash it actually is. The real megalopolis in ancient Greece was still residually an entity.' **2** A megalopolis is defined by EKISTICS as a settlement with a population of 150 million, and a 'small megalopolis' as having 25 million. **3** A large, high-density, mixed-use, urban development. Example: '...the High Paddington scheme: a megalopolis of houses, shops, churches and social facilities stacked above Paddington station.' See also SPRAWLOPOLIS.

megalopolitan Pertaining to a MEGALOPOLIS.

megapolis A huge city; a MEGALOPOLIS. John Holloway (1957) writes of the city depicted in Wyndham Lewis's 1936 painting 'The Surrender of Barcelona': 'Its vast flat windowless walls, round towers, simple inhuman masses, smoke stacks (as they seem) and grim gaping casemates can not be in anything but reinforced concrete. It is a Barcelona of the Maginot, the Siegfried line; insofar as it is a city, it is the megapolis of twentieth century war.' David Jones (1974) wrote in his poem 'The Tutelar of the Place': 'In the bland megapolitan light/ where no shadow is by day or by night/ be our shadow.'

megastructure A very large building comprising many individual units. Andrew Higgott (2000) defines a megastructure as 'a complex of various functions integrated into one three-dimensional form.' Reyner Banham suggested that the term should relate to a structure with a consistent section. In Martin Pawley's (1998) view, 'once upon a time all cities were megastructures, complex assemblies of spaces making the maximum use of shared structural walls, roofs and floors. The medieval city was like this, more like a nest of termites than a parade of palaces with boulevards and parks' (see HAV). Alison Ravetz dates the word's coinage to 1964.

megaturization See ARCOSANTI.

Megiddo See ARMAGEDDON.

Meidner, Ludwig (1884–1966) German expressionist painter. He is noted for his apocalyptic visions of cities being destroyed by fire, earthquakes and superhuman forces. Meidner wrote: 'The town which is our universe, the streets full of tumult, the elegance of its iron bridges, its gasometers hanging in mountains of clouds, the shrieking colours of its buses... the houses near us, which we can see with only half an eye – appear to wobble and collapse.' See GEORG HEYM, I AND THE CITY and URBAN DESTRUCTION.

Mellonta Tauta A story by Edgar Allan Poe in which New York is destroyed in 2050 by an earthquake. By 2848 the archaeological evidence suggests that the lost civilisation was addicted to building temples dedicated to Wealth and Fashion. See URBAN DESTRUCTION.

melting pot A place where people from different cultures and races are assimilated. Compare MOSAIC.

Melting Pot Suburb A report by William H Frey, published in 2001, using 2000 census data to analyse racial and ethnic changes in 102 large metropolitan areas in the USA. It found that minorities made up 27 per cent of suburbanites in these areas, up from 19 per cent a decade earlier.

Melville, Herman See REDBURN.

Memoirs of a Survivor, The Doris Lessing's novel, published in 1974, is set in an emptying city as civilisation crumbles. People huddle together in tribes for self defence and feral children live in the underground railway. The authorities turn a blind eye to all but the most serious outbreaks of disorder. The narrator recalls that 'the police ignored houses being lived in by people who didn't own them, gardens growing food for people who had no right to eat it, the ground floors of deserted houses accommodating horses and donkeys which were transport for the innumerable little businesses that illegally flourished, the little businesses themselves where all the riches of our old technology were being so ingeniously adapted and transformed, minuscule turkey farms, chicken runs, rabbit sheds – all this new life, like growth pushing up under old trees, was illegal. None of it should exist. None of it, officially, existed; and where "they" were forced into seeing these things, they sent in troops or the police to sweep it all away. Such a visit would be referred to in a headline, a broadsheet, a newscast as "Such and such a street was cleaned out today". And everyone knew exactly what had happened and thanked fortune it was someone else's street.'

Memorial Arch A soaring, stainless steel arch on the St Louis, Missouri, waterfront, designed by Eero Saarinen. It was built in 1965 to celebrate Thomas Jefferson's purchase of Louisiana and to symbolise St Louis' claim to be historically the gateway of the American west. Spiro Kostof (1987) records that 40 city blocks of the original commercial waterfront were razed to make room for it.

memory The writer Ken Worpole has described green spaces as 'reservoirs of collective memory'.

mental map The way a person conceives (and perhaps also draws) the layout of an area. Distances are likely to be distorted by the person's values, interests and experience. Asking people to draw mental maps can be useful in finding out how they perceive and use their locality.

mental mapping Recording how people perceive the spatial patterns of places with which they are familiar.

mentoring A person with experience in a particular field (the *mentor*) giving guidance to a newcomer to it (the *mentee*). The planning profession and several planning schools provide a mentoring service for new graduates.

Merchant City Glasgow's Merchant City is the area developed in the eighteenth and nineteenth century by the city's merchants. Johnny Rodger (1999) credits Charles McKean with coining the name in 1971 in place of its original name, the New Town. The new name had its critics. One pressure group, Rodgers records, campaigned against what it saw as the packaging and hype of the area's regeneration. It organised demonstrations and renamed the area *Workers' City*. 'One of the members of this group, the writer James Kelman, said this name was picked to highlight "the grossness of the fallacy that Glasgow somehow exists because of the tireless efforts of a tiny patriotic coalition of fearless eighteenth-century entrepreneurs and far-sighted politicians. These same merchants and politicians made the bulk of their personal fortunes by the simple expedient of not paying for the price of labour".'

Merry Hill An out-of-town shopping centre in the Black Country of England's West Midlands. It opened in 1989.

Mersey Tunnel See ONE-EYED CITY.

Merseyside Task Force Set up by environment secretary MICHAEL HESELTINE in 1981 after the Toxteth riots to promote urban regeneration.

Merville Garden Village A suburb of Belfast, built as a housing estate in the 1940s and '50s. See GARDEN VILLAGE.

mesh A network of connected streets and footpaths. A *fine mesh* has small street blocks and many connections compared to a *coarse mesh*.

meta-analysis Examines regeneration action in terms such as credibility, reliability and utility.

Metabolic Group Founded in the late 1950s to

promote the design of cities and buildings as living organisms. See ECOLOGICAL METABOLIC CYCLE THEORY, FLOATING CITY and HELIX CITY.

metabolism The organic approach to architecture and planning promoted by the METABOLIC GROUP.

metro (and metropolitan) *n.* **1** The international term for urban rapid transport. It derives from London's first underground line, the London Metropolitan Railway, which opened in 1863. **2** An underground railway system (also known in the USA as the *subway*). **3** A railway service so frequent not to need timetabling.

métro, boulot, dodo (French) Underground train, job, sleep. The phrase is used to sum up the bleak life of the urban commuter. *Boulot* is slang for job. *Dodo* – from *dormir*, to sleep – is the equivalent of the English child's phrase 'beddy-byes'.

MetroCentre A pioneering shopping mall that opened in Gateshead in 1987. John Hall was the developer.

metroland The areas of suburban London that developed in response to the building of railway lines, particularly in the 1920s and '30s, and celebrated by the poet John Betjeman. Example: 'The tentacles of post-war intercity "metro-land" now stretch across large parts of England' (Mars, 1998). The term was first used in 1914 as the name of an advertising booklet issued by the Metropolitan Railway (Burnett, 1986). See also LADY METROLAND.

métropole d'équilibre (French) A balancing metropolitan area, designated for regional economic development to reduce the domination of Paris and its region.

metropolis 1 A capital city or large urban centre, from the Greek for *mother* and *city*. Example: 'The United States has no metropolis, but it already contains several very large cities' (Alexis de Tocqueville writing in 1835, quoted in Bender, 2002). **2** EKISTICS defines a metropolis as a settlement with a population of four million, and a 'small metropolis' as having 500,000.

Metropolis 1 A classic silent science fiction film, directed by Fritz Lang, premiered in Berlin in 1927. Lang, trained as an architect, presents a dystopian vision of the twenty-first century. The ruling elite lives in a futuristic city, beneath which an enslaved underclass toils in an underground realm of giant machines, of which the workers seem to have become almost a part. The film was based on a novel of the same name by Thea von Harbou. The cast is said to have numbered 36,000. See also THINGS TO COME. **2** A town (with a population of around 6,700) in Illinois. **3** The city in which the comic book adventures and the film of 'Superman' are set.

metropolitan *adj.* Pertaining to a METROPOLIS.

Metropolitan Association for Improving the Dwellings of the Industrious Classes A charitable trust with dividends limited to five per cent, founded in 1841.

Metropolitan Board of Works Created in 1855 mainly to deal with drainage, sewerage and street improvements in London. Its achievements include the Victoria Embankment, Southwark Street, and Northumberland Avenue (linking the Embankment with Trafalgar Square).

metropolitan centralisation The tendency for activities to be concentrated in a metropolis. London is a striking example.

metropolitan centre A large shopping centre characteristic of outer parts of London, with a wide catchment area covering several boroughs (Greater London Authority, 2001).

metropolitan fragmentation See BALKANISATION.

metropolitan green belt An area of predominantly open land encircling London.

metropolitan open land Areas of predominantly open land within London that are significant to more than one borough.

metropolitan planning The planning of a metropolitan area.

metropolitan statistical area (MSA) A classification of urban areas. An urban area containing more than one MSA is a *primary MSA*, and an urban area containing more than one primary MSA is a *consolidated MSA*.

metroscope The landscape of a metropolitan area.

metrosexual An urban young heterosexual man who is interested in fashion and beauty, and rejects traditional male stereotypes (Quinion 2003).

Metzendorf, George See MARGARETENHÖHE.

mews 1 A short dead-end street. **2** A street or yard of stabling, often now converted to housing or other uses. The term comes from the Royal Mews at Charing Cross in London, which first kept hawks and later horses. See also CUL-DE-SAC.

Mexicà-Tenochititlán A city rebuilt after 1521 by Hernan Cortés to the first urban plan in the Spanish New World (Rykwert, 2000).

mezzanine finance An additional amount of loan charged at a higher rate of interest.

Mia Miami, Florida.

micro scale Relating to an area smaller than a town or city.

micro-conservation The CONSERVATION of such items as monuments, elements of a building's fabric, or a building's contents, as opposed to building conservation.

Microcosm The city of Wroclaw, so called in the 2002 book *Microcosm: portrait of a central European city* by Norman Davies and Roger Moorhouse. For over a thousand years control of the city has passed backwards and forward between the Germans and Poles – and anyone else who was passing that way. Its name has been variously Wrotizla, Vrestslav, Vratislava, Presslaw, Bresslaw, Bressla, Presslau, Bresslau and Breslau, among others.

microcredit A money-lending system that involves extending small amounts of money to people on low incomes who are considered unbankable.

micro-district The smallest unit (8,000–12,000 people) used by planners in the Soviet Union in their development plans, according to Ward and Dubos (1972). See NEIGHBOURHOOD.

microflat A very small flat intended to make living in central urban areas affordable to first-time buyers. The idea was promoted in 2001 by architects Piercy Conner. It borrowed from the concept of *pods*, like those in which Japanese business people have lived in the Nakagin Capsule Tower in Tokyo since the early 1970s (Gray, 2002). An owner selling a microflat would be required to make it available to another first-time buyer.

micro-spatial location A neighbourhood; a local area.

middle place See THIRD PLACE.

Ludwig Mies van der Rohe

Mies van der Rohe, Ludwig (1886–1969) German-born architect, later practising in the USA. Born Ludwig Mies (Mies means miserable), he added his matronymic van der Rohe. He was one of the most influential modernists of his generation, probably best known for the Seagram Building on New York's Fifth Avenue. From 1930–33 he was director of the BAUHAUS. Joseph Rykwert (2000) argues that Mies and his followers thought of each building 'as an individual object, never as part of, never an event in the urban fabric'. Later developers and architects 'took over his total disregard of urban form, with none of the virtues of Mies's obsessional care over detail, and between them produced one of the most devastating urban landscapes of the century.' See LESS IS MORE and MANSION HOUSE SQUARE.

Mildendo The miniature capital of the fictional island of Lilliput, described by Jonathan Swift in *Gulliver's Travels* (1726). The square city of half a million inhabitants is divided into four sectors by two main streets that cross at its centre.

Mile-High Sky-City A 1,609m-high skyscraper served by atomic-powered lifts, proposed in 1956 for the outskirts of Chicago by the architect FRANK LLOYD WRIGHT but never built.

milieu The setting of a building or space. The term is used particularly in the context of crime prevention, with regard to ways in which certain activities help to make a place safer.

Miliutin, Nikolai Politician and journalist. He was one of the DISURBANISERS.

milk-bar loungers A phrase used by FJ OSBORN in the journal *Town and Country Planning* in 1939 to describe city dwellers who do not experience 'normal community life'. See CAPPUCCINO CULTURE.

Millennium Dome Built as a year-long celebration of the new millennium, the Dome opened on 1 January 2000. The building, resembling a shallow dome, designed by architects the Richard Rogers Partnership (with Mike Davies [see DRESS SENSE] as the project architect) and engineers Buro Happold, was widely admired. The world's largest ever fabric-covered structure was supported by a structural net suspended from 12 masts. The government promised that visiting the Dome would be the experience of a lifetime, and while it was the most popular 'visitor attraction' of the year, it was still not popular enough to prevent it from being a financial disaster, due to extremely ambitious projections of visitor numbers. As the criticism mounted, the government increasingly stressed the project's benefits in terms of the regeneration of a rundown area of the capital, though the respective costs and benefits were too embarrassing to spell out.

Some critics said that the Dome's architects were at fault, first for helping to persuade the government to celebrate the millennium with a building when there was no clear idea of what it would be for, and second for designing it without a brief specifying how it would be used. Others retorted that the Dome was the equivalent of a marquee, and that it was reasonable for the architects to design a large, flexible space and leave others to decide what to use it for. RICHARD ROGERS himself laid the blame on the failure to appoint a person with vision to coordinate the Dome's content. The Dome's design was inspired by two structures at the 1951 Festival of Britain: the Skylon, a freestanding wire-stayed spire similar in shape to the Millennium

Dome's 12 masts, designed by architects POWELL AND MOYA, and the Dome of Discovery, an exhibition space designed by the architect Ralph Tubbs (demolished in 1952, though the site remained empty for decades).

millennium green One of the 250 open, green spaces created in a programme run by the COUNTRYSIDE AGENCY and funded by money from the national lottery.

Millennium Tower A 840m-high, mixed-use 'vertical city' for 50,000 inhabitants, proposed in 1989 but never built. Designed by NORMAN FOSTER, the structure was to have a cone-shaped, helical, steel outer frame, rising from the sea in Tokyo Bay. Internally it was to be organised as a series of distinct NEIGHBOURHOODS.

millennium village (or community) A government-sponsored, model development intended to set exemplary standards in design, planning and regeneration, celebrating the millennium in 2000. The first was launched in 1997 next to the MILLENNIUM DOME on the Greenwich peninsula in London. Other examples include those at Allerton Bywater, near Leeds, and the Cardroom estate in Manchester.

Milliard City A gridded city on the artificial Standard Island, near New Zealand, as described in Jules Verne's *Propeller Island* (1895). Originally populated by 10,000 American millionaires and equipped with moving pavements, the city was abandoned after the island was wrecked in a storm.

million city (or millionaire city) One with a million or more inhabitants.

Milton Keynes A new town, designated in 1967, halfway between London and Birmingham. In 2000 it was the UK's fastest-growing urban area. Milton Keynes was by far the largest product of the government's new towns programme (it was a Mark Three new town), and is the best known. Its name ('a neat marriage of two impeccable personalities,' Lord Esher joked) was in fact adopted from an actual village in the designated area. The masterplan was by Llewelyn-Davies, Weeks, Forestier-Walker and Bor. Lord Campbell of Eskan, known as a 'socialist businessman', was the development corporation's first chairman; the architect Fred Lloyd Roche the general manager; and Derek Walker, for the first six years, the chief architect and planner.

When people think of the qualities of town or city life, of the delights of URBANITY, they usually have in mind historic cities that were shaped in circumstances very different from those of today. Is it possible to create places with real urban qualities now, when the economy is dominated by multinationals, when many people choose to shop at superstores, and when using the private car for every conceivable journey is regarded as an essential freedom? Milton Keynes represents the most comprehensive attempt in the UK to answer that question. For 30 years its architects and planners have been trying to create the urban qualities that would justify its claim to be not just another new town but a 'new city' (although political circumstances have meant that since 1979 the planners have had to follow the market). Yet, despite all its qualities and a population of 150,000, Milton Keynes hardly feels urban. Strangely, many people who do not live there seem to find the place almost offensive. Perhaps they see it as an all-too-honest mirror of the priorities of today's consumer. The message is unpalatable, so they blame the messenger. But is urbanity really incompatible with modern life?

A closer look at Milton Keynes reveals that there is no mystery about what happened. The team that drew up the plan for Milton Keynes in the 1960s was advised by Melvin Webber, an influential American planning theorist. Webber was convinced that Los Angeles and southern California were the shape of the future. With the growth of private transport and telecommunications, it was no longer necessary to live near to work, leisure and friends. Instead, people were living in what Webber called a 'non-place urban realm' – not a localised part of a city, but a wide area over which they travelled for

Melvin Webber

specific purposes. Milton Keynes' master planners laid a loose grid of building-free main roads one kilometre apart over the rolling Buckinghamshire countryside. Intersecting at roundabouts, these roads fulfilled the role of the Californian freeways and provided the new city's basic structure. But when the master planners' work was done and that structure was fixed, different planners and architects were employed to implement the plan. They had other ideas.

Tim Mars (1992), a sceptical enthusiast for Milton

Keynes and a former resident, takes up the story. 'Derek Walker, its first chief architect and planner, promptly set out to build a scaled-down version of the sort of city – urban, visual, monumental – that Webber had shown to be both obsolete and irrelevant,' Mars writes. 'Bequeathed a Los-Angeles-inspired plan,

"MILTON KEYNES STANDS FOR THE IDEA THAT TOWNS ARE ASSEMBLAGES OF PARTS INTO A WHOLE"

Bill Hillier

Walker and his team of Europhile urbanists turned their backs on California and looked to the leafy squares of London, the axial boulevards of Paris, the canals and pedestrian squares of Venice, Milan's Galleria, the crescents of Bath, the quadrangles of Oxford and Cambridge. Respectable cities, unimpeachably urban places... Walker and his team set out to create islands of urbanity within the amorphous sea of the grid roads.' That attempt largely failed. BILL HILLIER of the University of London, who analyses cities and urban spaces, believes he knows why. Like Mars, he notes the contrast between the strategic decisions behind the planning of Milton Keynes ('taken with almost the single aim of avoiding traffic congestion') on the one hand, and the tactics of the city's design on the other. The tactics, Hillier (1992) says, 'belong to "romantic urbanism": the belief that the "good" things about cities and towns – pedestrian activity, informal use of public spaces, overlapping communities, the sense of local place, aesthetic stimulation, and so on – can be created piecemeal... More than anything, Milton Keynes is a town of parts, each spatially distinct and with its own idiosyncratic layout, the ultimate embodiment of the belief that good local places can be designed free-standing, then hierarchically combined to form an urban whole. In urban design terms, Milton Keynes stands for the idea that towns are assemblages of parts into a whole, rather than wholes in which good parts arise.'

Hillier points out that most of the pedestrian or vehicular movement in any urban space is accounted for, not by people who have come to that space for a particular reason (because their workplace is there or they are visiting a shop, for example), but because they are passing through on their way somewhere else. How lively a particular square, street or other space is will depend as much on what routes pass through it as on what happens in or beside it. This is important, as the presence of people in an urban space can be turned to economic, social and cultural advantage. Hillier writes: 'It is this that creates urban life out of everyday activity, and eventually turns collections of buildings into cities or towns... Unfortunately, twentieth century interventions in the urban fabric, especially housing, have tended to disrupt every aspect of this pattern...The relations between building entrances and public space, between local and global movement, and between inhabitants and strangers are systematically pulled apart. Obsessed with internal "layout" rather than the relation between internal and external structure, twentieth century disurbanism... creates zones that are so remote from the public realm that they no longer operate as urban space.'

The temptation for urban designers is to try to disguise this process by designing spaces which reflect popular romantic images of what successful urban places look like. These spaces may look good, on paper at least, but they do not come to life. In Milton Keynes, Hillier writes, everyday movement is canalised into specialised systems. Each aspect of movement is separated from all others and from the life that they could create together. He suggests that Milton Keynes is the first case of this being done on such a large scale. He sees it, not as the first town of a new kind of urbanism, but as the first whole-city expression of twentieth-century disurbanism disguised as romantic urbanism.

Milton, John Poet. See NOVA SOLYMA.

minerals plan Prepared by a local authority to control mineral workings in accordance with the special system of minerals control.

mini-brief A short DEVELOPMENT BRIEF setting out the basic design principles on which the development of a specific site should be based.

Miniland The first Lego World, created at Billund in Denmark in the 1960s.

mining the memory Drawing on the history of a place in designing improvements. The phrase has been used by the urbanist Pauline Gallacher.

Minister for Pedestrians See PEDESTRIANISATION.

ministerial design champion A minister in a government spending department who is responsible for promoting the design and procurement of better public buildings.

ministructure See ARCOSANTI.

minoritization (US) The condition by which most of the population of a city belongs to minority groups and feels distanced from the structure of power (Jencks, 1993).

misanthropic green A person who, in their support of the natural world, hates their fellow humans for intruding on it. The phrase is COLIN WARD's (1996).

Mischgebiet (German) A mixed zone.

Misérables, Les A novel by VICTOR HUGO. Peter Hall (1998) notes that *les misérables* originally referred to the criminal classes but came increasingly to denote the poor in general.

mission One of the religious and philanthropic initiatives in the poorest urban areas established in the nineteenth and twentieth centuries.

Mister Standfast See BIGGLESWICK GARDEN CITY.

Mitchell, Joseph (1908–1996) Author and journalist. See RATS.

mitigation Reducing the negative impact of a development.

mixed scanning An approach to planning proposed by AMITAI ETZIONI in the late 1960s. Mixed scanning, Nigel Taylor (1998) explains, 'distinguishes more fundamental or "strategic" decisions from more detailed decisions, and then advocates concentrating the process of rational decision-making on the more fundamental decisions. The mixed-scanning approach also involves "tracking" the detailed consequences of crucial, strategic decisions. In this way the capacity to oscillate – or "scan" – between more general or strategic and more detailed levels of thinking is developed.' Compare THE SCANNER.

mixed use A mix of complementary uses within a building, on a site or within a particular area. *Horizontal mixed uses* are side by side, usually in different buildings. *Vertical mixed uses* are on different floors of the same building. Places which have a mix of uses are likely to be lively at different times for different reasons, as different people use or pass through them. Such places will be unpredictable, not monotonous. They will be places where happy accidents happen. They will be versatile: when one activity closes for lunch, or for the night, or for ever, others will continue to provide life and a sense of security. Investors generally prefer to put their money into developments with single uses, regarding them as more straightforward.

Planners have tended to specify areas for mixed use, but urban designers point out that mixed uses will flourish only in certain conditions. The urban designer Kelvin Campbell (1999) has identified 10 factors that he suggests can help to create the conditions for mixed-use development. They are: a) A FINE-GRAIN scale of development. b) Diversity of ownership. c) Appropriate tenure. d) Sensitive planning of the process through time. e) Land values that are not excessively high. f) Location on streets that are sufficiently busy. g) Sufficient density. h) Buildings with a flexible form. i) An interface between two types of building or activity. j) Positive attitudes towards urban living.

Mob Town Mobile, Alabama. Compare MOBTOWN.

Mobilität (German) Mobility.

mobility 1 The ability of people and freight to travel where they want to go (Echenique, 2001). John Norquist (2002), mayor of Milwaukee, has summed up his view of the ever-increasing movement in the modern city region: 'people travel further and further between increasingly insignificant destinations.' **2** The ease with which people with or without disabilities (including carers of young children, older people, people with mobility or sensory impairments, or those encumbered with luggage or shopping) can move around a place. **3** The ease with which people can move from one home or workplace to another. COLIN WARD (1996) writes: 'Our most precious environmental possession, and the one which we lose least willingly, is mobility, whether this means personal, social, occupational or ideological mobility. Humans change. And their changing needs are not arbitrary. There are different habitats that they see as appropriate to changing roles in the family life cycle, quite apart from changes in the means of livelihood or employment.' That is something commentators on urban policy sometimes forget, Ward observes. 'I myself have known people who at the age of 21 had left the suffocation of their parents' suburban home, and were waiting for the revolt of the proletariat in the city, and who at the age of 31 were praising God and growing beans in the countryside. The problem is that when they are 41 they are back in the city, working as consultants, and propagating the view that it is axiomatic that we should live at high densities and walk to work. At 51 they are back in the suburbs, rearing a second family and waiting for early retirement.' See ACCESS AUDIT.

mobility hub A TRANSPORT INTERCHANGE.

Mobtown A town dominated by the Mafia ('the mob'); particularly the Chicago suburb of Cicero, Illinois. Al Capone moved to Cicero from Chicago in 1924, and its reputation for civic corruption has been maintained ever since. Its mayor Betty Loren-Maltese, widow of Tony 'Baldy' Maltese, was jailed in 2002 for a scam to siphon off city employees' health insurance. Compare MOB TOWN.

mockintosh Tourist knick-knacks, lettering or architectural features inspired by the designs and buildings of the Scottish architect, designer and artist Charles Rennie Mackintosh (1868–1928). One of the favourite architectural features of Mockintosh is the square-gridded oriel window, inspired by those on the west side of Mackintosh's Glasgow School of Art. The term was coined by the film-maker Murray Grigor and popularised by the architectural writer Gavin Stamp.

mockney A person who affects a COCKNEY accent.

mock-up A full-size representation of a proposed building or structure, used to test it or assess its visual impact. The Zuiderkerk, one of Amsterdam's architecture and planning centres, for example, builds mock-ups of social housing out of standard wooden components. A full-size mock-up of EDWIN LUTYENS' design for Castle Drogo on Dartmoor was erected to assess its impact and fine-tune the design.

modal convergence See TRIPLE CONVERGENCE.

modal shift A change in the MODAL SPLIT.

modal split How the total number of journeys in an area or to a destination is divided between different means of transport, such as train, bus, car and walking.

model *adj.* and *n.* **1** A simplified representation of reality. This may be in the form of a theory, a set of mathematical or statistical formulae, or a scaled-down, three-dimensional physical structure (in wood, card or polystyrene for example). Physical models can help people to understand urban form (and can also be a means of deception). Mathematical models enable calculations to be made about what is likely to happen in a range of different circumstances (and can be used to create a spurious sense of objectivity). Other models are expressions, in words, of ideas. **2** An example to be followed. PORT SUNLIGHT for example, is a model village. See also URBAN MODEL.

model cities program (US) The original aim of the federal programme was to designate and support a small number of *demonstration cities:* that term was abandoned when it became associated with urban riots (Cullingworth, 1997). The programme gave financial and technical assistance to 150 cities in the 1960s and '70s.

Model-Urban-Ecology Planning Game A participatory planning method that has been used in Altenburg, Thuringia (developing an urban greening programme), and in Saxony (drawing up a joint land-use plan for a group of towns, based on cooperation). The game, developed by the German Federal Building Ministry, encourages towns and cities to build on the experience of other places, and organises widely based support for urban renewal on ecological principles.

modern 1 Relating to recent times. **2** Characteristic of the present; up-to-date. **3** Of an advanced style; experimental. **4** In the architectural style of the modern movement. Peter Stewart (2003) of CABE writes: '"Modern" architecture is arguably, after nearly a hundred years, just a historical style like any other'. **4** Belonging to the period since the middle ages.

modern Athens Edinburgh. Like Athens, the Scottish capital has steep hills and a separate seaport, and it is a noted centre of cultural life. *Modern Athens* was the title of a book published in 1825 and another in 1829. Queen Victoria noted in her diary in 1842: 'I hear they sometimes call Edinburgh "The Modern Athens"' (Howard, 2001). The city has also been called the ATHENS OF THE NORTH.

moderne 1 Relating to art deco and similar design styles of the 1920s and '30s. **2** Pretentiously attempting to look modern.

Modernisierung (German) Modernisation.

modernism 1 An approach to the arts and literature that breaks with traditional forms and styles. **2** Experimental work in the arts between around 1890 and 1940. According to Marshall Berman (1982), the French philosopher Jean-Jacques Rousseau was the first to use the word *modernist(e)* in the ways in which the nineteenth and twentieth centuries were to use it. Compare MODERNISTIC and MODERNITY. See also BAUHAUS.

modernist architecture 1 A range of styles and approaches to architecture that, with origins in the late nineteenth century, developed in the early years of the twentieth as an avant garde. It has been a strong theme ever since. The movement was inspired, in some modernist architects at least, by a commitment to improving social conditions by designing better buildings. Some of the architects believed that a purely functional building, well designed and true to its materials, would be beautiful and would not need ornamentation (see FORM FOLLOWS FUNCTION). Others were more concerned with designing a building that looked starkly rational than with creating an external form that did truly express its structure. Typical features of early modernist buildings included flat roofs, rectangular forms and white external walls. Buildings tended to be laid out at right angles to each other, disregarding any existing pattern of streets and rarely creating new ones that had much sense of enclosure. By the 1970s many major developments were failing either to keep out the rain or to create agreeable places. Modernism was accused of creating forms inspired solely by architects' and planners' visions, with no understanding of the history or context of the site, or of how people would use and experience the buildings and their surroundings. The PRINCE OF WALES complained of a conspiracy by the architectural establishment to deny what he claimed most other people saw as common sense. The American NEW URBANISTS ridiculed the modernists

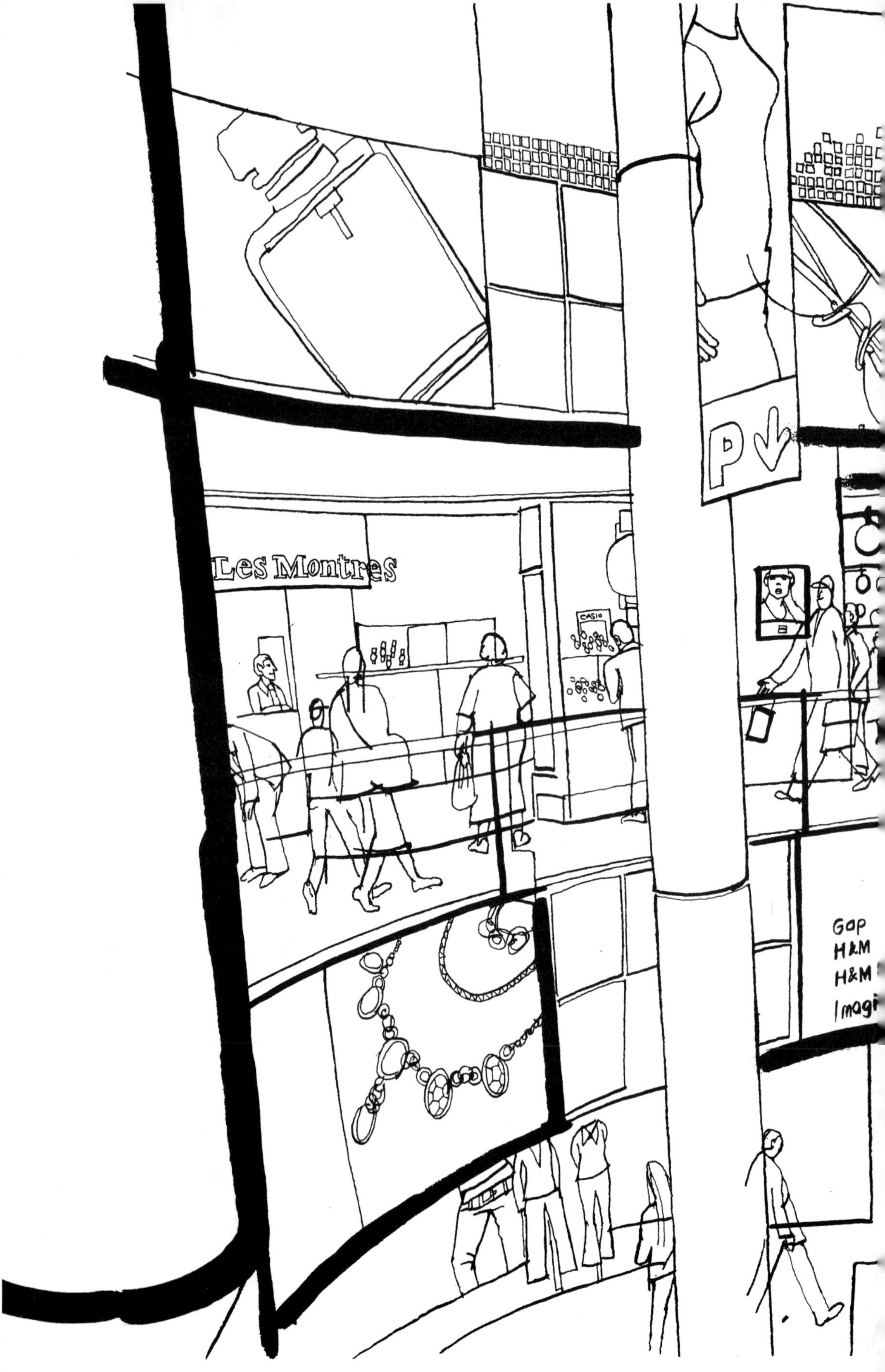
Les Montres
CASIO
P
Gap
H&M
H&M

mall

for their failure to understand how to make successful places. The backlash against modernism provided fertile ground for hi-tech architecture's exhuberant celebration of new building technologies, POST-MODERN architecture's playful popularism, and a classical revival. By the 1990s, though, modernism was making a comeback. The label no longer means anything very specific – if it ever did – but it denotes a determination by many architects to enjoy the latest building materials and techniques without feeling constrained by historical models. DoCoMoMo, the organisation devoted to promoting the documentation and conservation of works of architecture of the modern movement, naturally has to define the term, at least in relation to architecture. National DoCoMoMo groups define their own remits. 'Most countries initially depict modernism as the characteristic, flat-roofed, plain (often white), ribbon-windowed mode of the 1920s, followed by the more complex structures of the postwar period,' writes Dennis Sharp (2000). But in a country-by-country survey of modernist works published in 2000, Sharp notes, 'some countries kept rigidly to the 1920–30 period... DoCoMoMo UK came up to the 1960s... The French included the youngest building in the survey: Piano and Rogers' Centre Beaubourg (1977)... [and] Scotland decided its most recent example should be a North Sea oil rig (1978).' **2** An approach unconstrained by traditional forms and styles. See also COPY, INTERNATIONAL STYLE and MIES VAN DER ROHE.

modernistic 1 In tune with modern thought and practice. **2** Relating to art deco and similar design styles of the 1920s and '30s. The architectural modernists of the 1930s looked down on mere modernistic design, as Lord Esher (1981) recalls: 'It was mortifying and maddening that some laymen could not see the differences between modern and modernistic, the word progressives used for all the cubist-jazz-streamline derivatives of Art Deco... They little imagined that 40 years later it would be this, and not their hard-won architecture, for which the period would be affectionately remembered.'

modernity 1 The state of being modern or up-to-date. **2** Relating to MODERNIST ARCHITECTURE. Example: 'The failure of modernity is not that of architecture but that of ethics' (Rogers, 1988). **3** Relating to MODERNISM in culture and thought.

Marshal Berman (1982) explains what he sees as the distinction between *modernity, modernisation* and *modernism*. 'There is a mode of vital experience – experience of space and time, of the self and others, of life's possibilities and perils – that is shared by men and women all over the world today,' he writes. He calls this body of experience 'modernity'. 'To be modern is to find ourselves in an environment that promises us adventure, power, joy, growth, transformation of ourselves and the world – and, at the same time, that threatens to destroy everything we have, everything we know, everything we are.' Modern environments and experiences cut across all boundaries of geography and ethnicity, of class and nationality, of religion and ideology, Berman suggests. This pours all mankind into a maelstrom of perpetual disintegration and renewal, of struggle and contradiction, of ambiguity and anguish. The maelstrom of modern life has been fed from many sources, he notes: great discoveries in the physical sciences; the industrialization of production; immense demographic upheavals; rapid and often cataclysmic urban growth; systems of mass communication; increasingly powerful national states; mass social movements of people, and peoples; and an ever-expanding, drastically fluctuating capitalist world market. In the twentieth century, the social processes that bring this maelstrom into being, and keep it in a state of perpetual becoming, have come to be called 'modernization', he writes. 'These world-historical processes have nourished an amazing variety of visions and ideas that aim to make men and women the subjects as well as the objects of modernization, to give them the power to change the world that is changing them, to make their way through the maelstrom and make it their own.'

Over the past century, Berman writes, these visions and values have come to be loosely grouped under the name of 'modernism'. He divides the history of modernity, into three phases. In the first phase, roughly from the start of the sixteenth century to the end of the eighteenth, people are just beginning to experience modern life. The second phase begins with the great revolutionary wave of the 1790s. 'With the French Revolution and its reverberations, a great modern public abruptly and dramatically comes to life', though even the nineteenth-century modern public can remember what it is like to live, materially and spiritually, in worlds that are not modern at all. In the twentieth century, the third and final phase, 'the process of modernization expands to take in virtually the whole world, and the developing world culture of modernism achieves spectacular triumphs in art and thought'. On the other hand, as the modern public expands, Berman sees it as 'shattering into a multitude of fragments, speaking incommensurable private languages; the idea of modernity, conceived in numerous fragmentary ways, loses much of its vividness, resonance and depth, and loses its capacity to organize and give meaning to people's lives. As a result of all this, we find ourselves today in the midst of a modern age that has lost touch with the roots of its own modernity.'

Patsy Healey (1988) argues that the concept of 'modernity', as a primary intellectual/cultural influence in Western thought since the eighteenth century, needs to be distinguished from 'modernism' and 'post-modernism' in art and architecture. The latter, she writes, are specific tendencies or styles *within* western culture, developing from the late nineteenth century, with post-modernism gathering impetus from the 1960s. She sees a link between the challenge to 'modernity' and post-modernism, which lies in the rejection of rationalism, but warns that the link needs to be carefully spelled out rather than collapsing the one into the other.

modular home (US) One built in a factory and installed on site under regulations in the local building code. Compare MANUFACTURED HOME.

module See PREFAB.

modulor A system of proportion developed by LE CORBUSIER, based on the ratio between a man's standing height and the distance between his outstretched arms.

Mollison, Bill (b1928) He developed and promoted the theory and practice of permaculture, an integrated system of design encompassing not only agriculture, horticulture, architecture and ecology but also money management, land access strategies, and legal systems for businesses and communities. The aim is to create systems that provide for their own needs, do not pollute and are SUSTAINABLE. Conservation of soil, water and energy are central issues to permaculture. Mollison received the RIGHT LIVELIHOOD AWARD in 1981. 'All my life we've been at war with nature,' he writes. 'I just pray that we lose that war. There are no winners.'

Mo-mo DETROIT (*mo*tor town).

Monadnock building 'The first modern building in which the architect rejected ornament completely and expressed his vision sheerly through mass and structure,' according to Donald L Miller (1996). It was designed by Burnham and Root and built in Chicago in 1891.

Mondeo man A stereotype identified in the mid-1990s: a person whose possession of a smart but unexciting family car such as a Ford Mondeo symbolised his new prosperity. The Labour party sought the support of such people in planning its 1997 election victory, and was afterwards conscious of the risks of alienating them by transport policies which could be construed as being anti-car. Forerunners of the term include *Cortina man*, named after an earlier Ford car. *Vectra man* was a variant recorded in 2002.

money markets Markets for short-term debt securities. Compare CAPITAL MARKETS.

Montgomery of Skelmorlie, Robert (Sir) As governor of Carolina he prepared the unrealised plan for the colony of Azilia, centred on a new town (Rykwert, 2000).

mongoose architecture A pejorative term for a series of buildings that all face in the same direction (overlooking a river, for example) instead of contributing to a more thoughtful piece of urban design.

monitoring Assessing the effect of policy, guidance or action. Reyner Banham (1969), paraphrasing Melvin Webber, wrote: 'Planning is the only branch of knowledge purporting to be some kind of science which regards a plan as being fulfilled when it is merely completed; there's seldom any sort of check on whether the

> **"PLANNING IS THE ONLY BRANCH OF KNOWLEDGE PURPORTING TO BE SOME KIND OF SCIENCE WHICH REGARDS A PLAN AS BEING FULFILLED WHEN IT IS MERELY COMPLETED"**
>
> *Reyner Banham*

plan actually does what it is meant to do, and whether, if it does something different, this is for the better or for the worse.' See also IMPLEMENTATION.

monochronic space See POLYCHRONIC SPACE.

monocultural planning That which relates to an area for a single use (such as warehousing, offices or housing).

monotony Dull uniformity. In 1967 the American Institute of Architects applauded the *consistency* of CUMBERNAULD new town's 'grey monochrome with occasional colour relief', arguing that *monotony* had been avoided by variety in building types, siting and street landscaping (Glendinning and Page, 1999). The word was once used in a positive sense: in 1894 the architect Thomas Hastings wrote of the ideal streetscape as possessing 'a charming unity and monotony' (Goldberger, 1981).

Monstopolis The fictional setting of the animated film Monster Inc, released in 2002.

monstrous carbuncle The speech by the PRINCE OF WALES to the RIBA at Hampton Court Palace in 1984 famously described the competition-winning, proposed extension to the National Gallery in London's Trafalgar Square by architects Ahrends, Burton and Koralek as 'a monstrous carbuncle on the face of a much-loved and elegant friend'. The prince's criticism helped ensure that the design was not built, and the architects claimed that their reputation was permanently damaged. The prince was said by some to have got the phrase from his wife's stepmother, Lady Raine Spencer. A carbuncle is a dangerous and disfiguring inflammation of the subcutaneous tissue, as well as being (which was not what the prince had in mind) a precious gem of deep red colour. The word comes from the Latin *carbunculus*, meaning a little coal. Compare THE GREAT WEN.

MONTAGUE-BARLOW, ANDERSON

Montague-Barlow, Anderson (Sir) (1868–1951) See BARLOW COMMISSION.

monument See ANCIENT MONUMENT.

monumental architecture Buildings that symbolise power.

monumentenwacht (Dutch) Monument watch, a Dutch system under which teams of maintenance workers make regular visits to historic properties before specific problems arise. It inspired an equivalent organisation, Maintain UK.

moocher (US) A pejorative term for a beggar. See MOPER and VAGRANT.

moose in a city Toronto's equivalent of the COW PARADE programme.

moped mayor Fransesco Rutelli, the moped-riding Green politician who became mayor of Rome in 1993.

moper (US) A pejorative tem for a beggar. See MOOCHER and VAGRANT.

moral quadrilateral A type of quadrangle of buildings proposed by ROBERT OWEN, industrialist founder of New Lanark in Scotland. One side was a factory, and the others accommodated a dining room, rooms for meetings and recreation, and housing. Owen thought such an arrangement would benefit the workers' morals.

Morgan, Edwin Poet. He was made Glasgow's poet laureate in 1999. His poem 'Trio' is characteristic of his celebration of the city's life. Passing three youngsters in the street at Christmas – a boy with a guitar, a girl with a baby and another girl with a small dog, he comments: 'Orphean sprig! Melting baby! Warm chihuahua!/ The vale of tears is powerless before you./ Whether Christ is born or not born, you/ Put paid to fate.../ Monsters of the year go blank, are scattered back,/ Can't bear this march of three.'

morphogenesis The origins of form (of, for example, an urban area).

morphological frame A feature or set of features that play an important part in shaping a place's development.

morphological process One that shapes urban form.

morphological region An area of basically homogenous urban form. See MORPHOTYPE.

morphologist One who studies morphology.

morphology The study of form. The term was coined by Johann Wolfgang von Goethe (1749–1832), the German writer and polymath, whose scientific interests included geology. Goethe proposed morphology as a possible general science of outward description.

Morphopolis A small-scale replica of central Paris whose inhabitants are in the course of a 300-year sleep. The city was built and populated with volunteers following the invention of a drug capable of putting people in suspended animation. They are due to wake up in 2250. The story is told in Maurice Barrère's *The City of Sleep* (1929).

morphotype The smallest type of area of basically homogenous urban form. The term was used by MRG CONZEN. See MORPHOLOGICAL REGION.

William Morris

Morris, William (1834–96) Writer, designer and campaigner for socialism, and for high standards of craftsmanship and of urban, building and product design. See NEWS FROM NOWHERE.

Morrison, Arthur (1863–1945) Novelist. In *A Child of the Jago* (1896) and *The Hole in the Wall* (1902) he exposed the grim living conditions of London's East End.

Morrison, Herbert (1888–1965) Politician. As leader of the London County Council from 1934 he instituted a town planning scheme for the whole of London.

mosaic A place where people from different cultures and races live alongside one other. Compare MELTING POT.

Moseley, William See CRYSTAL WAY.

Moses, Robert (1888–1981) US public official responsible for large-scale infrastructure and urban renewal projects in New York, including 12 bridges, the Lincoln Center, Shea Stadium and numerous parks (together with the parkways that serve them). He was notorious for the huge public housing schemes he built in the 1940s and '50s, and for the expressways he constructed in New York City and State from the 1930s to the '60s. Moses ruthlessly ploughed through neighbourhoods on the expressways' routes. 'When you operate in an overbuilt metropolis,' he explained, 'you have to hack your way with a meat axe.' The writer Edmund Wilson, affirming the land rights of native Americans against Moses' electricity-generating projects, spoke of his 'blind will to build dams, indifference to the landscape, leaving devastation all around'.

Robert Moses

Mother Jacobs The derisive name LEWIS MUMFORD gave to JANE JACOBS, whose prescriptions for cities he characterised as a 'homemade poultice for the cure of cancer' (quoted by Johnson, 2001).

motherhood policy A planning policy so general and uncontroversial that almost no one could disagree with it. 'Development must be of high quality' is a typical example. They serve little purpose apart from conveying a vague idea of the local authority's aspirations. The term derives from the American phrase *motherhood and apple pie* (which refers to the only two supposedly indisputably good things in the US).

mother-in-law apartment (US) A small extension to a house, intended for an elderly relative. The UK equivalent is *granny flat*.

motion awareness Defined by KEVIN LYNCH (1960) as 'the qualities which make sensible to the observer, through both the visual and the kinaesthetic senses, his own actual or potential motion'.

motopia A place designed primarily to serve the interests of motor transport. Compare AUTOPIA.

motor city 1 DETROIT, centre of the USA's motor industry in the first half of the twentieth century. Noting its catastrophic industrial decline since the 1970s, Sir Peter Hall (1998) speculates that Detroit could become, 'before long, the first major industrial city in history to revert to farmland'. **2** Coventry, centre of the UK's motor industry until the 1980s.

motor *n.* A motor car. Shortening *motor car* to *motor*, rather than to the more usual *car*, is a specifically working class use in the UK. *v.* To drive. In contrast to the noun, the use of *motor* as a verb is specific to the upper classes in the UK.

motor slum (US) Poor-quality development and unplanned, assorted uses lining a busy road, where the traffic level makes residential use undesirable and significant business uses are not feasible. The term was used in the 1930s, particularly by advocates of FREEWAYS. Example: 'The motor slum in the open country is today as massive a piece of defilement as the worst of the old-fashioned urban industrial slums' (regional planner Benton MacKaye in 1932).

motor vehicle A mechanically propelled vehicle intended or adapted for use on roads.

motorisation The rate of car ownership and use; an increase in this.

motorway A high-speed road, reserved for motor vehicles only and uninterrupted by crossings (UK). Equivalents are *freeway* (US) and *autobahn* (German). Sir Peter Hall (1998) writes that the Long Island Motor Parkway, built 1906–11, 'could claim to be the first motorway'. In 1930 a Royal Commission in the UK concluded that there was no need for a system of 'Motor-Ways' (Hall, 1990). The UK's first motorway, the Preston bypass in Lancashire (now part of the M6), opened in 1958. The UK's first 1,000 miles were completed in 1971. See also URBAN MOTORWAY.

motorway box An urban motorway through inner London (later called Ringway 1) proposed by the Greater London Council in 1965. It was abandoned by a new political administration in 1973.

motorway city of the seventies Leeds and Rotherham both adopted this title. Leeds was still claiming it on postal franking at the start of the 1980s.

Motorways versus Democracy A book by JOHN TYME, published in 1978, on public inquiries into road proposals and their political significance as, he claimed, a threat to democracy.

Motown 1 DETROIT, in pop music parlance. **2** The Motown record label, founded and run in Detroit by Berry Gordy Jr (see DANCING IN THE STREET). Richard Williams (2000) notes that the Motown label was a unified creative force with a strong geographical identity from the early 1960s until it moved to Hollywood in 1972. 'To the people of Detroit, their lives already undermined by the slow decline of the American automobile industry, the departure had an altogether more intimate and profound significance,' Williams writes. The word is a contraction of motor town.

Mott, Seward The designer of the housing layouts promoted by the Federal Housing Administration in the USA after 1934.

Mount Laurel (US) A series of legal cases in the 1970s focusing on the use of zoning to exclude low-income housing from an area.

mousehole *v.* To enter a house by blowing a hole in a side wall instead of using the door. This method, used by soldiers in house searches to avoid triggering trip wires and having to show themselves in the street, has been a feature of modern urban warfare in Palestine and Iraq, among other places. It tends to cause civilian casualties. Mouseholing is also used by thieves ripping out fittings from streets of derelict houses. See also BREAK THE CHINA, FIBUA and MOUT.

mout (US) A military acronym for *military operations in urban terrain*. The UK equivalent is *fibua* (fighting in built-up areas). See also BREAK THE CHINA and MOUSEHOLE.

moveable feast, a The writer Ernest Hemingway's description of Paris. 'If you are lucky enough to have lived in Paris as a young man,' he told a friend in 1950, 'then wherever you go for the rest of your life, it stays with you, for Paris is a moveable feast.' Hemingway's autobiographical book *A Moveable Feast* was published in 1964.

movement People and vehicles going to and passing through buildings, places and spaces. The movement network can be shown on plans, by SPACE SYNTAX ANALYSIS, by highway designations, by FIGURE/GROUND DIAGRAMS, through data on origins and destinations or pedestrian flows, by DESIRE LINES, by details of public transport services, by WALK BANDS or by details of cycle routes.

The single most powerful influence on the density of building and the intensity of activity in any part of a city is the routes that pass through it. That was always so: villages grew where highways met, towns developed at river crossings, high streets flourished on busy roads. The vitality of a place and its potential to renew itself are determined in large part by people moving through it (on foot and by public transport, and to a lesser extent by car). The network of routes determines where people change from one mode of transport to another, where different people find themselves in the same place for different reasons, and where journeys are slowed or interrupted. All of these lead to people exchanging things: goods, information, money, favours, gossip, ideas and anything else. Exchange is the life of the city. Streets, squares and quarters will make lively places only if they are connected to the city's network of movement. If they are not connected, the efforts of even the best designers and planners will be frustrated.

The architectural critic Peter Buchanan (1988) has written: 'Movement in contemporary British planning and architecture is nearly always treated as circulation alone, as mere motion in the gaps and residual areas between buildings or blocks of development. Even when formalised as streets, these are little more than voids (even if in turn neatly furnished and landscaped). They merely provide access and form boundaries between neat parcels of development in which all functions, even shopping, are located at some remove from the street, each as a distinct and separate destination. The underlying model is at best suburban, which whether in its traditional residential form or in one of its contemporary manifestations as a business park is always characterised by the absence of a contiguous and active public realm. But it is only in historically recent times, with the coming of the railways and even more recently of limited access roads, that movement is found separated spatially and functionally in the city. Before that, and still today in any urban situation, movement is always inextricably linked with – and indeed usually generates – other activities, both adjacent and within the same external space. The various activities and the interactions between them that are allowed and shaped by the spaces of the movement network, and of course the spaces themselves, constitute the major part of any city's public realm. Together they give any city its particular flavour and identity, and much else besides.'

The architect and critic Michael Sorkin (1991) has questioned whether the increasing sameness of cities (see LOCAL DISTINCTIVENESS) – putting at risk 'the idea of cities as zones of the particular' – might make much movement redundant. 'One can easily imagine the day in which both the economic and the experiential basis for motion is altogether nullified,' he writes. 'As the whole world becomes nodalised – every place simply a station on an endless pilgrimage route to nowhere – urbanity, our greatest armature for the nurturing and accommodation of difference, would indeed be rendered obsolete' (compare TERMINAL ARCHITECTURE). Sorkin continues: 'We would then be reduced to perfect Cartesian subjects, enjoying our democratic rights of renunciation over all that distinguishes us, joining the lemming march to the melting pot of miserable, windowless, market-driven monads.'

movement economy The urban system consisting of a relationship between fixed elements (the physical and spatial structure) and movement elements (routes). The concept is central to SPACE SYNTAX ANALYSIS.

movers and shakers People of power and influence. The phrase was first used by Arthur O'Shaunessy in a song.

Moynihan, Daniel Patrick (1927–2003) Politician and an academic. Remarkably he served four successive Washington administrations: the Democrats under John Kennedy and Lyndon Johnson (whom he advised on urban affairs) and the Republicans under Richard

Nixon and Gerald Ford. At Harvard University he was director of the centre for urban studies. He was succeeded as senator for New York by Hillary Rodham Clinton.

MUDS Report The Minister's Urban Design Skills report, published in 2001, was commissioned by the DETR and chaired by CABE. It examined the need for more urban design skills and potential ways of meeting them.

muesli A metaphor for mixed-use development, used by the Civic Trust in commenting on the launch of an urban design competition for the MARSHAM STREET site in 1996. Mixed-use muesli should replace the 'toast rack' of the existing building (an image suggested by its three parallel blocks linked by a podium) that was, the Civic Trust suggested, 'a characteristic 1960s dog's breakfast'. The breakfast metaphors were offered in recognition of the media's taste for striking images to describe buildings in the news, though in this case without prompting any significant response. See also SPOTTED DICK and compare PORRIDGE.

mug To attack or threaten a person in the street with intent to rob. The term originally meant to punch in the face. The word 'mug' for 'face' derives from the drinking vessel. See also CHARITY MUGGER.

muggers' alley A popular name for any narrow passageway where people passing through feel unsafe, usually due to the route not being overlooked by people in nearby buildings or spaces, and the absence of other people on foot. See DEFENSIBLE SPACE and FOOTPADS' PARADISE.

Muir, John (1838–1914) Botanist, and founder of the USA's national parks and American conservation movement. He was brought up in an ultra-strict Presbyterian sect, in Scotland until the age of 10 and then in Ohio after his family emigrated. Muir rejected his father's belief that God had made nature for mankind to dominate. He valued the world's wild places as most valuable when mankind left them alone. 'In God's wildness lies the hope of the world, the great fresh unblighted, unredeemed wilderness,' he wrote. 'The galling harness of civilisation drops off, and wounds heal.' See also WILDERNESS.

Mulford Robinson, Charles (1869–1917). Architect. A leader of the American CITY BEAUTIFUL MOVEMENT.

multi (Scotland) *n.* A block of multi-storey housing.

multidisciplinary Involving people with different skills and experience working alongside each other. Compare INTERDISCIPLINARY, INTER-PROFESSIONAL and MULTIPROFESSIONAL.

multi-modal Relating to several different means of transport.

multi-modal transit station See TRANSPORT INTERCHANGE.

multi-neighbourhood centre (US) A shopping, services and employment centre serving more than one neighbourhood.

multiple deprivation The concentration in an area of characteristics such as unemployment, poor housing, ill health, crime, few facilities and poor public transport. See also POVERTY.

multiple use MIXED USE. FJ OSBORN suggested in 1963 that the *Architectural Review* had invented the then-current phrase (Hughes, 1971).

multiplex A multi-screen cinema complex. Stephen Barber (2002) evocatively, if not wholly convincingly, accuses this new urban form of destroying the relationship that he says once existed between filmic culture and the city. Travelling through Europe, he reports, 'I met identical multiplex architecture and the same blank faces. In those corporate hangers, the stultified populations vacillated between adhering displays of products and fast-food counters, until almost by malign accident they arrived in the rooms where Hollywood films composed almost entirely of digital effects battled in void, self-referential competition with one another, parallel universes away from their spectators. In these brutal multiplexes, the space of cinema stood infinitely removed from its former inhabitation of the city's central boulevards, where it had determined its spectators' intimate visual rapport with that place.'

multiplex city One with many networks of social and economic life.

multiplier The secondary effects of the economic activity generated by economic development or regeneration.

multiplier effect The indirect positive effects of a regeneration project.

multiprofessional Involving people from different professions working alongside each other. Compare INTERDISCIPLINARY, INTERPROFESSIONAL and MULTIDISCIPLINARY.

multi-screen/multiplex cinema Defined by the Scottish Office (1998) as a development of at least five cinema screens.

multivariate analysis A technique, developed in the 1960s, for comparing urban areas.

Mumford, Lewis (1895–1990) Writer and influential advocate of regional planning. Born in New York, Mumford was professor of humanities at Stanford University, and professor of city planning at the University of Pennsylvania. He studied American literature, the history of technology, urban and regional development, and the origins and history of cities. He was a passionate disciple of PATRICK GEDDES, though never as close a collaborator as Geddes hoped. Geddes saw in Mumford's literary talents the potential means of creating the accessible and popular books that he himself had never written. Mumford, though, found that he had to digest the master's teachings and develop the ideas in his own way, rather than act as his amanuensis.

Mumford's books included *The Story of Utopias* (1922), *Technics and Civilisation* (1934), *The Culture of Cities* (1938) and *The City in History* (1961). He campaigned against the appeasement of fascism in the 1930s, the nuclear arms race after the 1939–45 war, and the Vietnam war. He supported the UK GARDEN CITIES and NEW TOWNS movements, expressing his enthusiasm

Lewis Mumford

and occasional disagreements (particularly on what he saw as the new towns' excessively low housing densities) in a long correspondence with FJ OSBORN. He was an honorary member of the architectural and planning institutes in both the USA and the UK. See also GENERALIST, MOTHER JACOBS, NEW URBAN ORDER and REGIONAL PLANNING ASSOCIATION OF AMERICA.

Muncie, Indiana See PEOIRA.

Mundey, Jack See GREEN BAN.

municipal engineer See ENGINEER.

municipal housekeeping See JANE ADDAMS.

Municon Valley The Munich region in Bavaria since becoming the centre of the German microelectronics industry after the 1939–45 war (Hall, 1998). The analogy is with SILICON VALLEY.

murage A tax levied by a borough in medieval England to pay for building or maintaining town walls.

MURB (North America) Multi-unit residential building. The UK equivalent is HOUSE IN MULTIPLE OCCUPATION.

museumisation A pejorative term for the process of preserving a historic place for the benefit of visitors.

mushroom town One that sprang up to serve the needs of people building or operating canals or railways (Ward, 1998).

Music City Nashville, Tennessee.

music Many shops and other semi-public places use music to attract or relax customers, or to repel visitors deemed undesirable. A shopping mall near Sydney, Australia, for example, was reported in 2000 to have found a new role for piped music. 'We started playing Bing Crosby's records through the mall's PA system as an experiment,' a spokesman said, 'and quickly found that teenagers who normally hang around causing trouble couldn't stand the music or lyrics, and soon moved on. One song in particular, "My Heart is Taking Lessons", drove them up the wall, and even though most of the shopkeepers hate it too, that's a small price to pay for improved security.' In 2003 the City of Stoke-on-Trent Council decided to play Beethoven's ninth symphony continuously in a multi-storey car park in an attempt to rid it of ROUGH SLEEPERS. That same symphony had been the obsession of the central character Alex in *A Clockwork Orange* (see CLOCKWORK ORANGE CHIC), who was himself notably antagonistic to vagrants. See also CAPITAL OF ALL MUSIC, CHERYOMUSHKI, THE CLASH, DANCING IN THE STREET, DEAD CITIES, DOWNTOWN, EUPHONIA, CHARLES IVES, LIP-SYNC ARCHITECTURE, A LONDON OVERTURE, LONDON SYMPHONY, MAHAGONNY, MOTOWN, MUZAK, RAP, SUMMER IN THE CITY, URBAN MUSIC, WEST SIDE STORY and WHISTLING.

Musical City See EUPHONIA.

mutual aid agreement (US) Between two or more authorities who provide services (a fire service, for example) jointly.

mutuality Sharing benefits within a community. See also DEVELOPMENT TRUST.

muzak Deliberately bland MUSIC played in a shop, restaurant or other semi-public place with the aim of relaxing customers without being noticed. Some people, though, find it intensely irritating. The word was coined as a brand name by one company that supplied tapes of such music.

N

nabe (US) The NEIGHBOURHOOD.

Nachbarschaft (German) A neighbourhood.

nachhaltige Entwicklung (German) SUSTAINABLE development.

Nairn, Ian (1930–83) Writer. As the author of OUTRAGE, *The American Landscape*, *Nairn's London*, and *Nairn's Paris*, he communicated his passionate and personal responses to the world around him. His appreciation of architecture recognised no barriers. 'I don't believe in the difference between high- and lowbrow, between aristocracy and working class, between fine art and fine engineering,' he wrote in *Nairn's London* (1966). 'All are tilting horses erected by paper men because they can't or daren't recognise the golden thread of true quality.' Nairn was associated with TOWNSCAPE movement led by the *Architectural Review*.

Nakagin Capsule Tower See MICROFLAT.

names KEVIN LYNCH (1960) stresses the importance of names in giving meaning to and 'enhancing the IMAGEABILITY' of an urban ELEMENT. See also SILKINGRAD.

Napoleon of Notting Hill, The GK Chesterton's fable, published in 1904, imagines London in the future, with locales like Notting Hill enjoying a fairy-tale sovereignty.

narrative of use A written description of how a proposed development would be used. The description may reflect what would be the differing experiences of different types of user.

Nash, John (1752–1835) Architect, planner and developer. He laid out London's REGENT'S PARK and Regent Street after 1811, built Carlton House Terrace and began Buckingham Palace. See also ROYAL MILE.

National Evils and Practical Remedies See JAMES SILK BUCKINGHAM.

national fresh air tax See GREEN BELT.

national park authority (UK) Responsible for planning and management in a national park.

national park management plan (UK) Made by a NATIONAL PARK AUTHORITY, setting out its policies and management strategy.

national parks (UK) Set up under the National Parks Act 1949.

National Planning Basis, The A proposal, published in 1941 by the TOWN AND COUNTRY PLANNING ASSOCIATION and supported by a number of other organisations, calling for GREEN BELTS, NEW TOWNS, regional policy and a Ministry of Planning.

National Register of Historic Places (US) The federal government's list of properties worthy of preservation.

national scenic area (Scotland) An area for whose protection the local authority has special responsibility.

national strategy for neighbourhood renewal (England) A government programme aimed at combating SOCIAL EXCLUSION launched in 2000.

National Trust (England and Wales) Founded in 1895 to preserve places of historic interest or natural beauty permanently for the nation, the trust has the unique statutory power to declare land inalienable (such land can not be voluntarily sold, mortgaged or compulsorily purchased against the trust's wishes without special parliamentary procedure). Andrew Saint notes that the most significant single aim of the trust's founders (the housing reformer OCTAVIA HILL, the lawyer Robert Hunter and the clergyman – at one time of a London slum parish – Hardwick Rawnsley) was that of saving beautiful and historic landscapes for the recreation of the urban masses in what they called 'open-air sitting rooms for the poor'.

national/regional planning Large-scale, economic development planning, relating the development of each region to the progress of the national economy. Peter Hall (2002) uses the term to distinguish that type of planning from the smaller-scale, physical type he calls regional/local planning.

NATO (Narrative Architecture Today) A group of architects, formed in London in the early 1980s, promoting (mainly through journals and exhibitions) an approach to architecture that delighted in the messy complexity of cities. 'Only by metamorphosing the madness of life into the magic of architecture', the critic Brian Hatton wrote approvingly, 'are we going to get real cities, and not the monofunctionally zoned zombie/gnomescapes that the unholy alliance of the market and misunderstood modernism has produced in our midst' (quoted in Coates, 1988).

Natty Cincinnati, Ohio.

natural access control A means of controlling the movement of people or vehicles by the physical characteristics of buildings or space. See also NATURAL SURVEILLANCE.

natural capital Resources provided by natural systems.

natural capitalism A concept, described in 1999 by the environmentalist Amory Lovins, of an alternative to market capitalism. Natural capitalism, Lovins suggests, values the Earth as its largest source of capital, rather than liquidating it.

natural estate (Australia) Defined by the Australian Heritage Commission Act 1975 as 'those places, being components of the natural cultural environment of Australia, that have aesthetic, historic, scientific or social significance or other special value for future generations in terms of their scientific research, social aesthetic and life-support value.' See REGISTERED PLACE.

natural heritage area (Scotland) An area of outstanding value which needs particularly careful management.

natural light Combined skylight and sunlight. Also called *daylight*.

natural movement The movement through an urban space that is determined by the structure of the urban grid rather than by specific buildings or activities that attract people. Natural movement is an important concern of SPACE SYNTAX ANALYSIS.

natural presence The presence of users of a street or other public space, generally making it feel safer.

natural surveillance (also supervision) The discouragement to wrong-doing by the presence of passers-by or the ability of people to see out of windows. Also known as passive surveillance (or supervision). See EYES ON THE STREET, and compare FORMAL SURVEILLANCE and ORGANISED SURVEILLANCE.

nature conservation The protection and enhancement of the natural environment for the benefit of people and for its own sake.

Naturpark (German) A natural park.

Naturschutzgebiet (German) A nature protection area.

navel of the world Jerusalem, so regarded in the middle ages. The Mappamundi in Hereford Cathedral accordingly shows the city at the centre of the world. Biblical authority for this is provided by the Book of Ezekiel: 'This Jerusalem I have set in the midst of the nations round about her.'

navigable Easy to find one's way around. See LEGIBILITY.

Nazi architecture The Nazi regime in Germany in the 1930s and '40s favoured neo-vernacular architecture and, for public buildings, STRIPPED CLASSICISM (as did the Italian fascists). LÉON KRIER, an enthusiast for the classical architecture of ALBERT SPEER, regrets the negative associations that he sees classicism as having acquired. 'In Germany,' Krier (1983) writes, 'all traditional, classical architecture is still associated with tyranny and extermination under the Nazis. Architects consider that the erection of a column is more dangerous than a nuclear power station. The construction of a splendid classical colonnade alarms them much more than a line of tanks coming from the Krupp factories.' In Krier's view classicism is not inherently totalitarian. On the contrary, he argues, the Nazis' classical architecture was 'the civilized face, the aesthetic and cultured façade of this empire of lies, and was used by the regime to implant its totalitarian rule in the captivated soul of the masses. Classical architecture is quite simply incapable of imposing terror by the force of its internal laws. As a part of the totalitarian system, it was chosen only as an efficient form of lie and deceptive promise.' See also EQUILIBRIUM.

Nazi planning See HANS BERNHARD REICHOW.

nearness See PROPINQUITY.

neckdown A kerb extension at the corner of an intersections designed to slow vehicles and give pedestrians a shorter distance to cross. A BULBOUT is similar. See TRAFFIC CALMING.

neebourheid (Scots) A NEIGHBOURHOOD.

negative equity A situation in which the sum owed by the owner of a property on an outstanding loan or mortgage exceeds property's current value. Negative equity is created when property prices fall dramatically. Owners who have negative equity may be unable to afford to move home, even if they can no longer afford the cost of their present home.

negative site A piece of land that detracts from the quality of the area.

negative space That which is poorly defined, hardly enclosed, and difficult to make sense of. The opposite of *positive space*.

neighborhood traffic management plan Guidelines for managing traffic problems throughout an area. See also TRAFFIC CALMING.

neighbour A person who lives near another. The 1993 British Crime Survey found that one third of all home-based violence was caused by neighbours.

neighbour noise Unwanted noise from neighbours and from nearby activities such as building sites.

neighbourhood 1 A district or locality. 2 The area around some place or thing. 3 An identifiable part of an urban area; an area of mixed uses that is integrated into the structure of the city. The American Planning Association (1998) has defined a neighborhood as 'a diverse, dynamic social and economic entity with unique characteristics, which are recognized by residents of both the neighborhood and community at large'. **4** A planned 'urbanised area with a balanced mix of human activity... structured around a defined centre' (Duany and Plater-Zyberk, 1994). **5** A developer's term for a housing development. Example: 'Planning approval has been granted for the first phase of a brand-new neighbourhood outside Harlow, Essex, comprising 2,500 homes for about 7,000 people' (2001). **6** (Scots) Friendly, social relations (Warrack, 2000).

The concept of neighbourhood has its origins in distant history and has been central to much urban thinking in the past century. Runes and Schrickel (1946) note that 'the history of the neighbourhood unit goes back at least as far as about 793 AD, in Kyoto, Japan'. LEWIS MUMFORD (1961) wrote of Thomas More's 1516 book UTOPIA: 'Each Utopian city is divided into four quarters... But the more intimate organization, the neighbourhood, is based on the family... The basis of [the] whole system of representative government is the [neighbourhood of 30 families]'. Ebenezer Howard's original diagram of a garden city, published in 1898, showed it divided into WARDS (neighbourhoods) of around 5,000 people. The New York *Independent* newspaper argued in 1902 that large apartment houses destroyed 'neighborhood feeling, helpful friendships, church connections and those homely common interests which are the foundations of civic pride and duty' (Sennett, 1990). LETCHWORTH Garden City, begun in 1903, was designed with four 'neighbourhood units', each with public buildings, shops, schools and a green (Burnett, 1986). The sociologist Charles Horton Cooley stressed the importance of the *primary group* in cities: the family, the play-group of children and the neighbourhood (White, 1962). Writing in 1909, Cooley warned that: 'The intimacy of the neighborhood has been broken up by the growth of an intricate mesh of wider contacts which leaves us strangers to people who live in the same house... In our own cities the crowded tenements and the general economic and social confusion have sorely wounded the family and the neighborhood, but it is remarkable, in view of these conditions, what vitality they show; and there is nothing upon which the conscience of the time is more determined than upon restoring them to health.'

The neighbourhood as a planning concept was developed by the US planner Clarence Perry in around 1923, under the influence of RAYMOND UNWIN. Lewis Mumford (1961) wrote that Clarence Perry framed the concept of the neighbourhood unit 'after experiencing the benefits of a well-planned suburban environment as a resident of a model suburban development on Long Island, Forest Hill Gardens'. Perry had made 'more explicit, in a better defined structure, the life that he had there found rewarding.' Perry called in the New York Regional Survey of 1929 for neighbourhood units to be planned each with a quarter-mile radius, an area of around 160 acres, housing for enough people to require one elementary school, and 10 per cent of the area given over to recreation and park space. 'Neighborhood institutions' should be housed at its centre and its shape should be roughly circular.

Barry Parker's 1930 plan for WYTHENSHAWE divided the new town into neighbourhood units. The Federal Housing Administration in the 1930s published an influential pamphlet with the title *Planning Profitable Neighbourhoods*. The 1943 County of London Plan designated 11 'neighbourhoods' for comprehensive redevelopment. LANSBURY, the 1951 Festival of Britain's exhibition of 'live architecture', was one of them. The GREATER LONDON PLAN of 1944 also featured neighbourhood units. Miles Glendinning (2000) notes that in the 1940s 'there was much in common between the social-democratic and fascist replanning ideas: even at the height of the war, Hamburg's principal planner, Konstanty Gutschow, drew on the contemporary London neighbourhood-unit plans by PATRICK ABERCROMBIE as a model for rebuilding the city just incinerated by British bombers.' Many of the post-war NEW TOWNS in the UK were planned on neighbourhood principles. A study by the sociologist Ruth Glass (1948), though, cast doubt on the usefulness of the concept of neighbourhood to describe the social structure of working-class areas. Social networks and geographical areas did not coincide, she found. The new-town campaigner FJ OSBORN also had doubts about the neighbourhood concept. He told Lewis Mumford in 1952: 'I have not written much about the neighbourhood, but... I do not really believe in the Village within the Town; I mean that I do not believe it can be created by the physical structure of a neighbourhood and its centre... It is... the isolation – or rather the distance from other groups of people – that produces the more concentrated interchange between people in a village or small town; not its physical layout' (Hughes, 1971). Tim Mars (1998) notes that 'the residential areas in MILTON KEYNES [designated as a new town in 1967] were deliberately not called "villages" or even "neighbourhoods" but "grid squares" – a neutral, technical term for parcels of land carved up by the grid roads'. By the early 1970s John Parker (1973) was writing that 'town planners... have for many years been almost obsessively preoccupied with the idea of fostering "community feeling" following a brand of determinism strongly expressed in the neighbourhood unit concept, which was the characteristic feature of so many development plans...

The original neighbourhood unit idea has become largely discredited as a planning concept.'

Looking back at the history of neighbourhood planning, Donald Appleyard (1980) noted that: 'The neighborhood unit was conceived not only as a bounded social enclave, but also as a protection from traffic. Though attacked later for its social exclusiveness on the one hand and for its ineffectiveness in the socially and physically mobile world of the modern city on the other,... the concept endures with remarkable tenacity. The neighborhood concept is to be found in plans throughout the country and the world.' He added: 'While the original ideas of creating urban villages failed to materialize in the complete sense in which they were conceived, the concerns of the two groups of critics have to some extent cancelled themselves. Physically defined neighborhoods have not necessarily become exclusive because the social and physical mobility of their residents has not confined them within neighborhood boundaries.' Appleyard reported that, despite the internecine disputes of planning theorists, in 1980 the neighborhood concept was more popular than ever, both as 'the clarion call of a widespread political movement' and a plank in US national urban policy. 'The "new" neighborhood, however,' Appleyard wrote, 'is not the bounded social enclave of the old working class, though that mythical meaning still clings to the word, but is an active political entity dedicated to defending and upgrading its local territory.' Appleyard concluded that the revival of the concept of neighborhood as a basis for traffic management and other policies seemed justified, 'as long as some of the original social baggage is dropped.'

The ideas of neighbourhood planning resurfaced in the UK's URBAN VILLAGES movement in 1989: an urban village sounded very much like a planned urban neighbourhood. Michael Sorkin's proposed 'bill of rights' of 1991 included 'the right to live in a delineable neighbourhood which offers the means of satisfaction of all basic material and spiritual needs within easy compass of the dwelling place'. The contemporary NEW URBANISTS regard the neighbourhood as one of the fundamental organising elements of new urbanism (the others are the CORRIDOR and the DISTRICT). Andres Duany and Elizabeth Plater-Zyberk (2001) argue that in contemporary America 'there are two types of urbanism available: the neighborhood, which was the model in North America from the first settlements to the second world war, and SUBURBAN SPRAWL, which has been the model since then.'

A neighbourhood unit is often seen as focusing on a primary school and having a socially mixed population of 5,000–10,000. Clarence Perry (like Ebenezer Howard, as noted above) proposed around 5,000 as a suitable population for a neighbourhood. The first MARS PLAN for London, prepared in 1937, proposed one-mile long, linear neighbourhood units with 3,340 people each. Neighbourhood units would be connected to form linear strips. In the published MARS Plan of 1942, the neighbourhood units had a population of 6,000 each, and eight of them would constitute a borough. The 1952 General Plan for Stockholm proposed neighbourhoods of 4,000–7,000 people. Barbara Ward and René Dubos (1972) reported that planners in the Soviet Union used the *micro-district* of 8,000–12,000 people as the smallest unit in their development plans. The URBAN TASK FORCE (1999b) defined a neighbourhood 'in a city-scale urban area' as having a population of 5,000–15,000 people and a radius of 400–600m. Anne Power defines an urban neighbourhood as having around 2,000 homes and 5,000 people (Power, 2000). Hildebrand Frey (1999) defines the ideal neighbourhood as having a radius of about 600 metres, a 110–120 hectare built-up area (with some additional open land), an average gross population density of around 60 persons per hectare and a population of around 7,000. Frey suggests that, hardly surprisingly, the edges of existing neighbourhoods are often defined by railway lines, major traffic routes, canals, rivers, linear green spaces or breaks in the urban fabric. Where such features do not exist, he writes, it is more difficult to define the boundaries of a neighbourhood. The journal EKISTICS defines a neighbourhood as having a population of 1,500 and a *small neighbourhood* as having 250. To the Social Exclusion Unit (2000), a neighbourhood is 'the very local level (a single estate or a few hundred houses)'. The unit notes that 'neighbourhoods are difficult to define, but generally consist of areas of a few thousand people'. According to the UK Local Government Association (2000): 'In large towns and cities, neighbourhoods are the basic building blocks, defined by how people use and relate to their local area'. The Living Villages Trust has identified between 40 and 60 houses as the ideal number for a good neighbourhood (Lipman, 2002).

New urbanists tend to define a neighbourhood according the distance able-bodied people are able to walk comfortably to a local centre. This, they say, suggests a radius of around 400 metres, which creates an area of around 50 hectares. Such a neighbourhood is not intended to be self-contained, though: neighbourhoods should be connected with each other through a continuous network of urban movement. Andres Duany and Elizabeth Plater-Zyberk (in Katz, 1994) set out some physical conventions for creating new development in neighbourhoods on traditional patterns: a) A neighbourhood should have a centre and an edge. b) The optimal size of a neighbourhood is a quarter of a mile from centre to edge. c) Neighbourhoods should have a balanced mix of activities: dwelling, shopping, working, schooling, worshipping and recreating. d) A neighbourhood should structure building sites and traffic on a fine network of interconnecting streets. e) A neighbourhood should give priority to public space and to the appropriate location of civic buildings.

A single neighbourhood standing free in the landscape is defined by the new urbanists as a *village* (Duany and Plater-Zyberk, 1994). *A New Urbanist Lexicon* (McLaughlin, 2000) defines a neighborhood as an urbanised area having a diverse range of building types, thoroughfares and public open spaces accommodating a variety of human activity. McLaughlin insists that the physical form of an 'authentic' neighborhood must conform to at least nine of the following 10 principles: a) An area of 40–160 acres. b) A minimum density of five residential units per acre. c) An internal balance of housing, jobs and services. d) An identifiable neighborhood centre. e) Designated sites for civic buildings. f) A variety of public open spaces. g) A hierarchy of interconnected streets. h) Streets for both people and cars. i) Many separate and distinct buildings. j) OUTBUILDINGS as affordable housing units.

Andres Duany calls for a neighborhood to be defined 'by its area, which is constant, not by its density which must vary according to the local market or ethos. A New England village may be four units per acre, while a New York neighborhood approaches 200 units per acre'. A *planned neighborhood*, Duany (2000) states, 'is defined by an area generally circumscribed by a quarter-mile radius, which is the equivalent of a five-minute walk'. Hugh Barton (1998a) is typical of many contemporary critics of neighbourhood planning in calling for 'local high streets, not neighbourhood centres'. He writes: 'It is important to avoid urban forms that depend for their validity on fixed local catchments. Accessibility is more likely to be achieved with forms that offer innate flexibility over time, so that facilities can come and go, increasing or decreasing their catchments as appropriate.'

In the following example, from Robert Goodman's *After the Planners* (1972), the term neighbourhood is used four times. The first time it refers to the people, the second to the place and its people, the third to the place, and the fourth to the people. 'The plan would have removed the neighbourhood in order to build a new city-wide high school... While the residents favoured the high school, they said they also wanted a proper neighbourhood to live in... They demanded that 400 units of replacement housing be built in the same neighbourhood. Visibly affected by the neighbourhood's presentation, some members of the renewal board began discussions on housing.'

Toni Morrison in her 1973 novel *Sula* describes the transformation of a *neighborhood* into a *suburb*. 'In that place, where they tore the nightshade and blackberry patches from their roots to make room for the Medallion City Golf Course, there was once a neighborhood. It stood in the hills above the valley town of Medallion and spread all the way to the river. It is called the suburbs now, but when black people lived there it was called the Bottom... Generous funds have been allotted to level the stripped and faded buildings that clutter the road from Medallion up to the golf course. They are going to raze the Time and a Half Pool Hall, where feet in long tan shoes once pointed down from chair rungs. A steel ball will knock to dust Irene's Palace of Cosmetology, where women used to lean their heads back on sink trays and doze while Irene lathered Nu Nile into their hair. Men in khaki work clothes will pry loose the slats of Reba's Grill, where the owner cooked in her hat because she couldn't remember the ingredients without it.'

One of the many New Orleans neighbourhoods featured in John Kennedy O'Toole's comic novel *A Confederacy of Dunces*, published in 1980, is a former rural settlement swallowed – but not completely digested – by the city. 'Mattie's Ramble Inn was on a corner in the Carrollton section of the city where, after having run parallel for six or seven miles, St Charles Avenue and the Mississippi meet and the avenue ends. Here an angle is formed, the Avenue and its streetcar tracks on one side, the river and levée and railroad tracks on the other. Within this angle there is a separate little neighborhood. In the air there is always the heavy, cloying odor of the alcohol distillery on the river, an odor that becomes suffocating on hot summer afternoons when the breeze blows in from the river. The neighborhood grew haphazardly a century or so ago and today looks hardly urban at all. As the city's streets cross St Charles Avenue and enter this neighborhood, they gradually change from asphalt to gravel. It is an old rural town that has even a few barns, an alienated and microcosmic village within a large city.'

Neighbour comes from the Old English words for *near* and *dweller*. The word neighbourhood followed in the first half of the fifteenth century. *Nabe* is the US slang. The Scots word is *neebourheid*.

neighbourhood agreement A formalized arrangement between residents and those responsible for delivering local services (often a social housing landlord and often developed as part of a programme of neighbourhood regeneration) over standards, response times, targets and resources. Also known as *estate agreements* and *estate contracts*.

neighbourhood beautification (US) A local programme for improving an area's appearance.

neighbourhood centre Defined by the Scottish Office (1998) as a small group of shops, typically comprising a newsagent, small supermarket/general grocery store, sub-post office and other small shops of a local nature.

neighbourhood council A locally based committee set up by a local authority to decentralise consultation and decision making.

neighbourhood management Running local services in a way that ensures they are tailored to local needs and well coordinated; defined by the Local Government Association in 2000 as aiming 'to enable communities to improve local outcomes by improving, customising and joining up local services', and by the UK government as 'coordinating services at the very local level (a single estate or a few hundred houses)'.

neighbourhood management programme A way of encouraging stakeholders to work with service providers to help improve the quality of services delivered in deprived neighbourhoods.

neighbourhood regeneration organisation The Joseph Rowntree Foundation (2001b) describes them as including partnership organisations, development trusts and rural community councils as well as more focused agencies such as schools, health centres, housing providers and faith-based organisations.

neighbourhood renewal The government's social exclusion unit prepared the National Strategy for Neighbourhood Renewal in 2000. See also URBAN RENEWAL.

neighbourhood renewal assessment Carried out to establish the basis for a RENEWAL AREA.

Neighbourhood Renewal Community Chests A government fund providing small grants for community groups.

Neighbourhood Renewal Fund Government grants to support local services in deprived areas in association with local strategic partnerships.

neighbourhood space Public space in the places where people live, including pavements, paved areas, roads, playgrounds and small parks. Pauline Gallacher (2004) writes: 'If can we agree on anything, it's on the value of the life-affirming, casual, ordinary encounters we associate with life in this part of the public realm, the local neighbourhood. Differing in complexity and texture from the city centre, this localised public domain is just as much part of the "spatial experience of democracy", and arguably more important in its ubiquity and quotidian use. The challenge for designers is to construct the context in which these unspectacular encounters may take place.'

neighbourhood spine A neighbourhood's most important street. See MAIN STREET.

Neighbourhood Support Fund A government fund helping community groups to work with young people.

neighbourhood unit See NEIGHBOURHOOD.

neighbourhood warden A person (who may previously have been unemployed for a long period) employed to help prevent crime, support community development, improve management, and also to remove graffiti and fly-posters in a town centre or on a housing estate. See also STREET WARDEN.

neighbourhood watch A series of local crime prevention schemes, first introduced in the UK in the 1980s, involving neighbours keeping an eye out for, and reporting, opportunistic crime and receiving advice from the police. (The US equivalent is the BLOCK CLUB).

neighbourWood An urban woodland planned and designed with the participation of the local community. The term was used in a EU-funded research project in 1999.

Nelessen, Anton Urban designer. See VISUAL PREFERENCE SURVEY.

Nelson, Harriet (1914–94) Actor. See OZZIE AND HARRIET.

Nelson, Ozzie (1907–75) Actor, director, producer and writer. See OZZIE AND HARRIET.

neon metropolis Las Vegas, according to the title of a book by Hal Rothman, published in 2002. The city is famed for its neon signs advertising entertainment facilities.

neonscape The appearance of an illuminated city at night.

neo-schematic See URBAN SCHEMA.

neotechnic age The coming age when humankind

will use the earth's resources sustainably. The term was coined by PATRICK GEDDES. As the stone age was divided into the paleolithic and the neolithic, Geddes (1915d) wrote, so also could two phases of the industrial age be defined: the PALAEOTECHNIC AGE and the neotechnic age.

neo-traditional design and planning New applications of traditional approaches. See NEW URBANISM.

neo-traditional planning A name used around 1990 for what was later called NEW URBANISM, with which it is now used interchangeably. Andres Duany (2000) describes neo-traditionalism as the ethos of new urbanism, characterised by the pragmatic selection of available options.

neo-vernacular A new interpretation of a VERNACULAR style of building.

nerdistan An uninspiring landscape of uncreative technological activity. The term is used by the writer Joel Kotkin (Florida, 2002).

Nesbitt, Rab C See DEATH.

net density The number of people, rooms or housing units on an actual housing area, including local streets but excluding open space, public buildings or other uses.

net internal floor area Measured between the internal faces of external walls, and excluding common parts and services.

net present value The present value of benefits minus the present value of costs. NPV is used as a measure for assessing the economic viability of road schemes.

net residential area The area of land occupied by residential development. It includes any small public or private amenity space forming an integral part of the layout, and half the width of any adjoining street, up to a maximum of 6.1 metres (20 feet).

net site housing density A measurement of housing density that includes only those areas that will be developed for housing and directly associated uses. This includes access roads within the site, private garden space, car parking areas, incidental open space and landscaping, and children's play areas where these are to be provided. It excludes major distributor roads, primary schools, open spaces serving a wider area, and significant landscape buffer strips.

The UK government's *Planning Policy Guidance Note 3: Housing* notes that 'a net site density is the most commonly used approach in allocating housing land in development plans. It is appropriate for development on infill sites where the boundaries of the site are clearly defined and where only residential uses are proposed. It is also appropriate where phased development is taking place in a major development area (perhaps spanning different plan periods) and individual housing sites have been identified. Unlike gross, neighbourhood and town/district densities, the density assumption used does not need to reflect the inclusion of non-residential uses, but is solely based on the form of housing development envisaged.'

nether world The novelist George Gissing's (1857–1903) term for London.

Nettlefold, John As a councillor in Birmingham he was an influential advocate of town planning: 'We can not hope to make Birmingham into a garden city,' he wrote in 1906, 'although something can be done towards that end, but we can, if we will, create garden suburbs around Birmingham' (quoted in Cherry, 1982). Nettlefold played a leading part in campaigning for the Housing, Town Planning etc. Act 1909, and in ensuring that Birmingham used the act's planning powers more than any other local authority.

network city A series of urban centres with particularly good transport connections. The RANDSTAD is an example.

network density The number of routes that are linked together in an area.

network pattern A web of streets intersecting, not necessarily (unlike a conventional GRID pattern) at anything like right angles (Duany, 2000).

networking Making contact with and talking to individuals or groups.

Neulin 'Newlin' or the New Berlin. The term was used by planners in the 1920s and '30s, reflecting their hopes for the city (Nicolai, 2000).

Neutra, Richard (1892–1970) Architect. See RUSH CITY.

never trust air you can't see An unknown New Yorker explaining his dislike of the countryside. See also GREENERY.

Neverwhere A fictional candle-lit world beneath London, described in Neil Gaiman's *Neverwhere* (1996).

Neville, Ralph (Sir) (1865–1930) Lawyer and promoter of garden cities. He became the chairman of the GARDEN CITY ASSOCIATION in 1901, enhancing the young organisation's influence and credibility. Neville believed that garden cities offered a means of avoiding the destructive social conflict he thought the existing cities would otherwise cause. He later became a judge. See ANTI-URBANISM.

New Adam and Eve, The A story by Nathaniel Hawthorne presenting a vision of a dead city. Adam and Eve visit Boston after its inhabitants have all disappeared. The people's fate is apparently a consequence of the artificiality of their urban life being a 'revolt against nature'.

New Ash Green A new village built in Kent from the 1960s to the mid-1980s by the developer SPAN.

New Atlantis, The A description of a utopia written by Francis Bacon and published in 1627.

New Babylon The vision of the situationist artist Constant Niewenhuys, expressed from the mid-1950s to early '70s through models, montages, manifestos, films, drawings and paintings. In the unitary urbanism of New Babylon, the whole world is a single city. Everyone is an architect, nothing is fixed and everything changes in response to changing needs. In its 1960 version, multi-level structures of 5–10 hectares, their interiors artificially lit and air-conditioned, are strung together in a chain that spreads across the landscape (Wigley, 2001). New Babylon was, in the words of the writer Brian Hatton (1999), 'a proliferating megastructure, premised on automation and the end of labour, that would simultaneously resolve global mobility with spontaneous creation of intense local ambiences in the situationist game of "unitary urbanism"... Constant's pictures and constructions... exemplified the *modus operandi* of New Babylonian living, with a... drift through miles of open-plan labyrinths and galleries, all raised on pilotis above a limitless terrain of rapid transit... Constant's aim was to split the built environment into megastructure and "situation": rational support for the irrational act.' Compare BABYLON.

new brutalism See BRUTALISM.

New City, The A series of drawings of building and town planning ideas exhibited by the Futurist architect ANTONIO SANT'ELIA in 1914.

New Commitment to Neighbourhood Renewal The government Social Exclusion Unit's programme for neighbourhood renewal.

New Commitment to Regeneration An approach to tackling regeneration through partnership at a strategic level, developed by the Local Government Association with government support in the 1990s. LOCAL STRATEGIC PARTNERSHIPS are based on its experience.

New Commune, The A settlement of the future imagined by PAUL AND PERCIVAL GOODMAN.

New Deal for Communities (England) A government programme to help deprived neighbourhoods tackle SOCIAL EXCLUSION. It supports intensive regeneration schemes that deal with problems such as poor educational standards, unemployment, crime and poor standards of health in a small number of local authorities.

New Deal for Consultants A nickname for New Deal for Communities, used by people who feel that a disproportionate amount of the funding never reaches its target communities. Compare CAPACITY BUILDING and see also DAY TRIPPER.

New Delhi The new capital for India designed by Sir Edwin Lutyens and Sir Herbert Baker.

new downtown (US) An EDGE CITY.

New Earswick See RAYMOND UNWIN.

new economy, the A knowledge-based economy where information is a commodity (Caves, 2000).

new empiricism Modernism tempered by cosiness: an architectural style identified in 1947 by the *Architectural Review*. Its English exponents included FREDERICK GIBBERD and Basil Spence.

New Harmony A cooperative, utopian settlement in Indiana, USA, developed by ROBERT OWEN. It ruined him financially after two years.

New Heptarchy, the The name PATRICK GEDDES (1915d) gave to Britain's seven CONURBATIONS.

new industrial space In a specialised meaning coined by A Scott in 1988, new industrial spaces are agglomerations of certain industries in particular locations. SILICON VALLEY is a contemporary example. See INNOVATION and compare INDUSTRIAL AREA.

New Jerusalem The holy city that will be created at the Last Judgement, according to the Bible's Book of Revelations. It has also been referred to as the CITY OF THE SUN, the City on a Hill, Thelema, and Hygeia (Girouard, 1985).

New Moscow A 1938 film by Alexander Medvedkin about Stalin's plans for the city. The film's key sequence, Stephen Barber (2002) recounts, takes place at a prestigious cinema screening where the city's architects are presenting a film of their plans. 'The projector malfunctions, so that the images jam abruptly, layering on one another in the form of superimpositions, and then reverse in time, so that Stalin's ambitions are negated, and Moscow's archaic forms – its grand cathedrals and Tsarist buildings – become presciently resuscitated as the aberrant, contemporary Moscow. And when the malfunctioning projection of the city is corrected, and the celluloid begins to run smoothly forward through linear time, the forms of the new city appear even more untenable than before, surreal and insanely grandiose.' Stalin banned the film.

New Opportunities Fund The National Lottery fund for health, education and environmental projects.

New Paris The capital of the fictional land of Antarctic France, described in Robert-Martin Lesuire's *The French Adventurer* (1792). New Paris is a replica of the capital of France, but more beautiful and without the slums.

new parochialism A term used by the Chicago School sociologist ROBERT PARK for what he thought was needed to humanize cities. See also POSITIVE PAROCHIALISM.

new partnership, the (US) A major element of the Carter administration's urban policy in the 1970s.

new settlement A small new town, typically of around 10,000 population.

New Theory of Urban Design, A A book by CHRISTOPHER ALEXANDER and others, published in 1987. The authors argue that a process motivated and guided entirely by the search for wholeness produces an entirely different effect from current practice in urban design. An urban process can generate wholeness only when the structure of the city comes from the individual building projects and the life they contain, rather than being imposed from above. The principles of such a process include: a) Every new act of construction has just one basic obligation: it must create a continuous structure of wholes around itself. b) Every building increment must help to form at least one larger whole in the city, which is both larger and more significant than itself. c) Every project must first be experienced, and then expressed, as a vision that can be seen in the inner eye (literally). It must have this quality so strongly that it can also be communicated to others, and felt by others, as a vision. d) Every building must create coherent and well-shaped public space next to it. e) In the case of a large building, the entrances, the main circulation, the main division of the building into parts, its interior open spaces, its daylight, and the movement within the building must all be coherent and consistent with the position of the building in the street and in the neighbourhood. f) The structure of every building must generate smaller wholes in the physical fabric of the building, in its structural bays, columns, walls, windows, building base, and so on – in short, in its entire physical form and appearance. g) Every whole must be a 'centre' in itself, and must also produce a system of centres around it. See also CITY IS NOT A TREE, A.

new town 1 Twenty-eight new towns were designated in the UK between 1946 and 1970. They were built, not by local authorities (which did, though, retain planning powers), but by development corporations. Unlike the garden cities, the resulting increase in land values was recouped by the government, in the form of the Treasury. Some of the new towns were intended primarily to relieve population pressure ('accommodating OVERSPILL' was the phrase of the time) in London (Stevenage, Crawley, Harlow, Hemel Hempstead, Hatfield, WELWYN GARDEN CITY, Bracknell, Basildon, MILTON KEYNES, Northampton and Peterborough), the West Midlands (Telford and Redditch), Merseyside (Skelmersdale, Runcorn and Warrington), Greater Manchester (Central Lancashire), Tyne and Wear (Newton Aycliffe, Peterlee and Washington) and the Glasgow conurbation (East Kilbride, Cumbernauld and Irvine). Others provided a focus for regeneration (Cwmbran and Newtown in Wales, Corby in north-east England, and Glenrothes and Livingston in Scotland). In some ways the British new towns have been successful. They provide employment and decent homes, and they made a good financial return on the public investment. They have had their social problems, though probably less than much other public development at their time. Their design was, as was usual at the time, dominated by the excessive requirements of highway engineers at the expense of creating much sense of URBANITY. Most of their architecture was unexciting, but the new towns were settling down to a comfortable maturity when many of the more ambitious attempts at urban architecture in other places were being bulldozed. The new towns were bitterly criticised, particularly in the 1970s, for helping to strip the old cities of their employment and most economically active citizens. It is true that they were part of a planning policy that failed to nurture the complex workings of existing urban areas, but those mistakes would have been made whether there had been a new town programme or not. And the impact of planning policy can be overstated: powerful social and economic forces drove the urban exodus that planners helped along. In 2002 the government's view of new towns seemed unenthusiastic. 'Most of them are dormitories to the big cities,' deputy prime minister JOHN PRESCOTT told the URBAN SUMMIT, 'like Basildon which is suffering from deprivation. They are not sustainable communities.' See LEWIS SILKIN. **2** A large area with a major regeneration programme. Five large areas of inner Birmingham that were redeveloped in the 1960s were called 'new towns' at the time. In 2000 the New East Manchester partnership published a framework document entitled *A New Town in the City*. See also SPUR. **3** Any planned town. In Scotland alone, for example, more than 100 planned towns and villages were built in the late eighteenth and early nineteenth century. To take two other examples: London was designed in Rome as a new town on an uninhabited forested site, as the capital city of the Roman province of Britain, and Liverpool was laid out by King John's surveyors in 1207 as a base for launching attacks on Ireland. **4** A planned extension to a town or city. The New Town of Edinburgh is an example. John Summerson (1962) records that the developers of estates in GEORGIAN London often styled themselves 'new town'. Kensington New Town, Walworth New Town and Bromley New Town (all now known without the description) were examples.

new town blues A supposed social malaise identified by the popular press in the 1950s and '60s, resulting from what was seen as the new towns' failure quickly to become mature communities with extended family networks. The diagnosis may also have been partly a backlash against the new town campaigners' sometimes extravagant claims of what new town life would be like. By the 1970s the new towns in general had been replaced in the public's planning demonology by the new city of MILTON KEYNES. The term made a rare late appearance in a speech by the Prince of Wales in 1999. Calling for the regeneration of existing urban areas, the prince said that the post-war new towns programme had transformed lives for the better 'at a price... It took years for communities to become established and we had the phenomenon of "new town blues"' (Prince of Wales, 1999).

new town neurosis A variant of NEW TOWN BLUES. The term was current in the 1960s and '70s.

new towns within cities See NEW TOWN and SPUR.

New Townsmen, The A group of four GARDEN CITY activists (EBENEZER HOWARD, FJ OSBORN, CB PURDOM and WG Taylor) who in 1918 campaigned for the government to build 100 new towns.

New Urban Order LEWIS MUMFORD's proposal for regional development with planned communities of limited size.

new urbanism The approach to town planning and urban design advocated by the CONGRESS FOR THE NEW URBANISM and the COUNCIL FOR EUROPEAN URBANISM, emphasising the physical characteristics that traditionally have made successful NEIGHBOURHOODS, and the need for SMART GROWTH. The URBAN VILLAGES movement in the UK shares many of its ideas. Doug Kelbaugh (2000) describes new urbanism as 'utopian (or at least reformist), inspirational in style and structuralist in conception'. It is utopian, he explains, 'because it aspires to a social ethic that builds new or repairs existing communities in ways that equitably mix people of different income, ethnicity, race and age, and to a civic ideal that coherently mixes land of different uses and buildings of different types'. It is inspirational 'because it sponsors public architecture and public space that attempts to make citizens feel they are part, even proud, of a culture that is more significant than their individual, private worlds, and an ecology that is vertically and horizontally connected to natural loops, cycles and chains.' And new urbanism is structuralist, or at least determinist, Kelbaugh suggests, in the sense that 'it maintains that there is a direct, structural relationship between physical form and social behavior. It is normative in that it posits that good design can have a measurably positive effect on sense of place and community, which it holds are essential to a healthy, sustainable society.'

Elizabeth Moule and Stefanos Polyzoides, writing in *The New Urbanism* (Katz, 1994), set out some of the movement's physical conventions for creating new development on traditional patterns at the scale of the building, block and street: a) Buildings, blocks and streets are interdependent. b) The totality of the street, block and building should be shaped through design, not policy planning. c) Urban design should express the cultural variety inherent in climatic, social, economic and technical difference. d) Urban design should be an integration and collaboration of all architectural, engineering and design disciplines. e) The public should participate in the design process. f) The human scale should be preferred over that of the car. g) Any street should be part of a street network. h) Street blocks should be square, rectangular or irregular, with sides preferably between 250 and 600ft. i) Lobbies, major ground-floor interior spaces and public gardens should be regarded as an extension of the city's public space. j) Cars are best accommodated in the middle of blocks or underground. k) The ground floors of multi-storey car parks fronting pavements should be occupied by pedestrian-related uses. l) Multi-storey car parks should have significant public faces. m) Multi-storey car parks should be designed with future conversion to a different use in mind. n) Surface car parks should double up as significant public gardens. o) Street blocks should be lined with regularly planted trees. p) There are two kinds of buildings: fabric and monumental. Fabric buildings should conform to all street and block-related rules and be consistent in their form with all other buildings of their kind; monumental buildings should be free of all formal constraints. q) Regionally proven methods of building should be used wherever possible. r) Easily available local and recyclable materials should be used wherever possible. s) Labour-intensive building processes should be used where economically possible. t) Low-energy consumption and pollution-free operations should be pursued wherever possible. u) Buildings should be designed and built with a view to renovation and reuse over a long period. v) Specific street, block and building design rules for public and private developments should be designed and presented in the form of a code.

The new urbanists' critics include the architectural writer Michael Sorkin (2000). The new urbanists, Sorkin writes, 'romanticise the small town in a Disneyesque reverie of artificial halcyon, celebrating the captive nature of the front lawn, that perfect place of green. They celebrate urban interaction but their vision structures every arrangement along the contours of a scary fantasy of whitebread civility and order. Like the carefully managed landscapes of the eighteenth century, these are places that exclude the other, expunged like weeds. Deviance pent-up is released not in the jostling of the crowd but in solitary cellars with a garrotte around a little girl's neck.' Others have a different idea of new urbanism. 'If there is to be a "new urbanism",' write Rem Koolhaas and Bruce Mau (1995), 'it will not be based on the fantasies of order and omnipotence; it will be the staging of uncertainty; …it will no longer aim for configurations but for the creation of enabling fields that accommodate processes that refuse to be crystallized into definitive forms.'

A paper by Peter Gordon and Harry W Richardson (1998) sets out some typical criticisms of new urbanism: a) The stock of urban buildings is largely in place and changes very slowly, they write. 'Demonstration projects, the object of international study tours, a pleasant living environment for a few thousand households, well-paid lecture tours for a small clutch of somewhat immodest architects: the new urbanist communities amount to little more.' b) There is no evidence that most people want to live in new urbanism,

Gordon and Richardson argue. c) The scale and impact of the loss of agricultural land to suburban sprawl has been exaggerated. d) New urbanist communities rarely achieve their aims of having mixed uses. Their developers find difficulty in attracting shopping, consumer services and especially employment. e) New urbanism, despite its intentions, does little to promote equity, foster residential mixing, provide affordable housing, or reduce income differentials between city centres and the suburbs by infilling urban sites. Gordon and Richardson quote David Harvey (1997): 'New urbanism... builds an image of community and a rhetoric of place-based civic pride and consciousness for those who do not need it, while abandoning those that do to their "UNDERCLASS" fate.' f) Although most people would accept that our behaviour is sensitive to, and affected by, the surrounding physical environment, the new urbanists take the argument to extremes, they argue. 'Many new urbanist projects are so influenced by the nostalgic longing for the archetypical small town of the past that they fall into the trap of believing that recreating its physical structure (at least to some degree) can simultaneously recreate its social and civic behaviour.' g) There is little justification for the claims that new urbanism will reduce car dependence and increase transit (public transport) use, cycling and walking, according to Gordon and Richardson. A high proportion of trips is external to the community (for instance, almost all jobs are outside), cars remain vitally necessary for mobility, and new urbanist communities are unlikely ever to be sufficiently dense or large to justify significant transit services. h) New urbanists are merely tampering at the margins of urban problems, believing, 'at least implicitly, that social problems are remediable by architectural and design prescriptions rather than by economic development'. i) New urbanism is a threat to economic growth. 'If cities want to prosper, employment growth in their suburbs is to be welcomed,' Gordon and Richardson conclude from their analysis of economic trends. 'If suburban expansion is inevitably linked with sprawl, there are clearly serious risks in anti-sprawl actions.' j) The new urbanists correctly argue that the metropolitan region is the appropriate unit for analysis, but 'it is difficult to find any concrete details in new urbanist discussions as to how they will influence the future metropolitan region.' See also CELEBRATION, DECLARATION OF BRUGES, ANDRES DUANY, LÉON KRIER, NEO-TRADITIONAL PLANNING, POUNDBURY, PRINCE OF WALES, SEASIDE and STEPFORD WIVES.

New Vision for Planning Developed by the Royal Town Planning Institute in 2001. The vision sees planning as being: a) Spatial (dealing with the unique needs and characteristics of places). b) Sustainable (looking at the short, medium and long term issues). c) Integrative (in terms of the knowledge, objectives and actions involved). d) Inclusive (recognising the wide range of people involved in planning).

New Ways A house in Northampton, built in the 1926 to a design by the German architect Peter Behrens. It has been called England's first modernist house (Burnett, 1986).

New Winchelsea A Sussex town laid out on a gridiron pattern by Edward I (1272–1307) to replace Old Winchelsea, which was being destroyed by coastal erosion. The new town declined when its river silted up and is now half its original size.

New York See RUDOLPH GIULIANI, THE BIG APPLE, FUN CITY, URBANITY and WORLD TRADE CENTER.

New York Regional Plan Largely written by THOMAS ADAMS and published in two volumes in 1929–31. The plan proposed, most strikingly, a selective 'cull' of skyscrapers in order to 'thin out' Manhattan's urban forest, thus improving the daylighting and ventilation of the remainder while imposing a rational, ordered framework on the chaotic 'muddle' of the city's recent development. LEWIS MUMFORD attacked the plan at the time as 'a badly conceived pudding into which a great many ingredients, some sound, some dubious, have been poured and mixed: the cooks tried to satisfy every appetite and taste, and the guiding thought in selecting the pudding-dish was that it should "sell" one pudding to the diners, specially to those who paid the cooks.' Sir Peter Hall (1998) notes that in the plan 'are found the first applications of regional population forecasting, economic base theory and Clarence Perry's neighbourhood theory. It also pioneered in the way it related homes, jobs and transportation.' But, Hall concludes, 'this was quintessentially a big business plan to make New York City a bigger and better place to do business in.'

News from Nowhere A novel by WILLIAM MORRIS, published in 1890. The narrator, waking in the twenty-first century in an idealised socialist society, finds that London has become a semi-rural, cooperative paradise. Morris's 'utopian romance', as he called it, was a reaction to Edward Bellamy's LOOKING BACKWARD, whose vision Morris thought was bleakly machine-oriented.

Nicholl, Donald See SEGREGATION.

nickel sulphide inclusion See GLASS CANCER.

Niemeyer, Oscar (b1907) Brazilian architect. In the 1930s he collaborated with LE CORBUSIER and LUCIO COSTA on a new Ministry of Education and Health in Rio de Janeiro. He later collaborated with Le Corbusier on designing the United Nations Headquarters in New York. In 1956 he was asked to design the new capital of Brazil, BRASILIA. He agreed to design the principal government buildings but suggested a competition for the MASTER PLAN, which was won by his mentor Lucio Costa. From 1957 to 1959 Niemeyer was architectural advisor to Nova Cap, the organisation charged with implementing Costa's plan. After 1964 he spent some years as a political exile in Europe due to his communist sympathies. Edwin Heathcote (2003), interviewing Niemeyer at the age of 95, found him proud of Brasilia 'but saddened by its decline'. The great architect was still working, having been commissioned to design 'an entire cultural quarter' for the city of Niterói. 'The architect has approached it just as he did Brasilia,' Heathcote reported. 'No namby-pamby new urbanism for Niemeyer, this is unreconstructed modern – concrete objects in the landscape, green in between.'

Nietzsche, Friedrich (1844–1900) German philosopher. His writings were an important influence on the arts in the late nineteenth and early twentieth centuries, and in particular helped to inspire modernist architects to free themselves from the constraints of history.

Nieuwenhuys, Constant (b1920) Situationist artist, creator of the visionary NEW BABYLON.

Night and the City A novel by Gerald Kersh portraying the darkest side of London, published in 1938 and twice filmed. See VICE.

night architecture Buildings (often for entertainment) designed to impress at night.

night on the city (US) In jail. See also ONE ON THE CITY.

night-time economy Economic activities that take place at night, including culture, entertainment, eating, drinking, prostitution, shelf-stocking, cleaning and deliveries.

nimby (or NIMBY) A derogatory term for a person who objects to any development near where they live. The phrase was adopted in the UK in the 1980s from the US, where it is an acronym for 'not in my back yard', YARD being the American equivalent of the English GARDEN. Environment secretary NICHOLAS RIDLEY was particularly scathing of people who tried to obstruct development promoted by market forces. When development was proposed near his own country home, though, Ridley objected vigorously.

Terence Bendixson (1988) quotes the reaction of a parish councillor to the proposal to absorb his village into Peterborough new town. 'If we get these vandals and under-privileged coming from the pitholes of Liverpool and the slums of London, they will kick the hell out of this village... There are loads of other areas crying out for the expansion, like Yaxley and Thorney.' The poet William Wordsworth has been called 'the first NIMBY', though that protective instinct is no doubt as old as humankind. Wordsworth's *Guide to the Lake District* was published in 1810, but he campaigned in old age against tourism and railway building in the district. Also *NIMBY-ite*. Example: 'Many marginal constituencies are in NIMBY-ite rural or semi-rural areas [where] *the* political issue is housing pressure' (Breheny, 2001). See also BANANA, NIMTOO and YIMBY.

NIMTOO (US) Not in my term of office. A derogatory term applied to politicians who object to controversial developments for which they might be held answerable politically. A variant of NIMBY.

Nineteen Eighty-Four The title of George Orwell's 1949 novel, set in the bleakest of urban landscapes. Winston Smith, the central character, lives in London on the seventh floor of a grim block of flats. 'The ideal set up by the Party was something huge, terrible, glittering – a world of steel and concrete, of monstrous machines and terrifying weapons... The reality was decaying, dingy cities where under-fed people shuffled to and fro in leaky shoes, in patched-up nineteenth-century houses that smelt always of cabbage and bad lavatories. He seemed to see a vision of London, vast and ruinous, city of a million dustbins...'

nitrogen dioxide An air pollutant that increases the lung's vulnerability to infection. The main source is motor vehicle exhausts, though the combustion products of gas heating systems also contribute.

No Mean City A best-selling novel by Alexander McArthur and H Kingsley Long. Published in the 1930s, it reinforced the reputation of Glasgow's GORBALS district as a hotbed of gang violence. See also MEAN CITY.

no mean city An important city. The novelist Ford Madox Ford wrote in 1909: 'I doubt if... there are many Londoners who are proud of their home, if there are many to echo the excellent boast that they are citizens of no mean city' (Ford, 1909). PATRICK GEDDES used the phrase of Philadelphia in 1915. It comes from the Bible (Acts, chapter 21, verse 39), where Paul describes himself as 'a Jew of Tarsus, a city in Cilicia, a citizen of no mean city'.

no net loss of housing potential (US) A situation in which non-housing development is allowed on a site zoned for housing in return for arrangements being made to provide an equal or greater amount of housing elsewhere.

no place A place lacking LOCAL DISTINCTIVENESS.

Noddy box A pejorative term for a small house with no distinctive character, of the sort produced in large numbers by volume housebuilders. The reference is to Enid Blyton's stories of Noddy in Toytown. See also BARRATTIFICATION.

Noddyland A place of unreal simplicity of the sort where Noddy lives in Enid Blyton's stories. Example: 'The [so-called High Street at the Glasgow Garden Festival was] overwhelmingly reminiscent of Noddyland, a ghost borough of benevolent municipality' (Spring, 1990). Noddy actually lived in Toytown in TOYLAND.

Noddytown (A Glasgow term) Cumbernauld, so called because of the volume of boxy little houses spread across the landscape.

noisy architecture

node A place where activity and routes are concentrated; a point of interchange in a transport network. Also known as a *vertex*. KEVIN LYNCH (1960) defines nodes as 'points, the strategic spots in a city into which an observer can enter, and which are the intensive foci to and from which he is travelling. They may be primarily junctions, places of a break in transportation, a crossing or convergence of paths, moments of shift from one structure to another. Or the nodes may be simply concentrations, which gain their importance from being the condensation of some use or physical character, as a street-corner hangout or an enclosed square'. Richard Sennett (1990) has commented: 'In the development of the modern "megalopolis", it has become more reasonable to speak of urban "nodes" than of centers and suburbs. The very fuzziness of the word *node* indicates the loss of a language for naming environmental value: *center* is charged with meanings both historical and visual, while *node* is resolutely bland.'

no-go area A part of a town or city where the police, a particular ethnic, religious or political group, or people in general do not feel safe to go. The term is used in journalism. Example: 'Some areas of Oldham... are already no-go areas... [The presence of Asian teenagers at an underpass] is enough to unnerve the residents of two nearby blocks of flats: rather than walk through the underpass to reach the shops on the other side, many take a circuitous bus ride round' (Prentice, 2001). Judge Issard-Davies was quoted in the press in 2002 as saying that many parts of London had become 'no-go areas..., the sole province of the drunken, the violent and the drugged'. An official report into the 2001 riots in Oldham made a subtle distinction later in that year. 'There are areas where people, especially young people, of different communities feel uncomfortable... These might be considered "won't-go" areas; there are no "no-go" areas in Oldham.' The term is thought to have originated in Northern Ireland. See also SEGREGATION.

no-hatter See DRESS SENSE.

noise Unwanted sound. See also AMBIENT NOISE, AURAL PRIVACY, CLEAR ZONE, ENVIRONMENTAL NOISE, ENVIRONMENTALLY ENHANCED VEHICLE, FLANKING TRANSMISSION, GREEN WAVE, HARD GROUND, MUSIC, NEIGHBOUR NOISE, OCCUPATIONAL NOISE, RAILWAY BONUS, SENSITIVE RECEPTOR and SOUNDSCAPE.

noise breakout Unwanted sound being audible beyond the building from which it originates.

noise environment The whole experience of noise in a particular place, not only how loud it is but also how unwelcome or disturbing it might seem.

noise map A cartographic representation of acoustic data.

noise nuisance Defined by the World Health Organisation as 'a feeling of displeasure evoked by noise'.

noise pollution Excessive unwanted sound.

noise-sensitive development Housing, hospitals, schools and other development whose users are likely to be particularly disturbed by noise.

noisy architecture A pejorative term for buildings that overwhelm their neighbours by their size or design. Compare QUIET ARCHITECTURE.

noisy pedestrian environment One in which there is a relatively large potential for distractions, cross-flow movements and stopping. See also AMBIENT NOISE.

Nolan The Nolan Committee on Standards in Public Life defined the general principles of public life as selflessness, integrity, objectivity, accountability, openness, honesty and leadership. Chaired by Lord Nolan, it reported in the 1990s.

Nolen, John (1869–1937) City planner. His book *City Planning* was published in 1929.

noli me tangere design Building design which shows an extreme reluctance to disrupt historic fabric or context. Example: 'There is a tendency, even within the broadly modernist tradition, to go for safe, polite, "noli me tangere" solutions in which "respect" for historic fabric is paramount' (2003). The Italian phrase *noli me tangere*, meaning 'touch me not', is familiar as the title for many religious paintings (many of them Italian, but some by non-Italian painters who use the Italian title) since the fourteenth century. It comes from the Bible (John, chapter 20, verse 17), where Jesus appears to Mary Magdalene after his resurrection. 'Touch me not,' Jesus says, 'for I have not yet ascended to my father.'

Nolli diagram A FIGURE/GROUND diagram. The term comes from Giambattista Nolli, who prepared a famous plan of Rome.

nomadism The way of life of people who are not based at a specific place or places. Example: 'Nomadism comes naturally to the globe-trotting managers of multi-nationals.'

non-conforming use A land use that does not comply with the current rules, regulations or policies for that site.

non-governmental organisation (NGO) An agency having no statutory status.

non-market benefits Ones that result from a development but that do not accrue to the developer or investors.

non-participation See ARNSTEIN'S LADDER

non-place urban realm The term used by the Californian planner MELVIN WEBBER for what is a wide area over which people travel for specific purposes, rather than a localised part of a city. Webber (1963) writes: 'I contend that we have been searching for the wrong grail, that the values associated with the desired urban structure do not reside in the spatial structure *per se*. One pattern of settlement is superior to another only as it better serves to accommodate ongoing social processes and to further the non-spatial ends of the political community. I am flatly rejecting the contention that there is an overriding spatial or physical aesthetic of urban form.'

A little more than 30 years later Webber (1996) notes that 'social and economic activities that are the defining functions of urbanized society are no longer conducted in cities alone. With most specialized organizations now

> **"SOCIAL AND ECONOMIC ACTIVITIES THAT ARE THE DEFINING FUNCTIONS OF URBANIZED SOCIETY ARE NO LONGER CONDUCTED IN CITIES ALONE"**
>
> *Melvin Webber*

freed from locational constraints and able to interact with others anywhere, the organized complexity that is urban society no longer resides in cities exclusively. In turn, the concept of "urbanism" and the concept of "city" are no longer coterminous.' Yet he finds himself marvelling at how tenacious the traditional cities have proved, contrary to his expectations. 'What is the magnet that continues to attract firms and families into high-density, old-style, urban settlements?' he asks. 'Why do metropolitan areas continue to prosper? What is it that seems to make some people and some organizations immune to the space-lubricating effects of modern transportation and communication technologies?'

Webber notes some of the factors that seem to provide an explanation. 'The metropolis is the gathering place of growing arrays of business and consumer services that are ever-more narrowly focused... The complex interplay among specialized firms is encouraged by the access that proximity affords... Many people enjoy the sheer psychological and cultural stimulation that accompanies urban life lived at rather high densities.' The triumph of the non-place urban realm is, it seems, far from complete. See also ARCHITECTURAL DETERMINISM, CITY, COMMUNITY WITHOUT PROPINQUITY, THE EXPANDED TOWN, MILTON KEYNES and POST-URBANISM.

non-recourse finance Loans on property that are not supported by collateral unrelated to that property.

non-thematic building One that is a landmark, an exception to the general pattern of BACKGROUND BUILDINGS.

norm Something regarded as normal; a standard. The word derives from the Latin for a carpenter's square.

Norman, Al See SPRAWL-BUSTERS.

normative Based on specific models. Normative urban design, for example, is guided by forms of urban development that are known to be successful.

no-road building A prestige building designed by an architect to impress other architects through photographs in magazines, and likely to be ill-suited to its function and hard to adapt, according to the classification by Stewart Brand (1994). See HIGH-ROAD BUILDING and LOW-ROAD BUILDING.

North American Phalanx A short-lived utopian settlement founded at Red Bank, New Jersey, in 1843, inspired by the ideas of CHARLES FOURIER.

North Cornwall The planning service of this district council in south west England was the subject of a government-ordered investigation carried out by the planner Audrey Lees, published in 1993. The investigation confirmed that planning permission was being given on the basis of councillors' personal preferences, rather than on the council's planning policies and professional advice.

North Dallas special Defined by Andres Duany (2000) as 'a type of house laden with the architectural symbology of upper class inhabitation, displayed in grossly exaggerated form for the purposes of marketing.' See also KERB APPEAL and SIZZLE.

north of the Watford Gap (UK) A popular expression for any part of the UK north of London, based on the erroneous assumption that the Watford Gap (whose name is well known because it is a service station on the M1 motorway) is at the town of Watford at the northern edge of London. In fact it is at the village of Watford near Rugby in the English midlands.

north of Watford (UK) A popular expression, usually derogatory, for any part of the UK north of London. Watford is a town at London's northern edge. Among Londoners it has a pejorative sense of meaning a place of no significance.

Northampton A mark three UK new town (expanding an existing town), designated in 1968.

Northamptonshire County Hall competition Won by Jeremy and Fenella Dixon and Edward Jones with a controversial design (never executed) for a pyramid clad in mirror glass surrounded by water. A light chute was to be positioned to cast a shaft of sunlight on the county treasurer's desk on 5 April, the start of the financial year. The architects were formerly with the MILTON KEYNES development corporation, and the design can be seen as the culmination of a strand of neo-Platonic/new age thinking developed there.

Norton, Charles Dyer (1871–1923) A banker and, in the years after 1915, a promoter of regional planning in the USA. He was secretary of the RUSSELL SAGE FOUNDATION.

notation, the A method of townscape analysis devised by GORDON CULLEN in the 1960s.

notched terrace A row of houses with a regular rhythm of different heights.

Notes on Virginia A book, published in 1784, in which Thomas Jefferson warned of the dangers of cities: poverty, depravity, dependence and corruption. His view was that America should avoid the need for cities by leaving manufacturing to Europe and importing whatever was necessary. By 1816 he realised that political conditions made this impractical.

Nothing Gained by Overcrowding! The title of an influential pamphlet by RAYMOND UNWIN, published in 1912, arguing that housing should be developed at relatively low densities.

noun 'Most cities are nouns,' said John F Kennedy. 'New York's a verb.'

Nova Solyma, the Ideal City An anonymous utopian work in Latin of the mid-seventeenth century, subtitled *Jerusalem Regained*. It has been attributed to Milton but was probably written by Samuel Gott (Novak, 1995). Compare THE IDEAL CITY.

Nowa Huta An industrial new town near Kracòw in Poland.

Nowhere City, The Los Angeles, as portrayed in Alison Lurie's 1999 novel of that name. It explores two newcomers' responses to the city.

nowheresville (also nowhereville) (US) A place without interest or distinct identity.

nuclear family Spouses or partners with or without dependent children living in one household. Less than a quarter of all American households consist of a traditional nuclear family (Florida, 2002).

nucleated Grouped round a focal point.

Number 1 Poultry See MANSION HOUSE SQUARE and PRINCE OF WALES.

nurbanism NEW URBANISM. The term was in use in Australia in 2001.

O

O'Brien, Sean (b1952) Poet. Born in London and living in Newcastle, he bases much of his work on urban, social and political themes. He has been called 'the bard of urban Britain'.

O'Connor, Fergus (1794–1855) Founder of the CHARTIST COOPERATIVE LAND SOCIETY.

Oak and Eldon Gardens Two slab blocks of housing that were demolished by explosives by Birkenhead Council in 1979 – the first blow-down of municipal housing in the UK, inspired by the spectacular example of PRUITT-IGOE in the US. The demolition attracted large crowds and launched a new municipal craze. When built, Oak and Eldon Gardens were so highly regarded that the Ministry of Housing published a full colour brochure and distributed it to all local authorities urging them to follow their example.

Oakland, California See THERE IS NO THERE THERE.

object building 1 One that stands out from the BACKGROUND BUILDINGS of the urban fabric. **2** A pejorative term for one designed without consideration of its context. See TYPOLOGICAL CODE.

Objective 1 area A priority area for the allocation of European structural funds, where development is lagging behind the European norm.

Objective 2 area A priority area for the allocation of European structural funds, where there are structural difficulties such as the closure of traditional industries and high unemployment.

objective language See BIASED TERMINOLOGY.

object-positive building See SPACE-POSITIVE BUILDING.

occupation road A LANE, ALLEY or path providing side or rear access to a plot of land. The term was used by MRG CONZEN in his studies of urban morphology.

occupational noise That to which people are exposed in the workplace.

Octavia An imaginary city in Asia slung precariously from a net of ropes and chains stretched between two mountains. Italo Calvino describes it in INVISIBLE CITIES (1972).

octopus See BRITAIN AND THE OCTOPUS.

oecology See ECOLOGY.

öffentlicher Verkehr (German) Public transport.

offer What is provided by shops in terms of goods, services and hours of opening. Examples: 'There is great potential for expanding the evening offer' (that is, for providing more shops that are open in the evening); 'In the evenings the food offer [restaurants and fast food outlets] will attract people to the square'; 'The cities that succeed are those that have the offer that will attract creative people' (2003).

Office of the Deputy Prime Minister (ODPM) (UK) The government department's responsibilities include planning, urban policy, neighbourhood renewal, housing, social exclusion and the regions.

office village See VILLAGE.

offworld A secure and socially exclusive ENCLAVE. The term is used in the futuristic film BLADE RUNNER. Mike Davis (2002) applies it to, among other places, SUMMERLIN. See also GATED ESTATE.

Oglethorpe, James (1696–1785) The planner of SAVANNAH, Georgia. Born in England, Oglethorpe was appointed planner and builder of towns in the new colony of Georgia by George II.

oile See HOILE.

Okhitovich, Mikhail Sociologist. He was a major influence on town planning in the Soviet Union in the 1920s and '30s. See CITY and RED CITY OF THE PLANET OF COMMUNISM.

Ökologie (German) Ecology.

Ökosystem (German) An ecosystem.

Old Oak A pioneering cottage estate built by the London County Council in 1911.

Olmsted, Frederick Law (1822–1903) He was probably the first person to call himself a landscape architect, an occupation in which he was an influential pioneer. The historian Thomas Bender (2002) calls him 'America's first professional urban planner and city designer'. After studying engineering, Olmsted travelled in Europe and China before setting up in practice in the USA. With CALVERT VAUX he designed CENTRAL PARK, New York. See PARKWAY and URBAN VILLAGE.

Olmsted, Frederick Law, Junior Landscape architect and planner. Son of the above.

Olympia and York The Toronto-based developer of the World Financial Center in New York and CANARY WHARF in London. Its original partners were the brothers Paul, Albert and Ralph Reichmann. The name combined the names of two of the Reichmanns' previous companies. O&Y went bankrupt in 1992, but Paul Reichmann bought it back three years later.

On the Marble Cliffs A novel by the German writer Ernst Jünger (1895–1998), published in 1939. Jünger presents an image of urban destruction poetically and without much hint of regret. The narrator seems to think urban civilisation hardly worth preserving. From his viewpoint on the marble cliffs, 'the extent of the destruction could be read in towering flames, and far and wide the old and lovely towns along the Marina stood bright in ruin. They sparkled in fire like a chain of rubies, and from the dark depths of the waters there rose their shimmering image. Distant worlds flared up to delight our eyes in the beauty of their ruin... The palaces fell in ruins and from the harbour store-houses the cornstacks flew high into the air to scatter their glowing contents. Splitting the earth, the powder magazine at the Cock Gate blew up. The heavy bell, which had graced the belfry for a thousand years and had accompanied countless persons with its tolling in life and death, began to glow, darkly at first, and then with increasing brightness: finally it crashed from its bearings, wrecking the tower in its fall. I saw, too, the pediments of the pillared temples gleam in the red rays, and from their lofty pedestals the images of the gods with shield and spear bowed down, to sink without a sound into the raging flames.' See URBAN DESTRUCTION.

on the street HOMELESS.

on the streets Working as a prostitute. See also STREETWALKER.

One Book, One City A scheme in which a book is chosen for an entire city to read, to promote reading, discussion and a sense of community. The idea was born in Seattle, where *The Sweet Hereafter* by Russell Banks, which has a local setting, was the chosen book. New York, famously diverse, had trouble agreeing on which book to choose: an alternative scheme with a book for each borough was suggested instead (Burkeman, 2002).

one on the city (US) A drink of water. See also NIGHT ON THE CITY.

one-child policy The law that limits families in Chinese towns to one child. Rural dwellers are permitted two children.

one-eyed city Birkenhead, Merseyside. The name is given to it by people from Liverpool, which Birkenhead faces across the River Mersey. Local people give many explanations for the term, most of them implausible. Examples include: a) The town was thought to look in only one direction (towards Liverpool, thus showing its inferiority). b) A significant number of men had lost an eye through working as catchers of red-hot rivet ends in the shipyards. (The danger, it seems, was real enough. Ayn Rand in her 1947 novel *The Fountainhead* describes her hero Howard Roark working his way through architecture school by catching rivets on a skyscraper under construction in Boston: 'his eyes intent, and his right arm swinging forward, once in a while, expertly, without effort, to catch the flying ball of fire at the last moment, when it seemed that the hot rivet would miss the bucket and strike him in the face.') c) The nickname is short for *the one-eyed city of undiscovered crime*, so called because when the town was growing rapidly its police force was over-stretched. d) The one eye was the Mersey Tunnel (the road to Liverpool). e) The city slickers in Liverpool looked over their shoulders (with one eye) at their inferior neighbouring town. f) Only one illuminated clock in Birkenhead was visible from Liverpool at night. g) One-eyed means inferior (see ONE-HORSE TOWN); one-eyed yankee means a stupid person; one-eyed scribe [US Black slang] means an insignificant person). This explanation receives some support from Roderick Mackay's book *The One-eyed City*, published in 1983, which tells of the author's working life (only slightly fictionalised) in the Birkenhead police force. Mackay tells of an episode in which a detective from Liverpool crosses the river to Birkenhead to collect a prisoner caught in possession of butter stolen from the docks. The detective tells his Birkenhead colleagues that he hates their town and everyone in it. 'He tells us he can't understand why anybody would want to be a copper in this grotty dump – this one-horse town. "By Christ," he says, "it's no wonder they call it the One-eyed City."' The only other reference to the book's title comes in the introduction. Mackay (1983) writes: 'Slickers sometimes called it the One-eyed City – maybe to match the disdainful glances it got from across the river.'

If the term is an insult, which it certainly is, why call Birkenhead a city, which it is not? The Liverpool lexicographer Fritz Spiegel said that he had heard of other places called 'one-eyed city', including Oldham (presumably by people from nearby Manchester). Liverpudlians also have an insult for their neighbours in the other direction. They call people from Lancashire *woolly backs* (the term is also used elsewhere as a racist epithet), implying that they have only just come down from the trees. The people of Liverpool are, on the other hand, generally proud to be called SCOUSERS. A survey in 2002 showed that more people (29 per cent) in Birkenhead were divorced than in any other place in the UK 2002 (compared to fewer than seven per cent in Sevenoaks, Kent, the place with the lowest proportion). See also BIRKENHEAD PARK, CACTUSVILLE and WOOP WOOP, and compare BLIND-EYED CITY.

one-eyed city

one-horse town An insignificant place. The term, of US origin, derives from the low status of someone unable to afford a pair of horses to pull their cart. See also JERKWATER TOWN.

Oneida A nineteenth-century utopian settlement in New York State.

one-of-each syndrome Designing buildings so that each is strikingly different from its neighbours. See also ARCHITECTURAL ZOO.

one-way couplet A part of a suburban arterial road that splits into a pair of parallel, traffic-calmed, one-way roads, each with businesses on it, when it enters a VILLAGE CENTER. The new urbanist Peter Calthorpe proposes such an arrangement as being easier for pedestrians to cross.

open dialogue See DIALOGUE.

open environment Urban land that is predominantly undeveloped, including waste land, commons, parks, allotments, private sports grounds, private squares and publicly accessible open space (Greater London Authority, 2001).

Open House An annual event in which buildings are opened to the public for a day. The Scottish equivalent is Doors Open Day.

open housing Built according to a system that provides the basic structure but allows the occupiers to build everything else.

open space 1 Outdoor space. **2** A participation technique enabling groups of people (as few as five or as many as 800, and lasting between one and five days) to identify common interests, discuss ideas, share information and experience, and organise themselves into continuing working groups focusing on specific topics. FUTURE SEARCH is a similar technique.

Open Spaces and Footpaths Preservation Society The UK's first voluntary environmental organisation, founded in 1865.

open town One that is free of troops or military installations and so can not be attacked in accord with international law.

opening A street or road breaking the line of another. Compare BACK OPENING.

Operation Gomorrah A week-long air raid on Hamburg in 1943 by the RAF, supported by the United States Eighth Army Air Force, in which more than a third of all buildings in the city were destroyed, including most of the historic centre and its churches (Glendinning, 2000), with a loss of tens of thousands of lives. The operation was named after the Biblical city that God destroyed by fire and brimstone because of its wickedness. The novelist WG Sebald noted in his book *On the Natural History of Destruction* that Hitler had a similar fate in mind for British cities. 'Albert Speer describes Hitler at a dinner in the Reich Chancellery in 1940 imagining the total destruction of the capital of the British Empire: "Have you ever seen a map of London? It is so densely built that one fire alone would be enough to destroy the whole city, just as it did over 200 years ago. Goering will start fires all over London, fires everywhere... They will unite in one huge blaze over the whole area."' See also BAEDEKER RAIDS, BLITZ, CITIES OF THE PLAIN, CULTURAL BOMBING, THE DESTRUCTION OF SODOM AND GOMORRAH and ARTHUR 'BOMBER' HARRIS.

Operation Meetinghouse An American air raid on Tokyo in March 1945 – 'the most devastating air raid in world history', according to Mike Davis (2000). At the time the Americans believed the raid had killed a million people, though the real figure is probably around 100,000.

operational land Special planning arrangements apply to land used for the operations of STATUTORY UNDERTAKERS.

opportunity area Defined by the Greater London Authority (2001) as 'London's few opportunities for very large-scale, mixed-use development, important for regeneration'.

opportunity cost The value of the most valuable alternative use of a building or piece of land.

option 1 One of a set of choices to be considered. **2** An exclusive right to buy a piece of land within a specified period. Also known as a *call option*. In the case of a *put option*, the option holder is required to buy the land within the specified period if certain conditions (such as the granting of planning permission) are fulfilled. Compare CONDITIONAL CONTRACT.

option appraisal Weighing up the options intended to achieve a specific objective.

Orange County, California Mark Gottdiener and George Kephart (1991, quoted in Dear and Flusty, 1998) point to Orange County as 'the paradigmatic window on late-twentieth-century urbanism' – a prime example of *postsuburbia*. Orange County represents, they write, 'a new form of settlement space – the fully urbanized, multinucleated and independent county... formally separated from but adjacent to large well-known metropolitan regions.' Gottdiener and Kephart go so far as to suggest that this is the first new form of settlement space in 5,000 years of urban history.

orbital A road round a town or city.

orchard bourgeoisie Relatively wealthy people whose primary home is in the country, but whose livelihood is mainly urban and who get no closer to agriculture than tending some fruit trees. Anthony Barnett (1998) identifies them as a new class of people who live across the rural/urban divide but who 'would be bereft... if they had to leave their city-centred occupations and access to town culture'.

order Regular arrangement. Adrian Forty (2000a)

argues that 'the supposition that what looks ordered will be orderly has... been one of the great fallacies of the modern era, but it has nevertheless been taken for granted by exponents of urban design, from Alberti, to Baron HAUSSMANN, to DANIEL BURNHAM and to the master-planners of the 1950s and 1960s'. By contrast, Forty notes, KEVIN LYNCH calls for 'not a final but an open-ended order, capable of continuous further development'. The architects ROBERT VENTURI and DENISE SCOTT BROWN (in their 1972 book LEARNING FROM LAS VEGAS) quote Henri Bergson's definition of disorder as 'an order we can not see'. Richard Sennett (in *The Uses of Disorder*, published in 1970) castigates planners for isolating people in cities by seeking to reduce social conflict.

Ordering of Towns, The An anonymous pamphlet on the layout of agricultural towns, published in New England in 1635. A township should consist of six concentric rings around the meetinghouse: the first consists of housing; the second, common fields; the third, pasture. The fourth and fifth rings are reserved for later expansion (Kostof, 1991). See also ATLANTIS.

ordinance (US) A municipal regulation having the force of law.

ordinary people The phrase is sometimes used to refer to people who are not considered the main players in planning or regeneration processes, but whose needs should be taken account of. For example, a PLANNING AID leaflet published in the UK in 2000 asks rhetorically: 'Do you believe that ordinary people should have a say in planning decisions about their local environment?' *The British people*, by contrast, is a phrase used exclusively by politicians.

Ordnance Survey The government organisation responsible for making maps in the UK. *Ordnance* means military supplies: the maps were originally made for military purposes.

organic architecture Buildings whose design grows naturally from their environment and the nature of their materials. FRANK LLOYD WRIGHT used the term to describe his own approach.

organic town planning See HANS BERNHARD REICHOW and POUNDBURY.

organicism Treating cities as organic structures.

organised surveillance Closed-circuit television. Compare FORMAL SURVEILLANCE and NATURAL SURVEILLANCE.

orientation 1 The layout of a building in relation to the points of the compass. **2** Finding one's way.

originality See COPY.

orthogonal projection A standard way of drawing the facade of a building, without perspective. Every point is seen as if from a position perpendicular to it. This is, as Adrian Forty (2000a) points out, no less artificial and deceptive than a perspectival projection.

Frederic Osborn

Osborn, Frederic (Sir) (1885–1978) Propagandist for decentralisation, GARDEN CITIES and NEW TOWNS. As an office boy in London he continued his education at evening classes and as a member of the Independent Labour Party and the Fabian Society. After becoming a rent collector for a housing trust in London's east end, he moved to LETCHWORTH Garden City as secretary-manager of the Howard Cottage Society in 1912. During the war he was a conscientious objector. Afterwards he campaigned for new towns and urged the garden cities movement to avoid being diverted into building GARDEN SUBURBS. In 1920 he became company secretary of WELWYN Garden City Ltd, and Welwyn was his home for the rest of his life. Osborn was dismissed from the company in 1936 in one of its frenzied restructurings. From then on he combined the job of financial director of a Welwyn company with campaigning for the Golden Cities and Town Planning Association. He campaigned for low-density homes with gardens in new planned settlements, and against flats and suburban expansion.

In the 1940s Osborn worked to build a consensus for national planning action, but deep differences in policy were emerging on the wisdom of urban decentralisation. There was a major success, though, with the New Town Act 1946. By now Osborn was campaigning full-time with the TOWN AND COUNTRY PLANNING ASSOCIATION (as the organisation now was), and from 1949–65 he was editor of its journal, *Town and Country Planning*. He carried on a long transatlantic correspondence with his friend and ally LEWIS MUMFORD, who nevertheless thought Osborn excessively antagonistic to any but very low densities in housing. Osborn told Mumford: 'I can't think of a single element of civilisation or city "culture" that depends on densities higher than I would regard as all right for family living.' On reflection he did think of one: the value of houses without gardens for a visual sense of enclosure. But he did not think this worth sacrificing. In another letter to Mumford, he wrote: 'I don't think philanthropic housing people anywhere realise the irresistible strength of the impulse towards the family house and garden as prosperity increases; they think the suburban trend can be reversed by large-scale multi-storey buildings in the down-town districts, which is not only a pernicious belief from the human point of view, but a delusion... In a few years, the multi-storey method will peter out... Damage will be done to society by the trial; but probably all I can do is to hasten the date of disillusion. If I have underestimated the complacency of the urban masses, the damage may amount to a disaster' (Hughes, 1971).

The titles of Osborn's books reflect the consistent theme of his campaigning: *New Towns after the War* (1918), *Green Belt Cities* (1946) and (with Arnold Whittick) *The New Towns: the answer to megalopolis* (1963), and a book of light verse *Can Man Plan?* To the end he saw himself as the self-educated common man who understood the simple needs of ordinary families, and saw through the pretensions of architects and sociologists. He accused them of advocating high-density urban developments for the masses, while they themselves preferred to live in leafy suburbs. His friends and colleagues called him by his initials, FJO. See also EBENEZER HOWARD.

Other Side, The See PERLE.

Otis, Elisha Graves Inventor. He developed the safety LIFT (UK)/elevator (US) in the 1850s, installing the first of his passenger lifts in a New York store in 1857.

outbuilding A smaller building in the grounds of another. *A New Urbanist Lexicon* (McLaughlin, 2000) identifies using outbuildings as affordable housing units as one of the 10 principles of an authentic NEIGHBOURHOOD.

outcome One of the effects of a regeneration project. Compare OUTPUT.

outcome indicator A means of measuring when outcomes have been achieved.

outdoor classroom The term is sometimes applied to public green spaces.

outdoor room An enclosed urban space (such as a GEORGIAN square).

outer city (US) An area outside the centre and inner areas; an EDGE CITY. Compare INNER CITY.

outerclass (US) A variant of UNDERCLASS, current in the 1990s and preferred for its supposed political correctness.

outline planning application Permission for a limited range of matters relating to a proposed development, identifying others as RESERVED MATTERS to be considered in a subsequent DETAILED PLANNING APPLICATION.

outlook A view.

Outlook Tower Short's Observatory was a turret containing a camera obscura on a building at the top end of Edinburgh's ROYAL MILE. PATRICK GEDDES took the building over and renamed it the Outlook Tower, which he developed as a 'sociological museum and laboratory' and 'index museum of the universe'. Geddes intended the experience of visiting the tower (preferably with a guided tour by himself) to help visitors understand their local, regional and universal environment, and to inspire them to become involved in improving it. He thought every town should have a similar civic facility.

out-of-centre Defined by the Scottish Office (1998) as 'a location that is clearly separate from a town centre but is within the urban area, including programmed extensions to the urban area in approved or adopted development plans'.

out-of-town *adj.* Beyond the centre of a town or city. The Scottish Office (1998) defined out-of-town development as an OUT-OF-CENTRE development on a green field site, or on land not clearly within the current urban boundary.

ou-topia No place. See UTOPIA.

output A means by which an activity achieves its intended OUTCOME; a measurable, direct result or physical product of a regeneration project.

Outrage 1 The title of a special issue of the *Architectural Review* in 1955. Its author IAN NAIRN (1930–83) raged against the failure of planning to prevent the despoliation of Britain by thoughtless development. *Outrage* took its title from the writings of Sir George Stapleton (King, 1996). Compare BRITAIN AND THE OCTOPUS. **2** An exhibition held in Sydney, Australia, in 1964 protesting at the degradation of the visual environment, inspired by Nairn's writings (Gazzard, 1988).

outworn fabric Save Britain's Heritage noted at the time of the MANSION HOUSE SQUARE controversy that 'the terms "outworn fabric" and "a building at the end of its useful life" are frequently used by developers wishing to demolish worthwhile and usable historic buildings' (SAVE, 1982).

overage The amount by which the capital value of a development has grown.

overclass A small, homogeneous, elite group of individuals who run a nation's institutions. Michael Quinion (1996) comments: 'One of the defining characteristics of members of the overclass is their tendency towards isolation, using their resources to exclude themselves voluntarily from society, as the antithesis of the underclass, which is excluded by its poverty.' Compare UNDERCLASS.

overcrowded London Underground told a House of Commons committee in 2003 that there was no such thing as an overcrowded tube train. The term 'overcrowded' referred to a state of 'excess over a defined limit', a spokesperson said. As there was no set maximum number of passengers on a train, it was possible only to use the word 'crowded' (*Metro*, 2003). See SARDINE.

overpermeability An excess of access routes through an area, encouraging unwelcome visitors and making it hard to find one's way about. Compare PERMEABILITY.

overplan Planning things that should be left to chance. Example: 'Many places conceived as Utopian ideals end up as routine pieces of doctrinaire overplan. But then the logical, atomist designer can not leave anything to chance' (Smith, 1974).

overspacing See SOMETHING LOST BY OVERSPACING.

overspill People rehoused away from their home area to allow it to be cleared or redeveloped at a lower density. Like DECANTING, and for the same reasons, the term is now rare.

over-urbanisation A condition in which a city has more inhabitants than can be accommodated in its formal economy. Compare UNDER-URBANISATION.

Owen, Robert (1771–1858) Mill owner and social reformer. Born in Wales, Owen left school at the age of nine and worked his way up to become manager of a cotton mill in Manchester and a partner in the firm. In 1799 Owen persuaded his partners to buy the New Lanark mills in Scotland where David Dale had built a new settlement based on a complex of water-powered mills. Owen moved to New Lanark, married Dale's daughter and spent 25 years developing a model community. 'Man's character is made for, and not by him,' Owen believed. Hoping to prove it, he provided education, good housing and reasonable working hours at New Lanark. Later he moved to the USA to develop the Cooperative Community of New Harmony, Indiana. He returned home after it failed.

Owen, Robert Dale (1801–77) The son of ROBERT OWEN, he led the utopian community at New Harmony, Indiana.

Owenist (or Owenite) A follower of the ideas of ROBERT OWEN.

owner occupation People living in houses they own.

owner speculation People living in houses that they own and that appreciate in value at a faster rate than their owners earn salaries (Pawley, 2002).

ownership 1 Legal possession. **2** A sense of commitment to something, often due to the person having been involved in creating it or having been given responsibility for it. Example: 'The community association was given no authority or resources for the new public space. They could have helped maintain it, but the emotional ownership was not there'.

oyez The call of a town crier, attracting attention before making an announcement. From the Old French, meaning listen.

Oz See CUTTENCLIP and EMERALD CITY.

Ozzie and Harriet (US) The archetypal American suburban-living, nuclear family. Example: 'The traditional "Ozzie and Harriet" nuclear family continues to decline as a percentage of American households.' 'The Adventures of Ozzie and Harriet' ran as a radio show from 1944–54 and as a television sitcom from 1952–66, but the phrase is still current. Oswald 'Ozzie' Nelson (1907–75) led a dance band in the 1930s, with his wife Harriet (1914–94) as singer. Radio shows based on their musical careers gradually turned into a domestic comedy, directed, produced and largely written by Ozzie. After the first five years the couple's two sons played themselves. When they grew up and married, their wives joined the cast as themselves.

'Ozzie Nelson was able to conflate, reduce and transform the professional activities of his family's personal reality into a fictional domestic banality,' Nina Leibman (2001) writes. 'From the outset, "The Adventures of Ozzie and Harriet" had a nostalgic feel, resembling Ozzie's 1920s youth in New Jersey more than 1950s Los Angeles. The picket-fenced neighbourhoods, the corner drugstore and malt shop that featured weekly in this slow-paced half hour infiltrated American culture at a time of social unease and quiescent distress. In reality, most 1950s fathers were working 10-hour days and commuting long distances to isolated suburbs. For the Nelsons, however, neighbours still chatted over the back fence, and downtown was a brisk walk away. The Nelsons presented an America that never was, but always wished for, and through their confusion of reality and fantasy worked to concoct an image of American life that is, to this day, mistakenly claimed not only as ideal, but as authentic.'

The Nelsons lived at 822 Sycamore Road in the Los Angeles suburb of Hillsdale. In 2001 still nothing very much seemed to be happening in Hillsdale. The suburb's website offered visitors a long list of 'things you didn't know', including the facts that: a) Rubber bands last longer when refrigerated. b) Two-thirds of the world's eggplant is grown in New Jersey. c) It is impossible to sneeze with your eyes open. d) More people are killed by donkeys annually than in plane crashes.

Another sitcom with a musician and his family playing themselves appeared on television in the 2000s. The location of 'The Osbournes' was, once again, a family home in Los Angeles (though this time there was no pretence that this was normality), and the star the English (Birmingham-born) former heavy-metal rock star Ozzy Osbourne. See also TERRY AND JUNE.

public transport environment

P

pacer architecture Buildings whose design puts them just outside the normal limits of novelty and surprise. The term is borrowed from psychology. Example: 'The tendency of planners in towns and cities is to eliminate pacer architecture in favour of the schematic and neo-schematic' (Smith, 1974). See also URBAN SCHEMA.

package deal An arrangement by which a contractor supplies a building (often partly standardised) to a developer.

PAG report See PLANNING ADVISORY GROUP.

Page, Thomas See COTATI.

Paisley screwdriver A hammer. The term is used by people from Glasgow to suggest that the inhabitants of the nearby town of Paisley are not bright enough to know the difference.

palaeotechnic age The age of coal and steam, and of the unsustainable exploitation of the earth's resources. The term was coined by PATRICK GEDDES. See EOTECHNIC and NEOTECHNIC.

palimpsest A surface that has been wiped almost clear and is ready to be used again. The term, traditionally describing manuscripts that are to be reused, also describes the way in which continuous rebuilding in cities rarely quite obliterates the evidence of previous generations (despite some strenuous recent efforts). The word is from the Greek *palimpsestos*, meaning 'rubbed smooth again'. See also STRATIFICATION.

Palmanova An Italian new town on a radial plan, in the form of a nine-sided polygon, designed in 1593 and still surviving intact.

Palumbo, Peter (Lord Palumbo) Developer, patron of architecture and one-time chairman of the Arts Council of Great Britain. See MANSION HOUSE SQUARE.

PAN (Scotland) Planning Advice Note. A series of guidance documents produced by the Scottish Executive.

panellised home (US) See MANUFACTURED HOME.

panhandle (US) To beg.

panhandler (US) A beggar. See VAGRANT.

panopticon A type of building intended to accommodate people who need to be supervised: a prison, workhouse, asylum, hospital, or industrial or education institution. The design, proposed by Jeremy Bentham in 1784, allowed easy observation from a central point. James Stirling's 1968 History Faculty building at Cambridge applies the panopticon principle to the design of its library – all shelves are visible from the librarian's desk to deter would-be book thieves. The word is from the Greek for 'all seeing'.

Paolo Lins See CITY OF GOD.

paper architecture Designs of unbuilt buildings.

paper chase *n.* The process of tracking down all the relevant reports and other documents relating to a particular development opportunity or other project.

Papworth, John Buonarotti (1775–1847) Architect, planner and landscape designer. He proposed the unrealised town of HYGEIA (named after the Greek goddess of health) across the Ohio River from Cincinnati in 1827 (Rykwert, 2000).

Parable of the Sower A novel by Octavia Butler, published in 1993, in which those living within and without GATED enclaves are at war with one another in a futuristic Los Angeles.

parachute 1 *n.* A device, made of fabric and cord, that allows the wearer to float to the ground from a height. In 2002, responding to fears raised by the sight of people trapped in the burning buildings of the WORLD TRADE CENTER in the previous year, a US company marketed parachutes specially designed to allow office workers to jump to safety. **2** *v.* To come to a place with which one is unfamiliar to carry out consultancy work – on regeneration, for example. The term is pejorative. Example: 'It's always the same. Consultants parachute in, produce a report, and then disappear.' Compare HELICOPTER VIEW.

parade See SHOPPING PARADE.

paradigm A model to be followed; an example. Mervyn King of the Bank of England (later its governor) warned in 2002 that 'we should be cautious about those who speak of new paradigms… a word too often used by those who would like to have an idea but can not think of one.'

paradigm shift A significant and comprehensive change in circumstances. Example: 'The world is changing dramatically in ways that amount to a paradigm shift affecting the role of cities and how we run them... We need new skills well beyond new technological literacy, including new approaches to thinking about and running our cities' (Landry, 2000).

Paradise Moscow See CHERYOMUSHKI.

Paragon, The Georgian housing at Blackheath, London, designed by Michael Searles and built c1794–1805. Elain Harwood and Andrew Saint (1991) rate the Paragon as 'the equal of any of the Bath crescents or Regent's Park terraces, and one of Europe's most satisfactory set pieces of suburban planning'. Ian Nairn (1966) described the Paragon as 'perfect urbanity and perfect rurality meeting head-on. It is the Royal Crescent at Bath wearing a south London grin [with] cockney panache too'. John Summerson (1962) records three Paragons in London: one in Richmond, and another by Michael Searles on the New Kent Road. The word 'paragon' means a model of excellence or virtue.

parallel lives See SEPARATE PARALLEL LIVES.

parallel parking 1 Cars parked against the kerb, parallel to the road. **2** Sexual intercourse. See also LINE OF STEEL and compare ECHELON PARKING.

paranoiaburbia The safe residential area of the future, according to the humorist Ian Martin.

Parc de la Villette, Paris A park created in Paris in the 1980s as one of the GRANDS PROJETS. The design, by the Swiss-born deconstructivist architect Bernard Tschumi (b1944), is based on three superimposed patterns of lines, points and surfaces, and features a network of red-painted steel follies.

parcel See DEVELOPMENT PARCEL.

parcelisation (also parcellation) Bringing together sites in different ownership for development.

parent plot One from which secondary plots of land have been formed by partition. The term was used by MRG CONZEN.

pargeting 1 Ornamental rendered or plastered panels on the exterior of a building. **2** Cement lining on the interior of a chimney.

pariah city One whose reputation makes people want to avoid it.

Paris II The ship on whose cruise between Marseilles and Athens in 1933 CIAM's ATHENS CHARTER was drawn up.

Paris of the Amazon Manaus, Brazil, so called in the nineteenth century when it was immensely wealthy from its world monopoly in wild rubber.

Paris of the East Prague.

parish council (England) A parish council has the right to be consulted on planning applications in the parish. Some parish councils are called *town councils*. Scotland and Wales have *community councils* instead, without the statutory right to be consulted on planning applications.

parish mapping A process in which local people create a map or maps of their parish which express its character and what it means for them. This is 'a social exercise which can create an agenda for action', in the words of Sue Clifford (1997).

park 1 A piece of land reserved for public recreation. **2** A place where activities of a particular kind are concentrated, usually at a low density and served by large car parks. Examples include *business park, retail park, theme park* and *leisure park*.

park and fly Parking at an airport and continuing the journey by air.

park and glide A variant of *park and ride* where the second part of the journey is made by boat. Also known as *park and sail*.

park and ride An arrangement by which people who park at a specified location (or locations) outside a town or city centre are provided with public transport into the centre. The term was coined in the late 1960s. Compare KISS AND RIDE.

park and sweat A building containing a car park and fitness centre. Driving to a place where one exercises is a characteristically modern activity.

park belt A narrow strip of parkland encircling part of a large urban area (Pepper, 1978). Compare GREEN BELT.

Robert Park

Park, Robert (1864–1944) A leading urban sociologist (formerly a journalist) of the CHICAGO SCHOOL. See CITY, NEW PAROCHIALISM and URBAN ECOLOGY.

Parker Morris *Homes for Today and Tomorrow*, the report of a committee chaired by Lord Parker Morris, was published in 1961. Its recommended standards for all new housing were a major influence on housing design. They were made mandatory for all new public housing after 1967, but this was reversed by the Thatcher government in 1981.

Barry Parker

Parker, Barry (1867–1947) Architect and planner. He was responsible for the plans for LETCHWORTH, HAMPSTEAD GARDEN SUBURB and BRENTHAM (all with RAYMOND UNWIN) and WYTHENSHAWE.

parking *n*. **1** The act of leaving a vehicle in a particular place. **2** A space in which one or more vehicles can be parked. Example: 'The planners insisted on more parking being provided.' **3** (upper midwest and western US) A grass strip (often with trees) between a pavement (sidewalk) and a street (*American Heritage Dictionary*).

parking ratio The relationship between the amount of parking associated with a building and the building's size and use.

parking standard A prescribed level of car parking that must be provided for a specific development. For example a parking standard may specify a 100 per cent ratio (meaning that one parking space must be provided for each dwelling), or it may be expressed as the number of parking spaces per dwelling or in relation to office floorspace. The aim of a particular parking standard might be to ensure that enough parking is provided to meet the needs of a development's users, or the opposite: to ensure that the development does not generate excessive traffic. Parking standards should include cycle parking and disabled parking. In certain developments no parking or only visitor parking will be required.

park-once environment Development that makes it convenient to park once and visit a number of nearby locations on foot.

parkway (US) **1** A broad, tree-lined road. The term was coined by FREDERICK LAW OLMSTED and CALVERT VAUX, who built two in Brooklyn (Eastern Parkway and Ocean Parkway) (Hall, 1998). EDWARD M BASSETT defined a parkway as a strip of public land devoted to recreation over which the abutting property owners have no right of light, air or access (compare FREEWAY and HIGHWAY). **2** A euphemism for a six-lane suburban arterial road (Duany and Plater-Zyberk, 2001). Steven Pinker (1994) notes that 'one drives on a parkway and parks in a driveway'. **3** A railway station with extensive car parking, designed to persuade car-owning commuters to 'let the train take the strain'. Didcot Parkway, Bristol Parkway and Port Talbot Parkway are examples. See also BRESSEY REPORT.

parlour A small, secondary, living room. The TUDOR WALTERS REPORT of 1918 noted that most working-class households expressed a desire for a parlour. After the second world war, though, 'parlour' was no longer mentioned in the UK government's *Housing Manual* and other official housing guides (Markus and Cameron, 2002). Compare SCULLERY.

parochialism 1 Taking an inappropriately narrow and localised view. **2** Focusing effectively on community needs by taking a localised view. See NEW PAROCHIALISM and POSITIVE PAROCHIALISM.

partial uncertainty See CERTAINTY.

participation See PUBLIC PARTICIPATION.

participation exercise A term often used for consultation by a local authority or developer. It seems to imply merely going through the motions, which it often is. See ARNSTEIN'S LADDER.

participatory appraisal A technique for enabling the people of an area to decide what changes they want to initiate.

participatory democracy Government (usually at local level) through the direct involvement of the people; a process in which all citizens likely to be affected by a decision have an opportunity to take part in making that decision. See also DEMOCRACY.

partnership A shared enterprise. The DETR (1998) defined a partnership as 'the coming together of a range of different people, groups or bodies to take forward a strategy for a particular area'. Nigel Smith (2001) suggested a more specific motive when he defined a partnership as 'a loose collection of people and organisations with conflicting interests held together by the prospect of securing government money'. See ARNSTEIN'S LADDER and see also INNER CITY PARTNERSHIP.

partnership arrangement One made to allow a developer to develop land while the freeholder retains the land interest. The landowner grants a long lease to the developer.

Partnership Investment Programme Government support for reclaiming BROWNFIELD land.

party To judge from letters in the professional press, a invitation to a party fills a planner with dread. The problem is, planners complain, that admitting to being a planner is guaranteed to kill the conversation. This is hardly surprising. Planning is not a SIGNATURE PROFESSION. Many local authority planners are engaged in work that is bureaucratic and routine, and for which they are overqualified. This is the side of planning that the public mostly sees. Other planners are engaged in work that is positive and satisfying, but the public sees little of this except where it goes wrong. Other built environment professionals feel equally disadvantaged at parties. Urban designers complain that no one knows what urban design is, and conservation officers that they are expected to know about wildlife.

Jonathan Raban (1974) suggests that urban dwellers become particularly adapt at categorising people. 'People who live in cities become expert at making these rapid, subconscious decisions. At any large party, one can see people "reading" strangers with the abstracted speed of a blind man tracing over a book in Braille.' The planner is soon unmasked.

party's over, the Tony Crosland's tenure as ENVIRONMENT SECRETARY (1975–78) is remembered primarily for the phrase he used in telling local authorities that economic conditions required the government to restrict local authorities' spending. 'The party's over,' he said. Many people in inner city areas devastated by local authority clearance and policies asked: what party was over?

Pasmore, Victor (1908–98) Painter. As an adviser on the visual appearance of housing at Peterlee new town, he was asked to apply his painter's eye to layouts and exteriors. Alan Powers (2001a) records that, working with two architects, he 'devised a vocabulary of white-painted boarding and black or grey brick, in which windows were positioned with the eye of an abstract painter, although not always for the convenience of the inhabitants.' Powers notes that Pasmore made the layouts 'compressed, patterned on paper against winding roads to achieve something like the effect of certain of Pasmore's paintings and reliefs.' Pasmore also designed the Apollo Pavilion, named after the US space programme and completed in 1970. The concrete pavilion, which has no function except as a sculptural object and a space to experience, was soon vandalised. English Heritage proposed to list it in 1996, but the government turned it down in response to local lobbying. Alan Powers comments: 'It is unusual as a conservation case in that it offers no possibility for conversion to another use; neither is it in danger of collapse. Indeed, its demolition would be expensive and difficult.'

passage (French) A passage; an ALLEY; an ARCADE; a route. Glass-roofed arcades of shops called *passages* were fashionable in Paris in the first three decades of the nineteenth century and later more widely in Europe and in the USA (Girouard, 1985). One of them, the Passage Choiseul, provided the setting for Louis-Ferdinand Céline's novel *Death on the Instalment Plan*, and was where Céline himself grew up. Patrick McCarthy (1975) wrote in his biography of Céline that the Passage Choiseul 'stands, then as now, in a maze of little streets close to the opulent Avenue de l'Opéra but worlds apart. Tourists who admire the beauties of Paris know nothing of this neighbourhood, which is a hive of small shops and cafes, of bargains and basements. Ancient women hover behind dusty counters and haggle with customers. Gossip flies through the air. At lunchtime each café has its clientèle of harassed shopkeepers who devour their *croque-monsieur* and flee behind their narrow doors. The Passage, its glass roof admitting a murky light, offers to the shopper a cobbler's, a watch-maker's, a tailor's and a second-hand bookstore... It lives and breathes the fetid atmosphere of slim profits, fatigue and bankruptcy. It is a shrine to the most powerful of French gods – the *petit commerce*.' Hannah Arendt (1973) notes how the *passages* of Paris attracted the German cultural critic Walter Benjamin (1892–1940). 'The arcades which connect the great boulevards and offer protection from inclement weather exerted such an enormous fascination over Benjamin that he referred to his projected major work on the nineteenth century and its capital simply as "The Arcades" (*Passagenarbeit*),' she writes. 'These passageways are indeed like a symbol of Paris, because they clearly are inside and outside at the same time and thus represent its true nature in quintessential form.'

passeggiata Strolling; a stroll with friends or family in a public place. The term is borrowed from the Italian. Non-Italian observers admire Italians' ability to enjoy public space. Examples: 'Where were the families parading, passaggiata-style, up and down the streets of King's Lynn in the evening?' (2002); 'Quality of life in the centre of our cities has improved unbelievably. The idea of passeggiata is catching on' (the architect RICHARD ROGERS, quoted in *Building Design*, 2003b). See also CROWD-SOAKING, DÉRIVE, FLÂNEUR, GAZZARD'S LAW OF URBAN VITALITY and WALKING.

passenger car unit The equivalent of one private car. Other vehicles are converted to the same unit by applying an appropriate factor. PCUs are used as a unit for measuring traffic flow or road capacity.

passenger interchange The process of passengers changing between modes of transport. Compare TRANSPORT INTERCHANGE.

passenger transport authority Organisations set up (initially under the Transport Act 1968) to provide public transport in metropolitan areas (Merseyside Passenger Transport Executive, for example).

passive engagement Being involved in the life of a public space without doing anything active – watching people passing by, for example. Compare ACTIVE ENGAGEMENT.

passive solar gain See SOLAR GAIN.

passive surveillance (or supervision) The discouragement to wrong-doing by the presence of passers-by or the ability of people to see out of windows. Also known as *natural surveillance (or supervision)*. See EYES ON THE STREET.

pastiche A composition (in architecture, for example) drawing on parts of other works or elements of various styles. The word is used both with and without pejorative intent. Its use in recent years has been most often in association with POST-MODERN ARCHITECTURE. It comes from the French and Italian, deriving originally from the Italian *pasta*, meaning paste.

pasticheur One who designs in PASTICHE.

path 1 A footpath. **2** In the specialised sense described by KEVIN LYNCH (1960) in defining the elements of a city's image, paths are 'the channels along which the observer customarily, occasionally or potentially moves. They may be streets, walkways, transit lines, canals, railroads.'

pathiopolis A city representing the culture of deterioration. The term was used by PATRICK GEDDES.

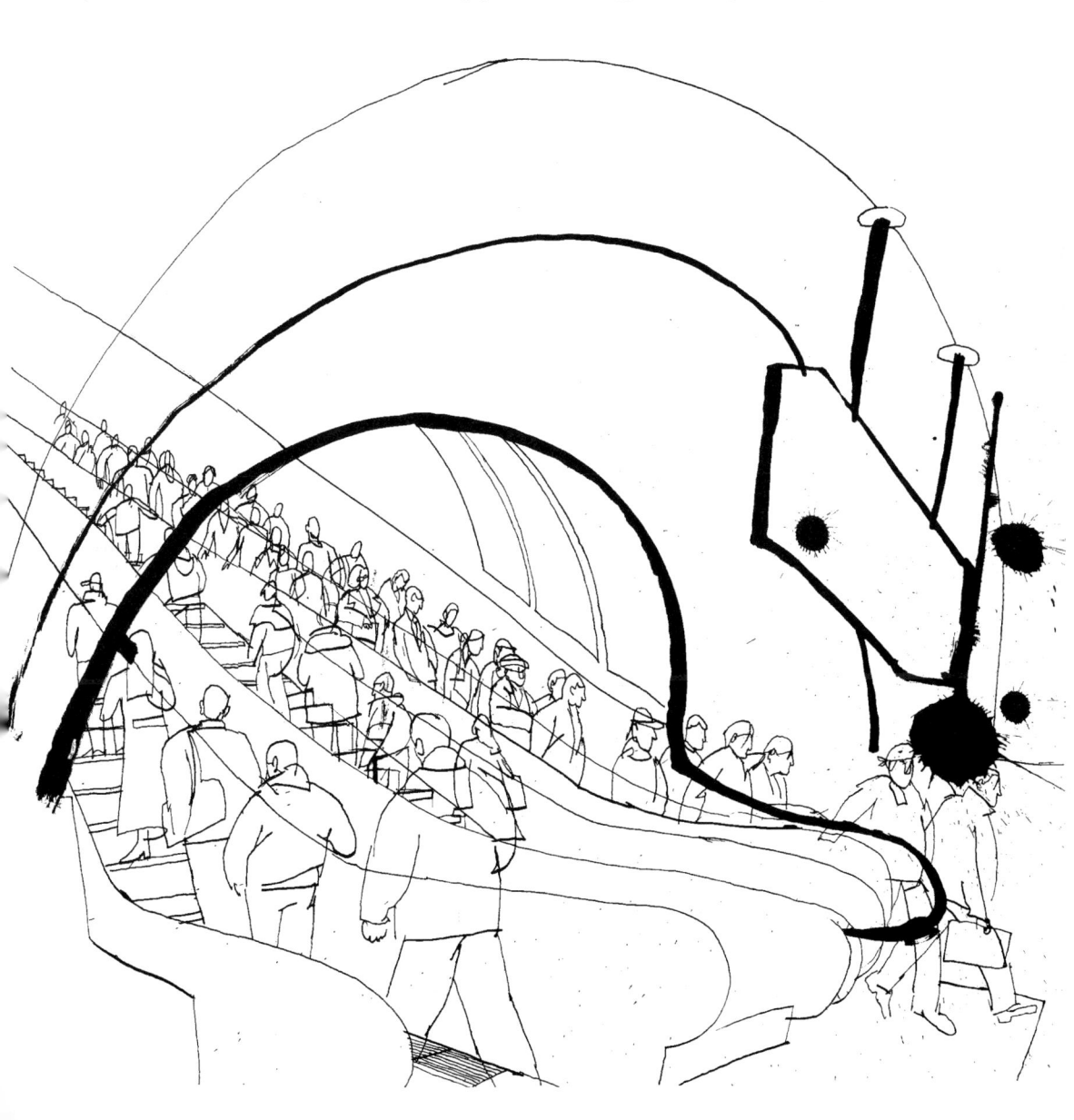

patron Andres Duany (2003) defines patrons of architecture as 'architectural sophisticates who commission buildings as conscious works of art'. They are, he suggests, 'willing to put up with additional costs, certain discomforts and some brickbats in support of the designer's conception' – unlike the typical CLIENT, CUSTOMER or VICTIM. The word comes from the Latin for 'father'. In ancient Rome a patron was the former master of a freed slave, who still enjoyed some rights over him or her.

Patten, Chris (b1944) Politician. As Conservative environment secretary in 1990 he made a significant move towards extending planning control to matters of urban design. He later became the last governor of Hong Kong and a European commissioner.

patter Glasgow dialect.

pattern book A guide illustrating popular ways of building, from which builders can select designs for an entire house or elements of it. Many were published in the nineteenth century. See also BATTY LANGLEY.

pattern language The basis of CHRISTOPHER ALEXANDER's system of participative design, using more than 200 'patterns' relating to aspect of design at scales ranging from a region to a room (Alexander, 1977).

pavement 1 (UK) The raised surface for pedestrians beside a street or road. The US equivalent is *sidewalk*, though pavement is used in some parts of the southern states (Bryson, 1990). **2** (US) The structure of a road, including its surface and underlying structure. The UK equivalent is *roadway*. **3** A paved surface.

From the Latin *pavire*, to beat hard. Apparently the novelist Arnold Bennett considered 'pavement' to be one of the most beautiful words in the English language (Pound, 1952). See also CAUSEY and PLAINSTONES.

pavement line The boundary where the pavement meets the road.

pavilion building One that stands away from any others and back from any street frontage; one with a prominent façade on each of its sides.

Pavillon de l'Arsenal A centre for architecture and urbanism run by the city of Paris, presenting information about the city and how it is changing. It has helped to inspire interest in ARCHITECTURE AND PLANNING CENTRES in the UK. The name comes from the historic building that houses it.

Paxton, Joseph (Sir) (1801–65) Designer and planner. Paxton began his working life as a gardener. By 1826 he was superintendent of the Duke of Devonshire's gardens at Chatsworth, where he designed green houses with innovative glass and metal roofs. He drew on this experience in designing the prefabricated iron and glass CRYSTAL PALACE for the 1851 Great Exhibition. He designed the village of Edensor on the Chatsworth estate and BIRKENHEAD PARK.

paying for growth A term sometimes used in the USA to describe IMPACT FEES. The principle is that the developer contributes to the cost of infrastructure that the development makes necessary.

Peabody Trust A philanthropic provider of housing, founded in the UK in 1862 by the American merchant George Peabody. The sombre, identikit tenements built by the trust in its early years are instantly recognisable all over inner London, as is the epithet 'Peabody' applied to them. In the 1990s the trust, still a major developer, gained a reputation for being at the forefront of new thinking about housing design.

peace wall (Northern Ireland) One separating areas occupied respectively by warring Loyalist and Republican communities. In 2002 the land beside peace walls was estimated to account for seven per cent of the entire area of Belfast (Booth, 2002b). See also BERLIN WALL and CUTTESLOWE WALL.

Peacock, Thomas Love (1785–1866) Novelist. See WOW FACTOR.

Pearl Delta Supercity A MEGAPOLIS in southern China incorporating Hong Kong, Guangzhou, Shenzen and Zhuhai. Terry Farrell and Partners (2002) have described it as 'an urban civilization without parallel on earth' and 'a giant landscape of car-based planning, commercial and residential complexes and shopping malls'.

Pearl of the Orient Manila.

pearl One of a series of concentrations of development on a transport corridor or other linear feature (the string of the string-of-pearls) such as a river.

Pearson, Charles Solicitor to the City of London. Ruth Rendell (1991) calls him the Father of the Underground. She writes: 'The idea of an underground railway running through a "spacious archway" came to Pearson in the 1840s along with other visions of creating garden suburbs and bringing London a gas supply.' The first line, from Farringdon to Paddington, opened in 1863, six months after Pearson's death.

pea-souper A London FOG, particularly in the 1920s and '30s (Ackroyd, 2000), so called because it was thick and greenish.

pebbledash A method of rendering exterior walls of buildings with pebbles set in mortar, sometimes to hide poor building work or to protect walls particularly exposed to wind, rain or sea spray. See BAYKO and HARLING.

pebbledash people Conservative party leader William Hague used the term in 2001 to describe one category of voter to whom he hoped to appeal: a typical resident of less affluent SUBURBIA, where houses are supposed to be commonly rendered in PEBBLEDASH. Compare BEDPAN MAN, MONDEO MAN and WHITE VAN MAN.

pedestrian 1 *n.* A person on foot. That meaning was coined in 1791 by William Wordsworth (Bryson, 1994). The degree to which account is taken of the interests of people on foot is fundamental in determining the effect of planning policy and practice. The Los Angeles planner quoted by Rebecca Solnit (2001) represents one extreme. 'The pedestrian,' he or she said, 'remains the largest single obstacle to free traffic movement'. **2** *adj.*

Reserved wholly or mainly for people on foot (as in *pedestrian precinct*). **3** *adj*. Dull and prosaic. This is the oldest meaning. In 2001 the Pedestrians Association adopted the campaigning name Living Streets. The organisation's original name had been tested on focus groups, who apparently gave it as negative a response as that previously received by the drilling specialists from the Boring Society. See also ELECTRONIC PEDESTRIAN.

pedestrian audit A systematic assessment of the conditions faced in a particular place by people on foot. Audits cover matters such as pedestrian flows; crossing points; pavement width and condition; street furniture; personal security and signage. See also ACCESS AUDIT.

pedestrian continuity A condition created by a network of safe and pleasant pedestrian routes.

pedestrian crossing (UK) A place where people on foot are encouraged or permitted to cross a road, with or without traffic lights. The US term is *crosswalk*.

pedestrian culture Ways of thinking, designing, planning and developing that give high priority to the interests of people on foot.

pedestrian flow The aggregate of people walking along a route; a measure of this.

pedestrian guardrail A fence erected at the edge of a pavement to prevent pedestrians crossing wherever they want. Designed to promote pedestrian safety and to prevent pedestrians from obstructing traffic, they make a major contribution to destroying the informality of shopping streets and to making people on foot subservient to those in vehicles. A planner in Swansea, Wales, suggested in 1999 – none too proudly – that his city ranked as having the greatest length of pedestrian guardrail per head of population in the UK. Westminster City Council's programme of street improvements to the Strand, completed in 1996, included the removal of all pedestrian guardrails.

pedestrian network diagram Shows all parts of an area that are accessible to pedestrians and inaccessible to vehicles.

pedestrian spine A main pedestrian route on to which others join.

pedestrian strategy One that coordinates measures to improve conditions for people on foot and to raise the priority of walking as a mode of travel.

pedestrianisation The creation of largely traffic-free streets or spaces. Also *pedestrianise*. London Road in Norwich was the first street in the UK to be closed to traffic and pedestrianised in 1957. When in 1971 the first public place in Sydney, Australia, was reserved for pedestrians only, the local politician responsible (Leo Port, who styled himself the Minister for Pedestrians) always insisted on saying positively that it was being opened to pedestrians, not closed to traffic (Gazzard, 1988).

pedshed The area within a 10-minute WALK BAND around a train station. The term was coined by planning and urban design consultants Llewelyn-Davies, who point to pedsheds as locations likely to be appropriate for relatively dense housing development. The analogy is with WATERSHEDS.

pedway 1 A paved route reserved for people on foot. The City of London Corporation planned a 32-mile Pedway network within the Square Mile in the 1960s. The plan was later abandoned, though fragments of the system of walkways 20 feet above pavement level are still in use today (Hebbert, 1998). **2** Supposedly the original name for Milton Keynes' *pede*strian cycle*way* network, it was accidentally mistyped as REDWAY. The new name stuck, and dictated the decision to surface the network with pink tarmac.

Peets, Elbert See CIVIC ART.

pencil A tall, thin TOWER BLOCK.

pend (Scots) An archway and passageway, suitable for vehicles, leading through to the back of a building.

penetrate To enter a densely built part of a city. Examples: '…you reached Seven Dials, which it was only safe to penetrate in the company of two top-hatted policemen'; 'Deeper and deeper the slums plunged into an East as impenetrable as a jungle' (both from Wolfe, 1938).

penetration Pedestrian or vehicular traffic entering a particular area.

Penn, William The founder and (with THOMAS HOLME) planner of Philadelphia.

William Penn

pentref (Welsh) Village. Compare DINAS and TREF.

people come where people are An old Scandinavian proverb quoted by the urban designer JAN GEHL (1987) in support of his assertion that people are attracted to busy places.

People of the Abyss, The A book by Jack London (pen name of John Griffith, 1876–1916) about the horrors of conditions in the east end of London. The American author lived near London's docks for two months in 1902 to investigate living conditions.

people policy (US) One that targets resources on people in need, rather than on places.

people power Effective action by people through means other than the normal political structures of government. Street demonstrations and community action campaigns are examples.

people-based planning Based on a social rather than physical perspective. Compare PLACE-BASED PLANNING.

people-friendly *adj.* Convenient and pleasant for people to use, and to pass by or through, particularly on foot. Example: 'The public space has been improved with lighting, seating and people-friendly materials' (2002).

people-oriented services Activities in the service sector, such as in leisure, hospitality, catering and retail.

peopling Taking measures to increase the number of people in a place (by making it more accessible or easier to find, or providing activities, for example), particularly to make it feel safer and more pleasant.

Peoria, Illinois The mid-west city, halfway between Chicago and St Louis, has been regarded as the traditional epitome of Middle America. Potential backers of a show would ask 'how will it play in Peoria?' Until the recession of the 1980s, Peoria was more or less the COMPANY TOWN of the Caterpillar tractor company. The Peoria were a Native American tribe. What is typical changes with the nation's changing demography. The town of Muncie, Indiana, where marketing consultants try out new products on the town's supposedly average Americans, is said to be a modern equivalent of Peoira.

George Pepler

Pepler, George (Sir) (1882–1959) Town planner and civil servant. He was successful in persuading local authorities to adopt town planning powers and put them into practice (under the planning acts of 1919, 1925 and 1932) He was the Town Planning Institute's first honorary secretary and twice its president.

pepper-pot 1 To carry out action at scattered locations rather than comprehensively throughout a whole area. Example: The UK's 2000 Urban White Paper declared that the government had 'put in place measures to use previously developed land to prevent urban sprawl and pepper-pot developments'. **2** To introduce a mix (of tenures or building types, for example); scattering one type of development among other types. Example: 'The affordable homes will be integrated by pepper-potting and indistinguishable from sale housing.'

The analogy is with the many holes in the top of a pepper-pot, compared to the single, larger hole in a salt-cellar.

per cent for art The practice of allocating a certain proportion of a development's budget (or of the SECTION 106 payments associated with it) to providing works of art or craft, or involving artists or crafts people in the process of construction. Some local authorities have planning policies encouraging this, although the government does not favour including such policies in development plans. LORD FOSTER of River Bank famously described per cent for art as 'lipstick on the face of the gorilla', implying that it is too often a futile attempt to compensate for a badly designed building (see also TURD IN THE PLAZA). In at least one place the art can be architecture. The council of Culver City, an area of Los Angeles, amended its per cent for art regulations in 1994 to permit architecture to be considered public art in some circumstances (Collings, 2000). In Culver City developers are excused from spending the specified one per cent on art or craft if the building is more than utilitarian and if its architect is recognised by the art world in exhibitions, museums and publications.

perceived height The height that a building appears to be, rather than its actual height. For example, the perceived height of a three-storey building may be two storeys if the top floor is incorporated in the roof and lit by dormer windows. This idea is taken to absurd lengths with some MANSARD ROOFS and roofs with oversize dormers, built with the claim that they will not be perceived, but in fact more obtrusive than a normal storey would have been. Even worse are flat-roofed buildings whose top floor is tile-hung – sometimes with a slight slope – to pretend it is a dormer or mansard roof.

perceived space See HENRI LEFEVBRE.

percentage for participation A short-lived campaign by the RIBA Community Architecture Group in the 1990s urging those promoting development to allocate a percentage (one per cent was the target) of the contract value to pay for community participation in the development process.

perception The subjective understanding that a particular person has of the environment. This will depend on such matters as their experience, mental state, social background and education.

perceptual plane The facade of a building.

Perec, Georges (1936–82) Writer. Much of his work explores the life of cities, especially his native Paris. His 1978 book *Life A User's Manual* (*Vie Mode d'Emploi*) focuses on a single apartment block, while his novel *A Void* (in both the original French and in its English translation) does not contain a single letter e.

performance criterion (plural *criteria*) A means of defining the extent to which a development must achieve a particular functional requirement (such as maintaining privacy), without having to set out precise physical standards (which specify more precisely how one aspect of a development is to be designed – by setting out minimum distances between buildings, for example). The art of urban design lies in balancing principles that may conflict with one another. Standards demand to be met, and may be too inflexible to be of use in achieving a balance. Performance criteria, on the other hand, make no prior assumptions about the means of achieving a balance. Planning policies based on criteria can be expressed as: 'Development will be permitted provided that...'. In the BEST VALUE system of appraisal, performance criteria for planning relate to processes rather than physical outcomes, probably because processes are easier to measure. The best value planning indicators include: a) The proportion of planning applications determined within the limits set by the government. b) The overall average time taken to determine applications. c) The proportion of applications that are a departure from the development plan. d) The cost of the service per head of population.

Pergamon The ancient Hellenistic capital of the Attalid dynasty (now Bergama, Turkey), built in the third and second centruries BCE, and noted for its library. Spiro Kostof (1991) describes Pergamon as 'still without peer as an articulate overall system of urban design'. This is all the more remarkable, Kostof notes, in that the city form did not result from a master plan worked out at the beginning, but rather from the responsive efforts of several generations of planners and architects. See BAROQUE.

perimeter block A street block each of whose frontages faces PUBLIC SPACE (usually a street), creating more or less continuous building frontages along the streets (the individual buildings may be semi-detached houses, terraced houses or blocks of flats). This layout is often characteristic of relatively dense urban development. Perimeter blocks are crucial to the configuration of urban space (see SPACE IS THE MACHINE) and offer the additional advantage that any back gardens and private areas are inaccessible to public spaces, making them less vulnerable to intruders.

Perinthia An imaginary city in Asia described by Italo Calvino in INVISIBLE CITIES (1972). It was laid out according to the detailed advice of astronomers to ensure that the influence of the stars would be in every way benevolent. As it happens, children born in Perinthia have turned out to be freakish and deformed. This shows either that such forms are, contrary to orthodox belief, eternally harmonious, or that the astronomers were wrong. Compare SPOROUNDIA.

peripheral estate A housing ESTATE on the edge of a town or city. Many suffer from problems of crime, poverty, deprivation and poor housing as bad as, and often worse, than some inner-city estates, as well as problems associated with lack of facilities, and inadequate or expensive public transport links.

périphérique (French) **1** *n.* A ring road. **2** *adj.* Outer.

periphery An area at the edge of a region, county or land mass that may suffer from economic problems due to its inaccessibility.

peri-urban At the outer edge (periphery) of an urban area; URBAN FRINGE.

Perle The dream city in which the artist Alfred Kubin's expressionist novel *The Other Side* (1907) is set, and which is finally utterly destroyed. '...The earth began to stretch and expand like rubber; a deafening roar, as though from hundreds of cannon, shattered the air. Slowly the facade of the Palace leaned forward, curved like a flag in the wind, and buried the Great Square under it. From all the towers in Perle the bells chimed melodiously, ringing out a majestic swan song for the dying city.' See also URBAN DESTRUCTION.

permanences A term used by Italian architect ALDO ROSSI for what are revealed through a city's monuments and basic layout. Through permanences, he argues, cities become historical texts.

permeability The degree to which an area has a choice of routes through it; the condition of being permeable. Permeability has long been considered as one of the central principles of urban design. A variety of pleasant, convenient and safe routes (as opposed to layouts in big blocks with no way through) is thought to make a place better suited to people on foot. (It may be possible to be spoiled for choice: the Australian Urban Design Forum [2001] has noted that in an area of 10 blocks x 10 blocks, if the diagonal corners of this super block are A and B, there are 184,756 different routes between A and B.) Permeability is sometimes spoken of as undesirable by people (such as the police) seeking to reduce the opportunities for crime. In this view a high degree of permeability, particularly in an area of housing, can provide a choice of escape routes for criminals. The reality is that, like any other principle of urban design, permeability is not an absolute. The desirable degree and type of permeability for a specific place will depend on local circumstances. See also ISOMETRIC PERMEABILITY and compare OVERPERMEABILITY.

permeable Allowing through movement; capable of being passed through.

permitted development That for which planning permission is given automatically by the GENERAL PERMITTED DEVELOPMENT ORDER. It includes minor house extensions and some agricultural buildings. See also ARTICLE 4 DIRECTION.

permitted parking regulations Applied in areas where parking is allowed for a limited period of time.

perpetual night syndrome The condition of some housing estates where people are scarcely more aware of other people during the day than in normal residential areas at night (Hillier, 1996).

Perry, Clarence Sociologist and town planner. See NEIGHBOURHOOD.

personal distance See INTIMATE DISTANCE.

personalisation Changing a building or place to reflect its owner's or users' taste; people putting their own stamp on their environment. This is one of the seven principles of urban design identified in *Responsive Environments* (Bentley et al, 1985). Examples of personalisation are as various as new Georgian front doors and garden gnomes, painting and planting. Personalisation is a sign that a place is cared for. Conversely, a place that people are able to personalise is more likely to be cared for. Andrew Saint (2001) writes: 'We want urban order, but there are other needs as well. People have got to have their ornament, all the more so because part of the price of worldwide urbanism is to deprive people of the daily work of their hands and their contact with the soil.' He asks: 'When are we going to learn that lesson, and appreciate that clients can be creative as well as architects? Perhaps more of the urban incident, sensation and individualism we crave should be left to the citizens themselves, while those who create the framework for them should stand further back and submit to a stricter urban discipline.' (For Michael Sorkin's contrasting view, see LOCAL DISTINCTIVENESS).

person-friendly *adj* See PEOPLE-FRIENDLY.

personification Attributing the character of a person to (for instance) a city. For example, Leslie Mitchell (better known as the novelist Lewis Grassic Gibbon) wrote in 1935: 'Glasgow is one of the few places in Scotland which defy personification. To image Edinburgh as a disappointed spinster, with a hare-lip and inhibitions, is at least to approximate as closely to the truth as to image the Prime Mover as a Levantine Semite. So with Dundee, a frowsy fish-wife addicted to gin and infanticide. Aberdeen a thin-lipped peasant woman who has borne 11 and buried nine. But no Scottish image of personification may display, even distortedly, the essential Glasgow. One might go further afield, to the tortured imaginings of the Asiatic mind, to find her likeness – many-armed Siva with the waistlet of skulls or Xipe of Ancient America, whose priest skinned the victim alive, and then clad himself in the victim's skin... But one doubts anthropomorphic representation at all. The monster of Loch Ness is probably the lost soul of Glasgow, in scales and horns, disporting itself in the Highlands after evacuating finally and completely its mother-corpse' (quoted in Spring, 1990).

The media sometimes dubs someone who is seen to dominate civic life as Mr New York, Mr London, or wherever. A fictional character can also personify a city, or at least one aspect of it. Millicent Harding in Henry James' 1886 novel *The Princess Casamassima* is

Henry James

an example. 'She was to her blunt, expanded finger-tips a daughter of London, of the crowded streets and the bustling traffic of the great city; she had drawn her health and strength from its dingy courts and foggy thoroughfares and peopled its parks and squares and crescents with her ambitions; it had entered into her blood and her bone, the sound of her voice and the carriage of her head; she understood it by instinct and loved it with passion; she represented its immense vulgarities and curiosities, its brutality and its knowingness, its good-nature and its impudence, and might have figured, in an allegorical procession, as a kind of glorified townswoman, a nymph of the wilderness of Middlesex, a flower of the clustered parishes, the genius of urban civilisation, the muse of cockneyism.'

perspective A drawing showing the view from a particular point as it would be seen by the human eye.

Peter ST PETERSBURG.

Peterborough A mark three new town, designated in 1967, expanding the existing city.

Peterloo Massacre An infamous episode in 1819 in which soldiers and yeomanry killed 11 people in dispensing a meeting of protesting handloom weavers in MANCHESTER.

petrol-head An enthusiast for motor cars. 'We are all petrol-heads now,' wrote the *Sun* newspaper in 2002. It was demanding a car-based transport policy in the light of the problems of the railways, following several fatal accidents.

Petronas Towers The 452m-high twin towers in Kuala Lumpur, Malaysia, designed by Cesar Pelli and built in the 1990s, were the world's tallest.

Pevsner, Nikolaus (Sir) (1902–83) Art and architectural historian. In Germany he specialised in the history of art in Great Britain. In England he combined his academic career with writing classics such as *A Outline of European Architecture* (see ARCHITECTURE), *The Englishness of English Art* (the 1955 Reith Lectures) and, his greatest achievement, the multi-volume *The Buildings of England*. See also FUNCTIONALISM, PLAN, LEWIS WOMERSLEY and JOHN WOOD THE ELDER.

Nikolaus Pevsner

peyzazh (Russian) Landscape in its subjective aspect; its poetic, pictorial and emotional associations. This contrasts with another Russian word, *landshaft*, meaning landscape in its more objective, technical aspects. The Dutch landscape designer Han Lorzing (2001, quoted in Mead, 2002a) writes: 'There is a landscape that we can measure, and there is a landscape that we can only feel. The former is seen by most people in the same way; the latter by some people and in different ways.'

phalanstery A communal palace housing 1,600 members of a utopian community called a *phalanx*, and including mixed leisure uses. The concept was proposed by the early nineteenth-century French writer CHARLES FOURIER. Joseph Rykwert (2000) comments that this, the only one of Fourier's terms to survive in French and Italian common parlance, 'has, ironically enough, come to mean a vast and barrack-like building rather than the highly articulated pleasure palace of Fourier's proposals.' The word combines *phalanx* and *monastery*.

phasing *n.* and *v.* Planning how land can be developed in stages.

Philadelphia Planned and founded in 1683 by William Penn as the 'city of brotherly love'.

philanthropy at five per cent Investing in a philanthropic cause (such as housing) in the expectation of receiving a limited return on the capital. The Metropolitan Association for Improving the Dwellings of the Industrious Classes, founded in London in 1841, was an early example.

photochemical smog A thick fog caused by the effect of sunlight on polluting chemicals in the air. See SMOG.

photomontage An image or images superimposed on to a photograph to show the visual effect of a proposed development or other change. See also CIVILIA.

photovoltaics The direct conversion of solar radiation into electricity by a semi-conductor device or cell (a *photovoltaic module*). Photovoltaics can be incorporated into the fabric of the building.

physical environment The built and natural, as distinct from the social or economic, environment.

physical exclusion The process by which dilapidated or badly designed physical environments exclude some people from a 'normal' lifestyle. Compare SOCIAL EXCLUSION.

physical planning That which focuses on the use of land and the form of development, rather than economic or social issues. This was the main type of town planning practised in the UK when Lewis Keeble wrote his influential book *Principles and Practice of Town and Country Planning* in 1952. 'Town and Country Planning might be described as the art and science of ordering the use of land and the character and siting of buildings and communicative routes,' Keeble wrote. 'Planning, in the sense with which we are concerned with it, deals primarily with land, and is not economic, social or political planning, though it may greatly assist in the realisation of the aims of these other kinds of planning' (quoted in Taylor, 1998). Compare SOCIAL PLANNING.

physicalist town planning Focuses on the physical planning and design of human settlements (Taylor, 1998).

Piacentini, Marcello (1881–1960) Italian rationalist architect. As state architect under Mussolini, Piacentini planned the grand boulevards that demolished medieval neighbourhoods in several Italian cities. See also HAUSSMANN.

piano nobile (Italian) The first floor above street level, often featuring higher ceilings and larger windows, containing the principal living and reception rooms of the dwelling, and providing privacy and some relief from the noise of the street.

Frank Pick

Pick, Frank The commercial manager of London Transport who in the 1920s and '30s played a major part in building the underground railway network. See also ALBERT STANLEY and CHARLES YERKES.

pigeon See FLYING RAT, GUTTER BIRD and THE LONDON PIGEON WARS.

Piggly Wiggly The first self-service store, opened by Clarence Saunders in Memphis in 1916 (Hall, 1998).

Pilgrim, Mr Politicians and the press blamed the planning system for the suicide of a Mr Pilgrim in the 1950s. He killed himself on realising that changes in government policy meant that compensation for a piece of land he had bought would be based on its existing use value, not its DEVELOPMENT VALUE, unlike the price he had paid.

piloti Stilts. LE CORBUSIER and other architects often raised their buildings on pilotis so that the landscape and sometimes motor traffic could flow through without interruption. Compare DINGBAT.

Piranesi, Giovanni Battista (1720–78) Architect, theorist and engraver. His engravings of imaginary views of ancient buildings powerfully evoke the classical civilisation that he imagined built them.

piranesiesque Fantastically and romantically dramatic; reminiscent of the etchings of *Imaginary Prisons* and other works by Piranesi.

pitch 1 The degree of slope of a roof, from shallow to steep. **2** A site allocated for a trader's stall (in a market, for example). **3** A piece of ground allocated to a tent, caravan or other moveable object. **4** A steep street or lane.

Pitsville A place devoid of any positive qualities; 'the pits'. Derived from the US practice of coining place names by adding -ville to some characteristic feature. Compare DULLSVILLE and JOYVILLE.

Pittsville There are towns called Pittsville in Maryland and Wisconsin, and other places with the name are found in Missouri, Pennsylvania and Virginia. The last residents of Pittsville in Texas moved away in 1947 after a new road bypassed it. A flourishing small town in 1860, this Pittsville had been named after the Pitt family, who ran a store. An abandoned cistern and a clump of trees mark the town's site.

Pittville 1 A district of Cheltenham, Gloucestershire, laid out by the developer Joseph Pitt in the 1820s. David Lodge describes it in his 2001 novel *Thinks...* as 'a delightful garden-city estate of fine houses and elegant terraces, set in landscaped parkland surmounted by a vast neoclassical spa'. **2** A district in North California.

placation See ARNSTEIN'S LADDER

place 1 A defined area; a distinct locality. A place is defined by the BURRA CHARTER as a site, area, building or other work, group of buildings or other works together with pertinent contents and surroundings. John Stephens (2002) describes a place as 'a location for which we have some regard'. A place is 'a space which has a distinct character', according to Christian Norberg-Schulz (1980). In the words of Sue Clifford (1997), a place is 'space with meaning'. She asks: 'What is it that turns a locality into a place? Places are not constructed, there is no formula: somewhere becomes a place because its people share knowledge about its stories, can read its subtle cues, understand their significances, they may feel relaxed in its physical forms, find it easy to congregate there, but the point is that ordinary or special, a place holds an accumulation of meanings. Moreover and paradoxically, places and their meanings are dynamic, but change is at a scale and pace which encourages apprehension. The permeability of the city, the town or the village, the ability to absorb and reinvent, keeps places vital.' Clifford (1990) notes that 'Ptolemy suggested that logic, precision and rationality give us one idea of place and that myth, magic and imagination give us another.'

The humanistic geographer YI FU TUAN said 'space is transformed into place as it acquires definition and meaning' (quoted in Clifford, 1990). Conversely, a place that loses meaning can be said to die. 'Places are vulnerable to slow change,' Sue Clifford (1990) has written. 'Many a small place has been lost through no leap of development, but a gentle weaving away of meaning

"SPACE IS TRANSFORMED INTO PLACE AS IT ACQUIRES DEFINITION AND MEANING"
Yi Fu Tuan

as road signs appear one after another, poles and wires push away the sky, a tree is cut down, the old seat is not replaced, a bus shelter takes up more room, cars force their way in and around, and so on. So a small symbolic gathering place is bleached of meaning and dies soulless. A place for social exchange and cultural reinforcement disappears.' The geographer Doreen Massey (1994) suggests that instead of thinking of places as areas with boundaries, a place can be imagined as the unique point of intersection of points in a network of social relations. 'A large proportion of those relations, experiences and understandings are constructed on a far larger scale than what we happen to define... as the place itself, whether that be a street, or a region or even a continent,' Massey writes. 'And this in turn allows a sense of place which is extroverted, which includes a consciousness of its links with the wider world, which integrates in a positive way the global and the local.' Adrian Forty (2000a) suggests that *place* replaced *space* as the buzzword in discussing architecture in certain circles in the early 1960s, through the influence of the German philosopher Martin Heidegger. As an example, Forty quotes the Dutch architect Aldo van Eyck, writing in 1961: 'Whatever space and time mean, place and occasion mean more, for space and time in the image of man is occasion. Split apart by the schizophrenic mechanism of determinist thinking, time and space remain frozen abstractions... A house should therefore be a bunch of places – a city a bunch of places no less.' Jonathan Raban (1974) wrote that 'place is important; it bears down on us, we mythicise it – often it is our greatest comfort, the one reassuringly solid element in an otherwise soft city. As we move across the square to the block of shops on the street, with pigeons and sweet-papers underfoot and the weak sun lighting the tarmac, the city is eclipsed by the here-and-now; the sight and smell and sound of place go to make up the fixed foot of life in the metropolis.' Raban concludes: 'Place, like a mild habitual pain, reminds one that one is; its familiar details and faces... assure us of a life of repetitions, of things that will endure and survive us, when the city at large seems all change and flux. Loyalty to and hunger for place are among the keenest of city feelings, reverenced and prized precisely because they go against the grain of that drift towards the formless and unstable which the city seems to encourage in us.' In the words of the urbanist Mike Franks, 'places are what people make, spaces are what designers make'. BILL HILLIER (1996) argues that 'the current preoccupation with "place" seems no more than the most recent of the urban designer's preference for the local and apparently tractable at the expense of the global and intractable in cities. However, both practical experience and research suggest that the preoccupation with local place gets priorities in the wrong order. Places are not local things. They are moments in large-scale things, the large-scale things we call cities. Places do not make cities. It is cities that make places. The distinction is vital. We can not make places without understanding cities.' **2** A street or public square. Example: Langham Place in Central London. **3** A short street open at only one end. **4** A building or area with a specific function or character. Examples: A place of worship; a place of ill repute. **5** (French) A SQUARE; a circus.

The word *place* comes from the Greek *plateia hodos*, meaning broadway, and the subsequent Latin *platea*, meaning broad street or open area. The Italian *piazza* and the Spanish *plaza* share that origin. See also GLOBALISATION and SENSE OF PLACE, and compare SPACE.

place management Coordinated action to improve a place by involving a wide range of people with a stake in it. See also TOWN CENTRE MANAGEMENT.

place manager The term is used in ROUTINE ACTIVITY THEORY in relation to crime prevention to describe people such as door staff, concierges and security guards.

place marketing The modern equivalent of BOOSTERISM.

place, work, folk The elements of the process of regional and urban development (representing environment, function and organism) in the analysis of PATRICK GEDDES.

place-based planning Based on a physical rather than social perspective. Gordon Cherry (1983) wrote: 'Whereas in the past town planning was "place based", it now has to be "people based"... In earlier decades this century town planning had a physical, spatial, environmental and visual base; social and other policies were somehow expected to fit these other criteria.' Compare PEOPLE-BASED PLANNING.

placecheck A type of urban design audit devised in 1998 and developed by the URBAN DESIGN ALLIANCE, based on the CONNECTED CITY APPROACH. A local collaborative alliance or partnership uses checklists to investigate the connections in the built environment, in its movement network and among the people who shape it. The placecheck becomes the first step in a continuing collaborative process of urban design. The placecheck may point to the need for a piece of supplementary planning guidance, in which case it will become the first step in drawing up that guidance. Alternatively, the placecheck may identify the need for some other type of response. The first step is for people with a stake in an area's future to come together in a local partnership or alliance (formal or informal) to agree to carry out or commission a placecheck. Local authorities are likely to be involved, but the initiative can come from anyone, in any organisation or sector. A placecheck can be carried out for a place as small as a neighbourhood or town centre, or as large as a city or county. The setting might be urban, suburban or a village.

placelessness The absence of distinct identity; lacking qualities of LOCAL DISTINCTIVENESS. See also THERE IS NO THERE THERE.

place-making Creating somewhere with a distinct identity; urban design.

place-making dividend The additional value that is thought to accrue to land developed so as to create a distinct place, rather than merely as an area occupied by a single use. The term was in use by the US Urban Land Institute in 2002.

place-sense A understanding of what is distinctive about a particular place; an ability to understand places; sense of place. PATRICK GEDDES used the term.

plainstones (Old Scots) A pavement.

Plan des Artistes A plan for Paris drawn up by a committee in the 1790s. Later it influenced the work of HAUSSMANN.

plan evaluation The stage in the planning process where alternative policies or plans are compared to decide which is preferable (Taylor, 1998).

plan *n.* **1** A scheme of doing or making something. The Local Government Association (2000) describes a plan as 'the tool we use in many different contexts to ensure that a desired outcome is achieved in an orderly and efficient way, coordinating the actions and resources needed to achieve it.' **2** A drawing or diagram (often to scale) showing a horizontal section of a building or area; a detailed map of a small area. Many writers on architecture emphasise the fundamental importance of the plan in shaping buildings and places. LE CORBUSIER wrote: 'Mass and surface are the elements by which architecture manifests itself. Mass and surface are determined by the plan. The plan is the generator.' Nikolaus Pevsner (1943) wrote: 'The history of architecture is primarily a history of man shaping space, and the historian must keep spatial problems always in the foreground. That is why no book on architecture... can be successful without ground plans.' In architecture of the Ecole des Beaux-Arts, according to Reyner Banham (1960), 'the elements of a building being of conventional form and structure, their distribution on plan did largely determine the appearance of the exterior.' Josef Kleihues (1990), director of the Internationale Bauausstellung (International Building Exhibition) in Berlin, called the ground plan 'the permanent gene structure of the city'. The word, dating from the 1670s, derives from the Latin *planus* meaning level. See also ACTION PLAN, BEST VALUE PERFORMANCE PLAN, CORPORATE PLAN, DEVELOPMENT PLAN, PLAN-LED SYSTEM and SERVICE PLAN.

plan *v.* Defined in Ambrose Bierce's *Devil's Dictionary* (published 1869–1906) as 'to bother about the best method of accomplishing an accidental result'.

Plan Voisin LE CORBUSIER's plan (to demolish a large part of the central business district of Paris and replace it with skycrapers, motorways and open space) was named after the Voisin Aircraft Company, whose motor-car division sponsored it.

plan, monitor and manage A UK government housing policy based on identifying proven need rather than following trends, and defining clear objectives (such as making better use of urban land and reducing the need to travel) to guide the planning of housing and the release of land for housing. The policy, introduced in the 1990s, replaced the discredited PREDICT AND PROVIDE.

planes of Id The central flatlands of LOS ANGELES, one of the four ecologies described by Reyner Banham (1973): 'an endless plain endlessly gridded with endless streets, peppered endlessly with ticky-tacky houses clustered in indistinguishable neighbourhoods, slashed across by endless freeways that have destroyed any community spirit that may have once existed'.

planetism Taking responsibility for the survival of the planet. The term was coined by the Australian futurist Peter Ellyard.

planification (French) Planning.

planimeter An instrument for measuring irregular areas on maps or plans.

plan-led system One in which planning applications that are in accordance with the development plan will be approved unless there are MATERIAL CONSIDERATIONS which suggest otherwise. Such considerations may be, for example, national policy statements issued after the plan was approved or changes in local circumstances. The UK government declared its commitment to a plan-led system of planning around 1990. This was supposedly not the tautology it seems. Market-led planning, which the new approach replaced, took some account of what a plan specified, but planners were expected to give market forces a major influence on what uses were allowed where.

plan-making Preparing plans, as opposed to exercising *development control*. Both are aspects of *planning*.

planned community (US) A form of homeownership in which the homeowners have a freehold interest in their homes and an interest in the owner's association that owns common areas. See COMMON INTEREST OWNERSHIP.

planned congestion Reducing road capacity in the interests of lower traffic speeds, safer streets, greater use of public transport or less pollution. See CONGESTION.

planned neighborhood development (PND) The preferred development type of US NEW URBANISM, based on the countryside, the corridor, the neighborhood and the district. PND is seen as the antithesis of CONVENTIONAL SUBURBAN DEVELOPMENT. A *planned neighborhood* is generally an area with a quarter-mile radius, equivalent to a five-minute walk.

planned unit development (US) A land-use zoning allowing a set of development standards to be adopted specifically for a proposed project. A PUD sets out criteria that a development must meet and sometimes also the legal framework for managing it.

planner In the popular mind 'the planners' are the people in the town hall who exercise planning control and promote development. They are credited with draconian powers, satanic vision and malicious intent so that the demolition of a cherished building, the construction of a brutal bypass or the erection of a carbuncular complex are invariably blamed on 'the planners', even though all three may have come about despite strenuous opposition from the local authority's planning department. There is little appreciation of the distinction between professionals and non-professionally qualified local authority staff, between council officers and council members (councillors), or between the respective powers of local and central government.

The professional body of town planners in the UK is the Royal Town Planning Institute (RTPI), though many planners are not members of it. Only corporate (full) members of the RTPI can call themselves *chartered town planners*, but anyone can call her- or himself (and practise as) a town planner, whether or not they have any relevant qualifications or experience. Some employers, such as local authorities, may require an applicant for a planning job to be a member of the institute. Others say only that the applicant must be eligible for election as a member of the institute, while others are not concerned one way or the other.

It is not possible to define precisely what a (town) planner is. Many of those who are professionally involved in running the statutory planning system under the Town and Country Planning Acts are clearly planners: local authority DEVELOPMENT CONTROL officers and the people who write local plans, for example. (This association with the statutory process is one reason for the profession's public image as being negative and bureaucratic). Other people in local authorities are on the margins of planning. They promote economic development, write policy, negotiate with developers, and deal with funding agencies; they may or may not have a planning education; their training may be in surveying, economics, management or one of a variety of other specialisms; they may be based in the chief executive's, economic development or urban regeneration department or section rather than the planning department; but much of their work is what the Royal Town Planning Institute would claim planning is all about.

planners' architecture Buildings designed to satisfy planners' criteria (usually relating to how the building fits into its context) rather than any more ambitious aim. See also PLANNING OFFICER'S GEORGIAN.

planning 1 PATRICK ABERCROMBIE defined planning as 'proposing to do, and then doing, certain things in an orderly, pre-meditated, related and rational way, having in view some definite end that is expected to be beneficial' (Williams-Ellis, 1937). Dahl and Lindblom (1953) describe planning as 'an attempt at rationally calculated action to achieve a goal'. Town or city planning is intended to provide: a) A framework offering a capacity for agreeing visions, analysing problems and opportunities, organising consultation and collaboration, setting policy, guiding design and implementing action, all within a dedicated legal structure. b) A flexible mechanism that can work with the timescales of 10 or 25 years that the processes of development and urban change often take, reconciling the need to think long-term with the more immediate requirements of grant regimes and politics. c) A process through which difficult decisions involving major conflicts of interest can be taken openly, fairly and accountably.

Peter Hall wrote in 1979 that the word planning 'is confusing in that it has two rather different but related meanings. First, it can refer to a set of *processes* whereby decision-makers engage in logical foresight before committing themselves. These include problem definition, problem analysis, goal and objective setting, forecasting, problem projection, design of alternative solutions, evaluation of alternative solutions, decision processes, implementation processes, monitoring, control and updating. Such processes are common to the planning of many public activities: defence, economic development, education, public order and welfare. Many of them are used in part, within different parameters and with different objective functions, by large private corporations. But secondly, the word can refer to processes that result in a *physical plan* showing the distribution of activities and their related structures (houses, factories, offices, schools) in geographical space.'

Patsy Healey (1988) has described planning as being 'about the mediation of conflicts of interest over environmental change'. The Royal Town Planning Institute defined planning in 2001 as 'the making of place, the mediation of space' (and added that curious slogan to its letterhead). The making of place involves questions of how much we value aspects of the environment. The mediation of space involves questions of social justice: of who benefits from change. The RTPI also defines planning as 'thinking spatially with a view to action'. In the same year a think tank of the institute (RTPI, 2001) provided another definition of planning as 'a management process which can deliver the spatial aspects of sustainable development, integrated agendas and inclusive communities anywhere in the world'. Andrew Saint (2001) notes that the word planning, 'quite different from a term like *urbanisme*, is dynamic yet insecure: it implies a longing to pin down and control events, places and peoples which can not be left to look after themselves.' Some critics of the planning system suggest that thinking of planning as a verb rather than a noun might concentrate the minds of planners on making the process proactive rather than reactive. **2** Short for planning permission: developers refer to 'going for planning' (applying for planning permission). See also CITY PLANNING, COMMUNITY PLANNING, SOCIAL PLANNING, SUSTAINABLE, TOWN AND COUNTRY PLANNING, TOWN PLANNING and URBANISM.

Planning Advisory Group Carried out a government review of the development plan system. Its report on *The Future of Development Plans*, known as 'the PAG report', was published in 1965. It recommended the two-tier structure of strategic STRUCTURE PLANS and LOCAL PLANS that was created by the Town and Country Planning Act 1968 and the Scottish equivalent in 1969.

planning aid Planners making their services available without charge to individuals or groups involved in the planning process. The government's green paper *Planning: delivering a fundamental change*, published in 2001, described planning aid as a service for 'individuals and community groups [who]... feel in need of independent and impartial advice about how to engage effectively with the planning process and lack the resources to be able to use planning consultants'. Planning aid is wider than this, though: sometimes it is a matter of supporting public participation and building community capacity in a way that few planning consultants would manage.

The planning profession used to claim that its job was 'rationally allocating land use in the public interest'. Planners said that part of their professional skill lay in knowing what the public interest was. The democratic political system had a role in setting priorities, of course, but the planners had a longer term and more objective view. The RTPI's report *The Management and Operation of RTPI Planning Aid Services*, published in 1992, painted a very different picture: 'The provisions in planning legislation for the role of the public are based on the twin assumptions that representative local democracy works effectively and that all sections of the population have equal access to knowledge and resources. Both assumptions are now generally recognised to be unfounded in fact. Elected members can not hope adequately to represent local views on specific issues. Experience has shown that the most articulate and resourceful sections of the population are most successful in having their views accepted.' Planning aid has been developed in response to that challenge. Every region of the UK now has a planning aid service, each independently organised and funded, either by or with the support of the local branch of the RTPI.

The organisation Urban Planning Aid was founded in the USA in the late 1960s. In the UK the term emerged from a discussion at the offices of the TOWN AND COUNTRY PLANNING ASSOCIATION in 1969. Legal aid was available to provide legal expertise to those who could not afford it. What was needed, it was suggested, was an equivalent for people who could not afford planning expertise. The TCPA appointed the first planning aid worker at the end of 1972, and its planning aid service opened in January 1973, though individual planners had worked in their free time with community organisations before that. See also INTERNATIONAL PLANNING AID.

planning appeal An appeal to the secretary of state against a refusal of a planning application, a failure to deal with it within the statutory time, or the imposition of unacceptable conditions.

planning approval 1 Formal approval, usually by a local authority, often with conditions, allowing development in respect of RESERVED MATTERS. **2** In common (though not strictly accurate) use, the terms *permission*, *approval* and *consent* tend to be used interchangeably, except by the government and the planning inspectorate. See PLANNING PERMISSION.

planning balance sheet A technique devised by economist planner Nathaniel Lichfield to measure the impact of development.

planning blight The shadow cast over a building, street or larger area by a planning decision concerning its demolition or redevelopment. The intervening period between the decision and its execution – which may be years or even decades – creates a sort of limbo where inward investment ceases, property values may collapse, business and residents move out, and buildings are abandoned. While these adverse effects may be unintentional, they are not unpredictable and are usually a consequence of considering outcomes but disregarding the processes by which they will be achieved. In the worst cases, changing circumstances mean that the planned outcome is never achieved, leaving blight as the only tangible consequence of the planners' intervention.

planning brief See DESIGN BRIEF.

planning by the rules A conventional approach to planning a development site or area. English Partnerships uses the term as a contrast to ENQUIRY BY DESIGN.

Planning Charter, The One of the UK government's citizen's charters, setting out timescales within which various categories of planning decision should be made.

planning committee (UK) Most commonly composed of elected councillors and carrying out certain of a local authority's statutory planning functions.

planning condition A planning authority can grant planning permission subject to conditions in any case where a proposed development would be unacceptable without them. The law requires that conditions are imposed only for a planning purpose, that they relate directly to the approved development, and that they are reasonable. The applicant has a right of appeal to the relevant secretary of state against any of the conditions.

planning consent 1 Formal approval, usually by a local authority, often with conditions, allowing development in respect of advertising, listed buildings and conservation area applications to proceed. **2** In common (though not strictly accurate) use, the terms *permission*, *approval* and *consent* tend to be used interchangeably in relation to planning, except by the government and the planning inspectorate. See PLANNING PERMISSION.

planning consultant A person or firm who hires her-, him- or themselves out as a specialist in planning. Some planning consultants appear as expert witnesses at public inquiries, giving their professional opinion of a planning application, for example. Often there will be planning consultants on opposing sides: for example one, representing a supermarket chain, may say that a particular planning application for a superstore is justified on objective planning grounds, while another, perhaps representing the local authority, may say that it is not. Is it a situation analagous to a legal trial, where (although lawyers are not meant to defend someone they *know* to be guilty) it is accepted that every defendant has the right to an advocate for their case? Presumably not: the planning profession has been based traditionally on the assumption that in relation to every development proposal there is such a thing as good planning, and that a profession planner has the skill to identify what it is.

In reality it is not that simple. Few cases are black and white, and reasonable people may make different technical judgements about the same issue. Many judgements are not technical, anyway. They depend on questions of value (the relative importance of different benefits and costs) and of politics (asking: in the face of conflicting interests, whose interests should be given priority?). All the same, the sight of some planning consultants selling their souls (or at least their professional integrity) to their clients is not pleasant. At the very least it raises questions about the status of what the planning profession traditionally claims to be objective judgements.

Planning for Real A participation technique that involves residents and other stakeholders making a model of their area and using it to help them determine priorities for the future. The technique was developed by Tony Gibson in the 1970s. It is now promoted by the Neighbourhood Initiatives Foundation (NIF), which Gibson founded. The NIF provides training in the use of Planning for Real and holds copyright for the use of the name. It acquired copyright as a way of preventing the reputation of Planning for Real being damaged by people who did not know how (or did not bother) to use it properly. Some local authorities and other organisations were finding it a cheap and easy way of going through the motions of public participation, ignoring the need for thorough preparation and skilled facilitation.

Planning for the Future The 1976 report of a Royal Town Planning Institute working party, chaired by SYLVIA LAW, that called for various types of planning to be integrated.

Planning Front A campaign for planning launched by the Garden Cities and Town Planning Association on the eve of the second world war in 1939.

planning gain Benefits for the community at large secured by a local authority through a SECTION 106 AGREEMENT. The official name for these benefits is now PLANNING OBLIGATIONS. The term planning gain, though widely used, is frowned on officially, being thought to be associated with suspicions that developers use the system to buy planning consents.

planning inks A range of standard ink colours that at one time were used by planners. Each colour denoted a particular land use.

planning inquiry See INQUIRY, PLANNING INSPECTOR and PUBLIC INQUIRY.

planning inspector A member of the planning inspectorate who conducts PUBLIC INQUIRIES into planning matters, and either informs the secretary of state or takes the decision on the secretary of state's behalf. The subjects of public inquiries include planning appeals, enforcement appeals, planning applications 'called-in' by the secretary of state, and development plans. Planning inspectors cover England and Wales; the Scottish equivalent is a *reporter*.

planning lawyer One who specialises in the law relating to the planning system. A lawyer is defined in Ambrose Bierce's *Devil's Dictionary* (published 1869–1906) as 'one skilled in circumvention of the law'.

planning obligation A legal instrument through which PLANNING GAIN is secured. Despite this distinction the two terms are often used interchangeably. A planning obligation is a binding legal agreement between a local authority and a developer, or unilaterally by a developer, for the purpose of restricting or regulating a development or the use of land, under Section 106 of the Town and Country Planning Act 1990. Such *section 106 agreements* are usually made in connection with the granting of planning permission, and may be used to enhance development proposals. They can 'enable a property owner to overcome obstacles which would otherwise prevent planning permission from being granted' (PPG1).

The Court of Appeal ruled in 1965 that a local authority did not have the power to impose a condition with a planning permission that would require a developer to contribute to the cost of off-site infrastructure. As a result a separate system has developed as a way of achieving the same effect through negotiating planning obligations. The system has been the subject of endless discussion over the years, and criticised for being confusing and open to abuse. It has survived because it serves a purpose; because no government has managed to find a workable alternative; and because it fills the gap left by the failure of three attempts by governments since 1945 to tax development values. The process of urbanisation raises the value of land. That increased value, according to one argument for justifying planning obligations, rightfully belongs to the community in general rather than to a landowner or developer.

planning officer's Georgian Bland, undemonstrative, vaguely vernacular, 'keeping-in-keeping' architecture which it is believed is more likely to be looked on favourably by the local authority planning department. A term of derision for a style of architecture designed to satisfy the local authority's requirements for a new building that looks reassuringly familiar. In the words of the architect and critic Michael Sorkin (1991): 'familiarity breeds consent.' Compare CONSERVATION-OFFICER GEORGIAN, KENTUCKY FRIED GEORGIAN and PLANNERS' ARCHITECTURE, and see GEORGIAN.

planning out crime Using the planning process to ensure that development is designed in ways that discourage crime. See NATURAL SURVEILLANCE and TARGET HARDENING.

planning permission Formal approval, usually by a local authority, often with conditions, allowing a proposed development to proceed. A full permission is usually valid for five years. Outline permission, where details are reserved for subsequent approval, is valid for three years. In relation to planning, the terms permission, approval and consent tend to be used interchangeably, except by the government and the planning inspectorate. Strictly speaking, planning *permission* is granted in respect of a development proposal, *approval* in respect of reserved matters, and *consent* in respect of advertising, listed buildings and conservation area applications.

planning policy guidance notes (PPGs) Government guidance on general and specific aspects of planning policy that local authorities must take into account in formulating development plan policies and in making planning decisions. They are: PPG1 *General Policy and Principles*, PPG2 *Green Belts*, PPG3 *Housing*, PPG4 *Industrial and Commercial Development and Small Firms*, PPG5 *Simplified Planning Zones*, PPG6 *Town Centres and Retail Development*, PPG7 *The Countryside: environmental quality and economic and social development*, PPG8 *Telecommunications*, PPG9 *Nature Conservation*, PPG10 *Planning and Waste Management*, PPG11 *Regional Planning*, PPG12 *Development Plans*, PPG13 *Transport*, PPG14 *Development on Unstable Land*, PPG15 *Planning and the Historic Environment*, PPG16 *Archaeology and Planning*, PPG17 *Sport and Recreation*, PPG18 *Enforcing Planning Control*, PPG19 *Outdoor Advertisement Control*, PPG20 *Coastal Planning*, PPG21 *Tourism*, PPG22 *Renewable Energy*, PPG23 *Planning and Pollution Control*, PPG24 *Planning and Noise*, and PPG25 *Development and Flood Risk*. PPGs are being replaced by *planning policy statements*.

planning policy statement See PLANNING POLICY GUIDANCE NOTES.

planning scheme A ZONING plan prepared by a UK local authority in the two decades after 1919.

planning system The arrangements by which central and local government carry out their statutory responsibilities to regulate the development and use of land in the public interest.

Planning-Programming-Budgeting Systems (PPBS) A system of management by objectives developed in the USA and used widely by central and local government in the UK in the 1970s.

plansmith A person without professional qualifications who is paid to prepare planning applications.

planted town A new town. The term is often used of towns begun in the middle ages.

plantscaping Designing the arrangement of plants in a building. Also *interiorscaping*.

Planung (German) Planning.

Planungspflicht (German) Planning obligations.

plat (US) *n*. **1** A plot of land. **2** A diagram showing the division of a settlement into individual plots. The word dates from the first half of the fifteenth century, originating from *plot* (a piece of land) and the Middle English *plat* (something flat). *v*. To divide into plots.

Plat of the City of Zion Joseph Smith's scheme for the ideal Mormon city. The plan was laid down twice before finally giving form to SALT LAKE CITY (Kostof, 1991).

Elizabeth Plater-Zyberk

Plater-Zyberk, Elizabeth Architect and town planner. In 1980 with her husband Andres Duany she co-founded Duany Plater-Zyberk, a leading NEW URBANIST practice, and was appointed dean of the University of Miami school of architecture in 1995. She helped write a groundbreaking TRADITIONAL NEIGHBORHOOD DEVELOPMENT ORDINANCE for Miami-Dade County, Florida.

Platz (German) A square.

playscape See URBAN PLAYSCAPE.

plaza A relatively formal public space. The term is of Spanish origin.

Pleasantville A film, directed by Gary Ross and released in 1998, in which two 1990s teenagers get trapped in a black-and-white 1950s soap opera called 'Pleasantville', featuring a small-minded American community where a woman's place is in the kitchen. The newcomers have a dramatic influence on the people of Pleasantville.

plot A small piece of land. The word comes from Old English.

plot holder A person who holds an allotment.

plot ratio The ratio of a building's floor space to the area of its site (gross floor area divided by the net site area). For example, a plot ratio of 5:1 means a building with a total floor area five times the area of the site on which it stands. The building could be a five-storey building

PLOT WIDTH

occupying the whole site, or a building of 10 storeys occupying half the site, or any other site/storey combination. Also called *site ratio* and (US) *floor area ratio*. Plot ratio is a measurement of density.

plot width The width of plots on a street is an important influence of the area's character. Narrower plots tend to provide variety, interest and a choice of routes.

plotland An area of farmland divided into small plots and sold as holiday homes or smallholdings, often without the usual infrastructure of paved roads, piped water and mains drainage. COLIN WARD (1998) writes: 'The word evokes a landscape of a gridiron of grassy tracks, sparsely filled with army huts, old railway coaches, sheds, shanties and chalets, slowly evolving into ordinary suburban development.' Plotland development was common in south-east England the few decades before 1939. The plots cost very little and their new owners built cheaply: in many cases a hut, chalet or railway carriage would be put in place and enlarged over the years by their owners' hands. Planners have generally regarded plotland development as a blot on the landscape and a professional affront. Plotlands at Laindon and Pitsea in Essex, for example, were a major reason for the designation of Basildon new town to sweep away the shacks and shanties. The clearance was accomplished with a good deal of sensitivity – plotland homes were often left standing in the middle of new development, waiting for the occupant to die or accept a place in an old people's home. Even so, 'Basildon was built on heartbreak' was a saying of older inhabitants. Ironically, by 1983 there were so few plotland homes left that they became regarded as HERITAGE. With the support of the Countryside Commission a plotland museum was established at Dunton Hills, with preserved bungalows and a waymarked trail.

Dennis Hardy and Colin Ward have celebrated the plotlands as valuable examples of how the right circumstances can give people the chance of continuously upgrading the place where they live, making owner occupation or running a smallholding a reality for people who start with nothing more than a plot of unserviced land. That has never ranked high as an objective of the planning system, particularly compared with the protection of the countryside. Anthony King noted in his history of the bungalow that, in the first four decades of the twentieth century, 'a combination of cheap land and transport, prefabricated materials, and the owner's labour and skills had given back to the ordinary people of the land the opportunity denied to them for over 200 years, an opportunity which, at the time, was still available to almost half of the world's non-industrial populations: the freedom for a man to build his own house. It was a freedom that was to be very short-lived' (King, 1984).

plug-and-play community One in which anyone can fit in quickly. RICHARD FLORIDA (2002) identifies these as places that attract creative people, 'where people can find opportunity, build support structures, be themselves, and not get stuck in any one identity'. The plug-and-play community 'is one that somebody can move into and put together a life – or at least a facsimile of a life – in a week'. The analogy is with a device that can be plugged in to the electricity supply without preparation.

plug-in city A proposal by ARCHIGRAM, published in 1964, for a city whose components could be added to or taken away from the basic 12-storey structure of services by crane or helicopter. The project had, in the words of design writer Peter Murray, 'a brashness that made LE CORBUSIER's Ville Radieuse look like a conservation project'.

plumb To design the traffic circulation for an area after the spaces themselves have been designed. Some urban designers (the authors of the ESSEX DESIGN GUIDE, for example) advocate plumbing new development as an alternative to designing a road network first, then designing development layouts to fit it. See also TRACKING.

pocket ghetto A low-income, high-security residential area (Dear and Flusty, 1998).

pod 1 An isolated, inward-looking complex or group of buildings with no through route. Examples include office and building parks, residential culs-de-sac, hotels and shopping malls. **2** A MICROFLAT.

poet See WALKING.

poetry See PROSE.

Pogatschnig, Giuseppe (1896–1945) Architect. See THE HORIZONTAL CITY.

point block A slim TOWER-BLOCK building. See also PENCIL.

Pointe Gourde principle The legal principle that the community in general shall not be required to pay the development value of any major planning scheme which is a public initiative.

Pol Pot planning Redevelopment or other action carried out with no concern whatsoever for its effect on people. Pol Pot led the Khmer Rouge, whose genocidal rule in Cambodia in the late 1970s left 1.5 million Cambodians dead. Planners frequently face the insult of being associated with dictators ('little Hitlers' is often heard) but the extraordinary brutality of Pol Pot seems to make him a favourite. Instances of planners in the UK being referred to as 'the Taliban' were recorded within a few days of the terrorist attacks of 11 September 2001 in the US. The attacks had been ascribed to supporters of the Taliban, the Islamic fundamentalists who ran the government of Afghanistan after the Soviet withdrawal.

polari The traditional argot of theatre, circus and the gay community, now considered to be a particularly urban language. Much of the vocabulary comes from Italian, Romany, Yiddish and slang words. The language may have developed from the nineteenth-century slang *parlyaree*, used by circus and fairground people, beggars and prostitutes, and from a variety of other slangs of marginalized groups such as sailors and thieves. See also LATTI.

pôle de développement (French) A growth pole.

polis Defined by EKISTICS as a settlement with a population of 75,000. A 'small polis' has 10,000.

polite Respectful of its context. Example: 'The Commission for Architecture and the Built Environment claimed that the original proposals were too "polite" and were "trying too hard to be unobtrusive". It called for some of the buildings to be more "striking"'(2002).

polite architecture Styles of architecture other than the VERNACULAR. Example: 'British polite architecture is one long story of imports from the Continent. It started with centuries of Roman rule bringing colonnaded forms better suited to sunny Italy.'

politogenics One of the terms used by PATRICK GEDDES (the other was *eu-politogenics*) for the science of good cities.

poll tax See TOLL TAX.

polluting development Development requiring statutory pollution control consent.

pollution The process of contaminating water, soil or the air; the state of being contaminated; something that contaminates. The UK Environment Agency estimated in 2002 that up to 24,000 people a year were dying prematurely due to air pollution in towns and cities (and double that number if deaths from cancers triggered by air particles were included), and as many again were hospitalised. This was due largely to pollutants – mostly from road traffic – such as nitrogen dioxide, sulphur dioxide and particulates. Jan Morris (1984) writes that Swansea in the 1860s, when its Metal Exchange was the copper centre of the world, 'seemed to have been visited by some horrific plague. Visitors approaching by train from the east, seeing for the first time the green sulphurous glow of its smelters, finding their carriages darkened by the black of its atmosphere, above all perhaps smelling its chemical fumes seeping and swirling all around, were sometimes terrified by the experience, so absolutely of another world did the place seem, and so poisoned by its own exhalations.' The writer VS Pritchett (1997) observed of London (probably writing in 1956): 'The city also is something you get on your lungs, which quickens and dries your speech and puts a mask on the face. We breathe an acid effluence of city brick, the odours of cold soot, the dead rubbery breath of city doorways, or swallow a mouthful of mixed sulfuric that blows off those deserts of railway tracks which are still called Old Oak Common or Nine Elms without a blade of vegetation in sight for miles – we breathe these with advantage. They gave us headaches when we were young, but now the poison has worked and is almost beneficent to those born to it. So herrings must feel when they have been thoroughly kippered.' See also FINE PARTICLES, FOG, HYBRID VEHICLE, LOW-EMISSION ZONE, NITROGEN DIOXIDE, RETROFIT TECHNOLOGY and SMOG.

Polomint City East Kilbride, west central Scotland, on account of its many roundabouts. The name, taken from the circular sweet with a hole in the middle, has also been applied to other towns.

polycentric (also polynuclear and polynucleated) Many-centred. Ebenezer Howard's SOCIAL CITY was one model of a many-centred urban structure. Modern urban regions vary in the degree to which they can be said to be polycentric. Peter Hall (1998) writes that ancient Rome was 'perhaps the first polycentric metropolis'. See CITY OF CITIES, POLYCENTRICITY, POLYCENTRISME and POLYNUCLEAR FIELD THEORY.

polycentricity Multi-centredness; a state of being many-centred. At a regional level the term describes the spatial structure of a region or territory, based on the analysis of where specific economic, social and environmental functions take place, and of the linkages between them. At the European scale, polycentricity is a spatial policy objective to achieve more balanced territorial development for the purposes of promoting economic competitiveness and SUSTAINABLE development (as set out in the European Spatial Development Perspective).

polycentrisme (French) An approach to analysing space and a process for developing spatial policies.

polychronic space That which is occupied at different times of the day – by office workers at lunchtime, people at leisure after work, and residents at weekends, for example. *Monochronic space* is fully used at only one time, probably because the buildings round it have only one use (Krietzman, 1999).

polygon A many-sided alternative to a SQUARE or CIRCUS. At least two were built (and so named) in GEORGIAN London (Summerson, 1962).

Polygon, The Despite its name (a polygon is a many-sided figure), the Polygon was a circle of 32 semi-detached four-storey houses built in 1793 at St Pancras, London. The campaigner Mary Wollstonecraft and her husband the political reformer William Godwin lived in a flat there. She died in the same year after giving birth to Mary, the author of *Frankenstein* and wife of the poet Shelley (Stamp, 1990).

polynuclear field theory An approach to regional development based on multiple centres spread across the landscape. A network of highways would be formed by an arterial road crossed by a series of tributary roads, each with a cluster of residential culs-de-sac at one end and an industrial hub at the other. Compare MARS PLAN.

Pombal, Marquis of (Sebastião José de Carvalho e Melo) (1699–1782) Statesman. As first minister to King José I of Portugal, Pombal was responsible for replanning Lisbon after the 1755 earthquake, which killed 40,000 people. He designed the lower town area, known as the Baixa, on a grid layout, with streets flanked by neoclassical buildings. Individual streets were allocated to specific crafts and trades. Pombal used a similar grid layout in replanning the town of Vila Real de Santo António on the Algarve in southern Portugal, which had been abandoned for several years after being destroyed by a tidal wave. Vila Real was rebuilt in five months. Pombal became the virtual dictator of Portugal, ruthlessly implementing a programme of modernising trade, administration, education and taxation, abolishing slavery, and limiting the power of the aristocracy and the church.

pomo POSTMODERNISM, particularly the 'postmodern' architectural style of the 1980s.

Pompey Portsmouth, England.

Pompidou Centre A major arts centre built in Paris in 1977, designed by Renzo Piano and RICHARD ROGERS, named after the French president. Famous for its brightly-coloured externally displayed service ducts and the escalator which snakes up the side of the building in a glazed tube, affording astonishing views across Paris, the uncompromisingly high-tech building is also notable for the lively public space created beside it. It underwent a major renovation in 1999. Also known as the *Beaubourg*.

Pontifex Maximus A nickname of THOMAS TELFORD (1757–1834), the great bridge builder.

Pontypandy The fictional South Wales village (a former coal-mining community) in which the children's animated television series 'Fireman Sam' is set. See also GREENDALE.

Pooleyville A nickname for a proposed new town promoted in the late 1950s by Fred Pooley, country architect of Buckinghamshire. Tim Mars (1998) describes it as 'modernist, impeccably urban and straight out of Sant'Elia – stepped "cluster blocks" interconnected by a figure-of-eight monorail'. The site – greatly enlarged, and with a very different design – later became MILTON KEYNES.

poor *adj.* and *n.* See POVERTY.

Pooter, Charles A City clerk and resident of The Laurels, Brickfield Terrace, Holloway, London, Pooter is the subject of *The Diary of a Nobody* by George and Weedon Grossmith. The comic classic, first published in book form in 1892, describes the minutiae of suburban life. Its humour derives mainly from the fact that Pooter himself has no sense of humour, a fact that is never so evident as when he tells a joke.

George Grossmith

pop architecture Based on making an aesthetic of the visual forms of popular culture.

popular planning A process in which local communities are actively involved in making decisions. The term was current in the 1980s.

porridge (Scotland) A nickname for render, which is thought to look like the food. Both are characteristic of Scotland. Render was traditionally applied to stone buildings. In the twentieth century, widely applied to brick-built council housing, it often failed, as the high potassium content in Scottish bricks made them explode when subject to the freeze-and-thaw cycle, forcing the render off. Today render is applied successfully to buildings made of concrete blocks.

Porridge Town VÄLLINGBY.

Port Sunlight A model community outside Birkenhead began in 1888 by soap manufacturer WH LEVER.

Port, Leo See PEDESTRIANISATION.

Porter, Dame Shirley See HOMES FOR VOTES.

Portland cement Made by cooking a mixture of chalk or limestone with clay. Invented by the Leeds stonemason Joseph Aspdin, it is named after Portland in Dorset, whose stone it is thought to resemble (Quinion, 2003). Compare ECO-CEMENT.

Portland, Oregon The city is celebrated for its recent achievements in planning, SMART GROWTH, NEW URBANIST development, and the promotion of cycling and walking.

Portmeirion A township on the north Wales coast designed and built by the architect Clough Williams-

Ellis from 1925–1972, and incorporating many rescued architectural elements (Williams-Ellis called it 'a home for fallen buildings' – the town hall is entered through a Norman Shaw fireplace, for example). The buildings, in a mix of architectural styles, achieve the effect of an Italianate hill village. They are all either part of the hotel or self-catering cottages. Portmeirion became well known in the 1960s as the location for the cult television series THE PRISONER. The place was earlier known as Port Meirion and Aber Ia.

positive covenant An obligation on the owner of a piece of land to do something. Compare RESTRICTIVE COVENANT.

positive parochialism Defined by London's deputy mayor Nicky Gavron in 2000 as 'speaking up for the interests of an area, but working within a strategic framework' (Baker, 2000). See also PAROCHIALISM and NEW PAROCHIALISM.

positive site A piece of land that adds to the quality of the area.

positive space That which is clearly defined, mostly enclosed, and easily understood. The opposite of *negative space*.

postcode snobbery (UK) The practice (particularly of estate agents) of identifying certain postcode areas as being especially desirable places to live.

post-fordism Flexible forms of organisation thought likely to be characteristic of POST-INDUSTRIAL SOCIETY, succeeding FORDISM.

post-historic man A person of the future who has been dehumanised by social forces that have developed through history. LEWIS MUMFORD (1961) described how he saw cities setting the scene for human development. 'When we finally reach our own age,' he wrote, 'we shall find that urban society has come to a parting of the ways. Here, with a heightened consciousness of our past and a clearer insight into decisions made long ago, which often still control us, we shall be able to face the immediate decision that now confronts man and will, one way or another, ultimately transform him: namely whether he shall devote himself to the development of his own deepest humanity, or whether he shall surrender himself to the now almost automatic forces he himself has set in motion and yield place to his dehumanized *alter ego*, "Post-historic Man". That second choice will bring with it a progressive loss of feeling, emotion, creative audacity, and finally consciousness.'

post-industrial society One in which traditional industries have been replaced by service industries and knowledge-based industries; one in which new social structures have replaced those of the industrial economy of the nineteenth and twentieth centuries. The concept of post-industrial society was described by the economist Daniel Bell in the 1960s.

Postman Pat See GREENDALE.

postmetropolis A POSTMODERN GLOBAL METROPOLIS.

postmodern The sociologist C Wright Mills wrote in 1959 of 'antiquity' being followed by 'the dark ages' (which were, he noted, a period of several centuries of oriental ascendancy), which were in turn followed by 'the modern age', which was being succeeded by a 'post-modern period' (Mills, 1959).

postmodern (also post-modern) architecture An approach drawing on a wide range of styles, symbols and imagery intended to appeal to a broad public. Timothy Mowl (2002) has called it 'applied architectural wit, a commentary on style, not an advance on it'. Charles Jencks' *The Language of Post-Modern Architecture*, published in 1977, helped to define the emerging style. Postmodernism flourished in the 1980s, at a time when the Prince of Wales was castigating modernist architects for failing to communicate with people who were not design professionals. Marshall Berman (1988) records that the phrase was being used in the USA by the 1970s. Jencks, the chronicler of the movement, writes that it was at its most creative between 1977 and 1985 (Jencks, 1991). See also LEARNING FROM LOS ANGELES.

postmodern global metropolis A new urban form as typified by Los Angeles. The term has been used by the theorist ED SOJA.

postmodernism An approach to design (and culture in general) based on the idea that different groups of people construct their own concepts of reality, all of which may be equally valid. In contrast to MODERNISM, it denies the objectivity of scientific method. David Kolb (1990) suggests that 'Arnold Toynbee (in 1946) seems to have been the first to use the word postmodern in anything like its current sense... [of describing] a breakdown of older unities and the transgression of prohibitions that had been set up by modernism'. According to Kolb, ROBERT VENTURI reported that Jean Lapatut at Princeton was using the word about architecture as early as the 1950s, and it became popular in architectural discussions due to the efforts of Charles Jencks and Robert Stern from 1977. Heinrich Klotz (1988) has suggested ten defining characteristics of postmodernism: 1) Regionalism (instead of internationalism). 2) Fictional representation (instead of geometric abstraction). 3) Emphasis on building an illusion (instead of functionalism). 4) Multiplicity of meanings (instead of the single machine metaphor). 5) Poetry (instead of utopianism). 6) Improvisation, spontaneity, and incompleteness (instead of finished perfection). 7) Memory and irony (instead of banishing history). 8) Historical and regional relativity (instead of autonomously valid form). 9) Variation of vocabulary and style (instead of one dominant style). 10) Aesthetic distance (instead of identifying architecture with life).

post-occupancy analysis A study of a newly completed and occupied building to determine how well it is working.

post-suburban development An EDGE CITY. See ORANGE COUNTY.

post-suburban metropolis One where traditional central-place functions (such as culture and sports, government, high-end shopping and corporate administration) are radically dispersed among different centres (Davis, 2002 and Olin et al, 1992).

post-taylorism Flexible approaches to the management of labour, succeeding TAYLORISM.

post-urbanism Forms of development that some commentators identify as replacing traditional towns and cities. EA Gutkind argued in *The Expanding Environment* (1953) that familiar urban forms were outdated. 'The conception "City" is an anachronism and even far-reaching reforms can not prevent its decay and final disappearance… It is just our technical advance that has made the very idea of the City obsolete. It has demolished all the ideal and material pre-conditions from which the early cities developed and from which the continuity of city life has drawn its vitalizing forces. Science and technique have destroyed the old scale, the old agents of material needs, and the old symbols. They have burst asunder the old units, the cities, and created the new units of whole countries and larger regions. They have opened they way to the creation of a new environment, neither city nor country, an environment for which we have not yet found a name but which is more than either city or country as we have known them in the past in their sterile antagonism and life-destroying degeneration. To uphold the conception "City" and to expect from timid improvements a revival of city life is the last relic, the last perversion of the first vision of urban civilisation'. Gutkind thought that the end of cities would lead to the rise of communities. 'The new structural unity will result in a free association of equally important communities and in a dismemberment of the metropolitan empires as well as in the abolition of the antagonism between town and country. A new landscape will emerge, a continuous green carpet interrupted by small community units'.

Deyan Sudjik (1992) suggests that the wider ownership of the car since the 1960s has finally transformed the nature of the city. 'The old certainties of urban geography have vanished, and in their place is this edgy and apparently amorphous new kind of settlement,' Sudjik writes. 'The chances are that the force field couldn't have come into being without a downtown, or historic crust, because massive amounts of resources are needed to achieve the critical mass required by this kind of city as a trigger. But in its present incarnation, the old centre is just another piece on the board, a counter that has perhaps the same weight as the airport, or the medical centre, or the museum complex. They all swim in a soup of shopping malls, hypermarkets and warehouses, drive-in restaurants and anonymous industrial sheds, beltways and motorway boxes.' Allen Cunningham (2000) has written: 'The city is an instrument of concentration, the car an instrument of dispersal; contrary to the received wisdom of modern movement urbanism, they are antithetical'. The Australian architect Glenn Murcutt predicted the fate of cities in the information age in a 1995 interview (quoted in Pawley, 1998). 'The fact that the computer is letting us link up with all over the world from a room in our house is going to make an immense difference to the way we operate in cities,' Murcutt said. 'It's going to break down urbanism as we've always understood it. It's going to reinforce suburbia and make the rural population able to survive much better than they ever survived before… Their biggest problem is the cost of transport to the cities. Once they ceased to have to do that, they could cut the cities off entirely and let them starve.'

Doug Kelbaugh (2000) identifies 'post-urbanism' – as distinct from EVERYDAY URBANISM and NEW URBANISM – with the work of REM KOOLHAAS and others who share that architect's approach. 'Post-urbanism is heterotopian, sensational and post-structuralist,' Kelbaugh writes: Koolhaas' urban projects 'welcome the disconnected hypermodern buildings and shopping mall urbanism. They are also heterotopic because they discount shared values or metanarratives as no longer thought to be possible in a fragmenting world composed of isolated zones of the "other" (eg the homeless, gays, communes, militia, prisoners, minorities, and so on), as well as mainstream zones of atomistic consumers, internet surfers, and free-range tourists.' Kelbaugh continues: 'Outside the usual ordering systems, these liminal zones of taboo fantasy and commercial zones of unfettered consumption are viewed as liberating because they allow for new forms of knowledge, new hybrid possibilities, new unpredictable forms of freedom. It is precisely this distrust of "ordering" that makes the post-structuralists so against conventional architecture and urbanism.' To post-urbanists, Kelbaugh suggests, traditional communities based on physical place and propinquity are stultifying, repressive, and no longer relevant in the light of modern technology and telecommunications. 'Post-urbanism is stylistically sensational because it attempts to wow an increasingly sophisticated consumer of the built environment with ever-wilder and more provocative architecture and urbanism. Like modernism, its architectural language is usually very abstract, with little reference to surrounding physical or historical context. It also continues the modernist project of avant-garde shock tactics, no matter what the building site or program. It is sometimes hard to know if it employs shock for its own sake or whether the principal motive is to inspire genuine belief in the possibility of changing the status quo, and resisting controls and limits that are thought to be too predictable and even tyrannical.' See also NON-PLACE URBAN REALM, RURAL CITY and URBAN COUNTRYSIDE.

Potemkin village A false façade or sham village of the type built by General Potemkin to impress Catherine II of Russia. In the short story *When Potemkin's Coach Went By* by the German writer Reinhard Lettau (1964), the workmen constructing a sham village for Potemkin build huts behind the structure to house themselves while the work is underway, and begin to replace the painted windows with real ones. The sham village begins to become a living one. That could be a problem, as unless there is a sham village to be seen, Potemkin might believe that the sham one he ordered was never built. The foreman gives instructions that 'the houses which face the street must quickly be given the candidly slipshod appearance of stage sets.'

Potter, Harry See PRIVET DRIVE.

Pottersville See BEDFORD FALLS.

Poulson, John Architect. He built his practice into what was said to be Europe's largest mainly through his persuasive way with public officials. In 1974 he was jailed for corruption in relation to building contracts and planning permissions, along with George Pottinger, a senior civil servant at the Scottish Office, and Andrew Cunningham, chairman of Durham County Council.

Pound, Ezra (1885–1972) Poet. See UNREAL CITY.

Poundbury A planned extension to the town of Dorchester, Dorset, begun in 1993 following a decision by the local planning authority to expand the town westwards on land owned by the Duchy of Cornwall and controlled by the PRINCE OF WALES in his capacity as Duke of Cornwall. The prince commissioned the Luxembourg architect and planner LÉON KRIER (who continues to supervise the planning of Poundbury) to prepare a master plan in 1998 for development that is intended to accommodate eventually 5,000 residents (between a third and a half of them in SOCIAL HOUSING) and provide 2,000 jobs. Krier's master plan set out four urban QUARTERS. As landowner, the Duchy of Cornwall exerts tight control over the design of buildings through a prescriptive DESIGN CODE. Buildings are in neo-vernacular or classical styles, and of traditional materials. Different land uses are mixed, not separated. In its early years, in a recession, the development of Poundbury was slow, and some of the prince's critics looked forward to celebrating its failure. By most criteria, though, the first phase has been highly successful. It has provided the UK with an influential example of NEW URBANISM and a demonstration of the residential road planning principles set out in the *People, Places and Movement*, the national design guide produced by Alan Baxter and Associates (the engineers for Poundbury) for the UK government. Poundbury's compact form and relatively high densities, unusual when they were first planned, now provide a standard that the government is urging other developers to emulate. It is more of a suburb – or an urban extension, to use the current term – than an 'urban quarter', being separated from the centre of Dorchester by a belt of inter- and post-war council housing and what will be a major road. See also AUTHENTICITY, FOOTPADS' PARADISE and THE STEPFORD WIVES.

poverty A state of being poor. More specifically: **1** The state of living on an income below half the national average (DETR, 2000b). **2** Lacking the essentials of life. This is known as *absolute poverty*. What the essentials of life are has to be defined in any particular situation. **3** Lacking the ability to enjoy the standard of living that most other people enjoy. This is known as *relative poverty*. Likewise, discussing relative poverty depends on defining it in terms of a specific proportion of the population.

Alternatively, poverty may be defined in relation to eligibility for particular welfare benefits such as income support. A survey carried out by the Joseph Rowntree Foundation in 2000 claimed that 26 per cent of the population of Britain could be defined as poor because of low income and a lack of necessities (defined as including an outfit for special occasions, a television set, an annual holiday and money to decorate the home). According to the survey, one person in six defined themselves as living in absolute poverty, as defined by the United Nations ('a severe deprivation of human needs', including severe deprivation of food, safe drinking water, sanitation facilities, health, shelter, education and information). A similar number considered themselves unable to heat their home, keep it free of damp and maintain a decent state of decoration. One person in four considered themselves in 'overall poverty'. A person's sense of being in poverty may be determined by the ratio between their resources and their expectations. In 2002 a study by the Child Poverty Action Group found that the UK's three poorest parliamentary constituencies were all in Glasgow. Others in the top ten were in Birmingham, Manchester, London and Liverpool. President Lyndon Johnson told Congress in 1964: 'For the first time in our history, it is possible to conquer poverty.'

University College London's Development Planning Unit (2001) writes that in cities and towns of the developing world 'poverty is occasioned (and characterised) by the lack of a secure and sufficient income to provide for the maintenance of a household's livelihood: food, clothing, shelter, health, education and development of each of its members.' But income and savings are not the only indices of urban poverty. 'Such poverty is exacerbated by physical and social insecurity; vulnerability to crises and shocks that may be caused by injury, illness, unemployment, eviction, natural disaster; and ethnic and cultural marginality and ostracism.' See also CULTURE OF POVERTY, INCOME DEPRIVATION and SOCIAL EXCLUSION.

poverty line The level of income or resources below which people can be said to be living in poverty.

Poverty: a study of town life Seebohm Rowntree's study of living conditions in York, published in 1901.

Powell and Moya An architectural practice led by Philip (later Sir Philip) Powell and John Hidalgo Moya. Its work included the celebrated council housing estate of Churchill Gardens in Pimlico, built in 1946, award winning buildings for Oxford and Cambridge collages and the Queen Elizabeth II conference centre in Westminster.

powergram A diagram showing the degree of influence that various categories of people (such as developers, landowners and planners) exert over urban form (McGlynn, 1993).

prairie planning A pejorative term, current in the 1950s, for low-density, suburban or new-town development. Also *prairified*. Examples: 'It was a great shock to planners and other philanthropists when hygienic, prairified new towns gave birth to a new medical phenomenon, NEW TOWN NEUROSIS' (Smith, 1974). In 1954 the poet Hugh MacDiarmid quoted an unnamed contemporary writer: 'The main concept [of new towns] is not in question... What has been questioned is the "wide and open" character of the towns and the "prairie planning" which leave these towns with so much of the aridity, the "spottiness" and economically impossible spaces of the old pre-war housing estates, and without either the urbanity or human warmth of the English village or market town. The charge against the new towns is not that they are wrong in principle, not that individual buildings are bad, but that – in reaction against anarchical nineteenth century overcrowding – they sprawl, undefined, over far more acres than they can ever need, maintain, use or even want' (quoted in Bold, 1984).

prairie style An architectural style characterized by roofs with shallow pitches and wide overhanging eaves, particularly as designed by FRANK LLOYD WRIGHT. The name came from a house plan published by Frank Lloyd Wright in the *Ladies Home Journal* in 1901 with the title 'A Home in a Prairie Town'.

pre-architecture Elements of the design of an area that are determined before any buildings are designed.

precautionary principle States that measures should be taken where a negative impact is suspected, even when there is as yet no actual proof.

precinct 1 An enclosed space, particularly one that is free of traffic. Examples: *pedestrian precinct* and *shopping precinct*. See ALKER TRIPP. **2** An urban QUARTER; a distinct local area; an area with a defined boundary.

Michael Young and Peter Willmott (1957) wrote in their study of Bethnal Green, east London: 'Sometimes a person's relatives live in the same turning [street], more often in another nearby turning, and this helps to account for the attachment which people feel to the precinct, as distinct from the street, in which they live.' Lewis Mumford (1961) noted that in Regensburg, as early as the eleventh century, 'the town was divided into a clerical precinct, a royal precinct and a merchant precinct, corresponding to the chief vocations, while craftsmen and peasants must have occupied the rest of the town.' **3** (US) A district within the jurisdiction or authority of a particular body.

precinctisation The process by which urban space becomes segregated into ENCLAVES. See also MALLIFICATION.

predict and provide 1 A government housing policy based on predicting the future number of households on the basis of past trends and requiring local authorities to provide sufficient land for new housing to accommodate them. The policy was discredited in the 1990s as being responsible for the development of unnecessarily large amounts of greenfield land. It was replaced by PLAN, MONITOR AND MANAGE. **2** A similar policy on transport.

prefab A prefabricated building, made in a factory and assembled on site. Prefabricated houses were made in the UK at the end of the second world war until 1948 in response to a shortage of building materials and spare capacity in former armament factories. More than 150,000 prefabs were built in the UK under the 1944 Temporary Housing Programme. Each bungalow had a fitted kitchen and bathroom. They were highly popular. Despite their intended life of around ten years, many lasted for decades. Around 500 were still in use in 2002, 32 of them (in Bristol and Birmingham) listed. In that year the government announced that prefabs (or *housing modules*) might be able to fulfil an important role in providing housing in inner urban areas, particularly for ESSENTIAL WORKERS who might not otherwise be able to afford a place to live. In 1968 the GREATER LONDON COUNCIL developed a prefab which was deployed as a stop-gap on many sites that the council was unable to develop. Some can still be found around London today.

preferred coastal conservation zone (Scotland) An area of coastline designated for special care. The zones cover a large part of Scotland's coastline.

preferred industrial location A strategic employment site normally suitable for general industrial, light industrial and warehousing uses (Greater London Authority, 2001).

pre-industrial city One without an industrial base. Spiro Kostof (1991) describes a pre-industrial city as one that is relatively small (rarely over 100,000 people), where land use is not specialised, where there is little social and physical mobility, and which has two classes (an elite and a lower class). The centre is taken up by government, religion and the residences of the elite. Compare INDUSTRIAL CITY.

pre-let *n*. An agreement to take a lease on a development that is not yet completed.

preliminary development review ordinance (US) Adopted by a city council to allow applicants to submit their development concept for review before formally submitting a development proposal.

pre-med A stage before MEDIATION, identifying common ground before a major planning inquiry. The term was used by Chris Shepley, chief planning inspector, in 2000.

Prescott, John (b1938) Politician. Deputy prime minister and SECRETARY OF STATE for environment, transport and the regions from 1997. Prescott's early attempts to promote integrated transport policies were frustrated by the government's unwillingness to curb car use. 'I will have failed if in five years' time there are not fewer journeys made by car,' he told the House of Commons in 1997. To that extent, at least, he failed. Prescott commissioned Richard Rogers' 1999 URBAN TASK FORCE report, but he was unable to get many of its recommendations implemented. He did become increasingly committed to raising standards of urban design and planning, calling variously for more of 'THE WOW FACTOR', and backing NEW URBANISM and the use of DESIGN CODES. The Office of the Deputy Prime Minister was made a department in 2002, with responsibilities for regional and local government, fire, housing, planning and regeneration. Prescott's plans for SUSTAINABLE COMMUNITIES would add up to a major HOUSEBUILDING programme in south-east England. He has enthusiastically promoted regional devolution. See TWO JAGS.

present value of benefits The future economic benefits (such as fewer accidents and savings in time) of a proposed road scheme, expressed in current prices.

present value of cost The capital cost of building a road, expressed in current prices.

preservation Maintaining a building or place unchanged. Defined by the BURRA CHARTER as maintaining the fabric of a place in its existing state and retarding deterioration, and defined by the US Department of the Interior as the act or process of applying measures to sustain the existing form, integrity and materials of an historic property. Michael Sorkin (2001) writes: '"Preservation" has been reduced to a battle of styles, an endless debate over the virtues of modern building versus the historicism that serves as the official default for building in old neighbourhoods... The discussion [has] lost sight of the ecology of place, that we needed to preserve not simply the sense of visual reliability in beloved environments but also to be sensitive to the far more consequential issues of established ways of living, of daily habits, of the need for human permanence in chosen habitats.' Compare CONSERVATION, PROTECTION, RECONSTRUCTION and REHABILITATION, and see also HISTORIC PRESERVATION.

preserve or enhance The meaning of the word 'or' in this phrase was the subject of legal dispute the Steinberg case in 1989, in relation to the statutory obligation for development in a conservation area to 'preserve or enhance' the area's character or appearance. The ruling was that development must do one or the other, but need not do both. The demolition of a building could be accepted if the quality of its replacement was such as to enhance the area.

preserved in aspic A pejorative term for a place whose positive features have led to its physical form being restored or maintained at a pitch of perfection most appropriate to a museum than to a living, changing, contemporary environment.

prestigious 1 Enhancing the prestige of the owner or occupant. **2** Overpriced. An estate agents' euphemism (Jennings, 2001). See also LUXURY and MARKETING.

preventer A person whose presence discourages crime. Also called a *guardian*.

previously developed land The government's emphasis on the need to concentrate development on previously developed ('BROWNFIELD') land in the interests of sustainability requires it to define the term. The DETR defined previously developed land rather tortuously in *Planning Policy Guidance Note No.3: Housing* (1999) as that which is or was occupied by a permanent (non-agricultural) structure, and associated fixed surface infrastructure. The definition, the DETR explained, covers the CURTILAGE of the development (although this does not mean that the whole area of the curtilage should be redeveloped). The definition excludes land and buildings that have been used for agricultural purposes, forest and woodland, and land in built-up areas that has not been developed previously (for example, parks, recreation grounds and allotments, even though these areas may contain certain urban features such as paths, pavilions and other buildings). Also excluded is land that was previously developed but where the remains of any structure or activity have blended into the landscape in the process of time (to the extent that it can reasonably be considered as part of the natural surroundings), or has subsequently been put to an amenity use and can not be regarded as requiring redevelopment.

primary group Defined by the sociologist CHARLES HORTON COOLEY in 1909 as being characterized by intimate face-to-face association and cooperation, such as the family, play-group and neighbourhood. These, he wrote, were the groups for which 'we' was the natural expression (White, 1962).

primary housing cooperative Formed to provide housing, as opposed to a secondary housing cooperative, which provides services to primary co-ops.

primary seating Benches and chairs, as opposed to SITTING LANDSCAPES (Gehl, 1987).

Prince Albert (1819–61) The husband of Queen Victoria. He promoted the 1851 Great Exhibition and the South Kensington museums in London, commissioned model housing and promoted housing reform. His death from typhoid fever in 1861 helped promote a positive change in attitudes towards regulation and municipal action to protect public health (Ward, 1989).

Prince of Wales (b1948) Prince Charles' influence on planning, urban design and architecture began in 1984 with his speech at a banquet at Hampton Court Palace, organised to celebrate the 150th anniversary of the Royal Institute of British Architects. Royal speakers on such occasions are expected to pat their hosts on the back. Instead the prince launched a bitter attack on planners and designers of the urban environment, and most of the architectural profession in particular, for designing ugly buildings, destroying communities, and ignoring 'the feelings and wishes of the mass of ordinary people' (see MONSTROUS CARBUNCLE). The public reaction to the prince's crusade, as it became, was largely positive. The professionals' response was mixed. Most planners, ironically, thought his analysis was more or less right, and their institute recruited him as its patron. The architects were divided between those who accepted his criticism of much recent architecture, on the one hand, and those who thought it unbalanced and a scandalous misuse of his unelected, highly influential position, on the other. RICHARD ROGERS (1989) wrote: 'By blaming the architect for the ugliness of the built environment the Prince has misguidedly chosen an easy target. He exonerates the real culprits – the commercial and political institutions that exercise architectural patronage – thereby frustrating the very debate he wishes to encourage and avoiding the political and financial realities... It is not an architectural style which is responsible for the disfigurement, much less the modern movement which has been made an easy scapegoat, but rather the subordination of public value to private greed.' The architect Piers Gough (1994) wrote: 'By suggesting that laymen should follow their instinctive dislike of modern architecture and distrust of professionals, the Prince supports the consumerist proud-to-be-philistine attitude to culture. The effect on practising architects is to make planning applications a much more precarious undertaking, where planning officers' advice has become castrated and skewed by the often unedifying prejudices of their committees. The result may be a more comfortable environment and a reduction of overtly ugly buildings, except that the now rampant mediocrity is a more insidious ugliness.'

The prince's onslaught continued with a television programme in 1988 and a best-selling book (on sale at supermarkets), both entitled *A Vision of Britain* (Prince of Wales, 1989). Architects could not escape responsibility for disastrous urban development, he wrote. 'It wasn't the local councillors, or the developers, who had read Le Corbusier and other apostles of modernism... Architects deliberately staged a revolution within their own system of education. It was the "great architects" of this period who convinced everyone that the world would be safe in their hands. Their descendants still retain prestige, and a kind of glamour among their peers; they set the style, control the curriculum, and have commanding positions in the Royal Institute of British Architects, the Royal Fine Arts Commission, and the Royal Academy. It is they who keep a tight grip on architectural education and who are the heroes of a largely sycophantic architectural press, and the focus of much uncritical attention from the media in general'. The prince continued to speak out, condemning a redevelopment proposal for the Paternoster site next to London's St Paul's Cathedral; James Stirling's design for No. 1 Poultry (see MANSION HOUSE SQUARE), also in the City of London ('like a 1930s wireless'); housing in Runcorn, also by Stirling ('a grubby launderette'); Colin St John Wilson's British Library ('an academy for the secret police'); the Building Design Partnership's Plessey factory in Plymouth ('a high-tech version of a Victorian prison'); and, some years later, the Swiss Re building by NORMAN FOSTER ('a giant glass shaggy ink-cap'). By contrast he praised community architecture. He put his money where his mouth was with a series of ambitious projects. He created a model development on Duchy of Cornwall land at POUNDBURY, on the edge of Dorchester, and founded the URBAN VILLAGES Forum, a school of architecture (the Prince's Institute of Architecture) and an architectural magazine (*Perspectives*). The institute and the magazine struggled and died, though the institute metamorphosed into the PRINCE'S FOUNDATION. In 2001 the government gave the Prince a role in overseeing the design of hospitals.

Prince's Foundation An educational charity founded in 1999 to bring together the Prince of Wales's interests in architecture, the arts and urban regeneration. The foundation incorporated, among other things, the Urban Villages Forum and the concerns of the Prince's Institute of Architecture. It pioneers the ENQUIRY BY DESIGN process and promotes traditional urbanism, SUSTAINABLE URBAN EXTENSIONS, URBAN VILLAGES, DESIGN CODES and PATTERN BOOKS. By 2004 it had become a major influence on the UK government's SUSTAINABLE COMMUNITIES programme.

The foundation explains its philosophy: 'From the fifth century BC to the 1940s, the practice of architecture and urban design in Western Europe was based on an evolving body of knowledge handed down from one generation to the next. This knowledge was founded on a set of carefully refined principles, which though articulated in different ways at different times, have remained fundamentally constant. No matter how each generation of architects and designers has interpreted these principles, whether it be the Georgian crescents of Bath or the Art Nouveau architecture of Glasgow, they continued to be observed because they recognise the needs of human beings and their rightful place at the centre of the design.'

In successful cities, the foundation argues, the proportions of the buildings, the way they relate to those around them, their density, and the mix of use and tenure have a unity and a humanity about them. 'These cities have stood the test of time functionally, economically and aesthetically. It is only in the last 80 years that these principles have been largely abandoned in favour of experimentation.' The foundation says it does not want to replicate the past, but to show 'how today's buildings, towns and cities might benefit from that body of knowledge'.

Principles and Practice of Town and Country Planning A standard textbook by Lewis Keeble, first published in 1952.

prior demolition The demolition of a building prior to planning permission or other necessary approval being obtained for the site's redevelopment. Landowners sometimes use prior demolition to pre-empt the refusal of planning permission in cases where the existing building's quality or usefulness makes approval less likely. The demolition of the FIRESTONE FACTORY was a notable example. An earlier instance was the developer NICHOLAS BARBON demolishing Essex House, south of the Strand in London, in the 1680s. Barbon worked in haste to clear the site for redevelopment before the King and Privy Council could insist on buying it to present to a political favourite (Summerson, 1962).

priority area Priority areas for financial assistance for development include assisted areas, rural development areas, European Union OBJECTIVE 1 AND 2 areas, and New Deal and neighbourhood renewal areas.

priority estate An area of public housing selected for treatment under the Priority Estates Project, set up by the Department of the Environment in 1979.

Prisoner, The A cult television series set in PORT-MEIRION, filmed in 1966–1967. The producer, Patrick McGoohan, also played the title role. The prisoner, who previously worked for some sort of spying organisation, has been taken hostage. The village is a repressive, self-contained unit with its own Council of Parliament. It is protected by a huge white balloon that threatens to suffocate any prisoner who tries to escape. Number 6, as the prisoner is known, does try in each of the seventeen episodes, and succeeds in the final one. 'I am not a number, I am a free man' is heard in each episode. The other villagers seem to accept with docility their lack of liberty, which has been destroyed by technology. Exactly, what is happening, and who is who, is never clear. Nor do the normal rules of logic seem to apply. The location is revealed as Portmeirion only in the final episode. The Prisoner cult holds its annual conference there (Davies, 2002).

Pritchard, Jack See ISOKON.

private affluence, public squalor The Canadian economist John Kenneth Galbraith's description of the USA in the twentieth-century.

privatisation The transfer of public responsibility (such as a local authority's development control service) or public assets (such as council housing) to private ownership.

privatism The tendency for people to live their lives in private rather than in public, making less use of public space and being less involved in community organisations.

privatopia An exclusive development enclave separated from the public realm.

privet A variety of hedge common in suburban areas, thought to be particularly dull and therefore typically suburban.

Privet Drive The fictional address in Little Whinging, Surrey, where Harry Potter (in JK Rowling's *Harry Potter and the Philosopher's Stone*, published in 1997, and its sequels) is brought up by his cruel and narrow-minded uncle and aunt. This is archetypal *suburbia*, 'silent and tidy under the inky sky, the very last place you would expect astonishing things to happen.'

proactive planning Taking positive action to bring about development that accords with planning policy, rather than merely reacting to developers' planning proposals. According to that definition it is not the tautology it might otherwise appear to be. The opposite of REACTIVE PLANNING. *Proactive development control* is any process by which a local authority works with planning applicants to improve the quality of development proposals as early as possible in period before a planning application is submitted.

probable sunlight hours The long-term average total number of hours during a year in which direct sunlight reaches the unobstructed ground, taking clouds into account.

problem estate (England and Wales) An estate of council housing with severe social and/or structural and/or environmental problems.

problem family A family living in a residential area whose activities are considered anti-social by their neighbours. Some commentators object that the term may stigmatise people whose problems are at least to some extent due to their home being in an area that is hard to live in. See also HARD TO LET.

procedural planning theory Concerns the process of planning rather than the nature of towns, cities and the environment, in contrast to *substantive planning theory* (Taylor, 1998).

process planning Working out collaboratively the process by which a plan or design will be developed.

procurement Obtaining buildings, goods or services; the process of getting a development designed and built.

producer-driven industry One that produces what suits the industry itself. The house-building industry is said to be one, preferring to build what has sold well before rather than see if there is a market for something different. Compare CONSUMER-DRIVEN INDUSTRY and see GEODEMOGRAPHY.

profession 1 A formal association of people whose occupation is based on a common body of specialised knowledge and skills; who define an aim that they claim is in the public interest, beyond their own and their clients' interests; who agree to abide by an ethical code; who guarantee their motivation and competence; who claim the public's trust; and who join the profession only after meeting rigorous entry requirements. **2** Such an occupation.

The role of the professions in the world of the built environment is increasingly difficult to define, as more and more specialisms emerge. There is a tendency for each identifiable variety of specialist to form some sort of professional institute, in order to bolster its members' professional identity and preserve the value of their specialism in the marketplace. This means, though, that it is increasingly difficult to define what body of knowledge a particular profession is claiming as its own. Many people are members of more than one, and perhaps several, professional institutes.

An ARCHITECT may once have been the person who designed and supervised the construction of a building. Today she may be one member of a team of perhaps dozens of different specialists, and not necessarily playing a lead role at all. The nature of the job is changing too, as computer software, new management systems and government regulations change the architect's relationship to the body of knowledge she possesses. Architects have a professional institute (the RIBA), but a different body (the Architects' Registration Board) is the one they have to be registered with to be legally permitted to call themselves an architect.

TOWN PLANNING has been agonising about its professional status for decades. The Town Planning Institute began as an association of members of other professions who had a common interest in planning. Only later did it become a profession most of whose members had no other professional affiliation. By the 1990s some of the leading members of the ROYAL TOWN PLANNING INSTITUTE (RTPI), as it had become, were asking whether the profession really could claim to posssess an identifiable body of knowledge and to be worthy of the public's trust, or if planners were valued solely because they knew how to manipulate the planning system. In 2002 the RTPI took the bold step of reinventing itself, redefining its sphere of interest as SPATIAL PLANNING and attempting to widen its reach beyond those people who pull the levers of bureaucracy.

The Institute of Historic Building Conservation developed in the 1990s out of the Association of Conservation Officers (see CONSERVATION OFFICER), but two of the existing professional institutes insisted that they could do the job just as well, and they now provide their own accreditation for conservationists. URBAN DESIGN raises yet more questions. Is urban design just another name for BIG ARCHITECTURE or PHYSICAL PLANNING? Or is it a new area of coherent professional activity? Or an umbrella term for place-making, an activity in which members of many different professions, and many non-professionals, are engaged? Or is urban design an activity that requires a particularly high level of skills and understanding, and a particular ability to work in multi-professional teams and to manage design-led development projects? Or is that something else, perhaps called URBANISM? And what is the role of multi-professional umbrella groups

> **"THE SELF-SUFFICIENCY OF THE SPECIALIST'S WORLD IS A PRISONER'S ILLUSION. IT IS TIME TO OPEN THE GATES."**
>
> *Lewis Mumford*

such as the URBAN DESIGN ALLIANCE? The answers to these questions are not yet clear. What is clear is that the professional landscape is rapidly changing. If the professions seem always to be in crisis, that may be because the skills needed to plan, manage, design, administer, build, engineer and survey the built envionment are too varied and variable to fit neatly into self-contained professional groupings. New – and flexible – ways of organising professionals are needed. 'The self-sufficiency of the specialist's world is a prisoner's illusion,' wrote LEWIS MUMFORD. 'It is time to open the gates.'

The rationale for formalised professions is that the public may benefit from being able to rely on the competence of professionals (supposedly guaranteed by standards of entry and education, and by disciplinary procedures). The professionals, for their part, may benefit from their profession's exclusiveness, resulting from what may be seen as its interest in making people rely on professionals even when they might otherwise be capable of helping themselves (hence George Bernard Shaw's description of a profession as a conspiracy against the laity). Gordon Cherry, a former president of the Royal Town Planning Institute, wrote that built environment professionals 'have been trained within a set of ideologies; they have their own ideas of ends or objectives which are right or wrong, desirable or undesirable, and they work towards these in ways which will gain them most credit from their peer group'. Some professionals allow these ideologies to render them incapable of seeing the world from any but their own perspectives, or of working creatively with anyone with different experience or values. The public's loss of confidence in architects and planners can be dated to the 1960s and '70s, when the professions' achievements were overshadowed by disasters in urban development and renewal. Planners and architects could have loaded more of the blame on to others, such as the building industry, politicians or highway engineers. But the architecture and planning professions were both continuing to claim pre-eminence in the development process. They could not claim convincingly to be simultaneously in charge and guiltless.

The URBAN TASK FORCE's report (1999) commented on the contemporary scene: 'There is a tendency in this country not to consider urban development schemes in an integrated way. Instead they are broken down too quickly to fit the interests of the different professions, whether it be the architect, the planner or the highway engineer... We would like to enhance the development profession by fostering the emergence of a new type of urban development professional who can promote, develop and manage complex development schemes and who appreciates how the various specialisms can work in tandem to achieve a coherent whole. There are few such people around.' See also JARGON and THREE MAGNETS.

professional generalist A professional with a wide remit. The traffic-calming pioneer DAVID ENGWICHT uses the term to describe himself. The new town campaigner FJ OSBORN called himself 'a specialist in things in general'.

professional institute An organisation that pursues the aims and interests of a particular professional group.

profit erosion An agreement between a developer and funder specifying that the developer will take a reduced profit if the development fails to let well enough. See also LEASE GUARANTEE.

programme authority A local authority area designated for treatment under the INNER URBAN AREAS ACT 1978.

programming plan Shows the stages at which various parts of a plan are intended to be implemented.

progression programme Helps people identify what they want to achieve in their lives and equips them with the means to succeed, as part of a regeneration initiative.

project 1 A defined task; a set of activities carried out to fulfil a defined aim; an individual element in a regeneration scheme. **2** (US) A public housing development. The equivalent in England and Wales is ESTATE and in Scotland SCHEME.

project appraisal An assessment of a regeneration project against specified criteria.

project execution plan Sets out how a project will be carried out, including detailed design and financial feasibility.

project finance Finance, provided for a property development, for example, for which the property is the principal or only security. Compare CORPORATE FINANCE.

Project for Public Spaces See WILLIAM H WHYTE.

project management The overall planning, control and coordination of a project.

projection A prediction based on data about the past and present.

promenade n. A leisurely walk for pleasure, particularly up and down. v. To do this.

promenader One who promenades. See FLÂNEUR.

property Buildings, land and infrastructure.

property agent One who markets and manages buildings or infrastructure.

property appraisal The valuation of property in terms of market price and analysis of its revenue-producing performance.

property developer One who invests in or procures buildings or infrastructure.

property finance 1 Money raised with property as security. **2** Money raised to spend on properties.

property investment company One receiving its income from rents. Compare PROPERTY TRADING COMPANY.

property management The care and maintenance of buildings.

property rights movement (US) The movement demands compensation for the diminution of property rights by public action or regulations.

property speculator One who buys buildings or infrastructure in the hope of selling at a profit, often without carrying out significant improvements.

property trading company One receiving its income from the sale of developments. Compare PROPERTY INVESTMENT COMPANY.

propinquity Nearness. The architect and critic Michael Sorkin (1991) declares: 'Computers, credit cards, phones, faxes and other instruments of instantaneous artificial adjacency are rapidly eviscerating historic logics of propinquity, the very cement of the city... The need for adjacency that created the densities of our traditional urban cores has been dissipated into altogether different logics of connection.' (This process began with the advent of the railways in the nineteenth century and the suburbs they brought about, and gathered speed with the increase in car ownership in the twentieth.) Sorkin continues: 'Electronic space has eroded the necessity for literal proximity even as the global air network has attenuated its possibility. This new city, designed to its precise specifications by the invisible hand, tends seemingly inexorably to an environment of universal equivalence. The condominium, the festive shopping mall, the highway interchange and, just over the horizon, the international airport, could as easily be located in Denver as Dacca or Dubai... Propinquity is the medium of urbanity. Cities acquire their indigenous styles by means of the mechanisms they invent to adjudicate questions of adjacency. Style, after all, isn't simply vocabulary, it's syntax, the mode of determining what goes with what. The first obligation of the designer of cities is to create, understand, and expand their logics of juxtaposition.' See also GLOBAL VILLAGE.

proportion The relationship between one element of a building (or part of a building) and another (height and width, for example).

proposals map (England and Wales) A DEVELOPMENT PLAN DOCUMENT illustrating the policies and proposals in a planning authority's other development plan documents. Its geographical base is at a scale that allows the policies and proposals to be illustrated in map form.

prose The architect LESLIE MARTIN called Georgian housing the 'good prose of architecture'. Churches and civic buildings, he said, represented its poetry. See also BACKGROUND BUILDING.

prospect A view; an outlook.

Prospect Hill A novel by Richard Francis, published in 2002, in which town councillors in Costford (a fictional town based on Stockport) in the 1970s argue about HIGH-RISE housing developments.

prostitution Apart from banking, virtually the only function of a modern city, according to FRANK LLOYD WRIGHT (Twombly, 1973). See ON THE STREETS, STREETWALKER, TRAMP and UNORTHODOX ENTREPRENEUR.

protect See BIASED TERMINOLOGY.

protection In the manifesto of the Society for the Protection of Ancient Buildings, written in 1877, WILLIAM MORRIS called for the protection, not RESTORATION, of ancient buildings. He called on those who dealt with historic buildings 'to stave off decay by daily care, to prop a perilous wall or mend a leaky roof by such means as are obviously meant for support or covering, and show no pretence of other art, and otherwise to resist all tampering with either the fabric or ornament of the building as it stands...'

Protopopov, Dmitrii A lawyer, he was a leading advocate of garden cities before the Russian revolution.

provider An organisation providing housing, health or social care support services, including registered social landlords, voluntary sector organisations, local authorities and the private sector.

Proving-Ground for World Destruction Vienna, in the words of the satirist Karl Kraus in 1914. See also CITY OF DREAMS.

provision That which is provided. In urbanistic jargon the term is usually redundant, as in *housing provision*.

provision-led project An element of an urban regeneration initiative that is provided to meet a per capita or per hectare requirement.

provost (Scotland) A mayor.

proxemics The study of how much space humans and animals need, how density affects their behaviour, and how people display what they perceive as the boundaries of their personal space. The term, derived from proximity, was coined in the early 1960s by the US anthropologist Edward T Hall. The novelist Tolstoy – a landowner, as Wyndham Lewis pointed out – wrote that the space a person needs is only six feet by two feet: the size of a grave.

proximity principle Specifies that waste should be collected, reprocessed and disposed of as close as possible to where it is produced, in order to reduce transport. See also HIERARCHY PRINCIPLE.

Prozorovka A town built for the Moscow-Kazan railway company as 'the first garden city in Russia' (Cooke, 1978).

Pruitt-Igoe A 14-storey, public housing block in St Louis, USA, designed by Minoru Yamasaki and built in 1955. It received a national award from the American Institute of Architects. By 1972 it had become a vandalised slum, and at 3.32pm on 15 July (the date is regarded as some as the 'death' of modern architecture and the loss of confidence in the hopes of public housing in the USA) the US army spectacularly demolished it with high explosive, inspiring a new municipal craze. Yamasaki was also architect of the WORLD TRADE CENTER, whose destruction was even more of a historical landmark. See also OAK AND ELDON GARDENS and QUARRY HILL, and URBAN DESTRUCTION.

PSSHAK (Primary System Support Housing Assembly Kit) A housing system developed in the late 1960s using standardised support elements and prefabricated modular partitions. The aim was to allow each tenant to design the layout of their home, using an instruction manual. The system was never widely used.

psychogeography Defined by the Situationist International Anthology as 'the study of the specific effects of the geographical environment, consciously organised or not, on the emotions and behaviour of individuals' (Knabb, 1981). The situationist GUY DEBORD used the term in the 1950s.

Psychoville A 1995 novel by Christopher Fowler set in the fictional suburban community of Invicta Cross, 'the town voted Britain's favourite'. It ends with the shopping mall and then the houses being destroyed by a couple of disaffected arsonists. 'Shelves dripped varnish, and mock-leather volumes of the *Readers Digest* combusted... Pale pink statues of prancing horses crackled and shattered.'

public *n.* The people. 'Making buildings of quality depends on clients who will accept nothing else,' writes the urban designer Leslie Gallery-Dilworth. 'The same is true of cities: there the client is the public.'

public art Art in a public place; permanent or temporary physical works created, selected or supervised by artists or craft workers for a building or site in a location visible to the general public, whether part of the building or free-standing. Public art includes sculpture (moulded, carved or assembled), paintings, mosaics, etched and stained glass, wall reliefs, gates and installations (including video and sound). It can be incorporated into street furniture, paving, railings and signs. STREET FURNITURE is sometimes described as being a form of public art when the hand of the designer is particularly evident. Example: 'If there has to be a security fence or grille, design it as a sculpture' (Llewelyn-Davies, 2000). Public art was first included as a funding category by the US National Endowment for the Arts in 1967 (Miles, 2000). See also PER CENT FOR ART and TURD IN THE PLAZA.

public distance See INTIMATE DISTANCE.

public domain PUBLIC REALM.

public goods Goods and services for which the public are not willing to pay and therefore the private sector is not motivated to provide (Hall, 1980).

public inquiry The Franks Committee in 1957 identified the purpose of a public inquiry as being 'to ensure that the interests of the citizens closely affected should be protected by the grant to them of a statutory right to be heard in support of their objectives and to ensure that thereby the minister should be better informed of the facts of the case.' A planning inquiry can last for anything from a day to more than a year. The longest, that into Heathrow Airport's proposed fifth terminal, lasted four years. The inspector took a further two years to write the inquiry report, and it was a further year before the government announced its decision that planning permission should be granted. See also INQUIRY and PLANNING INSPECTOR.

public interest That which will be to the collective benefit of society or of the inhabitants of a particular place. Both politicians and some professionals (town planners, for example) choose to see themselves as having a role in defining the public interest.

public meeting The most common method of involving people in planning issues. A public meeting is usually a poor start to a participatory process: it can help to get people fired up, but often in an unhelpful way. Public meetings can be intimidating for some of the participants; they can polarise attitudes and people into 'us' and 'them'; and they can focus too narrowly on a few issues.

public open space A familiar designation in plans, particularly in the second half of the twentieth century. Too often no thought had been given to what the space was for, or who would maintain and manage it. See also SLOAP.

public participation Any process in which members of the public are involved in the processes of urban change. PATRICK GEDDES advocated active public participation in planning and regeneration at the end of the nineteenth century, but the official planning system in the UK offered virtually no opportunities until the 1960s. A planner (Phillips, 2000) recalls working for a local authority in the early 1960s. 'Our only consultation was with the engineers in the county surveyor's department,' he writes. 'No parish councils, no amenity societies, no residents' associations and no neighbours. We made the judgement, we made the recommendation based on our judgement. If we called on a neighbour to assess a proposal from his property it was certainly not to seek any representation. It was purely to assist our decision making.'

In 1969 Sherry Arnstein wrote about her concept of a ladder of participation (see ARNSTEIN'S LADDER), helping to illuminate the political nature of the planning process. Such a perspective was far from the minds of a parliamentary committee chaired by Arthur Skeffington MP, which in that same year published its report *People and Planning*. Planning might reflect the public interest better, the report cautiously suggested, if the public were consulted. The Skeffington Report, as it was known, defined participation as 'the act of sharing in the formulation of policies and proposals'. Though some planners welcomed the report's proposals, to others it looked like a threat to their professionalism. In fact they had little cause to worry: Skeffington envisaged the public being kept firmly in its place, taking part in consultative exercises strictly on the planners' terms. For all its limitations, though, the Skeffington Report did give encouragement to those planners (some of them finding their inspiration in Geddes) who saw the potential of town planning as a popular activity.

Town planning as we know it today is unlike most other professions, being closely tied to the operation of a statutory process. In practice the process is confusing and confused: it involves professional judgements, which are meant to be the realm of the planners, and political decisions, which are meant to be taken by elected politicians (usually local councillors). As planning is inevitably a political process, there is no clear dividing line between where professional matters end and the stuff of politics begins. Ever since Skeffington, planners have been earnestly consulting the public on plans and development proposals. The public quickly finds that it is often impossible to make sense of the rules and regulations without an independent source of information and advice. The more enlightened local authority planners do their best to explain the process, but the fact that they are not seen as being independent is a real handicap. Besides, some of them say, local government today barely has sufficient resources to fulfil its basic statutory functions, let alone allow its officers time to make its deliberations accessible to a wider public.

In the 1970s it became clear that, whatever Skeffington might have believed, the formal planning system was an inadequate mechanism for widespread and effective public participation. People committed to making the planning process accessible looked for alternative ways to achieve it. One strategy was to use the education system to provide a structure that would enable children and adults to participate in planning. Environmental education developed in the 1970s, with URBAN STUDIES CENTRES and ARCHITECTURAL WORKSHOPS among its most impressive pioneering projects. Today, inspired teachers and planners still continue to pursue their vision of helping people to control their own surroundings through a process of learning, but with little official support. PLANNING AID is another initiative intended to make the planning process more accessible. A number of enlightened planners decided in the early 1970s that if local authority planners could not provide impartial advice to the public, independent services should be created to fill the gap.

An explosion of public participation in regeneration followed the growth of PARTNERSHIPS in the 1990s. Funded programmes of public involvement, serviced by a new breed of FACILITATOR and other participation professionals, aimed at building community capacity and reaching CONSENSUS. Many of the outcomes have been valuable. Others have suffered from the participation processes being badly timed or mismanaged, or from their initiators being concerned only with going through the motions. Commonly held principles of public participation include: a) People should be involved at an early stage in the processes of change. b) People should not be led into wasting their time if their involvement is unlikely to have an effect on what will happen. c) Participation should be continuous, giving time for trust and relationships to develop. d) Participatory structures should be linked to existing democratic structures, local agencies and partnerships. e) Special efforts are likely to be needed to involve groups of people who may otherwise be excluded, such as people with physical and mental disabilities, and black and minority ethnic communities. f) Participatory processes and methods need to be tailored to the particular locality. g) The programme, timing, funding and rules of engagement need to be established openly at the start. h) The process and the ability of people to participate in it must be adequately resourced. i) Clear measures of success for the participation process and the consequent action should be established from the start (Urban Green Spaces Taskforce, 2002).

public realm The parts of a village, town or city (whether publicly or privately owned) that are available, without charge, for everyone to see, use and enjoy, including streets, squares and parks; all land to which everyone has ready, free and legal access 24 hours a day. Also called *public domain* and *public space*. There are many alternative ways of classifying what is or is not public realm, and assessing its quality. Criteria include whether or when people are charged for being there; whether it is publicly or privately owned; whether there are restrictions on when or how it is used (whether photography is allowed or whether people are welcome who are not engaged in the space's primary function, for example, such as in the case of SHOPPING MALLS or EXCLUSIVE housing developments); and whether it is privately or publicly managed. Spaces that may or may not be classified as being public, depending on the circumstances, include shopping malls, shops, public transport, cinemas, pubs and private housing developments. In the words of Katherine Shonfield: 'All time spent outside the home and workplace is public time, and all places where that time is spent are public spaces.' The urban designer David Engwicht (2003) writes that cities are composed of two types of space: exchange space and movement space. 'The more space a city devotes to movement, the more the exchange space becomes diluted and scattered,' he writes. 'The more diluted and scattered the exchange opportunities, the more the city begins to lose the very thing that makes a city a city: a concentration of exchange opportunities.'

The urban design historian Spiro Kostof (1992) notes the decline of the public realm but thinks that the situation is not completely hopeless. 'Our public places were proud repositories of a common history,' Kostof writes. 'We have largely abandoned that sense of a shared destiny, and our public places show it. What is left may not be much, but it is crucial. We still want to be with other people, if not engaging them directly at least watching them stroll by. The public places unique to our time may be thoroughly privatised. Their motive may be no more noble than to lure us to buy. But having been drawn to the mall or boutiqued-up old town square for "recreational shopping" and the obligatory stop for food, we discover each other and might

public art

remember the place when we want to stage a public event, or celebrate a private event in public.' John Ruskin wrote: 'The measure of any great civilisation is in its cities, and a measure of a city's greatness is to be found in the quality of its public spaces, its parks and its squares.' Eric Hobsbawm (1968) notes that in the first half of the nineteenth century, UK cities' endless rows of houses and warehouses, cobbled streets and canals were generally unrelieved by fountains, public squares, promenades, trees or sometimes even churches. 'After 1848 the cities tended to acquire such public furniture, but in the first generations of industrialization they had very little of it, unless by chance they inherited traditions of gracious public building or open spaces from the past.' See also PUBLIC SPACE and RES PUBLICA.

public sector Organisations funded by and run by, or answerable to, national or local government. Often spoken of jointly with the private sector and the voluntary sector.

public space See PUBLIC REALM, and CRUSTY SPACE, JITTERY SPACE, SLIPPERY SPACE and STEALTHY SPACE.

public sphere The sociologist JURGEN HABERMAS' concept of the place where people talk about life. It is a sphere which 'mediates between society and state, and in which the public organises itself as the bearer of public opinion' (Habermas, 1962). He sees its growth in eighteenth-century England with the development of a new urban culture which flourished in, among other places, the coffee houses (see also CAPPUCCINO CULTURE).

public time See PUBLIC SPACE.

public transport (UK) A system of conveyance (typically bus, train or tram) provided collectively – by the public sector or the private sector, or a mixture of the two. The US terms are *transit* or *mass transit*.

public transport acceptability A measure determined by factors such as the attitude of staff, the quality of waiting facilities, the cleanliness of vehicles and the general character of other passengers (DETR, 2000).

public transport accessibility Defined by the DETR (2000) as a measure of the ease with which all categories of passenger can use public transport (DETR, 2000). This includes the quality of service, and the ease of getting to it and finding information about it. Price, frequency, reliability and punctuality would seem to be other obvious criteria.

public transport accessibility level (PTAL) A measure of ACCESSIBILITY to the public transport network at a particular point. Walk times are calculated from specified points of interest to all public transport access points, including bus stops, light-rail stations, underground stations and tram halts. The measure reflects walking time to the means of public transport; the reliability of services; the number of services available within an area; and average waiting time. It does not take account of the speed or usefulness of the services; of any overcrowding (including whether it is possible to get on board); or the ease of interchange. The PTAL method was developed in 1992 by the London Borough of Hammersmith and Fulham.

public transport availability A measure determined by the available routes, and the frequency and timings of services (DETR, 2000).

public transport environment The setting of a bus stop, or bus or train station, including the distance and quality of the route needed to reach it.

public urbanism Street layouts designed for ceremony, processions and promenading. See also GRAND MANNER.

public way A route or space along or through which people have a right to pass.

public/private interface The place where public areas and buildings meet private ones. In most successful places the interface is unambiguous.

pucka (also pukka) (Hindi) Strongly built (Vidal and Gupta, 1999).

Pugin, Augustus Welby Northmore (1812–52) Architect and designer. In *Contrasts*, published in 1836, he compared the meanness of the architecture of contemporary towns and cities to the glories of medieval gothic. His was a major influence on the widespread use of gothic. He collaborated with Charles Barry on the design of the Houses of Parliament although he felt his gothic detailing was merely cloaking what was essentially a classical building.

Pullman A model COMPANY TOWN south of Chicago built by George Pullman (1831–1897), maker of railway carriages.

pulse (US) To develop an area in regular concentrations of relatively high density, rather than at evenly low density. Example: 'Use key intersections to create walkable centers. Pulse the development instead of allowing low-density development to spread continuously' (2002).

pump-priming Giving a process support (a grant, for example) that will enable it to become self-supporting.

purchase notice Served by a landowner on a local authority, requiring it to buy a property on the grounds

> **"THIS WAS A LITTLE WORK BY A MAN WHO NEVER WROTE ANYTHING ELSE, WHICH NONE THE LESS IS ONE OF THE KEY BOOKS OF OUR CIVILIZATION"**
> *CB Purdom*

that a planning decision (such as a refusal of planning permission) has made it incapable of reasonably beneficial use.

purchase See BIASED TERMINOLOGY.

Purdom, Charles (CB) (1883–1965) GARDEN CITY pioneer, administrator and writer. 'Early in the new century when still a boy I had bought a second-hand copy of a book that contained a revelation, an event that has often happened to eager-minded lads,' he recalled (Purdom, 1951). 'This book was not a great masterpiece, however, but a little work by a man who never wrote anything else, which none the less is one of the key books of our civilization... Ebenezer Howard had written in *Tomorrow* a descriptive argument for the transformation of city life by building a new kind of town. To me, born and bred in London, which seemed a kind of hell, this was a wonderful idea'. FJ OSBORN wrote that 'in the 1917–19 period [Purdom], more than anybody, revived the garden city movement' (Hughes, 1971). It was a generous comment in view of the fact that Osborn complained that Purdom had libelled him in his autobiography.

pure planner One who has trained solely as a town planner, rather than turning to planning after training in another discipline, such as architecture, surveying or engineering. See also GENERIC TOWN PLANNER.

purified community One that seeks to segregate itself from groups it considers inferior. The term has been used by RICHARD SENNETT.

Purley See TERRY AND JUNE.

Purse-Seine, The A poem by Robinson Jeffers. See URBAN DESTRUCTION.

put option See OPTION.

Putnam, Robert D (b1941) Academic and writer on public policy, SOCIAL CAPITAL, and community and CIVIC RENEWAL. He is professor of public policy at Harvard University and was dean of the Kennedy School of Government at Harvard. See BOWLING ALONE.

Queen Anne style

Q

Quae publice utilia (Latin) (On Matters of Public Utility) A Papal Bull issued by Pope Gregory XIII (1571–85), setting out a building code for Rome. The code specified, among other things, that new streets should be lined with high walls, even if the particular plot were not yet developed (Kostof, 1991).

quaintspace A space of deliberate cuteness in an otherwise uncompromisingly modernist cityscape. The term has been used by Ted Relph (1987).

quality *n.* and *adj.* **1** A degree of excellence. British Standard 4778, published in 1987, states that quality should be seen as 'the totality of features and characteristics of a product or service that bear on its ability to satisfy stated or implied needs.' The Design Commission for Wales declares that quality 'should not be taken to relate only to the external appearance of buildings and their surroundings. It must also include matters of fitness for purpose, environmental performance, social and economic sustainability, responsiveness to user needs and the aspirations of the local and national community.' **2** High quality.

quality audit A review of its management of the design and planning process by a local authority or other organisation.

quality control The term is used by some planners to refer to ENFORCEMENT.

Quality in Town and Country A government campaign to promote high standards of design, launched by environment secretary JOHN GUMMER in 1994. At the same time the government revised its *Planning Policy Guidance Note 1*, to direct local authorities to take account of design in making planning decisions.

quality of life What quality of life a person enjoys in a particular place will depend to a large extent on their own circumstances and preferences. For purposes of public policy, though, it is useful to make assessments of what quality of life particular places offer in general, and to set objectives. The University of Westminster Transport Studies Group (1998) asked two categories of people (members of the public on the one hand, and professionals involved in developing indicators of the economy, the environment and the quality of life on the other), what were the qualities of a civilised city. The group reported that there seemed to be a consensus that the qualities were: a) Reduced crime or fear of crime. b) A cleaner and more attractive environment. c) Fulfilling employment opportunities. d) A healthier population. e) A reduction in poverty. f) Improved housing conditions. g) High-quality education. h) Good access to local services. i) Adequate social and leisure activities. j) More SUSTAINABLE consumption patterns. The group proposed a set of indicators to assess these qualities. These were: a) Crime (violent and non-violent). b) Safety (traffic accidents and perceived personal safety). c) Employment (unemployment rate). d) Wages (average gross weekly earnings). e) Education (educational attainment). f) Health (incidence of chronic heart disease and serious breathing problems). g) Air quality (local air quality measures). h) Noise (disturbance on street and in the home). i) Housing (condition and homelessness). j) Traffic (traffic levels, queue lengths, journey time variability). k) Economic vitality (empty buildings). l) Sustainability (CO^2 generation, waste recycling). m) Accessibility (amenities within walking distance, relative travel time by mode). n) Travel and activity (non-car trips, time spent out of home). o) Community (sense of involvement, provision of local leisure/recreation facilities). See also LIVEABLE.

quality of life capital The stock of assets that provide benefits for human life, now and in the future. The quality of life capital approach was introduced by the Countryside Agency, English Heritage, English Nature and the Department of the Environment Transport and the Regions in 2001 as a means of evaluating environmental, social and economic factors.

quality of life crime A minor offence that is thought to reduce people's quality of life. Dropping litter and street begging are cited as examples.

quango (quasi-autonomous non-governmental organisation) A body set up by the government, usually with a government-appointed board, to carry out a specific task, often including statutory duties. The number and powers of quangos have increased dramatically since the 1970s. Governments see them as a convenient means of avoiding more direct democratic control and of reducing their own accountability in sensitive areas.

quantity surveyor One who measures the amount and costs of materials to be used in a construction project, and who advises on the costs and economics of building.

Quarry Hill Built in the 1930s, the Quarry Hill housing development in Leeds became in 1975 the first major council housing scheme to be demolished for failing to provide tolerable living conditions. See also PRUITT-IGOE.

quantum A measurable quantity, particularly of development. Examples: 'You must define the density and quantum of development you propose for the site'; 'Density is a quantum that can be expressed in many different ways.'

quarter A distinct district of a city. Since the 1980s, UK planners and urban designers have taken to identifying quarters as a way of reinforcing local distinctiveness. Birmingham was an early example, with its Jewellery, Gun and Chinese Quarters. In this sense, there is no implication of it being a fourth part of anything. To the architect and urban designer LÉON KRIER, quarters are central to planning and designing cities. 'A large or a small city can only be recognised as a large or small number of urban quarters; as a federation of autonomous quarters,' Krier (1984) writes. 'Each quarter must have its own centre, periphery and limit. Each quarter must be a city within a city. The quarter must integrate all daily functions of urban life (dwelling, working, leisure) with a territory dimensioned on the basis of the comfort of a walking man; not exceeding 35 hectares in surface and 1,500 inhabitants'. In the context of POUNDBURY, Krier has defined a quarter as consisting of 700 dwellings.

Jonathan Raban (1974) is dubious about the practice of defining quarters. 'It is, perhaps, a symptom of our superstitious habitation of the city that we map it, quarter by quarter, postal district by postal district, into a patchwork quilt of differently coloured neighbourhoods and localities.' The urban dweller is less tied to rigid territorial boundaries than his country cousin, Raban suggests. 'The "Italian", or "Jewish", or "black" quarters are not exclusively inhabited by Italians, Jews and blacks; they are more or less arbitrary patches of city space on which several communities are in a constant state of collision. A colourful and closely-knit minority can give an area its "character", while its real life lies in the rub of subtle conflicts between all sorts of groups of different people, many of whom are visible only to the denizen.'

PATRICK GEDDES (1910) writes of focusing on the 'region and neighbourhood, quarter and city'. In Arnold Bennett's novel *The Card*, published in 1911, the speculative builder Councillor Cotterill is 'erecting several streets of British homes in the new quarter above the new municipal park'. The term comes from the French *quartier*. In HAUSSMANN's Paris a *quartier* was a fourth part of an *arrondissement*. See also LATIN QUARTER.

quarter framework An URBAN DESIGN FRAMEWORK for an urban QUARTER.

quartier (French) **1** Neighbourhood. **2** A fourth part of an *arrondissement*.

quartier de banlieue (French) A suburban area. See BANLIEUE.

Quartiere Triennale Otto (QT8) The district of the Eighth Triennale, an experimental development built to mark the 1948 exhibition in Milan. It was completed in the early 1960s.

quasi-public space That to which there is public access at specific times or under specific conditions.

Queen Anne style An eclectic, neo-vernacular approach to architecture, developed in England in the late nineteenth century. Joseph Rykwert (2000) suggests that it was named after a development of mansion flats at Queen Anne's Gate in Westminster.

Queen City of the World Paris, in the vision of Napoleon III in the 1850s and '60s (Hall, 1998). See CAPITAL OF THE NINETEENTH CENTURY.

Queen of the Suburbs Ealing, west London. The title is probably the relic of a campaign to market housing developments there.

quiet architecture Buildings that do not overwhelm their neighbours by their size or design. Compare NOISY ARCHITECTURE.

quiet lane The Department of Transport, Local Government and the Regions (2001) has proposed the following definition: 'Quiet lanes should be rural in character, though they do not necessarily have to be in rural areas. They should have no more than low flows of motor traffic after the authority has done whatever is needed to create the quiet lane. Any traffic should be kept to speeds appropriate to the mix of uses. Pedestrians, cyclists and horse riders would be encouraged to use quiet lanes. Uses might include recreation, play and education.' Compare HOME ZONE.

quoin A corner stone.

quotation The act of incorporating a copy or evocation of an element of an old building in the design of a new one.

quotidian Everyday; commonplace. From the Latin for 'each day'. In the urbanistic context the word is used mainly by academics.

quotidian space That which is used on an everyday basis in places where people live or work.

R

race All the people who have genetically inherited a particular set of characteristics. See RACISM.

race-coded street One that is generally thought of as the territory of one particular ethnic group. Example: 'Incorrect assumptions that streets are "race-coded" are causing damage' (2001).

Rachmanism The ruthless exploitation of tenants by slum landlords. The London landlord Peter Rachman was jailed in the 1960s for viciously harassing his tenants.

racism The belief that one RACE is biologically or culturally superior.

Radburn layout A type of housing layout segregating traffic and pedestrians. Culs-de-sac for vehicles serve one side of a line of houses, and footpaths serve the other side. The layout, used widely in the 1950s and '60s, was often unsuccessful. In many cases Radburn estates have been modified to provide combined vehicle and pedestrian access from one side, and the culs-de-sac have been linked to create connected routes. The name derives from the estate that pioneered it in the 1920s at Radburn, New York.

radiance The visual impact made on an observer by a building or work of public art.

radiant garden city JANE JACOBS' dismissive term for what she saw as the confused principles of two camps in the war of words about town planning: supporters of LE CORBUSIER's radiant city ideas on the one hand and supporters of EBENEZER HOWARD's very different GARDEN CITY ideas on the other.

rail booster (US) A mildly pejorative term for a person who promotes the use or construction of railways.

railroad (US) In the UK, where the equivalent is *railway*, the term railroad was current (alongside railway) until the 1830s, after which railway prevailed (Quinion, 2003).

railway *adj.* As an adjective, *railway* became 'a sort of synonym for ultra-modernity in the 1840s, as "atomic" was to be after the Second World War,' Eric Hobsbawm (1968) records. 'Their sheer size and scale staggered the imagination and dwarfed the most gigantic public works of the past.'

railway *n.* (UK) The US equivalent is *railroad*.

railway bonus The increased tolerance of people to noise created by a railway compared to a similar level of road noise. Whether this effect actually exists is a matter of dispute.

railway mania Eric Hobsbawm (1968) notes two extraordinary bursts of railway construction in the UK: 'the little "railway mania" of 1835–7 and the gigantic one of 1845–7. In effect, by 1850 the basic English railway network was already more or less in existence.' This transformation 'reached into some of the remotest areas of countryside and the centres of the greatest cities. It transformed the speed of movement – indeed of human life – from one measured in single miles per hour to one measured in scores of miles per hour, and introduced the notion of a gigantic, nation-wide, complex and exact interlocking routine symbolised by the railway time-table (from which all the subsequent "time-tables" took their name and inspiration).'

railway prose The Russian poet Osip Mandelstam (1891–1938) wrote (in his prose piece 'The Egyptian Stamp', published in 1928) of what he saw as the regrettable effect of the railway's monotous rhythm on writing. 'The railway,' he declared, 'has changed the whole course, the whole structure, the whole rhythm of our prose. It has delivered it over to... senseless muttering... Railway prose... is full of the coupler's tools, delirious particles, grappling-iron prepositions, and belongs rather among things submitted in legal evidence: it is divorced from any concern with beauty and that which is beautifully rounded.'

railway suburb One promised on and built contemporaneously with or after the construction of a railway linking the area to the city centre. Many such suburbs were built by the railway developers themselves, and in almost all cases the profitability of railway development depended on the sale or rent of convenient speculative housing.

raised crosswalk A pedestrian crossing area raised like a long, flat-topped speed hump to provide a better view of the crossing area and encourage drivers to slow down. See TRAFFIC CALMING.

Raleigh, Walter (Sir) See EL DORADO.

Ramapo system Growth management techniques designed to prevent URBAN SPRAWL, pioneered in Ramapo, New York.

Rand-McNally building, Chicago The world's first skyscraper completely supported by an all-steel skeleton frame, according to Donald L Miller (1996). Designed by Burnham and Root, it was built in the 1890s.

Randstad 1 (also *Randstad Holland*) The Netherlands' 'ring city' (actually a horseshoe), incorporating Rotterdam, the Hague, Leiden, Haarlem, Amsterdam and Utrecht. The idea was conceived in the 1930s. Within the horseshoe is the *Green Heart*, difficult to build on and containing Schiphol airport. **2** A group of neighbouring towns. Examples: 'To turn London progressively into Randstad England should be a primary aim of any strategic plan for the South East' (Peter Hall, 1989); 'Derby must see itself as a unique part of the East Midlands "randstad" with Nottingham, Leicester and Loughborough' (2002); 'Better transport could help create a Randstad in the Trans-pennine conurbation that incorporates Liverpool, Manchester, Leeds and Sheffield' (2002).

rank-size rule States that in some countries the population sizes of cities are related. The second largest city is likely to have half the population of the largest, the population of the third city will be a third of the size of the largest, and so on (Morris, 1989).

rap A form of popular music in which a highly rhythmical commentary is spoken over music with a heavy beat. Rap originated in the African American community in New York's South Bronx district in the mid-1970s as part of HIP HOP culture. Disk jockeys of Caribbean ancestry adapted the Jamaican style of using turntables to cut and mix records, adding their own commentary, derived from Jamaican 'toasting' (speaking a commentary based on boasting, joking and challenging), which has itself been traced to the West African singers and storytellers known as *griots*. Pioneers of the form included Jamaican-born KOOL HERC, who moved to the Bronx in 1967. His performances were associated with the development of BREAK DANCING, particularly by B-BOYS. Many rap lyrics express obscenity, violence, homophobia and misogyny, though there are plenty of exceptions and some successful women rap artists.

rape methyl ester A fuel (capable of being used for vehicles) made from oilseed rape. The question of how environmentally beneficial its use might be is controversial.

rapid transit A tram, light railway or guided bus system. Originally a US term, now used in the UK.

Rastrelli, Bartolomeo (1700–71) Italian architect, and court architect for ST PETERSBURG (appointed in 1738). His many works in the Russian city included the Winter Palace, built between 1754 and 1762.

rat run A short cut, often through a residential area, to avoid traffic congestion.

rat runner A driver using a RAT RUN.

ratchet basis An arrangement for sharing the profit from a development project on a variable basis.

rational nexus (US) The logical connection between a DEVELOPMENT CHARGE and the adverse impact of the development.

rational planning 1 Grid layouts. **2** Planned development, as compared to supposedly irrational, unplanned development.

rationalism An approach to architecture whose practitioners claim to base their work on the application of rationality, rather than drawing on historical styles. The group of seven architects who launched the Italian Rationalist Movement wrote in 1926: 'Architecture can not be individual, and in a coordinated effort to save it, to redirect it to a more rigid logic which stems directly from the needs of our time, we must sacrifice our very personalities... Against the elegant eclecticism of individuality, we set up the spirit of mass-produced construction' (quoted in Zevi, 1981).

rats According to a saying (clearly an exaggeration), 'in a city you are never more than 10 feet from a rat'. A local authority rat catcher in London told the *Evening Standard* in 2003: 'It's probably more like 30 feet.' Certainly in most cities rats well outnumber their human neighbours. New York has an estimated 28 million. The author and journalist Joseph Mitchell (1908–1996) wrote: 'Anyone who has been confronted by a rat in the bleakness of a Manhattan dawn and has seen it whirl and slink away, its claws rasping against the pavement, thereafter understands fully why this beast has been for centuries a symbol of Judas as the stool pigeon, of soullessness in general.' Jane Jacobs (1961) wrote of rats as 'one of the elementary evils that new housing is supposed to eliminate and the presence of old to perpetuate. But rats do not know that... The notion that buildings get rid of rats is worse than a delusion because it becomes an excuse for not exterminating rats. ("We are soon going to get rid of those rat-infested buildings.") We expect too much of new buildings, and too little of ourselves.' In Richard Jefferies' apocalyptic novel AFTER LONDON, the ruined city is overrun by rats before they in turn are controlled by birds of prey. In George Steward's EARTH ABIDES the rats that have found rich pickings in the dead city of San Francisco starve after they have consumed everything edible. Campaigners against urban pigeons call them 'flying rats'.

Rats, Posts and other Pests The title of a discourse by the architect Aldo van Eyck in 1981 discussing the style wars between rationalists, post-modernists and others.

railway mania

rattler (US) A train.
Raumordnung (German) Regional planning.
Raumplanung (German) Spatial planning.
Rawls, John (1921–2002) Political philosopher. See SOCIAL JUSTICE.
raze and rise Demolition and rebuilding. The phrase is associated particularly with slum clearance programmes of the 1960s.
Re:urbanism The title of a short book published by Urban Exchange in 2002 as a challenge to the government's Urban Summit of that year. It called for new ways of thinking about planning and designing cities. See also REURBANISM.
reactive planning 1 Reacting to developers' planning proposals rather than taking positive action to bring about development that accords with planning policy. **2** DEVELOPMENT CONTROL. Compare PROACTIVE PLANNING.
read (in relation to buildings or spaces, for example) To interpret; to understand. Example: 'The space is designed to be read from above just as much as from ground level.'
Reader for Those who Live in Cities An unfinished cycle of poems by Bertolt Brecht (1898–1956), written in Berlin in the 1920s.
real estate Immovable property such as land, buildings, ownership rights, businesses and leaseholds.
real property Immovable property such as land, buildings and ownership rights.
realo A person who takes a pragmatic ('realistic') view of a situation, as compared with a *fundi*, who takes a more fundamentalist view. Example: 'The local community was torn apart between realos and fundis. The former tried to adapt to the new exigencies of property development, while the latter formed a new grassroots movement.'
realtor (US) The UK term is ESTATE AGENT.
rear-view marketing Basing decisions about what will sell on what has sold in the past. Many housebuilders use this approach to justify poor design. They are building what people want, they say. The objection is that people are unable to show a market preference for an alternative product that does not exist.
reason See UNDERSTANDING.
reasoned justification Explanatory text that usually accompanies the policies in a DEVELOPMENT PLAN.
rebirth An uncommon synonym for urban renaissance, revival or regeneration. The historian Roy Porter in the Vision for London Lecture 1995 called for a 'rebirth of London's public places'. The CORE CITIES Group claimed in 2002 to be 'an important force in the drive for the "re-birth" of cities'.
rebrand Create a new identity. Example: 'We propose to rebrand Leicester as a sequence of activity islands, from exhibition and entertainment to love and fashion; from space and treasure to medicine and sport' (from Alsop Architects, writing in 2002). Sometimes the rebranding involves nothing more than changing a place's name. In around 2000 the South Bank Employers' Group decided to rebrand the South Bank (as the area on the south bank of the Thames in London is known) as 'South Bank', although this use does not seem to have caught on. In 2003 the mayor of London and the London Tourist Board announced that the EAST END was being rebranded 'Eastside' and parts of central London 'Cityside', apparently on the grounds that such names would be more familiar to American tourists. See also BRAND and CANTRIL FARM.
receiver site (US) One to which development rights or a right to higher density development is transferred in exchange for foregoing an equivalent right on another site.
recentralisation Increasing development densities in a city or city centre that has experienced dispersal of population.
receptor An aspect of the environment, or a particular group of people, that are affected by a particular change.
Reclaim the Streets An umbrella organisation, active in England in the 1990s, committed to mass protest against capitalism, GLOBALISATION and the poor quality of life in cities. See also URBAN ALLIANCE.
reconquered city See INVADED CITY.
reconstruction Defined by the BURRA CHARTER as returning a place as nearly as possible to a known state, while introducing materials (new or old) into the fabric. This, the charter warns, is not to be confused with either *recreation* or *conjectural reconstruction*. Compare RESTORATION. The US Department of the Interior defines reconstruction as the act or process of depicting by means of new construction, the form, features, and detailing of a non-surviving site, landscape, building, structure or object for the purpose of replicating its appearance at a specific period of time and in its historic location. Compare PRESERVATION and REHABILITATION, and see BIASED TERMINOLOGY.
recourse A lender drawing on assets of a defaulting borrower that are not immediately related to the development project funded by the loan.
recycled land Land that has been developed after the discontinuance of its previous use.
recycling 1 Re-using old buildings and structures. **2** The collection and separation of materials from waste and their subsequent processing to produce usable products. Recycling does not include the sale of second-hand books or clothes, the use of returnable or refillable bottles or containers, or by-products of waste treatment or disposal (such as landfill gas), according to the definition used by the Scottish Office (1996b).
Red City of the Planet of Communism The term

used by MIKHAIL OKHITOVICH for what he proposed would be the disurbanised region of the future.

red flag The legal obligation for motor vehicles to be preceded by a person carrying a red flag was abolished in England in 1896.

red line The boundary of an area designated for specific study, plan or action. Example: 'The success of a master plan is judged as much by its effect outside its time/space boundary as within its "red line"' (2002). See REDLINING.

red sneaker route A static form of the WALKING BUS. Instead of one adult walking with the children the entire length of the route, multiple individuals provide surveillance for very short sections of the journey (the adults stay static). Houses participating in the scheme are marked with a red sneaker. DAVID ENGWICHT claims to have invented the idea.

Redburn A novel by Herman Melville, published in 1849, in which the eponymous hero is shocked by the squalor and degradation of Liverpool, as the novelist himself had been when he arrived in the city as a sailor in 1839.

Redcliffe-Maud Report The Royal Commission on Local Government in England and Wales, chaired by Lord Redcliffe-Maud, reported in 1969. It recommended creating 58 single-tier, unitary authorities and a further three metropolitan authorities (for the Liverpool, Birmingham and Manchester areas). One commission member, Derek Senior, published a Memorandum of Dissent. His alternative recommendation was for a largely two-tier structure of regional and district authorities. The Labour government accepted the Redcliffe-Maud principles in 1970. The following year, though, the new Conservative government proposed a two-tier structure of county councils, six metropolitan councils (adding Tyne and Wear, Avon and Humberside to the original three) and district councils, all of which were to be planning authorities.

redevelopment The demolition and replacement of the buildings on a site. Developers often avoid the phrase in favour of more positive-sounding terms such as *renewal* or *regeneration*. The novelist Beryl Bainbridge wrote in 1986 of Liverpool's experience. 'When the grand scheme of redevelopment was started, the planners had enough cash to pull down all the buildings and make the motorways, and they hoped more would be found when the time came to erect houses,' she observed. 'But they didn't find it. There isn't the money to buy any more concrete or to maintain what remains. Liverpool isn't the wealthy port it was when my father went as a cabin boy to America. It should have been obvious to a blind moggie, but it wasn't to the planners. If I were a historian I could chart the reasons for all this chaos: decline of trade, loss of Empire, aeroplanes instead of ships, cars instead of railways, synthetics instead of cotton, the trade unions, the rise of the Japanese. If I were a politician I could blame the Conservatives for greed, the Liberals for lack of confidence, the Socialists for naivety and jumping on the bandwagon of progress. But it hardly matters now. It's too late. Someone's murdered Liverpool and got away with it' (quoted in Aughton, 1990).

redlining Designating a specified area for purposes such as refusing mortgage or grant applications, or giving outline planning permission. Example: 'The crude process of red-lining particular areas for development approval determines important design issues, offering little or no protection over the final design quality.' See RED LINE.

reductionism Explaining or dealing with a complex phenomenon in terms of what seem to be its component parts. The post-war traffic engineering approach to town planning is a good example. Compare HOLISM.

redways MILTON KEYNES' network of footpaths-cum-cycleway. The name is appropriate considering the surface's pink colour, but is said to have been coined accidentally by someone misreading from a plan the original term *pedway*. Naming urban places and features in error is not uncommon. In LETCHWORTH, for example, a place called Chaomans owes its name to a typing error (Chapmans was intended) in the early days of the garden city (Miller, 1989).

reed bed A natural system for filtering grey water or sewage using reeds growing in ponds.

reek (Scots) Smoke.

reekie (Scots) Smoky. See AULD REEKIE.

Rees Jeffreys, William (1871–1954) Roads lobbyist. He was administrative secretary to the Royal Automobile Club, secretary to the Motor Union and, from 1910 to 1918, secretary of the Road Board.

referencing Measuring and recording the size, density, accessibility, ground conditions, services, boundaries, legal restrictions and other matters in relation to land and buildings. In the development process, referencing is likely to be part of the job of a surveyor.

refurbish To renew. The word is used of buildings and, less often, spaces. *Furbish* (which has the same meaning, and also means to purify, polish or rub until bright) derives from the Old High German *furban*, to purify. Also *refurbishment*. See also IMPROVEMENT, REVAMP, URBAN REGENERATION, URBAN RENAISSANCE, URBAN RENASCENCE, URBAN RENEWAL, URBAN RESURRECTION and URBAN REVITALISATION.

refurbishment Walter Annenberg, US ambassador to Britain from 1969 to 1975, used the word on one occasion as a form of circumlocution and was never allowed to forget it. Receiving him for the first time at Buckingham Palace, the Queen asked Annenberg where he was living while his official residence was being redecorated. 'In the embassy,' he replied, 'subject of course, to some of the, um, discomfiture as a result of a need for, uh, elements of refurbishment.' The comment was captured by the BBC who happened to be filming the first royal documentary at the time, and was quoted for the rest of Annenberg's life (and in more than one obituary) as being characteristic of his way of speaking.

regenbabble The jargon of the urban regeneration industry. Also *regenspeak*.

regeneration See URBAN REGENERATION.

regeneration centre A regional centre for training, networking and information exchange set up in response to the report of the URBAN TASK FORCE.

regeneration practitioner A person who works for an urban regeneration initiative. Some have regretted the lack of a professional body tailored to their specific interests.

regenerator One who practises URBAN REGENERATION. The term was little used before 2002.

regenspeak See REGENBABBLE.

Regent's Park The London park and its associated development were designed by JOHN NASH and created mostly in the 1820s, though Nash's original conception was only partly realised. Elain Harwood and Andrew Saint (1991) have called Regent's Park 'at once the high point in European classicism, the acme of English picturesque achievement and the original of the middle-class garden suburbs'.

regime theory Describes how the effectiveness of government depends partly on the informal arrangements by which public bodies and private interests work together. The theory was developed in the USA by Clarence Stone in the 1980s (Taylor, 1998).

région (France) The largest unit of administration, consisting of a number of *départments*.

region An area between the size of a city and a nation. JANE JACOBS (1961) quotes the wry comment that 'a region is an area safely larger than the last one to which we found no solution.' The people who are classified as living in a particular region may not necessarily identify with it. A poll commissioned in 2000 by the East of England Development Agency found that fewer than 10 per cent of the residents of the official East of England region thought that they lived in the East of England. Thirty-five per cent identified with East Anglia and 23 per cent with the South-East of England. Tassilo Herrschel and Peter Newman (2002) suggest that the concept of the region has been rehabilitated 'after its demise during the 1980s in favour of the "locality".' See also DESIGNER REGION and VOLATILE REGION.

regional centre of excellence A centre, network or programme supported by a REGIONAL DEVELOPMENT AGENCY to promote regeneration skills. The idea for such initiatives was proposed in the report of the URBAN TASK FORCE.

regional chamber An organisation supporting the economic strategy of the REGIONAL DEVELOPMENT AGENCY in one of the eight English regions outside London. The chamber represents local authorities and other sectors.

regional city 1 (US) A concept, promoted in the 1920s by the REGIONAL PLANNING ASSOCIATION, of a planned network of urban settlements set among parks, farms and wilderness. It is the equivalent of Ebenezer Howard's SOCIAL CITY. **2** (US) A network of open space, economic activities and neighbourhoods, as distinct from the traditional, discrete towns and cities (Calthorpe and Fulton, 2000).

regional development agency Eight regional development agencies were created in England in 1999 under the Regional Development Agencies Act 1998 to coordinate regional economic development and regeneration, improve the regions' relative competitiveness and reduce regional imbalances. See also REGIONAL CHAMBER and SINGLE POT.

regional economic planning councils UK government-appointed advisory bodies set up by George Brown's Department of Economic Affairs in 1965, and abolished by environment secretary MICHAEL HESELTINE in the 1980s.

regional observatory A centre for intelligence gathering, monitoring and evaluation in support of regional development.

regional park Defined by Llewelyn-Davies (2000) as 'a large area (of around 400 hectares) or corridor of natural heathland, downland, commons, woodland and parkland, also including areas not publicly accessible but which contribute to the overall environmental amenity, primarily providing for informal recreation with some non-intensive active recreation uses.' In Scotland, a regional park is defined as an extensive area of land, part of which is devoted to public recreation. Compare DISTRICT PARK.

regional planning 1 Town planning on a regional basis. **2** Economic planning in support of regional development.

Regional Planning Association of America (RPAA) A small, influential group of promoters of planning and urban design. Its leading members included the financier Alexander Bing, the conservationist Benton Mackaye, CATHERINE BAUER, CLARENCE STEIN, LEWIS MUMFORD, Stuart Chase and HENRY WRIGHT. The RPAA was inspired particularly by the ideas of EBENEZER HOWARD, PATRICK GEDDES and RAYMOND UNWIN, and – from a wider field – Charles Horton Cooley, John Dewey and Thorstein Veblen. Michael Hughes (1971) writes of the association's work in 1923–33: 'The new RPAA concepts found concrete expression, directly or indirectly, in RADBURN, the greenbelt towns, the Appalachian Trail, the TOWNLESS HIGHWAY and the 1926 New York Housing and Regional Plan. Less specifically, their demonstrations of the region as the basic planning framework constitute one of the most important... chapters in American planning history.'

regional planning guidance Issued by the UK government as a broad but mandatory framework for structure plans and unitary development plans, until they were replaced by REGIONAL SPATIAL STRATEGIES in 2004. Guidance normally followed the advice given to the secretary of state by a regional planning conference, formed by unitary authorities and by county councils with representatives of their district councils.

Regional Selective Assistance A discretionary grant for projects with a capital expenditure of over £500,000, intended to create or safeguard jobs in ASSISTED AREAS.

regional shopping centre Defined by the Scottish Office (1998) as an OUT-OF-TOWN centre, generally of 50,000 square metres gross retail area or larger, typically enclosing a wide range of clothing and other comparison goods. Lakewood Contro near Long Beach, California, built in 1950–3, was one of the first (Hall, 1998).

regional spatial strategy (England and Wales) Prepared by a regional planning body, setting out policies relating to land use and development.

Regional Survey Association An informally structured, sporadically active organisation founded by PATRICK GEDDES in the 1920s (Novak, 1995).

regional transport strategy Coordinates major transport investment at regional level as an integral part of REGIONAL PLANNING GUIDANCE.

regional/local planning It attempts to relate the whole of an urban region to developments within each local part of it. Peter Hall (2002) uses the term to distinguish that type of planning from the larger-scale, economic development type.

regional/urban design assistance team (RUDAT) A form of ACTION PLANNING used by the American Institute of Architects (AIA). A team of professionals travels to a community where there has been little planning or urban design, spending four days working intensively with local people on a vision for the future. The method involves extensive preparation and follow-up work. The regional/urban in the title refers to the AIA committee that initiated the programme. DAVID LEWIS was one of the pioneers of RUDATs. UDAT was a UK equivalent. The practice of bringing a wide range of stakeholders and other local people for intensive working sessions has been influential on later methods of public participation in planning and development.

regioncity A CITY REGION. The term was suggested by PATRICK GEDDES in 1926 as an alternative to *region-city* or *regional city* (Novak, 1995).

registered place (Australia) One on the register of the NATIONAL ESTATE.

registered social landlord A housing association, housing trust, housing cooperative or housing company that provides SOCIAL HOUSING and is registered with the HOUSING CORPORATION.

regulating plan (or map) See TYPOLOGICAL CODE.

rehabilitation Improvement for reuse. In the UK the term was commonly used in the 1970s and '80s to describe bringing houses, and less often areas, up to a reasonable standard of repair and amenities, but its use declined in the 1990s. The US Department of the Interior defines rehabilitation as the act or process of making possible a compatible use for a property through repair, alterations and additions, while preserving those portions or features which convey its historical, cultural or architectural meaning. Compare PRESERVATION and RECONSTRUCTION, and see also IMPROVEMENT, REFURBISHMENT, REVAMP, URBAN REGENERATION, URBAN RENAISSANCE, URBAN RENASCENCE, URBAN RENEWAL, URBAN RESURRECTION and URBAN REVITALISATION.

Reichmann, Paul The developer (with his brothers) of CANARY WHARF, through their company Olympia and York. O&Y went bankrupt in 1992, but Paul Reichmann bought Canary Wharf back three years later.

Reichow, Hans Bernhard Architect and planner. After serving as an architect and town planner under the Nazi regime, he planned many towns in post-war West Germany. His 1948 book *Organic Town Planning, Organic Architecture, Organic Culture* explained his ideas, advocating the free organic growth of cities, and criticising urban forms based on grids and rigid layouts. Spiro Kostof (1991) sees this as reflecting the new thinking that was prevalent in Nazi planning circles after 1940. 'The traditional Nazi party doctrine of ruralism, with its fixation on the single family dwelling, was rather abruptly discarded when the rain of bombs over German cities brought home the urgency of future tasks – the rehousing of millions and the rebuilding of the urban infrastructure along more rational lines,' Kostof writes. 'Modernist tenets, once ostentatiously rejected, now seemed acceptable.' Plans now called for a massive programme of large, standardised apartment buildings set in parks and along gently curving streets – a softer modernism to suit Nazi tastes.

Reihenhaus (German) A TERRACED HOUSE.

Reilly green Houses grouped round an open space containing educational and social amenities. John Billingham (2002) writes that Reilly greens 'were intended to evoke the feeling of a village green idyll in an urban setting'. CHARLES REILLY, who developed the concept, used it in several plans, including that of 1944 for Birkenhead. See also URBAN VILLAGE.

Reilly, Charles (Sir) (1874–1948) Architect and writer. He was professor of architecture at the University of Liverpool from 1904 to 1933. His semi-architectural autobiography *Scaffolding in the Sky* was published in 1938. See REILLY GREEN.

re-image To create a new image for a place. See also RE-POSITION.

Reiss, Richard Housing reformer, town planner and campaigner for garden cities. See SILVER END.

John Reith

Reith, John (Sir) (Lord Reith) (1889–1971) Chairman of the committee set up in 1944 to advise on how to build new towns. Reith had been director general of the BBC and a wartime planning minister. His BBC experience persuaded him that the NEW TOWNS should be built, not by local authorities, but by development corporations funded and appointed by the government.

relict feature One left over from an earlier stage of an area's development.

relief The shape of the land surface and its height above sea level.

reluctant suburb A village swallowed up in the expansion of a city. The phrase is Colin Ward's (1977).

remediate To clean up contaminated land.

remediation statement Sets out how a piece of contaminated land is to be cleaned up, by whom and to what timetable.

remnant Defined by Andres Duany (2000) as a developable area that is left over when the site to be developed is larger than a full neighbourhood, as determined by maximum walking distance. NEW URBANISTS recommend that remnants be incorporated into adjacent neighborhoods. Compare FRAGMENT.

remote parking Car parking provided at a distance from the property it serves.

removable See CRAVED.

removal See HIGHLAND CLEARANCES.

renaissance See URBAN RENAISSANCE.

Renaissance town 1 One dating from the Italian renaissance. **2** One whose planners aspire towards meeting the expectations of the URBAN TASK FORCE report and the 2000 Urban White Paper. The regional development agency Yorkshire Forward launched a Renaissance Towns Initiative in 2002, with Barnsley, Doncaster, Halifax, Huddersfield, Grimsby and Scarborough as its first 'renaissance towns'.

renewal See URBAN RENEWAL.

renewal area Introduced by the Local Government and Housing Act 1989 to replace GENERAL IMPROVEMENT AREAS and HOUSING ACTION AREAS. The government hoped to encourage the demolition of bad housing where improvement was not thought appropriate.

rent gap The difference between current rents in a rundown area and the rents that would be likely to be chargeable following the building's or area's improvement.

rental void A period of time during which a completed development is unlet.

re-patterning Planning or carrying out a major restructuring of an urban area's physical layout.

repeated applications The government's green paper *Planning: delivering a fundamental change*, published in 2001, noted that some developers used repeated planning applications to wear down opposition to undesirable developments. It proposed that once a planning application has been refused and not appealed, or appealed and refused, no substantially similar planning application for the same site should be accepted unless there was a material change in circumstances.

replat *n*. The subdividing of an area once again. See PLAT.

repletion Gradually increasing the density of development in a particular area. The term was used by MRG CONZEN. See also REPLETIVE ABORPTION.

repletive absorption Gradually increasing the density of development in a particular area by one or more buildings or land uses expanding to take in neighbouring plots. The term was used by MRG CONZEN.

replication The creation of an exact copy – a replica – of a building or structure.

reporter (Scotland) The equivalent of a PLANNING INSPECTOR in England and Wales.

re-position To adapt the role or image of a city in relation to its competitors. See also RE-IMAGE and GLASGOW'S MILES BETTER.

representative democracy Government by elected representatives of the people. See also DEMOCRACY and PARTICIPATORY DEMOCRACY.

representativeness The degree to which a participant in a democratic political process can claim authority by virtue of speaking or acting on behalf of other people. In local government, elected councillors have the statutory authority to take planning decisions (although in some cases they can be overruled by the deputy prime minister) as representatives of their electors. To some councillors, that is where representation begins and ends, and they resent any attempt by planners or anyone else to consult people directly or through representative organisations. But councillors can never represent their electors fully. Even councillors with a deep understanding of the needs of the people they represent will find themselves asked to reflect conflicting views; and most will be bound to a greater or lesser extent by party political loyalties. A minority of councillors are hopelessly out of touch with the people they are meant to represent. Planners (whether councillors carrying out the council's planning function or planning officers) need to find additional and complementary ways of communicating with people and understanding their needs. Here again representativeness becomes an issue. The planners sometimes insist on dealing only with 'representative' organisations, which usually means those whose committees and officers have been elected at a general meeting. Such representativeness may well enhance such an organisation's authority, but it is never complete. Some views and interests are always likely to be represented more than others. Some may be excluded completely, often unintentionally. For planners to refuse to deal with 'unrepresentative organisations', as they often do, is absurd. Balancing competing interests depends on helping as many people as possible to become appropriately informed, advised and involved in the planning process, and on guiding elected councillors in making policy and taking political decisions to resolve otherwise irresolvable conflicts.

Repton, Humphry (1752–1818) Landscape gardener. He is said to have coined the term *landscape gardening*. Relatively intact examples of his work include Uppark in Sussex and Sheringham Hall in Norfolk.

res publica (Latin) A term used by LÉON KRIER for the PUBLIC REALM.

rescue archaeology Investigating, recording and occasionally removing archaeological remains that are due to be destroyed or covered by development.

reservation An enclave, disconnected from the continuous urban fabric, where few people go who do not have specific business there. The term has been used by Alison Ravetz (Hillier, 1996). Housing estates and business parks are examples. See ESTATE and PARK.

reserved matters Aspects of a development proposal, not covered by an OUTLINE PLANNING PERMISSION, that will be the subject of a subsequent DETAILED PLANNING APPLICATION.

resident services organisation A community-based enterprise, employing local residents to deliver local services. The model was developed in the 1990s with the aims of improving local services, tackling unemployment and empowering communities.

residential density The relationship between the amount of residential accommodation in a development and the area of the site. It can be calculated by dividing the number of HABITABLE ROOMS by the NET RESIDENTIAL AREA.

residential differentiation The tendency for distinct social groups or classes to live apart from each other. The growth of suburbs in the industrial revolution was an early example.

residential suburb See GARDEN SUBURB.

residual analysis Assessing the likely profit from a development by estimating revenue and subtracting likely costs of land, finance, construction and PLANNING OBLIGATIONS.

residual valuation An assessment of the profitability of a proposed development, derived by deducting the cost of the land and buildings, and the cost of development work, from the increased value of the land.

residualisation 1 The concentration of poor and unemployed people and people dependent on state benefits in a particular locality or tenure (such as council housing). **2** The process (brought about mainly through the RIGHT TO BUY and the end of council house-building programmes) of reducing the available council housing of less desirable buildings to a stock of less desirable buildings that houses only people with no other option.

resort town One where people go for holidays or days out.

resource centre Provides materials, facilities and services to support public participation.

resource flow analysis Identifies the resources consumed by a town or city and the waste produced.

resource(s) Something usable.

respond *v.* Be designed to relate to. Architects sometimes talk of a building (or its design) responding to its context. The nature of that response is often obscure. David Yeomans (2000) quotes an example from an exhibition caption: 'The window responds to the city, and the city responds to the window'. Catherine Croft (2002) reports 'a cheerfully laconic guide' at URBIS in Manchester explaining that, in the guide's words, 'the building responds organically to the surrounding streets – I don't know what that means, but it's what it says on the website.' See also ADDRESS.

Responsive Environments An influential primer of urban design by Bentley, Alcock, Murrain, McGlynn and Smith, published in 1985. The book sets out seven urban design principles: a) Permeability (there should be a choice of alternative ways through any environment). b) Variety (places should offer varied experiences through their range of uses). c) Legibility (people should be able to understand the layout of a place). d) Robustness (places should be usable for many different purposes). e) Visual appropriateness (the appearance of a place should make people aware of the choices it offers). f) Richness (detailed design, materials and construction techniques should contribute to increasing the sense-experiences users can enjoy). g) Personalisation (people should be able to put their own stamp on their environment).

restauration (French) Urban regeneration; restoration.

restoration 1 Repairing, rehabilitating and refurbishing a property. **2** The act or process of accurately depicting the form, features, and character of a property as it appeared at a particular period, by removing features from other periods in its history and reconstructing missing features from the restoration period. Defined by the BURRA CHARTER as 'returning the existing fabric of a place to a known earlier state, by removing accretions or by reassembling existing components without the introduction of new material'. In the manifesto of the Society for the Protection of Ancient Buildings, written in 1877, WILLIAM MORRIS condemned restoration as 'a strange and most fatal idea, which by its very name implies that it is possible to strip from a building this, that, and the other part of its history – of its life that is – and then to stay the hand at some arbitrary point, and leave it still historical, living, and even as it once was... A feeble and lifeless forgery is the final result of all the wasted labour.' Morris urged the PROTECTION of ancient buildings instead. Compare RECONSTRUCTION and see also VIOLLET-LE-DUC.

restrictive covenant A restriction on the use of land, written into the deeds.

retail The sale of goods directly to consumers.

retail anthropologist The consultants who adopt this name advise retailers on how to organise their outlets, claiming that retail anthropology is 'the science of shopping' (Quinion, 1999).

retail mall A covered shopping centre. Originally a North American term.

retail offer The amount, type and range of shopping available in a particular street or area.

retail park A large shopping development consisting of a number of retail buildings and a car park. Defined by the Scottish Office (1998) as a single development of at least three retail warehouses with associated car parking. See also PARK.

retail warehouse A large store specialising in the sale of household goods such as carpets, furniture and electrical goods, and bulky DIY items, catering mainly for car-borne customers and often in an OUT-OF-CENTRE location.

retail warehouse club (or discount club) Defined by the Scottish Office (1998) as generally comprising OUT-OF-CENTRE retailers specialising in bulk sales of reduced price, quality goods in unsophisticated buildings with dedicated car parks. The operator may limit access to businesses, organisations or classes of individual through membership restrictions.

retail-led regeneration project Where a building, area or complex of buildings is restored, refurbished and brought back into use principally as a shopping centre. Examples include COVENT GARDEN MARKET and the Great Western Designer Outlet Centre in Swindon's former railway works. Developers tended to use this term in place of *shopping centre development* in the UK in the late 1990s, in response to the call for mixed-use development.

retail-led urban quarter An area of mainly new, mixed-use development at least partly based on uncovered streets. The term was introduced in the 2000s by developers to describe the sort of development that was becoming more acceptable than the familiar shopping centre (a single-use megastructure based on pedestrian malls).

retirement community (US) A development devoted to the housing and support of elderly people.

retro design Evokes or imitates a past style. Compare AUTHENTICITY.

retrofit *v.* To provide facilities or other features in an area or building that was developed without them, or to a vehicle. An example of *retrofit technology* is cleaner technology fitted to older vehicles.

retrolutionary Concealing technical innovation beneath a traditional exterior.

retro-modern *adj.* A reinterpretation of MODERN MOVEMENT style.

retro-momo *n.* and *adj.* Modern movement revival architecture.

reurbanism Recreating the relationships that produce positive urban qualities; the opposite of DISURBANISM. William Hudnut, former mayor of Indianapolis, declared in 2002: 'The great task of the twenty-first century may prove to be re-urbanism – the inventive re-knitting of the frayed urban fabric at the core as we try to grow smarter, as we try to work better, and as we try to lead more inclusively' (CCM, 2002). See also RE:URBANISM.

revamp To improve; to give a facelift to. The term is in common currency, but is rarely used by urban specialists (though its brevity has led to it being used in the specialist press since the 1980s). The word originates from *vamp*, the upper front part of a shoe (which derives through Middle English from Old French *avant-pié*, meaning 'before foot'). To *revamp* a shoe meant to patch it up. See also REFURBISH.

revealed preference See STATED PREFERENCE.

reverse commuting Travelling to work against the usual suburb-to-centre flow.

revitalisation Bringing a place to life. Sometimes the term is used as a synonym for regeneration, but it is also used to refer to ways of bringing a place to life (such as finding new uses for old buildings or promoting cultural activities) that do not involve significant rebuilding. The URBAN TASK FORCE (1999) wrote of 'a projected increase of 3.8 million households over a 25 year period as an opportunity to revitalise our towns and cities'. In Dutch usage of the English words, *renewal* refers to physical regeneration and *revitalisation* to the process of ensuring that people live in the renewed place. *Revitalise* dates from the late 1850s.

revivance PATRICK GEDDES' (1915) term for the revival of urban and regional life.

Rekyavik of the South See ATHENS OF THE NORTH.

rez (US) A native American reservation.

rezoning (US) Amending a zoning map to permit a use prohibited by the zoning ordinance.

ribbon development Built along existing roads. This was a favourite form of development before the days of planning, particularly in the 1920s and '30s, as it allowed the developer to avoid the cost of road-building. After 1947 planners preferred compact towns with radial roads, and rejected ribbon development. It remains common, however, in the Republic of Ireland to this day. Recently some planners have argued that development along roads, properly planned, can be relatively democratic and SUSTAINABLE. John Summerson (1962) wrote that ribbon development was so called because the long strips of roadside house-building flew out from the centre of the map like loose ribbons. The term was coined by HJ Fleure and enshrined in the Restriction of Ribbon Development Planning Act 1935.

ribbon of settlement A concept of linear development proposed by DISURBANISTS in the Soviet Union in the 1920s and '30s.

ribbon park A PARKWAY linking several parks. The term was coined by ROBERT MOSES.

Richardson, Benjamin (Sir) A pioneer of public health. In the 1870s he published an unrealised proposal for a hygenic city called HYGEIA (Rykwert, 2000).

Richmond Riverside A mixed office and retail development built beside the Thames in Richmond, London, in 1988. Designed by the traditionalist architect Quinlan Terry, it incorporates some old buildings and conceals modern speculative office floorspace behind new facades (built in traditional materials) in a variety of historic styles. By day the overall effect is remarkably convincing, but in the evening the uniformly fluorescent-lit, suspended-ceiling interior becomes visible and gives the game away. The development was generally popular with the public but detested by a number of architects and critics as lacking AUTHENTICITY.

richness The visual interest of a building or space. One of the seven principles of urban design identified in *Responsive Environments* (Bentley et al, 1985).

Ricoeur, Paul See CRITICAL REGIONALISM.

ridesharing Two or more people travelling together.

Ridley, Nicholas (1929–93) Politician. Prime minister Margaret Thatcher's secretaries of state for the environment came and went. The first, Michael Heseltine, accused planners of 'locking up jobs in filing cabinets', and in the early years of her administration the rest were little more sympathetic. The planning profession kept its head down, and with each new environment secretary prayers of thanks were offered that at least the prime minister had not chosen her ideological soulmate Nicholas Ridley. Then, in 1986, she did. To Ridley, the free market was capable of allocating land uses in the most efficient way possible, so there was hardly any need for planners. If developers wanted to build out-of-town shopping centres (which they did), that was all right with him. He famously managed to confine his regional policy statement for planning in the south east of England to a mere four pages. The planning system survived, though: the government's supporters may have shared Ridley's opinion of planning in general, but they depended on it to protect the particular places where they, and their constituents, lived. Ridley, who condemned NIMBYISM, opposed a proposal to build housing near his own country home.

Riegl, Alois (1858–1905) Austrian architectural theorist and historian, author of *The Modern Cult of the Monument*, written in 1903, an important work on the idea of HERITAGE.

Right Bank (Rive Droite) An area of Paris on the north side of the River Seine (the right bank if you are going with the river's flow), associated with elegance and sophistication.

right livelihood The principle that each person should follow an honest occupation that fully respects other people and the natural world, being responsible for the consequences of their actions and taking only a fair share of the earth's resources.

Right Livelihood Award Known as 'the alternative Nobel prize', the award was established in 1980 to honour and support people who 'valiantly uphold' that principle. Its recipients include HERMAN DALY, HASSAN FATHY, FINNISH VILLAGE ACTION, EDWARD GOLDSMITH, LEOPOLD KOHR, MANFRED MAX-NEEF, BILL MOLLISON and JOHN TURNER. See also SUSTAINABLE.

right to bide The right to quiet enjoyment of a street or square as a public place, as opposed to the right to pass through it. Campaigners for the rights of pedestrians complain that the right to bide is not recognised in law.

right to buy Over the years many councils (usually Conservative) have offered tenants the right to buy their council homes. However, the right for *all* UK tenants to buy their council homes at a substantial *discount* was introduced by environment secretary MICHAEL HESELTINE in 1980. Local authorities were expressly forbidden from using the proceeds to build new low-cost housing.

right to light A legal right that a property may acquire over the land of another. It is not the same as a right to a *view*, to which many aggrieved householders discover they may not be entitled.

right to roam The right of access to all uncultivated land for walkers was granted in the Countryside and Rights of Way Act 2000. Ramblers from urban areas had been prominent among those who had campaigned for the legislation for decades. See BENNY ROTHMAN.

right to the city A collective human right, used as a guiding principal in reducing inequalities, eliminating discrimination and resolving conflicting interests of the use of natural resources, such as land and water. Such a right is included in the federal law of Brazil. See HENRI LEFEVBRE.

rights Michael Sorkin (1991) has proposed a 'bill of rights', setting out what he sees as being due to every resident of a city. 1) The right to a city conceived as a nation. Each city must be free to elaborate its own distinctiveness. Cities should have a clarity of limits defined by the interaction of location and the self-understanding of their citizens. Urban geography is both psychic and physical. 2) The right to a harmonious and visible relationship to nature. 3) The right of assembly, expressed in clear centres at all scales and throughout the city. 4) The right to tranquillity. 5) The right to a habitation that provides pleasurable comfort. At a minimum this must include space, sunlight, fresh air, sound construction, and access to available domestic technology. 6) The right to dwell in a chosen social arrangement, offering adequate scope for self-individuation. Anonymity and flamboyance both must be guaranteed. 7) The right to hygiene. No one should be obliged to confront the waste of another. 8) The right to free movement throughout the city. 9) The right to privacy, including the right not to participate. 10) The right to human locomotion as the privileged form of mobility. 11) The right to live in a delineable neighbourhood which offers the means of satisfaction of all basic material and spiritual needs within easy compass of the dwelling place. 12) The right to permanence, both of individual habitation and of the environment. 13) The right to change. 14) The right to memory, expressed in the retention of the city's authentic artefacts, not to be infringed either by arbitrary destruction or by the substitution of simulacra. 15) The right to architecture.

ring city See RANDSTAT.

Riley, Joseph P (b1943) Mayor of Charleston for seven terms, after first being elected in 1975. He has led the successful revitalisation of historic downtown Charleston through public-private partnerships and was the first receipient of the Urban Land Institute's prize for visionary urban development.

ring road (UK) A road which bypasses a village, town or city on all sides (compare BYPASS); one that encircles a town or city; an orbital motorway. Chris Upton (2001) has described a ring road as 'a road that goes nowhere. You travel for an hour then get back where you started: an idea so deep it's philosophical'. The US equivalent is BELTWAY.

Ringstrasse (German) **1** Vienna's ring BOULEVARD, built in place of the city walls after 1858. Its pretentious grandeur did not appeal to the philosopher Ludwig Wittgenstein (1889–1951), born to one of the wealthiest families in Vienna. David Edmonds and John Eidinow (2001) note that he frequently used the term 'Ringstrasse' for things he considered to be second-rate. 'To Wittgenstein it denoted a place of pomp and gesture, empty of content'. **2** Any ring road on the site of former city walls.

Ringway One See MOTORWAY BOX.

riot An outbreak of collective violence, often involving the destruction of property, and attacks on the police and other symbols of authority. See BROADWATER FARM, THE CLASH, DANCING IN THE STREET, DEAD CITIES, IT TOOK A RIOT, LYNDON JOHNSON, RODNEY KING, MERSEYSIDE TASK FORCE, MODEL CITIES PROGRAM, NO-GO AREA, LORD SCARMAN, SECOND CIVIL WAR, SEGREGATION, SEPARATE PARALLEL LIVES, URBAN REGENERATION, VAUIX-EN-VELIN and ZABRISKIE POINT.

riparian corridor A strip of land on the two sides of a watercourse and the vegetation dependant on that water.

Rippon, Geoffrey (Sir) (1924–97) Conservative politician, secretary of state for the environment (1973–74). His spot-listing of 100 buildings in COVENT GARDEN saved the area from demolition for a six-lane motorway and high-rise hotel and convention centre, and allowed it to evolve into the tourist honeypot it is today. See also SECRETARY OF STATE.

rising market The market conditions in an area where land and property values are increasing. These are the circumstances that developers favour.

risk 1 The possibility of an undesired outcome. **2** The possibility of an unexpected outcome. Where this second definition is being used (as in the world of property development), the possibility of an undesired outcome is referred to as *downside risk*. Compare CERTAINTY.

River City Memphis, Tennessee.

rivers of blood This was the image that stuck in the public mind from a notorious speech by Enoch Powell in 1968. Powell, then Conservative MP for Wolverhampton South West, and a former health minister, warned of the consequences of large-scale immigration to Britain's cities from Commonwealth countries. 'Like the Roman,' he declared, 'I seem to see "the River Tiber foaming with much blood".' A former classical scholar, he was quoting Virgil.

rizzi (US) Transportation.

road 1 A vehicle or vehicle and pedestrian route with few or no buildings along its route, or without a significant amount of pedestrian activity generated by adjoining buildings and public spaces. Compare STREET. In nineteenth-century America *road* was short for *railroad*, and *trail* was the usual word for what we call a road. In the UK the name of a road may alternate between having and not having a definite article, in cases where the name of the road is also the name of a place to which the road leads. Examples of this in London are Edgware Road ('the Edgware Road') and Finchley Road ('the Finchley Road'). **2** (Various English and Scots dialects) A direction. **3** (Yorkshire) A way; a means. Example: 'Look at it my road' (Look at it my way). *Any road up* in Yorkshire means 'however' or 'anyway'. The word road derives from the Old English word for a journey on horseback: a road was something one rode along.

road capacity A measure of the ability of a road to accommodate traffic, often expressed in PASSENGER CAR UNITS per hour.

road closure The legal closure of a highway and its pavement over which the public has a right of way.

road hierarchy 1 A classification of roads and streets according to their role in the network as carriers of traffic, and to the volume of traffic they can carry. This is the way in which highway engineers traditionally have understood the concept of a road hierarchy. Their hierarchy includes access roads, district distributors and primary distributors. **2** A classification of roads and streets according to their scale and to their role in relation to people on foot. This is the way in which urban designers tend to understand the concept of a road hierarchy. The hierarchy includes mews, residential streets, high streets and boulevards.

road kid (US) A young VAGRANT.

road passenger Defined by the Office of Economic Cooperation and Development as a person who makes a journey by vehicle, including the drivers of cars and taxis, but excluding staff of public transport or other vehicles.

road pricing Charging road users according to how much they use a road or roads. See also CONGESTION CHARGING.

Road to Wigan Pier, The A book by George Orwell, published in 1937, describing urban poverty in the north of England. Wigan Pier (in the town of Wigan), a structure used for tipping coal from railway wagons into barges, had been demolished some years earlier. It received only a passing mention in the book. Wigan Pier's memory, bolstered by the book's fame, has become a focus of the local heritage industry.

road traffic The movement of vehicles on a road network.

road train 1 (US/Australia) An articulated road vehicle comprising one or more tractor units and two or more trailers. **2** A line of vehicles whose distance from each other is controlled, perhaps electronically.

road transport The movement of goods and passengers on vehicles in a road network.

road warrior One who drives extensively. The term derives from the 1981 film 'Mad Max: the road warrior'.

roadbed (US) **1** The part of a road surface used by vehicles. **2** The foundation of a road.

roadman One who builds or maintains roads.

roadmap A written description or broad framework plan setting out options. The term became current in UK planning in 2003.

roadside urbanism Strips of buildings alongside – and serving – a road, such as filling stations, diners, drive-through restaurants, motels and retail sheds.

Roadtown A proposed linear city for New York State

described by the engineer Edgar Chambless in *Roadtown* (1910). Each house has direct access to an underground railway that lies beneath it and a glass-covered promenade on the roof. The Spanish engineer SORIA Y MATA had made a similar proposal in the 1890s.

roadway (UK) A surface used by vehicles. Compare CARRIAGEWAY.

Roberts, Henry (1803–76) Architect. He designed model housing and wrote *The Dwellings of the Labouring Classes*, published in 1850.

Robopolis An imaginary city described by Bob Jarvis (1983) in which everything that can be known is known; each activity can be located in time and space. 'Everyone shares this knowledge, and because the sharing itself is knowledge, the city of Robopolis is a single intelligence, always communicating exactly sufficient to understand and operate… Every event and every situation is foreseen, and each participant knows what to expect… Time loses its value just as space loses its meaning.' Robopolis is contrasted with EGOVILLE to help in understanding the real world, which is somewhere between the two.

Rochdale pioneers Twenty-eight workers who, inspired by ROBERT OWEN, opened a cooperative shop in Rochdale, Lancashire, in response to high prices in 1844. The initiative developed into the cooperative movement. By 1900 there were 1,400 cooperative retail societies with millions of members.

Rock, David Architect. See TOWN CHAMPION and VIVAT WARE.

Rockefeller, Nelson (1908–79) Politician. See ALBANY MALL.

Roe Green Village A picturesque development designed by FRANK BAINES and built in 1917 to house workers from the aircraft factories at Hendon, north London.

Roebling A company town in New Jersey, built between 1904 and 1906 by a son of John A Roebling, designer of the Brooklyn Bridge. Its design is admired by NEW URBANISTS.

Rogers, Richard (Lord Rogers of Riverside) (b1933) Italian-born British architect, the son of the architect Ernesto Rogers. He has been influential on urban policy, particularly as chairman of the URBAN TASK FORCE, which presented its report *Towards an Urban Renaissance* to the government in 1999. He is adviser on architecture and urbanism to the mayor of London. After a partnership in Team 4 with NORMAN FOSTER, Rogers designed the Beaubourg (Pompidou Centre) in Paris with Renzo Piano (1971–9) and the Lloyds Building in London (1979–85). He gave the 1995 BBC Reith Lectures on 'Cities for a Small Planet', later published as a book. Rogers (1989) has called for architecture to make the most of the technological revolution, rather than looking for support in nostalgic traditions and images of the past. 'The best buildings of the future will interact dynamically with people, adapting to the climate, for example, in order to better meet the user's needs. Closer to robots than to temples, these chameleon-like apparitions with their changing surfaces are forcing us once again to rethink the art of architecture. Architecture will no longer be a question of mass and volume but of lightweight structures whose superimposed transparent layers will create form so that architecture will become dematerialised… For the first time we have the knowledge and the means to create a paradise or a rubbish tip on earth.' See also AESTHETIC, ANTI-MONUMENT, ANYTOWN, BAROQUE-TECH, CAPPUCCINO CULTURE, DISNEYLAND, FORM FOLLOWS FUNCTION, MILLENNIUM DOME, PASSEGGIATA, POMPIDOU CENTRE, PRINCE OF WALES, RUPERT THE BEAR, SOD OFF! ARCHITECTURE, URBANISM and WOW FACTOR.

Richard Rogers

rolling back the state One of the stated objectives of the THATCHER governments (1979–90). For planning it meant letting the property market take the lead in urban regeneration, restricting the power of local government and imposing unelected QUANGOS such as urban development corporations. For all the rhetoric about 'rolling back the state', effectively power was further centralised in Whitehall.

rolling out the wallpaper Producing a colourfully patterned plan that is based on inadequate appraisal and analysis.

Romorantin See LEONARDO DA VINCI.

Ronan Point A tower block of 22 storeys containing 110 council flats in the London Borough of Newham, built using the Danish Larsen-Nielsen system of industrialised construction. Four people died when part of the block collapsed in 1968. The immediate cause was a gas explosion (the result of a DIY cooker connection), whose effects were aggravated by the block's heavy prefabricated concrete panel construction and incompetent workmanship. The disaster led to a national programme to strengthen system-built blocks and remove all gas appliances from them (thereby making many of them cripplingly expensive to heat), and it reinforced the case against HIGH-RISE HOUSING. The architect Theo Crosby (in 1973) called the collapse of Ronan Point 'the best thing that ever happened to British architecture' (quoted by Knevitt, 1986). The building was named in honour of a local councillor, who is said never to have recovered from his name being associated with what became the byword for disastrous housing. It was demolished in 1986 and the eight other tower blocks on the estate followed a few years later.

rond-point (French) **1** A roundabout. **2** A circus.

rookery A nineteenth-century term for SLUM tenements.

room PATRICK GEDDES (1918) wrote: 'I have to remind all concerned, first that the essential need of a house and family is *room*, and secondly that the essential improvement of a house and family is *more room*'.

room and kitchen (Glasgow) A small tenement flat with two rooms. Compare SINGLE END.

rosebay willow herb A flowering plant common on derelict urban sites. It was particularly common on bombsites after the 1939–45 war. See also BUDDLEIA.

Roseland The region known as ROSE (Rest Of The South East – that is, the south east of England excluding London).

Rosewell A company village built by the Lothian Coal Company in Lothian, Scotland, between 1860 and 1900.

Roskill Commission The inquiry into the location of London's third (after Heathrow and Gatwick) airport, chaired by Mr Justice Roskill, sat from 1968 to 1971. It reviewed alternative sites at great length, using cost-benefit analysis to weigh their respective impacts. Its report, published in 1971, recommended a site at Cublington near Leighton Buzzard in Buckinghamshire. A Note of Dissent by commission member COLIN BUCHANAN argued that the environmental impact of any of the three inland sites that had been considered would be unacceptable. At Cublington it would involve the demolition of a Saxon church at Wing, the moving of a Norman church at Stewkley to another site, the clearance of whole villages and the ruining of a large area of unspoilt Buckinghamshire countryside. The solution, Buchanan believed, was to build the airport at FOULNESS in South Essex, where it would contribute to the development of Essex and East London. Buchanan admitted that he did not really understand the intricacies of the commission's cost-benefit analysis. In effect he was saying that if Cublington was the answer it produced, the values built into it must be wrong. His message appealed to the government, which announced that the third London airport would be at Foulness and changed the place's unfortunate name to Maplin. Some commentators, though, could see that circumstances would lead, by default, to the site at Stansted becoming London's third airport, unless consistent planning and determined government policy intervened; and neither did. Others argue that it will never be possible to overcome public opposition to *any* new airport in the south-east, and expanding existing airports (like Stansted) is the only way forward. Today Stansted is London's third airport.

Rossi, Aldo (1931–97) Italian architect and theorist, and leader of the architectural movement La Tendenza. Rossi called (in *The Architecture of the City*, 1989, for example) for urban development to draw on the collective memory of the city. Rossi wrote in 1987: 'I have... a dream of great civil architecture; not the concordance of discords, but the city that is beautiful because of the wealth and variety it contains. I believe in the city of the future for this reason. It is a place where the fragments of something once broken are recomposed. In truth the recomposition does not seek a single, overall design but the liberty of a life of its own, a freedom of styles. A city that is free.' See also FRAGMENT.

Rossi, Karl Ivanovich (1775–1849) Architect. He was responsible for planning and designing a number of important buildings in St Petersburg.

rotary (US) A ROUNDABOUT.

Rothman, Benny (1911–2002) Campaigner. He led several hundred ramblers in the mass trespass on Kinder Scout in the Peak District in 1932, for which he was jailed for four months. The trespass was a landmark in attempts by city dwellers (Rothman was born into poverty in Manchester) to establish the RIGHT TO ROAM in the countryside.

Rotten Apple Harlem, New York – that is, the rotten part of the BIG APPLE.

Rotunda, The The circular 22–storey office tower, built in Birmingham in 1961 to a design by James A Roberts, is a well-known landmark in the city centre.

rough sleeper A homeless person who sleeps out of doors.

rough sleeper unit A government task force aimed at reducing the number of people sleeping rough.

Round City Baghdad in the eighth century. The city was planned around the caliph's palace, but the circular form was soon obliterated by the city's expansion (Kostof, 1991).

roundabout (UK) A rotary road intersection. The US term is *traffic circle* or *rotary*. When BARRY PARKER and RAYMOND UNWIN designed an early roundabout for the centre of LETCHWORTH garden city in 1908, Unwin described it as a *'carrefour à giration'* (Miller, 1989). The word *roundabout* was coined by Logan Pearsall Smith in the 1920s, as a member of an official committee charged with simplifying the language, to replace the former *gyratory circus* (Bryson, 1990). Compare GYRATORY and see also BRESSEY REPORT.

round-table workshop An event at which a wide range of stakeholders discuss an area's future.

Rousification Renewing a central urban location by developing it for high-quality shopping and leisure facilities, in the manner of the American developer James Rouse. The term was in use in 1989.

Rousseau, Jean-Jacques (1712–78) Writer and philosopher. See THE SOCIAL CONTRACT and WALKING.

route (French) A ROAD.

Route 66 Called the 'Main Street of America', Route 66 was designated in 1926 and decommissioned in 1985. It stretched 2,500 miles from Chicago to Los Angeles, stringing together one small town after another. 'Today,' Andrew Mead (2002) writes, 'sidelined by new highway systems and air travel, [it is] still part of the American psyche. It evokes both the open road of the automobile age and the pioneering movement west of a century before.'

route A road, footpath or cycleway (or a series of them) linking one place to another.

route corridor A broad band within which the precise route of a road will later be fixed.

route national (French) Part of France's state-maintained network of inter-city roads, but not including the AUTOROUTES.

routecheck An appraisal of a street or road, based on the PLACECHECK method.

routine activity theory An approach to crime prevention based on understanding the pattern of offenders' routine activities.

row house (US) One of at least three houses in a continuous row. The UK equivalent is *terraced (or terrace) house*.

Rowe, Colin (1920-99) English-born, US-based architectural and urban design theorist and critic. His book *Collage City* (with Fred Koetter, 1978) introduced the concept of *contextualism* which, according to the *Architectural Review*, he had originally intended to call *contextualization*.

Rowntree, Benjamin Seebohm (1871–1954) He commissioned the new community of New Earswick. He was the younger son of Joseph.

Rowntree, Joseph (1836–1925) Confectioner, reformer and philanthropist. He took over his father's grocery shop in York, and later joined his brother in manufacturing cocoa. Rowntree, a Quaker, pursued enlightened employment policies. He founded the model village of New Earswick, near York, for his workers. Among a number of several charitable and other trusts that he founded, what is now the Joseph Rowntree Foundation is the largest independent funder of social science research whose resources do not come from public funds.

Rows, The A network of two-tiered shopping streets of medieval origin in Chester. The upper pedestrian street runs above the ground floor shops. A variety of explanations have been given for this unusual form of street. Oliver Bott (2001) suggests that the lie of the land was an important factor. By the thirteenth century, when Chester's first Rows were built, the main streets were still at around the same level as they had been in Roman times. The ground level of much of the land behind the buildings, though, had risen due to rubble and rubbish accumulating during the Dark Ages. So, Bott writes, the lowest floor of a new building need be only a few steps down from the street if the next floor was to be level with the back yard. This meant that instead of having deep cellars, as in other medieval cities, Chester merchants had their storage at street level, with their shops or offices above. Richard Morriss (1993) records the theory that when the Saxon settlement took place the ruins of the Roman barracks and other buildings were converted into store rooms, and new shops and houses were built above them, connected by a raised walkway. Alternatively, Morriss suggests, owners were ordered to make their ground floors fireproof following a fire in 1278, which they did by building stone structures at ground level. It has also been suggested that the idea of the Rows came from builders from Constantinople (which had buildings in this form) who were based in Chester while constructing the chain of Welsh castles for Edward I after 1277. Whatever the explanation, Chester's Rows are a widely admired piece of urban design drawing in thousands of tourists each year, and arguably the most successful shopping environment ever constructed.

Royal Commission on the Housing of the Working Classes Chaired by Sir Charles Dilke, it sat from 1884–5, with the Prince of Wales taking part.

Royal Festival Hall The concert hall on London's South Bank, designed by SIR LESLIE MARTIN and Peter Moro and built for the 1951 Festival of Britain, was the first post-war building to be listed Grade I.

Royal Fine Art Commission (1924–99) An independent, government-appointed body with the power to call for the plans of any development proposal and issue its comment, but without any power to prevent development. After a long period under the chairmanship of Lord St John of Fawsley, it was replaced in 1999 by the COMMISSION FOR ARCHITECTURE AND THE BUILT ENVIRONMENT. The government promised that CABE would be less reactive than the RFAC. The RFAC was modelled on the American Arts Committee (Punter and Carmona, 1997).

Royal mile JOHN NASH planned Regent Street as a 'Royal mile' linking the Prince Regent's Carlton House with a Royal pleasaunce in Regent's Park (Summerson, 1962).

Royal Mile, The The street in Edinburgh that linked the royal castle to the royal abbey (and now the royal palace) of Holyrood.

Royal Town Planning Institute The Town Planning Institute was founded in 1913 'to advance the study of Town Planning and Civic Design and to secure the association of those engaged or interested in the practice of town planning.' Its aim was to coordinate people involved in planning (principally architects, engineers, lawyers and surveyors), not to create a new profession. The Royal Institute of British Architects, the Royal Institution of Chartered Surveyors and the Institution of Civil Engineers all opposed the planners' bid for professional status on the grounds that town planning was not separate from their own areas of work. The institute first recognised training for people without any other professional qualification in 1932. It was granted its Royal Charter in 1959 and its Royal prefix in 1970. In 2002 the RTPI launched its New Vision for Planning, describing it as 'a programme of radical change, leading to a body so different that it will be seen as a new institute'. The aim was to make it 'a more inclusive and effective organisation in order to promote a more inclusive and effective agenda for planning'. The institute declared: 'For too long we have had too narrow a view of who should make up the planning profession. Planning is not owned by or restricted to the planning profession, even with a broader definition of the profession.' The New Vision would involve reaching out beyond the profession 'to people who are not professional planners but whose involvement and interest in planning are just as real'. See PROFESSION.

RUDAT See REGIONAL/URBAN DESIGN ASSISTANCE TEAM.

ruderal ecology The scientific study of urban margins and abandoned land (Davis, 2002).

rue (French) A STREET.

rue-corridor (French) A corridor street; one lined with continuous buildings. 'Il faut tuer la "rue-corridor"!' LE CORBUSIER famously wrote ('We must kill the "corridor street"!').

ruelle (French) An ALLEY.

ruif (Scots) A roof.

ruimtelijke ontwikkeling (Dutch) Spatial development.

Ruined City, The A 1938 novel by Neville Shute about Sharples, a fictional northern town facing economic decline.

Ruinen Lust (German) A passion for ruins. The term was used by the writer Rose Macauley (Powers, 2001b).

rumble strip A change of texture in the road surface, signaling drivers to slow down. See TRAFFIC CALMING.

Rummidge The setting of several novels by David Lodge (b1935). Lodge describes Rummidge as 'an imaginary city, with imaginary universities and imaginary people, which occupies, for the purposes of fiction, the space where Birmingham is to be found on maps of the so-called real world'. *Nice Work*, published in 1988, for example, is set against the decline of Rummidge's heavy industry. Vic Wilcox, managing director of an engineering company, drives to work through a landscape 'so familiar that he does not really see it, an expanse of houses and factories, warehouses and sheds, railway lines and canals, piles of scrap metal and heaps of damaged cars, container ports and lorry parks, cooling towers and gasometers. A monochrome landscape, grey under a low grey sky, its horizons blurred by a grey haze'. Later in the book Robyn Penrose, a lecturer at Rummidge University, drives to Wilcox's works through the desolate suburbs. 'There are occasional strips of terraced houses, whose occupants seem to have given up the unequal struggle against the noise and pollution of the ring road, and retreated to their back rooms, for the frontages are peeling and dilapidated and the curtains sag in the windows with a permanently drawn look. Here and there an effort has been made at renovation, but always in deplorable taste, "Georgian" bay windows or Scandinavian-style pine porches clapped on to the Victorian and Edwardian facades. The shops are either flashy or dingy. The windows of the former are filled with cheap mass-produced goods, banks of conjunctival TVs twitching and blinking in unison, blinding white fridges and washing-machines, ugly shoes, ugly clothes, and unbelievably ugly furniture, all plastic veneers and synthetic fabrics. The windows of the dingy shops are like cemeteries for the unloved and unwanted goods – limp floral print dresses, yellowing underwear, flyblown chocolate boxes and dusty plastic toys.'

Runcie, Robert (1921–2000) Archbishop of Canterbury. See FAITH IN THE CITY.

rundown *adj.* Showing signs of severe urban decay.

Rupert the Bear A character in a series of children's books in which the story is told through pictures, prose and rhyming couplets. RICHARD ROGERS has compared his architecture to Rupert books on the grounds that it can be appreciated on several levels (which is true of all architecture).

rural The deputy chair of the Countryside Agency, Pam Warhurst, was reported in *New Start* (2001) as saying that the words *urban* and *rural* were tending to be replaced in discussions of policy by *places that are built up* and *places that are not built up*. 'Mud, hogs, and badly cooked food' was how Ambrose Bierce defined the word rural in his *Devil's Dictionary* (published 1869–1906). See COUNTRYSIDE.

rural belt A stretch of countryside around and between towns.

rural buffer A designation in a development plan of land which should not be developed, usually as a temporary measure. Like GREEN WEDGES and STRATEGIC GAPS, they are less formal than GREEN BELTS.

rural city One spread across its region; a CITY REGION. The term has been used by the architect Will Alsop (2003). See also URBAN COUNTRYSIDE.

rural connection The practice of keeping livestock in an urban back yard.

rural fringe See URBAN FRINGE.

rural planning An essential part of urban planning, as every urban area has a rural hinterland. *The European Spatial Development Perspective* has as one of its aims the 'development of a polycentric and balanced urban system, and strengthening the partnership between urban and rural areas.' This, it says, 'involves overcoming the outdated dualism between city and countryside.'

rural proofing A part of the formal policy-making process aimed at ensuring that all government policies take account of specific rural circumstances and needs.

rural/urban fringe (also rurban fringe) Rural fringe and URBAN FRINGE. Also called the EDGELANDS. Compare BORDERLANDS.

rurban Having both urban and rural attributes. The word was coined in 1918.

Rurisville A name considered and rejected, together with Unionville, by Ebenezer Howard for his GARDEN CITY concept. See also LETCHWORTH.

rus in urbe (Latin) The countryside in the town. The phrase, ascribed to the Roman writer Martial, was applied to suburbs in the nineteenth century.

Rush City A plan for a linear city designed by the US architect Richard Neutra in the late 1940s.

Ruskin, John (1819–1900) Writer, social commentator, and critic of art and architecture. His message, summed up in his motto 'no wealth but life', inspired a generation of social reformers. He wrote: 'I look upon those pitiful concretions of lime and clay which spring up, in mildewed forwardness, out of the kneaded fields about our capital – upon those thin, tottering foundationless shells of splintered wood and imitated stone – upon those gloomy rows of formalised minuteness, alike without difference and without fellowship, as solitary as similar – not merely with the careless disgust of an offended eye, not merely with sorrow for a desecrated landscape, but with a painful foreboding that the roots of our national greatness must be deeply cankered when they are thus loosely struck in their native ground; that those comfortless and unhonoured dwellings are the signs of a great and spreading spirit of popular discontent.' Of course, some of the Victorian suburban developments Ruskin so excoriated are today mature, cherished and sought-after residential areas.

The first intake of Labour MPs, asked in 1906 which author had most influenced them, all named Ruskin. RAYMOND UNWIN recalled: 'One who was privileged to hear the beautiful voice of John Ruskin declaiming against the degradation of *laissez faire* theories of life, to know William Morris and his work... could hardly fail to follow after the ideals of a more ordered form of society, and a better planned environment for it' (quoted in Miller, 1989). In 2002 JOHN PRESCOTT concluded his speech to the government's Urban Summit by quoting Ruskin (not quite accurately) as having said: 'When we build communities, let us build for ever.'

John Ruskin

Russell Sage Foundation Founded in the US in 1907, it developed model communities such as FOREST HILL GARDENS.

Russell, Bertrand (Lord Russell) (1872–1970) Philosopher. See UNREAL CITY.

rustication Masonry marked with deep joints or a rough surface (or stucco imitating this), particularly to make the lower part of a building look weightier. From *rustic*, meaning rural, rough and unrefined.

ruthlessness Jacob Polley aptly chooses this as a collective noun for umbrellas in his 2003 poem 'Saturday Matinee': 'Maybe it's raining and all the best shop doorways/ are sheltered in, a ruthlessness of umbrellas/ has taken to the streets...'

A Society for the Elimination of Umbrellas was formed in Glasgow in the 1970s, objecting to the hazards posed to pedestrians by the rib-ends of open umbrellas. Its plan to shock the public by surreptitiously sticking sheeps' eyes on to umbrella-users' rib-ends was never implemented, and the society was shortlived.

S

Sabsovich, Leonid An economic planner and a major influence on town planning in the Soviet Union in the 1920s.

Sack of Bath, the The demolition of Georgian and Victorian terraces in BATH from the late 1950s to the early 1980s to make way for new development, so called by the conservationists who eventually stopped it (Jeffreys, 1998).

Sacred City of the Sun Cuzco, the capital city of the Incas.

sacrificial A sacrificial building material is intended to decay before other elements of the building's fabric in order to ensure their long-term conservation.

safari See CITY SAFARI.

safety The relative absence of threats, real or imagined, to people. Compare SECURITY.

Saffron Park The setting of GK Chesterton's 1908 novel *The Man Who Was Thursday*, based on BEDFORD PARK.

Saguaro Seminar A periodical national workshop in the USA for civic leaders on CIVIC ENGAGEMENT, directed by ROBERT PUTNAM.

Saint-Simon, Henri (Comte de) (1760–1825) Utopian socialist. He proposed, among much else, a system of spatial planning.

Sakulin, Boris (1877–1952) Russian town planner and theoretician. He devised the *influentogram* concept and the *anatemoplanset* methodology (Cooke, 1978).

salami decision-taking A usually pejorative term for a type of INCREMENTALISM: taking a big (and often potentially unpopular) decision in small stages. As each slice is of barely significant width, the whole sausage has gone before anyone notices. Also known as STEALTH PLANNING. See ROSKILL COMMISSION.

sale leaseback An arrangement under which a homeowner sells their home to an investor but continues to occupy it on a lease.

Salem The capital city of the fictional South American republic of Cessares in James Burgh's *An Account of the First Settlement, Laws, Form of Government and Police of the Cessares* (1764). The city is a gridded one-mile square.

Salt Lake City, Utah Founded by the Church of Jesus Christ of Latter-Day Saints (the Mormons) in 1847 as the City of Zion to house the Chosen People until the Second Coming.

Saltaire A model COMPANY TOWN near Bradford, Yorkshire, built after 1851 by the Yorkshire alpaca manufacturer Sir Titus Salt. The name combined the name of the founder with that of the river beside which it stands. Saltaire was planned by the architects Lockwood and Mawson.

Salter, Alfred (1873–1945) Physician and radical politician. Salter and his wife Ada were closely associated with municipal enterprise in the slum district of Bermondsey. She was the first woman councillor in London and Mayor of Bermondsey. He left the Liberal Party in 1908 and became one of the founders of the Independent Labour Party, and in 1922 Bermondsey's MP. The Salters campaigned to redevelop much of the borough on GARDEN CITY lines, with wide avenues and detached and semi-detached houses. Their successful projects included a pioneering public health centre (with Britain's first municipal solarium for patients with tuberculosis), public recreation grounds, and public baths with a swimming pool and laundry.

salutogenesis The origins of health. Promoters of HEALTHY CITIES note that while enormous resources are devoted to studying disease processes and how they can be modified, little is spent on the study of health as a positive concept. *Pathogenesis* is the origins of disease or pathology.

sameness The opposite of DIVERSITY.

sampling Collecting examples (of building materials or photographs of buildings or places, for example) to help discussion of design options.

Samuel, Raphael (1934–96) Radical social historian, particularly of London life.

San Francisco See EARTH ABIDES and THE SCARLET PLAGUE.

San Gimignano An Italian hill town whose most striking feature is the 14 surviving extraordinarily high towers that some of its citizens built in medieval times to demonstrate their wealth. There were originally 72 towers at San Gimignano, but the other 58 have not survived. The image of San Gimignano's cluster of high towers has inspired many twentieth-century architects, planners and urbanists. See DISNEYLAND, RONAN POINT and SATELLITE TOWERS.

San Leucio A model silk-weaving town founded by Ferdinand IV of Naples in 1786.

Sandford, Jeremy (1930-2003) The author of CATHY COME HOME. He later developed a deep distrust of furniture after seeing Ionesco's play *Chairs*.

sandwich man People wearing sandwich board advertisements first appeared on the streets of London in the 1830s, according to Peter Ackroyd (2000). He claims that the term was coined by Charles Dickens, who described one as 'a piece of human flesh between two slices of pasteboard'.

Sandys, Duncan (Lord Duncan-Sandys) (1908–1987) Conservative minister for housing and local government 1954–57, responsible for the 1955 GREEN BELT circular. He founded the CIVIC TRUST in 1957 and was its first president. His private member's bill became the Civic Amenities Act 1967, which introduced CONSERVATION AREAS and placed an obligation on local authorities to remove abandoned vehicles and bulky household items.

Sane Planning in the South-East (Spise) An organisation set up in 1986 to oppose plans for 15 new towns in south east England. At a public meeting protesting against plans for a new settlement in Hampshire to be called Foxley Wood, Spise members burned an effigy of environment secretary NICHOLAS RIDLEY. Deciding in the cold light of morning that they had gone to far, they wrote to prime minister MARGARET THATCHER apologising. Their intention, they explained, had been merely to dump the effigy in a wheelie bin.

Sanierung (German) Redevelopment.

sanitary reform See ENGINEER.

sanitise To reduce the messiness of an urban place at the cost of its liveliness.

San-San The urbanised area stretching from San Francisco to San Diego, California.

Sant'Elia, Antonio (1888–1916) Italian architect associated with the Futurists. The *Manifesto of Futurist Architecture* (1914) appeared above his name, though he probably did not write it. In that same year he exhibited Città Nuova (New City), a series of drawings of architectural and town planning ideas. His vision of a city of gigantic buildings with step-back facades and external service towers, straddling a dense network of multi-level traffic conduits, was hugely influential. He was killed in the first world war.

Santos-Dumont, Alberto (1873–1932) A Brazilian pioneer of manned flight, he has been described as the only person to have used air transport for getting around town. At the end of the nineteenth century he is said to have visited cafés in his airship, handing the tethering rope to the doorman as he went in.

SAP The Standard Assessment Procedure required by the building regulations to ensure that new buildings are energy efficient.

sardine A person with many others in a confined space, like sardines in a can. Example: 'The sardine can is full to capacity. Please stand clear of the doors' (an announcement by the guard over the public address system of a crowded train on the London underground heard in 2003).

sardine city A pejorative term for excessively high-density development, where people are supposedly packed together like sardines. *Sunday Times* columnist Ferdinand Mount wrote in 2002: 'How scrumptious it is to hear these calls for Sardine City coming from such great magnates [government ministers]. At last count John Prescott had four dwellings to call on...'

Sarraz, La The French château that was the location of the meeting in 1928 which set up CIAM (Congrés Internationaux d'Architecture Moderne).

Sassen, Saskia Sociologist. Her books include *The Global City*, published in 1991. See GLOBAL CITY.

Satellite Towers Five functionless triangular towers of reinforced concrete, varying in height from 30 to 52 metres, marking the entrance to a suburb of Mexico City. The feature is intended to give the impression of SAN GIMIGNANO's towers or the skyline of Manhattan. The towers, designed by the architect LUIS BARRAGAN with the artist Mathias Goeritz, were built in 1957–58.

satellite town A new town that is at least to some extent dependent on a nearby larger, older town. LEWIS

Antonio Sant'Elia

MUMFORD wrote in a letter to FJ OSBORN in 1945 that he wondered whether the concept of a satellite town 'had taken on independently in England, or whether it owed its existence to a book Graham Taylor had written in 1915: *Satellite Cities*, though in that book the name refers only to the quasi-independent industrial suburbs of the big city'. Mumford added: 'I have always been reluctant to use the term, because it seemed to convey the notion that the solar central city would remain unaltered, and that it would remain a controlling influence. But I have spent 20 years trying to find a better name for the garden city and haven't succeeded' (Hughes, 1971). The term was first used in Britain in 1919, according to FJ Osborn (Pepper, 1976), as an alternative description of Welwyn Garden City because of the then prevalent misuse of the garden city label for GARDEN SUBURBS, and in recognition of Welwyn's special economic links with Greater London. See also GARDEN CITY. The German term is TRABANTENSTADT.

Sauk City See MAIN STREET.

Saunders, Clarence See SELF-SERVICE STORE.

sauvegarde (French) Conservation.

Savannah A city on the Savannah River, Georgia, laid out by JAMES OGLETHORPE (1696–1785) after 1732. The grid plan provided six *wards* (neighbourhood units), each with an open square at the centre. Public buildings fronted on to the squares. 'Among the densely gridded towns of America,' wrote Spiro Kostof (1987), 'the city stood out as a picture of gracious urbanity, and does still'.

Saxon Triangle The urbanised region of Germany based on Leipzig, Halle and Dresden.

scale 1 The link between a distance on a map and its real distance on the ground. See also KEY. **2** The size of a building in relation to its surroundings, or the size of parts of a building or its details, particularly in relation to the size of a person. Scale can be expressed in relation to surrounding buildings, or in terms of a maximum length of frontage or facade, maximum dimensions of a street block, or a ratio of building height to street or space width.

scale comparison diagram Compares the scale of a site or its proposed development to historical precedents.

scamscape (US) An area whose economy is noted for mail-fraud operations, savings and loan failures and country-government bankruptcy. ED SOJA (1992) has applied the term to Southern California's Orange County.

Scanner, The A technique of TOWNSCAPE analysis developed by GORDON CULLEN in the 1960s.

scanning See MIXED SCANNING.

scanscape An urban area under electronic surveillance by closed-circuit television and other means. The term has been used by the writer Mike Davis.

scarf *v*. To eat while driving. Probably a combination of *car* and *scoff*.

Scaricrotariparagorgouleo The capital of the fictional island of Letalispons, described by Abbé Pierre Desfontaines in *The New Gulliver* (1730).

Scarlet Plague, The A novel by Jack London, published in 1912, set in post-apocalypse San Francisco. See also EARTH ABIDES and URBAN DESTRUCTION.

Scarman, Lord (b1911) The government appointed the liberal judge Lord Scarman to report on the Brixton riots of 1981. His report (Scarman, 1981) ranged widely over law and order, and urban policy. Over the next few years Scarman frequently renewed his call for concerted government action to support urban regeneration.

scenario An attempt, less precise than a forecast, to simulate or assess what would happen in a particular set of circumstances; a representation of a possible future.

scenario planning A method of considering courses of action by examining possible alternative futures.

scenario testing Examining the outcomes of different sets of circumstances.

scenery See LANDSCAPE.

scenographic Contributing to the scene, as distinct (in architecture) from ARCHITECTONIC.

Scharoun, Hans Architect. See COLLECTIVE PLAN.

schedule of accommodation See ACCOMMODATION SCHEDULE.

scheduled monument See ANCIENT MONUMENT.

scheduled monument consent Permission from the secretary of state to carry out works to a *scheduled monument*. See ANCIENT MONUMENT.

schéma directeur (French) A development plan; a master plan.

schema See URBAN SCHEMA.

schematic See URBAN SCHEMA.

scheme 1 A development proposal. **2** (Scotland) A council housing estate. Compare PROJECT. **3** A package of projects where at the point of approval the individual projects remain largely unspecified. **4** (India) An area of town expansion (Vidal and Gupta, 1999). Compare COLONY.

schemie (Scotland, colloquial) **1** *n*. A tenant of a SCHEME. Example: 'They'd rather gie a merchant school old boy with severe brain damage a job in nuclear engineering than gie a schemie wi a PhD a post as a cleaner in an abbatoir' (TRAINSPOTTING, the novel by IRVINE WELSH, published in 1993). **2** *adj*. (Scotland, colloquial) Shabby, scruffy (*Scottish National Dictionary*).

Scherpenheuvel A seven-sided, star-shaped, radial city in the Netherlands built in honour of the Virgin Mary after 1603.

Schickhardt, Heinrich See FREUDENSTADT.

Schinkel, Karl Friedrich (1781–1841) German architect and painter who became state architect of Prussia in 1815. He designed in a variety of historical styles, from Greek to gothic revival. As city planner he laid out new boulevards and squares in Berlin.

Schmitthemmer, Paul See GARTENSTADT STAAKEN.

Schmoke, Kurt L See THE CITY THAT READS.

school run A car journey by which a child is taken to or collected from school. In 2003 such journeys were estimated to account for between 10 and 17 per cent of London's traffic between 8am and 9am.

Schuster Report In 1948 the government appointed the Committee on Qualifications of Planners, chaired by G Schuster, to find out if the profession was up to the job of using the powers of the Town and Country Planning Act 1947. The report, published in 1950, stressed the need for people skilled in developing social, economic and strategic policies, rather than in the traditional planning skills of design, engineering and surveying.

Schwartz, Martha (b1950) American landscape architect and artist. Her projects include master plans, public plazas, urban parks, reclamation and mixed-use developments.

science city A place designed to attract science- and technology-based industry. See SOPHIA ANTIPOLIS and TSUKUBA.

science fiction See HITCH-HIKER'S GUIDE TO THE GALAXY.

science of cities See CIVICS.

science park An industrial estate with predominantly science-based businesses. The first was set up in California in the 1950s by the 'father of Silicon Valley', Frederick Terman (Hall, 1998).

scoping 1 Carrying out a preliminary study to determine the scope of a subsequent study. **2** Identifying the likely effects of a development.

score An ALLEY.

Scots College See PATRICK GEDDES.

Denise Scott Brown

Scott Brown, Denise (b1931) African-born, American architect, planner and urban designer. ROBERT VENTURI is her husband and collaborator. See CELEBRATION, INDICATIVE SKETCH, LEARNING FROM LAS VEGAS, MAIN STREET IS ALMOST ALL RIGHT and ORDER.

Scott Report The UK government's Committee on Land Utilisation in Rural Areas, chaired by Lord Justice Scott, published its report in 1942.

Scottish Enterprise Scotland's economic development agency, formerly the Scottish Development Agency.

Scottish Executive The devolved government for Scotland, responsible for planning, transport, health, education, justice and rural affairs, among other matters.

Scottish Homes Formed in 1988 from the Housing Corporation in Scotland and the Scottish Special Housing Association.

Scottishness The distinctive characteristics of Scottish buildings. What these are, and how (or whether) they should be reflected in new buildings, is a matter of controversy. Features often thought to be characteristically Scottish include (depending on the region): steep roof pitches, small windows with a vertical emphasis, stone, HARLING (often tinted in a colour characteristic of the locality), white walls, pantiles, trimmed eaves and verges (without large overhangs and barge boards), small dormers, chimneys on (and flush with) gable ends, baronial turrets, and porches. The TENEMENT tradition is also distinctly Scottish. Compare WELSHNESS.

scourge of suburbia See CUPRESSOCYPARIS LEYLANDII.

scouse The local dialect of Liverpool. The word is derived from *lobscouse*, the name of a dish of meat, vegetables and hardtack eaten by sailors (*lob* meaning bubbling and scouse possibly deriving from *course*).

scouser A person from Liverpool. See also ONE-EYED CITY.

scrape See LANDSCRAPE.

screenager A technically proficient young person, reared on television and computers. The term was coined in 1997 by Douglas Rushkoff in his book *Playing the Future* (Quinion, 1998).

screever A pavement artist. George Orwell quoted a London one in *Down and Out in London and Paris*, published in 1933. 'I'm what they call a serious screever. I don't draw in blackboard chalks like these others, I use proper colours the same as what painters use.' Orwell reported: 'At that time there was a screever almost every 25 yards along the Embankment – 25 yards being the recognised minimum between pitches.' One screever, Orwell noted, was said to have been drawing the same picture (of a dog pulling a child out of the water) every day for ten years.

scullery The back kitchen, a room for cooking, dish washing, food preparation and clothes washing, occasionally containing a fixed bath (otherwise a tin bath was sometimes stored there) in both middle-class and working-class housing. In a house without a kitchen, cooking would usually be done over the fire or on the hob grate in the living room. Markus and Cameron (2002) report that by the second world war the term scullery was no longer mentioned in the UK government's housing manuals in relation to working-class housing. *Working kitchen* appeared instead. Compare PARLOUR.

Seagram Building Designed by MIES VAN DER ROHE and built in 1956–57, the New York skyscraper is said to have been the first with floor-to-ceiling glass walls. Mies surprised many orthodox modernists by mounting non-structural I-beams on the mullions, from the top to the bottom of the façade.

seagull Increasing numbers of herring gulls and lesser black-backed gulls are attracted to Britain's cities by food waste, higher temperatures (see URBAN HEAT ISLAND) and the street lighting that enables them to feed at night.

Seahaven Island The fictional idyllic island community where the film *The Truman Show* (directed by Peter Weir and released in 1998) is set. Truman Burbank, played by Jim Carrie, is the star of the world's most popular soap opera, broadcast 24 hours a day, and he has been ever since he was born. He is oblivious of that fact, unlike everyone else who appears in the programme, who are all actors. Seahaven Island is a vast film set, covered by a dome, and even the weather is artificial. Truman eventually discovers the deception and manages to escape. Seahaven Island is set in the NEW URBANIST community of SEASIDE in Florida.

seam The line where two areas of the urban fabric meet which have significantly different characteristics, but where there is no impermeable barrier.

seaport AJ Liebling wrote: 'New Orleans resembles Genoa or Marseilles, or Beirut or the Egyptian Alexandria more than it does New York, although all seaports resemble one another more than they can resemble any place in the interior. Like Havana and Port-au-Prince, New Orleans is within the orbit of a Hellenistic world that never touched the North Atlantic. The Mediterranean, Caribbean and Gulf of Mexico form a homogenous, though interrupted, sea' (quoted in Toole, 1980).

search sequence The method of using the SEQUENTIAL APPROACH to select housing sites for development plans.

Searles, Michael (1751–1813) Architect. He designed speculative housing in south London, including the PARAGON in Blackheath (c1794–1805).

Seaside A resort town in Florida built to a master plan by LÉON KRIER and an urban and design code by architects and planners DUANY PLATER-ZYBERK. Seaside was a celebrated early example of NEW URBANISM. See SEAHAVEN ISLAND.

seasonal suburbanisation The changing pattern of housing occupation in an area due to the intermittent occupation of second homes.

Seattle, Chief The native American tribal leader after whom the city of Seattle was named. His 1854 oration is one of the most widely quoted statements of the principles of sustainability (see SUSTAINABLE). If his words sound strikingly in accord with modern concerns, that is probably because they are not his own. A translation of the speech was published by Chief Seattle's friend Henry Smith in 1887, over 30 years after he gave it. In 1970 Ted Perry heard a revised version of this being read at the Earth Day festivities, and he used it as the basis for a television script for the Southern Baptist and Television Commission, which the producer further revised. The words that the script put into Chief Seattle's mouth are what he is famous for, even though they contain several glaring anachronisms and errors of geography. Some commentators have regretted this episode as an example of Native American culture being appropriated and exploited.

second city of the Empire 1 Calcutta, in the days of British imperial rule over India. **2** Glasgow, when it was the largest city in the UK after London. See also WORKSHOP OF THE EMPIRE. **3** Dublin, when what is now the Republic of Ireland was part of the British Empire. **4** Liverpool and Birmingham have recently advanced utterly spurious claims to the title.

second civil war The USA's urban riots of the late 1960s (Davis, 2002).

second contradiction of capitalism The fact that capitalistic processes externalise their social and environmental costs (to local workforces and communities, for example), which later return as a threat to capital (in the form of sprawl, pollution, deforestation and global warming, for example), which eventually become constraints of global profitability (Davis, 2002). The syndrome has been described by James O'Connor.

second home A property owned, leased or rented on a long-term basis as the occasional or holiday home of a household that usually lives elsewhere.

second unit (US) A self-contained home on the same plot as a primary home. Also called a *granny flat* or *in-law unit*.

secondary housing cooperative A cooperative formed to provide services to primary housing cooperatives, rather than (unlike primary co-ops) providing housing directly.

secondary impact See INDIRECT IMPACT.

secretary of state A succession of secretaries of state and currently the deputy prime minister have been responsible to Parliament for the planning system in England. The responsibilities include issuing national

JAMES WILSON
MERCHANT, GLASGOW

second city of the empire

policy guidance, exercising the power to call in and decide on planning applications of major importance, and making decisions (with the PLANNING INSPECTORATE) on planning appeals. The secretaries of state responsible for urban issues since 1970 have headed, successively, the Department of the Environment; the Department of the Environment Transport and the Regions; and the Department of Transport, Local Government and the Regions. Two Conservatives, Peter Walker (appointed 1970) and GEOFFREY RIPPON (1973) were followed by Labour's PETER SHORE (1974) and ANTHONY CROSLAND (1975), and Peter Shore again in 1978. Six Conservatives followed in quick succession: MICHAEL HESELTINE (1979), Tom King (1983), Patrick Jenkin (also 1983), KENNETH BAKER (1985), NICHOLAS RIDLEY (1986), Chris Patten (1989) and Michael Heseltine again in 1990. JOHN GUMMER was the last of the run of Conservative secretaries of state, followed by Labour's JOHN PRESCOTT (1997) and Stephen Byers. John Prescott took over the responsibilities once more in 2002, heading the new Office of the Deputy Prime Minister.

secteur sauvegardé (French) Conservation area. The concept was introduced by André Malraux as minister of culture in 1962.

section A drawing showing a slice through a building or site.

section 106 agreement An agreement or instrument entered into by a person with an interest in a piece of land, either with the local planning authority or unilaterally, normally before the grant of planning permission. The agreement may restrict the development or use of the land in a specified way; require specific operations or activities to be carried out in, on, under or over the land; require the land to be used in a specified way; or provide for a specific payment to the local authority or other public body to secure benefits to the community. The legal term for such restrictions or requirements is *planning obligations*. More often they are known by the informal term (now frowned on officially) *planning gain*. The statutory basis for such agreements is section 106 of the Town and Country Planning Act 1990. Government policy insists that planning obligations must be necessary; relevant to planning; directly related the proposed development; fairly and reasonably related in scale and kind to the proposed development; and reasonable in all other respects. A *unilateral undertaking* under section 106 can be proposed by a developer in circumstances where a local planning authority can not or will not advance section 106 negotiations and determine a planning application; these are usually sought as part of an appeal but are rarely used.

section 38 agreement Used by a local highway authority to secure planning advantages and PLANNING GAIN under section 38 of the Highways Act 1980.

section 52 agreement They became known as SECTION 106 AGREEMENTS on a change of the law.

section 75 agreement (Scotland) The equivalent of a SECTION 106 AGREEMENT.

sector 1 A generic word for such terms as neighbourhood and district. Andres Duany (2000) defines a sector as 'a portion of an urbanized area'. **2** A SUPERBLOCK at the new town of Chandigarh.

Secured by Design The corporate title of a family of national police projects aimed at reducing crime by designing buildings and developments to create fewer opportunities for criminals. The initiative is managed by the Association of Chief Police Officers and supported by the UK government. Some local authorities insist in their development plans that relevant development must meet Secured by Design criteria. Aspects of the criteria, particularly relating to the layout of housing schemes, are controversial.

The section of the official document *Secured by Design* on new homes says that 'a key element in the security of any [housing] development is to discourage casual intrusion by non-residents through the development'. This can not be true of a mixed development (houses and shops, for example) or of housing on a street that leads somewhere. Yet accepted good practice is that as much housing development as possible should be of one of these two types (see SPACE SYNTAX ANALYSIS). There also is a more fundamental issue, which explains why security is such a contentious urban design issue. Urban design is a matter of balancing conflicting interests. Successful urban development is likely to respond to local character, enclose space, contribute to the quality of the public realm, promote ease of movement, be welcoming and adaptable, promote diversity, make good use of resources, and promote safety and security. There are many design principles that can be followed to achieve these qualities, but no development can adopt all of the principles to an equal extent. The conflicts are not just between objectives but also between ways of achieving objectives. For example, a tall fence may serve to increase security by making access more difficult, but reduce security by preventing overlooking. That is why design is a process of achieving balance rather than simply a matter of ticking items on a checklist. (Checklists have a valuable role as part of the agenda-setting stage at the start of the design process, as with PLACECHECKS).

Achieving the appropriate balance in a particular circumstance depends on fully understanding the local context. Security is an important issue in urban design, and in some settings it might even be the most important, so people who understand about security (such as the police) should be involved in the design process. But security is not (except in certain special circumstances) an absolute, and problems can arise when anyone tries to be prescriptive about how to design for it. Design guidance on security should distinguish between non-prescriptive *principles* (on matters which have to be balanced with other objectives), on the one hand, and prescriptive *standards* (which must always be met), on the other. See CRIME PREVENTION.

securitisation Creating tradable securities from a property asset.

security 1 Freedom from risk; the relative absence of threat to property. Compare SAFETY. **2** Measures taken to minimise risk. See also PUBLIC SPHERE and STARBUCKS AND STADIA.

seeing is believing Visits that enable people involved in the planning and design process to learn about relevant experience elsewhere, and in particular to have higher expectations about what might be possible.

Segal method The method of self-build housing devised by WALTER SEGAL.

Segal, Walter (1907–85) Architect. He devised the successful Segal method of self-build housing in 1962, originally as a means of providing a temporary home (built in two weeks) for his own family. The method simplifies the process of building by using timber frames to avoid bricklaying, standard sizes of plywood panels and other components to avoid cutting, plasterboard to avoid plastering, and concrete pads in place of foundations. The method has been used by self-builders throughout the country, most notably in Lewisham in the 1970s, where the approach was adopted to develop sites that were uneconomic for mainstream local authority house building.

segregation The separation of urban functions, such as pedestrians and vehicles on a street, different uses in different parts of a town; the tendency for particular groups to live apart from one another, usually as a result of social, economic or political pressures. Sir Peter Hall (2003) writes: 'In Bengali East London... some children grow up on estates so segregated that they might well be in another continent.' The high degree of segregation in some UK towns was highlighted by studies investigating the causes of riots that took place in a number of northern towns in the summer of 2001. The report of the Oldham Independent Review, published later that year, found in Oldham 'a community more polarised on racial lines than anything seen before in the UK'. It noted that one of Oldham's communities – the indigenous white population – could trace its ancestry in the town longer than others, but that it had always been a town of immigrants, from the rest of northern England in the nineteenth and twentieth centuries, from Poland, the Ukraine and elsewhere after the second world war, and from the Caribbean in the 1950s and '60s. All had been accepted, even if in some cases this took time. More recently, though, Pakistani and Bangladeshi Oldhamers had not become integrated.

'The divisions are now such that we have had to ask the question whether people in the different communities actually want to have much to do with one another,' the report said. 'For many white people the attitude seems to be that we would rather the Asians were not here, we will have as little to do with them as possible, and so we pretend that the Asians are not here. For many Asians, the attitude seems to be that this is a difficult and alien environment in which we find ourselves, we must protect ourselves from it and its corrupting influences, and we can do that best by creating largely separated communities in Oldham modelled on what we have left behind in Pakistan and Bangladesh... Many policies pursued by the council and other agencies over the years have reinforced the separateness between the communities.' Warning of how dangerous might be the long-term consequences, the report quoted the Christian spiritual writer Donald Nicholl. Describing the relationship between different parts of society in Germany after the first world war, Nicholl had commented: 'The different religious and political groupings in Germany were so deeply divided that it would have been almost unthinkable – even impertinent – for a representative of one group to have spoken up on behalf of another group. To begin with, these groups virtually never met one another socially; Catholics went to Catholic schools and Protestants to Protestant schools; socialists had their comics for socialist children and communists had theirs for their children; Jews went to Jewish doctors and Catholics to Catholic doctors; all along the line they tended to meet only people of their own political or religious colour, whether they were worshipping or playing or being ill; and so they harboured the strangest notions about those outside their own community.' Divisions in Oldham had not reached that level, the report noted, but the lessons needed to be kept in mind. 'The fact that it is mainly self-segregation makes the task all the more challenging.' The report's authors could have found examples of deep segregation closer to home than inter-war Germany: in Northern Ireland, as well as in the USA. See also CLUSTERING, SEPARATE PARALLEL LIVES, GHETTO, SUBURB and ZONING, and compare CONGREGATION.

Segway Human Transporter A battery-powered scooter, with two wheels side by side, controlled by body movements with the help of computers and gyroscopes. Invented by Dean Kamen, it went on sale in 2003.

Seifert, Richard (1910–2001) Architect. Colonel Seifert (as he was known, following his wartime army service) was probably the UK's most commercially successful architect in the 1950s, '60s and '70s. His particular skill was in manipulating the planning and other regulatory systems to pile more development on a site than anyone else would have been able to manage. His best-known buildings were the NatWest Tower in the City of London (the UK's tallest building at the time) and CENTRE POINT on London's Oxford Street (constructed in 1961–5 as the world's tallest prefabricated building, now listed). Both these were built with the engineers Pell Frischmann. Seifert's other buildings included hotels, hospitals, high-rise housing and more than 500 office blocks.

Richard Seifert

seismic retrofit Strengthening a building to make it better able to survive an earthquake.

self-build 1 Buildings (usually houses) physically constructed (completely or in part) by their owners. **2** Buildings whose owners commission contractors to build them. **3** Buildings constructed by groups of people pooling their expertise and resources.

self-help People or communities taking responsibility for improving their living conditions, rather than relying on local or central government. At times (such as the 1980s) self-help has been associated with right-wing politics, on the grounds that it reduced the need for state intervention. At other times it has been seen as the most local level of community organisation, without necessarily any ideological implications.

self-referential *adj.* A pejorative term used to describe a building that fails to respond to its context. Example: 'Much commercial building is self-referential and devoid of public value.'

self-service store The first, Piggly Wiggly, was opened by Clarence Saunders in Memphis in 1916 (Hall, 1998).

Sellafield See WINDSCALE INQUIRY.

Sellier, Henri (1883–1943) Politician. A socialist, he was a leading figure in the French housing, planning and garden cities movement.

semi-detached house (UK) A house attached to its neighbour on one side. The end house of a TERRACE is technically semi-detached, but the term is more usually applied to pairs of houses, which comprise one of the most common forms of suburban development in England. Semis are a compromise between the cheapness and small plot size required for a terraced house and the larger plots required for detached houses. Semi-detached houses also have the advantage over terraced housing of allowing direct access to the back door and garden from the front, disposing of the need for an alley or lane at the bottom of the garden and the concomitant problems of security and squalor. Among the earliest semi-detached houses were those built in Sir Robert Walpole's model village at Houghton, Norfolk, in 1729 (Girouard, 1985) and on the Eyre Estate in London's St John's Wood in 1794 (Burnett, 1986). John Summerson (1962) suggested that an engraved map of the Eyre Estate, dated 1794, is the earliest record of a scheme consisting of pairs of semi-detached houses. The US term is a *double* or DUPLEX.

semilattice The structure of a natural city, according to CHRISTOPHER ALEXANDER.

Semionov, Vladimir (1874–1960) A leading planner in the Soviet Union, he is said at one time to have worked for RAYMOND UNWIN in England (Cooke, 1978).

semi-public space Open to the public (or at least some of the public, some of the time) but under private control. Examples include retail malls, corporate office podiums and leisure complexes.

send to Coventry To refuse to speak to or acknowledge someone. The phrase may derive from the way in which soldiers garrisoned in Coventry were at one time shunned by the civilian population, or from the fact that Royalist soldiers were imprisoned in the fiercely Parliamentarian city during the English civil war.

senior debt The debt that has first charge on a security. Compare JUNIOR DEBT.

Senior, Derek Journalist and writer on planning. See REDCLIFFE-MAUD REPORT.

Sennett, AR Engineer and author. He submitted an unsuccessful entry for the competition to design Letchworth garden city – on a hexagonal grid resembling a giant honeycomb, Mervyn Miller (1989) records – and wrote *Garden Cities*, a two-volume chronicle of the garden city movement, published in 1905.

Sennett, Richard (b1943) Sociologist and writer. In the *Uses of Disorder* (1970), Sennett criticises planners' attempts to avoid the consequences of conflict and disorder. People learn to live together by confronting and resolving conflict themselves, he argues. Decisions should be taken at a neighbourhood level, and without depending on professionals to avoid making difficult choices. *The Fall of Public Man* (1977) explores the distinction between public and private life in terms of public behaviour as a kind of ritual. The public realm lost its life when it lost these rituals, Sennett argues. A novel *Palais Royal* (1986) takes the theme of how a city's complexity enriches the lives of individuals who, in the eyes of the world, are failing. Born on a public housing project in Chicago, where white tenants lived rent-free in an attempt to secure a racial mix, Sennett began his career as a cellist. He teaches at the London School of Economics and New York University. See also ANTI-URBANISM, CITY and GRAFITTI.

sense of arrival The sense of reaching a distinct place.

sense of place A feeling of appreciation for the distinct CHARACTER of a locality. This will depend on characteristics (gender, ethnic group, beliefs and values, for example) of the observer as well as those of the place. See GENIUS LOCI and compare NON-PLACE URBAN REALM.

sensitive receptor (US) A land use (such as housing or a hospital) particularly sensitive to noise.

sensitivity analysis An examination of the effects on an appraisal of varying the projected values of important variables.

sensitivity testing Investigating the effects of small changes in certain costs of a proposed development on its expected profitability.

separate parallel lives The phrase used in the report of one of the official investigations into the riots in towns such as Bradford, Burnley and Oldham in 2001, describing the SEGREGATION between different ethnic groups. It was reported that in Oldham, for example, most primary schools were single race, and many secondary schools were 99 per cent white or 99 per cent Asian.

sequential approach Setting out the sequence in which particular sites will be developed.

sequential design Taking advantage of an extended period of development to allow different designers to design phases of an area's development at different times, allowing variety and flexibility.

sequential test Examining a planning proposal to determine if there are preferable alternative sites (*brownfield* rather than *greenfield*, closer to the centre of town, or offering better pedestrian or vehicular access, for example) that should be developed first.

serial vision A series of drawings showing what a person would see at a succession of viewpoints when walking through an area. The technique was devised by the architect and illustrator GORDON CULLEN as a way of visualising what exists or is proposed.

Sert, Jose Luis See URBAN DESIGN.

service plan Defines the aims and objectives of a specific local authority service, and explains how they will help to achieve the aims of the CORPORATE PLAN and the indicators against which success can be measured.

service road A subsidiary road often parallel to a more important road, providing vehicular access to properties.

service-dependent ghetto A concentration of users of social and health services round a place where those services are available. Also called ASYLUM-WITHOUT-WALLS.

service-learning Learning about architecture, urban design or planning while providing a service to the public, for example through a COMMUNITY DESIGN CENTRE.

setback The horizontal distance between a building and the general building line of the street.

setting The context or environment in which something sits.

settlement 1 A place where people live, at any scale from a hamlet to a city. **2** A small community. **3** Subsidence (due to a building settling over time). **4** A base for philanthropic and social work set up in a poor urban area, particularly in the nineteenth and early twentieth century: in the words of LEWIS MUMFORD (1961), 'forming a centre for the spiritual and cultural life of the neighbourhood, as the church had once done.' HULL HOUSE and TOYNBEE HALL are examples.

settlement pattern The distinctive way in which the roads, fields, paths and buildings are laid out in a particular place.

settlement unit A variation of the neighbourhood unit, proposed by the architect and planner LUDWIG HILBERSHEIMER. The units would be separated by park belts.

seven clamps Jon Rouse, then secretary to the URBAN TASK FORCE and later chief executive of CABE, identified 'the seven clamps of urban design' in a talk at the Urban Design Alliance's conference in 1998 (echoing the Seven Lamps of Architecture described in the book of that name by JOHN RUSKIN). The clamps preventing successful urban design were: 1) Strategic vacuum 2) Reactivity 3) Over-regulation 4) Meanness 5) Design illiteracy 6) Smallmindedness 7) Short-termism.

seventy feet See TWENTY-TWO METRES.

seventy-two suburbs See LOS ANGELES.

sewerage The pipes and other services that carry and process *sewage*.

sex The writer Angela Carter suggested that 'cities have sexes: London is a man, Paris a woman and New York a well-adjusted transsexual' (Brandes Gratz, 2002). See also DRESS SENSE and THE FOUNTAINHEAD.

sezain The word means a town on the continent of Terra Australe (Southern Lands), as described by Gabriel Foigny in *The Adventures of Jacques Sadeur* (1676). Terra Australe (consisting of the countries of Hube, Hüed, Hüod, Hump, Hulg, Hug, Huff, Gurf, Durf, Iurf, Surf,

Burf, Turf, Pulg, Mulg, Pure, Trum, Sum, Burd, Purd and Sub) is home to, among many other curiosities, the blue carrot (Manguel and Guadalupi, 1999).

Sforzinda An imaginary city conceived by Antonio Averlino in the late fifteenth century.

shade tree Planted to provide shade.

shahar-ashoob (Urdu) A lament for the city: a genre of poetry in Urdu, evoking the destruction or decline of a great city (Vidal and Gupta, 1999). See also URBAN DESTRUCTION.

shahari gaon (Persian and Hindi) URBAN VILLAGE; a village whose land use has changed from rural to urban (Vidal and Gupta, 1999).

shallow green A pejorative term for a person who, unlike a *dark green* or *deep green*, sees the need for reducing environmental impacts but who does not favour a radical or fundamentalist approach (Quinion, 1997). See also ECOLOGISM.

shallow plan A characteristic of a building whose depth from front to back is less than its width; one in which no part of the floor area is far from a source of natural light. The opposite of *deep plan*.

sham (Ireland) A name used by a country person in addressing a city dweller. Compare JACKEEN.

Shame of the Cities, The A book by Lincoln Steffens exposing municipal corruption in the USA, published in 1904.

shanty town A collection of makeshift homes. The word *shanty*, meaning a small, crudely built hut, was first recorded in 1820 in the USA. Its origin (possibly from the French *chantier*, a timber yard or storage place) is uncertain (Quinion, 1999). See SQUATTER SETTLEMENT.

shapemaker An architect who is more concerned about a building's external appearance and image than about its other functions. Example: '[The Irish Republic] is still a small country, and it's not in the mood for the showy flamboyance of the blob-builders and bombastic shapemakers' (Deyan Sudjic in 2002). See also FORMALISM.

shared equity Where the ownership of a dwelling is split between more than one person or more usually between the occupier and a landlord (a housing association, for example). This allows the occupier to have a stake in the (anticipated rising) value of a property for which they are unable to buy outright, paying rent to the landlord and servicing a mortgage on their share. The equity can be split 50/50 or any other proportion. In some arrangements the occupier is entitled progressively to buy out the landlord's as their financial circumstances permit. This is sometimes known as 'staircase ownership' – a means of, to mix metaphors – setting a foot on the housing ladder.

shared ownership See SHARED EQUITY.

Sharp, Evelyn (Dame) (Lady Sharp) The influential permanent secretary of the Ministry of Housing and Local Government in the 1960s. She was an enthusiastic promoter of SYSTEM BUILDING.

Thomas Sharp

Sharp, Thomas (1901–78) Town planner and writer. Sharp was born into a mining community near Durham. His book *Town and Countryside* (1932) argued that town and country should be distinct and different. In his view EBENEZER HOWARD, in promoting a fashion for low-density GARDEN CITY development, had created 'a hermaphrodite, sterile, imbecile, a monster, abhorrent and loathsome to the Nature which he worships'. Sharp's passion was for a countryside free of urban sprawl, and towns with streets. He had nothing against new towns, but argued they should be urban in character. His paper *Town Planning*, published in 1940, sold a quarter of a million copies in 10 years. It was followed in 1946 by his classic *Anatomy of a Village* in which he developed the concept of TOWNSCAPE, an idea that was being promoted by the *Architectural Review*. Sharp made plans for several historic towns including Exeter, Salisbury, Chichester, Durham and Oxford. He was Town Planning Institute president in 1945–6 and president of the Institute of Landscape Architects in 1949–50. In the Town Planning Institute he challenged the profession's move from PHYSICAL PLANNING to socio-economic planning. His opposition was successful for a while within the institute, but it had little impact on planning practice. In 1966 Sharp bitterly criticised the new system of strategic planning which, he said, made an impossible distinction between policies in a plan and the physical form that they would lead to. Any planner who refused to provide a drawing could not be said to be planning in any meaningful way. 'Either they have the plans worked out or they've got a nonsensical document,' he told a Town Planning Institute conference.

Sharples The fictional northern town in Neville Shute's 1938 novel *The Ruined City*.

shatter zone An area on the edge of a city centre where city centre uses are not viable and land values are low.

Shaw, Geoff (1927–78) Glasgow community worker, church minister and politician. He was convenor of Strathclyde Regional Council from 1975 until his early death. See STREET.

Shaw, George Bernard (1856–1950) Writer, dramatist and socialist. Shaw was a local councillor in London and an early supporter of the GARDEN CITY movement.

shed 1 A cheaply built structure, usually for storage. **2** A cheaply constructed, single-storey building providing a large, uninterrupted floor area, for manufacture, warehousing or retailing. Also called a *big shed* or *big box*. The word is a variant of *shade*.

shed city An area of large SHEDS, often for retail uses, usually served by road.

shed on a roundabout A pejorative term for a building of standard design sited with no concern for anything except easy access to a road.

sheep-pen crossing An arrangement of pedestrian barriers in the middle of the street that prevents people crossing the street in one go. The sheep pen is the fenced area, parallel to the road, that the people must walk through.

shell and core The structure and services of a building, prior to being fitted out. Compare DEVELOPER'S FIT OUT.

shells An element of EKISTICS. Shells are housing, service facilities, shops, offices, factories, and cultural and educational units.

Shelter Neighbourhood Action Project Set up in Liverpool's Granby area in 1969 to help residents improve their homes. The pioneering project provided a free technical advice service.

Shepheard, Peter (Sir) (1913–2002) Architect, landscape architect and town planner. He trained at Liverpool School of Architecture under CHARLES REILLY, attended lectures by his godfather PATRICK ABERCROMBIE and in 1942 joined the Town Planning Institute. After war service as an engineer, he worked with Abercrombie on the GREATER LONDON PLAN. Later he worked with WILLIAM GRAHAM at the Ministry of Town and Country Planning before moving to Stevenage Development Corporation. After that he formed a private practice whose projects included designing London housing estates (disdaining the fashion for HIGH-RISE housing) and a campus for Lancaster University. He was president of the Landscape Institute and the RIBA, and in the 1970s spent half of each year at Pennsylvania University.

Shevky technique In the 1950s the sociologist E Shevky introduced a technique for studying urban social structure according to three elements: social rank, urbanisation and segregation.

Shimizu The shorthand term for a legal case in 1997 (Shimizu [UK] Ltd v Westminster City Council) that had important implications for the law on the control of listed buildings.

sholopolis The city of leisure. The term was used by PATRICK GEDDES.

shop Premises falling within class A1, as defined by the Town and Country Planning (Use Classes) Order 1987. This includes use for the retail sale of goods other than hot food, a post office, for the sale of tickets or as a travel agency, for the sale of sandwiches or other cold food for consumption off the premises, for hairdressing, for the direction of funerals, for the display of goods for sale, for the hiring out of domestic or personal goods or articles, for the cleaning or washing of clothes or fabrics on the premises, for the reception of goods to be washed, cleaned or repaired, in all cases where the sale, display or service is to visiting members of the public.

shopmobility A scheme providing electric buggies for shoppers who find walking difficult or impossible as a result of injury, illness, disability or obesity.

shopping arcade Joseph Rykwert (2000) notes that 'the possibility of covering a whole street with glass had first been exploited in Paris, toward the end of the eighteenth century, in Palais-Royal... The shopping arcades round the palace garden... were supplemented by a glazed wooden structure that crossed the gardens, to be replaced after 1828 by the glass-roofed masonry building which became a model for such constructions.' The Victor Emmanuel II arcade in Milan, built in 1865–67, is frequently cited as a model for the twentieth-century SHOPPING MALL.

shopping centre A planned group of shops. Peter Hall (1998) writes that the forum and market of the Roman emperor Trajan, built in the second century, included 'what can only be described as a vast shopping centre embracing a covered hall and some 150 individual shops'. The Roland Park Shopping Centre (six shops and parking space) opened in Baltimore, US, in 1907. Market Square in Lake Forest, Illinois, built in 1916, was the first planned shopping mall, according to Bill Bryson (1994); County Club Plaza in Kansas City followed in 1922 and Highland Parking Shopping Village in Dallas (1931) was the first to segregate shoppers from cars completely and ignore the street. Shopping centre development boomed in the 1950s. Catherine

Croft (2001) names the LANSBURY in London's Tower Hamlets, built in 1951, as having Britain's first pedestrianised shopping centre.

shopping centre development See RETAIL-LED REGENERATION PROJECT.

shopping mall A covered shopping centre where people on foot are segregated from traffic. Market Square in Lake Forest, Illinois, built in 1916, was the first planned shopping mall, according to Bill Bryson (1994). Spiro Kostof (1987) characterises the shopping mall as a 'sanitised and disembodied replica of Main Street... Excluded are bars and second-hand stores, and the kind of people who would patronise them, and instead of bustle and dirt and traffic, we are presented with tasteful landscaping and Muzak.' The writer and mall-watcher Margaret Crawford fears that Americans, at least, are losing the ability to function outside protected, controlled and unchallenging environments. 'People now are accustomed to being in malls, and they feel increasingly uncomfortable when they are not in mall-like situations... The three experiences of being in a mall, driving in a car, and watching television are remarkably similar. They really constitute an entirely different mode of perception, based on the idea of discontinuity, quick cuts, and the blurring of vision and reality. It creates a hyper-reality in which there is no memory.' A covered shopping street was a feature of the future city of Boston described in EDWARD BELLAMY'S novel *Looking Backward*, published in 1888. In EBENEZER HOWARD's original conception of the GARDEN CITY, published in 1898, the central park was surrounded by a glazed shopping arcade to be called the Crystal Palace. See also DISNEYLAND, FUTURE MALL and MALL.

shopping parade A short row of shops along a street. It was a popular form of retail development in suburban areas after the first world war, often set back from the main road fronting a SERVICE ROAD with kerbside parking. The US equivalent is *strip mall*.

Shore, Peter (Lord Shore) (1924–2001) Labour politician. He was the secretary of state for the environment in 1974 and from 1978–79, responsible for the Inner Urban Areas Act 1978, which changed the focus of the government's urban policy from decentralisation to rebuilding inner areas.

Short's Observatory The turret containing a camera obscura on a building at the top end of Edinburgh's Royal Mile that PATRICK GEDDES took over and renamed the OUTLOOK TOWER.

short-life housing That which is being used in the short term prior to its demolition or rehabilitation. Short-life housing may be improved or brought up to a minimum basic standard commensurate with its limited life expectancy.

Shostakovich, Dmitri (1906–1975) Composer. See CHERYOMUSHKI.

shoulder height The general height of buildings in an area, above which LANDMARK buildings stand out.

shuffleability The quality of the surface of a footway that is negotiable by people whose limited mobility means that they are able only to shuffle along, without lifting their feet clear of the ground.

shute An ALLEY or passageway.

Shute, John (d1563) Architect and painter. His *The First and Chief Groundes of Architecture*, published in 1563, has been called the first English architectural book.

Shute, Nevil (1899–1960) Novelist. Pen name of Nevil Shute Norway. See SHARPLES.

shuttering See BÉTON BRUT.

Sicheng, Liang Architect and town planner. He was chief planner of Beijing under Mao in the 1940s.

sick building syndrome A tendency to illness allegedly caused by the internal environment of certain modern buildings. The syndrome was named in 1983, though what its causes are and even whether it exists have been hotly debated.

sidewalk (US) The raised surface for pedestrians beside a street or road. The UK term is *pavement*.

sidewalk surfer (US) A SKATEBOARDER.

Siedlung (German) 1 A housing estate. 2 A settlement.

Siedlungsstruktur (German) Settlement structure.

Siena A walled medieval city in Tuscany, Italy, preserved unspoilt and intact in its entirety. Probably no town or city has been more admired for its urban form. Edward Hutton (1955) writes: 'I think perhaps there is nothing in the world quite like Siena, no other place, at any rate, that has just her piercing beauty, her quality of joy, of passion, of sheer loveliness.' Siena was particulary frequently cited as a model of urban design in the 1980s, before BARCELONA took some of the limelight in the 1990s. See URBAN DESIGN FRAMEWORK.

sieve A set of criteria. For example, the Urban Villages Forum devised (but never used) a sieve which was intended to test whether an actual or proposed development merited the name URBAN VILLAGE.

sieve map Shows which parts of an area are unsuitable for a particular use due to one or more local circumstances.

sight distance The distance at which an object becomes visible to an observer. Sight distance is important in laying out roads, for example.

sight line The direct line from a viewer to an object. Sight lines from a travelling vehicle will help to determine how fast vehicles are likely to move, as the further drivers can see ahead, the faster they are likely to feel safe driving. Traditionally road engineers have favoured long site lines, whereas many urban designers have argued that shorter sight lines tend to make safer places.

sign ordinance (US) Local regulations governing the display of signs.

signature architect One whose name is thought to add value to his or her buildings.

signature building One whose value, fame or ease in gaining planning permission is enhanced by the name of its celebrated designer.

signature profession One in which the name of the practitioner adds value to the product. Signature professions have glamour and famous practitioners. Architecture and fashion design are signature professions, planning and surveying are not. The fact that a building is credited to a particular architect does not necessarily means that he or she designed it, though. Apart from the fact that many buildings are designed by teams of different professionals (including many varieties of engineer, for example), a particular building may have been designed by other architects in the famously named practice, with little or no input from the big-name star (who may be busy appearing in the media, touting for jobs or running the business). See also STARCHITECT and TROPHY ARCHITECTURE.

Silent Spring A book by biologist Rachel Carson (1907–1964), published in the USA in 1962, on threats to the environment, particularly from pesticides. 'Over increasingly large areas of the United States,' Carson writes, 'spring now comes unheralded by the return of the birds, and the early mornings are strangely silent where once they were filled with the beauty of bird song.' *Silent Spring* was an important inspiration to the GREEN movement.

Silicon Alley A neighbourhood in lower Manhattan with a concentration of internet, multi-media and computer firms. The nickname, dating from the 1990s, echoes California's SILICON VALLEY.

Silicon Valley The Santa Clara Valley, centre of the California microelectronics industry. The name was coined in 1971. It is nicknamed *Siva*. Sir Peter Hall (1998) records that in 1950 the Santa Clara Valley was the prune capital of America.

Silkin, Lewis (Lord Silkin) (1889–1972) Politician and lawyer. He was responsible for the New Towns Act 1946 as minister of town and country planning in Clement Attlee's Labour government. See SILKINGRAD.

Silkingrad The railway stations signs at Stevenage in Hertfordshire were changed by irate residents to read Silkingrad on the occasion of a visit to the town in 1946 by Lewis Silkin, planning minister in Clement Attlee's Labour government. The protest – at Silkin's proposal to make Stevenage the first designated NEW TOWN – was unsuccessful. The analogy is with Stalingrad, the name used between 1925 and 1961 for the Russian city of Volgograd (which had earlier been called Tsaritsyn) in honour of the Soviet dictator Joseph Stalin, as Joseph Vissarionovich Dzhugashvili (1879–1953) called himself. (The Soviet cities of Donetsk, Dyushambe and Novokuznetsk, and Katowice in Poland, were similarly renamed, respectively, Stalino, Stalinabad, Stalinsk and Stalinogrod.)

silo A unit of a large organisation that works in isolation from other parts of the organisation. Example: 'The council's corporate management strategy is aimed at ending the silo mentality.'

silo initiative One that is carried out in isolation, usually in consequence of a *silo* or *bunker mentality*.

silver city, the Aberdeen (more often called the granite city), apparently so called because of the way in which sunlight reflects on the granite, particularly after rain.

Silver End A model town of modernist houses (particularly for disabled ex-servicemen) built by metal window manufacturer Francis Crittall in Essex in the 1920s. The brick-built houses were (and still are, the town being a conservation area) painted cream, had (not surprisingly) metal windows and were mostly flat-roofed. The picturesque layout was by RICHARD REISS, a leading garden city campaigner.

SimCity A computer game of US origin in which players simulate the development of a city. 'The program appears capable only of generating garbitecture and the worst kind of US strip mall development,' Tim Mars writes. 'Whatever you do it ends up looking uncannily like the Merryhill shopping centre in the West Midlands.'

Simon, Ernest (Lord Simon of Wythenshawe) (1879–1960) Industrialist and politician. In Manchester he organised the city's purchase of the Tatton estate for suburban development and the building of WYTHENSHAWE GARDEN SUBURB.

simplified planning zone An area in which the secretary of state could specify particular uses for which further planning permission is not required. The concept was introduced in the UK in 1987, but only rarely used. Compare ENTERPRISE ZONE.

Sims, The Will Wright's semi-sequel computer game to SIMCITY. It was launched in 1999.

simulacrum (plural *simulacra*) Something seemingly historic – a townscape, for example – that has been created and never actually existed in the past. See also INVENTED PLACE.

simultaneous flush The predicted effect of all the toilets in building being flushed simultaneously is sometimes used as a metaphor for planning for the maximum possible (even if rare or highly unlikely) use of a system. Other examples are providing a car park for a shopping mall to accommodate demand on the busiest day of the year or, in Andres Duany's (2000) phrase, 'a road width such that a fire truck can pass two automobiles stalled in tandem'.

Sin City The first of the Sin City series of comic novels written and drawn (in black and white) by Frank Miller.

Published in 1992, it is a story of violent revenge set in a violent and seedy city.

sin city Las Vegas. The city's convention centre advertised Las Vegas in 2001 as the city 'where you can do what you want, when you want'. The *Financial Times* of London commented that this was unlikely to refer to children being able to ride a big wheel at 3am, despite Las Vegas' tentative steps to presenting itself also as a place for families.

Singapore See LOCAL DISTINCTIVENESS.

single end A one-room apartment in a tenement, purpose-built or 'made down' from a larger apartment. Many were built in Glasgow in the second half of the nineteenth century. Compare ROOM AND KITCHEN.

single pot The regeneration funds available for distribution by REGIONAL DEVELOPMENT AGENCIES.

single regeneration budget A UK government funding programme launched in 1994 by bringing together 20 existing regeneration and economic development programmes. SRB funds were allocated on the basis of competitive bids by local partnerships, which set out the outputs (such as people trained, jobs created, land improved) they expected to achieve. In the years after 1994 there were six rounds of competition for the budget.

single-occupancy (also single-occupant) vehicle A car with a driver and no passenger.

single-room occupancy (US) A dwelling unit consisting of one room with a basin, with or without bathroom and kitchen facilities.

sink A SLUM. Example: '232,000 people are packed into three and a half square miles in Harlem. Apart from letting the sink run its course and destroy the city, there is an alternative solution: introduce design features that will counteract the ill effects of the sink but not destroy the enclave in the process' (from the USA, 1966).

sink estate (UK) A housing estate where conditions (physical, social, economic) have deteriorated so much that the only people who live there are those who have no choice.

Sironi, Mario (1885–1961) Artist. His work between 1914 and 1920 included many urban landscapes. He was a signatory of the 1915 Futurist manifesto *Italian Pride* and later became an enthusiastic Fascist.

site An area of land with a defined boundary.

site of special scientific interest (SSSI) A site designated by English Nature as being of national importance due to its plants, animals, geology or other natural features. SSSIs are protected under the National Parks and Access to the Countryside Act 1949. See also AREA OF SPECIAL SCIENTIFIC INTEREST.

site ratio See PLOT RATIO.

site value rating See HENRY GEORGE.

site-specific art A public art work made for a particular site. Alternative terms are *site-determined*, *site-oriented*, *site-referenced*, *site-related* and *community-specific* art.

Sitte, Camillo (1843–1903) Austrian urban design theorist, architect and planner. In his book *City Planning According to Artistic Principles (Der Städtebau)*, published in 1889, Sitte pioneered the study of TOWNSCAPE and the principles of composition.

sitting landscape A multi-purpose element in a city space that doubles as a seat (a step, for example) (Gehl, 1987).

situational *adj.* Embedded in a physical or cultural setting.

Situationism The political theory and practice of the Situationist International (1957–72). The avante-garde artistic and political movement was inspired by what its members saw as the possibilities for people to recreate themselves, in the words of writer Brian Hatton (1999), 'free from alienated work and the false goals of advertisers and planners'. Hatton writes: 'The city of marvellous, irrational density was the SI ideal, and it led them as much against CIAM as against capitalism.' The name comes from the phrase of the philosopher Jean-Paul Sartre, 'being-in-situation' (a preferable state for the theorist or philosopher, he argued, than merely analysing a situation). See also GUY DEBORD, DÉRIVE and NEW BABYLON.

Siva See SILICON VALLEY.

six hundred feet The farthest distance an American will walk before getting into a car, according to the accepted wisdom of US developers in the 1990s.

six-acre standard Proposed by the National Playing Fields Association, the standard specifies six acres of outdoor playing space for each 1000 people. In 2002 the Urban Green Spaces Task Force called for the standard to be dropped in favour of local authorities assessing their own needs.

Sixteen Principles of Urbanism A policy document issued in East Germany in 1949. The principles refuted the major premises of modernist planning, calling instead for mixed uses, traditional street blocks and building styles inspired by historic precedent (Kostof, 1992).

sizzle *n.* Features that supposedly make something easy to sell. Example: 'Liverpool is the sizzle that sells the sausage, which is the rest of Merseyside' (from a discussion in 2003 of regional promotional campaigns). The term is used particularly to describe superficial design features on a house that have no purpose other than to help attract a buyer (see also KERB APPEAL and NORTH DALLAS SPECIAL).

skate geezer A relatively elderly skateboarder, roller skater or rollerblader (in their 30s, perhaps).

skate park A place designed specifically for skateboarding, roller skating or rollerblading.

skate spot Any place where people skateboard, roller skate or roller blade.

skateboard *n.* A narrow board mounted on small wheels for riding and acrobatics, mainly used by males. The sport of skateboarding uses urban space in ways its designers never intended (except perhaps in MILTON KEYNES, where urban designers consider the needs of skateboarders). The consequence is sometimes that a space which would otherwise be unnoticed is used and enjoyed. In other instances, though, skateboarders effectively requisition public space which would otherwise be available for strolling or sitting. The manoeuvre known as 'grinding', where a skateboard is driven along a sharp edge on its chassis, discolours and sometimes damages stone stops, copings and ledges. Ian Borden (2001) notes that skateboarding was banned completely in Norway in 1979, and that some cities in California have imposed curfews or banned skateboarding in public areas. Skateboarding, said to have developed from surfing in California in the 1950s, became popular in the UK in the late 1970s. Many skateboard parks where built at the time, but most were closed within a few years (Bordern, 2001). Skateboarding is also called (in the US) SIDEWALK SURFING. See also TRICKABILITY.

skate-proof *v.* To make a place unattractive to skateboarders and skaters. Methods include fixing bumps to otherwise smooth surfaces such as handrails and the tops of walls, and making other surfaces unridable by means of gravel, sand or rubber.

Skeffington Report *People and Planning* was the official title of the report of the Committee on Public Participation in Planning, published in 1969. Arthur Skeffington MP was its chairman. The committee's brief was to advise on how to promote PUBLIC PARTICIPATION in preparing development plans.

Skem Nickname of Skelmersdale, Lancashire. See SO GOOD THEY NAMED IT TWICE.

skid rogue (US) An untrustworthy VAGRANT.

skid row (US) An area where VAGRANTS, and homeless, very poor and addicted people live. The term may come from *skid road*, where loggers dragged timber and beside which they lived in some squalor.

skin architecture Standard forms of building, easily adaptable, with distinctive exterior facings. The term has been used by the architectural critic Ada Louise Huxtable. Compare BLOB ARCHITECTURE.

Skladanowsky, Emil and Max Film-makers. The two brothers held the first-ever screening of films for a public audience on 1 November 1895 in Berlin. The show included short films of urban landscapes of Berlin made by Max (Barber, 2002).

sky The writer VS Pritchett (1997) observed (writing in 1956): 'London generates its own sky – a prolonged panorama of the battle between earth and heaven. For if the lower sky is glum over London and sometimes dark brown or soupy yellow, it is often a haze of violet and soft, sandy-saffron colours. If the basis is smoke and the next layer is smoke and fog banked up, the superstructure of cloud is frequently noble. White cumulus boils up over the city against a sky that is never blue as the Mediterranean knows blue, but which is fair and angelic. The sky space in our low city is wide.'

skyglow Light pollution reflected in the night sky.

skyhouse A skyscraper of flats, high-rise gardens and health clubs proposed by the architects David Marks and Julia Barfield (designers of the giant wheel the London Eye) in 2003. The buildings, up to 600 feet high, would be built in clusters. 'We reinvented the wheel,' Marks said, 'and now we are reinventing the tower block' (Browne, 2003).

skyline The appearance of the upper parts of buildings against the sky. Spiro Kostof (1991) notes that this meaning was not current before 1876, but was common by the 1890s. Example: 'The Manhattan skyline shimmered in the imaginations of all the nations, and people everywhere cherished the ambition, however unattainable, of landing one day upon that legendary foreshore' (Morris, 1987). In the USA until 1896, according to Bill Bryson (1994), the term was a synonym for *horizon* – the line where earth and sky meet.

skyline building One that makes a significant impact on the skyline. Example: 'The people of New York rejected the early proposals to redevelop the World Trade Center site with squat office blocks. They insisted on having a skyline building' (2003).

skyplane A floating glass roof used to cover a street or other space without visible fittings to the tops of the building facades. Such a structure was used at Birmingham's 2003 BULLRING development, at a time when the building of roofed shopping malls was being criticised for destroying the urban qualities of town and city centres.

skyscape The appearance of buildings against the sky.

skyscraper A very tall building. The term was originally used to describe the topmost sail of a square-rigged ship and, by analogy, any tall structure (such as a factory chimney). It was first used to describe a building in 1888. The word first appeared in a dictionary (Maitland's *American Standard*) in 1891, defined as a 'very tall building such as now are being built in Chicago' (Girouard, 1985). The first skyscraper, according to Bill Bryson (1994), was the Home Insurance Building in Chicago, built 1883–5. The Empire State Building in New York, 102 storeys and 1,250 feet high, was the world's tallest building from 1931 to 1974. Henry James (1907) saw skyscrapers as an unattractive face of the market economy. 'One story is good until another is told,' he wrote, 'and skyscrapers are the last word of economic ingenuity only till another word be written. This shall be possibly a word of still uglier meaning, but the vocabulary of thrift at any price shows boundless resources, and the consciousness of that truth, the consciousness of the infinite, the menaced, the essentially *invented* state, twinkles ever, to my perception, in the thousand glassy eyes of the mere market.' To the poet WH Auden, skyscrapers had sinister associations. In his political poem 'September 1st 1939', he writes of 'the lie of Authority/ Whose buildings grope the sky'. Katherine Solomonson (2001) suggests that 'in the 1920s the Gothic skyscraper was variously perceived and represented as an up-to-date expression of the advanced steel structure and a mitigation of the ills of the machine age; an attestation of commercial might and the embodiment of spiritual ideals; a monument to unified democratic society and a reinforcement of the hegemony of the ruling elite; a testimony to the United States' triumphant role in the war and a commemoration of monuments that had been desecrated and soldiers who had died.'

The architect REM KOOLHAAS (1978) writes of New York: 'Only the skyscraper offers business the wide-open spaces of a man-made Wild West, a frontier in the sky.' The architectural critic Katherine Shonfield (2002) comments: 'Skyscrapers are for wannabe cities,' meaning that some aspiring cities – or towns aspiring to be cities – see them as a way of enhancing their status. To Paul Finch (2002) of the Commission for Architecture and the Built Environment (and others who have made the same comment), 'tall buildings are just like any other buildings, but taller.' This means, Finch says, that they should not be obliged to comply with anything beyond the normal planning requirement that, in his words, 'the bigger the building is, the better the architecture should be and the more rigorous the planning.' Frank Duffy, the architect and authority on office design, sees the skyscraper as a seductive architectural form rarely justified functionally: 'the perfect example of a solution in search of a problem' (Duffy, 2000). Steven Johnson (2001) writes: 'Metropolitan space may habitually be pictured in the form of skylines, but the real magic of city living comes from below.' The Prince of Wales (2001) has denounced tall buildings as 'overblown phallic structures and depressingly predictable antennae that say more about an architectural ego than any kind of craftsmanship.' Skyscrapers, he claims, are 'utilitarian and commercial, so-called statement buildings that are self-referential and fulfil no communal purpose whatsoever.' The *Guardian* in 2002 defined a skyscraper hotel as being one of over 12 storeys. See also CANARY WHARF, CONTINUOUS MOVEMENT, ECOLOGICAL SKYSCRAPER, ERNEST FLAGG, HAIRY BUILDING, LEVER HOUSE, MILE-HIGH SKY-CITY, MILLENNIUM TOWER, NEW YORK REGIONAL PLAN, PETRONAS TOWERS, RAND-MCNALLY BUILDING, SEAGRAM BUILDING, VERTICAL URBAN DESIGN, VIRTUAL SKYSCRAPER, WORLD TRADE CENTER and KEN YEANG.

skyway An interconnecting second-storey link between buildings, avoiding traffic or bad weather.

Slam-dunking Wal-Mart See SPRAWL-BUSTERS.

slap (US) A street or expressway.

Slaughterhouse 5 A novel by Kurt Vonnegut, published in 1969, based on his experience as a prisoner of war during the firebombing of Dresden. See also URBAN DESTRUCTION.

Sleeper Awakes, The A novel by HG Wells, published in 1898, set in Britain in 2048. It is an almost completely urbanised world. 'Nearly all the towns in the country and almost all the villages had disappeared. Here and there only a gigantic hotel-like edifice stood amid square miles of some single cultivation and preserved the name of a town... The cities had drawn away the workers from the countryside with the gravitational force of seemingly endless work... There was a vision of city beyond city. Cities on great plains, cities beside great rivers, vast cities along the sea margin, cities girdled by snowy mountains... Everywhere now through the city-set earth the same cosmopolitan social organisation prevailed and everywhere, from Pole to Equator, the whole world was civilised. The whole world dwelt in cities.'

sleeping policeman A hump across a road intended to slow down traffic. See also TRAFFIC CALMING.

sleeving development Buildings erected in front of or around a large development to create a greater variety of facades and uses, and more interaction with the street.

sliced income approach A method of carrying out a property appraisal by identifying elements of the income that carry varying degrees of risk. *Core income* is less risky and the *top slice* more risky.

slicing The division of income from a property development. See also TOP SLICE and FOUR-SLICING.

slip road A length of road at a junction connecting two roads, usually at different levels. The US term is *onramp* or *offramp*, according to whether the slip road allows vehicles to join or leave.

slippery space Described by Dear and Flusty (1998) as 'passively aggressive... space that may be reached only by means of interrupted or obfuscated approaches'. Compare STEALTHY SPACE.

slipping area One that is in the early stages of decline – slipping from one state to the next.

sloane ranger A pejorative term for an affluent young woman who lives in or who frequents the fashionable London district around Sloane Square, pursued by her male equivalents, *hooray Henries*. The LONE RANGER was the hero of a 1940s and '50s radio and television Western series.

SLOAP Space left over after planning. A pejorative term for space in a planned environment that has no apparent use, it was in use particularly in the 1960s and '70s.

slopopolis The shapeless SUBDIVISIONS that spring up to house the rapidly growing populations of places such as California. The term was coined by San Francisco architect Herbert McLaughlin (McDowell, 1988).

Slough of Despond, The London, according to WILLIAM BOOTH, who borrowed the name from John Bunyan's *Pilgrim's Progress*.

Slough See JOKE TOWN.

slow city A place belonging to the *slow city movement*. The aim is to maximise the quality of life without harming the environment, focusing on the quality, rather than the quantity of development, and emphasising local identity. The movement began in Tuscany. Fifty Italian cities were signed up to it by 2001, and others elsewhere. The coining is by analogy with the *slow food movement*, set up in opposition to the increasing dominance of fast food.

sluis (Dutch) A traffic-calming device that allows buses through while obstructing other traffic. The sluis combines a road depression and road hump.

slum An area of unfit, squalid or overcrowded housing. This sense of the word originated in the 1820s, although it seems to have been a slang term for a squalid room before then. It probably derives from *slump*, a wet mire. Originally the term slum referred to housing built on marshy or unsound ground. Only later did it come to be a more general label for areas of unsatisfactory housing regardless of the state of the ground. Its use in relation to cities of the developed world has declined since the 1970s, generally being thought insulting to the people who live there. For a while (and still, to some extent) INNER CITY served as a euphemism for it.

UK housing law defined slums according to physical criteria. The Housing Act 1957 stated that 'a house shall be deemed unfit for human habitation if and only if it is so far deficient in one or more of the following matters as to be not reasonably suitable for occupation: repair, stability, freedom from damp, natural lighting, ventilation, water supply, drainage and sanitary conveniences, facilities for storage, preparation and cooking of food, and the disposal of waste water.' The Act also defined *clearance areas* in which the houses were unfit for human habitation, or 'are by reason of their bad arrangement or narrowness or bad arrangements of the street, dangerous, or injurious to the health of the inhabitants of the area, and that of the other buildings, if any, in the area, are for a like reason dangerous or injurious to the health of the said inhabitants'. Clearance areas were identified by local authority public health inspectors, without taking account of social factors such as poverty, crime or delinquency, or of positive factors such as family ties. In later years official definitions of slums widened in response to concerns about living conditions in dwellings that were structurally sound but which had become slums through over-use and overcrowding (Parker, 1973).

Some definitions of a slum, by contrast, focused on the people rather than the buildings. The Scottish poet Edwin Muir wrote in 1935 of how he saw the experience of living in slums marking those who suffered it. 'The best way I can put it is that these people seemed to have all passed through the slums, and to bear the knowledge of the slums within them,' he wrote. 'On their faces, which were different from the faces I had known before, I thought I could see, quite clearly displayed, a depraved and shameful knowledge, a knowledge which they could not have avoided acquiring, I can see now, but of which they were for the most part unaware... This depraved knowledge which I found in people's faces was frightening mainly, I think, because the knowledge was concealed from its possessors, and was like a dangerous thing, always within them, whose existence they ignored' (quoted in Spring, 1990). One American writer (Clinard, 1966) suggested that slum dwellers exhibited 'a subculture with a set of norms and values which is reflected in poor sanitation and health practices, deviant behaviour, and characteristic attitudes of apathy and social isolation. People who live in slum areas are isolated from the general power structures and are regarded as inferior, and slum dwellers, in turn, harbour suspicions of the outside world.' Such descriptions helped to ensure that the concept of slums, however defined, stigmatised the people who lived in them. This no doubt contributed to the term eventually falling virtually into disuse. But by then the damage had been done. Spiro T Agnew, who as President Nixon's vice-president from 1969 had a special responsibility for urban affairs, was castigated for commenting (in the *Detroit Free Press* in 1968): 'If you've seen one city slum, you've seen them all'. Some commentators (Mayne, 1993, for example) have suggested that the slums were given mythical status to suit the press and reformers. The concept of slums, according to this argument, was a means of popular entertainment and a useful image to contrast to the reformers' utopias.

At one time the saying 'You can take the person out of the slum, but not the slum out of the person' had currency. In an interview the Liverpudlian dramatist Alan Bleasdale (2001) gave a positive spin to an updated variant of the saying. 'There's an expression up here that you can take the man out of KIRKBY but not Kirkby out of the man,' he said. 'That's appropriate to any area that can be considered rough. There are qualities in people from those areas that shouldn't be taken out, though – the sense of identity and spirit that helps them come through in great crises.' See THE CLASSIC SLUM, COALS IN THE BATH, MOTOR SLUM, ROOKERY, STEW and UNSLUM.

slum clearance The slum clearance programmes of the first three quarters of the twentieth century tackled the appalling legacy of Victorian towns and cities: large areas of housing which had been designed, built or maintained to unacceptably low standards, or which had declined to unacceptable standards through subdivision and overcrowding. That, at any rate, is the official explanation. Some commentators have pointed out that the selection of one area for clearance over another seemed to have more to do with SOCIAL CLEANSING than the physical condition of the houses. Clearance was used as a means of breaking up and scattering 'difficult', 'unruly', 'lawless' areas, often with high concentrations of Irish immigrants.

Some planners saw this as the explicit purpose of clearance. Wilfred Burns (1963), chief planner of Newcastle-upon-Tyne under T DAN SMITH, and later the government's chief planner, argued: 'The dwellers in a slum area are almost a separate race of people, with different values, aspirations and ways of living... Most people who live in slums have no views on their environment at all... When we are dealing with people who have no initiative or civic pride, the task, surely, is to break up such groupings even though the people seem to be satisfied with their miserable environment and seem to enjoy an extrovert social life in their own locality'.

Fifteen years later Sir Wilfred, as he had become, seemed to have changed his mind and was speaking of the need to involve communities in making the decisions about their future (Ward 1989). By the early 1970s the social costs of slum clearance in terms of the destruction of social networks were being recognised, and local authorities began rehabilitating unfit housing (see EVANGELISTIC BUREAUCRAT and compare DANGEROUS CLASSES).

slum networking Developing networks in slums (particularly in the developing world) as a way of improving the city as a whole, instead of regarding slums as a blight on the city. The approach was pioneered by the engineer Himanshu Parikh in Indore, India, in the 1980s.

slumism US vice president Hubert Humphrey used the term in 1966, defining it at conference of mayors. 'It is poverty; it is illiteracy; it is disease; it is discrimination; it is frustration and it is bitterness,' he said. 'It is a virus that spreads, that races like a malignancy through our cities, breeding disorder, disillusionment, and hate' (quoted in Goodman, 1972).

slumland Slums and their people, as evoked by writers.

slumming Visiting slums to satisfy one's curiosity about slum life; uncharacteristically being in a slum. Example: 'The new library seems almost embarrassed to be slumming it in downmarket Peckham, such is its disdain for the real heart of this South London community' (2001).

Slump City A book on the politics of mass unemployment by Andrew Friend and Andy Metcalf, published in 1987.

slurb See SLURBIA.

slurbia (US) Suburban development at the urban fringe oozing out into the countryside beyond. 'Since nowadays it is the developer who builds the streets and provides the services, not the municipality,' writes Spiro Kostof (1987), 'subdivisions tend to be small, scattered, and randomly shaped. They create a spotty carpet of even-grained parcels around an irregular rural road net'. Alan Loomis has credited the term *slurb* to the architectural critic Ada Louise Huxtable.

slype A passage between walls, particularly between a cathedral transept and chapter house. The word, dating from the nineteenth century, may come from the Dutch *slijpe*, a secret path. See also ALLEY.

small family house Defined in the UK as a house with fewer than six habitable rooms and smaller than 115 sq m (1,238 sq ft) gross internal area.

Small is Beautiful An influential book by EF Schumacher, published in 1974. Subtitled 'a theory of economics as though people mattered', the book challenged prevailing political and economic nostrums like 'economies of scale' and the obsession with advanced technology, and showed the economic (as well as human) advantages of keeping things small, local and simple. Schumacher's work inspired the intermediate technology movement.

small polis Defined by EKISTICS as a settlement with a population of 1,000 million.

Smallville The fictional town in the American mid-west where the cartoon character Superman was brought up. See also CACTUSVILLE.

smart 1 Responsive to changing conditions. Example: 'Consider two "smart" cars converging on a vacant "smart" parking space... The system controlling and charging for the space (a descendent of the primitive parking meter) might run an automated auction and sell it to the highest bidder. Motorists could set their bid limits according to how urgently they needed to park, or how long they had been looking for a space' (Mitchell, 2001). **2** SUSTAINABLE. See SMART GROWTH.

smart city One with a significant concentration of high technology industry.

smart community Defined by city planning theorist Roger Caves as 'a geographical area, ranging in size from a neighbourhood to a multi-county region, whose residents, organisations and governing institutions are using information technology to transform their region in significant ways'. John Eger of the California Institute for Smart Communities describes it as a matter of using information technology to transform life and work in more than just incremental ways. Eger (2003) identifies ten steps to becoming a smart community: 1) The smart community concept must be well understood. 2) Ownership of the smart community concept must be broadly communicated. 3) A new decision-making mechanism must be created. 4) The needs of the community must be assessed and the community defined. 5) A vision and mission statement must be developed. 6) Specific goals and priorities must be established. 7) A strategic plan for the smart community concept needs to be drafted. 8) Responsibilities must be clearly defined and timelines established. 9) Community linkages must be made. 10) Metrics (relating to such things as the development of a new GIS system, or linking the schools and the libraries, or launching a request for proposal to develop a broadband grid) must be established and progress constantly monitored.

smart (also smarter) growth (US) SUSTAINABLE development; development that is based on mass transit and whose environmental impact is limited. The US Environmental Protection Agency identifies 10 principles of smart growth: 1) Mix land uses. 2) Take advantage of compact building design. 3) Create a range of housing opportunities and choices. 4) Create walkable neighbourhoods. 5) Foster distinctive, attractive communities with a strong sense of place. 6) Preserve open space, farmland, natural beauty and critical environmental areas. 7) Strengthen and direct development towards existing communities. 8) Provide a variety of transportation choices. 9) Make development decisions predictable, fair and cost effective. 10) Encourage community and stakeholder collaboration in development decisions. The term became current in the 1990s. See also NEW URBANISM, SUSTAINABLE COMMUNITY, SUSTAINABLE and URBAN VILLAGE.

smart home One using technology that helps residents to manage and control how their home functions.

smart technology In the home, smart technology can keep residents in contact with carers or wardens, detect falls or lack of movement in vulnerable people, or cut off the water to an overflowing bath, for example.

smaze (US) Smog and haze.

smile A survey in 2003 investigated the likelihood of a smile at a stranger being returned in various British cities. The most cheery citizens were in Bristol, with 70 per cent returning a stranger's smile. The most dour were in Edinburgh, where the response rate was four per cent (though Glasgow was the second friendliest, with 68 per cent). 'We do smile a lot in Bristol,' one native of the city explained. 'But sometimes it's not really a smile. We're just a little bit constipated' (Seenan, 2003). Another survey in the same year identified Liverpool as the city that produces the most famous comedians per head of population, followed by Manchester in second place.

Smith, T Dan Politician. As Labour leader of Newcastle City Council from 1958 to 1967 he energetically pursued plans to transform Newcastle into his vision of a new BRASILIA, promoting large-scale redevelopment and developing the regional economy. 'During my career,' he wrote in his autobiography *Dan Smith*, 'I have always been exposed to accusations of dictatorship and ruthlessless' (Smith, 1970). He was imprisoned for bribery and corruption.

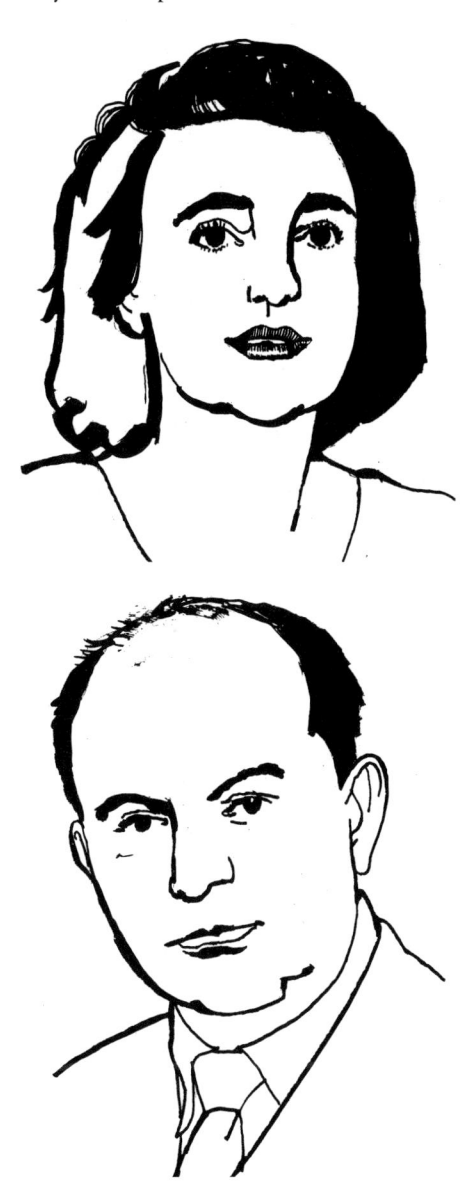

Alison and Peter Smithson

Smithson, Alison and Peter (1928–1993 and 1923–2003) Architects. The couple set up in practice together in 1949 when they won the competition to design Hunstanton School in Norfolk. That building, inspired by MIES VAN DER ROHE and constructed of glass and exposed steel, was celebrated as a notable example of the new BRUTALISM. Unfortunately it was uncomfortably cold in winter and hot in summer. The Smithsons' office building for the Economist, built in 1965 in London's west end, has been greatly admired. As leading modernists, the Smithsons were active in CIAM, trying to use their influence to interest its members in streets rather than buildings set in parkland. At CIAM's 1953 meeting they urged architects to create a sense of 'neighbourliness'. Three years later they and their fellow members of TEAM X left CIAM.

The Smithsons reinvented the street as 'streets in the sky', open corridors on each floor serving long blocks of flats, as at their Robin Hood gardens estate in London's Tower Hamlets. This, an arrangement traditionally used in prisons, turned out to be the least successful of all forms of housing. In later decades Alison and Peter Smithson built little, but were influential as teachers and writers.

smog Smoke plus FOG. The word was coined in 1905 by London physician H A Des Voeux, first president of the National Smoke Abatement Society, to describe the atmospheric conditions over many British towns and cities due to the burning of coal (Potter, 1950). There are two types of smog: *sulphurous smog* (due to coal burning) and *photochemical smog* (caused by hydrocarbons and nitrogen oxides emitted by cars and other sources). James Howard Kunstler (2001) recalls a drive to Atlanta: 'The sky was blue, well, bluish-brownish-ochre really, due to the ozone-producing nitrogen oxides and carbon particulate matter issuing from scores of thousands of other cars like mine similarly plying the overloaded freeway system of greater Atlanta that same moment. But this was Atlanta every day nowadays: one big-ass parking lot under a toxic pall...' See also ELECTROSMOG.

smoke The life-shortening, building-blackening smoke of the nineteenth-century city was not universally condemned. The painter Benjamin Robert Haydon wrote in the 1840s: 'So far from the smoke of London being offensive to me, it has always been to my imagination the sublime canopy that shrouds the City of the World. Drifted by the wind or hanging in gloomy grandeur over the vastness of our Babylon, the sight of it always filled my mind with feelings of energy such as no other spectacle could inspire.' See also BIG SMOKE and NEVER TRUST AIR YOU CAN'T SEE.

smoke, the 1 London. **2** Any big city. See AULD REEKIE and BIG SMOKE.

smokestack city A nineteenth- or early twentieth-century city heavily dependent on manufacturing industry.

SNAP SHELTER NEIGHBOURHOOD ACTION PROJECT.

snicket An ALLEY (see that entry for regional variants), particularly used as a shortcut. The term is used in Yorkshire, among other places.

snout house (US) A house whose garage is incorporated into the main body of the building.

Snow, John (1813–54) Physician and epidemiologist. He demonstrated in the 1840s that cholera was borne by water and plotted on a map an outbreak in London in 1854, showing that all victims had drunk from a single contaminated well in Golden Square.

snuburbanism Defined by the humorist Ian Martin (2002) as 'stubborn non-compliance with "urban life" by living elsewhere'.

so good they named it twice New York, New York, according to the song, the name of the city and its state being the same. Also Cantril Farm, according to an ironic reference in the poem 'The Sleep of Estates' by Paul Farley (1998). The poem ends by evoking: 'Skem and Speke and Stockie/*née* Cantril Farm, so good they named it twice.' Skem (local nickname for the new town of Skelmersdale), Speke and Stockie (Stockbridge Village) are areas of originally public housing on the outskirts of Liverpool. Stockbridge Village was built as the council estate Cantril Farm, but was renamed in the 1980s as part of a privatisation and regeneration programme in an attempt to avoid the stigma that had become attached to its inappropriately bucolic name. In other words, they named it twice not because it was so good, but because it was so bad. See also BRAND and BROADWATER FARM.

John Soane

Soane, John (Sir) (1753–1837) Architect. His schemes for public buildings included the unrealised design of a ceremonial processional route for the state opening of

Parliament. The route, to be lined by buildings in an appropriately rich classical style, began with a Grand National Entrance into the Metropolis at Kensington Gore. On more utilitarian buildings Soane used a stripped-down classical style with incised ornament in place of moulding and carved stone, leading some commentators to call him the first modern (or modernist) architect. Among his best-known buildings are Dulwich Collage Picture Gallery and his own house at 13 Lincoln's Inn Fields (now part of the Soane Museum).

Soapsuds Island Kensal New Town in London, so called because at one time its people took in the washing of the fashionable districts of Bayswater and Belgravia (Ward, 1998).

soccer mom (US) A parent who habitually acts as chauffeur for a child or children. Example: 'Suburban sprawl condemns us to the role of soccer mom.'

sociability Openness to social contact with others. See also DISSOCIATION.

sociable city A type of polycentric urban cluster, based on transport corridors, proposed for sites on the south east of England by the Town and Country Planning Association in 1998. The name was inspired by Ebenezer Howard's SOCIAL CITY.

social Relating to life in an organised group.

social architecture Buildings accommodating public services, including education, health and public housing.

social area An area with a homogenous social structure.

social auditing Estimating the social impact of a profit-driven organisation.

social balance A mix of different types of people in a particular area that is considered appropriate in the light of criteria (proportions that match the national average, for example) that may or may not be made explicit.

social capital An area's social assets, principally intangible like voluntary associations, community networks, social stability and other 'feelgood factors', but also including concrete elements such as the range and quality of housing, schools, hospitals, shops and other facilities. ROBERT D PUTNAM defines it as 'features of social organisation, such as networks, norms and social trust, that facilitate coordination and cooperation for mutual benefit' (New Economics Foundation, 2000) and as 'the extent to which people in communities engage with one another and outside agencies that affect the quality of their lives' (Palmer, 2001). The New Economics Foundation defines the four components of social capital as 'trust, norms, reciprocity, and networks and connections'. The Social Exclusion Unit (2000) defines social capital as 'the contact, trust and solidarity that enables residents to help, rather than fear, each other', with vital resources such as COMMUNITY SPIRIT. The concept of social (or cultural) capital was earlier used by the French sociologist Pierre Bourdieu. Critics of the social capital approach include RICHARD FLORIDA. In *The Rise of the Creative Class* Florida writes: 'A number of serious social commentators in recent years have urged us to recultivate and rebuild the old forms of "social capital" found in these communities. Such efforts are fruitless, since they fly in the face of today's economic realities. A central task ahead is developing new forms of social cohesion appropriate to the creative age.' See also BOWLING ALONE.

social city A cluster of GARDEN CITIES, as proposed by EBENEZER HOWARD. He envisaged that when each garden city's population had grown to 32,000, another would be started nearby, eventually creating a cluster linked by railways. A social city would have a population of around a quarter of a million people.

social class A means of categorising people according to measures such as their position in the economic system, their status in society and their power.

social cleansing Taking action that leads to a particular social group moving out of the area where they live (see GENTRIFICATION), or to certain types of street user (such as rough sleepers, drinkers or street vendors) being moved on in the name of creating better public spaces. The term, coined in the late 1990s, is used in the UK by those who claim that such action is being taken, perhaps as a consequence of a local authority's policy. Example: 'The council stunned locals by announcing a brutal five-year housing regeneration scheme. Some 1,700 households were to be forcibly decanted... Angry letters were published in the local press complaining about "social cleansing"' (London, 2001). The analogy is with *ethnic cleansing*, the euphemism used by those in former Yugoslavia who forced certain ethnic groups from their home areas.

social cohesion See COHESIVE COMMUNITY.

social condenser A place where the people of a neighbourhood meet socially. John Willett (1978) records the term being used in the Soviet Union in the 1920s, when it was 'a concept peculiar to Soviet society, meaning certain new institutions intended to absorb and transform the individual'. See THIRD PLACE.

Social Contract, The A book by JEAN-JACQUES ROUSSEAU, published in 1762, proposing the idea that the state is based on a contract in which free individuals entrust it with part of their freedom.

social Darwinism Applying theories of natural selection and evolution to the study of society.

social distance See INTIMATE DISTANCE.

social economy Economic activities carried out to meet social needs.

social engineering Planning with the aim of determining where and how particular groups and types of people will live. An example is development that mixes expensive and less expensive (or owner-occupied and rented) housing.

social enterprise zone Proposed in a 1998 report by the Joseph Rowntree Foundation, the zones would allow rules and regulations to be rewritten locally to promote regeneration in deprived communities. A consortium of public sector agencies, businesses and the local community would be created to run a zone. The authors said that there were lessons to be learned from business ENTERPRISE ZONES, which encouraged private development by applying planning laws flexibly.

social entrepreneur A person who initiates and develops projects with direct social benefits. One social entrepreneur – Liam Black (2001) of the Liverpool Furniture Resource Centre – has defined such a person as 'someone who not only simultaneously achieves a financial and social return on their investment, but was pursuing both objectives'.

social exclusion Poverty. Social exclusion has been defined by the DETR (1998) as people being 'socially excluded from what most people would regard as the usual lifestyle', and by the Department of Culture, Media and Sport (2002) as 'a combination of linked problems such as unemployment, poor skills, low incomes, poor housing, high-crime environments, bad health, poverty and family breakdown'. The Joseph Rowntree Foundation (2000) defines social exclusion as 'the process by which some forms of disadvantage, including unemployment, poor skills and poverty, can interact to push people out of mainstream society, and the effect that lack of income and lack of work have on people's ability to participate in society'.

The term became widely used in government in the UK following the election of New Labour in 1997. Deputy prime minister John Prescott (2002) noted that the term social exclusion was once confined to academic circles. 'A few years ago... we talked about "poverty" or "the underclass"... Nowadays, "social exclusion" is part of the everyday language of policy-makers, politicians and professionals such as teachers and social workers.' This change in the language, he wrote, 'indicates a fundamental shift in the government's approach to tackling this significant social issue. It indicates that we have developed a sharper understanding of social problems and the complex links between them.'

The sociologist Anthony Giddens points to the 'voluntary exclusion of the elites' (wealthy people opting out of mainstream institutions of education, health and local government, and living in gated communities, for example) and the 'involuntary exclusion of the excluded' (Minton, 2002). The UK-based sociologist Zygmunt Bauman (b1925) relates feelings of exclusion to the high level of communications in the modern world. 'In a consumer society,' Bauman says, 'people wallow in things, fascinating, enjoyable things. If you define your value by the things you acquire and surround yourself with, being excluded is humiliating. We live in a world of communication... There is universal comparison and you don't just compare yourself with the people next door, you compare yourself to people all over the world and with what is being presented as the decent, proper and dignified life. It's the crime of humiliation' (quoted in Bunting, 2003).

Some commentators argue that the term is a deliberate attempt to avoid confronting politically sensitive issues like the regressive nature of the tax system, inadequate levels of benefit and the minimum wage, and the perverse incentives built into the current structure of the benefit system itself. To paraphrase Basil Fawlty: 'Don't mention the poor!' The campaigner Jimmy Reid (2001) has commented: 'The poor now suffer from social exclusion, as if they were lacking social skills, and not money'. Compare PHYSICAL EXCLUSION.

social housing Housing provided for social purposes (rather than for profit), usually by local authorities, housing associations or housing trusts. In the UK the term's wide currency dates from the early 1980s. It was coined by the then Conservative government as a more appropriate description than 'council housing', which the government planned effectively to abolish by discounted sales to tenants and transfers to housing association.

social inclusion The opposite of SOCIAL EXCLUSION.

social indicator A feature that is regularly measured as one of those used to describe social change.

social justice The condition in which people get from society what they justly deserve. What they deserve and how they should get it are of course matters of controversy. The political philosopher John Rawls (1921–2002) suggested imagining a group of individuals brought together to decide on the constitution of a society of which they were about to become part. Suppose, he said, that they were ignorant of the gender, race, class, abilities, religion and values that they would have. However self-interested they might be, their decision was bound to be fair. They would choose to be governed by two principles of justice. First, each person should have as much liberty as is compatible with the liberty of others. Second, social and economic inequalities should be arranged so that they disadvantage those who are in other respects best off.

Social Logic of Space, The A book by Bill Hillier, pioneer of SPACE SYNTAX ANALYIS, published in 1984, presenting a general theory of how people relate to space in built environments.

social mobility Moving between social classes (from working to middle, for example).

social planning This approach to planning was common in the late 1960s and early '70s. David Eversley (1973), one time chief strategic planner of

social space

the Greater London Council, defined it as 'the total effort by all agencies to achieve changes in the physical environment, and in the economic and social structure which exists within that environment, in pursuit of improvements in the living standards of an urban population Eversley noted: 'This form of planning is an entirely different activity from traditional physical planning which was mainly concerned with the tangible shortcomings of the urban environment, consisting of such activities as slum clearance, road improvements and the creating of open spaces. Social planning is still concerned with the quality of the housing stock, with safety and amenity and with environmental quality in the form of the control of air and water pollution. But it is also concerned with health and education in the wider sense, with community relations, with real incomes and with problems of disadvantaged groups in society... Social planning is really a form of urban management. Its objectives are social, its methods avowedly political (it aims at redistributing goods, services and amenities, that is, real incomes, between different sections of society).'

social polarisation The process by which people tend to become segregated into income or ethnic groups. See SEGREGATION.

social provision Providing social facilities such as shops, schools and doctors' surgeries.

social regeneration Tackling an area's social problems, such as crime and drug abuse.

social science The study of SOCIETY.

social space Where the public and cultural life of a society takes place. It can include outdoor spaces like parks, squares and streets as well as indoor places such as restaurants, cafes, pubs and bars.

social stratification 1 Allocating people to social categories for the purpose of sociological study. **2** People with different levels of income living in different parts of an urban area.

social structure The networks of social relationships. SOCIOLOGY is the science of social structure.

social town planning Brendan Gleeson and Bill Randolph (2002) have described social town planning as 'a sub-discipline of SOCIAL PLANNING that has emerged within urban planning as a specialism'. Much of this work, they write, focuses on 'issues of process and participation, and... the translation of some health and safety issues to urban design'.

social usage approach A method of urban design analysis focusing on how people use space. It was employed by, among others, the urban designer David Thomas (Jarvis, 2002).

social value A generic term for the political, cultural, traditional and other values held by people in general, or by a specific group in a place.

socially mixed community One in which a number of social classes or occupational groups are represented (Little and Mabey, 1973).

societarian 1 Pertaining to fashionable society. **2** Socialist; Fourieristic (see CHARLES FOURIER).

society 1 The body of people as a whole. **2** The members of the community who consider themselves an elite. **3** Companionship.

The then prime minister MARGARET THATCHER famously said in an interview with *Woman's Own* in 1987 that 'many people have been given to understand that if they have a problem, it's the government's job to cope with it. They're casting their problem on society. And, you know, there is no such thing as society. There are individual men and women and there are families.' She believed that attempts to change behaviour by improving an abstraction called 'society' could never work: they merely created jobs for unnecessary government officials, professionals (including planners) and academics (including, worst of all in her mind, sociologists). Instead, individuals and families should be the focus for government action. Thatcher agreed with her one-time education secretary Sir Keith Joseph that 'social science' was not science at all. Under her government the Social Science Research Council became the Economic and Social Research Council. In 2002 a series of essays by Conservative politicians and thinkers was published with the title *There is Such a Thing as Society* and an introduction by the then party leader Iain Duncan Smith. Thatcher remained adamant, though. She wrote in her book *Statecraft* of the quotation: 'There are a number of things I have said in my political life which I would have liked to rephrase. These words are not among them.'

Society for the Improvement of the Condition of the Labouring Classes A charitable trust with dividends limited to five per cent, founded in 1844 to build dwellings for skilled workers. See also PHILANTHROPY AT FIVE PER CENT.

Society for the Protection of Ancient Buildings Founded by WILLIAM MORRIS in 1877 to campaign for the sensitive repair of historic buildings in the face of a fashion for radical restoration.

socio-economic mixing See GENTRIFICATION.

sociologism An explanation based on considering social factors only.

sociology The study of SOCIAL STRUCTURE and social change. The term was coined by Auguste Comte (1798–1857).

sociospatial dialectic A process by which people shape and are shaped by their surroundings. The term is used by theorist ED SOJA.

sod off! architecture Buildings designed without concession to popular taste or historical and architectural context. The phrase refers to a comment made in the 1980s by Owen Luder, then president of the RIBA, on RICHARD ROGERS' entry to the competition for an extension to the National Gallery in Trafalgar Square, London. The design's uncompromising message to its neighbours and the unappreciative public was, Luder said approvingly, 'sod off!' The phrase has also been applied in other contexts, for example: 'There used to be "sod off" railings here. But this park is about welcome and inclusiveness' (2002).

Sodom 1 One of the Biblical 'CITIES OF THE PLAIN'. **2** Any place of depravity. See also BABEL, DESTRUCTION OF SODOM AND GOMORRAH and URBAN DESTRUCTION.

soft architecture The process or product of designing the setting for urban life, other than buildings and structures. This might include collaborations, programmes, initiatives and organisations. The term is used by the urban designer Leslie Gallery-Dilworth. See also SOFT CITY, SOFTWARE and compare GENTLE ARCHITECTURE.

Soft City A book by Jonathan Raban, published in 1974, exploring and celebrating the intangible elements of urban life. Raban argued that cities were now wilder, more organic places than the countryside which had been almost entirely tamed, ordered and controlled. 'Decide who you are, and the city will again assume a fixed form round you,' Raban writes. 'Decide what it is, and your own identity will be revealed, like a position on a map fixed by triangulation. Cities, unlike villages and small towns, are plastic by nature. We mould them in our images: they, in their turn, shape us by the resistance they offer when we try to impose our own personal form on them. In this sense, it seems to me that living in cities is an art, and we need the vocabulary of art, of style, to describe the peculiar relationship between man and material that exists in the continual creative play of urban living.' For a fictional treatment of the same idea, see DESPINA.

soft end use A use such as open space for reclaimed land. See HARD END USE.

soft landscaping See LANDSCAPING.

soft outcome One that can not easily be measured or that can not be predicted.

soft separation A distinct but gentle difference between road and pavement (softer than the usual kerb) where the whole carriageway is shared between pedestrians, cyclists and vehicles in traffic-calmed areas. Soft separation (which may involve a small step between the road and pavement) is an alternative to indicating the two shared surfaces by changing the material. A further alternative is not to distinguish between the two at all.

soft space See HARD SPACE.

soft urban renewal Improving an area and rehabilitating its buildings without the residents having to move away.

software In regeneration such features as local education services and social development programmes are referred to as the software. Compare HARDWARE.

SoHo A district in New York. The former industrial area was blighted by urban renewal and highway proposals, occupied by artists looking for cheap space, and gradually renewed over 30 years. LOFT living was pioneered there in the 1970s. The name was coined in the 1960s from its location south of Houston Street. The area is noted for its nineteenth-century cast-iron buildings. 'Some of the moulding is so good,' write Tiesdell, Oc and Heath (1996), 'that the only way to tell a cast-iron façade from a masonry façade is with a magnet.'

Soho A district of London, famous for its former bohemian atmosphere, range of ethnic restaurants and concentration of porn shops, and known for its café and night life. Its name (written SoHo in the seventeenth century) apparently comes from a hunting call (like tally-ho) heard when the area was open country.

SoHo loft 1 A LOFT in SoHo, New York. **2** An apartment (in any city) marketed as offering the lifestyle associated with lofts in SoHo.

Soja, Edward (Ed) Geographer, and theorist of planning and urban political economy. Soja has researched and written widely about Los Angeles, focusing particularly on how issues of class, race, gender and sexuality relate to the spatial expression of social life. See CAPITAL OF THE TWENTIETH CENTURY, COSMOPOLIS, EXOPOLIS, HENRI LEFEVBRE, POSTMODERN GLOBAL METROPOLIS, SCAMSCAPE, SOCIOSPATIAL DIALECTIC and SPLINTERED LABYRINTH.

Sokol A garden village built on the edge of Moscow in 1924–6 to a design by Nikolai Markovnikov (Cooke, 2001).

solar building Laying out development to maximise (in cold climates) or minimise (in hot ones) solar gain.

solar city One to which one or more SATELLITE TOWNS relates. LEWIS MUMFORD used the term in 1945 (Hughes, 1971).

solar design Designing buildings to make the most of light and energy from the sun.

solar gain A rise in the temperature of a building's fabric due to the sun shining on it. This can provide a welcome boost to ambient indoor temperatures in winter, but can cause a building to become uncomfortably warm in summer where there are no mitigating measures (design or air conditioning).

Where a building is consciously designed and orientated to make the most of the sun's warmth, this is usually referred to as *passive solar gain* to distinguish it from the *active* use of solar energy (by such means as solar or photovoltaic panels).

solar urbanism Defined by Bill Dunster, architect of BEDZED, as large-scale development orientated towards the sun to minimise the use of energy.

Soleri, Paolo (b1919) Italian-born architect, inventor of

ARCOLOGY, designer of ARCOSANTI and an associate of FRANK LLOYD WRIGHT.

solid-to-void ratio A measure of the proportion of a building's façade accounted for by wall (solid) on the one hand, and doors and windows (void) on the other.

something lost by overspacing A comment by LEWIS MUMFORD (1961) on Raymond Unwin's famous pamphlet NOTHING GAINED BY OVERCROWDING! Mumford admired Unwin's pamphlet but was warning about what he saw as excessively low suburban housing densities. See also PRAIRIE PLANNING.

Sommer, Robert Environmental psychologist. See HARD ARCHITECTURE.

Song of Speed, A The poem by William Ernest Henley, published in 1903, was the first to celebrate the joys of motoring.

sonic sketchbook A recording of sounds, commentary and interviews, used in appraising a place.

Sophia Antipolis A SCIENCE CITY in southern France.

Soria y Mata, Arturo (1844–1920) Engineer and town planner. In 1894 he proposed his concept of a linear city, *ciudad lineal*. A corridor, centred on a road, electric railway and cycle track, would be lined by low-rise, high-density housing to a depth of 200 metres. Beyond that would be an agricultural belt at least four kilometres wide. Such a city might extend from Madrid to St Petersburg, 'urbanising the country and ruralising the town'. A five-kilometre stretch was built near Madrid in 1897 (Rykwert, 2000).

Sorkin, Michael Architect and critic. See LIP-SYNC ARCHITECTURE, MOVEMENT, PLANNING OFFICER'S GEORGIAN, PROPINQUITY, RIGHTS and TELEVISION.

souk (also suk, sukh and suq) An Islamic market or bazaar. Planners and developers in the west, particularly in the 1980s, sometimes referred to a proposed space as a souk to convey their (invariably disappointed) hopes of its bustling liveliness.

soul Life, spirit or distinctive character. Researchers for the Urban Task Force (1999) found that 'soul' was seen as a very desirable attribute that applied to areas as well as buildings, and that there was a feeling that places that had developed over a long period in a natural or unplanned way had more soul.

soulless Without life, spirit or distinctive character. The word, Sue Clifford (1990) suggests, is 'one of the common ways of describing a city place which draws negative feelings'.

soundscape The overall acoustic environment; a representation of this.

sous les pavés, la plage UNDER THE PAVEMENT, THE BEACH.

South East Study Published in 1964, the report of the study highlighted the expected population pressure on south east England and recommended that further new towns be built to help accommodate it.

South Woodham Ferrers A new town (though not designated under the New Towns Act) built in Essex between 1970 and 1990 according to the principles of the ESSEX DESIGN GUIDE. Most of the houses were built for sale.

Southway A proposal by PETER HALL for building a major new toll road in south London (Hall, 1989). It would have been almost entirely underground, and much of it would have been double decked in order to use the route of former railway lines.

Soylent Green A film, directed by Richard Fleischer, and starring Charlton Heston and Edward G Robinson, released in 1973. A future Los Angeles is desperately overcrowded and short of food. Artificial protein-rich foods are marketed under the names Soylent Red and Green. Aged citizens are encouraged to die to reduce overcrowding. They are put to sleep gently to the strains of Beethoven's Pastoral Symphony, watching projected images of flowers, grass and other natural features that no longer exist. Their bodies are processed to provide a rich source of protein (Soylent Green) for the rest of the population. The film is based on the novel *Make Room, Make Room*.

Spa Green Estate Three slab blocks – two straight and one sinuously curving – of council flats on Rosebery Avenue in Finsbury, London, designed by BERTHOLD LUBETKIN and Tecton in 1938, and built in 1946–9. 'The obsessive pattern-making of the facades is as arbitrary as the arrangement of the blocks,' according to Jones and Woodward (1983).

space 1 An empty area. 'We are in the habit of thinking that open space is precious in the city,' observes Robert Venturi (1966). 'It is not. Except in Manhattan perhaps, our cities have too much open space in the ubiquitous parking lots, in the not-so-temporary deserts created by urban renewal and in the amorphous suburbs around.' Example: 'Urban design is concerned with more than just the space between buildings'. **2** The three-dimensional region in which matter exists. Example: 'Architecture is about enclosing space'. Adrian Forty (2000a) suggests Seigfried Giedion's *Space, Time and Architecture*, published in 1941, as probably being the work that introduced *space* in English as a term to describe the chief concern of architecture. **3** The extent of a surface. 'So much space was taken by retail uses that there was no room left for housing'. **4** An area set aside for a specific purpose: *a parking space or storage space, for example*.

The thirteenth-century word space comes from the Latin *spatium* meaning distance or space. See HENRI LEFEVBRE, NEGATIVE SPACE and POSITIVE SPACE.

Space City HOUSTON, Texas, a centre of space research and travel since the 1960s.

Space is the Machine A book by Bill Hillier (1996) presenting 'a configurational theory of architecture', of

SoHo

which SPACE SYNTAX ANALYSIS is an important element. With the right theory, Hillier believes, architects will build in towns and cities in a way that encourages patterns of movement that society needs. He argues that 'the considered strangeness of genuine architecture' depends on architects having, not only a body of correct theoretical knowledge, but also creative freedom in which to innovate. 'Without the protection of an analytic theory,' he writes, 'architecture is inevitably subject to more and more externally imposed restrictions that substitute social ideology for architectural creativity. Analytic theory is necessary in order to retain the autonomy of creative innovation on which the advance of architecture depends'.

Hillier suggests that, in the act of designing, an architect is thinking about possible configurations of space. As a configuration is a whole entity, not an accumulation of unconnected parts, the properties of the whole will change every time the configuration is changed in any way. This means, he believes, that design must be a holistic, intuitive process, generally done from the top down. Design 'can not... follow a reasoned procedure, nor can it proceed additively from the bottom up.'

At its worst, Hillier warns, 'the takeover of areas of architecture by ideological formulations instead of analytic theories can lead architecture into its opposite: a kind of degenerate quasi-vernacularism...' He concludes: 'Lesser architects assert that they create. Great architects believe they discover. This difference is due to the intervention of that peculiar brand of reflective thought which stands on the foundation of theory, yet when applied in creative mode breaks bounds and changes the architecture of the past into the architecture of the future.'

The book's title comes from a phrase coined in 1994 by Nick Dalton, a computer programmer colleague of Hillier's. Le Corbusier's statement 'a house is a machine for living in' was mentioned in conversation with a student. 'But I thought all that functional stuff had been refuted,' the student said. 'Buildings aren't machines.' Dalton's response was: 'You haven't understood. The building isn't the machine. Space is the machine.'

space of uncertainty A leftover space used for informal and temporary uses.

space syntax analysis A technique for analysing movement through urban space and predicting the amount of activity likely to result from that movement. Space syntax is based on the idea that, other things being equal, urban movement is based on the CONFIGURATION of urban space. The technique has been developed by Bill Hillier and his colleagues at the Bartlett School of Architecture and Planning, University College London. Some of its main ideas (as explained in Hillier's book SPACE IS THE MACHINE) are: a) Movement in the urban grid is, other things being equal, generated by the configuration of the grid itself. (The urban grid is the organisation of groups of contiguous buildings in outward-facing, fairly regular clumps, among which is defined a continuous system of space. The grid's configuration is the way it is put together). b) The relation between grid and movement underlies many other aspects of urban form: the distribution of land uses, such as retail and residence, the spatial patterning of crime, and the evolution of different densities. The structuring of movement by the grid leads, through multiplier effects, to dense patterns of mixed-use encounter that characterise the spatially successful city. c) The structure of the urban grid determines how much potential each location has for generating contact between people. A location with more potential will tend to have higher densities. These higher densities will generate more contact between people, which will in turn attract new buildings and uses, and give rise to urban buzz. d) Places are not local things. They are moments in the large-scale things we call cities. Places do not make cities. It is cities that make places. e) Movement largely dictates the configuring of space in the city and, in terms of the effects of spatial form, movement is largely determined by spatial configuration. f) How much movement passes along a particular route will be strongly influenced by the position of the route with respect to the urban system as a whole. g) Urbanity is not so mysterious. Good space is used space. Most urban space use is movement. Most movement is through movement, that is, the by-product of how the grid offers routes from everywhere to everywhere else. h) The positive benefits of urbanism depend on, among other things, the relation between buildings and public space, the relation between scales of movement, and the interface between inhabitant and stranger. i) Urbanism is disrupted by replacing continuous urban structure with specialised enclaves (destinations which people do not pass through on their way to somewhere else); lowering densities, reducing spatial scale; and separating and restricting different forms of movement. j) Successful urban space, even in predominantly residential areas, is characterised by multiple interfaces: between inhabitant and stranger, between men and women, between old and young, and between adults and children. k) A local sense of place (and with it the sense of safety, the development of social networks and the distribution of crime, among other things) arises from the way in which a part of a town or city is integrated into the whole through natural movement, which brings people together in the same place for different reasons. l) Successful urban places depend on the humanising influence of the public realm. m) Our view of the city in the recent past has been afflicted by conceptions of space which are at once too static and too localised. We need to replace these by concepts which are dynamic and global.

There has been extensive discussion of what space syntax analysis reveals about everyday developments. According to Hillier's theories, for example, culs-de-sac have configurations which should tend to make them, all other things being equal, more likely to suffer from crime. Yet the police and Home Office have long advocated such layouts as being relatively free from crime (see SECURED BY DESIGN). More recent research by Hillier's Space Syntax Laboratory at the Bartlett School has correlated actual crime figures to the type of layout of the housing to which they relate. The researchers claim that the results show that culs-de-sac are indeed the worst housing layouts for crime. The laboratory has developed software programmes that help designers, local authorities and developers to create safer street layouts.

space use The use of a space.

space-positive building Where the spaces between buildings are lively and useful, unlike *object-positive buildings* (Terry Farrell and Partners, 2002). The terms were used by COLIN ROWE in *Collage City*.

space-time distanciation See DISTANCIATION.

Spaghetti Junction In the UK the name is given to the Gravelly Hill motorway interchange, where the M6 motorway meets the A38(M) and other roads northwest of Birmingham in a symphony (or nightmare, depending on your point of view) of slip roads, viaducts, overpasses and underpasses. It is the most spectacular multi-level interchange in the UK.

spaghetti The looped, interlinked roads of an interchange between motorways.

Spam Valley (a Glasgow term) Any suburban area whose young residents are said to have to eat cheap canned meat (Spam) to be able to afford the cost of the mortgage. The term may date from the 1960s.

Span developments Small developments of flats or houses, fitted in among existing buildings and trees, designed by the architect Eric Lyons and built by his company Span Developments from the 1950s. See GEOFFREY TOWNSEND and NEW ASH GREEN.

spatial Of or relating to space. The nineteenth-century word was coined from the Latin *spatium*.

spatial convergence See TRIPLE CONVERGENCE.

spatial definition An outdoor space being made to seem contained by the height of buildings or trees that enclose it.

spatial determinism The belief that reorganising the distribution and configuration of development is an effective way of achieving certain social goals. The theorist David Harvey (1997) has accused NEW URBANISTS of it.

spatial development strategy 'The management of place-specific issues in all aspects of public policy' (Local Government Association, 2000). The LGA comments: 'Spatial development strategies are joined-up where conventional plans are tunnel-visioned.' In London, the term refers to the strategy – renamed THE LONDON PLAN – prepared by the mayor in 2002/03 to replace the previous strategic planning guidance.

spatial displacement The movement of an activity, anything from crime to car parking, from one place to another. It can occur 'organically' or as a result of deliberate intervention (anything from police activity to parking charges).

spatial equity The degree to which people in different places benefit from change. Compare INTERGENERATIONAL EQUITY.

spatial integration 1 A mix of different types of people (in terms of wealth or ethnic origin, for example) in an area. **2** The elements and functions of a particular place working together in a co-ordinated way.

spatial master plan See MASTER PLAN.

spatial plan 1 A series of LOCAL DEVELOPMENT DOCUMENTS contained in a LOCAL DEVELOPEMENT FRAMEWORK. **2** An outcome of the SPATIAL PLANNING process. **3** A two-dimensional plan, showing the layout of an area, as opposed to a policy plan. Planners often to use the term in this sense, and may also describe it as a MASTER PLAN. **4** A three-dimensional plan, showing the layout and massing of an area, as opposed to a two-dimensional plan. Architects often use the term in this sense, and may also describe it as a SPATIAL MASTER PLAN. In a sense, then, professionals use spatial to mean 'one more dimension than we usually deal with'.

spatial planning Methods used to inform actions, taken by both the public and private sectors, that influence the location of activities in two-dimensional space and the linkages between them; focusing public policy and action on making the most of the potential of particular places at every scale, from local communities to regions, the nation and Europe; town and country planning; urban and regional planning. Unlike land-use planning, spatial planning is not solely concerned with land uses, but also with the wider activities of sectors such as health and education. The phrase is in official use in relation to the EU's activities and is becoming more widely used in the UK. Dick Williams (2000) has proposed that the term be officially adopted by the UK planning profession. A spatial planning profession could be defined as offering, he suggests, 'expertise in public policy and actions intended to influence the location and distribution of activities in space and the linkages between them'. The essential characteristics of spatial planning are, Williams writes, that it can occur at any spatial scale, for example from that of the EU (the European Spatial Development Perspective) to national, regional, local and site planning, and that it is concerned with the integration and coherence of different sectoral policies. By contrast many of the alternative titles for planning 'seek to define a spatial scale or

SPATIAL STRATEGY

context (eg regional, urban, rural), and are therefore limited and not universally applicable.'

spatial strategy 1 A plan that shows the proposed physical form of development (in two or three dimensions). **2** A statement of SPATIAL PLANNING. See REGIONAL SPATIAL STRATEGY.

spatial vortex An urban design concept used by the architect BERTHOLD LUBETKIN. *Spatial vectors* (urban AXES) were designed to pass beyond the buildings towards the natural environment beyond, rather than pointing towards landmark buildings (Allan, 2000).

spatiality The human ability to perceive space.

spec development SPECULATIVE DEVELOPMENT.

special blue ribbon zone A designation for the River Thames proposed by London mayor KEN LIVINGSTONE in 2000 to protect it against unsympathetic development. See also BLUE BELT.

special development order Made by the relevant secretary of state, specifying special requirements for planning permission for a particular place.

special district (US) **1** An area covered by an amendment to a zoning ordinance. **2** A government agency with a specific function.

special parking area Makes parking offences a matter for a local authority rather than the criminal law.

specially protected wildlife species Badgers and other species protected under the Wildlife and Countryside Act 1981.

species Related biological organisms sharing common characteristics and capable of interbreeding within the group but not usually outside it. Some local authority planning policies insist that planting which accompanies development should be of species that are already common locally. The reasons for such policies are generally that planting locally common species will help development harmonise with its context, that plants of such species are more likely to flourish, and that local flora are more likely to support local fauna. See also BIODIVERSITY.

specific plan (US) One indicating land uses, open spaces and infrastructure for a specific area, as a step towards implementing the local general plan.

speculative development Carried out without a particular customer in mind. Compare BESPOKE DEVELOPMENT.

speed The rate at which a distance is covered.

speed board (US) A large electronic sign that displays the measured speed to a driver. It may be carried by a *speed wagon*. See TRAFFIC CALMING.

speed hump (or bump) A raised strip of roadway designed to slow traffic. See TRAFFIC CALMING.

speed merchant A person who drives excessively fast.

speed order Authorises the local traffic authority to take measures to reduce the speed of motor vehicles or cycles, or both, on a specified road.

speed table A raised area of roadway at an intersection, designed to slow traffic. See TRAFFIC CALMING.

speed wagon See SPEED BOARD.

speed watch (US) A programme in which volunteers with radar guns record the licences of cars that speed through their neighbourhood. The municipality subsequently sends speeding drivers a letter reminding them to drive more slowly. See TRAFFIC CALMING.

speedway sculpture See FREEWAY ART.

Speer, Albert (1905–81) German architect. Appointed chief city planner of Berlin by Hitler in 1937, he produced grandiose neo-classical plans for its transformation into Germania, capital of Hitler's thousand year Reich, including a Three Mile Avenue which out-Haussmanns HAUSSMANN. In London he designed the interior of the pre-war German Embassy at 7–9 Carlton House Terrace. He later became armaments minister. On trial by the Nuremburg Tribunal after the 1939–45 war, Speer managed to escape a death sentence by claiming, among other things, to have defied Hitler's orders to raze Germany's cities before the advancing allies could capture them. He served a long prison sentence. See also OPERATION GOMORRAH.

Speke See SO GOOD THEY NAMED IT TWICE.

Spence, Thomas EBENEZER HOWARD acknowledged the influence of this late eighteenth-century radical from Newcastle-upon-Tyne, who advocated the parish ownership of land as a universal tenure (Miller, 1989).

Spengler, Oswald Historian. See ANTI-URBANISM.

sphere of influence (US) A designated planning area covering all the land that is expected ultimately to be within the city's boundaries. In some cases it will be defined by the city's existing boundaries.

spider web A layout in which streets run at right angle to radial streets.

spikey *n*. A person who engages in or supports violent mass protest against capitalism and globalisation. The term became current in the 1990s. Compare FLUFFY.

spill-out space Open space used in association with an adjacent building (tables and chairs on the pavement outside a café, for example). Also known as *capturing space*.

spindelform A medieval form of town plan, similar in shape to a weaver's bobbin, in which streets parallel to the main axis curve at the ends to join at the city gate (Kostof, 1991).

spine A street or streets along which activity is concentrated.

spiritual ownership Rights that a person may have over something despite not owning it. For example, some architects claim that their spiritual ownership of buildings they have designed gives them a right to be consulted about any proposals to change them.

Spirn, Anne Whiston Landscape architect. See THE LANGUAGE OF LANDSCAPE.

splintered labyrinth An extreme form of social, economic and political polarisation characteristic of the post-modern city. ED SOJA uses the term (Dear and Flusty, 1998).

splintered urbanism Urban space broken up into inward-looking islands and ENCLAVES, surrounding by the infrastructure of roads and car parks. Steve Graham and Simon Marvin describe the phenomenon in their book *Splintering Urbanism*, published in 2001.

spontané (also urbanisme spontané) (French) Urban sprawl.

Sporoundia Otherwise known as the City of the Deformed, Sporoundia is the capital city of Sporoumbia, a fictional country set on a river island in Australia. All the country's deformed people live in the city, as Denis Veiras recounts in *History of the Sevarambes* (1677–79).

sport action zone A deprived area in which Sport England promotes participation in sport to reduce SOCIAL EXCLUSION and promote community development.

spot zoning (US) Allowing a single lot or small area to enjoy an relaxation of zoning requirements.

spotted dick Particular kinds of land uses scattered among otherwise homogenous development, rather than being concentrated in certain areas. The analogy is with the fruit in the sponge or suet pudding so nicknamed. See also MUESLI.

sprawl See SUBURBAN SPRAWL.

sprawl index (US) Relates population growth to the rate of urbanisation or suburbanisation.

Sprawl-busters A US organisation that helps local community coalitions design and implement campaigns against megastores and other locally unwanted large-scale developments. Its leader is Al Norman, author of *Slam-dunking Wal-Mart! How you can stop superstore sprawl in your hometown* (slam-dunking is a basketball term for jumping up and placing the ball in basket, rather than throwing it in from a distance).

sprawlopolis A low-density MEGALOPOLIS. The Australian architectural writer Elizabeth Farrelly has used the term.

sprawlscape The landscape of urban sprawl. James Howard Kunstler writes in *The Geography of Nowhere*, published in the 1990s, of 'the tragic sprawlscape of cartoon architecture, junked cities and ravaged countryside'. The mess that Americans have made of their everyday environment is not merely the symptom of a troubled culture, Kunstler writes, but one of the primary causes of the nation's troubles. 'We created a landscape of scary places, and we became a nation of scary people.'

spread city Urban development sprawling over a region. Alan Loomis has credited the term to the REGIONAL PLANNING ASSOCIATION. See also SUBURBAN SPRAWL.

springboard project An innovative project that provides a model for other similar ones in the same area.

Springfield 1 The fictional American town where the eponymous family of the television cartoon 'The Simpsons' lives in a detached house at 742 Evergreen Terrace, an undistinguished suburban street. Homer Simpson works at the local nuclear power station. Notable episodes in Springfield's civic life include eight-year-old Lisa Simpson becoming mayor. Noticing that traffic moves fastest through traffic lights when they are at amber, she decrees that they should be set at amber permanently. The resulting decrease in congestion helps Springfield to move up to 299th place in the list of America's 300 most livable cities, ahead of East St Louis, Illinois. Springfield is probably the second most common name for a city in the USA, after Fairview. Springfield, Illinois, for example, is the capital of that state. Aficionados of 'The Simpsons' try to work out where the Simpsons' Springfield is, but the programme's evidence is contradictory. See also BROOKSIDE, CORONATION STREET, EASTENDERS and OZZIE AND HARRIET. **2** A new settlement (advertised as 'Australia's largest master-planned community' and 'an "edge city" in the making') whose construction began in 1992 on a site near Brisbane. The intended population is 55,000.

SPUD STRUCTURED PLANNED URBAN DEVELOPMENT.

SPUR The Society for the Promotion of Urban Renewal, formed in 1958 and dissolved six years later. It campaigned against dispersal from the cities and for 'new towns within cities' to be built by development corporations. SPUR's chairman was Lionel Brett, later Lord Esher.

square *n.* **1** A landscaped or paved space of roughly rectangular shape enclosed, wholly or partly, by buildings. **2** An urban space enclosed, wholly or partly, by buildings (see also STREETS AND SQUARES). Leeds' civic architect described the city's millennium project in 2001 as being a plan with a layout consisting of 'a triangular square, a rectangular square and a square square.'

Adrian Forty (2002) notes that the English word square describes what in some other European languages is known variously as *place*, *platz* or *praça*. He asks: 'Why should the English have opted for this idiosyncratic term, which bears no relation to the common route of all the other European words? The mystery deepens on discovering that when the word was introduced in the 1660s (Bloomsbury Square was the first so designated), English already had at least seven other perfectly good words for describing enclosed urban spaces – close, court, yard, quadrangle, piazza, fields and walks – so why yet another one?' Forty adds: 'Squareness, or even four-sidedness, turns out not to be a feature common to all places called squares – there are three-sided squares, five-sided ones, squares with circular sides, and so on.' See also JOHN WOOD (THE ELDER).

squatter One who claims rights to land or a building to which they have no formal legal title (such as deeds of ownership or lease). In England the term dates from the second half of the nineteenth century. English common law has long recognised certain 'squatters' rights'. For example, if a squatter is able to construct a dwelling on common land in the space of a single day, to the extent of having a fire burning in the hearth by sundown, the house may remain and they are entitled to live there. Similarly, if a squatter occupies a vacant dwelling and is not asked to leave or notified of his trespass by the owner after seven years, they are entitled to consider the property their own.

squatter settlement An unofficial, unauthorised and often unserviced concentration of rudimentary self-built houses built on land to which the occupants have no legal title, usually on the edge of a town or city. Also known as a *barong-barong* (Philippines), *barraca* (Tripoli), *barriada* (Latin America), *bidonville* (North Africa), *bustee* (India), *callampas* (Chile), *favela* (Brazil), *jhuggi* (India), *kampong* (Indonesia) and SHANTY TOWN.

squeegee merchant A person who offers to wash (often with a squeegee wiping instrument) the windscreens of cars stopped at traffic lights in return for payment. They became common in the UK and the US in the 1990s. RUDOLPH GIULIANI in New York and home secretary Jack Straw in the UK (in 1997) branded them as undesirable in view of the fact that many drivers found them intimidating. As with beggars, they said, the streets should be kept clear of them. 'Does anybody even remember the squeegee men,' asks the architecture critic Paul Goldberger (2001), 'who once seemed the bane of city existence?'

St John's Wood, London The first English SUBURB, according to Mark Girouard (1985).

St Martin's Cottages, Liverpool A tenement block built by the local authority in 1869. It was the first council housing in the UK outside London.

St Petersburg Peter the Great first gave the city the Dutch name Sankt Pieter Burkh on its foundation in 1703 but soon renamed it St Petersburg. In 1924 it was renamed Petrograd and later, on the death of Lenin in 1924, Leningrad. It reverted to St Petersburg in 1991 on the dissolution of the Soviet Union, following a public vote (nearly half the population voted for Leningrad, and many still call it that), but the city is widely known as Peter (Glancey, 2003). See CHARLES CAMERON, BARTOLOMEO RASTRELLI and DOMENICO TREZZINI.

stabilisation Defined by the BURRA CHARTER as maintaining the FABRIC of a place in its existing state, and retarding or slowing deterioration.

stable community See HOMES FOR VOTES.

stad (Swedish) A city.

Stadt (German) A town or city.

Stadtbaukunst (German) The art of town building.

Städtebau (German) Town building; urban design. See JOSEPH STÜBBEN.

Stadtkern (German) A town or city centre. Also *Stadtmitte*.

Stadtkrone (German) City crown. A type of civic building of indeterminate use proposed by Bruno Taut and other German expressionist architects around 1919. Several were planned, but not built, under the Nazi regime in Germany in the 1930s and '40s. By their central location, height, bulk and scale, they were to act as the dominant visual focus of the city, in the same way that the cathedral had done in the middle ages.

Stadtplanung (German) Urban planning.

Stadtraud (German) The outskirts.

Stadtraum (German) Urban space.

Stadtteil (German) A district.

Stadtzentrum (German) A town or city centre.

Stahlstadt A fictional, model steel-making city in the USA described by Jules Verne in *The Begum's Fortune* (1879). This City of Steel was zoned in concentric rings. Stahlstadt went into decline and was abandoned after its founder, Professor Schultze, was killed accidentally when he fired a huge gun at a neighbouring city. See also STEELTOWN.

staircase ownership See SHARED EQUITY.

stakeholder 1 A person or organisation with an interest in or concern for a particular place; one who affects or is affected by the processes of urban change. The term came into currency in urbanism in the 1980s, but became less widely used in the world of urban regeneration when the opposition Labour party announced its commitment to promoting a *stakeholder economy*. David Blackman (2001) notes: 'Tony Blair made stakeholding the centre of a keynote speech... in 1995, only to drop it quietly when his advisers realised the idea entitled giving rights to workers. Stakeholding's only mark on the Blair government's policy has been as a description of a new type of pension.' The association with party politics made it seem unwise to use the term in applying for funding from the Conservative government. The term came back into wide currency in urban regeneration following the election of a New Labour government in 1997. **2** A person or organisation with a financial or legal interest (owning property or running a business, for example) in a particular site or area. This second meaning is less often used in relation to urbanism and regeneration, but the existence of two meanings makes stakeholder a somewhat ambiguous term.

Stalin, Josef (1879–1953) Soviet dictator. See NEW MOSCOW and SILKINGRAD.

Stalin-Allee One of Europe's last large-scale beaux-arts boulevards (Hebbert, 2000), built in East Berlin in the 1950s, named after Josef Stalin.

Stalingrad See SILKINGRAD.

Stalinstadt (Eisenhüttenstadt) East Germany's first planned new town, built in the 1950s.

stalk To lavish with unwanted attention. Daskalakis, Waldheim and Young (2001) title their book of essays, images, design projects and critiques of one particular city as *Stalking Detroit*. Charles Waldheim and Marili Santos-Munné (2001), in their contribution, find one of the more compelling cultural images for Detroit's vast areas of vacant land in Andrey Tarkovsky's film *Stalker*. In the film's imagined post-industrial wilderness, Tarkovsky's protagonist, the Stalker, 'displays a post-urban intelligence capable of divining a trajectory across an otherwise inhospitable and foreboding landscape.'

stall riser The panels below a shopfront's window cill, also called an *undercill*. Insisting that shopfronts should have stall risers (rather than the window glass going down almost to the ground) is a common instruction in shopfront design guides.

Albert Stanley

Stanley, Albert (Lord Ashfield) As chairman of London Transport in the 1920s and '30s he played a major part in building the underground railway network. The crime writer Ruth Rendell (1991) records that Stanley was godfather to a child born in a Bakerloo line train and gave her a silver christening mug when she was baptized Thelma Ursula Beatrice Eleanor: TUBE. 'I hope people won't make a habit of this,' Lord Ashfield said, 'as I am a busy man.' See also FRANK PICK and CHARLES YERKES.

Stansted London's third airport, designed by NORMAN FOSTER. See ROSKILL COMMISSION.

Stapleton, Sir George See OUTRAGE.

StarCity The home of the Russian Space programme.

Starbucks and stadia The phrase is used as shorthand for the most simplistic view of the sort of economic activity that constitutes urban regeneration. The term became current in 2003. Some local authorities and development agencies are supposed to look no further than coffee shops as evidence of streetlife and big building projects as means of economic development. See also CAPPUCCINO CULTURE.

starchitect A star architect; one who is well known in the profession or more widely. See also SIGNATURE PROFESSION and TROPHY ARCHITECTURE.

starter home A very small house or flat, intended as the first step on the housing ladder for young people.

state of the art defence A defence in terms of European Union directives on environmental liability. It specifies that there is no liability in a case where emissions or activities were not considered harmful according to the state of scientific and technical knowledge at the time they took place, if the operator had taken due care in managing them.

state, the The institutions that govern society. See also LOCAL STATE and KARL MARX.

stated preference The answer given by people who are asked how much they would be willing to pay for some specified change (in the environment, for example). Finding out about stated preferences is one way by which economists assess the value of matters on which the market does not put a value, or which it does not fully value. The method has been used in assessing the value of protecting historic buildings. An alternative is to infer the value from *revealed preference*, indicated by actual behaviour. The term 'stated preference' can also be used in a wider sense. Thus the stated preference of most people that they would use public transport if it were convienient, available and reliable is, when such conditions exist, contradicted by the 'revealed preference' that they continue to use their cars.

statement building One whose image is intended to advertise its architect, developer, owner or occupier. Example: 'Skyscrapers are... so-called statement buildings that are self-referential and fulfil no communal purpose whatsoever' (the Prince of Wales in 2001).

statement of community involvement (England and Wales) Sets out the standards that a council intends to achieve in involving the public in preparing, altering and reviewing all LOCAL DEVELOPMENT DOCUMENTS and in development control decisions, and how it will achieve them.

states of mind Former New York mayor Ed Koch (in the *Observer* in 1999) described being a New Yorker as 'a state of mind'. He explained: 'If, after living there for six months, you find that you walk faster, talk faster and think faster, you are a New Yorker.' Ernest Hemingway

STATIONNEMENT

wrote something similar of Paris: 'If you are lucky enough to have lived in Paris as a young man, then wherever you go for the rest of your life, it stays with you, for Paris is a moveable feast.'

stationnement (French) Parking.

statue 1 A sculpture in the likeness of a person or persons. **2** An ICONIC building. Example: 'The terrorists destroyed "statues" which represented a way of life' (a conference leaflet from the Pratt school of architecture, New York, referring to the towers of the WORLD TRADE CENTER, 2002). The word comes from the Latin *statuere*, to set up.

statutory body An organisation set up under an Act of Parliament.

statutory lighting That which is provided by statutory authorities to make streets and public spaces safe and secure. Compare AMENITY LIGHTING.

statutory undertaker A provider of public utilities and services such as electricity, gas, water, and sewage disposal. A statutory undertaker does not need planning permission for certain types of development necessary to do their job.

staying put Growing old at home rather than in an institution. Also called *aging in place*.

steak and kidney (Australian rhyming slang) Sydney.

stealth planning Taking action in small increments so that change is barely noticeable. An example is significantly reducing the amount of car parking in an area by removing only a small number of spaces each year. Also known as INCREMENTALISM and SALAMI DECISION-TAKING.

stealth vehicle 1 One with a relatively low impact on the environment. **2** A vehicle fixed with photo-opaque number plates and/or radar detection equipment so as to speed with impunity.

stealthy space Described by Dear and Flusty (1998) as 'passively aggressive space concealed by intervening objects or grade changes'. Compare SLIPPERY SPACE.

steaming Moving quickly through an area as a team, robbing and sometimes assaulting people who happen to be there.

Steeltown 1 Pittsburgh, Pennsylvania (also known as 'Steeltown, USA'). **2** Hamilton, Ontario. **3** Magnitogorsk, the previously forbidden Soviet city in the Urals, built under Stalin as a centre of steel production and a model 'garden city'. Stephen Kotkin has described it in his 2001 book *Steeltown, USSR: Soviet society in the Gorbachev era*. **4** Any other steel-making (or former steel-making) town or city. **5** The grim fictional industrial town that is the setting for the radical play *The Cradle Will Rock*, written by the composer Marc Blitzstein (1905–64) in 1936 and produced by the young Orson Welles in the following year. The police tried to prevent the show from opening, prompting Welles to organise a protest march up Broadway. The story of that first production is the subject of Tim Robbins' 1999 film *Cradle Will Rock* [sic]. The play's subjects – of unionism and corruption – had been suggested to Blitzstein by BERTOLD BRECHT, to whom *The Cradle Will Rock* is dedicated. See also STAHLSTADT.

Clarence Stein

Stein, Clarence (1882–1975) Architect and planner. He was chairman of the New York State Housing and Regional Planning Commission from 1923 to 1926 and was a founder of the REGIONAL PLANNING ASSOCIATION in 1923. His designs, inspired by the GARDEN CITY movement, included RADBURN, New Jersey; GREENBELT, Maryland; GREENDALE, Wisconsin; and Greenhills, Ohio. Stein was awarded the Gold Medal of the American Institute of Architects.

Stein, Gertrude (1874–1946) Writer. See THERE IS NO THERE THERE.

stem (US) To beg. See VAGRANT.

stems and webs Forms of street layout used in some organic approaches to urban design. The disastrous design by Shadrac Woods for the new town of Toulouse-Le Mirail in France is an example (Kostof, 1991).

Stepford Wives A pejorative term for women who choose to live in physically controlled, model communities such as CELEBRATION and POUNDBURY, and are consequently judged to have violated natural instincts. The classic film *The Stepford Wives*, based on Ira Levin's 1972 novel, is set in a fictional suburban community that seems the ideal of the American dream: well-manicured, peaceful, prosperous and happy. It turns out that Stepford's men have had their wives turned into automatons with no purpose but to gratify their husbands. The term was also applied disparagingly to the supposedly ultra-loyal young female intake of Labour MPs at the 1997 UK general election (Quinion, 1998). See also SEAHAVEN.

step-in rights Ones that allow the funder of a development to complete it if the developer is unable to.

stepping down The height of a tall building decreasing in steps, so that the part nearest a lower neighbour is at a similar height to it.

Stevenage The first new town (in Hertfordshire) built under the New Towns Act 1946. It was begun in 1946.

Stevin, Simon (1548–1620) Dutch urban theorist and planner of port cities.

stew An obsolete term for an overcrowded SLUM or ROOKERY. The term comes from the old French for an artificially stocked fishpond – *estuier*, meaning to shut up (Ackroyd, 2000).

stewardship The careful management of the environment.

stick-on *n.* Meaningless detail on a building. Example: 'Architects must refuse to work for clients who have no interest in making a building that is relevant to its context (except perhaps for a few last-minute, neo-vernacular stick-ons)' (2002). See also GOB-ON.

stim A briefly existing point in time and space of intensity, interaction and interest: 'a flickering essentially fluid non-form' (Jarvis, 2000) that the Swedish architectural writer Lars Lerup sees as coming *After the City* (to quote the title of a book of his).

Stimmann, Hans Chief planner of Berlin in the 1980s. He insisted that the reconstruction of the city after the fall of the BERLIN WALL should be based on urban BLOCKS.

stitching Designing or carrying out small-scale development that draws together disconnected parts of the urban fabric. Also called *knitting*.

Stockbridge Village See SO GOOD THEY NAMED IT TWICE.

Stockley Park A BUSINESS PARK built to the west of London in the 1980s, noted for many of the buildings having been designed by well-known architects. Deyan Sudjic (1992) writes: 'There are service roads, but no streets and no pedestrians. A bus service does skirt the edges of the scheme, to bring in cleaners and the occasional secretary and canteen worker, but as much as possible the individual buildings are kept away from the roads. Rather they are focused on the landscaping, and hidden away from one another.'

Stockport See PROSPECT HILL.

STOLport An airport for *short take-off and landing* planes.

Stone, Clarence See REGIME THEORY.

Stonehouse A proposed new town designated in 1973 in Lanarkshire, Scotland. The project was cancelled in 1976 when the government changed the focus of its policy from new towns to inner cities. Personnel and resources were switched to the Glasgow Eastern Area Renewal (GEAR) project.

Stones of Venice, The A three-volume study by JOHN RUSKIN, published in 1851–3, setting the city's architecture in its social context. It is one of the most influential books on architecture ever written, inspiring people as diverse as WILLIAM MORRIS and Marcel Proust. Mary McCarthy's *The Stones of Florence* is named in homage.

stop notice Issued by a local authority to halt unauthorised development that is having an unacceptable impact.

Stoppard, Tom (b1937) Playwright. See ARCADIA and ATHENS OF THE NORTH.

storey/story (UK/US) A floor of a building. Some design codes or planning regulations specify a maximum number of storeys rather than a maximum height. This allows a developer to build high by providing more generous floor-to-ceiling heights. See also LÉON KRIER.

Stow, John (1525–1605) The author of *A Survey of London*, published in 1598 and 1603.

straight-space The space of a canyon street between skyscrapers. The term has been used by Ted Relph (1987).

strangeness The theologian Paul Tillich thought the essential value of the city was that it provided contact with things that were 'strange' and could otherwise be experienced only by travelling. Tillich wrote (in the 1950s, source unknown): 'Since the strange leads to questions and undermines familiar tradition, it serves to elevate reason to ultimate significance... There is no better proof of this fact than the attempts of all totalitarian authorities to keep the strange from their subjects... The big city is sliced into pieces, each of which is observed, purged, and equalised. The mystery of the strange and the critical rationality of men are both removed from the city.'

stranger danger The potential risk that strangers pose to children in public places. The catchy phrase is used in alerting children to the risk. The approach may be almost entirely counter-productive. Children understand the word 'stranger' to mean a strange-looking adult rather than an unfamiliar one. And in any case children are most at risk from *familiar* adults, and their nearest and dearest. The social policy researcher and transport campaigner Meyer Hillman notes that many more children are killed by strangers behind the wheels of motor vehicles than by strangers on foot. He concludes that danger should be removed from children rather than children from danger (Karpf, 2002).

strap-hanging Standing as a passenger on a bus or train. The reference is to the leather straps that used to be provided for the passengers to hang on to. Also *strap-hanger*.

strata See DENYS LASDUN.

strata title (Australia) See CONDOMINIUM.

strategic centre A town centre of strategic importance for shopping, employment, arts, culture, entertainment and other activities.

strategic gap A designation in a development plan of land which should not be developed, usually to prevent settlements merging into one another. As with GREEN WEDGES and RURAL BUFFERS, they are less formal than GREEN BELTS.

strategic referral A planning application of potential strategic importance referred to London's mayor.

strategic view The line of sight from a particular point to an important landmark or skyline.

strategolopolis The war city. The term was used by PATRICK GEDDES.

strategy A systematic plan of action. The word derives from the Greek *strategos*, meaning a general.

stratification The physical or metaphorical layering of a city's fabric. The architect GIANCARLO DE CARLO wrote: 'To design in a historic place one should read its architectural stratification and try to understand the significance of each layer before superimposing a new one' (quoted in MacCormac, 1991). See also PALIMPSEST.

Straw, Jack (b1946) Politician. See SQUEEGEE MERCHANT.

street 1 A public space used as a pedestrian or pedestrian and vehicle route (with pavements or shared surfaces) on to which buildings or public spaces open. Compare ROAD. **2** A public thoroughfare and the houses along it. **3** The surface of a thoroughfare as distinct from the pavement. Example: 'It was so quiet the children played in the street.' **4** The culture and way of life of people who spend much of their time hanging around on the streets. Example: 'In East Harlem you bring up each child for 14 years wondering all the time whether you will win them or the street will win them, but knowing that almost certainly the street will win them' (an East Harlem parent, 1970s). *On the street* means HOMELESS. *On the streets* means working as a prostitute. *The word on the street* is public opinion. *The Arab street* (for example) is public opinion in the Arab world (compare STREET ARAB). The American political activist Abbie Hoffman (1968) wrote: 'The street has always been an interesting symbol in middle-class American life. It was always the place to avoid. There is "violence in the streets", "bad people in the streets" and "danger in the streets", as honkie America moved from outside to inside. It is in the streets that we will make our struggle. The streets belong to the people!'

The Glasgow youth worker and church minister (and later convenor of Strathclyde Regional Council) Geoff Shaw was also thinking positively about the streets in the late 1960s. Ron Ferguson (1979) remembers: '[Geoff Shaw] was not interested in "keeping people off the streets". He wanted the streets of the Gorbals to be full of interesting life. His vision for the Gorbals youngsters was that of a "university of the streets", in which young people would learn new skills, excel in sport, become involved in community service, learn to analyse their own situation and solve their own problems, and to experience moments of "unconditional joy".' **5** A way of life, as in *civvy street* (civilian life), *Grub Street* (the world of London's literary hacks), easy street (the comfortable life). **6** The focus of danger, menace and excitement in the urban realm as in *street crime, streetwise, street language* and *walking the streets.*

The engineers Alan Baxter and Associates identify five functions of a street, as providing for a) Movement. b) A conduit for services and utilities. c) Access to buildings for people, light and air. d) Social life. e) Storage (parked cars, and the delivery and collection of goods). The planner David Lock writes: 'The street is the city. Its public buildings are an extension of the street. Everything else – the buildings that frame the street – can come and go to meet the needs of the moment. The wise builder, understanding this, will build a structure that can be adapted every time life changes' (quoted in Campbell and Cowan, 2002). The writer and philosopher TE Hulme (1911), described a street as 'a place for strolling and walking in' (see also BOLOGNA). The modernist architect Peter Moro favoured streets when other architects were designing estates of houses and flats in green spaces. His was a distinctly architectural view: 'The street gives you a proper progression of spaces from the public to the inner sanctum,' he explained (Melhuish, 2002). Spiro Kostof (1992) defines the traditional purposes of the street as 'traffic, the exchange of goods, and social exchange and communication'. He suggests that the first conscious street in history may have been one at Khirokitia in Cyprus, dating from the sixth millennium BC. The Old English word street derived from the Latin *via strata*, meaning a paved road. See also CHELM and FIELD OF WHEAT.

street agreement Sets out how the occupiers of buildings along a street will contribute to improving it.

street arab (also arab or city arab) 1 A child living on the streets. **2** Someone skilled at surviving and thriving in the streets of the city.

street boy, street girl One who spends much of their time hanging about on the streets.

Street Boys A novel by Lorenzo Carcaterra, published in 2002, set in Naples in 1943. The only people left in the shattered, bombed-out city are abandoned children. With the German army advancing with the intention of destroying Naples, the armed children are determined to resist and save it, or die trying.

street canyon A street lined with buildings that are tall relative to its width.

street champion A person who takes a leading role in improving the quality of a street in relation to such matters as lighting, litter, paving, crime and anti-social behaviour. Compare DESIGN CHAMPION and TOWN CHAMPION.

street excellence model A method of promoting coordinated action to improve the public realm. It was developed by the URBAN DESIGN ALLIANCE from the *business excellence model* (a business management system) in 2000.

street furniture Structures adjacent to the highway, such as bus shelters, litter bins, seating, lighting and signs. Well designed, integrated and carefully sited, they can contribute to the amenity and attractiveness of a street. Too often the opposite is the case. Mostly there is just too much of the stuff cluttering up the place.

street game One played by children in the street, passed on from each generation of children to the next. In 1999 one housing cooperative in Glasgow found that the children seemed no longer to know the street games that had been the common culture of Glaswegians for generations. The co-op provided the props and a rota of local women who took it in turn to play with the children, teaching them the games.

street grid ANDRES DUANY advocates a system of zoning based not on use, but on the quality and PEDESTRIAN-FRIENDLINESS of street frontage. 'Develop your street grid with a rhythm of "A" streets and "B" streets,' he advises. 'Designate those streets like your Walnut Street as "A" streets, where every building on these blocks must be high-grade, pedestrian-oriented and reinforce continuity: no parking lots, no curb cuts. Then assign all your anti-pedestrian frontages to your "B" streets, your service streets. There is absolutely nothing worse for a city than to make every street excellent.' Duany concludes: 'If you try to make every street excellent, every street will be mediocre.'

street in the air LE CORBUSIER used the term to refer to a skyscraper, and particularly its lift shaft.

street life Activities that take place on or beside streets. Ken Worpole (1992) has written: 'Street life is essentially about short journeys. The more interesting the activities in the street the longer the journey will take and the less it will become "traffic movement", as the planners might call it.'

street of asses (*le chemin des anes*) A street that is not straight, according to the definition of LE CORBUSIER, as opposed to *le chemin des hommes*, a straight street. Reyner Banham (1960) observed that Le Corbusier was apparently 'under the impression that to travel in straight lines is to reveal the ability to reason and a sense of purpose peculiar to *homo sapiens*', despite the fact that, given a reasonably flat surface, a donkey would do the same.

Street of Ink Fleet Street, London in the years before the 1980s when it was the centre of the newspaper industry.

Street People An art project by the Detroit artist Tyree Guyton, consisting of hundreds of discarded shoes scattered in the street, with the intention that they would be run over by cars and battered by the elements. This was, Guyton felt, a poignant analogy to the plight of homeless people. Guyton's many large-scale installations of selected items of rubbish displayed in his neighbourhood in the 1980s and '90s inspired heated controversy about whether they were worthwhile art-specific artworks or unwelcome garbage (Arens, 2001).

street person A homeless person who lives and perhaps sleeps on the streets. See VAGRANT.

street pharmacist (US) A drug dealer.

street reclaiming Reusing the space saved through reduced car use to enhance the social, cultural and economic life of a neighbourhood (Engwicht, 2003).

street repair 1 Remedying deficiencies in the form of the buildings whose activities give life to a street and whose structure creates a sense of enclosure (by, for example, filling gaps in an otherwise continuous frontage). **2** Mending holes in the roadway.

street warden A uniformed person patrolling a neighbourhood or a town or village centre, tackling matters such as litter, graffiti, dog fouling and ANTI-SOCIAL BEHAVIOUR. See also NEIGHBOURHOOD WARDEN.

Street, Dancing in the See DANCING IN THE STREET.

Street, The CORONATION STREET.

streetage (US) A toll for street facilities.

streetcar (US) The UK equivalent is *tram*.

streetcar suburb (US) **1** A suburb served by a streetcar (tram). **2** A suburb made attractive to new residents by the developer providing or subsidising public transport.

streetdoor One that opens on to the street.

streeted Having streets.

streetholder A person with an interest in or concern for a particular street; one of a street's STAKEHOLDERS.

street-keeper One who plays a part in maintaining or improving a street and the streetscape.

street-level bureaucrat (US) An official who has direct contact with the public, such as a police officer or neighbourhood housing manager.

street-making Creating streets with continuous urban form and pedestrian routes.

streets and squares A generic term for the non-green, urban PUBLIC REALM.

streets in the air (also streets in the sky) See ALISON AND PETER SMITHSON.

streetscape 1 The appearance of a street. The Department of Transport, Local Government and the Regions and CABE (2001) defined streetscape as 'the hard and soft landscape' of a place. **2** A street and all the elements associated with it. Example: 'When things [for a cyclist] get really bad, there is an escape route: get off, shelter behind bits of streetscape and kerbs' (Eley, 2001).

streetscene The roadways, pavements, street furniture, signage and other elements that together comprise the street environment.

streets-for-people Areas subject to measures aimed at improving the street environment by increasing neighbourliness, improving public transport and reducing poverty.

street-smart (US) STREETWISE.

streetspace Public space on and around streets.

streetspace audit A systematic assessment of the streetspace and how it could be improved.

street-talking Professionals engaging people in conversation in the street as a way of making contact with people who would be unlikely to come to formal consultative events in a regeneration project (Rook, 2002).

streetwalker A prostitute who solicits in the street. An anonymous writer in London in 1758 noted that there was a 'gradation of whores in the metropolis: women of fashion who intrigue, demi-reps, good-natured girls, kept mistresses, ladies of pleasure, whores, park-walkers, street-walkers, bunters, bulk-mongers' (quoted in O'Connell, 2003). See also ON THE STREETS, TRAMP and UNORTHODOX ENTREPRENEUR.

streetward Facing the street.

streetway (US) The roadway.

streetwise *adj.* Familiar with the ways and culture of people who spend much of their time hanging around on the streets; capable of surviving in difficult, urban conditions.

streetwork Urban fieldwork. The term was coined by the environmental educationalist Anthony Fyson in 1972 and was in currency during that decade. See also URBAN STUDIES CENTRE.

streety Characteristic of streets.

stretch *v.* To extend the facade of a building in a similar style, often debasing that style in the process. See FACADISM.

stretcher A brick placed lengthwise in a wall. Compare HEADER.

stretcher bond An arrangement in which all the bricks in a wall are placed lengthwise.

striking See POLITE.

strip (US) A shopping and commercial street, usually following an important route.

strip development (US) Commercial buildings lining a highway, usually with undeveloped land behind.

strip mall (US) The UK equivalent is SHOPPING PARADE.

stripped classicism A style of neo-classical architecture without fine detail. It was popular in the 1920s and '30s, not only by the Nazi and fascist regimes. See CLASSICAL, NAZI ARCHITECTURE and JOHN SOANE.

stroke city A colloquial name for Derry/Londonderry in Northern Ireland (or, depending on your politics, the north of Ireland). The city, originally Doire and anglicised to Derry, was renamed Londonderry by its London-financed settlers. Irish nationalists call it Derry, while unionists call it Londonderry. Those not wanting to display a political affiliation call it Derry/Londonderry, or drop the two contentious parts and call it after its non-partisan oblique stroke.

strongpoint of sale A commercial area fortified against wrongdoers (Dear and Flusty, 1998).

structure Adrian Forty (2000a) identifies three uses of the term in relation to architecture: **1** Any building, in its entirety. **2** The system of support of a building (as distinct from other elements such as decoration, cladding or services). **3** A schema through which a drawn project, building, group of buildings, entire city or region becomes intelligible. Forty comments that definition 2 is really no more than a particular case of definition 3, and he illuminates brilliantly what is going on. '"Structure" is a *metaphor* which, while it may have started in building, only returned to architecture after much foreign travel. Furthermore, "structure" is not one, but *two* metaphors, each borrowed from a different field: first from natural history, which gave it its nineteenth-century meaning; and second, from linguistics, which provided its twentieth-century meanings. Whereas in other fields – ethnography for example – when the new linguistic sense of structure was introduced, there was a vigorous campaign to cleanse the other biological metaphor from the discipline, in architecture this never happened; what has been remarkable in architecture has been the prolonged coexistence within a single word of two essentially hostile metaphors. No doubt this has much to do with the original, first sense of "structure", which has permitted architects to claim a privilege in matters of "structure"'. Forty comments: 'Were the third, linguistic sense of "structure" to be upheld to the exclusion of the others, this right would vanish, for an architect could no more claim to "make" structure than might an individual by speaking a language.'

structure model A description of the development process in terms of the relationship between economic factors. Compare EQUILIBRIUM MODEL.

structure plan The strategic element of what, with the associated local plans, constituted the development plan for an area. A structure plan set out broad land-use policies by means of a written statement and a diagram (not a map). It did not specify what use was appropriate for a specific site. A structure plan was based on projections of future need and demand, particularly for housing, employment and shopping, and described the requirement for transport, schools and services. Its strategic framework guided policies in local plans. Where there was no county council, part 1 of the unitary development plans dealt with similar issues. A local plan was required to conform to the relevant structure plan. The green paper *Planning: delivering a fundamental change*, published in 2001, announced the government's intention to abolish structure plans.

structured planned urban development (SPUD) In the 1990s the Urban Villages Group proposed SPUD as a designation for sites suitable for URBAN VILLAGES.

Struth, Thomas (b1954) A Dusseldorf-based photographer known for his urban landscapes.

Strutt, Jedediah (1726–1797) Industrialist. After building the first water-powered cotton-spinning mill at CROMFORD in Derbyshire in 1771 as a partner of Richard Arkwright, Strutt built his own first mill a few miles away in 1776 at BELPER, which he developed as an industrial town.

Stübben, Joseph Town planner. His popular manual *Städtebau* (Town Building) was published in 1890.

stucco A hard plaster used particularly on the exterior of buildings.

studio apartment/studio flat (US/UK) Living accommodation without a separate bedroom; a bedsitter/bedsit. Estate agents prefer the terms to the alternative *bedsit*.

Styal A company village in Cheshire built by the textile manufacturer Samuel Gregg after 1783 to house workers at Quarry Bank Mill.

style A distinctive way of designing. The nineteenth century was dominated by the 'war of the styles' between advocates of *gothic* and *classical* as the 'appropriate' style for new buildings. The architect William Lethaby dismissed the empty debates about style. 'Notwithstanding all the names,' he wrote, 'there are only two modern styles of architecture: one in which the chimneys smoke, and the others where they do not' (quoted in Ward, 1991).

style police 1 A pejorative term for anyone who uses their position of authority to insist on specifying a development's architectural style. **2** Taste-makers and fashion gurus in the (architectural) past.

subdivision 1 The process of dividing unbuilt land into building plots by laying out blocks, streets and areas for public space. **2** A product of this.

subdivision control (US) The division of a piece of land into two or more parts, in order to subject it to controls which enable local government to impose conditions relating to the form of its physical development (usually for housing). As Cullingworth (1997) notes, subdivision controls must comply with the zoning ordinance and can not be used to amend it.

sublimation See GORDON CULLEN.

submerged tenth The term used by CHARLES BOOTH in IN DARKEST ENGLAND AND THE WAY OUT for what he saw as an urban UNDERCLASS.

subscraper An extensive building wholly or partly buried underground. In some cases the roof might be planted or made use of in some other way. The Malasian architect KEN YEANG has used the term to describe some of his buildings. The most notable example in the UK is the British Library beside St Pancras station in London. Compare GROUNDSCRAPER and SKYSCRAPER.

subsidiarity The principle of taking decisions at the lowest level possible, never taking a decision at a higher level when it could be taken more locally. The term was introduced to the UK from the EU.

substantive planning theory Concerns the nature of towns, cities and the environment rather than the process of planning itself, in contrast to *procedural planning theory* (Taylor, 1998).

substitution 1 Taking a particular action in a regeneration project, instead of another that may be no less beneficial, in order to take advantage of available funding. **2** The movement of activity from one place to another. For example, the economic activity promoted by urban regeneration in one place may be at the cost of a loss of customers in another.

sub-tolerable (Scotland) Below the TOLERABLE standard.

subtopia A landscape degraded by badly designed suburban development and sprawl. The word, coined by Ian Nairn in the *Architectural Review* in 1955, combines *suburb* and *utopia*. Nairn described subtopia as 'the annihilation of the site, the steamrolling of all individuality of place to one uniform and mediocre pattern.' He warned: 'If what is called development is allowed to multiply at the present rate, then by the end of the century Great Britain will consist of isolated oases of preserved monuments in a desert of wire, concrete roads, cosy plots and bungalows.' Example: 'What is being built here, for all the fine words spluttered in the name of Thames Gateway, is low-grade subtopian housing: isolated, boring, and a nesting ground for future disaffected teenagers' (Glancey, 2003).

suburb 1 An area at the edge of a town or city; low-density urban development. The Greater London Authority (2001), for example, estimates that three in every five Londoners live in a suburb. **2** An irrelevant backwater. Example: 'The House of Commons has become an irrelevant suburb, miles away from the real action' (2003).

Peter Hall (1998) notes that 'the Romans always described the area around the city as the *suburbium*, which certainly did not mean what we mean by the term, but rather a comfortable day's journey for regular trading: 35 to 40 kilometres seems to have been the limit'. An early suburb might have been a slum where unpleasant or noxious activities could flourish beyond the reach of the city authorities. Later the suburb was where those who could afford it lived within easy access of both the city centre and the countryside. The growth of suburbs marked the separation of the home from the workplace. Improved transport can extend the distance from suburb to urban centre. In 1895, for example, Brighton, Hastings and Eastbourne on the south coast of England were described as 'isolated suburbs of London' (quoted in Morris, 1989). Today we are less surprised by such a close relationship to such distant places, and the towns would be more likely to be described as part of London's city region. An early expression of the case for suburban expansion was presented in AN APOLOGY FOR THE BUILDER, published in 1685. Clapham became an early suburb of London after a daily coach service to the City of London was established in 1690 (Girouard, 1985). RAYMOND UNWIN wrote in 1901 of the 'festering suburb' interposed between town and country (quoted in Miller, 1989). In the USA, SUBURBAN SPRAWL was encouraged in the years after the second world war by major highway building programmes, and by loan programmes offered by the Federal Housing Administration and the Veterans Administration (which favoured the development of single-family suburban homes rather than terraced houses, mixed-use buildings, or renovations). David Harvey (1989) sees suburbanisation as having been essential to the survival of capitalism. 'Though suburbanisation had a long history,' he writes, 'it marked post-war urbanisation to an extraordinary degree. It meant the mobilisation of effective demand through the total restructuring of space so as to make the consumption of the products of the auto, oil, rubber, and construction industries a necessity rather than a luxury.' Harvey argues that, for nearly a generation after 1945, suburbanisation was part of a package of moves (the global expansion of world trade, the reconstruction of the war-torn urban systems of Western Europe and Japan, and a more or less permanent arms race being the other key elements) to insulate capitalism against the threat of crises of underconsumption. 'It is now hard to imagine that postwar capitalism could have survived, or to imagine what it would have now been like, without suburbanisation and proliferating urban development.'

To some commentators, a suburb represents the absence of positive urban qualities. CIAM (1933) called suburbia 'a kind of scum, churning against the walls of the city' and 'one of the evils of the century'. The novelist J G Ballard has called suburbs 'the death of the soul'. Jim Kunstler (2000) writes: 'Suburbia, the anti-place,... is a dangerously provisional collective hallucination, nourished by a sado-masochistic idiot pop culture, which can fall apart at the slightest provocation. (We have a name for this collective hallucination, by the way: The American Dream, a sort of mega-lie stating that this sort of ghastly provisional collective hallucination is the ultimate state of being worth aspiring to).' Kunstler continues: 'The provisional order of the anti-place is continually being subverted by an array of logical human responses. Most are self-defense mechanisms of one sort or another. For instance, teen drug use as a social phenomenon exists because the ecology of the anti-place is so deeply unrewarding, corrosive and degrading that the spirit demands analgesia. Teen drug abuse is really self-medication gone awry. Likewise, teen violence is a logical response to the deep sense of purposelessness generated by the American Dream. Just as young adults begin to acquire some inkling of their physical and mental power as human beings, and lacking any notion as to how these might be used to construct a purposeful life, the kids squander their poorly understood personal power in a single reckless act intended to destroy the legitimacy of their everyday environment and everything that it represents.' ANDRES DUANY describes suburban places as 'a lesser or permanently incomplete version of urbanism'.

COLIN WARD (1977) explains that a suburb is 'the child-rearing sector of the city: its nursery. But it is precisely this aspect of the suburb which makes it seem an intolerable place for those who are neither nurses or nurslings.' Ward writes: 'To the adolescent or the young man or woman who is not involved in the family nest, the suburb is a place of tedium and monotony where nothing ever happens'. Cyril Connolly agreed. He wrote in *The Unquiet Grave*, published in 1945, that 'slums may well be breeding-grounds of crime, but middle-class suburbs are incubators of apathy and delirium'. Graham McInnes (1965) described a suburb of Melbourne, Australia, where he grew up. 'Each little red-brick terra-cotta roofed house, or more modest weatherboard tin-roofed house, has its own paling or wire fence and neat hedge, and its own little garden with a few standard roses, its own circumambient space and air and light, the absence of which in most European suburbs might seem to make them poor indeed. But these immense deserts of brick and terra-cotta, or wood and galvanised iron induce a sense of overpowering dullness, a stupefying sameness, a worthy, plodding, pedestrian, middle-class, low church conformity.' The novelist Jeanette Winterson (2001) writes: 'The suburbs may muffle the pain of urban living, but they neuter the pleasure too... Life worth living is in the city or the country... Fleeing to the suburbs is not an inevitable part of growing up, anymore than is buying your clothes at Marks and Spencer'.

LEWIS MUMFORD (1961) wrote of the development of the suburb in the first half of the twentieth century: 'In the mass movement into suburban areas a new kind of community was produced, which caricatured both the historic city and the archetypal suburban refuge: a multitude of uniform, unidentifiable houses, lined up inflexibly, at uniform distances, on uniform roads, in a treeless communal waste, inhabited by people of the same class, the same income, the same age group, witnessing the same television performances, eating the same tasteless prefabricated foods, from the same freezers, conforming in every outward and inward respect to a common mould, manufactured in the central metropolis. Thus the ultimate effect of the suburban escape in our time is, ironically, a low-grade uniform environment from which escape is impossible.' Mumford warned that what had happened to the suburban exodus in the United States now threatened, through the same mechanical instrumentalities, to take place, at an equally accelerating rate, everywhere else – unless the most vigorous counter-measures were taken. 'But before we confront this final caricature of the unfettered suburban life, lived according to nature, for the sake of health and child nurture, let us consider more closely the actual development of the suburban container. For we shall see that out of this break-up of the old urban forms, out of the chaotic freedom and spatial looseness of the suburban community, came the first substantial changes in urban structure, which matched, unconsciously, the changes that have been taking place in our whole conception of the cosmos. The open basket-work texture of the suburb bears little resemblance to the solid stone container of late neolithic culture. Though the suburb lacked many of the attributes of the ancient city, it has served as an experimental field for the development of a new type of open plan and a new distribution of urban functions.'

Alan Powers (2002) has written: 'The physical suburb and the ideological suburb are not the same thing. The *Urban Task Force Report* appeared to conflate the two, and add the converse, that when you put people in dense urban situations with plenty of pavement cafes, they will automatically lose their alienation and become citizens of an active democracy. Apart from a serious question about whether the present government would really welcome an active participatory democracy, the assumption is deterministic and manipulative to a dangerous degree. The suburb is in your head, and travels wherever you go' (see also A MOVEABLE FEAST).

Suburbs featured in a speech in 1993 in which prime minister John Major sought to reassure his party about the survival of British identity in the face of European integration. 'Fifty years on,' he promised, 'Britain will still be the country of long shadows on county cricket grounds, warm beer, invincible green suburbs, dog lovers, and – as George Orwell said – old maids bicycling to Holy Communion through the morning mist.' The poet Edwin Muir (1887–1959) wrote in 'Suburban Dream' of suburbs as places liberated by the absence ('in offices,/ Committee-rooms, laboratories, banks...') of their menfolk. Left to themselves, the women and children can be gently creative. 'The massed unanimous absence liberates/ The light keys of the piano and sets free/ Chopin and everlasting youth,/ Now with the masters gone.' It is, Muir writes, 'a child's dream of a grown-up world', disrupted only when, with a 'fanfare of motor horns', the men come noisily home.

The word suburb is recorded as early as 1380, when it referred to parts of a town or city outside, and beyond the protection of, the city walls. The word combines the Latin *urbanus*, derived from *urbs*, city, with the prefix *sub-*, meaning under or close to (Quinion, 1997). See also LOS ANGELES and VILLA.

suburbain (French) Suburban.

suburban 1 Pertaining to a suburb; characteristic of suburbs. The adjective dates from the early 1600s. The Urban Task Force wanted to know what sort of terms to use in trying to persuade the general population of the advantages of living in urban areas. Their researchers organised focus group workshops to find out. They reported (URBED *et al*, 1999) that the term suburban 'meant space, large houses, wide streets, peace, quiet and trees.' But 'to many suburbia was also boring, a place where parents lived, lacking in facilities and socially oppressive.' **2** Lacking the qualities of town or country. **3** Narrow, small-minded and smug, as in *suburban attitude*.

suburban city One that is dependent on the car. See also AUTOMOBILE CITY and MILTON KEYNES, and compare WALKING CITY.

suburban creep The relentless spread of suburban development across the countryside; SUBURBAN SPRAWL.

suburban downtown (US) A shopping and services centre at the periphery of a city.

suburban exploitation Residents of suburbs consuming services paid for by inner urban local authorities, not their own.

suburban retrofit Adding new uses to mainly single-use suburban areas.

suburban sprawl 1 Low-density, mainly housing development built as the outward expansion of an urban area. **2** Development that is not within comfortable walking distance of a shop.

ANDRES DUANY (2001) has set out what he sees as the physical attributes of suburban sprawl. a) Sprawl is disciplined only by isolated *pods*, which are dedicated to single uses such as *shopping centers*, *office parks*, and *residential clusters*. All of these are inaccessible from each other except by car. Housing is strictly segregated in large clusters containing units of similar cost, hindering socio-economic diversity. b) Sprawl is limited only by the range of the automobile, which easily forms catchment areas for retail often exceeding 50 miles. c) There is a high proportion of cul-de-sacs and looping streets within each pod. Through traffic is possible only by means of a few 'collector' streets which, consequently, become easily congested. d) Vehicular traffic controls the scale and form of space, with streets being wide and dedicated primarily to the automobile. Parking lots typically dominate the public space. e) Buildings are often highly articulated, rotated on their lots, and greatly set back from streets. They are unable to create spatial definition or sense of place. Civic buildings do not normally receive distinguished sites. f) Open space is often provided in the form of *buffers, pedestrian ways, berms*, and other ill-defined residual spaces.

Duany argues that the destructive process of sprawl continues because of its seductive simplicity, which derives from the fact that it consists of five basic components, each strictly segregated from the others. The components are: a) *Housing subdivisions*, also called *clusters* and *pods*. These places consist only of residences. They are sometimes called *villages*, *towns* and *neighborhoods* by their developers, which is misleading, since those terms denote places which are not exclusively residential and which provide an experiential richness not available in a housing tract. Subdivisions can be identified as such by their contrived names, which tend toward the romantic and often pay tribute to the natural or historic resource they have displaced. b) *Shopping centers*, also called *strip centers*, *shopping malls* and *big-box retail*. These are places exclusively for shopping. They come in every size, from the Quick Mart on the corner to the Mall of America, but they are all places to which one is unlikely to walk. The conventional shopping center can be easily distinguished from its traditional main-street counterpart by its lack of housing or offices, its single-storey height, and its parking lot between the building and the roadway. c) *Office parks* and *business parks*. These are places only for work, Duany explains. Derived from the modernist architectural vision of the building standing free in the park, the contemporary office park is usually made of boxes in parking lots. Still imagined as a pastoral workplace isolated in nature, it has kept its idealistic name and also its quality of isolation, but in practice it is more likely to be surrounded by highways than by countryside. d) *Civic institutions*. The fourth component of suburbia is public buildings: the town halls, churches, schools and other places where people gather for communication and culture. In traditional neighborhoods, these buildings often serve as neighborhood focal points, but in suburbia they take an altered form: large and infrequent, generally unadorned owing to limited funding, surrounded by parking, and located nowhere in particular. e) *Roadways*. The fifth component of sprawl, Duany writes, consists of the miles of pavement [paved road] that are necessary to connect the other four disassociated components. Since each piece of suburbia serves only one type of activity, and since daily life involves a wide variety of activities, the residents of suburbia spend an unprecedented amount of time and money moving from one place to the next.

The urban designer Anne Vernez-Moudon (2002) points to the role of regulation in continuing to create suburban sprawl in the USA. 'Take the suburban edge as it exists and has existed over the last 50 years. I think we all find problems with this kind of environment – little houses, subdivisions, multi-family apartments, retail, big box, small box, and so on. The fact is that this is the most highly regulated environment that has ever existed. We may all say we hate it, but our society has created this environment. Not only have we created it with an amazingly well-engineered, finely tuned system, but if we say we don't like it, we're still going to return to that system because we invented it. And we invented it only 50 years ago.'

In the USA sprawl has its advocates as well as its critics. They argue, for example, that the amount of land taken by sprawl is acceptable (and over-estimated by the critics), and that controlling sprawl raises the price of land and homes, which particularly limits the opportunities of people on relatively low incomes. Example: 'If Europeans want to drive Mini Coopers, fine. That isn't America. We subsidise big oil, big autos and big sprawl' (2002).

In 1937 Earle Draper, director of planning for the Tennessee Valley Authority, looked for the right term to describe the spread of suburban development. 'Perhaps diffusion is too kind a word... In bursting its bounds, the city actually sprawled and made the countryside ugly' (quoted on PlannersWeb, 2001). See also AN APOLOGY FOR THE BUILDER and SPREAD CITY.

suburban village The term was applied to Riverside, Illinois, the GARDEN SUBURB designed by FREDERICK LAW OLMSTED and CALVERT VAUX in 1869.

suburbanisation 1 The spread of relatively low density development at the urban fringe and into rural areas. See also EXTENDED SUBURBANISATION. **2** Moving out to the suburbs (in relation to a group of people or an industry, for example).

suburbanise To make suburban.

suburbanism The social characteristics of suburban residents. Sociologists argue about whether there are any such common characteristics.

suburbanite One who lives in a suburb.

suburbanity Suburban quality.

suburbia A generic term for SUBURBS, dating from the 1890s. See also SUBTOPIA.

subway 1 A pedestrian tunnel under a road. **2** (US) An underground railway. See also METRO.

success factor One of the characteristics of a place (or places in general) that tends to make it attractive to live in, work in, or visit.

SUDS SUSTAINABLE URBAN DRAINAGE SYSTEM.

sufficient density A density of development high enough to support specified facilities or uses. The phrase is sometimes used in place of *high density*, on the grounds that the latter is only relative, whereas *sufficient* can be more usefully descriptive.

Suicide City A fictional underground city near Paris where people live who have made a failed suicide attempt. Robert Louis Stevenson described it in *New Arabian Nights* (1882).

suitable for use The 'suitable for use' approach recognises that the risks presented by a given level of land contamination will vary according to what the land is used for. Consequently the amount of cleaning up required will depend on the final use.

suk, sukh, suq See SOUK.

SULEV (US) Super-ultra-low emission vehicle.

Louis Henry Sullivan

Sullivan, Louis Henry (1856–1924) An architect of the Chicago School and designer of some early pioneering SKYSCRAPERS. He coined the phrase FORM FOLLOWS FUNCTION and was the teacher of FRANK LLOYD WRIGHT.

Summer Holiday A poem by Robinson Jeffers (1887–1962). See URBAN DESTRUCTION.

Summer in the City A successful pop song released in July 1966 by the Lovin' Spoonful: 'hot town, summer in the city, girls walking by, looking so pretty...'. The urban, New York equivalent of the Beach Boys' California surf sound, 'Summer in the City' included the sound of car horns, traffic and a pneumatic road-drill. See also DANCING IN THE STREET and DOWNTOWN.

Summerlin A new settlement near Las Vegas, named after one of its joint developers (the Summa corporation) and one of Howard Hughes' grandmothers. 'When Summerlin is finally completed,' writes Mike Davis (2002), 'a population of more than 200,000 living in 26 income- and age-differentiated "villages" will be hermetically sealed in Las Vegas' own upscale version of Arizona's leaky Biosphere'.

SUN SUSTAINABLE URBAN NEIGHBOURHOOD.

Sunday towns VILLAS DO DOMINGO.

sunrise industry Serving a growing market, often using new technology.

sunset industry Serving a declining market, often using obsolete technology.

super high rise A building more than 150 metres high.

super profit A profit greater than was expected when the level of GAP FUNDING was calculated.

super-icon A building or structure of particular significance and distinctiveness; a LANDMARK. The increasing popularity of the word ICON, which now sometimes seems used to describe any building not specifically designed to be self-effacing, has made room for another term for buildings or structures of real significance. Super-icon was heard in 2003.

superblock 1 A large street block consisting of houses that face inwards on to a traffic-free green. Spiro Kostof (1991) traces the concept back to PORT SUNLIGHT in 1887. **2** A site composed of several contiguous URBAN BLOCKS; the area contained within one rectangle of a SUPERGRID.

supercity (US) A sprawling, car-based conurbation; a MEGALOPOLIS or MEGA-CITY. The term dates from the early 1920s, was current in the USA in the 1950s and '60s, and was revived in the 2000s. See also PEARL DELTA SUPERCITY.

supergrid A large-scale grid that organises the overall structure of a town. Milton Keynes' grid of kilometre squares is an example. Also known as a *maxigrid*. See also SUPERBLOCK.

supermarket A large retail self-service store, usually located in a town or city centre. Defined by the Scottish Office (1998) as a single-level, self-service store selling mainly food, with a trading floorspace of between about 500 and 2,500 square metres, often with its own car park. The UK retailing group Sainsbury's defined a supermarket in 2000 as having up to 15,000 product lines.

The term dates from the early 1920s. The first supermarket in the UK opened in Wimbledon, south London, in 1962. 'Store which brought avocado to the masses closes its door' announced the local paper when the site was redeveloped in 2001.

supermodernism Architecture that deliberately pays no regard to its historic surroundings. The term is credited to the critic Hans Iblings.

superstore A very large self-service retail store, often located out-of-town or at the edge of a town or city centre. Defined by the Scottish Office (1998) as a single-level, self-service store selling mainly food, or food and non-food goods, usually with at least 2,500 square metres trading floorspace with a dedicated car park at surface level. Defined by the retailing group Sainsbury's in 2000 as having around 25,000 product lines. The term dates from the first half of the 1940s.

superstore sprawl See SPRAWL-BUSTERS.

supplementary planning document (England and Wales) A piece of guidance supplementing the policies and proposals in DEVELOPMENT PLAN DOCUMENTS.

supplementary planning guidance (SPG) Additional advice provided by the local authority on a particular topic, 'elucidating and exemplifying' policies in a development plan. SPG included urban design frameworks, development briefs, design guides and village design statements. It had to be consistent with the plan (and cross-referenced to the relevant policy or proposal), prepared in consultation with the public, and formally approved by the council. SPG status gave guidance additional weight as a MATERIAL CONSIDERATION in the planning process. SPG is replaced by SUPPLEMENTARY PLANNING DOCUMENTS in the post-2004 planning system.

supported housing Where there is an element of personal care and supervision, for people who for one reason or another are unable to live wholly independently. Supported housing may or may not be specially designed or adapted.

surfurbia Beach cities. Reyner Banham (1973) used the term to describe one of the FOUR ECOLOGIES of LOS ANGELES.

surveillance Discouragement of wrong-doing by the presence of passers-by, CCTV cameras or the ability of people to see out of windows. See also DEFENSIBLE SPACE and EYES ON THE STREET.

survey before plan The approach to planning adopted by IDELFONSO CERDÁ and later by PATRICK GEDDES.

Survey of London, A (1525–1605) Written by John Stow and published in 1598 and 1603.

Survey of London, The Started by the architect CR Ashbee (1863–1942) and others at the end of the nineteenth century. Andrew Saint notes that Ashbee began the *Survey* not as a dry art-historical record, but to draw attention to old buildings of beauty which, by their very survival, could remind Londoners of the saner social order which once had been.

survey, analysis, plan PATRICK GEDDES' dictum, which became an orthodox planning approach.

surveyor The Institution of Surveyors was founded in 1868. Today the Royal Institution of Chartered Surveyors represents a wide range of practitioners concerned with land, property, construction and associated environmental issues.

Suschitzky, Wolfgang (b1912) Photographer and film-maker. He left Austria in 1933 and later settled in London. Among his photographs from the 1930s to the 1950s were many of life in Glasgow, Edinburgh and Aberdeen. His films include *Children of the City* (1944), filmed mainly in Dundee, and GET CARTER (1971).

sustainable 1 Likely to have a positive impact on the social, economic and environmental conditions of people in the future and/or in other places. The UK government defined sustainable development in 2003 as 'social progress which recognises the needs of everyone, effective protection of the environment, prudent use of natural resources, and the maintenance of high and stable levels of economic growth and employment' (McNulty, 2003).

The language of urbanism is awash with over-used words that stand for ill-defined concepts. Never, though, has a word been so quickly adopted, so widely used and so ill-defined as sustainability. 'If sustainability is the new religion,' writes Tim Mars (1998), 'then planners are its priests and the compact city the new Jerusalem.' Heather Cruickshank of Cambridge University has found around 500 definitions of sustainability (Guthrie, 2002), though few of these are likely to be usefully precise. Often the word is used as a placebo, free of any real content but intended to give a sense of comfort to the writer or the reader. People completing funding applications or writing brochures about regeneration initiatives have sometimes said that they use the words *sustainable* or *sustainability* as they know they are terms their target audiences will expect to read. In cases where the word is intended to carry some specific meaning, the alternatives are many. In addition to the definition given above, *sustainable* is also used to mean one or more of the following (which are not mutually exclusive): **2** Minimising the use of non-renewable resources. **3** Considerate of the environment's capacity. Bill Dunster, architect of BEDZED, defines 'true sustainable development' as that which, if practiced generally, would require the resources of the equivalent of one planet (compared to the equivalent of three planets that the present use of resources requires). **4** Considerate of the needs of future generations. In 1966 George Ewart Evans recalled the countryside adage 'a farmer should live as though he were going to die tomorrow, but he should farm as though he was going to live forever'(Reynolds, 2003). **5** Considerate of the needs of people in other places who may suffer the impact of development or who may be deprived of resources. **6** Concerned with the general quality of life. **7** Concerned with social equity and justice. **8** Respectful of social, economic, biological and cultural diversity. **9** Considerate of the rights and responsibilities of citizens. **10** Achieved through collaborative and participatory democratic processes. **11** Responsive to social, economic and environmental interdependence, locally and globally. **12** Finding an acceptable balance between the environmental, economic and social factors involved. (This, used in the City of London's 2001 study *Tall Buildings and Sustainability*, must rank as one of the least taxing tests of sustainability). **13** Likely to have a positive impact on the social, economic and environmental and cultural conditions of people in the future and/or in other places. The explicit cultural aspect is a relatively newcomer to meanings of 'sustainable'. The National Trust in 2003 defined 'four broad components' of sustainability: 1) Environmental well-being. 2) Cultural well-being. 3) Economic well-being. 4) Social well-being.

Sustainability was one of the most frequently used words in discussions of urbanism in the 1980s and '90s. The most common definition is that set out in the World Commission on Environment and Development's report, *Our Common Future* (1987), known as the Brundtland Report. Sustainable development, the report says, 'meets the needs of the present without compromising the ability of future generations to meet their own needs'. The comment attributed (apocryphally) to the native American Chief SEATTLE is also often quoted: 'We do not inherit the world from our ancestors: we borrow it from our children.' The Scottish Executive has defined sustainable development as 'development which avoids harming the long-term needs of people, the economy or the environment'; the Local Government Association (2000) as 'acknowledging that economic, social and environmental resources are finite and fragile'. In the Planning and Compulsory Purchase Bill 2002 the UK government identified the statutory purpose of the planning system as being sustainable development, defining it as 'a high and stable level of economic growth and employment, social progress, effective protection of the environment and prudent use of resources'. When a House of Commons select committee pressed at the beginning of 2003 for a more precise definition, the government refused. Junior planning minister Tony McNulty insisted, evocatively, that defining sustainable development more precisely would 'run the risk of opening up a Pandora's box with lots of Trojan horses jumping out of it'. Lord Rooker, the housing and planning minister, took the same line. 'We don't feel there is a need for a definition,' he said. 'We think people know what you mean by sustainable development. If we start trying to define it we'll be here till the cows come home' (Donati, 2003).

Development that is more sustainable is built in forms that produce less pollution and use less energy in both construction and use; minimise the need for travel, particularly by car; and make the most of the potential for public transport. The American Planning Association (2000) notes that global indications of unsustainability include global warming, soil degradation, deforestation, species extinction, declining fisheries and economic inequity. US indications of community unsustainability include suburban sprawl, segregation and unequal opportunity, loss of agricultural land and open space, depletion and degradation of water resources, loss of wetlands, traffic congestion and air pollution, and disproportionate exposure to environmental hazards. The APA identifies major contributors to unsustainability as over-consumption, population growth, dependence on non-renewable resources, pollution, environmentally and socially destructive development patterns, inequities in resource distribution, and limited public participation. In 2002 the authors of the draft *South East of England Regional Sustainability Checklist for Developments* wrote of 'planning "sustainability" into a development plan' and of 'planners specify[ing] "sustainability" in supplementary planning guidance'. Their 90-page checklist set out the many elements that would determine whether a development could be considered sustainable or not.

Sustainability is not an absolute: it is only possible to say that one development seems more likely to be more sustainable than another. Nor is it an exact science. We can predict with complete accuracy neither the impact of a development nor the ability of future generations to remediate it. Some critics of the concept of sustainability argue that advances in technology are likely to solve problems that at present seem insuperable. They point out that at the end of the nineteenth century there were warnings that horse-drawn travel was unsustainable due to the enormous growth in the amount of equine excrement being produced. As it happened, that did not turn out to be a problem for future generations. Of course the fact that the future can not be predicted accurately is no reason not to plan for it.

A number of the principles declared at the Rio Earth Summit concerned economic and social issues. For example, the summit urged that 'all people shall cooperate in the essential task of eradicating poverty as an indispensable requirement for sustainable development'. But many of the principles concern environmental issues, and it is clear that these are seen as criteria that must be achieved, not just as a set of factors to be weighed in the balance against various social and economic factors. Peter Jackson (2000) notes that 'we appear to have shied away from engaging in a constructive debate about how to reconcile the various aspects of sustainable development and the relative priority that should be given to each of them. Rather, we have taken the easy route and assumed that sustainable development can somehow encompass the objectives of a wide range of different interests'. By assuming that we can find a balance between this range of objectives, without clarifying the priorities, Jackson argues, we have been able to avoid a number of difficult choices implicit in the declaration. 'This has had the benefit of enabling a wide range of interests to "sign up" to sustainability, but it has also led to confusion and lack of clarity about what it means in practice. This is very much in evidence when we think about road and air transport, which are major contributory factors in air pollution, climate change, resource depletion and the use of non-renewable energy. Increasingly, measures to manage the impact of road and air transport on the environment are met with hostility, on the grounds that they may harm the economy or may affect individual choice. Does potential harm to the economy mean that measures to reduce the impact of traffic on the environment are not "sustainable"?'.

Gillen (2000) suggests that 'there is an argument that sustainable development is being used as a mediating term to bridge the gulf between developers and environmentalists and it is therefore deliberately vague and has an inherently contradictory tone... Today, many commentators, academic and professional, are of the opinion that the term... is so extensively used and imprecisely applied that it has been devalued to a token term. Some environmentalists openly despise the concept of sustainable development'.

The World Conservation Union defined sustainable development in 1991 as 'improving the quality of life while living within the carrying capacity of supporting ecosystems'. In 2000 the UK House of Commons Select Committee on Environment, Transport and Regional Affairs painted a picture of what it saw as unsustainable development. 'The patterns of development characteristic of most of the last century can not continue,' the committee wrote. 'They have been socially unstable, concentrating the poor in inner city areas; environmentally damaging, destroying the countryside and creating a car-dependent society; economically harmful, since they have undermined our core urban areas which remain the essential centres of the English economy; and wasteful because schools, shops, even houses, lie waste in urban areas while new infrastructure is provided at great expense outside.' The architect Richard (Lord) Rogers wrote of sustainability in his book *Cities for a Small Planet* (drawing on the ideas of Amory Lovins) in 2000: 'The core of this concept is the redefining of wealth to include natural capital: clean air, fresh water, an effective ozone layer, a clean sea, fertile land and the abundant diversity of species.'

These ideas were not new in the second half of the twentieth century. The philosopher John Locke (1632–1704) argues in his *Second Treatise of Government*, published in 1690, that people have a duty to improve the earth and a right to private property, as long as they do not prejudice other people's ability to use land. We have a responsibility to ensure that there is 'still enough and as good left,' he writes. 'For he that leaves as much as another can make use of does as good as take nothing at all. Nobody could think himself injured by the drinking of another man, though he took a good draught, who had a whole river of the same water left him to quench his thirst' (Reynolds, 2003). In 1864 George Perkins Marsh, the US ambassador to Italy, warned in his book *Man and Nature* of the danger of humans overturning 'the harmonies of nature' (Worster, 2001). LEWIS MUMFORD recalled in 1955 that 'the great George Perkins Marsh, in the final revised edition of *The Earth and Man,* published in 1907 after his death, inserted a footnote on the effect of cities in modifying the climate'. Mumford noted that research had been carried out to investigate this, but that 'there has been no serious investigation on the effect of uncontrolled urban growth on the water supply, or on the general ecological balance' (Hughes, 1971). The capacity of the environment to sustain human activity was an essential element of PATRICK GEDDES' approach. Geddes warned in *Cities in Evolution* (1905) that 'such swift multiplication of the quantity of life, with corresponding swift exhaustion of the material resources on which life depends, has been too much.' He called for environmental protection and social organisation to be integrated in urban design, ending the 'waste and dissipation of nature and community'. Noting the corrosive effects of industrialisation on geographical community, Geddes (1915) observed that such 'swift multiplication of the quantity of life, with corresponding swift exhaustion of the material resources on which life depends' has been too much.' The novelist Ford Madox Ford wrote in 1909: 'We are the tyrants of the men to come; where we build roads, their feet must tread; the traditions we set up, if they are evil, our children will find it hard to fight against; if for want of vigilance we let beautiful places be defiled, it is they who will find it a hopeless task to restore them' (Ford, 1909). The Russian poet Anna Akhmatova seemed to warn of the possible consequences of human intervention in the natural world in a short, untitled poem of the late 1950s. 'Distance collapsed in rubble and time shook/ and accelerated and diabolically stamped on the brows/ of great mountains and reversed the river's flow./ The seed lay poisoned in the earth,/ the sap flowed poisoned in the stem' (translation by Richard McCane). Norbert Wiener wrote in *The Human Use of Human Beings,* published in 1954: 'The more we get out of the world the less we leave, and in the long run we shall have to pay out debts at a time that may be very inconvenient for our own survival.' Marya Mannes wrote in *More in Anger,* published in 1958: 'The earth we abuse and the living things we kill will, in the end, take their revenge; for in exploiting their presence we are diminishing our future.' Helen Hoover declared in 'The Waiting Hills' (published in 1963 in *The Long-Shadowed Forest*): '[Man] thinks of himself as a creator instead of a user, and this delusion is robbing him, not only of his natural heritage, but perhaps of its future'. In the UK the Ecology Party (later the Green Party) was formed in 1973. These concerns were central to the conservation movement in the 1960s and '70s. Conservationists campaigned against the unthinking exploitation of the world's resources, and in many cases they found it necessary to oppose development. This made any government favouring development (as almost all governments do) suspicious of conservation. The term 'sustainable development' avoided that problem. The assumption was in favour of development, and the issues became what its impact would be. The later adoption of the term *economic, environmental and social sustainability* allowed governments to argue that environmental concerns must be balanced with the other two types. 'Sustainable development' was being discussed in academic circles and in writings of some radical environmentalists in the 1970s. Barbara Ward and René Dubos, though, wrote comprehensively about issues of sustainable development in their book *Only One Earth: the care and maintenance of a small planet,* published in 1972, without using the term. Nor did Ronald Higgins use it in his book *The Seventh Enemy: the human factor in the global crisis,* published in 1978. The term was formally introduced in the World Conservation Strategy (1980), popularised by the Brundtland Report (1987) and diplomatically embraced at the Earth Summit 1992 (Mazmanian and Kraft, 1999). In 2002 the broadcaster Jonathan Dimbleby, vice-president of the Campaign for the Protection of Rural England (as it then was), declared himself committed to sustainable development, but thought it was 'the most boring phrase in the whole world... Two long, Latinate words'. He tried to come up with something for his own use that would bore him less, he explained, 'but there's no substitute'. Apparently *SusDev* and *SD* were options he considered (Taylor, 2002) Sooner or later, no doubt, the phrase will go out of fashion. By 2002 the Scottish Executive seemed to have replaced the terms social, economic and environmental sustainability by social justice, economic competitiveness and environmental quality. Economic, environmental and social sustainability is sometimes referred to as COMMUNITY WELL-BEING, ECONOMIC VITALITY and ENVIRONMENTAL INTEGRITY. See also AALBORG CHARTER and LOCAL AGENDA 21.

sustainable architecture Defined by environmental campaigner Jonathan Porritt (2000) as 'architecture which meets human needs and respects the diversity of human culture, as well as the world's natural resources'.

Sustainable Communities Programme A partnership of EnCams, Forward Scotland and the Sustainable

Northern Ireland Programme, investigating ways of involving people in local action on sustainable development.

sustainable community The term originated in the USA in the 1990s, being defined as widely – and usually as vaguely – as its components SUSTAINABLE and COMMUNITY. The 1994 the annual conference in Chicago of the International City/County Management Association included a session entitled 'Planning Sustainable Communities'. The term has been defined by US NEW URBANISTS as 'a viable human environment within a protected ecology'.

The UK government adopted the term in 2003 as the focus for its housebuilding programmes, and in 2004 the Office of the Deputy Prime Minister (ODPM) adopted the slogan 'building sustainable communities'. The Egan Review on Skills for Sustainable Communities, which reported to the ODPM in 2004, offers a definition of the term. 'Sustainable communities,' the review states, 'meet the diverse needs of existing and future residents, their children and other users, contribute to a high quality of life and provide opportunity and choice. They achieve this in ways that make effective use of natural resources, enhance the environment, promote social cohesion and inclusion, and strengthen economic prosperity.'

The Egan Review identifies the 'components' of a sustainable community as: 'Governance (effective and inclusive participation, representation and leadership); social and cultural (vibrant, harmonious and inclusive communities); housing and the built environment (a quality built and natural environment); economy (a flourishing and diverse local economy); environmental (providing places for people to live in an environmentally friendly way); and services (a full range of appropriate, accessible, public, private community and voluntary services)'.

sustainable human development A conception of substainable development that emphasises issues such as gender equality, participation in decision-making, and access to education and health.

sustainable mobility service A system providing access to and information on a range of transport options, so that people can choose which to use.

sustainable regeneration The Sustainable Development Commission described it in 2002 as an approach 'which not only considers social and economic inequalities within society, but also environmental inequalities and the link between the quality of the local environment and poverty'.

sustainable residential quality Defined by the Greater London Authority (2001) as 'the design-led approach and urban design principles by which dwellings can be built at higher density, while maintaining urban quality and fostering sustainable development'.

sustainable rural development The Countryside Agency (2000) has illuminated the debate in suggesting what planning for sustainable rural development could mean. 'Rural areas need the right sort of development as much as they need protection. Both are essential but plans too often see them as stark alternatives: do we have new houses, or do we protect the landscape? We can, and should, have both... The challenge for planners is to use the government's definition of sustainable development to ensure that development and protection can proceed together. Policies should promote development which responds to social and economic needs, makes wise use of non-renewable resources and protects environmental quality. This means that plans and development control decisions consider not just the traditional location of development, but the nature of that development, too. So, for example, planners should consider whether a new business in a converted farm building meets sustainable development criteria as a whole, such as the design of the buildings, its contribution to the local economy, its support of local services, and the prudent use of non renewable resources, rather than focusing purely on location and access criteria... Decisions within the planning system have traditionally been based on the idea of "balance". The economic advantages of a particular proposal, for example, might be deemed to be more important than the local environment so the development goes ahead: in other words, the balance of the argument favours the development even though there is an acknowledged loss.' A balanced approach is widely used and easy to comprehend, the Countryside Agency points out, but the inevitable result is that there is a 'winner' and a 'loser'. 'For instance, major town expansion has meant that attractive countryside has been the loser; while tight restraint on village development has meant that affordable homes for local people have often gone unprovided. We believe a better approach is to require development to show a net gain (or at least a neutral effect) for the social, environmental and economic interests of the area, with no significant losses to any of them.' Policy integration can achieve this if decision making at the plan level uses the following sequential approach, the Countryside Agency explains. 'The first stage is to identify those solutions for meeting development needs which achieve social, economic, and environmental objectives together – for example, a high proportion of affordable housing on a brownfield site as part of the wider regeneration of a market town; or encouraging the reuse of vernacular farm buildings close to villages for new employment uses and housing. The second stage is to make sure that any significant losses from meeting remaining needs for development are mitigated or compensated through associated measures. In the example of a greenfield site, development might need to retain the benefits of the current landscape – perhaps hedgerows or woodland – or to provide new landscape features offering a similar benefits. Informal recreation sites might also be kept or re-created, or new habitats developed so that the wildlife in the area is retained.'

sustainable social city region A concept of regional development advocated by the TOWN AND COUNTRY PLANNING ASSOCIATION in 1997, updating EBENEZER HOWARD's concept of the SOCIAL CITY.

sustainable tourism Attempts to minimise the use of resources and adverse impacts on local ecosystems and indigenous cultures, while maximising the benefit to local people. See also ECOSERT.

sustainable urban drainage system (SUDS) Physical structures built to receive surface water run-off, including constructed wetlands, detention basins, infiltration devices, permeable surfaces, retention ponds and SWALES. SUDS are designed to reduce pollution and flood risk in watercourses and wetlands, and to improve biodiversity in urban areas.

sustainable urban extension An approach to extending urban areas developed by ENGLISH PARTNERSHIPS and the PRINCE'S FOUNDATION in 1999. Its features include a collaborative planning and design process (based on a four-day design workshop for each site), and providing MIXED USES, public transport and SUSTAINABLE URBAN DRAINAGE.

sustainable urban neighbourhood The Sustainable Urban Neighbourhoods Initiative advocates SUNs as urban building blocks suitable both for creating new neighbourhoods and repairing the fabric of existing urban areas. The concept, promoted by consultants URBED, has much in common with an URBAN VILLAGE, a planned NEIGHBOURHOOD and aspects of NEW URBANISM. A SUN was defined in 1996 as having: buildings and spaces that are human in scale but urban in nature; a network of streets and squares serving as routes and public places; a mix of uses and tenures; a density of uses sufficient to animate streets and public places, and sustain facilities; a minimal environmental impact; qualities of integration and permeability; a sense of place; and means of encouraging people to feel a sense of responsibility towards the area.

sustainagility Defined by the humorist Ian Martin (2002) as 'the ability to deliver loud, impromptu lectures in a restaurant on such diverse issues as the Kyoto Protocol, domestic windows and the correct use of trees'.

SUV (US) Sports Utility Vehicle. A four-wheel-drive vehicle, capable of going off-road but rarely (if ever) used for this purpose, favoured by affluent suburban households for trips to the supermarket and taking their children to school. The suburbanite in an SUV is a common object of derision in NEW URBANIST polemic. A leading article in the *Financial Times* in 2003 argued that, as well as being a danger to their occupants due to their high centre of gravity, 'SUVs cause disproportionate death and damage when they hit other vehicles. They seem to encourage aggressive driving. And they consume absurd amounts of petrol… Sooner or later, anti-SUV sentiment will sweep the world, and these vehicles of destruction will reap the whirlwind. Their drivers still pursue all those exciting off-road opportunities in Manhattan and the West End. But the SUV will not be around for long' (Financial Times, 2003). UK examples include the Range Rover and the Land Rover Discovery. See also HUMMER.

swagman (or swaggie) (Australia) A tramp. A *swag* is the bedding roll a swagman carries. See BINDLE STIFF and VAGRANT.

Swain, Henry (1924–2002) Architect. See CLASP.

swale A linear depression (often beside a road) that allows rainwater to soak away. See SUSTAINABLE URBAN DRAINAGE SYSTEM.

swamp *v.* To overwhelm. The word became politically sensitive after Conservative leader MARGARET THATCHER used it in 1978 to describe Wolverhampton as an example of Britain being 'swamped' by an alien culture. Home secretary David Blunkett was castigated in 2002 for claiming that some schools were being 'swamped' by the children of asylum seekers.

Swampy The nickname of Daniel Hooper, a young environmental campaigner active in the 1990s. He and others hid in tunnels they dug under the proposed routes of the Newbury bypass and other new roads to obstruct the builders. Swampy, renowned for occupying the deepest, wettest and muddiest of them, became a celebrity for a few months. The name lives on: a report by MPs in 2002 warned that government proposals to reduce the number of planning inquiries into major development projects could create 'a new generation of Swampies'.

sweat equity Occupiers earning a share in the value of their home by building it themselves, helping to build it or fitting out. The proportion of the equity 'earned' will depend on the extent of the 'sweat' contributed.

swept path The area of highway (wider than the vehicle itself) over which a vehicle passes as it turns a corner.

Swindon Railway Village Designed by the Great Western Railway's engineer IK Brunel in 1840 and built (using stone spoil from a railway tunnel) in 1842–55 to house railway workers and ancillary facilities beside the company's locomotive works. The village has since been absorbed into the town of Swindon.

Swinging London The phrase was popularised by a cover story in *Time* magazine in 1965, celebrating the city as a centre of fashion and youth culture.

Swiss cheese syndrome The condition of an urban block with many alternative routes through it. The analogy is with the holes in the cheese. See PERMEABILITY.

switch lanes To leave one street gang and join another.

SWOT analysis A method of assessing an area in terms of its strengths, weaknesses, opportunities and threats.

Sybil, or the Two Nations A novel by Benjamin Disraeli (1804–81) (later prime minister), published in 1845, recording the squalor of life for the Victorian urban poor and describing a model settlement built by a philanthropic mill-owner. The book inspired TITUS SALT, among others. Its subtitle suggested the name adopted by members of the liberal wing of the UK Conservative party who call themselves *one-nation conservatives*. See also ATHENS OF THE NORTH.

Benjamin Disraeli

synergy The condition where the whole is greater than the sum of its parts. In chemotherapy *synergism* describes the combined effects of two drugs that produce different particular effects that are greater than those of each drug alone. From the Greek for 'working together'.

synoecism The administrative coming together of several villages to form a town. The term, meaning living together, was used by Aristotle (Kostof, 1991).

system building Any method of housing construction using factory-made prefabricated components. Such building methods were enthusiastically promoted (and subsidised) by governments in the 1960s and '70s, particularly for council housing. The results were often disastrous, dampness being one of the major problems. Defects were often due to poor design, careless building, or both. As a council officer recalled years later: 'You've got a guy standing 20 floors up with a crane hoisting a big panel towards him. If he can't locate the various bars in the floor and wall panels that need to line up, he'll make it fit quickly by flattening a few.' *Building Design* humorist Ian Martin summed up the problem in 1999: 'Apparently, sudden loads – an aerobics tumble, a frisky Labrador skidding on a loose rug – could take out a flank wall...' Some supporters of system building point out that such methods are widely and successfully employed in mainland Europe. The problem in the UK was that untried methods were used on too large a scale, systems designed for hot, dry climates were imported without modification for use in wet, windy conditions, and systems were abandoned, instead of being modified in the light of experience. In 2002 the UK government announced its intention once again to pursue a large-scale programme of systems-built house-building.

systems analysis Mathematical techniques for viewing many consequences of a particular action. Developed during the 1939–45 war to examine alternative military strategies (Goodman, 1972), these techniques were the basis of the SYSTEMS APPROACH to planning.

systems approach An approach to planning based on analysing and controlling regions, cities and towns as systems. It was developed from SYSTEMS ANALYSIS and SYSTEMS THEORY. It was widely used in the UK in the 1960s and '70s (in the planning of MILTON KEYNES, for example), but by 2001 Bob Jarvis was noting that 'the systems view of planning has been so discredited that it gets only a one-line dismissal in a recent text on planning theory' (Jarvis, 2001).

The approach was described in *Urban and Region Planning: a systems approach* by Brian McLoughlin, published in 1969, and *A Systems View of Planning* by George Chadwick, published in 1971. Peter Hall (1979) has summarised the elements of a systems approach. First, 'the present environment is scanned to isolate main problems. A hierarchy of goals and objectives is set up, and is edited to manageable proportions. An inventory of available resources is established. Alternative ways of meeting the objectives are hypothesized and then evaluated in terms of some common metric of costs and benefits, generally associated with the achievement of the objectives. Usually, some calculation is made of probabilities of different courses of action; the preferred course is the one that maximizes the net expectation (probability multiplied by utility). The choice is translated into managerial action and implemented. The implementation is constantly monitored and, if unexpected outcomes are discovered, appropriate modifications are introduced.'

systems theory Describes the relationship between the elements that make up a whole social or geographical unit.

T

tag The signature of a GRAFFITI artist.
Tai Cymru The Welsh equivalent of England's HOUSING CORPORATION.
taigh (Gaelic, Scotland) A house.
taking (US) Regulating property to the extent that the act infringes the Fifth Amendment to the Constitution (which specifies that private property shall not be taken for public use without just compensation).
Tale of Johnny Town-Mouse, The A story by Beatrix Potter which concludes that some people are suited to the town and others to the country. Horace's satire of 30 BC *The Town Mouse and the Country Mouse* explored the same theme (Barnett, 1998).
Taliesin The house FRANK LLOYD WRIGHT built for himself in Wisconsin in 1911, named after the Welsh poet. Wright later developed Taliesin as a design school with up to 60 apprentices, and constructed a second complex, Taliesin West, in Arizona, where he and his entourage would overwinter.
tall building (also high building) Defined variously as a building significantly higher than most of its surrounding buildings, or a building of more than six storeys or 25 metres. A tall building was defined by the Commission for Architecture and the Built Environment and English Heritage in 2001 as one that is 'substantially taller than its neighbours and/or which significantly changes the skyline'. The architectural critic Martin Pawley (2002) has noted that 'tall buildings are just small buildings, only taller.' He was arguing that they did not need special treatment outside the normal planning process. The architect Louis Sullivan made a different point in 1896: 'What are the chief characteristics of the tall office building?' he asked. 'At once we must answer, it is lofty.' His argument was that the great height of such a building was the main feature that the design should express – 'rising in sheer exultation that from bottom to top it is a unit without a single dissenting line' (quoted in Bender, 2002). See also HIGH RISE and SKYSCRAPER.
Tammany Hall politics Municipal government founded on political corruption. Tammany Hall was the headquarters of New York City's Democratic Party.

Tamoe The fictional capital city of a Pacific island of the same name where a model society has been established by a French deserter from a passing ship. The city is circular and laid out on a gridded plan. The houses, two storeys high, are painted in pink and green squares. Tamoe is described by the Marquis de Sade in *Aline and Valcour* (1795).
tandem development Carried out at the back of an existing building, from whose frontage it is accessed.
target attractiveness The potential for being chosen as a target by enemy weapons. The development of nuclear weapons in the 1940s led to governments considering the value of low-density urban forms as ways of reducing vulnerability to attack. See DOUGHNUT CITY.
target hardening Modifying a building to reduce opportunities for committing crime. Compare FORTRESS MENTALITY.
Tarzana A development in California financed by Edgar Rice Burroughs, author of the Tarzan books. Burroughs bought the site, near Hollywood, in 1919 in order to be near the filming of his Tarzan stories.
Taut, Bruno (1880–1938) German expressionist architect. In 1919 he proposed abandoning cities and building utopian communities. The public buildings of these garden cities would be made of glass. See STADTKRONE.
tax *v.* To MUG. The term is used by muggers, with the implication that robbing people in the street is a justifiable way of redistributing wealth to those who need it most.
taxonomy Classification by type or based on structure. Also TYPOLOGY.
Tayler and Green The architectural practice of Herbert Tayler and David Green was noted for sensitively fitting neo-vernacular cottage housing into Norfolk villages in the years between 1938 and 1973.
Taylor, Graham See SATELLITE TOWN.
Taylor, William See BRIGHTFIELD SITE.
taylorism A system of scientific management of labour devised by US engineer and inventor Frederick Taylor (1856–1915). It is based on 'time and motion' studies of workers and workplace practices.

Team X (Team Ten) An international group of modernist architects formed in 1954 to promote a programme of ideas for urban development, including streets in the air and grids of urban expressways. ALISON AND PETER SMITHSON and Aldo van Eyck were among its members. The group broke away from CIAM in 1956.

technobabble Technical JARGON. Example: 'Every direct question about the Los Angeles uprising or the cities' fiscal cries was met with neutered technobabble about "micro-enterprise zones" and "infrastructure"' (Davis, 2002).

technobelt A belt of planned high-technology industry.

technoburb 1 Residential and economic development whose existence on the periphery of urban areas is made possible by advanced information technology. **2** Robert Fishman's (1987) term for an EDGE CITY. Also *technoburbia*.

technology park Defined by the Greater London Authority (2001) as 'a strategic employment site providing high quality business space, particularly for research and development, possibly building on links with university and research institutions'.

techno-pessimist One who believes that technology is dehumanising society and causes more problems than it solves.

technopole A concentration of technologically innovative activity at the edge of a city; a planned centre for the promotion of high-technology industry. Such places include science parks, science cities, and technobelts (Castells and Hall, 1994).

technosphere See BIOSPHERE.

techno-utopia A UTOPIA based on the use of new technologies.

techno-utopian One who believes in the capacity of technology to solve social, economic and enviromental problems.

telecommunications equipment Equipment (including masts and satellite dishes) relating to any form of communication by electrical wire, optical cable or radio signals. Telecommunications equipment is the subject of some local authority DESIGN GUIDES.

telecommuter A person who maintains contact with their employing organisation largely by means of electronic communication from home. Steven Johnson (2001) writes that in the mid-1990s 'most digital-savvy social critics predicted that the rise of the Web and various telecommuting appliances would deliver the death blow to city living, finishing a 40-year process that had begun with the suburban flight of the post-war years. We'd all be living on our Wyoming ranches in 10 years, dialing into the office instead of straphanging on an overcrowded subway.' The prediction was unfounded. 'Industries driven by ideas naturally gravitate toward physical centres of idea generation, even in an age of instant data transmissions. Bright minds with shared interests still flock together, even when they have wireless modems and broadband in their living rooms.'

telesprawl Decentralisation from cities resulting from the growth of TELEWORKING.

televillage A place comprehensively supported by information and computer technological infrastructures and services.

television The architect and critic Michael Sorkin (1991) has called television 'the central technology of the new city. It's the major agent in inventing this new placelessness, the coming softer, gentler, post-Orwellian dystopia.' See also GAZZARD'S LAW OF URBAN VITALITY and NON-PLACE URBAN REALM.

teleworking People working at home using information technology. See HOMEWORKING.

telezone A place where advanced office and business space is combined with sophisticated telecommunications facilities (Graham and Marvin, 1995).

Telford, Thomas (1757–1834) Engineer. The son of a Scottish shepherd and trained as an architect, he built the greatest roads, bridges and canals of his age. His works included the London to Holyhead road (including the Menai Bridge, opened in 1826) and the Caledonian Canal. He was the first president of the Institution of Civil Engineers. Telford lived to see the first steam locomotives, but he was dubious about the prospects for railways. The future, he thought, lay with motorised road vehicles (Rolt, 1958). The great railway age came and went before he was – perhaps – finally proved right. See also THE COLOSSUS OF ROADS and PONTIFEX MAXIMUS.

Temple Bar, Dublin The location of a celebrated regeneration initiative. In the 1980s the area just south of the Liffey was blighted by a proposal for a bus station. The proposal lowered property prices, and artists' studios, galleries, bookshops, pubs and restaurants flourished. The bus station proposal was abandoned and replaced by a policy of improving the area for mixed uses. Tax incentives encouraged businesses to improve their properties. An urban design framework was successfully implemented in the early 1990s, creating new squares and routes in what was now declared to be a new 'cultural quarter'.

tenement A single building containing a number of separate flats or apartments. The first blocks to which the form was applied were built in Edinburgh in the sixteenth century, and Scottish cities have a long and rich tradition of tenement building to this day. However, the word also has a pejorative connotation when applied to dwellings which have been 'made down' into flats or declined into multiple occupation. Example: 'The street is made up of eighteenth century houses which had, by 1900, decayed into tenements.' The term is rarely used in England, even to describe blocks of flats, the exception being the blocks built by the PEABODY TRUST in London in the nineteenth century. In the USA in the nineteenth century a tenement was legally a unit of housing occupied by more than three families, though late in the century it was generally used to describe working-class flats (Girouard, 1985).

tentative plan (US) A legal plan of subdivision.

tenure The conditions on which a property is held. Examples are owner occupation, renting and shared ownership (see SHARED EQUITY).

ten-year rule (UK) Allows for any building begun more than 10 years ago to be considered for LISTING if: a) It is threatened with alteration or demolition. b) It qualifies as an 'outstanding' example at either Grade II* or Grade I.

Terminal 5 The planning inquiry into a fifth terminal for London's Heathrow airport was Britain's longest. The secretary of state granted planning approval for the terminal in 2001.

terminal architecture The future architecture of the information age, according to Martin Pawley, who used the term as the title of a book. Pawley (1998) argues that art history stops people understanding architecture. The value of a building should be judged not by its aesthetic pedigree, but by its usefulness as a terminal in the new networks of communication and distribution. The failure to understand this, he writes, is leading to urban life being destroyed by planners, politicians, art historians, and the heritage and tourist industries. Authentic architecture, in Pawley's view, survives only in the shape of buildings like distribution centres, factories and petrol stations that are designed as instruments, not monuments. Architecture is in a 'terminal' condition now, in the sense of being a dying patient. In the future it will be 'terminal' in the sense of providing the terminals for the complex systems of modern life.

Terra Australis (Southern Lands) A land of ideal cities described by Gabriel Foigny in *The Adventures of Jacques Sadeur* (1676). See SEZAIN.

terrace 1 A row of houses where each is attached to its neighbour on either side by means of a common or 'party' wall. **2** A street on to which such houses face. **3** A paved area beside a building. **4** A raised level area, natural or artificial.

terraced (also terrace) house (UK) One of at least three contiguous houses. The US equivalent is *row house*. Andrew Saint (2001) describes the London terraced house after 1774 (see the BLACK ACT) as 'more or less the clauses of the building regulations turned into bricks and mortar and put up for sale... A minimal machine for tolerably safe living...' John Summerson (1962) notes that, with exception of the aristocrats' palaces and the ROOKERIES of the 'unemployable and criminal classes', practically the whole population of GEORGIAN London lived in 'their narrow slices of building, now called, for no very good reason, "terrace-houses"'. The probable reason for the term was, in fact, that the roadway in front of and between two terraces would often be built up, creating semi-basements at the front of the houses (which would be at garden level at the back) and sometimes cellars under the road. In such cases the road could be said to be in the form of a raised terrace. Compare TERRASSENHÄUSER.

terracotta 1 A facing material widely used (in a variety of colours) for Victorian and Edwardian buildings. Terracotta is clay that has been pressed into absorbent moulds before being fired. The blocks are usually hollow, and filled with concrete. When glazed the material is called *faience*. Terracotta was relatively cheap, light and resistant to the acidic urban atmosphere of the time. It was a convenient means of mass-producing elaborate detail and was extensively used on the facades of banks, offices, pubs and civic buildings. **2** A brownish-orange colour. *Terra cotta* is Italian for baked earth.

terraform To create a self-sustaining atmosphere and ecology to support human habitation on a planet such as Mars. The word was coined by the science fiction writer Jack Williamson in 1942 (Quinion, 1998). See WORLDSCAPE and compare ECOPOESIS.

terrain model A representation on computer or in solid material of the configuration of a site's ground surface.

terrain vague (French) The post-urban residual spaces of the abandoned industrial city (Daskalakis and Perez, 2001). The semi-abstract 1973 painting 'Terrain Vague' by the artist CONSTANT NIEWENHUYS (see NEW BABYLON) depicts an urban wasteland. Ignasi de Solà-Morales Rubió used the term in 1995 to describe residual space (Rubió, 1995).

Terrassenhäuser (German) A block of flats built on a hillside, each flat having a terrace on the roof of the one below. The word is often misleadingly translated as TERRACED HOUSES, for which the German word is *Häuserreihe*.

territorial impact assessment Assessing the impact of development against policy objectives.

territorial justice The allocation of resources across an area according to the specific needs of its individual parts.

territorial planning SPATIAL PLANNING.

territorial reinforcement Creating a sphere of influence by physical design so that the users of a building or space develop a sense of ownership over it.

territoriality 1 The setting of spatial boundaries by institutions. **2** Expressing a sense of belonging to a particular place. **3** The sense felt by residents that a building or space is theirs, or by outsiders that they are not welcome. Oscar Newman (1973) defined territoriality as 'the capacity of the physical environment to create perceived zones of territorial influence'. See also BOUNDARY DEFINITION.

Terry and June (UK) Archetypal suburban dwellers. Example: 'These days it's unfashionable to plan for the Terry and June of the suburbs' (2002). The UK television sitcom 'Terry and June' ran in nine series from 1979 to 1987, with Terry Scott as Terry Medford and June Whitfield as his wife June. The fictional couple lived in Purley, Surrey, in the outer suburbs of London. It was more or less a continuation of an earlier sitcom 'Happy Ever After', in which the same principals played a similar couple, also called Terry (Fletcher) and June. See also OZZIE AND HARRIET and THE GOOD LIFE.

Terry Street Douglas Dunn's first collection of poems, published in 1967. It describes life in a run-down, working-class neighbourhood of Hull.

Terry, Quinlan Architect. See GOOD DESIGN and RICHMOND RIVERSIDE.

Tesco Transylvanian See VERNACULAR.

test map A diagram showing the essentials of a proposed development's physical form.

Tetra-City A proposal by BUCKMINSTER FULLER for a floating city of one million people in the form of a tetrahedron (a four-sided pyramid) with each side a mile long.

Texas option A means by which one party in a joint venture can buy out another in a case where they have unequal interests.

Thames Gateway A development corridor to the north and south of the River Thames, extending from the Blackwall Tunnel in east London eastwards into Kent and Essex, incorporating the new high-speed rail link to the Channel Tunnel and including Stratford, Dartford, Chatham, Gravesend, Rainham Marshes and Barking Reach. A major urban regeneration project for the area was announced by environment secretary MICHAEL HESELTINE in 1991, originally under the name the East Thames Corridor. In February 2003, John Prescott, the deputy prime minister, unveiled plans to build up to 200,000 new homes over the next 15 years, together with 325,000 new jobs and all the necessary infrastructure. This will be the largest exercise of its kind since the creation of the NEW TOWNS in the 1960s and '70s. It will not be a gigantic piece of SUBURBAN SPRAWL, we are assured, but an exercise in 'town making', building sustainable, living communities in a series of URBAN VILLAGES. All the currently fashionable buzz words are being displayed with a vengeance.

Thamesmead A new town on the windswept Erith marshes on the south bank of the Thames estuary. Weinreb and Hibbert (1983) describe it as 'AWARD-WINNING'. It was planned by the London County Council and built by the Greater London Council from the late 1960s onwards. The early stages of development were SYSTEM BUILT. The new towns movement was always anxious to dissociate itself from such places: not being built under the New Towns Act, they were not considered new towns, though that was often what they were called. Stanley Kubrick chose Thamesmead as the setting for his film *A Clockwork Orange*, portraying it a place of menacing modernity (see CLOCKWORK ORANGE CHIC). A development trust has been responsible for Thamesmead since the 1980s.

Thatcher, Margaret (Baroness Thatcher of Kesteven) (b1925) UK prime minister, 1979–90. Nicknamed the Iron Lady for her image of being unwilling to compromise, her policies included privatising public utilities, rate capping (reducing local authorities' control of expenditure) and introducing the community charge (called the 'poll tax' by its opponents). Her cabinet forced her resignation in 1990. She entered the House of Lords in 1992. See also BACK-TO-BACKS, BARRATT, BUS, ALICE COLEMAN, COMMUNITY ENTERPRISE, COMMUNITY LAND ACT, CONSENSUS, CONSORTIUM DEVELOPMENTS, COUNCIL HOUSING, THE ELDONIANS, FAITH IN THE CITY, GREATER LONDON COUNCIL, FRIEDRICH HAYEK, INNER CITY, IT TOOK A RIOT, LIFTING THE BURDEN, KEN LIVINGSTONE, MARXISM, PARKER MORRIS, NICHOLAS RIDLEY, ROLLING BACK THE STATE, SANE, SOCIETY and URBAN DEVELOPMENT CORPORATION.

theatre A report by the Theatres Trust (2002) illustrated the decline in theatre-going how the theatrical life of towns and cities has been diminished: 28 theatres lost in Liverpool, 21 in Birmingham, 18 in Glasgow, and 183 in London. Even a modest town like Aldershot has lost 13 theatres, and now has none.

thee-thou A person from Sheffield, so called from the traditional use of the second person singular pronoun forms 'thee' and 'thou' in that city. Stoddart, Upton and Widdowson (1999) note that thee and thou were 'traditionally male preserves in the locality and largely eschewed by women... [who] strongly objected to men using these pronouns to address them'.

Thekla A city in Asia that is permanently under construction. Italo Calvino explains in *Imaginary Cities* (1972) that its people never want to finish it as they know that it will begin to decay as soon as they do.

Thelema See NEW JERUSALEM.

theme park An entertainment facility, usually covering an extensive area and serving mainly car-borne families, offering a range of attractions on a common theme. Disneyland, Alton Towers and Legoland are well-known examples. An unnamed American commentator quoted by Spiro Kostof (1987) called theme parks 'the meeting ground between the automobile culture and the television culture'.

themed space A shopping mall, leisure facility or historic place wholly designed or restored on a theme or themes to attract visitors. An example is the Orient Leisure Dome at the Trafford Centre, whose 'sensational world theming', according to its brochure, 'will allow you to have breakfast in New York, lunch in Paris and dinner in Egypt, Morocco or Italy'. At the opposite end of the spectrum is the chinoisification of the Gerrard Street area in London's west end, where Westminster City Council has built Chinese arches, installed pagoda-style phone boxes and translated the street names into Chinese.

Theodora An imaginary city that fought invasions of one insect or animal pest after another over many years. After their triumph over a plague of rats, the city's people thought they were finally free of pests, only to find themselves challenged by a variety of mythical beasts. Italo Calvino tells the story in INVISIBLE CITIES (1972).

theory of contacts The suggestion by the Town Planning Committee of the MARS GROUP in 1937 that cities should be seen as centres that facilitated human contacts and transactions of all types: intellectual, social and commercial (Gold, 2000).

theory of loose parts The theory states that the degree of inventiveness and creativity, and the possibility of discovery in an environment, are directly proportional to the number and kind of variables in it. Simon Nicholson, formulating the theory in the 1970s, argued that the imposed environment (the one in which the citizen has only a passive part to play) results from cultural elitism. Colin Ward (1996) comments: 'The missing cultural element is the aesthetic of a variable, manipulable, malleable environment: the aesthetic of loose parts. The missing political element is the politics of participation, of user control and of self-managing, self-regulating communities.'

therapy See ARNSTEIN'S LADDER.

there goes the neighborhood (US) A comment that people are said to make when something happens in an area (such as supposedly undesirable residents moving in) that will lead to people the speaker considers desirable moving out, and the neighborhood's character eventually changing dramatically for the worse. See also BLOCKBUSTING and WHITE FLIGHT.

there is another way The slogan of COIN STREET Community Builders, pointing to their experience as an example of an alternative to commercial development.

there is no there there The writer Gertrude Stein's (1874–1946) comment on her home town of Oakland, California, in her book *Everybody's Autobiography*, published in 1937. Peter Hall (1989) notes 'the California Department of Transportation's lesser-known but equally devastating words, "Oakland: Next Eleven Exits"'. See also LOS ANGELES.

thermal movement The expansion and contraction of building materials caused by changes in temperature. Buildings and structures may need to be designed to compensate for this (by providing expansion joints in walls, for example).

Thiel, Phillip See EXPERIENTIAL ENVIROTECTURE.

Things to Come A film adaptation of the book by HG Wells. Released in 1936, it tells of a war that destroys Everytown (based on London) in 1940.

thinking machine See PATRICK GEDDES.

third age technology Makes life better for elderly people.

Third City See MAGNETIC CITY.

third city The French urban designer Christian Devillers refers to the traditional city as *Ville I*; the twentieth-century, functionally separated city as *Ville II*; and the new urbanist street-based city *Ville III*. The German theorist Dietrich Hoffmann-Axthelm calls on urban designers to build *der dritte Stadt* (the third city) (Hebbert, 2000).

Third Coast, the HOUSTON's name for itself, challenging the West Coast and the East Coast of the USA.

Third Garden City A proposal by the Town and Country Planning Association, outlined in a prospectus published in 1979, with the aim of bringing the garden city concept up to date. It did not lead to any new settlements being built, although it did inspire a small experimental development at Lightmoor, Telford. The concept was partly inspired by a 1975 idea of COLIN WARD's for a do-it-yourself new town. The first two garden cities were LETCHWORTH and WELWYN.

third party rights Rights of the public to appeal against the granting of planning permission. Such rights do not exist in the UK, except in relation to maladministration (through the Ombudsman) or on a point of law (through judicial review), even if permission is given contrary to the local authority's policies and development plan. The other two parties are the applicant (who has the right of appeal against refusal of permission) and the local authority. A case for third party rights has often been argued.

third place 1 An informal gathering place where people meet socially. Ray Oldenburg uses the term in his book *The Great Good Place*, published in 1989, to describe the setting for informal public life (also called a *social condenser*), providing a change from the other two settings, the home and the workplace. Oldenburg argues that third places are the bedrock of community life. The first place is the home, the second is the workplace. Also called a *middle place*. **2** Appropriated by Starbucks to describe their coffee bars. **3** Appropriated by Sony to market its Playstation 2 games console.

third world A term first used to describe developing countries in the 1950s or '60s. Raymond Williams (1983) suggests that the phrase originated as *Tiers Monde* in France in the early 1950s, by analogy with the

Third Estate of the French Revolution. The other worlds were the capitalist (first) and communist (second). The term does not reflect the complexity of cities, though. Janice Perlman of New York University has written: 'Every first-world city has within it a third-world city of malnutrition, infant mortality, homelessness and unemployment. And, conversely, every third-world city has within it a first-world city of high tech, high fashion and high finance' (quoted in Ward, 1996).

thirty-year rule (UK) Allows for any building begun more than 30 years ago to be considered for LISTING.

Thomas, David Urban designer. See TOPOGRAPHICAL PLANNING DESIGN.

Thoreau, Henry David (1817–62) See WALDEN.

Thornton Hough A model housing scheme built after 1888 by WH Lever on the Wirral, Cheshire, for workers on his estate. The architects included William and Segar Owen, who adopted a black-and-white vernacular style. See also PORT SUNLIGHT.

thoroughfare A road open at both ends. The *thorough-* is a variation of *through*.

thoroughness Careful attention to detailed design. The DTLR and CABE (2001) write of *thoroughness* as an essential of good housing design: it results in 'richness and sense of quality'.

three-city test The test – 'if at least 50 per cent of the American public can't identify at least three cities in a given country, we shouldn't bomb it' – was devised by the American writer Ted Rall in *To Afghanistan and Back*, published in 2004.

three Es See TRAFFIC CALMING and TRIPLE BOTTOM LINE.

Three Graces Three famous landmark buildings on Liverpool's waterfront: the Liver Building (1908–11), a twin-towered office building with one of the world's first reinforced-concrete frames; the Mersey Docks and Harbour Board offices (completed 1907, with an immense central dome); and the Cunard Building (1914–16).

The collective name seems not to have been widely used, if at all, before a 'fourth grace' (a concept as meaningful as a fourth side to a triangle) was proposed in the 1990s. The pre-eminent Liverpool architectural writer Quentin Hughes (1920–2004), for one, confirmed (in conversation with Paul O'Keeffe in 2003) that he had not come across the term before the proposal for a fourth. In his authoritative book *Liverpool* (published in 1969 and in a revised edition in 1999) Hughes refers to the three buildings as 'the Pier Head group'. An architectural competition for the design of a 'fourth grace' on an adjacent site was won in 2003 by WILL ALSOP, as part of the city's successful bid to be awarded the title of European Capital of Culture, but the project was later abandoned.

In Greek mythology, the Three Graces were Aglaia (splendour), Euphrosyne (mirth) and Thalia (good cheer), daughters of the god Zeus. They presided over social events, sang to the gods, danced to the music of Apollo, and inspired artists and poets. Together (and they were almost always portrayed together, dancing in a circle) they embodied grace and beauty.

In 2004 a Moscow developer dubbed his scheme 'the eighth grace', the city apparently having seven graces (landmark buildings) already, of which Moscow university is one.

Three Magnets, The EBENEZER HOWARD drew what is now probably the best-known planning diagram for his book *Tomorrow: the peaceful path to real reform* (1898). The diagram shows two magnets made up of those features which Howard saw as attracting people to the town, on

> **"TOWN AND COUNTRY MUST BE MARRIED, AND OUT OF THIS JOYOUS UNION WILL SPRING A NEW HOPE, A NEW LIFE, A NEW CIVILISATION"**
>
> *Ebenezer Howard*

the one hand, and the country, on the other; and a third magnet, which Howard believed his GARDEN CITY concept would create, of 'town-country'. The town offered attractions such as 'social opportunity' and 'high money wages', but disadvantages such as 'closing out of nature' and 'distance from work'. The country offered 'fresh air' and 'low rents', but also 'low wages' and 'lack of society'. Town-country, by contrast, would offer the best of both worlds, including 'beauty of nature, social opportunity, bright homes and gardens, no smoke, freedom [and] cooperation'. 'Town and country must be married,' Howard wrote in *Tomorrow*, 'and out of this joyous union will spring a new hope, a new life, a new civilisation.'

The diagram has been updated several times by other hands, including the TOWN AND COUNTRY PLANNING ASSOCIATION and SUSTAINABLE URBAN NEIGHBOURHOODS. The urban designer Kelvin Campbell (1995) suggests that built environment specialists have three magnets of their own. Planners are generally concerned with a *process*, architects with a *product* and road engineers with *structure*. Between these three magnets swings a pendulum representing *policy and action on cities*. The force of each magnet is determined by the strength of its associated professions, philosophies, programmes, theories, practices, mechanisms and agencies. The pendulum swings drunkenly between the magnets. Faith in a particular architectural style will swing it towards *product*; the development of new decision-making techniques will favour *process*; and the balance of opinion on the role of private transport will be one factor influencing the attraction of *structure*.

three ugly sisters, the The three 19-storey slabs of the former Department of the Environment headquarters in MARSHAM STREET, London. See also MUESLI and compare THE THREE GRACES.

threshold costs These occur when current services and infrastructure reach capacity, or where renewal and major investment is required before further development can take place.

threshold definition A design feature that emphasises where two parts of a building meet.

threshold limit The level of pollution above which damage is likely to occur.

throbbing Extremely VIBRANT. Example: 'the throbbing hub of the financial and commercial world is reflected in the townscape' (SAVE, 1982).

througate (Scots) An ALLEY (see that entry for regional variants); a passageway; a lane.

through traffic That which has its origin and destination outside a specified area.

through-movement (US) Traffic passing by (and possibly stopping at) shops and other facilities. Compare TO-MOVEMENT.

through-terrace A through-terrace house has a door and windows at both the front and back (unlike a BACK-TO-BACK), with a garden or yard at the back leading on to an alley or lane that runs behind the terrace.

Tibbalds, Francis (1941–92) Town planner, urban designer and architect. Tibbalds was influential in introducing American urban design ideas to the UK, in his city centre design strategy for Birmingham (1990), for example. He was a founder and chairman of the Urban Design Group and the only president of the Royal Town Planning Institute (1988) in recent years to have made an impact outside the profession. Tibbalds set out his 'Ten Commandments for Urban Design' in various articles in 1988: 1) Consider places before buildings. 2) Have the humility to learn from the past and respect your context. 3) Encourage the mixing of uses in towns and cities. 4) Design on a human scale. 5) Encourage freedom to walk around. 6) Cater for all sections of the community and consult with them. 7) Build legible (recognisable or understandable) environments. 8) Build to last, and adapt. 9) Avoid simultaneous change on too great a scale. 10) Promote intricacy, joy and visual delight in the built environment.

TICCIH The International Committee for the Conservation of the Industrial Heritage. Jim Douet has noted that it is pronounced to rhyme with Mickey, though around the Mediterranean it is sometimes Titchie or Ticksey.

time In the words of Sue Clifford (1997): 'It has been the curse of our age that we have been seduced more by time than by place. "Modernity" and "Progress" have been fine smokescreens for those who saw gain in change which needed clean slates, and for whom the only context was fashion within their own profession. They carried no responsibility for those physically and socially displaced, for the longer term or for sustaining those who would have to make things work. Much of the aftermath has left lost souls and places bleached of meaning, indistinguishable from anywhere else.' PATRICK GEDDES (1905) explained the importance of understanding cities in the dimension of time.

'A city is more than a place in space, it is a drama in time,' he wrote (see also DRAMA). 'The ideals and the achievements of one day and generation and city are ever melting away, and passing out of sight of the next... we have no continuing city... Upon all these degrees of dying, all these faint and fading steps between immortality and oblivion, we may arrange what we call our historic cities. Obviously in the deeper and more living sense the city exists only in actualising itself; and thus to us it is that the ideal city lies ever in the future. Yet it is the very essence of this argument that an ideal city is latent in every town.'

LEWIS MUMFORD wrote: 'Cities are a product of time. They are the moulds in which men's lifetimes have cooled and congealed, giving lasting shape, by way of art, to moments that would otherwise vanish with the living.' The novelist Peter Ackroyd (2001) has written: 'Just as the city creates its own weather, with a distinctive pattern of "HEAT ISLANDS", so it creates its own time. The innumerable lives and dwellings within the city make time shift and bend in unpredictable ways; like a lava flow from some unknown source, time moves more slowly or quickly in the ambience of certain districts. If artists understood this better, it might become a wonderful source of inspiration'. COLIN ROWE and Fred Koetter asked in COLLAGE CITY whether the ideal city might not 'at one and the same time, behave as both theatre of prophecy *and* theatre of memory'. The urban designer Bob Jarvis (2001) has warned against supposing that a place can be described fully in three dimensions. 'You could dance a place in four dimensions as easily as draw it in three.' The architect Aldo Van Eyck wrote: 'I dislike a sentimental antiquarian attitude towards the past as much as I dislike a sentimental technocratic one toward the future. Both are founded on a... clockwork notion of time' (quoted in Curtis, 1996).

The words of Marcus Aurelius (AD 120–180) from his *Meditations* are sometimes quoted by urban conservationists: 'One thing hastens into being, another hastens out of it. Even while a thing is in the act of coming into existence, some part of it has already ceased to be. Flux and change are forever renewing the fabric of the universe, just as the ceaseless sweep of time is forever renewing the face of eternity. In such a running river, where there is no firm foothold, what is there to value among all the many things that are racing past us?' See also GLOBALISATION, INVISIBLE CITIES, PLACE and X-URBIA.

time bank An arrangement by which people and local organisations can build up credits for the time they put into voluntary activities in their local area. The concept of using time as a currency was pioneered by the Time Dollar Institute in the USA. See also LETS.

time convergence See TRIPLE CONVERGENCE.

Time for Design 1 A booklet published by English Partnerships in 1996, calling for better design. **2** The title of an earlier, unconnected project run by the National Planning Forum.

time limit A planning permission lapses if the development has not been begun within five years, unless the local authority or the secretary of state has specified a longer or shorter period. See also TIME-LIMITED CONSENTS.

time management Organising the activities in an area to accommodate different uses at different times of the day and night.

time series Defined by KEVIN LYNCH (1960) as 'series which are sensed over time, including both simple item-by-item linkages, where one element is simply knitted to the two elements before and behind it (as in a casual sequence of detailed landmarks), and also series which are truly structured in time and thus melodic in nature'.

time-budget study Analyses how people use their time, often based on questionnaires. Such studies are used in assessing, for example, the amount of SOCIAL CAPITAL.

time-limited consents The government's green paper *Planning: delivering a fundamental change*, published in 2001, noted that permissions and consents normally lasted for five years and were often automatically renewed, effectively preventing the use of potentially developable land for other purposes. The government said it would limit permissions and consents to three years and that they should automatically lapse thereafter.

time-space convergence The decreasing significance of duration and distance in the light of modern technologies of transport and communication.

tin shed A cheap. simple, utilitarian building entirely or predominately clad in corrugated iron or its modern equivalent, plastic-coated profiled steel cladding. Almost every town in the UK is now ringed by extensive collections of them, leading to the phrase 'tin sheds on the bypass'. Also known as 'crinkly tin sheds'. See also BIG BOX.

Tin Town A temporary model village built around 1900 by the Derwent Valley Water Board to house 900 workers constructing two dams. The buildings, made of corrugated iron and weatherboarding, were dismantled during the first world war, many of them being reused in a prisoner-of-war camp near Wakefield. Other similar villages elsewhere bore the same name.

TINA A transport infrastructure needs assessment, reporting to the EU in relation to a prospective new member country.

Tinseltown Hollywood, California, so called because of the superficial glitter of its celebrity culture. The famous hillside 'Hollywood' sign originally read 'Holly-woodland'. It was erected in 1923 to advertise homes in the Hollywood

Hills being built by Hollywoodland Realty Co. The sign was sold to the city in 1944. See also CITY OF THE STARS.

tipping point The moment at which a series of small urban improvements suddenly leads to major regeneration. The analogy is with a pair of scales, and the effect is the opposite of the straw that broke the camel's back. See COMPLEXITY.

tissue study A comparison of the scale and layout of different settlements. The technique makes use of overprinting or tracing maps of successful and familiar places over the proposed development site or area, at the same scale. This provides clues as to the capacity of a place and how it might be structured.

Titfield Thunderbolt, The See BEECHING CUTS.

toast rack The headquarters of the DEPARTMENT OF THE ENVIRONMENT in MARSHAM STREET, Westminster, London, until the late 1990s, so called for its uncompromising form of three slab blocks linked by a podium. See MUESLI.

toby A tramp; a VAGRANT.

TOD TRANSIT ORIENTED DEVELOPMENT.

toft 1 A homestead; a private house plot; an enclosed piece of land with a house, outbuildings, garden, yards and small enclosures belonging to one person. The toft is the basic structural building block for most medieval villages. The normal length of a toft (the distance between the street frontage line and the back of the plot) is between 50 and 150m (Roberts, 1987). **2** A hillock.

togetherness Jane Jacobs (1961) called it 'a fittingly nauseating name for an old ideal in planning theory. This ideal is that if anything is shared among people, much should be shared. "Togetherness", apparently a spiritual resource of the new suburbs, works destructively in cities. The requirement that much shall be shared drives city people apart.'

toid A unique identifier or tag used to attribute data to a map. The use of toids was part of the Ordnance Survey's programme of making the UK's maps into an integrated data system. The term became widely known in 2004.

toilet The availability of toilets is proposed by the British Toilets Association and the World Toilets Organisation as an important measure of the quality of public space. The Victorians, understanding this, provided an extensive network of lavishly appointed surface and underground public conveniences in their towns and cities. Many of these have been closed in recent years, sometimes converted to other uses such as bars, restaurants and tanning salons. In some cases they have been replaced by a usually inadequate number of coin-operated concrete-pillbox 'superloos'. The alternative term *lavatory* is used by an increasingly narrow upper social class and the National Trust.

tokenism See ARNSTEIN'S LADDER.

Tokyo Fist See ANTI-URBANISM.

tolerable standard The Scottish equivalent of the term 'unfit', designating sub-standard houses.

toll road One for which users must pay a charge.

toll tax A pejorative term for CONGESTION CHARGING, used in 2002 by opponents of plans by mayor KEN LIVINGSTONE to introduce congestion charging in central London. It echoes *poll tax*, the term used for the *community charge* (the forerunner of council tax) in the 1980s by its opponents. A charge is thought of as being paid in exchange for a benefit. A tax, by contrast, has no such redeeming feature.

to-movement (US) Traffic generated by a specific destination, particularly for shopping. Compare THROUGH-MOVEMENT.

tontine A system of annuities in which the benefits pass to the surviving subscriber until only one is left. It was used to fund buildings and other public works in France, Britain and the USA. There are still several buildings with the word in their name. The system was banned to avoid the temptation for subscribers to murder one another. It is named after Lorenzo Tonti, a Neapolitan banker who started such a scheme (though not the first) in France in 1653 (Quinion, 1998).

top slice The riskiest, least certain element in the expected income stream from a property development. See also FOUR-SLICING.

topic workshop A participative event at which stakeholders or members of the public discuss the future of an area in relation to one or a series of important issues.

topographical planning design A method of 'thinking creatively about realities as features of localities' devised by the urban designer David Thomas (Jarvis, 2001).

topography 1 A description or representation of artificial or natural features on or of the ground. **2** Mapping the shape of the land surface. From the Greek for 'place' and 'to describe'.

Topolobampo A nineteenth-century utopian colony in Mexico. Its failure helped to persuade EBENEZER HOWARD that his garden cities should not emulate its attempt at centralised economic control.

topology A topographical study of a particular place. From the Greek for 'place' and 'discourse'. Compare TYPOLOGY.

toponymy The study of place names.

topophilia The affective bond between people and place or setting. The term was coined by the American geographer YI-FU TUAN (Jarvis, 1998).

Tornado Alley Oklahoma City.

tornado bait (US, jocular) A mobile home park.

total architecture The architectural design of whole places, rather than piecemeal improvements. The phrase was used by the architect WALTER GROPIUS. Compare BIG ARCHITECTURE.

total uncertainty See CERTAINTY.

total urbanisation See CONTINUOUS MOVEMENT.

totalitarian architecture See NAZI ARCHITECTURE.

Totterdown Fields The site of the London County Council's first cottage estate, in Tooting, begun in 1900.

toucan crossing An unsegregated signal-controlled crossing for cyclists and pedestrians. A place where *two* (modes) *can* cross together, it is a variant of another type of crossing named after a bird: the pelican.

Toulouse-Le Mirail See STEMS AND WEBS.

toun (Scots) A TOWN.

Towards a New Architecture The title of the first English translation (published in 1927) of Le Corbusier's *Vers Une Architecture*. A reviewer in the *Architects' Journal* objected to the change of meaning: 'Le Corbusier, one believed, made a plea for an architecture, meaning that the present thoughtless copying of forms of forgotten significance is not architecture at all'.

tower block A HIGH RISE building (usually housing) whose height is significantly greater than its width. The term dates from the late 1960s.

tower-in-the-plaza A type of layout of a city centre building. The tower is set back in an open space rather than continuing the BUILDING LINE along the street.

town 1 A substantial collection of dwellings, together with commercial civic and ancillary buildings, on a scale larger than a VILLAGE but not designated as a CITY. **2** *A New Urbanist Lexicon* (McLaughlin, 2000) defines a town as 'the aggregate of two or more complete neighborhoods, with a central commercial area.' **3** NEW URBANISTS sometimes use the noun without its indefinite article, to mean traditional urban development. Example: 'We do not want another housing estate. The developer should be building town.' The word derives from the Old English *tun*, an enclosure or town. **4** (Scots) A farmstead. The Scots for the English word 'town' is *toun*.

Town and Country Planning Association Founded in 1899 as the Garden City Association, it became the Garden Cities and Town Planning Association in 1907 and adopted its current name in 1941. The TCPA has consistently campaigned for new settlements and dispersal policies, and since the 1970s for public participation in planning and urban regeneration. In 2003 it was calling itself 'the sustainable development charity'. See also ENVIRONMENTAL EDUCATION, EBENEZER HOWARD, FREDERIC OSBORN, PLANNING AID, TOWN CRAMMING and COLIN WARD.

town and country planning The phrase was enshrined in legislation (in place of TOWN PLANNING) in the Town and Country Planning Act 1932. A careers booklet published by the Royal Town Planning Institute in 2002 notes that town and country planning is 'often called town planning for short'. The title of the longstanding annual Town and Country Planning Summer School was changed to the Planning Summer School in 2002. See URBAN AND REGIONAL PLANNING.

town architect Appointed to ensure that the buildings of a town or a development (often designed according to the principles of NEW URBANISM) are constructed according to the urban or urban design code. He or she may be a developer's representative or a local government officer. Compare CITY ARCHITECT.

town centre The Scottish Executive (2000) defines town centres as 'city, town and district centres, irrespective of size, which provide a broad range of facilities and services, and which function as a focus for both the community and public transport', excluding 'RETAIL PARKS, NEIGHBOURHOOD CENTRES and small PARADES of shops of purely local significance'.

town centre health check Planning Policy Guidance Note 6 *Town Centres and Retail Development* proposes the use of 'health checks' as a measure of the vitality and viability of a town centre.

town centre management Treating all the components of a town centre – its shops, signage, street furniture, traffic management and all its facilities – as a single entity, the better to coordinate action to improve the quality of a town centre through such means as removing fly-posting and graffiti, street-cleaning, shopfront improvements, re-paving, providing seating, re-imaging, civic pride campaigns, publicity, shop-mobility schemes, providing crèches, lighting, and holding festivals and other events. The DETR (1998) defined it as 'the reactive and proactive work aimed at ensuring the future success and therefore survival of town and city centres'. Deborah Peel (2002) notes that town centre management emerged in the 1980s and took off in the 1990s.

town centre management plan See TOWN PLAN.

town champion An independent professional or public figure appointed to raise standards of a town's design and development. The concept was promoted in 1999 by David Rock as president of the Royal Institute of British Architects. He drew on his own experience in the Hertfordshire town of Ware (see VIVAT WARE) and that of the architect Gordon Michell at Calne in Wiltshire and Wirksworth in Derbyshire. Rock described a town champion as 'an independent enabler, a banger together of heads, who by bringing together existing agencies and individuals, and by drawing on local goodwill, can make things happen... For "champion" read "animateur", "enabler" or, in the broadest meaning of the word, "architect"'. Compare DESIGN CHAMPION and STREET CHAMPION.

town clerk 1 (UK) An official (usually a lawyer) responsible for a town's affairs. In the UK they have generally been replaced by chief executives. **2** (US) An official who keeps a town's records.

town cramming A pejorative term for high densities or DENSIFICATION. The Town and Country Planning

Association (particularly FJ OSBORN) used the term frequently in the 1960s in its campaigning. It argued that redeveloping existing urban areas at excessively high densities would reduce the quality of life they offered. Decentralisation was essential and inevitable, according to the TCPA, and a programme of new and expanded towns was required to accommodate it. The term fell out of use but was revived in the 1990s as the debate continued. The need to avoid town cramming was mentioned in government policy in 1992 (Planning Policy Guidance Note 12 on *Development Plans and Regional Planning Guidance*). The London Borough of Bromley used the term several times in its draft unitary development plan, but the government's planning inspector in 2001 ordered that each reference be removed.

town crier An official who makes official announcements in a public place. The historic post has been revived in several towns and cities in recent years as a tourist attraction. The town crier generally wears historic costume and carries a hand bell.

town design FREDERICK GIBBERD used the term in the title of a book, published in 1953. See also CIVIC DESIGN and URBAN DESIGN.

Town Development Act 1952 The basis for the planned expansion of small towns, complementing the new towns programme. The largest *expanded towns* were Andover, Basingstoke and Swindon.

town extension A planned addition to the edge of an urban area.

Town for the Motor Age, A The phrase RADBURN used to describe itself.

town house 1 A terraced house (often a euphemism for this), particularly one on three floors, with the main reception room on the first floor, and a garage on the ground floor or in a basement. **2** The urban home of someone who has another home in the country.

town improvement zone Proposed areas modelled on US BUSINESS IMPROVEMENT DISTRICTS.

town manager The chief executive officer of a town. The term was coined in the early 1920s.

town map One of the first generation of British post-war development plans (Taylor, 1998).

town plan Described by the Civic Trust Regeneration Unit as an opportunity to supplement or compliment the statutory planning process, by producing a more detailed and place-specific document. The plan might be adopted as SUPPLEMENTARY PLANNING GUIDANCE and therefore taken into account when determining planning applications. The plan can be economic/business-led (a town centre management plan, for example), community-led (such as a social and cultural action plan) or environment-led (such as an urban design framework, streetscape studies or a bio-diversity action plan). More often than not, the town plan will be a combination of these, instigated by a partnership of interests in the town.

town planning (UK) The common generic term for planning urban areas. The US equivalent is CITY PLANNING. The term town planning dates from around 1900–05. RAYMOND UNWIN was using it by 1906 (Cherry, 1981). Its first use in legislation in the UK was in 1909, though the law has never defined it. The Royal Town Planning Institute, in relation to its professional indemnity insurance scheme, requires its members to declare whether their work involves providing town planning services, but the institute notes – unhelpfully – that '"town planning" is not defined, and includes the full range of work typically undertaken by members'. The architect BERTHOLD LUBETKIN described town planning as 'the art of expressing a social vision in an urban ensemble' (Allan, 2000). In his book on planning theory, Nigel Taylor (1998) consistently uses the term *town planning* 'because it is probably the most widely used term the world over to describe the activity... But... I take it to refer also to what some people (especially in the USA) call "urban" or "city" planning.' Strangely his book's title is *Urban Planning Theory Since 1945*. The Royal Town Planning Institute's *New Vision for Planning*, conceived in 2001, suggested a change in the institute's name. PLANNING or SPATIAL PLANNING looked likely to replace town planning. In 2002, though, a survey of RTPI members found that, of 15 possible proposals for renewing the institute, replacing the term town planning in the institute's name was the least popular of all. See also CITY PLANNING, TOWN AND COUNTRY PLANNING, TRADITIONAL TOWN PLANNING and URBAN AND REGIONAL PLANNING.

town scheme An area where the conservation of buildings and the environment is promoted with grants from English Heritage and the local authority.

town square The civic, commercial and social centre of a town, often used for markets, public events and festivals. Andres Duany and Elizabeth Plater-Zyberk (2001) note that 'town square' is often a euphemism for a strip mall (shopping parade). See also SQUARE.

town team A group of local people who take responsibility for a town's strategic planning. The approach was used in Yorkshire in the regional development agency's Renaissance Towns initiative in 2001.

Town That Was Murdered, The A book by Ellen Wilkinson, published in 1939, about the economic decline of the ship-building town of Jarrow on Tyneside (which had already been dramatised by the Jarrow March of unemployed workers to London).

town tidying The architect WR Lethaby called for a 'movement' of town tidying in 1916 in an essay for the Arts and Crafts Society (reprinted in Lethaby, 1922): 'not the affair of a few but of everyone... Order, tidiness, the right way of making things and the right way of doing things, especially the public things of our towns and cities.'

town, to go up to To go to London.

townhouse See TOWN HOUSE.

townless highway (US) One avoiding the smaller towns near its route. The term was current in the 1940s.

townlet CLOUGH WILLIAMS-ELLIS wrote of LANSBURY: 'One welcomed this brave baby townlet, peeping hopefully out, as if it were like a little kangaroo from the pouch of its old mother borough of Poplar' (quoted in Croft, 2001).

townling A town dweller.

Towns and Cities: Partners in Urban Renaissance Initiative A scheme run by the Office of the Deputy Prime Minister's URBAN POLICY UNIT in which 24 partner towns in England promoted positive change in inner urban areas. Also called the Working with Towns and Cities Initiative.

townscape 1 Urban form and its visual appearance; the appearance of streets, including the way the components of a street combine in a way that is distinctive to a particular locality. GORDON CULLEN wrote: 'One building is architecture, but two buildings is townscape'. **2** An approach to urban design that focuses on this. Whistler and Reed (1994) note that the *Oxford English Dictionary* cites 1880 for the first use of the word *townscape* and 1889 for its specific use in this sense. They quote THOMAS SHARP reinventing the term 'by an analogy with an equivalent art practised by the eighteenth century improver of land, it might be christened townscape' (Sharp, 1948). The use of the term was developed through writers (like Sharp) associated with the *Architectural Review*, including Ivor de Wolfe (*nom de plume* of its proprietor, HUBERT DE CRONIN HASTINGS) and Gordon Cullen (author of *Townscape*) in the 1940s and 50s. IAN NAIRN, also of the *Architectural Review*, wrote of 'the missing art of townscape midway between town planning and architecture' (quoted in King, 1996). **3** Part of a town that can be seen in a single view.

townscape audit In Scotland the phrase is used in government policy to denote a conservation area character statement.

Townscape Heritage Initiative The Heritage Lottery Fund's grant-giving programme for the repair and regeneration of the historic environment in towns and cities throughout the UK.

Townsend, Geoffrey (1911–2002) Developer. With the architect Eric Lyons he built SPAN housing developments in the 1950s and '60s. Townsend established the binding legal agreements that created residents' associations committed to maintaining the buildings and the spaces between them.

townsfolk (US) The people of a town.

township 1 A village. **2** (US) A unit of government found principally in the north east and north central United States. It is a subdivision of a country and is usually 36 square miles in area. Township functions vary but the major services most commonly provided are the maintenance of local roads and the administration of public assistance. **3** (Scots) A farm occupied by two or more farmers in common or separately. 4 (Highland Scots) A small crofting community (Warrack, 2000).

townsman A person who lives in a town.

toxocara canis See DOG FOULING.

Toxteth diamonds Small heaps of shattered glass on Liverpool kerbsides, evidence of car windows smashed by opportunist thieves. The term was coined by the writer Paul O'Keeffe in 2001.

Toyland The setting of Noddy's Toytown tales featured in Enid Blyton's *Noddy goes to Toyland* (1929) and subsequent books. Beneath Toyland is the frightening Bogeyland. See NODDY BOX, NODDYLAND and TOYTOWN.

Toynbee Hall A SETTLEMENT in the Whitechapel slums of east London, founded by the Oxford academic

track

Arnold Toynbee. A visit there in the 1880s inspired JANE ADDAMS to found Hull House in Chicago.

toytown (also Toytown) A pejorative term for a place that seems to have been designed childishly. In 1986 the architectural critic EM Farrelly described 'standard postmodern architects' as 'PASTICHEURS' and 'toytown tarter-uppers' indulging in 'an aesthetic of least resistance'. The architect Nigel Coates called post-modern architecture (in 1988) 'Toytown classic'. See also LEGO.

Toytown The home town of Noddy in the eponymous series of children's books by Enid Blyton. See NODDYLAND and TOYLAND.

Trabant The most common car in East Germany from 1955 to 1989, the Trabbi (as it was nicknamed) was widely ridiculed as typifying the poor quality of the regime's consumer goods.

Trabantenstadt (German) A SATELLITE TOWN. Trabant means satellite.

track The line of a canal, including its cuttings, embankments, locks, tunnels, bridges and towpaths as well as the water channel itself.

tracking *n.* The linear area of roadway along which vehicles pass. The tracking may be a more regular and narrower area than the roadway's entire road surface, for example where the latter is an irregular urban space.

trackless *n.* (Yorkshire) A trolley bus.

tract (US) A section of a municipality by which the Census Bureau counts.

Traction City Another name for London in the children's novel *Mortal Engines* by Philip Reeve, published in 2001. The book is set in a future when towns and cities roam the countryside on wheels, consuming each other. 'It was a dark, blustery afternoon in spring,' it begins, 'and the city of London was chasing a small mining town across the dried-out bed of the old North Sea.' Compare WALKING CITY.

tradition A belief or practice handed down from one generation to another; a continuously developing set

> **"TRADITION IS IN THE LIFE OF THE COMMUNITY WHAT MEMORY IS FOR ITS INDIVIDUAL UNITS"**
>
> *Patrick Geddes*

of beliefs or practices. PATRICK GEDDES (1905) wrote: 'Tradition is in the life of the community what memory is for its individual units'.

traditional neighborhood development (TND) ordinance A document that sets out the enforceable local requirements of TND: 'a genetic code for urbanity', in the words of Spiro Kostof (1992). The use of these regulatory tools is advocated by NEW URBANISTS. See also ELIZABETH PLATER-ZYBERK.

traditional town planning (US) The term is used by some NEW URBANISTS to describe their work, making the point that neighbourhood-based planning is not an innovation. On the contrary, they claim, urban sprawl is a 50-year aberration marring an otherwise consistent history of sound planning.

traffic Users of a THOROUGHFARE. The word's origin is obscure.

traffic calming Measures to reduce the speed of motor traffic, particularly in residential areas. They include education, enforcement and engineering ('the three Es'). A distinction is sometimes made between *volume control measures*, which generally divert traffic to streets better able to handle it, and *speed control measures*, which alter the roadway to reduce speeds. The term was introduced as a translation of the German *Verkehrsberuhigung* by the transport planner Carmen Hass-Klau. She traced the concept back to COLIN BUCHANAN's advocacy of environmental areas (which were themselves inspired by the work of ALKER TRIPP), the first of which were designated in British towns in the 1960s.

DAVID ENGWICHT (2003) insists that traffic-calming initiatives must be considered in a wider context. Everyone has had their quality of life diminished by excessive traffic, he argues, even those who live in quiet cul-de-sacs or on traffic-calmed streets. 'They must breathe poisoned air; endure noise and fumes when shopping; send their children to schools located on major roads; be mired in traffic congestion; become a full-time chauffeur to their children; drive more than they need because public transport is inadequate; or take their life in their hands every time they want to walk or cycle. Our entire society has paid a very high social and cultural price for the loss of the street as the epicentre of community life.' The most common objection Engwicht hears to widely based action to tame traffic is that it is not the local residents that are the problem, but 'rat runners' (people using back streets to avoid hold ups on major roads). Or the critics will argue that it is people from outer suburbs who are causing all the traffic. He insists, though, that local problems (like rat-running) must be devised within a city-wide context. 'It is legitimate for the people who live on a rat-run to say that it is other people who are causing the traffic problems on their street. But this ignores the fact that when the people who live on this rat-run street drive their cars, they probably do to others what others are doing to them. Some people think that traffic-calming measures such as speed bumps and chicanes are the solution, forcing traffic back on to major roads where it rightfully belongs. But this also ignores the fact that major roads are where other people live, where everyone shops, and where most schools are located.'

Engwicht strongly rejects the notion that some streets are for living and others are for driving. 'It is true that some streets must carry more traffic than others. But because of the historical development of our cities, major arterials are also part of their living fabric. Simply diverting traffic out of some streets and concentrating them on major arterials does not address the fundamental issue of how this extra traffic on the major arterial will directly undermine livability for those people who live there, and for those who shop, work, recreate or go to school on these roads. Some people living on rat-run streets, particularly in the inner urban areas, say: "Yes, but it is the people who live on their acreages on the outskirts of town who are causing our problem. We don't drive past their houses but they drive past ours".' Again, there is some validity in this argument, Engwicht concedes. 'But the way you get these people to modify their behaviour is not by throwing bricks and speed bumps at them. First and foremost what is needed is a city-wide cultural change where everyone reduces their car use to an absolute minimum and everyone respects the neighbourhoods through which they drive.' A *traffic reduction treaty* is one means that Engwicht proposes as 'a mechanism for facilitating a collective solution to something which is a collective problem'. See BULBOUT, CHICANE, CHOKER, DIVERTER, DIAGONAL DIVERTER, ENTRY TREATMENT, MEDIAN, NECKDOWN, NEIGHBORHOOD TRAFFIC MANAGEMENT PLAN, RAISED CROSSWALK, RUMBLE STRIP, SPEED BOARD, SPEED HUMP, SPEED TABLE, SPEED WAGON, SPEED WATCH and WARRANT.

traffic circle (US) The UK term is ROUNDABOUT.

traffic evaporation The failure of traffic to reappear on a road from which it was earlier excluded by the road being closed.

Traffic in Towns See COLIN BUCHANAN.

traffic jam Extreme congestion. In the USA the term dates back at least to 1917 (Flavell and Flavell).

traffic management Adapting the use of roads to improve the environment, access, safety or traffic flow.

traffic movement See STREET LIFE.

traffic restraint Discouraging the use of roads by traffic management, fiscal measures, or transport and planning policy.

traffic serial zone (US) A small area in which traffic data is collected.

Trafford Park Built in 1896 following the construction of the MANCHESTER SHIP CANAL, it has been called the world's oldest and largest industrial estate (Middleton, 1991). A major regeneration programme followed the creation of the Trafford Park Development Corporation in the 1980s.

trail 1 A tour through an area with a fixed route, guided by human or written guides, or by signs. **2** (US) A beaten or marked path through wooded land or open countryside.

train à grande vitesse (TGV) (France) A high-speed electric train, travelling at speeds of up to 300 kph on dedicated stretches of track.

train station The term is now common in the UK. A few decades ago it was largely an American term, the UK term being *railway station*. Train station itself superseded an earlier American usage, *railroad station* (Quinion, 2003).

training and enterprise council The TECs were set up in the early 1990s to run youth and employment training services, with private business playing a major role.

Trainspotting A novel by Irvine Welsh (b1961), published in 1994, and subsequently a play and a successful film (directed by Danny Boyle), set against a background of urban squalor and drug abuse in the author's home city of Edinburgh. Welsh (1996) explains that he was motivated to write the book by hearing people discussing Edinburgh's familiar image. 'That image was a lie,' he writes. 'It was at best just a small constituent part of the culture of that city. That of the middle-class, festival city. Yet it had hegemony over all the other images of this urban, largely working-class but multi-cultural city. Other realities existed, had to be shown to exist.' See SCHEMIE.

train-wreck layout A type of layout where buildings (usually houses) are laid out independently of the road and in rotation relative to each other, reminiscent of the carriages of a train that has left the tracks (Duany, 2000). See also DROWNED WORM and LOOPS AND LOLLIPOPS.

trajectory A plan's consequences that evolve through time, as distinct from an end-state, which a different kind of plan might envisage. The trajectory can be adjusted as circumstances change. Compare BLUEPRINT PLAN.

tram (UK) A public transport vehicle running on rails set in the carriageway. Trams were originally horse-drawn, then steam-powered, but since the early years of the twentieth century they have worked by electric traction, drawing power from an overhead cable. Blackpool boasts a celebrated historic system, but most British towns and cities took up their tram tracks in favour of buses (and occasionally TROLLEY BUSES) in the 1950s and '60s. European cities retained and developed their tram systems, however, and in the last 20 years trams have returned to Manchester, Sheffield, Wolverhampton and elsewhere, with more planned. The characteristic clanging and screeching of a tram inspired the Italian futurist Carlo Carrà to celebrate the city's rhythm and movement in his 1911 painting *What the tram said to me*. Tram is a shortening of tram-car.

Originally the word tram referred to the shaft of a barrow. It derives from the Low German word *traam*, a beam or shaft. The US equivalent term is *streetcar*.

tramp 1 A homeless person who travels around on foot. See VAGRANT. **2** A prostitute. The word derives from their walking the streets. **3** A promiscuous woman, by extension from *prostitute*. See also ON THE STREETS, STREETWALKER and UNORTHODOX ENTREPRENEUR.

trance (Scots) An ALLEY (see that entry for regional variants); a lane; a passage.

tranquil zone Defined by the CAMPAIGN TO PROTECT RURAL ENGLAND as anywhere that lies at least three kilometres from a large power station, major motorway, major industrial area or large city; two kilometres from other motorways, trunk roads or smaller towns; one kilometre from busy local roads carrying more than 10,000 vehicles per day, or the busiest main-line railways; and beyond the interference of civil and military aircraft.

Richard MacCormac

transaction The architect Sir Richard MacCormac (1994) has analysed commercial development in terms of those involved in *local transactions* (such as shops and small business) and those involved in *foreign transactions* (such as large corporate organisations). In large commercial developments, MacCormac suggests, the former should be designed to front on to the public realm, while the latter can be placed on upper floors or away from the street frontage. Locating the foreign transaction on the street, on the other hand, will tend to deaden the public realm.

transaction encounter An occasion on which two or more people meet, and exchange or do business of some sort, formal or informal, economic, social or recreational. Spitalfields Market Under Threat defined BRIGHTFIELD SITES in 2002 as 'places where transaction encounters are local rather than global, personal rather than virtual.'

transect A system of classification devised by American NEW URBANISTS. The transect orders development on a range from more rural to more urban: its zones are classified as edge (the least urban), general, centre, core and district (the most urban). See also URBAN TRANSECT.

transfer of development rights (US) A legal mechanism allowing developers to develop at higher than normal project densities in growth areas if they buy or trade rights with people who own land in other places.

transfer station A facility for sorting and compacting waste, and transferring it to its means of final disposal.

Transforming Communities Grants from the New Opportunities Fund for environmental projects.

transfrontier metropolis A large urban area that straddles the border between two countries (Mexico and the USA, for example).

transgressive activities Defined in 2001 by an action group called Transgressive Architecture as unauthorised (and in its view unjustly marginalized) activities such as rough sleeping, street vending, cruising for sex, and squatting.

transit (US) The UK equivalent is *public transport*. From the Latin *transire* meaning to go across.

transit boulevard (US) A rail transit route running within a boulevard's vehicular right-of-way.

transit mall (US) A pedestrian street, closed to general traffic, that carries buses, trams or light rail.

transit node A point where two or more forms of transport meet. See NODE.

transit-oriented development (TOD) A NEW URBANIST development concept pioneered by the California-based, English urban designer Peter Calthorpe. Development is concentrated around public transport stops at a scale that encourages walking, with some workplaces and local services. Terraces of family housing are served by on-street car parking.

transit village (US) One of a series of relatively high-density, mixed-use developments on a public transport route. The planners Michael Bernick and Robert Cervero have promoted the concept. The term is also used in relation to Bay Area Rapid Transport (BART).

transition space Space at a point were two functions meet, with characteristics of both. An area with tables on a pavement outside a café is an example.

transitional housing (US) Provided for homeless people for an extended period, with support from social services, to help them find jobs and prepare to move on to permanent housing. See also FOYER.

transmitted deprivation A tendency to suffer poverty, inherited from parents' poor education and skills, and their low expectations.

transport Means of travelling.

transport channel A generic term for roads, railways and waterways.

transport demand management Agreements between employees, employers and other agencies to limit numbers of vehicle journeys.

transport development area An area of mixed uses and relatively high density with good access to public transport. A local authority can grant planning permission for development in a TDA at higher density than the development plan would allow, if the developer contributes to improving transport locally. See also LIVING CENTRE.

transport interchange A planned facility for changing between different modes of transport (bus/rail, rail/underground, car/train or any other combination). See also PASSENGER INTERCHANGE.

transport policies and programme (TPP) A statement by the local highway authority that was submitted annually to the Department of the Environment, Transport and the Regions. Its estimates of annual expenditure were used in distributing government grants and setting a local authority's capital allocations. This system, by which local authorities drew up annual transport strategies, was replaced in 1998 by a new system of five-yearly *local transport plans*.

transport poverty A measure determined by factors such as car ownership and distance from a bus stop (DETR, 2000).

transportation Transport; being transported; a means of transporting. Pedants in the UK used to insist that the term (its new meaning was imported from the USA) was valid only as a description of what was once inflicted on convicts, but its wider use is now generally accepted.

transportation demand management Programmes aimed at reducing the number of people who drive alone.

trapped countryside A green space in an urban area; an urban park.

trattoria trickle See CAFÉ CREEP.

traveller An itinerant person. See also GYPSY.

Travelstead, G Ware A Texan developer who proposed the CANARY WHARF development in 1985, but pulled out two years later.

tree See A CITY IS NOT A TREE and FIXED HAZARDOUS OBJECT.

tree preservation order (TPO) Made by a local authority under the Town and Country Planning Act 1990 to protect trees of importance for amenity, landscape and nature conservation. A TPO requires consent for the lopping or cutting down of a tree or group of trees.

Treen City The home of the alien Treens in the cartoon strip 'Dan Dare' in the 1950 and '60s *Eagle* comic.

tref (Welsh) Town. Compare DINAS and PENTREF.

trenchless technology Enables underground services and pipelines to be installed and maintained without the need for excavation.

trendism Following trends rather than trying to shape the future. LEWIS MUMFORD warned: 'Trend is not destiny.'

Treppenstrasse (German) A long, open staircase that functions as a street, featured in some BAROQUE examples of set-piece urban design. See also INCLINED PLAZA.

Trezzini, Domenico (1670–1734) Swiss-born architect and engineer. He designed a street plan for ST PETERSBURG in 1717.

triangulation The combination of different activities in a public space; the process by which an external stimulus prompts strangers to talk to one another (Whyte, 1980).

trickability The quality of a HARD LANDSCAPE that provides a wide variety of suitable and challenging surfaces and features to skaters and skateboarders. See SKATEBOARDING.

trickle-down effect One of the supposed consequences of allowing market forces a free rein. The political right traditionally relies on the benefits of market-led development trickling down to the sector of the population unable to afford to buy into it. The political left, on the other hand, tends to favour urban regeneration strategies targeted on those unable to afford what the market offers.

trip reduction Discouraging people from driving alone, in order to reduce congestion.

trip-end activity Using a particular means of transport at either the start or the end of a journey. The term distinguishes this from transport used as the sole means of getting from one place to another. Campaigners for walking argue that walking should be more than a trip-end activity.

triple bottom line, the Economy, (social) equity and environment, said to be the three aims of urban regeneration. In accountancy the bottom line is the final figure.

triple convergence A theory proposed by Anthony Downs in *Stuck in Traffic*, published in 1992, to explain how new roads generate traffic. Drivers converge on a new road in three ways: spatially (changing to the new route), in time (driving at a time that suits them better) and by mode (abandoning public transport). Downs calls these respectively *spatial convergence, time convergence* and *modal convergence*.

triple R (Australia) Roads, rates and rubbish: three of the most basic concerns of local government.

Triple X (US) Amsterdam, the Netherlands.

triple-decker (US) A three-storey building with one apartment on each floor; a *triplex*.

triplex (US) An apartment on three floors.

Tripp, H Alker (Sir) (1883–1954) Swedish-born urbanist. His influential *Town Planning and Road Traffic*, published in 1942, proposed a hierarchy of roads and pedestrian-only precincts. It was an important influence on COLIN BUCHANAN's report *Traffic in Towns*. Alker Tripp was assistant commissioner of police (traffic) in London. See COMMUNITY UNIT and TRAFFIC CALMING.

trivium (Latin) A place where three radial streets meet at a piazza.

trojan horse A respected architect whom a developer uses to design TROJAN-HORSE ARCHITECTURE.

trojan-horse architecture A seducive design by a well-known architect that helps to get planning permission for a development but is later abandoned by the developer in favour of a cheaper, pedestrian design. Compare DELIVERY ARCHITECT.

trolley bus An electric, rubber-tyred passenger road vehicle connected to overhead conductors. The term comes from the connection between the cable and the vehicle, originally a *troller* (Hall, 1998).

trophy architecture Buildings (or designs) by famous architects. See also SIGNATURE PROFESSION and STARCHITECT.

Truman Show, The See SEAHAVEN ISLAND.

trust Defined by Francis Fukayama (1996) as 'the expectation that arises within a community of regular, honest and cooperative behaviour, based on commonly shared norms, on the part of other members of that community'.

trustafarian A young person relying on inherited wealth to live a in an impoverished part of an inner city (*Collins Concise Dictionary*).

Truth Against the World The defiant motto of the architect FRANK LLOYD WRIGHT (a translation of the Welsh *Y Gwir yn erbyn y Byd*).

Tschumi, Bernard (b1944) Swiss architect. See ARCHITECTURE, EVENT-CITIES and PARC DE LA VILLETTE.

Tsukuba A SCIENCE CITY near Tokyo.

Tuan, Yi-Fu (b1931) Chinese-American humanistic geographer. Tuan pioneered the study of humans' emotional ties to PLACE.

Tudor-Walters Report Published in 1918 by the committee of inquiry into 'questions of building construction in connection with the provision of dwellings for the working classes in England and Wales and Scotland and... upon methods of securing economy and despatch in the provision of such dwellings', chaired by Sir John Tudor-Walters. The report, largely written by RAYMOND UNWIN, came down strongly in favour of the 'self-contained cottage' as the most suitable type of accommodation for the working classes. This type of dwelling, the report pointed out, had continued to be the customary means of housing in Britain despite the rapid growth of large towns and cities, and the consequent 'freedom from tenement dwellings' characteristic of the British Isles had been 'regarded with envy by those countries and cities which have had the misfortune to adopt the tenement system to any great extent' (see THE UNIQUE CITY). The Housing and Town Planning Act 1919 (the Addison Act) adopted most of the report's recommendations and design guidelines for dwellings to be built by local authorities, with the result that estates of 'self-contained cottages' became the inter-war norm.

Rexford Tugwell

Tugwell, Rexford (1891–1979) Economic planner and public servant. He was a leading organiser of the GREENBELT TOWNS programme while working at the US Resettlement Administration in the 1930s. He was appointed chairman of the New York Planning Commission in 1938.

tunnel-backs Terraced houses whose rear alleyways are accessed by tunnel-like passageways leading from the front of the terrace to the back. One such passageway serves several houses. Compare BACK-TO-BACKS.

turd in the plaza A (usually abstract) work of art sited in a public place in a desperate attempt to compensate for the miserable architecture around it. The term, which may have been coined by James Wines, has also been used by the PRINCE OF WALES. See also PER CENT FOR ART.

turf politics Political life at its most local, neighbourhood level.

Turner, John (b1927) Trained as an architect, he is noted for developing the theory, practice and tools for self-managed home and neighbourhood building in Peru, the USA and the UK. His books include *Uncontrolled Urban Settlement* (1966), *Freedom to Build: dweller control of the housing process* (with Robert Fichter, 1972) and *Housing by People* (1976). He received the RIGHT LIVELIHOOD AWARD in 1988. 'When dwellers control the major decisions and are free to make their own contributions in the design, construction or management of their housing,' Turner and Robert Fichter write in *Freedom to Build*, 'both this process and the environment produced stimulate individual and social well-being. When people have no control over nor responsibility for key decisions in the housing process, on the other hand, dwelling environments may instead become a barrier to personal fulfilment and a burden on the economy.' See also ALICE COLEMAN, HASSAN FATHY and COLIN WARD.

turning A street. Michael Young and Peter Willmott (1957) recorded this use in their study of Bethnal Green, east London: 'the streets are known as "turnings", and the adjoining ones as "back-doubles"'.

turning the corner The way the joint between two adjoining faces of a building is made to create a sense of continuity between them.

turnkey contract An arrangement by which a contractor supplies a building and arranges the finance to build it.

turnover rent (US) Varies in relation to the tenant's turnover (usually in a shopping centre).

turnpike 1 (UK) A toll road built under an eighteenth-century Act of Parliament. **2** (US) A high-speed toll road. The first, the Pennsylvania Turnpike, opened in 1940.

Tweed, William 'Boss' (1823–78) New York City commissioner. Under his control the Democratic party machine at TAMMANY HALL became a byword for political corruption. He was jailed for fraud.

Twelve A novel by Nick McDonell, published in 2002, about the life of rich kids from Manhattan's Upper East Side and their poor counterparts in Harlem. Twelve is the name of a new designer drug. The central character, a dropout called White Mike, seems to have been inspired to become a drug dealer by the film AMERICAN BEAUTY, in which a youth takes up drug dealing to escape suburbia.

Twentieth Century Society Founded in 1979 as the Thirties Society, from the start its remit was to protect post-1914 British art and design. It changed its name in 1992 – not only, as Alan Powers observed, because it was occasionally mistaken for a dating agency for the over-thirties. Powers (2000b) notes that, for some founder members, 'the 1930s offered a field on which the battle of the styles, current in the 1970s when modernism was under attack, could be investigated in historical terms'.

twentieth-century city The planning historian Laurence Gerckens (2000) has identified 10 events, 10 successes and 10 failures that shaped the twentieth-century American city. First, the ten events. 1) 1847: the beginning of massive immigrations. 2) 1885: the introduction of the steel-framed skyscraper. 3) 1886: the invention of the electric trolley car. 4) 1893: the Columbian Exposition. 5) 1908: the introduction of the inexpensive automobile. 6) 1916: the adoption of the New York city zoning code. 7) 1929: the stock market crash. 8) 1940–45: the second world war. 9) 1950 and after: the cold war. 10) 1958: the introduction of commercial jet aircraft. Second, ten successes: 1) The provision of pure water and effective sewage treatment. 2) The isolation of dangerous and disharmonious land uses. 3) The abolition of corrupt boss governments. 4) The development of integrated roadway systems. 5) The electrification of cities and regions. 6) The advent of universal communications. 7) The widespread extension of home ownership. 8) The realisation of metropolitan and regional park systems. 9) The control of land subdivision. 10) The environmental movement.

Finally, Gerckens' list of 10 failures that shaped the twentieth-century American city: 1) The demise of community-oriented design and development. 2) The lost vision of regional planning. 3) The fragmented nature of metropolitan governance. 4) The unfulfilled promise of high-tech housing. 5) The landscape of racial and economic segregation. 6) Disinvestment in public transit. 7) Defaulting on the promise of public housing. 8) The abandonment of the quest for a 'great society'. 9) Narrowing the mission of HUD (the US Department of Housing and Urban Development). 10) The constraining of comprehensive planning.

twenty-three skidoo (US) **1** Clear off! The phrase is said to have originated in the shouts of policemen charged with clearing New York's 23rd Street of men watching out for women's dresses being blown up by the winds caused by the down draughts from the FLATIRON BUILDING, built in 1903 (Goldberger, 1981). **2** Wow! An appreciative expression of mild surprise popular in the first decade of the twentieth century.

twenty-two metres A standard sometimes specified by planners as the required distance between dwellings. An earlier equivalent was 70 feet. Richard Silson (2002) suggests the standard originated in a 1908 report into the welfare of working-class families. The distance allowed at least one hour of sunlight into a ground floor south-facing window in central London on the shortest day of the year. The alternative belief that 22 metres was chosen as being the shortest distance at which it was impossible to see a nipple is erroneous.

twilight area (also zone) An area, between a town or city centre and the suburbs, showing symptoms of decline. The term was widely used in the 1960s and '70s. Walter Bor, Liverpool's city planning officer, wrote in 1964: 'The whole of the inner crescent of "twilight" areas and two thirds of the Central Area are due to be rebuilt by the turn of the century.' (Often a twilight area would be identified as a ring round the central area: in Liverpool it was a crescent as the city centre is on the waterfront.)

The term suggests a natural process, with the sun setting on an area's buildings when they have come to the end of their natural life. Example: 'Social services are at their least adequate in the "twilight zones" of our major cities where the housing stock is sinking to the end of its useful life' (1973). The concept of traditionally built housing having a natural life is a dubious one, though. Many twilight zones have had a new lease of life thanks to the efforts of housing associations and cooperatives in rehabilitating the stock, through local authority ENVELOPING schemes, environmental improvements or when a change in the local housing market begins the process of gentrification.

Houses decay only when their repair and maintenance is neglected, or when they come to be seen by their occupants as undesirable or unsatisfactory, or when social factors cause an area to be abandoned wholesale. Anne Hathaway's Cottage in Stratford-upon-Avon, hundreds of years old and intensively used, will look as good as ever, long after the last fragment of its original fabric has been inconspicuously replaced. The 1990s US television science fiction series 'The Twilight Zone' has given the phrase a new meaning relating to bizarre occurrences. See MAIN STREET.

twin cities, the Minneapolis and St Paul, two cities in Minnesota joined in one metropolitan area.

Twin Towers, the See WORLD TRADE CENTER.

twin tracking The government's green paper *Planning: delivering a fundamental change*, published in 2001, noted that it was not unusual for housebuilders and other larger developers to twin-track identical applications so that one could be submitted to appeal once the statutory period for determination of an application had been passed. It proposed to supplement authorities' powers so that they could refuse to accept a substantially similar application for the same site if they were still considering a previous one or if it was at appeal or had been called-in.

twinkle An initial development idea (at the stage when it is no more than a twinkle in the developer's eye) (Spencer, 2003).

twitten (also twitting) *n.* (northern England) An ALLEY (see that entry for regional variants) or narrow LANE between two walls or hedges. Compare SLYPE.

Two Cities, The A book by St Augustine (AD 354–430). The two cities are the earthly, where most of the human race live, and the heavenly, where some people live pure lives on earth.

Two Jags A nickname for Labour MP JOHN PRESCOTT, deputy prime minister (appointed 1997) and environment secretary (1997–2001). A keen advocate of public transport while environment secretary, he owned two Jaguar cars. Prescott was ridiculed for such episodes as using a car to take him and his wife the 250 yards from their hotel to the venue of the 1999 Labour party

> **"THE GREEN BELT IS ONE OF NEW LABOUR'S FINEST ACHIEVEMENTS AND WE'RE GOING TO BUILD ON IT"**
> *John Prescott*

conference, where he gave a speech urging motorists to leave their cars at home. An incident where he punched an egg-throwing protestor in the 2001 general election campaign briefly earned him a new nickname: Two Jabs. The media got into the habit: when planning and regeneration were once again added to his portfolio in 2002 (he had previously been relieved of them), he was named Two Jobs. Prescott is known for his mangled syntax and some memorable sayings. 'The green belt is one of New Labour's finest achievements,' he told an interviewer, 'and we're going to build on it.'

Two Nations See SYBIL.

Twopeny, Richard (1857–1915) Editor and author. His book *Town Life in Australia*, published in London in 1883, was a frank assessment of colonial life.

two point four children The average number of children in a family is jokingly said to be 2.4. After the figure was once quoted as an official statistic, the notion of 0.4 of a child proved memorable. Example: 'New Ash Green is the epitomy of middle-management, 2.4 children, Stepford-Wives, Brookside-on-acid, *Daily Mail* reading, suburban hell'. By 2002 the figure had declined to 1.64.

twocking (also twocing) Taking (a car) without consent. The term for this crime of disaffected urban youth derives from the acronym used in police records.

two-envelope system Requires tenderers to submit their tenders in two parts. The client first assesses the parts concerned with technical matters. The second envelopes (containing the financial proposals) of all technically acceptable proposals are then opened. The system is intended to prevent proposals that are technically deficient (buildings being badly designed, for example) being accepted on the grounds of cheapness.

two-line logic A space has *two-line logic* if, when a pedestrian walks down a route that is visible from the main network of streets, the next route to a directly visible destination takes them either out of the back area again or to a significant larger space or building. The concept is central to SPACE SYNTAX ANALYSIS.

Two-R meters The name given to the first parking meters when they were installed in Oklahoma City in 1935. The two Rs stood for what the meters were expected to provide: *regulation* and *revenue*.

two-track planning system One providing a fast-track route to approval for applications that conform to specified design (or other) principles. Western Australia has such a system.

Tyme, John A campaigner against motorway construction in the 1970s. Tyme, a polytechnic lecturer, argued that road inquiries were unjust, as there was neither a national transport policy nor any parliamentary approval of road-building programmes, and the Department of Transport was in thrall to the roads lobby. Tyme made a major impact on public opinion by disrupting public inquiries into road proposals by such means as chaining himself to a table and by publishing in 1978 a book provocatively titled *Motorways Versus Democracy*.

Tyneside flats TERRACED HOUSING divided horizontally, so that the ground floor and first floor are separate flats. Two flights of stairs, at front and back, serve each upper flat. This house type was common on Tyneside in the nineteenth and early twentieth centuries. LONDON COTTAGE FLATS are similar.

type New urbanists tend to organise neighbourhoods, blocks, buildings, streets and open spaces by type rather than by use. 'By choosing from a selection of proven types,' Andres Duany and Elizabeth Plater-Zyberk (2001) write, 'urban designers can work more efficiently to create places that are consistent with existing neighbourhoods.'

typological code Describes the components of a neighbourhood, usually with diagrams of types of buildings, streets and open spaces. The code may be accompanied by a *regulating plan* or map showing where the components are placed. Andres Duany and Elizabeth Plater-Zyberk (2001) explain: 'Unlike typical ZONING practices, typological codes allow the designer to specify the various "types" of buildings, streets and open spaces that will be featured in the plan. After the street network has been laid out, each parcel and thoroughfare in the plan is assigned one of the selected types. Public buildings such as churches, libraries and city halls are often not coded, since these "object buildings" are meant to stand out as special within the urban fabric.'

typology Classification by type (of building or urban element, for example). Also *taxonomy*. Compare TOPOLOGY.

Tyrannopolis PATRICK GEDDES' term for state socialism.

tything See WARD.

Tzonis, Alex See CRITICAL REGIONALISM.

urban

U

UDAL THE URBAN DESIGN ALLIANCE.

UDAT Urban design assistance team. A UK name for the equivalent of the US REGIONAL/URBAN DESIGN ASSISTANCE TEAM. See also CUDAT.

Ugine A cooperative settlement in southern France founded in 1910 to house workers at a steel works.

ugly sister See CINDERELLA EFFECT.

ultra vires (Latin) Beyond legal powers. A local authority action can be challenged in the courts if it has acted beyond its powers.

Umgebung (German) Surroundings; environment.

Umgehung (German) A bypass.

Umweltplanung (German) Environmental planning.

Umweltverträglichkeitsprüfung (German) Environmental impact assessment.

unbuilding The systematic removal of built structures from a site or area. '"Unbuilding",' writes Dan Hoffman (2001) of DETROIT, 'has surpassed building as the city's major architectural activity.'

uncertainty See CERTAINTY.

under the pavement, the beach (sous les pavés, la plage) A slogan of (sometimes paving-slab throwing) protesters in Paris in 1968.

undercill See STALL RISER.

underclass A group of people excluded by poverty, class, race, belief, social dysfunction or disaffection (or any combination of these) from the wider society. Whether some people do constitute an underclass is hotly debated and a matter of definition. The term seems inappropriate in the UK at least. Colin Ward (1989) identifies 'several reasons why it is dangerous and socially destructive to categorise the city poor as a self-perpetuating underclass. The first is that it is not true... The children will keep wandering off into independence and out of the stigmatised group. The second is that it encourages an easy fatalism: the syndrome known as blaming the victims... The third is that it encourages fear... This particular fear perpetuates a grotesque and wounding racial stigma, and adds one more burden to the problems faced by the poor, non-academic urban young.' Sir Peter Hall (1998) records that the term underclass can be traced back to the 1960s.

In 1857 the writer Charles Kingsley alarmed an audience of women with a lurid picture of the lowest level of society. 'We have... to face the existence of a dangerous class... into which the weaker as well as the worst members of society have a continual tendency to sink,' he warned. 'A class which, not respecting itself, does not respect others; which has nothing to lose and all to gain by anarchy; in which the lowest passions, seldom gratified, are ready to burst out and avenge themselves by frightful methods' (quoted in Raban, 1974). See also DANGEROUS CLASSES and OVERCLASS.

Underground, the London London's underground railway network, 146 of whose 259 miles total length are in the open. Its first line (the Metropolitan Railway between Paddington and Farringdon, the world's first operating underground system) opened in 1863. The word 'underground' first appeared on the stations in 1908. The network is also called the Tube.

underneath the pavement the beach A slogan of (sometimes paving-slab throwing) protesters in Paris in 1968.

underpass 1 A section of road passing under another or under a railway. **2** A pedestrian tunnel under a road; a subway.

understanding The American writer Ralph Waldo Emerson (1803–82) writes that mere *understanding* is the urban faculty, whereas the more valuable *reason* is characteristically exercised in the country. 'The city delights the Understanding. It is made up of finites: short, sharp, mathematical lines, all calculable. It is full of varieties, of successions, of contrivances. The Country, on the contrary, offers an unbroken horizon, the monotony of an endless road, of vast uniform plains, the melancholy of uniform and infinite vegetation; the objects on the road are few and worthless, the eye is invited ever to the horizon and the clouds. It is the school of reason' (quoted in White, 1962).

under-urbanisation A condition in which there is insufficient housing and urban infrastructure to serve an area's industry. Compare OVER-URBANISATION.

underutilized parcel (US) Land that could be redeveloped for a more productive use.

unexpectedness See WOW FACTOR.

unfit A house officially designated as 'unfit for human habitation' would be classified as a SLUM. See also TOLERABLE STANDARD.

Unhealthy Areas Committee Chaired by NEVILLE CHAMBERLAIN. In its *Interim Report* (1920) it proposed a plan for London and became the first government committee to call for a policy of decentralisation for the capital.

uniform building code (US) Sets out national building standards.

uniform See DRESS SENSE.

uniformity The quality of not varying. Henry Skene wrote of Edinburgh in 1793: 'We were most agreeably surprised to find ourselves transported into the most regular and superb city that any country can boast; the streets all intersect each other at right angles, and the buildings are of finest stone, constructed in the most perfect uniformity.'

unilateral undertaking See SECTION 106 AGREEMENT.

Unionville A name considered and rejected by EBENEZER HOWARD, together with Rurisville, for his GARDEN CITY concept. See also LETCHWORTH.

unique See MARKETING.

unique city, the London, according to the Danish architect Steen Eiler Rasmussen, whose book *London: the unique city* was published in 1937. It is unique among European cities in being a low-rise city of houses rather than blocks of flats, he writes. Rasmussen wrote the book to warn his compatriots to an alternative and, in his view, more successful and desirable model of urban development to the apartment-block continental model. In the preface to the English edition, Rasmussen notes that London was now enthusiastically importing the very continental model which he believed had failed and considered inferior to the indigenous English tradition. Jonathan Raban (1974) echoes him. 'London is unique among capital cities,' Raban writes, 'in that its middle class regard it as a right to live in a whole house and not in an apartment'. See also ALICE COLEMAN.

unit (Australia) A flat or apartment.

unitary development plan (UDP) Produced by a unitary authority. A UDP states the local authority's general policies for the development and use of land in its area (like a *structure plan*), and detailed proposals (like a *local plan*). Design policies in a unitary development plan set both the strategic and more detailed framework for the local authority's design control and guidance.

unitary urbanism The situationist artist Constant Niewenhuys' vision of the urbanism of the future when the world is a single city. See GLOBAL VILLAGE and NEW BABYLON.

Unité d'Habitation A type of apartment block designed by LE CORBUSIER. The first Unité d'Habitation de Grandeur Conforme, providing housing for 1,600 people and community facilities (including shops, a laundry, post office, hotel, restaurant, school and, on the roof, a kindergarten, running track and sun terrace), was built in Marseilles in 1952. It became a major influence on housing design, though most of its imitators were mere blocks of maisonettes with none of the Unité's communal facilities. Its expressively board-marked or heavily textured concrete finish became a major stylistic influence on subsequent buildings of all kinds.

United Parking Lot of America See ZONING.

universal design (US) Creates buildings or places that are usable by people with a wide range of abilities. In the 1990s this concept was widely used in place of the concept of designing for specific levels of disability.

university of the streets See STREET.

unknowing urban design Described by Carmona, Heath, Oc and Tiesdell (2003) as the continuing 'accumulation of relatively small-scale, often trial-and-error decisions and interventions'. Compare KNOWING URBAN DESIGN.

unorthodox entrepreneur A beggar, prostitute or drug dealer in a Vancouver park. The usage was noted in 2002 by the American Dialect Society.

unreal City The phrase is from TS Eliot's poem *The Waste Land*, published in 1928, where the image is a metaphor for the disintegration of the human soul. It is

T S Eliot

occasionally quoted in planning documents (and elsewhere). What its use in relation to planning is intended to convey is rarely explained, but the phrase is clearly evocative. *The Waste Land* presents the contemporary city as offering a fragmenting, dislocating experience. In the words of the poet Ezra Pound, who edited the poem for Eliot: 'The life of the village is narrative... In the city the visual impressions succeed each other, overlap, overcross, they are cinematographic' (quoted in Timms and Kelley, 1985). 'City' has an initial capital in the poem as it refers to the City of London, the capital's financial district. Eliot's heavily annotated manuscript/typescript (reproduced in Eliot, 1971) shows that he originally wrote 'Terrible City'. The idea of unreality occurs again in a later section of the poem. 'What is the city over the mountains/ Cracks and reforms and bursts in the violet air/ Falling towers/ Jerusalem Athens Alexandria/ Vienna/ London/ Unreal.' Those lines reminded the philosopher Bertrand Russell that he had once told Eliot about a nightmare in which he had dreamed of London as an unreal city, its people as hallucinations, its bridges collapsing and its buildings dissolving into mist.

Max Beckmann (1884–1950), the twentieth century's greatest German painter, wrote in a letter from the western front in 1915 of 'those holes and sharp trenches. Those ghostly passageways and artificial forests and houses. That fatal hissing of the rifle bullets and the roar of the big guns. Strangely unreal cities, like lunar mountains, have emerged there' (Beckmann, 1997).

unsaleable A word erroneously used to describe a house that has been on the market for a long time. The correct term is *overpriced*.

unslum To cease being a SLUM. Jane Jacobs (1961) used the term to describe the process of neighbourhoods spontaneously improving themselves.

unspoiled The word became a term of praise for landscape in the 1920s (Mullan, 2000).

unsustainability See SUSTAINABLE.

unsystematic risk A property development's risk relating to factors over which the developer or investor has some control, such as the property, its location and the method of financing.

Unthank 1 The imaginary, unreal city in which much of Alasdair Gray's novel *Lanark* (published in 1981) is set. Lanark, the protagonist, seems to be in an afterlife. Unthank is the dystopian nightmare in which he finds himself. The rest of the novel is set in Glasgow, of which Unthank is a weirdly distorted representation. **2** Villages in Cumbria, Derbyshire and Northumberland.

Unwin, Raymond (1863–1940) Housing reformer and pioneer of town planning. Unwin, brought up in Oxford, was inspired in the 1870s and 80s by the socialism of JOHN RUSKIN and WILLIAM MORRIS. He began his career as an engineering apprentice. In 1896 he

Raymond Unwin

set up in partnership with the architect BARRY PARKER (his brother-in-law) designing houses and housing estates. In 1902 he prepared plans for New Earswick, a model village outside York. Two years later Parker and Unwin's plan for Letchworth, the first garden city, was approved. Unwin planned HAMPSTEAD GARDEN SUBURB, adopting garden city layouts to a suburban setting. In *Nothing Gained by Overcrowding!* (1912) he argued for low-density housing (he favoured 12 houses to the acre of building land, excluding all roads) and garden city-type layouts. His other influential writings included *Town Planning in Practice* (1909). He became chief town planning inspector in 1914 and was an influential member of the TUDOR-WALTERS committee, whose advice helped determine the sort of housing local authorities built after 1919. By then Unwin was chief housing architect of the Ministry of Health. He was appointed visiting professor of architecture at Columbia University, USA, in 1930.

Andrew Saint (2001) writes that 'Unwin's importance as an urbanist lay less in his designing than in his willingness to get to grips with building regulations in detail, at the level of traffic, roadway, frontage, external appearance and internal planning. Unwin was the first major British architect to give up design for a position in modern government, because he could see that this was where the far-reaching decisions about cities were being taken.' Unwin's career is a reminder that there need be nothing anonymous or uncreative about building legislation, Saint observes. 'It just needs to be in the right hands. It is a field that demands the attention and dedication of first-rate architects today.'

upgrade See BIASED TERMINOLOGY.

uplift *v.* To improve (an area).

upskilling Improving skills.

upstream Earlier in the development process. For example, design is *upstream* of building. See also DOWNSTREAM.

uptown See DOWNTOWN.

upzoning (US) Changing the zoning of an area to a use of higher intensity.

Ur The 4,600–year-old Sumerian city (also known as Ur of the Chaldees) was hailed as the world's oldest when it was excavated in the 1920s, and the name is still used as a prefix meaning 'the original' (see UR-URBANISM). But there are older cities – nearby URUK, for example. The Bible cites Ur as the birthplace of Abraham, the father of the three great monotheistic religions. The site, which was on the River Euphrates until the river shifted its course, is in what is now southern Iraq. See also CATAL HÜYÜK and VARANASI.

Uralmash A post-revolutionary showpiece new town near Sverdlovsk in Russia (Cooke, 2000).

Uranopolis The imaginary City of Heaven in Macedonia, described by Pliny the Elder in *Natural History* (first century).

urb A suburban area. The word, coined in the late 1960s, is a shortening of *suburb*. Compare URBS.

URBAN An urban regeneration programme of the EU.

urban *adj.* **1** Pertaining to a town or city; the converse of RURAL. In the 2001 Urban White Paper the UK government defined an urban area as a settlement with a population of 10,000 or more. United Nations research in 1972 defined urban populations as living in towns of more than 20,000 people (Ward and Dubos, 1972), and in 1999 the URBAN TASK FORCE defined as 'urban' any settlement with a population of more than 10,000, but generally much smaller places are considered urban as well. **2** Pertaining to relatively dense, mixed-use development and streets that are well used by people on foot, as distinct from SUBURBAN. The sociologist Ray Pahl writes that 'in an urbanised society, "urban" is everywhere and nowhere; the city can not be defined'. Jonathan Raban (1973), who quotes this, thinks that Pahl's comment 'smacks of a certain academic blindness to a very real imaginative experience... the knowledge that... in the metropolis, if not first in "the city", one is in a realm of thought and action quite different from that of the suburb, the small town, the provincial city'. Deyan Sudjic (1992) suggests that some modern airports can almost be classified as urban. 'Along with a handful of other international airports, Heathrow has reached the critical mass that makes it much more than simply an interchange between passengers, aircraft and cargo. If not actually a city in its own right, it has become a vital constituent of the city as a whole. Despite the fact that large areas of the airport are restricted to people who have tickets, it has authentically urban qualities that self-consciously fabricated tourist traps such as New York's South Street Seaport or London's Covent Garden do not.' **3** Pertaining to a place. At the government's URBAN SUMMIT in 2002, deputy prime minister JOHN PRESCOTT defined the Summit's remit as including villages and rural areas. The DETR and CABE (2000) used the term 'urban design' to mean the design of groups of buildings and the space between them, even if the setting was rural; and the Scottish Executive (in its 2001 policy statement *Designing Places)* defined urban design as 'the collaborative process of shaping the setting for life in cities, towns, villages and rural areas'.

The term urban is regarded as positive in some contexts but negative in others. When the Urban Task Force wanted to know what sort of terms to use in trying to persuade the general population of the advantages of living in urban areas, their researchers organised focus group workshops to find out. 'The impression gained from listening to the discussions at the workshops was that many participants had quite positive impressions of urban areas,' they reported (URBED *et al.*, 1999). 'However, reading through the transcripts it is very difficult to find any positive quotes that use the word *urban*... except when used in the phrase *urban lifestyle*, which is thought of as positive.' In describing positive aspects of urban places people were more likely to use the word *city*.' The journalist Will Hutton (2002) has written: 'We need to think not of the depressing notion of "urban" but rather the celebratory notion of the city – and to make re-energising our cities part of the... revitalisation of all dimensions of British civilisation.'

A note in the *Guardian* in 1998 observed that *urban*, which it suggested formerly sometimes had negative connotations, was 'now used to mean sophisticated, or expensive, or with considerable design content, or all three. 'As in urban village ("a period three-bedroom cottage in the urban village of South Kensington") or urban sportswear ("camouflage linen drawstring running pants, £255")'. In 2000 Dulux launched three new ranges of paint in the UK: Oriental Living, African Living and Urban Living. The latter offered a choice of 11 shades 'to turn your home into a chic city dwelling': manhattan view, quartz frost, city limit, chalk stone, dot com, café latte, loft, madison mauve, plaza, shale and cracked slate. Two years later the Dulux offered a paint range called simply 'Urban'. Several of the colours – or at least the names – survived from the Urban Living range, but city limit, dot com and café latte had gone, and city view and mochaccino had been introduced. (In his poem 'Glasgow' from his collection *Lucky Poet*, published in 1943, the poet Hugh MacDiarmid offered his own list of the colours he hoped would characterise

the modernist architecture of a future Glasgow: 'Strange subtle colours hard to name,/ –Schooner, terroco, graphite, matelot,/ Sphinx-like fawn and putty, string and carbon blue –...') The humorist Ian Martin (2003b) muses that 'it is a fact that 87 per cent of conferences on architecture now have the word "urban" in the title'.
4 Black; pertaining to black people (usually with positive connotations). Compare COMMUNITY.

The term *urban* was first used around 1610–20. It is derived from the Latin *urbanus*, which itself came from the Latin *urbs*, meaning city. Joseph Rykwert (2000) notes that *urbs* was related to the word for ploughing, since the Romans ritually ploughed around the outline of a new city. See also URBAN AREA.

urban agglomeration The concentration of people, activities and development in towns and cities.

urban aid programme Created in the 1960s to help meet social need in deprived areas, it later became the URBAN PROGRAMME.

Urban Alliance An organisation, active in England in the 1990s, committed to mass protest against capitalism, globalisation and the quality of life in cities. See also RECLAIM THE STREETS. Compare URBAN DESIGN ALLIANCE.

Urban America A report by the President's Commission on a National Agenda for the Eighties, published in 1980. President Reagan approved of its wholehearted confidence in the ability of market forces to promote positive urban change.

urban and regional planning The term was in common use as an alternative to TOWN AND COUNTRY PLANNING, particularly in academia, by the 1960s. It is favoured perhaps to denote a wider focus than that of the Town and Country Planning Acts, and perhaps because it is thought to sound more impressive (see also MARRIAGE OF TOWN AND COUNTRY).

urban architecture 1 Buildings in an urban setting. **2** The overall design of an urban area. The *Urban Design Compendium* (Llewelyn-Davies, 2000) describes urban architecture as 'buildings and open space considered as a totality'.

urban area A generic term for the whole or part of a town, city or conurbation. In the 2001 Urban White Paper the UK government defined an urban area as a settlement with a population of 10,000 or more.

urban armature See ARMATURE.

urban artefact A physical part of a city with its history, geography, structure and connection with the life of the city. The term is a translation (by Sir John Summerson, among others) from the Italian *fatto urbano*, which itself comes from the French *faite urbaine* (Rossi, 1982).

urban autonomy Development that requires minimal connection to mains services such as water, sewage, gas and power.

urban block See BLOCK.

Urban Bus Challenge Fund Provides bus services to deprived areas and isolated estates.

urban buzz A sense of liveliness, particularly that created by people being in a place for a variety of different purposes. The 2003 bid by Newcastle/Gateshead to be City of Culture 2008 was titled 'Newcastle/Gateshead Buzzin' [sic]. See also GAZZARD'S LAW OF URBAN VITALITY and SPACE SYNTAX.

urban capacity study An assessment of how much development a particular area can accommodate.

urban capacity The amount of development that an urban area is likely to be able to accommodate in terms of physical space, road space, public transport capacity, shops and other facilities.

urban choreography See CHOREOGRAPHY.

urban composition An aspect of the visual appearance of urban form. It can be described in terms such as axiality, rhythm, scale and symmetry.

urban consolidation Making the form of a place more compact. Example: 'With Australia experiencing major bushfires, the role of urban design and planning in reducing fire risk is on the agenda. Urban consolidation could reduce the spread of low density into bushland' (from Australia in 2003).

urban containment Preventing the spread of urban areas. See GREEN BELT.

urban countryside A landscape, no longer fundamentally agricultural, across which factories, offices, schools, stores and housing developments are scattered. KEVIN LYNCH originally used the term as a positive prescription for an alternative to the dense, urban city of the European tradition which, in his view, dangerously obsessed contemporary architects and planners. 'Imagine an urban countryside, a highly varied but humanised landscape,' he wrote. 'It is neither urban nor rural in the old sense, since houses, workplaces and places of assembly are set among trees, farms and streams. Within that extensive countryside, there is a network of small intensive urban centres. This countryside is as functionally intricate and interdependent as any contemporary city.' The commentator Tim Mars (1998) includes the new city of MILTON KEYNES and many parts of supposedly rural England in the category of urban countryside. See also RURAL CITY.

Urban Decay A range of cosmetics launched in 2001, apparently aimed at the young and streetwise. The brand logo is in the style of a graffito, hastily applied with an overloaded paintbrush. The eye shadow goes by the name of Oil Slick. The nature of the fragrance can only be imagined. Compare URBAN HEALING.

urban decay The process and the product associated with economic decline, poverty, poor management and maintenance, and obsolete buildings.

urban degradation The deterioration of an urban area; the act of causing such an area to deteriorate.

urban design The collaborative and multi-disciplinary process of shaping the physical setting for life in cities, towns and villages; the art of making places; design in an urban context. Urban design involves the design of buildings, groups of buildings, spaces and landscapes, and the establishment of frameworks and processes that facilitate successful development.

Peter Webber (1988a) defines urban design as 'the process of moulding the form of the city through time'. Jerry Spencer (2003) has described it as 'creating the theatre of public life'. To Carmona, Heath, Oc and Tiesdell (2003) it is 'the process of making better places for people than would otherwise be produced'. The urban designer Doug Paterson has defined urban design as 'merging *civitas* and the *urbs*: building the values and ideals of a civilized place into the structure of a city'. Peter Batchelor and DAVID LEWIS (1986) define urban design as 'design in an urban context'. They use the word design 'not in its traditional narrow sense, but in a much broader way. Economic projections, packaging new developments, negotiating public/private financial partnerships, setting up guidelines and standards for historic revitalisation, forming non-profit corporations that combine citizens with public and private sector financing resources, all are considered as design.'

In the words of the writer and critic Peter Buchanan (quoted in Cowan, 1997a): 'Urban design is about how to recapture certain of the qualities (qualities which we experience as well as those we see) that we associate with the traditional city: a sense of order, place, continuity, richness of experience, completeness and belonging... Urban design lies somewhere between the broad-brush abstractions of planning and the concrete specifics of architecture. It implies a notion of citizenship: life in the public realm. It is not just about space, but time as well. Much of what passes for urban design is conceived only for one moment. Good urban design... is more than just knitting together the townscape. Urban designers should be configuring a rich network in which buildings come and go: a framework of transport, built fabric and other features, which will create natural locations for things. Urban design structures activities.' Buchanan (1988) has written that 'urban design is concerned with analysing, organising and shaping urban form so as to elaborate as richly and as coherently as possible the lived experience of the inhabitants. In essence it is about the interdependence and mutual development of both city and citizen. And at its core is the recognition that, just as the citizen is both biological organism and self-consciously acculturated persona, so the city too is an organism shaped by powerful intrinsic, almost natural, forces (that must be understood and respected in any successful intervention) and a wilfully, even self-consciously, created cultural artefact. Interventions of the creative will have always guided the city's growth and change, elaborated its identity in many ways large and small as well as conceived and realised those crowning glories that make great cities so special. Urban design is essentially about place making, where place is not just a specific space, but all the activities and events that it makes possible. As a consequence the whole city is enriched. Instead of a city fragmented into islands of no place and anywhere, it remains a seamlessly meshed and richly varied whole. In such a city, daily life is not reduced to a dialectic between city centre and one of the similar suburbs: instead the citizen is encouraged to avail himself of the whole city, to enjoy all its various parts and so enrich his experience and education (become street-wise) in the ways only real urban life allows.'

Some urban designers define urban design as 'the design of the spaces between buildings', presumably to distinguish it from architecture, which they define as the design of the buildings themselves. This definition excludes urban design's proper concern with the structure of a place; it ignores the fact that to a significant extent the characteristics of the spaces between buildings are determined by the buildings themselves; and it encourages architects in any tendency they may have to ignore the context in which they are designing. The question of where urban design should or does fit into the landscape of urban professions – whether it should be regarded as a distinct profession itself, or as a way of thinking, or as common ground between a number of professions or between a wide range of people involved in urban change, for example – is widely discussed.

Barry Young (1988) has suggested one set of stages for the urban design process. These are: a) Define physical design principles. b) Identify performance criteria. c) Develop design options. d) Evaluate the options in terms of design principles and performance criteria. e) Develop the preferred option.

Abercrombie and Forshaw wrote in their 1943 County of London Plan of the 'low level of urban design' in pre-war London. Urban design was being discussed in the American planning profession in the 1950s. What is generally said to have been the first urban design conference was held at Harvard University's Graduate School of Design in 1956, its participants including LEWIS MUMFORD, JANE JACOBS, VICTOR GRUEN and EDMUND BACON. Its organiser, Jose Luis Sert, announced urban design as a new academic field, which he defined as 'the part of planning concerned with the physical form of the city' (Kahn, 2002). The first university course in urban design was established at Harvard in 1960. LEWIS MUMFORD wrote in 1957 from the USA accusing FJ OSBORN (in a letter to him) of identifying new towns with 'only one kind of urban design' (Hughes, 1971). In 1959 the American Institute of Planners' policy statement on urban renewal stated: 'Renewal offers an opportunity to secure superior urban design when relatively large areas

urban buzz

of land are improved under coordinated design leadership, and relatively uniform site and building controls' (quoted in Goodman, 1972). The American Institute of Architecture established a Committee on Urban Design in 1960 and it published Paul D Spreiregen's book *Urban Design: the architecture of cities and towns* in 1965. The Joint Centre for Urban Design at Oxford Polytechnic (later Oxford Brookes University) was established in 1972. The UK URBAN DESIGN GROUP was formed in 1978. Punter and Carmona (1997) note that in the UK the term urban design 'had been conspicuous by its absence' in government publications and guidance until the publication of John Gummer's *Quality in Town and Country* in 1994. The Department of the Environment, Transport and the Regions gave a definition (in *Planning Policy Guidance Note 1*) that was broad in describing what urban design covered but, despite its length, said little about what sort of activity urban design was. Urban design, said PPG1, was 'the relationship between different buildings; the relationships between buildings and the streets, squares, parks, waterways and other spaces which make up the public realm; the relationship of one part of a village, town or city with other parts; patterns of movement and activity which are thereby established; in short, the complex relationship between all the elements of built and unbuilt space.' See also KNOWING URBAN DESIGN and UNKNOWING URBAN DESIGN.

urban design action team The UK equivalent of a REGIONAL/URBAN DESIGN ASSISTANCE TEAM. Several were organised by voluntary organisations in the 1980s.

Urban Design Alliance (UDAL) A group of professional and campaigning bodies committed to improving the quality of life through urban design, particularly through collaboration between professional and their institutes. Founded in 1997, its foundation members are the Civic Trust, the Institution of Civil Engineers, the Institution of Highways and Transportation, the Landscape Institute, the Royal Institute of British Architects, the Royal Institution of Chartered Surveyors, the Royal Town Planning Institute and the Urban Design Group. It took the initials UDAL rather than UDA to distinguish it from the paramilitary Ulster Defence Association. Compare URBAN ALLIANCE.

Urban Design Council A proposal made by UDAL (the URBAN DESIGN ALLIANCE) in 1998 for a national advisory body on urban design. The government created an advisory body with a rather different remit in the COMMISSION FOR ARCHITECTURE AND THE BUILT ENVIRONMENT.

urban design framework 1 (UK) A document describing and illustrating how planning and design policies and principles should be implemented in an area where there is a need to control, guide and promote change. It includes a two-dimensional vision of future infrastructure requirements. Such areas include urban quarters, transport interchanges and corridors, regeneration areas, town centres, urban edges, housing estates, conservation areas, villages, new settlements, urban areas of special landscape value, and suburban areas identified as being suitable for more intensive development. The area may be one that is likely to be developed in several phases and by several developers. An urban design framework often covers an area only part of which is likely to be developed in the near future. Urban design frameworks are used to coordinate more detailed development briefs and master plans. These frameworks are also called a variety of other names, including *urban design strategy, area development framework*, and *planning and urban design framework*.
2 Any set of principles that shapes the physical form of urban development. Peter Webber (1988b) notes how a framework for urban design was created in medieval SIENA, 'one of the most admired of cities for its urban qualities, its artistic qualities, the consistency yet variety in its public streets and places and its integrity as a total spatial composition'. We tend to suppose, Webber writes, that the formal delights of the medieval city were due to the exquisite good taste of the ruling class and the exquisite sensibility of the medieval craftsmen. 'Evidence of the political structure of thirteenth century Siena demonstrates otherwise... Each year in May a great assembly was held devoted to building and public works.' The scholar Wolfgang Braunfels (1975), quoted by Webber, explains: 'The citizens of Siena considered each project within the framework of the town as a whole. Many of the resolutions make it clear that no one was free to build at will, and that very strict regulations were enforced. But, from the wording of the texts, we learn that this sense of order in town planning arose from a general idea of what a strong, good, beautiful and pious city should be. For the Sienese, the ordering of the town was directly connected with the order of life which, in its turn, was a mirror of the order of the Celestial City.'

Urban Design Group A membership organisation that campaigns to promote effective action in improving towns and cities. The UDG believes that urban design is not the job of any single profession: making successful places depends on breaking down professional barriers, on building collaborations between the people with the power to make things happen, and making sure that they all (including professionals, developers, councillors and communities) have the necessary skills and understanding. Founded in 1978 as Architects in Planning, the group soon gave itself its current name, describing itself as 'a forum for architects, landscape architects and designers in planning' for a while, until its focus widened still further.

urban design guidance There are four types of guidance that can usually be distinguished one from another. a) Guidance relating to specific places. There are three main types of these: URBAN DESIGN FRAMEWORKS (for areas), DEVELOPMENT BRIEFS (for sites) and MASTER PLANS (for sites). b) Guidance relating to specific topics. These, usually called design guides, cover topics such as shopfronts, house extensions, lighting and cycling. c) Guidance relating to specific policies. Examples are policies on conservation areas, transport corridors, waterfronts, promenades and green belts. d) Guidance relating to a whole local authority area. Such documents may give general urban design guidance for the whole district or county.

urban design strategy A document setting out how urban design principles should be applied in a specific area.

urban designer 1 A professional with a range of knowledge and skills relating mainly to shaping the physical setting for life in villages, towns and cities. A study by the University of Reading in 2000 suggested that such knowledge and skills included: a) Contextual knowledge (the city: urban change, form, issues and policies; property development processes; urban design theory and principles). b) Analysis/appraisal (physical setting, for example townscape/site analysis; activity/user analysis; movement analysis; meaning and association). c) Design policy formulation (development strategy and policy; regeneration strategy and policy; conservation strategy and policy). d) Design (building, landscape and engineering design; site planning; masterplanning; framework design; illustrative design and visioning). e) Implementation (design and development briefing; design and development control; development appraisal; project funding; planning and development law; project delivery and management). f) Collaboration (participative approaches and techniques). g) Selected generic skills (creativity and innovation; design awareness and visual literacy; graphic communication; inter-disciplinary team-working; market awareness and business sense; negotiation skills; ability to visualise and interpret plans). Most professional urban designers are also qualified as town planners, architects or landscape architects. The term *urban designer* was in use in the UK by 1970. **2** A person who contributes to shaping the built environment in any way, such as by designing, writing briefs, making policy, setting standards, commissioning professionals and influencing expectations.

urban destruction Cities start to decay as soon as the processes of maintaining their buildings lapse. The processes of decay are as complex and fascinating as the processes of creation that are their counterpoint. 'Nature is constantly straining against its chains: probing for weak points, cracks, faults, even a speck of rust,' writes Mike Davis (2002). 'The forces at its command are of course as colossal as a hurricane and as invisible as baccilli.'

The destruction of cities has been a popular subject for writers, to whom it has been variously a symbol of transitoriness, the vanity of human aspirations, the cleansing of sinfulness, and much else. The poet Shelley imagined the distant time when 'St Paul's and Westminster Abbey shall stand, shapeless and nameless ruins in the midst of an unpeopled marsh' (Ackroyd, 2000). In a poem about the 1871 Great Fire of Chicago, John Greenleaf Whittier suggested that the fire had cleansed the city of its evils: 'How shrivelled in thy hot distress/ The primal sin of selfishness' (quoted in Smith, 1984). On at least one occasion, JOHN RUSKIN evoked destruction as a necessary remedy. Invited to lecture in Glasgow, he retorted: 'First burn your city, and cleanse your river.' (Less than 100 years later the city fathers seemed to take him at his word – see THE GORBALS.) In his 1908 novel *The War in the Air*, HG Wells portrays Lower Manhattan as 'a furnace of crimson flames, from which there was no escape. Cars, railways, ferries, all had ceased, and never a light lit the way of the distracted fugitives in that dusky confusion but the light of burning. Dust and black smoke came pouring into the street, and were presently shot with red flame' (quoted in Davis, 2002). With the destruction of the WORLD TRADE CENTER in 2001, Wells' vision seems to have been eerily prescient. The protagonist of DH Lawrence's novel *Kangaroo*, written in 1922 and set in Australia, reacts to what he sees as Sydney's complacent suburbs by wishing that 'the sea would send a wave about 50 feet high round the whole coast of Australia'.

Rainer Maria Rilke, writing his 1930 autobiographical fiction *The Notebooks of Malte Laurids Brigge*, can still sense the life which inhabited the former houses that are now gap sites. 'The stubborn life of these rooms had not allowed itself to be trampled out. It was still there; it clung to the nails that had been left in the walls; it found a resting-place on the remaining handsbreadth of flooring; it squatted beneath the corner beams where a little bit of space remained... The breath of these lives came forth – the clammy, sluggish, fusty breath, which no wind had yet scattered. There were the midday meals and the sicknesses and the exhalations and the smoke of years, and the sweat that breaks out under the armpits and makes the garments heavy, and the stale breath of mouths, and the oily odour of perspiring feet. There were the pungent tang of urine and the stench of burning soot and the grey reek of potatoes, and the heavy, sickly fumes of rancid grease. The sweetish, lingering smell of neglected infants was there, and the smell of frightened children who go to school, and the stuffiness of the beds of nubile youths. To these was added much that had risen from the pit of the reeking street below, and more that had oozed down from above with the rain, which over cities is not clean. And much the feeble, tamed, domestic winds, that always stay in the same street, had borne thither; and much more was there, the sources of which were not known.'

With the coming of the second world war, urban destruction on a vast scale became a reality. William Woods (1969) describes the fate of the Polish capital of Warsaw. 'Hitler had ordered it levelled to the ground, and that is very nearly what the German army did. All civilians left alive were marched westward out of the city, either to camps in Poland or to forced labour in Germany itself. With the methodical industry of termites, Germans began ranging through the deserted buildings, seizing anything that could conceivably be said to have a value.' Street by street as the houses were cleared, other troops went through with flame-throwers and set the buildings on fire. 'Houses that still had a wall or two standing were planted with mines,' Woods writes. 'And when the Germans were finished they simply cleared out to the west. Warsaw was never liberated. When the Red Army was ready to advance again it simply moved forward into the vacuum the Germans had left. Poles who came back to the city in January 1945 say that the most terrible thing was to walk down the well-beloved streets, piled sometimes shoulder high with rubble, and to see familiar facades of all the many houses. So that at first one felt that perhaps the damage was not so bad after all. But then one realized that there was nothing except a cold January daylight shining behind the empty window-frames. Yes, the facades were there. But nowhere was there anything beyond them.' Parts of the medieval centre of Warsaw were rebuilt in facsimile after the war, but generally the second world war's destruction paved the way for reconstruction according to new theories of town planning (see DONALD GIBSON). The Australian poet Les Murray (2002) notes in 'The Machine-Gunning of Charm': 'Happy the city that stayed poorish/ or unbombed through the twentieth century/ and never rebuilt itself then/ ...The twentieth century grew such icy/ ambition and scorn that it built marvels/ or else crap...'

In his 1960 autobiographical novel *North*, the novelist Louis-Ferdinand Céline describes Berlin in the last days of the 1939–45 war (translation by Ralph Manheim; the triple dots are Céline's characteristic punctuation). 'The city was all stage sets... whole streets of façades, the insides had caved in, sunk into holes... not all, but pretty near... much cleaner, I hear, in Hiroshima, neat, clipped... decoration by bombing is a science, it hadn't been perfected yet... here the two sides of the street still created an illusion... closed shutters... another curious thing was that on every sidewalk the rubble – beams, tiles, chimneys – was neatly piled up, no disorder, every house had its wreckage outside the door, one or two storeys high... everything numbered!... If the war ended tomorrow all of a sudden, they wouldn't need a week to put everything back in place... in Hiroshima it couldn't be done, progress has its drawbacks... there in Berlin, a week and they'd fix it all up!... the beams, the drain pipes, every brick, already classified and numbered, painted yellow and red... which gives you an idea... a nation with an innate sense of order... that house is good and dead, one big crater, all its bowels and pipes outside, its skin, heart, bones, yes, but the innards nicely grouped, in perfect order on the sidewalk... as if an animal in the slaughterhouse... a stroke of the wand! presto!... were to pick up its guts! giddyap!... and gallop away!' The novelist Rose Macauley wrote in *Pleasure of Ruins* of how ruined buildings and streets evoke the people who once lived there. Her 1950 novel *The World My Wilderness* was set in the blitzed ruins of London. Macauley herself had lost all her belongings when her London flat was bombed in 1941.

Stephen Barber (2002) notes how some film-makers responded to the war's aftermath. 'In the films of the late 1940s,' he writes, 'the monochrome images of Europe's impoverished or ruined cities appear as incitements to act – to invent new cities, to destroy the residue of the old ones still further, to instigate physical or social upheavals. Human figures are shown trapped within suffocating urban environments that work to exact repetition and subjugation. Only film images of the city capture that moment's unique, contrary substance of urban paralysis and insurgence.' In her 1947 novel *The Fountainhead*, Ayn Rand describes her architect hero Howard Roark blowing up a public housing development that he designed but whose design has been compromised. 'The upper part of the... building... tilted and hung still while a broken streak of sky grew slowly across it. As if the sky was slicing the building in half. The streak became turquoise-blue light. Then there was no upper part, but only window frames and girders flying through the air...'

The poet Robinson Jeffers (1887–1962) described cities as locking people together into interdependence. He wrote in 'The Purse-Seine' that the great cities 'have gathered vast populations incapable of free survival, insulated/ From the strong earth, each person in himself helpless, on all/ dependant'. The future promised 'inevitable mass-disasters... surely one always knew that cultures decay...' In his characteristically unfestive poem 'Summer Holiday', Jeffers imagined a time when 'the towered-up cities/Will be stains of rust on mounds of plaster'. In her poem 'The City Planners', Margaret Atwood describes what she feels is an offensively sane and sanitary suburb. It seems doomed: she imagines 'the landscape behind or under/ the future cracks in the plaster/ when the houses, capsized, will slide/ obliquely into the clay seas, gradual as glaciers'. In 'Peace in the

Welsh Hills' by the poet Vernon Watkins (1906–67), the city is a metaphor representing, perhaps, human spirit and faith. The natural landscape soon comes to life after a storm: 'Rivers fly faster, and upon their banks/ Birds preen their wings, and irises revive./ Not so the cities burnt alive with fire/ Of man's destruction: when their smoke is spent,/ No phoenix rises from the ruined walls.' But the tranquillity of the countryside keeps alive hope and faith. 'There is a city we must build with joy/ Exactly where the fallen city sleeps.'

Much post-war planning and redevelopment has been characterised by its critics as urban destruction. In the 1978 the punk band THE CLASH sang in 'Clash City Rockers' about 'burning down the suburbs with a half-closed eye'. Their song 'Up in Heaven' forsees the fate of high-rise housing estates (see also HIGH RISE). 'The towers of London, these crumbling rocks/...You can piss in the lifts which have broken down/ You can watch from the debris the last bedroom light/... When the wind hits this building this building it tilts/ One day it will surely fall to the ground'. See also AFTER LONDON, BAEDEKER RAIDS, BERLIN EXPRESS, BLITZ, CHELYABINSK-40, CITY BY THE SEA, CITY IN THE SEA, THE CITY OF DREADFUL NIGHT, CREATIVE DESTRUCTION, THE DAY OF THE TRIFFIDS, DEAD CITIES, DEBRIS SURGE, DESTRUCTION OF SODOM AND GOMORRAH, EARTH ABIDES, EARTHQUAKE, EVERYTOWN, GENETIC BLUEPRINT, GERMAN VILLAGE, ARTHUR 'BOMBER' HARRIS, GEORG HEYM, I AND THE CITY, INDEPENDENCE DAY, ALBERT KAHN, LUFTWAFFE, THE MARBLE FARM, LUDWIG MEIDNER, MELLONTA TAUTA, OAK AND ELDON GARDENS, ON THE MARBLE CLIFFS, OPERATION GOMORRAH, OPERATION MEETINGHOUSE, PERLE, PRUITT-IGOE, QUARRY HILL, RATS, THE SCARLET PLAGUE, SECOND CIVIL WAR, SHAHAR-ASHOOB, ALBERT SPEER, STREET BOYS, THEKLA, THINGS TO COME, UNREAL CITY and WORLD TRADE CENTER.

urban development corporation (UDC) The Thatcher government created urban development corporations through the Local Government, Planning and Land Act 1980 to buy and redevelop land. What new towns had achieved largely on greenfield sites, UDCs were intended to do in rundown urban areas. It was in fact the chairmen of new town development corporations who had long lobbied the government to set up urban development corporations, though the Thatcher model differed in some ways from their prescription. UDCs were set up in central Manchester, London Docklands, Cardiff Bay and elsewhere. The UDCs were, like those for the new towns, independent of local government, their boards accountable to Parliament through the secretary of state for the environment (at that time, the entrepreneurial MICHAEL HESELTINE). They were given large tracts of land previously owned by local authorities and statutory undertakers. Unlike the new town corporations, they had the power to give planning permission in their designated areas. In their early days, the UDC boards generally responded enthusiastically to their brief that local authorities were part of the problem, not the solution, and that consulting the public was an unnecessary cause of delay. The UDCs had lives of around 10 years.

urban diabetes Defined in 2002 by James Jones, Bishop of Liverpool, as a social disease that pumps a large quantity of blood into city-centre projects so that there is nothing left for the urban extremities, which rapidly deteriorate.

urban diplomacy Cities engaging with one another in competition or collaboration.

urban domain The planner and political scientist Maarten Hajer and the sociologist Arnold Reijndorp (Hajer and Reijndorp, 2001) describe urban domain as semi-public space that is privately owned and managed but used as a public space (a retail mall, art gallery, airport or stadium, for example). Compare their definition of URBAN REALM.

urban ecology The study of patterns of urban development according to principles inspired by biology. The term was coined by Ernest Burgess and ROBERT PARK. Also called *human ecology*.

urban engineering A working group on URBAN DESIGN skills convened by the Commission for Architecture and the Built Environment suggested in 2001 that this, or something similar, might be a more compelling title for a course than 'urban design' if an institution were seeking to attract engineers on to it.

urban entrepreneurialism Towns and cities competing for economic development.

urban exodus The movement of people from towns and cities to suburbs or settlements in the countryside.

urban extension A planned development at the edge of and continuous with an existing urban area.

urban fabric The physical, built form of an urban place.

urban fallow land Land in an urban area that is no longer in permanent use; BROWN LAND. The term is a translation from the French *friches industrielles* and *friches urbaines* (Hebbert, 2000). Also known as *urban fallows*.

urban false memory syndrome Designing buildings and places which reflect a history that is more imagined than real. See also AUTHENTICITY.

urban field 1 A polycentric urban region. **2** The sphere of influence of an urban centre.

urban first The principle of reusing urban sites before developing in green fields. See BROWNFIELD.

urban forest (US) The trees in a city's street, parks and gardens.

urban form See URBAN FABRIC.

Urban Forum An umbrella body for community and

voluntary groups with interests in urban and regional policy, especially regeneration.

urban fringe The zone where town and countryside meet. It may be as logical to call such zones *rural fringe*, as Tunbridge Wells' planners have done in order to emphasise the importance of the fringe remaining rural as long as possible (Punter and Carmona, 1997). Also called the EDGELANDS. Compare BORDERLANDS.

urban governance The methods by which an urban area is governed and administered by local government and a variety of other agencies.

urban grain The pattern of the arrangement and size of buildings and their plots in a settlement; and the degree to which an area's pattern of street-blocks and street junctions is respectively small and frequent, or large and infrequent. Compare URBAN STRUCTURE.

urban green spaces The Urban Green Spaces Taskforce (2002) defines them rather opaquely as being 'increasingly understood to mean the green areas within the overarching term of open space'. This includes, the taskforce notes: a) Public parks and gardens. b) Play spaces (playgrounds, play areas, adventure playgrounds and play centres). c) Natural green spaces (urban wildlife, ecology and woodland areas). d) Amenity green spaces (residential squares and public spaces around buildings. e) Functional green spaces (publicly accessible cemeteries, allotments, community gardens, sports fields, publicly accessible school grounds, churchyards and urban farms). f) Green corridors (including river banks, canals and waterfronts). g) Greening of urban vacant and derelict land. h) Private green spaces which benefit the public. See also AMENITY GREEN SPACE and URBAN OPEN SPACE.

urban greenfield Urban land that has never been built on, including playing fields, parks, other public open space and landscaped areas, flood plain and land too small or inaccessible (due to being hemmed in by railway lines, for example) to have been developed. Compare BROWNFIELD.

urban grid A network of intersecting streets. BILL HILLIER (1996) describes the urban grid as 'the organisation of groups of contiguous buildings in outward-facing, fairly regular clumps, amongst which is defined a continuous system of space in the form of intersecting rings, with a greater or lesser degree of overall regularity'.

urban guerrilla A member of an organised group committed to fighting in an urban area against the authorities. Examples include the Angry Brigade in the UK, the Red Hand Commando in Japan and the Baader-Meinhoff Fraction in West Germany.

Urban Healing A range of cosmetic products by Farmacia. British Airways issued them in 2001 to their female first-class passengers. For that particular clientele, the marketing specialists seemed to assume, the word urban had sophisticated, positive associations, but its tough grittiness was also something that one needed help in recovering from. Compare URBAN DECAY.

urban healing Sympathetically renewing an area while making the most of the physical fabric that already exists.

urban heat island An area of warmer temperatures associated with urban development. The effect is caused by the urban fabric retaining and storing heat; by industry, heating, air conditioning and transport; by pollution reducing the radiation of heat; and by drainage reducing the amount of cooling by the evaporation of surface water. Mike Davis (2002) notes that the nightly temperature in Las Vegas, for example, is frequently five to 10 degrees hotter than the surrounding desert. Example: 'Sparrows… are small birds which can lose body heat very quickly, so they are perfectly adapted to the "heat island" of London' (Ackroyd, 2000). See also SEAGULL.

urban homesteading 1 Taking on the ownership of a rundown, derelict or abandoned house for little or no payment in exchange for a commitment to improving it and bringing it back into use. **2** Making houses available for this purpose. The term dates from the early 1970s. It was one of the housing policy initiatives of the Conservative Greater London Council in that decade.

urban husbandry Managing an urban place in a way that makes good uses of resources.

urban ideology Defined by Karl Mannheim (quoted in Fishman, 1971) as plans for large-scale reconstruction that seek to preserve and glorify an already powerful class. See HAUSSMANN.

urban infrastructure Systems of services such as water supply, sewerage, surface water drainage, highways and other transport facilities, telecommunications facilities, energy distribution networks; also health and education facilities, leisure facilities, open space and systems relating to law and order, public health, welfare and public administration.

urban integration The quality of a place being connected at both local and wider scales. For example, in the words of the Urban Task Force (1999), 'to achieve urban integration means thinking of urban open space not as an isolated unit… but as a vital part of the urban landscape'. See also INTEGRATION.

urban intensity A concentration of activity promoted by the proximity of people and a mix of uses. It is a quality that is 'lost like a fire which dies down when the logs are separated,' according to the architect Erik Gunnar Asplund.

urban intervention See INTERVENTION.

urban jack-boot A term used in the 1990s by the countryside lobby to describe the supposed oppression of country people by urban populations.

urban jungle A place where people feel unsafe and

urban fabric

where they have difficulty in finding their way around. To people marketing gas-guzzling SUVs, a city is more than a jungle. 'Admittedly, there are no boulders, crevasses or bears to deal with,' says a 2003 newspaper advert for the Jeep Cherokee. 'Just Camden High Street, speed bumps and couriers with short fuses.' The advert continues (moving swiftly on from boulders, crevasses and bears): '"It's a jungle out there" they say. Well they're wrong. In the jungle, you'd know what to expect. So while the Cherokee 2.8 CRD Automatic gives you all the mod cons you'd want, you also get all the Jeep ruggedness that, in a better world, you wouldn't need.' Also CONCRETE JUNGLE. Compare LEGIBILITY.

urban legend See URBAN MYTH.

urban livelihoods approach A method of understanding the opportunities and assets available to poor people.

urban living In 2002 business leaders in Maidstone, Kent (home of the liquorice allsort, apparently) distributed a pamphlet *Maidstone: alternative urban living*. It claimed that the town offered urban attractions such as loft-style apartments, lively night-life and designer shops at a much lower cost than London.

urban malaise Multiple problems facing an urban area.

urban marker A feature that acts as a landmark in the streetscene. Example: 'Its primary function was as an urban marker, an emphatic stop to the vista along the road'.

urban metabolism The process by which an urban area takes in resources such as water, food and raw materials, and puts out products and wastes. The metabolism may be *linear* or to some extent *circular*. A natural ecosystem such as a forest has a circular metabolism, the falling leaves providing nutrients for the trees.

urban millennium The second millennium, 1901–2000.

urban model The pattern of land use in a town.

urban monoculture An area devoted mainly to a single use. Compare MIXED USES.

urban morphology The study of urban form. See MORPHOLOGY.

urban motorway A MOTORWAY in a built-up area. Sir Peter Hall (1998) describes Henry Hudson Parkway in New York state, begun in 1934, as 'the world's first true urban motorway'.

urban music Black or underground popular music (as distinct from 'pop' music), particularly that which reflects cultural diversity and cross-fertilisation. Examples: 'In the USA, urban music is just a euphemism for black music, and it's really hard for us to get our white artists played on urban radio' (2002); 'The music industry in the UK is quite multicultural and mixed up. An artist can be both a popstar and an urban, underground star' (2002). *Country music*, by contrast, is largely made and enjoyed by white people, though its roots are in cities (Memphis and Nashville, for example) as much as the country.

urban myth (also legend) An often-repeated story of unknown origin and dubious veracity, often humorous or horrific. They are called 'urban' perhaps because they are generally set in familiar, everyday places, rather than in a far-off country, long ago.

urban networks for innovative cluster area (unica) A type of high-tech business cluster proposed by the UK Department of Trade and Industry in 1999. Technology parks would be developed at four or five growth points in each cluster, with good road and commuter links to a university town up to an hour's drive away.

urban open space Defined by the Urban Green Space Taskforce (2002) as comprising a mixture of private and public, formal and informal landscape and townscape within designated urban boundaries, and including streets, boulevards, plazas, pedestrian areas, footpaths, cycleways, squares, parks and green space. See also URBAN GREEN SPACE.

urban playscape The bars, clubs and other places that provide the setting for young people's night-life.

urban plume A persistent cover of smoke over a city (Ackroyd, 2000).

urban policy Attempts to order, control and manage the forces shaping urban areas. Satirical columnist Ian Martin (2000) sums up his impression of UK government urban policy: 'City folk are to be encouraged to stay where they are and clock up enough income tax to subsidise rural services.'

Urban Policy Unit Set up in the Department of the Environment, Transport and the Regions in 2000, it was transferred to the new Department of Transport, Local Government and the Regions in the following year, and later to the Office of the Deputy Prime Minister.

urban practitioner A generic term for a professional engaged in matters of urban change. The term was newly current in the UK in 2002.

urban prairie A derogatory term for green but featureless open space of minimal ecological value. Also known as ECOLOGICAL DESERT.

urban priority area The Urban Task Force (1999) proposed *urban priority areas* with streamlined planning processes.

urban professional 1 A professional person leading an urban lifestyle. **2** An URBAN PRACTITIONER.

Urban Programme A government grant regime set up in 1978. It was replaced by the SINGLE REGENERATION BUDGET and later the SINGLE POT.

urban quality consultant An URBAN DESIGNER; an URBAN PRACTITIONER. The urban designer JAN GEYL describes his practice in this way.

Urban Question, The 1 Russia's first journal devoted to town planning, launched in St Petersburg in 1909. Its principal editor was DMITRII PROTOPOPOV (Cooke, 1978). **2** An influential book by Manuel Castells, published in 1977, presenting a Marxist analysis of cities as 'spaces for collective consumption'.

Manuel Castells

urban realm The planner and political scientist Maarten Hajer and the sociologist Arnold Reijndorp (Hajer and Reijndorp, 2001) describe urban realm as public space owned and controlled by the city. Compare PUBLIC REALM and their definition of URBAN DOMAIN.

urban reconstruction (US) URBAN REGENERATION.

urban refacement Superficial improvements. Example: 'Only a block deep and intended for easy access from suburban highway systems, these superficial surfaces of urban refacement... simultaneously erase both the guts and guilt of what had been one of the largest and wealthiest cities in the modern world [Detroit]' (Daskalakis, Waldheim and Young, 2001).

urban regeneration The term became current in the 1980s (and more widely after 1995) as a replacement for URBAN RENEWAL, a term that had become associated with wholesale clearance and comprehensive redevelopment. It was used initially by the private sector and was later applied to all kinds of positive urban change. English Partnerships defined regeneration in 2003 as 'the holistic process of reversing economic, social and physical decay in areas where it has reached a stage when market forces alone will not suffice'. David Donnison's and Alan Middleton's (1987) book *Regenerating the Inner City* used the terms regeneration and renewal interchangeably. Urban regeneration was the banner under which MICHAEL HESELTINE launched his personal crusade against urban problems, focusing on Liverpool, after the 1981 inner-city riots. *The Connected City* (1997) defines urban regeneration as 'spending a large sum of money over a short period on an area that has failed so disastrously as to be embarrassing'. By 2000 the term was being used to distinguish improvements to the physical environments from social improvements in urban neighbourhoods (URBAN RENEWAL). The 2000 Urban White Paper wrote of 'regeneration and urban renaissance', seeming to make a distinction between the two but not spelling it out. The context suggested that *regeneration* was being used to mean economic development. (Chris Couch [1990] defined urban regeneration as 'something more than urban renewal... in essence we are talking about economic growth'.) Planners at the South East England Regional Assembly said in 2002 that they regarded urban regeneration as a subset of URBAN RENAISSANCE. The latter, they considered, embraced environmental, social and economic policy objectives, and was applicable to all urban (including suburban) areas, not just those requiring economic intervention. Regeneration's use in the urban context draws on the word's biological meaning of new growth and repairing damaged tissue, and its theological meaning of spiritual rebirth. The word dates from the first half of the fourteenth century. See also IMPROVEMENT, RECONSTRUCTION, REFURBISHMENT, REVAMP, URBAN RENASCENCE, URBAN RESURRECTION and URBAN REVITALISATION.

urban regeneration company (England) A not-for-profit company set up by local authorities, regional development agencies and ENGLISH PARTNERSHIPS, among others, to promote physical and economic regeneration. The aim is to combine the freedom of URBAN DEVELOPMENT CORPORATIONS from bureaucracy and their ability to act commercially, on the one hand, with the active involvement of local authorities, on the other. The first were set up in Liverpool, Sheffield and east Manchester, in response to a recommendation in the report of the URBAN TASK FORCE in 1999.

urban region A city (or conurbation) and its hinterland. Planners increasingly see the urban region, as opposed to just the city, as the appropriate scale for their activities and deliberations. The novelist HG WELLS, writing in 1902, foresaw 'urban regions' or 'town provinces' replacing towns and cities. 'It is not too much to say that the London citizen of the year AD 2000 may have a choice of nearly all England and Wales, south of Nottingham and east of Exeter as his suburb'. In Wells' utopian vision this region would combine the best of town and country. See also CITY REGION.

urban renaissance The phrase adopted by Tony Blair's first Labour government for what had previously been called *urban regeneration* (particularly around 1995–1998), and before that, *urban renewal* (common until around 1995). Promoters of urban change rebrand their activities from time to time so as to distance themselves from previous calamities. *Urban regeneration* emerged as the preferred phrase of the private sector, conveying a suggestion of some sort of natural rebirth engendered by market forces. *Urban renaissance*, in its turn, was heralded by Lord Rogers' URBAN TASK FORCE in 1999. The phrase and its historical overtones hinted at a design-led approach which would inspire an upsurge of creativity and a rediscovery of what urban life could offer. English Partnerships defined urban renaissance in 2003 as 'the process of making towns, cities and other areas liveable'. A committee of the American Institute of Architects, in presenting their 'Architects' Plan for Boston' in 1961, talked of 'the coming renaissance of our cities' (Goodman, 1972). The term was used in 1980 in a Council of Europe campaign for improving historic towns (URBED and UCL, 2000), and in the south east England regional planning agency SERPLAN's *Sustainable Development Strategy for the Southeast*, published in 1998 (Punter, 2000). What would constitute an urban renaissance is rarely defined. Lord Heseltine (2002), former environment secretary, claimed in 2002 that 'in the 1980s and 1990s we saw an urban renaissance the like of which has not been seen since the nineteenth century'. The term takes its power from the more general use of renaissance to describe the fourteenth to seventeenth century revival of the arts and learning in Europe. The English usage of the word *renaissance* dates from the 1830s. Writers in the renaissance themselves used the Italian term *rinascimento*, meaning rebirth.

urban renaissance manager The regional development agency Yorkshire Forward advertised such a post in 2002. It was looking for someone with 'a track record in urban design and community engagement' to help develop its RENAISSANCE TOWNS programme.

urban renaissance zone Proposed by the Institute of Historic Building Conservation in 2002 in response to a government proposal for business planning zones, they were intended to focus on land assembly, master planning and providing transport, public realm and infrastructure, and to be 'design-led and heritage-led'.

urban renascence In the urban context as well as in general use, renascence is less common than the alternate spelling *renaissance*. Renascence is older, dating from the 1720s.

urban renewal 1 Social improvements in urban neighbourhoods. English Partnerships defined renewal in 2003 as 'improvement in the situation of the most disadvantaged places and their communities, including the level and quality of the services they receive. Renewal objectives may be wide ranging but will seek to deliver improved work and business opportunities, improved residential attractiveness and improved public services' (compare URBAN REGENERATION). **2** Redevelopment and improvement in towns and cities. This use of the term is less common since 'urban renewal' was displaced by URBAN REGENERATION in the 1980s and since it acquired its new social connotations in the 1990s, but it still survives. For example, the Sustainable Urban Renewal Expo of 2003 was devoted to 'urban planning, design and conservation, and sustainable materials' rather than social issues. **3** (Netherlands) Renewing the physical fabric. In this Dutch usage the corresponding term for bringing people to live in such renewed areas is URBAN REVITALISATION. Though the words are taken directly from the English, their use differs from that in the UK.

The term has been in use since the 1940s. THOMAS SHARP used the term 'renewal' in 1946 in his book *Exeter Phoenix*: 'The watchword for the future should be – not restoration, but renewal.' LEWIS MUMFORD (Hughes, 1971) 'had a vague remembrance' that he himself had coined the phrase. In 1958 he wrote to FJ OSBORN: 'Your remarks about the betrayal of the Urban Renewal programme awakens very heartfelt echoes: all the more because... I feel a little guilty at having even invented a phrase that has lent itself to such perverse misuse. Perhaps one should always in future use that term in quotation marks. As I predicted in 1940, some of our skyscraper housing projects have become filthy slums.' In another letter in 1958 Mumford wrote to Osborn: 'What has happened to [the term urban renewal] gives no cause for anything but shame and indignation. In America it has simply become a policy of lending government aid to assemble land for the private investor, who gets a further government subsidy in acquiring the land at a lower price than the market would demand. The whole business is scandalous: socialisation for the sake of the rich accompanied by the expropriation and the expulsion of the poor! This use of the term has made renewal a filthy word – like "love" or "creativity" in the mouth of an advertising copy writer' (Hughes, 1971). Lionel Esher (1981) had a similar feeling, recalling that 'the words Urban Renewal had by 1963 been appropriated by the developers and were no longer in radical currency, except satirically'. Peter Webber (1988b) notes of the first International Seminar on Urban Renewal, held in the Hague in August 1958, that 'despite the platitudes and the cautions that "urban renewal must be applied with great caution, sympathy and understanding", the overwhelming mood of the papers was in favour of massive clearance and rebuilding projects... The seminar programme director proclaimed with chilling confidence: "Cities mirror the will and wisdom, the ideas and ideals of men. The structural fabric of the community has little value apart from the satisfaction it affords human functions, needs and desires. The life of the city is in the life of its people, and the physical structure of the city must be renewed in order to nurture the life of a contemporary society".' Urban renewal has been defined by Chris Couch (1990) as 'the physical change, or change in the use or intensity of use of land or buildings, that is the inevitable outcome of the action of economic and social forces upon urban areas'. He adds: 'Since urban areas are never static, urban renewal is going on everywhere all the time'. The term's appearance in the title of the weekly journal *Regeneration and Renewal*, launched in 2000, confirmed its revival and its new meaning. The journal's publishers regarded *regeneration* as referring mainly to physical change, while *renewal* referred more to social change, as reflected in the NEIGHBOURHOOD RENEWAL STRATEGIES being proposed at that time by the government. The term made at least one appearance in the 2000 Urban White Paper, as – oddly – 'a key objective of the Heritage Lottery Fund, particularly in its Urban Parks and Townscape Heritage Initiatives'. The word *renewal* dates from around 1675–85.

urban repair Piecemeal changes to the extant fabric (Kostof, 1991).

urban reserve (US) An area, beyond a serviced urban area, which lies within an urban growth boundary in which future development and extended services are planned.

urban resurrection Miraculously bringing back to life a place that was dead. The phrase is an uncommon synonym for *revival* or *regeneration*. Roy Porter in his Vision for London Lecture 1995 called the revival of Covent Garden 'an object lesson in urban resurrection'.

urban revitalisation Bringing new life to an urban area. See REVITALISATION.

urban schema A person's idea of what towns or cities, or parts of them, or particular types of buildings, will generally be like. A building or a part of a city, for example, may be described as *schematic* if it accords with a schema, *neo-schematic* if it diverges a little (perhaps due to its novel architecture) or *a-schematic* if its form is totally unfamiliar (Smith, 1974). See also PACER ARCHITECTURE.

urban service area (US) That in which the services of a town or city and its public agencies are generally available.

urban service boundary (US) An agreed limit beyond which a state will not finance infrastructure extensions.

urban sociability Enjoying living alongside strangers in towns and cities.

urban sociology The study of social relationships and structures in towns and cities.

urban soldier (US) A person who fights for justice.

urban sports Ones that are practiced in streets and other urban spaces, such as SKATEBOARDING, roller-blading and break dancing.

urban sprawl Unplanned, low-density, development; SUBURBAN SPRAWL. John Norquist (2002), the new-urbanist mayor of Milwaukee, notes: 'there are two things Americans don't like: urban sprawl and density.' Mike Davis (2000) credits the term to the sociologist WILLIAM WHYTE who, in an article in *Fortune* magazine in 1958, described how 'flying from Los Angeles to San Bernardino – an unnerving lesson in man's infinite capacity to mess up his environment – the traveller can see a legion of bulldozers gnawing into the last remaining tract of green between two cities.' Whyte called this 'urban sprawl'. Compare NEW URBANISM, SMART GROWTH and TRADITIONAL TOWN PLANNING.

urban structure The framework of routes and spaces that connect locally and more widely, and the way developments, routes and open spaces relate to one another. Compare URBAN GRAIN.

urban studies centre COLIN WARD and Anthony Fyson of the TOWN AND COUNTRY PLANNING ASSOCIATION published an article in the *Bulletin of Environmental Education* in 1973 arguing for a creation of urban studies centres as an equivalent of the existing *rural and field studies centres*. The Council of Urban Studies Centres (CUSC) was set up later in the year to promote the idea. By 1984 CUSC identified 37 centres, some of which were also ARCHITECTURE WORKSHOPS. CUSC identified the possible functions of an urban studies centre as: a) A base for local schools and colleges to study the local environment. b) A venue for involvement in local issues and with the local community. c) A teaching resource centre. d) A base for teacher training in the field of urban studies. e) A base for visiting the town or city. f) A centre which could be the focus for public consultation in planning and other government activities. g) A venue for community forums and a force for community action. h) The catalyst of large-scale projects that bring about meaningful change in the local area (Newcastle Architecture Workshop, 1990). The urban studies centre movement declined later in the 1980s, though CUSC survived into the new century.

Urban Summit A major conference organised by the UK government in 2002 to discuss urban regeneration. Held in Birmingham and attracting 1,600 participants, it was presided over by deputy prime minister JOHN PRESCOTT. A second was planned for 2005.

urban surgery LE CORBUSIER's term for the drastic treatment he said was necessary to create urban order: the antithesis of the CONSERVATIVE SURGERY advocated by PATRICK GEDDES. Since 1945 the scalpel has been much in evidence.

Urban Task Force Lord Rogers of Riverside (the architect RICHARD ROGERS) had identified himself as a supporter of the Labour party and as a prominent advocate of URBAN RENAISSANCE (a term he helped to popularise) before the 1997 general election. After New Labour's victory, he pressed the new government to fulfil its promised support for urban regeneration and the development of BROWNFIELD rather than GREENFIELD sites. Environment secretary JOHN PRESCOTT bought himself some time by commissioning Rogers to chair an Urban Task Force that would report on how urban renaissance might be achieved. Its brief was to 'identify causes of urban decline in England and recommend practical solutions to bring people back into our cities, towns and urban neighbourhoods. It will establish a new vision for urban regeneration founded on the principles of design excellence, social well-being and environmental responsibility within a viable economic and legislative framework.'

The task force's report *Towards an Urban Renaissance*, presented to the government in June 1999, was generally well received, though the government was reluctant to commit itself to action. It was not until November 2000 that the government issued its formal response, in the form of an Urban White Paper that promised to implement only some of the task force's recommendations. Lord Rogers welcomed the white paper as 'one important step along a very long road' but regretted that it fell short 'of what is going to be required to engender a real urban renaissance'. The following year he said of the task force and the government's response to its report: 'I feel like the wind has been taken out of my sails'. In 2002 he reconvened the task force to review the government's performance. The Urban Task Force's secretary Jon Rouse later became chief executive of CABE, and later of the HOUSING CORPORATION.

urban transect A description or diagrammatical representation in cross-section of the buildings and structures on a route through an urban area. See also TRANSECT.

urban typology The study of types of urban form. At various scales they may be types of city, quarter, block, building, or building element.

urban use A use of a sort characteristic of urban areas. In the UK government's usage, the term does not relate only to uses actually in urban areas. For example, official figures on the amount of development carried out on 'land previously in urban uses' includes industrial sites in rural areas (Breheny, 2001). The distinction is significant in relation to the question of how much urban and BROWNFIELD land is being reused.

urban villa (US) A building similar to a large house, able to accommodate a wide variety of uses, including conventional apartments, single-room occupancy units (like a boarding house), a bed and breakfast inn, a small professional office or restaurant. The model is the old, converted mansion of the inner city (Duany, 1998). Compare VILLA.

urban village 1 A part of a town or city with a distinct identity and a mix of different uses, including housing; an urban neighbourhood; an urban quarter. For example, English Heritage wrote in 2000: 'London is a collection of vibrant urban villages.' The Terry Farrell Partnership (2002) described Swiss Cottage as both 'an existing urban village' and 'a genuine town centre', and wrote that its master plan for the area would create 'one of London's most positive urban villages' and a 'new urban quarter'. **2** A development model advocated by the Urban Villages Group in the 1990s. **3** A village whose land use has changed from rural to urban (Vidal and Gupta, 1999).

The Urban Villages Group was formed in 1989 as the result, it said, of 'the Prince of Wales's wish to investigate and promote the concept of planned mixed-use, mixed-tenure developments which would provide a more civilised and sustainable environment for the people living and working in them'. The Urban Villages Group (1992) explained its use of the term. 'For want of a better label, we have called our proposed development model *urban village*. It is what continental Europeans would recognise as an "urban quarter" – a mixed-use neighbourhood within a wider urban area. The word "village" is, to be sure, much abused and over-used. But real villages have many of the essential characteristics we are arguing for; and, in a British context, urban village is convenient shorthand for what we are aiming at.' An urban village, the group stated, should be big enough to support a wide range of uses and amenities (including primary and nursery schooling), yet small enough (about 40 hectares) for all its buildings to be within easy walking distance. It should have a combined working and resident population of around 3,000–5,000, a variety of sizes and types of building, and a mixture of tenures both for housing and employment uses. It should be promoted by a single body made up of land-owning, developer and other interests, managed by a purpose-made management company, and developed and managed with public involvement (perhaps through a development trust). It should be ecologically balanced. Preferably a single individual or organisation should control all the land. The urban village should be designed with a master plan, supported by detailed design codes. The movement helped to promote the cause of mixed-use development, and a number of urban village developments were built, with and without the approval of the Urban Villages Group. Urban villages have been advocated by the Greater London Authority (2001) which defines them as 'a development concept, based on higher density mixed-use development and

urban open space

redevelopment underpinned by improved accessibility through public transport investment'.

Like GARDEN CITY before it, the urban village label was appropriated by some developers and housebuilders interested in it only as a marketing device. 'Many of the schemes advertising themselves as urban villages are in fact no more than glorified housing estates,' complained David Lunts, then chief executive of the PRINCE'S FOUNDATION, in 1999, the year in which that new organisation incorporated the Urban Villages Forum (formerly the Urban Villages Group). Miles Glendinning and David Page (1999) noted that in Scotland 'peripheral urban extensions, council housing scheme regenerations, housing areas in new towns, even multiplex complexes' were being 'hailed as "urban villages"'. The consensus against the term was hardening. In 2000, Jon Rouse (2000), chief executive of CABE and former secretary of the URBAN TASK FORCE, put the case against it. '"Urban village". Were ever two words so horribly conjoined?' he asked. 'And now I can not get away from the indecipherable idiom. Every local newspaper is replete with house builders advertising the damned things.' Rouse noted that, on inspection, these places were neither urban nor villages. 'They are housing estates. "Urban village" is a phrase adopted by people who perhaps do not like cities at all, delivering, as it appears to, an instant judgement that the city must be sanitised and cleansed – the goodness of "rus" breathed into the horrors of "urbe". [The phrase] perpetuates the myth that our towns and villages were once made up of villages. The reality is that small cities were once surrounded by villages. They industrialised and enveloped those villages and now everything is a wonderfully messy mix of quarters, districts, neighbourhoods, linear commercial routes and so on.' In 2002 a report by Mike Biddulph, funded by the Economic and Social Research Council, argued that urban village had become a virtually meaningless term. An attempt to devise a set of prescriptive development principles had failed, rendering the concept 'a loose, fuzzy and ambiguous set of ideas and associations' (Biddulph, 2002).

In the 1850s FREDERICK LAW OLMSTED and his partner CALVERT VAUX described their development at Riverside, outside Chicago, as 'a village in a park' designed for 'urban villagers' (Kostof, 1987). Morton and Lucia White (1962) noted that American urban reformers of the late nineteenth and early twentieth centuries were opposed to the giantism of the cities and wanted to cut them down to manageable size. 'Their conception of size was affected by a certain degree of nostalgia for the American village. They did not flee the metropolis for this village, but they wanted to decompose the city into spiritual units that would emulate village life.'

Supporting the positive attributes of village life was a keynote of PATRICK GEDDES' approach to planning. He used the phrase 'urban village' in his celebrated planning reports on Indian cities. In one he noted: 'when I examined the draft of the "improvement" plan I found it did not even include the main mosque of the neighbourhood, which should, of course, have been made the nucleus of the new urban village' (Geddes, 1915b). In another, Geddes (1915c) wrote that, in cities of the East or the West, 'health and prosperity can not be restored by herding [people] into... mean streets of standardised houses... It can only come by again evoking the constructive powers of the people themselves... in the building of their own homes in a real, though urban village plan' (see also JOHN TURNER). Patrick Abercrombie developed the urban village concept in his London plans in the 1940s. CHARLES REILLY developed the concept of 'Reilly greens' (where houses were grouped round an open space containing educational and social amenities) and used it in several plans, including that of 1944 for Birkenhead. John Billingham (2002) writes that 'they were intended to evoke the feeling of a village green idyll in an urban setting'. Herbert Gans' book *The Urban Villagers* was published in 1962. The villagers Gans described were people who, having moved from the countryside to a big city, still retained a distinct social structure. The 1972 plan for the centre of Los Angeles (*Central City LA, 1972–90*) proposed a mixed-income 'urban village' at South Park (Davis, 2002). Donald Appleyard (1980) identified the creation of 'urban villages' as being one of the original ideas behind the concept of NEIGHBOURHOOD planning, though he noted that the urban villages had failed to materialize.

The UK Department of the Environment, Transport and the Regions and its development agency English Partnerships strongly supported urban villages in the late 1990s, but the term urban village did not appear in the 2000 Urban White Paper. A survey in 2001 identified 55 developments termed 'urban villages'. They varied from just over one hectare to nearly 300, and from a projected population of 160 to 15,000 (Biddulph *et al*, 2002). Plans to develop Wales' first urban village were announced in 2003. The project, with the Prince's Foundation as one of the partners, would create a 'SUSTAINABLE COMMUNITY' of 2,500 homes and 3,200 jobs at Llandarcy near Swansea: 'the first in the UK on such a large scale', the press reported. See also SUBURBAN VILLAGE.

urban wallpaper Buildings of no great architectural merit or integrity whose facades are designed to be make a pleasant and inoffensive contribution to the townscape.

Urbana, Illinois See COMMUTERVILLE.

urban-centric Focused on urban areas. Example: 'The proposed changes to planning law highlight the cavalier attitude of this urban-centric government to democratic process' (2002).

urbane Smooth and sophisticated. The word developed from the Latin *urbanus* by way of Old French. It originally meant what URBAN means today, and developed its current meaning after urban replaced it.

urbanisation 1 A rise in the proportion of people living in urban settlements. In Britain in 1750 there were two cities (London and Edinburgh) with more than 50,000 inhabitants. In 1801 there were eight and in 1851 29, including nine of more than 100,000 (Hobsbawm, 1968). The 1851 census was the first to show Britain as a country with more than 50 per cent of the population living in urban areas. Half the population of the USA was urban by 1920 and 75 per cent by 1990. **2** The changes that occur in social structures when people move to towns and cities. Eric Hobsbawm (1968) writes that the city of the industrial revolution 'destroyed society': there was much less personal communication between an industrial master and his workers than between a member of the aristocracy and the workers on his estate. 'The city was a volcano, to whose rumblings the rich and powerful listened with fear, and whose eruptions they dreaded. But for its poor inhabitants it was not merely a standing reminder of their exclusion from human society. It was a stony desert, which they had to make habitable by their own efforts.' Compare DISURBANISATION.

urbanism 1 The study or appreciation of the processes of change in towns and cities; making towns and cities work; town (UK) or city (US) planning. Charles Landry (2000) describes urbanism as 'the discipline which helps understand the dynamics, resources and potential of the city in a richer way'. **2** The process of becoming urban (as a result of development on formerly rural land, for example). **3** The product of town planning or development. ANDRES DUANY (2000) describes urbanism as 'the created habitat of humanity'. As a NEW URBANIST, Duany refuses to accept suburban places as being anything but 'a lesser or permanently incomplete version of urbanism'. Duany and Elizabeth Plater-Zyberk (2001) argue that in contemporary America 'there are two types of urbanism available: the NEIGHBORHOOD, which was the model in North America from the first settlements to the second world war, and SUBURBAN SPRAWL, which has been the model since then.' PATRICK ABERCROMBIE wrote: 'Let urbanism prevail and preponderate in the town and let the country remain rural. Keep the distinction clear' (Hall, 1994). **4** Patterns of social life characteristic of urban areas. Sir Terry Farrell writes: 'Urbanism is a culture: the culture of place' (Terry Farrell and Partners, 2002). **5** Architecture in an urban context. The term is used in this sense by some architects. **6** A building's characteristic of having internal spaces that create something of the sense of being in a street, square or other external urban space. Example: 'The new theatre's urbanism is more successful. Moving into the intermediate space of the foyer and bar from the street is akin to entering a public square from a side street... The final stage of the theatre-goers' quasi-urban experience leads them into what feels like a private space – the auditorium' (a review in *Building Design* in 2003).

The term, adapted from the French *urbanisme*, was first used in the UK in the late 1880s. The architect Peter F Smith called his 1974 book on design and perception *The Dynamics of Urbanism*. In it he describes urbanism as 'a portmanteau term which embraces the concept of architecture in its external and internal manifestations as well as the wider aspects of townscape', and notes that 'perception of urbanism does not recognise intellectual compartments'. Smith suggests that 'new towns are, to varying degrees, deficient in that indefinable quality called urbanism' (Smith, 1974). The term was still rare enough in 1992 for Mark Fisher MP to write that 'on the Continent there is a word for the issues that affect the built environment, "urbanism"' (Fisher, 1992). The term was not widely used in the UK before 2001. A symptom of its wider currency was the Greater London Assembly's naming in that year of its newly formed Architecture and Urbanism Unit, headed by RICHARD ROGERS. Rem Koolhaas and Bruce Mau (1995) suggest a paradox: 'that urbanism, as a profession, has disappeared at the moment when urbanization everywhere... is on its way to establishing a definitive, global "triumph" of the urban condition.' They comment: 'What makes this experience disconcerting and (for architects) humiliating is the city's defiant persistence and apparent vigour, in spite of the collective failure of all agencies that act on it or try to influence it – creatively, logistically, politically.'

The subject matter of urbanism is as wide as history and as deep as the human imagination, but there are some major common themes. The changing language recorded in this dictionary reflects the difficulty of finding the right words with which to describe the complexities of towns and cities, and the processes of shaping and managing them. Some of the more common concepts that are reflected in the language of urbanism include: 1) The aim of the planning and regeneration processes, described in terms such as amenity, social justice, the good city and sustainability. 2) The process of positive environmental change, described in terms such as urban renewal, urban regeneration and urban renaissance. 3) The overarching discipline that manages change, described in terms such as town planning, social planning, physical planning, civic design, architecture, sustainable urban management, urban design, urbanism and spatial planning. 4) A set of guiding principles about urban form, described in terms such as modernism, new urbanism and sustainable development. 5) The geographical unit that is the focus for planning, described in terms such as ward, micro-spatial location, neighbourhood, neighbourhood unit, community, community area, urban village and sustainable community. 6) The corresponding social group, described in terms such as community and local people. 7) The means of involving that group in the processes of change, described in terms such as democracy, public participation, consultation and collaboration. 8) The valued and defining characteristics of an area, described in terms such as character, identity, local distinctiveness, sense of place and genius loci. 9) The process of placemaking, described in terms such as town or city planning, civic design, urban design, town and country planning, urban and regional planning, spatial planning and masterplanning. 10) An attitude to the traditional city, described in terms such as urbanism, anti-urbanism and post-urbanism.

It seems that at any time at least one term relating to each of these 10 concepts will be in fashion. Whenever a term goes out of fashion, at least one more relating to the same concept will come in to fashion to replace it. See also ANTI-URBANISM, EVERYDAY URBANISM, NEW URBANISM, POST-URBANISM and SPLINTERED URBANISM.

urbanisme (French) **1** Urbanism. **2** Town planning. In France *urbanisme* is more common than the English word is in the UK.

Urbanisme A book by LE CORBUSIER, published in 1924, advocating RATIONAL PLANNING. It was later published in English as *The City of Tomorrow*.

urbanisme spontané (French) Urban sprawl.

Urbanist A Franciscan nun following the rule instituted by Pope Urban IV in 1263.

urbanist One who studies or seeks to influence the processes of change in human settlements. In UK professional life the word was rarely used before the late 1990s, usually by practitioners looking for a word other than *planner* or *urban designer* with which to describe themselves. What was probably the first job advertisement in the UK for an urbanist (an 'urbanist/urban designer') was posted by the regional development agency Yorkshire Forward in 2002. Brown, Claydon and Nadin (2002) write of urbanists as having 'their base in architecture and urban design'. The term was first used around 1515–25. Joseph Rykwert (2000) notes that the term urbanism 'and the notion of a separate discipline concerned with both the making and the study of towns' were first launched in the book by IDELFONSO CERDÁ, *The General Theory of Urbanisation*, published in 1867. The French Society of Urbanists was founded in 1909. The Institute of Urbanism was founded at the University of Paris in 1919.

urbanist-disurbanist debate The phrase is used to refer to discussions in the Soviet Union in 1929–31 about whether the proper form of the Soviet, socialist town was a relatively unchecked metropolis, or a union of town and country through dispersed settlements (Cooke, 1978). A similar debate has been raging in the UK and US throughout most of the twentieth century – and continues to the present day – between centrists and decentrists, town crammers and garden city advocates, urban boosters and suburban apologists, and Radiant City proseletisers and Broadacrists.

urbaniste 1 (French) An urbanist; a town planner (UK); a city planner (US). **2** (UK) An URBANIST. The French spelling has been used occasionally by UK professionals (as recently as 2003), presumably regarding the English term *urbanist* as not yet an established use.

urbanitarian FJ OSBORN used the term pejoratively in 1963 to denote people who promoted urbanity and what he considered to be housing development at excessively high densities (Hughes, 1971).

urbanite A person who lives in a town or city, particularly one who enjoys living in an inner urban (rather than suburban) area. Example: 'Brick Lane [in the East End of London, near to the City]... buzzes with young urbanites, nipping into "@Coffee" to grab a café latte on their way to work' (2002).

urbanity 1 The quality of being well-mannered. **2** The condition of life in a city. This meaning became current around 1900 (Forty, 2000). **3** The positive qualities of the social and collective life of cities; a quality of vitality and diversity possessed by successful towns and cities, resulting from a wide range of people coming together in the same place for different purposes. This third sense was introduced by LEWIS MUMFORD in around 1953 (Forty, 2000). Ambrose Bierce's *Devil's Dictionary* (published 1869–1906) defines urbanity as 'the kind of civility that urban observers ascribe to dwellers in all cities but New York'. **4** A type of urbanism. Example: 'The contemporary urban environment can be thought of as a field of parallel urbanities'.

urbanoid mishmash See MEGALOPOLIS.

urbanology The study of towns and cities.

urbatecture The architectural theorist Bruno Zevi has used the term to describe a concept that 'bridges the gap between architecture and urban planning'.

urbiculture The way of life of people in cities. The term dates from the early 1950s.

Urbis A museum in Manchester celebrating life in cities and exploring the process of URBANISATION. Designed by architect Ian Simpson, it opened in 2002. See also RESPOND.

urbs (Latin) A city. Compare URB.

Uruk At 6,000 years old, the Sumerian city (like nearby UR but with more justification) has been called the world's first. The modern town of Tall al Warka occupies the site on the River Euphrates in what is now southern Iraq. See also CATAL HÜYÜK.

ur-urbanism The earliest forms of urban development. Example: 'For Le Corbusier, the origins of the city itself could be found in the ur-urbanism of the military encampment.' See UR, URBANISM, URUK and VARANASI.

use class One of the categories of use of buildings and land defined in the Town and Country Planning (Use Classes) Order 1987. A change of use to one that falls within the same class as the existing use does not constitute DEVELOPMENT, and so will not need planning permission.

Use Classes Order Categorises uses and sets out what changes within groups of uses do not constitute DEVELOPMENT and so do not require planning permission.

use order Permits the use of a road for purposes other than passage. Compare USE CLASSES ORDER.

use value The value of a commodity in use, as distinct from its *market value* (*exchange value*).

use variance (US) A zoning variance permitting a departure from a zoning ordinance in relation to the use of a site.

useful life See OUTWORN FABRIC and TWILIGHT ZONE.

uselessness One of the distinguishing features of architecture, as distinct from mere building, according to JOHN RUSKIN. In *The Seven Lamps of Architecture* he describes a plain building, and comments: 'But if these projecting masses be carved beneath into rounded courses, which are useless, and if the headings of the intervals be arched and trefoiled, which is useless, *that* is Architecture'.

user 1 A person who occupies or passes through a building or space. The term was unknown before about 1950, Adrian Forty notes. Its use became widespread in the late 1950s and '60s, waned in the 1980s and returned to currency in the 1990s (Forty, 2000a). **2** A drug addict. **3** A person who uses a public service.

Usonian City, The FRANK LLOYD WRIGHT's original term for the concept he later called BROADACRE CITY. The word *usonia*, which Frank Lloyd Wright used from the 1920s, was the novelist Samuel Butler's fictional name for the USA.

Uthwatt Report The report, published in 1942, of the government's Expert Committee on Compensation and Betterment, chaired by Mr Justice Uthwatt.

utility 1 An organisation providing a basic service such as water, electricity or gas. **2** Usefulness.

utility walking Walking as a means of getting from one place to another, rather than for enjoyment or in the course of shopping. The term is used by the UK Department of Transport (2004).

Utopia A book by Thomas More (written in Latin and published in 1516) recounting an imaginary discussion about the relative merits of England and the island of Utopia (from the Greek 'no-place'), where land is communally owned. The island, about 500 miles long and 200 miles wide, has 54 cities, 'all large and well built'. All the cities are designed 'as near to the same manner as the ground on which they stand will allow'. None is less than 24 miles from its nearest neighbour, 'and the most remote are not so far distant, but that a man can go on foot in one day in it, to that which lies next it'. When the population of a city grows, the people of Utopia 'fill up the lack in other cities' or 'build up a town... in the next land where the inhabitants have much waste and unoccupied ground'. The roofs of the buildings are flat. Every tenth year people change houses, seemingly to prevent any feeling of ownership. Bertrand Russell (1946) thought that More's vision was 'in many ways astonishingly liberal'. He commented that 'it must be admitted, however, that life in More's Utopia, as in most others, would be intolerably dull. Diversity is essential to happiness, and in Utopia there is hardly any. This is a defect of all planned social systems, actual as well as imaginary.'

Joseph Rykwert (2000) notes that More's title is often translated as 'no-place', 'but it can also be understood as the good place, and that is perhaps the way the title had originally been intended'. Rykwert (2002) writes that the name Utopia, coined by More, 'was not merely a Latinized form of *outopos*, no-place, as it is usually understood, but also sounding the same as *eutopos*, good-place – "the best state of a publique weal" – since Anglicised Greek allowed both *ou* and *eu* to be pronounced as "u".'

utopia Defined by Karl Mannheim (quoted in Fishman, 1971) as a coherent programme for action arising out of thought that transcends the immediate situation, the programme's realisation being likely to break the bonds of the established society. Oscar Wilde wrote (in *The Soul of Man under Socialism*): 'A map of the world which does not include utopia is not worth even glancing at.' The writer Jane Jacobs thought that town planners' tendency to imagine utopias often insulated them from the real world. 'Cities are an immense laboratory of

> **"PLANNERS ARE GUIDED BY PRINCIPLES DERIVED FROM THE BEHAVIOUR AND APPEARANCE OF SUBURBS, TUBERCULOSIS SANATORIA, FAIRS AND IMAGINARY DREAM CITIES – FROM ANYTHING BUT CITIES THEMSELVES"**
>
> *Jane Jacobs*

trial and error, failure and success, in city building and city design,' she wrote. 'This is the laboratory in which city planning should have been learning and testing its theories. Instead the practitioners and teachers of this discipline (if such it can be called) have ignored the study of success and failure in real life, have been incurious about the reasons for unexpected success, and are guided instead by principles derived from the behaviour and appearance of... suburbs, tuberculosis sanatoria, fairs and imaginary dream cities – from anything but cities themselves' (Jacobs, 1961). Isaiah Berlin (1990), writing about utopian ideas, quotes the philosopher Immanuel Kant: 'Out of the crooked timber of humanity no straight thing was ever made.' Berlin comments: 'For that reason no perfect solution is, not merely in practice, but in principle, possible in human affairs, and any determined attempt to produce it is likely to lead to suffering, disillusionment and failure.' The word was coined by Thomas More. See also AMOUROT, CITY OF THE SUN, DRESS SENSE, EDEN VALE, UTOPIAN and UTOPUS.

Utopia on Trial A book by the geographer ALICE COLEMAN, published in 1985.

utopian 1 Based on a vision of a perfect society. **2** Hopelessly over-optimistic.

Utopus The designer of the city of AMOUROT in Thomas More's book UTOPIA.

V

vacation land The open countryside between PAUL AND PERCIVAL GOODMAN's imaginary CITY OF EFFICIENT CONSUMPTION.

vagrant A homeless person who wanders from place to place or lives on the street. See also BAG LADY, BINDLE STIFF, BOSTON BUM, BUM, DERELICT, DERO, DOSSER, DOWN-AND-OUT, DUMMERER, GAGGER, GENTLEMAN OF THE ROAD, HOBO, HOBOHEMIA, HOME GUARD, LIZZIE TRAMP, MAIN STEM, MOOCHER, MOPER, PANHANDLER, ROAD KID, SKID ROGUE, SKID ROW, STEM, STREET PERSON, SWAGMAN, TOBY, TRAMP, WALLY and WINO.

Valadier, Giuseppe (1762–1839) Architect and town planner. He redesigned the Piazza del Popolo in Rome in 1794.

Valdrada A lakeside city in Asia, described by Italo Calvino in INVISIBLE CITIES (1972). Its people are aware that it is, in effect, a double city, the other half being its reflection in the lake.

valley section A way of conceiving a valley in cross-section (sometimes with a diagram) from the mountains down through the countryside to the city and finally the sea, with its related human activities. The valley section was central to how PATRICK GEDDES thought about regions.

Valleys Initiative A government programme for the regeneration of the valleys of south Wales, launched in 1988.

Vällingby A SATELLITE TOWN to Stockholm, Sweden, built in the 1950s. The name apparently means Porridge Town (Hall, 1998).

valuation Ascribing a monetary value to something.

value The architectural commentator Paul Finch (2002) has suggested that, in the context of development economics, value is satisfaction minus price. See VIVA.

valued environment A place that holds personal meaning for a particular person or group of people.

values The beliefs, emotions and preferences on which people base their opinions and actions. Each person has a different set of values, although any group of people will have many values in common.

vandalism The act of deliberately damaging a place. It ranges from relatively trivial nuisance (such as GRAFFITI), through varying degrees of damage (broken windows, demolished boundary walls) to serious assaults on buildings and structures (sabotaging lifts, deliberate flooding, damaging structural components). In 2001 culture secretary Tessa Jowell turned the word on its head when she branded a council estate in Camden, London, as a 'monstrosity which vandalised the lives of people' (a use similar to referring the houses being hard to live in rather than HARD TO LET). The Vandals (their name meant *wanderers*) were the Germanic tribe that sacked Rome in 455AD. See also OAK AND ELDON GARDENS and PRUTT-IGOE.

Vandreuil A new settlement near Rouen, France, designed as a pollution-free industrial city (Ward and Dubos, 1972).

Vanity Fair A town on the route from the CITY OF DESTRUCTION to the CELESTIAL CITY, described in John Bunyan's *The Pilgrim's Progress* (1684). Vanity Fair is devoted to all forms of low life, though Bunyan writes of it as being rather less uncivilised than it once was.

Varanasi (called Kasi by Hindus, and formerly called Benares) A holy city (to Hindus, Buddhists and Muslims) in Uttar Pradesh state, north central India, on the River Ganges. It is said to be one of the world's oldest cities (see also UR and URUK).

variance 1 A statistical measure of dispersion around the mean, used in property development as a measure of RISK. **2** A ZONING VARIANCE.

vasectomy zoning (US) ZONING to ensure that development in an area accommodates few children.

Vauix-en-Velin A housing estate in Lyons, France, the scene of rioting in 1990 immediately after undergoing a major programme of renovation.

Vaux, Calvert (1824–1895) Landscape architect. Vaux worked as an architect in London, his birthplace, before moving to New York to work with the architect ANDREW JACKSON DOWNING. His popular PATTERN BOOK *Villas and Cottages* was published in 1857. With his partner FREDERICK LAW OLMSTED he designed New York's Central Park and Brooklyn's Prospect Park.

Vectra man See MONDEO MAN.

vegetarianism The vegetarian advocate of social or

urban reform (possibly also bearded and sandal-shod – see DRESS SENSE) was a common stereotype in the first decades of the twentieth century. Wyndham Lewis writes in his 1954 novel *Self Condemned* of one such resident of Welwyn Garden City: 'One of a group of families who had collectively evolved a strongly marked mannerism, suggestive of the coy shyness of a retiring herbivore. If you can imagine a phenomenally smart, forever quietly amused yak, standing quite still, slyly self-conscious, its big knowing eye shining with quiet, self-satisfied humour, standing almost as if it expected to be stroked or hugged, for being so entirely *understanding* an animal, if you can summon to stand there in your fancy such a curious beast, always *sideways*, always one-eyed, not looking at you, but at some mesmerically absurd thought which bemused and transfixed it, *then* you would, by the same token, be in the presence of Percy Lamport Esq. In a street in Welwyn, to this day, a herd of these animals may be encountered: a whole tribe of people, neighbours and friends, who stand quietly like obedient ponies, or like yaks on a secluded hillside, or in the cages of a zoo, presenting you with a profile in which is a big, amused, contemplative eye.'

vehicle kilometre A unit of measurement for the amount of travel on a road.

velodrome A cycling stadium.

Venice Charter A statement of the principles of conservation of monuments and sites, the Venice Charter for the Conservation and Restoration of Monuments and Sites was approved by the Second International Congress of Architects and Technicians of Historic Monuments in 1964. See ATHENS CHARTER, HISTORIC MONUMENT and KRAKOV CHARTER.

Venice of the North 1 ST PETERSBURG. **2** Birmingham, England, according to some of its BOOSTERS (somewhat confusingly considering that, though it is in northern Europe, the city is in the English midlands). Birmingham has a network of canals more extensive than Venice, although the effect is somewhat different. Compare ATHENS OF THE NORTH.

vennel (Scots) An ALLEY (see that entry for regional variants). From the Latin *vennella*, a lane.

Venturi, Robert (b1925) Architect and theorist. His book *Complexity and Contradiction in Architecture* (1966), hailed by Vincent Scully as the most important since LE CORBUSIER's *Vers une Architecture*, is a 'gentle manifesto' for complexity and contradiction (as against simplification or picturesqueness), ambiguity, 'both/and' rather than 'either/or', and 'the obligation toward the difficult whole'. It includes some remarkable re-evaluations of (among others) LUTYENS, LE CORBUSIER, GAUDI and MIES VAN DER ROHE. Venturi's work helped to lay the foundations for POSTMODERN ARCHITECTURE. DENISE SCOTT BROWN is his wife and collaborator. See also CELEBRATION, GAZZARD'S LAW OF URBAN VITALITY, LEARNING FROM LAS VEGAS, MAIN STREET IS ALMOST ALL RIGHT and ORDER.

Robert Venturi

Vergara, Camilo Chilean-born writer and photographer. His New American Ghetto Archive chronicles the process of urban decay in the ghettos of New York, Chicago, Detroit and New Jersey (Davis, 2002).

Verkehr (German) Traffic.

Verkehrsberuhigung (German) TRAFFIC CALMING.

Verkehrsentwicklungsplan (German) A transport development plan.

Verkehrsmittelwahl (German) MODAL SPLIT.

vernacular *adj.* and *n.* The way in which ordinary (rather than monumental) buildings were (or are) built in a particular place before local styles, techniques and materials were (or have been) superseded by imports. The word can be used as an adjective (*vernacular buildings*) or a noun (*the vernacular*). Today *vernacular style*, when used to describe new buildings, is likely to mean buildings designed to look like vernacular buildings of a particular place at a time in the past. *Neo-vernacular* refers to buildings which attempt to use local styles, materials and characteristic forms in an authentic or original way. *Pseudo-vernacular* describes those buildings replete with vernacular materials and devices which are not indigenous to the locality but borrowed promiscuously from all over. The new buildings at the Royal Agricultural College, Cirencester, are fine examples of the former. The Tesco Transylvanian style is a ghastly and ubiquitous example of the latter.

vertex A point of interchange in a transport network. Also known as a NODE.

vertical city See MILLENNIUM TOWER.

vertical cooperation Between organisations at different levels, such as local, regional and national bodies. See HORIZONTAL COOPERATION.

vertical garden city A term used by LE CORBUSIER to describe some of his development proposals. The planning historian Dennis Hardy (1991) calls it 'a complete contradiction of terms.'

vertical integration Different land uses mixed one above another in a building of two or more storeys. Also called *vertical mixed use*.

vertical kerb/curb (UK/US) One whose sharp right angle discourages parking on the pavement.

vertical mixed uses See MIXED USES.

vertical rhythm The frequency and arrangement of vertical elements on a building's façade or along a street.

vertical town The architect Renzo Piano's description in 2002 of his proposed 'shard of glass' skyscraper at London Bridge.

vertical urban design The term used by the architect KEN YEANG for building SKYSCRAPERS that, in his words, 'recreate in the sky what we find pleasurable on the ground'.

vet, vigilance, verify Three actions that some council officers bear in mind to ensure their personal safety when visiting sites or premises in connection with enforcement action over breaches of planning control.

via principalis (Latin) One of the two parallel streets of a Roman camp, at right angles to a major cross-axis. The other was the *via quintana* (Kostof, 1991). See also CARDO.

viability The ability (of a commercial development, for example) to survive. See also VITALITY AND VIABILITY.

vibrancy Liveliness. Example: 'Affluent British travellers always enjoyed the fruits of density: crowded late-night streets, restaurants, bars and general urban vibrancy' (Travers, 2001).

vibrant Buzzing with life. The word is a favourite of urban designers, planners and policy makers in describing successful places or, more often, their aspirations for a place. Example: 'The urban renaissance will benefit everyone, making towns and cities vibrant and successful, and protecting the countryside from development pressure' (from the Urban White Paper, 2002). See also THROBBING.

vice Immorality; depravity. E Porter Belden wrote in his otherwise enthusiastic 1849 guide to New York (quoted in White, 1962): 'Large cities never present a pleasing view to the eye of the moralist. Where multitudes of all opinions, characters and pursuits, congregate, vice is more open in appearance and more successful in operation. Companions are found to suit every taste, and individual turpitude escapes, in the mass, its merited disgrace.' Gerald Kersh – variously a nightclub bouncer, short-order cook, wrestler, soldier, journalist and novelist – portrayed the darkest side of London in his twice-filmed novel *Night and the City*, published in 1938. Typical is his evocation of the low life to be found in a drinking club owned by an egregious character by the name of Bagrag. 'Bagrag's Cellar is a dragnet through which the undercurrent of night-life continually filters. It is choked with low organisms, pallid and distorted, unknown to the light of day, and not to be tolerated in healthy society. It is on the bottom of life; it is the penultimate resting-place of the inevitably damned. Its members comprehen addicts to all known crimes and vices. Mingling with them there circulate indefinable people, belonging to no place or category, creatures begotten of decay and twilight, enslaved by appetites so vile that even text-books never mention them, drifting in silent putrefaction to their unknown ends.' *Night and the City* closes on an optimistic note, though, with the hero discovering his vocation as a sculptor, and the promise of a new day. 'The night bursts open. Blood and life soak into the sky. Torn at the edge of the black silhouettes of spiky spires, and cold chimneys – polluted but bright, ragged but triumphant – dawn breaks over the city.'

victim In the context of housing design, Andres Duany (2003) defines a victim as one who has no choice. 'Due to limited income or a very tight housing market, victims are grateful for any place of their own. They will accept good or bad housing.' The absence of choice, Duany suggests, is one of the reasons that some affordable housing can be so good. 'Such quality is not just a matter of talent, but of a consumer that has little choice in the matter. Some lucky victims are forced to accept very good housing that they will surely grow to appreciate, even if they would not have chosen to do so in the first place.' Compare CLIENT, CUSTOMER and PATRON.

Victoria A model town proposed in 1849 by JAMES SILK BUCKINGHAM.

Victorian Dating from the reign of Queen Victoria (1837–1901).

Victorian Society A campaigning conservation group founded in 1958.

view What is visible from a particular point. Compare VISTA.

view (also viewing) corridor The area of land where development of a certain height would block a valued view.

view cone A representation of the area visible from a particular spot by a viewer looking in a specified direction.

view-shed 1 A view protected from intrusive development. **2** The area within which a particular television station is viewed. This is one way of defining a region. Compare PEDSHED and WATERSHED.

Vigo, Jean (1905–34) French film-maker. His documentary portrait of the resort town *A Propos de Nice*

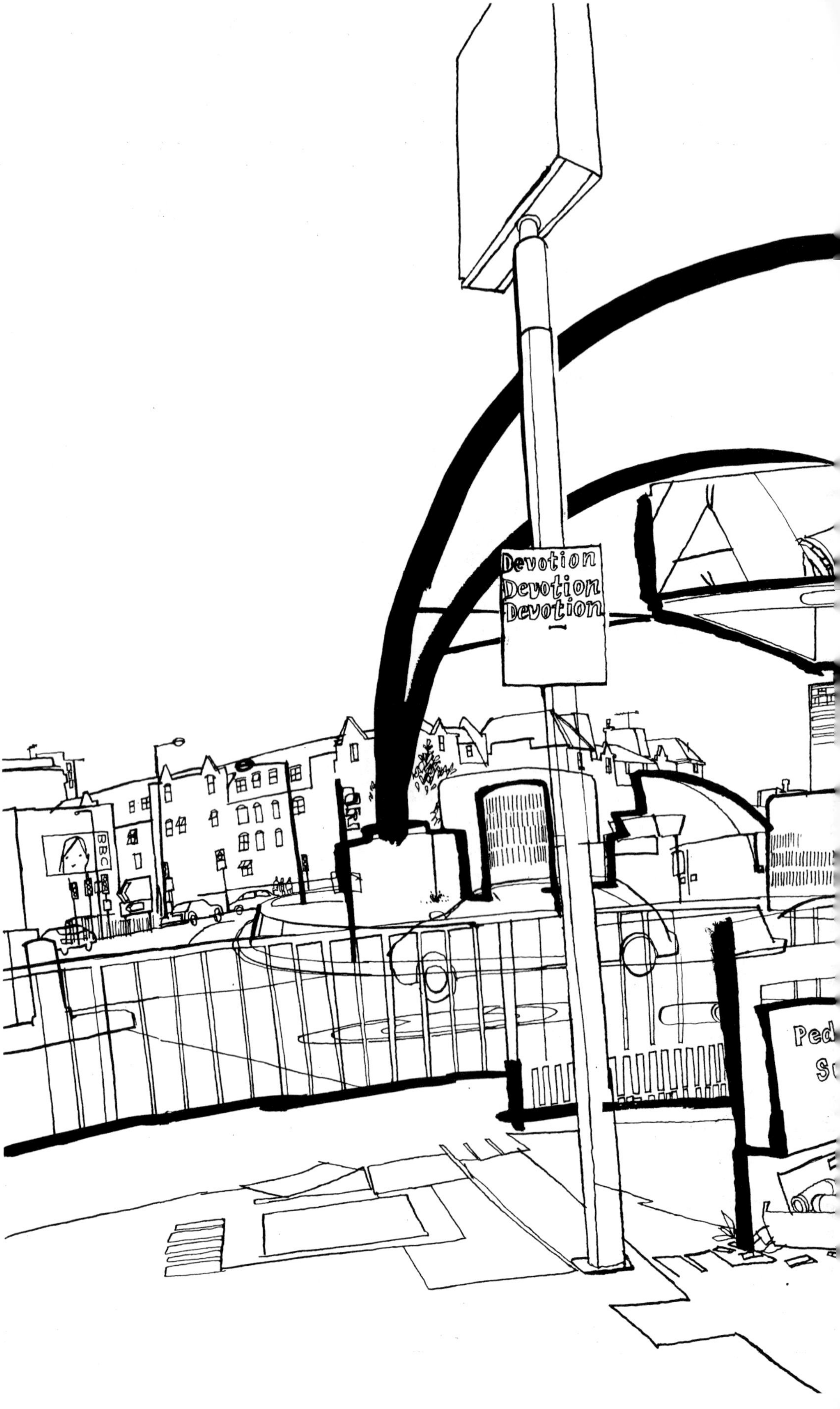

visual clutter

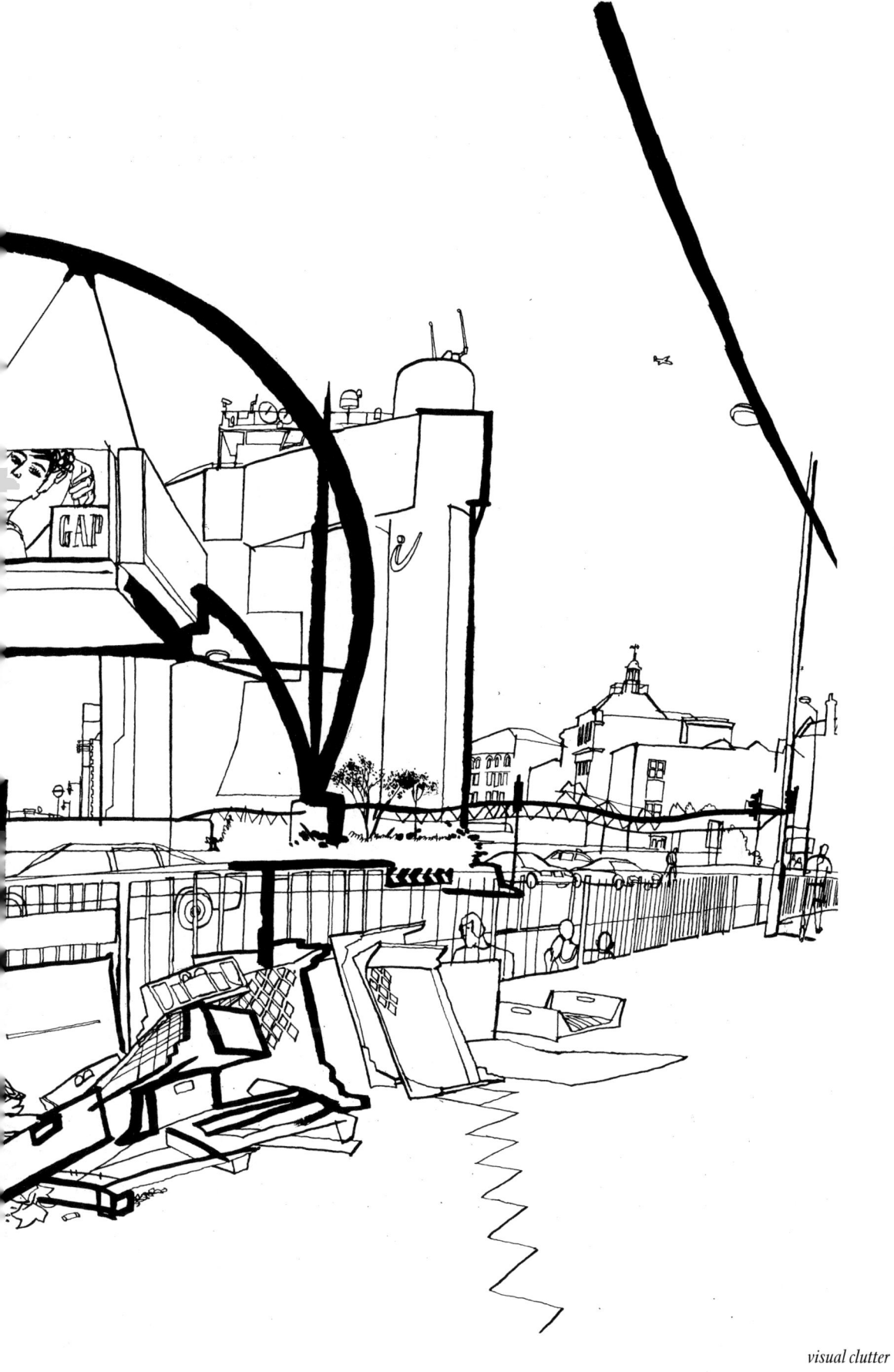

(*Concerning Nice*) contrasts the lives of the wealthy tourists with the poverty-stricken local population.

Vila Piloto A new town, concentric in form, built in Brazil in the 1960s to house construction workers for a hydroelectric plant. It had a model farm at its centre and was designed to become a model agricultural community when the plant was complete. Its upkeep proved to be too expensive, though. Eventually half was taken over by the army and half was demolished (Kostof, 1991).

Vila Real de Santo António See Marquis of POMBAL.

villa 1 (UK) A suburban house of some pretension to elegance. A villa might be detached, semi-detached or in a terrace. John McKean (1994) has written of mid-nineteenth-century Glasgow: '[The] flight to suburban "villas" invokes anti-urban memories right back to VITRUVIUS, who talks of the *villa suburbana* as the urban man's resort. The first-century Romans, with their clear urban types of *domus* and *insula*, invented the *villa* as an escape from their teeming city of a million inhabitants, a city seen as unhealthy and dangerous.' McKean notes that 'the new Victorian reinterpretation of the suburb of villas had the twin aims of show and separation, of pomp and privacy'. John Summerson (1962) suggests that the true villa character in GEORGIAN London was that of being 'smallish..., strikingly symmetrical and decidedly classical'. Mark Girouard (1992) notes that the term villa dropped out of fashion in England and America largely because it had become vulgarised. After about 1850, Girouard writes, American houses in the country of any pretensions ceased to be called villas. **2** (French) A detached house. See also VILLE.

villadom Extensive areas of VILLAS, particularly in Victorian suburbs.

village *n.* **1** A small settlement in the countryside. Some NEW URBANISTS define a village as 'a single neighborhood standing free in the landscape' (Duany and Plater-Zyberk, 1994). According to *A New Urbanist Lexicon* (McLaughlin, 2000) a village should be 'a compact urban settlement within the countryside, with the essential characteristics of a complete neighborhood, including commercial services used on a daily basis.' Jonathan Raban (1974) suggests that 'in a village, most of the people you deal with have been known to you (or to someone in your family circle) for a long time... You will probably have seen them in more than one role.' Andres Duany and Elizabeth Plater-Zyberk (2001) complain that 'village' is often a euphemism for 'COOKIE-CUTTER' housing subdivisions. George Ferguson said the same on becoming president of the RIBA. 'There has been a terrible misuse of the term "village collection",' he complained, 'which is really just a load of naff, little houses all pushed together in a slightly villagey form but with no village sense at all' (quoted in Moye, 2003). **2** A small part of an urban area that has a distinct identity. Sometimes this identity derives from the place having been a rural village before it was engulfed by urban development. The Congress for the New Urbanism (2001) has described New York's physical form as ranging 'from the towering skyscrapers of Midtown to the fine-grained urbanism of the outer borough villages'. Michael Young and Peter Willmott (1957) wrote in their study of Bethnal Green, east London: 'The residents of the turning [street], who usually make up a sort of "village" of 100 to 200 people, have their own places to meet, where few outsiders ever come.' The writer VS Pritchett (1997) observes (writing in 1956): 'London is an agglomeration of villages which have been gummed together in the course of centuries.' **3** (US) In some states a village is an incorporated community smaller in population than a town. **4** One of several groups of offices, each with its own distinct identity, in a large office building. This use was current by 2001. Example: 'The 11 three-storey office "villages" in the skyscraper will be breathtaking places to work'. **5** A community of people in a particular place. Example: 'The government is hoping that the rumours in the Westminster village will soon fizzle out'. **6** *v.* To aspire to the simulcrum of a bucolic, rural lifestyle while living in a city. Example: 'Villaging is a recreation for the very rich indeed; if you can buy a house with trellis and cottage-garden in Highgate Village, you could probably afford Cannes and polo ponies too' (Raban, 1974). See also SUV.

The word village (deriving from the Latin *villaticus*, meaning belonging to a villa) dates from the second half of the fourteenth century. The Scots for village is *clachan*. See also GARDEN VILLAGE, MAIN STREET and URBAN VILLAGE.

village appraisal A study identifying a local community's needs and priorities. The Civic Trust Regeneration Unit describes a village appraisal as a comprehensive survey carried out by the community, for the community. Through a locally compiled questionnaire distributed to each household, the appraisal offers local people the opportunity to comment on issues that affect their lives. The information gathered from the survey can be used both to celebrate LOCAL DISTINCTIVENESS and to put together community action plans for a village, parish or town.

village center (US) A form of development proposed by the new urbanist Peter Calthorpe, comprising a retail cluster containing 100,000 square feet of retail, including a 50,000-square-foot supermarket. Such a centre would require a catchment of at least 10,000 people, Calthorpe suggests, and preferably would be laid out with a grid of arterial roads. See also ONE-WAY COUPLET.

village design statement An advisory document, usually produced by a village community, showing how development can be carried out in harmony with the village and its setting. A village design statement can be given weight by being approved as *supplementary planning guidance*. The use of village design statements is promoted by the Countryside Agency.

Village of Tomorrow, The An exhibit of modernist houses at the 1934 Ideal Homes Exhibition. 'They proved extremely difficult to sell,' writes John Burnett (1986).

village urbain (French) An urban village.

Village, The A city in Oklahoma.

villas do Domingo (Spanish) Sunday towns, built in remote parts of Brazil as social centres for scattered rural populations (Kostof, 1991).

ville (French) A town. In France the word *villa* (referring originally to a building of importance to local agriculture) developed into ville, meaning a town (Girouard, 1992).

-ville (suffix) **1** A town, or part of one. See CACTUSVILLE, CELESTEVILLE, CIRCLESVILLE, COLEVILLE, COMMUTERVILLE, DULLSVILLE, EGOVILLE, GREENVILLE, JOYVILLE, LEADVILLE, NOWHERESVILLE, PITSVILLE, PITTSVILLE, PITTVILLE, PLEASANTVILLE, POOLEYVILLE, POTTERSVILLE, PSYCHOVILLE, RURISVILLE, SMALLVILLE and UNIONVILLE. **2** A particular condition; a state of mind (-city, following a descriptive word, is used with a similar sense). Examples: 'Don't bother coming. It's grimsville'; '"We [the team of toymakers relaunching the My Little Pony range] could tell you where Ponyville is," she continues, stroking the mane of Lemondrop with obvious love, "but we'd have to kill you. It's just Pony-perfect – wherever the little girl and her Pony are"' (Thompson, 2003).

ville nouvelle (French) A NEW TOWN.

ville-dortoir (French) A dormitory town.

Viollet-le-Duc, Eugène-Emanuel (1814–79) Architect and scholar. He specialised in restoring buildings and explaining gothic architecture, which he saw as the functional equivalent of the innovative iron buildings of his own time that he also admired. He wrote in 1866: 'to restore a building is not to preserve it... it is to reinstate it in a condition of completeness which may never have existed at any given time' (quoted in Glendinning, 2000).

virgin aggregates Previously unused natural granular material used in construction.

virtual community People interacting with like-minded internet users. See COMMUNITY.

virtual skyscraper One which is proposed by a developer, negotiated with the planners, eventually winning planning permission and so raising the value of the site, but which may not actually be built.

visibility See VIVA.

visibility map Shows how a site (or a proposed development) is (or will be) visible from particular viewpoints.

vision An imaginative perception of how things could be in the future. Franklin D Roosevelt drew on the Bible in declaring in his inaugural presidential address in 1933: 'They have no vision, and where there is no vision the people perish.' The sentence has often been quoted in planning documents, without intentional irony.

Vision for London A membership organisation active in the early 1990s providing a focal point, through its events and publications, for information and debate about London's future. Its network helped to link London's communities, local and central government, business, arts, education and research, architecture, planning, urban design and transport. Vision for London was launched in 1990 following widespread concern that, with the abolition of the Greater London Council and the absence of any London-wide strategic body, the capital was losing out to other cities, particularly as regards planning, transport and urban design.

Vision of Britain, A A book by the PRINCE OF WALES presenting his personal view of architecture and urban design. Published in 1989, it sold well at (among other places) supermarkets.

visioning The process of conceiving and agreeing a collective VISION for a place, particularly through involving a large number of people in imagining how the future could be. The term is of US origin.

visitable housing Housing whose high standards of access make it convenient for people with a wide range of abilities.

vista A narrow view past a series of landmarks. In planning documents it is usually part of the phrase 'views and vistas'. The term dates from the 1650s. Compare VIEW.

vista-stopper A building or structure that acts as the end point of a vista.

visual appropriateness The degree to which the appearance of a building or place reflects its use and structure. One of the seven principles of urban design identified in *Responsive Environments* (Bentley *et al*, 1985).

visual clutter A profusion of often poorly designed and coordinated elements of the street scene (such as advertisements, signage and street furniture) that detract from the appearance of the townscape.

visual envelope 1 The extent to which a specific feature or area can be seen from a particular point. **2** The extent of what is visible from a particular point.

visual literacy An understanding of the grammar and syntax of the built environment and the elements that go to make it up. Everyone should possess (but sadly many do not) a basic literacy simply by walking around with their eyes open. Designers, planners, councillors and commentators should possess a much higher level of literacy, including a knowledge of architectural

VISUAL LOGIC

history and local vernaculars. The evidence of the contemporary built environment suggests that this is too rarely the case.

visual logic A situation in which the appearance of a place matches the way it works. For example, what looks like the entrance is the way in, and what appears to be the route across a space actually is. See also AUTHENTICITY and LEGIBILITY.

visual plan KEVIN LYNCH (1960) envisioned a visual plan for a city or metropolitan region as a set of recommendations and controls concerned with visual form on the urban scale.

visual pollution Ugly buildings or structures. Example: 'Glass, steel and concrete monuments to sterile imaginations, erupting between those precious interstices between urban motorways, rank high among contemporary pollutants' (Smith, 1974).

visual preference survey A technique, patented by the American urban designer Anton Nelesson, that involves showing people slides of places and asking them to rate them on a scale of plus 10 to minus 10.

visual scope Defined by KEVIN LYNCH (1960) as 'qualities which increase the range and penetration of the visual, either actually or symbolically. These include transparencies (as with glass or buildings on stilts); overlaps (as when structures appear behind others); vistas and panoramas which increase the depth of vision (as on axial streets, broad open spaces, high views); articulating elements (foci, measuring rods, penetrating objects) which visually explain a space; concavity (as of a background hill or curving street) which exposes farther objects to view; clues which speak of an element otherwise invisible (as the sight of activity which is characteristic of a region to come, or the use of characteristic detail to hint at the proximity of another element).'

visualisation A representation (such as a drawing, photomontage or computer simulation) of a proposed development or other change.

visually sensitive area Land in a green belt, in a conservation area, in a local area of special character, or adjacent to a listed or locally listed building.

Vital Villages A Countryside Agency programme providing funding and advice to help people in rural communities and small market towns meet local needs.

vitality and viability The mantra of successful town and city centres. According to the Scottish Office (1998), the vitality of a town centre is a reflection of how busy it is at different times and in different parts, whereas viability is a measure of its capacity to attract investment for maintenance, improvement and adapting to changing needs. See also VIABILITY.

Vitruvius (Marcus Vitruvius Pollio) (c90–20BC) Roman architect and writer. His treatise *De architectura* was influenced by earlier Greek works. See COMMODITIE, FIRMENES AND DELIGHT.

VIVA A mnemonic, used in CRIME PREVENTION, for four factors that influence a target's risk of criminal attack: value (of the item to the offender), inertia (how difficult it is to move the item), visibility (of the target to the offender) and access. Compare CRAVED.

Vivat Ware The report of a study into the regeneration of the small Hertfordshire town of Ware by the architect David Rock with GORDON CULLEN, published in 1974. Rock recalled later: 'Importantly, and unusually for the time, the report included three-dimensional sketch schemes, rather than the broad zoning and land-use plans that were then the norm' (quoted in Bone, 1999). This work led to Rock becoming, in effect, Ware's TOWN CHAMPION over a period of 12 years.

vivendo discimus (Latin) We learn by living. The motto of PATRICK GEDDES.

vocal local A pejorative term for those residents of an area who are most forthright and persistent in expressing their opinions, regardless of whether their views are those of the majority or command significant support.

voice of the site See GENIUS LOCI.

void 1 An element of urban form other than a building or structure (a street, square, park, or space within a block, for example) (see CONTEXTUALISM). **2** An element of a building's façade that it not a solid wall (a window or door, for example) (see SOLID/VOID RELATIONSHIP and SOLID-TO-VOID RATIO). **3** The space contained within a building, as opposed to its *elements*. **4** An unused building or part of a building (an empty flat, for example). **5** Space that would be part of an upper floor were it not for the fact that it forms the 'headroom' of a room or rooms on the floor below which are more than one storey in height (particularly used in this sense as an annotation on a plan). **6** A period of time during which a completed development is unlet.

void for vagueness (US) A legal ground for challenging a ZONING.

void space See LANDFILL CAPACITY.

void-filling Developing undeveloped sites to create or restore continuous urban form and pedestrian routes.

voisinage (French) A NEIGHBOURHOOD.

volatile region Defined by Herrschel and Newman (2002) as one that exists as a REGION merely on paper and depends on collaboration between dominant local urban centres.

voluntary environmental agreement An agreement among the corporate, government and/or non-profit sectors, not required by legislation, that aims to improve environmental quality and the use of natural resources.

von Harbou, Thea (1888–1954) The author of the novel METROPOLIS, on which the film of the same name was based.

W

Wagner, Martin Chief planner of Berlin, 1926–33. He planned major housing estates of modernist design.

Wakefield, Edward Gibbon EBENEZER HOWARD acknowledged the influence on his own ideas of Wakefield's proposals, published in 1849, for an organised migratory movement of population (Miller, 1989).

Walden HENRY DAVID THOREAU's famous 1854 book (subtitled *Life in the Woods*) espousing life as an isolated individual communing with nature and escaping the horrors of city life. Walden was the place where Thoreau enjoyed the rural life. See also ANTI-URBANISM.

Wales, Prince of See PRINCE OF WALES.

walk band A line on a map or plan showing the furthest distance that can be walked from a particular point at an average pace in a certain time (usually five or ten minutes).

walkability The ease with which it is possible to walk around an area, from one point to another, or from housing to local facilities. Factors reducing walkability include distance, roads that are difficult to cross, and large street blocks with no routes through them. The consultant Space Syntax, commissioned by Transport for London in 2001 to develop a *walkability index* for London, identified a number of factors influencing walkability. These included footway quality, width and gradient; proximity of walking to road traffic; lighting; weather; proximity to transport facilities; signage; ground level activity; pedestrian crossing design; traffic signal phasing; time of day; and axial depth (a measure based on the average number of changes of direction required to reach a location from any other point in the network – see SPACE SYNTAX ANALYSIS).

walkable neighbourhood An area where local facilities are within walking distance; for example, a post box or telephone box within two to three minutes (250 metres), a newsagent within five minutes (400 metres), and local shops, a bus stop, a health centre and perhaps a primary school within 10 minutes (800 metres) (Llewelyn-Davies, 2000).

walkabout 1 (Australia) Movement, usually on foot, from here to an unspecified place and back again, often for the purpose of being stimulated by, or contemplating, the environment. Examples: 'He's gone walkabout'; 'I'm on walkabout'. Compare FLÂNEUR and GO BUSH. **2** (UK) A group of residents and others with a concern for an area walk around it discussing how it can be improved and recording their observations and conclusions. Walkabouts are often used in carrying out PLACECHECKS, for example.

Walker, Peter (Lord Walker) (b1932) Politician. First secretary of state, in 1970, of the newly created DEPARTMENT OF THE ENVIRONMENT (which as originally set up included responsibility for transport). See SECRETARY OF STATE.

walkers Walkers have been identified as an INDICATOR SPECIES for successful places. The suggestion is that the success of a place or a public space can be measured by the number of people on foot.

walking CABE (2001) has suggested that 'it is no accident that those British cities which are regarded as highly successful in urban design terms (Oxford, Cambridge, Bath and York, for example) were laid out when walking was a primary means of locomotion and have retained their basic plan ever since'. In fact walking is still the primary means of movement in towns and cities. What has happened is that it is too rarely allowed to shape them. In the words of Michel de Certeau (1974), 'the act of walking is to the urban system what the speech act is to language'. Jean-Jacques Rousseau said that he could 'meditate only when I am walking. When I stop, I cease to think: my mind works only with my legs' (quoted in Solnit, 2001). The novelist Martin Amis once defined a poet as 'someone who does not drive a car'. The view of one council official (in Glasgow) towards walking was illustrated by a comment quoted by Johnny Rodger (1999). The

> **❝I CAN MEDITATE ONLY WHEN I AM WALKING. WHEN I STOP, I CEASE TO THINK: MY MIND WORKS ONLY WITH MY LEGS❞**
>
> *Jean-Jacques Rousseau*

council was considering a planning application for a tall building. It could not be considered too tall for the site, the official assured the committee, 'as there is no view down Pitt Street anyway, because Pitt Street is one way'. Since the second world war transport planning has been fixated on motorised modes of transport, private (the car) and public (buses, trams, trains). Often walking (and cycling) are not even mentioned, not treated as 'transport' at all and consequently poorly provided for. York City Council is one that has consciously tried to address this motorised tunnel vision by adopting a new 'transport hierarchy' which puts walking first, cycling second, public transport third and the car last (see also BIASED TERMINOLOGY). Ivan Illich wrote in *Energy and Equity*: 'People move well on their feet. This primitive means of getting around will, on closer analysis, appear quite effective when compared with the lot of people in modern cities... People on their feet are more or less equal. People solely dependent on their feet move on the spur of the moment, at three to four miles per hour, in any direction and to any place from which they are not legally or physically barred. An improvement on this native degree of mobility by new transport technology should be expected to safeguard these values' (compare SEGWAY HUMAN TRANSPORTER). Peter Ackroyd (2000) notes that 'in the 1850s, 200,000 people walked into the City [of London] each day'. The novelist Henry James explained in his preface to *The Princess Casamassima* (1886) that 'this fiction proceeded quite directly, during the first year of a long residence in London, from the habit and interest of walking the streets'. The book's hero, he wrote, 'sprang up for me out of the London pavement'. See also FLÂNEUR, PEDESTRIAN and PROMENADE.

walking bus A group of children, escorted by teachers and/or parents, walking to school. The 'bus', which leaves at a regular time and takes on 'passengers' at timetabled stops, ensures that the children do not walk on their own and frees some parents from the need to accompany them. It is designed to reduce the number of cars crowding the roads ferrying children to school, as well as offering children the benefits of exercise and sociability. DAVID ENGWICHT claims to have invented the idea. See also RED SNEAKER ROUTE.

walking city A city (or part of one) where walking is the dominant mode of movement. Compare AUTOMOBILE CITY and SUBURBAN CITY.

Walking City Proposed by ARCHIGRAM, the legs of the megastructure would enable it to move from place to place. Compare TRACTION CITY.

walking distance A distance comfortable for most people to walk as an attractive alternative to driving. *A New Urbanist Lexicon* (McLaughlin, 2000) defines it as a quarter of a mile or a five-minute walk. Andres Duany (2000) defines walking distance as 'the distance which may be covered by a five-minute walk at an easy pace from the outer limit of the neighborhood proper to the edge of the neighborhood centre'. This, he argues, is the distance most people will walk rather than drive, providing that the environment is pedestrian-friendly. Duany defines this dimension as one quarter of a mile or 1,320 feet, though he accepts that it may be adjusted to a median distance of half a mile or 2,640 feet for a PLANNED NEIGHBORHOOD DEVELOPMENT of low density, or by calculating an average of the various edge-to-centre distances for a planned neighborhood development that has an eccentrically-located centre. Walking distance is an important factor in new urbanist planning. See also SIX HUNDRED FEET.

walking-friendly *adj.* Convenient and pleasant for people on foot to use, and to pass by or through. KEN LIVINGSTONE, mayor of London, declared in 2002 his aim 'to make London one of the world's most walking-friendly cities for pedestrians by the year 2015'. See also PEOPLE-FRIENDLY.

walking-talker A person (who may be a local resident) employed to walk round an area covered by a regeneration initiative, talking to people about it. Such people help to build the informal networks on which programmes of public participation depend.

Walkman (plural *Walkmans*) The first personal stereo. It was launched by Sony in Japan in 1979, originally with the name Stowaway. It began the change in relationship between pedestrians and their environment that developed further with the spread of mobile phones in the 1990s. The Académie Française urges the use in French of the alternative *baladeur* (Quinion, 2003).

walkover survey Recording features of a site while walking over it. Compare DESK STUDY and WINDSCREEN SURVEY.

walk-up A block of flats without a lift.

walled development See GATED ESTATE.

Walled Towns See BEAULIEU.

wally (US) A VAGRANT who stays within a town or city (in sight of its walls, as it were). Also *home guard*.

wally close (Glasgow, rhymes with *valley*) A tenement close (hallway) that is tiled (and thus superior to a painted one. Wally means china and derives from 'walloon'.

Walnut Whip London mayor KEN LIVINGSTONE planned a council tax rise of 44p a week in 2002. That was no more than 'the price of a Walnut Whip' (a chocolate confection), he explained.

ward 1 An administrative division of a city. The administrative wards of the City of London date back to the early ninth century (Ackroyd, 2000). The city grid of Savannah, Georgia, laid out in 1733, was organised into wards. A ward consisted of four *tythings*, and ten freeholders formed a tything. The plan, Spiro Kostof (1991) notes, was the blueprint of a political system.

EBENEZER HOWARD used the term for the NEIGHBOURHOODS of his proposed GARDEN CITIES. The city would have six wards, each with around 5,000 people.

Ward, Colin (b1924) Anarchist, writer, editor and environmental educationalist. After leaving school at 15 he worked in the council housing department and later as an architectural draughtsman. He was converted to anarchism while in the armed forces in the second world war (which led to him being imprisoned for 56 days). From 1947 to 1960 Ward was an editor of the anarchist magazine *Freedom*, and he later edited the monthly *Anarchy*. He worked as an architectural technician and then as a liberal studies teacher. In the 1970s he pioneered ENVIRONMENTAL EDUCATION at the Town and Country Planning Association. He has written widely on the informal environments that people make for themselves, such as ALLOTMENTS and PLOTLAND settlements. His books include *Anarchy in Action; The Child in the City; Welcome, Thinner City; Housing: an anarchist approach*; and *Talking to Architects*. 'The fact there is no route-map to utopia,' Ward (1991) writes, 'does not mean that there are no routes to more accessible destinations.' See ANARCHY.

warrant (US) One of the minimum criteria necessary to justify a traffic measure such as a road sign or a TRAFFIC CALMING device. Commonly used warrants include the results of speed surveys, traffic volume studies and accident counts.

waste Defined by the Scottish Office (1996b) as any substance that constitutes a scrap material or an effluent or other unwanted surplus substance arising from the application of any process, and any substance or article that needs to be disposed of as being broken, worn out, contaminated or otherwise spoiled. The consultants Llewelyn-Davies (2000) define waste as 'what we have not found a use for'. See also COMMERCIAL WASTE, CONTROLLED WASTE, HIERARCHY PRINCIPLE, HOUSEHOLD WASTE, LEONIA, PROXIMITY PRINCIPLE and PLANNING POLICY GUIDANCE NOTES.

waste stream The process that extends from the generation of waste to its disposal.

watercourse A canal, cut, culvert, drain, passage, river, sluice or stream (but not a sewer or water main) carrying or designed to carry water, together with the banks, bed, pipes, walls or other works containing it.

Waterloo, Stanley Novelist and journalist. He called for a literature that reflected the rough energy of his city of Chicago in the 1890s.

watershed 1 (UK and sometimes US) The imaginary dividing line between two river systems (drainage basins). **2** (US) The whole area of land that drains into a particular river. The word is borrowed from the German *Wasserscheide*, which has the first of the two meanings (Quinion, 1999). The relationship of watersheds to land form, drainage and watercourses

makes them an important consideration in planning and urban design. The US term is *divide*. **3** A dramatic and significant change of direction.

way-finding Helping people find their way by means such as signs, landmarks and a clear urban structure. The term, of US origin, became current in the UK in the 1990s.

We A novel by Yevgeny Zamyatin (1884–1937), which circulated in manuscript form in the Soviet Union but was never published there. An English translation was published in the USA in 1924. It portrays a planners' utopia where workers live in glass houses, have numbers rather than names, wear identical uniforms, eat chemical food and enjoy rationed sex. They are ruled by a planner called 'the Benefactor' who is unanimously and perpetually re-elected. The novel's hero is inspired to revolt by seeing the House of Antiquity in a city of otherwise relentless order. See PRIMARY GROUP.

wealth creation Cullingworth and Nadin (1997) suggest that wealth creation was identified as an aim of urban policy for a short time in the mid-1980s, but that its use in that way declined in the face of the impossibility of defining wealth.

Webb, Mike See ARCHIGRAM.

Webber, Melvin Planner. See also COMMUNITY WITHOUT PROPINQUITY, NON-PLACE URBAN REALM and MILTON KEYNES.

wedding cake A building whose upper floors are progressively stepped back, sometimes to conform with planning or ZONING regulations, designed to maximise the amount of daylight reaching street level.

weedjie A pejorative term for a Glaswegian, used by Scots from elsewhere.

weighting and scoring A method of combining a number of a regeneration initiative's outputs (which can not be valued in monetary terms) into a single overall measure of output.

weightless economy Knowledge-based economic activities, often heavily if not exclusively dependent on the internet and independent of heavy infrastructure. The term was coined by Danny Quah at the London School of Economics around 2000.

Weill, Kurt (1900–50) Composer. Born in Germany, he moved to the USA in 1935 and became an American citizen. See MAHAGONNY.

Weir, Peter See SEAHAVEN ISLAND.

Weissenhof estate A showpiece collection of 33 houses by many of Europe's leading modern architects, built by the Deutscher Werkbund in Stuttgart in 1927, under the direction of MIES VAN DER ROHE. The aim, Mies explained, was to display a new architecture based on 'the struggle for a new way of habitation, together with a rational use of new materials and new structures.' John Willett (1978) observes that 'to judge from the surviving photographs the estate's inhabitants were to consist mainly of healthy-looking women in swimsuits'. Willett recalls seeing a German postcard in the late 1930s which showed gummed-in lions and camels among the Weissenhof's flat-roofed, mainly white buildings, intended to mock it as an 'Arab village' alien to the architecture of the master race.

Well Hall A GARDEN SUBURB built in 1915 at Eltham, London, to house workers at Woolwich Royal Arsenal. Simon Pepper and Mark Swenarton (1978) called it 'a *tour de force* of picturesque design, in which the components of the "Old English Village" were assembled with a virtuosity exceeding anything attempted by Unwin.' Ewart Culpin (1917), one of the early campaigners for garden suburbs, wrote that it was 'from the architectural standpoint, without equal in the world'. It inspired much inter-war housing design, but nothing comparable was ever built, not least due to budgetary constraints. Being a defence-related housing project, Well Hall was built with almost unlimited funds. The architect was Frank (later Sir Frank) Baines.

Weller Streets Housing Cooperative The pioneering cooperative in Liverpool opened its new homes in 1982. Faced with the prospect of years of blight before the area was redeveloped, the residents fought hard for land, finance and planning permission for the new homes, designed as they wanted. One of their more orthodox and effective techniques was to hire a minibus and tour the leafy wards of councillors voting against the co-op's plans, letting it be known that they were from Liverpool 8 (their district which had a notorious reputation) and were prospecting for a suitable place to live. The Weller Streets had been named after characters in Dickens.

Wells, HG (1866–1946) Novelist. He supported the GARDEN CITY movement, becoming vice president of the Garden Cities Association in 1900. His 1900 essay on 'The probable diffusion of great cities' predicted that technological developments would soon make them obsolete. See URBAN REGION.

Welsh Development Agency The economic development agency for Wales.

Welsh Historic Monuments Agency See CADW.

Welsh, Irvine (b1958) Writer. See SCHEMIE and TRAINSPOTTING.

Welshness The distinctive characteristics of Welsh buildings. Dewi Prys-Thomas was among many architects who have tried to develop an architecture combining modernism and the Welsh VERNACULAR. Slate is often used as a characteristic Welsh building material.

Weltstadt (German) A WORLD CITY.

Welwyn Garden City EBENEZER HOWARD bought the site for his second garden city 20 miles from London with borrowed money at an auction in 1919. Welwyn was planned and designed, in neo-Georgian style, by Louis de Soissons. It grew slowly until the 1940s, when it was taken over by the government and became a Mark 1 NEW TOWN.

wen See DISPERSAL and GREAT WEN.

west end The fashionable side of a city. At first glance it seems an extraordinary coincidence that the west end is the fashionable side of so many UK cities – London, Newcastle, Glasgow to name just some. The explanation appears to be that, as the prevailing winds in the UK blow from the west, the east side suffers the worst of the smoke, dust and smells. With characteristic canniness the rich moved west to breath purer air. The first use of the term referred to London. Compare EAST END.

West Side Story A musical adapting the Romeo and Juliet story to the youth of New York's ghettoes, first staged in 1957 and later filmed. Leonard Bernstein was the composer, Stephen Sondheim the lyricist and Jerome Robbins the director.

wetland An area whose ground is frequently or permanently waterlogged due to a high water table. Wetlands provide valuable habitats for rare species, but many are threatened by drainage or peat removal.

Wheatley Act The Housing Act 1924, named after John Wheatley, the minister for health in the first Labour government. It offered increased subsidies to local authorities, with the aim of securing the construction of 2.5 million dwellings within 15 years. While only 520,000 houses were completed by 1939, in terms of production it was the most successful housing act of the inter-war years. See also ADDISON ACT and CHAMBERLAIN ACT.

whistling The sound of whistling is a much less common urban sound than it was a few decades ago. Reasons may include the greatly increased playing of recorded music and changing fashions. American Messenger Service, forerunner of United Parcel Service, banned its errand boys from whistling when it was founded in 1907.

Whitby, Mark See ENGINEER.

White City 1 The World's Columbian Exposition, held in Chicago in 1893 to celebrate the 400th anniversary of Columbus's discovery of America, so called for its white neoclassical buildings laid out in a 686 acre park along the city's south lakefront. DANIEL BURNHAM was chief planner and FREDERICK LAW OLMSTED the landscape architect. See CITY BEAUTIFUL MOVEMENT. **2** The area in north west London that was the site of the 1908 British-Franco exhibition (and subsequent exhibitions until 1914). The Hungarian designer Imry Kiralfy created 20 palaces and around 120 exhibition halls, in neo-rococo style and painted white, in 200 acres of landscaped grounds and waterways. The population of the area is now predominately black. Compare SYMZONIA.

white flight (also white exodus) The movement of relatively prosperous white people from inner urban

walking

areas out to the suburbs (see also DOUGHNUT EFFECT); the movement of white people out of a neighbourhood that members of a different ethnic group have moved in to. Example: 'When Asian people moved out to other areas, this prompted "white flight" from those areas to other neighbourhoods' (2001). The social researcher Anne Power reported to the URBAN SUMMIT in 2002 that estate agents in Birmingham, East London, and towns such as Burnley and Rochdale in north west England were encouraging 'white flight' by provoking fears that members of ethnic minorities were moving into certain areas. The estate agents calculated that they would profit from the increased volume of house sales.

white gloves See DRESS SENSE.

white land Underdeveloped land for which there are no specific planning proposals.

white paper A statement of UK government policy and proposed legislation. Compare GREEN PAPER.

white shoe brigade (Australia) Wealthy developers with no concern for cultural values or the quality of what they build. Example: 'Someone from the white shoe brigade is most likely a property developer carrying a brown paper bag full of crisp dollar bills, who is just as likely to despoil a pristine view of the ocean by throwing up a 12–storey apartment block made out of balsite and spit.'

white van man A stereotype of a driver of a white Transit-type van who is taken to represent, literally, the man in the street. White Van Man is the title of an occasional column in the *Sun* newspaper, in which a succession of drivers of white vans give their views on a current issue. White van man is sometimes thought of as an inconsiderate driver, as he may not mind a little damage to his vehicle as he does not own it. See also MONDEO MAN and PEBBLEDASH PEOPLE.

Whiteways A cooperative community inspired by the ideas of LEO TOLSTOY, founded in 1897 near Stroud in Gloucestershire by the journalist Samuel Bracher (Quail, 1978). The deeds to the land were burnt to prevent an open market in property, and to this day houses at Whiteways are unmortgagable. See also COOPERATIVE COLONY.

whole-life costing Assessing the likely costs of a development throughout its life, rather than just the cost of designing and building it; assessing the most cost-effective balance between the capital costs of a building and its maintenance and running costs. Compare LIFE-CYCLE COSTING.

wholism See HOLISM.

Whyte, William H 'Holly' Urbanist and sociologist. His influential studies based on close observation of how people used streets and plazas include *The Social Life of Small Urban Spaces*. 'It's hard to design a space that will not attract people,' he wrote. 'What is remarkable is how often this has been accomplished.' His work is continued by Project for Public Spaces, a nonprofit group that puts his principles to work in retrofitting problematic parks, plazas, shopping strips and streets across America.

wic As an element in English place-names, wic commonly indicates a place with a specialised function, as in Droitwich (salt production) and Butterwick (dairy farming) (Morris, 1989). The word comes from the Latin *vicus*, meaning a small town.

widened See BIASED TERMINOLOGY.

widow cleansing A pejorative term for persuading widows and other single occupiers of houses to move into smaller accommodation in order to make better use of the housing stock. Compare SOCIAL CLEANSING.

Wiener, Norbert (1894–1964) Mathematician and cyberneticist. His work on CYBERNETICS was influential on the development of the SYSTEMS APPROACH to planning. He was a professor at the Massachusetts Institute of Technology from 1919 to 1960.

wilderness A region barely touched by the presence of people. Some commentators and campaigners have valued wilderness as a source of moral or spiritual regeneration for people who visit it, and perhaps even of value to those who do not. Some of those who most value wilderness have seen big cities, by contrast, as sources of spiritual emptiness and moral degeneration (see ANTI-URBANISM), though there is no necessary connection between loving wilderness and hating cities. Conservationists campaigning to protect wilderness have been criticised by some who point to the human cost of their actions, borne by indigenous populations who have been driven off their land or whose opportunities have been otherwise restricted. The beneficiaries of wilderness conservation, these critics claim, tend to be white and wealthy.

Willebrand, IP The author of a 1775 book on the aesthetics of planning, *The Layout of a Beautiful City*.

Williamsburg A community in Virginia, USA, preserved from the 1920s onwards as it is supposed to have been in the 1790s. John D Rockefeller funded the project. Most buildings dating from after the 1790s were demolished and new ones in colonial style replaced them. Buildings were stripped of alterations made after the 1790s. Williamsburg has become an open-air museum, with people in period costume demonstrating daily life in colonial times. To many conservationists it is the prime example of an inauthentic approach to conservation. See AUTHENTICITY.

Williams-Ellis, Clough See PORTMEIRION.

Willian A model estate village in Hertfordshire, built by Charles Frederick Hancock after 1867. It was later incorporated into LETCHWORTH Garden City. Its architect, Owen Jones (1809–74) is now better known as the authority on decorative design. Mervyn Miller (1989) notes that the overall character of the white, rendered cottages in short blocks, set in generous gardens, 'anticipated the development of the garden city 40 years later'.

willingness-to-engage The attitude of the people of an area positively inclined to take part in a regeneration process.

Willis Faber Dumas building A celebrated early work by architect NORMAN FOSTER, built in the mid 1970s in Ipswich. The office building's black glass front (transparent at night) approximates the undulating line of a historic street. Its colour and shape have suggested it local nickname: 'the big black grand piano'.

Willmott, Peter Sociologist. See FAMILY AND KINSHIP IN EAST LONDON.

Wilson, James See BROKEN WINDOWS.

WIMBY! *Welcome into my backyard* was the theme of the 2001 International Building Exhibition in Rotterdam, whose aim was to overcome NIMBY attitudes.

Wind Singer, The See ARAMANTH.

wind tunnel A configuration of buildings that creates strong winds.

windae-hinger (Glasgow) One who hangs out of the window of a tenement block, passing the time of day with neighbours on the street and at other windows.

windfall (US) A substantial increase in the value of property due to public action or regulation. Compare WIPEOUT.

windfall site One unexpectedly becoming available for redevelopment (such as when a local factory or business folds). Some commentators argue that local and structure plans make no allowance for windfalls, and therefore over-designate greenfield sites for housing when brownfield sites will become unexpectedly available.

window-dominated architecture Buildings a large part of whose facades are windows.

Windrush See EMPIRE WINDRUSH.

Windscale inquiry British Nuclear Fuels applied for planning permission for a plant for processing irradiated oxide spent nuclear fuel at its Windscale site on the Cumbrian coast. The subsequent public inquiry lasted for several months in 1977. It gave environmental campaigners the chance to challenge an industry that had had a significant impact on the environment for decades without effective public scrutiny. The inspector recommended approval, though, and the plant was built. 'Windscale' having been demonised in the public mind, British Nuclear Fuels renamed it Sellafield.

windscreen survey A derogatory term for an area survey carried out without the trouble of getting out of the car. See also DESK STUDY.

Windy City (also Big Wind and Big Windy) Chicago. The origin of the nickname is controversial. Generally it is said to refer to the city's fondness for boasting about itself, dating back to when it was competing with New York to host the World's Columbian Exhibition of 1893 (see also BOOSTER). Michael Quinion (2001) records the name in use as early as 1885. He suggests that it originated in a scheme by the *Chicago Tribune* in the early 1880s to promote the city as a pleasant summer resort, cooled by the breezes of Lake Michigan. It seems likely that the name did begin as a reference to the wind, and has persisted for more than a century as a reference both to the wind and to its boosters' oratorical windiness, as well as out of habit. Before it acquired its new nickname, Chicago was known as GARDEN CITY. Its Latin motto is 'urbs in horto' (city in a garden).

Wine City The Greenock and Port Glasgow area, so called by Glaswegians who stigmatise it as the home of heavy drinkers of cheap wine. See also GARDEN PARTY.

winner-takes-all society One in which the distribution of rewards for economic activity is so unequal that those at the top receive most of the cake while those at the bottom scrabble for crumbs.

wino A person suffering from alcoholism, particularly one living on the streets. See VAGRANT.

wipeout (US) A substantial reduction in the value of a property due to public action or regulation. Compare WINDFALL.

wirescape The wires, aerials and related features that appear on the skyline.

Wirth, Louis (1897–1952) Chicago-based urban sociologist and author of *The Ghetto* (1928) and *Urbanism as a Way of Life*. Wirth argued that urbanism is not just a matter of buildings, infrastructure and concentrations of people but, more importantly, about a distinctive culture and consciousness unknown among and unattainable by rural and small town dwellers.

Wisconsin Phalanx A short-lived utopian settlement founded in Southport, Wisconsin in the 1840s, inspired by the ideas of CHARLES FOURIER.

Wohnbaufläche (German) A residential development zone.

Wohnfolgeeinrichtungen (German) Local amenities.

Wohngebiet (German) A built up area; a residential zone.

Wohnung (German) A flat or dwelling.

women See GENDER.

Womersley, Lewis (b1910) City architect of Sheffield, 1953–64. He was responsible for the vast council housing complexes at Park Hill (1960) and Hyde Park (1966). The design of these developments began in 1953 under the influence of LE CORBUSIER'S UNITÉ D'HABITATION, through the latter's internal corridor was replaced at Park Hill by a 'street deck' open on one side and wide enough to accommodate a milk float. The decks link all the blocks together and, as a result of the topography of the site, each deck starts at ground level. If Park Hill is overwhelmingly horizontal – a wall half a mile long – Hyde Park by contrast is overwhelmingly vertical, self-consciously designed as a motte to Park Hill's bailey. Its rooftop gardens were eventually closed after someone walking close to the block was killed by a television set thrown from them. As part of Sheffield's preparations for the world student games in 1991, the tallest block, the curiously named St John's Gardens, was demolished and the other Hyde Park blocks refurbished to accommodate the athletes. When the games finished the blocks were passed to housing associations for a variety of uses (including sheltered housing for the elderly). Park Hill remains council housing. It has been listed by English Heritage along with a tranche of other post-war buildings. Lord Esher (1981) recalls Nikolaus Pevsner writing soon after the scheme was complete: 'There can alas be no doubt that such a vast scheme of closely set high blocks will be a slum in half a century or less, but hopefully a cosy slum'.

won't-go area See NO-GO AREA.

Wood, John, the Elder (1704–54) Architect and planner, notably of Queen Square (built 1729–36) and the Circus (built after 1754) in Bath. The architectural historian Nikolaus Pevsner (1943) notes that Wood was the first architect after Inigo Jones to impose Palladian uniformity on an English square as a whole. 'All the squares in London and elsewhere laid out since 1660 had left it to each owner of a house to have it designed as he liked, and it was due only to the rule of taste in Georgian society that not one of these houses ever clashed violently with its neighbours,' Pevsner explains. 'John Wood now made one palace front with central portico and secondary emphasis on the corner blocks out of his Queen Square in Bath.'

Wood, John, the Younger (1721–81) Architect and planner, the son of the above. His work in Bath included the Royal Crescent (built 1761–5). The crescent was built as a freestanding façade with owners free to construct their own houses behind it. This explains why some of the houses are not full height, leaving the top storey as just a façade and, in contrast to the meticulous uniformity of the front elevation, the bewildering jumble of the back elevation to the mews.

Woodward, Augustus B (Judge) The designer of the 1805 Baroque plan for Detroit (Kostof, 1991).

woolly back See ONE-EYED CITY.

woonerf (Dutch, literally 'living [or residential] yard', pronounced *vone-airf*, plural *woonerven*). A small, highly traffic-calmed residential area, often with road and pavement integrated into a single surface. The term was coined by Dutch academic Niek De Boer in 1963 (Kostof, 1992). The UK equivalent is a 'home zone', though the woonerf concept was introduced (and the word became current) in the UK some years before 'home zone' was coined. See also ERF.

Woop Woop (Australia) A name given to any insignificant town. See also CACTUSVILLE, ONE-EYED CITY and PITSVILLE.

Wordsworth, William (1770–1850) Poet. See NIMBY and PEDESTRIAN.

work *n.* See JOBS.

work *v.* (of the whole or part of a building, or a place) To perform its intended function; to be successful. Tim Brindley of De Montfort University notes that, used in relation to architecture, the term is vague, highly generalised and untestable: part of a set of implicit meanings that may be widely shared within the architectural profession, but not outside it.

workable Capable of performing its intended function. Example: 'The problem of organising socially "workable" public space has bedevilled even the best attempts to provide successful public housing' (2002).

Workers' City See MERCHANT CITY.

working kitchen See SCULLERY.

working with the grain Building with a layout that has a grain similar to that of previous development or the surrounding area.

Working with Towns and Cities Initiative See TOWNS AND CITIES: PARTNERS IN URBAN RENAISSANCE INITIATIVE.

workmen's fares Cheap early-morning train, bus and ferry fares available in the UK between around 1860 and 1960. They were encouraged by the Cheap Trains Act 1883 and often made a condition of parliamentary approval to construct a railway line.

workplace parking levy A charge imposed by a local authority on every car-parking space at a place of work.

Workshop of the Empire/the World The description has been applied to both Glasgow and Birmingham in the nineteenth and early twentieth centuries. See also ATHENS OF THE NORTH, CANCER OF EMPIRE, SECOND CITY OF THE EMPIRE and VENICE OF THE NORTH.

workshopper A volunteer worker at ARCOSANTI.

world citadel A self-contained cluster of defensive office towers (Dear and Flusty, 1998).

world city One that is of strategic importance in international terms. The mayor of London defines a world city as 'a globally successful business location paralleled only by a small number of the world's other great cities, measured on a wide range of indicators such as financial services, government, business, higher education, culture and tourism'. NICKY GAVRON (2000), then deputy mayor of London, called London 'one of only three genuine "world cities"'. She had in mind the world financial centres of London, New York and Tokyo. Professor Brendan Nevin told the URBAN SUMMIT in 2002: 'There is no such thing as London any more. There is a world city in the south east of England and it is growing all the time.' Whether London – or any other city – should seek to become a world city, or to maintain that status, is controversial. Opponents assume that making a city attractive to international business will be at the expense of the interests of the city's local communities. The writer VS Pritchett (1997), writing in 1956, tells a story of a Cockney being asked whether the London he came from was London, Ontario. 'The Cockney groaned: "Nah! London the whole bloomin' world".' Pritchett comments: 'Truculent, proud, even sentimental, yet the old hypocrite was piously complaining of the weight of the world upon the London mind.' Many second-line cities noisily claim the distinction of being a world city, as CJ Fox points out. See also WELTSTADT.

world heritage site The sites are designated by UNESCO to highlight their value and the need to protect them. The designation draws attention to the sites' international importance, but does not give any additional protection. Sites in the UK include Ironbridge Gorge, Stonehenge and the city of Bath.

world in one city, the Liverpool, according to the slogan used in 2003 in its successful campaign to be European Capital of Culture 2008. The reference is to Liverpool's cultural diversity.

World Society of Ekistics A society that studies human patterns of living and their physical expression in the past, present and future. See EKISTICS.

World Squares for All A master plan for public spaces at Trafalgar Square, Parliament Square and Whitehall in central London. The first phase, involving the partial pedestrianisation of Trafalgar Square, was completed in 2003.

World Trade Center Designed by MINORU YAMASAKI (in collaboration with Emery Roth and Sons) and completed in 1970, the centre was the world's largest commercial complex until it was destroyed by terrorist action on 11 September 2001 with the loss of around 3,000 lives. It consisted of two 110-storey towers and five smaller buildings. The two biggest towers were popularly mocked as the boxes the Empire State and Chrysler buildings came in, on account of their severe minimalism (in contrast to the expressive shapes and exuberance of the Chrysler and the Empire State buildings).

The towers were unusual in that the steel mullions of the façade were load-bearing, along with the central lift and stair core, allowing column-free interiors. It is possible that this factor allowed the two towers to collapse in such a self-contained way, with less damage to surrounding buildings than would have been the case with a more conventional column and curtain wall construction.

The aftermath of the World Trade Center's destruction saw architects, urban designers and other commentators pointing to what they saw as its lessons. Some hoped that the increased awareness of safety and security would lead to fewer SKYSCRAPERS being built. Some called for technology to help defend high buildings from terrorist attack, and to find ways of evacuating them more quickly. Others argued that to give up building skyscrapers would be to give in to terrorism. 'We can't hide behind anonymous buildings,' the architect Peter Eisenman wrote. 'Urban living is about density and we're still going to need skyscrapers. We have to live our life and carry on building symbols worth attacking' (Eisenman, 2001).

The view from the top of the World Trade Center inspired some writers to hyperbole. Michel de Certeau (1984) writes: 'To be lifted to the summit of the World Trade Center is to be lifted out of the city's grasp. One's body is no longer clasped by the streets that turn and return it according to an anonymous law; nor is it possessed, whether as player or played, by the rumble of so many differences and by the nervousness of New York traffic... It transforms the bewitching world by which one was "possessed" into a text that lies before one's eyes. It allows one to read it, to be a solar Eye, looking down like a god. The exaltation of a scopic and gnostic drive: the fiction of knowledge is related to this lust to be a viewpoint and nothing more... The desire to see the city preceded the means of satisfying it. Medieval or Renaissance painters represented the city as seen in a perspective that no eye had yet enjoyed. This fiction already made the medieval spectator into a celestial eye. It created gods.' De Certeau asks: 'Have things changed since technical procedures have organized an "all-seeing power"? The totalizing eye imagined by the painters of earlier times lives on in our achievements. The same scopic drive haunts users of architectural productions by materializing today the utopia that yesterday was only painted. The 1,370-foot high tower that serves as a prow for Manhattan continues to construct the fiction that creates readers, makes the complexity of the city readable, and immobilizes its opaque mobility in a transparent text.' See also BATTERY PARK CITY, ICONIC, PARACHUTE and PRUITT-IGOE.

world wide web See X-URBIA.

worldscape *v.* To make another planet or a moon fit for human life. The word was coined by Roger Zelazny (Quinion, 1998). See TERRAFORM and compare ECOPOESIS.

worm's-eye view The view from absolute ground level. The term was coined by HUBERT DE CRONIN HASTINGS around 1932 in a caption to a photograph in the *Architectural Review*.

worsement The harmful impact of development (the opposite of betterment). The inelegant term is rarely used.

Wotton, Sir Henry (1568–1639) Diplomat and cultural commentator. See COMMODITIE, FIRMENES and DELIGHT.

wow factor A feature or aspect of a building or place that surprises at first sight. A character in Thomas Love Peacock's satirical 1816 novel *Headlong Hall*, a landscape gardener of the picturesque school, explains that he aims to give his layouts the character of *unexpectedness*. His companion asks in reply: 'Pray, sir, by what name do you distinguish this character, when a person walks round the grounds for the second time?' The same can be asked of the wow factor. Designers of buildings that are intended to have the wow factor seem often to use it as a substitute for designing something that works in its urban context. There are, however, a small number of buildings which both work in their urban context and seem to have an inexhaustible wow factor. Richard Rogers' Lloyds of London building is perhaps the most spectacular example.

wrapping Placing buildings that contribute to street life round the perimeter of a block that is mainly occupied by a use offering little to the street (a car park, for example).

wrapping paper architecture See SKIN ARCHITECTURE.

Wren, Christopher (Sir) (1632–1723) Architect. His plan for rebuilding London after the Great Fire of 1666 was rejected in favour of less ambitious proposals. These were preferred as they allowed the city's economic life to be resumed more quickly, with new buildings being constructed on old plots and along the line of the old streets. Wren designed St Paul's Cathedral (1675–1711) and more than 50 other churches in London. In a poll carried out for the COMMISSION FOR ARCHITECTURE AND THE BUILT ENVIRONMENT in 2002, Wren was the third most frequently named living architect, despite having been dead for 279 years.

Wrenaissance An architectural style inspired by that of Christopher Wren. The term was coined by the architect EDWIN LUTYENS, who used it to describe some of his own buildings (Darley, 2001).

Wright, Frank Lloyd (1867–1959) Architect and visionary. Martin Pawley (2002) is one critic who is willing to accept Wright's claim to have been advocating a new form of city. 'Frank Lloyd Wright was an urbanist,' Pawley writes, 'but entirely different to today's postmodern urban regenerators. The difference can be demonstrated by one shattering paradox. Wright was in favour of high-rise buildings but against high-density living. His urban vision was not exclusive but inclusive, encompassing everything from the spectacular 1956 "Mile High Illinois" skyscraper project – with its 528 storeys, outrigged helipads and 56 "atomic-powered elevators" – to the tiny Usonian self-build houses he continued to design for private clients until his death.' Wright was indeed an enthusiast for skyscrapers, but he wanted them as stand-alone objects in the landscape, visible from miles around. He disapproved of agglomerations of tall buildings (like Manhattan), but did not appear to understand the economic rationale that causes concentrations of skyscrapers to be built – scarce and expensive land coupled with potentially high rental yields. Neither condition applies in a field in the middle of Illinois. See ANTI-URBANISM, BROADACRE CITY, ORGANIC ARCHITECTURE, PRAIRIE STYLE, TALIESIN and THE USONIAN CITY.

Frank Lloyd Wright

Wright, Henry (1878–1936) Community planner, architect and landscape architect. His book *Re-Housing Urban America* was published in 1935.

Wright, Will The designer of the computer games SIMCITY and THE SIMS.

written representation A statement of a case relating to a planning appeal, submitted to a planning inspector for his or her decision. The written representations procedure avoids the need for a public inquiry in relatively straightforward cases.

Wunderwaffe (German) A magic weapon. Example: 'Traffic calming is not a *Wunderwaffe* against road congestion. It is just one tool and has limitations...'

Wurster, Catherine Bauer See CATHERINE BAUER.

wynd (Scotland) An ALLEY (see that entry for regional variants); a narrow, winding street.

Wyndham, John See DAY OF THE TRIFFIDS.

Wythenshawe A suburb of Manchester designed by BARRY PARKER. It was built in 1927–41 as Wythenshawe Satellite City by Manchester Corporation. In 2003 the press named it as the most expensive place in Britain for car insurance.

X, Y

X A vast and strangely indeterminate city, half ruined, half unbuilt, described by Tibor Déry in *Mr G.A. in the City of X* (1963). The city's president is chosen according to the length of his arms (Manguel and Guadalupi, 1999).

xeriscape A landscape whose species require little or no water or maintenance. From the Greek *xeros*, meaning dry.

x-list To designate a building as detrimental to the appearance and character of a CONSERVATION AREA. Such a designation was proposed in 2003 by George Ferguson, president of the RIBA. He suggested that x-listing would make a building eligible for a government grant towards its alteration or demolition.

x-urbia The contemporary American fringe city. The term was coined in 1999 by the US academic Mario Gandelsonas. He describes the x-urban city as 'the latest restructuring of the American city where the "formless" in the plan seems to dominate, where architectural concerns stop at the level of the building, and where the urban forces resist any attempts to see architectural form imposed. The emphasis seems to have shifted from the spatial dimension, where the ordering devices have been substantially impoverished, to the temporal dimension, where new and complex ordering structures have been introduced. A symptom of this situation is the fact that there is a lot more experimentation in the world wide web as public sphere than in the "reality" of urban space' (Gandelsonas, 1999). See also EDGE CITY, EXURBIA and LEARNING FROM LAS VEGAS.

Y Drenewydd (Welsh) The new town; the Welsh name for Newtown in mid-Wales.

yaird (Scots) A YARD; a GARDEN.

Yamasaki, Minoru (1912–1986) Japanese-American architect. He designed the AWARD-WINNING but later notorious PRUITT IGOE housing in St Louis (1955, demolished in 1972) and the WORLD TRADE CENTER in New York (built 1966–72, destroyed by terrorism in 2001). He wrote in 1952: 'As an architect, if I had no economic or social limitations, I'd solve all my problems with one-story buildings' (quoted in Goodman, 1972).

yard 1 (UK) A paved, utilitarian area beside a house.

2 (US) A space next to a house that is largely given over to grass. The equivalent word in the UK is GARDEN. See also LAWN.

Yay Oakland, California.

Yeang, Ken (b1948) Architect. Born in Malaysia, he has pioneered the *bioclimatic skyscraper*, designed to save land and energy, and put urban people in touch with nature. See GROUNDSCRAPER and SUBSCRAPER.

Yellowstone National Park The world's first national park, in Wyoming, USA, designated in 1872.

Yerkes, Charles Tyson (1837–1905) An American financier who built New York subways and much of the London underground. He was imprisoned for embezzlement in Philadelphia and was hounded out of Chicago (where he had been financing and constructing the Loop railway) for corrupt financial dealings, before moving to London. Theodore Dreiser fictionalised him in three novels.

YIMBY (US) Acronym for 'yes in my backyard', the opposite of NIMBY. The YIMBY approach involves proposals to deal with hazardous waste in the area in which it was produced.

yob A lout. The word, current since the 1850s for a familiar urban stereotype, is back-slang for *boy*, perhaps deriving from the sense of a yob being a backward boy. Compare YOUTH.

Yorkshire Development Group Set up by a consortium of local authorities in the 1960s in order to achieve economies of scale in the construction of council housing, the group developed its own heavy concrete panel building system. This was used to construct flats in Leeds, Sheffield and Hull – all now demolished.

Young, Michael (Lord Young of Dartington) (1916–2002) Social entrepreneur, researcher and reformer. He wrote the Labour party manifesto for the 1945 general election, and founded the Institute of Community Studies and the Consumers Association. His FAMILY AND KINSHIP IN EAST LONDON, written and researched with Peter Willmott, was a classic of social research and reportage. 'It had a political purpose,' Sir Peter Hall (2002) notes, 'which was to question the dispersal of the East End working class into satellite estates and new towns... He believed that the old working class communities of Bethnal Green, with their extended family structures, embodied the values he so assiduously sought... As the nuclear family that replaced it has come under threat, one senses that he was more troubled still.'

Young, Raymond See ASSIST.

youth 1 A state of being young, but not a child. Eric Hobsbawm (1968) suggests that '"youth" as a recognisable group, and not merely as a period of transition, to be got through as quickly as possible, between childhood and adult life... emerged in the 1950s; both commercially as the "teenage market", and in habits and behaviour.' **2** With an indefinite article, *a youth* is usually a young male, and the term is generally pejorative. Compare YOB.

youth shelter A small pavilion provided to give young people a place to hang out (usually in a residential area), located in a place where they are thought unlikely to cause a nuisance.

Ys A fictional ruined city under the sea off Finistère, France, whose church bells can still sometimes be heard. It was protected from the sea by a dam until one day, hundreds of years ago, the king's daughter gave away the key to the sluice gates to a stranger. The story is told in *The King of Ys*, a play by Edouard Blau and Edouard Lalo, first performed in 1926 (Manguel and Guadalupi, 1999).

ystryd (Welsh) A street.

yumpie (US) A young, upwardly mobile person. See YUPPIE.

yuppie A young upwardly mobile professional person; a young urban professional. The latter meaning is more common in the US, though both are heard in the US and UK. Yuppie is sometimes a pejorative term – 'yuppie values encompass greed, ambition, selfishness,' writes Sam Whimster (1992) – though as late as 2000 a letter to the etiquette correspondent of *The Times* began: 'My wife and I are expecting our first child and, post-yuppies that we are, wish to have a proper birth announcement printed...' In the UK, thrusting young people with large amounts of disposable income seemed to be the image of Thatcherism. Whimster found that foreign-exchange dealers in London spoke of eurobond dealers (who tended to come from middle-class backgrounds and be highly educated) as yuppies, and the eurobond dealers called the foreign exchange dealers yuppies. The use of the word peaked in the late 1980s. Two more recent examples lack the pejorative connotation: 'Will Alsop's team has produced architectural collages, splashed all over the magazines, which look a bit like Daniel Libeskind on ecstasy: a great wheeze, but will it sell to the yuppie punters?' (Sir Peter Hall on Urban Splash's proposals for East Manchester, in 2002); 'There exists a "them and us" divide [in POUNDBURY, Dorset] between Porsche-driving yuppies and retired professionals... and the subsidised housing association tenants... Graduate high flier Emma Heron says: "The village is a little lifeless and dull. I'm hoping more yuppies will move in"' (*Daily Express*, 2002). The yuppie lifestyle featured in novels such as Jay McInerney's *Bright Lights, Big City* and Tom Wolfe's THE BONFIRE OF THE VANITIES.

The word's US antecedents include YP (signifying a young professional, a term from the west coast of the USA), *preppie* (a product of an expensive private school), *hippy* (a follower of the 1960s and '70s counterculture) and yippy (a member of the radical Youth International Party). An early use of yuppie has been recorded in a story in the *Chicago Tribune* in 1983. The transformation from yippy to yuppie mirrors the decline of the counterculture (which, as Whimster notes, represented a rejection of the values of career, suburban life and conventional politics) and some young peoples' enthusiastic embrace of all that the counterculture had opposed. The acronym yuppie spawned many variants of the species, such as *dinky* (dual income, no kids yet).

yuppify *v.* To make a place attractive to YUPPIES (by, for example, ensuring a profusion of coffee bars, Poggenpohl kitchen outlets and designer clothes shops). See also CAPPUCCINO CULTURE.

Z

Z Cars A TV police series (1962–78) set in the fictional old port of Seaport (based on Liverpool's Seaforth) and the new housing estates of Newtown (based on the Liverpool overspill town of KIRKBY). See DIXON OF DOCK GREEN.

Zabriskie Point A film directed by Michelangelo Antonioni, released in 1970, aimed at the counterculture youth market. The grim face of urban dysfunction in Los Angeles is presented as a metaphor for the exploitative capitalist consumer society that the protagonists rebel against. Daria (played by Daria Halprin) is an anthropology student working as a secretary to a property developer who is building a village in the desert. Her boyfriend Mark (Mark Frechette) is being hunted by the police on suspicion of killing a policeman during a student riot. The film climaxes with the blowing-up, in Daria's mind, of the Death Valley retreat of her boss. The film was a critical and box-office failure.

Zähringer towns A series of twelfth-century planned towns in Germany and Switzerland founded by the Dukes of Zähringer, perhaps on the model of St Gallen. Alan Stones (2001) notes that the towns share a common set of planning principles. 'Each town is based on a broad market street intersected by a narrower principal cross street. The rest of the space is covered by parallel longitudinal and transverse streets. The streets are fronted by standard plots of 60 feet by 100 feet which were devised for taxation purposes but can be subdivided. Public buildings are placed away from the main street, and the castle is in one corner of the town, whose perimeter was not originally designed to be enclosed by defensive walls. Water supply and drainage channels were provided down the middle of the wider streets and to the side of the narrower streets.'

Zeilenbau (German) Parallel rows of slab housing blocks. Pioneered in Germany in the 1920s, the layout aligned blocks north-south so that their east- or west-facing windows would receive the maximum sunlight (Gold, 2000). There are arguments in favour of this arrangement if the principal habitable rooms are on *both* sides of the block. However, in the northern hemisphere the maximum sunlight on *one* elevation is achieved by a south-facing orientation. Most SOLAR BUILDING follows this pattern, placing the principal habitable rooms on the south-facing side of the building.

Zemrude An imaginary city in Asia that people perceive in different forms according to their different moods. ITALO CALVINO describes it in INVISIBLE CITIES (1972).

Zenobia An imaginary city in Asia (also described by ITALO CALVINO in INVISIBLE CITIES, 1972) that is built, for no reason anyone can recall, on stilts.

zero tolerance See BROKEN WINDOWS.

zero-friction society The supposed result of transport technology making moving between places exceptionally easy. Also known as *hypermobility*.

Zetetical Society Its debates on social issues in the early 1880s influenced EBENEZER HOWARD. The society's members included GEORGE BERNARD SHAW and Sidney Webb. The word comes from the Greek and means 'proceeding by inquiry'.

Zhanjiagang China's official model National Sanitation City, a river port on the Yangtze, 125km north west of Shanghai.

Zholtovsky, Ivan His plan for Moscow, commissioned by Lenin in 1918, proposed a number of GARDEN CITIES outside the industrial ring (Cooke, 2001).

Zlin The company town built by the Bata Shoe Company in south-eastern Bohemia in the decades after 1900. The company's owner, Tomas Bata, was also the town's mayor. The design combined garden city layout with modernist architecture. After the end of the second world war the city was renamed Gottwaldov after the first communist president of Czechoslovakia, Klement Gottwald.

Zola, Émile (1840–1902) Writer. His novel *Work*, published in 1900, described a utopian manufacturing town.

zonage (French) Zoning.

zone of change Six such zones were identified in 2002 by the Greater London Authority as focuses for regeneration. They incorporated established town centres, industrial and transport infrastructure, or large areas of BROWNFIELD land.

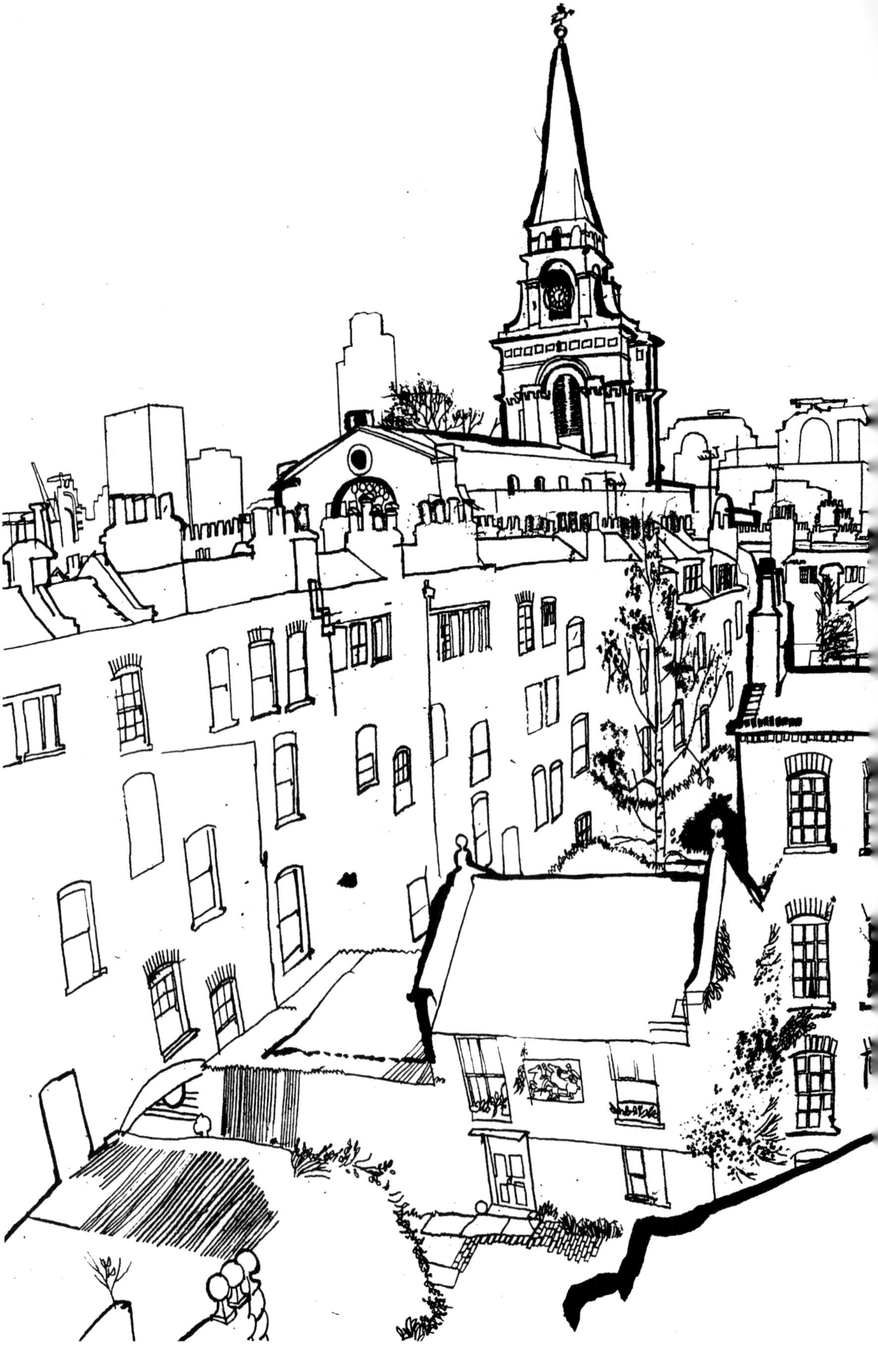

zone of transition

zone of transition 1 A TWILIGHT AREA. **2** An area with a high turnover of population and businesses. Example: 'Spitalfields remains a "zone of transition", as people continue to move in and out of the area. New buildings go up, old buildings are renovated. Businesses move out as new ones appear' (2002).

zone of visual influence An area within which a development has a visual impact.

zone piétonniére (French) A PEDESTRIAN area.

zoning 1 A system of allocating land for different uses and/or densities. Zoning is common throughout the world (but is not used in the UK) as the basis for controlling the use of land. The main aim of zoning is the protection of property rights by excluding uses thought to be undesirable. In the USA the system of VARIANCES provides the necessary flexibility. Zoning is thought to suit a nation such as the USA where the political climate is generally hostile to more positive planning. The earliest modern application of land-use zoning in the USA was initiated in San Francisco to isolate obnoxious land uses from existing houses. Laurence Gerckens (1994) notes that 'the physical separation and isolation of dangerous, odiferous or unsightly practices, such as tar boiling, soap making, fat rendering and dead carcass cremation, was viewed at that time as a reasonable governmental response to the unacceptable impositions of one otherwise legal activity upon another. Both the residences and these businesses had their right to exist, it was held, but not necessarily in close proximity to each other. Thus, the legal separation and isolation of land uses began.'

Jim Kunstler (2003) has condemned zoning as 'the systematic disassembly of the complex civic organism into less than the sum of its parts'. Kunstler writes: 'Zoning may have started as a reasonable response to the novelty of industrialism, but it has evolved into an abstract scheme which fragments daily life and makes car dependency mandatory. Under the bonehead logic of zoning, benign activities like shopping are given the same treatment as glue factories and detached from the places where people live, with the result that we have become a United Parking Lot of America.'

The 1916 New York City zoning ordinance is usually regarded as the first comprehensive zoning ordinance in the USA (Cullingworth, 1997). The concept was introduced in the UK by the Town Planning Act 1932, which allowed local authorities to schedule districts for development at specific densities (see PLANNING SCHEME), but the system was replaced in 1947. See also EDWARD M BASSETT, CONTRACT ZONING, CLUSTER ZONING, DOWNZONING, INCENTIVE ZONING, INCLUSIONARY ZONING, LARGE-LOT ZONING, REZONING, SPOT ZONING, STREET GRID and UPZONING. **2** In the UK the term zoning is sometimes used in a non-technical (and usually pejorative) sense to refer to plans allocating land for particular uses, but technically UK planning is not a system of zoning. **3** The supposed tendency of a city to be disposed in concentric residential districts around either a central business district or a government core. The existence of such a tendency was identified by sociologists ROBERT PARK and ERNEST BURGESS in Chicago in 1923. Aldo Rossi (1982) suggests that zoning in this sense made its first appearance in studies by Reinhard Baumeister in 1870 and was also applied to the plan of 1925 for the city of Berlin. 'But in Berlin it was used in an entirely different way,' Rossi writes. 'It indicated five zones in the city (residential, parkland, commercial, industrial, mixed), but the disposition of these zones was not radiocentric'.

zoning appeal (US) Made to a board of adjustment or board of appeals, or to the legislative body, or to the courts seeking to revoke or vary a zoning ordinance.

zoning ordinance (US) Passed by a municipality or other legislative body allocating land for different uses and/or densities.

zonitis Declaring an excessive number of zones designated for a variety of area-based regeneration initiatives.

zoomorphic architecture Buildings that resemble animals. THE ARMADILLO in Glasgow is an example.

Zwink, Oliver (b1967) A Berlin-based painter whose work features imaginary cityscapes.

> **"UNDER THE BONEHEAD LOGIC OF ZONING, BENIGN ACTIVITIES LIKE SHOPPING ARE GIVEN THE SAME TREATMENT AS GLUE FACTORIES"**
>
> *Jim Kunstler*

References

Ackroyd, P. (2000) *London: the biography*, Chatto and Windus, London.
Ackroyd, P. (2001) 'The life of the city' in *Century City* (brochure to the exhibition), Tate Modern, London.
Adam, R. (2003) 'How heritage dogma destroys living history', *Context*, London, May.
Adams, J. (1974) 'And how much for your grandmother?' *Environment and Planning*, A6, London.
Adams, J. (1998) 'Carmageddon' in Barnett, A. and Scruton, R. (eds.) *Town and Country*, Jonathan Cape, London.
Adamson, P. (2000) 'Looking back on our future: conflicting visions and realities of the modern American city' in Deckker, T. (ed.) *The Modern City Revisited*, Spon Press, London.
Alexander, C. (1965) 'A city is not a tree', *Architectural Forum*, April.
Alexander, C. et al. (1977) *A Pattern Language*, Oxford University Press, Oxford.
Allan, J. (2000) 'Lubetkin and Peterlee' in Deckker, T. (ed.) *The Modern City Revisited*, Spon Press, London.
Alsop, W. (2003) 'A beautiful place…', *Architects Journal*, London, 13 March.
American Planning Association (1998) *Policy Guide on Neighborhood Collaborative Planning*, American Planning Association, New York.
American Planning Association (2000) *Policy Guide on Planning for Sustainability*, American Planning Association, New York.
Appadurai, A. (1991) 'Global ethnoscapes: notes and queries for a transnational anthropology' in Fox, R. (ed.) *Recapturing Anthropology*, School of American Research Press, Santa Fe.
Appleyard, D. (1980) *Livable Streets*, University of California Press, Berkeley.
Architectural League of New York (2001) Announcement of the exhibition 'Ten shades of green', New York.
Arendt, H. (1973) Introduction to Benjamin, W. *Illuminations*, Fontana Press, London.
Arens, R. (2001) 'The Heidelberg Project' in Daskalakis G., Waldheim, C. and Young, J. (eds.) *Stalking Detroit*, ACTAR, Barcelona.
Arnstein, S. (1969) 'A ladder of citizen participation', *Journal of the American Institute of Planners*, July.
Ash, J. (1980) 'The rise and fall of high-rise housing in England' in Ungerson, C. and Karn, V. *The Consumer Experience of Housing*, Gower, Farnborough.
Aughton, P. (1990) *Liverpool: a people's history*, Carnegie Publishing, Preston.
Bailey, A. (1967) *Through the Great City: impressions of megalopolis*, Macmillan, New York.
Baker, L. (2000) 'Power to the people', *Planning*, London, 7 April.
Banham, R. (1960) *Theory and Design in the First Machine Age*, Architectural Press, London.
Banham, R. (1965) 'The Great Gizmo', reprinted in *Design by Choice*, Academy, London, 1981.
Banham, R. (1971) *Los Angeles: the architecture of four ecologies*, Penguin, London.
Banham, R., Barker, P. and Price, C. (1969) 'Non-plan: an experiment in freedom', *New Society*, London, 20 March.
Barber, S. (2002) *Projected Cities: cinema and urban space*, Reaktion Books, London.
Bareham, G. (2001) 'A round peg in a square hole', *Building Design*, London, 19 October.
Barnett, J. (1995) *The Fractured Metropolis*, Icon Editions, New York.
Barton, H. (1998a) 'Design for movement' in Greed, C. and Roberts, M. (eds.) *Introducing Urban Design*, Addison Wesley Longman, Harlow, Essex.
Barton, H. (1998b) 'Going green by design', *Urban Design Quarterly*, Oxford, January.

Batchelor, P. and Lewis, D. (ed.) (1986) *Urban Design in Action*, Student Publication of the School of Design at North Carolina State University, Raleigh, North Carolina.
Beaman, M. (2001) 'The property professional in the community', *Planning in London*, London, January.
Bech, H. (1992) 'Living together in the (post)modern world', paper presented to the European Conference on Sociology in Vienna, August.
Beer, A. (1993) 'Landscape planning and environmental sustainability', *Town Planning Review*, 64(4).
Bender, T. (2002) *The Unfinished Metropolis*, New Press, New York.
Bendixson, T. (1988) *The Peterborough Effect*, Peterborough Development Corporation, Peterborough.
Benevolo, L. (1993) *The European City*, Blackwell, Oxford.
Benjamin, W. (1938) 'The Paris of the Second Empire in Baudelaire', in Benjamin, W. (1997) *Charles Baudelaire: a lyric poet in the era of high capitalism*, Verso, London.
Bennett, A. (1911) *The Card*, Methuen, London.
Bennun, D. (1996) 'Hell out there', *Guardian*, London, 1 November.
Bentley I. et al (1985) *Responsive Environments: a manual for designers*, Architectural Press, London.
Berlin, I. (1990) 'The decline of utopian ideas in the West' in *The Crooked Timber of Humanity*, John Murray, London.
Berman, M. (1982) *All That Is Solid Melts into Air*, Simon and Schuster, New York.
Berman, M. (1988) 'The experience of modernity' in Thackara, J. *Design after Modernism*, Thames and Hudson, London.
Biddulph, M. (2000) 'Homes zones initiatives', *Urban Design Quarterly*, London, October.
Biddulph, M. (2001) *Home Zones: a planning and design handbook*, Policy Press, Bristol.
Biddulph, M. (2002) *The Urban Village: a real or imagined contribution to sustainable development?* Economic and Social Research Council, London.
Biddulph, M., Tait, M. and Franklin, B. (2002) 'The Urban Village: an obituary?' *Urban Design Quarterly*, 81, London.
Billingham, J. (2002) Review of *Marketing Modernisms* in *Urban Design Quarterly*, London, Spring.
Black, L. (2001) 'Are these jobs really necessary?' *Regeneration and Renewal*, London, 14 September.
Blackler, Z. (2003) 'Frank talking', *Architect's Journal*, 20 March.
Blackman, D. (2001) 'The space between us', *New Start*, London, 3 August.
Bleasdale, A. (2001) Interview in *Metro*, London, 25 September.
Blowers, A. (1976) *Reform or Revolution?* Open University Press, Milton Keynes.
Bohigas, O. (1999), 'Ten points for an urban methodology', *Architectural Review*, London, September.
Bold, A. (ed.) (1984) *The Thistle Rises: an anthology of poetry and prose by Hugh MacDiarmid*, Hamish Hamilton, London.
Bone, D. (1999) *Town Champions*, RIBA, London.
Booth, R. (2002a) 'Sue me, campaigner goads regulator', *Building Design*, London, 5 April.
Booth, R. (2002b) 'Designers' block', *Building Design*, London, 5 April.
Bordern, I. (2001) *Skateboarding Space and the City: architecture and the body*, Berg Publishers, London.
Bott, O. (2001) 'Medieval boom town', in Langtree, S. and Comyns, A. *2000 Years of Building: Chester's architectural legacy*, Chester Civic Trust, Chester.
Boussel, P. (undated) *Da Vinci*, Alpine Fine Arts Collection, London.
Brand, S. (1994) *How Buildings Learn: what happens after they're built*, Penguin/Viking, New York and London.

REFERENCES

Brandes Gratz, R. (2002) 'New word lessons', *Guardian*, London, 31 October.
Brassaï (1993) *Graffiti*, publisher unknown, Paris.
Braunfels, W. (1975) 'Institutions and their corresponding ideals: an essay on architectonic form and social institutions' in *Quality of Man's Environment*, Voice of America, Washington DC.
Breheny, M. (2001) 'Densities and sustainable cities: the UK experience' in Echenique, M. and Saint, A. (eds.) (2001) *Cities for the New Millennium*, Spon Press, London.
Brennan, T. (1959) *Reshaping a City*, House of Grant, Glasgow.
Bridson, D. (1971) *Prospero and Ariel*, Victor Gollancz, London.
Briggs, A. (ed.) (1962) *William Morris: selected writings and designs*, Penguin, Harmondsworth, Middlesex.
Broady, M. (1966) 'Social theory in architectural design', *Arena*, London, January.
Brody, H. (1998) 'Nomads and settlers', in Barnett, A. and Scruton, R. (eds.) *Town and Country*, Jonathan Cape, London.
Brown, C., Claydon, J. and Nadin, V. (2002) 'Planning, planners and professionalism', RTPI Education Commission papers, RTPI, London.
Browne, A. (2003) '60s tower blocks are reborn as skyhouses', *Times*, London, 11 February.
Bryson, B. (1990) *Mother Tongue*, Hamish Hamilton, London.
Bryson, B. (1994), *Made in America*, Secker and Warburg, London.
Buchanan, P. (1988) 'What city? A plea for place in the public realm', *Architectural Review*, London, November.
Buenger, B. (ed.) (1997) *Max Beckmann, Self-portrait in Words: collected writings and statements 1903–1950*, University of Chicago Press, Chicago.
Building Design (2003a) 'Great expectations', *Building Design*, London, 10 January.
Building Design (2003b) 'Rogers brings back task force', *Building Design*, London, 25 July.
Bunting, M. (2003) 'Passion and pessimism', *Guardian*, London, 5 April.
Burchill, J. (2001) Column in the *Guardian*, London, 6 January.
Burkeman, O. (2002) 'It's a novel idea, but nothing can get New York reading from the same page', *Guardian*, London, 27 February.
Burnett, J. (1986) *A Social History of Housing (1815–1985)*, Methuen, London.
Burns, W. (1963) *New Towns for Old*, Leonard Hill, London.
Burrows, E. and Wallace, M. (1998) *Gotham: a history of New York City to 1898*, Oxford University Press, New York and Oxford.
Calthorpe, P. and Fulton, W. (2000) *The Regional City*, Island Press, California.
Campbell, B. (1993) *Goliath: Britain's dangerous places*, Methuen, London.
Campbell, K. (1995) 'Urban design in the Age of Unreason', *Urban Design Quarterly*, Oxford, July.
Campbell, K. (1999) 'Mixed-use city centres', *Urban Design Quarterly*, Oxford, April.
Campbell, K. and Cowan, R. (2002), *Re:urbanism*, Urban Exchange, London.
Carmona, M., Heath, T., Oc, T. and Tiesdell, S. (2003) *Public Space – Urban Spaces: the dimensions of urban design*, Architectural Press, Oxford.
Castells, M. and Hall, P. (1994) *Technopoles of the World*, Routledge, London and New York.
Cavanagh, S. (1998) 'Women and the urban environment' in Greed, C. and Roberts, M. (eds.) *Introducing Urban Design*, Addison Wesley Longman, Harlow, Essex.
Caves, R. (2000) 'What is a smart community?', *Insight*, San Diego, California, Fall.
CCM (2002) 'Our challenge is to rebuild our cities', Connecticut Conference of Municipalities website, 11 October.
Chandler, B. (2001) 'The HIs and LOs of urban design', *Urban Forum*, Melbourne, December.
Chapman, T. (2002) Letter in *Architects' Journal*, London, 31 October.
Cherry, G. (ed.) (1981) *Pioneers in British Planning*, Architectural Press, London.
Clark, G. (2000) 'The gifts of women', paper given to a symposium on 'The Age of Theodora', *Hugoye: Journal of Syriac Studies*, New London, Connecticut.
Clarke, C. (1951) in the *Journal of the Royal Statistical Society*, Part 4.
Clifford, S. (1990) 'Places: the city and the invisible', talk at the PADT Creative City seminar, February.
Clifford, S. (1997) 'The tick-tock of the new', Local Distinctiveness in Design Conference, Nottingham University, 19 March.
Clinard, M. (1966) *Slums and Community Development*, Free Press, New York.
Clouston, B. (2002) 'Lessons in bronze', letter in *Landscape Design*, London, March 2002.
Coates, N. (1988) 'Street signs' in Thackara, J., *Design after Modernism*, Thames and Hudson, London.

Coleman, A. (1985) *Utopia on Trial*, Hilary Shipman, London.
Collings, J. (2000) 'Los Angeles per cent for art', *Urban Design Quarterly*, London, October.
Collins, R. (1980) 'Changing views on historical conservation in cities', *Annals of the American Academy of Voice and Social Science*, September.
Congress for the New Urbanism (2001) Flyer for its ninth annual meeting, published in San Francisco.
Cook, P. (1966) Editorial in *Archigram 7*, London.
Cooke, C. (1978) 'Russian responses to the garden city idea', *Architectural Review*, London, June.
Cooke, C. (2000) 'Cities of socialism' in Deckker, T. (ed.) *The Modern City Revisited*, Spon Press, London.
Cooke, C. (2001) 'Extensive or intensive development? A century of debates and experience in Moscow' in Echenique, M. and Saint, A. (eds.) (2001) *Cities for the New Millennium*, Spon Press, London.
Cooley, M. (1988) 'From Brunelleschi to CAD-CAM' in Thackara, J. (ed.), *Design after Modernism*, Thames and Hudson, London.
Corner, J. (2001) 'Landscraping' in Daskalakis, G., Waldheim, C. and Young, J. (eds.) *Stalking Detroit*, ACTAR, Barcelona.
Corr, O. Casey (1999) 'The hiring of Rem Koolhaas and the shock of the shoes', *Seattle Times*, 16 June.
Couch, C. (1990) *Urban Renewal*, Macmillan, London.
Couclelis, H. (2003) 'The social construction of the digital city' on www.geo.ucsb.edu, Department of Geography, University of California, Santa Barbara.
Countryside Agency (2000) *Planning Tomorrow's Countryside*, Cheltenham.
Cowan, R. (1995) *The Cities Design Forgot*, Urban Initiatives, London, 1995.
Cowan, R. (1997) *The Connected City*, Urban Initiatives, London, 1997.
Cowan, R. (1997a) 'The new urban design agenda', *Urban Design Quarterly*, Oxford, July.
Cowan, R. (2001) *Placechecks: a users' guide* (second edition), Urban Design Alliance, London.
Cowan, R. (2002) *Urban Design Guidance: urban design frameworks, development briefs and master plans*, Thomas Telford, London.
Cowan, R. and Delaney, A. (1993) *London After Dark*, Phaidon Press, London.
Cox, D. (1967) 'Ralph Vaughan Williams' in Simpson, R. *The Symphony*, Volume 2, Penguin, Harmondsworth, Middlesex.
Crawford, M. (1992) 'The World in a Shopping Mall' in Sorkin, M. (ed.) *Variations on a Theme Park: the new American city and the end of public space*, Noonday.
Crimson with Michael Speaks and Gerard Hadders (1999) *Mart Stam's Trousers: stories from behind the scenes of Dutch moral modernism*, 010 Publishers.
Croft, C. (2001a) 'Rhapsody in red', *Building Design*, London, 1 June.
Croft, C. (2001b) 'Best intentions', *Architects' Journal*, London, 6 September.
Croft, C. (2002) 'Unfulfilled potential', *Building Design*, London, 5 July.
Cruickshank, D. (1994) 'Picking up the pieces of Euston Arch', *Perspectives*, London, September.
Cullen, G. (1971) *The Concise Townscape*, Architectural Press, London.
Cullingworth, B. (1997) *Planning in the USA*, Routledge, London.
Cullingworth, B. and Nadin, V. (1997) *Town and Country Planning in the UK* (twelfth edition), Routledge, London.
Culpin, E. (1917) 'The remarkable application of town-planning principles to the war-time necessities of England', *Journal of the American Institute of Architects*, Vol. 4, No. 4.
Cunningham, A. (2000) 'Envoi' in Deckker, T. (ed.) *The Modern City Revisited*, Spon Press, London.
Curtis, W. (1996) *Modern Architecture Since 1900* (third edition), Phaidon, London.
Dahl, R. and Lindblom, E. (1953) *Politics, Economics and Welfare*, Harper and Row, New York.
Dalley, J. (2002) 'Bonds and building societies', *Financial Times*, London, 22 June.
Darley, G. (2001) 'Stamp of authority', *Architects' Journal*, London, 16/23 August.
Daskalakis, G. and Perez, O. (2001) 'Projecting Detroit' in Daskalakis, G., Waldheim, C. and Young, J. (eds.) *Stalking Detroit*, ACTAR, Barcelona.
Daskalakis, G., Waldheim, C. and Young, J. (eds.) (2001) *Stalking Detroit*, ACTAR, Barcelona.
Davies, S. (2002) *The Prisoner Handbook*, Boxtree, Basingstoke and Oxford.
Davis, M. (2002) *Dead Cities*, New Press, New York.
De Bono, E. (1985) *Conflicts: a better way to resolve them*, Harrap, London.
De Castella, T. (2003) *CABE Annual Report*, CABE, London.
De Certeau, M. (1984) *The Practice of Everyday Life*, University of California Press, Berkeley.
De Costa, R. (2002) Review of *No Logo* in *Urban Policy and Research*, Basingstoke, March 2002.

REFERENCES

De Mare, H. and Vos, A. (eds.) (1993) *Urban Rituals in Italy and the Netherlands,* Van Gorcum, Assen, Netherlands.

Dear, M. and Flusty, S. (1998) 'Postmodern urbanism', *Annals of the Association of American Geographers,* Blackwell Publishers, Malden, Massachusetts, and Oxford.

Debord, G. (1981) 'Theory of the Dérive', republished in Knabb, K. (ed.) *Situationist International Anthology,* Bureau of Public Secrets, Berkeley, California.

Deckker, T. (2000) 'Brasilia: city versus landscape' in Deckker, T. (ed.) *The Modern City Revisited,* Spon Press, London.

Department of Culture, Media and Sport (2002) *People and Places: social inclusion policy for the built and historic environment,* DCMS, London.

Department of the Environment, Transport and the Regions (1998a) *The Impact of Large Foodstores on Market Towns and District Centres,* DETR, London.

Department of the Environment, Transport and the Regions (1998b) *Urban Exchange Initiative* on www.detr.gov.uk.

Department of the Environment, Transport and the Regions (2000), *Social Exclusion and the Provision and Availability of Public Transport,* London.

Department of the Environment, Transport and the Regions (2001) *UK Fuel Poverty Strategy: consultation draft,* DETR, London.

Department of the Environment, Transport and the Regions and Commission for Architecture and the Built Environment (2000) *By Design: urban design in the planning system – towards better practice,* Thomas Telford Publishing, London.

Department of Transport, Local Government and the Regions (2001) *Home Zones and Quiet Lanes: consultation on statutory guidance and regulations,* DTLR, London.

Department of Transport, Local Government and the Regions and the Commission for Architecture and the Built Environment (2001) *Better Places to Live: by design,* Thomas Telford Publishing, London.

Development Planning Unit (2001) *Implementing the Habitat Agenda: in search of urban sustainability,* Department for International Development and Development Planning Unit, University College London, London.

Dixon, R. and Muthesius, S. (1978) *Victorian Architecture,* Thames and Hudson, London.

Donati, M. (2003) 'Committed reformer', *Planning,* London, 24 January.

Donnison, D. and Eversley, D. (eds.) (1973) *London: urban patterns, problems and policies,* Heinemann, London.

Donnison, D. and Middleton, A. (eds.) (1987) *Regeneration the Inner City: Glasgow's experience,* Routledge and Kegan Paul, London.

Downs, R. and Stea, D. (eds.) (1973) *Image and Environment: cognitive mapping and spatial behavior,* Aldine Publishing, Chicago.

Drewett, R. (1980) 'Changing Urban Structures in Europe', *Annals of the American Academy of Political and Social Science,* September.

Duany, A. (1998–2003a) on www.dpz.com

Duany, A. (2003b) 'In defense of traditional architecture', *The American Enterprise,* July/August.

Duany, A. and Plater-Zyberk, E. (1994) in 'The neighborhood, the district and the corridor', in Katz, P. (ed.) *The New Urbanism: toward an architecture of community,* McGraw-Hill, New York.

Duany, A. and Plater-Zyberk, E. (2001) on www.dpz.com

Duffy, F. (2000) Review in *Architectural Review,* London, May.

Dunnett, J. (2000) 'Le Corbusier and the city without streets' in Deckker, T. (ed.) *The Modern City Revisited,* Spon Press, London.

Durack, R. (2002) 'Community design centres', *Urban Design Quarterly,* London, Spring.

Dyckhoff, T. (2003) 'The memorial man', *Times,* London, 4 March.

Echenique, M. (2001) 'Mobility and space in metropolitan areas' in Echenique, M. and Saint, A. (eds.) (2001) *Cities for the New Millennium,* Spon Press, London.

Echenique, M. and Saint, A. (eds.) (2001) *Cities for the New Millennium,* Spon Press, London.

Edmonds, D. and Eidinow, J. (2001) *Wittgenstein's Poker,* Faber and Faber, London.

Edwards, P. (2000) *Wyndham Lewis: painter and writer,* Yale University Press, New Haven.

Eger, J. (2003) 'Cyberspace and cyberplace: building the smart communities of tomorrow', *San Diego Union-Tribune,* San Diego, California, 26 October.

Eisenman, P. (2001) quoted in *Regeneration and Renewal,* London, 9 November.

Eley, M. (2001) 'A view from the saddle', *Urban Design Quarterly,* London, 78.

Eliot, T.S. (1948) *Notes Towards the Definition of Culture,* Faber and Faber, London.

Eliot, V. (1971) *The Waste Land: a facsimile and transcript of the original drafts,* Faber and Faber, London.

Elson, M. (1986) *Green Belts,* Heinemann, London.

English Heritage (2000) *Streets for All,* English Heritage, London.

Engwicht, David (2003) on www.lesstraffic.com

Esher, L. (1981) *The Broken Wave,* Penguin Books, Harmondsworth, Middlesex.

Eversley, D. (1973) 'Problems of social planning in inner London' in Donnison, D. and Eversley, D. (eds.) *London: urban patterns, problems and policies,* Heinemann, London.

Farley, P. (1998) *The Boy from the Chemist is Here to See You,* Picador, London.

Farmer, J. (1996) *Green Shift,* Butterworth-Heineman, Oxford.

Farrelly, E. (1986) 'The New Spirit', *Architectural Review,* London, 180.

Ferguson, R. (1979) *Geoff: the life of Geoffrey M. Shaw,* Famedram Publishers, Gartocharn.

Financial Times (2003) 'End of the road', *Financial Times,* London, 20 January.

Finch, P. (2000) 'London swings again', *Planning in London,* London, April.

Finch, P. (2002a) 'BCO: Getting best value out of office design', *Architects' Journal,* London, 14 March.

Finch, P. (2002b) at the Urban Design Alliance 'Tall Buildings' conference, London, 25 November.

Fisher, M. (1992) in Rogers, R. and Fisher, M., *A New London,* Penguin, London.

Fishman, R. (1971) *Urban Utopias in the Twentieth Century,* Basic Books, New York.

Fishman, R. (1987) *Bourgeois Utopias: the rise and fall of suburbia,* Basic Books, New York.

Flavell, L. and R. (1999) *The Chronology of Words and Phrases,* Kyle Cathie, London.

Florida, R. (2002) *The Rise of the Creative Class,* Basic Books, New York.

Ford, F. M. (1909) 'The future in London' reprinted in Stang, S. (1986) *The Ford Madox Ford Reader,* Carcanet, Manchester.

Forty, A. (2000a) *Words and Buildings: a vocabulary of modern architecture,* Thames and Hudson, London.

Forty, A. (2000b) 'Material word', *Building Design,* London, 6 September 2002.

Forty, A. (2001) Review in *Architects' Journal,* London, 6 September.

Forty, A. (2002) 'Square, but not square', *Building Design,* London, 24 May.

Fowler, H. (1926) *A Dictionary of Modern English Usage,* Oxford University Press, London.

Frampton, K. (1988) 'Place-form and cultural identity' in Thackara, J., *Design after Modernism,* Thames and Hudson, London.

Fraser, M. (2001) 'Angels with dirty traces', *Architects' Journal,* London, 29 November.

Frey, H. (1999) *Designing the City: towards a more sustainable urban form,* E. and F.N. Spon, London.

Frieling (2001) 'Deltametropolis: an exercise in strategic planning' in Echenique, M. and Saint, A. (2001) *Cities for the New Millennium,* Spon Press, London.

Fukayama, F. (1996) *Trust,* Penguin, London.

Fuller, P. (1988) 'The search for a postmodern aesthetic' in Thackara, J. (ed.), *Design after Modernism,* Thames and Hudson, London.

Galilee, B. (2003) 'Voice in the wilderness', *Building Design,* 17 January.

Gallacher, P. (2003) *Looking Again at the Five Spaces,* unpublished report.

Gallacher, P. (2003) Paper presented at the 'Commonplace' conference at the Lighthouse, Glasgow, 30 May.

Gandelsonas, M. (1999) *X-Urbanism: architecture and the American city,* Princeton Architectural Press, New York.

Gard'ner, J. (2003) 'Informed conservation: principles and practice', *Context,* London, March.

Gargus, J. (1981) 'From Futurism to Rationalism', *Architectural Design* 51.

Garlick, R. and Loney, N. (2001) 'London tower policy still stands', *Regeneration and Renewal,* London, 21 September.

Garreau, J. (1994) *Edge City: life on the new frontier,* Anchor/Doubleday.

Gates, C. (2003) 'The price of fame', *Building Design,* London, 11 April.

Gavron, N. (2000) 'London, World City', *Urban Design Quarterly,* 78.

Gazzard, D. (1988) 'The "Peoples' Promenade"' in Webber, P. (ed.) *The Design of Sydney: three decades of change in the city centre,* Law Book Company, Sydney.

Geddes, P. (1905) *Civics as Applied Sociology II,* reprinted in Mellor, H. (1979) *The Ideal City,* Leicester University Press, Leicester.

Geddes, P. (1910) 'The Civic Survey of Edinburgh', *Transactions of Town Planning Conference,* London.

Geddes, P. (1915a) *Report on the Towns in the Madras Presidency: Ballary* reprinted in Tyrwhitt, J. (1947) *Patrick Geddes in India,* Lund Humphries, London.

Geddes, P. (1915b) *Report on the Towns in the Madras Presidency, 1915: Madura* reprinted in Tyrwhitt, J. (1947) *Patrick Geddes in India,* Lund Humphries, London.

REFERENCES

Geddes, P. (1915c) *Report on the Towns in the Madras Presidency: Coimbatore* reprinted in Tyrwhitt, J. (1947) *Patrick Geddes in India*, Lund Humphries, London.

Geddes, P. (1915d) *Cities in Evolution*, Williams and Norgate, London.

Geddes, P. (1918) *Town Planning Towards City Development: a report to the Durbar of Indore* reprinted in Tyrwhitt, J. (1947) *Patrick Geddes in India*, Lund Humphries, London.

Gehl, J. (1987) *Life Between Buildings*, Van Nostrand Reinhold, New York.

George, H. (1886) *Social Problems*, publisher unknown, New York.

Gerckens, Laurence (1994) 'American zoning and the physical isolation of uses', *Planning Commissioners Journal*, Burlington, Vermont, Summer.

Gerckens, Laurence (2000) 'Ten events, ten successes and ten failures that shaped the twentieth-century American city', *Planning Commissioners Journal*, Burlington, Vermont, Spring.

Gibson, J. (1977) 'The theory of affordances' in Shaw, R. and Bransford, J. (eds.) *Perceiving, Acting and Knowing*, Erlbaum, New Jersey.

Gillen, M. (2000) *Sustainable Development Research Report* (source unknown).

Girardet, H. (1999) *Creating Sustainable Cities*, Green Books, Totnes, Devon.

Girouard, M. (1985) *Cities and People*, Yale University Press, New Haven and London.

Girouard, M. (1992) *Town and Country*, Yale University Press, New Haven.

Glancey, J. (2003) 'Window on the west', *Guardian*, London, 24 May.

Glass, R. (1948) *The Social Background of a Plan*, Routledge and Kegan Paul, London.

Glazebrook, M. (1967) 'Some artists of Bedford Park', *London Magazine*, London, June.

Gleeson, B. and Randolph, B. (2002) 'Social disadvantage and planning in the Sydney context,' *Urban Policy and Research*, March.

Glendinning, M. (2000) 'The conservation movement: a cult of the machine age', paper presented to the Institute of Historic Buildings Annual School, June, and published in three parts in *Context* 68, 69 and 70, London.

Glendinning, M. and Page, D. (1999) *Clone City: crisis and renewal in contemporary Scottish architecture*, Polygon, Edinburgh.

Gold, J. (2000) 'Towards the functional city' in Deckker, T. (ed.) *The Modern City Revisited*, Spon Press, London.

Goldberger, P. (1981) *The Skyscraper*, Alfred A. Knopf, New York.

Goldberger, P. (2001) 'The malling of Manhattan', *Metropolis*, New York, March.

Goodman, R. (1972) *After the Planners*, Simon and Schuster, New York.

Gottdiener, M. and Kephart, G. (1991) 'The multinucleated metropolitan region: a comparative analysis' in Kling, R. and Poster, O. (eds.) *Postsuburban California: the transformation of Orange County since World War II*, University of California Press, Berkeley.

Gough, P. (1994) 'The end of innocence', *Building Design*, London, 3 June.

Graham, S. and Marvin, S. (1999) 'Planning cyber-cities? Integrating telecommunications into urban planning', *Town Planning Review*, January.

Grant, R. (1998) 'Heritage, tradition and modernity', in Barnett, A. and Scruton, R. (eds.) *Town and Country*, Jonathan Cape, London.

Gray, C. (2002) 'Microflats may be solution to city housing shortages', *Independent*, London, 19 January.

Greater London Authority (2001) *Towards the London Plan: initial proposals for the mayor's spatial development strategy*, GLA, London.

Gropius, W. (1965) *The New Architecture and the Bauhaus*, MIT Press, Cambridge, Mass.

Gustafson, K. (1999) Interview in *Landscape Design*, London, February.

Guthrie, P. (2002) 'Urban engineering for sustainable development', *RSA Journal*, London, 1/6.

Gutkind, E. (1953) *The Expanded Environment*, Freedom Press, London.

Habermas, J. (1962) *The Structural Transformation of the Public Sphere*, Polity, London.

Hague, C. (2001) 'The music of our era', *Planning*, London, 20 April.

Hajer, M. and Reijndorp, A. (2001) *In Search of the New Public Domain*, MAI Publishers, Rotterdam.

Hall, E. (1966) *The Hidden Dimension*, Doubleday, New York.

Hall, P. (1972) 'Planning and the environment' in Townsend, P. and Bosanquet, N. (eds.) *Labour and Inequality*, Fabian Society, London.

Hall, P. (1980) *Great Planning Disasters*, Weidenfeld and Nicolson, London.

Hall, P. (1989) *London 2001*, Unwin Hyman, London.

Hall, P. (1994) *Abercrombie's Plan for London 50 Years On: a vision for the future*, Vision for London, London.

Hall, P. (1995) 'Planning and urban design in the 1990s', *Urban Design Quarterly*, Oxford, October.

Hall, P. (1998), *Cities in Civilisation*, Weidenfeld and Nicholson, London.

Hall, P. (2001) 'Searching for a good city in the United States', *Regeneration and Renewal*, London, 24 August.

Hall, P. (2002a) 'Lord Young of Dartington', *Regeneration and Renewal*, London, 25 January.

Hall, P. (2002b) 'Time to market fresh farm food to the masses', *Regeneration and Renewal*, London, 8 November.

Hall, P. (2002c) *Urban and Regional Planning* (fourth edition), Routledge, London and New York.

Hall, P. (2003a) 'Regeneration lessons from a man of action', *Regeneration and Renewal*, London, 7 March.

Hall, P. (2003b) 'Unenviable task for new head of London schools', *Regeneration and Renewal*, London, 21 February.

Hardy, D. (1991) *From Garden Cities to New Towns: campaigning for town and country planning, 1899–1946*, E. and F.N. Spon, London.

Harridge, C. and Silvera, I. (2001) 'Goals of global planning aid', *Planning*, London, 23 November.

Harvey, D. (1989) *The Urban Experience*, Basil Blackwell, Oxford.

Harvey, D. (1997) 'The New Urbanism and the Communitarian Trap', *Harvard Design Magazine*, Cambridge, Massachusetts, Winter/Spring.

Harwood, E. (2000) *Something Worth Keeping: post-war architecture in England*, English Heritage, London.

Harwood, E. and Saint, A. (1991) *London*, HMSO, London.

Hatton, B. (1999), 'A dazzling vision', *Architects' Journal*, London, 20 May.

Haydon, B. R. (ed. Blunden, E.) *Autobiography of Benjamin Robert Haydon*, The World's Classics, Oxford University Press, Oxford.

Healey, P. (1988) 'Imaging the city: projects or policies', *Urban Design Quarterly*, Oxford, April.

Heathcote, E. (2003) 'Old master', *Architects' Journal*, London, 22 May.

Hebbert, M. (1998) *London*, Wiley, Chichester.

Hebbert, M. (1999), 'New urbanism and the climacteric of 1900', presentation to the Congress of the New Urbanism.

Hebbert, M. (2000) 'Twenty-first century places: comparative and international perspectives', Urban Design Alliance conference, Manchester, September.

Hellman, L. (2002) 'Paradigm lost?' *Architects' Journal*, London, 17 October.

Herron, J. (2001) 'Three meditations on the ruins of Detroit' in Daskalakis, G., Waldheim, C. and Young, J. (eds.) *Stalking Detroit*, ACTAR, Barcelona.

Herrschel, T. and Newman, P. (2002) *Governance of Europe's City Regions*, Routledge, London.

Heseltine, M. (2002) 'The next step', *Regeneration and Renewal*, London, 1 November.

Higgott, A. (2000) 'Birmingham: building the modern city' in Deckker, T. *The Modern City Revisited*, Spon Press, London.

Hillier, B. (1988) 'Against enclosure' in Teymur, Markus and Woolley (eds.) *Rehumanising Housing*, Butterworth, London.

Hillier, B. (1992) 'Look back to London', *Architects' Journal*, London, 15 April.

Hillier, B. (1996) *Space is the Machine: a configurational theory of architecture*, Cambridge University Press, Cambridge.

Hillier, J. and Rooksby, E. (eds.) (2002) *Habitus: a sense of place*, Ashgate Publishing, Aldershot.

Hobsbawm, E. (1968) *Industry and Empire*, Weidenfeld and Nicolson, London.

Hoffman, A. (1968) *Revolution for the Hell of It*, Dial, New York.

Hoffman, D. (2001a) 'Erasing Detroit' in Daskalakis, G., Waldheim, C. and Young, J. (eds.) *Stalking Detroit*, ACTAR, Barcelona.

Hoffman, D. (2001b) 'The best the world has to offer' in Daskalakis, G., Waldheim, C. and Young, J. (eds.) *Stalking Detroit*, ACTAR, Barcelona.

Holloway, J. (1957) 'Wyndham Lewis: the massacre and the innocents', *Hudson Review*, Summer.

Holmgren, S. and Svensson, O. (2001) 'Urban architecture in urban renewal – in dialogue between professionals and residents', *Urban Design International*, Oxford, Volume 6, Number 1.

Horsey, M. (1990) *Tenements and Towers: Glasgow working-class housing 1890–1990*, Royal Commission on the Ancient and Historical Monuments of Scotland, HMSO, Edinburgh.

Hough, M. (1990) *Out of Place: restoring identity to the regional landscape*, New Haven and London.

Hough, M. (1995) *Cities and Natural Process*, Routledge, London.

Howard, D. (2001) 'Edinburgh' in Echenique, M. and Saint, A. (2001) *Cities for the New Millennium*, Spon Press, London.

Huang, T. (2000) 'Hong Kong Blue: flâneurie with the camera's eye in a phantasmagoric global city', *Journal of Narrative Theory* 30.3, Fall.

Hughes, M. (ed.) (1971) *The Letters of Lewis Mumford and Frederic J. Osborn*, Adams and Dart, Bath.

Hughes, R. (1980) *The Shock of the New*, BBC, London.

Hulme, T.E. (1911) 'Notes on the Bologna Congress', *New Age*, Hulme, 27 April.

Hutchinson, M. (1989) *The Prince of Wales: right or wrong?* Faber and Faber, London.

Hutton, W. (2002), 'Put the cities in charge', *Observer*, London, 7 July.

REFERENCES

Hutton, W. (2003) 'Political stakeholder', *Planning*, London, 17 January.
Hvattum, M. (1995) 'Gottfried Semper: towards a comparative science of architecture', *Architectural Research Quarterly*, Cambridge.
Illich, I. (1973) *Tools for Conviviality*, Harper and Row, New York.
Jack, I. (1989) 'Reinventing Glasgow', *Independent Magazine*, London, 4 February.
Jackson, P. (2000) 'Defining terms for sustainable growth', *Planning*, London, 28 July.
Jacobs, A. and Appleyard, D. (1987) 'Toward an urban design manifesto', *American Planning Association Journal*.
Jacobs, J. (1961) *The Death and Life of Great American Cities*, Random House, New York.
James, H. (1907) *The American Scene*, Charles Scribner's Sons, New York.
Jarvis, B. (1983) 'Readers, travellers, visitors, inhabitants and storytellers: notes for an existential urban design', Gloucestershire Papers in Local and Rural Planning, Cheltenham, No. 18.
Jarvis, B. (1998) 'Being there', *Urban Design Quarterly*, Oxford, January.
Jarvis, B. (2000) Review of *After the City* in *Urban Design Quarterly*, Oxford, October.
Jarvis, B. (2001) 'Just passin' thru: considerations of the city as an event', unpublished paper.
Jarvis, B. (2002) 'Place and performance', *Urban Design Quarterly*, London, Spring.
Jeffreys, S. (1998) 'Planning and the citizen' in Barnett, A. and Scruton, R. (eds.) *Town and Country*, Jonathan Cape, London.
Jencks, C. (1991) 'Post-modern triumphs in London', *Architectural Design*, London.
Jencks, C. (1993) *Heteropolis: Los Angeles – the riots and the strange beauty of heteroarchitecture*, Academy Editions, London.
Jenkins, S. (2003) 'Brum looks to a giant bottom to save its soul', *Times*, London, 5 September.
Jennings, C. (2001) 'Talk of the Devil', *Guardian*, London, 5 May.
Johnson, S. (2001) *Emergence*, Penguin, London.
Joiner, R. (2002) 'Home: designing the future' conference in Glasgow, organised by the Lighthouse, 22 May.
Jones, D. (1974) 'The Tutelar of the Place' in *The Sleeping Lord and other Fragments*, Faber and Faber, London.
Joseph Rowntree Foundation (2000) 'The reality of social exclusion on housing estates', *Findings*, York, November.
Joseph Rowntree Foundation (2001a) 'The future of community investment by housing associations', *Findings*, York, October.
Joseph Rowntree Foundation (2001b) 'The contribution of large, independent neighbourhood regeneration organisations to regeneration', *Findings*, York, October.
Kahn, A. (ed.) (2002) 'Urban Design: practices, pedagogies, premises', discussions at Columbia University, New York, 5–6 April.
Karpf, A. (2002) 'A chain reaction', *Guardian Weekend*, London, 2 November.
Katz, P. (ed.) (1994) *The New Urbanism*, McGraw-Hill, New York.
Kayden, J. (2000) *Privately Owned Public Space: the New York City experience*, John Wiley and Sons, New York.
Kelbaugh, D. (2000) *The Essential Common Place*, University of Washington Press, Washington DC.
Kelbaugh, D. (2002) in Kahn, A. (ed.) 'Urban Design: practices, pedagogies, premises', discussions at Columbia University, New York, 5–6 April.
Kelling, G. and Wilson, J. (1982) 'Broken windows', *Atlantic Monthly*, March.
Kelsall, F. (2001) 'Dating old buildings' in *Building Conservation Directory 2001*, Cathedral Communications, Tisbury.
King, A. (1984) *The Bungalow: the production of a global culture*, Routledge and Kegan Paul, London.
King, G. (1996) 'Ian Nairn: the missing art of townscape', *Urban Design Quarterly*, London, July.
Kleihues (1990), *Project Report*, Internationale Bauausstellung, Berlin.
Klotz, H. (1988) *The History of Postmodern Architecture*, MIT Press, Cambridge, Mass.
Knabb, K. (1981) (ed.) *Situationist International Anthology*, Bureau of Public Secrets, Berkeley, California.
Knevitt, C. (1986) *Perspectives*, Lund Humphries, London.
Koolhaas, R. (1978) *Delirious New York*, Momacelli Press, New York.
Koolhaas, R. (1994) in the *New York Times*, 11 September.
Koolhaas, R. (1996) 'From Bauhaus to Koolhaas', interview with Katrina Heron, *Wired*, London.
Koolhaas, R. (2000) on the BBC Radio 3 series 'Sounding the Century', date unknown.
Koolhaas, R. (2002) Interview on www.wired.com
Koolhaas, R. and Mau, B. (1995) *S, M, L, XL*, Office for Metropolitan Architecture.

Koscevic, Z. (2002) in Benson, T. (ed.) *Central European Avant-Gardes: exchange and transformation 1910–30*, MIT Press, Boston, Massachussetts.
Kostof, S. (1987) *America by Design*, Oxford University Press, New York.
Kostof, S. (1991) *The City Shaped: urban patterns and meanings through history*, Thames and Hudson, London.
Kostof, S. (1992) *The City Assembled*, Thames and Hudson, London.
Kraebel, T. (1997) 'Sacred realm: the emergence of the synagogue in the ancient world', *Biblical Archaeological Review*, London, September/October.
Krier, L. (1983) 'Krier on Speer', *Architectural Review*, London, Volume 173.
Krier, L. (1984) 'Houses, palaces, cities', *Architectural Design*, London, Profile No. 54.
Krier, L. (2001) *The Future of Cities: the absurdity of modernism*, interview by Nikos Salingaros on www.planetizen.com
Krietzman, L. (1999) *The 24-Hour Society*, Profile Books, London.
Kunstler, J. (2000) 'The Spirit of Place', a presentation at the seventh Congress for the New Urbanism, on the CNU website.
Kunstler, J. (2001) 'Does edge city have a future?' on www.kunstler.com
Kunstler, J. (2003) on www.kunstler.com
La Ferla, R. (2003) 'Fashion and style', *New York Times*, New York, 9 February.
Landry, C. (2000) 'The Creative City', *Streetwise* 42, Brighton, November.
Landscape Institute (with the Institute of Environmental Management and Assessment) (2002) *Guidelines for Landscape and Visual Impact Assessment*, Spon Press, London.
Laurence, R. (1999) *The Roads of Roman Italy*, Routledge, London.
Law, H. (2002) 'Tax message', *Building Design*, London, 8 March.
Lehrer, E. and Zinmeister, K. (2002) Interview with Andres Duany, *The American Enterprise*, October/November.
Leibman, N. (2001) on www.mbcnet.org
Lethaby, W. (1922) *Form in Civilisation*, Oxford University Press, Oxford.
Lettau, R (1964) 'When Potemkin's coach went by' in *German Short Stories*, Penguin, Harmondsworth, Middlesex.
Lewis, M. (2002) *The Gothic Revival*, Thames and Hudson, London.
Lewis, W. (1948) *America and Cosmic Man*, Nicholson and Watson, London.
Lipman, C. (2002a) 'Villages made to measure', *New Start*, London, 8 February.
Lipman, C. (2002b) 'In search of the mainstream', *New Start*, London, 24 May.
Little, A. and Mabey, C. (1973) 'Reading attainment and social and ethnic mix of London primary schools' in Donnison, D. and Eversley, D. (eds.) *London: urban patterns, problems and policies*, Heinemann, London.
Littlejohn, G. (2002) 'Homes face the cappuccino test', *Metro*, London, 13 March.
Llewelyn-Davies (2000) *Urban Design Compendium*, English Partnerships and the Housing Corporation, London.
Local Government Association (2000) *Reforming Local Planning: planning for communities*, LGA, London.
Loew, S. (1996) 'A book that changed my life', *Urban Design Quarterly*, Oxford, July.
London County Council (1961) *The Planning of a New Town*, London County Council, London.
Lorzing, H. (2001) *The Nature of Landscape: a personal quest*, 010 Publishers.
Lynch, K. (1960) *The Image of the City*, MIT Press, Cambridge, Massachusetts.
MacCormac, R. (1991) 'The pursuit of quality', *RIBA Journal*, London, September.
MacCormac, R. (1994) 'Understanding transactions', *Architectural Review* 194 (1165), London.
MacDiarmid, H. (1966) *The Company I've Kept*, Hutchinson, London.
Mackay, R. (1983) *The One-eyed City*, Countyvise, Birkenhead.
Maddox, B. (2003) 'Spirits of the bush', *Guardian*, London, 26 July.
Manguel, A. and Guadalupi, G. (1999) *The Dictionary of Imaginary Places*, Bloomsbury, London.
Markus, T. and Cameron, D. (2002) *The Words Between the Spaces: buildings and language*, Routledge, London.
Mars, T. (1992) 'Little Los Angeles in Bucks', *Architects' Journal*, London, 15 April.
Mars, T. (1998) 'The life in new towns' in Barnett, A. and Scruton, R. *Town and Country*, Jonathan Cape, London.
Martin, I. (2000) Column in *Building Design*, London, 9 October.
Martin, I. (2002) Writing under the name of Eric Ericsson in the Astragal column, *Architects' Journal*, London, 13 June.
Martin, I. (2003a) Column in *Building Design*, London, 10 January.
Martin, I. (2003b) Column in *Building Design*, London, 23 May.
Massey, D. (1994) *Space, Place and Gender*, Polity Press, Cambridge.

REFERENCES

Mayne, A. (1993) *The Imagined Slum*, Leicester University Press, Leicester.
McAuslan, P. (1980) *The Ideologies of Planning Law*, Pergamon Press, London.
McCarthy, P. (1975) *Céline: a critical biography*, Allen Lane, London.
McGlynn, S. (1993) 'Reviewing the rhetoric' in Hayward, R. and McGlynn, S. (eds.) *Making Better Places: urban design now*, Butterworth, London.
McGrath, M. (2003) 'History in the dock', *Evening Standard*, London, 11 June.
McInnes, G. (1965) *The Road to Gundagai*, Hamish Hamilton, London.
McKean, C. (1994) 'In search of purity' in Stamp, G. and McKinstry, S. *'Greek' Thomson*, Edinburgh University Press, Edinburgh.
McKean, J. (1994) 'Thomson's city' in Stamp, G. and McKinstry, S. *'Greek' Thomson*, Edinburgh University Press, Edinburgh.
McLaughlin, R. (2000) *A New Urbanist Lexicon* on Planning Minnesota On Line.
McNulty, T. (2003) Speech at a RTPI Conference on the Planning and Compulsory Purchase Bill, London, 4 March.
Mead, A. (2002a) 'Points of reference', *Architects' Journal*, London, 31 January.
Mead, A. (2002b) Review in *Architects' Journal*, London, 21 March.
Meades, J. (2003) 'Our affection for maypoles and morris men...', *Independent*, London, early February.
Melhuish, C. (2001) 'A stroll through the socio-economic history of Spitalfields', *Architects' Journal*, London, 16/23 August.
Melhuish, C. (2002a) 'Ian Buruma's thoughts on anti-urban thinking', *Architects' Journal*, London, 7 February.
Melhuish, C. (2002b) 'Blonski's retrospective on architect Peter Moro', *Architects' Journal*, 28 March 2002.
Meller, H. (1981) 'Patrick Geddes' in Cherry, G. (ed.) *Pioneers in British Planning*, Architectural Press, London.
Mencken, H. L. (1921) in the *Baltimore Evening Sun*, Baltimore, 3 January.
Mencken, H. L. (ed.) (1925) *Americana 1925*, Martin Hopkinson, London.
Metro (2003) 'Crowded carriages are "all in the mind"', *Metro*, London, 24 January.
Middleton, M. (1991) *Cities in Transition*, Michael Joseph, London.
Miles, Malcolm (2000) 'Public art, urban space and democracy', *Urban Design Quarterly*, London, October.
Miller, D. (1996) *City of the Century: the epic of Chicago and the making of America*, Simon and Schuster, New York.
Miller, M. (1989) *Letchworth: the first garden city*, Phillimore, Chichester.
Mills, C.W. (1959) *The Sociological Imagination*, Oxford University Press, New York.
Ministry of Housing and Local Government (1962) *Residential Areas: high densities*, Planning Bulletin 2, HMSO, London.
Minton, A. (2002) *Building Balanced Communities*, Royal Institution of Chartered Surveyors, London.
Mitchell, W. (2001a) Urban Design Alliance annual lecture, London, September.
Mitchell, W. (2001b) 'Electronic cottages, wired neighbourhoods and smart cities', *Planning in London*, London, October.
Molinaro, M., McLuhan, C. and Toye, W. (eds.) (1987) *Letters of Marshall McLuhan*, Oxford University Press, Toronto.
Moore, W. (1949) *A Dictionary of Geography*, Penguin, Harmondsworth, Middlesex.
Morris, J. (1984) *The Matter of Wales*, Penguin, Harmondsworth, Middlesex.
Morris, J. (1987) *Manhattan '45*, Faber and Faber, Boston.
Morris, R. (1989) *Churches in the Landscape*, J.M. Dent and Sons, London.
Morrison, M. (2002) 'The fascination of white gloves', paper given to the conference 'Where conservation meets conservation', De Montfort University, Leicester, 9 September.
Morriss, R. (1993) *The Buildings of Chester*, Alan Sutton, Stroud.
Morton III, B. (2000) Speaking at the Institute of Historic Building Conservation School, Glasgow.
Mowl, T. (2002) 'Desperate love', *Times Literary Supplement*, London, 21 June.
Moye, C. (2003) 'The gospel according to George', *Daily Telegraph*, London, 21 June.
Mullan, J. (2000) 'Country Codas', *The Guardian*, London, 7 October.
Mumford, L. (1938) *The Culture of Cities*, Martin Secker and Warburg, London.
Mumford, L. (1961) *The City in History*, Harcourt, Brace, Jovanovich, New York.
Mumford, L. in Tyrwhitt, J. (1947) *Patrick Geddes in India*, Lund Humphries, London.
Murray, L. (2002) *Poems the Size of Photographs*, Carcanet, Manchester.

Muthesius, S. (1982) *The English Terraced House*, Yale University Press, New Haven and London.
Nagashima, C. (1998) in *Streetwise*, Brighton, No. 33, April.
Nairn, I. (1966) *Nairn's London*, Penguin, Harmondsworth, Middlesex. New edition (1988), revised by Peter Gasson, Penguin, Harmondsworth, Middlesex.
Neville, R. (1909) 'The Divorce of Man from Nature', *Garden Cities and Town Planning*, London, August.
Nevin, T. (1996) *Ernst Jünger and Germany: into the abyss, 1914–1945*, Duke University Press, Durham, North Carolina.
New Economics Foundation (2000) *Prove It! Measuring the effect of neighbourhood renewal on local people*, NEF, London.
New Start (2001) 'Neighbourhood Watch', column in *New Start*, London, 30 November.
New Urban News (2001) 'Celebration's downtown: how successful is it?' *New Urban News*, Ithaca, New York, December.
Newcastle Architecture Workshop (1990) *National Review of Architecture Workshops, interim report*, unpublished.
Newman, O. (1973) *Defensible Space: crime prevention through urban design*, National Institute of Law Enforcement and Criminal Justice, Washington DC.
NHS Executive, King's Fund, Government Office for London and Association of London Government (2000) *London's Health Strategy: statistical supplement*, London.
Nicolai, B. (2000) 'The symphony of the metropolis' in Deckker, T. (ed.) *The Modern City Revisited*, Spon Press, London.
Nolen, J. (1916) *City Planning: a series of papers presenting the essential elements of a city plan*, D. Appleton and Company, New York.
Norberg-Schulz, C. (1980) *Genius Loci*, Academy Editions, London.
Norquist, J. (2002) Speech to the Urban Summit, Birmingham (England), 31 October.
Novak, F. (1995) *Lewis Mumford and Patrick Geddes: the correspondence*, Routledge, London and New York.
O'Carroll, G. and Barcia, M. (2003) 'Brave old world', *Building Design*, London, 28 February.
O'Connell, S. (2003) *London 1753* (exhibition catalogue), British Museum Press, London.
Olin, S. *et al* (1992) *Postsuburban California*, Berkeley, California.
Osborn, F. (1926) in the journal *Garden Cities and Town Planning* (p. 194), London.
Osborn, F. (1938) in the journal *Town and Country Planning* (p. 55), London.
Osborn, F. (1939) in *Town and Country Planning* (p. 115).
Osborn, F. (1949) in *Town and Country Planning* (p. 104).
Osborn, F. (1952) in *Town and Country Planning* (p. 496).
Osborn, F. (1953) in *Town and Country Planning* (p. 225).
Osborn, F. (1966) in *Town and Country Planning* (p. 23).
Osborn, F. (1970) *Genesis of Welwyn Garden City*, Town and Country Planning Association, London.
Owen, S. (1997) speaking at the Local Distinctiveness in Design Conference, Nottingham University, 19 March.
Palmer, H. (2001) 'Global guru chronicling community breakdown', *Regeneration and Renewal*, London, 13 April.
Park, R. (1952) *Human Communities: the city and human ecology*, publisher unknown, Glencoe, Illinois.
Parker, J. (1973) 'Some sociological implications of slum clearance programmes' in Donnison, D. and Eversley, D. (eds.) *London: urban patterns, problems and policies*, Heinemann, London.
Pawley, M. (1998) *Terminal Architecture*, Reaktion Books, London.
Pawley, M. (2002a) 'EH and CABE come out fighting as tall buildings debate rumbles on', *Architects' Journal*, London, 21 February.
Pawley, M. (2002b) 'You could make a career out of building absolutely nothing at all', *Architects' Journal*, London, 11 April.
Pawley, M. (2002c) 'Why there's no place like home when it comes to making money', *Architects' Journal*, London, 9 May.
Pawley, M. (2002d) 'Beware the great tide of waste that is coming to engulf us all', *Architects' Journal*, London, 11 July.
Pearman, H. (2002) Introduction to Terry Farrell and Partners *Ten Years, Ten Cities: the work of Terry Farrell and Partners 1991–2001*, Laurence King Publishing, London.
Peel, D. (2002) 'Town centre management: multi-stakeholder evaluation', unpublished paper, University of Westminster, London.
Pepper, S. (1978) 'The garden city legacy', *Architectural Review*, London, June.
Pepper, S. and Swenarton, M. (1978) 'Home front: garden suburbs for munition workers', *Architectural Review*, London, June.

REFERENCES

Pevsner, N. (1943) *An Outline of European Architecture*, Pelican, London.

Pharoah, T. (2001) 'Why traffic management in town centres?' *Planning in London*, London, January 2001.

Phillips, J. (2000) 'Planning practice', presentation at the Town and Country Planning Summer School, St Andrews.

Pivaro, A. (2003) 'Tower Struggle', *Building Design*, London, 6 June.

PlannersWeb (2001) on www.plannersweb.com

Planning (2000) 'Living Places: urban renaissance in the south east', *Planning*, London, date unknown.

Plumb, J. (1961) *The Horizon Book of the Renaissance*, Collins, London.

Porritt, J. (2000) Hepworth Lecture given at the Royal Institute of British Architects, London, June.

Potter, S. (1950) *Our Language*, Pelican, Harmondsworth, Middlesex.

Pound, R. (1952) *Arnold Bennett: a biography*, William Heinemann, London.

Powell, K. (2001), '"Kilted crusader" [Roderick Gradidge] dies, aged 71', *Architects' Journal*, London, 11 January.

Power Drawing Newsletter 1 (2001) Drawing Power (the Campaign for Drawing), London, May.

Power, A. (2000) 'Social exclusion', *RSA Journal*, London, 2/4.

Powers, A. (2000a) 'The Twentieth Century Society comes of age', *Context*, London, June.

Powers, A. (2000b) 'Sir Leslie Martin: an appreciation', *Twentieth Century Society Newsletter*, London, Autumn.

Powers, A. (2001a) 'New town artistry', *Architects' Journal*, London, 11 October.

Powers, A. (2001b) 'Reputation in ruins', *Building Design*, London, 2 November.

Powers, A. (2002a) 'The suburb in our mind', *Building Design*, London, 1 March.

Powers, A. (2002b) 'Revolution thinking', *Building Design*, London, 22 March.

Powers, A. (2003) 'Demolish and be damned', *Building Design*, London, 10 January.

Prentice, E-A. (2001) 'No go: whites not welcome', *Times*, London, 20 April.

Prescott, J. (2002) 'The heart and soul of the nation', *Guardian*, London, 16 January.

Prince of Wales, The (1989) *A Vision of Britain*, Doubleday, London.

Prince of Wales, The (1999) Speech reported in *Proceedings of the Making Heritage Industrial Buildings Work conference*, Swindon, Business in the Community, London.

Prince of Wales, The (2001) Speech at the 'Building for the Twenty-first Century' conference, London, 11 December.

Pritchett, V. (1997) *The Pritchett Century*, Modern Library, New York.

Punter, J. (1995) 'Edge city leaves private sector in design control', *Planning*, Cheltenham, 28 April.

Punter, J. and Carmona, M. (1997) *The Design Dimension of Planning: theory, content and best practice for design policies*, E. and F.N. Spon, London.

Punter, L. (2000) 'The Urban White Paper', a paper presented at the Town and Country Planning Summer School, St Andrews.

Purdom, C. (1951) *Life Over Again*, J.M. Dent, London.

Pye, M. (1991) *Maximum City: a biography of New York*, Sinclair-Stevenson, London.

Quail, J. (1978) *The Slow Burning Fuse: the lost history of British anarchists*, Paladin, London.

Quinion, M. (1997–2003) on www.worldwidewords.org

Raban, J. (1974) *Soft City*, Hamish Hamilton, London.

Raine, K. (1970) *William Blake*, Thames and Hudson, London.

Rakoki, C. and Lloyd-Jones, T. (2002) *Urban Livelihoods*, Earthscan, London.

Regeneration and Renewal (2002) 'The new name on the planning block', *Regeneration and Renewal*, London, 25 January.

Reid, J. (2001) 'Snipping away the safety net strands', *Scotsman*, Edinburgh, 2 July.

Reilly, C. (1938) *Scaffolding in the Sky: a semi-architectural autobiography*, George Routledge and Sons, London.

Relph, E. (1987) *The Modern Urban Landscape*, John Hopkins, University Press, Baltimore.

Rendell, R. (1991) 'Underworld', in Fisher, M. and Owen, U. *Whose Cities?* Penguin, Harmondsworth, Middlesex.

Reynolds, F. (2003) 'Planning for a small island', lecture to the Environmental Law Foundation, 21 May.

Richards, E. (2000) *The Highland Clearances*, Birlinn, Edinburgh.

Richardson, H. and Gordon, P. (2001) 'Compactness or sprawl: America's future vs. the present' in Echenique, M. and Saint, A. (eds.) *Cities for the New Millennium*, Spon Press, London.

Roberts, B. (1987) *The Making of the English Village*, Longman, Harlow, Essex.

Roberts, G. (2001) 'Change here for the 21st century', *Planning*, London, 20 April.

Rodger, J. (1999) *Contemporary Glasgow: the architecture of the 1990s*, Rutland Press, Edinburgh.

Rodwell, D. (2002) 'From accolade to responsibility', *Context*, London, November.

Rogers, R. (1988) Speech to the Royal Society of Arts, London, April.

Rogers, R. (1989) Foreword to Hutchinson, M. *The Prince of Wales: right or wrong?* Faber and Faber, London.

Rogers, R. (1998) 'People at the heart of urban design', *Times*, London, 22 September.

Rogers, R. (2001) 'The fear of beauty is destroying our urban environment', *Independent*, London, 2 April.

Rolt, L. (1958) *Thomas Telford*, Longman, London.

Rook, A. (2002) 'The changing use of the street and community involvement', paper to the Urban Design Alliance Conference, Cardiff, 19 September.

Ross, A. (2000) *The Celebration Chronicles: life, liberty and the pursuit of property value in Disney's new town*, Verso, London.

Rossi, A. (1982) *The Architecture of the City*, MIT Press, Cambridge, Massachusetts.

Rossi, A. (1987) *Aldo Rossi: architect*, Electra, Milan.

Rouse, J. (2000) Column in *Planning*, London, 2 June.

Rouse, J. (2001) 'Architecture: where's the bottom line?' *Planning in London*, London, January.

Rowntree, D. (2001) 'Sir Denys Lasdun' (obituary), *Guardian*, London, 12 January.

RTPI (2001) *We can do better: opportunities for the planning profession*, Report of the RTPI think tank on modernising local government, Royal Town Planning Institute, London.

Rubió, I. (1995) 'Terrain Vague' in *Anyplace*, MIT Press, Cambridge, Massachusetts.

Rudlin, D. (1998) *Tomorrow: a peaceful path to real reform – the feasibility of accommodating 75 per cent of new homes in urban areas*, Friends of the Earth, London.

Runes, D. and Schrickel, H. (eds.) (1946) *Encyclopedia of the Arts*, Philosophical Library, New York.

Russell, B. (1946) *History of Western Philosophy*, George Allen and Unwin, London.

Rutherford, S. (2002) 'English Heritage's Parks and Gardens Register', *Context* 74, Tisbury, May.

Rykwert, J. (2000) *The Seduction of Place: the city in the twenty-first century*, Weidenfeld and Nicholson, London.

Rykwert, J. (2002) 'Heaven on earth', *Times Literary Supplement*, London, 27 December.

Saarinen, E. (1956) in *Time* magazine, 2 July.

Saint, A. (2001) 'Lessons from London' in Echenique, M. and Saint, A. (eds.) *Cities for the New Millennium*, Spon Press, London.

Sassen, S. (2000) 'Detecting the global inside the national', University of Chicago Magazine, Chicago.

SAVE (1982) *The Mansion House Square Scheme: stop it*, Save Britain's Heritage, London.

Scarman, Lord (1981) *The Brixton Disorders, 10–13 April 1981: report of an inquiry*, HMSO, London.

Schoon, N. (2001) *The Chosen City*, Spon Press, London.

Schumacher, P. and Rogner, C. (2001) 'After Ford', in Daskalakis, G., Waldheim, C. and Young, J. (eds.) *Stalking Detroit*, ACTAR, Barcelona.

Scott Brown, D. (2002) in Kahn, A. (ed.) 'Urban Design: practices, pedagogies, premises', discussions at Columbia University, New York, 5–6 April.

Scottish Executive (2000) *National Planning Policy Guidelines 1: the planning system*, Scottish Executive, Edinburgh.

Scottish Executive (2001) *Designing Places: a policy statement for Scotland*, Scottish Executive, Edinburgh.

Scottish Office (1995) *National Planning Policy Guidelines 7: planning and flooding*, Scottish Office, Edinburgh.

Scottish Office (1996a) *National Planning Policy Guidelines 3: land for housing*, Scottish Office, Edinburgh.

Scottish Office (1996b) *National Planning Policy Guidelines 10: planning and waste management*, Scottish Office, Edinburgh.

Scottish Office (1998) *National Planning Policy Guidelines 8: town centres and retailing (revised)*, Scottish Office, Edinburgh.

Scruton, R. (1979) *The Aesthetics of Architecture*, Methuen, London.

Seenan, G. (2003) 'Lack of city smiles is no laughing matter', *Guardian*, London, 18 February.

REFERENCES

Sennett, R. (1978) *The Fall of Public Man: on the social psychology of capitalism*, Vintage Books, New York.
Sennett, R. (1990) *The Conscience of the Eye: the design and social life of cities*, Faber and Faber, London.
Sennett, R. (2001) 'Capitalism and the city' in Echenique, M. and Saint, A. (eds.) *Cities for the New Millennium*, Spon Press, London.
Seymour-Smith, Martin (1975) *Guide to Modern World Literature*, Hodder and Stoughton, London.
Shallcross, G. (2000) 'Andres Duany shares the principles and practices of new urbanism' on Planning Minnesota Online.
Shama, S. (2003) 'A world of their own', *Guardian*, London, 5 April.
Sharp, D. (2000) 'Global conquest', *RIBA Journal*, London, October.
Sharp, T. (1932) *Town and Countryside: some aspects of urban and regional development*, Oxford University Press, London.
Sharp, T. (1946) *Exeter Phoenix*, publisher unknown.
Sharp, T. (1948) *Oxford Replanned*, Architectural Press, London.
Shepheard, P. (1997) *The Cultivated Wilderness*, MIT Press, Cambridge, Massachusetts.
Shields, R. (1994) 'Fancy Footwork: Walter Benjamin's notes on flânerie' in Tester, K. (ed.), *The Flâneur*, Routledge, New York.
Shonfield, K. (1998) *At Home with Strangers: public space and the new urbanity*, Comedia/Demos.
Shonfield, K. (2002) quoted at the Urban Design Alliance 'Tall Buildings' conference, London, 25 November.
Silson, R. (2002) Letter in *Planning*, London, 8 November.
Smith, C. (1984) *Chicago and the American Literary Imagination 1880–1920*, University of Chicago Press, Chicago.
Smith, D (1970) *Dan Smith*, Oriel Press, Newcastle-upon-Tyne.
Smith, J. (2003) Letter in *Times Literary Supplement*, London, 7 March.
Smith, N. (2001) 'Our language has been hijacked by the government', *Planning*, London, 13 April.
Smith, P. (1974) *The Dynamics of Urbanism*, Hutchinson Educational, London.
Social Exclusion Unit (2000) *National Strategy for Neighbourhood Renewal: a framework for consultation*, Cabinet Office, London.
Social Market Foundation (2002) 'Safe Haven or Social Division? Gated communities and social balance in the United Kingdom', seminar invitation.
Soja, E. (1992) 'Inside Exopolis: scenes from Orange County' in Sorkin, M. (ed.) *Variations on a Theme Park*, Noonday Press, New York.
Solnit, R. (2001) *Wanderlust: a history of walking*, Verso, London.
Solomonson, K. (2001) *The Chicago Tribune Tower Competition*, Cambridge University Press, Cambridge.
Sorensen, C. (1996) *London on Film*, Museum of London, London.
Sorkin, M. (1991) 'The Politics of Propinquity', RIBA Annual Discourse, London.
Sorkin, M. (2000) Foreword in Deckker, T. (ed.) *The Modern City Revisited*, Spon Press, London.
Sorkin, M. (2001) in the *Architectural Record*, New York, November.
Sorkin, M. (2002) in Kahn, A. (ed.) 'Urban Design: practices, pedagogies, premises', discussions at Columbia University, New York, 5–6 April.
Spencer, J. (2003) Speaking at the CABE regional development agency design champions seminar, London, 26 February.
Spirn, A. (1996) (edited by Thomas Møller Kristensen), *Deep Structure: on process, form, design in the urban landscape in city and nature*, Odense University Press, Odense, Denmark.
Spring, I. (1990) *Phantom Village: the myth of the new Glasgow*, Polygon, Edinburgh.
Stamp, G. (1990) 'From Battle Bridge to King's Cross: urban fabric and change' in Hunter, M. and Thorne, R., *Change at King's Cross*, Historical Publications, London.
Stapleton, C. (2002) 'Learning curve', *Urban Design Forum*, Melbourne, December.
Starr, K. (1990) *Material Dreams: Southern California through the 1920s*, Oxford University Press, New York.
Steiner, G. (1975) *After Babel*, Oxford University Press, Oxford.
Stephens, J. (2002) 'Karalee Rock: the formation of place and identity', *Urban Policy and Research*, Basingstoke, March.
Stewart, P. (2003) 'Building in context: the CABE casebook', *Context*, London, March.
Stones, A. (2001) 'Strasbourg and Zähringer towns', *Urban Design Quarterly*, London, Autumn.
Streetwise (2001) 'Citizenship follow up', *Streetwise 46*, Brighton.
Stringer, G. (1995) Speaking at the launch of Manchester's *Draft City Development Guide*, 8 June.
Stubbs, S. (2002) 'Don't underrate people-power', *Regeneration and Renewal*, London, 1 March.

Sudjic, D. (1992) *The Hundred-mile City*, Andre Deutsch, London.
Sugrue, T. (1996) *The Origins of the Urban Crisis: race and inequality in postwar Detroit*, Princeton University Press, Princeton, New Jersey.
Sullivan, L. (1949) *The Autobiography of an Idea*, publisher unknown, New York.
Summerson, J. (1962) *Georgian London*, Pelican Books, Harmondsworth, Middlesex.
Summerson, J. (1994) 'On discovering "Greek" Thomson' in Stamp, G. and McKinstry, S. *'Greek' Thomson*, Edinburgh University Press, Edinburgh.
Swenarton, M. (1981) *Homes Fit for Heroes: the politics and architecture of early state housing in Britain*, Heinemann, London.
Tate Modern (2001) *Century City* (brochure of the exhibition), London.
Taylor, A.J.P. (1957) in *Encounter*, London, March.
Taylor, D. (2002) 'Foreseeing and forestalling', *Architects' Journal*, London, 2 May.
Taylor, N. (1998) *Urban Planning Theory since 1945*, Sage, London.
Taylor, W. (2000) *This Bright Field: a travel book in one place*, Methuen, London.
Terry Farrell and Partners (2002) *Ten Years, Ten Cities: the work of Terry Farrell and Partners 1991–2001*, Laurence King Publishing, London.
Tester, K. (ed.) (1994) *The Flâneur*, Routledge, London.
Thiel, P. (1961) 'A sequence space notation', *Town Planning Review*, Liverpool, April.
Thompson, J. (2003) 'My little *what?*' *Independent on Sunday*, London, 20 July.
Tiesdell, S., Oc, T. and Heath, T. (1996) *Revitalizing Historic Urban Quarters*, Architectural Press, Oxford.
Times, The (1991) An article quoting Richard Rogers, *Times*, London, 13 February.
Timms, E. and Kelly D. (1985) *Unreal City: urban experience in modern European literature and arts*, Manchester University Press, Manchester.
Toole, J. (1980) *A Confederacy of Dunces*, Louisiana State University Press.
Towers, G. (1995) *Building Democracy*, UCL Press, London.
Trachtenberg, M. and Hyman, I. (1986) *Architecture*, Academy Editions, London.
Travers, T. (2001) 'Density means better cities' in Echenique, M. and Saint, A. (eds.) *Cities for the New Millennium*, Spon Press, London.
Travers, T. (2002) 'Would zero tolerance work here?' *Evening Standard*, London, 13 February.
Treasury Taskforce (2000) *Technical Note 7*, London.
Twombly, R. (1973) *Frank Lloyd Wright*, Harper and Row, New York.
University of Westminster Transport Studies Group (1998), *Civilising Cities: the contribution of transport and land use*, RAC Foundation for Motoring and the Environment, Feltham.
Upton, C. (2001) 'Herbert Manzoni: a lesson from the past', paper to the Urban Design Alliance annual conference in Birmingham, September.
Urban Design Forum (Australia) (2001) *Urban Design Forum*, June.
Urban Green Spaces Taskforce (2002) *Green Spaces, Better Places*, DTLR, London.
Urban Task Force (1999a) *Shaping Attitudes to Urban Living*, Urban Task Force, London.
Urban Task Force (1999b) *Towards an Urban Renaissance*, Department of the Environment, Transport and the Regions, London.
Urban Villages Group (text by Tony Aldous) (1992) *Urban Villages*, Urban Villages Group, London.
URBED and the Bartlett School of Planning, University College London (2000) *Living Places: urban renaissance in the south east*, Government Office for the South East and Department of the Environment, Transport and the Regions, London.
URBED, MORI and the University of Bristol (1999) *But Would You Live There? Shaping attitudes to urban living*, Urban Task Force, London.
Venturi, R. (1966) *Complexity and Contradiction in Architecture*, Museum of Modern Art, New York.
Venturi, R. and Scott Brown, D. (1984) *A View from the Campidoglio: selected essays 1953–1984*, Harper, New York.
Vernez-Moudon, A. (2002) in Kahn, A. (ed.) 'Urban Design: practices, pedagogies, premises', discussions at Columbia University, New York, 5–6 April.
Veyne, P. (1990) *Bread and Circuses: historical sociology of political pluralism*, Penguin, Harmondsworth, Middlesex.
Vidal, D. and Gupta, N. (1999) 'Urban vocabulary in Northern India' on www.unesco.org
Wade, R. (2002) 'America's empire rules an unbalanced world', *International Herald Tribune*, 3 January.
Waldheim C. and Santos-Munné, M. (2001) 'Decamping Detroit' in Daskalakis, G., Waldheim, C. and Young, J. (eds.) *Stalking Detroit*, ACTAR, Barcelona.

REFERENCES

Walsh, J. (2000) 'It does exactly what it says on the tin', *Independent*, London, 2 December.

Wannop, U. and Leclerc, R. (1987) 'Urban renewal and the origins of GEAR' in Donnison, D. and Middleton, A. (eds.) *Regeneration the Inner City: Glasgow's experience*, Routledge and Kegan Paul, London.

Ward, B. and Dubos, R. (1972) *Only One Earth: the care and maintenance of a small planet*, Penguin, Harmondsworth, Middlesex.

Ward, C. (1973) *Anarchy in Action*, George Allen and Unwin, London.

Ward, C. (1977) *The Child in the City*, Architectural Press, London.

Ward, C. (1989) *Welcome, Thinner City*, Bedford Square Press, London.

Ward, C. (1990) *Talking Houses*, Freedom Press, London.

Ward, C. (1991) *Influences: voices of creative dissent*, Green Books, Bideford, Devon.

Ward, C. (1996) *Talking to Architects: ten lectures*, Freedom Press, London.

Ward, C. (1998) 'The unofficial countryside' in Barnett, A. and Scruton, R. (eds.) *Town and Country*, Jonathan Cape, London.

Ward, C. (2002) 'People and ideas', *Town and Country Planning*, London, September.

Warrack, A. (2000) *The Scots Dialect Dictionary*, Waverley Books, Lanark.

Watkin, D. (1984) *Morality and Architecture*, Univrsity of Chicago Press, Chicago.

Weaver, M. (1995) 'Forensic conservation and other current developments in the conservation of heritage resources and the built environment', *Journal of Architectural Conservation*, Vol. 1, No. 3.

Webber, M. (1963) 'Order and diversity: community without propinquity' in Wingo L. *Cities and Space: the future use of urban land*, John Hopkins University Press, Baltimore.

Webber, M. (1996) 'Tenacious cities', *Conference Research Notes: spatial technologies, geographical information and the city*, Baltimore, September.

Webber, M. (2003) at www.hevanet.com/oti

Webber, P. (1988a) Preface in Webber, P. (ed.) *The Design of Sydney: three decades of change in the city centre*, The Law Book Company, Sydney.

Webber, P. (1988b) 'The nature of the city' in Webber, P. (ed.) *The Design of Sydney: three decades of change in the city centre*, The Law Book Company, Sydney.

Weinreb, B. and Hibbert, C. (1983) *The London Encyclopaedia*, Macmillan, London.

Wells, H.G. (1902) *Anticipations*, Chapman and Hall, London.

Welsh, I. (1996) 'City tripper', *Guardian*, London, 16 February.

Weston, R. (2002) 'Plazas and plants', *Architects' Journal*, London, 31 January.

Whimster, S. (1992) 'Yuppies: a keyword of the 1980s' in Budd, L. and Whimster, S. (eds.) *Global Finance and Urban Living*, Routledge, London.

Whistler, W. and Reed, D. (1994) 'Townscape as a philosophy of urban design', *Urban Design Quarterly*, Oxford, October.

Whitby, M. (2001) 'Urban design education: engineering', *Urban Design Quarterly*, London, Autumn.

White, M. and L. (1962) *The Intellectual versus the City*, Harvard University Press, Cambridge, Massachusetts.

Whittick, A. (1987) *FJO, practical idealist: a biography of Sir Frederic Osborn*, Town and Country Planning Association, London.

Whyte, W. (1980) *The Social Life of Small Spaces*, Conservation Foundation, Washington DC.

Wigley, M. (2001) 'The great urbanism game', *Architectural Design*, London, June.

Willett, J. (1978) *The New Sobriety 1917–1933: art and politics in the Weimar period*, Thames and Hudson, London.

Williams, A. (2001) 'Masterplanning a getaway', *Architects' Journal*, London, 11 January.

Williams, A. (2002) 'Green saviour or eco-maniac?' *Architects' Journal*, London, 25 April.

Williams, D. (2000) 'The scope and definition of the planning profession', *Planning*, London, 2 June.

Williams, R. (1983) *Keywords*, Fontana Press, London.

Williams, R. (2000) 'It's what happened, baby', *Times Literary Supplement*, 3 March.

Williams-Ellis, C. (1937), *Town and Country Planning*, Longman, London.

Winterson, J. (2001) 'Reclaim the city', *Building Design*, London, 29 June.

Woods, W. (1969) *Poland: phoenix in the east*, André Deutsch, London.

Worpole, K. (1992) *Towns for People*, Open University Press, Milton Keynes.

Worpole, K. (2000) *The Value of Architecture*, RIBA Future Studies, London.

Worster, D. (2001) 'On the planet of the Apes', *Times Literary Supplement*, London, 13 July.

Yeang, K. (2003) 'Vertical urban design', Urban Design Group Annual Lecture, London, 11 July.

Yeomans, D. (2000) 'Failing to communicate', *Architectural Research Quarterly*, London, Vol. 4, No. 1.

Young, B. (1988) 'Darling Harbour: a new city precinct' in Webber, P. (ed.) *The Design of Sydney: three decades of change in the city centre*, The Law Book Company, Sydney.

Young, M. and Willmott, P. (1957) *Family and Kinship in East London*, Routledge and Kegan Paul, London.

Zevi, B. (1981a) 'Gruppo 7: the rise and fall of Italian rationalism', *Architectural Design*, 51, London.

Zevi, B. (1981b) 'Lines of Futurism', *Architectural Design*, 51, London.

List of places illustrated

Page		Page	
Cover	6th Avenue and 16th Street, Manhattan	219	Birds Hill, Letchworth
7	Mudchute Farm, Isle of Dogs, London	224	Gadebridge Park, Hemel Hempstead
13	Ferry Lane, Tottenham Hale, London	243	Milton Keynes station
24	Aldersgate Street, Barbican, London	246	Place du Havre, Paris
43	Arnold Circus, Bethnal Green, London	260	Stratford Road, West Ham, London
46	London Bridge station	267	Holborn Viaduct, London
48	Coffee@157, Brick Lane, London	273	Castle Street, Birkenhead
53	Churchill Way flyover, Liverpool	278	Tottenham Hale stations, London
59	East 43rd Street, Manhattan	283	Liverpool Street station, London
65	Lime Street, Liverpool, in 2003	313	Town Square, Stevenage
71	Globe Road, Stepney, London	316	Queen Anne's Gate, Victoria, London
77	Eldonian Village, Vauxhall, Liverpool	321	Clapham Junction station, London
83	Cathcart Road, Gorbals, Glasgow	330	Pitfield Street, Hoxton, London
111	Old Compton Street, Soho, London	342	The Necropolis, Glasgow
124	St Enoch Square, Glasgow	361	Spitalfields Market, London, in 2000
128	Walthamstow marshes, London	365	Greene Street, SoHo, Manhattan
137	St Paul's Churchyard, London	375	The Broadway, Stratford, London
148	The North Circular at Woodford, London	394	Pier Head, Liverpool
157	McClellan Avenue, Newark, New Jersey	399	Fellows Court, Hackney, London
162	Gorbals Street, Glasgow	401	Grand Union Canal, Limehouse, London
164	Northampton Road, Finsbury, London	410	6th Avenue and 16th Street, Manhattan
176	A12, Saxmundham, Suffolk	417	Times Square, Manhattan
183	Alexander Thomson's St Vincent Street church, Glasgow	423	Singer Street, Shoreditch, London
193	Trafalgar Way, Isle of Dogs, London	429	Trafalgar Square, London
195	Golden Lane, St Luke's, London	438	Old Street roundabout, Shoreditch, London
200	Bryant Park, Manhattan	447	Victoria Square, Birmingham
202	Outside Slough station	454	Stratford station, London
206	Lea Bridge Road, London	456	Spitalfields, London, in 2001

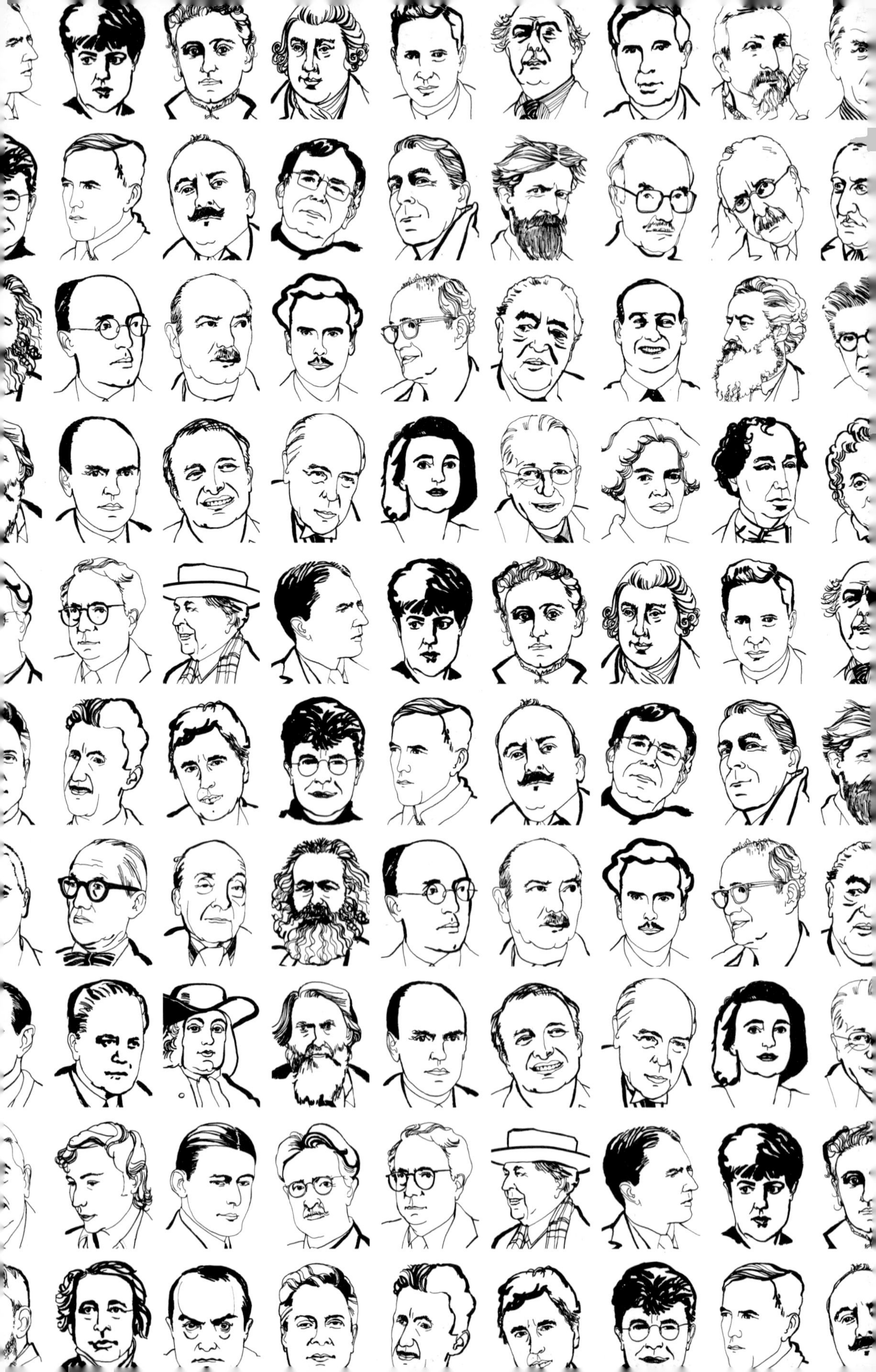